Microsoft®

Microsoft® Project 2010 Inside Out

Teresa S. Stover
with Bonnie Biafore
and Andreea Marinescu

Published with the authorization of Microsoft Corporation by:
O'Reilly Media, Inc.
1005 Gravenstein Highway North
Sebastopol, California 95472

ISBN: 978-0-7356-2687-4

1 2 3 4 5 6 7 8 9 TG 6 5 4 3 2 1

Printed and bound in Canada.

Microsoft Press books are available through booksellers and distributors worldwide. If you need support related to this book, e-mail Microsoft Press Book Support at mspinput@microsoft.com. Please tell us what you think of this book at http://www.microsoft.com/learning/booksurvey.

Acquisitions and Developmental Editors: Juliana Aldous and Kenyon Brown
Production Editor: Holly Bauer
Editorial Production: Dessin Designs
Technical Reviewers: Ulhas Samant and Thuy Le
Copyeditor: John Pierce
Proofreader: Octal Publishing, Inc.
Indexer: Denise Getz
Cover Design Twist Creative • Seattle
Cover Composition: Karen Montgomery
Illustrator: Robert Romano

Contents at a Glance

Table of Contents

Part 2: Developing the Project Plan

Part 3: Tracking Progress

Part 4: Reporting and Analyzing Project Information

Part 5: Managing Multiple Projects

Part 6: Integrating Project 2010 with Other Programs

Part 8: Customizing and Managing Project Files

Part 9: Appendixes

Introduction

Welcome to Microsoft Project 2010 Inside Out. This book is your comprehensive Project 2010 reference, in which you can learn not only the essentials, but also the intermediate topics and advanced techniques for using Project 2010 like a power user.

Who This Book Is For

This book is designed for intermediate to advanced computer users who manage projects. Depending on where you are on the spectrum of project management experience, this book can help you in the following ways:

- If you are completely new to project management and Project 2010, this book will give you a solid grounding in the use of Project 2010 as well as basic project management practices and methodologies. It will help you understand the phases of project management, including the controlling factors in the project life cycle.

- If you're an experienced project manager, this book integrates common project management practices with the use of the software tool. This helps you see how you can use Project 2010 to carry out the project management functions you're accustomed to.

- If you're already an experienced Microsoft Project user, this book will help you better understand the inner workings of Project 2010 so that you can use it more effectively to do what you need it to do. In many ways, Project 2010 is like an entirely new project management information system. It departs in several ways from how things were done in previous versions, and it provides many more choices to consider that have an impact on your project throughout its phases. This book also extensively covers the striking new features in Project 2010 and provides the necessary guidance and "gotchas" regarding whether, when, and how to use those features.

Assumptions About You

Even if you have never used Microsoft Project 2010 or managed a project before, this book assumes you have experience with Microsoft Windows and at least a couple of programs in Microsoft Office—for example, Microsoft Word, Microsoft Excel, or Microsoft Visio.

How To Use This Book

Regardless of your previous experience, this book serves as a facilitator in helping you work with Project 2010 for your project's processes and phases. Read the chapters and parts you feel are appropriate for your needs right now. Familiarize yourself with the topics available in the other chapters.

Then, as you continue to manage your projects with Project 2010, keep the book within arm's reach so that you can quickly find the answers to questions and problems as they come up.

As you achieve mastery in one level of knowledge, use this book to help you attain the next level, whether it's working with multiple projects at one time, customizing Project 2010, or programming Project 2010 functions to automate repetitive activities. This book is your comprehensive Project 2010 reference, in which you can quickly find answers and then get back to work on your project plan, and more importantly, doing the vital work of managing your projects.

How This Book Is Organized

The book is organized into the following parts:

- **Part 1: Project Fundamentals (Chapters 1–2)** If you want a primer on project management in general or Project 2010 in particular, read the chapters in this part. Here, you find an overview of Microsoft Project, including what's new in Project 2010. There's an overview of project management processes and how Project 2010 facilitates those processes. You also find a discussion of the various kinds of people involved in your project, as well as some keys to successful project management.

- **Part 2: Developing the Project Plan (Chapters 3–10)** Everything you need to know about starting a new project and creating a new project plan is found here. You get details about working with the Project 2010 workspace, scheduling tasks, setting up resources and assigning them to tasks, establishing costs, and adjusting the project plan to be an accurate model of your project's reality.

- **Part 3: Tracking Progress (Chapters 11–12)** After you create the perfect project plan, you're ready to execute it. To keep the project plan working for you, it needs to be up to date. This part provides details about setting and working with baselines so that you can track and compare your progress toward deadlines. It covers important aspects of updating and tracking costs as well as adjusting the schedule, resource workload, and costs to reflect ongoing changes in your project.

- **Part 4: Reporting and Analyzing Project Information (Chapters 13–14)** Project 2010 provides a wide range of options for setting up and printing views and reports. This part outlines these methods—from simply printing your current view to generating a built-in report to designing and running your own custom report. This part also describes how you can export data to Microsoft Excel or Microsoft Visio to generate visual reports for analysis, as well as how you can use earned value data to analyze progress and costs.

- **Part 5: Managing Multiple Projects (Chapters 15–16)** As a project manager, it's likely that you're managing more than one project at a time, working with a collection of smaller projects that feed into a large project, and working with various groups of resources who contribute to different projects. This part explains the concepts and practices of master projects, subprojects, and resource pools. It also explains how you can exchange information between different project plans; copy or link information; and leverage customized views, reports, groups, and other Project 2010 elements you might have created.

- **Part 6: Integrating Project 2010 with Other Programs (Chapters 17–21)** Project 2010 is designed to work seamlessly with other programs. You can copy, embed, link, hyperlink, import, and export information. This part describes these methods in detail and also devotes chapters to the specific integration techniques for working with Microsoft Excel, Microsoft Visio, Microsoft Outlook, and Microsoft SharePoint.

- **Part 7: Managing Projects Across Your Enterprise (Chapters 22–27)** Project 2010 helps to facilitate collaboration in project teams across your enterprise. If you're using Microsoft Project Professional 2010, Microsoft Project Server 2010, and Microsoft Project Web App, you and your organization have access to robust features for enterprise project management, portfolio management, and team collaboration. In this part, you learn how to set up and use the enterprise features to standardize and customize Project 2010 and project management processes throughout your organization. Project managers and resource managers can assign tasks, obtain task progress updates, and receive status reports from team members. A chapter each is devoted to the duties and capabilities of different stakeholders in the enterprise project management structure: the project server administrator, the project manager, the team member or team lead, the executive or other managing stakeholder, and the portfolio manager.

- **Part 8: Customizing and Managing Project Files (Chapters 28–32)** With Project 2010, you can create and customize your own views, tables, groups, reports, formulas, macros, and more. You can also customize the Office ribbon. This part covers the details of these custom elements. This part also discusses methods for closing a project at the end of its life cycle and continuing to use what you learn by creating templates that can become the basis for the next project of its kind. Along these lines, this part details project file-management issues, including file locations, backups, and multiple versions.

- **Part 9: Appendixes** This part includes ancillary information you'll find useful in your work with Project 2010. For example, there are installation guidelines and a list of online resources to expand your knowledge of Project 2010 and project management. Also included is a handy keyboard shortcut reference.

Throughout the book, you'll find tips that provide shortcuts or alternative methods for doing certain tasks. The Inside Out tips give you information about known issues or idiosyncrasies with Project 2010 and possible methods of working around them.

There are also Troubleshooting tips that alert you to common problems and how to avoid or recover from them.

This book is designed so that you can quickly find the answers you need at the time you have the question. The comprehensive table of contents is a good starting point. Another excellent place to start finding your solution is in one of the two indexes at the end of the book. Use the special Troubleshooting index to solve specific problems. Use the master index to help you find the topics you're looking for when you need them.

Features and Conventions Used in this Book

This book uses special text and design conventions to help you find the information you need more easily.

Text Conventions

Convention	Meaning
Commands for navigating the ribbon	When referring to commands on the ribbon, this book points to the tab, group, and button. For example, "On the Task tab, in the Insert group, click the Task button."
Abbreviated commands for navigating the ribbon	In some cases, you'll see abbreviated commands. For example, "Click Task, Insert, Task" means click the Task tab on the ribbon, then in the Insert group, click the Task button.
Boldface type	Boldface indicates text that you type.
Initial Capital Letters	The first letters of the names of tabs, dialog boxes, dialog box elements, and commands are capitalized. Example: the Save As dialog box.
Italicized type	Italicized type indicates new terms.
Plus sign (+) in text	Keyboard shortcuts are indicated by a plus sign (+) separating key names. For example, Ctrl+Alt+Delete means that you press the Ctrl, Alt, and Delete keys at the same time.

Design Conventions

INSIDE OUT This statement illustrates an example of an "Inside Out" heading

These are the book's signature tips. In these tips, you get the straight scoop on what's going on with the software—inside information about why a feature works the way it does. You'll also find handy workarounds to deal with software problems.

Sidebar

Sidebars provide helpful hints, timesaving tricks, or alternative procedures related to the task being discussed.

TROUBLESHOOTING

This statement illustrates an example of a "Troubleshooting" problem statement.

Look for these sidebars to find solutions to common problems you might encounter. Troubleshooting sidebars appear next to related information in the chapters. You can also use "Index to Troubleshooting Topics" at the back of the book to look up problems by topic.

Cross-references point you to locations in the book that offer additional information about the topic being discussed.

CAUTION!

Cautions identify potential problems that you should look out for when you're completing a task or that you must address before you can complete a task.

Note

Notes offer additional information related to the task being discussed.

About the Companion Content

The companion content for this book includes sample files that you can use as the basis for practicing Project 2010 techniques throughout this book. Additionally, the companion content for this book includes a list of online resources regarding Microsoft Project 2010 and project management. The following table lists the sample files and online resources.

To access and download the companion content, visit:

http://go.microsoft.com/FWLink/?Linkid=218006

Chapter or Topic	Content
Chapter 1	01WebDev.mpp
Chapter 3	03WebDev.mpp 03aWebDev.mpp 03RecurringTask.mpp 03Training-WBS.mpp
Chapter 4	04WebDev.mpp 04aWebDev.mpp
Chapter 5	05WebDev.mpp 05aWebDev.mpp
Chapter 6	06WebDev.mpp
Chapter 7	07Resources.mpp
Chapter 8	08Home.mpp 08aHome.mpp 08WebDev.mpp 08aWebDev.mpp 08bWebDev.mpp
Chapter 9	09Costs.mpp 09WebDev.mpp
Chapter 10	10Home.mpp 10WebDev.mpp
Chapter 11	11WebDev.mpp
Chapter 12	12NewBiz.mpp 12ProgressLines.mpp
Chapter 13	13NewBiz.mpp

Chapter or Topic	Content
Chapter 15	15Prototype.mpp 15VendorRFP.mpp 15Consolidated.mpp 15Consolidated2.mpp 15ResourcePool.mpp 15ResourcePool1.mpp
Chapter 16	16NewBiz.mpp 16OfficeMove.mpp
Chapter 17	17AnnualRpt.mpp 17AnnualPlan.pptx 17AnnualRpt.docx 17CopyTimeline.docx 17LogoS.bmp
Chapter 20	20OutlookTasks.mpp 20OutlookTasks_Routing.mpp 20TasksToExchange.mpp
Chapter 21	21ContosoWeb.mpp 21ContosoWeb2.mpp 21WebDev.mpp
Chapter 28	28OfficeMove.mpp
Chapter 31	31WebDev.mpp 31DirectMailCampaign.mpp
Chapter 32	32DirectMailCampaign.mpp 32DirectMailCampaign1.mpp 32ComparisonReport.mpp
Online Resources	Microsoft-Sponsored Resources for Project 2010 Project Desktop Basics Project Server Basics Discussion Forums and Social Media Developer Information Project Certification Independent Resources for Project 2010 Organizations Experts and Resources Blogs and Discussions

Acknowledgments

Work on this book was marked by layers of transition: Microsoft Project transitioning to a new paradigm, Microsoft Press and O'Reilly Media transitioning into a new partnership, me transitioning into a new way of working and thinking.

Thanks go out to Andreea Marinescu for her hard work and enthusiasm while writing the enterprise project management chapters under a tight deadline. I'm especially grateful to Bonnie Biafore for writing several other chapters and for being expert, clone, friend. She assured me that everything would be fine, and as always, she was right.

Much appreciation to Ulhas Samant and Thuy Le for their insightful technical editing. Their comments made this book accurate and more usable. Many thanks go to Brian Kennemer for his technical review of certain chapters.

Thanks to O'Reilly acquisitions editor Kenyon Brown for keeping the train moving steadily forward. I'm grateful for my agent Claudette Moore, with her cheerful encouragement and creative thinking. I'm indebted to John Pierce, copyeditor, and Holly Bauer, production editor. Their professionalism and precision is a world I love to inhabit.

Scott Chapman and Ron Luchansky at Project Hosts graciously provided me with a invaluable enterprise project management hosted setup.

My friends gave me so much encouragement and always said or did exactly the right thing for me. Thanks to my mom, Song Ai Soon Remhof, and to my brother, Lester Remhof.

Thanks most of all to my wonderful husband and traveling companion through life's journey, Craig Stover. He knew when to ask the tough questions and when to just empathize. He knew how to prevent procrastination and when to make me stop and get some sleep. He's my biggest fan—it's pretty cool when he shows off my books.

Finally, thanks to you, reader and project manager. Your projects can and do change the world. Remember, there's no end to the incredible things you can do with a well-planned and well-run project.

Support and Feedback

The following sections provide information on errata, book support, feedback, and contact information.

Errata & Support

We've made every effort to ensure the accuracy of this book and its companion content. If you do find an error, please report it on our Microsoft Press site at oreilly.com:

1. Go to *http://microsoftpress.oreilly.com*.
2. In the Search box, enter the book's ISBN or title.
3. Select your book from the search results.
4. On your book's catalog page, under the cover image, you'll see a list of links.
5. Click View, Submit Errata.

You'll find additional information and services for your book on its catalog page. If you need additional support, please e-mail Microsoft Press Book Support at

mspinput@microsoft.com

Please note that product support for Microsoft software is not offered through the addresses above.

We Want to Hear from You

At Microsoft Press, your satisfaction is our top priority, and your feedback our most valuable asset. Please tell us what you think of this book at

http://www.microsoft.com/learning/booksurvey

The survey is short, and we read every one of your comments and ideas. Thanks in advance for your input!

Stay in Touch

Let's keep the conversation going! We're on Twitter: *http://twitter.com/MicrosoftPress*.

How to Access Your Online Edition Hosted by Safari

The voucher bound in to the back of this book gives you access to an online edition of the book. (You can also download the online edition of the book to your own computer; see the next section.)

To access your online edition, do the following:

1. Locate your voucher inside the back cover, and scratch off the metallic foil to reveal your access code.
2. Go to *http://microsoftpress.oreilly.com/safarienabled*.
3. Enter your 24-character access code in the Coupon Code field under Step 1.

(Please note that the access code in this image is for illustration purposes only.)

4. Click the CONFIRM COUPON button.

A message will appear to let you know that the code was entered correctly. If the code was not entered correctly, you will be prompted to re-enter the code.

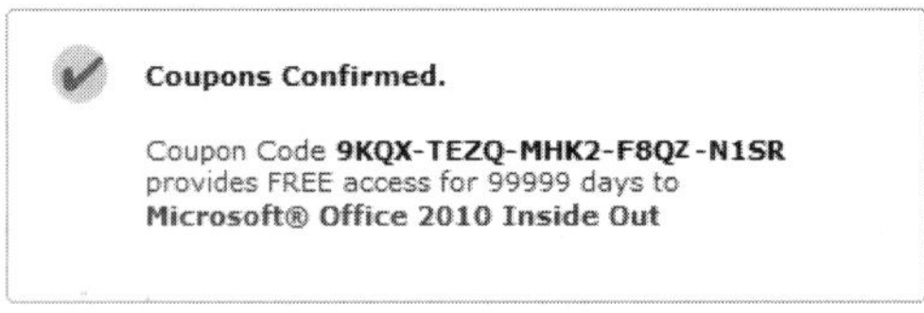

Coupons Confirmed.
Coupon Code 9KQX-TEZQ-MHK2-F8QZ-N1SR
provides FREE access for 99999 days to
Microsoft® Office 2010 Inside Out

5. In this step, you'll be asked whether you're a new or existing user of Safari Books Online. Proceed either with Step 5A or Step 5B.

5A. If you already have a Safari account, click the EXISTING USER – SIGN IN button under Step 2.

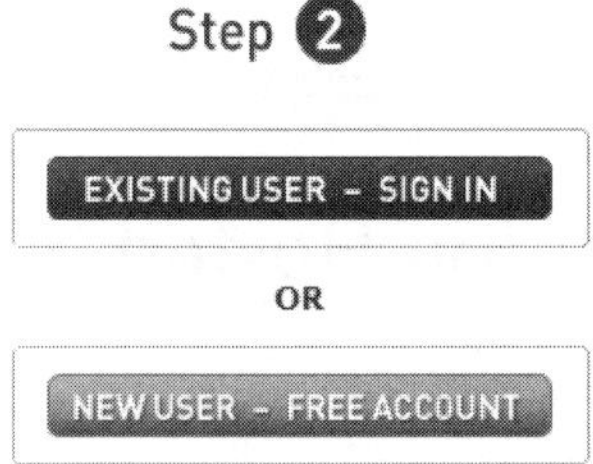

5B. If you are a new user, click the NEW USER – FREE ACCOUNT button under Step 2.

- You'll be taken to the "Register a New Account" page.
- This will require filling out a registration form and accepting an End User Agreement.
- When complete, click the CONTINUE button.

6. On the Coupon Confirmation page, click the My Safari button.

7. On the My Safari page, look at the Bookshelf area and click the title of the book you want to access.

How to Download the Online Edition to Your Computer

In addition to reading the online edition of this book, you can also download it to your computer. First, follow the steps in the preceding section. After Step 7, do the following:

1. On the page that appears after Step 7 in the previous section, click the Extras tab.

2. Find "Download the complete PDF of this book," and click the book title.

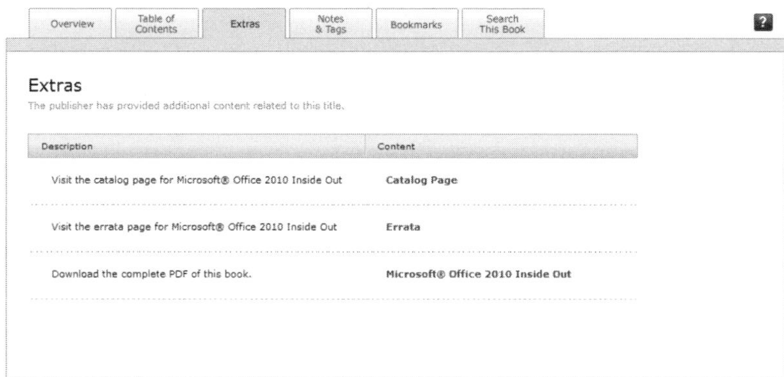

A new browser window or tab will open, followed by the File Download dialog box.

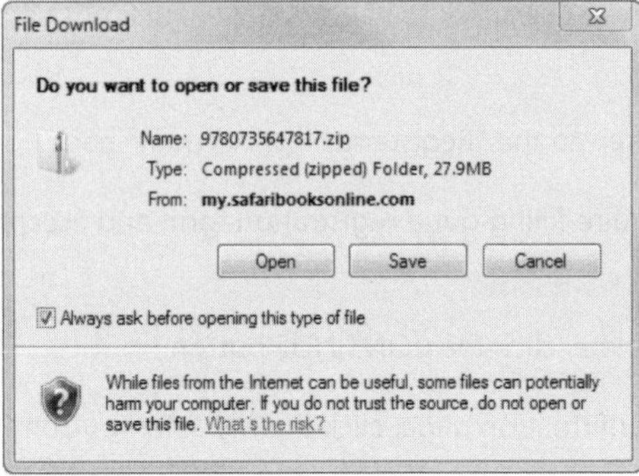

3. Click Save.

4. Choose Desktop and click Save.

5. Locate the .zip file on your desktop. Right-click the file, click Extract All, and then follow the instructions.

> **Note**
> **If you have a problem with your voucher or access code, please contact *mspbooksupport@oreilly.com*, or call 800-889-8969, where you'll reach O'Reilly Media, the distributor of Microsoft Press books.**

PART 1

Project Fundamentals

Before you can use the sample files for Chapter 1, you'll need to install them from this book's companion content website. For more information about downloading and installing the sample files, see "About the Companion Content" on page xxviii.

CHAPTER 1

Introducing Microsoft Project 2010

Let's say you are a supremely multitasking product specialist for an up-and-coming startup company. You handle research, development, material procurement, and marketing for your suite of products. On top of all this, you now have the responsibility of managing the project for the launch of your company's newest product.

On the other hand, we could say that you are an accomplished project management professional who manages projects for several departments in your organization at any given time. You're responsible for managing thousands of tasks, hitting hundreds of deadlines, and assigning scores of resources. You need to plan and monitor each project, work with different managers, and make the best use of resources—some of whom might work on only one project and others who might be shared among several of your projects.

As these two scenarios illustrate, project management is a process and a discipline that can be the full focus of your career or one of many aspects of your job description.

Numerous industries rely on sound project management for their success. Here are just a handful:

- Construction
- Filmmaking
- Computer system deployment
- Logistics
- Engineering
- Publishing
- Events planning
- Software development

Across different industries, there are common project types, for example:

- New business startup
- New product development
- New service rollout
- Computer system deployment
- Training development and delivery
- Website development
- Conference and trade show exhibition
- Office move
- Marketing campaign

Regardless of the size of your organization, the scope of your projects, or even the number of projects you find yourself managing simultaneously, effective project management is vital at the start of a project. This is when you determine what needs to be done, when, by whom, and for how much money. Effective project management is also essential after you kick off the project, when you are continually controlling and managing project details. You frequently analyze the project—tracking the schedule, the budget, resource requirements, and the scope of tasks. In addition, you manage the level of quality in the project, plan for risks and contingencies, and communicate with the members of the project team as well as with upper management or customers.

Throughout this intricate process of planning and tracking your project, Microsoft Project 2010 is a smart and trustworthy assistant that can help you manage the many responsibilities associated with your project. Many software applications can help you work toward producing a specific result that you can print, publish, or post. And it's true that you use Project 2010 to set up a project schedule and print reports that reflect that schedule. However, Project 2010 goes far beyond just the printed outcome. This is a tool that helps you brainstorm, organize, and assign your tasks as you create your schedule in the planning phase. Project 2010 then helps you track progress and manage the schedule, resources, and budget during the execution phase. All this so you can reach your real objective—to successfully achieve the goals of your project on schedule and under budget.

Using Project 2010—An Overview

Project 2010 is a specialized database that stores and presents thousands of pieces of data related to your project. Examples of such data include tasks, durations, links, resource names, calendars, assignments, costs, deadlines, and milestones.

These pieces of information interrelate and affect each other in a multitude of ways. Underlying this project database is the scheduling engine, which crunches the raw project data you enter and presents the calculated results to you, as shown in Figure 1-1. Examples of such calculated results include the start and finish dates of a task, resource availability, the finish date of the entire project, and the total cost for a resource or for the project.

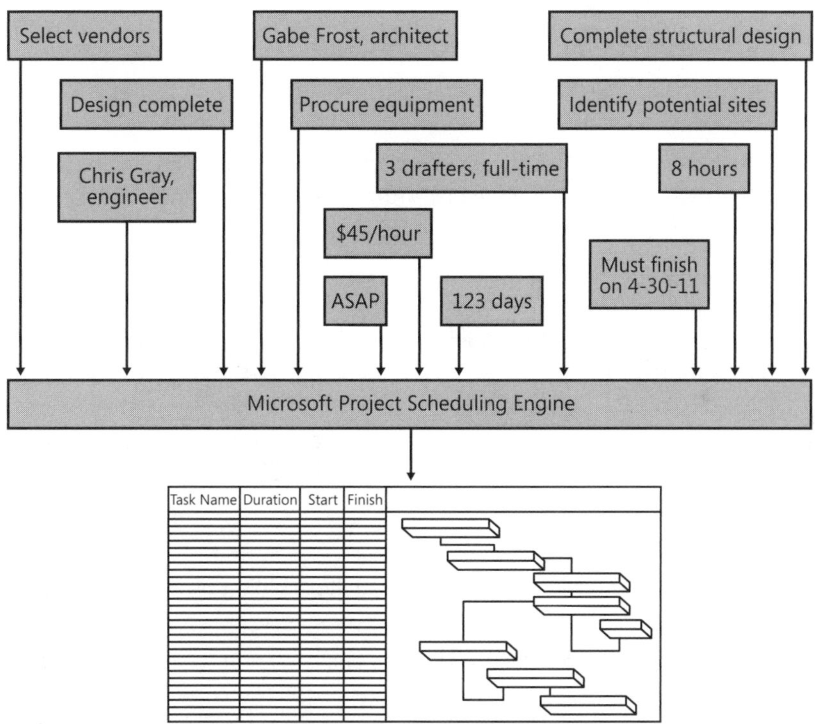

Figure 1-1 Use Project 2010 as your database of project management information.

You can then manipulate and display this calculated data in various views to analyze the planning and progress of your project. This information helps you make decisions vital to the project's success.

You can also communicate your progress and provide the feedback necessary to keep your team and other stakeholders informed of essential project information. You can create and print reports for status meetings or distribution to stakeholders, and you can print or publish certain views or reports to your team's website.

Different Project 2010 editions and companion products are available for you and your organization to get the project management features you need.

Project Standard 2010

Microsoft Project Standard 2010 is the basic desktop edition. Project Standard 2010 has all the essential features for individual project management, including the following:

- Task scheduling
- Resource management
- Tracking
- Reporting
- Customization

With this substantial tool set, you can start planning, managing, and reporting your project information "straight out of the box"—that is, immediately upon installation. (See Figure 1-2.)

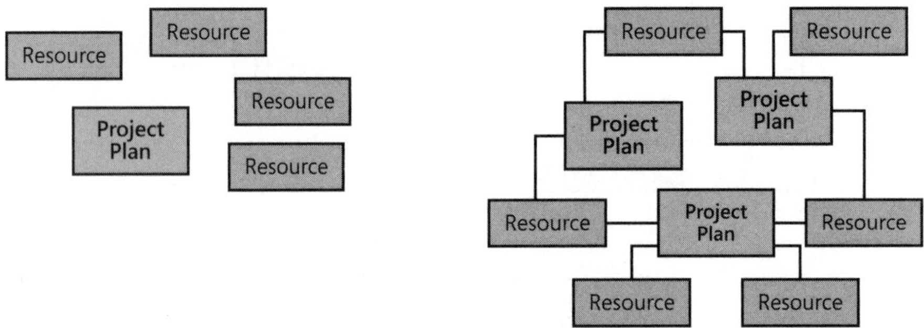

Figure 1-2 Develop and execute single or multiple project plans with Project Standard 2010.

Project Professional 2010

Project Professional 2010 provides everything that Project Standard 2010 does, with some notable additions. Project Professional includes the Team Planner view, the ability to show deactivated tasks for what-if scenarios, and workgroup collaboration features through Microsoft SharePoint Foundation 2010.

In addition, if you're working with Project Server 2010 and Project Web App, Project Professional serves as the client for a complete enterprise project management solution. This solution includes enterprise capabilities for project standardization, resource management, team collaboration, communication, executive analysis, and portfolio management. With Project Professional, project management is fully scalable across multiple departments and divisions in an organization, as shown in Figure 1-3.

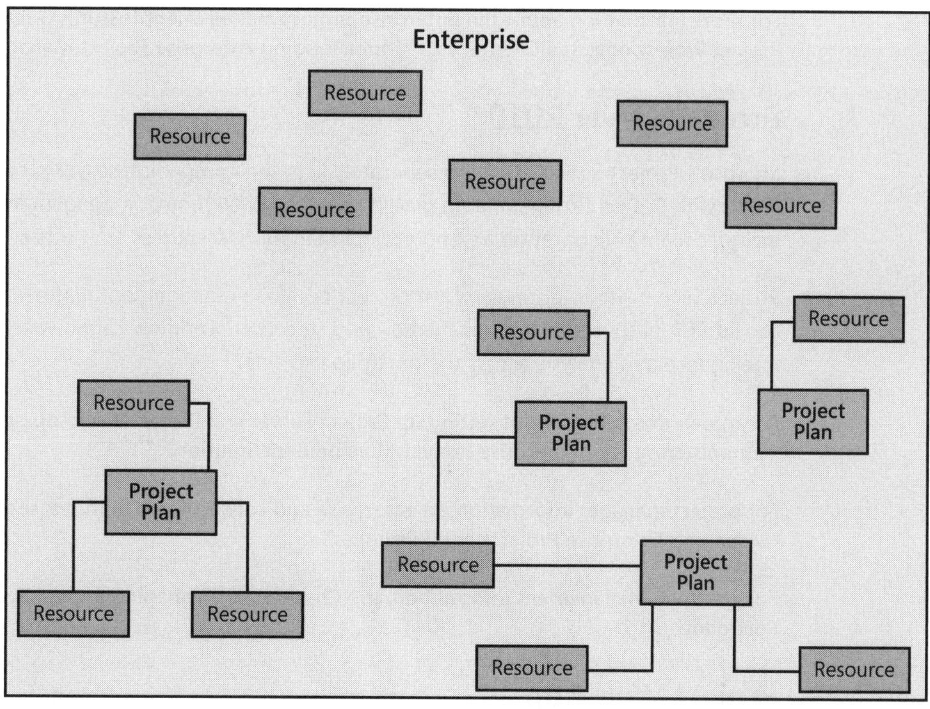

Figure 1-3 Develop and execute project plans across an enterprise with Project Professional.

Project Professional, as connected to Project Server, includes the following features:

- Team collaboration through Project Web App, which is built on Microsoft SharePoint Server 2010. From Project Professional, the project manager can submit assignments to the organization's project server, and resources can view and update their assignments by using Project Web App, the web-based project management interface.
- Global templates, enterprise fields, and other elements that enable your project administrator to standardize and customize the use of Project 2010 for the way your enterprise manages projects.
- The ability to choose and manage resources from the pool of a specific group or the entire company. You can see resource availability across multiple projects and have Project 2010 automatically find resources that will appropriately fill project team requirements.

Project managers use Project 2010 to enter, store, and update project information. They can then send project information such as assignments or task updates to specific resources or grouped team resources through Project Server.

For more information about the enterprise project management features provided through Project Professional, see Chapter 22, "Understanding Enterprise Project Management."

Project Server 2010

Microsoft Project Server 2010 is a separately licensed companion server product that works with Project Professional to provide an enterprise project management solution that includes team collaboration among project managers, resources, and other stakeholders.

Project Server also integrates robust project portfolio management features. These tools provide for proposed project evaluation and selection, workflow capabilities, and business intelligence and analysis across the portfolio projects.

For more information about setting up Project Server and Project Web App, see Chapter 23, "Administering Your Enterprise Project Management Solution."

For project manager information on enterprise and collaboration features, see Chapter 24, "Managing Enterprise Projects and Resources."

For portfolio management information, see Chapter 27, "Managing and Analyzing Project Portfolios."

Project Web App

Microsoft Project Web App is a web-based client application to Project Server. Project Web App provides the user interface for enterprise project management and team collaboration functions for project managers, resources, executives, portfolio managers, and other stakeholders.

Resources and other associated stakeholders in the project can view and work with the information held in Project Server. Resources can review their assigned tasks and other project information in Project Web App. In addition, they can add tasks, update progress information, and submit status reports through Project Server. Upon approval, this information ultimately updates the project plan being maintained by the project manager.

Executives can view high-level project overviews as well as detail information. They can examine projects within a particular program, analyze several projects within a portfolio for resource usage or cost, and make strategic decisions about proposed projects. All information is gathered, organized, and reported consistently throughout the organization, providing a complete and accurate picture of all projects.

For more information about functions for resources and resource managers, see Chapter 25, "Participating on a Team Using Project Web App." Upper managers and other stakeholders should see Chapter 26, "Making Executive Decisions Using Project Web App." Portfolio managers can refer to Chapter 27.

What's New in Project 2010

Project 2010 represents a dramatic step forward in the product's evolution. This is evident from the introduction of user-controlled scheduling and workgroup collaboration features in the desktop version of the product, all the way to the fully realized project portfolio management system in the enterprise version. The way projects are scheduled has made a sizable shift, and in some cases this new approach is much more than just a departure, because it contradicts the way project managers have used previous versions of Microsoft Project. Many new features provide more flexibility and user control, but with that flexibility is needed knowledge of consequences in various aspects throughout the project life cycle.

This section is the first step, providing an overview of the new features throughout Project 2010. As you gain more experience with the features and processes described in this and succeeding chapters, we hope that you'll learn how best to approach the product's new paradigm and tap into the power of the "new Microsoft Project" and use it to your advantage as you manage your projects effectively.

As in previous versions of Microsoft Project, there are two editions of Project 2010: Project Standard and Project Professional. Both versions can be used as a standalone desktop project management application for a single project manager, although Project Professional has a few more features available than Project Standard. Furthermore, with the implementation of Project Server for enterprise project management, a host of additional features becomes available in Project Professional.

Throughout the different configurations of Project 2010, you'll see new features and significant improvements in the following areas:

- Controlling the project schedule
- Analyzing and troubleshooting the schedule
- Collaborating on project details
- Viewing project information
- Working with commands and tools

In Project 2010 enterprise project management, you'll see additional changes in the following areas:

- Managing portfolios, including demand management and workflow
- Planning projects and resource capacity

- Tracking project status and timesheets
- Viewing project information, including the use of new business intelligence tools
- Working with commands and tools
- Managing the project server

This section summarizes the new features in Project Standard, Project Professional, Project Server, and Project Web App. Cross-references indicate where these features are explained in detail elsewhere in this book.

What's New in Project Standard 2010

A major highlight of the new version of Project Standard is the introduction of manually scheduled tasks, which provide more freedom and flexibility when creating a project. New ways to share information, including the use of SharePoint and PDF, provide for better collaboration among team members. You can highlight and focus on the most important tasks and phases using the new Timeline. Making commands easier to find and use, the Office ribbon is now part of Project 2010. The many Microsoft Project menus and toolbars are now a thing of the past.

Controlling the Project Schedule

You now have more choices when it comes to how tasks are created and scheduled:

- **Manually scheduled tasks** You can select whether the tasks in a project are scheduled manually or automatically, as shown in Figure 1-4. With manually scheduled tasks, you can enter durations, start dates, and finish dates without having those entries recalculate other aspects of the schedule. You can enter notes in the duration and date fields. You can even leave those fields blank, as placeholders, until you have more information. You can still designate other tasks in the same project as automatically scheduled tasks, and you can convert manually scheduled tasks to automatically scheduled tasks. This gives you greater flexibility and lets you control the schedule, which can be particularly beneficial in the beginning stages of a project and for phases that are further out and have many unknowns.

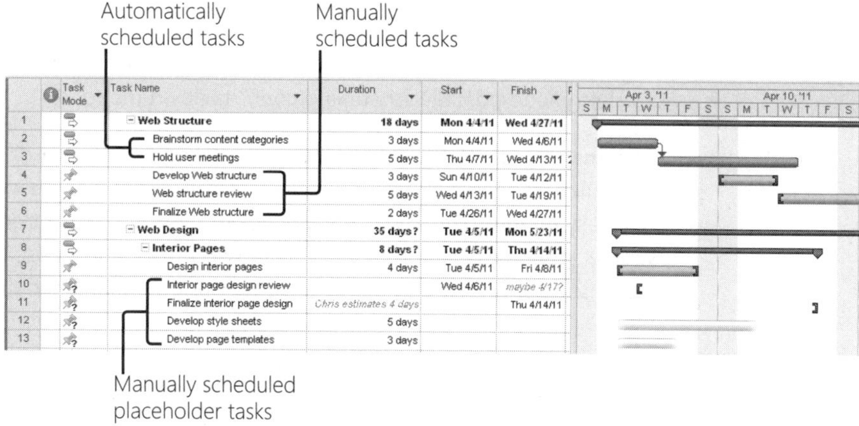

Figure 1-4 Tasks can be automatically or manually scheduled, depending on the needs of the project and the information currently available.

For more information, see "Manually Scheduling Tasks" on page 184.

- **Top-down summary tasks** In past versions of Microsoft Project, you could create a summary task only by making subtasks out of tasks beneath it. You can still do this in Project 2010, but you can also now create a summary task out of the gate. You can insert a summary task above an existing task, or you can create a summary task at the end of the task list. In the latter case, a new subtask is automatically added beneath the new summary task, as shown in Figure 1-5.

Task Mode	Task Name	Duration	Start	Finish
	<New Summary Task>	**1 day**	**Mon 4/4/11**	**Mon 4/4/11**
	<New Task>			

Figure 1-5 Create top-down summary tasks and then add subtasks under them.

For more information, see "Organizing Tasks into an Outline" on page 115.

Analyzing and Troubleshooting the Schedule

In Project 2010, tools are at your disposal to help you see why a task is scheduled the way it is and to alert you to possible scheduling conflicts down the road.

- **Task Inspector** This tool lists all the scheduling factors that drive how a task is scheduled, as shown in Figure 1-6. Such factors might include whether the task is manually or automatically scheduled, its duration, any dependency links, date constraints, resource calendars, overallocated resources, and so on. In some cases, the Task Inspector provides solutions to current or potential scheduling problems.

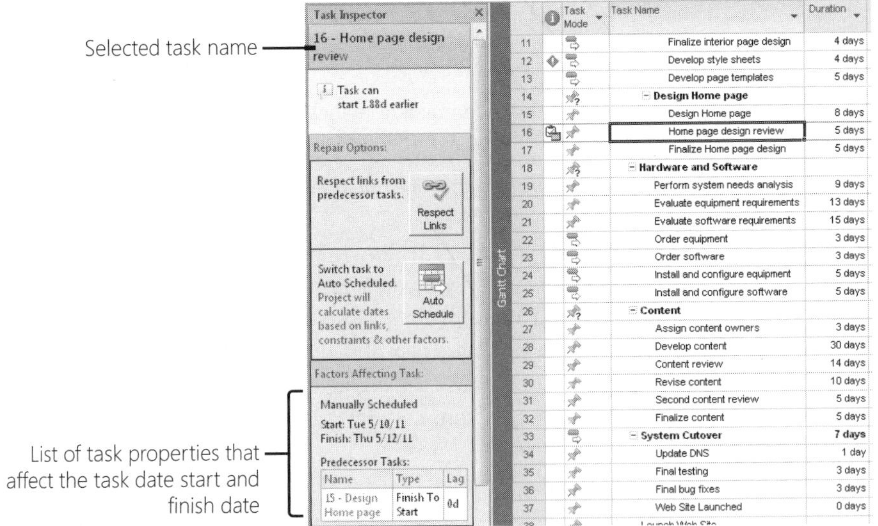

Figure 1-6 The Task Inspector lists all schedule "drivers" for a selected task.

For more information, see "Reviewing the Factors That Affect a Task Start Date" on page 240.

- **Schedule warnings and indicators** If Project 2010 detects a condition in the schedule that is causing a current or potential schedule conflict, a visual cue appears in the task information at the point of the problem. You can click that visual cue to get more information, and then use the Task Inspector to see more details and resolve the problem.

- **Compare project versions** In previous versions of Microsoft Project, the Compare Projects feature was an add-in. Now it's built in to Project 2010, and provides a comprehensive view that shows differences between two projects, line by line, as shown in Figure 1-7. This can be useful in a variety of situations—for example, when building a new project and taking input from several sources, or when you've based a new project on an existing project and you want to compare detailed information between the two.

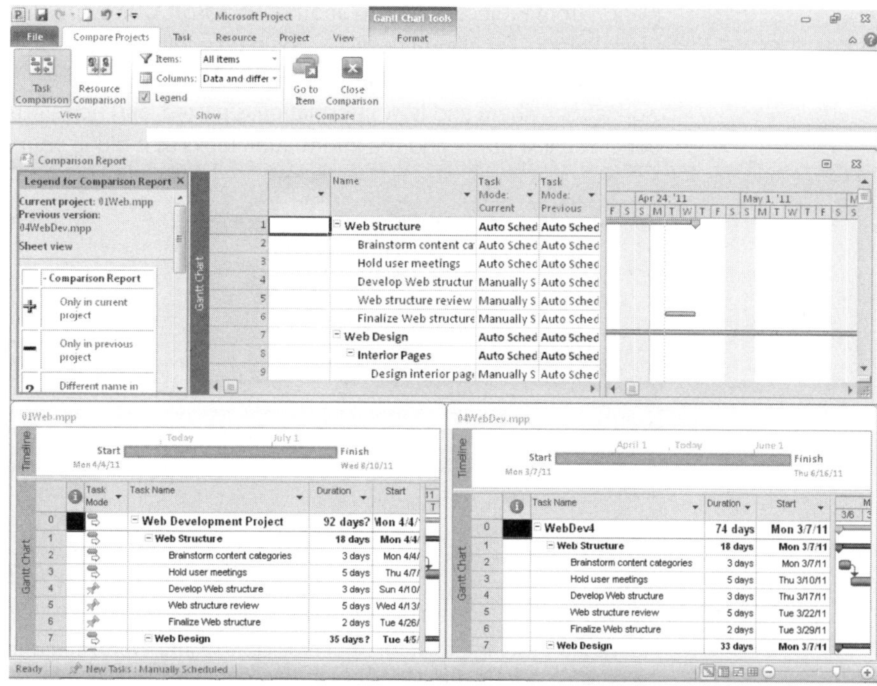

Figure 1-7 The Compare Projects report shows differences between two project files.

For more information, see "Comparing Project Plans Side by Side" on page 1223.

Collaborating on Project Details

Project collaboration among team members and other stakeholders is always an essential component to effective project management. Project 2010 adds new functionality with its integration with SharePoint. Project 2010 also lets you copy and paste information between applications and provides additional file formats to add to its set of robust collaboration features.

- **Save to SharePoint** You can facilitate more collaboration by saving (although not synchronizing) a project file to a site created with SharePoint Foundation or SharePoint Server.

For more information, see "Save a project to SharePoint by using Project Standard 2010" on page 789.

- **Enhanced copy and paste to other applications** When you copy and paste information from Project 2010 into another Microsoft Office application such as Microsoft PowerPoint or Excel, outline levels, column headings, and formatting are maintained as they were in the project file, as shown in Figure 1-8. There's no longer any guesswork about where and how information is pasted, and no reformatting has to be done. You just paste, and the information looks as it did in your project file.

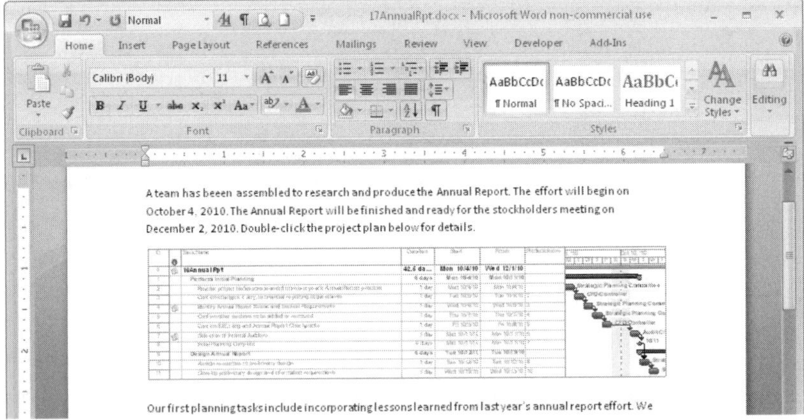

Figure 1-8 Paste information from Project 2010 into Word, and the outline levels, column headings, and formatting look just as they did in the project plan.

For more information, see "Copying from Project 2010 to Another Application" on page 647.

- **Save to PDF/XPS** You can save a project view or report as a PDF (Portable Document Format) or XPS (XML Paper Specification) file without needing to install any other program, as shown in Figure 1-9. With either of these formats, you can be sure that your file preserves its original formatting and is not editable. The files are also easy to open and read on any computer. This is especially important because you can't assume that everyone who needs to see your project information has access to Project 2010.

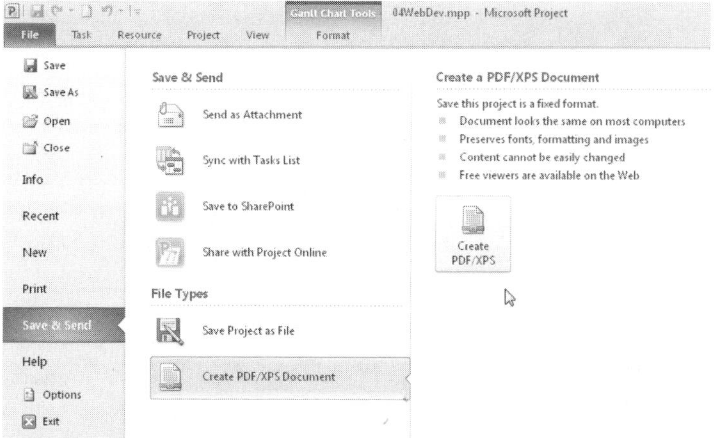

Figure 1-9 Save a view as a PDF or XPS file to ensure that it looks exactly as you intended when your recipients open the file on their computers.

For more information about PDF and XPS, see "Working with Common Cross-Application File Formats" on page 1221.

- **Backward compatibility** Project 2010 readily opens files created in previous versions of Microsoft Project. This means that a converter is not necessary to open files created in earlier versions.

- **Scalable 64-bit compatibility support** Project 2010 is offered as a 32-bit or 64-bit installation. The 64-bit compatibility provides improvements in performance, which is particularly helpful for project managers who regularly work with very large projects or complex structures of master projects and subprojects.

Viewing Project Information

The new Timeline lets you see key phases or tasks, keeping you focused on the big picture. If you're familiar with Excel, you'll like how text wraps and columns are added in any sheet view. There are new ways to zoom, draw, and color elements in your plan.

- **Timeline view** You can see the highlights of your entire schedule or review specific dates and deadlines with the new Timeline, available at the top of every view throughout the project plan, as shown in Figure 1-10. You can select which tasks, phases, or milestones to include in the Timeline, making it easy for you to control the content and present the most relevant information for your own everyday reference or for your audience. With its rich formatting and visual effects, the Timeline is a prime candidate for copying and pasting into other applications, like Outlook, PowerPoint, or Visio, for sharing key project information with stakeholders.

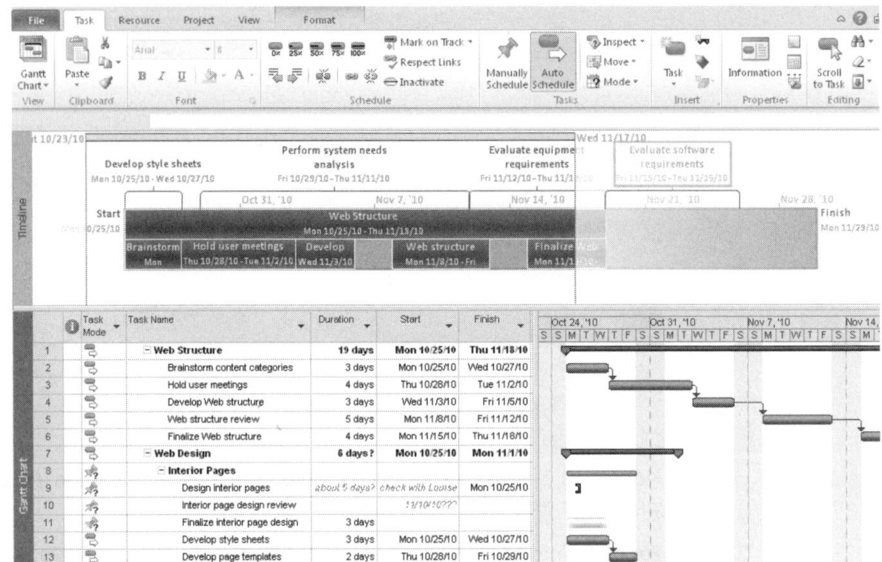

Figure 1-10 Use the Timeline to view the highlights or milestones you want to keep at the forefront.

For more information, see "Highlighting Tasks with the Timeline" on page 134.

- **Add new columns quickly** Every table throughout Project 2010 includes a blank column into which you can simply enter data without first defining the column's data type, as shown in Figure 1-11. This provides for a more intuitive way to add new columns, especially columns for custom project information.

Resource Names	*Add New Column*
Designer	
Yolanda Sanchez	
Designer	
Designer	
Designer	
Designer	
Yolanda Sanchez	

Figure 1-11 Use the Add New Column column to quickly customize a table.

For more information, see "Hiding and Showing Columns" on page 158.

- **Text wrap** Row heights now adjust automatically to displa cell, as shown in Figure 1-12. This makes it easy to see all the in especially Task Name or Resource Name cells, with minimal colun

Task Name	Duration
Define the Opportunity	**13 days**
Research the market and competition	3 days
Interview owners of similar businesses	5 days
Identify needed resources	2 days
Identify operating cost elements	2 days

Figure 1-12 Long task names can now easily be accommodated because of text wrapping.

- **Zoom slider** You can use the Zoom slider in the lower-right corner of the Project 2010 window to zoom the timescale of a time-based chart in or out, as shown in Figure 1-13. This makes working with the Gantt Chart or Resource Usage view so much more convenient.

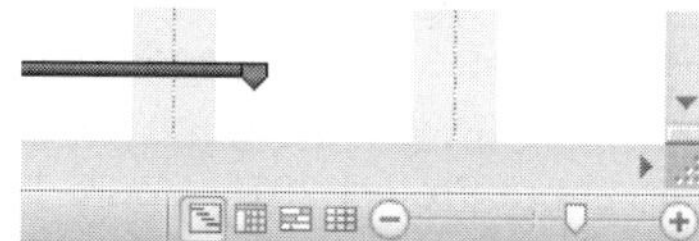

Figure 1-13 Use the Zoom slider to adjust the timescale to more or less detail.

- **Expanded color palette and formatting** More colors are now available for bar styles, font colors, and backgrounds. Gantt chart color schemes can help personalize your project, and the new drawing tools help you emphasize important schedule details.

For more information about the drawing tools, see "Marking Up a Schedule with Drawing Tools" on page 1080.

Working with Commands and Tools

Like the other Microsoft Office applications, Project 2010 now incorporates the ribbon, Quick Access Toolbar, Backstage view, and context-sensitive right-click menus and toolbars. These all make working with Project 2010 more familiar and intuitive, and allow power users to work even faster.

- **Ribbon interface** Part of what's known as the *Office Fluent user interface,* used throughout Microsoft Office, the ribbon is now integrated into Microsoft Project. Instead of arranging commands in drop-down menus and toolbars, the ribbon arranges commands logically in tabs and groups and presents them graphically, as shown in Figure 1-14. The ribbon can change dynamically depending on which view of the project plan you're showing.

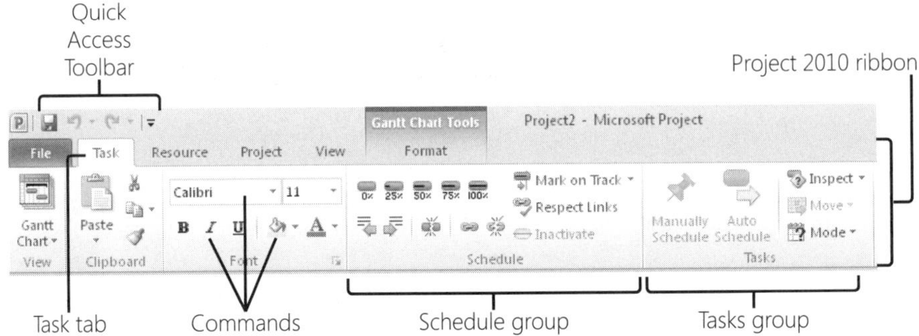

Figure 1-14 Use the ribbon to find and use Project 2010 commands and tools.

For more information about the ribbon, see "Using the Project Ribbon" on page 30.

- **Quick Access Toolbar** The Quick Access Toolbar is another aspect of the Fluent user interface. This toolbar is always present in the upper-left corner of the Project 2010 window, and it can be customized with your most frequently used commands.
- **Backstage view** Tools, templates, and program options are available in the new Backstage view. The Backstage view is where you save and print files, create new project plans or open existing ones, and set your program preferences and options. It's also where you go to get Help about Project 2010. Figure 1-15 shows the Print Backstage view.

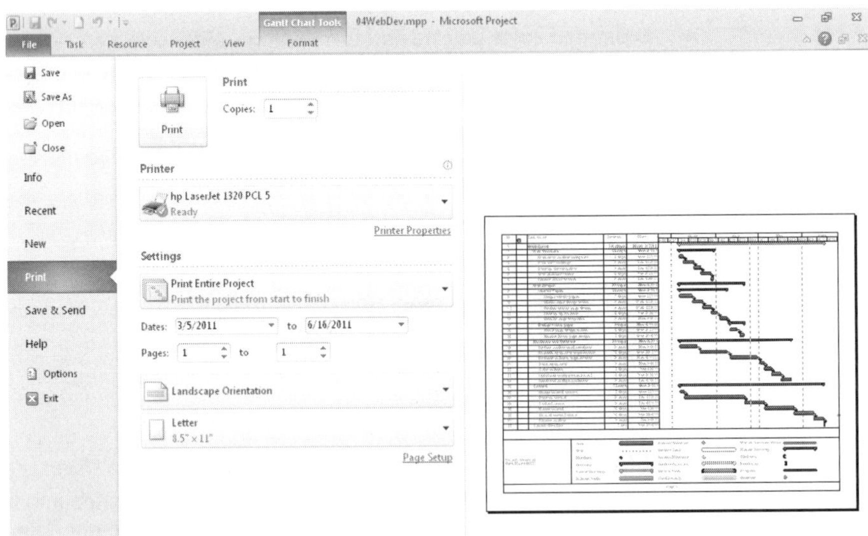

Figure 1-15 Several pages of the Backstage view help you set file preferences and manipulate your project files.

- **Context sensitive menus and mini-toolbars** You can quickly find the most commonly used commands in a particular context with a well-placed right-click on the Project 2010 window. In most places, a menu appears that shows commands that apply to the area or content where you clicked. In some places, a mini-toolbar also appears to provide even more context-sensitive options. (See Figure 1-16.)

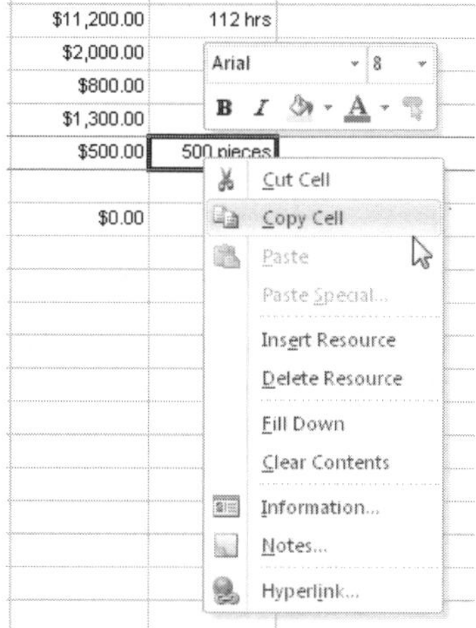

Figure 1-16 Right-click an area of the Project 2010 window to see a menu of context-sensitive commands, and sometimes a mini-toolbar.

What's New in Project Professional 2010

Project Professional 2010 includes all the new features of Project Standard 2010. In addition, Project Professional 2010 includes features for managing resource teams and deactivating tasks.

You can look at your schedule in different ways by using the Team Planner, by synchronizing project workgroup information in SharePoint, and by inactivating and reactivating tasks in Project Professional 2010.

- **Team Planner** Visually arrange the scheduling and assignment of tasks along a graphical timeline by using the new Team Planner view. You can assign tasks, reassign tasks, or reschedule tasks to when resources are available by dragging and dropping on a resource timeline grid, shown in Figure 1-17. Use the Team Planner view not only to rearrange tasks and assignments, but to understand how much resources are underworked or overworked or where tasks are bunching up.

INSIDE OUT Some features from previous versions are discontinued in Project 2010

The following is a list of Project 2007 features that are no longer available in Project 2010.

- **Project guides** Previous versions included a set of project guides to help set up tasks and resources, to track progress, or to generate reports. Although these are discontinued, you can use Microsoft Visual Basic for Applications (VBA) to enable any custom project guides you might have created.
- **Double-click to enable task splitting** Task splitting is still available; you just single-click to enable it instead.

  For more information, see "Splitting Tasks" on page 420.
- **Resource availability graphs from the Assign Resources dialog box behave differently** You can only see the graph of one resource at a time. However, using the combination view that appears, you can still page through multiple resources assigned to a single task, or see the resources assigned to a different task.

  For more information, see "Finding the Right Resources for the Job" on page 290.
- **Former add-ins are now built-in features** The Copy Picture, Adjust Dates, and Compare Project Versions commands are now built in to Project 2010, and add-ins are no longer needed for these functions.
- **Save as Excel PivotTable** You cannot save Project 2010 data as an Excel PivotTable file. However, you can still create Excel visual reports that use your project data in an Excel PivotTable format. You can export earned value information and see S-curves of this data in Excel. You can also now save Project 2010 data in other Excel formats, including .xlsx and .xlsb.

  For more information about visual reports, see "Generating the Right Reports" on page 541. For more information about saving project information in an Excel file format, see "Saving and Opening with Different File Formats" on page 1214.
- **Add-ins and sample macros** Add-ins and sample macros provided with Project 2007 are no longer available. These include the PERT Analysis, Format_Duration, ResMgmt_TaskEntry, Rollup_Formatting, Toggle_Read_Only, and Update_File functions.
- **Custom forms** The ability to create custom forms (typically used to create custom dialog boxes or data entry forms) is no longer available. However, you can still use VBA to create such forms.

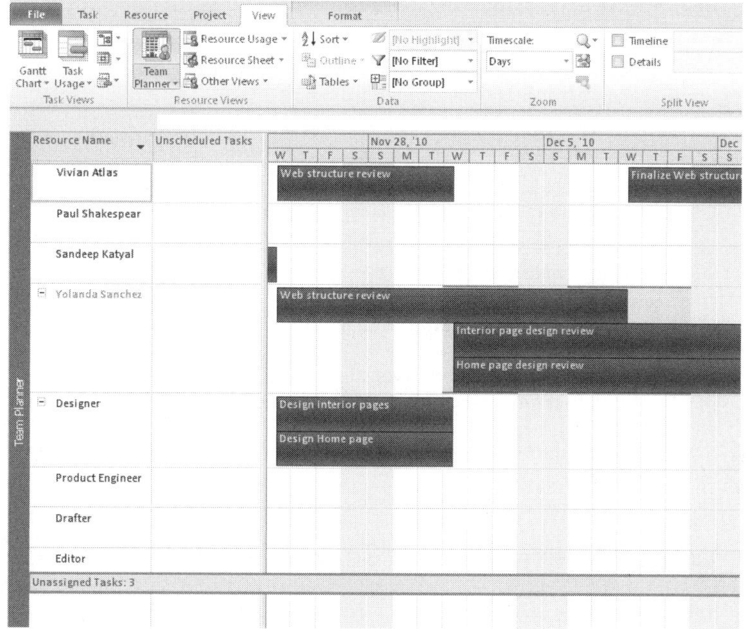

Figure 1-17 The Team Planner provides another view into your tasks, resources, and assignments.

For more information, see "Reviewing Assignments with the Team Planner."

- **SharePoint integration for workgroup collaboration** With Project Standard 2010, you can save a project file to a SharePoint site. Project Professional 2010 takes this further with the ability to publish a project schedule to a SharePoint task list. You can also create projects from a SharePoint task list or convert a list into a Project 2010 schedule. Either way, the schedule information in SharePoint and Project 2010 are synchronized. In addition, you can receive task updates from team members, and those updates are also synchronized.

  For more information, see Chapter 21, "Collaborating as a Team by Using SharePoint."

- **Inactive and active tasks** You can remove tasks from the active schedule while still keeping the task information intact in the project plan. By making tasks inactive, you can run what-if scenarios to see the impact of removing tasks. If you decide to keep those tasks in the plan, you can reactivate them with a single click. The information for inactive tasks is dimmed, as shown in Figure 1-18, and is removed from the schedule calculations. Reactivated tasks have their information recalculated in the schedule as they were before they were made inactive. Keeping inactivated tasks in the project plan is also a good way to record scope cuts, which can be useful information for project archives and future projects.

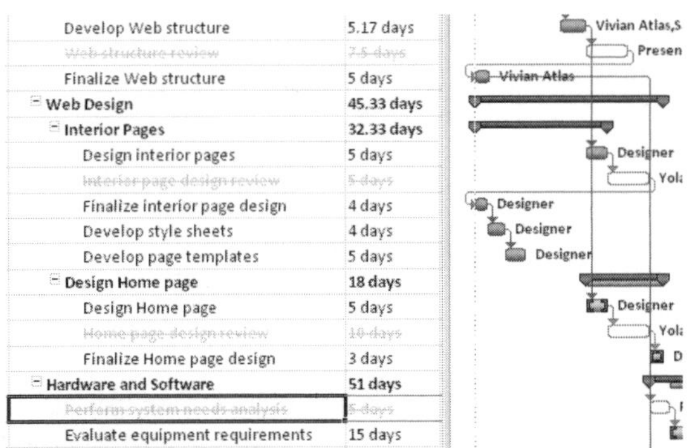

Develop Web structure 5.17 days
Web structure review 7.5 days
Finalize Web structure 5 days
Web Design 45.33 days
Interior Pages 32.33 days
Design interior pages 5 days
Interior page design review 5 days
Finalize interior page design 4 days
Develop style sheets 4 days
Develop page templates 5 days
Design Home page 18 days
Design Home page 5 days
Home page design review 10 days
Finalize Home page design 3 days
Hardware and Software 51 days
Perform system needs analysis 5 days
Evaluate equipment requirements 15 days
Vivian Atlas
Designer

Figure 1-18 Inactivated tasks still show as "ghost" images in your project plan. You can reactivate them later if needed, or just keep them for archival purposes.

For more information about deactivating tasks, see "Changing Project Scope" on page 436.

What's New in Project Server 2010 and Project Web App

In Project Server 2010 and Project Web App, a multitude of new features work together to facilitate portfolio analysis and decision making, project scheduling, resource management, and reporting. Built on the Microsoft SharePoint Server 2010 platform, this provides complete start-to-finish enterprise project management (EPM) and project portfolio management (PPM) solutions on a single server, with a familiar and consistent user interface.

Managing Portfolios

Project portfolio management (PPM) encompasses the methods by which an organization can analyze, prioritize, and maximize proposed projects, and then execute the selected projects while being ever mindful of the overall progress, cost, and resource utilization throughout. The objective of project portfolio management is to achieve the ideal mix of projects that can enable the organization to achieve its strategic goals.

- **Integrated project and portfolio management** In Project 2007, the portfolio management features were handled on a separate, add-on server platform. In Project 2010, project portfolio management functionality is now completely integrated with enterprise project management in the Project Web App user interface. The result is a common and interconnected user experience throughout the entire project portfolio management life cycle.
- **Demand management system** The heart of the project portfolio management capabilities implemented in Project Server 2010 is the demand management system. In this context, *demand management* is the system for selecting project proposals against the organization's strategic business objectives, and then governing the

execution of selected projects against a defined workflow that ensures the fulfillment of key indicators at identified checkpoints in the project life cycle. Different enterprise project categories can be defined and associated with a workflow, a project, and a template.

- **Workflow configuration** As a major component of the demand management system, the *workflow* defines each step in the life cycle of a project. In fact, the workflow essentially implements the demand management system. The portfolio manager can configure all aspects of the workflow to reflect the characteristics of the organization and to ensure the appropriate level of governance. The workflow typically begins with the initial project proposal and includes all approval steps along the way, through to project selection, execution, and closure. The project manager can track the status of the project in all the steps of the workflow. You can use the Project Web App workflow module to define one or more workflows for the different categories of projects in your organization, as shown in Figure 1-19. New enterprise custom fields provide the flexibility that portfolio managers need to customize their workflows.

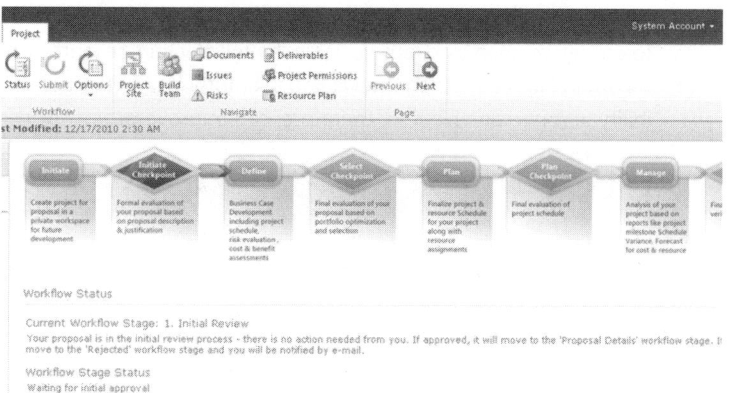

Figure 1-19 New in Project Web App is the ability to view the project workflow.

- **Business driver definition** The identification and prioritization of key business objectives or development areas for an organization is another significant component of the demand management system. Examples might include increasing profit, expanding into new markets, or increasing customer satisfaction. The portfolio manager and others in the leadership team can objectively weigh and prioritize proposed projects against business objectives and more quickly come to a consensus about which projects have the most merit and have the most potential for fulfilling the organization's strategic goals. As shown in Figure 1-20, Project Web App includes an intuitive visual interface for defining and prioritizing business drivers.

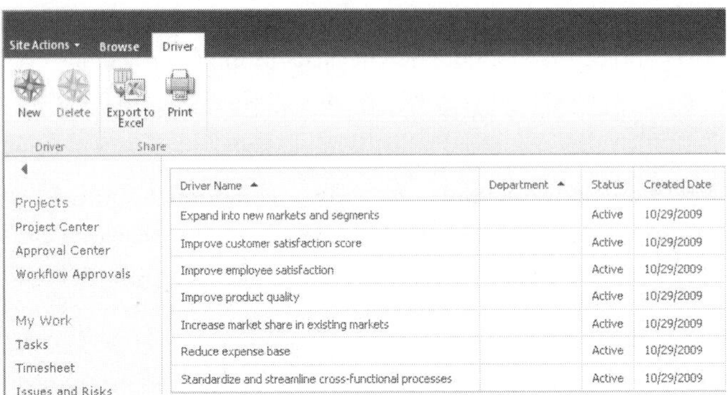

Figure 1-20 An organization can define and prioritize business drivers to help analyze which projects will work toward strategic goals.

- **Portfolio analysis tools** In Project Web App, portfolio managers and executives can use business drivers, the optimizer, and planning tools to analyze the projects in the portfolio. They can see which projects hit the target for key business drivers and can analyze which projects are best meeting the business drivers for that function, within given cost and resource constraints. They can optimize portfolios based on different filters, such as strategic value, financial value, resource utilization, and risk. As shown in Figure 1-21, the views and user interface in Project Web App provide flexibility and perspective and, therefore, can improve project portfolio decision making.

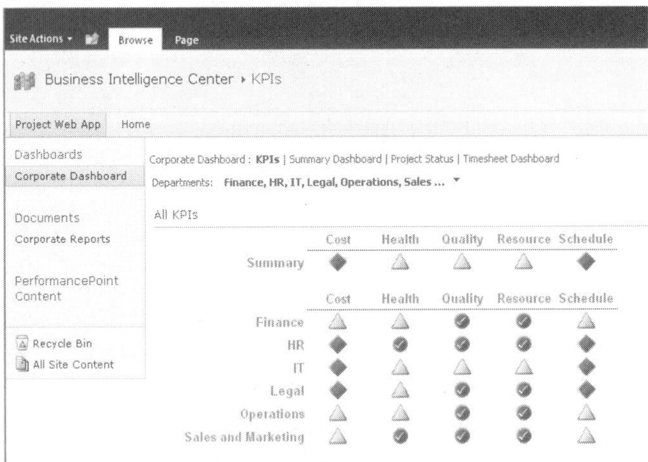

Figure 1-21 In Project Server 2010, visibility and reporting of key performance indicators are now available.

For more information about project portfolio management and demand management, see Chapter 27.

Planning Projects and Resource Capacity

Project managers can now use Project Web Access to edit projects in ways similar or identical to editing projects in the Project Professional user interface. As a result, updating project information is more intuitive and efficient and can be performed wherever project managers have a web browser and Internet access. In addition, a new resource capacity planning feature set makes it possible to maximize resource utilization across the organization.

- **Schedule creation and update** Project managers can build a new schedule and also make simple edits and updates from within Project Web App. In addition, change highlighting and multiple-level undo features are also now available in Project Web App.

- **More robust projects in Project Web App** Project managers can now create projects with more than 100 tasks, a previous limitation in Project Server. Project managers can also assign multiple resources, define task hierarchy in outlines, and set dependencies with task links, all working in Project Web App. (See Figure 1-22.)

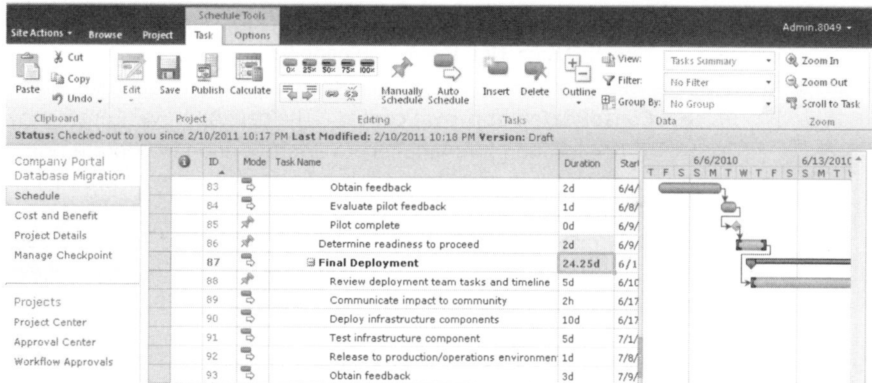

Figure 1-22 Project managers now have much more scheduling flexibility and power when creating and updating schedules in Project Web App.

- **Manual or automatic task scheduling** As in the Project 2010 desktop version, in Project Web App, project managers can now choose whether tasks are scheduled manually or automatically. With manually scheduled tasks, you can set durations, start dates, and finish dates without having those entries recalculate other aspects of the schedule. With automatically scheduled tasks, you can have Project 2010 calculate dates and durations as before. You can have a mix of manually and automatically scheduled tasks, and you can convert one to the other.

- **Resource capacity planning** Project and portfolio managers can view resource capacity across the organization, ensuring maximum resource utilization. This provides insight into demand and availability of generic resources over time. Projects can be rescheduled to maximize resource utilization while maintaining the set schedule dependencies. What-if scenarios regarding staffing levels can be modeled and compared.

For information about managing project schedules and doing resource capacity planning using Project Server 2010 and Project Web App, see Chapter 24.

Tracking Project Status and Timesheets

In Project 2010, time and task progress tracking, status reporting, approvals, and Microsoft Exchange Server integration have been improved.

- **Time reporting enhancements** If teams prefer, task status and timesheet updates can be unified by enabling single entry-mode through a consistent yet flexible user interface. This can save time for team members as well as project managers.

  For more information about submitting task status updates and timesheets, see "Logging Time by Using Timesheets" on page 992.

- **Consolidated approval center** The new Approval Center provides a convenient all-in-one location for managers to approve and incorporate task status and timesheet updates.

- **Delegate approvals** With the enhanced user delegation features, you can easily delegate task status and timesheet approvals to another individual, such as a resource manager or team lead.

  For more information about approving task status updates and timesheets, see "Exchanging Task Progress Information" on page 948.

- **Exchange Server integration** Team members can choose to receive and update their task status and other notifications through Microsoft Outlook or Outlook Web App. Project tasks are shown as Outlook tasks grouped by project name. No Outlook add-in is required.

  For more information about working with task updates and notifications through Outlook, see "Working with Project Tasks in Outlook" on page 998.

Viewing Project Information

You can now easily create reports and dashboards through the reporting layer built on the Microsoft Business Intelligence platform through SharePoint Server. Through the Project Web App interface, you can use these tools to better visualize and track key project performance indicators.

- **Highly customizable** The reporting and dashboard functionality is highly customizable. With the ability to set up summary and detail project information exactly as you need, you can more quickly respond to changing conditions in projects and portfolios.

- **PerformancePoint Services** PerformancePoint, part of the Microsoft Business Intelligence platform, gives you a dashboard designer with a variety of indicators. (See Figure 1-23). Create different dashboards for different purposes and audiences to help you effectively monitor and present portfolio performance.

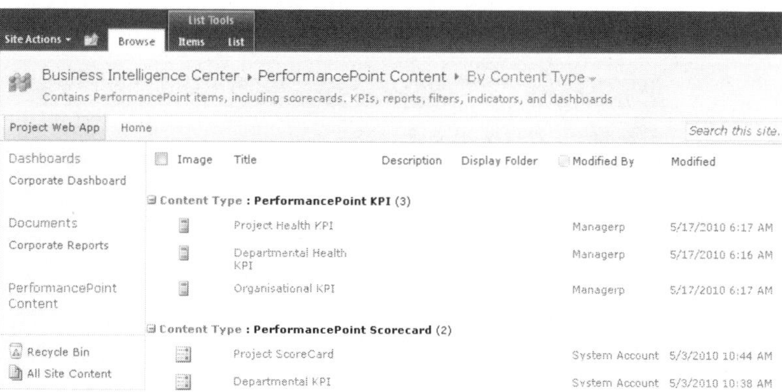

Figure 1-23 Use PerformancePoint content to create dashboards that help you or your audience see key project and portfolio status at a glance.

- **Office reporting services** In addition to PerformancePoint Services, you can use Excel Services, Visio Services, PowerPivot for Excel 2010, and SQL Reporting Services to publish information from a Microsoft Office application.

- **Predefined report templates** You can choose from a variety of predefined report templates that reflect project reporting best practices. Examples include reports on key performance indicator by department, project costs, resource capacity, issues and risks, workflow chart, and more.

For more information about creating and using reports and dashboards, see "Analyzing and Reporting on Project Information" on page 1021.

Working with Commands and Tools

With Project Server 2010 built on the SharePoint Server 2010 platform and the adoption of the ribbon in Project Web App, users experience a more consistent user interface as they move between Project Professional 2010, other Microsoft Office applications, and other SharePoint sites to work in Project Web App.

- **Built on SharePoint Server 2010** Project Web App uses the familiar SharePoint Server interface. In addition, SharePoint enterprise search makes it easy to find project information, including tasks, resources, documents, and more. In addition, teams can be connected and communication enhanced through the use of all the capabilities of SharePoint. This includes wikis, blogs, discussion forums, My Sites, document libraries, and more.
- **Ribbon interface** In Project Web App, the menus and toolbars have been replaced with the ribbon for easier access and grouping of major functions. As shown in Figure 1-24, commands are logically arranged in tabs and groups that are presented graphically and dynamically, depending on which area of Project Web App you're working in.

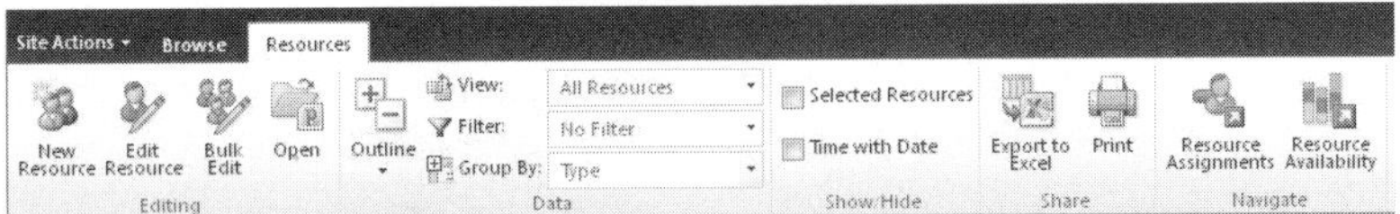

Figure 1-24 Project Web App now uses the ribbon to present commands graphically and dynamically.

For more information about the ribbon, see "Using the Project Ribbon" on page 30.

- **Microsoft Visual Studio Team Foundation Server** Through interoperability with Visual Studio, the world of application development can be easily connected with that of project and portfolio management.

Managing the Project Server

Project server administration functions are simplified in Project Server 2010 and Project Web App. User setup, Project Web App configuration and customization, and security features are centralized for project and portfolio administration.

- **Centralized project server administration** The server settings console provides all project server administration functions in one centralized location for both project and portfolio management capabilities, as shown in Figure 1-25. This includes everything from setting up users and their permissions to setting up project workflow settings.

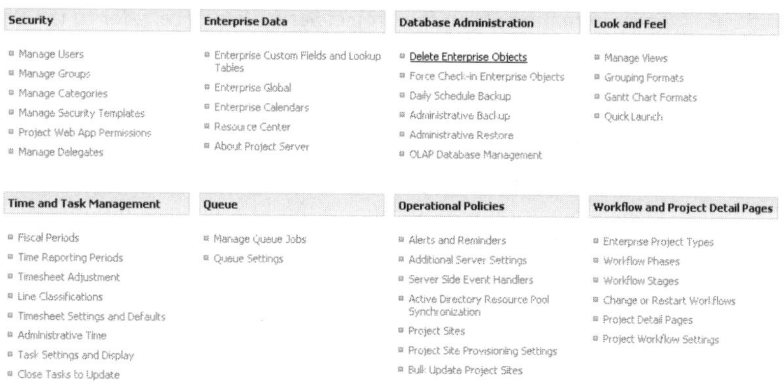

Figure 1-25 Use the Server Settings page in Project Web App to carry out most project server administrator functions.

- **Project access permissions** Within the Project Web App Permissions function, project managers can expand on what the security model allows to create and modify resources and set basic view permissions to better control who has the rights to view or edit projects.

- **Delegate users** With enhanced delegation, users can identify colleagues to act as their delegate when needed. The project server administrator no longer needs to set up delegation rights between users.

- **Custom enterprise fields** Project server administrators and portfolio managers can use custom enterprise fields to customize enterprise project templates the way they're needed throughout the organization. With the custom departmental fields, users in specific departments can focus on their own data, filtering out information that doesn't apply to them. With these custom departmental fields, enterprise project types, resources, and custom fields can be associated with specific departments to maintain the relevancy of project data.

- **Administer reporting cubes** Through the improved interface for working with reporting cubes, project server administrators and portfolio managers can easily add, edit, copy, refresh, and delete reporting cubes.

- **Enhanced customization and scalability** To extend functionality and integrate project information with other applications, Project Server 2010 uses the applications programming interface (API) called the *Project Server Interface (PSI)*. With the PSI, you can access the properties of objects such as Project, Task, and others, and thereby integrate information between your project server and other organizational systems that interact with project management processes, such as accounting, procurement, or human resources. In Project 2010, enhancements to the PSI provide for easier customization to Project Server and Project Web App. Customization is also enhanced by SharePoint Server 2010 and Visual Studio 2010.

For information about the Project Server Interface, refer to the Project 2010 Software Development Kit (SDK), available on the Microsoft Developer Network (MSDN) at *msdn.microsoft.com/en-us/library/ms457477.aspx*.

- **Hosted Project Server solutions** Through one of several Microsoft Project partners, you can access and configure web-based hosting for your enterprise project management solution. Through a third-party hosting provider such as Project Hosts, you can speed up enterprise project management deployment for your organization and reduce your IT infrastructure costs.

For more information about third-party hosting partners, see "Analyzing Your Project Server Requirements" on page 1241.

Using the Project Ribbon

With Project 2010, the Microsoft Office ribbon and Quick Access Toolbar are introduced to the Project user interface. This is a substantial change to the way you access Project 2010 features and tools. If you've been working with any other Microsoft Office applications that use the ribbon and Quick Access Toolbar, you have a head start in understanding how commands are organized. Instead of arranging commands in menus and toolbars, the ribbon presents commands graphically and logically organized in tabs and groups, as shown in Figure 1-26. Often the tabs change depending on which view you're showing. The Quick Access Toolbar shows a handful of the most commonly used commands.

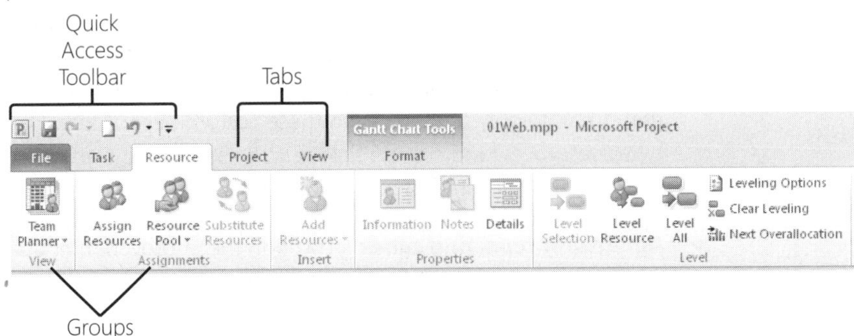

Figure 1-26 Use the ribbon to find and use Project 2010 commands and tools.

Throughout the procedures in this book, directions to find a command are given in the following format: "On the Task tab, in the Schedule group, click Link Tasks." Sometimes the directions are abbreviated to something like "Click Task, Schedule, Link Tasks."

> **Note**
>
> **The look of the ribbon adjusts according to the resolution of your screen and the size of your Project 2010 window. Narrower screens show all groups, but the buttons might be smaller or moved to a drop-down menu instead of appearing directly on the ribbon.**

Minimizing and Expanding the Ribbon

You can hide the ribbon so that only the tab labels are showing, without a tab's groups or buttons. When you click a tab in the minimized ribbon, the full ribbon appears. After you click a button, the ribbon is minimized again. This is a great way to give yourself more working space in the project plan, either temporarily or after you're familiar with where commands are on the ribbon.

Minimize The Ribbon

Expand The Ribbon

In the upper-right corner of the Project 2010 window, click the Minimize The Ribbon icon.

To show the full ribbon again, in the upper-right corner of the Project 2010 window, click the Expand The Ribbon icon.

Using Keyboard Shortcuts to Access Commands

Even though menus are gone, you can still quickly apply commands with keyboard shortcuts, called *access keys*. Every command on the ribbon can be executed by using access keys, which get you to a command in two to four keystrokes. To use access keys to execute a command on the ribbon, follow these steps:

1. Press and release the Alt key.

   KeyTips are displayed above each feature in the current view, as shown in Figure 1-27.

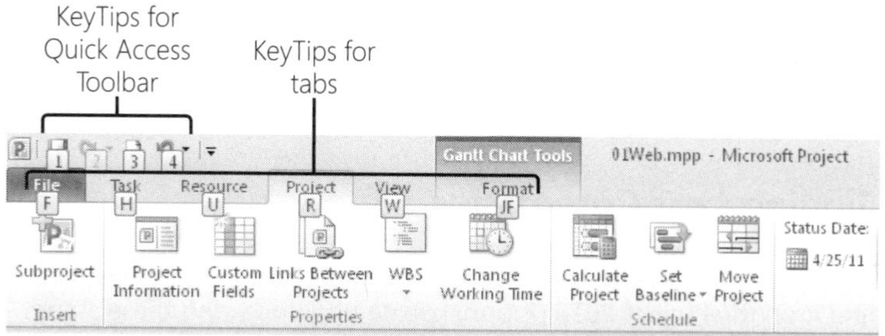

Figure 1-27 Press and release the Alt key to show the KeyTips on the ribbon and Quick Access Toolbar.

2. Press the letter shown in the KeyTip that corresponds with the tab you want to use. Do this even if the tab you want is already showing.

   The tab you select becomes active, and the KeyTips for the features on that tab appear, as shown in Figure 1-28.

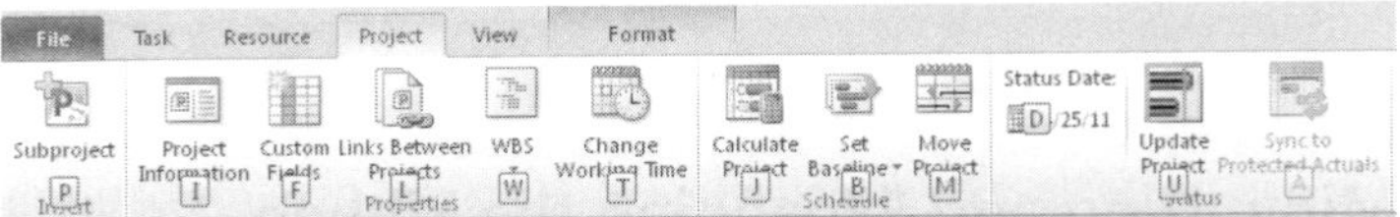

Figure 1-28 KeyTips appear for all features on the selected tab.

3. Press the letter shown in the KeyTip that corresponds with the command you want.

   Depending on the command, a dialog box might open, a drop-down menu might appear, or the command might be executed.

> **Note**
>
> **To cancel the use of the KeyTips, press and release the Alt key or the Esc key.**

To use access keys to execute a command on the Quick Access Toolbar, follow these steps:

1. Press and release the Alt key.
2. Press the KeyTip number that corresponds to the command you want.

   The command is executed.

> **Note**
>
> **KeyTips do not work in the Project Web App ribbon. Because Project Web App is a web-based application, when you press the Alt key, it activates the browser menu for the keyboard instead of showing KeyTips in the ribbon.**

Finding Lost Commands

Suppose that you used a certain command in earlier versions of Project, and now you can't find it on the Project 2010 ribbon. Locate it by following these steps:

1. On the File tab, click Options.

   The Project Options dialog box appears.

2. In the left pane, click Customize Ribbon or Quick Access Toolbar.

   A list of commands appears in the Project Options dialog box.

3. In the Choose Commands From box, click All Commands.

   All commands throughout Project 2010 are listed.

4. Scroll through the list to find the command you want.

5. To find where the command is located on the ribbon, rest the mouse pointer over the command name.

   The location of the command appears, including the name of the tab, group, and command.

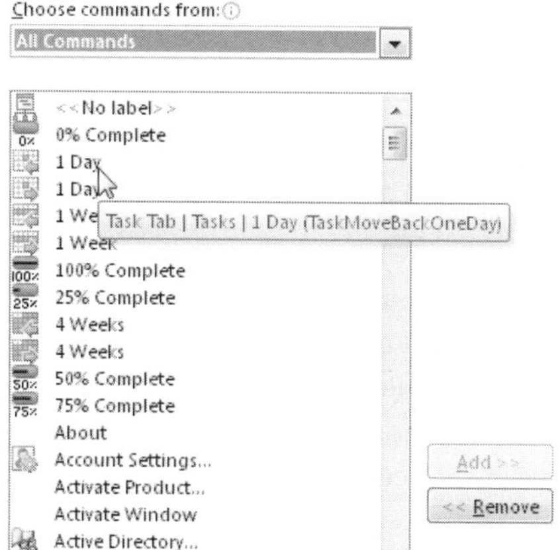

The commands are listed in alphabetical order. You might need to look in a couple different places if you're not sure of the exact command name.

You might also try clicking Commands Not In The Ribbon in the Choose Commands From box. If you need to use a command that's not on the ribbon, you can add it to the Quick Access Toolbar or to a custom group.

For more help on finding commands, use the interactive ribbon guide in Project 2010 online Help at *www.microsoft.com/project/en/us/ribbon_guide.aspx*. Click a graphic of the toolbars and menus from Microsoft Project 2007 to learn where those commands are located on the Project 2010 ribbon.

Customize the Ribbon and Quick Access Toolbar

You can customize the ribbon in a variety of ways. You can add a custom group with the commands you want to an existing tab. You can even create your own custom tab with custom groups arranged on them. For details, see "Customizing the Project 2010 Ribbon" on page 1153.

You can also customize the Quick Access Toolbar with commands you use most frequently. For details, see "Customizing the Quick Access Toolbar" on page 1146.

Learning as You Go

As you work in your project plan, you can quickly get assistance and other information when you need it—from online Help, from discussion forums, and from Project 2010 feedback while you're working.

Note

Previous versions of Microsoft Project included a set of project guides that provided instructions, controls, and wizards to help set up tasks and resources, track progress, or generate reports. Project guides are discontinued in Project 2010. The ribbon takes on some functionality that was previously carried out by the project guides. In addition, you can use Visual Basic for Applications (VBA) to enable any custom project guides you created.

Getting Help

You can find Help topics to assist you with your project plan. A set of Help topics is installed and available with Project 2010 on your local computer. A more comprehensive set of Help topics and other forms of assistance are available on the web through Office.com. You can:

- Browse Project Help contents.
- Search for topics using key words or phrases.
- Browse for more Project Help on Office.com.
- Join and ask questions from a Microsoft Project discussion forum.

Browsing Project Help Contents

If you want to see a list of Help topics, follow these steps:

1. In the upper-right corner of the Project 2010 window, click the Help icon.

   You can also press F1 or, on the File tab, click Help, and then click Microsoft Office Help.

   Project Help appears in a separate window, as shown in Figure 1-29.

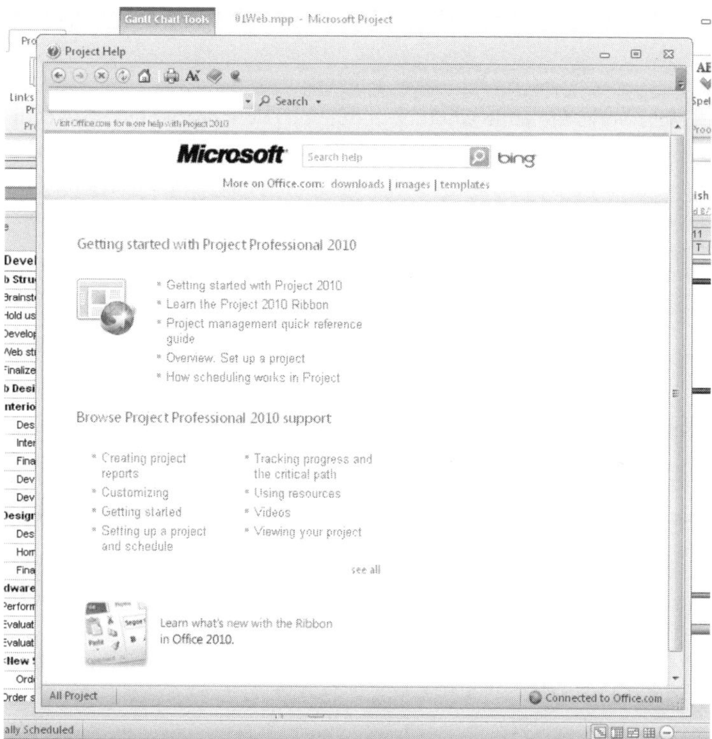

Figure 1-29 Browse through the list of Project Help topics.

2. Click the name of the category you want. If necessary, click a topic under the Subcategories section.

3. Under Topics, click the link for the Help topic you want to view.

If you're connected to the Internet and Office.com, you see even more categories and topics listed in the Project Help window.

INSIDE OUT Get better Help results by connecting to Office.com

You can toggle whether Project 2010 presents Help from your local computer or from Office.com on the web. The current mode shows in the lower-right corner of the Project Help window. If you click the mode button, a menu appears with other choices.

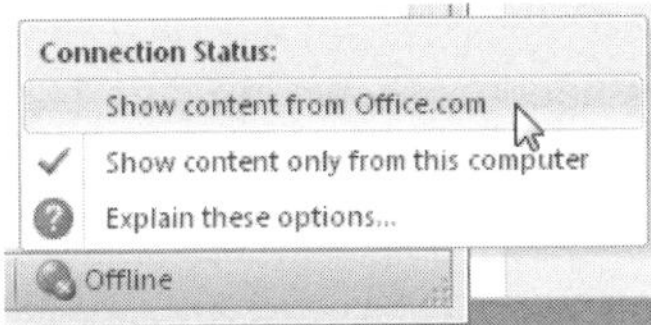

Help works the same whether or not you're connected to Office.com. You can browse categories and topics as usual; the difference is that more categories and topics are available on Office.com because more are being added over time. Also, when you search on a certain word or phrase, you tend to see better results when you're connected to Office.com.

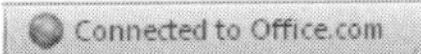

Searching for a Specific Topic

Rather than going through a hierarchical list of topics, sometimes it's faster to just ask a direct question and get a direct answer. If you prefer to get your help that way, search using a question or phrase as follows:

1. In the upper-right corner of the Project 2010 window, click the Help icon.
2. Near the top of the Project Help window, click in the search box.

Search

3. Type the word, phrase, or question in the search box, and then click Search.

   The Project Help window appears with a list of Help topics related to your question, as shown in Figure 1-30.

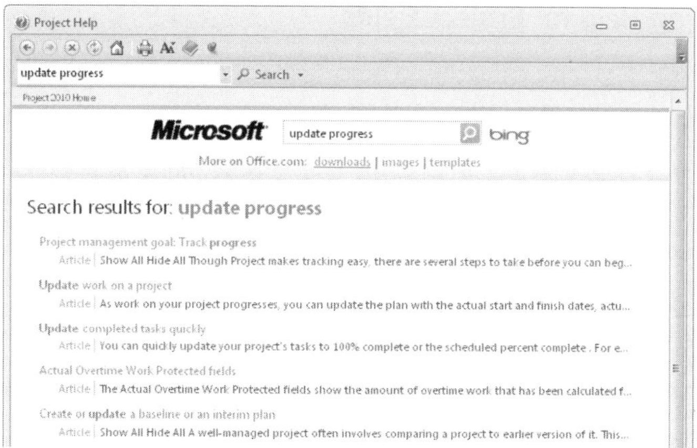

Figure 1-30 The Project Help window lists topics related to your search question.

4. Click a topic that matches what you're looking for, and then read the article about your question.

Back

5. To read a different Help topic that was listed, click the Back button to return to the list of topics, and then click the other topic.

TROUBLESHOOTING

The Project Help window is obstructing your work

When you search for help, the Project Help window appears and floats over the top of your Project 2010 window. Even when you click in the Project 2010 window, the Project Help window stays on top.

The window is designed to stay on top like this because you might want to follow a procedure in a Help topic while working in Project 2010. If this is the case, resize the Project Help window and drag it to the side so that you can still read it but it's out of the way of your work.

If you don't need the Project Help window showing right this minute but want to keep it handy, click its Minimize button to temporarily move it out of the way.

Chapter 1

Getting Help for Project Fields

There is a Help topic for each and every field in Project 2010. One way to find such topics is by browsing the Project Help contents, as follows:

1. In the upper-right corner of the Project 2010 window, click the Help icon.

   Home

   If the Project Help window is already open, click the Home button in the Project Help toolbar.

2. If you're accessing Project Help through Office.com, under the categories, click See All, and then click Reference.

   If you're accessing Project Help from your offline computer, click General Reference.

3. Under Subcategories, click Available Fields Reference.

4. Click the topic for the field you want to learn more about.

   Each field reference topic includes best uses, examples, calculations if applicable, and particular issues to be aware of when working with this field.

You can also open a field reference Help topic if the field is showing in a table. Position your mouse pointer over the column heading; a ScreenTip pops up that provides a brief description of the field. Press F1 while the ScreenTip is showing to display a Help topic for the selected field in a separate Help window.

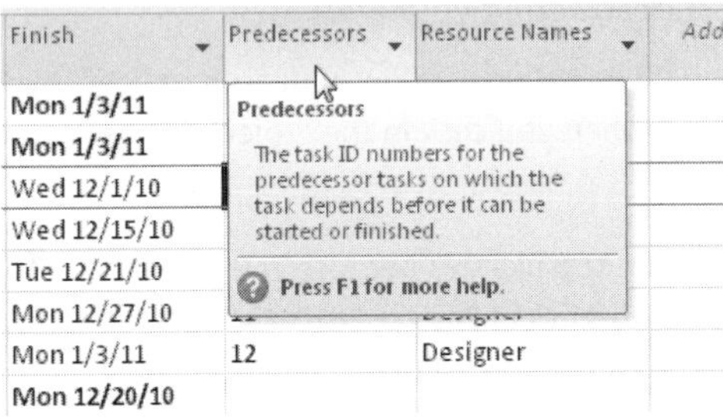

INSIDE OUT **Help for dialog boxes doesn't help**

Many of the more complex dialog boxes in Project 2010 include a Help button. In previous versions of Microsoft Project, you could click that button and read an associated Help topic.

In Project 2010, however, the main Project Help window appears, showing the Home-level Help categories. You have to find the appropriate Help topic yourself.

Your best bet is to browse through those categories to find the topics that seem most related to the dialog box.

Finding Project Assistance on the Web

You have already seen how you can search on a keyword or browse the contents of Project Help topics on Office.com on the web. As long as you're connected to the Internet, you can also simply open Office.com in a full web browser window. To do this, follow these steps:

Getting Started

1. On the File tab, click Help, and then click Getting Started.

   Even if you don't want to see the Getting Started Help topic, this step gets you to the right place quickly.

   The Office.com website appears in a separate web browser.

2. To show just the resources available for Project 2010, in the path showing under the menu bar, click Project, as shown in Figure 1-31.

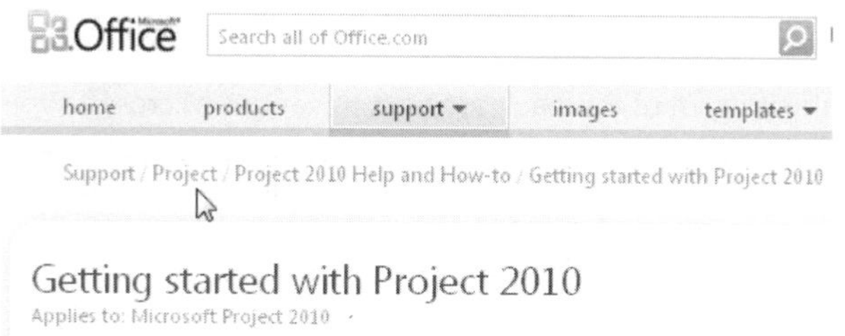

Figure 1-31 Click Project to see more resources for Project 2010 on Office.com.

The Project page appears, as shown in Figure 1-32. This page includes links to videos, demos, top issues, and training courses, in addition to the Help topic categories listed on the right side of the page.

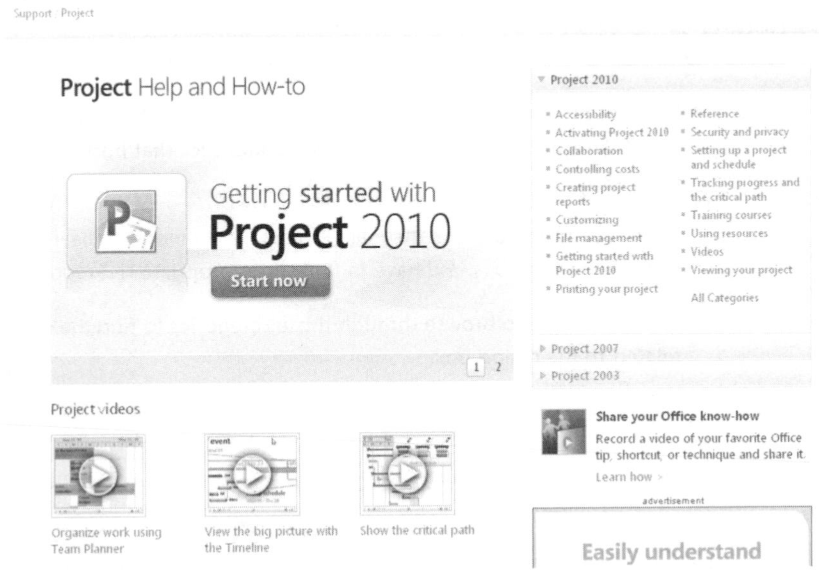

Figure 1-32 The Project page on Office.com includes a variety of online resources from which to learn more about Project 2010.

The following are some highlights of the Project page on Office.com:

- Getting started with Project 2010
- Get to know Project 2010
- Microsoft Project basics
- Introduction to project management
- Project roadmap

  Near the bottom of this page are links to various Microsoft Project community sites, including expert blogs. There is a link to the Project Developer Center, which includes the Project 2010 Software Development Kit and access to Project 2010 topics on Microsoft TechNet.

Following Project 2010 through Social Media

You can keep up with tips, techniques, and news about Project 2010 through the following social media channels:

- **Facebook** *www.facebook.com/pages/Microsoft-Project/95221953802*
- **Twitter** *twitter.com/ProjectHelpTeam*
- **MSDN blog for Microsoft Project** *blogs.msdn.com/b/project/*

For more information about these and other resources, see the Microsoft Project 2010 Inside Out companion website at *oreilly.com/catalog/9780735626874/*.

Joining a Project Forum

It's often easiest to learn from your more experienced buddies. A built-in group of knowledgeable friends willing to help can be found on Office.com. There you will find a Project 2010 discussion forum that can help you find answers to your questions and where you can also learn from questions posed by other users. To find and join a Project 2010 discussion forum:

1. In the address bar of your web browser, enter **www.answers.microsoft.com**.
2. Under Microsoft Office, click More Office Products.
3. Under Answers By Forum, in the Visio, Project, InfoPath, And Access line, click Project.

   The forum page for Microsoft Office For Business Users: Visio, Project, InfoPath, And Access appears, with the discussion items filtered for Microsoft Project.
4. Click in the Office Version box, and then click Office 2010.

   The discussion items are now filtered for Project 2010, as shown in Figure 1-33.

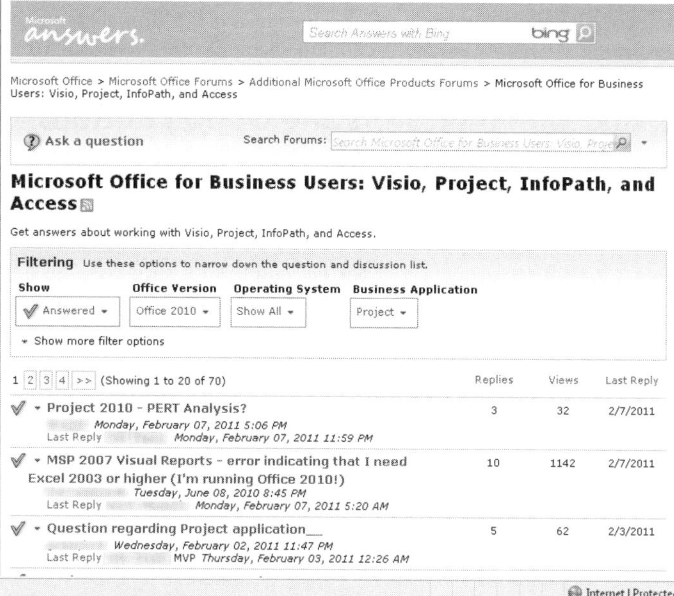

Figure 1-33 The Project discussions page represents a community of Project users and experts who ask and answer questions.

You can search for a particular topic or browse through a list of topics.

5. Before you ask a question, check whether your question has been asked (and answered) previously. Enter a keyword or phrase in the Search Forums box.

   It's a great idea to do this before posting a new question, especially if you're a newer user.

6. If you don't find anything in the archives that answers your question, click the Sign In button to sign in with your Windows Live ID, and then click Ask A Question. A form appears in which you can type your question and post it to the discussion forum.

You'll find that you get great answers to your questions, often quite quickly. If you stick around long enough, you'll soon find that you're knowledgeable enough to answer others' questions. To reply to an existing question, click the Reply button. Enter your answer and post it to the discussion forum.

More advanced Project 2010 users might find the TechNet discussion forums useful.

1. In the address bar of your web browser, enter **www.technet.microsoft.com**.
2. In the menu bar, click Forums.
3. Scroll down and click one of the forum categories under Project Professional or Project Server.

For more information about discussion forums and additional resources to help you learn and use Project 2010, see Appendix B, "Online Resources for Project 2010."

Working with Indicators and Option Buttons

When you make certain types of adjustments to your project plan, Project 2010 presents an indicator with an option button, as shown in Figure 1-34. This is interactive feedback that specifies the action you've just taken, along with implications that the action might have. You see information, especially in certain ambiguous situations, to ensure that the result is really your intention. You also see options to switch to a different action if you intended a different outcome.

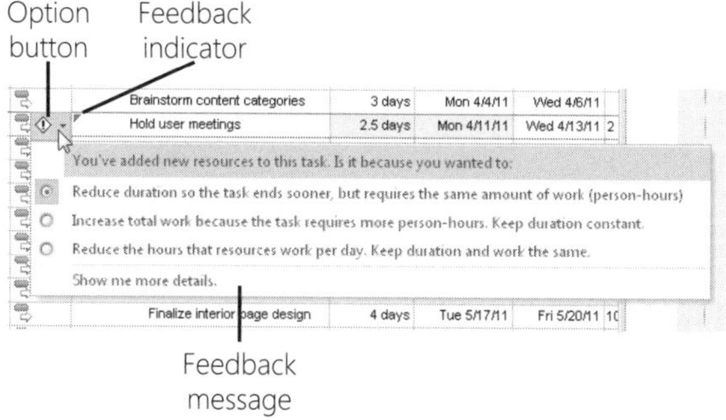

Figure 1-34 An indicator shows as a green triangle in a cell that contains a potential issue that Project wants to confirm. When you move your mouse pointer over the green triangle, the option button appears. Click the button to display the options in a drop-down menu.

Indicators and option buttons might appear for four operations:

- Changing resource assignments
- Changing start or finish dates
- Changing work, duration, or units
- Deleting a task or resource in the Name column

The indicator appears in the cell as long as the edit is available for an Undo operation. After you make a new edit, the indicator disappears.

You can turn off the display of indicators and option buttons. On the File tab, click Options, and then click Display in the left pane. Under Show Indicators And Option Buttons For, clear the check boxes for the categories of changes for which you don't need indicators.

For more information about using the indicators and option buttons for scheduling feedback, see "Changing Resource Assignments" on page 314.

Chapter 1

CHAPTER 2

Understanding Projects and Project Management

You use a word-processing program to create a text document. You use a spreadsheet program to calculate sales and other types of numerical data. You use a publishing program to design and lay out a brochure. In these cases, the application helps you create the end result.

With Microsoft Project 2010, this isn't so. Although Project 2010 helps you create a *project plan*, the actual project is executed by your team, which carries out tasks to fulfill the overarching goals of the project. It's up to you, as project manager, to track and control the actual project, using the project plan as your essential road map. When effectively maintained, the project plan is a model that provides an accurate picture of what's currently going on in your project, what has happened in the past, and what will happen in the future.

This chapter describes project basics and the stages of the project management process. It also outlines how Project 2010 fits into the world of your project. You'll learn how you can use Project 2010 as your project information system—that is, the indispensable tool for modeling your project and helping you efficiently and successfully manage it.

If you're new to project management, read this entire chapter. If you're an experienced project manager but new to Microsoft Project, skip ahead to "Facilitating Your Plan with Project 2010" on page 53.

Understanding Project Management Basics

Although project management might overlap other types of management, it entails a specific set of management processes.

What Is a Project?

Organizations perform two types of work: operations and projects. A great way to define a project is to say what it is *not*, and a project is *not* an operation. An *operation* is a series of routine, repetitive, and ongoing tasks that are performed throughout the life of the organization. Operations are typically necessary to sustain the business. Examples of operations are accounts receivable, employee performance reviews, and shipping and receiving. Employee performance reviews might take place every six months, for example, and although the names and circumstances of employees and supervisors might change, the process of preparing and conducting employee reviews is always the same. In addition, it's expected that employee reviews will be conducted throughout the life of the organization.

On the other hand, *projects* are not routine or ongoing. That is, projects are unique and temporary and are often implemented to fulfill a strategic goal of the organization. A project is a series of tasks that will culminate in the creation or completion of some new initiative, product, or activity by a specific end date. Some examples of projects include an office move, a new product launch, the construction of a building, and a political campaign. The same project never occurs twice—for example, this year's product launch is different from last year's product launch. There's a specific end date in mind for the launch, after which the project will be considered complete. After the project is complete, a new and unique product will be on the market.

Projects come in all sizes. One project might consist of 100 tasks; another, 10,000. One project might be implemented by a single resource; another by 500. One project might take 2 months to complete; another might take 10 years. Projects can contain other projects, linked together with a master project consolidating them all. These subprojects, however, are all unique and temporary, and they all have a specific outcome and end date.

What Is Project Management?

Project management is the coordinating effort to fulfill the goals of the project. The *project manager*, as the head of the project team, is responsible for this effort and its ultimate result. Project managers use knowledge, skills, tools, and methodologies to do the following:

- Identify the goals, objectives, requirements, and limitations of the project.
- Coordinate the different needs and expectations of the various project stakeholders, including team members, resource managers, senior management, customers, and sponsors.
- Plan, execute, and control the tasks, phases, and deliverables of the project following the identified project goals and objectives.
- Close the project when it is completed and capture the knowledge accrued.

Project managers are also responsible for balancing and integrating competing demands to implement all aspects of the project successfully, as follows:

- **Project scope** Articulating the specific work to be done for the project.
- **Project time** Setting the finish date of the project as well as any interim deadlines for phases, milestones, and deliverables.
- **Project cost** Calculating and tracking the project costs and budget.
- **Project human resources** Signing on the team members who will carry out the tasks of the project.
- **Project procurement** Acquiring the material and equipment resources, and obtaining any other supplies or services, needed to fulfill project tasks.
- **Project communication** Conveying assignments, updates, reports, and other information to team members and other stakeholders.
- **Project quality** Identifying the acceptable level of quality for the project goals and objectives.
- **Project risk** Analyzing potential project risks and response planning.

While project managers might or might not personally perform all these activities, they are always ultimately responsible for ensuring that they are carried out.

Balancing scope, time, and money is often among the biggest responsibilities of the project manager. These factors are considered the three sides of the *project triangle*. (See Figure 2-1.)

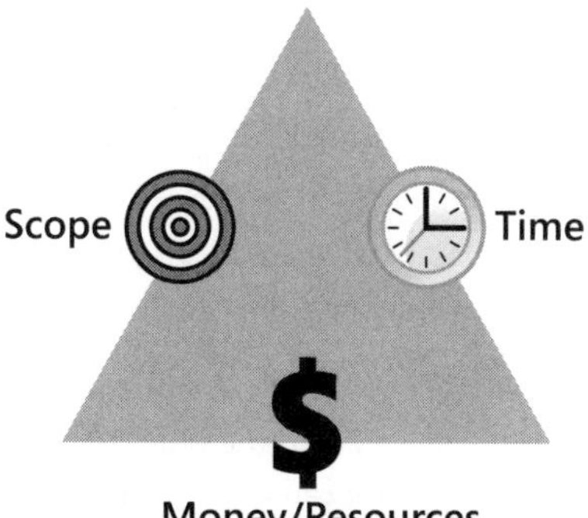

Figure 2-1 The project triangle is an effective model for thinking about your project's priorities.

INSIDE OUT Project 2010 and the project management disciplines

Project 2010 supports many but not all of the management areas associated with project management. That is, while Project 2010 does a great job with project time and cost, it provides only glancing support for project procurement and project quality.

However, you can combine Project 2010 with other tools to create for yourself the full package of project management support. Use Project 2010 to capture the lion's share of project information, including the schedule, milestones, deliverables, resources, costs, and reporting. Then draw upon other tools when needed to more fully handle responsibilities specifically associated with procurement or quality. Finally, come full circle with Project 2010 by adding notes to tasks or resources, inserting related documents, or hyperlinking to other locations.

For example, use Project 2010 to help estimate your initial equipment and material resource requirements. Work through your organization's procurement process and compile the relevant data. Add the equipment and materials as resources in your project plan and add notes as appropriate, making the information easy to reference. Use a tool such as Microsoft Excel 2010 to help track the depletion of materials to the point where reorder becomes necessary. Even though Project 2010 can't manage every aspect of your project, it can still be the central repository for all related information.

If you increase the scope, the time or money side of the triangle will also increase. If you need to reduce time—that is, bring in the project finish date—you might need to decrease the scope or increase the cost through the addition of resources.

Is It Really a Project Rectangle?

There's some debate about how to accurately describe the key controlling elements that make up a project. Some believe that a project is best described as a triangle—the three sides representing scope, time, and money. Others say that it's a square—with scope, time, money, and resources being the four sides, each one affecting the others. Additional debate suggests a hexagon of scope, time, money, resources, quality, and risk.

This book approaches money and resources as synonymous in this context because resources cost money. Adding resources adds money, and the only thing you'd need more money for would be resources. Quality and risk can arguably be considered part of scope. So in this book, the key demands for a project are conceptualized as a triangle with the three sides being scope, time, and money.

For information about working with the project triangle and other competing demands to help control your project, see Chapter 12, "Responding to Changes in Your Project."

Project Management Practices: Balancing and Integrating Competing Demands

Whether you keep the project triangle, rectangle, hexagon, or other shape in mind as you manage your project depends largely on the priorities and standards set for your project and by your organization, and on the weight placed on certain demands over others. Knowing these priorities and standards can help you make appropriate decisions about the project as the inevitable issues arise. Although scope, time, and cost tend to be the most prevalent demands, the following is the full list of project controls:

- Scope
- Human resources
- Quality
- Time
- Procurement
- Risk
- Cost
- Communications

These project controls are also referred to as *project knowledge areas*. An additional knowledge area is project integration management—balancing the demands of these other project controls to succeed in meeting the goals of the project.

Understanding Project Management Stages

It might seem daunting when you realize that, as a project manager, you're responsible for such a tremendous balancing act throughout the life of the project. However, this responsibility can be broken down into the following four key stages:

1. Initiating and planning the project
2. Executing the project
3. Monitoring and controlling the project
4. Closing the project

Most of the chapters in this book are structured with these four stages in mind. For each stage, you use Project 2010 in specific ways. Standard project management practices are also related to planning, executing, controlling, and closing the project. Throughout this book, the Project 2010 procedures as well as the project management practices are described in the context of the relevant project stage.

The following sections detail the key elements of each of the four project management stages.

Initiating and Planning the Project

You're ready to begin the planning stage after an authoritative stakeholder, such as an executive or customer, decides to initiate this project with you as the project manager. The outcome of this planning stage will be a workable project plan and a team ready to start working on the project. When planning the project, do the following:

- **Look at the big picture** Before you get too far into the nuts and bolts of planning, you need a comprehensive vision of where you're going with your project. You shape this vision by first identifying the project goals and objectives. This practice helps you set the scope of the project. You learn the expectations, limitations, and assumptions for this project, and they all go into the mix. You also identify possible risks and contingency plans for the project. Much of the information you need can come from the project proposal or other such preliminary document that might have helped bring this project into existence.

- **Identify the project's milestones, deliverables, and tasks** Subdivide the project into its component tasks and then organize and sequence the tasks to accurately reflect the project scope.

- **Develop and refine the project schedule** To turn the task list into a workable project schedule, specify task durations and relate tasks to each other. You can create task dependencies—that is, a model of how the start of one task depends on the completion of another task, for example. If you have any specific dates for deliverables, you can enter them as deadlines or, if really necessary, task constraints. With this plan, you can accurately forecast the scope, schedule, and budget for the project. You can also determine which resources are needed, how many, and at what time.

- **Identify skills, equipment, materials, supplies, and services needed** After the tasks are identified, you can determine the skills, equipment, and materials needed to carry out the work for those tasks. You obtain the needed human, equipment, and material resources and assign them to the appropriate tasks. You also factor in supplies, services, and other cost items that will be incurred and assign those cost resources to tasks as well. You can now calculate when the project can be completed and how much it will cost. If it looks like you're exceeding the allowable deadline or budget, you can make the necessary adjustments.

Note

Some project managers refer to the "project plan" as the text-based document in which the broad goals and methodologies of the project are defined. Throughout this book, however, we refer to the Project 2010 file as the project plan. Although some refer to this file as the project schedule, more goes on in this file than the schedule. For example, it can include resource definitions, cost information, reports, and attached documents.

Executing the Project

The second project management stage is execution. At this point, you have your project plan in hand. The tasks are scheduled and the resources are identified. Everyone's at the starting gate waiting for you to say "Go!"

You give the word, and the project moves from planning to the execution and controlling stage. In the course of executing the project, you communicate project information. You need to communicate task assignments to the team members and get their feedback. You also need to communicate requirements, budget, and progress to upper management, customers, and other stakeholders.

Monitoring and Controlling the Project

At the same time that your project team is executing the tasks, you're continually monitoring all task activities and comparing the plan to actual progress, making sure that the project stays within the prescribed deadline and budget while the scope of the project is being completed as outlined in the project goals. As part of these efforts, you're controlling the project—making the adjustments necessary to keep the project on the right track. To monitor and control the project, you do the following:

- **Save a baseline plan for comparison** To maintain reliable tracking information, you keep a copy of certain project plan information so that you can compare original plan information to actual progress as the project moves along.
- **Monitor the resources as they carry out their assigned tasks** As the project manager, you keep an eye on the progress resources make in completing their tasks.
- **Track task progress** You can track progress in terms of percentage complete, how long a task takes from beginning to end, or how many hours a resource spends on a task. As you collect this information, you can see whether tasks and milestones will finish on time. You can also gather information about costs of resources, tasks, and the project as a whole.

Project Management Terminology

The following is a list of terms related to project management:

- **Baseline** A snapshot of key project information for tasks, such as task start dates, finish dates, durations, and costs. With baseline information, you have a means of comparison against actual progress on tasks.
- **Date constraint** A specific date associated with a specific task. A date constraint dictates that a task must be finished by a certain date, for example, or started no earlier than a certain date.
- **Deliverable** A tangible outcome, result, or item that must be produced to mark the completion of a project or a project phase. Often, the deliverable is subject to approval by the project sponsor or customer.
- **Dependency** The reliance of one task upon another. When one task cannot start or finish until a related task starts or finishes, the tasks are dependent on one another, or related. Also referred to as a *task link* or *task relationship*.
- **Gantt chart** A graphic representation of a project. The left half of a Gantt chart is a table listing task names and other task-related information. The right half of the Gantt chart is a bar chart along a timeline in which each bar represents a task, its start and finish date, and its duration. Links to other tasks can also be represented.
- **Milestone** A significant event in the project, often the completion of a major deliverable or phase. Milestones are represented as part of a project's task list.
- **Network diagram** A graphic representation of a project, characterized by nodes representing tasks and link lines showing the relationships among the tasks. Also sometimes called a PERT (Program Evaluation and Review Technique) chart.
- **Phase** A grouping of tasks that represents a major stage in the life cycle of the project. The outcome of a phase is typically a major deliverable.
- **Portfolio** A collection of projects, typically related in some way, either by discipline or organizational management. A portfolio manager oversees multiple projects being handled by project managers.
- **Scope** The specific work that needs to be done in a project to deliver the product or service.
- **Stakeholders** Individuals or organizations who have a vested interest in the outcome of the project and who can influence those project outcomes. Stakeholders include the project manager, portfolio manager, members of the project team, the sponsoring organization, and customers.

- **Analyze project information** Analyze the information you're gathering and use this analysis to solve problems and make decisions. Often, you need to decide how to recover a slipped schedule or readjust for a budget overrun. Sometimes, you're in the happy position of deciding what to do with extra time or money.
- **Report** Throughout the execution of the project, you must constantly report various levels of information to your team members and other stakeholders. You need to keep upper management, customers, and other stakeholders informed of any potential problems, new decisions, corrective actions, and your overall progress.

Closing the Project

In the final stage of the project, you have successfully fulfilled the goals of the project, and it's now complete. Before you move on to the next project, you want to capture the knowledge you gained from this one. When closing the project, you do the following:

- **Identify lessons learned** Work with your project team and conduct a "postmortem" review meeting to learn what went well and what could be improved. You can therefore articulate problems to avoid in future projects and also capture details of efficiencies gained that should be replicated in future projects.
- **Create a project template** Save the project plan along with tasks, duration metrics, task relationships, resource skills, and the like so that the next time you or one of your colleagues manages a similar project, your wheel will not need to be reinvented.

Facilitating Your Plan with Project 2010

Because a project involves a myriad of tasks, resources, assignments, dates, and more, it's obvious that you need some kind of tool to help you track the details. By using a spreadsheet or a word-processing program, you could create a table that lists your tasks, durations, start and finish dates, and assigned resources. In fact, that might very well get you started. But it's likely that you'll end up working harder than you have to in an attempt to make the tool work right, especially when changes have to be made during the project. Such a table would not be able to:

- Calculate the start and finish dates for you.
- Indicate whether assigned resources are actually available.
- Inform you if assigned resources are underallocated or overworked.
- Alert you if there's an upcoming deadline.

- Understand how much material you've depleted or how much you're spending on supplies and services.
- Calculate how much of the budget you've spent so far.
- Draw your project tasks as a Gantt chart or network diagram so you can visualize your project.

To do this and more, you can create a table in Project 2010. You can then use the project database, schedule calculation, and charting capabilities to help facilitate your project management processes, as shown in Figure 2-2.

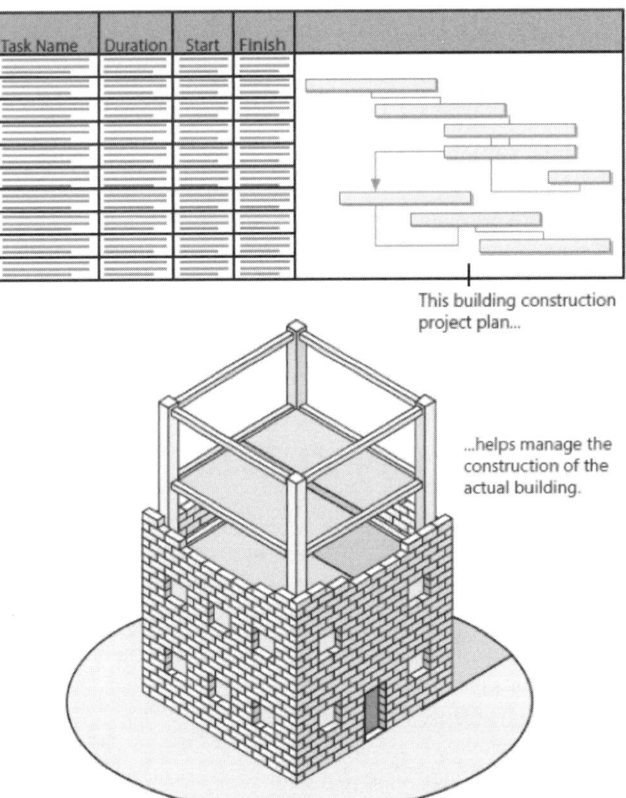
Task Name
Duration
Start
Finish
This building construction project plan...
...helps manage the construction of the actual building.

Figure 2-2 The project plan helps you manage your project.

Although Project 2010 can't negotiate a more reasonable finish date, it can help you determine what you have to sacrifice to make that date. Although Project 2010 won't complete a difficult and time-consuming task for your team, it will help you find extra time in the schedule or additional resources for that task. And although Project 2010 can't motivate an uninspired team member, it can tell you if that team member is working on critical tasks that will affect the finish date of the entire project.

In short, Project 2010 can help you facilitate all processes in the project management life cycle, from developing your scope, modeling your project schedule, and tracking and communicating progress, to saving knowledge gained from the closed project. Furthermore, with Microsoft Project Professional 2010, project management standards can be established and disseminated throughout your enterprise.

Creating a Model of Your Project

You can use Project 2010 to create a model of your project. This model reflects the reality of your project. You enter your tasks, resources, assignments, and other project-related information into Project 2010. You can then organize and manage the copious and very detailed bits of project information that otherwise can be quite overwhelming.

With all the necessary information stored in Project 2010, the exact project information you need at any given time is always at your fingertips. You can manipulate and analyze this information in various ways to solve problems, make decisions, and communicate progress to successfully manage the project. As you take action and move forward in your project, you update information in Project 2010 so that it continues to reflect reality. (See Figure 2-3.)

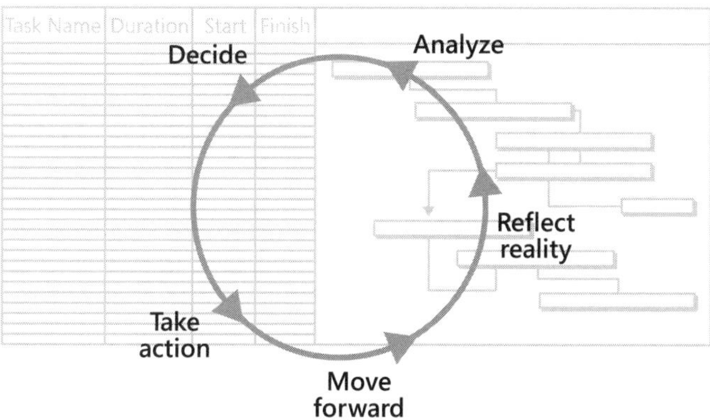

Figure 2-3 Model your project's reality.

Planning with Project 2010

Specifically, in the planning stage, you use Project 2010 to do the following:

- **Create your project phases, milestones, and task list** Project 2010 uses your task list as the basis for the project database it creates for you. You can organize tasks within phases or subtasks within summary tasks so that you can break your project down into manageable segments.

- **Estimate task durations** One task might take two hours to complete; another might take four days. Unless you're scheduling manually, Project 2010 uses these durations to help build your schedule.

- **Link tasks with their appropriate relationships to other tasks** Often, a task cannot begin until a previous task has been completed. For example, for an office move project, you schedule the "Design office space" task before the "Order new furniture" task. The two tasks are linked because the second task cannot be done until the first task is complete. Unless you're using manual scheduling, Project 2010 uses these task relationships to build your schedule. The durations and task relationships are also shown in the Gantt Chart and Network Diagram views of your project.

- **Enter any imposed deadlines or other date constraints** If you know that you must vacate your current office space by the end of August, for example, you work with that date as one of the important constraints of your project. Project 2010 can automatically schedule according to such constraints and inform you of a conflict between a constraint and the durations or task relationships you have also set.

- **Set up the resources and assign them to tasks** Resources can be employees, vendors, or equipment that are responsible for carrying out tasks. Not only does Project 2010 keep track of which resources are assigned to which tasks, it also schedules work on assignments according to the resource's availability and lets you know whether a resource is overloaded with more tasks than can be accomplished in the resource's available time. Resources can also include materials consumed or special costs incurred in the execution of a task, so you can plan for how much lumber you need, for example, or how much you're going to have to spend on travel costs throughout the life of the project.

- **Establish resource costs and task costs** You can specify hourly, monthly, or per-use rates for the employees or equipment being used to complete tasks. You can specify the cost for consumable materials or other special costs for items such as trade show registration, printing, or travel. When your human, equipment, material, and cost resources are assigned to tasks, Project 2010 calculates and adds these costs so that you can get an accurate view of how much your project will cost to execute. You can often use this calculation as a basis for the project budget.

- **Adjust the plan to achieve a targeted finish date or budget amount** Suppose that your project plan initially shows a finish date that's two months later than required or a cost that's $10,000 more than the allocated budget. You can make adjustments to scope, schedule, cost, and resources to bring the project plan in line. While working through your inevitable project tradeoffs, Project 2010 can recalculate your schedule automatically until you have the result you need.

For information about using Project 2010 to plan your project, see the chapters in Part 2, "Developing the Project Plan."

Executing with Project 2010

In the execution stage of the project, planning is complete and you give the green light for the project team members to start work on their assigned tasks. Communication is a huge part of the execution stage. Use Project 2010 to communicate in one or more of the following ways:

- **Print to-do lists** You can print a to-do list for each team member, or print a report of tasks coming due within the next month.

  For more information, see "Using Views to Report Project Information" on page 528 and "Working with Text-Based Reports" on page 534.

- **Send e-mail messages containing task lists** You can send task lists to team members over e-mail. If they use Microsoft Outlook or another MAPI-based e-mail program, they can integrate the items into their e-mail task list.

  For more information, see "Adding Project 2010 Tasks to Outlook Tasks"on page 771.

- **Communicate task assignments and progress with your SharePoint workgroup** Use Microsoft SharePoint 2010 to post task lists and updates for communication and collaboration among your team members.

  For more information, see Chapter 21, "Collaborating as a Team by Using SharePoint."

- **Communicate task information with Microsoft Project Server 2010** Use the power of enterprise project management and Microsoft Project Web App to exchange task and progress information with team members.

  For more information, see "Collaborating as a Project Team" on page 816.

Monitoring and Controlling with Project 2010

In the execution and control stage of the project, use Project 2010 to do the following:

- **Save the baseline plan** For comparison and tracking purposes, you need to take a snapshot of what you consider your baseline project plan. As you update task progress through the life of the project, you can compare current progress with that snapshot of your original plan. These comparisons provide valuable information about whether you're on track with the schedule and your budget.

- **Update actual task progress** With Project 2010, you can update task progress by entering percentage complete, work complete, work remaining, and more. As you enter actual progress, the schedule can be automatically recalculated.

- **Compare variances between planned and actual task information** Using the baseline information you saved, Project 2010 presents various views to show your baseline against actual and scheduled progress, along with any variances. For example, if your initial project plan shows that you had originally planned to finish a task on Thursday, but the resource actually finished it on Monday, you'd have a variance of three days in your favor.

- **Review planned, actual, and scheduled costs** In addition to seeing task progress variances, you can compare baseline costs against actual and currently scheduled costs and see the resulting cost variances. Project 2010 can also use your baseline and current schedule information for *earned value* calculations that you can use for more detailed analyses.

- **Adjust the plan to respond to changes in scope, finish date, and budget** What if you get a directive in the middle of the project to cut $10,000 from your budget? Or what if you learn that you must bring the project in a month earlier to catch a vital marketing window? Even in the midst of a project, you can adjust scope, schedule, cost, and resources in your project plan. With each change you make, Project 2010 can recalculate your schedule automatically.

For more information about using Project 2010 to track and control your project, see the chapters in Part 3, "Tracking Progress."

- **Report on progress, costs, resource utilization, and more** Using the database and calculation features of Project 2010, you can generate a number of text-based and visual reports. For example, reports can show the project summary, milestones, tasks starting soon, over-budget tasks, resource to-do lists, and other information. The visual reports send Project 2010 data to Microsoft Excel 2010 or Visio 2010, which lets you see the data as a column chart or flow diagram, for example. You can modify these built-in reports to suit your needs or create custom reports entirely from scratch.

For more information about using Project 2010 to report progress, see Chapter 13, "Reporting Project Information."

Closing with Project 2010

In the closing stage of the project, use Project 2010 to accomplish the following tasks:

- **Capture actual task duration metrics** If you tracked task progress throughout the project, at the end of the project you have solid, tested data for how long certain tasks actually take.
- **Capture successful task sequencing** Sometimes, you're not sure at the outset of a project whether a task should be performed sooner or later in the cycle. With the experience of the project behind you, you can see whether your sequencing worked well.
- **Save a template for the next project of this kind** Use your project plan as the boilerplate for the next project. You and other project managers will have a task list, milestones, deliverables, sequence, durations, and task relationships already in place, and this template can easily be modified to fit the requirements of the new project.

For more information about closing the project and creating templates, see Chapter 31, "Standardizing Projects by Using Templates."

You can also use Project 2010 to work with multiple projects—and even show the task or resource links among them. In the course of modeling your project in this way, Project 2010 serves as your project information system. Project 2010 arranges the thousands of bits of information in various ways so that you can work with it, analyze your data, and make decisions based on coherent and soundly calculated project management information. This project information system carries out three basic functions:

- It stores project information, including tasks, resources, assignments, durations, task relationships, task sequences, calendars, and more.
- If you so choose, it calculates information such as dates, schedules, costs, durations, critical path, earned value, variances, and more.
- It presents views of information you're retrieving. You can specify the views, tables, filters, groups, fields, or reports, depending on what aspect of your project model you need to see.

Working with Your Team Through Project 2010

In addition to helping you create your project plan, Project 2010 helps with resource management, cost management, and team communications. With Project 2010 resource management features, you can perform the following tasks:

- Enter resources in the Project 2010 resource list.

- Enter resources from your organization's e-mail address book, Active Directory service, or Project Server 2010 accounts.
- Maintain a reusable pool of resources available across multiple projects.
- Specify skills required for a task and have Project 2010 search for available resources with those skills.
- Schedule tasks according to the availability of assigned resources.
- See which assignments all resources are working on, and also identify resource overload or underutilization at a glance and make adjustments accordingly.
- Book a proposed resource in your project (using Project Professional 2010).

For more information about managing resources, see Chapter 7, "Setting Up Resources in the Project," and Chapter 8, "Assigning Resources to Tasks."

With the cost management features of Project 2010, you can do the following:

- Enter periodic or per-use costs for human, equipment, and material resources, including multiple rates for different task types.
- Enter costs for fees, supplies, or services that will be incurred on a task; for example, permit fees or travel costs.
- Enter fixed costs for tasks.
- Estimate costs for the project while the project is still in the planning process.
- Compare planned cost variances to actual cost variances.
- Compare planned, actual, or scheduled costs against your budget.
- View cost totals for tasks, resources, phases, and the entire project.
- Analyze earned value calculations, including budgeted cost of work performed (BCWP), schedule variance (SV), and earned value (EV).

For more information about setting and managing costs, see Chapter 9, "Planning Resource and Task Costs," and Chapter 12, "Responding to Changes in Your Project." For information about working with earned value, see Chapter 14, "Analyzing Progress Using Earned Value."

Your communications requirements might be as simple as printing a Gantt chart or resource list for a weekly status meeting. Or you might prefer to electronically exchange task updates with your resources every day and publish high-level project information to your company's intranet.

With Project 2010, you can communicate with others in just the way you need, as follows:

- Print a view as it looks on your screen.
- Generate and print a predesigned text-based report.
- Generate and print a predesigned visual report by using Project 2010 data in Excel or Visio 2010.
- Create a custom view, text-based report, or visual report.
- Copy a project view as a static picture to another Microsoft Office application.

For more information about working with views and reports, see Chapter 13.

Being able to collaborate summary and detailed project information with team members and project stakeholders is essential, whether or not you're using enterprise capabilities.

- Use SharePoint 2010 to collaborate with your team by posting and synchronizing task lists as well as making project updates.
- Exchange task assignments, updates, and status reports with your team members through Project Server and Project Web App.
- Allow team leads to delegate tasks to other team members.
- Track issues and documents through SharePoint Server, Project Server, and Project Web App.
- Publish the project through Project Server and Project Web App for review by team members, senior management, customers, and other stakeholders.

For more information about working with project information by using SharePoint, see Chapter 21. For more information about working with resources across an enterprise, see Chapter 24, "Managing Enterprise Projects and Resources."

Using Project 2010 in Your Enterprise

Through the use of Project Server, as accessed by Project Professional and Project Web App, an entire portfolio of projects can be standardized across your enterprise. Numerous Project 2010 elements, including views, filters, groups, fields, and formulas, can be designed and included in the enterprise global template that reflects your organization's specific project management methodology. This customization and design is done by a *project server administrator*. This project server administrator is the person who sets up and manages the installation of Project 2010 for your organization. The project server administrator knows the requirements of project management and the features of Project 2010 well enough to design custom solutions and is often a programmer or other information technology professional. The project server administrator might also be a technically oriented lead project manager.

When your project server administrator designs a common enterprise project template, all project managers in the organization can then work with the same customized project elements that support organizational initiatives. In addition, senior managers can review summary information from multiple projects throughout the organization.

The project server administrator also sets up the *enterprise resource pool*, which contains all the resources available to the enterprise, and from which the various project managers draw to staff their projects. The enterprise resource pool includes key resource information such as cost, availability, and skill set.

Some organizations might divide the duties between a project server administrator and *portfolio manager*. The project server administrator can handle installation, server, network, and database issues, and the portfolio manager can be responsible for designing custom project elements, managing the enterprise resource pool, and setting up users and permissions.

For more information about enterprise capabilities, see Part 7, "Managing Projects Across Your Enterprise."

Working with the Project Stakeholders

Every project has a set of stakeholders associated with it. *Project stakeholders* are individuals or organizations who are connected to the project in one way or another and can influence the project's outcome. As the project manager, you need to work with different types of stakeholders in various ways. A stakeholder can do the following:

- Be actively involved in the work of the project.
- Exert influence over the project and its outcome (also known as *managing stakeholders*).
- Have a vested interest in the outcome of a project.

A variety of stakeholder categories exist, and each is supported in its own way by Project 2010. The categories are as follows:

- **Project manager** Project 2010 directly supports the project manager with its scheduling, tracking, and communication capabilities.
- **Team members** The project resources who are executing the project can be supported through SharePoint or Project Web App, where they can view their assigned tasks, send and receive assignment progress updates, send status reports, and review the project as a whole.
- **Team leads** Team leads can use Project Web App to reassign and manage tasks.
- **Project resource manager** A resource manager might work in concert with the project manager to help acquire and maintain necessary resources. Through Project Web App, a resource manager can analyze resource utilization information, build project teams, make assignments, and approve timesheets.
- **Senior managers, portfolio managers, executives, or sponsors** People who lead the organization in implementing the project or supply the project budget or other resources can use Project Web App to review high-level project summaries. Collectively, they can make up a project management office (PMO). In an enterprise environment, executives can review a summary that compares multiple projects being carried out throughout the organization.

INSIDE OUT Project support for customers and end users

Other possible stakeholders include customers or end users. Project 2010 does not provide direct support for such stakeholders. However, you can provide them with access to information via Project Web App or periodically publish a view designed for them on a website.

For more information about Project Web App, see Chapter 25, "Participating on a Team Using Project Web App," and Chapter 26, "Making Executive Decisions Using Project Web App." For more information about publishing project information, see Chapter 13.

Managing stakeholders can influence the planning processes of a project and help set the expectations and assumptions of the project. Sometimes the expectations of different stakeholders conflict with one other. It's the job of the project manager to balance and reconcile these conflicts well before project execution begins.

Managing stakeholders might also impose new requirements that necessitate adjustments to the finish date, budget, or scope. Even if this happens in the midst of execution, you can use Project 2010 to make adjustments responding to the new demands.

Keys to Successful Project Management

Being well versed in project management processes and using a powerful tool such as Project 2010 puts you well ahead in the project management game. For an even greater edge toward a successful project, follow these guidelines:

- **Develop the goals and objectives** Know the broad goals as well as the specific, measurable objectives of your project. They are your guiding principles.
- **Learn the scope** Know the scope (including tasks, quality, and deliverables) of your project and exactly what is expected of it. The scope includes how much you're doing (quantity) and how well you're doing it (quality).
- **Know your deadlines** Seek out any deadlines—final as well as interim milestone and deliverable deadlines. If these deadlines are up to you to suggest, lucky you. But often you don't have this luxury. Often, you might propose one reasonable date, only to have upper management or your customers suggest another, not-so-reasonable date. The sooner you learn about these dates, the better you can plan for them by adjusting the scope, the budget, and the resources.
- **Know your budget** If the project finish date is not your limitation, the budget might very well be. Again, it might be up to you to tell upper management how much the proposed project will cost. But it's also likely that the budget will be imposed on you, and you'll need to fulfill the goals of the project within a specific and firm dollar amount. The sooner you know the definitive budget of the project, the more realistic and accurate your plan can be. You can adjust scope, time, and resources to meet the budget.
- **Find the best resources** Gather input about the best candidates for certain tasks so that you can get the best resources. Although more experienced resources will likely be more expensive, they'll also be more apt to complete tasks quickly and with a higher level of quality. Similar principles might also apply to equipment and consumable material resources. Focus on value rather than price, and your budget will go further with better results. Determine the acceptable level of quality for the project, balance this determination with your budget constraints, and procure the best you can get.
- **Enter accurate project information** You can enter tasks and durations, link the tasks, and assign them to resources, which makes it seem like you have a real project plan. But suppose the data you enter doesn't reflect the real tasks that will be done, the amount of time resources will really be spending on these tasks, or the activities

that really need to be done before each task can start. In this case, all you have is a bunch of characters and graphics on a colorful screen or an impressive-looking report. You don't have a project plan at all. The "garbage-in, garbage-out" maxim applies. As you're planning the project, draw on previous experience with a similar type of project. Solicit input from resources already earmarked for the project—they can provide excellent information about which tasks need to be done, how long they take, and how tasks relate to each other.

- **Adjust the project plan to meet requirements** Look at the plan's calculated or estimated finish date and the total cost. See if they match your limitations for project deadline or budget. If they do not, make the necessary adjustments and do the necessary negotiations. This must all be done before you actually start the project—probably even before you show the project plan to any of your managing stakeholders.

- **Save a baseline and go** After you have a project plan that solidly reflects reality, save the plan's baseline information and begin project execution. This baseline is the means for determining whether you're on track and how far you might have strayed if you need to recover the schedule later.

- **Track progress** Many project planners only go so far as to enter and calculate tasks, durations, relationships, and resources so that they can see a schedule and budget. They say "Go" and everyone charges, but the plan is left behind. As project variables change (and they always do), the project plan becomes useless as a blueprint for managing the project. If you want the project plan to be useful from the time you first enter, assign, and schedule tasks until the time you close the project on time and on budget, you need to maintain the project plan as a dynamic tool that accompanies you every step of the way. Maintaining the plan means tracking progress information. Suppose a task planned for 5 days takes 10 days instead. You can enter that the task actually took 10 days, and the schedule can be recalculated. Your plan will still work, and you'll still be able to see when succeeding tasks should be completed.

- **Make necessary adjustments** As project variables change during project execution, you can see whether an unplanned change affects key milestones, your resources' schedules, your budget, or your project finish date. For example, suppose that 5-day task took 10 days to complete, and it changes the project finish date and also causes the project to exceed its budget. If this happens, you can take steps well ahead of time to make the necessary adjustments and avert the looming crisis. You can use the power of Project 2010 to recalculate the project plan when actual project details vary from the plan. Then you can analyze the plan, decide on the best course of action to keep the project on track, and take action. This action might be within the project plan or outside the confines of the plan in the real world of the project itself.

- **Communicate** Make sure that your team members know what's expected of them and stay focused. Pay attention when they alert you to potential problems with their tasks. Keep upper management and customers informed of your progress and of any changes to the original plan.
- **Close the completed project and capture information** When a project goes well, we're often so pleased with ourselves that amidst the congratulations and celebrations we don't think to capture all the information we should. When a project is completed with much difficulty, sometimes we're just relieved that we're done with it and can't wait to get on with the next project and forget about such an unhappy nightmare. But whether a project is simple or difficult, a radiant success or a deplorable failure, much can always be learned. Even if you're not to be involved in any other projects of this type, other people might be. It's important to record as much information about the project as possible. Narrative and evaluative information can be captured through a postmortem or "lessons learned" document. Project information such as tasks, resources, durations, relationships, and calendars can be recorded in a project plan itself. If the project went very well, you can even save your project plan as a template to be used for similar projects in the future, thereby enabling other project managers to benefit from your hard-won experience.

PART 2

Developing the Project Plan

Before you can use the sample files for Chapters 3–10, you'll need to install them from this book's companion content website. For more information about downloading and installing the sample files, see "About the Companion Content" on page xxviii.

CHAPTER 3

Starting a New Project

BECAUSE the heart of project management is planning, it's no wonder that the planning processes for a new project require you to do a significant amount of work just to set the stage. You define the big picture and obtain stakeholder approval for the specifications of the product or service you're creating and for the boundaries defining the overall scope of the project itself.

After this vision is in place, you're ready to create your project blueprint—the project plan—using Microsoft Project 2010. You create a new project file and enter foundation information.

Then you break down your project goals and objectives into the actual phases, milestones, and tasks that form the backbone of your project information system. You sequence the phases and tasks and organize them into a hierarchy that maps to your project.

If your project or organization has more specialized or advanced requirements, you can use work breakdown structure codes that organize your task list by each deliverable.

You can add your supporting documentation, such as the vision or strategy document, to the project plan. Likewise, you can add supplementary information such as notes or hyperlinks to individual tasks, milestones, and phases. All this information makes your project plan the central repository of project information.

Getting from Idea to Proposal to Project

Many projects begin life as a bright idea. Maybe it's a new product idea, a new service, or a new community fundraising event. The new project can be the solution to a specific problem that has arisen—for example, a factory retooling, a marketing initiative, or a training program. The new project might be generated from a client company that puts out a request for proposal.

Often the normal cycle of business dictates the creation of a new project. If you're in the software development business, for example, you live with a product cycle that begins with a project plan and ends with the software launch. If you're in the construction business, you work within a building process that starts with a project plan and ends with the ribbon-cutting ceremony. Whatever the project—another office move, another trade show, or another system deployment—you know you need to start with the project plan.

Before you get to the project plan, however, the idea needs to be given the green light by the powers that be, especially if it's an entirely new idea. This is true whether a new project idea is conceived from the normal course of business, is the solution to a problem, or is a brilliant flash of inspiration. The skeleton of the idea is fleshed out in the form of a project proposal or business case. In the proposal or business case, the project is described along with the rationale for carrying out the project.

The largest part of this rationale is often the cost-benefit analysis. The proposal outlines the expected cost of implementing the project, the resources and time needed, the risks involved, and any assumptions and limitations. The proposal then explains the resulting benefits of the project, such as increased customer satisfaction, more efficient processing, or increased profitability.

The proposal is assessed by upper management. This group examines whether the proposal is compelling and workable, whether the organization has the necessary capacity, and most importantly, whether the expected benefits are greater than the expected costs. If these conditions are met, upper management gives the project the go-ahead, and the project can be implemented.

With all the preliminary thinking that goes into the proposal, you're likely to be well aware of everything from scope to risks for the new project.

Focusing the Project Vision

You might already have a clear picture in your mind of what your project is about and what it will be when it is complete. On the other hand, the project might still seem a little fuzzy, at least around the edges. It's not uncommon for other stakeholders to have a clear vision when you're not sure if you get it just yet.

And don't be surprised if one stakeholder's expectations seem clear enough, but another stakeholder's expectations sound entirely contradictory.

The challenge at this important starting point is to define the project without ambiguity, so that everyone involved is talking about the same project, has the same expectations, and wants the same results. Defining the vision clearly at the beginning prevents redirection (and the attendant wasted effort) in the middle of the project. More importantly, a lucid articulation of the project vision prevents disappointment (which can often cost big bucks) at the end.

So how do you create a vision? You work with key stakeholders, such as the customers, potential users, sponsors, executives, and project team members, to collect their expectations of the project. You might have to reconcile conflicting views and opposing agendas. Throughout this process, you identify the goals of the project as well as their measurable objectives. You identify project assumptions, spell out potential risks, and make contingency plans for those risks. You also identify known limitations, such as budget, time, or resources.

By the time you finish this high-level project planning and get the necessary approval, everyone involved knows exactly what they're signing up for.

Defining Scope

A defined scope articulates the vision of the product you're creating and the project that will create it. As your project is executed and issues arise, your defined scope can help you make decisions. The scope definition is your guideline for whether the direction you're considering is really the job of this project. If you don't stay focused on the agreed-upon scope of the project, you're likely to experience "scope creep," in which you end up spending time, money, and resources on tasks and deliverables that are not part of the original vision.

This is not to say that scope can't change during the course of a project. Business conditions, design realities, budgets, time, resource availability, and many other factors can necessitate changing project scope midway through. In addition, as members of your project team work on their tasks, they are likely to generate great new ideas. Nonetheless, your scope document helps you make decisions and manage any changes so that you turn in the proper direction—in line with your organization's overall strategy, the project's reason for being, and the project's goals.

Understanding Product Scope and Project Scope

There are two types of scope: product scope and project scope. First, you define the product scope, unless it has been defined for you. The *product scope* specifies the features and functions of the product that will be the outcome of the project. The product scope might well be part of the product description in your charter. The product can be tangible, such as the construction of a new office building or the design of a new aircraft. The product can also be the development of a service or event—for example, deploying a new computer system or implementing a new training initiative.

Regardless of the type of product, the product scope indicates the specifications and parameters that paint a detailed picture of the end result. For example, the product scope of the construction of a new office building might include square footage, number of stories, location, and architectural design elements.

The *project scope* specifies the work that must be done to complete the project successfully, according to the specifications of the associated product scope. The project scope defines and controls what will and will not be included in the project. If product development will have multiple phases, the project scope might specify which phase this project is handling. For example, a computer system deployment project might specify that its scope encompass the infrastructure development and installation of the new computer system, but not the documentation and training for new system users. Or it might specify that the project handle all aspects of the product, from concept through completion of the final stage.

Developing the Scope Statement

To define the project scope and communicate it to other key stakeholders, you develop and record the *scope statement*. Depending on your organization's planning methods, certain elements of the scope statement might be defined very early, sometimes even before you are assigned as project manager. Other elements might be defined just before you begin identifying and sequencing the project's tasks. Your scope statement should include the following:

- **Project justification** The scope statement should define the business need or other stimulus for this project. This justification provides a sound basis for evaluating future decisions, including the inevitable tradeoffs. This information can come straight from the project proposal or business case that initiated the original formation of the project.
- **Product description** The scope statement should characterize the details of the product or service being created. The project justification and product description together should formulate the goals of the project.
- **Project constraints or limitations** The scope statement should include any factors limiting the project. Factors that can limit a project's options include a specific budget, contractual provisions, the availability of certain key personnel, a precise end date, and so on.

> **Note**
> **Because we use the term *constraints* throughout this book to mean task scheduling constraints, in this chapter we're using the term *limitations* to refer to overall project constraints.**

- **Project assumptions** The scope statement should list any elements considered to be true, real, or certain—even when they might not be—for the purposes of continuing to develop the project plan and move forward. By their nature, assumptions usually carry a degree of risk. For example, if you don't know whether the building for a commercial construction project will be 10,000 or 15,000 square feet, you have to assume one or the other for the sake of planning. The risk is that the other choice might end up being correct. You can adjust the plan after the facts are known, but other project dependencies might already be in place by then.

> **Note**
> **Although certain aspects of your scope statement might remain unchanged through the iterative planning process, that's not necessarily the case with project limitations and assumptions. As the scope becomes more tightly defined, the limitations and assumptions come to light and are better exposed. Likewise, as you continue down the road in the planning process, the entire project scope tends to become more and more focused.**

- **Project deliverables** The scope statement should list the summary-level subproducts created throughout the duration of the project. The delivery of the final subproject deliverable marks the completion of the entire project. This list might bring into focus major project phases and milestones, which will be valuable when you start entering tasks into your project plan.

- **Project objectives** The scope statement should enumerate the measurable objectives to be satisfied for the project to be considered successful. The objectives map to the deliverables and are driven by the project goals, as described by the project justification and product description. To be meaningful, the project objectives must be quantifiable in some way; for example, a specific dollar amount, a specific timeframe, or a specific level of quality. In fact, think "SMART" when setting project objectives to ensure that they are Specific, Measureable, Attainable, Relevant, and Time-Bound.

> **Note**
> **Your scope statement might also address other project planning issues, such as communications, quality assurance, and risk management. It can define the reporting requirements and the collaboration tools that the team will use. The scope statement can also specify the minimum level of quality acceptable, define the potential risks associated with the itemized limitations and assumptions, and stipulate methods of countering the risks.**

Product scope and project scope are intricately linked. The project scope relies on a clear definition of the product scope. The project scope is fulfilled through the completion of work represented in the project plan. In the same way, product scope is fulfilled by meeting the specifications in the product requirements.

With the draft of the scope statement in hand, you have a document you can use to clearly communicate with other project stakeholders. This draft helps you ferret out any cross-purposes, mistaken assumptions, and misplaced requirements. As you continue to refine the scope statement, the project vision is honed to the point where all the stakeholders should have a common understanding of the project. And because all the stakeholders participated in the creation of the vision, you can feel confident that everyone understands exactly what they're working toward when you begin to execute the project plan.

Creating a New Project Plan

You're now at the point where you can start Project 2010 and actually create your project plan. When you create a new project file, you first decide whether to schedule from a start date or finish date. You then set your overall project calendar that the tasks will be scheduled against. If you want to, you can attach project documentation such as your all-important scope statement and possibly other project-related documents.

Creating a Project File

To begin creating your new project plan, start Project 2010 and choose whether you're creating a new project from scratch, from a template, or from an existing project plan.

If you haven't installed Project 2010 yet, refer to Appendix A, "Installing Microsoft Project 2010," for installation guidelines and details.

To start Project 2010, click the Windows Start button. Point to All Programs, click the Microsoft Office folder, and then click Microsoft Project 2010. You'll see a blank project file, as shown in Figure 3-1.

> **Note**
>
> **If you're working with enterprise projects using Microsoft Project Professional 2010, you might first be prompted to enter your account name and password to connect to Microsoft Project Server 2010.**

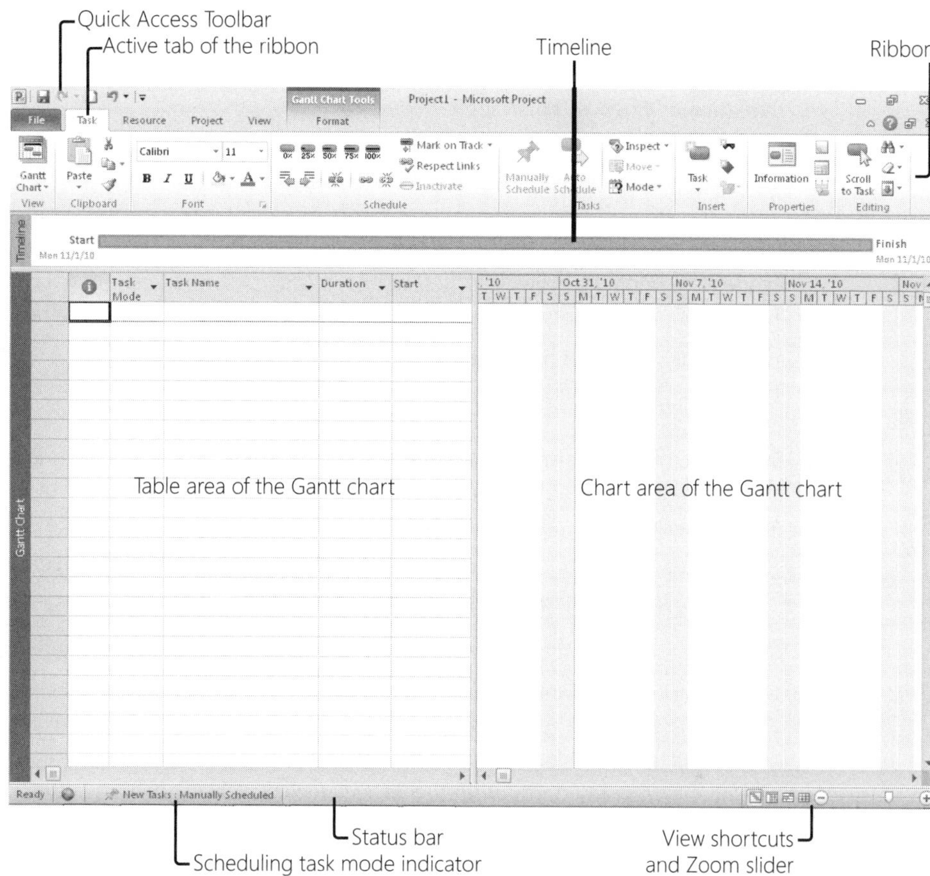

Figure 3-1 A blank project file appears in Project 2010.

> **Note**
>
> **Depending on how you customize your setup, you might also be able to open Project 2010 by double-clicking its icon on the Windows desktop.**

The Project 2010 workspace is called the *view*, and the view that appears by default when you first open Project 2010 is the Gantt Chart. The Gantt Chart is made up of a task table on the left and the chart showing Gantt bars on the right.

For more information about working with the Gantt Chart and the other views available in Project 2010, see "Using Views" on page 131.

Creating a New Project from a Blank Project File

If you want to create your new project plan from scratch, you can use the blank project file that appears when you first open Project 2010.

If you already have another project file open, and you want to create a new project from scratch, follow these steps:

1. On the File tab, click New.

   The Project 2010 Backstage view appears.

2. Under Available Templates, double-click Blank Project.

   A blank project appears.

By default, new blank projects are set for manually scheduled tasks. For more information about manual versus automatic scheduling, see Chapter 5, "Scheduling Tasks Manually or Automatically."

Add the New Button to the Quick Access Toolbar

If you frequently create new projects from scratch, consider adding the New button to the Quick Access Toolbar, located in the upper-left corner of the Project 2010 window. Click the arrow at the right edge of the Quick Access Toolbar, and then click New. The New button is added. When you click the New button on the Quick Access Toolbar, you don't need to go through the Backstage view; a blank project is created in one quick step.

For more information, see "Customizing the Quick Access Toolbar" on page 1146.

Creating a New Project from a Template

You can also create a new project from a template. A *template* is a type of project file that contains project information that helps you start your project more quickly. The template usually contains a list of tasks, already sequenced and organized. The task list might be further detailed with phases, milestones, and deliverables. There might be additional task information in the template as well, such as task durations and task dependencies. You can use this task list as the basis for your project. You can add, remove, and rearrange tasks, adapting the task information as needed to correspond to your project requirements. A template can also include resource information, customized views, calendars, reports, tables, macros, option settings, and more.

A template file has the extension .mpt, indicating that it is the Microsoft Project template file type. When you open and modify a template file, it is saved as a normal .mpp (Microsoft Project plan) file by default.

For more information about file types and project file management, see Chapter 32, "Managing Project Files."

NEW!

As of Project 2010, all Microsoft Project templates are downloadable from Office.com, rather than built directly into Project 2010. Although you need to be connected to the Internet to access the available templates, you can download and store the ones you use more frequently on your local computer. You also have ready access to new templates as they are added to Office.com from various sources.

In Project 2007, 41 templates were built in to the product. In Project 2010, through Office.com, about twice that number are available, and more are being added. These templates reflect various types of product, service, or activity projects in different industries and organizations, and they are based on widely accepted industry standards. Table 3-1 shows a sampling of the types of templates available.

Table 3-1 **Project Templates**

Business Development	Startup business plan
	New product plan
	New product launch
	Marketing campaign planning
Customer Service	Customer feedback monitoring
	Customer service ramp up
	Post-manufacturing customer service planning
Construction and Facilities	Commercial construction project plan
	Engineering project plan
	Office move plan
	Residential construction project plan
Finance and Accounting	Finance and accounting system implementation
	Audit preparation process
	Financial service offering launch
General Business	Annual report preparation
	Training rollout initiative and plan
	Proposal development plan
	Vendor evaluation and consolidation
Human Resources	Human resources interview plan
	Performance reviews
	Evaluating offshoring strategy for HR functions

Information Technology	Software development plan
	Security infrastructure
	Software localization plan
Standards and Process	Project office plan
	Project Management Institute process
	ISO 9001 management review
	Six Sigma DMAIC cycle
	Sarbanes-Oxley (SOX) compliance and technology options

Search for Templates Online

New Microsoft Project templates are continually being added to Office.com, and you can see those additions from the Project 2010 Backstage view or by going to the Office.com website. These templates are created not only by Microsoft, but also by project management consultants, solution providers, and everyday users.

Although the list is the same when you browse templates from the Project 2010 Backstage view, when you go to the Office.com website, you have the added convenience of sorting or searching for templates.

For the easiest way to open Office.com from Project 2010, follow these steps:

Help

1. In Project 2010, click the Help button in the upper-right corner.
2. Near the top of the Help screen, under the search box, click Templates.

   The Microsoft Office Templates page appears in your Internet browser.
3. On the Templates page, click See All Categories, and then click Plans.

Click the subcategory you want—for example, Business. The list of Microsoft Office planning templates appears. Browse through the list, looking for the Microsoft Project templates. You can sort the listed templates by title or rating.

Also on this web page, you can enter keywords for the type of template you're looking for in the search box. It might help to use "Project" as one of the keywords, because templates for various Microsoft Office programs are included here.

Click the thumbnail for a template, and a preview of the template appears. If you want to download the template, click the Download button, and then follow the instructions. When the download is finished, the template is loaded into Project 2010 as a new file based on that template.

To create a new project from a template, follow these steps:

1. On the File tab, click New.

   The Available Templates Backstage view appears, shown in Figure 3-2.

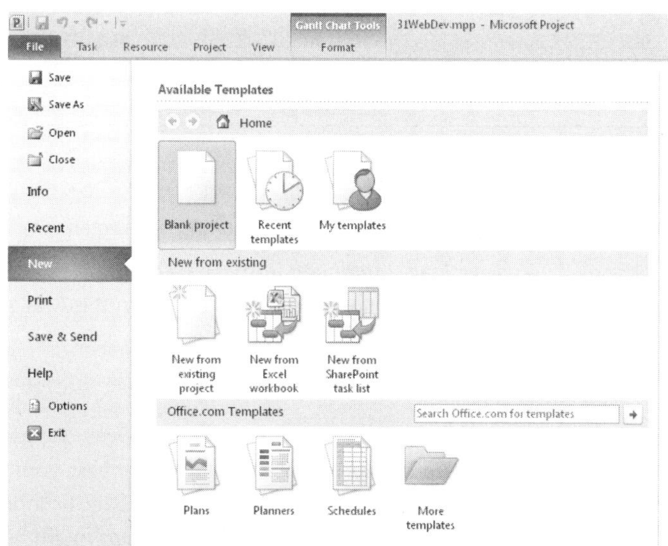

Figure 3-2 Available templates either on your computer or on Office.com are listed on the Backstage view.

2. If the template you want is already on your computer, you can find it by clicking Recent Templates or My Templates.

   Otherwise, click one of the categories under Office.com Templates and browse through the templates from Office.com.

3. When you find the template you want, click Download, Create, or OK, and the template opens as a new project plan. (See Figure 3-3.)

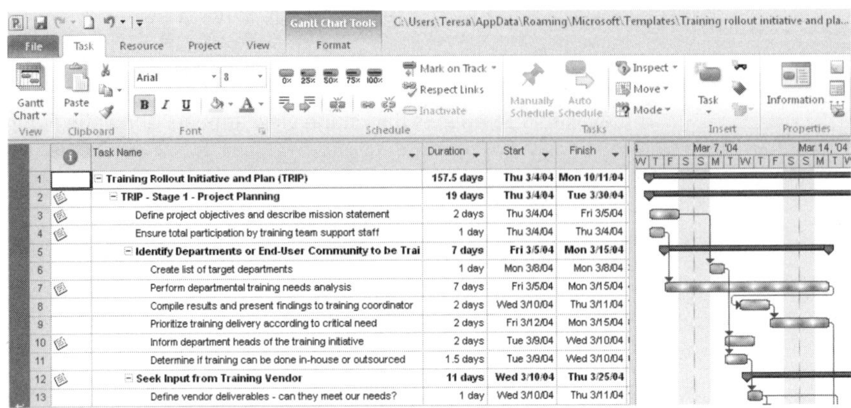

Figure 3-3 A new project file is created based on the selected template.

My Templates

Whenever you download a template from Office.com, it becomes available on your computer, and you can find it under My Templates on the Available Templates Backstage view.

Other Sources for Templates

Office.com isn't the only source for templates on which to base your new projects. You can also look for templates that reflect standards in your specific industry. Professional organizations, standards organizations, and industry groups might have resources, often downloadable from their websites, which include such templates for use with Project 2010.

You can even create your own project templates from previous projects. For more information about using completed projects as templates, see "Creating Your Own Project Template" on page 1198.

Note

If you use the enterprise features of Project Professional 2010, you use the enterprise global template, a different kind of template, which is set up by your project server administrator. The enterprise global template can include elements such as customized views, tables, and fields that reflect the project standards for your organization.

Creating a New Project from an Existing Project

If you have an existing project that you want to use as a starting point for your new project, you can simply copy and modify it for your current purposes. You save it under a different file name, creating a completely new file. Follow these steps:

Open

1. On the File tab, click Open.
2. In the Open dialog box, browse to the project file, and then click Open.

Saving Your New Project

Whether you are creating a new project from scratch, from a template, or from an existing project file, your next step is to save your new project. To do this, perform the following steps:

Save As

1. On the File tab, click Save As.

> **Note**
> **If you're creating a new project from scratch or from a template, you can simply click the Save button on the Quick Access Toolbar to open the Save As dialog box.**

2. In the Save As dialog box, choose the drive and folder in which you want to save the new project file.

   If you're set up for enterprise project management using Project Professional 2010 and Project Server 2010, you'll see the Save To Project Server dialog box instead.

3. In the File Name box, enter a descriptive name for your project, and then click the Save button.

   If you're working with Project Server and you want to save the project to the server, click the Save button. Depending on how your organization has set up enterprise project management standards, you might need to add information in custom enterprise fields.

   If you want to save the project locally on your own computer instead, click the Save As File button.

   For more information about working with enterprise projects, see "Creating a New Enterprise Project" on page 905.

> **Note**
>
> **Previous versions of Microsoft Project included the Define The Project Wizard, which walked a user through the setup of a new project. This wizard was part of the Project Guide and is no longer available in Project 2010.**

Scheduling from a Start or Finish Date

Your first scheduling decision is whether Project 2010 should calculate the schedule of your new project from a start date or from a finish date. Often, you have a finish date in mind, but you can still schedule from the start date and then make sure you hit the targeted finish date. You'll get more predictable results when you schedule from a start date.

For example, suppose you set up a project with 100 tasks to be scheduled from the start date. You specify task durations and sequence, link the tasks in the order they are to be performed, and indicate whether any tasks have specific dates by which they must be completed. With automatic scheduling, when you do not enter specific task start or finish dates, Project 2010 schedules tasks to be completed as soon as possible. Using task durations, links, and date constraints, Project 2010 schedules the first task to start on your project start date and the remaining tasks from that point forward until the last task is completed. If that last task is finished on a date that is too late for your project requirements, you can adjust the duration and sequencing, as well as the scope and resources assigned, to bring in the finish date to where you need it to be.

However, you might know the project finish date but not when your project will begin, because you're receiving work from another source that could be delayed. Or the project management methodology you use might require you to schedule from a finish date.

Consider that same project of 100 tasks. In a project scheduled from the finish date, any tasks that do not require a specific date are scheduled to be done as late as possible, rather than as soon as possible. Project 2010 schedules the last task to be finished on your project finish date and works backward from that point until the first task is started. If that first task is scheduled before the current date or too early for your project requirements, you can adjust the tasks and other aspects of the schedule.

INSIDE OUT **Beware of scheduling from the finish date**

If you must schedule from the finish date, be aware that your task dependencies, task constraints, and leveling tools will behave differently than in a project that is scheduled from the start date.

For more information about task constraints, see "Scheduling Tasks to Achieve Specific Dates" on page 219. For more information about resource leveling, see "Balancing Resource Workloads" on page 403.

To set up your project plan to be scheduled from the project start date, follow these steps:

Project Information

1. On the Project tab, in the Properties group, click Project Information.

   The Project Information dialog box appears, as shown in Figure 3-4.

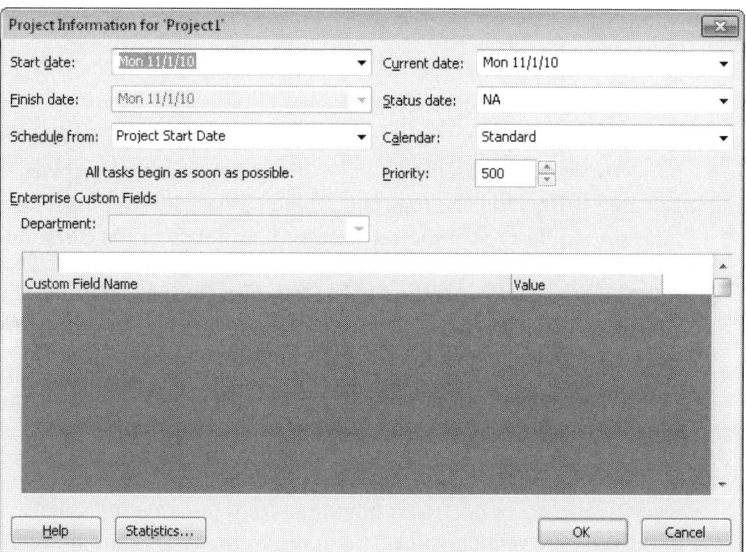

Figure 3-4 Use the Project Information dialog box to specify settings for the entire project.

2. In the Start Date box, enter the project start date.

   By default, the Start Date box shows today's date.

3. In the Schedule From box, click Project Start Date.

   Note that the date in the Finish Date box is dimmed, so you cannot edit it. Because you chose to schedule from the project start date, Project 2010 will calculate the finish date for you later. This is true whether the project is manually or automatically scheduled, particularly because projects can have a mix of manually and automatically scheduled tasks.

To set up your project plan to be scheduled from the project finish date, follow these steps:

1. On the Project tab, in the Properties group, click Project Information.
2. In the Schedule From box, click Project Finish Date.
3. In the Finish Date box, enter the project finish date.

   The date in the Start Date box is dimmed, so you cannot edit it. Because you chose to schedule from the project finish date, Project 2010 will calculate the start date for you later.

NEW!

Automatically Schedule from the Project Start Date or Today's Date

In previous versions of Microsoft Project, new tasks were always scheduled from the project start date (or from the project finish date if the project was set to be scheduled from the finish date). In Project 2010, you can specify whether automatically scheduled tasks should start at the project start (or finish) date or the current date.

To specify this preference, on the File tab, click Options, and then click Schedule in the left pane. Under Scheduling Options For This Project, in the box labeled Auto Scheduled Tasks Scheduled On, select Project Start Date or Current Date.

Setting Your Project Calendar

With the *project calendar*, you establish the working days and times for your project and its tasks. The project calendar also becomes the default calendar for any resources working on your project. The project calendar indicates when your organization typically works on project tasks and when it's off work. By setting your project calendar, you establish one of the fundamental methods for scheduling the tasks in your project.

You choose a *base calendar* to become your project calendar. You can create your own base calendar, or you can choose one of the three base calendars that come with Project 2010. A base calendar is rather like a calendar template that you can apply to a set of resources, a set of tasks, or the project as a whole. Table 3-2 describes the working days and times specified in the base calendars provided by Project 2010.

Table 3-2 Base Calendars

Standard	Working time is set to Monday through Friday, 8:00 A.M. until 5:00 P.M., with an hour off for lunch between noon and 1:00 P.M. each day. This is the default base calendar used for the project, for tasks, and for resources.
Night Shift	Working time is set to an 11:00 P.M. until 8:00 A.M. night shift, five days a week, with an hour off for lunch from 3:00 A.M. until 4:00 A.M. This base calendar is generally used for resources who work a graveyard shift. It can also be used for projects that are carried out only during the night shift.
24 Hours	Working time is set to midnight until midnight seven days a week; that is, work never stops. This base calendar is typically used for projects in a manufacturing situation, for example, that might run two or three back-to-back shifts every day of the week.

Applying a Base Calendar to the Project Calendar

If you want to use the Standard base calendar as your project calendar, you don't need to do much—the Standard calendar is the project calendar by default. If you want to use a different base calendar, you must select it as your project calendar. To do so, follow these steps:

1. On the Project tab, in the Properties group, click Project Information.
2. In the Calendar box, select the name of the base calendar.
3. Click OK.

You can use any of the three base calendars (Standard, Night Shift, or 24 Hours) as the basis for the project calendar, resource calendars, or task calendars. In fact, you could use all three within the same project. For example, you might apply the Standard calendar to the project as a whole, the Night Shift calendar to a certain group of resources, and the 24 Hours calendar to tasks being carried out by automated equipment.

For more information about the task calendar, see "Working with Task Calendars" on page 234. For more information about resource calendars, see "Setting Working Times and Days Off for Work Resources" on page 267.

Modifying a Base Calendar

You can modify the project calendar to reflect your team's normal working times and days off, including any holidays you'll all be taking and other one-time calendar exceptions. You can also specify recurring exceptions in your working times calendar.

To modify the project calendar, you change the base calendar that the project calendar is using as its starting point. Any of the base calendars can be customized to reflect specialized working days and times.

Specifying the Normal Work Week for a Base Calendar

As specified earlier in Table 3-2, the three base calendars that come with Project 2010 have their default working days and times. You might apply one of these base calendars to your project to make it the calendar on which your project is based. When you do this, your schedule is governed by the working days and times in that base calendar.

You can change the default working days and times of the normal work week. To do this, follow these steps:

Change Working Time

1. On the Project tab, in the Properties group, click Change Working Time.
2. In the For Calendar box, click the name of the base calendar you want to modify. (See Figure 3-5.)

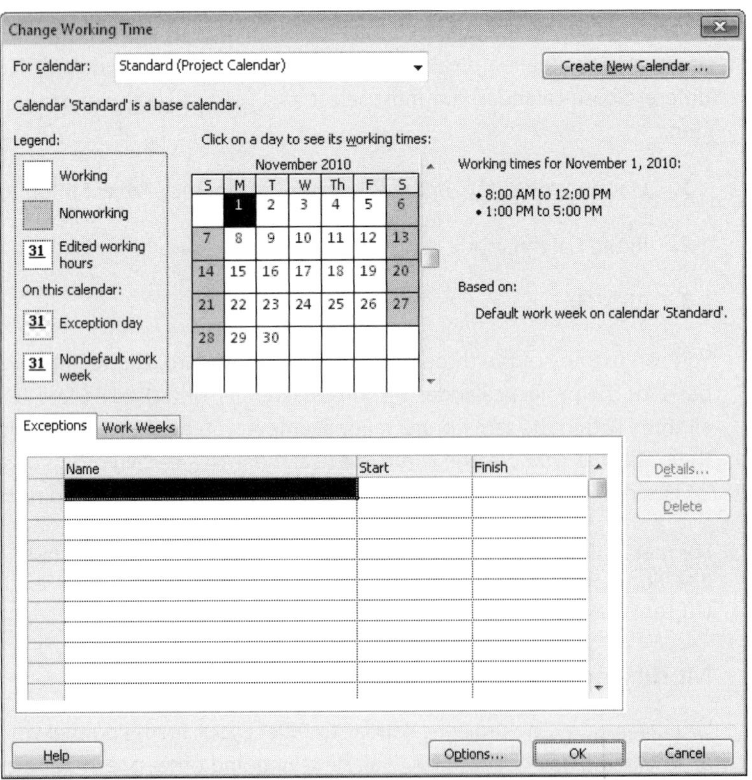

Figure 3-5 Use the Change Working Time dialog box to modify a base calendar.

3. Click the Work Weeks tab, shown in Figure 3-6.

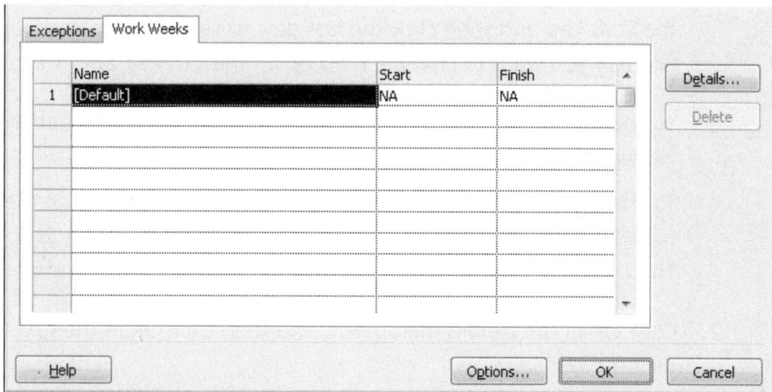

Figure 3-6 Use the Work Weeks tab to change the default work week or to create alternative work weeks.

Notice that row 1 contains the text [Default] with NA in both the Start and Finish fields. This indicates that the default working days and times are to be used whenever an alternative work week is not scheduled.

4. Be sure that the Default row is selected, and then click the Details button to open the Details for '[Default]' dialog box, shown in Figure 3-7.

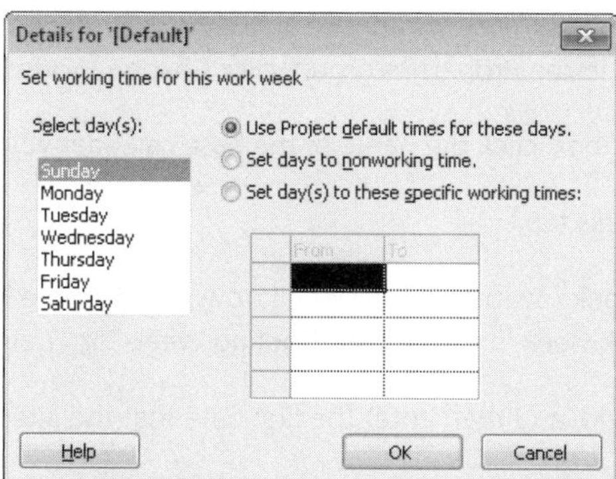

Figure 3-7 The work week Details dialog box shows the working days and times for the selected work week.

If you click a day of the week in the Select Day(s) box, its working times appear in the From/To table to the right. If no working times appear in the table, this indicates that the selected day is a nonworking day. Above the table, the option labeled Use Project Default Times For These Days is selected.

Chapter 3

5. In the Select Day(s) box, click the day of the week you want to change.

   You can drag to select consecutive days. You can also click the first day, hold down the Shift key, and then click the last day. To select several nonadjacent days, click the first day you want to change, hold down the Ctrl key, and then click the other days.

6. To change the day(s) to nonworking time, click the option labeled Set Days To Nonworking Time.

   To change a nonworking day to a working day, or to change the working times of a working day, click the option labeled Set Day(s) To These Specific Working Times. Then, in the From/To table, type the start and finish working times.

7. Click OK in the Details dialog box, and then click OK in the Change Working Time dialog box.

Setting Up an Alternative Work Week

Your project might need an alternative work week specified for a particular period of time. One example might be a construction company working an accelerated schedule to complete exterior work before winter. Another example might be a training project in which the default work week is used for curriculum development and testing and a different, temporary work week is used when actual training takes place.

You can specify any number of alternative work weeks to make sure your project scheduling reflects such situations. To specify an alternative work week, follow these steps:

1. On the Project tab, in the Properties group, click Change Working Time.
2. In the For Calendar box, click the name of the base calendar you want to modify.
3. Click the Work Weeks tab.
4. Click in the next blank row below the Default row. In the Name field, type a name for the alternative work week, for example, "Roofing Week" or "Training Week."
5. Click in the Start field, and then enter the first date that the alternative working times should be in effect.
6. Click in the Finish field, and then enter the last date that the alternative working times should be in effect.
7. With the row for the new work week still selected, click the Details button.
8. In the Select Day(s) box, click the day(s) of the week you want to change.

9. To change a nonworking day to a working day, or to change the working times of a working day, click the option labeled Set Day(s) To These Specific Working Times. Then, in the From/To table, type the start and finish working times.

   To change the selected day(s) to nonworking time, click the option labeled Set Days To Nonworking Time.

10. Click OK in the Details dialog box, and then click OK in the Change Working Time dialog box.

> **Note**
>
> **To delete an alternative work week, on the Work Weeks tab in the Change Working Time dialog box, click the name of the work week and then click the Delete button. You cannot delete the Default work week.**

Setting Up Holidays and Other One-Time Calendar Exceptions

To make a one-time exception to an existing base calendar, follow these steps:

1. On the Project tab, in the Properties group, click Change Working Time.

2. In the For Calendar box, click the name of the base calendar you want to modify.

3. Click the day in the calendar thumbnail whose working times you want to change.

   When you click a day in the calendar thumbnail, information about that day's working times appears to the right. This tells you whether the day is a working or nonworking day, and what the working times are. It also indicates which calendar the selected day is using and whether there's a exception or alternative work week applied.

   To change the working time of a day in another month, use the scroll arrow in the calendar thumbnail until you see the correct month.

4. Be sure the Exceptions tab is selected, click in the first available row in the Name column, and then enter the name of the calendar exception. Press Enter or Tab when you finish.

   Although entering a name for the exception is not required, it can be useful for distinguishing the reason for the exception. Examples might include "Martin Luther King, Jr. Holiday" or "Department Offsite."

   After you press Enter or Tab, the name is entered and the Start and Finish dates are entered, defaulting to the date you clicked in the thumbnail calendar.

5. If necessary, change the date in the Start or Finish field.

   When you enter an exception for a working day, by default it changes to a nonworking day.

> **Note**
>
> **By default, the Start and Finish dates are the same—the date selected in the thumbnail calendar. If the date of an exception is several months in the future, it's easier to enter the date in this field rather than scroll to it in the thumbnail calendar.**
>
> **Also, if the exception goes across a series of days, enter the last day of the exception in the Finish field. This can be useful for entering a two-week holiday shutdown, for example.**

6. If the exception is a change other than switching a working day to a nonworking day, click the Details button to open the Details dialog box. (See Figure 3-8.)

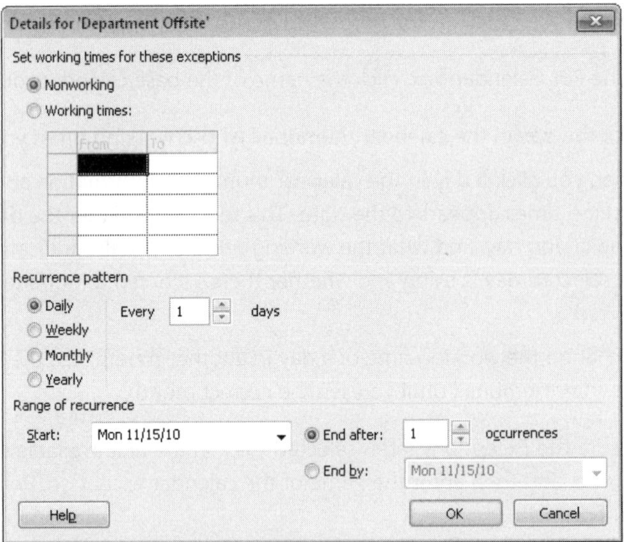

Figure 3-8 Use the Details dialog box to specify the details about the working times calendar exception.

7. If you're changing working time to nonworking time, select the Nonworking option.

8. If you're changing the working time to something other than the default, select the Working Times option, and then change the times in the From and To boxes as needed.

9. Click OK to close the Details dialog box, and then click OK to close the Change Working Time dialog box.

Setting Up a Recurring Calendar Exception

You can set up a calendar exception to take place on a recurring pattern. For example, if you're developing the plan for a three-year project, you'll probably want to show that the New Year's Day holiday exception takes place on January 1 each year, or that the Thanksgiving holidays take place on the fourth Thursday and Friday of November each year.

In the same way, if you know that no work on the project will take place from 9:00 to 11:00 A.M. on the first Monday of every month because of the monthly divisional staff meeting, you can build that into your project's working times calendar.

Recurring Calendar Exceptions vs. Recurring Project Tasks

If company or department events will take place and affect progress on project tasks—for example, meetings or offsites that don't have a direct bearing on the project work itself—it's best to handle the time for these events using a calendar exception.

However, if you know you have a recurring project status meeting every Wednesday morning, for example, you can build that into your project tasks schedule and assign resources to it. For more information, see "Entering Recurring Tasks" on page 107.

To set up a recurring calendar exception to an existing base calendar, follow these steps:

1. On the Project tab, in the Properties group, click Change Working Time.
2. In the For Calendar box, click the name of the base calendar you want to modify.
3. Click the day in the calendar thumbnail whose working times you want to change.
4. On the Exceptions tab, click in the first available row in the Name column, and then enter the name of the calendar exception. Press Enter or Tab when you finish.
5. If necessary, change the dates in the Start or Finish field.
6. Click the Details button.
7. If you're changing working time to nonworking time, select the Nonworking option.

8. If you're changing the working time to something other than the default, select the Working Times option, and then change the times in the From and To boxes as needed.

9. Under Recurrence Pattern, specify how often the calendar exception takes place; that is, daily, weekly, or monthly.

   Also specify the details of when the recurring calendar exception is to take place during that frequency—for example, every other Thursday or the first Monday of every month.

10. Under Range Of Recurrence, specify the number of times the recurring calendar exception is to take place or the date when the recurring calendar exception is to end.

11. Click OK to close the Details dialog box, and then click OK to close the Change Working Time dialog box.

Note

To delete an exception, on the Exceptions tab in the Change Working Time dialog box, click the name of the exception, and then click the Delete button.

Set Up a Weekly Working Times Exception

In Microsoft Project 2003 and earlier versions, if a working times exception occurred on a particular day of the week, you selected the day heading in the calendar thumbnail and then changed the working times.

To do the same thing in Project 2010, you select the first day that this exception occurs and give the exception a name. Then, in the Details dialog box, you specify the recurrence pattern of every week. You also specify how long that recurrence pattern takes place. If this exception will be happening throughout the life of the project, use the project finish date as a guideline.

If the project finish date changes, remember to come back to this dialog box and change this setting. In fact, it doesn't hurt to have such recurring working times calendar exceptions overshoot the project finish date by a month or so. Then, when you need to adjust your project schedule for the inevitable changes that will take place, you'll have one less adjustment to worry about.

Creating a New Base Calendar

If you need to apply a common working calendar to your project, a group of resources, or a set of tasks that isn't built in to Project 2010 already, you can create your own base calendar.

To create a new base calendar, follow these steps:

1. On the Project tab, in the Properties group, click Change Working Time.
2. Click the Create New Calendar button. The Create New Base Calendar dialog box appears, as shown in Figure 3-9.

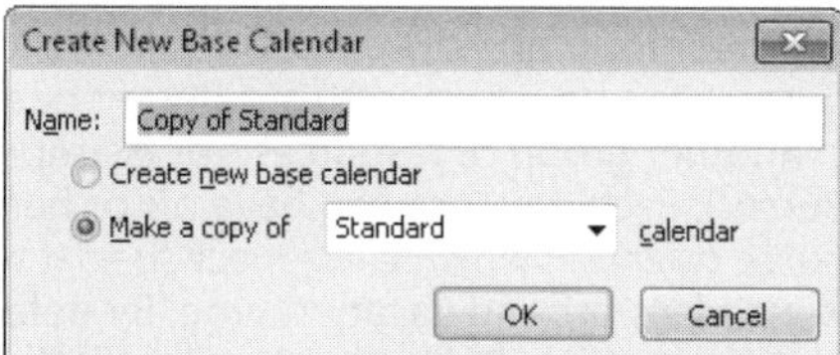

Figure 3-9 You can create a new base calendar from scratch or adapt an existing one.

3. In the Name box, type the name you want for the new base calendar (for example, Swing Shift).
4. Select the Create New Base Calendar option if you want to adapt your calendar from the Standard base calendar.

   Select the Make A Copy Of option if you want to adapt a different base calendar, such as the Night Shift calendar, to create the new calendar. Click the name of the existing calendar you want to adapt, and then click OK.
5. Make the changes you want to the working days and times of individual days or for a particular day of every week, as needed.
6. When you finish with your new base calendar, click OK.

Organizer

Note

You can delete a base calendar you have created, but you cannot do it within the Change Working Time dialog box. Instead, you need to use the Organizer. On the File tab, click Organizer, and then click the Calendars tab. In the box on the right, you'll see a list of base calendars used by the current project. Select the base calendar you want to delete, click the Delete button, and then click Yes. Click the Close button to dismiss the Organizer dialog box.

For more information about the Organizer, see "Sharing Customized Elements Among Projects" on page 1138.

Project, Resource, and Task Calendars

Project 2010 uses three types of calendars as tools for scheduling the project, as shown in Table 3-3.

Table 3-3 **Calendars in Project 2010**

Project calendar	Governs when tasks are scheduled to be worked on and when resources are scheduled to work on assigned tasks. See "Setting Your Project Calendar" on page 84.
Resource calendar	Governs when resources are scheduled to work on assigned tasks. One group of resources (for example, day shift resources) can be assigned to a different base calendar than another group of resources (for example, swing shift resources). Each resource can have his or her own individual resource calendar, which can reflect special work schedules, personal days off, and vacation time. By default, the resource calendar is the Standard calendar. See "Setting Working Times and Days Off for Work Resources" on page 267.
Task calendar	Governs when tasks are scheduled to be worked on. As a rule, tasks are scheduled according to the project calendar and the calendars of any assigned resources. However, sometimes a task has special scheduling requirements that are different from the norm. For example, a task might be carried out by a machine running 24 hours a day. In such a case, it's useful for a task to have its own calendar. See "Setting Up the Task Calendar" on page 234.

Attaching Project Documentation

You can make Project 2010 the central repository for all your important project documentation. For example, you might want to attach or link your scope statement to your project plan, as well as other documents, such as the needs analysis, market study, and product specifications.

Showing the Project Summary Task

To attach planning documentation to your project, the first step is to display the project summary task. Not only does the project summary task eventually provide summary date and cost information for the project as a whole, but it can serve as the location for your attached or linked planning documents.

There's a quicker, more direct route to displaying the project summary task than in previous versions of Microsoft Project. On the Format tab, in the Show/Hide group, select the Project Summary Task check box.

A summary task appears in Row 0 of the Gantt Chart (see Figure 3-10), adopting the name of the file as the project summary task name. If you want to change the name, click twice in the Task Name field for the project summary task. Edit the name and then press Enter.

Figure 3-10 Use the project summary task to attach or link planning documents.

The project summary task appears in any task view for this project—for example, the Task Usage view or the Network Diagram.

Copying a Document to Your Project File

You can include planning documents created in other programs within Project 2010. Although this can significantly increase the size of your project file, you'll know that all your project information is stored in one place. To include the documents, follow these steps:

1. Select the project summary task.

Notes

2. On the Task tab, in the Properties group, click Notes.

   You can also double-click the project summary task to open the Summary Task Information dialog box.

Insert Object

3. On the Notes tab, click the Insert Object button.
4. In the Insert Object dialog box, select the Create From File option, and then click the Browse button.
5. In the Browse dialog box, select the project planning document you want to attach to or *embed* in your project file. Click the Insert button.

6. Back in the Insert Object dialog box, select the Display As Icon check box. (See Figure 3-11.)

   If the document is small, consider clearing the Display As Icon check box. Clearing this check box embeds the content of the file in your project Notes box, so you can read it directly from there.

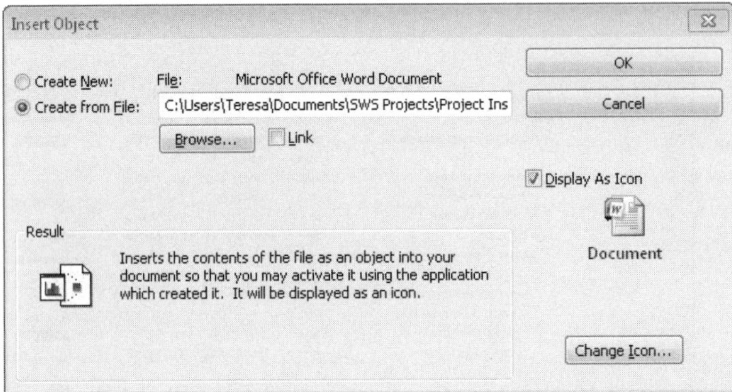

Figure 3-11 The selected document will be embedded in your project plan.

7. Click OK.

   The document's icon appears in the Notes area of the Summary Task Information dialog box, as shown in Figure 3-12.

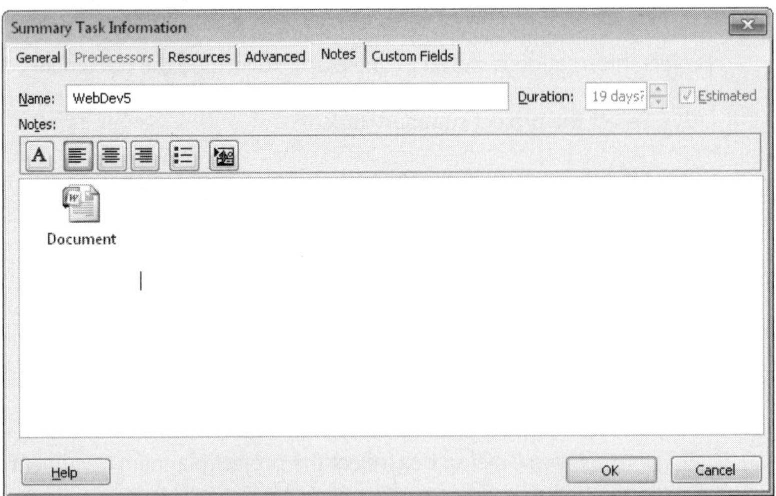

Figure 3-12 Double-clicking the icon opens the file in its originating application.

8. In the Summary Task Information dialog box, click OK.

   The Note indicator appears in the Gantt Chart, as shown in Figure 3-13.

	ⓘ	Task Mode	Task Name	Duration
0			− **WebDev5**	**19 days?**
1			− **Web Structure**	**19 days**
2			Brainstorm content categories	3 days
3			Hold user meetings	4 days

Figure 3-13 When you store something in a Notes tab, the Note indicator appears in the corresponding row of the Gantt Chart.

Now, whenever you need to review the document, just double-click the Note indicator to open the Notes tab of the Summary Task Information dialog box. Then double-click the document icon.

For more information about embedding, see "Embedding Information" on page 656.

Note

In addition to attaching documents to the project summary task, you can attach documents to summary tasks and individual tasks. This can be useful when you have specifications or drawings that further define the scope of a particular subphase or task. You can also attach deliverables or milestone reports to milestone tasks.

Hyperlinking a Document or Website to Your Project File

Hyperlinking is another way to include planning documents or web references with your project file. Hyperlinking is a preferred method for attaching files when you want to keep the size of your project file trimmer and you know that your project plan and associated planning documents will always be in the same place. It's also a very efficient method for opening associated documents quickly.

Adding a hyperlink to a document or website on the project summary task ensures that the content is associated with the project as a whole, rather than with an individual task.

Note

In addition to hyperlinking to documents from the project summary task, you can create a hyperlink from summary tasks and individual tasks.

To insert a hyperlink to a project planning document or website, follow these steps:

Hyperlink

1. Right-click the project summary task, and on the shortcut menu that appears, click Hyperlink.

   The Insert Hyperlink dialog box appears.

2. In the Text To Display box, type a descriptive name for the document to which you are linking—for example, Project Scope Statement or Web Dev Team Site.

3. If you're hyperlinking a project planning document, be sure that Current Folder is selected, and browse through your computer's file system to find and select the document. (See Figure 3-14.)

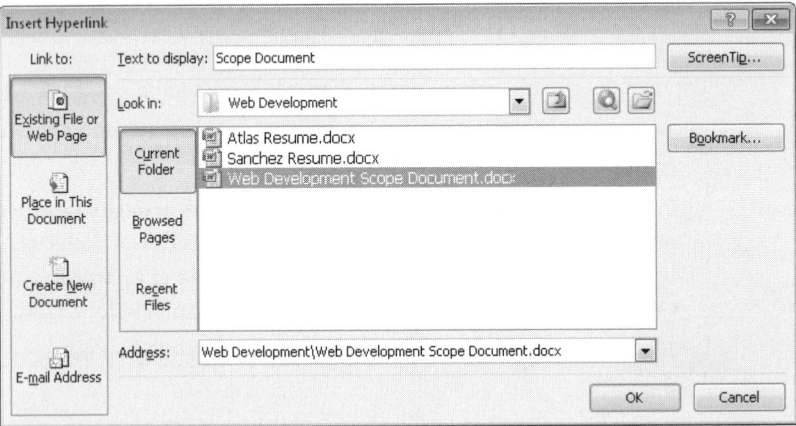

Figure 3-14 The path and name of the selected document appear in the Address box.

   If you're hyperlinking a web page, select all existing text in the Address box and replace it with the address for the website to which you want to hyperlink. (See Figure 3-15.)

4. Click OK.

   The Hyperlink indicator appears in the Indicators field of the Gantt Chart, as you can see in Figure 3-16.

   Now, whenever you need to review the document or go to the website, just click the Hyperlink indicator. The document opens in its own application window, or the website opens in your web browser.

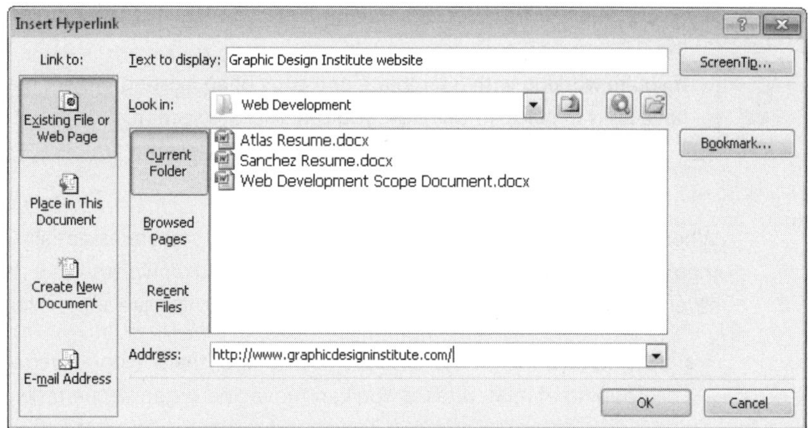

Figure 3-15 Enter the address of the website in the Address box.

		Task Mode	Task Name	Duration
0			**WebDev5**	**19 days?**
1			**Web Structure**	**19 days**
2			Brainstorm content categories	3 days
3			Hold user meetings	4 days

Figure 3-16 When you hyperlink a document to a task, the Hyperlink indicator appears in the corresponding row of the Gantt Chart.

For more information, see "Hyperlinking to Websites or Other Documents" on page 674.

If you're using Project Professional with Project Server for enterprise project management, the preferred method for keeping all project documents together is to use the *document library* that's part of Microsoft Project Web App 2010. With the document library, you can set up, maintain, and share documents with the project team and other stakeholders. This way, everyone involved can view the documents through their web browsers. They can also check documents in and out, which provides vital version control.

For more information about setting up a document library in Project Web App 2010, see "Controlling Project Documents" on page 959.

Entering Tasks

Now that you've created the foundation for your new project plan, with the project start date and the project calendar, you're ready to get down to the real business of entering tasks.

Note

If you're working with a template or a copy of an existing project plan, you already have tasks in place. In this case, you can skip this section.

When entering tasks and filling in the Gantt Chart, you are essentially entering the elements and the hierarchy reflected in your *work breakdown structure (WBS)*. You can take several approaches to develop your WBS. The following are some examples:

- **Brainstorming** Enter tasks as you think of them, without regard to sequence or grouping of related tasks. You can move and organize the tasks later.
- **Sequential** Think through the project from beginning to end, and enter tasks sequentially.
- **Phases** Think of the overall phases of the project. For example, in a commercial construction project, you might enter the phases of Procurement, On-Site Mobilization, Site Grading, Foundations, Steel Erection, and so on. After those phases are in place, you can add tasks and subtasks beneath them.
- **Milestones and deliverables** Consider what the project is producing in terms of the milestones and deliverables. Enter those events as tasks and then add tasks and subtasks beneath them to flesh out the project. Your scope statement can be a valuable guide in this process.
- **Team collaboration** Ask team members to list the tasks they believe will be necessary for the areas under their responsibility. This assumes, of course, that you already have team members in place and available. Team members can submit tasks and estimated durations in several ways. They can use a simple e-mail message or a document. They can use a Microsoft Outlook task list, a Microsoft Excel spreadsheet, or a Microsoft SharePoint task list. If you're using Project Server, team members can send you tasks from Project Web App, and then you can incorporate them automatically into your project plan.

For more information about these collaboration methods, see "Importing Tasks from an Excel Worksheet" on page 102; Chapter 20, "Integrating Project 2010 with Outlook;" and Chapter 21, "Collaborating as a Team by Using SharePoint." For information about creating new tasks through automated team collaboration, see "Assigning Tasks to Enterprise Resources" on page 941.

- **Archived projects** Review completed projects of a similar type in your organization. With such historical information, you might find that much of the legwork—in terms of phases, task sequencing, resource assignments, and more—has been done for you. If the archived projects contain solid tracking information, you'll have excellent data on durations and costs.

  For more information about using an old project as a starting point for a new one, see "Starting a New Project from a Template" on page 1192. For more information about saving a completed project for future reference, see "Closing a Project" on page 1202.

- **Expert consultation** Ask known experts what tasks are needed for various aspects of the project. This is particularly useful if you're the manager of a project in which you're not necessarily an expert. This happens frequently enough, and it's not necessarily a bad thing, but you need dependable experts to help provide reliable task information. Even if you're well versed in the project knowledge area, you might not know all the nitty-gritty details for each phase. Experts can come from within your own group, from stakeholders, from other groups or project managers within your organization, or from colleagues in your profession or industry.

Project Management Practices: Activity Definition

The stage of the project management process in which you're entering tasks is often referred to as activity definition. Here, the planning team identifies the specific activities, or tasks, that must be done to produce the project deliverables and meet the project objectives as specified in the scope statement.

Activity definition is typically performed with the guidance provided in the scope statement and the work breakdown structure. The deliverables, or work packages, described in the WBS are divided and subdivided into smaller tasks that can be better managed and controlled in the project.

For more information about work breakdown structures in Project 2010, see "Setting Up Your Work Breakdown Structure" on page 119.

In some organizations, the project management methodology dictates that the WBS is developed first and the task list is developed next. Other organizations develop both at the same time.

In any case, the task list must include all activities that will be performed in the project, but it does not include any activities that are not required as part of the project scope. Each task should be descriptive enough to communicate to responsible team members what is required by the task.

Adding Tasks to Your Project Plan

To enter tasks directly into your project plan, follow these steps:

1. Make sure you're working in the Gantt Chart.

   Gantt Chart

   You can see the name of the current view in the Active View bar that runs vertically along the left edge of the view. If it isn't labeled *Gantt Chart,* on the View tab, in the Task Views group, click Gantt Chart.

   You can enter tasks in any task view, of course. For more information about views, see Chapter 4.

2. Type the name of the task in the Task Name field.

3. Press Enter or the Down Arrow key to move to the next row.

   The task name isn't recorded, and other commands remain unavailable, until you press Enter.

4. To edit a task that's already entered, click the task name, and then click it again until the cursor appears in the cell. Be sure to make the two clicks slowly so that they are not interpreted as a double-click, in which case a dialog box appears. Edit the task name.

   By default, new tasks are manually scheduled. Tasks can easily be changed to be automatically scheduled, and the default scheduling method can be changed as well.

   For more information, see Chapter 5, "Scheduling Tasks Manually or Automatically." For more information about entering durations, links, and start and finish dates, see Chapter 6, "Building Your Schedule."

Importing Tasks from an Excel Worksheet

Many project managers find that they can more quickly build an accurate task list for their project plan by having others on the team develop a task list for their specific areas of responsibility. Even if a team isn't in place yet, you can still ask the advice of those with the necessary expertise. If these individuals are not Microsoft Project users, a great way to automate this process is to have them use Excel to create their task lists. You can then import the worksheets into the Project 2010 Gantt Chart.

The easiest way to import tasks from Excel into Project is to use the Project Task List Import Template. This Excel template contains columns that are mapped to specific Project 2010 fields to ensure that the right information ends up in the right places in your Gantt Chart task table.

What Happened to the Entry Bar?

In previous versions of Microsoft Project, an entry bar was shown by default. In Project 2010, if you want to use the entry bar, follow these steps:

1. On the File tab, click Options, and then in the left pane, click Display.
2. Under Show These Elements, select the Entry Bar check box.
3. Click OK.

   The entry bar appears between the bottom of the ribbon and the top of the view in all views throughout the project and in any other project files you open.

Use the entry bar to enter or edit tasks. When you type in the entry bar, the cancel and enter buttons appear.

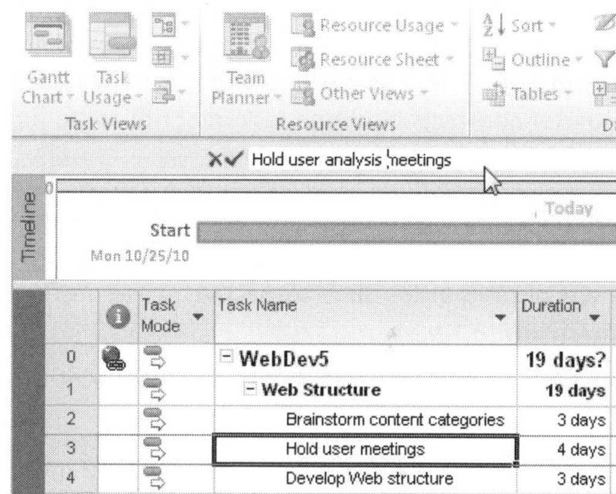

You can cancel an entry by pressing Esc on the keyboard and enter changes by pressing the Enter key.

Tips for Entering Tasks

Keep the following suggestions in mind while you enter tasks:

- Don't be overly concerned about sequence when you first enter tasks. You can worry about that after you have a "first draft" of tasks in place.
- Don't get into the scheduling aspects of the tasks just yet. Leave the duration, start, and finish fields blank, at least until you learn more about your project scheduling options.
- Name the task with sufficient description to communicate to team members and stakeholders what the task is about. A task called simply "Review" or "Edit" might not provide enough information.
- Decide whether you want the context of the task to be understood if it's ever separated (by being in a separate view, report, filter, or grouping, for example) from its surrounding tasks. For example, you might have several tasks in different phases for "Administer contracts." But one task might relate to procurement, one to the architects, and another one to the builders.
- Note whether you have sets of tasks that are repeated in different phases of the project. You might want to give them more general names so that you can copy and paste these sets of tasks under their respective phases instead of repeatedly typing them individually.

To use the Project Task List Import Template, Excel and Project 2010 must be installed on the same computer.

Follow these steps to find the Project Task List Import Template in Excel and enter tasks:

1. Start Microsoft Excel 2010. On the File tab, click New.
2. Near the top of the Available Templates Backstage view, click Sample Templates.

Sample Templates

3. Click the Microsoft Project Task List Import Template.

INSIDE OUT Don't feel obligated to complete the other fields

In previous versions of Microsoft Project, we regularly cautioned users not to complete the Start and Finish fields when entering tasks, no matter how tempting it might be. It really felt intuitive to fill in the blank fields on the Gantt Chart, which by default includes the Task Name, Duration, Start, Finish, Predecessors, and Resource Names fields as columns.

However, at this stage of project planning, it's best to focus just on entering tasks. If you happen to know durations off the top of your head, it's okay to enter those as well. But leave the Start and Finish fields as they are for now. These dates and other scheduling information can be added a little later.

That said, with the choice of manual or automatic scheduling in Project 2010, and with manual scheduling being the default, most adverse impacts of entering start and finish dates in your plan are eradicated.

If you fill in the Start and Finish fields for manually scheduled tasks, no harm is done. The manually entered dates are in place for you to use as you wish. If you decide to switch to automatic scheduling, those dates are removed and replaced with the automatically scheduled dates.

Just take special care if you have switched the default for all new tasks in your project to be automatically scheduled. In this case, the old warnings still apply. In automatic scheduling, if you enter dates in the Start and Finish fields, Project 2010 interprets those as hard-and-fast date constraints that can put undue restrictions on your schedule. This not only can impact scheduling flexibility, but it can also create scheduling conflicts, and actually cause quite a mess in your project.

The best approach is to enter the task names first and then the durations if you know them. For automatically scheduled tasks, leave the Start and Finish fields as they are for now and let Project 2010 calculate them as you add other project information, such as durations and links between tasks. If you then need to constrain the dates, you can edit them as you need to.

The differences between manually and automatically scheduled tasks are detailed in Chapter 5. The various controls available for scheduling the project—including durations, task links, and date constraints—are covered extensively in Chapter 6.

4. Click the Create button.

   The template appears, showing information about the template.

5. Read the template information, and then click the Task_Table tab at the lower-left corner of the worksheet. The template appears with columns similar to standard Project 2010 fields, as shown in Figure 3-17.

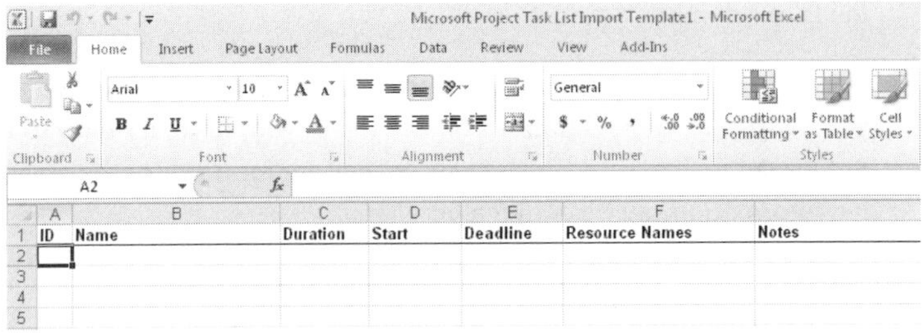

Figure 3-17 Share the Excel Task List Import template with your team to help build your project plan.

6. Save this file and provide it to your team members to use to enter tasks and other task information. Have them save the information and send the electronic file to you when they finish.

You can also provide the template to others on your team who might not have Project 2010 installed on their computers. The template is typically located on your computer in the C:\Users*username*\AppData\Roaming\Microsoft\Templates folder and is named Tasklist.xlt. You can copy and e-mail this file to your team members. They should save this file to the same Templates folder on their computers. It will then appear in the Sample Templates list on the Available Templates Backstage view.

INSIDE OUT Find the template in earlier versions of Excel

If you're working with earlier versions of Microsoft Excel, you can still find the Microsoft Project Task List Import template.

In Excel 2007, click the Microsoft Office Button, and then click New. In the New Workbook dialog box, under Templates, click Installed Templates. Double-click the Microsoft Project Task List Import Template.

In Microsoft Excel 2003 or earlier, click File, New. In the task pane, click the On My Computer link. Click the Spreadsheet Solutions tab. Double-click the Microsoft Project Task List Import Template.

When you're ready to import the task list into your project plan, follow these steps:

1. Open the project plan in which you want to import the Excel task list.
2. On the File tab, click New.
3. In the Available Templates Backstage view, under New From Existing, click New From Excel Workbook.

New From Excel Workbook

4. Use the Open dialog box that appears to browse to the location on your computer or network where the task list from Excel is saved.

   By default, Excel Workbooks (*.xlsx) are listed. If the task list was created using Excel 2003 or an earlier version, change the file type being searched. To the right of the File Name box, click the arrow on the button labeled Excel Workbook (*.xlsx), then click Excel 97-2003 (*.xls) in the drop-down menu.

   The task list appears in the list of folders and files.
5. Click the task list workbook, and then click Open.

   The Import Wizard appears.
6. Click Next.
7. Click Project Excel Template, and then click Next.
8. Specify whether you want to import the file as a new project, append the tasks to the currently active project, or merge the data into the active project.
9. Click Finish.

   The tasks are imported into Project 2010 as you specified.

For more information about using Project 2010 with other applications, see "Importing and Exporting Information" on page 676 and Chapter 18, "Integrating Project 2010 with Excel."

Entering Recurring Tasks

You might have certain project tasks that need to be scheduled at regularly occurring intervals. For example, your project team might meet every Thursday morning, or perhaps you gather information and generate a resource management report the first Monday of each month. Instead of entering the same task every week or every month throughout the span of the project, you can create a *recurring task*. To do this, follow these steps:

1. Make sure you're working in the Gantt Chart.

   If necessary, on the View tab, in the Task Views group, click Gantt Chart.

2. In the Task Name field, click in the row above which you want the recurring task to appear.

3. On the Task tab, in the Insert group, click the arrow under Task, and then click Recurring Task.

4. In the Recurring Task dialog box, type the name of the recurring task in the Task Name field; for example, **Generate resource management report**. (See Figure 3-18.)

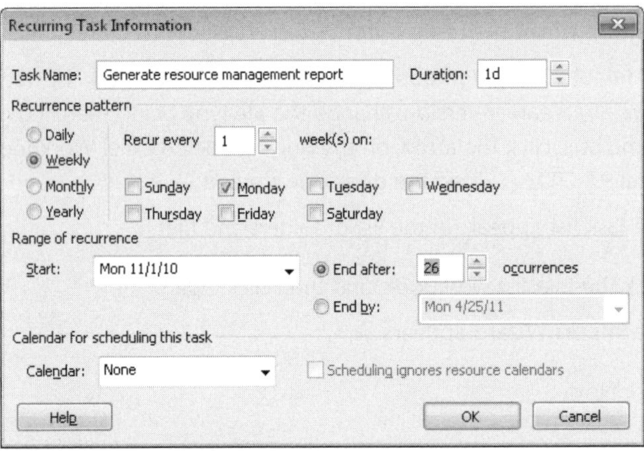

Figure 3-18 Specify the name and scheduling details of your recurring task.

5. Under Recurrence Pattern, specify how often the task is to be scheduled; for example, daily, weekly, or monthly.

6. Specify the details of when the task is to take place during that frequency; for example, every other Thursday or the first Monday of every month.

7. Under Range Of Recurrence, specify when the recurring task is to start and end.

   By default, the End By option is selected, with today's date in the box. If you leave this default, no recurring tasks are created. Be sure to enter an end by date or change the option to End After and enter a number of occurrences.

8. If this recurring task is to be scheduled according to a base calendar that's different from the project calendar, in the Calendar box, select the name of the base calendar to be used.

9. When you have finished, click OK.

Recurring indicator

The recurring task is marked with a Recurring Task indicator. It's formatted as a *summary task* with all occurrences of the task as *subtasks*. (Information about summary tasks and subtasks can be found in "Organizing Tasks into an Outline" on page 115.)

View Recurring Task Information

You can view recurring task information in different ways, as follows:

- **Click the + icon next to the recurring summary task to see each occurrence of the recurring task.**
- **Review the recurrence range by resting your pointer over the Recurring Task indicator.**
- **Double-click the recurring task to open the Recurring Task Information dialog box.**

Sequencing and Organizing Tasks

With the Gantt Chart in your project file now full of tasks, it's time to put these tasks in a logical order. It's also time to add any forgotten tasks or delete duplicate ones.

Moving Tasks

To move a task from one row to another, follow these steps:

1. In the table area of the Gantt Chart, select the entire task row by clicking the gray row heading, which includes the task number.
2. With your mouse pointer still over the row heading (the pointer should appear as a black crosshair), drag the task to the location in the Gantt Chart where you want to place it.

   A gray line along the row border follows your mouse movements, indicating where the task will be inserted when you release the mouse button. (See Figure 3-19.)

INSIDE OUT Recurring tasks are automatically scheduled, however...

The summary task for a recurring task (or for any set of subtasks, for that matter) is always set as an automatically scheduled task, regardless of the default task mode of your project plan. This scheduling mechanism is used because summary task information is calculated from the aggregate of the subtasks, so by its nature it cannot be manually scheduled.

Note, however, that the subtasks of the recurring task adopt the default task mode, whether it's manual or automatic scheduling.

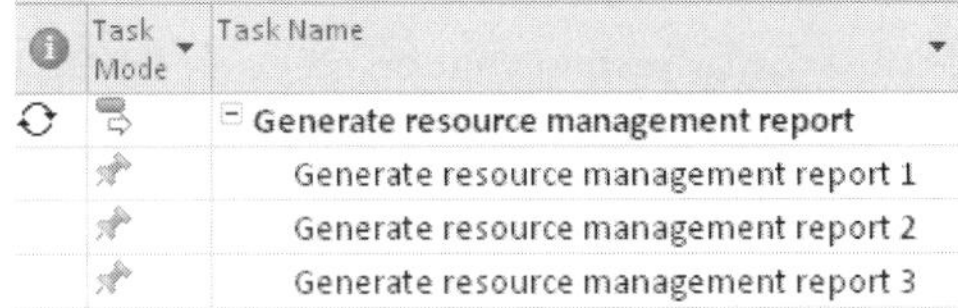

By their nature, recurring tasks are automatically scheduled according to your specifications. But whether a recurring subtask is set to be automatically or manually scheduled, you can easily change its date without adverse impact on the other recurrences of the task.

Recurring tasks that are set as automatically scheduled are marked with a Start No Earlier Than date constraint set to the date of the recurrence.

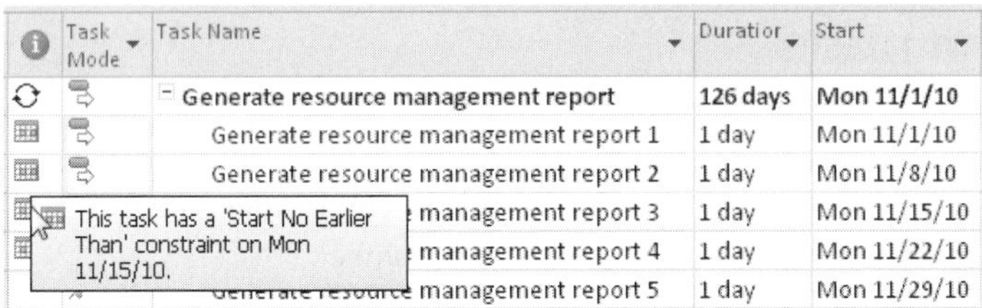

TROUBLESHOOTING

You enter information in a Gantt chart and your ribbon has turned gray

When you're in the middle of entering any task information in a Gantt chart, the ribbon and its commands become temporarily unavailable and are therefore dimmed.

Finish entering the task by pressing Enter. If you want to do something to that task, click it to select it again, and then choose the command or button you want.

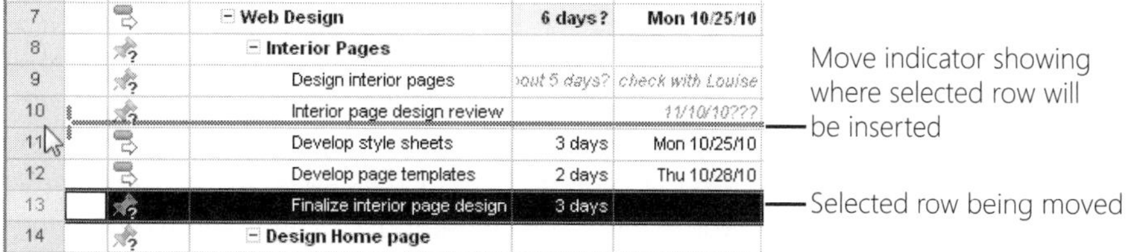

Figure 3-19 As you drag, a gray indicator shows where the selected row will be inserted when you release the mouse button.

3. Release the mouse button to insert the task in the new location.

> **Note**
>
> **Dragging tasks is the best method for reordering tasks in your project plan. If you use the Cut and Paste commands (on the Task tab in the Clipboard group), the Task Unique ID field for a task is renumbered, and this can cause problems if you integrate the project with other applications, including third-party timesheet systems.**

Inserting Additional Tasks

To add a new task between other existing tasks, follow these steps:

1. In the table area of the Gantt Chart, click anywhere in the row above which you want the new task to be inserted.

2. On the Task tab, in the Insert group, click Task. (You can also simply press the Insert key.)

   A new row is added above the selected row.

Task

3. Click in the Task Name field for the new row, type the name of the new task, and then press Enter.

Copying Tasks

You can copy one or more tasks to use as the basis for other tasks. The following list describes the various copying techniques:

Copy

- **Copy a single task name** Click in the Task Name field, and then on the Task tab, in the Clipboard group, click Copy. Click the Task Name field in a blank row, and then on the Task tab, in the Clipboard group, click Paste.

- **Copy multiple adjacent task names** Click the first task name you want to select, hold down the Shift key, and then click the last task name. All task names between the first and last are selected. On the Task tab, in the Clipboard group, click Copy. Click the first Task Name field where you want the selected tasks to begin. On the Task tab, in the Clipboard group, click Paste. You can also simply drag to select the tasks. If you want to copy a series of selected tasks to empty rows directly under a particular task, drag the fill handle in the lower-right corner of the cell into those empty rows. (See Figure 3-20.)

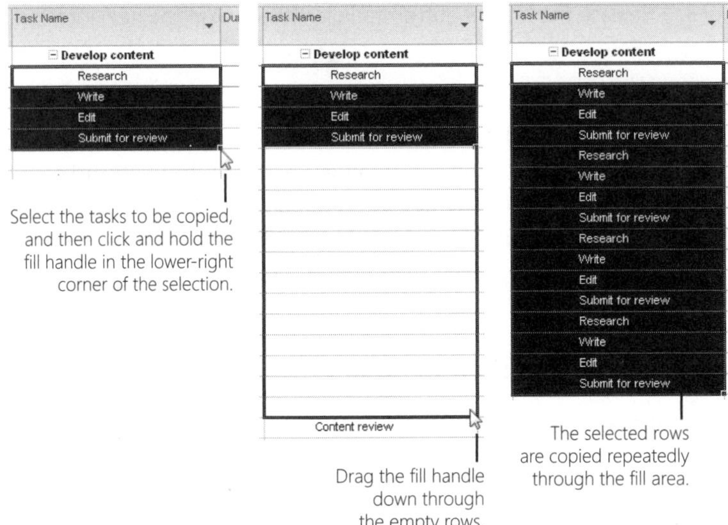

Figure 3-20 Copy tasks using the fill handle.

- **Copy multiple nonadjacent task names** Click the first task name you want to select, hold down the Ctrl key, and then click any additional task names you want to add to the selection. (See Figure 3-21.) On the Task tab, in the Clipboard group, click Copy. Select the Task Name field where you want to add the selected tasks. On the Task tab, in the Clipboard group, click Paste. The tasks are added in the order that you selected them.

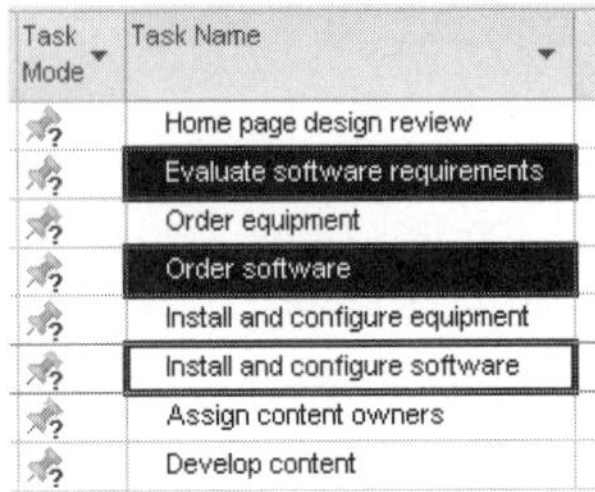

Figure 3-21 Copy multiple task names at once to save yourself some keyboard entry.

- **Copy a single task and its task information** Click the row heading of the task you want to copy, which selects the entire task and its associated information. On the Task tab, in the Clipboard group, click Copy. To add the task to an empty row, select the row and then on the Task tab, in the Clipboard group, click Paste. To insert the task between two existing tasks, select the lower task and then on the Task tab, in the Clipboard group, click Paste. The copied task is pasted into a new row above the selected task.

- **Copy multiple adjacent tasks and their task information** Click the row heading of the first task you want to copy. Hold down the Shift key, and then click the row heading of the last task. (See Figure 3-22.) On the Task tab, in the Clipboard group, click Copy. Select the task above which you want to add the copied tasks. On the Task tab, in the Clipboard group, click Paste.

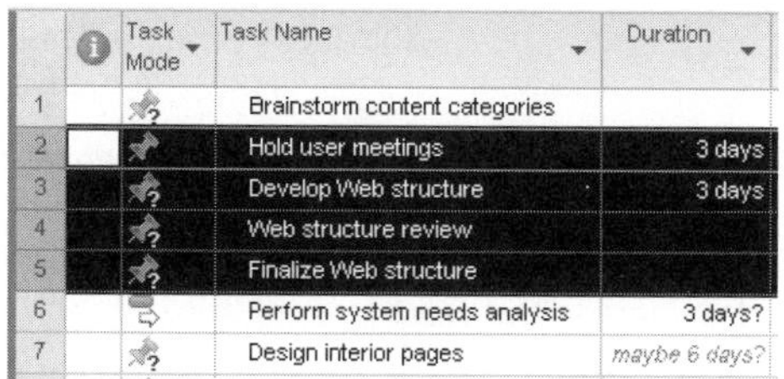

Figure 3-22 Copy multiple tasks along with all their associated information.

- **Copy multiple nonadjacent tasks and their task information** Click the row heading of the first task you want to copy. Hold down the Ctrl key, and then click the row headings of all the tasks you want to copy. On the Task tab, in the Clipboard group, click Copy. Select the task above which you want to add the copied tasks. On the Task tab, in the Clipboard group, click Paste. The tasks are added in the order that you selected them.

If you're doing a lot of copying and pasting, you might find it quicker to right-click the selection and then click Copy Cell or Paste from the drop-down menu. You can also press Ctrl+C to copy and Ctrl+V to paste.

Deleting Tasks

To delete a task you don't need, select the row heading and then press Delete.

When you click a manually scheduled task name (rather than the row heading) and the press Delete, the task name is cleared.

When you click an automatically scheduled task name and then press Delete, the Delete indicator appears in the Indicators column. Choose whether to delete the entire task or just the task name. (See Figure 3-23.)

Deleting a manually scheduled task name brings up no further prompts.

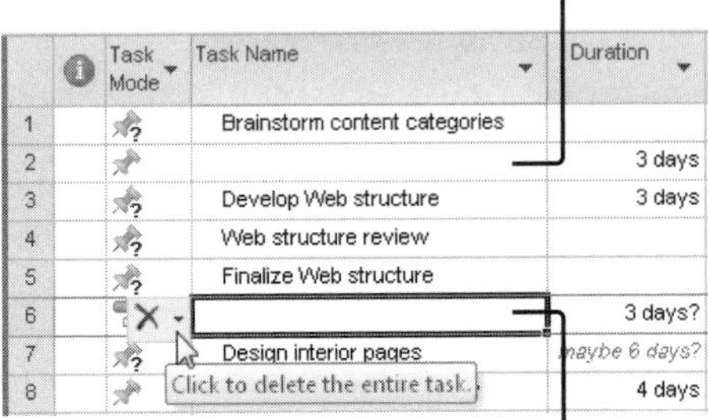

Deleting a automatically scheduled task name displays the Delete indicator for more choices.

Figure 3-23 Click the arrow next to the Delete indicator to choose what you want to delete.

If you want to delete the entire task, click the indicator. If you simply want to clear the task name, press Enter or click elsewhere in the view.

Clear

If you want to clear certain items from a task, you can use the Clear commands. On the Task tab, in the Editing group, click the arrow next to the Clear button. You can clear hyperlinks, notes, or formatting from the selected task(s). You can clear all three elements from the selected task(s) by clicking Clear All. To delete the task altogether, click Entire Row.

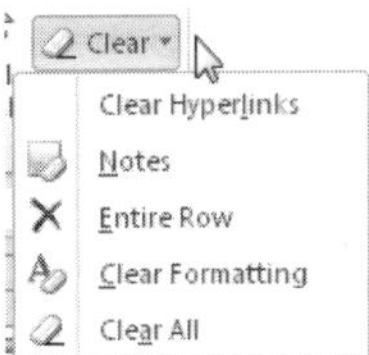

Undoing Multiple Edits

Undo

In Project 2010, you can undo multiple edits. To undo recent edits, click the Undo button on the Quick Access Toolbar at the upper-left corner. Each time you click Undo, the previous edit is undone in the reverse order from which you made them.

Other ways to work with the Undo command are as follows:

- You can press Ctrl+Z to reverse the last edit.
- To undo a series of edits all at once, click the arrow next to the Undo button on the Quick Access Toolbar. In the drop-down menu that appears, select the point at which you want to undo. All edits between the current state and the selected edit are undone.

Redo

- To redo an edit that you've undone, click the Redo button on the Quick Access Toolbar.
- You can also press Ctrl+Y to redo undone edits.
- To redo a series of undone edits all at once, click the arrow next to the Redo button on the Quick Access Toolbar. Select the point at which you want to redo the edits. All edits between the current state and the selected edit are redone.

  You can redo only those edits that you have previously undone. The Redo command does not repeat commands or edits.
- You can set the maximum number of undo operations. On the File tab, click Options, and then in the left pane click Advanced. Under General, enter the maximum number of undo operations you want in the Undo Levels box. The default is 20, and the maximum is 99.

Note

If the Undo or Redo button is not showing on the Quick Access Toolbar, you can easily add it. Click the arrow at the right edge of the Quick Access Toolbar, and then click Undo or Redo in the drop-down menu.

Organizing Tasks into an Outline

Now that your task list is sequenced to your satisfaction, you're ready to organize the tasks into a structure representing the hierarchy of tasks, from a broad perspective to the deep and detailed perspective where the real work actually takes place.

A task at a higher outline level than other tasks is called a *summary task*; the tasks beneath that summary task are called *subtasks*. (See Figure 3-24.) Summary tasks typically represent phases in a project. For example, in a website development project, you might have summary tasks for creating the web structure, designing the site, determining the hardware and software needed, and developing the content.

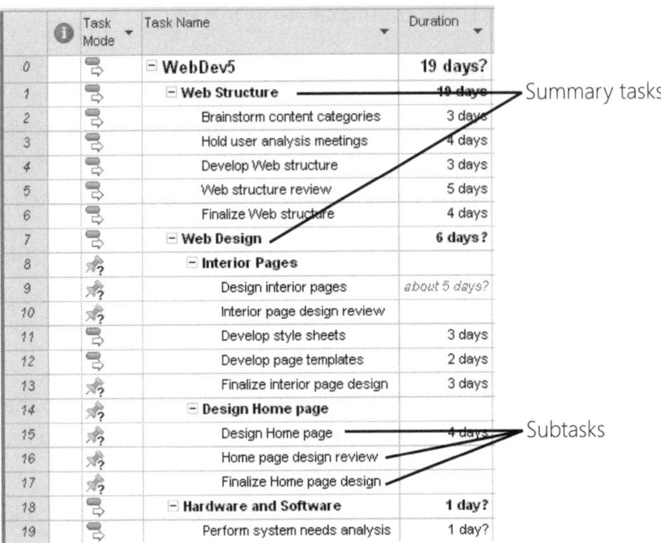

	Task Mode	Task Name	Duration
0		WebDev5	19 days?
1		Web Structure	19 days
2		Brainstorm content categories	3 days
3		Hold user analysis meetings	4 days
4		Develop Web structure	3 days
5		Web structure review	5 days
6		Finalize Web structure	4 days
7		Web Design	6 days?
8		Interior Pages	
9		Design interior pages	about 5 days?
10		Interior page design review	
11		Develop style sheets	3 days
12		Develop page templates	2 days
13		Finalize interior page design	3 days
14		Design Home page	
15		Design Home page	4 days
16		Home page design review	
17		Finalize Home page design	
18		Hardware and Software	1 day?
19		Perform system needs analysis	1 day?

Figure 3-24 Use summary tasks and subtasks to combine related tasks into manageable chunks.

The subtasks under those phases can be actual tasks that are assigned to resources, or they could be another set of summary tasks. For example, the "Web Design" summary task could have subtasks such as "Design interior pages" and "Design Home page." These subtasks in turn can be summary tasks to still more subtasks.

> **Note**
>
> **As of Project 2007, the number of available outline levels became unlimited. Earlier versions of Microsoft Project had a limit of nine outline levels.**

Many project managers use the outline levels to correspond to their WBS, in which the lowest-level subtask corresponds to the work package.

For more information about the WBS in Project 2010, see "Setting Up Your Work Breakdown Structure" on page 119.

As you create the outline structure in your task list, you might find that you need to refine the task list even more by inserting, moving, and deleting tasks.

All your tasks are initially at the first outline level. To make a summary task, you need to indent subtasks beneath it. The following list describes various outlining techniques:

Indent Task

- **Make a task a subtask** Click the task. On the Task tab, in the Schedule group, click Indent Task. The task is indented, and the task above it becomes its summary task. Summary tasks are highlighted in bold in the table area of the Gantt Chart and are marked with a black bar spanning the summary tasks in the chart area of the Gantt Chart.

Task Name	Duration	Start	Finish	Oct 24, '10 S S M T W T F S
Web Structure	**4 days**	**Mon 10/25/10**	**Thu 10/28/10**	
Brainstorm content categories	3 days	Mon 10/25/10	Wed 10/27/10	
Hold user analysis meetings	4 days	Mon 10/25/10	Thu 10/28/10	

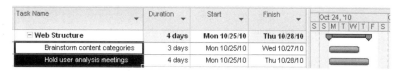

Regardless of your default task scheduling mode, summary tasks are always set as automatically scheduled tasks because summary task information is calculated from the aggregate of its subtasks.

NEW!

Summary

- **Insert a summary task** Click the task above which you want to insert a new summary task. On the Task tab, in the Insert group, click Summary. A new summary task is inserted above the selected task, and that selected task becomes the first subtask for the new summary task. This method of creating a top-down summary task is new for Project 2010.

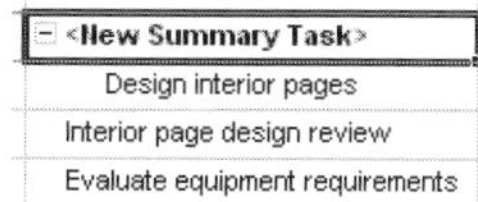

If you insert a summary task above a blank row, the new summary task row appears with a new subtask beneath it.

- **Create a subtask under a subtask** Click a task under a subtask. On the Task tab, in the Schedule group, click Indent Task twice. This task is now at the third outline level, as a subtask of a subtask.

Outdent Task

- **Move a subtask to a higher level** Click a subtask. On the Task tab, in the Schedule group, click Outdent Task.
- **Indent several tasks at one time** Drag the mouse pointer across several adjacent tasks to select them, or use the Ctrl key to select several nonadjacent tasks at once. On the Task tab, in the Schedule group, click Indent Task. This method also works to create subtasks under different summary tasks.

Show Subtasks

- **Hide or show the subtasks for a selected summary task** Next to each summary task is a plus or minus sign. The plus sign indicates that there are hidden subtasks for this summary task. Click the plus sign, and the subtasks appear. You can also select a summary task, and then on the View tab, in the Data group, click Outline, and then click Show Subtasks.

Hide Subtasks

  The minus sign indicates that the subtasks are currently displayed. Click the minus sign, and Project 2010 hides the subtasks. You can also select a summary task, and then on the View tab, in the Data group, click Outline, and then click Hide Subtasks.

Outline

- **Show all tasks at a specified outline level** You can make visible only those tasks at the first and second outline levels, for example, throughout your entire project plan. On the View tab, in the Data group, click Outline. In the drop-down menu that appears, click Outline Level 2. You can select any level from Outline Level 1 through Outline Level 9.

All Subtasks

  To show all levels again, in the Outline drop-down menu, click All Subtasks.

- **Delete a summary task** If you decide to delete a summary task, just be aware that all of its subtasks will be deleted as well. If this is indeed what you want to do, select the summary task's row heading and then press Delete.

  However, you might really just want to change the task's level from a summary task to a subtask or a nonoutlined task. To do this, click somewhere in the summary task row, and then on the Task tab, in the Schedule group, click Indent until the task is showing at the level you want.

  Likewise, you can make a summary task a subtask or a nonoutlined task by outdenting its subtasks. Select all the subtasks under the summary task, and then on the Task tab, in the Schedule group, click Outdent until the summary task and subtasks are at the levels you want.

Summary tasks show rolled-up task information that is an aggregate of the information in the associated subtasks. For example, if each of four subtasks has an associated cost of $100, the summary task shows the total of $400. You can also see rolled-up summary information for total elapsed duration for all subtasks, the earliest start date and the latest finish date for all subtasks, and other such information.

You can also display a summary task for the project as a whole. The project summary task shows rolled-up summary information for the entire project; for example, total costs, total duration, project start, and project finish.

To show the project summary task, on the Format tab, in the Show/Hide group, select the Project Summary Task check box. The project summary task name is adopted from the project file name. You can change this summary task name if you want.

Setting Up Your Work Breakdown Structure

As mentioned earlier in this chapter, many project managers and organizations use a work breakdown structure (WBS) as an essential element of their project management methodology. Similar to the outline structure of your project task list, the WBS is a hierarchical chart view of deliverables in a project in which each level represents an increasingly detailed description of the deliverables.

WBS levels can be associated with a particular code set, such as 2.1.3.a. Levels in the hierarchy represent summary tasks, subtasks, work packages, and deliverables. You can define a project's scope and develop its task lists with the WBS.

Industries, application areas, and organizations experienced with a particular type of project tend to develop WBSs to represent the life cycles of their typical types of projects—for example, the design of a new vehicle or the construction of an office building.

Understanding Work Breakdown Structure Codes

Each item and level in a WBS is described by a unique WBS code. Each digit in the code typically represents a level in the structure's hierarchy, such as 2.1.4.3 or 5.B.c.3. A WBS code such as 1.2.3 might represent the third deliverable for the second activity in the first phase of the project.

Note

In some industries or application areas, the work breakdown structure is also known as the *project breakdown structure,* or *PBS.*

Showing Outline Numbers as Basic WBS Codes

In Project 2010, any outline structure you set up for your tasks is assigned a set of unique outline numbers. The outline number for the first summary task is 1; the outline number for the first subtask under the first summary task is 1.1, as you can see in Figure 3-25.

Outline Number	WBS	Task Name
0	0	Training Rollout Initiative and Plan (TRIP)
1	1	TRIP - Stage 1 - Project Planning
1.1	1.1	Define project objectives and describe mission statement
1.2	1.2	Ensure total participation by training team support staff
1.3	1.3	Identify Departments or End-User Community to be Trained
1.4	1.4	Seek Input from Training Vendor
1.5	1.5	Perform End-User Skill Assessment
1.6	1.6	Stage 1 - TRIP - End project initiation
2	2	TRIP - Stage 2 - Project Commencement
2.1	2.1	Prepare Rollout Schedule and Create Awareness
2.2	2.2	Training Sessions Registration
2.3	2.3	Schedule Instructors
2.4	2.4	Courseware Evaluations
2.5	2.5	Stage 2 - TRIP - End project commencement
3	3	TRIP - Stage 3 - Project Implementation and Control
3.1	3.1	Conduct training and track attendance
3.2	3.2	Daily Conference Call (Hold Daily Call to Address Issues)
3.3	3.3	Collect feedback and compile results

Figure 3-25 The outline number specifies the task's position in your project plan's task outline hierarchy.

As seen in this example, if no other WBS code pattern, or mask, is set for the project, the WBS code is the same as the outline numbers. If the outline numbers are enough of a WBS code for you, you can display them in their own column, or you can make the outline number the prefix to the task name.

Follow these steps to display the outline numbers in their own column:

1. Show the view and table to which you want to add the outline number column; for example, the default Entry table in the Gantt Chart.

   For more information about switching views and tables, see "Accessing Your Project Information" on page 127.

2. Click anywhere in the column to the left of which you want to insert the new outline number column.

3. On the Format tab, in the Columns group, click Insert Column.

   A new column is inserted to the left of the selected column, along with a long drop-down menu of all available fields.

4. Type **o** to move quickly to the fields that start with the letter O, and then click Outline Number.

   The inserted column is defined as the Outline Number field, and the outline numbers generated by Project 2010 are filled in.

It's much quicker to append the outline number as a prefix to the task name. On the Format tab, in the Show/Hide group, select the Outline Number check box. The outline numbers are added to the beginning of each task name, as shown in Figure 3-26.

Figure 3-26 Selecting the Outline Number check box adds the outline number as the prefix to every task name throughout the project.

Creating a Custom WBS Code

By default, Project 2010 creates WBS codes that are derived from the automatically generated outline numbers, and you can't change the code scheme of the outline numbers. However, if you and your organization have a specific WBS coding scheme, you can change the WBS numbering. When working with WBS codes, keep the following in mind:

- You can have only one set of WBS codes. However, if you use additional coding schemes, you can create up to 10 sets of outline codes and then sort or group your tasks by those codes.

> **Note**
>
> **Certain project management methodologies use other structured and hierarchical codes that can describe your project from different viewpoints. Examples include the *organizational breakdown structure (OBS)*, the *resource breakdown structure (RBS)*, and the *bill of materials (BOM)*.**
>
> **For more information about outline codes, see "Working with Outline Codes" on page 1116.**

- You can include ordered numbers, uppercase letters, and lowercase letters as part of your custom WBS code format. You can also include unordered characters in the code format.
- You can automatically generate your custom WBS codes for tasks as you add them.

Setting Up Work Breakdown Structure Codes

To set up your custom WBS code scheme, including any prefix and *code mask,* follow these steps:

1. On the Project tab, in the Properties group, click WBS, and then click Define Code.
2. If you use a prefix for the project in front of the WBS code to distinguish it from other projects using the same code format, enter that prefix in the Project Code Prefix box.
3. In the Sequence field in the first row, select whether the first digit of the code (representing the first level of the hierarchy) is an ordered number, ordered uppercase letter, ordered lowercase letter, or unordered character.
4. In the Length field in the first row, specify whether there is a length limit for the first code.
5. In the Separator field in the first row, specify the character that separates the first and second code—for example, a period or a dash.
6. Repeat the procedure in the Sequence field in the second row.

   Continue these steps until all the levels of your custom WBS code are set up. (See Figure 3-27.) As you enter the code mask for each succeeding level, the Code Preview box shows an example of the code.

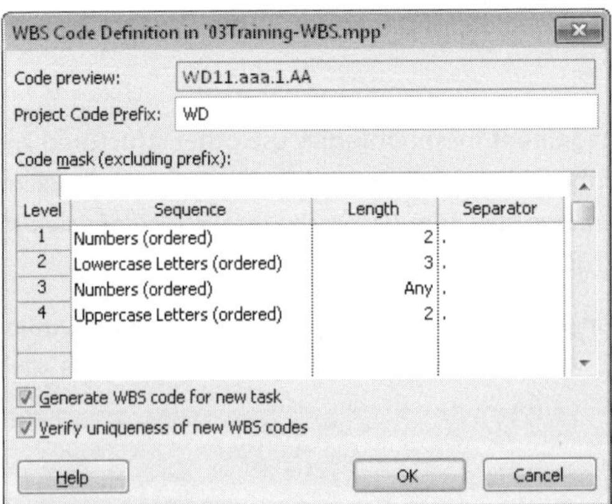

Figure 3-27 Define your organization's WBS code format.

7. When you finish, click OK. The WBS codes for your tasks are reset to conform to your custom structure, as shown in Figure 3-28.

Outline Number	WBS	Task Name
0	WD	Training Rollout Initiative and Plan (TRIP)
1	WD01	TRIP - Stage 1 - Project Planning
1.1	WD01.aaa	Define project objectives and describe mission statement
1.2	WD01.aab	Ensure total participation by training team support staff
1.3	WD01.aac	Identify Departments or End-User Community to be Trained
1.4	WD01.aad	Seek Input from Training Vendor
1.5	WD01.aae	Perform End-User Skill Assessment
1.6	WD01.aaf	Stage 1 - TRIP - End project initiation
2	WD02	TRIP - Stage 2 - Project Commencement
2.1	WD02.aaa	Prepare Rollout Schedule and Create Awareness
2.2	WD02.aab	Training Sessions Registration
2.3	WD02.aac	Schedule Instructors
2.4	WD02.aad	Courseware Evaluations
2.5	WD02.aae	Stage 2 - TRIP - End project commencement
3	WD03	TRIP - Stage 3 - Project Implementation and Control
3.1	WD03.aaa	Conduct training and track attendance

Figure 3-28 Your newly defined WBS codes replace the default WBS codes derived from the outline numbers.

Follow these steps to display the WBS column:

1. Show the view and table to which you want to add the WBS column.

2. Click anywhere in the column to the left of which you want to insert the new WBS column.

3. On the Format tab, in the Columns group, click Insert Column.

   A new column is inserted to the left of the selected column, along with a long drop-down menu of all available fields.

4. Type **w** to move quickly to the fields that start with the letter *W*, and then click WBS.

   The inserted column is defined as the WBS field, and the WBS codes for your tasks are filled in according to the code mask you created.

Adding Supplementary Information to Tasks

You can annotate an individual task by entering notes. To add a note to a task, do the following:

1. Click the task to which you want to add a note.

2. On the Task tab, in the Properties group, click Notes.

   The Task Information dialog box opens to the Notes tab.

3. In the Notes area, type the note.

4. When you are finished, click OK.

   A note icon is added to the Indicators column in the table area of the Gantt Chart.

Note Indicator

You can insert an entire document as a note associated with an individual task. For more information, see "Copying a Document to Your Project File" on page 95.

To read the note, or at least part of it, rest your mouse pointer over the Note indicator. To read the note in its entirety, or to change the existing note, double-click the note indicator. Make the change you want.

If you want to remove the note altogether, first select the content in the Notes box by dragging across the content or by clicking in the Notes box and pressing Ctrl+A. Press Delete, and then click OK. The note is gone, along with the note icon in the task's Indicators field.

Note

You can also hyperlink from a task to a document on your computer or on a website. For more information, see "Hyperlinking a Document to Your Project File" on page 97.

CHAPTER 4

Viewing Project Information

To plan, track, and manage your project with Microsoft Project 2010, you enter a variety of detailed information regarding tasks, resources, assignments, durations, resource rates, and more. Project 2010, in turn, calculates certain entries to create even more information, including start dates, finish dates, costs, and remaining work. In Project 2010, more than 400 distinct pieces of information, including your own custom information, are available for tasks, resources, and assignments. The more tasks, resources, and assignments you have in your project, and the more custom capabilities you use, the more these pieces of information are multiplied.

There's no way you could look at this mass of project information at one time and work with it in any kind of meaningful or efficient way. To solve this problem, Project 2010 organizes and stores the information in a *database*. All information associated with an individual task, for example, is a single *record* in that database. Each piece of information in that record is a separate *field*. (See Figure 4-1.)

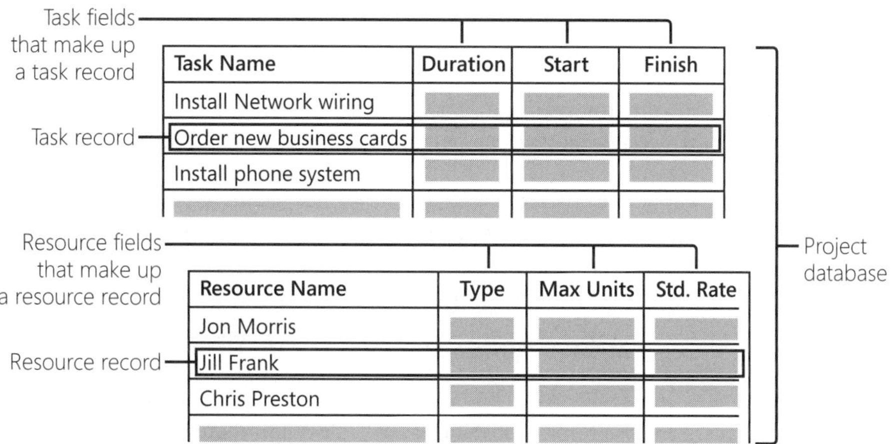

Figure 4-1 Each task represents a single record in your project database, with all associated information represented by individual fields.

When you need to look at or work with a particular set of information, you choose a particular *view* to display in the Project 2010 window. A view filters the project information according to the purpose of the view and then presents that layout of information in the Project 2010 window so that you can easily work with it. More than 25 different views are built into Project 2010.

You can rearrange the project information presented in a view. You can sort information in many views by name, date, and other values. You can group information in different categories—for example, by complete tasks versus incomplete tasks. You can filter information to see only the information you want—for example, only tasks that are assigned to a particular resource. These concepts and techniques are all presented in this chapter, which serves as a guided tour as well as a reference of views and other ways of viewing project information.

Understanding Project Information Categories

The means for organizing, managing, and storing the thousands of pieces of project information is the Microsoft Project database. There are three major categories in the project database:

- Task information
- Resource information
- Assignment information

When you start entering project information, typically you enter tasks and associated information, such as duration, date constraints, deadlines, and task dependencies. These all fall under the task information category.

Then you enter resource names and associated information, such as standard rate, overtime rate, and available working times. These all fall under the resource information category.

As soon as you assign a resource to a task, this creates a new entity—the assignment, which is the intersection of task and resource. Information associated with an assignment includes the amount of work, the assignment start and finish dates, the cost for the assignment, and so on. These fall under the assignment information category.

Note

There are also three subcategories of project information: task-timephased, resource-timephased, and assignment-timephased. These subcategories are covered in "Timesheeting with Usage Views" on page 142.

Understanding these three categories is important when viewing project information. There are task views and resource views. The individual fields that make up all views are also classified as task, resource, or assignment fields, and they can be seen only in their respective views. Likewise, there are filters and groups designed just for task views and other filters and groups designed just for resource views.

Accessing Your Project Information

You view and work with information in Project 2010 by selecting a specific view to display in your Project 2010 window. Of the many views built into Project 2010, some have to do with tasks, others with resources, and still others with assignments. Certain views are a spreadsheet of tables and columns. Others are graphs or forms. Other views are a blend—for example, the Gantt Chart includes both a sheet and a graph.

You can switch tables in a view and add and remove fields shown in a table, and so modify these views to present your project information exactly the way you need.

Switching Between Views

When you first start using Project 2010, typically the first view you use is the Gantt Chart, which is the default view. Here, you enter information such as tasks, durations, and task relationships. Then you might use the Resource Sheet, in which you enter resource information. As you continue to plan your project, your requirements become more sophisticated, and you find you need other views. For example, you might want to see all your tasks with their current percent complete along with the critical path. Or you might need a graph showing a particular resource's workload throughout April and May.

Note

By default, the view that appears when you first open Project 2010 is the Gantt Chart topped by the Timeline. You can change this default view. On the File tab, click Options, and then click General in the left pane. Under Project View, in the Default View box, click the view you want to appear first whenever you create a new project file.

This setting changes the view only for any new project files. The view that appears when you open an existing project file is the one that was last showing when you saved and closed the file.

For more information about other view options, see the "Arranging Your Project 2010 Window" on page 165.

Switching to Frequently Used Views

There are three ways to see and select the most commonly used views:

NEW!

Other Views

- On the View tab, in the Task Views or Resource Views group, click the button for the view you want. If you don't see the name of the view you're looking for, click the arrow next to a related view name to see other options. For example, in the Task Views group, click the arrow next to Gantt Chart, and you'll see the Detail Gantt and Tracking Gantt. If you still can't find the view you want, click Other Views, and then click More Views.

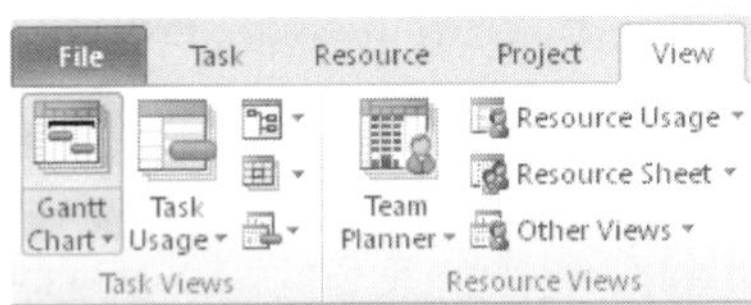

- Right-click the Active View bar (showing the name of the current view) at the left edge of the Project window. The shortcut menu that appears shows about half of the available views, so this is often the quickest way to get to another view. If the view you want is not listed on the shortcut menu, click More Views to display the full list.

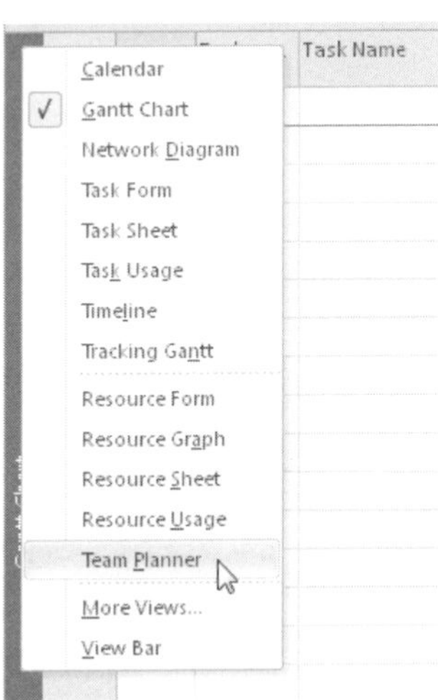

Chapter 4

NEW!

- Click one of the four view shortcuts in the lower-right corner of the Project 2010 window, next to the Zoom slider. These are considered the four most commonly used views: the Gantt Chart, Task Usage, Team Planner, and Resource Sheet.

It's a great idea to experiment and click through all the available views, just to see how they present your project information in various ways. This tour of views can become even more meaningful as you add more task information, add resources, and assign resources to tasks.

Seeing the List of All Available Views

All views are listed in the More Views dialog box. To see the full list of views built in to Project 2010 and switch to a different view, do the following:

1. On the View tab, in either the Task Views group or the Resource Views group, point to Other Views, and then click More Views.

   The full list of available Project 2010 views appears. (See Figure 4-2.)

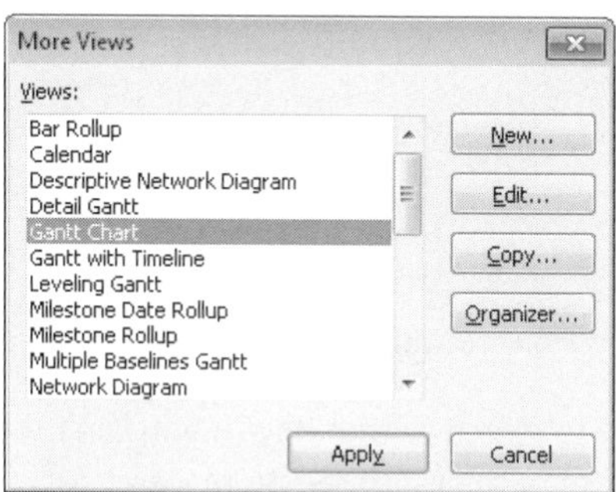

Figure 4-2 The More Views dialog box lists all available views in alphabetical order.

2. Click the view you want, and then click Apply.

   The selected view replaces the previous view in your Project 2010 window.

Keep in mind that when you switch from one view to another, the data doesn't change; you just get a different look at the data in your project database.

Showing the View Bar

If you display the View bar, you can use it to quickly switch views. To show the View bar, do the following:

1. Right-click the Active View bar (showing the name of the current view) at the left edge of the Project window.

2. At the bottom of the shortcut menu that appears, click View Bar.

   The View bar appears on the left edge of the Project 2010 window, as shown in Figure 4-3. The same views that appear on the shortcut menu are listed on the View bar.

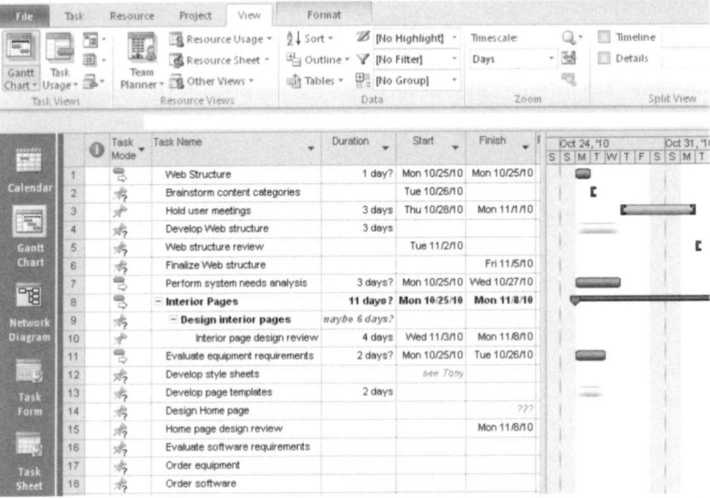

Figure 4-3 The View bar lists icons for about half the available Project 2010 views.

3. Click a view's name or icon to switch to that view. If you can't see the view's name, click the arrow at the bottom of the list to see more views.

   If the view isn't listed on the View bar, click More Views at the bottom of the View bar to see the full list.

> **Note**
>
> **To hide the View bar, right-click in the View bar, and then click View Bar to turn it off. When the View bar is hidden, it's replaced by the gray Active View bar, which shows the name of the current view.**

Chapter 4

INSIDE OUT **Add your favorite views to the View bar menu and View bar**

Although the most commonly used views are listed on the View bar menu and the View bar itself, they might not be *your* most commonly used views. For example, you might use the Task Entry view and the Detail Gantt every day, and it would be cumbersome to have to click More Views every time you need one of these.

NEW!

Now Project 2010 dynamically adds views that you apply to the various menus. For example, if you apply the Detail Gantt, its name appears in the Active View bar shortcut menu and in the View Bar. It also appears on the Gantt Chart menu (View, Task Views, Gantt Chart). This ensures that your frequently used views are always quickly available, whether you like to use the View tab or the View bar.

You can also add a frequently used view to the View tab and View bar menu by editing the view definition as follows:

1. On the View tab, in the Task Views group, click More Views.
2. Click the view you want to add to the View tab and View bar menu, and then click Edit.
3. In the View Definition dialog box, select the Show In Menu check box.

You can use this technique to remove views you never use from the View tab and View bar menu as well. Simply select the view, click Edit, and then clear the Show In Menu check box.

You can fully customize your views and create entirely new views. For more information, see "Customizing Views" on page 1062.

Using Views

You can think of Project 2010 views in the following categories:

- Gantt charts
- Network diagrams
- Sheet views
- Usage views
- Forms
- Combination views

There are also several one-of-a-kind views that defy categorization. They tend to be more graphically oriented, but because they're unique and specialized, we'll discuss them separately throughout this section. These special views are the following:

- Timeline
- Calendar
- Team Planner
- Resource Graph

Scheduling with Gantt Charts

Gantt charts are a special type of view that are used extensively in project management. The left side of a Gantt chart contains a sheet view, and the right side contains a bar graph along a timescale. (See Figure 4-4.)

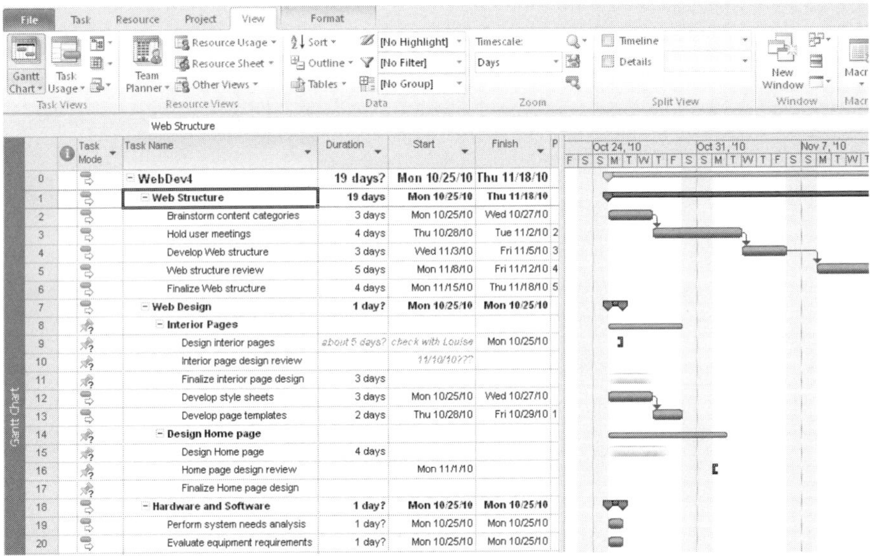

Figure 4-4 A Gantt chart shows task information in the sheet area of the view; the corresponding bar graph shows the task's duration, start and finish dates, and task relationships along a zoomable timescale.

Gantt Chart

To display the Gantt Chart, on the View tab, in the Task Views group, click Gantt Chart.

You can also quickly switch to the Gantt Chart by clicking its icon in the view shortcuts area on the status bar next to the Zoom slider.

To display a different Gantt chart view, click the arrow under the Gantt Chart button. The menu lists recent Gantt chart views you've accessed. If the Gantt chart you want is not listed, click More Views, and then click it from the list.

Table 4-1 describes the default Gantt charts that are built in to Project 2010.

Table 4-1 **Project 2010 Gantt Charts**

Gantt chart	How you can use it	For more information
Detail Gantt (task view)	View tasks and associated information in a sheet and see slack and slippage for tasks over time in a bar graph on a timescale. Use the Detail Gantt to check how far a task can slip without affecting other tasks.	Chapter 10, "Checking and Adjusting the Project Plan"
Gantt Chart (task view)	View tasks and associated information in a sheet and see tasks and durations over time in a bar graph on a timescale. Use the Gantt Chart to enter and schedule a list of tasks. This is the view that appears by default when you first start new projects.	"Creating a New Project Plan" on page 74
Leveling Gantt (task view)	View tasks, task delays, and slack in a sheet, and the before-and-after effects of the Project 2010 leveling feature. Use the Leveling Gantt to check the amount of task delay caused by leveling.	"Balancing Resource Workloads" on page 403
Multiple Baselines Gantt (task view)	View different colored Gantt bars for the first three baselines (Baseline, Baseline1, and Baseline2) on summary tasks and subtasks in the chart area of the view. Use the Multiple Baselines Gantt to review and compare the first three baselines you set for your project.	"Saving Original Plan Information Using a Baseline" on page 445
Tracking Gantt (task view)	View tasks and task information in a sheet and a chart showing a baseline and scheduled Gantt bars for each task. Use the Tracking Gantt to compare the baseline schedule with the actual schedule.	Chapter 11, "Setting a Baseline and Updating Progress"

INSIDE OUT **Obsolete Rollup Gantt charts**

In the list of views, there are three Gantt charts that are vestiges of previous versions of Microsoft Project: the Bar Rollup, Milestone Date Rollup, and Milestone Rollup views. These views were used together with the Rollup_Formatting macro to label summary Gantt bars with certain types of task information. The Rollup_Formatting macro is not provided with Project 2010, so these Gantt charts are essentially obsolete.

TROUBLESHOOTING

You can't find the PERT analysis views

Previous versions of Microsoft Project included functions for PERT (Program Evaluation and Review Technique) analysis. PERT analysis was an add-in to help statistically estimate task durations, but it is no longer available with Project 2010, and its associated views—PA_Expected Gantt, PA_Optimistic Gantt, PA_Pessimistic Gantt, and PA_PERT Entry Sheet—are also no longer available.

For information about estimating durations, see "Setting Task Durations" on page 196.

You can change the look and content of bars on a Gantt chart. You can:

- Change the pattern, color, and shape of the Gantt bar for a selected task.
- Change the text accompanying the Gantt bar for a selected task.
- Change the format and text for all Gantt bars of a particular type.
- Change the text style for all Gantt bars of a particular type.
- Change the layout of links and bars on a Gantt chart.
- Change the gridlines in the view.

For more information about changing the look and content of Gantt bars, see "Formatting a Gantt Chart View" on page 1071. To change the timescale in a Gantt chart, see "Adjusting a Timescale" on page 167. You can also change the content or look of the sheet area of a Gantt chart. For details, see "Customizing Views" on page 1062. You can print views with the content and format you set up in the Project 2010 window. For more information, see "Setting Up and Printing Views" on page 528.

Highlighting Tasks with the Timeline

NEW!

The Timeline is a new graphical view available in Project 2010 that you can use to summarize selected project information along a timeline. By default, the Timeline appears above all other views, as shown in Figure 4-5. This is true whether you're showing a task or resource view. You can select specific tasks to add to the timeline and specify how those tasks appear. This is particularly helpful to highlight project phases and key milestones and deliverables.

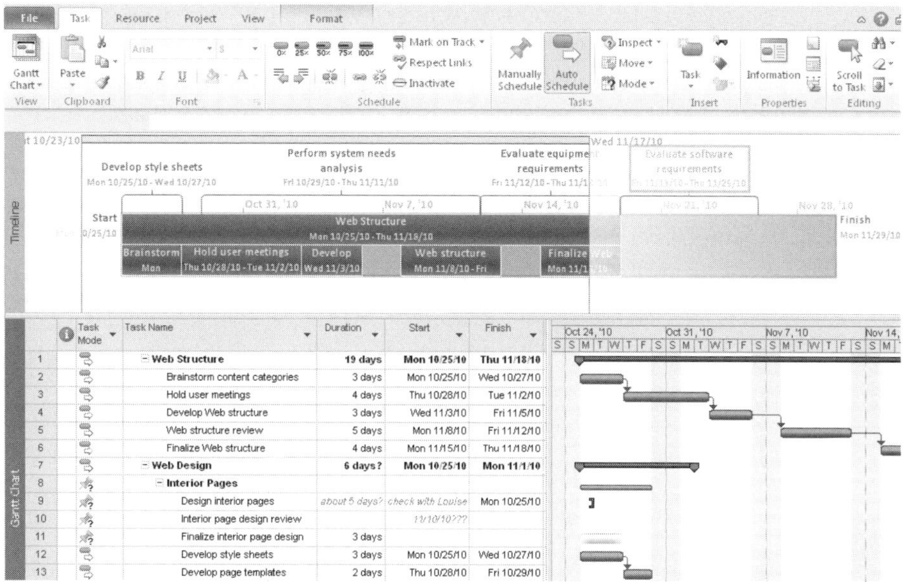

Figure 4-5 The Timeline typically appears above all other task or resource views.

The Timeline is great for communicating higher-level project information to others, especially because it's easy to copy the Timeline graphic to an e-mail message or a PowerPoint presentation, for example.

Although the Timeline appears by default above other views, you can also display it as a view on its own, as shown in Figure 4-6. To do this, on the View tab, in the Task Views group, click Other Views, and then click Timeline.

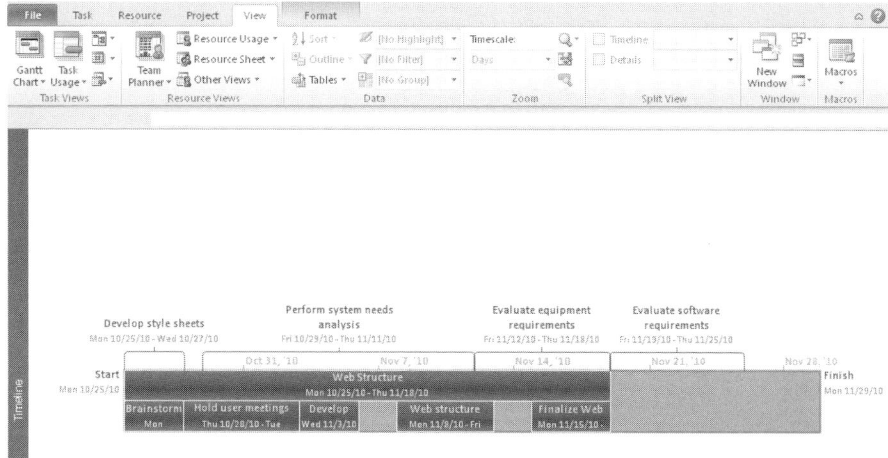

Figure 4-6 You can apply the Timeline as a view on its own instead of having it appear above other views.

Chapter 4

When you switch to another view after reviewing the Timeline as its own view, the Timeline doesn't appear above the other view as it did before. This is also true when you switch from a combination view such as the Task Entry view. To display the Timeline above other views, on the View tab, in the Split View group, select the Timeline check box.

You can add any regular task, summary task, milestone, or deliverable to the Timeline. The task must be automatically scheduled or have at least some estimated schedule information to be added to the Timeline. If a manually scheduled task has a task mode indicating that it needs more information, it cannot be added to the Timeline. To add a task to the Timeline, follow these steps:

1. Display any task view; for example, the Gantt Chart or Calendar.
2. Right-click the task name, and then click Add To Timeline on the shortcut menu that appears.

   If you're working in a task sheet view such as the Detail Gantt or Task Usage view, you can select the task row by clicking the row number and then dragging from the row number to the Timeline to add that task to the Timeline.

After you add a task to the Timeline, you can specify whether it should be displayed as a callout instead of as the default bar. If you're using the Timeline to show major phases and summary tasks, for example, you might want to display the phases as callouts and the summary tasks as bars, as shown in Figure 4-7.

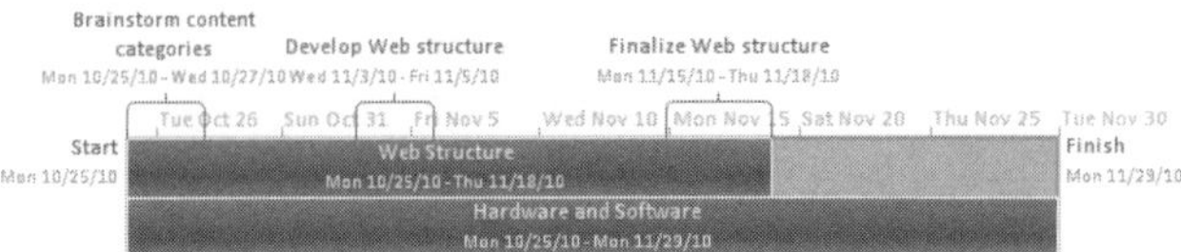

Figure 4-7 Use a combination of callouts and bars to differentiate between different types of tasks on the Timeline.

To change a Timeline bar to a callout, follow these steps:

1. Click anywhere in the Timeline area of the view.

   The ribbon changes to show the Timeline Tools Format tab.
2. Click the task whose bar you want to change to a callout.
3. On the Format tab, in the Current Selection group, click Display As Callout.

   You can also right-click a task in the Timeline and then click Display As Callout in the shortcut menu that appears.

For details on using the Timeline to help create graphical reports, see "Using Views to Report Project Information" on page 528. For details on changing text and bar styles in the Timeline, see "Modifying the Timeline" on page 1081.

Flowcharting with Network Diagrams

Network diagrams are a special type of graph view that presents each task and associated task information in a separate box, or *node*. The nodes are connected by lines that represent task relationships. The resulting diagram is a flowchart of the project. Network Diagram views (see Figure 4-8) are also referred to as PERT (Program Evaluation and Review Technique) charts.

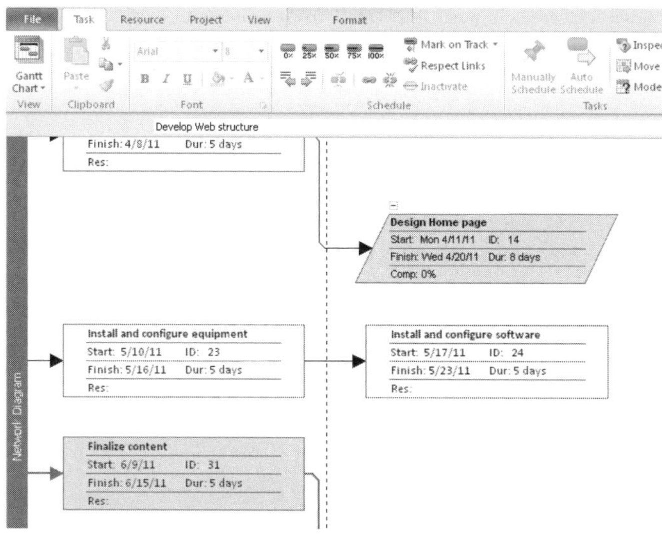

Figure 4-8 You can enter, edit, and review tasks and their dependencies in the Network Diagram view.

Network Diagram

To display a network diagram, on the View tab, in the Task Views group, click the arrow next to Network Diagram. Select the network diagram you want to display. If the one you want is not listed, click More Views, and then select it from the list.

Table 4-2 describes the Project 2010 network diagram views.

Table 4-2 **Project 2010 Network Diagram Views**

Network diagram	How you can use it	For more information
Descriptive Network Diagram (task view)	View all tasks and task dependencies. Use the Descriptive Network Diagram to create and fine-tune your schedule in a flowchart format. This view is similar to the regular Network Diagram, but the nodes are larger and provide more detail.	"Establishing Task Dependencies" on page 206
Network Diagram (task view)	Enter, edit, and review all tasks and task dependencies. Use the Network Diagram to create and fine-tune your schedule in a flowchart format.	"Establishing Task Dependencies" on page 206
Relationship Diagram (task view)	View the predecessors and successors of a single selected task. In a large project or any project with more complex task linking, use this task view to focus on the task dependencies of a specific task.	"Establishing Task Dependencies" on page 206

To learn about modifying the content or format of a network diagram, see "Modifying a Network Diagram" on page 1083.

Visualizing the Project with the Calendar

Use the Calendar to view tasks and durations for a specific week or range of weeks in a monthly calendar format, as shown in Figure 4-9.

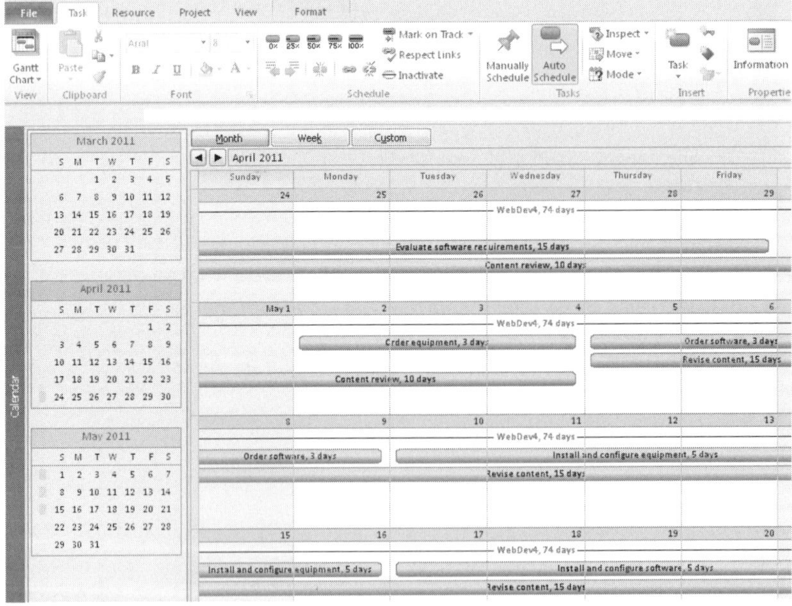

Figure 4-9 In the Calendar view, you can quickly see which tasks are scheduled for particular days, weeks, or months.

Calendar

To display the Calendar, on the View tab, in the Task Views group, click Calendar.

For more information about setting up schedule information, see Chapter 6. For information about modifying the Calendar view, see "Modifying the Calendar" on page 1096.

Reviewing Assignments with the Team Planner

NEW!

The Team Planner is a new view in Microsoft Project Professional 2010 that you can use to graphically visualize how your resources are scheduled during a selected time period, as shown in Figure 4-10.

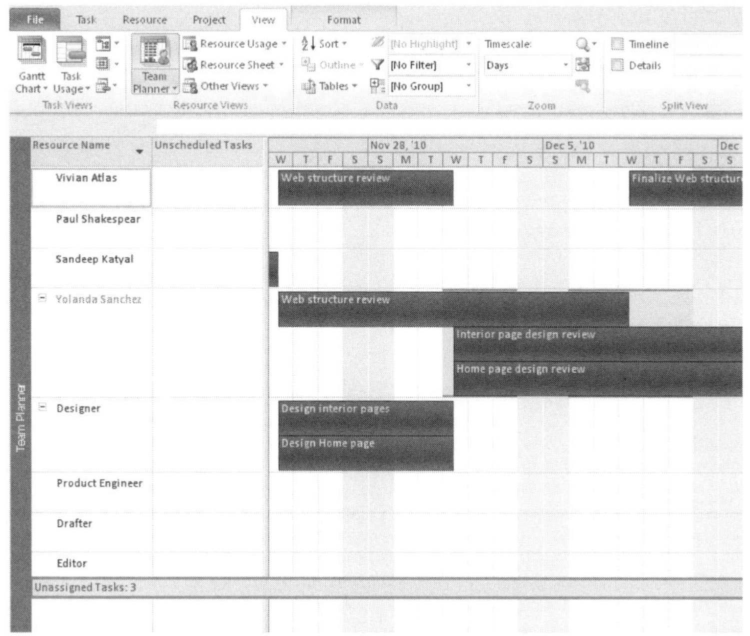

Figure 4-10 Use the Team Planner to review assignments and to assign and reassign tasks.

You can see which team members have availability to work during the time period that a task needs to be done and then drag the task to assign it to that person. You can reassign tasks from one resource to another to resolve overallocations or improve the schedule. You can also drag tasks along the timesheet to change the assignment scheduling.

Team Planner

To display the Team Planner, on the View tab in the Resource Views group, click Team Planner.

You can also quickly switch to the Team Planner by clicking its icon in the view shortcuts area on the status bar (next to the Zoom slider).

In the Team Planner, you can manipulate task information through the Task Information dialog box. You can format bars to show actual work or late tasks.

For more information about using the Team Planner to assign resources to tasks, see "Assigning Work Resources to Tasks" on page 283. For information about customizing the Team Planner, see "Modifying the Team Planner" on page 1089.

Charting Team Availability with the Resource Graph

With the Resource Graph, you can view resource allocation, cost, or work over time for a single resource or group of resources. Information is displayed in a column graph format, as shown in Figure 4-11.

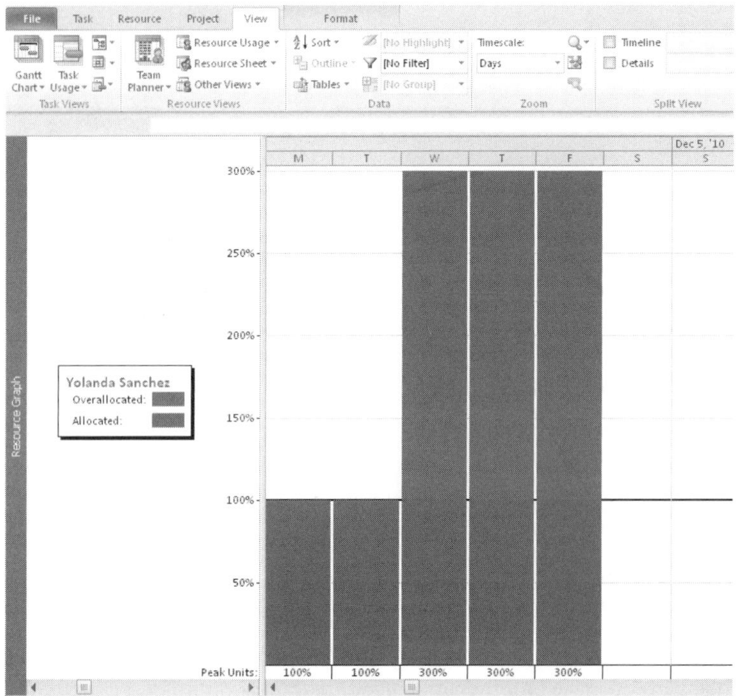

Figure 4-11 You can use the Resource Graph to review resource allocation levels.

When used in combination with other views, the Resource Graph can be very useful for finding resource overallocations.

To display the Resource Graph, on the View tab, in the Resource Views group, click Other Views, and then click Resource Graph.

The Resource Graph shows peak units by resource, including the percentage of allocation and overallocation. You can change the type of information being shown in the Resource Graph by doing the following:

1. Display the Resource Graph.
2. On the Resource Graph Tools Format tab, in the Data group, click the arrow in the Graph box.

   The drop-down menu lists the various categories of information that the Resource Graph can chart, such as Cost, Percent Allocation, and Work.
3. Click the category of information you want to chart on the Resource Graph.

For more information about using the Resource Graph, see "Viewing Resource Workloads"on page 404. For information about customizing the Resource Graph, see "Modifying the Resource Graph" on page 1091.

Tabling with Sheet Views

Sheet views are spreadsheet-type views that are divided into columns and rows and in which each individual field is contained in a cell. An example is shown in Figure 4-12.

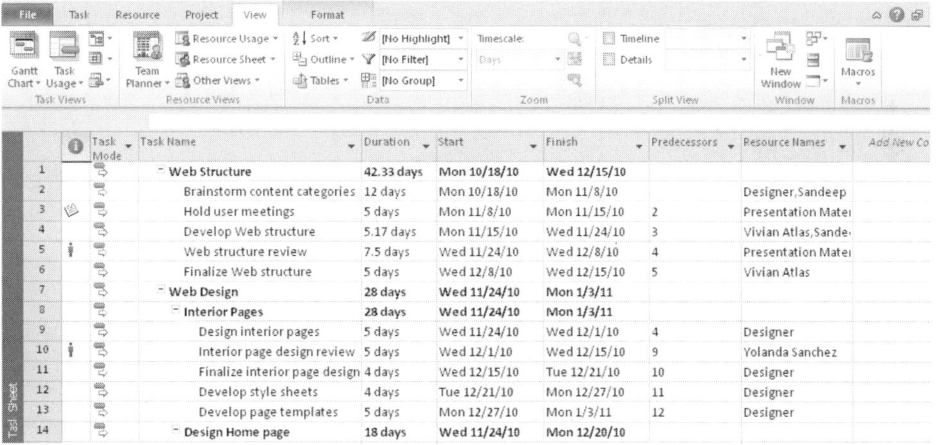

	Task Mode	Task Name	Duration	Start	Finish	Predecessors	Resource Names	Add New Co
1		Web Structure	42.33 days	Mon 10/18/10	Wed 12/15/10			
2		Brainstorm content categories	12 days	Mon 10/18/10	Mon 11/8/10		Designer,Sandeep	
3		Hold user meetings	5 days	Mon 11/8/10	Mon 11/15/10	2	Presentation Mate	
4		Develop Web structure	5.17 days	Mon 11/15/10	Wed 11/24/10	3	Vivian Atlas,Sande	
5		Web structure review	7.5 days	Wed 11/24/10	Wed 12/8/10	4	Presentation Mate	
6		Finalize Web structure	5 days	Wed 12/8/10	Wed 12/15/10	5	Vivian Atlas	
7		Web Design	28 days	Wed 11/24/10	Mon 1/3/11			
8		Interior Pages	28 days	Wed 11/24/10	Mon 1/3/11			
9		Design interior pages	5 days	Wed 11/24/10	Wed 12/1/10	4	Designer	
10		Interior page design review	5 days	Wed 12/1/10	Wed 12/15/10	9	Yolanda Sanchez	
11		Finalize interior page design	4 days	Wed 12/15/10	Tue 12/21/10	10	Designer	
12		Develop style sheets	4 days	Tue 12/21/10	Mon 12/27/10	11	Designer	
13		Develop page templates	5 days	Mon 12/27/10	Mon 1/3/11	12	Designer	
14		Design Home page	18 days	Wed 11/24/10	Mon 12/20/10			

Figure 4-12 Use the Task Sheet to enter tasks and durations and to review calculated start and finish dates.

To display the Task Sheet, on the View tab, in the Task Views group, click Other Views, and then click Task Sheet.

Resource Sheet

To display the Resource Sheet, on the View tab, in the Resource Views group, click Resource Sheet.

You can also quickly switch to the Resource Sheet by clicking its icon in the view shortcuts area on the status bar, next to the Zoom slider.

The Project 2010 sheet views are described in Table 4-3.

Table 4-3 **Project 2010 Sheet Views**

Sheet view	How you can use it	For more information
Resource Sheet (resource view)	Enter, edit, and review resource information in a spreadsheet format.	Chapter 7, "Setting Up Resources in the Project"
Task Sheet (task view)	Enter, edit, and review task information in a spreadsheet format.	"Creating a New Project Plan" on page 74

For information about modifying the content or format of a sheet view, see "Modifying a Sheet View" on page 1099.

Timesheeting with Usage Views

Usage views are made up of a sheet view on the left side and a timesheet on the right. Together with the timescale, the timesheet can show work, cost, availability, and other data broken out by time—that is, *timephased.* (See Figure 4-13.)

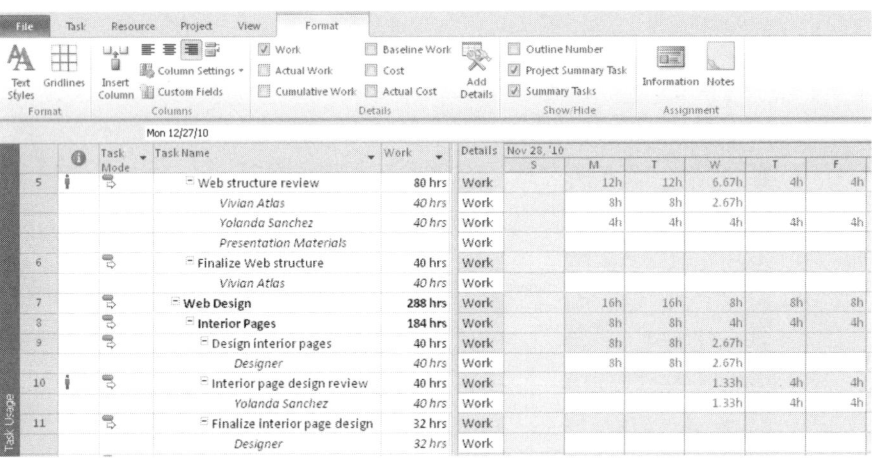

Figure 4-13 Display the Task Usage view to review assignments by task.

Task Usage

To display the Task Usage view, on the View tab, in the Task Views group, click Task Usage.

You can also quickly switch to the Task Usage view by clicking its icon in the view shortcuts area on the status bar.

To display the Resource Usage view, on the View tab, in the Resource Views group, click Resource Usage.

The Project 2010 usage views are described in Table 4-4.

Table 4-4 **Project 2010 Usage Views**

Usage view	How you can use it	For more information
Resource Usage (assignment view)	Review, enter, and edit assignments by resource. In the sheet area of the Resource Usage view, each resource is listed with all associated task assignments indented beneath it. (See Figure 4-14.) In the timesheet area of the view, information such as work or costs for the resource and the assignment is listed according to the timescale—for example, by week or month.	Chapter 8
Task Usage (assignment view)	Review, enter, and edit assignments by task. In the sheet area of the Task Usage view, each task is listed with the assigned resources indented beneath it. (See Figure 4-15.) In the timesheet area of the view, information such as work or costs for the task and the assignment is listed according to the timescale—for example, by day or by week.	Chapter 8

Vivian Atlas	130.67 hrs
Develop Web structure	*26.67 hrs*
Web structure review	*40 hrs*
Finalize Web structure	*40 hrs*
Assign content owners	*24 hrs*
Paul Shakespear	408 hrs
Perform system needs analysis	*40 hrs*
Evaluate equipment requirements	*120 hrs*
Evaluate software requirements	*120 hrs*
Order equipment	*24 hrs*
Order software	*24 hrs*

Figure 4-14 In the Resource Usage view, each resource is listed with its assigned tasks.

Develop Web structure	40 hrs
Vivian Atlas	*26.67 hrs*
Sandeep Katyal	*13.33 hrs*
Web structure review	80 hrs
Vivian Atlas	*40 hrs*
Yolanda Sanchez	*40 hrs*

Figure 4-15 In the Task Usage view, each task is listed with its assigned resources.

Because the timesheet area of the usage views breaks down information from certain fields and from specific time periods, there are three subcategories to the major field categories of tasks, resources, and assignments:

- Task-timephased
- Resource-timephased
- Assignment-timephased

You can review task-timephased and assignment-timephased fields in the timesheet area of the Task Usage view. You can review resource-timephased and assignment-timephased fields in the timesheet area of the Resource Usage view.

> **Note**
>
> **Timephased information is used in many earned value analysis calculations. For more information about earned value, see Chapter 14, "Analyzing Progress Using Earned Value."**

The Work field is shown by default in the timephased fields in the timesheet area of a usage view. Multiple fields of information can be stacked in the view at one time. To change the type of information shown, do the following:

1. Display one of the usage views.
2. On the Format tab, in the Details group, select the check box for the timephased details you want to show in the timesheet area of the usage view.

   This group shows the various timephased fields that the timesheet area of the current usage view can display—for example, Actual Work, Baseline Work, and Cost. Any fields currently displayed are noted with a check mark.

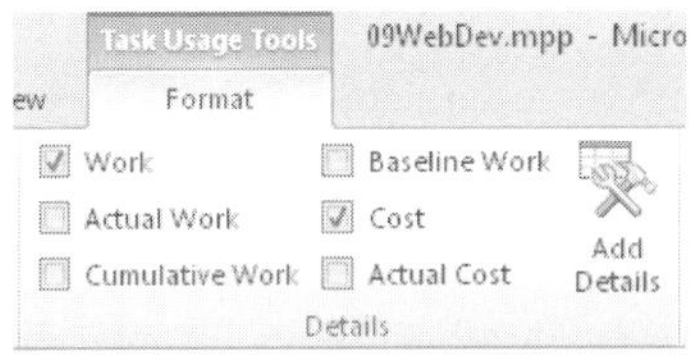

When you select a check box, another row of timephased information is added to the timesheet for each task.

Work	12h	12h	6.67h	4h
Cost	$500.00	$500.00	$246.67	$120.00
Work	8h	8h	2.67h	
Cost	$360.00	$360.00	$120.00	
Work	4h	4h	4h	4h
Cost	$120.00	$120.00	$120.00	$120.00
Work				
Cost	$20.00	$20.00	$6.67	

3. To remove a row of information from the timesheet, on the Format tab, in the Details group, clear the check box of the field you want to remove.

For information about modifying the format of a usage view, see "Modifying a Usage View" on page 1100.

Seeing Details with Forms

Forms are specialized views that include text boxes and grids in which you can enter and review information as you do in a dialog box. (See Figure 4-16.) Although you can display a form on its own and click the Previous and Next buttons to cycle through the different tasks or resources in your project, a form is most useful when it's included as part of a combination view. (See "Working with Combination Views" in the next section.)

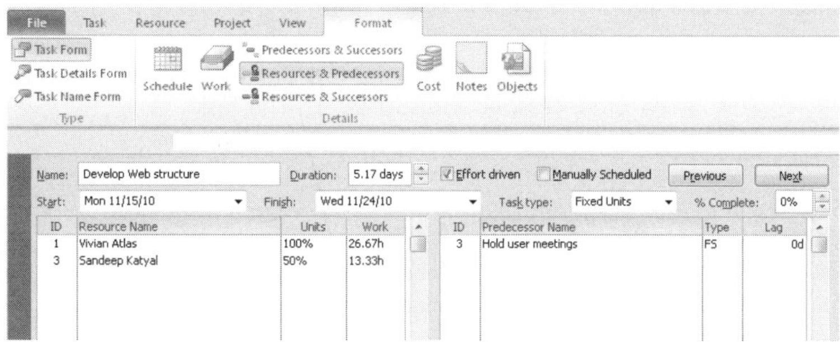

Figure 4-16 This Task Form shows fundamental information about the task, along with information about assigned resources and predecessor tasks.

To display a task form, on the View tab, in the Task Views group, click Other Views, and then click More Views. Click the name of the form in the dialog box, and then click Apply.

To display a resource form, on the View tab, in the Resource Views group, click Other Views, and then click More Views. Click the name of the form in the dialog box, and then click Apply.

Remember, after you apply any form, it appears on the Other Views drop-down menu so you don't have to drill all the way into the More Views dialog box every time you need it.

The Project 2010 forms are described in Table 4-5.

Table 4-5 **Project 2010 Forms**

Form	How you can use it	For more information
Resource Form (resource view)	Enter, edit, and review all resource, task, and schedule information about a selected resource, one resource at a time. The grid area can show information about the resource's schedule, cost, or work on assigned tasks. It is most useful when used as part of a combination view. (See Figure 4-17.)	Chapter 8
Resource Name Form (resource view)	Enter, edit, and review the selected resource's schedule, cost, or work on assigned tasks. The Resource Name Form is a simplified version of the Resource Form.	Chapter 8
Task Details Form (task view)	Enter, edit, and review detailed tracking and scheduling information about a selected task, one task at a time. The grid area can show information about assigned resources, predecessors, and successors.	Chapter 6
Task Form (task view)	Enter, edit, and review information about a selected task, one task at a time. The grid area can show information about the task's assigned resources, predecessors, and successors.	Chapter 6
Task Name Form (task view)	Enter, edit, and review the selected task's assigned resources, predecessors, and successors. The Task Name Form is a simplified version of the Task Form.	Chapter 6

You can change the categories of information shown in a form view. To do this, follow these steps:

1. Show the form whose categories of information you want to change.
2. On the Format tab, in the Details group, review the different types of information that can be shown in the form. The item currently shown in the form is highlighted in yellow.
3. Click the information you want to display in the form. You can choose only one item from the shortcut menu at a time.

Cross-Referencing with Combination Views

Combination views are groupings of two views in a split screen. The information in one portion of the split screen controls the content in the other portion, as shown in Figure 4-17.

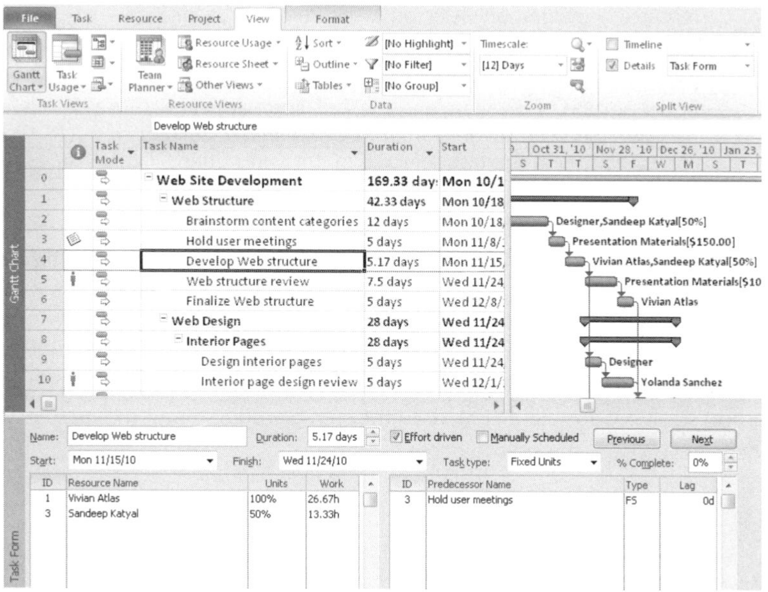

Figure 4-17 When you click a task in the Gantt Chart portion of the Task Entry view (at the top), the task, assignment, and predecessor information for that selected task appear in the Task Form portion of the view (at the bottom).

To apply the Task Entry combination view, on the View menu, in the Task Views group, click Other Views, and then click More Views. Click Task Entry, and then click Apply.

To apply the Resource Allocation combination view, on the View menu, in the Resource Views group, click Other Views, and then click More Views. Click Resource Allocation, and then click Apply.

The predefined Project 2010 combination views are described in Table 4-6.

Table 4-6 **Project 2010 Combination Views**

Combination view	How you can use it	For more information
Resource Allocation (resource view)	Review and resolve resource overallocations. The Resource Usage view appears in the upper portion of the view, and the Leveling Gantt appears in the lower portion. The information shown in the Leveling Gantt corresponds with the resource or assignment selected in the Resource Usage view.	"Balancing Resource Workloads" on page 403
Task Entry (task view)	Enter, edit, and review detailed information about the task selected in the Gantt Chart. The Gantt Chart appears in the upper portion of the view, and the Task Form appears in the lower portion. The information shown in the Task Form corresponds with the task selected in the Gantt Chart.	Chapter 6

You can create your own combination view by simply splitting the view. For example, if you split the Gantt Chart view, the Task Form appears in the lower pane, instantly resulting in the Task Entry view. Likewise, if you split the Resource Sheet, the Resource Form appears in the lower pane.

The split bar is located in the lower-right corner of the Project 2010 window, just below the vertical scroll bar. To split a view, drag the split bar up to about the middle of the view or wherever you want the split to occur.

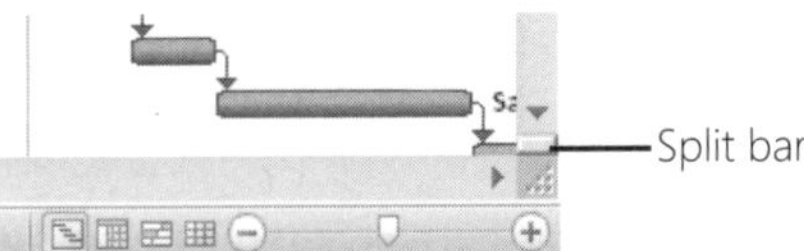

To remove the split and return to a single view, double-click the split bar, which is now the gray dividing bar between the two views. Or, on the View tab, in the Split View group, clear the Details check box.

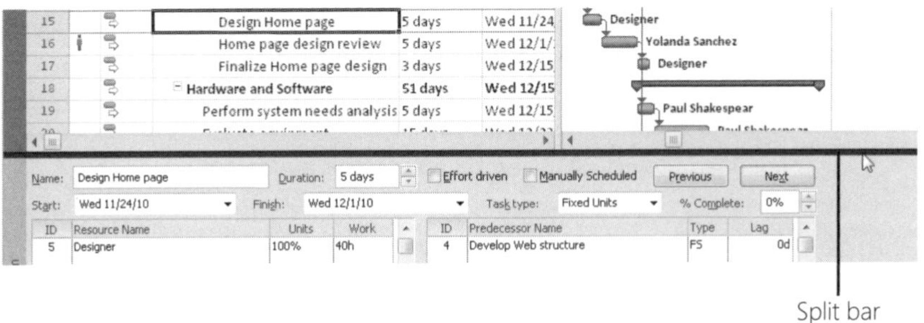

To modify a combination view, simply modify one component of the combination view as if it were in its own view.

For more information about combination views, see "Customizing Views" on page 1062.

TROUBLESHOOTING

The current view doesn't have a split bar

By their nature, graph views and forms do not have a split bar. However, you can still create a combination view with these views in the upper pane. On the View tab, in the Split View group, select the Details check box. If a task view is showing, the Task Form appears at the bottom of the split screen. If a resource view is showing, the Resource Form appears at the bottom.

You can change the form that appears. On the View tab, in the Split View group, click the arrow in the box next to the Details check box, and then select a different view under Detail Panes.

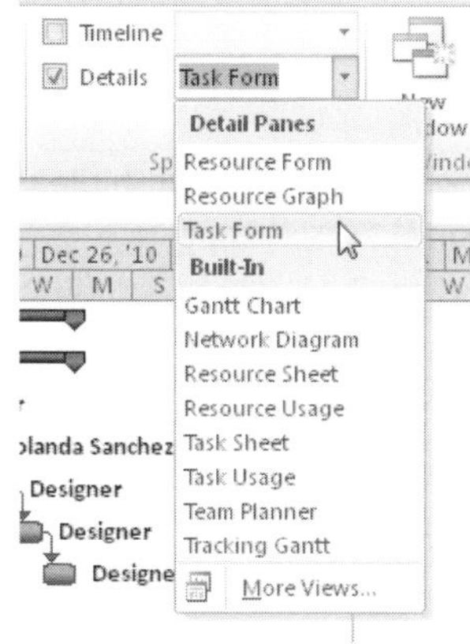

TROUBLESHOOTING

You can't get the combination view to be a single view again

In a combination view such as Task Entry or Resource Allocation, one of the two views always has focus; that is, it's the currently active view. When you switch to another view, only the active view switches.

Before switching to another view, make the combination view a single view. To do this, double-click the split bar—the gray dividing bar between the two view. Or, on the View tab, in the Split View group, clear the Details check box, and then switch to the other view.

Using Tables

All sheet views, including the sheet area of any Gantt chart or usage view, have a table applied. Although every sheet view is associated with a default table, you can change the table in the sheet view to accommodate the kind of information you need to see.

Each table is made up of columns containing field information relevant to the job of the table and its view. You can rearrange the order of these columns, hide columns you don't need, and add other columns you do need.

Sheet and Table Reference

There is a default table defined for each sheet view in Project 2010. Table 4-7 lists all sheet views and their default tables.

Table 4-7 **Sheet Views and their Default Tables**

Sheet view	Default table	View	Default table
Bar Rollup	Rollup Table	Resource Allocation	Usage (Resource Usage view) Delay (Leveling Gantt view)
Detail Gantt	Delay	Resource Sheet	Entry
Gantt Chart	Entry	Resource Usage	Usage
Leveling Gantt	Delay	Task Entry	Entry
Milestone Date Rollup	Entry	Task Sheet	Entry
Milestone Rollup	Rollup Table	Task Usage	Usage
Multiple Baselines Gantt	Entry	Tracking Gantt	Entry

Table Definition Reference

Although every sheet view has a default table, that table can easily be switched with another. There are 17 built-in tables for task sheets and 10 built-in tables for resource sheets.

Table 4-8 lists a description of the available task tables and the fields that make them up by default.

Table 4-8 **Task Tables and Their Default Fields**

Task table	Default fields included	For more information
BASELINE		
Specific baseline values reflecting the schedule as originally planned	ID, Task Name, Baseline Duration, Baseline Start, Baseline Finish, Baseline Work, and Baseline Cost	"Saving Original Plan Information Using a Baseline" on page 445
CONSTRAINT DATES		
The specific constraint types for each task, along with associated dates where applicable; you can use these fields to review or change the constraint type and date	ID, Task Name, Duration, Constraint Type, and Constraint Date	"Scheduling Tasks to Achieve Specific Dates" on page 219
COST		
Cost information for each task, which helps you analyze various types of cost calculations	ID, Task Name, Fixed Cost, Fixed Cost Accrual, Total Cost, Baseline, Variance, Actual, and Remaining	"Monitoring and Adjusting Costs" on page 502
DELAY		
Information to help you determine how long it will take to complete your tasks given the resources you have and the amount of time they have for a given task	ID, Indicators, Task Name, Leveling Delay, Duration, Start, Finish, Successors, and Resources	"Balancing Resource Workloads'" on page 403
EARNED VALUE		
Earned value information that compares the relationship between work and costs based on a status date	ID, Task Name, Planned Value – PV, Earned Value – EV, AC (ACWP), SV, CV, EAC, BAC, and VAC	Chapter 14
EARNED VALUE COST INDICATORS		
Earned-value cost information, including the ratio of budgeted to actual costs of work performed.	ID, Task Name, Planned Value – PV, Earned Value – EV, CV, CV%, CPI, BAC, EAC, VAC, and TCPI	Chapter 14
EARNED VALUE SCHEDULE INDICATORS		
Earned-value schedule information, including the ratio of work performed to work scheduled	ID, Task Name, Planned Value – PV, Earned Value – EV, SV, SV%, and SPI	Chapter 14
ENTRY		
Fundamental information regarding tasks; this table is useful for entering and viewing the most essential task information	ID, Indicators, Task Mode, Task Name, Duration, Start, Finish, Predecessors, and Resource Names	"Entering Tasks," in Chapter 3

Task table	Default fields included	For more information
EXPORT		
A large set of fields from which to export task fields to other applications, such as Microsoft Excel or Microsoft Access	ID, Unique ID, Task Name, Duration, Type, Outline Level, Baseline Duration, Predecessors, Start, Finish, Early Start, Early Finish, Late Start, Late Finish, Free Slack, Total Slack, Leveling Delay, % Complete, Actual Start, Actual Finish, Baseline Start, Baseline Finish, Constraint Type, Constraint Date, Stop, Resume, Created, Work, Baseline Work, Actual Work, Cost, Fixed Cost, Baseline Cost, Actual Cost, Remaining Cost, WBS, Priority, Milestone, Summary, Rollup, Text1–10, Cost1–3, Duration1–3, Flag1–10, Marked, Number1–5, Subproject File, Contact, Start1–5, and Finish1–5	"Importing and Exporting Information" on page 676
HYPERLINK		
Hyperlink information to associate linked web pages or file shortcuts with your tasks	ID, Indicators, Task Name, Hyperlink, Address, and SubAddress	"Hyperlinking to Websites or Other Documents" on page 674
SCHEDULE		
Detailed scheduling information that can help you see when a task is scheduled to begin and how late it can actually begin without jeopardizing the project's finish date	ID, Task Mode, Task Name, Start, Finish, Late Start, Late Finish, Free Slack, and Total Slack	"Understanding Slack Time and Critical Tasks" on page 369
SUMMARY		
Overview of project information to analyze durations, dates, progress, and costs	ID, Task Mode, Task Name, Duration, Start, Finish, % Complete, Cost, and Work	"Bringing In the Project Finish Date" on page 383
TRACKING		
Actual progress and cost information, as contrasted with scheduled or baseline information	ID, Task Name, Actual Start, Actual Finish, % Complete, Physical % Complete, Actual Duration, Remaining Duration, Actual Cost, and Actual Work	"Updating Task Progress" on page 462
USAGE		
The most fundamental task schedule information	ID, Indicators, Task Mode, Task Name, Work, Duration, Start, and Finish	Chapter 6

Task table	Default fields included	For more information
VARIANCE		
Gaps between baseline start and finish dates and the actual start and finish dates, enabling a comparison between your original planned schedule and actual performance	ID, Task Mode, Task Name, Start, Finish, Baseline Start, Baseline Finish, Start Variance, and Finish Variance	Chapter 12
WORK		
A variety of measurements for analyzing the level of effort for each task	ID, Task Name, Work, Baseline Work, Variance, Actual Work, Remaining Work, and % Work Complete	"Updating Task Progress" on page 462

Table 4-9 lists a description of all resource tables and their default fields.

Table 4-9 **Resource Tables and Their Default Fields**

Resource table	Default fields included	For more Information
COST		
Cost information about resources in a project	ID, Resource Name, Cost, Baseline Cost, Cost Variance, Actual Cost, and Remaining Cost	"Monitoring and Adjusting Costs" on page 502
EARNED VALUE		
Earned value information that compares the relationship between work and costs for resources based on a status date	ID, Resource Name, Planned Value – PV, Earned Value – EV, AC (ACWP), SV, CV, EAC, BAC, and VAC	Chapter 14
ENTRY		
Essential information regarding resources; this table is most useful for entering and viewing fundamental resource information	ID, Indicators, Resource Name, Type, Material Label, Initials, Group, Maximum Units, Standard Rate, Overtime Rate, Cost/Use, Accrue At, Base Calendar, and Code	Chapter 7, "Setting Up Resources in the Project"
ENTRY – MATERIAL RESOURCES		
Essential information about consumable material resources	ID, Resource Name, Type, Material Label, Initials, Group, Standard Rate, Cost/Use, Accrue At, and Code	"Adding Material Resources to the Project" on page 258
ENTRY – WORK RESOURCES		
Essential information about work (people and equipment) resources	ID, Resource Name, Type, Initials, Group, Maximum Units, Standard Rate, Overtime Rate, Cost/Use, Accrue At, Base Calendar, and Code	"Adding Work Resources to the Project" on page 250

Resource table	Default fields included	For more Information
EXPORT		
A large set of fields from which to export resource fields to other applications, such as Excel or Access	ID, Unique ID, Resource Name, Initials, Maximum Units, Standard Rate, Overtime Rate, Cost Per Use, Accrue At, Cost, Baseline Cost, Actual Cost, Work, Baseline Work, Actual Work, Overtime Work, Group, Code, Text1–5, and Email Address	"Importing and Exporting Information" on page 676
HYPERLINK		
Hyperlink information to associate linked web pages or file shortcuts with your resources	ID, Indicators, Resource Name, Hyperlink, Address, and SubAddress	"Hyperlinking to Websites and Other Documents" on page 674
SUMMARY		
Overview of resource information	ID, Resource Name, Group, Maximum Units, Peak, Standard Rate, Overtime Rate, Cost, and Work	Chapter 7
USAGE		
The most essential resource scheduling information	ID, Indicators, Resource Name, and Work	Chapter 8
WORK		
A variety of measurements for analyzing work (level of effort) for resources and their assigned tasks	ID, Resource Name, % Complete, Work, Overtime, Baseline, Variance, Actual, and Remaining	"Using Resource Work to Update Progress" on page 470

In addition to the default fields, every table has a last column called Add New Column. You can click the Add New Column heading and see all available task or resource fields. Click a field to add it to the table. The selected field is added to the table, and a new Add New Column column appears.

Note

You can quickly see the name of the current table. Simply rest your mouse pointer in the All Cells box where the row and column headings intersect. The ScreenTip containing the table name (and view name) appears.

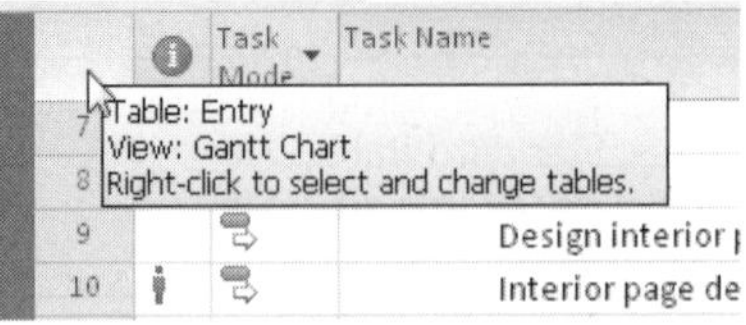

Chapter 4

Changing the Table in a View

To switch to a different table, follow these steps:

1. Display the view containing the table you want to change. This view could be the Task Sheet, Resource Sheet, Gantt Chart, Task Usage view, and so on.

Tables

2. On the View tab, in the Data group, click Tables.

   If the current view is a task sheet, only task tables are listed. Likewise, if the current view is a resource sheet, only resource tables are listed. You cannot apply a resource table to a task view, and vice versa.

   Because there are only 10 resource tables, all of them are listed in the drop-down menu. However, only nine of the most commonly used task tables are listed. The others are available in the More Tables dialog box.

3. If the table is listed on the submenu, click it. If the table is not listed on the submenu, click More Tables (see Figure 4-18), and then double-click the table you want.

   The table is replaced by the table you select.

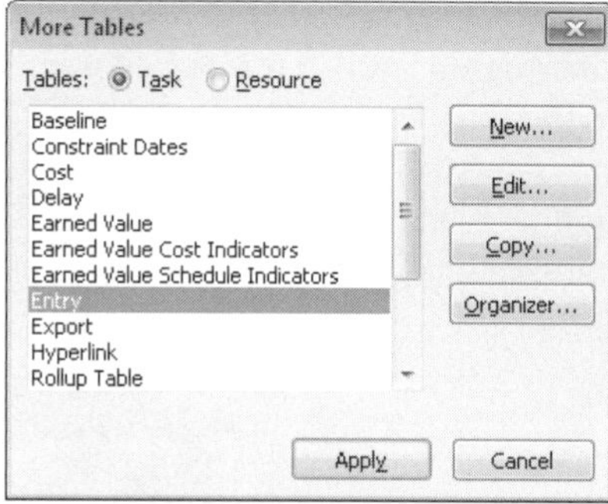

Figure 4-18 The More Tables dialog box contains the full list of built-in tables.

Note

Another method for changing tables is to right-click the All Cells box where the row and column headings intersect. The Tables shortcut menu appears.

Modifying a Table

Suppose that the Entry task table provides all the information you need except baseline values. You can easily add another column to any table, and you can just as easily remove superfluous columns. You can also make certain changes to the columns themselves.

> **Note**
>
> **When working with columns in a table, you're working with fields in your project database. Fields are discussed in more detail in "Using Fields" on page 160.**

To add a column to the right edge of a table, follow these steps:

1. Apply the table to which you want to add a new column.
2. If necessary, scroll to the far right edge of the table until you see the column labeled Add New Column.

NEW!

3. Click the Add New Column heading.

   All relevant task or resource fields are listed in the drop-down menu in alphabetical order, as shown in Figure 4-19.

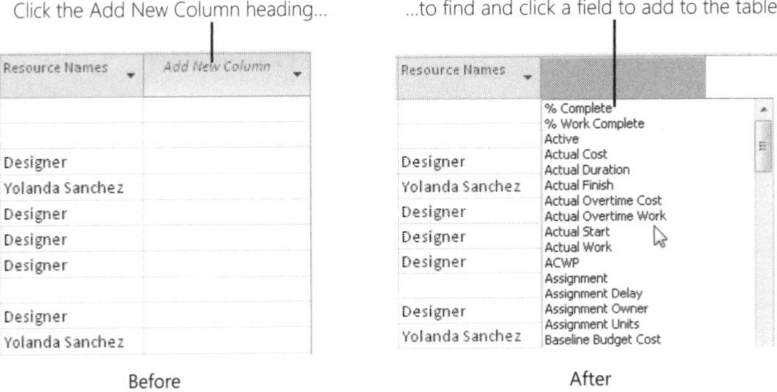

Figure 4-19 Click the Add New Column heading in any table to add a new field to the current table.

4. Scroll down as necessary to find the field you want.

   To move quickly to a field, type the first one or two characters of its name.

5. Click a field to add it to the table.

   The selected field is added to the table, and a new Add New Column column appears to the right.

To add a column to a specific place in a table, follow these steps:

1. Display the view and table to which you want to add a column.
2. Click the column heading that will be to the right of the new column.
3. On the Format tab, in the Columns group, click Insert Column.

Insert Column

   A new column is created to the left of the selected column and the fields drop-down menu appears.
4. Find the field you want, either by scrolling or by typing the first one or two characters of its name.
5. Click a field to add it to the table.

   The selected field is added to the new column.

To replace an existing column with a different field, follow these steps:

1. Display the view and table to which you want to add a new field.
2. Double-click the column heading you want to replace.

   The fields drop-down menu appears.
3. Click the field you want to use as a replacement.

TROUBLESHOOTING

The field you're looking for is not in the Field Name list

When you display a task view and table, only task fields are listed in the column drop-down menu. Likewise, when you display a resource view and table, only resource fields are listed. Assignment fields are available only in the Task Usage and Resource Usage views.

To remove a column from a table, follow these steps:

1. Display the view and table from which you want to remove a column.
2. Right-click the heading of the column you want to remove, and then click Hide Column.

   The column is removed. The field and its contents still exist in the database, however, and can be displayed again in this or other tables.

Note

Here's another way to remove a column. Select the column heading, and then click Format, Columns, Column Settings, Hide Column. You can also simply select the column heading and press the Delete key.

Hiding and Showing Columns

You can hide a column in your table while keeping it in place. Position your mouse pointer over the right edge of the column heading border. The mouse pointer changes to a black crosshair. Drag the right border past the column's left border. The column disappears.

To show the column again, position your mouse pointer on the edge where your column is hidden. Drag to the right, and your column appears again.

Using this method is a bit tricky. You need to know where you hid the column because there's no visual indication that it's there.

You can change the title of the column to something other than the actual field name. You can also modify the column text alignment and the column width. To modify a column, follow these steps:

1. Display the view and table whose column settings you want to change.
2. Click the heading of the column you want to change.
3. On the Format tab, in the Columns group, click Column Settings, and then click Field Settings.

   Column Settings

   You can also right-click anywhere in the column you want to change and then click Field Settings on the shortcut menu.

   The Field Settings dialog box appears, as shown in Figure 4-20.

Figure 4-20 Use the Field Settings dialog box to change the field, name, alignment, or width of a field in a column.

4. To change the field information appearing in the column, in the Field Name list, click the field you want.
5. To change the title of the column heading, type a new title in the Title box.

   This changes the title of this column only in this table. It does not permanently change the field name itself.
6. Use the Align Title list to change the alignment of the column title.
7. Use the Align Data list to change the alignment of the field information itself.
8. Enter a number in the Width box to change the column width.

   If you prefer, you can click the Best Fit button to adjust the column width to its widest entry.
9. By default, the column heading title wraps onto two or more lines as necessary. If you want the title to stay all on one line, clear the Header Text Wrapping check box.
10. Click OK.

    Your changes are made to the field in the selected column.

Note

You can also change the column width directly on the table, exactly as you do in Excel. Click the column's heading to select the column. Then move the mouse pointer to the right edge of the column until the pointer changes to a black crosshair. Drag to the right to widen the column; drag to the left to make the column narrower. Double-click the edge to widen the column to the same size as the longest entry in the column.

You can move a column to another location in the table simply by dragging. To move a column, follow these steps:

1. Display the view and table containing the column you want to move.
2. Click the heading of the column you want to move.
3. With the black crosshair mouse pointer over the column heading, drag to the new location for the column. As you drag, a gray line moves with the mouse pointer to indicate where the column will be inserted when you release the mouse button.

Note

In addition to adding and removing columns in existing tables, you can also create entirely new tables. For more information, see "Customizing Tables" on page 1103.

Using Fields

Tables are made up of columns, and columns contain field information. The previous section describes how to add, remove, and manipulate columns in a table. This section provides more detail about the fields used throughout Project 2010.

Fields are the smallest piece of data in the vast collection of information that makes up your project database. For example, one task comprises a single record in this database. This record consists of a number of task fields, such as the task name, duration, start date, finish date, assigned resource, deadline, and more.

Whether you see them in a view or not, there are numerous fields for your tasks, resources, and assignments, as well as for the project as a whole.

Some fields are entered by you, such as task name and duration. Other fields are calculated for you by Project 2010, such as start date, finish date, and total cost. Still other fields can be entered by you or calculated by Project 2010.

From the discussion of views, tables, and the fields in those tables earlier in this chapter, you should already be familiar with the different *field categories*:

- Task fields
- Task-timephased fields
- Resource fields
- Resource-timephased fields
- Assignment fields
- Assignment-timephased fields

The timephased fields break down field information—such as work, costs, and availability—by time periods. This breakdown gives you more information to work with in your project. In the Task Usage and Resource Usage views, for example, you can see task cost by day or resource work by week. You can break either of those down further into the component assignments. The timephased fields also give you more tools for analysis through earned-value calculations.

For more information about earned value analysis, see Chapter 14.

Another way that fields are categorized is by *data type*. The data type indicates how a field can be used—for example, as a currency-type field, or a text-type field. The following are the field data types:

- **Cost or Currency** Information is expressed as a cost.
- **Date** Information is expressed as a date.
- **Duration** Information is expressed as a span of time.
- **Enumerated** Information is selected from a list of predefined choices.
- **Indicator** Information is shown as graphical indicators, or icons, about a task, resource, or assignment.
- **Integer** Information is expressed as a whole number.

- **Outline code** Information is defined with a custom tag for tasks or resources that enables you to show a hierarchy of tasks in your project.
- **Percentage/Number** Information is displayed as a value that can be expressed as either a percentage or decimal number, such as 100 percent or 1.00.
- **Text** Information is expressed as unrestricted characters of text.
- **Yes/No** Information is set to either Yes or No, that is, a True/False or Boolean value.

Fields make up your project database, the whole of which you might never see, or even have a need to see. You do see various fields throughout your project plan, in the following locations:

- Columns in a table
- Rows in a timesheet
- Bars in the Timeline
- Resources and tasks in the Team Planner
- Information in a network diagram node
- Gantt bars and associated text in a Gantt chart
- Fields in a form view
- Fields in a dialog box

Some of these locations, such as columns in a table and rows in a timesheet, can be changed to suit your needs. Others, such as the fields in a dialog box, are fixed.

In addition to adding built-in fields wherever you might need them, you can also create your own custom fields and add them to tables in your views. There are custom fields you can define for currency, dates, durations, finish dates, start dates, text, numbers, outline codes, and more. Project Professional 2010 includes an additional set of enterprise custom fields as well, so an organization can design a robust set of fields that standardizes project management data collection and display across the enterprise.

For more information about defining custom fields, see "Customizing Fields" on page 1107. For information about working with enterprise custom fields, see "Working with Custom Enterprise Fields" on page 919.

Learn More About Project 2010 Fields

You can immediately get comprehensive information about any field in a table. Position your mouse pointer over the column heading, and a ScreenTip pops up that provides a brief description of the field. Press F1, and the Help topic for the selected field appears in a separate Help window.

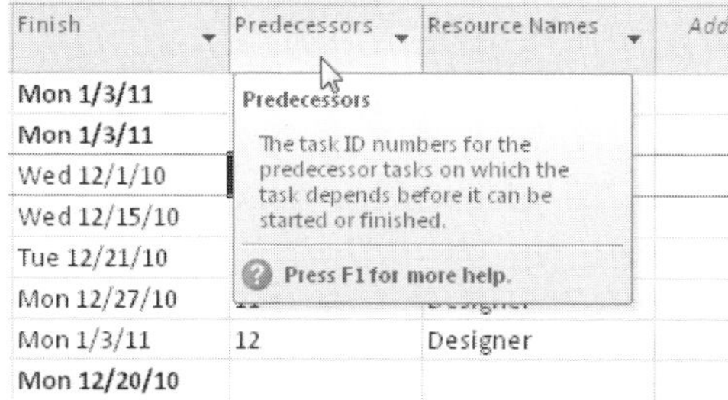

You can also get Help about fields by following these steps:

Help

1. In the upper-right corner of the Project window, click the Help icon.

   You can also press F1 or, on the File tab, click Help, and then click Microsoft Office Help.

2. Under Browse Project 2010 Support, click See All.
3. In the Categories list, click Reference.
4. On the Reference page, click Available Fields Reference.
5. Click one of the field categories—for example, Task Fields or Assignment Fields. A complete list of fields in that category appears, along with a short description of each.
6. Click a field name, and its Help topic appears. (See Figure 4-21.)

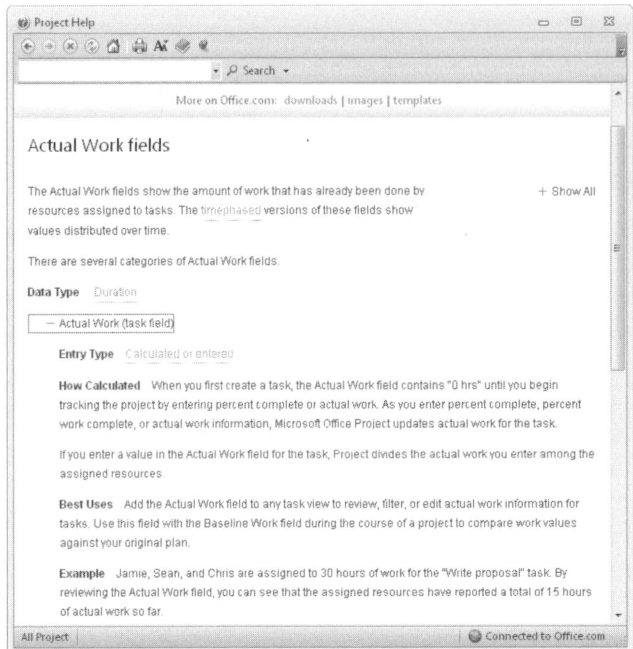

Figure 4-21 The Fields Reference Help topics contain comprehensive information about the fields.

These online Help topics about the fields contain the following information:

- Data Type (duration, cost, text, and so on)
- Entry Type (entered, calculated, or both)
- Description (a general overview of the field's function)
- How Calculated (for calculated fields)
- Best Uses (the purpose of the field)
- Example (how this field might be used to facilitate a project plan)
- Remarks (any additional information)

Arranging Your Project 2010 Window

The more you work with Project 2010, the stronger your preferences become about how you want elements laid out in the window. You can make changes to the Project 2010 window that will persist across your working sessions with the project plan as well as to other projects you create. For example, you can reset which view should be the default when you first start a new project plan. You can also show or hide different elements in the default Project 2010 window. In making these changes, you can set up your Project 2010 window to be the most efficient for your own working methods.

On the other hand, sometimes you need to rearrange the Project 2010 window temporarily to accomplish a specific task. For example, you can zoom the window or the timescale. You can arrange one window in two different panes. You can also easily switch between multiple open projects.

Setting Your Default View

The Gantt Chart is the default view that appears whenever you start Project 2010 or create a new project file. This is because project managers use this view most often, at least as a starting point. However, if a different view is your favorite, you can make that one the default view. To do this, follow these steps:

1. On the File tab, click Options, and then click General in the left pane.
2. Under Project View, in the Default View box, click the view you want to appear first whenever you create a new project file.

INSIDE OUT **Not always the default view**

Setting the default view does not control the view that appears when you open an existing project plan. When you open an existing project plan, it displays the last view you were working with when you closed the file. If you want your project plan to open in a particular view each time, be sure you end your working session in that view.

Using the Zoom Slider

NEW! The Zoom slider is the control on the status bar in the lower-right corner of the Project 2010 screen.

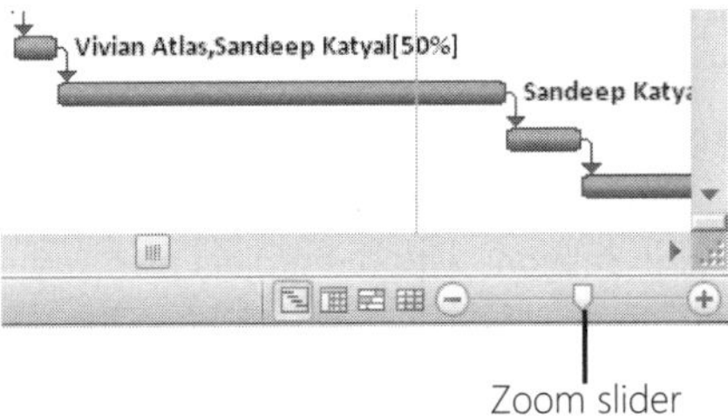

Use the Zoom slider to see more or less detail in your view. If you're working in a view with a timescale, such as a Gantt chart or usage view, use the Zoom slider to expand or contract the time periods shown. If you're working in a graphical view such as the Calendar or a network diagram, the Zoom slider expands or shrinks the entire current view.

You can click the plus button or drag the slider to the right to see more detail. Or, you can click the minus button or drag the slider to the left to see more in the window at one time.

The Zoom slider is not available in views that don't need to be zoomed in or out, such as sheet views and forms.

TROUBLESHOOTING

You can't find the Zoom slider

If the status bar is not showing at all along the bottom of your Project window, you need to turn it on to see the Zoom slider. On the File tab, click Options, and then click Advanced in the left pane. Under Display, select the Show Status Bar check box.

If the status bar is showing, but the Zoom slider is not, right-click the status bar. Near the bottom of the shortcut menu that appears, click Zoom Slider to turn it on.

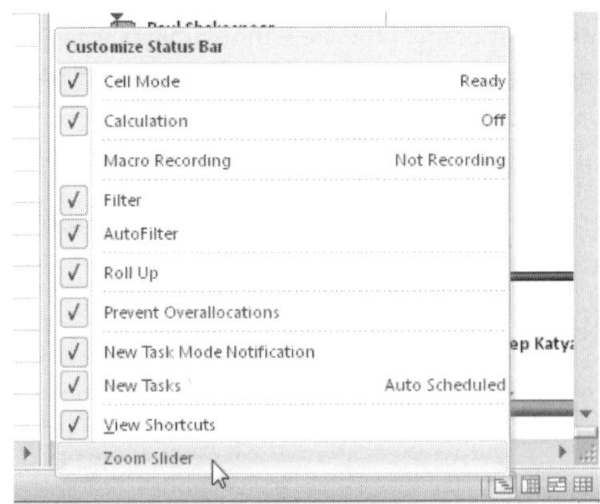

After turning the Zoom slider on, click off the shortcut menu to dismiss it.

Adjusting a Timescale

Many Project 2010 views, including Gantt charts and usage views, use a timescale to indicate time in the project. The timescale appears above the chart or timesheet area of a view. You can display up to three timescales (see Figure 4-22), with each timescale in a tier. The highest tier shows the broadest period of time, and the lowest tier shows the most detailed period of time. For example, you can show days within weeks within months, or you can show weeks within quarters.

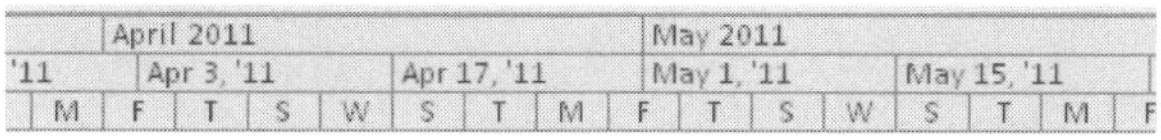

Figure 4-22 You can zoom your timescales up or down while you're working.

The default timescale is two tiers: days within weeks. To set your timescale options, do the following:

1. Show a view that contains a timescale, for example, the Gantt Chart, Task Usage view, or Resource Graph.
2. On the View tab, in the Zoom group, click the arrow in the Timescale box, and then click Timescale in the drop-down menu.

   The Timescale dialog box appears, providing four tabs: Top Tier, Middle Tier, Bottom Tier, and Non-Working Time. The Middle Tier tab is displayed by default.
3. Under Timescale Options, in the Show box, click the number of timescale tiers you want to display (one, two, or three).
4. Under Middle Tier Formatting, in the Units box, specify the time unit you want to display at the middle tier—for example, quarters, months, or weeks.
5. In the Label box, click the format in which you want to display the time unit—for example, January 28, Jan 28, Sun 28, and so on. If necessary, scroll to see more time unit formats to find the one you want.
6. If you choose to display more than one tier, click the Top Tier and/or Bottom Tier tabs and repeat steps 4 and 5.

Showing and Hiding Screen Elements

Certain screen elements are displayed by default in the Project 2010 window. Figure 4-23 shows these screen elements. To expand your working area, you can hide elements that you don't use much or that you just want to get out of the way temporarily. (You can still use these elements when you need them.)

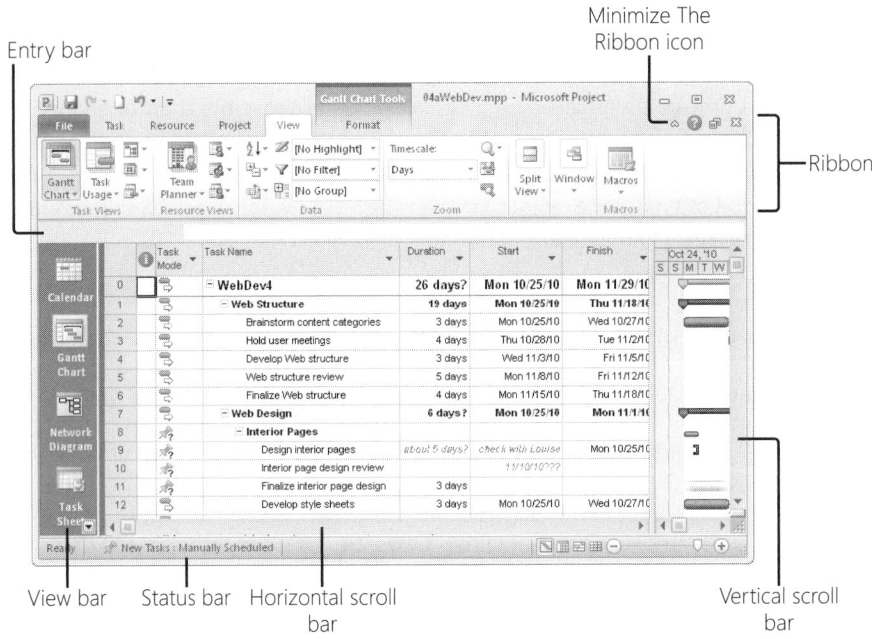

Figure 4-23 You can display or hide various screen elements on the Project 2010 window.

Table 4-10 lists the screen elements you can show or hide, along with the procedure for doing so.

Table 4-10 Screen Elements

Screen element	How to display or hide it
Ribbon Minimize The Ribbon Expand The Ribbon	You can hide the ribbon to the extent that only the tab names are showing. In the upper-right corner of the Project 2010 window, click the Minimize The Ribbon icon. To show the ribbon again, click the Expand The Ribbon icon.
View bar	To show the View bar, right-click the Active View bar—the gray bar at the left edge of the Project 2010 window that shows the name of the current view. At the bottom of the drop-down menu, click View Bar. To hide the View bar, right-click the View bar, and then click View Bar.
Status bar (the bar below the view)	On the File tab, click Options, and then click Advanced in the left pane. Under Display, select or clear the Show Status Bar check box.
Scroll bars (horizontal and vertical)	On the File tab, click Options, and then click Advanced in the left pane. Under Display, select or clear the Show Scroll Bars check box.
Entry bar (the bar above the view)	In Project 2010, the Entry bar above the current view does not show by default. On the File tab, click Options, and then click Display in the left pane. Under Show These Elements, select or clear the Entry Bar check box.

> **Note**
>
> **Previous versions of Microsoft Project included the Project Guide, which was a prominent screen element that could be turned on or off. As of Project 2010, the Project Guide is no longer available.**

Splitting a Window

You might be familiar with the Split function in Microsoft Excel or Microsoft Word, with which you can divide a single window into two panes and scroll each pane independently. In Project 2010, you might need to refer to different parts of the same Project 2010 view. Perhaps you want to show different parts of the same view in a split screen because you're modeling a new section of a project on an existing section farther up the view. Or maybe you want to see two different views at the same time.

The problem is that when you split a screen in Project 2010 (by dragging the split bar), a form appears in the lower portion of the split that gives you a combination view. You can switch to a different view, but the lower view is designed to show information relevant to the information selected in the upper view.

The solution is to open a second instance of the same window and then arrange them side by side in your Project 2010 window. To see your project plan in two independent panes at the same time, follow these steps:

1. Display the project plan you want to see in a split screen format.

New Window

2. On the View tab, in the Window group, click New Window.
3. In the New Window dialog box, click the name of your project plan, and then click OK.

   This opens a second instance of your project plan. The two instances are marked in the title bar with a ":1" and ":2" after the file name, indicating that these are separate windows for the same project file. Any changes you make in one window are simultaneously made in the other.

Arrange All

4. On the View tab, in the Window group, click Arrange All.

   Any open project plans are tiled in your project window. (See Figure 4-24.)

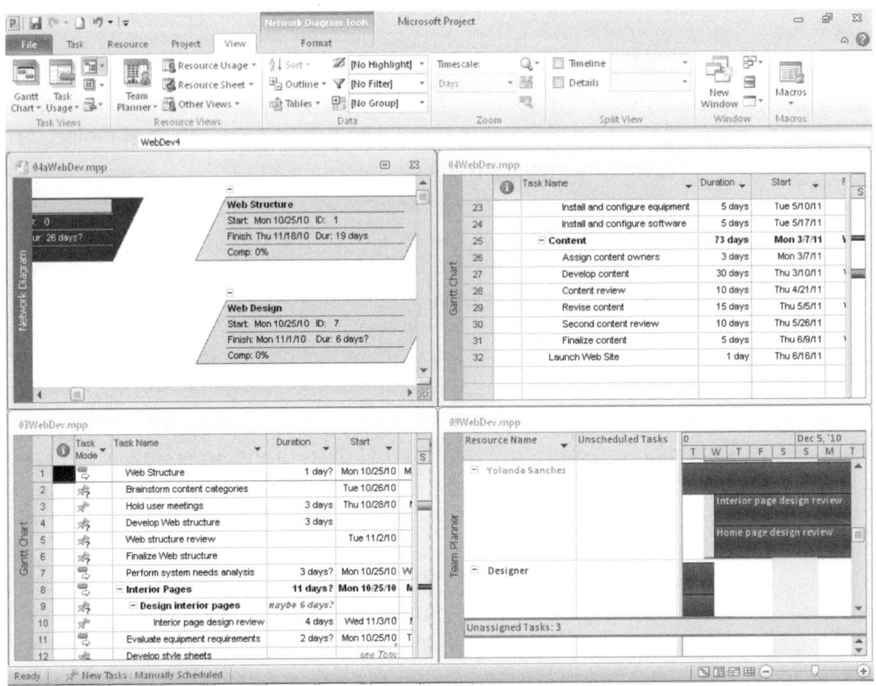

Figure 4-24 Clicking Arrange All makes all open projects visible.

Hide

5. If you have other project plans open besides the two you want to work with, close or hide them. To hide an open window, select it, and then on the View tab, in the Window group, click Hide, and then click Hide again.

6. When only the two instances of the project plan are displayed, click Window, Arrange All again. The two open projects are tiled horizontally: one above, and the other below, as shown in Figure 4-25. Now you can scroll the two windows independently of each other and also look at different views independently.

7. To return to a full-screen view of a single project file, close the file in one of the panes and maximize the file in the remaining pane.

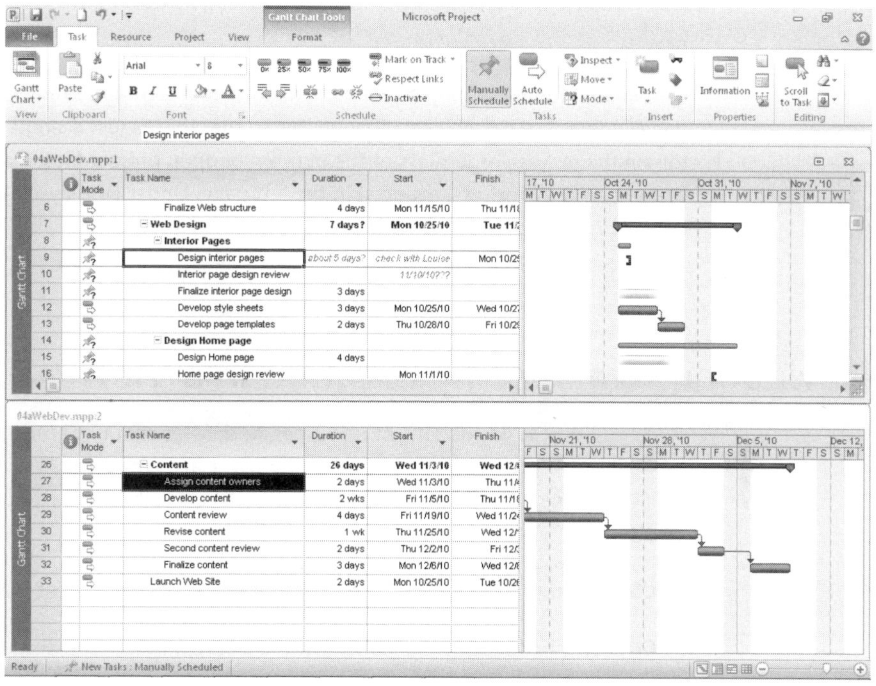

Figure 4-25 You can independently scroll or change views in the two tiled project windows.

Note

To give yourself more working space while viewing two project windows at one time, minimize the ribbon. Click the Minimize The Ribbon icon in the upper-right corner of the Project window. The tabs of the ribbon still show, so you still have access to commands. To restore the ribbon, click the Expand The Ribbon icon.

Switching Between Open Projects

If you have multiple projects open at the same time, there are several ways to switch between them. You can do the following:

- Click the project's button on the Windows taskbar
- Press Alt+Tab to cycle through all open programs and windows
- Press Ctrl+F6 to cycle through all open projects

> **Note**
>
> **By default, multiple open Project 2010 files are represented as individual buttons on the Windows taskbar. You can change this so that there's just a single Project 2010 button on the taskbar, regardless of the number of open project files. On the File tab, click Options, and then click Advanced in the left pane. Under Display, clear the Show Windows In Taskbar check box.**

Navigating to a Specific Location in a View

With a long list of tasks, dozens of resources, and dates spanning months or even years, the different views in your project plan probably cover a lot of space. When you're trying to get to a specific place in a view, you can always scroll vertically or horizontally. But there are shortcuts, as follows:

- **Ctrl+Home** Moves to the first cell in the first row in a sheet view.
- **Ctrl+End** Moves to the last cell in the last row in a sheet view.
- **Alt+Home** Moves to the beginning of the project timescale (Gantt Chart, Resource Graph, usage view).
- **Alt+End** Moves to the end of the project timescale (Gantt Chart, Resource Graph, usage view).
- **Alt+Left Arrow** Moves the timescale to the left.
- **Alt+Right Arrow** Moves the timescale to the right.

Scroll To Task

- **Scroll To Task button, or Ctrl+Shift+F5** Moves the timescale area of a view (Gantt chart or usage view) to the location of the task or assignment selected in the sheet area of the view. On the Task tab, in the Editing group, click Scroll To Task.
- **Go To command, F5** Goes to the Task ID or Resource ID entered in the ID box. Or, if used in a timescaled view (Gantt chart, Timeline, usage view, or Resource Graph), moves the chart area of the timescaled view to the location of the date entered in the Date box.

By default, the Go To command is available only by pressing F5. However, if you prefer, you can add it to the Quick Access Toolbar or to a custom group on the ribbon. To learn how, see Chapter 29, "Customizing the Project 2010 Interface."

Rearranging Your Project Information

The ability to switch from one view to another, to switch tables in a sheet view, and to add or remove fields in a view gives you tremendous versatility in how you see your project information. You can take it a step further by sorting, grouping, and filtering the information in a view.

Ordering Project Information with a Sort

By sorting information in a table, you can arrange it in alphabetical or numerical order by a particular field. For example, you might sort your tasks by start date so that you can see tasks that are due to start next week. Or you might sort your tasks by duration so that you can see the tasks with the longest durations and how you might break them up and bring in the project finish date.

You can also sort resources. For example, in the Resource Sheet, you might have originally entered all resources as they came on board, but now you want to see them in alphabetical order. You can easily sort by the resource name. Better yet, you can sort by department or group name and then by resource name.

To sort items in a sheet view, do the following:

1. Display the sheet view containing the information you want to sort.

   The sort operation applies only to the current view.

Sort

2. On the View tab, in the Data group, click Sort.
3. In the submenu that appears, commonly used sort fields are presented. For example, if you're working in the Gantt Chart, you can quickly sort by Start Date, Finish Date, Priority, Cost, or ID. If you're working in the Resource Sheet, you can quickly sort by Cost, Name, or ID.
4. If you want to sort by a different field than what's presented in the submenu, click Sort By. The Sort dialog box appears, as shown in Figure 4-26.
5. Under Sort By, click the name of the field you want to sort by, and then specify whether you want the sort to be ascending (lowest to highest) or descending (highest to lowest). If you want to sort within the sort, add another field in one or both of the Then By boxes.

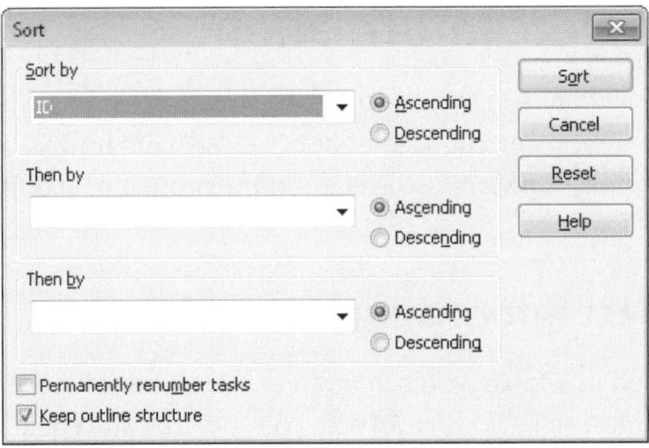

Figure 4-26 Use the Sort dialog box to choose the fields by which you want to order information.

6. Make sure that the Permanently Renumber check box is cleared. In the majority of cases, you will want this check box cleared. However, if you really want this sort to be permanent, and you're certain that you won't ever want to return to the original order of the tasks or resources, select this check box. This causes the ID numbers for the tasks or resources to be changed, and the tasks or resources are always sorted by order of their ID numbers when you don't have any other sort order applied.

7. Click Sort.

   The current sheet view is sorted according to your specifications.

If you sort tasks by duration, start date, or finish date, and if you have manually scheduled tasks that don't have that information filled in yet, those tasks will be sorted at the bottom.

INSIDE OUT Don't accidentally renumber tasks when sorting

If you select the Permanently Renumber Tasks or Permanently Renumber Resources check box for the current sort operation, the check box remains selected for your subsequent sort operations for this or any other project plans. This is true whether your next sort operation is for resources or tasks. This can be a problem if you want to do a temporary sort—which is likely to be the case most of the time—and you're not in the habit of looking at that check box.

To prevent unwittingly jumbling up your project plan, whenever you do a permanent renumber sort, immediately open the Sort dialog box again, clear the Permanently Renumber check box, and then click Reset.

To return a sorted sheet view to its original order, click View, Data, Sort, By ID.

> **Note**
>
> **If you choose to permanently renumber your tasks or resources according to a new sort order, remember that this renumbering affects the order of tasks and resources in all other task or resource views. This is not the case with temporary sorting operations.**

Grouping Project Information into Categories

Think of grouping as a more sophisticated kind of sorting, in which a graphical layout is applied to a sheet view to segregate the groupings you've chosen. For example, suppose that you group your task sheet by complete and incomplete tasks. Tasks that are 0 percent complete (not started yet) are grouped first and marked by a yellow band (see Figure 4-27). Tasks that are 1–99 percent complete (in progress) are grouped next, bounded by another yellow band. Tasks that are 100 percent complete are grouped last.

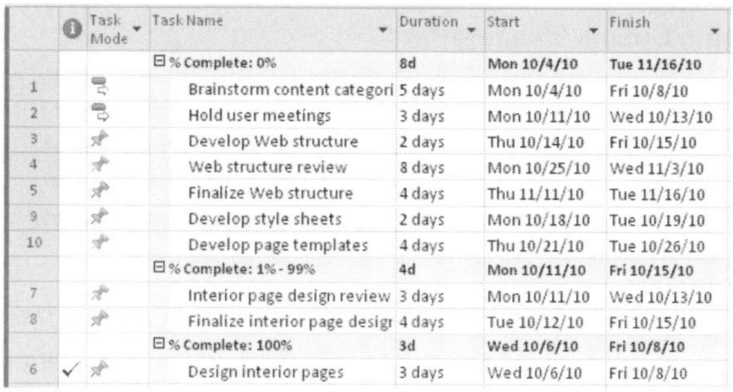

		Task Mode	Task Name	Duration	Start	Finish
			% Complete: 0%	**8d**	**Mon 10/4/10**	**Tue 11/16/10**
1			Brainstorm content categori	5 days	Mon 10/4/10	Fri 10/8/10
2			Hold user meetings	3 days	Mon 10/11/10	Wed 10/13/10
3			Develop Web structure	2 days	Thu 10/14/10	Fri 10/15/10
4			Web structure review	8 days	Mon 10/25/10	Wed 11/3/10
5			Finalize Web structure	4 days	Thu 11/11/10	Tue 11/16/10
9			Develop style sheets	2 days	Mon 10/18/10	Tue 10/19/10
10			Develop page templates	4 days	Thu 10/21/10	Tue 10/26/10
			% Complete: 1% - 99%	**4d**	**Mon 10/11/10**	**Fri 10/15/10**
7			Interior page design review	3 days	Mon 10/11/10	Wed 10/13/10
8			Finalize interior page desig	4 days	Tue 10/12/10	Fri 10/15/10
			% Complete: 100%	**3d**	**Wed 10/6/10**	**Fri 10/8/10**
6	✓		Design interior pages	3 days	Wed 10/6/10	Fri 10/8/10

Figure 4-27 Groups graphically separate categories of information in a view.

The grouping band shows the title of the group—for example, Percent Complete: 0%. Where appropriate, the grouping band also rolls up information summarized from the group, such as the total duration for the grouping, the earliest start date for all tasks in the grouping, the latest finish date for all tasks in the grouping, and so on.

NEW!

Built-in Task Groups

When a task view is showing, all built-in task groups appear on the View tab, in the Data group, in the Group By box. These built-in task groups are:

- Active V. Inactive
- Auto Scheduled V. Manually Scheduled
- Complete And Incomplete Tasks
- Constraint Type
- Critical
- Duration
- Duration Then Priority
- Milestones
- Priority
- Priority Keeping Outline Structure
- Resource
- Status

You can also group resources in a resource sheet. For example, you might want to group resources by their department or code or by resource type (work or material).

Built-in Resource Groups

When a resource view is showing, all built-in resource groups appear on the View tab, in the Data group, in the Group By box. The following is a complete list of these built-in resource groups:

- Assignments Keeping Outline Structure
- Complete And Incomplete Resources
- Resource Group
- Resource Type
- Standard Rate

You can also group nodes in the Network Diagram view, as shown in Figure 4-28.

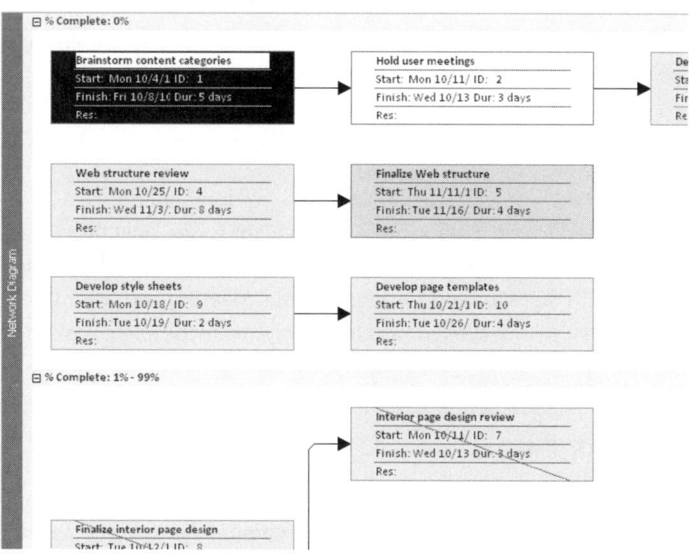

Figure 4-28 Nodes are collected and rearranged when you group them by a particular category.

To group task or resource information in a sheet view or the Network Diagram view, follow these steps:

1. Display the view in which you want to show the grouping.

   The group operation applies only to the current view.

Group By

2. On the View tab, in the Data group, click the arrow in the Group By box.
3. In the drop-down menu that appears, click the grouping you want.

   The view is grouped according to the category you selected.

If you group tasks by duration, start date, or finish date, and if you have manually scheduled tasks that don't have that information filled in yet, those tasks are grouped at the bottom under the No Value subcategory.

The groupings are not interactive; that is, if you change task information that makes the task belong in another group, it doesn't automatically move to that other group. You need to reapply the grouping.

To remove a grouping, on the View tab, in the Data group, click the arrow in the Group By box, and then click No Group.

You can customize built-in groups and create entirely new groups as well. You can group by fields, including custom outline codes that you create.

For more information about changing existing groups or creating your own, see "Customizing Groups" on page 1124.

Seeing Only What You Need by Filtering

When you filter a view, you exclude information you don't need to see so you can focus on what you do need to see. For example, if you want to see only tasks that use a particular resource so that you can more closely analyze the workload, you can apply the Using Resource filter. Or if you're about to attend a status meeting and want to discuss tasks that are either in progress or not started, you can apply the Incomplete Tasks filter to a task sheet.

Built-in Task Filters

When a task view is showing, the most commonly used task filters appear on the View tab, in the Data group, in the Filter box. These commonly used filters are:

- Active Tasks
- Completed Tasks
- Critical
- Date Range
- Incomplete Tasks
- Late Tasks
- Milestones
- Summary Tasks
- Task Range
- Tasks With Estimated Durations
- Using Resource

All built-in task filters are accessible in the More Filters dialog box.

You can also apply filters to a resource sheet. If you want to examine all resources that are running over budget, for example, you can apply the Cost Overbudget filter. Or if you want to see only your material resources, you can apply the Resources—Material filter to a resource sheet.

Built-in Resource Filters

When a resource sheet is showing, the most commonly used resource filters appear on the View tab, in the Data group, in the Filtered For box. The following is a complete list of the most commonly used resource filters:

- Budget Resources
- Cost Overbudget
- Group
- Non-Budget Resources
- Overallocated Resources
- Resource Range
- Resources—Cost
- Resources—Material
- Resources—Work
- Work Overbudget

All built-in resource filters are accessible in the More Filters dialog box.

To filter information in a view, follow these steps:

1. Display the view in which you want to show filtered information.

   You can filter information in all views. However, the filter operation applies only to the current view.

2. On the View tab, in the Data group, click the arrow in the Filter box.

   Filter

3. If the filter you want is listed in the drop-down menu, click it. If the filter is not in the submenu, click More Filters, and then find and click it in the More Filters dialog box. (See Figure 4-29.) Click Apply.

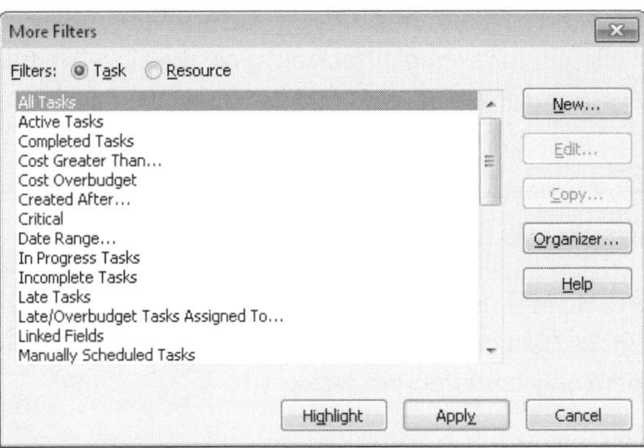

Figure 4-29 The More Filters dialog box lists all built-in filters.

4. If a filter requires additional information, enter that information in the dialog box that appears, and then click OK.

   For example, if you select the Date Range filter, you are prompted to enter dates for the tasks you want to see. If you're filtering a resource view by Group, you are prompted to enter the resource group name.

   The view is filtered according to your specifications.

Highlight

Note

A filter excludes tasks or resources that do not meet the conditions of that filter. If you prefer, you can instead have the filter highlight tasks or resources that do meet the filter conditions while leaving the other tasks or resources visible. On the View tab, in the Data group, click the arrow in the Highlight box, and then click the criteria for the highlighting.

To remove a filter and show all tasks or all resources again, on the View tab, in the Data group, click the arrow in the Filter box, and then click No Filter.

Using AutoFilter, you can quickly filter tasks or resources by a value in a particular field or column. In Project 2010, the AutoFilter arrows are already displayed for all columns in sheet views.

To filter information using AutoFilter, follow these steps:

1. Display the sheet view whose information you want to autofilter.

Display AutoFilter

2. If the AutoFilter arrows are not showing in the column headings, on the View tab, in the Data group, click the arrow in the Filter box, and then click Display AutoFilter.

   The AutoFilter arrows appear in each column heading in the sheet view.

Task Mode	Task Name	Duration	Start	Finish
	Brainstorm content categories	5 days	Mon 10/4/10	Fri 10/8/10
	Hold user meetings	3 days	Mon 10/11/10	Wed 10/13/10
	Develop Web structure	2 days	Thu 10/14/10	Fri 10/15/10
	Web structure review	8 days	Mon 10/25/10	Wed 11/3/10
	Finalize Web structure	4 days	Thu 11/11/10	Tue 11/16/10
	Design interior pages	3 days	Wed 10/6/10	Fri 10/8/10

3. Click the arrow in the column whose information you want to filter by, and then click the value you want to filter by.

   For example, suppose that you are displaying the Gantt Chart with the Entry table applied. If you want to filter for all tasks scheduled to start in April, click the AutoFilter arrow in the Start column, clear the Select All check box, and then select the April check box.

   When AutoFilter is applied, the AutoFilter icon appears in the column heading.

Task Name	Duration	Start	Finish
Brainstorm content categories	5 days	Mon 10/4/10	Fri 10/8/10
Hold user meetings	3 days	Mon 10/11/10	Wed 10/13/10
Develop Web structure	2 days	Thu 10/14/10	Fri 10/15/10
Web structure review	8 days	Mon 10/25/10	Wed 11/3/10

4. To show all tasks or resources again, click the AutoFilter icon in the column heading, and then select the Select All check box.

The AutoFilter arrows remain handy in the column headings for all views throughout your project plan unless you turn AutoFilter off. If you want to turn AutoFilter off, on the View tab, in the Data group, click the arrow in the Filter box, and then click Display AutoFilter.

TROUBLESHOOTING

Some of your project information is missing

It's easy to apply a filter, work with your project information for a while, and then forget that the filter is applied. Then, when you look for certain tasks or resources that you know are there, you can't see them.

Check whether a filter is applied. On the View menu, in the Data group, look at the Filter box. If it says No Filter, you know you're seeing all the information that's there. If, on the other hand, it says Critical, for example, you know you have a filter applied. In the Filter box, click No Filter to show all information again.

The Filter box might say No Filter if you have an AutoFilter applied. Review the column headings and find the one that shows the AutoFilter icon. Click the AutoFilter icon, and then select the Select All check box. Or, on the View menu, in the Data group, click the arrow in the Filter box, and then click No Filter. Clicking No Filter in the Filter box not only clears regular filters but also AutoFilters.

You can customize built-in filters and create entirely new filters as well. You can also create custom AutoFilters. For more information, see "Customizing Filters" on page 1129.

Learn More About Project Views, Tables, Groups, and Filters

In Project 2010 online Help, you can get more information about all available views, tables, filters, and groups. To do this, follow these steps:

1. In the upper-right corner of the Project window, click the Help icon.

   You can also press F1 or, on the File tab, click Help, and then click Microsoft Office Help.

   Project Help opens in a separate window.

2. Under Browse Project 2010 Support, click Viewing Your Project.
3. Click the subcategory and topic you want to read.

You can also learn more about customizing views, tables, groups, and filters in Chapter 28.

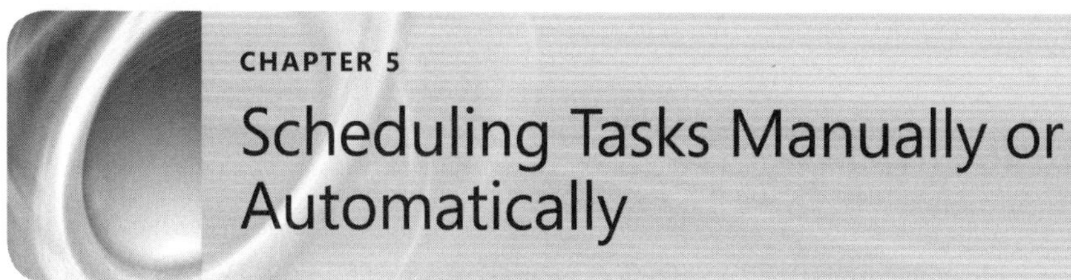

CHAPTER 5

Scheduling Tasks Manually or Automatically

Some project managers want or need more scheduling control over their projects. That is, they want to be able to manually enter durations, start dates, and finish dates without having those entries recalculate other aspects of the schedule.

Other project managers need a scheduling engine that automatically calculates dates as soon as they enter or change task information. When they enter a task duration, they want the tool to figure the task's finish date, and when they make a change, they don't want to have to manually compute all the ripple effects throughout the schedule.

New in Microsoft Project 2010 is the ability to choose whether a task is scheduled manually or automatically. By default, all new tasks are set for manual scheduling, although this default setting can easily be changed. Manually scheduled tasks can be switched to automatic scheduling, and vice versa. You can have a mixture of manually and automatically scheduled tasks within a project plan. Whether you schedule manually or automatically or use a mixture of both can depend largely on your project planning style, the development stage of the plan, and the complexity of your project.

Controlling the scheduling yourself or letting Project 2010 calculate the schedule for you gives you the flexibility you need as a project manager. But with this flexibility, more awareness and responsibility are needed. Like many other choices you make in Project 2010, your selection of manual or automatic scheduling for some or all of your tasks can significantly affect how you use other aspects of Project 2010. Such issues will be pointed out where relevant in this chapter and throughout the book.

Manually Scheduling Tasks

NEW!

With *manually scheduled tasks*—also known as *user-controlled scheduling*—when you type a task name, no duration, start date, or finish date is assumed or calculated for you by Project 2010. In fact, the Duration, Start, and Finish fields are blank. You are free to leave them blank until you have more information. You can enter a duration without dates. You can enter a start date without a finish date. You can even enter text in the Duration, Start, and Finish fields. (See Figure 5-1.)

	Task Mode	Task Name	Duration	Start	Finish
1		Brainstorm content categories		Tue 10/26/10	
2		Hold user meetings	3 days	Thu 10/28/10	Mon 11/1/10
3		Develop Web structure	3 days		
4		Web structure review		Tue 11/2/10	
5		Finalize Web structure			Fri 11/5/10
6		Design interior pages	maybe 6 days?		
7		Interior page design review	4 days	Wed 11/3/10	Mon 11/8/10
8		Develop style sheets		see Tony	
9		Develop page templates	2 days		
10		Design Home page			???
11		Home page design review			Mon 11/8/10

Figure 5-1 Enter as much or as little scheduling information as you like for a manually scheduled task.

Manually scheduled task icon

Manually scheduled tasks are marked with the pushpin icon in the Task Mode field of the Gantt Chart. If you enter two out of three bits of scheduling information—such as the duration and finish date or the start and finish date—the task is marked with a pushpin icon. If you enter no scheduling information, or maybe just one bit—such as just the duration or just the start date—the task is marked with a pushpin icon with a question mark.

More information needed icon

The chart area of the Gantt Chart also provides visual cues about the information entered for a manually scheduled task. (See Figure 5-2.)

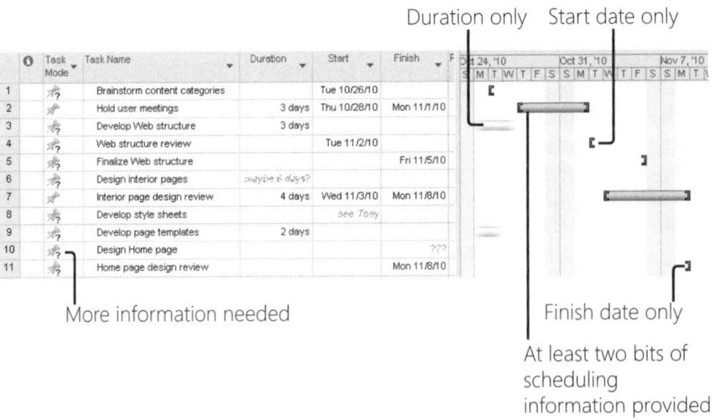

Figure 5-2 The Gantt Chart shows any manually scheduled information in the chart area.

Chapter 5

Even for manually scheduled tasks, Project 2010 does do a little calculation, but it's the calculation that Project assumes you want. As you can see, the three bits of scheduling information Project 2010 is looking for are duration, start date, and finish date. If you have any two of these three, Project 2010 extrapolates the third. That is, if you enter duration and start date, Project 2010 fills in the finish date. If you enter duration and finish date, the start date is provided for you. If you enter start and finish dates, Project 2010 fills in the duration.

INSIDE OUT **Project 2010 is like a spreadsheet on scheduling steroids**

If you've ever used Microsoft Excel to set up a project schedule, manual scheduling in Project 2010 will feel comfortable and familiar. Enter your tasks and as much or as little scheduling information as you want. You don't need to worry about calculations getting out of your control. As a bonus, Project 2010 draws Gantt bars and calculates a third bit of scheduling information from any two that you enter.

With manual scheduling, you get the control you had when you used Excel for certain tasks or projects. Project 2010 does only minor calculations and makes some "educated guesses" about your scheduling information without getting in your way. Then, if you decide you want Project 2010 to take over the headache of figuring dates and durations, you can simply convert the task to automatic scheduling. This way, you're getting the best of both worlds, and as much (or as little) flexibility, control, and scheduling power as you might want in a given situation.

You can even add new columns as though you were using Excel. In Project 2010, you can insert a column and label it whatever you want. You don't have to go through a lot of steps to create a custom field and then add the column, which was necessary in previous versions of Microsoft Project.

For more information about adding new columns to a table view in Project 2010, see "Using Fields" on page 160.

Automatically Scheduling Tasks

If you have used previous versions of Microsoft Project, you're already familiar with *automatically scheduled tasks*. When you type the name of a task that's identified for automatic scheduling, the default estimated duration of 1 day is entered, the default start date is the same as the project start date, and the finish date is calculated from the start date and duration. (See Figure 5-3.)

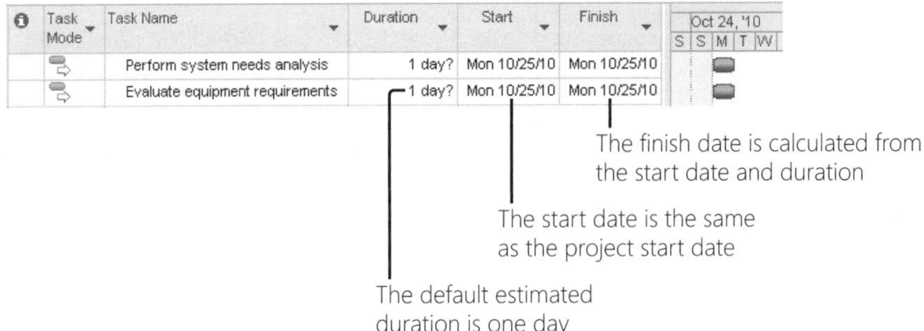

Figure 5-3 Default scheduling information is filled in for automatically scheduled tasks.

As you refine the durations, link tasks, and possibly enter date constraints or assign resources, Project 2010 calculates your schedule to reflect those controls.

Automatically scheduled task icon

Automatically scheduled tasks are marked with the Gantt bar icon in the Task Mode field of the Gantt Chart. You can also add this field to other sheet views when you need to distinguish between manually and automatically scheduled tasks.

The chart area of the Gantt Chart shows traditional Gantt bars in their default medium blue. This is in contrast with the various visual cues associated with a manually scheduled task, which might show a start date marker, a finish date marker, a duration, or some combination of the three in a variegated light blue (by default). (See Figure 5-4.)

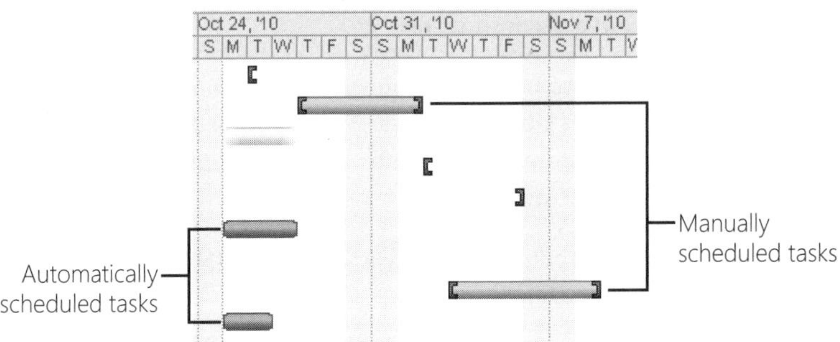

Figure 5-4 By default, the Gantt bars of automatically scheduled tasks are medium blue without start or end markers.

Mixing Manual and Automatic Tasks in a Project Plan

More likely than not, you have tasks with different scheduling requirements or that need differing levels of control or flexibility. To accommodate this in Project 2010, you can easily mix manually scheduled tasks and automatically scheduled tasks in the same project plan.

For example, suppose you're starting a new project. The five tasks in the first phase of the project are well defined and standard to many of your projects. From experience, you know how long each of the tasks should take. You also know that the first phase starts with the project start date and how the tasks are interrelated. You can enter the first phase tasks as automatically scheduled tasks.

On the other hand, six out of the eight tasks in the second phase of the project have few details or are too far in the future to be able to firm up those details. You want to update them yourself as information becomes available, without any repercussions from automatic calculation. You have durations for some and target finish dates for others. You'd rather not link any of the tasks or set date constraints on them. You retain the default for the six tasks as manually scheduled tasks, and you switch the other two to automatically scheduled tasks. (See Figure 5-5.)

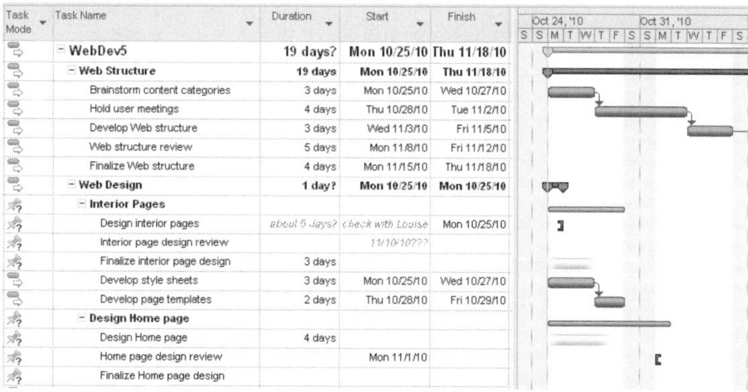

Task Mode	Task Name	Duration	Start	Finish
	WebDev5	19 days?	Mon 10/25/10	Thu 11/18/10
	Web Structure	19 days	Mon 10/25/10	Thu 11/18/10
	Brainstorm content categories	3 days	Mon 10/25/10	Wed 10/27/10
	Hold user meetings	4 days	Thu 10/28/10	Tue 11/2/10
	Develop Web structure	3 days	Wed 11/3/10	Fri 11/5/10
	Web structure review	5 days	Mon 11/8/10	Fri 11/12/10
	Finalize Web structure	4 days	Mon 11/15/10	Thu 11/18/10
	Web Design	1 day?	Mon 10/25/10	Mon 10/25/10
	Interior Pages			
	Design interior pages	about 5 days?	check with Louise	Mon 10/25/10
	Interior page design review		11/10/10???	
	Finalize interior page design	3 days		
	Develop style sheets	3 days	Mon 10/25/10	Wed 10/27/10
	Develop page templates	2 days	Thu 10/28/10	Fri 10/29/10
	Design Home page			
	Design Home page	4 days		
	Home page design review		Mon 11/1/10	
	Finalize Home page design			

Figure 5-5 Set your tasks to be manually or automatically scheduled as suits your purpose.

You might make such decisions throughout your project, allowing automatic scheduling for certain tasks and retaining manual scheduling for other tasks. Your criteria for choosing the task mode might have to do with how closely you want to control a task, how solid the task scheduling information is, or whether a task is still in the planning stages or has moved into the execution stage. Whatever criteria you choose, you have full flexibility over how you allow your tasks to be scheduled.

Switching Task Scheduling Modes

By default, any new tasks added in Project 2010 are manually scheduled. You can easily convert a task to automatic scheduling. To do this, follow these steps:

1. Select the manually scheduled task you want to convert to automatic scheduling.

   A manually scheduled task is marked with the pushpin icon in the Task Mode column.

Auto Schedule

2. On the Task tab, in the Tasks group, click Auto Schedule.

   The task is converted to an automatically scheduled task. Any start or finish dates already entered are discarded. However, any durations are retained and used as part of the automatic scheduling calculation.

When you open a project file that was created in Microsoft Project 2007 or earlier, all tasks come in as automatically scheduled tasks, even if your default for new tasks is set to manually scheduled tasks. This occurs because Project 2007 and earlier versions have no option for manually scheduled tasks; all tasks are automatically scheduled. But just as in any project plan, you can convert an automatically scheduled task to a manually scheduled task, and vice versa.

To convert an automatically scheduled task to manual scheduling, follow these steps:

1. Select the automatically scheduled task you want to convert to manual scheduling.

   An automatically scheduled task is marked with the Gantt bar icon in the Task Mode column.

Manually Schedule

2. On the Task tab, in the Tasks group, click Manually Schedule.

   The task is converted to a manually scheduled task. Any previously entered duration is retained, and any start or finish constraint dates are retained in the Start and Finish fields.

> **Note**
>
> **The ribbon highlights the current state of the selected task: Auto Schedule or Manually Schedule.**

If you're working in the Entry table of a task sheet (or any task table to which the Task Mode column has been added), you can also quickly switch a task between manual and automatic scheduling by clicking in the Task Mode field for the task. Click the arrow that appears, and then click Manually Scheduled or Auto Scheduled.

You can change multiple tasks to automatically or manually scheduled tasks at once. To select multiple adjacent tasks, click the first task, hold down the Shift key, and then click the last task. All tasks from the first to the last are selected. To select multiple nonadjacent tasks, click the first task, hold down the Ctrl key, and then click the other tasks. On the Task tab, in the Tasks group, click Manually Schedule or Auto Schedule.

If you're changing several attributes of one or more tasks, you can use the Task Information dialog box to also specify whether a task is manually or automatically scheduled. To do this, follow these steps:

1. Select the task(s) you want to change.

Information

2. On the Task tab, in the Properties group, click Information.

   The Task Information (or Multiple Task Information) dialog box appears, as shown in Figure 5-6.

   You can also simply double-click a single task to open the Task Information dialog box.

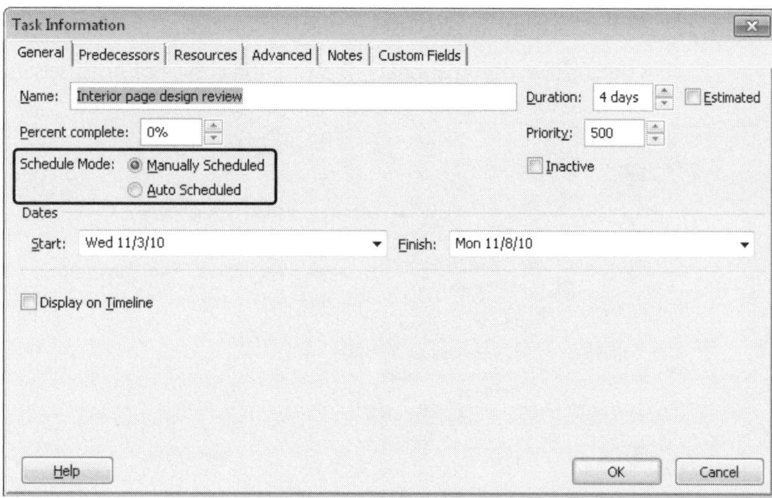

Figure 5-6 Use the Task Information dialog box to change various properties of a task.

3. On the General tab, next to Schedule Mode, select Manually Scheduled or Auto Scheduled. Make any other changes you want, and then click OK.

   If you're working with multiple tasks, not all fields are available for multiple update.

Changing Scheduling Defaults

Consider your scheduling style and your habits, and determine whether your default task mode should be manually scheduled or automatically scheduled tasks. If you're fairly new to Microsoft Project, or if you have previously used Microsoft Excel to manage your projects, you might want to retain the manually scheduled task default.

However, if you're an experienced Microsoft Project user, and if you like the way the scheduling engine automatically calculates and updates your schedule as you make changes, it would be most efficient for you to change the default task mode to automatic scheduling. You can change the default for new tasks added to an existing project plan, for new tasks in a newly created project plan, or for all new project plans.

Switching the Task Mode Default for New Tasks in a Plan

Suppose you've been working on a project plan, and you find that you keep changing the task mode from manual to automatic (or automatic to manual) scheduling. You can change the default for new tasks to your preferred task mode. To do this, follow these steps:

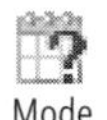

Mode

1. On the Task tab, in the Tasks group, click Mode.

   A drop-down menu appears, showing the choice of Auto Schedule or Manually Schedule for new tasks. The current default is highlighted.

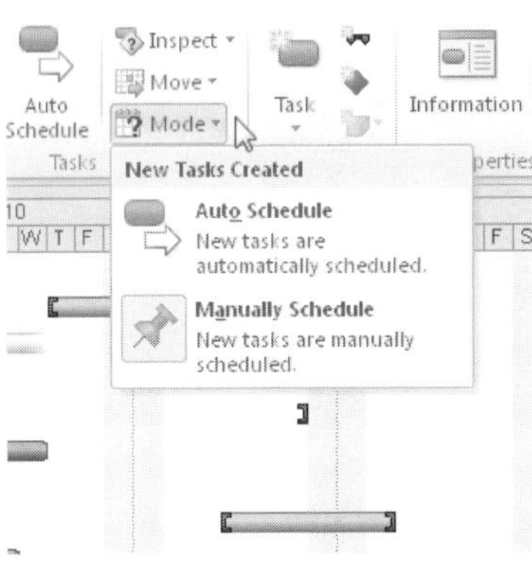

2. Click the task mode you want new tasks to adopt.

   The button in the lower-left corner of the Project 2010 status bar shows the new default mode for this project plan.

   All new tasks are created in the task mode you select.

> **Note**
>
> **Remember, even after changing the task mode default, you can always switch a task to the other task mode as needed. On the Task tab, in the Tasks group, click Manually Schedule or Auto Schedule.**

Switching the Task Mode Default for a New Project Plan

When you begin a new project plan, it's a good time to decide whether your predominant task mode will be manual or automatic scheduling. To change the default task mode when you create a new project, follow these steps:

1. On the File tab, click New.
2. In the Available Templates window that appears, double-click Blank Project.

   The new blank project appears, along with a pop-up notification near the status bar at the lower left of the screen. The notification indicates the default task mode; for example, "New tasks are created in Manually Scheduled mode."

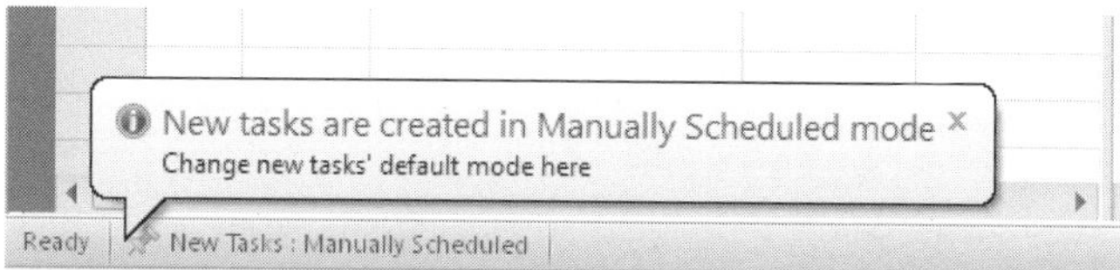

3. If you want to keep the task mode shown in the notification, you don't need to do anything. (The notification disappears after a few seconds.)

   If you want the other task mode, click the button on the status bar labeled New Tasks: Manually Scheduled or New Tasks: Auto Scheduled. In the menu that appears, click the task mode you want to use for new tasks in your new project.

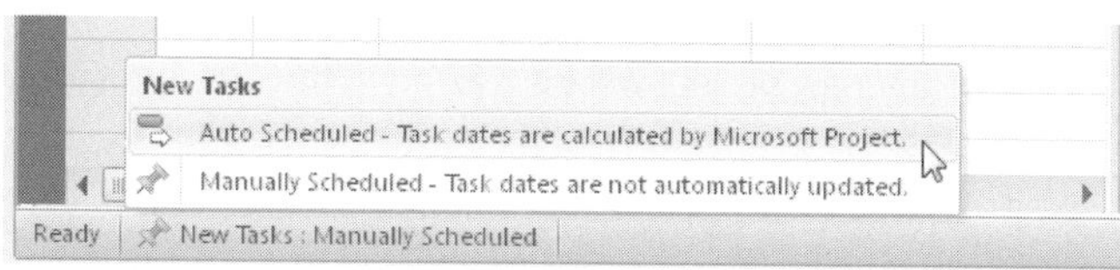

> **Note**
>
> **Click the New Tasks button on the status bar anytime you want to change the default task mode for new tasks being added to the project.**

Switching the Task Mode Default for All New Project Plans

You can change the task mode default for all new project plans. To do this, follow these steps:

1. On the File tab, click Options, and then click Schedule in the left pane.
2. In the box next to the section title labeled Scheduling Options For This Project, click All New Projects.
3. In the New Tasks Created box, choose how you want new tasks to be scheduled: Manually Scheduled or Auto Scheduled. (See Figure 5-7.)

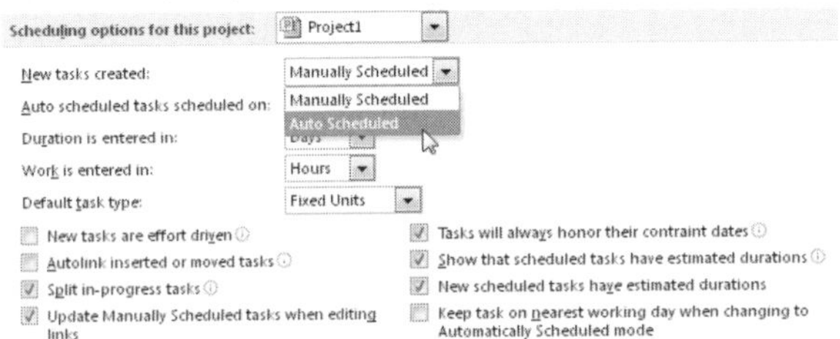

Figure 5-7 Change the project plan's scheduling options if you want to switch the task mode default for all new project plans.

4. Click OK.
5. Be sure to click Save on the File tab to save the settings you just changed for all new projects.

   All tasks in any new project will be created in the selected task mode.

TROUBLESHOOTING

You changed the default task mode for new projects, but Project is still using the old task mode

When you change options that apply to all projects, those new options don't take effect until you save the project file in which you changed the options.

Open the Options dialog box again, and change the options for all new projects. After clicking OK to close the Options dialog box, click Save on the File tab.

Now when you create a project, it should include the new options you set.

Whether a task is scheduled manually or automatically affects various aspects of scheduling; for example, setting durations, linking task dependencies, identifying start and finish dates, setting baselines, tracking progress, and more. The relevant chapters that cover these topics discuss the differences and how they can affect your task scheduling and overall project plan.

CHAPTER 6

Building Your Schedule

YOU'VE developed your work breakdown structure, and your task list is now sequenced and outlined. You have a good work breakdown structure now, but you don't have a schedule...yet.

There are many knowledge areas (including scope management, cost management, and resource management) that contribute to successful project management. However, the time management knowledge area is most relevant to the development of your project schedule—your roadmap for completing tasks, handing off deliverables, marking milestones, and achieving the goals of your project in a timely manner.

To develop an accurate and workable schedule that truly reflects how your project will run, you need to do the following:

- Enter task durations.
- Identify the relationships, or dependencies, among tasks.
- Schedule certain tasks to achieve specific dates when necessary.

When you've done these three things, you begin to see the basic outline of a real project schedule. You have not yet added and assigned resources, which further influence the schedule. Nor have you refined the project plan to make the project finish date and costs conform to your requirements. However, at this point, you can start to see how long certain tasks will take and how far into the future the project might run.

To learn about adding and assigning resources, see Chapter 8, "Assigning Resources to Tasks." For information about refining your project, see Chapter 10, "Checking and Adjusting the Project Plan."

New in Microsoft Project 2010 is the ability to turn off automatic scheduling and completely control the durations, start dates, and finish dates yourself, somewhat as if you were entering schedule information in a spreadsheet. With manual scheduling, you can build your schedule using the information you have, completely at your control. The automatic calculation done by Project 2010 is suspended for manually scheduled tasks. You can easily switch between manual and automatic scheduling for some or all tasks within a project plan.

For more information about working with automatically and manually scheduled tasks, see Chapter 5, "Scheduling Tasks Automatically or Manually."

Whether you use manual or automatic scheduling controls in your plan, you can use a variety of scheduling tools and cues to help keep you focused and on track as you and your team work your way through the project. You can do the following:

- Create reminders to alert you as deadlines are approaching.
- Add milestones to your schedule as conspicuous markers of producing a deliverable, completing a phase, or achieving another major event in your project.
- Apply a calendar to a task that is independent of the project calendar or the calendars of resources assigned to the task so that the task can be scheduled independently.
- See the effects of scheduling changes while you work, and review the factors that affect the scheduling of a task.

Setting Task Durations

When your task list is entered, sequenced, and outlined in Project 2010 (see Figure 6-1), you're ready to start the work of creating a schedule.

To create a realistic schedule, you can start by entering the length of time you believe each task will take to complete; that is, the task *duration*.

When you create an automatically scheduled task, Project 2010 assigns it an estimated duration of 1 day. You can easily change that duration. At this beginning point, this estimated duration is shown with a start date the same as the project start date and a finish date one day later.

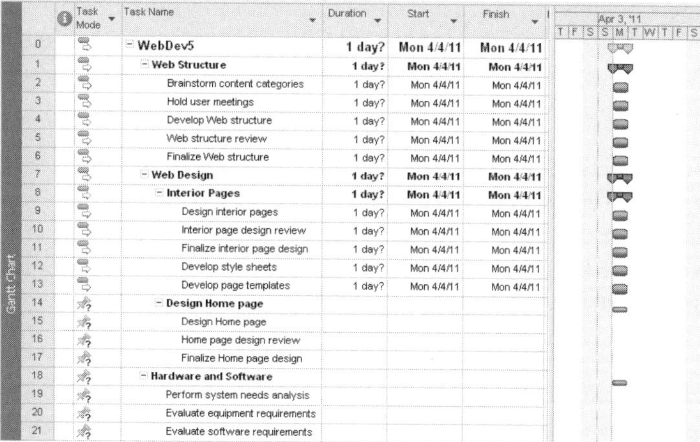

Figure 6-1 Your project schedule shows any automatically scheduled tasks starting on the project start date, each with an estimated duration of 1 day.

Entering accurate duration estimates is very important for creating a reliable project schedule. For automatically scheduled tasks, Project 2010 uses the duration to calculate the start and finish dates for the task. If you assign resources, the duration is also the basis for the amount of work for each assigned resource.

When you create a manually scheduled task, Project 2010 makes no assumptions and keeps the Duration, Start, and Finish fields clear. If you enter a value in the Duration field, a bar is drawn in the chart area of the Gantt Chart.

Developing Reliable Task Duration Estimates

As the project manager, you can start building the schedule by entering a broad duration estimate based on your own experience. Then, you can refine the estimate by soliciting input from others who are more directly involved or experienced with the sets of tasks. The following are some good sources for developing reliable task durations:

- **Team knowledge** Suppose that you're managing a new business startup project, and you already have your team in place. The business advisor can provide durations for tasks such as creating a market analysis, researching the competition, and identifying the target market niche. The accountant can provide durations for tasks such as forecasting financial returns, setting up the accounting system, and obtaining needed insurance. Team members ready to work on the project can also provide duration estimates for tasks based on their previous experience as well as their projection of how long they expect the tasks to take for this particular project.

- **Expert judgment** If you have not yet assembled a team from whom you can obtain durations, or if you want reliable input from impartial specialists in the field, you might call upon experts such as consultants, professional associations, or industry groups. These can help you establish task durations for projects common to your field.
- **Past projects** Similar projects that have been completed in your organization can be an excellent source of accurate durations. If archived Microsoft Project files are available, you can see the initial durations. If the project manager maintained the project plan by tracking actual information throughout the life of the project, you have at your disposal invaluable data about how long certain tasks actually took, as well as any variances from their planned durations.
- **Industry standards** Historical duration information for tasks typical to an industry or discipline is sometimes available commercially through professional or standards organizations. You can adapt such information for tasks and durations to fit the unique requirements of your project.

You might use a combination of these methods to obtain durations for all the tasks in your project. It's often very useful to have durations based on established metrics. For example, suppose that you know the industry standard for the number of hours it takes to develop certain types of architectural drawings as well as the number of those drawings you need. You can multiply these figures to develop a reasonable duration for your specific task.

Note

You can also use these methods to obtain work amounts for resources assigned to tasks. While duration is the span of time from task start to finish, work is the amount of time a resource has to complete the task. Sometimes duration and work are the same; many times they are not, depending on the type of task and the number and type of resources assigned.

TROUBLESHOOTING

You can't find the PERT analysis views

Previous versions of Microsoft Project included functions for PERT (Program Evaluation and Review Technique) analysis. PERT analysis was an add-in to help statistically estimate task durations, but it is no longer available with Project 2010.

Project Management Practices: Building in a Buffer

Building in a duration *buffer* is a method that many project managers use as a contingency against project risk. Some say that the durations should be as "real" and accurate as possible, already taking into account any possible risk. Others say it just isn't realistic to believe that you can account for all possible problems while you're still in the project planning processes. To build in a buffer, also known as *reserve time,* you can add a "buffer task" close to the end of the project, with a duration that represents either a percentage of the total project duration or a fixed work period (for example, two weeks).

The reserve time can later be reduced or eliminated as more precise information about the project becomes available. For example, suppose you initially enter a duration of 5 days to set up the accounting system. Later on, more concrete information indicates that it will actually take 8 days. You can "transfer" that time from your buffer without pushing out your project finish date.

Understanding Estimated vs. Confirmed Durations

For automatically scheduled tasks, any value in the Duration field that's followed by a question mark is considered an *estimated duration*. Technically, all planned durations are only estimates because you don't know how long a task takes until it's completed and you enter an *actual duration*. However, the question mark indicates what you might consider an "estimate of a duration estimate." Estimated durations are calculated into the schedule the same as confirmed durations; they simply serve as an alert that a duration is still more of a guess.

Note

If you have no use for the estimated durations question mark, you can turn it off. On the File tab, click Options, and then click Schedule in the left pane. Under Scheduling Options For This Project, clear the check boxes labeled Show That Tasks Have Estimated Durations and New Scheduled Tasks Have Estimated Durations.

Typically, these settings take effect for the current project. If you want them to be in effect for all projects you create, in the box next to the Scheduling Options For This Project section heading, click All New Projects.

For automatically scheduled tasks, a duration estimate of 1 day is entered by default for any new task (**1d?**). Use this value as a flag to indicate that the duration still needs to be entered for this task. For either automatically or manually scheduled tasks, you can also enter a question mark (?) after a duration, for example, **2w?**. Any durations with question marks can serve as flags to indicate that the duration is still under consideration and might change after you receive more solid information. When you remove the question mark from a duration, the duration is confirmed; that is, you're now confident of this duration.

Note

You can sort, group, or filter tasks by whether a task has an estimated or confirmed duration. For more information, see "Rearranging Your Project Information" on page 173.

Entering Durations

You can enter duration in different units of time, as follows:

- Minutes (**m** or **min**)
- Hours (**h** or **hr**)
- Days (**d** or **dy**)
- Weeks (**w** or **wk**)
- Months (**mo** or **mon**)

Whether you type **h**, **hr**, or **hour** in your duration entry, by default Project 2010 enters "hr". You can change which abbreviation of the time unit appears in the Duration field. On the File tab, click Options, and then click Advanced in the left pane. In the duration fields under Display Options For This Project, set the abbreviation you want to display for the time unit.

Note

By default, this setting applies to the current project file only. If you want it to apply to all new projects you create, in the box next to the Display Options For This Project heading, click All New Projects.

You can use different duration units throughout your plan. One task might be set with a duration of 2w, and another task might be set for 3d.

> **Note**
>
> **If you enter a duration value in an automatically scheduled task but don't specify a duration unit, by default Project 2010 assumes that the unit is days and automatically enters "days" after your duration value. If you want the default duration unit to be something different, such as hours or weeks, you can change it. On the File tab, click Options, and then click Schedule in the left pane. Under Scheduling Options For This Project, in the box labeled Duration Is Entered In, select the time unit you want as the default.**
>
> **By default, this setting applies only to the current project file. If you want to apply it to all new projects you create, in the box next to the Scheduling Options For This Project heading, click All New Projects.**

To enter a duration, follow these steps:

1. Display the Gantt Chart.
2. In the Duration field for each task, type the duration—for example, **1w** or **4d**.
3. If a duration is an estimate, add a question mark after it—for example, **1w?** or **4d?**.

   If you enter any value other than a value and accepted time period abbreviation in the Duration field of an automatically scheduled task, you get an Invalid Duration error message. However, you can enter any value or text in the Duration field of a manually scheduled task. Project 2010 interprets such entries as a note rather than a duration.
4. Press Enter. The Gantt bar is drawn to represent the time period for the task. (See Figure 6-2.)

   For automatically scheduled tasks, the Finish field is recalculated for the task. Project 2010 adds the duration amount to the Start date to calculate the Finish date.

   For manually scheduled tasks, the duration amount is drawn in the chart area of the Gantt Chart. If a start or finish date is entered, the duration amount is drawn from that date; otherwise the duration is drawn from the project start date by default.

   > **Note**
   >
   > **In a Gantt chart, you can also drag the right edge of a Gantt bar to change the task duration.**

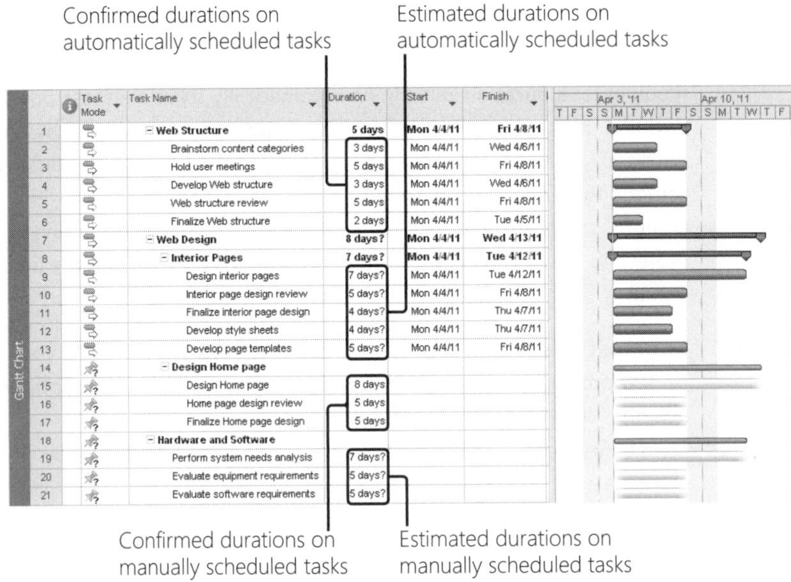

Figure 6-2 Confirmed as well as estimated durations are drawn with the Gantt bars. The color of the Gantt bars are different for automatically scheduled tasks and manually scheduled tasks.

Task Information

> **Note**
>
> **You can change the estimated durations of multiple tasks to confirmed durations. Select all the tasks containing estimated durations. On the Task tab, in the Properties group, click Information. On any tab in the Task Information dialog box, clear the Estimated check box.**

Understanding How Durations Affect Scheduling

When you enter a duration, the task is scheduled according to its assigned calendar. Initially, this is the project calendar. When resources are assigned, the task is scheduled according to the resource's working times calendar. If a task calendar is applied, the task is scheduled according to the task's working times calendar.

For more information about task calendars, see "Working with Task Calendars" on page 234.

For example, suppose that you enter a 2-day duration for the automatically scheduled "Create market analysis plan" task, and the task starts Monday at 8:00 A.M. Based on the default Standard calendar and its options, and assuming that the resource is assigned full-time to the task, Project 2010 counts the 16 working hours in the 2-day duration to arrive at a finish date of Tuesday at 5:00 P.M.

Where Do Start and Finish Dates Come From?

Until you set task dependencies by linking predecessors and successors or explicitly enter start or finish dates, the start date of all your tasks is by default the same as the project start date.

You can make any new tasks adopt the current date (today) as the start date. On the File tab, click Options, and then click Schedule in the left pane. In the Schedule Options For This Project box, specify whether this change should apply only to this project or to all new projects. In the box labeled Auto Scheduled Tasks Scheduled On, click Current Date.

In a project being scheduled from the finish date, start and finish dates are calculated the opposite way as those in a project being scheduled from the start date. In a project scheduled from the finish date, the finish date of all tasks starts out the same as the project finish date. As you enter task durations, Project 2010 subtracts the duration amount from the task finish date to calculate the task start date.

If you want a task to take a set amount of time regardless of any working times calendars, you can enter an *elapsed duration.* An elapsed duration can be useful for tasks such as "Paint drying" or "Cement curing" that can't be stopped after they've started or that are independent of project schedules or resource assignments. Elapsed durations are scheduled 24 hours a day, 7 days a week, until finished. That is, one day is always considered 24 hours long (rather than 8 hours), and one week is always 7 days (rather than 5 days). To specify an elapsed duration, simply enter an **e** before the duration unit—for example, **3ed** for 3 elapsed days or **2ew** for 2 elapsed weeks. (See Figure 6-3.)

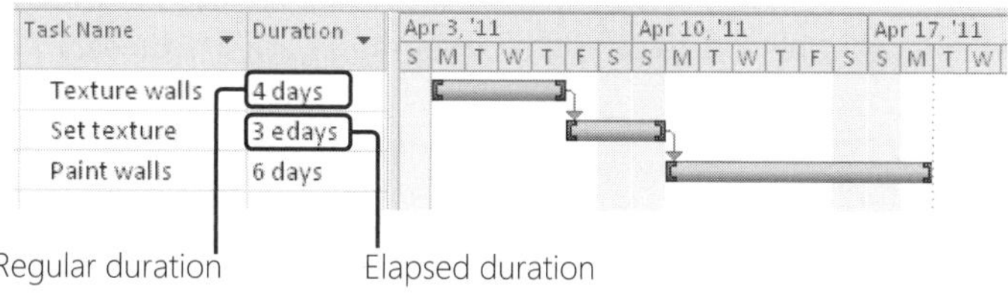

Figure 6-3 Regular durations are scheduled according to applied working times calendars, whereas elapsed durations are based on 24 hours per day, 7 days per week. Notice that weekend days are counted as two of the three elapsed duration days for the "Set texture" task. However, weekend days are not counted as part of the duration for the "Paint walls" task, which has a regular duration.

For regular (nonelapsed) durations, you need a way to specify the number of working hours in a day and week, the number of working days in a month, and so on. This way, when you specify 2 weeks as a duration, for example, you can be assured that this means the same thing as 80 hours or 10 days. To set these options, follow these steps:

1. On the File tab, click Options, and then click Schedule in the left pane. (See Figure 6-4.)

   Change Working Time

   An alternative method is to click Project, Properties, Change Working Time, and then click the Options button.

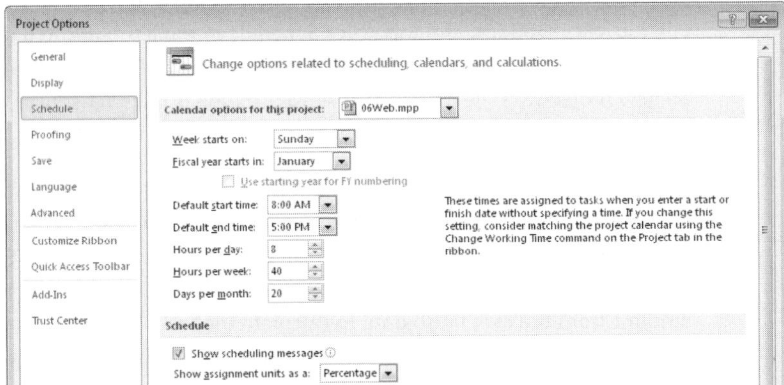

Figure 6-4 Set the calendar options to specify the details regarding the hours, days, and weeks that your team works.

2. Under Calendar Options For This Project, specify your preferences for working time units to reflect how your team works.

   The Default Start Time (8:00 A.M.) and Default End Time (5:00 P.M.) are assigned to tasks when you enter a start or finish date without specifying a time.

   The Hours Per Day, Hours Per Week, and Days Per Month values serve as your time unit specifications when needed. If you specify that a task has a duration of 1 month, does that mean 20 days or 30 days? These settings are used in conjunction with the working times calendars to dictate how your tasks are scheduled.

TROUBLESHOOTING

You set the calendar for 20 hours per week, but the tasks are still being scheduled for 40 hours per week

Or you thought you set the calendar for 8:00 A.M. to 12:00 P.M., for the project to be scheduled only in the mornings, but the tasks are still being scheduled 8:00 A.M. to 5:00 P.M.

Sometimes, the calendar options are more confusing than helpful. The Hours Per Day, Hours Per Week, and Days Per Month settings can easily be misinterpreted to make you think you're using them to set the schedule for the project. What you're actually doing is setting start and end times and specifying how duration entries are converted to assignment work.

Suppose that you want to specify that work on this project should be scheduled only in the mornings, from 8:00 A.M. until 12:00 P.M. To affect actual task scheduling in this way, you'd need to edit the working times for each day in the Change Working Time calendar. The Default Start Time field specifies the time that Project 2010 should enter if you enter a start date without a corresponding start time. The Default End Time field specifies the time that Project 2010 should enter if you enter a finish date without a corresponding finish time. Most project managers don't go to the level of detail in their project plans to enter the time of day that a task is to start or finish, so in this way, Project 2010 fills those times in as needed.

Also, suppose that you want to specify that work on this project should be scheduled only 20 hours per week because your team is working on another project at the same time. If you enter 20 in the Hours Per Week box and then enter a duration of 2 weeks, work on this project is scheduled for 40 hours—according to the project calendar. That means if the project's working times calendar is still set for Monday through Friday, 8:00 A.M. through 5:00 P.M., the 2 weeks is scheduled as two sets of 20 hours back to back, resulting in "2 weeks" taking place in 1 actual week in your schedule—probably not what you intended. The solution is to make the corresponding change in the working times calendar. Set the working and nonworking times in the Change Working Time calendar so that there are 20 hours of working time per week. Then, when you enter 2 weeks as a duration, the first 20 hours are scheduled in the first week, and the second 20 hours are scheduled in the second week.

The calendar options settings also determine how durations are translated into work time units when you assign resources to tasks. Think of these as "time unit conversion" settings, and it will probably become more clear.

Reviewing Durations

Any Gantt chart view can give you a closer look at your task durations graphically across the timescale. The Calendar, as shown in Figure 6-5, also displays each task as a bar on the days and weeks in which it's scheduled.

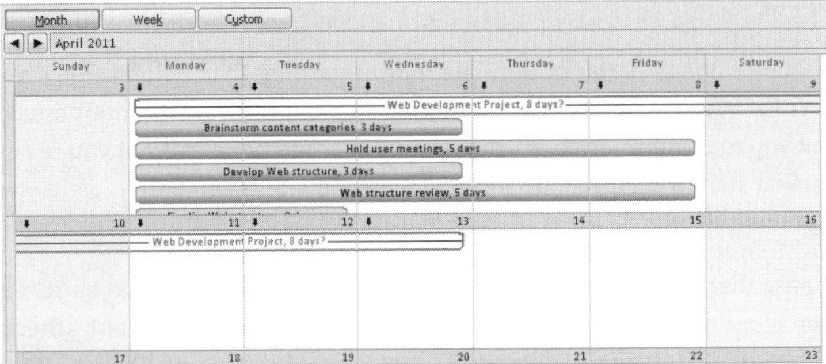

Figure 6-5 In addition to any Gantt chart, you can use the Calendar to see your task durations graphically laid out over time.

Establishing Task Dependencies

At this point, your tasks all have what you hope are realistic durations. What is not realistic is that the tasks might look like they're all starting on the project start date. (See Figure 6-6.)

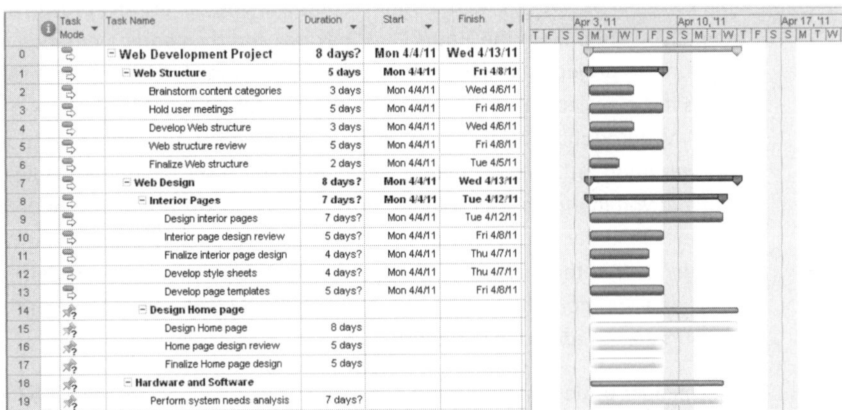

	Task Mode	Task Name	Duration	Start	Finish
0		Web Development Project	8 days?	Mon 4/4/11	Wed 4/13/11
1		Web Structure	5 days	Mon 4/4/11	Fri 4/8/11
2		Brainstorm content categories	3 days	Mon 4/4/11	Wed 4/6/11
3		Hold user meetings	5 days	Mon 4/4/11	Fri 4/8/11
4		Develop Web structure	3 days	Mon 4/4/11	Wed 4/6/11
5		Web structure review	5 days	Mon 4/4/11	Fri 4/8/11
6		Finalize Web structure	2 days	Mon 4/4/11	Tue 4/5/11
7		Web Design	8 days?	Mon 4/4/11	Wed 4/13/11
8		Interior Pages	7 days?	Mon 4/4/11	Tue 4/12/11
9		Design interior pages	7 days?	Mon 4/4/11	Tue 4/12/11
10		Interior page design review	5 days?	Mon 4/4/11	Fri 4/8/11
11		Finalize interior page design	4 days?	Mon 4/4/11	Thu 4/7/11
12		Develop style sheets	4 days?	Mon 4/4/11	Thu 4/7/11
13		Develop page templates	5 days?	Mon 4/4/11	Fri 4/8/11
14		Design Home page			
15		Design Home page	8 days		
16		Home page design review	5 days		
17		Finalize Home page design	5 days		
18		Hardware and Software			
19		Perform system needs analysis	7 days?		

Figure 6-6 Until you enter task dependencies, start dates, or finish dates, all tasks appear to start on the project start date.

Although many tasks in a project are likely to begin on the project start date, most other tasks cannot begin until another task has finished. Sometimes, several tasks are dependent upon the completion of one task; sometimes, several tasks must finish before a single later task can begin.

So, the next step in creating your schedule is to link tasks that are dependent on each other. You can link the previous, or *predecessor* task, to its succeeding, or *successor* task, and thereby set up the *task dependency* between the two.

Note

A task dependency is also referred to as a *task relationship* or a *link*.

When your task dependencies are combined with your durations, your project plan starts to look like a real schedule. You can begin to see possible start dates and finish dates not only for the individual tasks, but also for major phases, milestones, and the project as a whole. When you create a link between two tasks, Project 2010 calculates the successor's start and finish dates based on the predecessor's start or finish date, the dependency type, the successor's duration, and any associated resource assignments. There's still more information and refinement to be done, but you're getting closer to a schedule that starts to reflect reality.

Project Management Practices: Real vs. Preferred Task Dependencies

When building your project schedule, bear in mind whether the task dependencies you create are really required or whether they simply reflect a preference on your part.

For example, in a construction project, a task such as "Install siding" *must* be the predecessor to "Paint house." This is a true task dependency.

On the other hand, you might make a task such as "Finish interior" a predecessor to "Install landscaping." They don't need to be linked to each other but might only reflect a preference you or your team has for a variety of reasons.

Be careful of these kinds of preferred but unnecessary dependencies, because they can cause unnecessary problems later when you're trying to fine-tune the project plan or respond to problems that arise in the midst of tracking the project. At that point, you want as much scheduling flexibility in the project as possible. Any artificial task dependencies reduce that flexibility.

Creating the Finish-to-Start Task Dependency

The most typical link is the finish-to-start task dependency. With this link, the predecessor task must finish before the successor task can begin. To link tasks with the finish-to-start task dependency, follow these steps:

1. Display the Gantt Chart.

   You can set task dependencies in any task sheet, but you can see the effects of the links immediately in the Gantt Chart.

2. In the task sheet, select the two tasks you want to link. Drag from the predecessor to the successor task if they are right next to each other. If they are not adjacent tasks, click the predecessor, hold down the Ctrl key, and then click the successor.

Link Tasks

3. On the Task tab, in the Schedule group, click Link Tasks.

   The tasks are linked in the chart area of the Gantt Chart as shown in Figure 6-7. In addition, the Predecessor field of the successor task lists the task number for its predecessor.

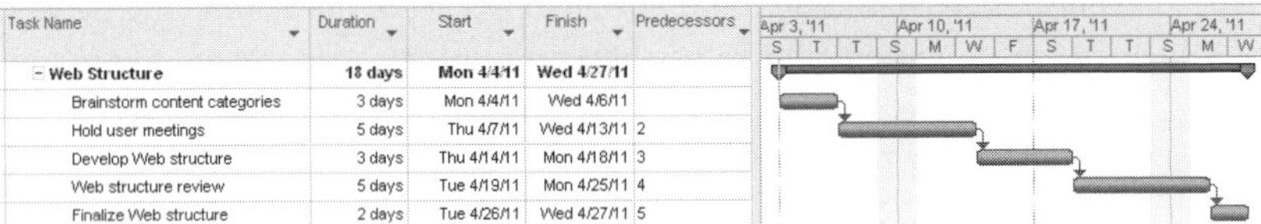

Task Name	Duration	Start	Finish	Predecessors
Web Structure	**18 days**	**Mon 4/4/11**	**Wed 4/27/11**	
Brainstorm content categories	3 days	Mon 4/4/11	Wed 4/6/11	
Hold user meetings	5 days	Thu 4/7/11	Wed 4/13/11	2
Develop Web structure	3 days	Thu 4/14/11	Mon 4/18/11	3
Web structure review	5 days	Tue 4/19/11	Mon 4/25/11	4
Finalize Web structure	2 days	Tue 4/26/11	Wed 4/27/11	5

Figure 6-7 See how tasks are linked in the chart area of a Gantt chart.

Tips and Techniques for Linking Tasks

- **You can link multiple tasks at one time, as long as they all have the same type of task dependency. Select all the tasks that are to be linked, either by dragging across adjacent tasks or by clicking nonadjacent tasks while holding down the Ctrl key. On the Task tab, in the Schedule group, click Link Tasks.**

- **You can have multiple links to and from a single task. One task might be the predecessor for several other tasks. Likewise, one task might be the successor for several tasks. There's no difference in how you set the links. Select the two tasks, and then click Task, Schedule, Link Tasks. Or, select the successor, and then set the predecessor and link type on the Predecessors tab in the Task Information dialog box.**

- **In the chart area of a Gantt chart, drag from the middle of the predecessor Gantt bar to the middle of the successor Gantt bar. Before you drag, be sure that you see a crosshair mouse pointer. As you drag to the successor, the mouse pointer changes to the link icon. This method creates a finish-to-start task dependency between them.**

Linking Manually Scheduled Tasks

Linking manually scheduled tasks with a finish-to-start relationship produces similar results as linking automatically scheduled tasks. Even when you link manually scheduled tasks that have little or no information, Project 2010 extrapolates and fills in new schedule information, as follows:

- **Linking tasks with no schedule information** After the tasks are linked, the previously empty Duration field changes to an estimated duration of 1d?. The previously empty Start field changes to the project start date (by default), and the previously empty Finish field changes to 1d after the start date.
- **Linking tasks with only duration entered** After the tasks are linked, the previously empty Start field changes to the project start date (by default), and the previously empty Finish field changes to the start date plus the entered duration value.
- **Linking tasks with only a start date entered** After the tasks are linked, the previously empty Duration field changes to an estimated duration of 1d?. The previously empty Finish field changes to 1d after the entered start date.
- **Linking tasks with only a finish date entered** After the tasks are linked, the previously empty Duration field changes to an estimated duration of 1d?. The previously empty Start field changes to the finish date minus 1d.

When you link manually scheduled tasks that include information that might conflict with the linking, the linking takes precedence, and the manually entered information changes accordingly. If you change the manually entered start or finish date to the point that there's a potential conflict with the link relationship, the task is flagged as a potential scheduling problem. This problem and its possible solutions are explained in the Task Inspector.

Note

When you edit the scheduling of a task—for example, its duration or a task dependency—you might affect other tasks that are linked with a task dependency to this task. When this happens, by default the changed cells are temporarily filled with a background color so that you can immediately see how your edit changed the scheduling for other tasks. This change highlighting changes or disappears when you make the next scheduling edit.

For more information about change highlighting, see "Highlighting the Ripple Effects of Schedule Changes" on page 238.

INSIDE OUT Link in or out of order

When you drag across a series of tasks and then click Link Tasks, the tasks are linked in order from the task higher in the task list (lower Task ID number) to the task lower in the task list (higher Task ID number). It doesn't matter whether you drag from top to bottom or bottom to top—the resulting links are the same. This is also true if you select adjacent tasks using the Shift key—the order of selection does not matter.

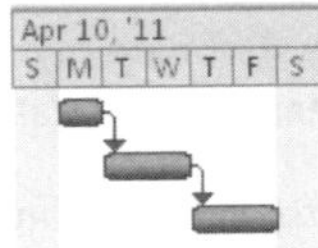

However, if you hold down Ctrl and click each task, the tasks are linked in precisely the order in which you select each individual task. Using this method, you can make a task lower in the list the predecessor of a task higher in the list.

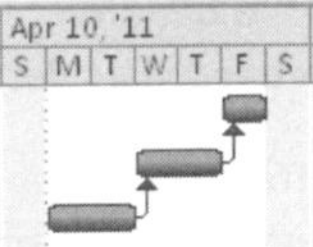

Understanding the Dependency Types

Although the finish-to-start task dependency is the most common, there are four types of dependencies that help you model your task relationships. These dependency types are as follows:

- **Finish-to-Start (FS)** As soon as the predecessor task finishes, the successor task can start.

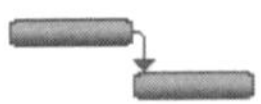

- **Finish-to-Finish (FF)** As soon as the predecessor task finishes, the successor task can finish.

- **Start-to-Start (SS)** As soon as the predecessor task starts, the successor task can start.

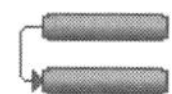

- **Start-to-Finish (SF)** As soon as the predecessor task starts, the successor task can finish. This type of link is rarely used, but still available if you need it.

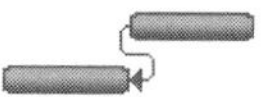

Note

By default, when you move a task from one location to another in your task sheet or when you insert a new task, that task is automatically linked like its surrounding tasks. You can control this behavior. On the File tab, click Options, and then click Schedule in the left pane. Under Scheduling Options For This Project, select or clear the check box labeled Autolink Inserted Or Moved Tasks.

You've already seen that to quickly apply a Finish-To-Start task dependency, all you have to do is select the tasks in the task sheet, and then click the Link Tasks button. But what about applying one of the other types of task dependencies?

You can still work directly in the Gantt Chart—you just need to take it one step further. After linking the tasks, double-click the task link line in the chart area of the Gantt Chart. The Task Dependency dialog box appears, as shown in Figure 6-8. In the Type box, change the dependency type, and then click OK.

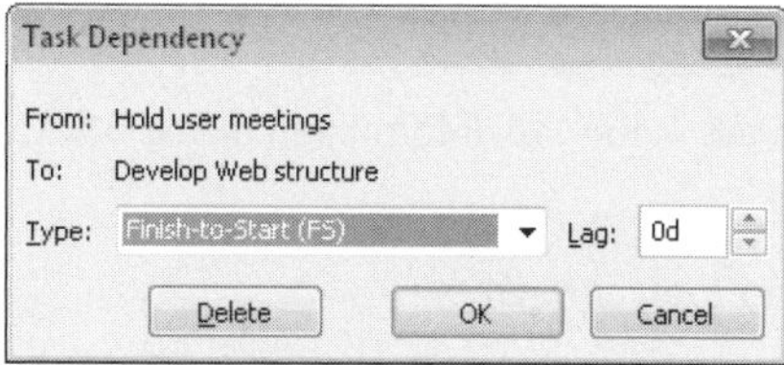

Figure 6-8 Double-click the task link line to open the Task Dependency dialog box and change the dependency type.

An alternative, which doesn't require such a steady hand with the mouse, is to change the task dependency by using the Task Information dialog box. To do this, follow these steps:

1. Display the Gantt Chart or other task sheet view.
2. Link the tasks using the Link Tasks button as usual.
3. Click anywhere in the row for the successor task for the linked pair whose link type you want to change.
4. On the Task tab, in the Properties group, click Information.

   You can also simply double-click the successor task to open the Task Information dialog box.
5. Click the Predecessors tab.

   The Task Name field shows the name of the predecessor task to the current task, and the Type field shows that it's a finish-to-start (FS) link.
6. Click in the Type field, and then click the arrow that appears in the field.

   The four link types are listed in the drop-down menu that appears, as shown in Figure 6-9.

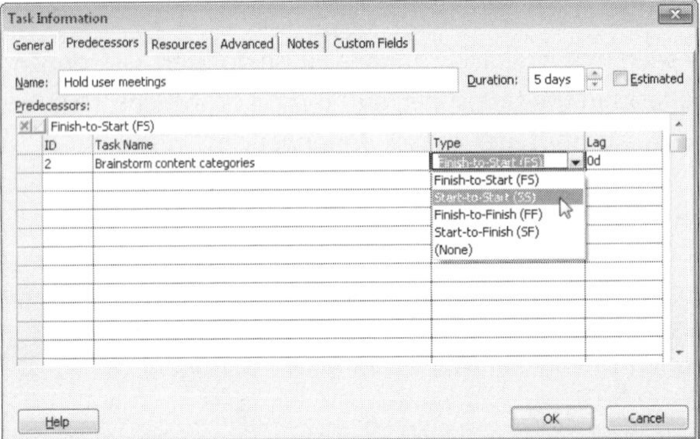

Figure 6-9 Use the Predecessors tab in the Task Information dialog box to set different types of task dependencies.

7. Click the link type you want, and then click OK.

   The link between the Gantt bars is redrawn to reflect the new link type, and the notation in the Predecessors field is also updated.

Note

Not only can you link tasks within one project, you can link tasks in different projects. For more information, see Chapter 16, "Exchanging Information Between Project Plans."

Delaying Linked Tasks by Adding Lag Time

Suppose that you have a pair of tasks with a finish-to-start link. Then you realize that the successor really can't start when the predecessor is finished—there needs to be some additional delay. This is usually the case when something needs to happen between the two tasks that isn't another task.

For example, suppose the "Order equipment" task is the predecessor to the "Install equipment" task. Although the equipment cannot be installed until after the equipment is ordered, it still cannot be installed immediately after ordering. Some *lag time* is needed to allow for the equipment to be shipped and delivered. In such a case, the successor needs to be delayed. You can enter lag time in the schedule to accurately reflect this condition.

Lag time can be expressed as a percentage of the predecessor; for example, **75%**, or as a specific time period; for example, **16h** or **3ed**.

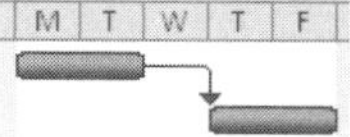

Lag Time vs. Assignment Delay

Don't confuse the delay afforded by lag time with assignment delay. With lag time, the delay is from the end of the predecessor to the beginning of the successor task. With assignment delay, there is a delay from the task start date to the assignment start date.

For more information about adjusting assignments using delay, see "Adjusting Assignments" on page 412.

To enter lag time for a linked task, follow these steps:

1. Display the Gantt Chart or other view with a task sheet.
2. Select the successor task that is to have the lag time.

3. On the Task tab, in the Properties group, click Information.

4. In the Task Information dialog box, click the Predecessors tab.

5. In the Lag field for the existing predecessor, type the amount of lag time you want for the successor. Use a positive number, and enter the lag time as a percentage or duration amount.

Overlapping Linked Tasks by Adding Lead Time

One way to make your project schedule more efficient is to overlap linked tasks where possible. Suppose you have a task that isn't scheduled to begin until a previous task is finished. You realize that the predecessor doesn't actually have to be finished—the successor can really begin when the predecessor is only 50 percent complete. The successor essentially gets a 50-percent head start, hence the term *lead time*. For example, "Construct walls" is the predecessor to "Plaster walls." Although plastering cannot be done until the walls are constructed, the final wall does not need to be constructed before plastering of the first wall can begin. You can set an amount of lead time for the "Plaster walls" task.

Lead time is expressed as a negative value. If you think of it as reducing time in the schedule, the minus sign makes sense. Lead time can be expressed as a percentage of the predecessor; for example, **-25%**, or as a specific time period; for example, **-4d** or **-1ew**.

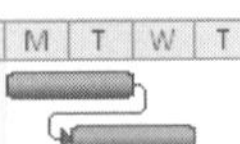

To enter lead time for a linked task, follow these steps:

1. Display the Gantt Chart or other view with a task sheet.

2. Select the successor task that is to have the lead time.

3. On the Task tab, in the Properties group, click Information.

4. In the Task Information dialog box, click the Predecessors tab.

5. In the Lag field for the existing predecessor, type the amount of lead time you want for the successor. Use a negative number, and enter the lead time as a percentage or duration amount.

Note

Although it might seem strange to use the Lag field to enter lead time, "lag time" and "lead time" are essentially the same idea. They express the amount of time that should pass before the successor task should start (or finish). Lag time adds time between the performance of predecessor and successor tasks, so it is expressed as a positive number. Lead time subtracts time between the performance of predecessor and successor tasks, hence the negative number.

Enter Lead or Lag Time Directly in the Gantt Chart

There are two other methods for entering lead or lag time for a pair of tasks.

One method uses the sheet area of the Gantt Chart. Click in the Predecessors field for the successor task. The field should already contain the Task ID of the predecessor task. After the Task ID, enter the code representing the link type, and then enter the amount of lead time—for example, **9FS-1 day** or **14FF-20%**—or lag time—for example, **9FS+1 day** or **14FF+20%**.

The other method uses the chart area of the Gantt Chart. Double-click the link line between the predecessor and successor tasks. In the Task Dependency dialog box, enter the lead or lag time in the Lag box. Remember to express lead time as a negative number and lag time as a positive number.

Changing or Removing Links

To remove all predecessor and successor links on a task, follow these steps:

1. In any task view, click the task.
2. On the Task tab, in the Schedule group, click Unlink Tasks.

   Unlink Tasks

   All predecessor and successor links to and from the selected task are removed.

To change or remove an existing task dependency by using the link line in the chart area of the Gantt Chart, follow these steps:

1. Display the Gantt Chart or other Gantt view.

2. In the chart area of the Gantt view, double-click the link line representing the link you want to change or remove.

3. In the Task Dependency dialog box, use the Type or Lag box to make the changes you want.

   If you want to remove the link altogether, in the Type box, click None.

To change or remove an existing task dependency by using the Task Information dialog box, follow these steps:

1. Display the Gantt Chart or other view with a task sheet.

2. Select the successor task whose link you want to change.

3. On the Task tab, in the Properties group, click Information.

4. In the Task Information dialog box, click the Predecessors tab.

5. Click in the Type field for the predecessor you want to change, and then select the type of task dependency you want it to be: Finish-to-Start (FS), Start-to-Start (SS), Finish-to-Finish (FF), Start-to- Finish (SF), or None. If you select None, the link is removed entirely.

CAUTION!

Removing a link from a task can move the scheduling of the task back to the project start date. Always check the new start and finish dates on a task when you have removed a link or changed the link type to be sure that the task is scheduled the way you expect.

Note

As with setting dependency types or entering lead or lag time, you can use the Predecessors field in the sheet area of the Gantt Chart to change or remove a link.

TROUBLESHOOTING

You're trying to remove just the predecessor link from a task, but the successor link is removed at the same time

When you click Task, Schedule, Unlink Tasks, all links are removed: predecessor, successor, and any multiples. As a result, the scheduling of this task returns to the project start date or a start date entered as a constraint.

To remove just a single predecessor, click the task, and then click Task, Properties, Information. In the Task Information dialog box, click the Predecessors tab. Click the task name of the predecessor you want to delete, and then press the Delete key.

Note

Undo

To undo recent edits, click Undo on the Quick Access Toolbar in the upper-left corner of the Project 2010 window. Each time you click Undo, the previous edit is undone in the reverse order in which it was performed. You can also press Ctrl+Z to undo edits.

Redo

To redo an edit that you've undone, click Redo on the Quick Access Toolbar. You can also press Ctrl+Y.

Reviewing Task Dependencies

When more details are needed, the following views can give you a closer look at the task dependencies in your project:

- The Gantt Chart shows task dependencies with link lines between the Gantt bars. In fact, all Gantt views show task dependencies this way.

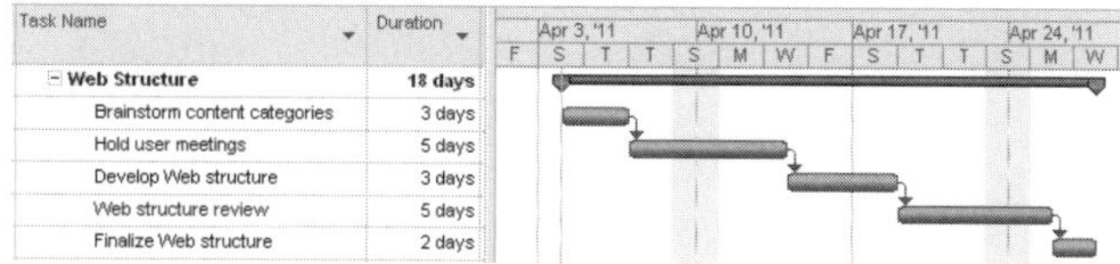

- The Network Diagram shows each task as an individual node with link lines between them. The Descriptive Network Diagram shows the same view, but the nodes are larger and provide more detail.

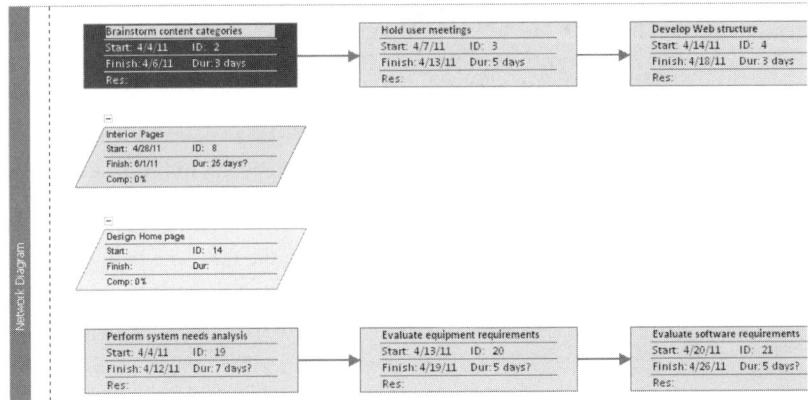

- The Relationship Diagram shows the predecessors and successors of a single selected task. This view is particularly useful for a large project or any project with complex linking.

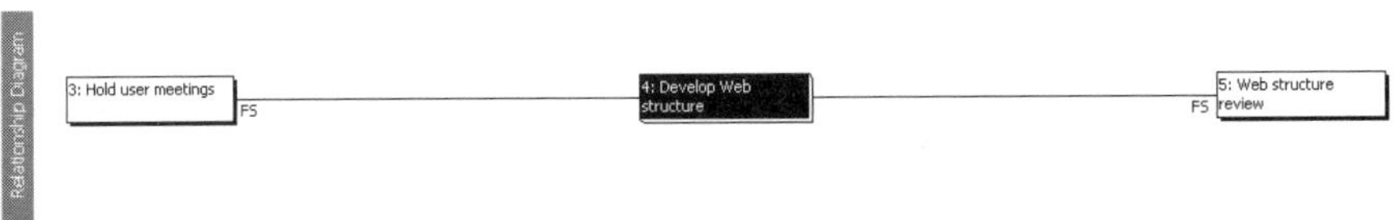

Predecessors & Successors

- The Task Details Form, Task Form, and Task Name Form can show predecessors and successors of a single selected task as part of a combination view. For example, you can display the Gantt Chart in the upper pane, and one of the task forms in the lower pane. In fact, the Task Entry view is the built-in combination view of Gantt Chart and Task Form. By default, these forms show assigned resource information in the left grid, and the predecessor information in the right grid. To show predecessor and successor information in the form, first click the form pane and then on the Format tab, in the Details group, click Predecessors & Successors.

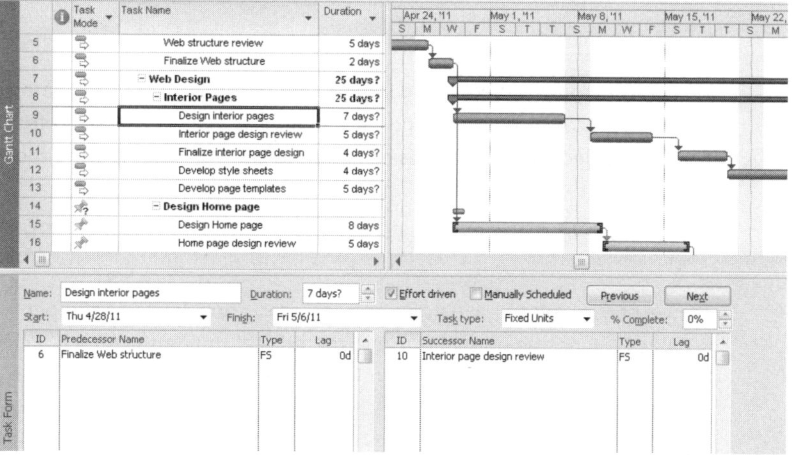

Scheduling Tasks to Achieve Specific Dates

With task dependencies established, your project schedule is taking shape and looking more and more like a realistic model of your project, as shown in Figure 6-10.

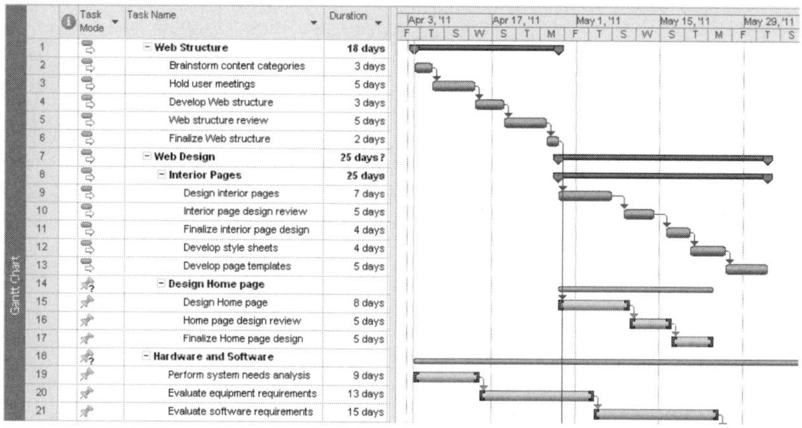

Figure 6-10 With durations entered and tasks linked, the Gantt Chart shows more meaningful schedule information.

Project 2010 uses the task information and controls that you enter to schedule your project from start to finish. By default, Project 2010 schedules each task to start "as soon as possible."

> **Note**
>
> **For a standard project being scheduled from the project start date, Project 2010 applies a default constraint of As Soon As Possible. If you're scheduling from the project finish date, Project 2010 schedules each task to start by default using the As Late As Possible constraint.**

However, you might have additional dates to consider. For example, maybe certain pivotal supplies will not be ready for use in the project until after April 6. Perhaps an important review meeting is taking place on June 29 that will set the stage for work toward the final milestones. Maybe one of your deliverables is a presentation at a key professional conference held on August 22.

To schedule around these important dates, you can set a *constraint*, which is a restriction on the start or finish date of a task. All automatically scheduled tasks have a constraint applied—at the very least, the default As Soon As Possible constraint. The As Soon As Possible constraint indicates that the task should be scheduled according to its working times calendars, duration, task dependencies, and any resource assignments—without regard to any specific date.

> **Note**
>
> **Manually scheduled tasks are set to the As Soon As Possible (or As Late As Possible) constraint. This constraint type cannot be changed as long as the task is in manually scheduled mode. Also, unlike with automatically scheduled tasks, entering start and finish dates does not cause date constraints to be set.**

Understanding Constraint Types

The As Soon As Possible (ASAP) constraint is applied by default to all tasks in a project scheduled from the start date. In a project scheduled from the finish date, the As Late As Possible (ALAP) constraint is applied. The As Soon As Possible and As Late As Possible constraints are considered flexible constraints.

> **Note**
>
> **Different types of constraints are applied in certain situations, depending on whether you're working with a project scheduled from the start date or from the finish date. For example, entering a date in the Start field of an automatically scheduled task in a project scheduled from the start date causes a Start No Earlier Than constraint to be applied. Doing the same thing in a project scheduled from the finish date causes a Start No Later Than constraint to be applied.**

When an automatically scheduled task needs to be scheduled relative to a specific date, there are additional constraints you can apply, each of which is associated with a date. The following is a list of all the date constraints you can use to refine your project schedule:

- **Start No Earlier Than (SNET)** A moderately flexible constraint that specifies the earliest possible date that a task can begin. For projects scheduled from a start date, this constraint is automatically applied when you enter a start date for a task.
- **Finish No Earlier Than (FNET)** A moderately flexible constraint that specifies the earliest possible date that this task can be completed. For projects scheduled from a start date, this constraint is automatically applied when you enter a finish date for a task.
- **Start No Later Than (SNLT)** A moderately flexible constraint that specifies the latest possible date that this task can begin. For projects scheduled from a finish date, this constraint is automatically applied when you enter a start date for a task.
- **Finish No Later Than (FNLT)** A moderately flexible constraint that specifies the latest possible date that this task can be completed. For projects scheduled from a finish date, this constraint is automatically applied when you enter a finish date for a task.
- **Must Start On (MSO)** An inflexible constraint that specifies the exact date a task must begin. Other scheduling controls such as task dependencies become secondary to this requirement.
- **Must Finish On (MFO)** An inflexible constraint that specifies the exact date on which a task must be completed. Other scheduling controls such as task dependencies become secondary to this requirement.

INSIDE OUT Beware of entering dates for automatically scheduled tasks

If you enter a date in the Start field (in a project scheduled from the start date) of an automatically scheduled task, the Start No Earlier Than constraint is applied. The finish date is recalculated based on the new start date and the existing duration.

If you then enter a date in the Finish field of the same task, the constraint changes to Finish No Earlier Than. The start date remains as you set it, but the duration is recalculated to reflect the difference between the start and finish dates you entered.

These kinds of constraints can prevent your schedule from taking advantage of time saved by a task finishing earlier than expected. For example, suppose that the 8-day task "Construct walls" is scheduled to finish on October 3. It is the predecessor to the "Plaster walls" task which has a Start No Earlier Than constraint of October 4. If the "Construct walls" task finishes 2 days early, on October 1, the schedule for the "Plaster walls" task does not change to October 2 but maintains that the task not be started until October 4.

Always be aware that any dates you enter change the As Soon As Possible or As Late As Possible constraints to something more inflexible. If you enter both the start and finish dates for a task, Project 2010 recalculates the duration.

Entering your own start and finish dates imposes often unnecessary restrictions on the capability of Project 2010 to create the best possible schedule. It can also adversely affect results when you have Project 2010 level overallocated resources. In the majority of cases, you get the best results when you enter durations and task dependencies and then let Project 2010 figure out the best start and finish dates for tasks to be done as soon as possible. Use date constraints only when there is a specific calendar date that you must work toward, such as an event or a fixed deliverable due date that has no possibility of changing.

Project Management Practices: Working with Date Constraints

When developing your project schedule, you might contend with one of two major categories of date constraints: externally imposed dates and milestone dates.

An externally imposed date reflects a situation outside the project that influences the project schedule. Examples include the following:

- A shipment of material needed for the project
- A market window for a new product
- A product announcement date at a trade conference
- Weather restrictions on outdoor activities
- A special event important to the project but scheduled by forces outside the project

You can reflect externally imposed dates as constraints on the tasks they affect. You can also add a task note as a reminder of the source of this date.

Milestone dates are typically dates set internally, often used to mark the end of phases or "chunks" of work in your work breakdown structure. As the project manager, you might set them yourself as goals to work toward. The project sponsor, customer, or other stakeholder might request certain dates for certain milestones, deliverables, or events being produced by the work of your project. You can set constraints on milestones as well as on regular tasks.

Changing Constraints

Remember, tasks always have a constraint applied—even if it's just As Soon As Possible or As Late As Possible. So you should never think of *adding* or *removing* constraints. When changing constraints in an automatically scheduled task, you are typically changing a constraint from a flexible one to a more inflexible one or vice versa.

Note

You can change constraints only in automatically scheduled tasks. Manually scheduled tasks have only one constraint applied—As Soon As Possible or As Late As Possible.

There are several methods for changing constraints, as follows:

- In the Gantt Chart or similar view with a task sheet, type or select dates in the Start or Finish fields. In a project scheduled from the start date, this causes a Start No Earlier Than or Finish No Earlier Than constraint to be applied. In a project scheduled from the finish date, this causes a Start No Later Than or Finish No Later Than constraint to be applied.

- In any task view, double-click the task whose constraint you want to change to open the Task Information dialog box. In the dialog box, click the Advanced tab as shown in Figure 6-11. In the Constraint Type box, click the constraint type you want to apply to this task. If applicable, enter the date in the Constraint Date box.

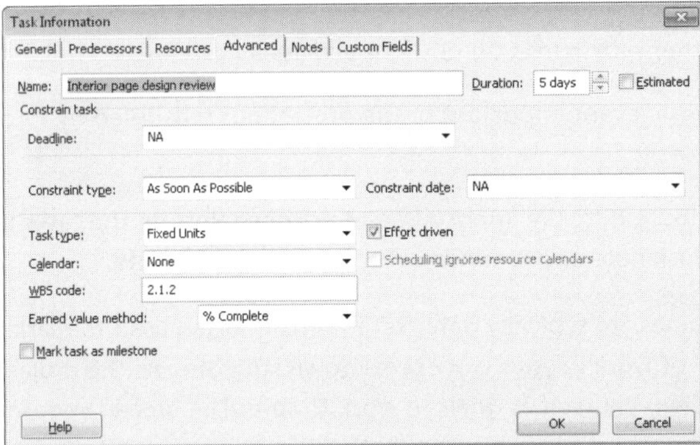

Figure 6-11 You can set constraints on the Advanced tab of the Task Information dialog box, in addition to deadlines, milestones, and task calendars.

Note that when you look at the Advanced tab for a manually scheduled task, the Constraint Type box shows As Soon As Possible (or As Late As Possible), and the Constraint Type and Constraint Date boxes are not editable. This indicates that the constraint type cannot be changed for manually scheduled tasks.

Tables

- In the Gantt Chart or other view with a task sheet, apply the Constraint Dates table. To do this, click View, Data, Tables, More Tables. In the More Tables dialog box, click Constraint Dates, and then click the Apply button. The table is applied to the view. (See Figure 6-12.) In the Constraint Type field, click the constraint type you want to apply to this task. If applicable, enter the date in the Constraint Date field.

	Task Name	Duration	Constraint Type	Constraint Date
1	**Web Structure**	**18 days**	**As Soon As Possible**	**NA**
2	Brainstorm content categories	3 days	As Soon As Possible	NA
3	Hold user meetings	5 days	Must Finish On	Wed 4/13/11
4	Develop Web structure	3 days	As Soon As Possible	NA
5	Web structure review	5 days	Must Finish On	Mon 4/25/11
6	Finalize Web structure	2 days	As Soon As Possible	NA
7	**Web Design**	**25 days?**	**As Soon As Possible**	**NA**
8	**Interior Pages**	**25 days**	**As Soon As Possible**	**NA**
9	Design interior pages	7 days	Start No Earlier Than	Thu 4/28/11
10	Interior page design review	5 days	As Soon As Possible	NA
11	Finalize interior page design	4 days	As Soon As Possible	NA

Figure 6-12 Apply the Constraint Dates table to review or change constraint types and dates.

CAUTION!

If a task has no predecessors, changing the constraint to an As Soon As Possible (or As Late As Possible) constraint can move the scheduling of the task back in time to the project start date. Always check the new start and finish dates on a task after you change constraint types to be sure the task is scheduled the way you expect.

Change Constraints for Multiple Tasks at Once

In a task sheet, select all the automatically scheduled tasks that will have the same constraint applied. Drag across adjacent tasks to select them, or hold down Ctrl while clicking nonadjacent tasks. Click Task, Properties, Information. In the Multiple Task Information dialog box, click the Advanced tab. Change the Constraint Type and, if applicable, the Constraint Date, and then click OK. The constraint is changed for all selected tasks.

This method works best if you're changing date constraints to As Soon As Possible or As Late As Possible because it's rare for multiple tasks to have the same constraint date.

TROUBLESHOOTING

You can't delete a constraint

By their nature, constraints are not deleted. A constraint is applied to every task. If you're thinking of deleting a constraint, what you probably mean to do is change it from a date constraint such as Must Start On or Finish No Later Than to a flexible, non-date-dependent constraint such as As Soon As Possible.

Double-click the task to open the Task Information dialog box, and then click the Advanced tab. In the Constraint Type box, click As Soon As Possible or As Late As Possible.

Working with Flexible and Inflexible Constraints

When thinking of task constraints, it's helpful to keep in mind the three levels of flexibility: flexible, moderately flexible, and inflexible.

Flexible Constraints

The flexible constraints are As Soon As Possible and As Late As Possible. These constraints work with task dependencies to schedule a task as soon or as late as the task dependency and other scheduling considerations will accommodate. These default constraints give Project 2010 maximum flexibility in calculating start and finish dates for the tasks. For example, a task with an As Soon As Possible constraint and a finish-to-start dependency is scheduled as soon as the predecessor task finishes.

Moderately Flexible Constraints

The moderately flexible constraints—Start No Earlier Than, Start No Later Than, Finish No Earlier Than, and Finish No Later Than—have a range of dates to work within. That is, the task is restricted to starting or finishing before or after the date you choose, which provides some room for flexibility, even though a date is in place. For example, a task with a Start No Later Than constraint for November 14 and a finish-to-start dependency to another task can begin any time its predecessor is finished up until November 14, but it cannot be scheduled after November 14.

Inflexible Constraints

The inflexible constraints—Must Start On and Must Finish On—have an absolute single date that the schedule must accommodate, which means that other scheduling considerations must fall by the wayside if necessary to meet this date. By default, constraints take precedence over task dependencies when there's a conflict between the two. For example, a task with a Must Finish On constraint for April 30 and a finish-to-start dependency to another task is always scheduled for April 30, regardless of whether the predecessor finishes on time.

INSIDE OUT

Conflicts between dependencies and constraints

If you set a moderately flexible constraint, such as Start No Earlier Than, or an inflexible constraint, such as Must Finish On, you run the risk of a conflict with task dependencies. Suppose the "Hang wallpaper" task has a Must Finish On constraint for June 25. Because of various delays, the task's finish-to-start predecessor task, "Install drywall," actually finishes on June 29.

This situation creates a scheduling conflict. According to the task dependency, you can't hang wallpaper until the drywall is installed, which won't finish until June 29. But according to the constraint, the wallpaper must be hung by June 25.

By default, where there's a conflict like this between a task dependency and a constraint, the constraint takes precedence. In this case, there would be 4 days of *negative slack,* which essentially means that the predecessor task is running 4 days into the time allotted to the successor task. You might see a Planning Wizard message regarding this, especially if you're still in the planning processes and are setting up tasks with such a conflict before actual work is even reported.

To prevent this situation during the planning phase, review your project for places where predecessors and successors either overlap or have lag. In those cases, check to make sure there is a nonzero lag on that link. If there is not, then there is a potential constraint problem or conflict on that link.

To resolve the scheduling conflict, you can change the constraint to a more flexible one, such as Finish No Earlier Than. You can change the Must Finish On date to a later date that will work. You can also change the scheduling precedence option. If you want task dependencies to take precedence over constraints, on the File menu, click Options, and then click Schedule in the left pane. Under Scheduling Options For This Project, clear the check box labeled Tasks Will Always Honor Their Constraint Dates, which is selected by default.

Reviewing Constraints

With the right constraints in place, you have the beginnings of a schedule. The Gantt Chart can provide a great deal of information about your constraints and other scheduling controls.

You can sort tasks by Start Date, Finish Date, Constraint Type, or Constraint Date. You can group tasks by Constraint Type. You can filter tasks by the Should Start By date or the Should Start/Finish By date.

Such task arrangements can provide overviews of the big picture of start and finish dates across many tasks at a time. If you want to review details, you can review the Task Information dialog box for a task. The General tab includes the scheduled start and finish dates, and the Advanced tab includes the constraint type and constraint date.

You can apply the Task Entry view. Although the Task Form does not reflect constraints, other task details for any task you select in the Gantt Chart in the upper pane are shown in the Task Form in the lower pane. The default Resources & Predecessors details show task dependencies as well as any lead or lag time. (See Figure 6-13.)

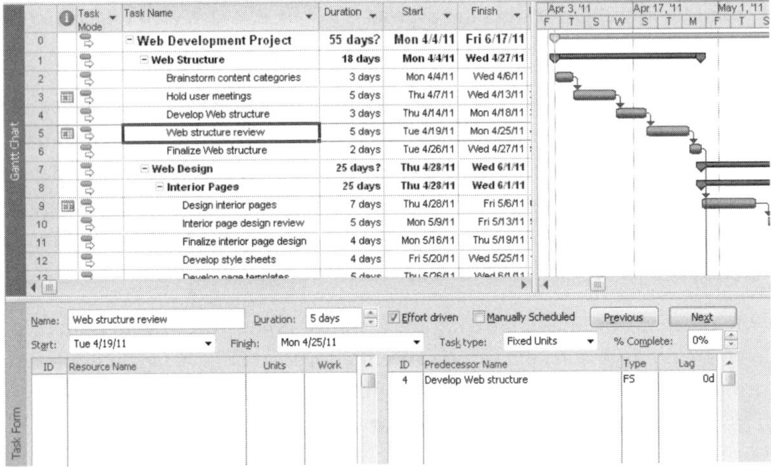

Figure 6-13 With the Task Entry view, you can review many details of an individual task selected in the Gantt Chart.

Setting Deadline Reminders

You might be tempted to enter a finish date on an automatically scheduled task or a Must Finish On constraint when you want a task to be completed by a certain date. But instead of a date constraint that might unnecessarily restrict the schedule, what you really need is a reminder or target toward which to move your schedule.

So rather than set a date constraint in such situations, set a *deadline* instead. A deadline appears as an indicator on your Gantt Chart as a target or goal, but it does not affect the scheduling of your tasks.

To set a deadline, follow these steps:

1. Select the task for which you want to set a deadline.
2. On the Task tab, in the Properties group, click Information.

3. In the Task Information dialog box, click the Advanced tab.
4. In the Deadline box, enter or select the deadline date.

   The deadline marker appears in the chart area of the Gantt Chart, as shown in Figure 6-14. Repeat steps 1 through 4 to change or remove a deadline if necessary. If you're removing a deadline, select the date, and then press the Delete key.

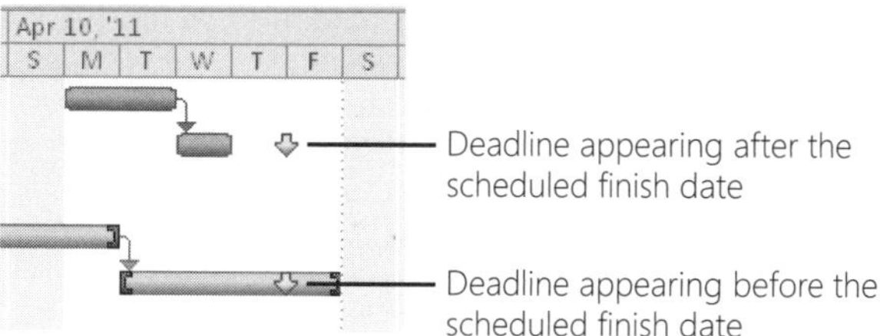

Figure 6-14 The deadline provides a guide for important dates.

Adjust Your Schedule to Hit Your Deadlines

When you have deadline flags set up in your project plan, you can graphically see the differences between your deadlines and the scheduled finish dates.

So what do you do when you have a discrepancy between the two?

The first thought is that the project schedule might simply give you the sanity check you needed to see whether your deadlines are realistic. If you think the task durations, dependencies, and constraints are all exactly as they should be, then the deadline might just need to be adjusted.

If you still really want to try to hit that deadline, there are various techniques to modify scope, refine the schedule, and change resource allocations to make the adjustments necessary to schedule the finish date closer to the deadline.

For more information about shortening the schedule for certain tasks or the project as a whole, see "Bringing in the Project Finish Date" on page 383.

You can show deadlines in your task sheet as well by adding the Deadline field as a column. Follow these steps:

1. Right-click the column heading to the right of where you want to insert the Deadline column, and then click Insert Column.

   Or, click the column heading, and then click Format, Columns, Insert Column.

   A new column is created and a drop-down list of available fields appears.

Chapter 6

2. In the list, click Deadline. You can type the first one or two characters to go straight to it in the list.

   The Deadline field shows any deadline dates that are already set and shows "NA" for tasks without deadlines. You can enter deadlines directly in this field.

If the schedule for a task moves beyond its deadline date, either because of normal scheduling calculations or because of actual progress information entered, an alert appears in the Indicators field, specifying that the task is scheduled to finish later than its deadline. (See Figure 6-15.)

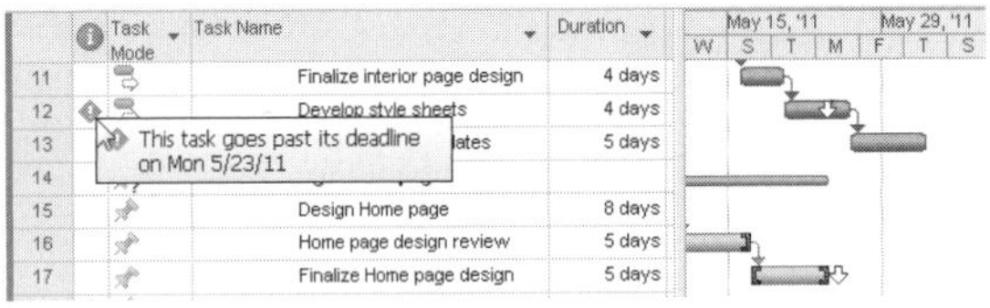

Figure 6-15 If a deadline will be missed, the Deadline indicator provides the details.

You can set deadlines for manually as well as automatically scheduled tasks. You can also set deadlines for summary tasks as well as individual tasks. If the summary task's deadline conflicts with the finish dates of any of the subtasks, the Deadline indicator specifies a missed deadline among the subtasks. You can also set deadlines for milestone tasks.

INSIDE OUT A deadline might affect scheduling after all

There are two instances in which a deadline can indeed affect task scheduling. The first is if you enter a deadline that falls before the end of the task's *total slack*. The total slack is recalculated using the deadline date rather than the task's late finish date. If the total slack reaches 0, the task becomes critical.

The second instance is if you set a deadline on a task with an As Late As Possible constraint. Suppose the task is scheduled to finish on the deadline date. However, if any predecessors slip, the task could still finish beyond its deadline.

For more information about the critical path, slack, and late finish dates, see "Working with the Critical Path and Critical Tasks" on page 367.

Creating Milestones in Your Schedule

You can designate certain tasks as *milestones* in your project plan. Having milestones flagged in your project plan and visible in your Gantt Chart helps you see when you've achieved another benchmark. Milestones often indicate the beginning or end of major phases or the completion of deliverables in your project. As you complete each milestone, you come ever closer to completing the project. Milestones are also excellent reporting points.

A milestone, as such, has no additional calculation effect on your schedule. However, you typically link a milestone to other tasks. You might also set a date constraint or deadline on a milestone.

The simplest method for entering a milestone is to create a task that's worded like a milestone (for example, "Website launched") and enter a duration of 0. Any task with a 0 duration is automatically set as a milestone. The milestone marker and date are drawn in the chart area of the Gantt Chart, as you can see in Figure 6-16.

	Task Mode	Task Name	Duration	Start
33		System Cutover	7 days	Mon 8/1/11
34		Update DNS	1 day	Mon 8/1/11
35		Final testing	3 days	Tue 8/2/11
36		Final bug fixes	3 days	Fri 8/5/11
37		Web Site Launched	0 days	Wed 8/10/11

Figure 6-16 Project 2010 interprets any task with a 0 duration as a milestone.

NEW!

Milestone

Another easy way to create a milestone task is to use the Milestone button. In a task sheet, click where you want the milestone task to be inserted. On the Task tab, in the Insert group, click Milestone. A task labeled "<New Milestone>" is added above the selected row. The task has a duration of 0 days, and its date is set as the project start date. To correct the date of the new milestone task, link it as appropriate with its surrounding tasks or enter a start or finish date to correct the milestone date.

Note that a milestone doesn't have to have a 0 duration. You might want to make the final task in each phase a milestone, and these are likely real tasks with real durations.

CAUTION!

Before you make tasks with durations into milestone tasks, be aware that you might be creating a new set of problems. The Gantt bar is replaced by a milestone marker at the finish date, so the duration is not shown unless you create a custom Gantt bar for this purpose. Also, if you export task data to other applications or copy task data between different projects, the milestone tasks are not likely to appear as you expect.

To change a regular task into a milestone, follow these steps:

1. Select the task you want to become a milestone.
2. On the Task tab, in the Properties group, click Information.
3. In the Task Information dialog box, click the Advanced tab.
4. Select the Mark Task As Milestone check box, and then click OK.

   The Gantt bar for the task changes to the milestone marker at the finish date in the chart area of the Gantt Chart. (See Figure 6-17.)

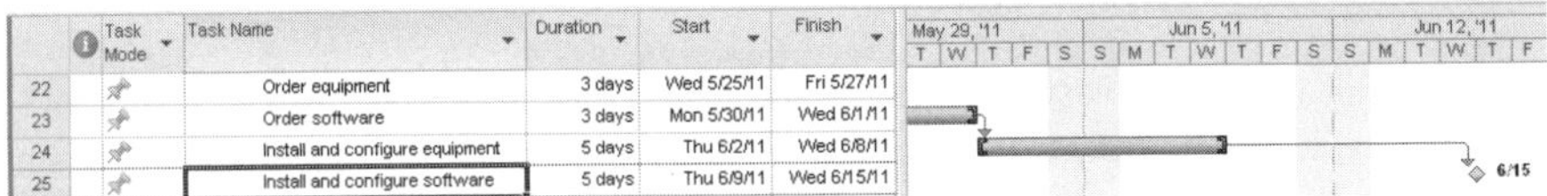

Figure 6-17 You can set any task as a milestone.

INSIDE OUT Create Gantt bars to show milestones with duration

If all your milestones have a duration and if you never use a milestone with a 0 duration, you might consider creating a milestone Gantt bar that shows duration from the start to the finish of the milestone task, with the milestone marker sitting on the finish date.

To do this, follow these steps:

1. **Display the Gantt Chart (or other Gantt view for which you want to create the milestone Gantt bar).**
2. **On the Format tab, in the Bar Styles group, click Format, and then click Bar Styles.**

3. **In the table listing the Gantt bar styles, find the Milestone style.**

   Modify the Milestone style for milestones on automatically scheduled tasks. Modify the Manual Milestone style for milestones on manually scheduled tasks.
4. **Click the arrow in the From field for the Milestone style, and then click Task Start.**
5. **Be sure the To field shows Task Finish.**
6. **In the Bars tab below the table, under Start, change the Shape box to show a blank instead of the diamond-shaped milestone marker.**

7. Under Middle, select the shape, pattern, and color for the Gantt bar you want to use to represent the milestone bar.
8. Under End, change the Shape box to show the diamond-shaped milestone marker, as shown in Figure 6-18.

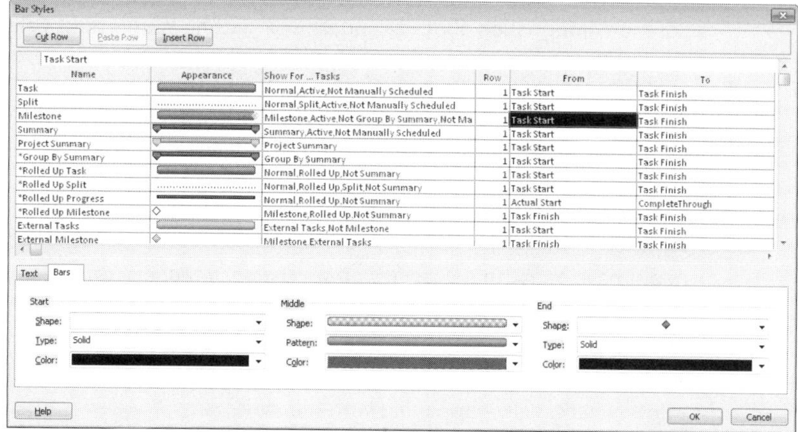

Figure 6-18 Change the look of milestones in the chart area of the Gantt Chart by using the Bar Styles dialog box.

The resulting Gantt bar appears in the Milestone row of the dialog box under Appearance. Click OK. This produces a Gantt bar showing the duration of the milestone task as well as a symbol to mark the end of the task and the completion of the milestone, as shown in Figure 6-19.

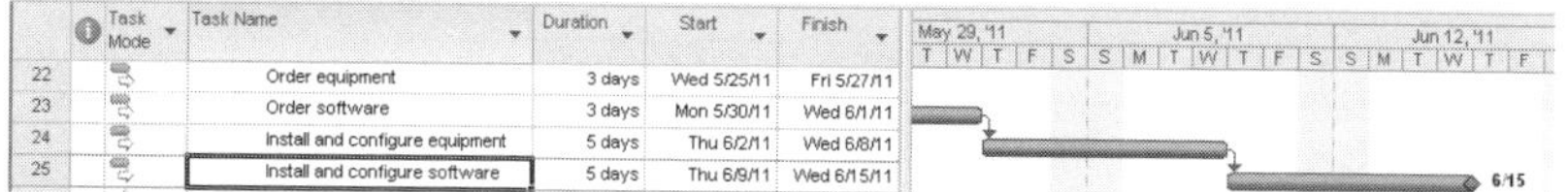

Figure 6-19 You can change the bar style for milestones from a single marker on the Start date to a Gantt bar with the diamond-shaped marker on the Finish date.

However, remember that if you create a milestone Gantt bar to show the start and finish dates, there will be no marker if you create a milestone with 0 duration.

For more information about changing Gantt bar styles, see "Formatting the Layout of Gantt Bars" on page 1079.

Working with Task Calendars

The scheduling of your tasks is driven by task duration, task dependencies, and constraints. It's also driven by the project calendar. If your project calendar dictates that work is done Monday through Friday, 8:00 A.M. until 5:00 P.M., initially that's when your tasks are scheduled.

For more information about calendars, see "Setting Your Project Calendar" on page 84.

However, if a task is assigned to a resource who works Saturday and Sunday, 9:00 A.M. until 9:00 P.M., the task is scheduled for those times instead. That is, the task is scheduled according to the assigned resource's working times calendar rather than the project calendar.

Sometimes, you have a task that needs to be scheduled differently from the working times reflected in the project calendar or the assigned resource calendars. For example, you might have a task that specifies preventive maintenance on equipment at specified intervals. Or you might have a task being completed by a machine running 24 hours a day. In any case, the task has its own working time, and you want to schedule it according to that working time rather than the project or resource working time so that you can accurately reflect what's really happening with this task.

Keep in mind that there's an order of precedence when it comes to calendars that govern the scheduling of tasks throughout the project. All tasks start out being scheduled by the project calendar. When resources are assigned, the calendars of the assigned resources take precedence in the scheduling of the tasks. If a task calendar is assigned to a task, its scheduling information is combined with that of any assigned resource calendars to determine when the task should be scheduled.

Note

Unlike project or resource calendars, which are essential to the accuracy of your schedule, task calendars are more of an optional scheduling feature. Create and apply task calendars only in those special situations when a task has its own unique schedule that tends to be independent of the project or assigned resource calendar.

Setting Up the Task Calendar

To schedule a task according to its own working times, you must first set up the calendar. You can use or adapt a built-in base calendar. Think of the base calendar as a kind of calendar template that can be applied to the project as a whole, to resources, or to tasks. If the task's working times are quite different from anything available in the existing base calendars, you can create your own.

For specific procedures on modifying an existing base calendar, see "Modifying a Base Calendar" on page 85. To create a new base calendar, see "Creating a New Base Calendar" on page 93.

INSIDE OUT Take care modifying a built-in base calendar

When you have the need for a task calendar, it's usually because the task has a schedule that's quite different from the project working times calendar or the assigned resource working times calendar.

Be careful when modifying an existing base calendar to use as a task calendar. If that base calendar is used for a particular resource, for example, the scheduling of that resource will change to reflect what you are intending just for the task calendar.

If you're certain that the base calendar in question will not be used for anything except as the task calendar, then modify away. Otherwise, create a new base calendar. You can always create a new base calendar from an existing one. You can also name it in such a way as to make your intentions for this calendar crystal clear.

But suppose that you inadvertently modify a base calendar being used to schedule resource working time, or even the entire project's working time. How do you return it to its default settings? Follow these steps:

1. On the Project tab, in the Properties group, click Change Working Time.
2. Click the Work Weeks tab, and then click the Details button.
3. In the Select Day(s) box, in which Sunday is already selected, hold down the Shift key and click Saturday so that all seven days are selected.
4. Click the Use Project Default Times For These Days option, and then click OK.

If you have a set of tasks that are carried out entirely by equipment on the equipment's own schedule, an alternative to creating a task calendar is to set up the equipment as a work resource. You can then apply a working times calendar to the equipment resource and assign the equipment resource to the appropriate tasks.

For more information about creating work resources, see "Adding Work Resources to the Project" on page 250.

> **Note**
>
> **When you create a base calendar to use as a task calendar, give the new base calendar a specific name that indicates its role as a task calendar. This clarifies the differences among the base calendars (for you and possibly other project managers) to prevent confusion and the application of the wrong calendars for the wrong purposes.**

Assigning a Base Calendar to a Task

To assign a base calendar to a task, follow these steps:

1. Double-click the task to which you want to assign a base calendar.
2. In the Task Information dialog box, click the Advanced tab.
3. In the Calendar box, click the name of the calendar you want to assign to this task. All base calendars are listed, including any that you have created yourself.
4. Click OK.

   Task Calendar indicator

   A task calendar icon appears in the Indicators column. If you rest your mouse pointer over the indicator, a ScreenTip displays the name of the assigned calendar. (See Figure 6-20.) Follow this same procedure to switch to a different task calendar or to remove the task calendar.

	Task Name	Duration
4	Develop Web structure	3 days
5	Web structure review	5 days
6	The calendar 'Review Task Calendar' is assigned to the task.	2 days
7		**25 days?**
8	**Interior Pages**	**25 days**
9	Design interior pages	7 days

Figure 6-20 Assign a calendar to a task to schedule it independently from the project or resource calendars.

Don't make the mistake of confusing the task calendar with the Calendar view. A task calendar reflects working days and times for one or more selected tasks. The Calendar view is a graphical representation of tasks and durations in a monthly calendar format.

For more information about the Calendar view, see "Visualizing the Project with the Calendar" on page 138.

TROUBLESHOOTING

You assigned a task calendar, but it's not scheduling tasks in all the times it should

The task probably also has a resource assigned, and the resource calendar is conflicting with what you want the task calendar to accomplish.

When you assign a task calendar, it takes the place of the project calendar. However, suppose resources are assigned to the task, as well. Resources are all associated with their own resource calendars. Although a resource's calendar might be the same as the project calendar, it can be customized for the resource's specific working times.

When resources are assigned, the task is scheduled not just for the working times indicated in the task calendar. By default, Project 2010 schedules the task according to the common working times between the task calendar and the resource calendar.

For example, suppose that the 24-hour base calendar is assigned to a task that's also assigned to a resource who works Friday through Sunday, 9:00 A.M. until 7:00 P.M. The only times the two calendars have in common are Friday through Sunday, 9:00 A.M. until 7:00 P.M., so by default, those are the only times when work will be scheduled for this task.

If you apply a task calendar to a task with a resource assigned, and there are few to no common working times between the task calendar and the resource calendar, an error message appears, as shown in Figure 6-21.

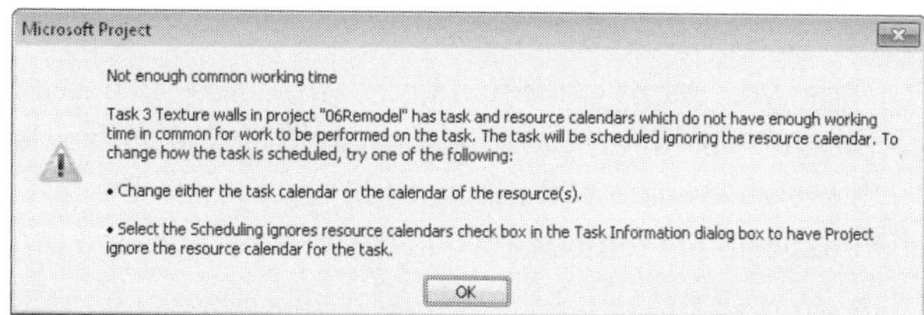

Figure 6-21 The Not Enough Common Working Time error message offers two suggestions for making sure your task is scheduled the way you want.

You can change the working times in the resource calendar to ensure enough common time, or you can change the working times in the task calendar. You might also remove the resource if that's possible for the task.

If you want the resource calendar to be ignored on a task, open the Task Information dialog box for the task and click the Advanced tab. Select the check box labeled Scheduling Ignores Resource Calendars.

For more information about resource calendars, see "Setting Working Times and Days Off for Work Resources" on page 267. For information about resource assignments, see "Assigning Work Resources to Tasks" on page 283.

Seeing Feedback on Scheduling Changes

Have you ever thought you were making a simple change to a task, only to find out it caused an unexpected change to several surrounding tasks? You might just increase a duration, change a task link, or add a date constraint to one task, and you find, much to your frustration, that undesirable ripple effects have happened throughout the project.

Such ripple-effect changes happen in your schedule whether tasks are scheduled automatically or manually. With automatically scheduled tasks, it's important that Project 2010 provide you with needed information when it recalculates aspects of your schedule, or when you have choices as to how a change is to be interpreted in your schedule. With manually scheduled tasks, you need to know when a scheduling change you enter might cause a conflict or ambiguity that will be problematic.

This is where Project 2010 feedback information comes in handy. The change highlighting and Task Inspector pane both provide information to help you see exactly what is changing in your schedule and to help you make the decisions appropriate for your project.

For more information about changing your schedule, see Chapter 10.

Highlighting the Ripple Effects of Schedule Changes

When you change a duration in a task that's in the middle of a series of linked finish-to-start tasks, that one task's change in duration will affect the start and finish dates for all of its successor tasks.

Likewise, other changes you might make to a task's schedule—such as a task dependency or a start date constraint—can affect other tasks that are linked with a dependency to this task. To be sure you see the impact of these kinds of changes on the rest of your schedule, by default the changed cells are temporarily filled with a background color, as shown in Figure 6-22.

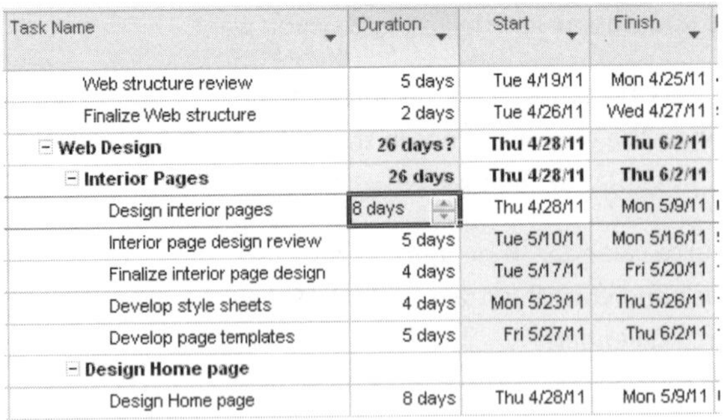

Task Name	Duration	Start	Finish
Web structure review	5 days	Tue 4/19/11	Mon 4/25/11
Finalize Web structure	2 days	Tue 4/26/11	Wed 4/27/11
Web Design	**26 days?**	**Thu 4/28/11**	**Thu 6/2/11**
Interior Pages	**26 days**	**Thu 4/28/11**	**Thu 6/2/11**
Design interior pages	8 days	Thu 4/28/11	Mon 5/9/11
Interior page design review	5 days	Tue 5/10/11	Mon 5/16/11
Finalize interior page design	4 days	Tue 5/17/11	Fri 5/20/11
Develop style sheets	4 days	Mon 5/23/11	Thu 5/26/11
Develop page templates	5 days	Fri 5/27/11	Thu 6/2/11
Design Home page			
Design Home page	8 days	Thu 4/28/11	Mon 5/9/11

Figure 6-22 See the ripple effects of scheduling changes you make by reviewing the highlighted cells in a task sheet.

This change highlighting shows only in sheet views such as the Gantt Chart, the Task Usage view, or the Resource Sheet. There is no change highlighting for graphically-oriented task views such as the Calendar view or Network Diagram.

The change highlighting remains in effect until you make the next edit that affects scheduling, at which time the highlighting shifts to those cells affected by the new change. The last set of change highlighting is cleared when you save the project.

By default, change highlighting is light blue. To change the color of change highlighting, follow these steps:

1. Display the view whose change highlighting color you want to change.
2. On the Format tab, in the Format group, click Text Styles.

Text Styles

3. In the Item To Change box, click Changed Cells, as shown in Figure 6-23.

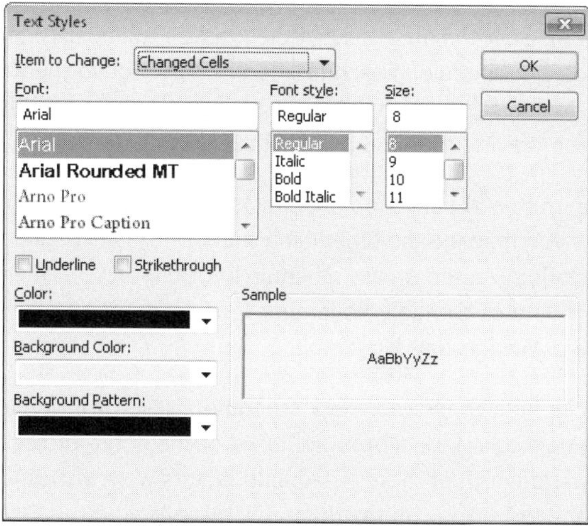

Figure 6-23 Change the color and pattern for change highlighting in a task sheet view by using the Text Styles dialog box.

4. In the Background Color box, select the change highlighting color you want.
5. If you also want to change the background pattern, select one in the Background Pattern box.

> **Note**
>
> **If you don't want to use change highlighting, you can turn it off by adding the Display Change Highlighting command to the ribbon.**
>
> **For information about adding commands to the ribbon, see "Customizing the Project 2010 Ribbon" on page 1153.**

Reviewing the Factors That Affect Task Scheduling

When you first create your project schedule, you start by entering a project start date and setting up a project working times calendar. You add tasks to the project, and then you add scheduling information about those tasks, such as task duration, dependencies, constraints, and task calendars.

In a project made up of automatically scheduled tasks, Project 2010 takes this information and calculates the schedule of each task to ultimately build the full project schedule, complete with start dates and finish dates. Because you've entered this other information, you're freed up from having to figure out the start dates of each task yourself.

In a project made up of manually scheduled tasks, Project 2010 takes a mostly hands-off approach and lets you manage the scheduling. However, it still makes educated guesses about your expectations, based on the schedule information you've entered. For example, if you enter a start date of Monday, November 1, and a duration of 2 days, Project 2010 will fill in a finish date of Wednesday, November 3.

If you're contemplating a change to a task schedule, particularly if you're trying to shorten the schedule of a particular task, a group of tasks, or the entire project, it's tremendously helpful to understand which of these scheduling factors were instrumental in determining the start date of the tasks. You can see this easily by reviewing the Task Inspector.

The Task Inspector shows factors responsible for controlling the start and finish dates of the selected task and also indicates whether the task can start any earlier. (See Figure 6-24.)

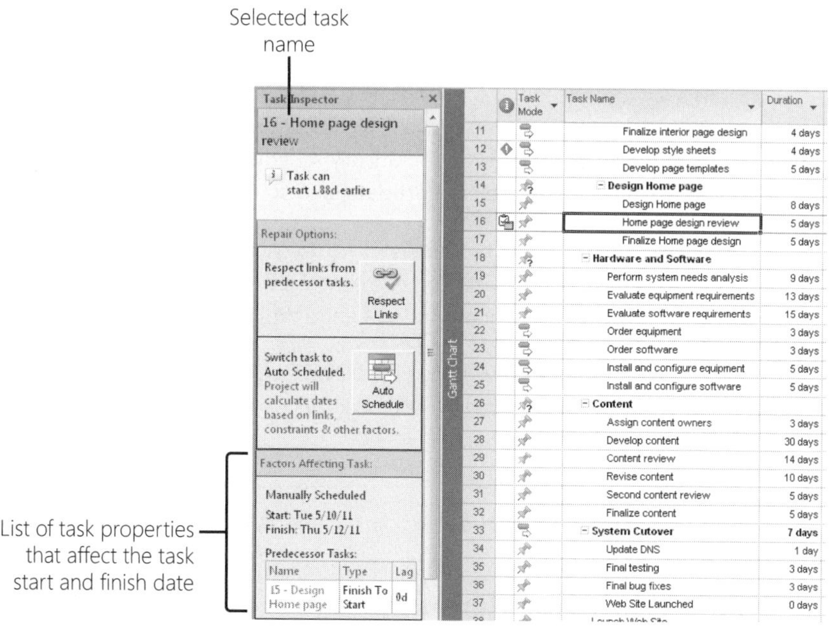

Figure 6-24 Show the Task Inspector to see a list of the factors responsible for setting a task's start and finish dates.

You can inspect any task in your project. A task might have just a single factor, or it might have three or four. Examples of common task drivers are:

- Project start date
- Project calendar
- Predecessor tasks
- Constraint date
- Resource calendar
- Task calendar
- Actual start date

To inspect a task and its scheduling factors, follow these steps:

1. Display any task view, such as the Gantt Chart, Task Usage view, or Network Diagram.
2. Click the task whose scheduling factors you want to see.

Inspect

3. On the Task tab, in the Tasks group, click Inspect.

   The Task Inspector appears in the left pane. The upper portion of the Task Inspector lists any opportunities for shortening the schedule. Below, under Factors Affecting Tasks, the task properties responsible for the task's scheduling are listed—for example, whether it's manually or automatically scheduled, the start and finish dates, the predecessor tasks, the project start date, and so on.

You can click the name of a predecessor task to go to that task in the view and see the scheduling factors for that task. You can click the name of a calendar listed in the Task Inspector to open that calendar in the Change Working Time dialog box.

Keep the Task Inspector open while you click different tasks and review their task drivers. When you're finished inspecting tasks, click the X in the upper-right corner of the pane to close it.

Seeing Scheduling Feedback on Assigned Tasks

Another source of feedback in Project 2010 are the indicators and option buttons that appear when you edit the project plan in certain ways, such as:

- **Changes to resource assignments**
- **Changes to start and finish dates**
- **Changes to work, units, or duration**
- **Deletions in the Name field**

When you make these kinds of changes, a green triangle might appear in the corner of the edited cell of a sheet view such as the Gantt Chart or Task Usage view.

Task Name	Duration	Start
Brainstorm content categories	3 days	Mon 4/4/11
Hold user meetings	2.5 days	Mon 4/11/11
Develop Web structure	3 days	Thu 4/14/11
Web structure review	5 days	Tue 4/19/11

Scheduling feedback triangle

When you move your mouse pointer over the cell containing the feedback indicator, an option button appears.

Task Name	Duration	Start
Brainstorm content categories	3 days	Mon 4/4/11
Hold user meetings	2.5 days	Mon 4/11/11
Develop Web structure	3 days	Thu 4/14/11
Web structure review	5 days	Tue 4/19/11

Option button

Click the option button. A message explains the scheduling ramifications of your edit. The message usually gives you the opportunity to change the edit so that the result is closer to your expectation.

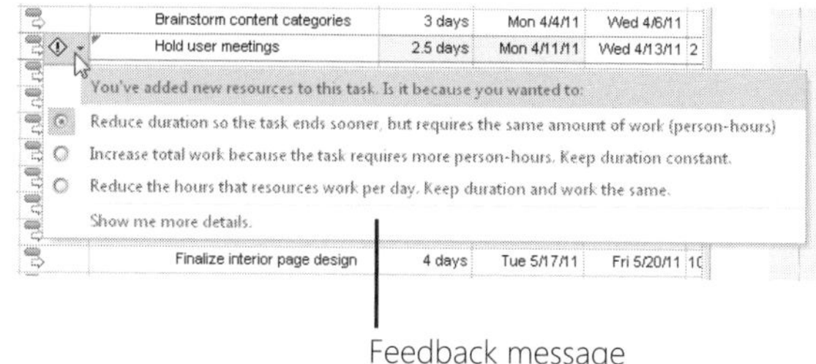

An indicator and button usually appear after a potentially ambiguous edit and provide choices to ensure that you understand the schedule ramifications of the change you're making.

For more information about using the indicators and option buttons for scheduling feedback, see "Changing Resource Assignments" on page 314.

CHAPTER 7

Setting Up Resources in the Project

As soon as you've been assigned as manager of the project, certain resources might come to mind whom you know are right for the project. As the scope becomes more defined, and as you develop the task list along with the milestones and deliverables, you're likely to have even more ideas. If you have specific people in mind, you might start inquiring about their availability. You might also start investigating sources, specifications, and prices for material and equipment. You're likely to have a particular budget, and you might start thinking about the kinds of costs the tasks in your project are likely to incur.

By the time you define the durations of the tasks, you have very concrete information in front of you—you now know exactly which tasks need to be done and what kinds of resources you need to do them.

A team might be in place already—the full-time members of a department who are waiting to sink their teeth into a good project. There might be no team at all, and you'll have to hire some people and borrow others from another group. Or you might have a core staff, but for this project you'll need to contract additional temporary workers to fill out the skills needed for the team.

You can add the names of resources who will be working on this project as you acquire them. These might be the names of actual people, or they might be generic resource names that describe the skills and competencies needed to fulfill the task. Where applicable, you can enter the names of equipment or material resources that will also help implement the project. You can specify cost resources such as equipment rentals or travel fares, and you can enter additional resource information, such as work schedule, availability, cost, and notes.

How Many Resources Do You Need?

Although you know the tasks that need to be done and the kinds of resources you need to be able to do them, you might not know how many of a particular type of resource you need just yet.

Here's the process: first, identify the tasks that need to be done. Second, identify the resources needed to do those tasks. Third, assign resources to the tasks. At that point, you can see whether the resulting schedule meets your target date or target budget.

You need to have tasks in place to find out how many resources you need. You also need resources to assign to those tasks to create an accurate schedule and cost estimate. After you assign resources, if the schedule calculates a finish date later than the target finish date, you might have to go back and add more resources to your team. Or, if the project costs are over budget and you haven't even started work yet, you might have to forego additional resources or scramble to replace expensive resources with less expensive ones.

As you can see, tuning your project plan to get the right number of resources to meet your schedule, costs, and workload requirements is an iterative process. You might need to go through several cycles of refinement before you arrive at the perfect plan.

For more information about refining the project plan to meet a target date or budget, see Chapter 10, "Checking and Adjusting the Project Plan."

Understanding the Impact of Resources in the Plan

Resources carry out the work of your project or model the expenditure of costs or consumption of materials. However, with your tasks defined and scheduled, why is it necessary to actually specify resources in your project plan? You could just print the schedule and tell people which tasks they're responsible for: here are your due dates; now go make them happen.

This approach might seem like a simple way of managing a project, but if you do it this way, you'll miss out on the tremendous scheduling, tracking, and communication capabilities provided by Microsoft Project 2010. By adding resources to your project, you can do the following:

- Increase the accuracy of your schedule. If you use automatic scheduling, Project 2010 already takes into account the project calendar, durations, task dependencies, and constraints to build an accurate model of your project. When you assign resources, Project 2010 takes this schedule a significant step further by adding the working times and availability of your resources to the scheduling calculations.
- Know ahead of time whether any resources are overloaded with too much work in the allotted time. You can also see whether anyone is underallocated and shift responsibilities accordingly as you refine your schedule. Later, when work is being done and you're getting progress information on each task, you can find bottlenecks or any new overallocations or underallocations due to shifts in the schedule.
- Track progress according to resource work. Your resources can tell you how much time they've spent on their tasks for a given week and how much more time they will need. This tracking can help you make any necessary adjustments to keep the project moving in the right direction. Recording actual progress data also captures historical information that will be invaluable for future projects.
- Record the use, cost, and consumption of materials in your project. These details can help you monitor your budget performance as well as give you advance notice about when you need to reorder supplies.
- Track some of the largest expenses in the project, including costs for labor, equipment, materials, travel, rentals, software, and so on.
- Exchange task assignments, task updates, progress information, and status reports with your resources via Microsoft Project Server 2010 and Microsoft Project Web App. If you're not set up for enterprise project management, you can share project information using Microsoft SharePoint.
- Make sure that all tasks are assigned to a responsible and accountable resource so that nothing inadvertently slips through the cracks and is forgotten until it's too late.

Adding Resources to the Project

The following types of resources can be assigned to your tasks:

- People or equipment, referred to as work resources
- Consumable materials, referred to as material resources
- Cost items incurred in the performance of a task, referred to as cost resources

Chapter 7

Entering Resources in the Resource Sheet

To add resources to your project by simple data entry, follow these steps:

Resource Sheet

1. On the View tab, in the Resource Views group, click Resource Sheet to switch to the Resource Sheet view, shown in Figure 7-1.

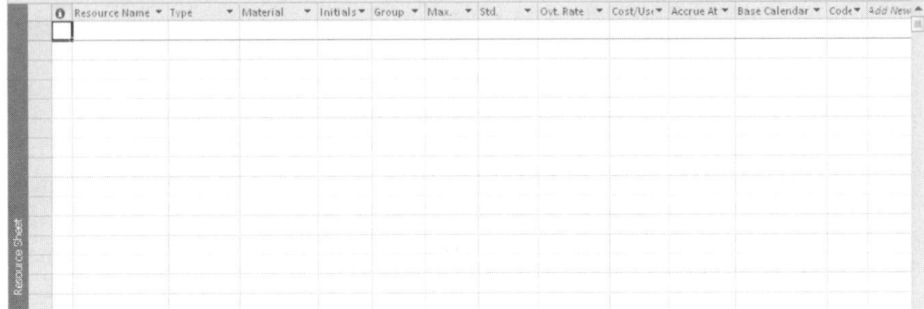

Figure 7-1 Enter resource information on the Resource Sheet.

Tables

2. Make sure the Entry table is applied. If necessary, on the View tab, in the Data group, click Tables, and then click Entry.

> **Note**
>
> **You can check which table is applied to a sheet view by resting your mouse pointer over the All Cells box, where the row and column headings intersect. The ScreenTip containing the table name (and view name) appears.**

3. In the first Resource Name field in the top row, type the name of a resource, and then press Enter.

4. Enter the names of other resources in the same way.

If a piece of equipment will be integral to the successful completion of a task, enter its name as a work resource, just as you would a human resource.

Sort Your Resource Names

When you have all the resources entered, you might want to sort them in a particular order and keep them in that order. To do this, follow these steps:

Sort

1. With the Resource Sheet showing, on the View tab, in the Data group, click Sort, and then click Sort By.
2. In the Sort By field, click the field you want the resources sorted by; for example, Name or Group.
3. Select the Permanently Renumber Resources check box, and then click Sort.

   The resources are sorted, and this order is made permanent because Project 2010 renumbers the unique identifier (Unique ID) for each resource.

By permanently renumbering the resource order, your resources will always appear in this order by default.

Whenever you select the Permanently Renumber Resources check box and click Sort, you should always open the Sort dialog box again, click Reset, and then click Cancel. This process clears the Permanently Renumber Resources check box, so the next time you sort your resources for some temporary need, you won't inadvertently renumber the resources again.

TROUBLESHOOTING

You have duplicate resource names, and information is being tracked separately for each instance

When you enter resource names, be aware that Project 2010 allows duplicate entries; for example, Adam Carter in row 3 and Adam Carter in row 20. Because a Unique ID is used for each resource record you enter, the duplicate entries appear unique to the Microsoft Project database. A problem occurs if you assign tasks to the duplicated resource—for example, you assign some tasks to the row 3 instance of Adam Carter and other tasks to the row 20 instance. Project 2010 tracks the resource and assignment information as though it applied to separate resources, so your information is skewed. That is, it might look like Adam has plenty of availability when in effect he's actually overallocated.

If you enter a long list of resources, it's a good idea to sort the Resource Sheet by name and check for duplicates. With the Resource Sheet showing, on the View tab, in the Data group, click Sort, and then click By Name.

Adding Work Resources to the Project

Work resources consist of people and equipment that use time as a measure of effort on a task. Add resources to your project simply by entering their names into your project plan as described in the previous section. To automate the process, you can select resource names from your company's e-mail address book. If you have a resource list in a Microsoft Excel workbook, you can import it into your project plan. After your resources are in place, you can add information regarding their availability, costs, notes, and more.

Note

If you're entering a significant number of work resources, or if you don't expect to enter any material resources, apply the Entry–Work Resources table. This table has only those resource fields applicable to work resources.

With the Resource Sheet showing, on the View tab, in the Data group, click Tables, and then click More Tables. Click Entry–Work Resources, and then click Apply.

Project Management Practices: Staffing Management

Ongoing operations such as accounts payable or shipping and receiving always need to be staffed "forever." In projects, however, that's not the case: because true projects always have a specific start and finish date, there's a distinct point when you begin to need resources. There's also a distinct point when resources are no longer needed because the project is complete. In between the project start and finish dates, there are likely to be ramp-up and ramp-down periods, which often take place at a variety of times for different phases or functions.

Given this condition of project staffing, it's important to have a clear sense of when you actually need people to work on projects, what you need them for, when you don't need them anymore, and what happens to them after that point.

A staffing management plan is considered a subset of your project plan. It describes when and how your human resources will be brought on and taken off your project team. An excellent way to develop your staffing management plan is to use Project 2010 to develop your task list and preliminary schedule using generic resources. This preliminary schedule can help you determine your staffing needs based on specific tasks in the schedule.

Adding Resources from Your E-Mail Address Book

If Project 2010 is installed on the same computer as your organization's MAPI e-mail connection (for example, Microsoft Exchange Server 2010 or Microsoft Outlook 2010), you can add resources to your project plan from the e-mail address book. To do this:

1. Be sure that the Resource Sheet is displayed.

Add Resources

2. On the Resource tab, in the Insert group, click Add Resources, and then click Address Book.

   If the Choose Profile dialog box appears, click the profile name for your e-mail system. (This dialog box appears only if you have more than one profile set up in your e-mail system.)

   The Select Resources dialog box appears.

3. Click the resources you want, and then click the Add button to add the selected resources to your project plan.

   You can add all resources contained in a group or distribution list. Add the name of the group to your list, just as you would add an individual resource. When you click OK, Project 2010 asks whether you want to expand the group to list the individual resources in the project plan.

> **Note**
>
> **If you're connected to Project Server 2010 to use the enterprise features, you have access to all existing resources identified on the server. On the Resource tab, in the Insert group, click Add Resources, and then click Build Team From Enterprise. The Build Team dialog box appears. In the Build Team section, in the Enterprise Resource table on the left, select the team members you want to add to your project. Use the Ctrl or Shift key as needed to select multiple resources. Click Add. The names you selected are added to the Project Resource table on the right. When you are finished, click OK.**

TROUBLESHOOTING

You get an error message when trying to display your e-mail address book

If you try to add resources from your e-mail address book, and you get an error message saying the address list could not be displayed, click OK in the error message. The Select Resources dialog box appears with no resources listed. Click the arrow in the box labeled Show Names From The to see which address lists are available in the drop-down menu. If another Address Book or Contacts subfolder is listed, click it.

If you still do not see contacts from your address book, go to your e-mail system's online Help for other ideas. Remember that you can import contact information to your Project 2010 resource sheet only from a MAPI-compatible e-mail program.

Using Resource Information from Excel

Suppose you have a list of resources in an Excel workbook. You can easily use it to populate your project's Resource Sheet. You can copy information or you can import the file.

To copy a resource list from an Excel workbook, follow these steps:

1. Open the Excel workbook that contains the resource list you want to copy to Project 2010.
2. Select the cells containing the resource list.
3. On the Home tab in Excel, in the Clipboard group, click Copy.

Copy

4. Open the project plan. If necessary, on the View tab, in the Resource Views group, click Resource Sheet.

   In the Resource Name column, click the cell where you want to begin inserting the copied resources.
5. On the Task tab in Project 2010, in the Clipboard group, click Paste.

Paste

You can also use the Microsoft Project Plan Import Export Template to import resources from Excel to Project 2010. The standard Excel import process involves mapping the Excel columns to the corresponding Project 2010 columns to ensure that the right information ends up in the right location in your Resource Sheet. The Microsoft Project Plan Import Export Template is set up so that you can enter detailed resource information in the format needed by Project 2010. To do this, make sure that Excel and the Microsoft Project Plan Import Export Template are installed on the same computer as Project 2010 and then follow these steps:

1. Start Excel.
2. On the File tab, click New.
3. Under Available Templates, click Sample Templates. (See Figure 7-2.)

Sample Templates

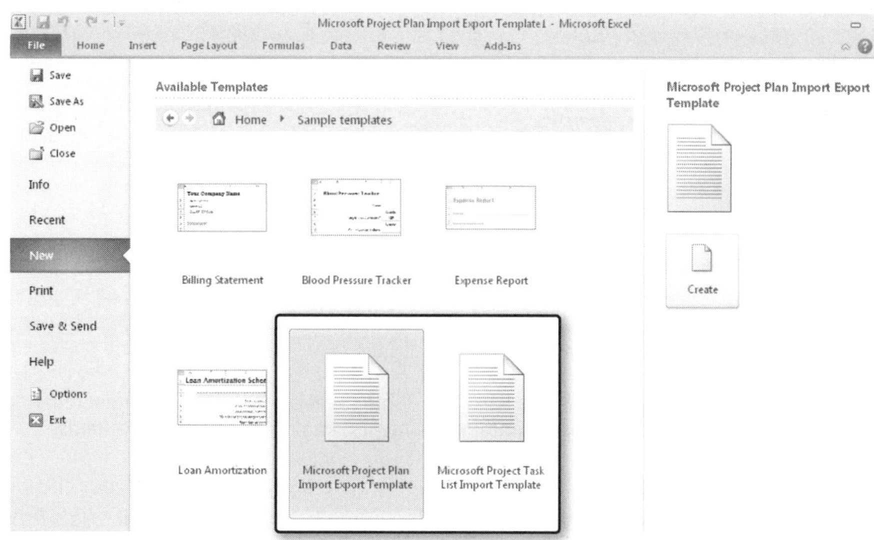

Figure 7-2 Two templates are available in Excel to facilitate entering information in Project 2010.

4. Double-click the Microsoft Project Plan Import Export Template.

   A new workbook opens showing a sheet that explains the use of this template.

5. At the bottom of the workbook window, click the Resource_Table tab.

   The Resource_Table tab includes columns that correspond to the fields in the Project 2010 Resource Sheet.

6. Enter resource names and any other resource information in the columns provided. (See Figure 7-3.)

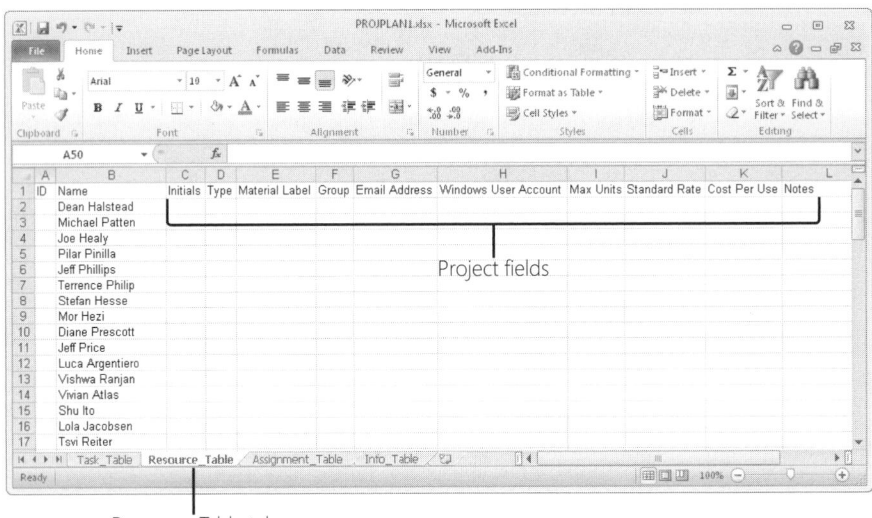

Figure 7-3 The Resource_Table sheet of the Microsoft Project Plan Import Export Template in Excel contains the most commonly used resource fields.

Save

7. On the File tab, click Save. Browse to the location on your computer where you want to save the file, change the name from the default Microsoft Project Plan Import Export Template.xlsx if you want to, and then click Save.

Note

If you save your file as an .xls file—for example, if you're working with Microsoft Excel 2003—be aware that you must first change your security settings for the import process to be successful. See the Troubleshooting note "Project 2010 will not let you import the older .xls file format" on page 257.

When you're ready to import the resource list into your project plan, follow these steps:

Open

1. In Project 2010, on the File tab, click Open.
2. In the Open dialog box, go to the location on your computer or network where the Excel workbook is saved.
3. Next to the File Name box, click the Microsoft Project Files (*.mp*) button.

4. In the list that appears, click Excel Workbook (*.xlsx).

   The workbook appears in the list of folders and files.

5. Click the name of the workbook, and then click the Open button.

   The Import Wizard appears, as shown in Figure 7-4.

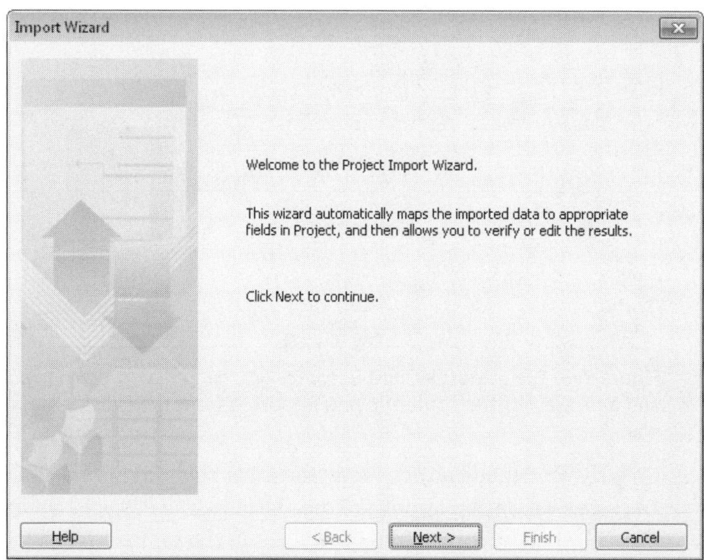

Figure 7-4 The Import Wizard helps you import the resource information from your Excel workbook to your project plan.

6. In the first wizard page, click Next.

7. Ensure the New Map option is selected, and then click Next.

8. Specify whether you want to import the file as a new project, append the resources to the currently active project, or merge the data into the active project. Click Next.

9. Select the Resources check box, and then click Next.

   The Import Wizard Resource Mapping dialog box appears, showing the fields and contents of the resource information from the Resource_Table sheet. (See Figure 7-5.)

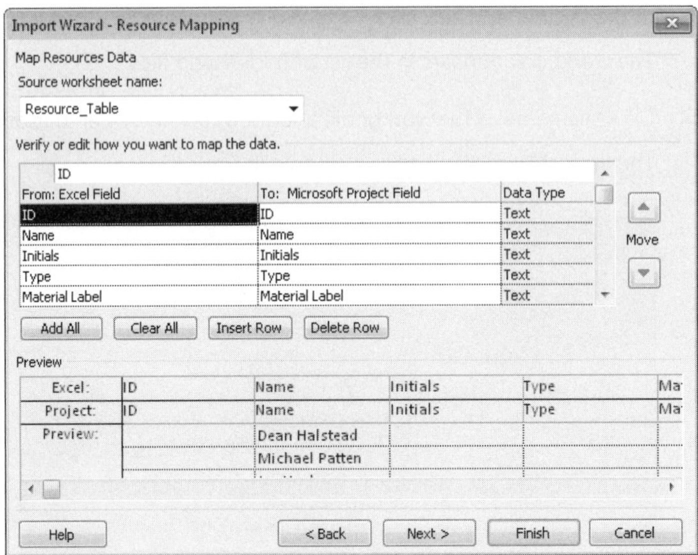

Figure 7-5 The Import Wizard Resource Mapping dialog box shows the field mapping and a preview of the content being imported from the Excel template into your project plan.

Unless you've made any changes, the Excel fields and Project 2010 fields should show an exact relationship to one another, because the Project Plan Import Export Template is set up to contain the same fields in the same order as the default Entry table on the Resource Sheet.

10. Click Finish.

    The resource information is imported, as shown in Figure 7-6. If necessary, display the Resource Sheet to see the results.

		Resource Name	Type	Material	Initials	Group	Max.	Std.	Ovt. Rate	Cost/Us	Accrue At	Base Calendar
1		Dean Halstead	Work				100%	$0.00/hr	$0.00/hr	$0.00	Prorated	Standard
2		Michael Patten	Work				100%	$0.00/hr	$0.00/hr	$0.00	Prorated	Standard
3		Joe Healy	Work				100%	$0.00/hr	$0.00/hr	$0.00	Prorated	Standard
4		Pilar Pinilla	Work				100%	$0.00/hr	$0.00/hr	$0.00	Prorated	Standard
5		Jeff Phillips	Work				100%	$0.00/hr	$0.00/hr	$0.00	Prorated	Standard
6		Terrence Philip	Work				100%	$0.00/hr	$0.00/hr	$0.00	Prorated	Standard
7		Stefan Hesse	Work				100%	$0.00/hr	$0.00/hr	$0.00	Prorated	Standard
8		Mor Hezi	Work				100%	$0.00/hr	$0.00/hr	$0.00	Prorated	Standard
9		Diane Prescott	Work				100%	$0.00/hr	$0.00/hr	$0.00	Prorated	Standard

Figure 7-6 The resource information is imported into the Resource Sheet of Project 2010 as you specified.

TROUBLESHOOTING

Project 2010 will not let you import the older .xls file format

If you try to import a template that was saved in the older .xls format from Microsoft Excel 2003, you might see the following error message after finishing with the Import Wizard:

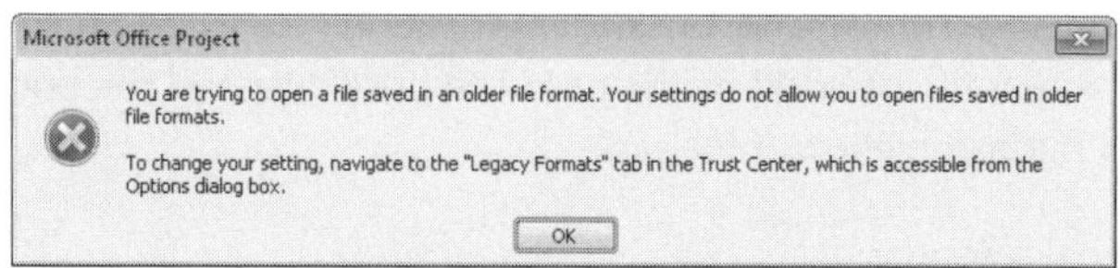

Options

If you see this message, click OK. On the File tab, click Options, and then click Trust Center in the left pane. Under Microsoft Project Trust Center, click Trust Center Settings. In the left pane, click Legacy Formats, and then select either the Prompt When Loading Files With Legacy Or Non-Default File Format or the Allow Loading Files With Legacy Or Non-Default File Formats option. Click OK, and then OK again.

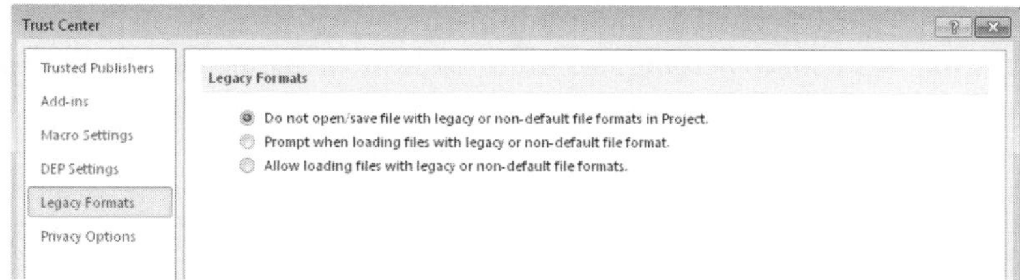

Run through the Import Wizard process again. If you selected the Prompt When Loading Files With Legacy Or Non-Default File Format option, you'll see the following prompt:

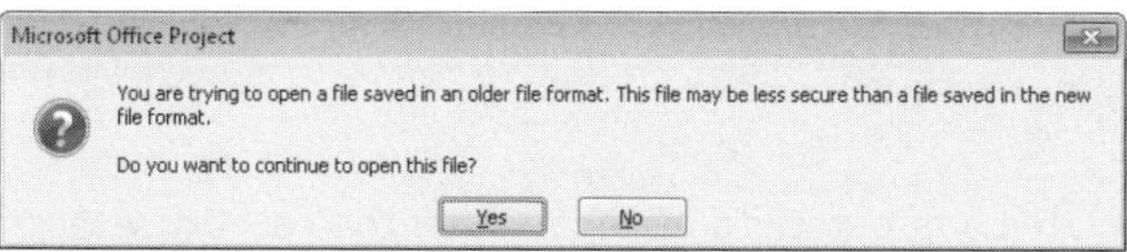

Click Yes. The information from the Excel Project template appears in your project file.

For more information about using Project 2010 with other applications, see "Importing and Exporting Information" on page 676 and Chapter 18, "Integrating Project 2010 with Excel."

For more information about adding resources to your project plan from a shared resource pool file, see "Sharing Resources by Using a Resource Pool" on page 614.

For more information about adding resources from the enterprise resource pool, see "Building Your Enterprise Project Team" on page 927.

Adding Material Resources to the Project

Material resources are consumable supplies that use quantity as a measure of effort on a task. Any supplies that are integral to completing tasks can be added to your project plan as material resources. Examples of such material resources might be steel for a building structure, roofing material for a home, or bricks for a landscaping project. You might have a task "Lay brick sidewalk," to which a bricklayer is assigned for a certain amount of time. You can also assign a quantity of bricks to the task. The bricklayer and the bricks are both essential resources to the completion of the task.

To enter a material resource:

1. Display the Resource Sheet with the Entry table applied.
2. In the next available Resource Name field, type the name of the material resource (for example, **Bricks**).
3. In the Type field, click Material.
4. In the Material Label field, enter the unit of measurement for the material.

   This measurement differs depending on the nature of the material. It might be tons, yards, feet, cartons, and so on.

> **Note**
> **The field might just show a heading of "Material," but if you drag to increase the column width or row depth, or if you rest your mouse pointer over the Material heading, you'll see that the label is indeed "Material Label."**

When you specify that a resource is a material rather than a work resource, be aware of the following points:

- Maximum units (or resource units) and the associated variable availability are not applicable to material resources. You specify units (for example, 50 yards or 100 feet per day) when you assign the material resource to a task. With these assignment units, you can track the usage of materials and possibly the depletion rate of materials.

  Note that if you enter units with a per-time period specification, for example, **yards/day**, that calculation is not made when the material resource is assigned. To ensure that proper calculations are made for a variable consumption rate, always specify the rate in the Units field in the Assign Resources dialog box.

For more information about material resource assignments, see "Assigning Material Resources to Tasks" on page 303.

- Resource calendars are not available for material resources.
- Workgroup fields such as Workgroup and Windows Account are not available for material resources. The Overtime field is also disabled.

If you're entering a significant number of material resources, apply the Entry–Material Resources table. This table has only those resource fields applicable to material resources. With the Resource Sheet showing, on the View tab, click Tables, and then click Entry–Material Resources.

Another way to apply the table is to right-click the All Cells box that sits between the first column and first row. In the shortcut menu that appears, click Entry–Material Resources.

Adding Cost Resources to the Project

If you rely on Project 2010 for tracking costs and adhering to your project budget throughout the life of the project, you'll find cost resources a most convenient tool.

What Are Cost Resources?

A *cost resource* is a cost item that contributes to the completion of a task but does not affect the duration or work of a task. When you include a cost resource with a task or a set of tasks, you can be assured that not only are you tracking the cost of human resources or equipment resources with their cost per hour or per use, but you are also tracking any cost items incurred as a result of carrying out the task.

Suppose you have several tasks, such as "Hold user meetings," "Staff conference booth," or "Train trainers at client site." These might be at different locations and handled by different team members. However, they all involve cost items such as airfare and lodging. They might also involve room rentals or equipment fees. You can create cost resources named Airfare, Lodging, Booth Rental, Conference Fees, Printing, and so on.

Unlike work or material resources, you do not enter a cost amount in the Resource Sheet or Resource Information dialog box. You only create the resource and identify it as a cost resource.

Only when you have assigned a cost resource to a task do you deal with the cost. At that point, you can enter the cost for the airfare, for example, associated with the task to which the airfare cost resource is assigned.

For example, you might have the Airfare cost resource assigned to the "Hold user meetings" and the "Staff conference booth" tasks. The "Hold user meetings" task needs one person to travel from Portland to Chicago in the spring and costs $330. The "Staff conference booth" task needs three persons to travel from Raleigh to Las Vegas in the fall and costs $720 total. You're using the same cost resource but entering different cost amounts on the different task assignments.

Identifying a Resource as a Cost Resource

To set up a cost resource, do the following:

1. Display the Resource Sheet.
2. In the next available Resource Name field, type the name of the cost resource. Good examples include Car Rental, Client Entertainment, Software Purchase, Airfare, Lodging, and so on.

   Make the cost resource name specific enough that you know what the resource is for when you assign it to a particular task, but make it general enough that you can use it for multiple tasks. You might find it helpful to use your organization's budget category names. Later you can view information about how much you're spending throughout the project on all car rentals, for example.
3. In the Type field, click Cost.

Because cost resources do not rely on working time to accomplish their tasks, they are not associated with max units, base calendars, or availability dates. Also, because specific costs are entered for the task to which the cost resource is assigned, costs are not entered on the cost resource itself. Therefore, these fields in the Resource Sheet and Resource Information dialog box are not available for cost resources.

Removing a Resource from the Project

If you add a resource by mistake or find duplicates of the same resource, you can delete a resource.

> **Note**
>
> **If you're working with enterprise features using Microsoft Project Professional 2010 and Project Server, you cannot delete an enterprise resource from your project. Enterprise resources can be deleted only by the project administrator by using Project Web App.**

TROUBLESHOOTING

You can't enter costs for your cost resource

When you identify a resource as a cost resource, you might be surprised that the resource cost fields—Std. Rate, Ovt. Rate, and Cost/Use—suddenly become unavailable to you, both in the Resource Sheet as well as on the Costs tab of the Resource Information dialog box.

However, because cost resources are intended to be assigned to different tasks in which the cost amounts are likely to be different from assignment to assignment, the cost information is actually entered in the Assignment Information dialog box available from the Task Usage or Resource Usage view.

First, assign the cost resource to a task. Then open the Task Usage or Resource Usage view. Double-click the assignment of the cost resource on the task to open the Assignment Information dialog box. On the General tab, in the Cost box, enter the cost for this cost resource as it pertains to the selected task assignment. You can also enter the cost in the Assign Resources dialog box or in the Cost field added to the Task Usage or Resource Usage view.

For more information about working with cost resources, see "Assigning Cost Resources to Tasks" on page 306 and "Entering Costs for Cost Resource Assignments" on page 332.

To completely delete a resource:

1. Display the Resource Sheet.
2. Right-click anywhere in the row of the resource you want to delete.
3. In the drop-down menu that appears, click Delete Resource.

   The resource row, along with any associated resource or assignment information, is removed from your project.

   You can also delete a resource by clicking the row header for the resource to select the entire row and then pressing Delete.

Identifying Tentative, Generic, or Budget Resources

As you add work, material, or cost resources to the Resource Sheet, you can set up these resources with additional characteristics that provide you with more flexibility in managing resources. You can identify any resource as a proposed rather than a committed resource.

You can specify that a resource is generic. You can set up a resource as a budget resource to help you compare project costs against the established budget.

Proposing Tentative Resources

If you're using Project Professional 2010, you can specify that a resource be either proposed or committed to your project. Adding proposed resources and assigning them to tasks can help you decide whether a particular resource is needed without locking up their availability for other projects. You and other project managers and resource managers can search for resources and include or exclude proposed resources. This helps you build and preassign your team, and is particularly helpful in bidding situations.

All resources you add are booked as *committed* to your project by default. To specify that a resource be *proposed* rather than committed, follow these steps:

1. Display the Resource Sheet.
2. Click the resource you want to specify as proposed.
3. On the Resource tab, in the Properties group, click Information to open the Resource Information dialog box, shown in Figure 7-7.

Information

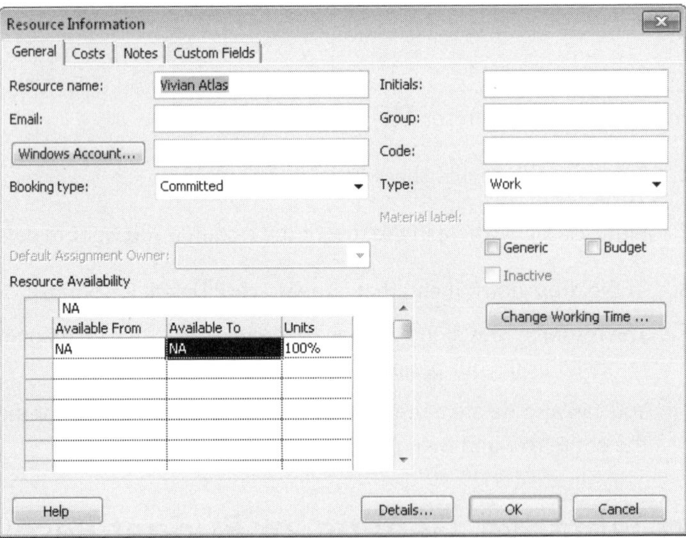

Figure 7-7 Use the Resource Information dialog box to view or enter details about a resource.

4. In the Resource Information dialog box, be sure that the General tab is showing.
5. In the Booking Type list, click Proposed.
6. Click OK.

Update Several Resources at Once

If you want to switch several resources to the Proposed status, you can do this in one step by selecting the resources before you open the Resource Information dialog box.

Click the first resource you want to change, and then use Shift or Ctrl to select the other resources you want to change. On the Resource tab, in the Properties group, click Information.

The Multiple Resource Information dialog box appears. (See Figure 7-8.) Only those fields that can be changed for multiple resources at once are available.

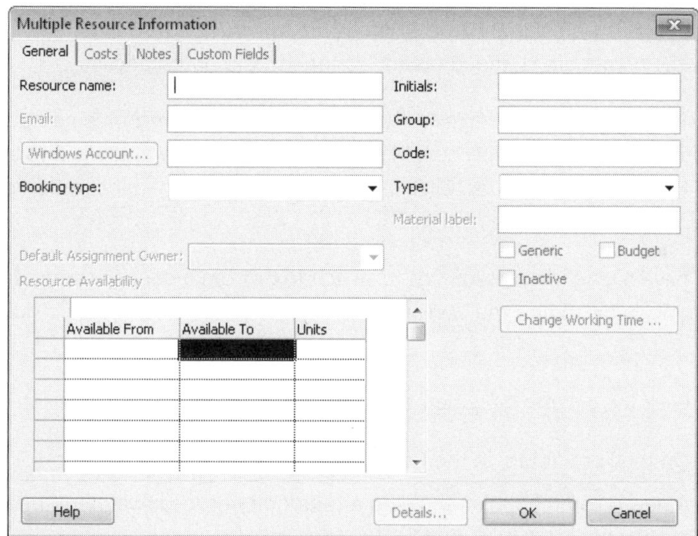

Figure 7-8 Use the Multiple Resource Information dialog box to make a global change to all selected resources.

In the Booking Type list, click Proposed, and then click OK. All the selected resources are changed to the proposed booking status.

Using Generic Resources as a Placeholder

You can enter actual names of resources or you can enter *generic resources*. A generic resource is listed by a title or other similar description instead of an actual name; for example, Accountant, Marketing Specialist, or Sales Representative. (See Figure 7-9.)

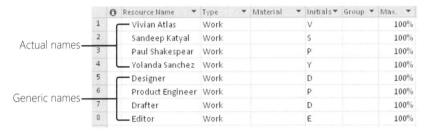

		Resource Name	Type	Material	Initials	Group	Max.
1		Vivian Atlas	Work		V		100%
2		Sandeep Katyal	Work		S		100%
3		Paul Shakespear	Work		P		100%
4		Yolanda Sanchez	Work		Y		100%
5		Designer	Work		D		100%
6		Product Engineer	Work		P		100%
7		Drafter	Work		D		100%
8		Editor	Work		E		100%

Actual names (rows 1–4)
Generic names (rows 5–8)

Figure 7-9 Use either actual resource names or generic categories of resources to get started.

As you bring resources into the project, you can leave the generic names or replace the generic names with actual names. Whenever you change resource names in the Resource Sheet, the names are changed on any assigned tasks automatically.

Generic Resource indicator

You can mark generic resources as such. Double-click the resource name to open the Resource Information dialog box. Make sure that the General tab is displayed, and then select the Generic check box. Click OK, and you'll see the generic resource icon appear in the Indicators field for the resource.

If you have a long list of resources to switch to or from a generic status, you can do this more quickly by adding the Generic column to the Resource Sheet. To do this, follow these steps:

1. Click the column heading next to where you want to insert the Generic column.

Insert Column

2. On the Format tab, in the Columns group, click Insert Column.

   A new column appears showing a temporary drop-down menu of all available resource fields. (See Figure 7-10.)

> **Note**
>
> **You can also right-click the column heading and then click Insert Column.**

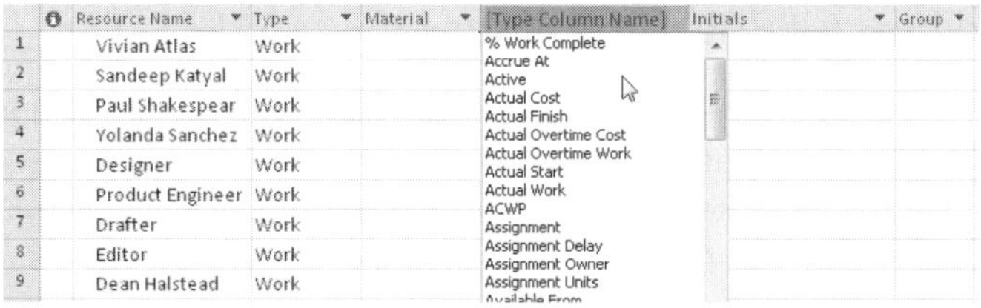

Figure 7-10 When you add a new column, the list of all available fields temporarily appears.

3. Type **g** to quickly go to Generic in the list, and then click it to apply the field to the column and dismiss the drop-down menu.

   If the list disappears before you can choose Generic from the list, select the column heading, which is labeled [Type Column Name], and type **generic**. The column appears as the Generic field.

4. Click Yes or No in the Generic field for the resources listed on the Resource Sheet.

Whether the Generic column is showing or not, you can use the Generic field to sort, group, or filter your resources to quickly find all your generic resources. Arranging the resource list in this way can help you determine any outstanding resource requirements.

For more information about sorting, grouping, or filtering resources by a particular field, see "Rearranging Your Project Information" on page 173.

Estimating with Generic Resources

Entering generic resources can help you estimate which resources and how many of a type of resource you need to meet your project finish date within a targeted budget. Enter your generic resources in the Resource Sheet, and then assign them to tasks.

For more information about associating resources with specific tasks, see Chapter 8.

Check the calculated project finish date to see whether you need additional resources to meet the targeted date. Check the total project costs to see if you need to change your resource mix to meet your budget.

When you finish tweaking your project plan to meet your requirements, you'll know which resources you need.

Specifying a Budget Resource

A *budget resource* is one that you will use specifically to capture a budget amount for a particular category related to the project as a whole. You create a resource that represents that project budget category; for example, Travel Budget, Equipment Cost Plan, or Project Materials. You can identify any work, material, or cost resource as a budget resource.

When you designate a resource as a budget resource, it can then be assigned only to the project summary task. This restriction is in place because the purpose of a budget resource is to reflect the planned budget for that category for the overall project.

For more information about the project summary task, see "Showing the Project Summary Task" on page 94.

You can use this information to compare your planned budget amounts for both costs and amounts of work against what is being scheduled or carried out in your project.

For more information about using budget resources to help monitor and control the project budget, see "Setting Up and Reviewing a Project Budget" on page 346.

Setting When Resources Are Available for Work

It's likely that many of your work resources will work full-time on your project. However, you might have many others who don't, for example:

- Resources who work part time.
- Resources who work part time on your project because they're being loaned from another group.
- Multiple individuals or machines (work resources) that perform the same function.
- A resource who will work full-time on your project until October, at which time she will be shared half time with another project that is ramping up then.

All of your work resources will take company holidays off, and most of them will take vacations and other days off throughout the year.

In Project 2010, you can account for these different types of resource availability and working times to schedule resources most effectively and accurately for your project.

Setting Working Times and Days Off for Work Resources

The basis of setting the availability of resources on the project is the resource's working time calendar, also simply known as the *resource calendar*. Each work resource has an individual resource calendar, which is initially based on the project calendar. You can customize each resource calendar as necessary to reflect the individual resource's specific working times and days off. Because the resource calendar indicates when a resource is available to work on assigned tasks, it affects the manner in which tasks are scheduled.

For more information about the project calendar, see "Setting Your Project Calendar" on page 84.

> **Note**
>
> **If you're working with enterprise projects and enterprise resources, the calendars are set by the project administrator. In this case, your ability to assign different calendars to resources might be limited.**

Viewing a Resource Calendar

As soon as you create a resource, the project calendar is assigned by default as the resource's working time calendar. To view a resource's working time calendar:

1. Display the Resource Sheet or other resource view.
2. Click the resource whose working time calendar you want to view.
3. On the Resource tab, in the Properties group, click Information.

   You can also simply double-click a resource to open the Resource Information dialog box.
4. On the General tab in the Resource Information dialog box, click the Change Working Time button.

   Change Working Time

   You can also open the Change Working Time dialog box from the ribbon. On the Project tab, in the Properties group, click Change Working Time.

   The working time calendar for the selected resource appears, as shown in Figure 7-11. The resource calendar is identical to the project calendar until you change it.

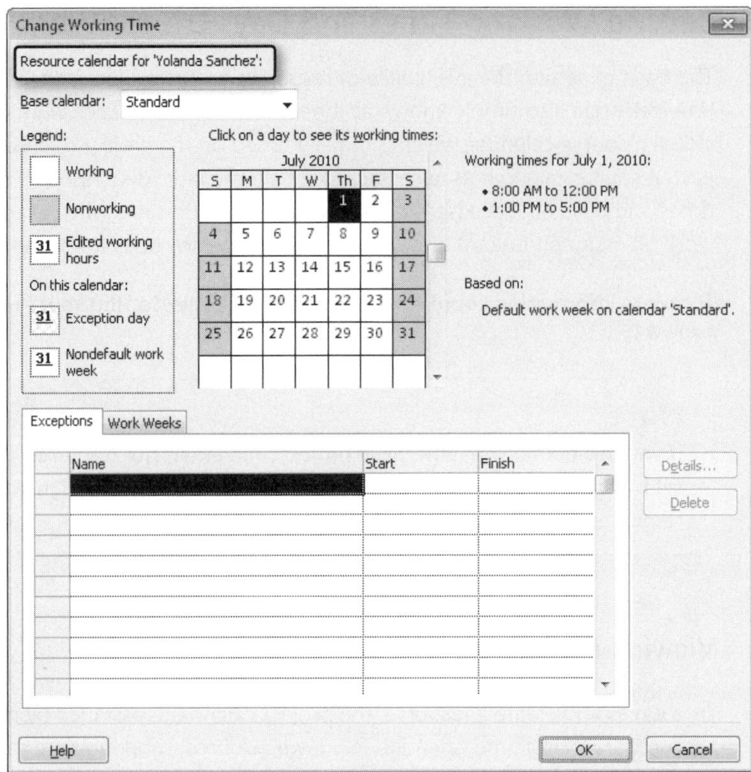

Figure 7-11 Use the Change Working Time dialog box to view or modify an individual resource's working times. These are the days and times when work on assigned tasks can be scheduled for this resource.

5. To see the working times for a particular day, click the date in the calendar thumbnail. The working times for that day appear to the right of the calendar.
6. To see the working times and days off for a typical week, click the Work Weeks tab. Be sure that the [Default] row is selected, and then click the Details button. In the Select Day(s) box, click the day of the week to see the working times in the grid to the right. When you are finished, click OK or Cancel.
7. Click OK or Cancel in the Change Working Time dialog box, and then click OK or Cancel in the Resource Information dialog box.

Applying a Different Base Calendar to a Resource

Project 2010 comes with three *base calendars*: Standard, Night Shift, and 24 Hours. These base calendars are like calendar templates that you can apply to a set of resources, a set of tasks, or the project as a whole.

You can apply the base calendar you want for a resource. If most of your team work a standard 8:00 A.M. to 5:00 P.M. day shift, you can keep the Standard calendar as the basis for their working time calendar. If others on your team work a graveyard shift, you can apply the Night Shift base calendar to those resources. To change which base calendar is applied to a resource, follow these steps:

1. In the Resource Sheet or other resource view, double-click the resource whose base calendar you want to change.
2. On the General tab in the Resource Information dialog box, click the Change Working Time button.
3. In the Base Calendar box, click the name of the base calendar you want to use as the basis of the current resource's calendar.
4. Click OK in the Change Working Time dialog box, and then click OK in the Resource Information dialog box.

Modifying a Resource Calendar

You can change an individual resource's calendar to reflect a different work schedule from others on the project team. For example, most everyone on your team might work Monday through Friday, 8:00 A.M. until 5:00 P.M. But suppose one team member works just three days a week, and another team member works weekend nights. You can change their resource calendars to fit their actual work schedules. This way, their assigned tasks will be scheduled only when they're actually available to work on them.

A resource might need an alternative work week specified for a particular period of time. One example might be a trainer working a combination of day, swing, graveyard, and weekend shifts throughout the next two weeks to train individuals on those shifts.

You can also update resource calendars to reflect team member work week exceptions such as vacation time, personal time off, sabbaticals, and so on. Updating the resource calendars helps keep your schedule accurate.

For more information about changing base calendars, including specifying the normal work week, alternative work weeks, one-time calendar exceptions, and recurring calendar exceptions, see "Modifying a Base Calendar" on page 85.

Creating a New Base Calendar for Resources

If you find you're making the same modifications to individual resource calendars repeatedly, you might do well to create an entirely new base calendar and apply it to the applicable resources. If you have a group of resources who work a different schedule—for example, a weekend shift or "four-tens"—create a new base calendar and apply it to those resources.

For details, see "Creating a New Base Calendar" on page 93.

When you create a new base calendar, it becomes available in any of the three calendar applications: project calendar, task calendar, or resource calendar. To apply the new base calendar to a resource, follow these steps:

1. Display the Resource Sheet or other resource view.
2. Double-click the resource to whom you want to assign the new base calendar.
3. In the Resource Information dialog box, click the Change Working Time button.
4. In the Base Calendar field, select the base calendar you want to apply to the selected resource.
5. Make any additional changes to the calendar as needed for this resource.

   These changes apply only to the selected resource; they do not change the original base calendar.

Note

Previous versions of Microsoft Project had a Project Guide to walk users through the definition of resource working times. Project Guides have been discontinued in Project 2010, so this method is no longer available.

INSIDE OUT **You cannot apply a base calendar to multiple resources**

You have to select each resource individually and then switch to the other base calendar you want. A faster way to apply base calendars is to work in the Resource Sheet. For each resource, select the new calendar in the Base Calendar field.

If you are changing the base calendar for many contiguous resources to the same base calendar, an even quicker method is to use the fill handle. Change the base calendar for the first resource, and then drag down the fill handle in the lower-right corner of the Base Calendar field for that resource and through the fields of the other resources.

Here's still another way to apply a base calendar quickly to multiple resources. Use this method when you want to make a few other changes to each resource's working time calendar in addition to changing the base calendar:

1. On the Project tab, in the Properties group, click Change Working Time.
2. In the For Calendar box, click the name of the resource whose base calendar you want to change.
3. In the Base Calendar box, click the name of the base calendar you want to apply to the selected resource.
4. Make any other changes to the working time calendar for the selected resource.
5. In the For Calendar box, click the name of the next resource whose base calendar you want to change.
6. In the message that appears, click Yes to save the changes you made to the previous resource's calendar.
7. Repeat steps 3 through 6 for the other resources.

Use whichever of these methods is most efficient for your purposes.

Specifying Resource Availability with Max Units

Suppose that your team includes three full-time resources, one half-time resource, and another who is available three days each week or 60 percent of the time.

You can specify this kind of resource availability by setting the resource's *maximum units*, which you might also think of as *resource units*.

By definition, the full-time resources are each available at 100% max units. The half-time resource is available at 50% max units. The other part-timer is available at 60% max units.

When you assign resources to tasks, those tasks are scheduled according to that resource's availability and indicates the point when the resource is considered overallocated.

But 100 percent or 50 percent of what, you might ask? The max units setting is multiplied by the availability shown in the resource calendar of working time and days off to determine the maximum level of availability of this resource for this project. If a resource calendar reflects a 40-hour work week, then 100% max units means a 40-hour work week for this project, while 50% max units means a 20-hour work week for this project. (See Figure 7-12.)

Resource Name	Max Units	Work	Details	M	T	W	T	F
Vivian Atlas	50%	20 hrs	Work	4h	4h	4h	4h	4h
Design interior pages		*20 hrs*	Work	4h	4h	4h	4h	4h
Paul Shakespear	100%	40 hrs	Work	8h	8h	8h	8h	8h
Perform system needs analysis		*40 hrs*	Work	8h	8h	8h	8h	8h

Figure 7-12 Given the same 40-hour-per-week resource calendar, a 100% max units resource works 8 hours per day, and a 50% max units resource works 4 hours per day.

Likewise, if a resource calendar reflects a 20-hour work week, then 100% max units means a 20-hour work week while 50% max units for this resource is a 10-hour work week. Again, max units play against the resource calendar. Figure 7-13 illustrates the schedules for these two scenarios.

Resource Name	Max Units	Work	Details	M	T	W	T	F
Sandeep Katyal	50%	20 hrs	Work	2h	2h	2h	2h	2h
Design Home page		*20 hrs*	Work	2h	2h	2h	2h	2h
Yolanda Sanchez	100%	40 hrs	Work	4h	4h	4h	4h	4h
Develop Web structure		*40 hrs*	Work	4h	4h	4h	4h	4h

Figure 7-13 Given the same 20-hour-per-week resource calendar, a 100% max units resource works 4 hours per day, and a 50% max units resource works 2 hours per day.

Here's another scenario: suppose that you have three engineers, two architects, and four drafters, all working a full-time schedule. Instead of naming them individually, you decide you want to name your resources by their functions and consolidate them into a single resource representing multiple individuals. You can do that with max units as well. The three engineers together are available at 300 percent, the two architects at 200 percent, and the four drafters at 400 percent.

If you have three full-time drafters and one half-time drafter, your **Drafter** resource is available at 350% max units.

To enter max units, simply type the percentage in the Max. Units field in the Resource Sheet. (See Figure 7-14.) The default for the Max. Units field is 100%.

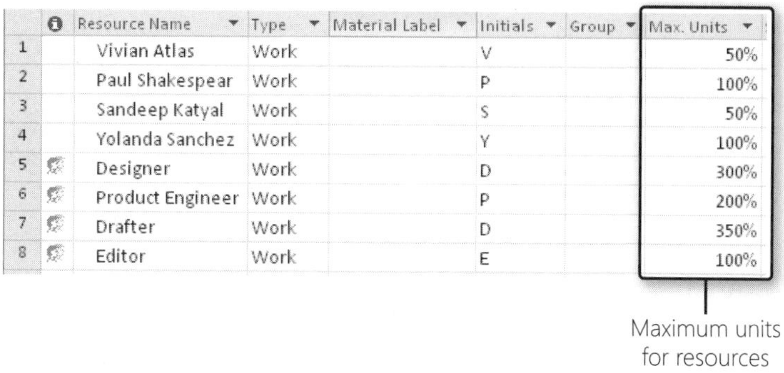

		Resource Name	Type	Material Label	Initials	Group	Max. Units
1		Vivian Atlas	Work		V		50%
2		Paul Shakespear	Work		P		100%
3		Sandeep Katyal	Work		S		50%
4		Yolanda Sanchez	Work		Y		100%
5		Designer	Work		D		300%
6		Product Engineer	Work		P		200%
7		Drafter	Work		D		350%
8		Editor	Work		E		100%

Maximum units for resources

Figure 7-14 You can enter max units when you enter resource names, or come back to it later.

Now suppose that your staffing plan specifies that you'll start the project life cycle needing four drafters. After three months, you'll need only three drafters. Two months later, you'll need only one. To specify variable resource quantity or availability over time, follow these steps:

1. In the Resource Sheet, double-click the resource whose maximum units you want to adjust.

   The Resource Information dialog box appears. Make sure the General tab is displayed.

2. In the Resource Availability table, enter the first date range for the resource's first max units specification.

   That is, enter the beginning date in the first Available From field, the ending date in the first Available To field, and the max units that will be available during those dates in the Units field. For example, in the first row enter **5/2/11** under Available From, enter **7/29/11** under Available To, and enter **400%** under Units.

3. In the second row, enter the second date range for the resource's max units specification.

   For example, enter **8/1/11** under Available From, enter **9/30/11** under Available To, and enter **300%** under Units.

4. Continue in this manner until your entire resource availability specification is set.

   For example, enter **10/3/11** under Available From, leave **NA** in the Available To field, and enter **100%** under Units. (See Figure 7-15.)

   NA in the Available From field indicates that there is no start date to the availability. Likewise, NA in the Available To field indicates that there is no set end date to the availability. NA is the default availability specification.

Available From	Available To	Units
5/2/2011	7/29/2011	400%
8/1/2011	9/30/2011	300%
10/3/2011	NA	100%

Figure 7-15 Use the Resource Availability table in the Resource Information dialog box to specify multiple levels of max units throughout the project.

INSIDE OUT Resources with variable max units show as 0% max units

Resources whose quantity or availability are set to change over time show max units of 0%. There's really no other situation in which you'd have max units of 0% (otherwise, why add the resource to the project?).

So when you see a resource with 0% max units, double-click it to open the Resource Information dialog box, and you'll see the whole story in the Resource Availability table.

If this doesn't work for you, or if you want to provide additional information for others who might view the project plan, you can also add a note to the resource. With the resource selected, on the Resource tab, in the Properties group, click Notes. Enter a note such as "This resource is set for varying availability over time" or "Check the Resource Availability table for details about max units." The note icon appears in the Indicators field. You can rest your mouse pointer over the Note indicator to read the reminder.

For more information, see "Adding a Note Regarding a Resource" on page 279.

Note

By default, max units are expressed as a percentage. You can represent them as a decimal if you prefer. On the File tab, click Options, and then click Schedule in the left pane. In the Schedule section, in the Show Assignment Units As A box, select Decimal. Now, instead of 100%, one full-time resource is shown as having 1 max unit.

INSIDE OUT **Allow for nonproject work**

It's a reality that your resources are not likely to spend every minute of every work day devoted to project tasks. To allow for department meetings, administrative tasks, and other nonproject work, you can adjust the project calendar, the resource calendar, or max units.

First, determine how much nonproject work there is. If you're thinking of the project as a whole, adjust the project calendar. If you think of nonproject work in terms of individual resources, adjust the individual resource calendars. For example, instead of defining a day as 8 hours long, you might define it as 6 or 7 hours. Changing the calendar directly affects the days and times when tasks are scheduled.

You can also adjust max units for resources. Instead of setting up full-time resources with 100% max units, set them up with 75% max units. This method distributes task scheduling over time, without regard to specific days and hours.

With either method, you can keep from having every single hour of the day being scheduled for project work and allow for the realities of a normal workday.

If you're set up for enterprise project management using Project Professional and Project Server, you can use the timesheets and administrative time to formalize and track resources' nonproject activities.

For more information about administrative projects, see "Reviewing and Approving Administrative Time" on page 956.

Note

You can enter max units with varying availability and a customized resource calendar for equipment resources just as you can for human resources. Both equipment and human resources are considered work resources. Setting equipment working times and availability can help account for other projects using the same equipment at different times and can schedule downtime for preventive maintenance.

Adding Detailed Resource Information

Along with the basic resource information such as the resource name, type, units, and calendar, you can add supplementary information to work, material, or cost resources. This data can include additional fields of resource information, notes, or hyperlinks.

Working with Supplemental Resource Fields

You can add initials, group designations, or a code to a resource by using the appropriate field in the Resource Sheet or on the General tab in the Resource Information dialog box. The following list provides examples of how you might use these fields:

- **Initials** If you want a resource's initials, rather than his or her entire name, to appear in certain fields in your project plan, enter the initials in the Initials field in the Resource Sheet or on the General tab in the Resource Information dialog box.
- **Group** Use the Group field to specify any categories of resources that might be useful for sorting, grouping, or filtering. For example, you can specify the department the resources come from, such as Product Development or Marketing. If you are using contracted resources, you can enter their company's name in the Group field, or you can use the Group field to specify the resource's title or skill set—for example, Engineer, Architect, or Designer.

> **Note**
>
> **You cannot assign a group name to a task. The group simply provides more information about a resource so that you can sort, group, or filter resources.**

- **Code** Enter any code meaningful to you or your company in the Code field. It can be any alphanumeric designation you want. In fact, you can use it the way you use the Group field. You can enter job codes or skill codes, for example. Like the Group field, you can then sort, group, or filter these codes.

Cost-related fields are an important part of the Resource Sheet. The Resource Information dialog box also includes a Costs tab.

For more information about resource cost information and using the cost fields in the Resource Sheet and the Resource Information dialog box, see "Planning Resource Costs" on page 323.

In addition to the default Entry table on the Resource Sheet, other tables containing different collections of resource fields are available. To apply a different table to the Resource Sheet:

1. Display the Resource Sheet.

2. On the View tab, in the Data group, click Tables. Click the table you want.

   If the table you want is not listed, click More Tables. Click the table in the list (see Figure 7-16), and then click Apply.

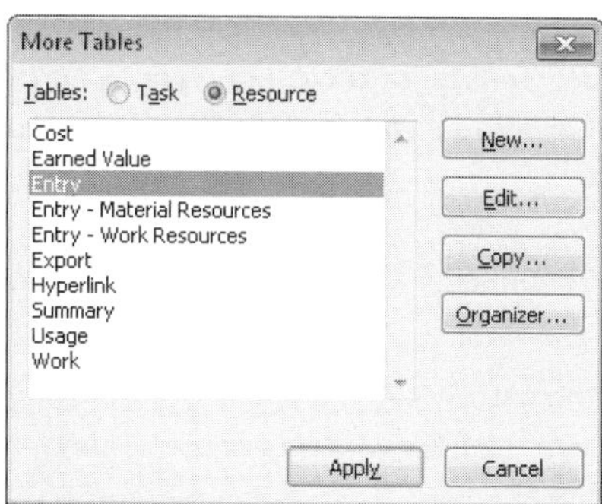

Figure 7-16 Apply any table that fits what you're trying to do.

Dozens of additional resource fields are available to add to your Resource Sheet. Some examples include Available From, Booking Type, Cost Center, and many more. To add a new field to your current table:

1. Click the column heading next to where you want to insert the new column.
2. On the Format tab, in the Columns group, click Insert Column.

   A new column appears showing a temporary drop-down menu of all available resource fields.
3. Click a field to apply it to the new column.

   The fields listed are all resource fields. You can quickly move to a field by typing the first one or two letters of its name.

To hide a field you don't need, follow these steps:

1. Click the column heading you want to hide.

Hide Column

2. On the Format tab, in the Columns group, click Column Settings, and then click Hide Column. You can also simply press the Delete key.

   The column is hidden, but the information is not deleted. It's still in the project database and can be shown again whenever you display its column.

Hide a Column by Making It Very Narrow

You might frequently hide and insert certain columns, for example, when you print a view for presenting at a status meeting. If you grow tired of constantly hiding and then re-inserting these columns, you can just make them very narrow. Position your mouse pointer on the right edge of the heading for the column you want to hide. When the pointer becomes a black crosshair, drag to the left to narrow the column until the contents cannot be seen.

If you drag past the left column edge, the column will be completely hidden, although it is actually still there.

When you're ready to display the narrow column again, drag the edge of the column heading to the right until you can read the contents of the column.

There's no indication that a column you hid completely is there—you just have to remember...and then be rather dexterous with your mouse.

Specifying Contact Information

If you plan to communicate project information to resources electronically, you might need to complete one or more of the following fields on the General tab in the Resource Information dialog box:

- **E-mail** Specifies the resource's e-mail address, which is essential if you exchange e-mail messages, schedule notes, or project files with team members. If the resource is outside your company—that is, the resource uses a different e-mail system than you—be sure to specify the full e-mail address; as in someone@example.com. If you added resources from your MAPI e-mail address book (Resource, Insert, Add Resources, Address Book), the resources e-mail addresses are already filled in.

  For more information about communicating project information through e-mail, see Chapter 19, "Integrating Project 2010 with Outlook."

- **Windows account** Finds the resource's user account in the local address book and places it in that resource's Windows User Account field. Click the Windows Account button. In the alert that appears, click Allow. If there is more than one match, click the entry you want in the Check Names dialog box. Click OK. This field is useful if you're working in an enterprise project management environment, and the enterprise resources are set up in Project Server with Windows user account names.

Adding a Note Regarding a Resource

Use notes to add comments regarding a resource. Notes might include information about the skills or experience of the resource or anything you believe is pertinent to this resource working on this project. To add a note to a resource:

1. Display the Resource Sheet or other resource view, and then click the name of the resource to which you want to add a note.

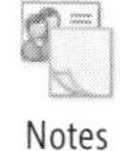

Notes

2. On the Resource tab, in the Properties group, click Notes

   The Resource Information dialog box appears with the Notes tab open, as shown in Figure 7-17.

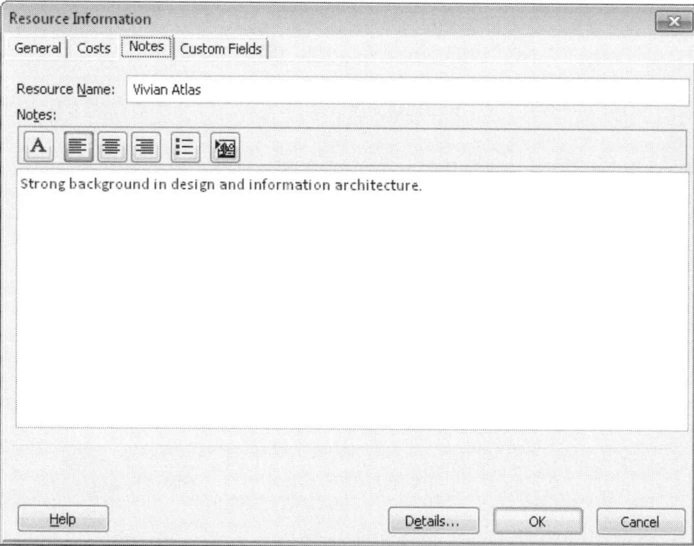

Figure 7-17 Enter relevant notes about a resource on the Notes tab of the Resource Information dialog box. You can also attach outside documents by using the Notes tab.

3. In the Notes area, type the note.

4. When you are finished, click OK.

Note indicator

   The Note indicator appears next to the resource name in the Indicators field of the Resource Sheet. (See Figure 7-18.) You can double-click this icon when you want to read the note.

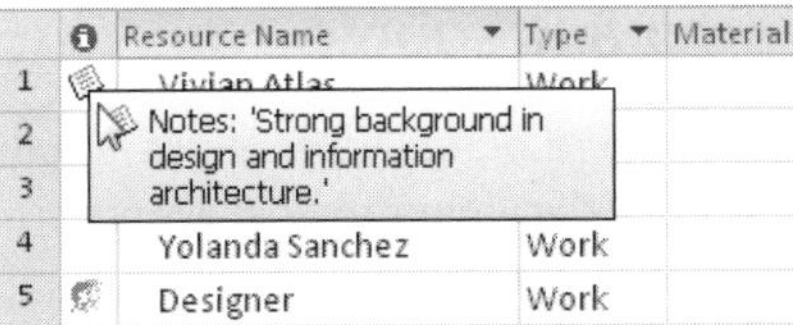

Figure 7-18 Position your mouse pointer over the Note indicator to read the note. Double-click the indicator to open the Notes tab in the Resource Information dialog box.

Hyperlinking to Resource Information

If there's a document or website relevant to a resource, you can insert a column containing a hyperlink to reference it. This technique is a very efficient method for opening associated documents quickly. To insert a hyperlink, follow these steps:

1. Display the Resource Sheet or other resource view.
2. Right-click the resource to which you want to link a web page or document.
3. On the drop-down menu that appears, click Hyperlink.

   Hyperlink

   The Insert Hyperlink dialog box appears.
4. In the Text To Display box, type a descriptive name for the document to which you are linking; for example, **Quarterly Goals**.
5. Find and select the document or site you want to link to your project file. (See Figure 7-19.)

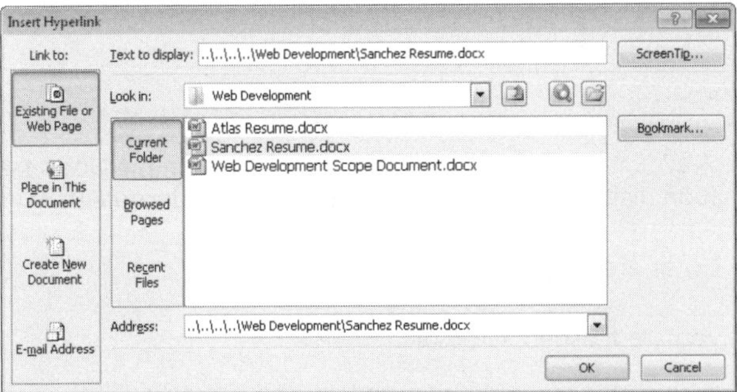

Figure 7-19 The path and name of the selected document or website appear in the Address box.

6. Click OK.

   The Hyperlink indicator appears in the Indicators field of the Resource Sheet, as shown in Figure 7-20.

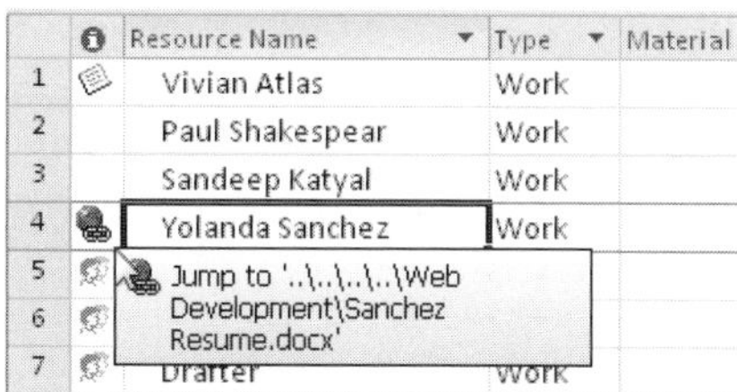

Resource Name
Type
Material
1
Vivian Atlas
Work
2
Paul Shakespear
Work
3
Sandeep Katyal
Work
4
Yolanda Sanchez
Work
5
6
7
Jump to '..\..\..\..\Web Development\Sanchez Resume.docx'

Figure 7-20 Position your mouse pointer over the Hyperlink indicator to read the link. Click the indicator to jump to the link's location.

Whenever you need to review the target of the hyperlink, just click the Hyperlink indicator. The content opens in its own application window.

If you have difficulty clicking the Hyperlink indicator or getting the target to open, right-click anywhere in the resource row, point to Hyperlink, and then click Open Hyperlink. If a security message appears, click Yes to continue.

CHAPTER 8

Assigning Resources to Tasks

You have tasks. You have resources. Now you need to get them together. Tasks + resources = assignments. With human and equipment resources assigned to tasks, Microsoft Project 2010 can create a project schedule that reflects not only the project calendar, task durations, dependencies, and constraints, but also the calendars and availability of assigned resources. With material and cost resources assigned to tasks, you can track the depletion of project-related inventory as well as specific cost items to ensure that you have what you need to accomplish tasks when needed.

Assigning Work Resources to Tasks

When you assign a work resource, you are attaching the resource name to a task and then indicating how much of the resource's total availability is to be devoted to this task.

When you first add a resource to the project plan, through the use of max units (you might also think of them as *resource units*), you specify how available this resource will be to this project. For example, if the resource is available full time on the project—say, 40 hours per week—you would probably specify that the resource has 100% max units. If another resource is available 20 hours per week, you would probably specify that this resource has 50% max units. If you have three of the same type of resource (for example, three graphic designers), you could indicate that they have a total of 300% max units.

When you assign these resources to tasks, you take the idea of availability a step further by using *assignment units*. With max units, you specify resource availability to the project as a whole. With assignment units, you specify resource allocation to the specific task to which the resource is assigned.

For example, one resource might be available full time to perform one task. When that's finished, she'll be assigned full time to the next task, and so on. Upon assigning this resource to the task, you indicate 100% assignment units for this resource.

On the other hand, you might have another full-time resource who is spending 40 percent of his time on one task and 60 percent of his time on another task that takes place during the same period. For the first task you specify 40% assignment units; and for the second task, 60%. The assignment units specify the percentage of the full 100% max units being used for the task in question.

Now, take the case of a half-time resource (50% max units) who is spending all available time on one task. If you specify assignment units greater than 50% for this resource, the resource will be marked as overallocated because of that task. If this resource is spending half her time on one task and half on another, the assignment units are 25% for each task.

Note

If this resource is assigned to other tasks at the same time, Project 2010 allows it but flags the resource and the assignment as overallocated—that is, having more work than there is time, or availability, to do the tasks.

Project 2010 does not flag overallocations on resources assigned to placeholder tasks—that is, manually scheduled tasks that don't have enough scheduling information (two out of three of duration, start date, or finish date) entered yet.

Finally, let's look at the case of the three graphic designers whose max units are 300%. When you start to assign tasks to a *consolidated resource* such as this one, by default Project 2010 does not assume that you want to use all three on one task. You can, but the default assignment units are 100%. You can change those units to any increment up to 300%.

Creating Work Resource Assignments

By creating an assignment, you specify both the resources assigned to a task as well as their associated assignment units. Using the Assign Resources dialog box, you can assign one resource to a task, multiple resources to a task, or multiple resources to multiple tasks. To assign a work resource to a task, follow these steps:

1. In the Gantt Chart or other task sheet, click the task to which you want to assign resources.
2. On the Resource tab, in the Assignments group, click Assign Resources.

   Assign Resources

   The Assign Resources dialog box appears, as shown in Figure 8-1.

INSIDE OUT Max units vs. assignment units

Because max units and assignment units are both called "units," the terms can be confusing. They're related but different. It would be nice if the respective names were a little more different and a little more descriptive. However, they're vital to your assignment scheduling, and they're what you have to work with. So you need to keep them straight in your mind.

The Max. Units field applies to resources. Think of max units as total *resource units*. The value you enter in the Max. Units field tells Project 2010 how much of a particular resource you have available for work on this project, whether it's half of full time (50%), full time (100%), or three full-time equivalents (300%). Also remember that this percentage is based on the available time reflected in the resource's working time calendar.

The Units field applies to assignments. Think of the Units field as *assignment units*. The value you enter in the Units field tells Project 2010 how much of the resource you can use to work on this specific assignment.

Another way to differentiate the two kinds of units is to pay attention to the context in which you see them. If you see a Units field in the Resource Sheet, it's referring to the resource's availability on the entire project. If you see a Units field in the Assign Resources dialog box or the Assignment Information dialog box, it's referring to the resource's availability on the individual assignment.

Note

Max units and assignment units can be expressed in either percentages or decimals. The default is to express them as percentages.

To change the units to decimals, on the File tab, click Options, and then click Schedule in the left pane. Under Schedule, in the box labeled Show Assignment Units As A, click Decimal.

A resource working full time on an assignment is shown as having 1 assignment unit instead of 100%. A resource that has 450% max units in the Resource Sheet is shown as having 4.5 max units.

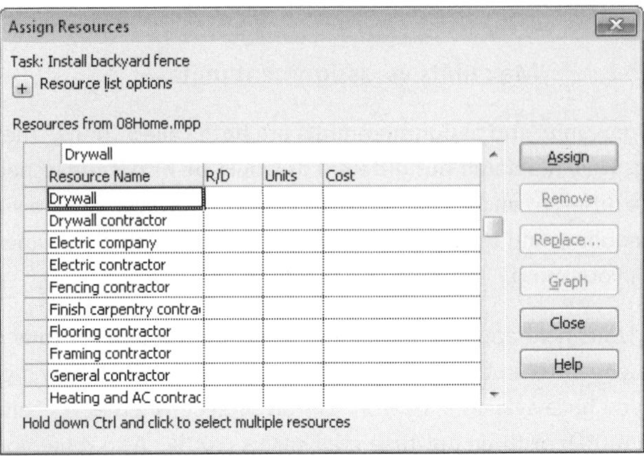

Figure 8-1 Use the Assign Resources dialog box to designate details about task assignments.

3. In the dialog box, click the name of the work resource you want to assign to the selected task, and then click the Assign button.

   The resource name moves to the top of the Resources list in the table, and a default percentage appears in the Units field for the resource. For individual resources, the default assignment units are the same as the resource's max units. For consolidated resources with more than 100% max units, the default assignment units are 100%.

4. If you want to assign a second resource, click that resource's name, and then click the Assign button.

5. Modify the Units field for any assigned resources as necessary.

> **Note**
>
> **You can select all resources to be assigned to a task and assign them at once. Click the first resource, hold down Ctrl, and then click all other resources. Click the Assign button.**

6. Repeat steps 4 and 5 for all resources you want to assign to the selected task.

7. To assign resources to a different task, click the next task for which you want to make assignments.

   You don't have to close the Assign Resources dialog box to select a different task.

8. Repeat steps 3 through 6 to assign resources to all tasks as necessary.

9. When you are finished assigning resources to tasks, click the Close button.

> **Note**
>
> **Unlike with other dialog boxes, you can switch back and forth between the task sheet and the Assign Resources dialog box. It's handy to keep the dialog box open while you're working out all the details you need to finish making your assignments.**

Adding and Assigning Resources at the Same Time

Suppose that you want to assign a specific resource to a task, but that resource isn't listed in the Assign Resources dialog box because you haven't added her to your Resource Sheet yet. You can add new resources to your project plan while working in the Assign Resources dialog box and then immediately assign the resource to tasks. You can then go to the Resource Sheet and complete any detailed resource information you want. To add new resources in the Assign Resources dialog box, follow these steps:

1. In the Gantt Chart or other task sheet, click the task to which you want to assign resources.

2. On the Resource tab, in the Assignments group, click Assign Resources to display the Assign Resources dialog box.

3. In the Resources table, type the new resource name in the first blank Resource Name field, and then press Tab to enter the name and stay in the same field.

4. Click the Assign button.

   The resource name moves to the top of the Resources list in the table, and 100% appears in the Units field for the resource.

5. Adjust the assignment units if necessary. Assign any additional tasks you want.

6. When you are finished, click the Close button.

Resource Sheet

7. Switch to the Resource Sheet. The quickest way is to click the Resource Sheet shortcut in the lower-right corner of the status bar (next to the Zoom slider).

   The new resource you added in the Assign Resources dialog box is listed. Modify any resource fields as necessary; for example, Max. Units, Calendar, or Group.

Project Management Practices: Assigning the Right Resources

As the project manager, you consider several factors when deciding who to assign to which tasks. One of the most important factors is the resource's skill set, competencies, and proficiencies. His ability to carry out the assigned task is essential to the success of the task. You can set up your resources in Project 2010 so that you can find and assign resources based on their skill sets.

Another important factor is the resource's availability. If the perfect resource is 100 percent committed to another project during the same timeframe as your project, you can't use this resource. Project 2010 can help you find resources that are available to work on your project.

There are other factors as well:

- **Experience** Have the resources you're considering for the assignment done similar or related work before? How well did they do it? Perhaps you can use this assignment as an opportunity to pair a more experienced team member with one who has less experience. This pairing can set up a mentoring situation in which both team members can benefit, and your team is strengthened in the long run.
- **Enthusiasm** Are the resources you're considering personally interested in the assignment? A resource with less experience but more enthusiasm can often be more effective than a seasoned but bored resource.
- **Team dynamics** Do certain tasks require several resources to work together? If so, are the resources you're considering likely to work well together? Do they have a history of conflicts with each other? Do certain team members have good synergy with one another?
- **Speed** Is alacrity important to your project, all other things being equal? Some resources work faster than others. This speed can be a function of experience, or it can be a function of working style or level of quality. Determine how important speed is to your project and assign tasks accordingly.
- **Cost** Are you hiring contractors for the project? If you have specific budget limitations, cost is definitely a factor. Sometimes, any rework required by an inexpensive but also inexperienced resource can negate any cost savings. Conversely, sometimes more expensive resources can be a bargain, especially if they work faster than the norm.
- **Quality** What are your quality standards for the project? Try to assign resources who can match those standards.

Note

If you double-click any resource name in the Assign Resources dialog box, and the Resource Information dialog box appears for that resource. You can then enter detailed resource information as needed.

You can add an entire group of resources from your e-mail address book, Microsoft Project Server 2010, or your network's Active Directory listings to the Assign Resources dialog box, just as you can in the Resource Sheet. To add resources from a server, follow these steps:

1. With any task sheet open, on the Resource tab, in the Assignments group, click Assign Resources.

2. If necessary, click the + button next to Resource List Options to expand the dialog box, as shown in Figure 8-2.

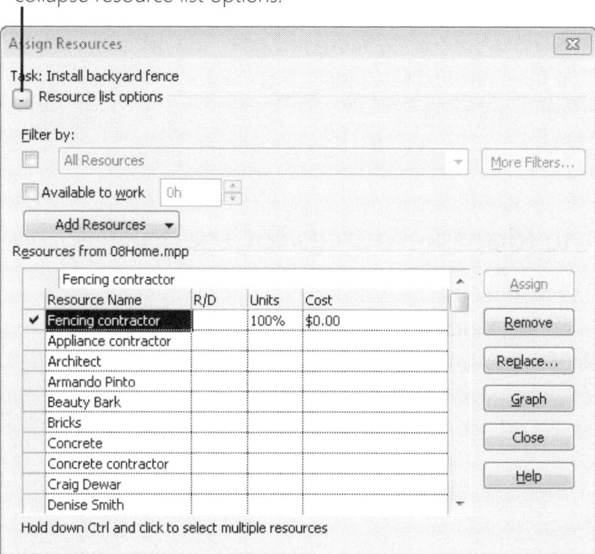

Figure 8-2 Click the - button next to Resource List Options to collapse the Assign Resources dialog box; click the + button next to Resource List Options to expand it.

3. Click the Add Resources button.

4. Click From Active Directory if you are working with Windows Server and want to add resources from the Active Directory service.

   Click From Address Book if you want to add resources from your e-mail program's address book.

   Click From Project Server if you want to add the resources who are listed as Project Server 2010 users.

5. Click the resources you want from the source you choose, and then click the Add button to add the selected resources to the Assign Resources dialog box.

6. After the resources are added, you can immediately assign them to tasks.

Avoid Assigning Resources to Summary Tasks

Be very careful about assigning resources to summary tasks. Technically you can do it, and in some cases it might be beneficial. However, having resources assigned to summary tasks can cause confusion when you review rolled-up values for work, actual work, cost, and so on. By default, the summary task Gantt bar does not show the resource name, which can cause still more confusion.

Also take care when you create additional tasks and make them subtasks under existing tasks that have resources assigned. This creates a situation where resources are now assigned to summary tasks.

Finding the Right Resources for the Job

You can use the Assign Resources dialog box to narrow your list of resources to only those who meet the criteria needed for the tasks you're assigning. For example, you can filter the resource list to show only those resources who belong to the marketing department or only those resources who have a particular job code or skills definition. Using resource fields such as Group or Code comes in handy in these scenarios.

If you create and apply resource outline codes, you can also filter for a particular outline code level.

To find resources that meet certain criteria, follow these steps:

1. With any task sheet displayed, on the Resource tab, in the Assignments group, click Assign Resources.

2. If necessary, click the + button next to Resource List Options.

   The Assign Resources dialog box expands to show the Filter By box.

3. Select the check box immediately under Filter By.

4. Click the arrow in the All Resources box, and then scroll to and click the filter that applies to the type of resource you want to find—for example, Group or Resources–Material, as shown in Figure 8-3.

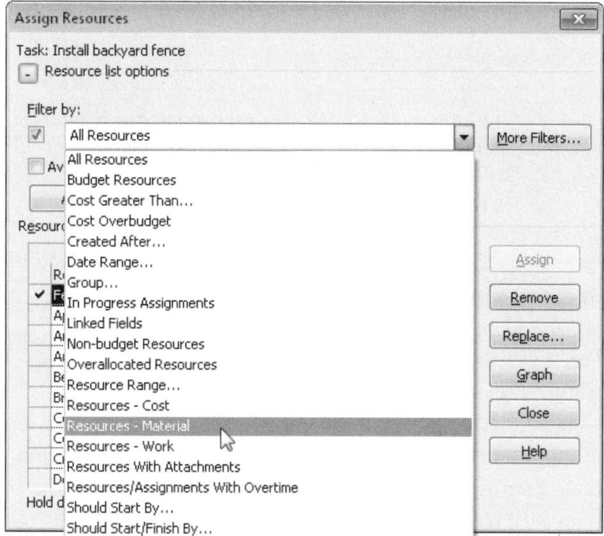

Figure 8-3 Select the check box under Filter By, and then click the name of filter that describes the type of resource you're seeking.

Any filter that requires additional information includes an ellipsis (...) after its name. Click the filter, enter the requested information in the dialog box that appears, and then click OK.

As soon as you select a filter, the list in the Resources table changes to show only those resources that meet the filter's criteria, as shown in Figure 8-4.

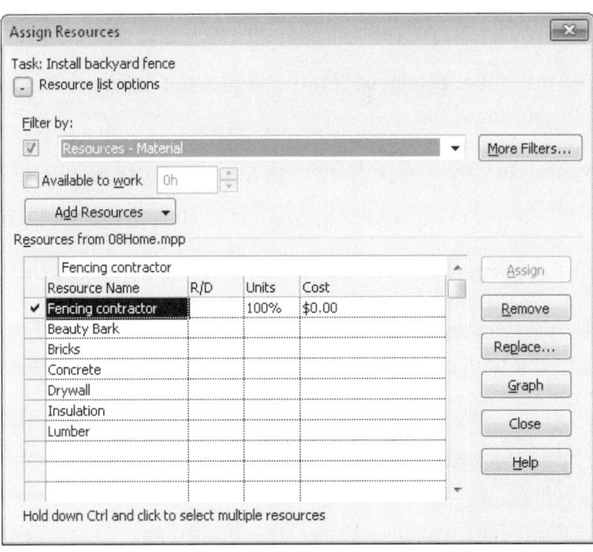

Figure 8-4 By filtering your resource list, you can choose from a set of targeted resources that meet the criteria for the tasks you are currently assigning.

5. Assign resources to tasks as usual.

6. When you want to review the full list of resources again, click All Resources in the Filter By list, or simply clear the Filter By check box.

INSIDE OUT Missing resource filters

There is no built-in resource filter for Code or Outline Code, but you can create your own filters. To do this, in the Assign Resources dialog box, click the More Filters button, and then click New in the dialog box. Specify the field name, test, and value that defines your new filter. For example, you can create a filter that finds all resources that have a Code field greater than 9100. Or you can create a filter that finds all resources that have an outline code equal to Engineer-1.

If you're using Microsoft Project Professional 2010, you might have added certain resources to your project as *proposed resources*. It would be nice, therefore, to have a filter to find only confirmed resources or to find just proposed resources when setting up assignments. But such filters are not built-in, and you need to create them yourself.

For more information about adding proposed resources, see "Proposing Tentative Resources" on page 262. For more information about creating your own filter, see "Customizing Filters" on page 1129.

Define Resource Roles

If you set up a resource field that defines certain roles, job titles, or skill sets, you can use the Assign Resources dialog box to filter for resources with specific criteria. For example, you can use the Group field in the Resource Sheet to specify the type of resource, for example, Writer, Editor, Designer, or Programmer. To assign writing tasks, you can filter for Writer in the Group field. To assign programming tasks, you can filter for Programmer in the Group field. Filtering by the Group field can be especially useful if you have a large number of resources.

Other fields you can use to define roles or skill sets include Code and Outline Code. You can also use custom fields such as Text1 or Number1 to specify skills descriptions or job title numbers. The Code field is present by default on the Entry table of the Resource Sheet. You can enter any alphanumeric string you like in the Code field. Enter the set of skill codes that correspond with how you identify skills in your organization or develop your own scheme. For example, you can have a set of codes for Designer-1, Designer-2, Programmer-1, and so on. As long as you enter your codes consistently for your resources, you can successfully sort, group, and filter resources by their code.

For a more sophisticated and hierarchical code scheme, set up an outline code for skill sets. With an outline code, you can have a higher level, such as Designer, and sublevels of 1, 2, and 3. You can then filter or group on the upper-level Designer or find just designers at level 3. First set up your outline code, and then apply the appropriate outline code to resources.

With all your custom codes, you can create a lookup table (also known as a *pick list*), so that you don't have to remember the exact wording or format for entering the code.

For more information about working with fields, see "Customizing Fields" on page 1107. For more information about outline codes, see "Working with Outline Codes" on page 1116.

You can filter to see only those resources who have time to take on more work. For example, suppose that you assigned all your resources to tasks. Then you add several more tasks, and you want to assign only resources who have time for them. To filter for resources with a certain amount of available time, do the following:

1. With any task sheet open, select the task to which you want to assign resources with available time.
2. On the Resource tab, in the Assignments group, click Assign Resources.

3. If necessary, click the + button next to Resource List Options to expand the Assign Resources dialog box.
4. Select the Available To Work check box.

   In the Available To Work box, enter the amount of time needed for the task you're about to assign. For example, if you need a resource with 4 days of available time, enter **4d** in the box. As soon as you enter the amount of time, the list in the Resources table changes to show only those resources who have the specified availability.
5. Assign resources to the selected task as usual.
6. If you click another task, the filter is applied to that task as well. The list of resources available to work for the specified amount of time might change, depending on the task dates and the resource availability during those dates.
7. When you want to see the full list of resources again, simply clear the Available To Work check box.

Note

You can find resources in the category you want who have the right amount of available time for your assignments. Under Resource List Options in the Assign Resources dialog box, select both check boxes under Filter By. Select the resource filter you want to use in the first box, and then enter the amount of time in the Available To Work box.

You can review graphs of resource availability from within the Assign Resources dialog box. This can help you decide which work resource should be assigned to a task. To review the resource availability graph, follow these steps:

1. With any task sheet displayed, on the Resource tab, in the Assignments group, click Assign Resources.
2. In the Assign Resources dialog box, click the work resource whose availability graph you want to view. Note that availability applies only to work resources, not to material or cost resources.
3. Click the Graph button.

   The view changes to a combination view with the task sheet in the upper pane and the Resource Graph in the lower pane, as shown in Figure 8-5. If necessary, move the Assign Resource dialog box out of the way.

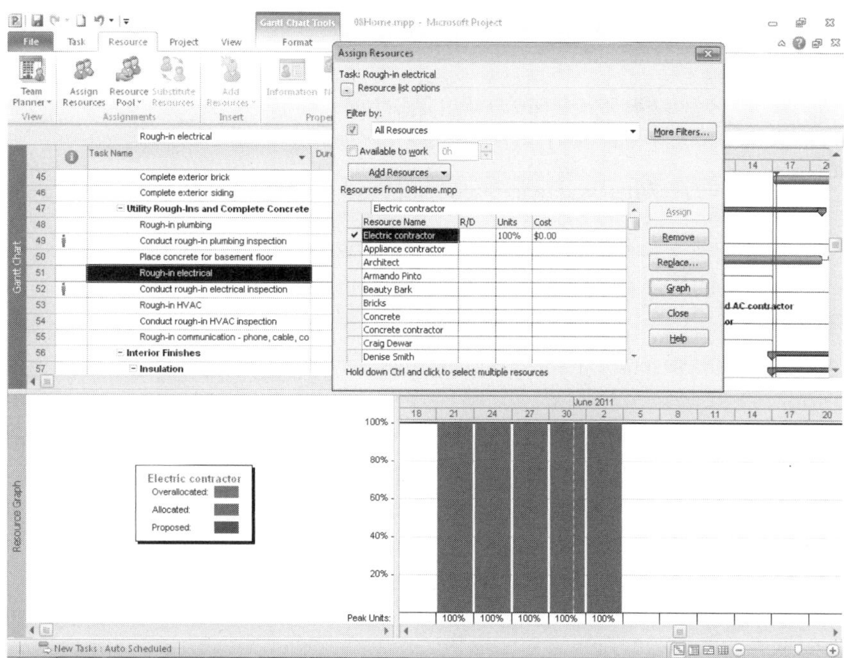

Figure 8-5 In the default Peak Units version of the Resource Graph, you can review how much the selected resource is assigned to tasks over time.

4. To change the field on which the graph is based, on the Format tab, in the Data group, click the arrow in the Graph box, and then click another field—for example, Remaining Availability or Work.

Graph:

Peak Units

The Remaining Availability graph shows when the selected resource has any available time for more assignments. The Work graph shows the total work for all the selected resource's assignments.

5. If you want to zoom the graph up or down, you need to click in the task sheet in the upper pane. Then use the Zoom slider or, click View, Zoom, click the arrow in the Timescale box, and then select the timescale zoom level you want. The zoom level in the task sheet is adopted by the Resource Graph in the lower pane.

Timescale:

Days

Previous Resource

Next Resource

6. To switch the graph to other resources assigned to the same task, click Format, Navigate, and then click Previous Resource or Next Resource.

   You cannot switch the graph to a different resource by clicking another name in the Assign Resources dialog box.

7. When you're finished with the Assign Resources dialog box, click Close.

8. To restore your task sheet to the full screen again, double-click the pane divider.

For more information about the Resource Graph, see "Charting Team Availability with the Resource Graph" on page 140, "Viewing Resource Workloads" on page 404, and "Modifying the Resource Graph" on page 1091.

Using the Team Planner to Assign Resources

NEW!

The Team Planner is a new view in Project Professional 2010 that you can use to interactively arrange the scheduling of tasks along a graphical timeline.

Assigning Resources in the Team Planner

To assign resources using the Team Planner, follow these steps.

Team Planner

1. On the View tab, in the Resource Views group, click Team Planner.

   You can also click the Team Planner view shortcut in the lower-right corner of the screen, next to the Zoom slider.

   As shown in Figure 8-6, the resources are listed along the left side, with the project timeline stretching out horizontally from there. Unassigned tasks are listed in the Unassigned Tasks pane that appears at the bottom of the view.

2. Drag an unassigned task to the place along a resource's timeline to assign it to that person. Where you place it along the timeline specifies when the assignment is scheduled.

   If you drag a manually scheduled task to a different place on the timeline, its manual scheduling is adjusted accordingly. If you drag an automatically scheduled task to a different place, you set a date constraint, such as Start No Earlier Than.

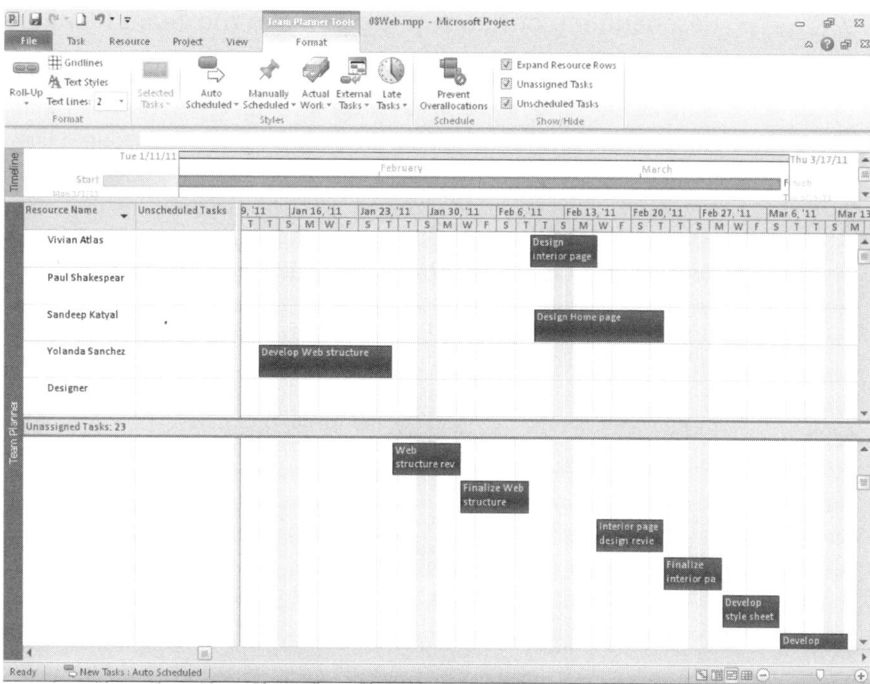

Figure 8-6 Use the Team Planner to graphically assign tasks along a timeline.

After you've assigned all the unassigned tasks, or if you don't want to see them, you can hide the Unassigned Tasks pane. On the Format tab, in the Show/Hide group, clear the Unassigned Tasks check box.

Scheduling Tasks in the Team Planner

In addition to assigning tasks, you can schedule unscheduled tasks by dragging them into place in the Team Planner. An unscheduled task is a manually scheduled placeholder task that doesn't have a start and finish date yet. Such tasks are also known as *placeholder tasks*.

In the Team Planner, unscheduled tasks are shown in the Unscheduled Tasks column. To schedule an unscheduled task, drag the task bar to the location along the assigned resource's timeline to specify when the task should be performed. When you drag an unscheduled task onto the timeline, it adopts the start and finish date accordingly.

After you've scheduled all unscheduled tasks, or if you just don't want to see them, you can hide the Unscheduled Tasks column. On the Format tab, in the Show/Hide group, clear the Unscheduled Tasks check box.

Rescheduling or Reassigning Tasks in the Team Planner

When reviewing the Team Planner, you can easily see when resources are overallocated or underallocated. You can also easily see when tasks are scheduled, and you can adjust their scheduling simply by dragging the task bar. You can reschedule a task on the same resource by dragging the task bar to a time when that resource is not overallocated. You can reassign a task to another resource by dragging the task to the other resource.

Preventing Overallocations by Using the Team Planner

Overallocations happen when you assign a resource to more than one task at the same time. An overallocation is a situation in which a resource is assigned to more tasks in a time period than she has time available. In the Team Planner, if you see multiple tasks assigned to the same resource assigned in the same time period, that resource is overallocated, and her name shows in red, as shown in Figure 8-7.

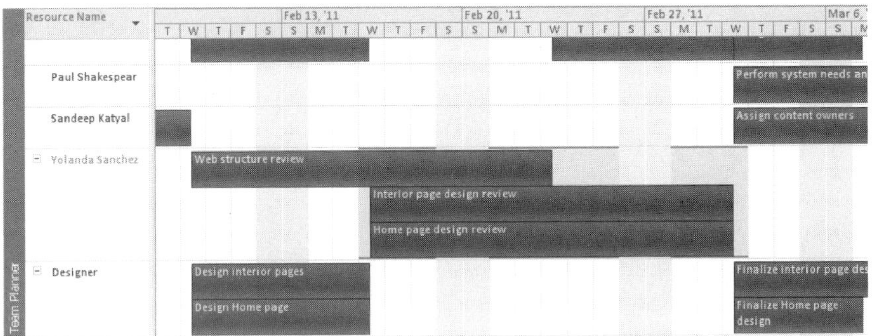

Figure 8-7 Yolanda Sanchez is shown as overallocated in the Team Planner.

> **CAUTION!**
>
> **You'll get better results if you just note the resources who are flagged as overallocated and then take more controlled steps to review and resolve the overallocations. If you leave the Prevent Overallocations mode set, you could cause unintended rescheduling that is difficult to undo. The mode is best used in a what-if scenario to see how Project 2010 might resolve overallocations. Always turn the Prevent Overallocations mode off before leaving the Team Planner for another view.**

You can use the Team Planner to prevent overallocations. To do this, follow these steps:

1. Be sure the Team Planner is displayed.

2. On the Format tab, in the Schedule group, click Prevent Overallocations.

   The button changes color to indicate that Team Planner is in the prevent overallocations mode. Any tasks causing overallocations are rescheduled for later times when the assigned resource has time for them, as shown in Figure 8-8. This is true for manually scheduled tasks as well as automatically scheduled tasks.

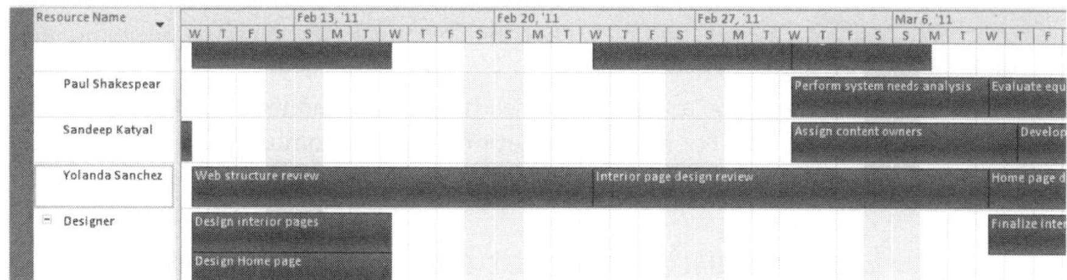

Figure 8-8 The tasks assigned to Yolanda Sanchez that were causing the overallocation are now rescheduled to other times.

As long as you have the Prevent Overallocations button set, whenever you review your schedule in Team Planner, Project 2010 automatically reschedules tasks so that there are no overallocations. This rescheduling happens as soon as you display the Team Planner. Because of this, it's best to turn Prevent Overallocations off before leaving the Team Planner for another view.

For more information about resolving resource overallocations, see "Balancing Resource Workloads" on page 403.

Reviewing Task Details in the Team Planner

To see scheduling details about a task, rest your mouse pointer over the task bar in the timesheet area. A pop-up window indicates whether the task is manually or automatically scheduled, its duration, start and finish dates, and more.

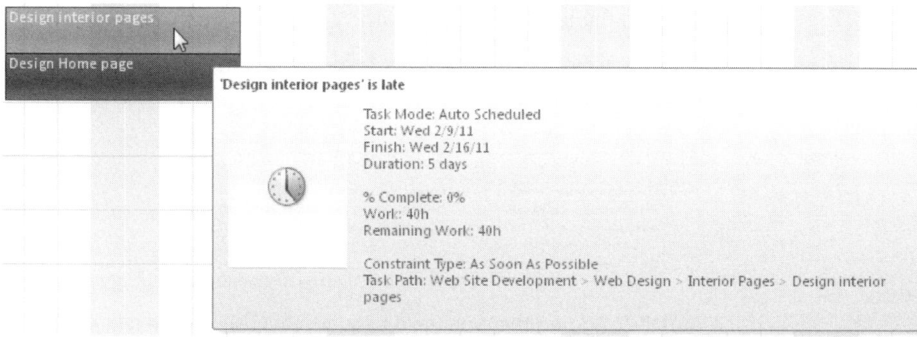

To see even more information, double-click the task bar, and the Task Information dialog box opens, showing all information about the task. You can also change task information in the dialog box as usual. For example, you can change the duration of a task or assign additional resources.

You can change properties of a task by right-clicking its task bar in the Team Planner. Using the drop-down menu that appears, you can switch between automatic and manual scheduling, reassign the task to another resource, add it to the Timeline, and more.

For information about working with the Team Planner, see "Highlighting Tasks with the Timeline" on page 134. For more information about customizing the Team Planner, see "Modifying the Team Planner" on page 1089.

Understanding Assignment Calculations

Work is the amount of effort it takes to complete a task. As soon as you assign a resource to a task, the duration is translated into work. A simple example: If you have a task with a 3-day duration, and you assign a single full-time resource to it, that resource now has an assignment with 24 hours of work spread across three days (assuming default calendar settings).

You can see how duration is used to calculate work amounts by adding the Work field to the Gantt Chart or other task sheet, as follows:

1. Display the Gantt Chart or other task sheet that contains the Duration field.
2. Click the heading of the column to the right of the Duration field. For example, if you are working with the default Gantt Chart with the default Entry table applied, click the Start column heading.

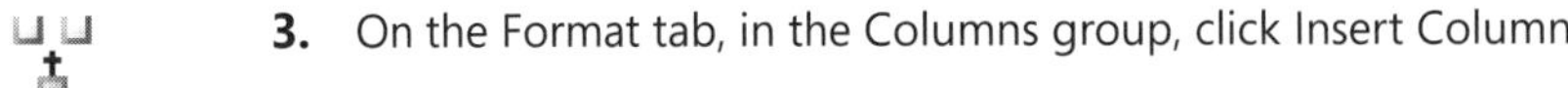

Insert Column

3. On the Format tab, in the Columns group, click Insert Column.
4. In the drop-down menu that appears in the newly inserted column, type **w** to move quickly to the fields that begin with W, and then click Work.

   As shown in Figure 8-9, the Work field appears next to the Duration field, and you can now compare the two.

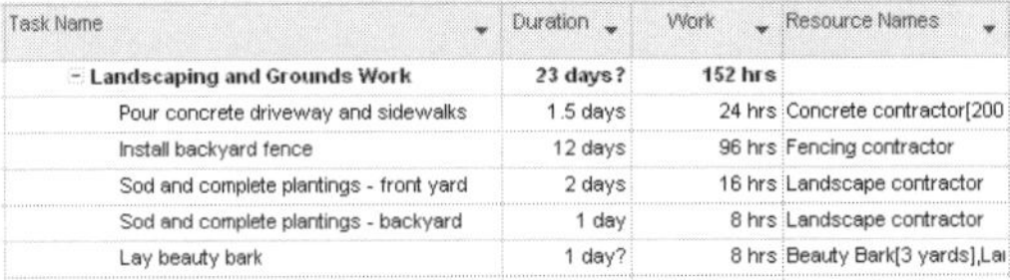

Task Name	Duration	Work	Resource Names
− **Landscaping and Grounds Work**	**23 days?**	**152 hrs**	
Pour concrete driveway and sidewalks	1.5 days	24 hrs	Concrete contractor[200
Install backyard fence	12 days	96 hrs	Fencing contractor
Sod and complete plantings - front yard	2 days	16 hrs	Landscape contractor
Sod and complete plantings - backyard	1 day	8 hrs	Landscape contractor
Lay beauty bark	1 day?	8 hrs	Beauty Bark[3 yards],La

Figure 8-9 Adding the Work field to a task sheet shows the relationship of task duration to task work, based on how tasks are assigned to resources.

That task with a 3-day duration and a single full-time resource assigned translates (by default) to 24 hours of work. Another task with a 3-day duration and two full-time resources assigned translates to 48 hours of work. Another task with a 3-day duration and three full-time resources assigned translates to 72 hours of work.

Duration is the length of time it takes from the start to the finish of the task, but work equates to person-hours for the resources assigned.

Note

Duration is used to calculate work amounts for both manually and automatically scheduled tasks. This is even true for placeholder tasks that have only duration entered.

If you assign a resource to a placeholder task that has no duration entered, Project 2010 enters an 8-hour work amount. This is based on the premise that placeholder tasks have a default duration of 1 day, and by default, 1 day equals 8 hours.

These calculations are based on the *initial assignment*; that is, assigning one, two, or six resources at one time to a task that previously had no assigned resources. In other words, if you assign two full-time resources to that same 3-day task, both resources are assigned 24 hours of work, also spread across 3 days. You can see how the assignment work is spread across the days by reviewing the Task Usage view as shown in Figure 8-10. When you assign multiple resources *initially*, Project 2010 assumes that you intend for the resources to have the same amount of work across the original task duration. You can also see assignment work over a time period by using the Resource Usage view.

Task Name	Work	Duration	Details	M	T	W	T	F
Pour concrete driveway and sidewalks	24 hrs	1.5 days	Work	16h	8h			
Concrete contractor	*24 hrs*		Work	16h	8h			
Install backyard fence	96 hrs	6 days	Work		8h	16h	16h	16h
Thomas Andersen	*48 hrs*		Work		4h	8h	8h	8h
Jon Morris	*48 hrs*		Work		4h	8h	8h	8h

Figure 8-10 In the first task with a single resource assigned, the total work is 24 hours. In the second task with two resources assigned, the total work is 96 hours, split into 48 hours for each of the two assigned resources.

Note

Instead of entering duration and having Project 2010 calculate work amounts when you assign tasks, you can do this the other way around. You can enter tasks, assign resources, and then enter work amounts from estimates those resources provide. From those work amounts, Project 2010 can calculate duration.

Just as work is calculated from the duration and assigned resource availability, duration can be calculated from work amounts and assigned resource availability.

Translate Duration to Work Amounts

You have some control over how Project 2010 translates duration to work amounts. By default, if you specify a 1-day duration, Project 2010 translates this to 8 hours of work. However, if you want 1 day to mean 6 hours to account for nonproject work, you can change your calendar options.

On the File tab, click Options, and then click Schedule in the left pane. Under Calendar Options For This Project, change the settings in Hours Per Day, Hours Per Week, or Days Per Month as needed to fit your requirements.

If you want the project or resource calendar to reflect these calendar options, you must change the appropriate working time calendars to match. If the calendars don't match the calendar option settings, you'll see odd results.

For more information about changing the project calendar, see "Setting Your Project Calendar" on page 84. For information about resource calendars, see "Setting Working Times and Days Off for Work Resources" on page 267.

TROUBLESHOOTING

You assign two resources to a task, but the work is doubled rather than halved

When you assign multiple resources initially, Project 2010 assumes that you intend for the same amount of work to be applied to all assigned resources across the time span represented by the task duration.

If you want the duration to be reduced because multiple resources are assigned, set the duration accordingly. Or start by assigning just one resource, and then assign the additional resources in a separate operation. As long as the task is not a *fixed-duration task*, the duration is reduced based on the number of additional resources you add.

The calculations for work and duration can change if you assign one resource initially and then later assign a second resource. This might also be true if you initially assign two resources and later remove one of them.

For more information about these schedule recalculations, see "Changing Resource Assignments" on page 314.

> **Note**
>
> **If you don't specify a work unit, Project 2010 by default assumes the unit to be hours and automatically enters hrs after your work amount. You can change the default work unit if you like. On the File tab, click Options, and then click Schedule in the left pane. Under Scheduling Options For This Project, in the Work Is Entered In box, select the time unit you want as the default for this project.**

Assigning Material Resources to Tasks

When you assign a material resource, you are attaching the material resource name to a task and then indicating the quantity of material to be used in fulfilling this task.

Material resources are supplies consumed in the course of fulfilling a task. As with work resources, there are units of measurement to specify how much of the resource is available to carry out the task. With work resources, this measurement is time: number of hours or days, for example. With materials, however, the measurement, and therefore the material resource assignment units, is quantity. When you assign a material resource to a task, you specify the quantity of resource that this task will consume.

For example, suppose that you have a landscaping project that includes the "Lay down beauty bark" task. The material resource for this task is obviously beauty bark. Because beauty bark is measured in cubic yards, you would have set the material's unit of measurement, or label, as **cubic yards** when you added beauty bark as a material resource in the Resource Sheet. Now, when you assign beauty bark as a material resource to the "Lay down beauty bark" task, you can specify the assignment units as **6**, to indicate 6 cubic yards of beauty bark.

Other examples of material labels include tons, linear feet, packages, cartons, pounds, and crates. You can make the label be any unit of measurement you want.

The quantity of material consumed in the course of performing a task can be fixed or variable, based on duration. That is, if the same amount of material will be used whether the task takes 2 days or 2 weeks, the material is said to have a *fixed material consumption*. However, if more material will be used if the duration increases and less material used if the duration decreases, the material is said to have a *variable material consumption*. To specify variable material consumption, enter a per-time period specification in the assignment Units field: for example, 1/week or 3/day. This is translated with the material's label: for example, 1 ton/week or 3 yards/day.

For more information on setting up a material resource, see "Adding Material Resources to the Project" on page 258.

INSIDE OUT Specify a variable consumption rate

You might think that a material with a variable consumption rate can be set as such in the Material Label field of the Resource Sheet. Not so. You can enter any string you want in the Material Label field, including something like yards/day. But when you assign the material to a task, the expected per-day calculations are not made.

To specify the variable consumption rate, always specify it in the Units field in the Assign Resources dialog box rather than in the Material Label field in the Resource Sheet.

To assign a material resource to a task, follow these steps:

1. In the Gantt Chart or other task sheet, click the task to which you want to assign a material resource.
2. On the Resource tab, in the Assignments group, click Assign Resources.
3. In the Assign Resources dialog box, click the name of the material resource you want to assign to the task, and then click the Assign button.

   The material resource name moves to the top of the Resources list in the table, and the label appears in the Units field, defaulting to a quantity of 1—for example, **1 yards**.
4. Change the *1* in the Units field to the correct quantity for this assignment—for example, **3 yards**. (See Figure 8-11.)

   If you change the quantity directly in the Units field, press Tab or Enter when you're finished, or click another field to enter the change and exit edit mode.
5. If necessary, change the units value from the default fixed consumption rate to a variable consumption rate, as shown in Figure 8-12. After the units value, enter a slash and time period abbreviation—for example, **3/d**. Project 2010 adds the unit of measurement label, such as yards or cartons, to make it **3 yards/d**.

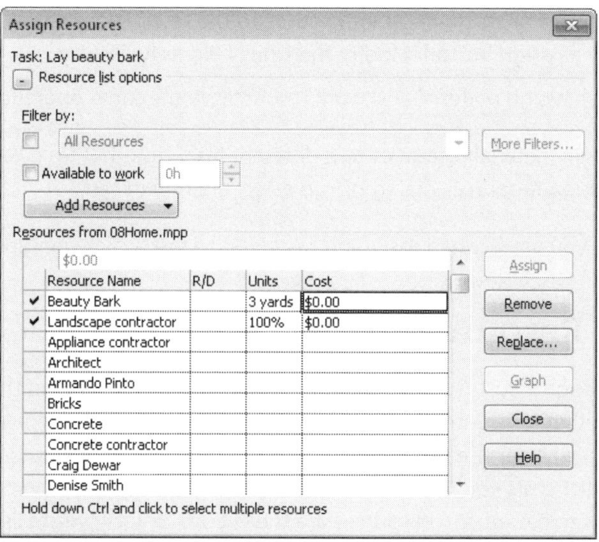

Figure 8-11 Change the default of 1 unit to the appropriate quantity of material to be used to complete the selected task.

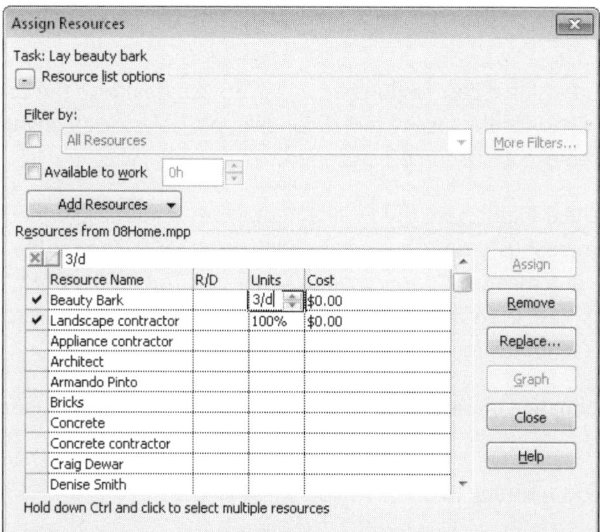

Figure 8-12 Use the standard time period abbreviations (h, d, w, and so on) to specify the quantity per time period for a material resource with a variable consumption rate.

6. If you want to assign another resource to the selected task, click the name, and then click the Assign button. Modify the Units field as necessary.

   You can assign material and work resources in the same operation.

7. To assign material resources to a different task, click that task. You don't have to close the Assign Resources dialog box to select a different task.

8. When you are finished assigning resources to tasks, click the Close button.

Assigning Cost Resources to Tasks

When you assign a cost resource to a task, you associate a cost item that must be incurred to complete that task. Entering costs for work resources, such as an hourly rate for a human resource or a cost per use for an equipment resource, certainly helps you track some of the biggest project costs you're likely to encounter. Cost resources help you track other significant costs. Examples of cost resources are travel costs or facility rentals associated with the fulfillment of a task.

Unlike for work or material resources, you do not enter a cost amount in the Resource Sheet or Resource Information dialog box. You only create the resource there and identify it as a cost resource.

Only after you assign a cost resource to a task do you deal with the cost. At that point, you can enter the cost for the facility rental, for example, as associated with the task to which the Facility Rental cost resource is assigned.

For example, you might have the Facility Rental cost resource assigned to the "Conduct focus group meetings" and "Conduct usability tests" tasks. The facility used for the "Conduct focus group meetings" task costs $200 per day. The facility used for the "Conduct usability tests" task costs $400 per day. You're using the same cost resource but entering different cost amounts for the different task assignments.

For more information on setting up a cost resource, see "Adding Cost Resources to the Project" on page 259.

To assign a cost resource to a task, follow these steps:

1. In the Gantt Chart, Task Usage view, or other task sheet, click the task to which you want to assign the cost resource.

2. On the Resource tab, in the Assignments group, click Assign Resources.
3. In the Assign Resources dialog box, click the name of the cost resource you want to assign to the task.
4. Click in the Cost field for the cost resource, and then type the cost amount for this resource on this task.

   For cost resources, the Units field is not available.
5. Click the Assign button.
6. To assign the same cost resource to a different task, click that task. Enter the cost for that cost resource on the newly selected task, and then click the Assign button.
7. When you are finished assigning resources to tasks, click the Close button.

   By default, the name of the cost resource as well as the cost amount for the assignment is shown next to the Gantt bar for the task, as shown in Figure 8-13.

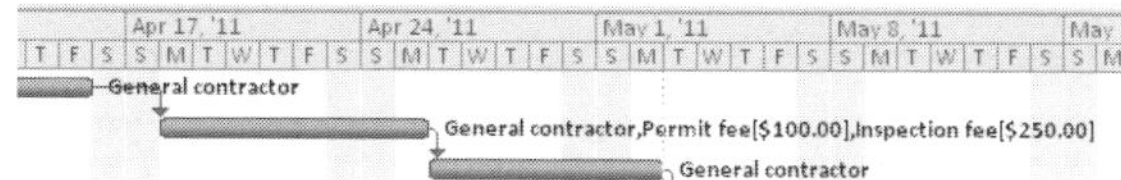

Figure 8-13 The default Gantt bar shows the name of the cost resource as well as the cost amount for the task to which the cost resource is assigned.

You can change the cost you enter on a cost resource assignment. This is helpful if the cost for the resource on the task has changed or if you didn't have that information at all when you first made the assignment. There are several ways to change the cost on a cost resource assignment:

- In the Gantt Chart or any other task sheet, select the task. On the Resource tab, in the Assignments group, click Assign Resources. Click in the Cost field for the assigned cost resource and change the amount.

Task Information

- In any task sheet, click the task. On the Task tab, in the Properties group, click Information. In the Task Information dialog box, click the Resources tab. In the Cost field for the cost resource, change the amount, as shown in Figure 8-14.

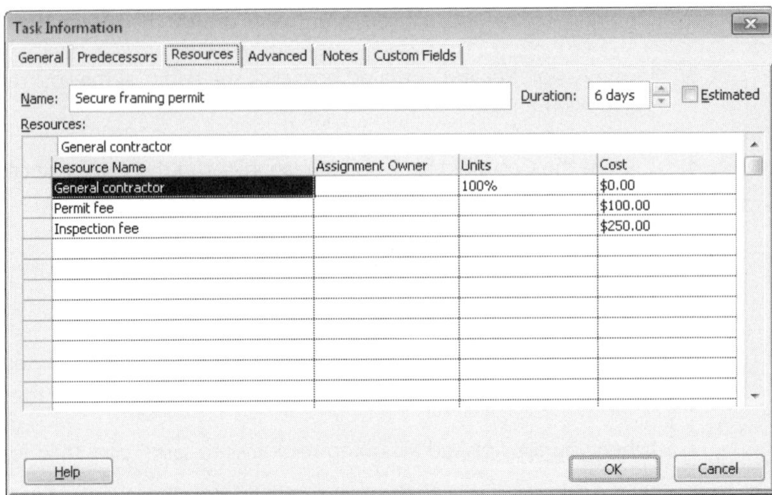

Figure 8-14 The Resources tab of the Task Information dialog box shows the cost amount for an assigned cost resource.

- In the Task Usage view, double-click the assignment—that is, the name of the cost resource under the task to which it is assigned. In the Assignment Information dialog box, on the General tab, change the amount in the Cost box.
- In the Resource Usage view, double-click the assignment—that is, the name of the task under the cost resource name assigned to that task. In the Assignment Information dialog box, on the General tab, change the amount in the Cost box.
- In either the Task Usage or Resource Usage view, add the Cost column to the sheet area of the view. Right-click any column heading, and then click Insert Column on the shortcut menu. In the drop-down menu that appears in the inserted column, type cost to move to the Cost field. Click the Cost field. In the Cost column that's inserted, change the amount next to the assignment, as shown in Figure 8-15.

Task Name	Work	Cost
Secure framing permit	24 hrs	$350.00
General contractor	*24 hrs*	*$0.00*
Permit fee		*$100.00*
Inspection fee		*$250.00*

Figure 8-15 Add the Cost field to the Task Usage or Resource Usage view to review or modify the amount for a cost resource assignment.

For more information about working with project costs, see "Reviewing Planned Costs" on page 339.

> **Note**
>
> **Project 2010 also includes a cost-related resource type called *budget resources*. Budget resources are assigned only to the project summary task for the express purpose of tracking project costs and project work for the overall project budget. For more information about working with budget resources, see "Setting Up and Reviewing a Project Budget" on page 346.**

Reviewing Assignment Information

There are several ways to look at resource assignments. You can switch to a usage view, which shows assignments for each task or assignments for each resource. You can also add a form to your Gantt Chart or other task view and review assignment information in relation to selected tasks.

Showing Assignments by Task or Resource

Task Usage

You can see work assigned to resources in either the Task Usage or Resource Usage views. As shown in Figure 8-16, the Task Usage view lists assignments by tasks. The information for each assignment is rolled up, or summarized, in the row representing the task. To switch to the Task Usage view, click View, Task Views, Task Usage.

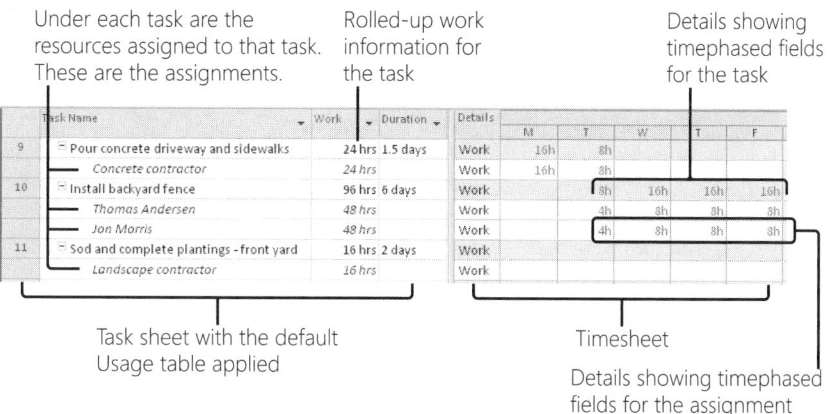

Figure 8-16 The Task Usage view shows task duration as well as assignment work.

Resource Usage

As shown in Figure 8-17, the Resource Usage view lists assignments by resources. The information for each assignment is rolled up, or totaled, in the row representing the resource. To switch to the Resource Usage view, click View, Resource Views, Resource Usage.

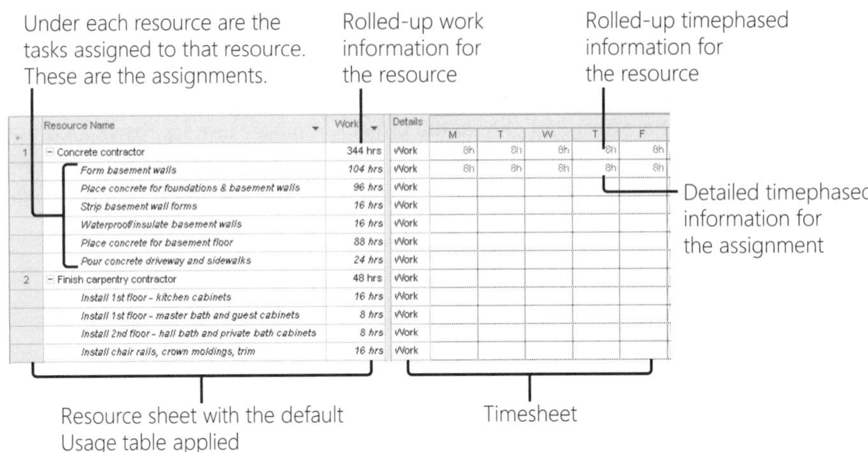

Figure 8-17 The Resource Usage view focuses on resource and assignment work.

Either usage view is great for reviewing assignment information. Which one you use depends on whether you want to see assignments within the context of tasks or resources.

Assignment Information

The usage views are the only two views in which you can see detailed assignment information. From these two views, you can also access the Assignment Information dialog box, shown in Figure 8-18. To display the dialog box, click the assignment for which you want to see detailed information, and then click Format, Assignment, Information.

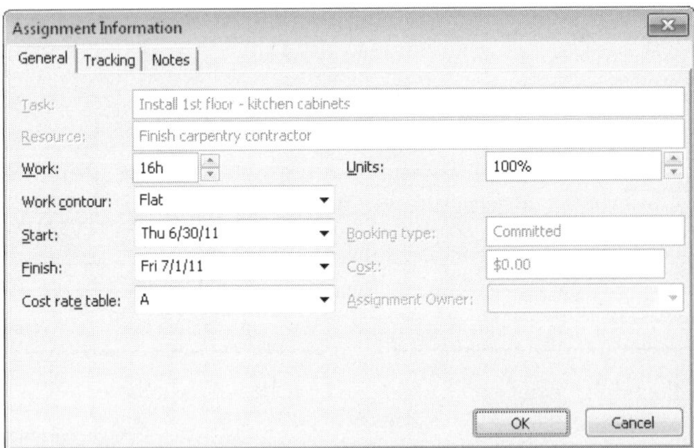

Figure 8-18 You can open the Assignment Information dialog box by double-clicking an assignment in the Task Usage or Resource Usage view.

Note

Assignment Notes

You can enter a note about an individual assignment. In the Task Usage or Resource Usage view, click the assignment. On the Format tab, in the Assignment group, click Notes. The Notes tab in the Assignment Information dialog box appears. Type the note, and then click OK. The Notes indicator appears in the Indicators column of the usage view.

TROUBLESHOOTING

The Assignment Information dialog box does not open

If you're working in the Task Usage view or Resource Usage view and you want to open the Assignment Information dialog box, be sure that you actually have selected an assignment. In the usage views, assignments appear under the task name or resource name. If you double-click the task or resource name at the summary level, the Task Information or Resource Information dialog box opens.

Instead, double-click the assignment under that summary level. In the Task Usage view, the summary level shows the task name, and the subordinate assignment level shows the resource names. Those are the resources assigned to the task; that is, the task's assignments. If you double-click a resource name in the Task Usage view, the Assignment Information dialog box appears.

In the Resource Usage view, the same principle applies. The summary level shows the resource name, and the subordinate assignment level shows the task names. Those are the tasks to which this resource is assigned; that is, the resource's assignments. If you double-click a task name in the Resource Usage view, the Assignment Information dialog box appears.

Show and Hide Assignments

You can hide and show assignments for individual tasks or resources. Click the minus (–) sign next to the summary task or resource to hide the assignments under that task or resource. To show the assignments again, click the plus (+) sign.

Showing Assignment Information Under a Task View

You can use different types of forms under the Gantt Chart or other task view to see detailed information about assignments. To do this, first display the task view you want. Then on the View tab, in the Split View group, select the Details check box. As shown in Figure 8-19, the Task Form appears as the lower pane.

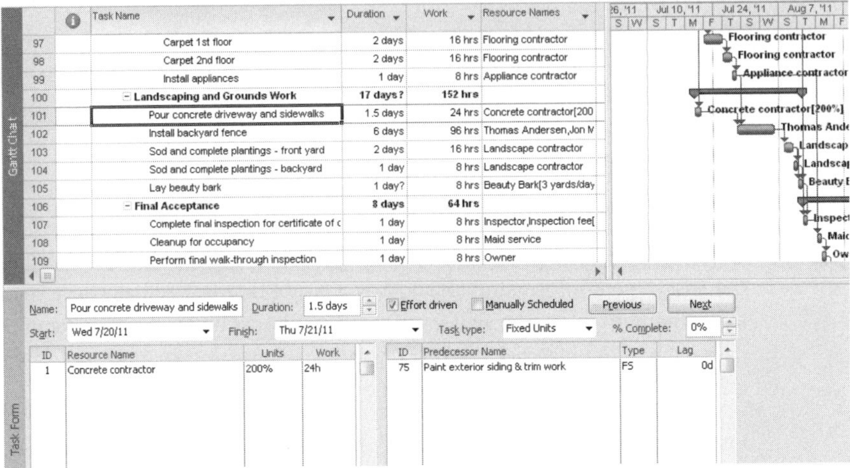

Figure 8-19 Detailed task and assignment information is shown in the Task Form in the lower pane for the task selected in the Gantt Chart in the upper pane.

Other Views

> ### Note
>
> **Adding details to the Gantt Chart produces the same result as applying the Task Entry view, which is a built-in combination view made up of the Gantt Chart and the Task Form. On the View tab, in the Task Views group, click Other Views, and then click More Views. In the dialog box, click Task Entry, and then click Apply.**

With the Task Form, you can easily see all schedule-related information—including duration, task type, units, assigned resources, and work—for the selected task in the Gantt Chart. Click the Previous or Next button to move to different tasks.

In the Task Form, the default table information includes resources on the left and predecessors on the right. You can change which categories of information are shown. To do this:

1. Click in the lower pane to make the form the active pane.

2. On the Format tab, in the Details group, click the information you want to see in the form—for example, Schedule or Work.

   You can also simply right-click in the form, and then click the categories of information you want to see.

You can see more detailed information about resources assigned to the selected task by applying the Resource Form as the lower pane under a task sheet. To apply the Resource Form:

1. In the lower pane, right-click the view title bar.
2. In the drop-down menu, click More Views.
3. In the dialog box, click Resource Form, and then click Apply.

In the Resource Form, you can review detailed information about the resources assigned to the task selected in the task sheet in the upper pane, as shown in Figure 8-20. This data includes availability and cost information.

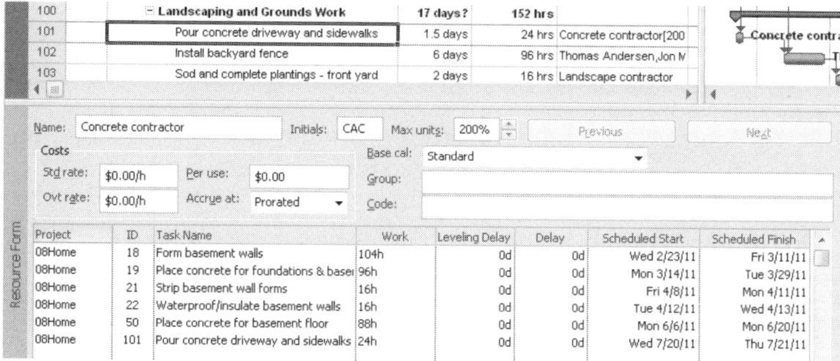

Figure 8-20 Use the Resource Form to review detailed information about assigned resources.

By default, schedule information is shown in the table area. To change the category of table information, right-click the form, and then click a category such as Cost or Work. Click the Previous or Next button to move to the resources assigned to the current task.

> **Note**
>
> **To return to a single-pane view, double-click the split bar dividing the two panes. Another method is to right-click in the form, and then click Show Split to turn it off. And here's a third method: On the View tab, in the Split View group, clear the Details check box.**

Show Assignment Information Under a Resource View

You can also show details about resources and assignments under a resource view. Display the Resource Sheet, which is often the most useful view to be paired with a resource form. On the View tab, in the Split View group, select the Details check box. The Resource Form appears as the lower pane under the Resource Sheet. The information in the Resource Form corresponds with the selected resource in the Resource Sheet.

Changing Resource Assignments

You can change existing resource assignments in three ways:

- You can add more resources to the existing resources assigned to a task.
- You can replace one resource with another.
- You can remove a resource from a task.

To add more resources to the existing ones initially assigned to a task, follow these steps:

1. In the Gantt Chart or other task sheet, click the task to which you want to add more resources.
2. On the Resource tab, in the Assignments group, click Assign Resources.

   The Assign Resources dialog box appears, showing a check mark next to the names of resources already assigned.

   You can also open the Assign Resources dialog box by right-clicking a task name and then clicking Assign Resources.
3. Click the name of the resource you want to add to the task, and then click the Assign button.

   The resource name moves to the top of the Resources list in the table, and the default percentage appears in the Units field for the resource.
4. Review the Units field and be sure that it's appropriate for this assignment.

   If you change the Units field, press Enter or click another field to set your change and exit edit mode for the field.
5. When you are finished working with resource assignments, click the Close button.

In the task sheet, you'll see that the task has been updated to include the new resource. You'll also see certain cells highlighted so that you can see which fields have changed as a result of the assignment change.

If the task is automatically scheduled, you might see changes in the duration, work amount, or finish date as a result of the newly assigned resource. The nature of the changes depend on the task type (fixed units, fixed work, or fixed duration) and whether the task is effort-driven. Learn more about this in "Controlling Schedule Changes with Task Types" on page 337.

See Feedback on Schedule Changes

After you assign automatically scheduled tasks to resources, Project 2010 provides scheduling feedback. When you make certain kinds of changes that affect scheduling—such as changes to duration, start date, or finish date—a green scheduling feedback triangle might appear in the corner of the edited cell in a Gantt Chart, task sheet, or usage view.

When you move your mouse pointer over the cell containing the feedback triangle, the option button appears. An option button might also appear when you delete a task, assign an additional resource to a task, or remove a resource from a task.

Click the option button. A message explains the scheduling ramifications of your edit. The message usually gives you the opportunity to make a choice or change the edit so that the result is closer to your expectation.

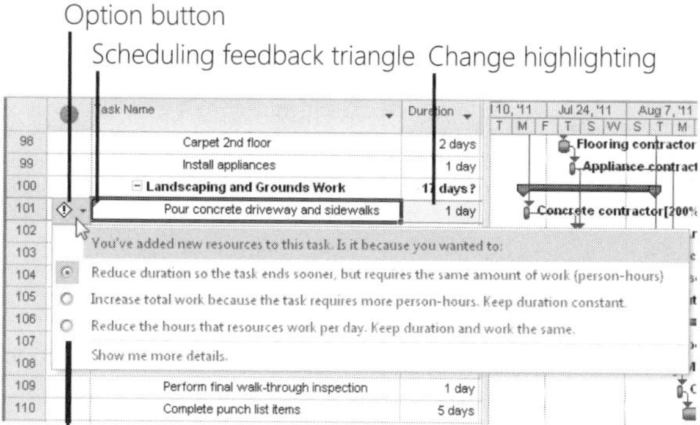

The indicator appears in the cell as long as the edit is available for an Undo operation. After you make a new edit, the indicator disappears.

Option buttons provide feedback for users who are still getting used to the ways in which Project 2010 schedules tasks. This feedback helps users understand the impact of their scheduling changes.

If you understand the impact of your scheduling changes, you might not need or want to see the feedback triangles or option buttons. In this case, you can turn them off. On the File menu, click Options, and then click Display in the left pane. Under the section labeled Show Indicators And Option Buttons For, clear the categories for which you do not want to see feedback.

To replace one resource with another, follow these steps:

1. In the Gantt Chart or other task sheet, click the task for which you want to replace a resource.
2. On the Resource tab, in the Assignments group, click Assign Resources.

   The Assign Resources dialog box appears, showing a check mark next to the names of resources already assigned.
3. Click the name of the assigned resource you want to replace, and then click the Replace button.

   The Replace Resource dialog box appears, showing the same resources that are displayed in the Assign Resources dialog box, according to any filters you might have applied.
4. Click the name of the replacement resource, and then click OK.

   The name of the replacement resource moves to the top of the Resources list in the table, and the default percentage appears in the Units field for the resource.
5. Review the Units field and be sure that it's appropriate for this assignment.
6. When you are finished replacing resources, click the Close button.

To remove a resource assignment, follow these steps:

1. In the Gantt Chart or other task sheet, click the task from which you want to remove a resource.
2. On the Resource tab, in the Assignments group, click Assign Resources.

   The Assign Resources dialog box appears, showing a check mark next to the names of resources already assigned.
3. Click the name of the assigned resource you want to remove, and then click the Remove button.
4. When you are finished working with resource assignments, click the Close button.

Note

When you remove a resource assignment, you remove only the assignment, not the resource itself. The resource is still assigned to other tasks and is available for assignment to other tasks.

In the task sheet, you'll see that the task has been updated to exclude the deleted resource. If multiple resources were assigned, and you removed one of them but left others intact, you'll also see the green scheduling feedback triangle in the task cell. Position your mouse pointer over the triangle to display the option button in the Indicators field. Click the option button, and a menu appears.

> **Note**
>
> **As an alternative to using the Assign Resources dialog box, you can double-click a task to open the Task Information dialog box, and then click the Resources tab. Although the Task Information dialog box doesn't have all the options of the Assign Resources dialog box, you can still assign, replace, and remove assigned resources (as well as set the assignment units) for a single task.**

Contouring Resource Assignments

When you assign a work resource to a task, the work time allotted for the task is usually spread equally across the task duration. For example, if Pat is the only resource assigned full time to a 4-day task, Pat is assigned 8 hours of work in each of the 4 days.

If you want to adjust how the hours are assigned, you can shape the work amounts. You can assign 1 hour on the first day, 2 hours on the second day, 5 hours on the third day, 8 hours on the fourth and fifth day, 5 hours on the sixth day, 2 hours on the seventh day, and 1 hour on the eighth day. You still have 32 hours of work, but the duration has stretched to 8 days. The assignment is shaped like a bell, as shown in Figure 8-21: It has a ramp-up period, a full-on period, and a ramp-down period. A shape applied to the work is called a work *contour*.

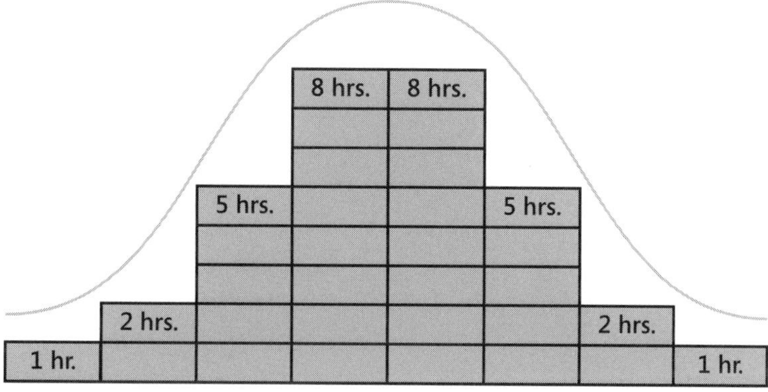

Figure 8-21 Apply the Bell work contour to shape the work amounts to reflect ramp-up, peak, and ramp-down periods in the shape of a bell.

You can apply this shape by manually adjusting work amounts for the assignment in the timesheet area of the Task Usage view. You can also apply the built-in bell contour, which converts the default flat contour into different shapes of time, such as back loaded, front loaded, early peak, and more.

The available built-in work contours are the following:

- Flat (the default)
- Back Loaded
- Front Loaded
- Double Peak
- Early Peak
- Late Peak
- Bell
- Turtle

To apply a built-in work contour to an assignment, follow these steps:

1. Display the Task Usage or Resource Usage view so that you can see assignments.
2. Click the assignment to which you want to apply a work contour.
3. On the Format tab, in the Assignment group, click Information.

   The Assignment Information dialog box appears.
4. In the Assignment Information dialog box, click the General tab if necessary.
5. In the Work Contour box shown in Figure 8-22, click the work contour you want to apply.

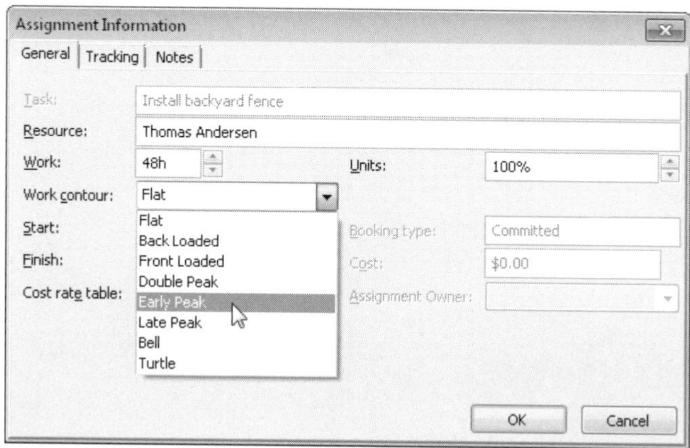

Figure 8-22 Use the General tab in the Assignment Information dialog box to set work contours.

Work for the assignment is redistributed to match the shape of the contour you select, and the specific contour icon appears in the Indicators column of the Task Usage or Resource Usage view, as shown in Figure 8-23.

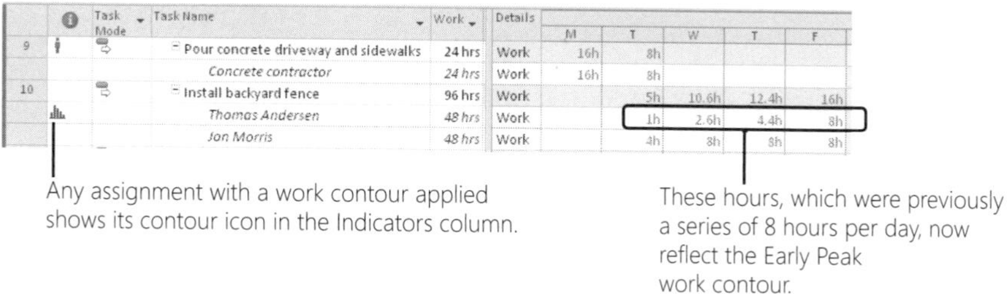

Figure 8-23 When you apply a work contour to an assignment, the assigned hours are distributed across the assignment's time span, according to the shape of the contour.

Edited work contour indicator

You can also manually reshape the work for an assignment by editing work amounts in the timesheet area of the Task Usage or Resource Usage view. When you do this, an icon appears in the Indicators column, alerting you to the fact that work amounts have been edited.

Note

Although work contours do not apply to cost resources, you can apply a work contour to material resources. In this case, the quantity of material used is distributed over the task span according to the selected contour.

CHAPTER 9

Planning Resource and Task Costs

MICROSOFT Project 2010 can help you plan, forecast, and track costs associated with the performance of the project. The bulk of your costs is likely to be generated by the resources assigned to tasks. Costs are often also directly related to the tasks themselves, independent of the assigned resources.

To set up your project plan so that it reflects costs, you can:

- Enter unit costs for work and material resources and assign those resources to their tasks.
- Assign and quantify cost resources such as travel costs, facility rentals, permit fees, and equipment or software purchases.
- Specify any fixed costs for tasks.

When you have entered all applicable cost items and associated them with your project tasks, Project 2010 calculates the cost forecast for each assignment, each resource, each task, and the project as a whole. You can therefore see costs in detail or at a high-level as you need to for various purposes.

While you're in the planning stage of the project, you can use this cost forecast to develop your project's budget. If a budget has been imposed on you, your forecast can help you clearly see whether the project plan is in line with the realities of the budget. You can use the budget resource feature to help you compare your project's planned costs against your allocated budget.

If your planned costs go beyond your budget, use the data you have in Project 2010 to lobby for additional funding or adjust project scope, schedule, or resources to match the cost forecast to the allocated budget.

As soon as you start executing the project, you start tracking and managing costs. At that point, you can compare actual costs to your original planned costs and analyze any variances between the two.

For more information about adjusting the project plan to conform to the budget, see "Reducing Project Costs" on page 396. For information about tracking costs, including setting cost baselines and entering actual costs, see Chapter 11, "Setting a Baseline and Updating Progress." For information about managing costs, see "Monitoring and Adjusting Costs" on page 502.

Project Management Practices: Cost Management

Project cost management is one of the many disciplines required for successful project execution. Simply put, effective project cost management ensures that the project is completed within the approved budget. In fact, the benchmark of a successful project is its completion not only on time, but also within the allocated budget.

Processes associated with project cost management include the following:

- **Resource planning** After you determine the types and quantities of resources needed for the project, you can estimate costs for those resources. You obtain work resources by hiring staff through human resources processes. You obtain contract staff, material resources, and equipment resources through procurement processes. You then enter those resources into your project plan and assign them to tasks.
- **Cost estimating** Top-down cost estimating is the practice of using the actual cost of a similar project as the basis for estimating the cost of the current project. Bottom-up cost estimating involves estimating the cost of individual tasks and then summarizing those estimates to arrive at a total project cost. The estimate should account for labor, materials, supplies, travel, fees, and any other costs. With Project 2010, you can see the planned costs of resources, as well as the fixed costs associated with tasks. Project 2010 can total all costs to give you a reliable estimate of how much it will cost to implement the project.
- **Cost budgeting** The budget can allocate certain amounts to individual phases or tasks in the project. Or the budget can be allocated to certain time periods in which the costs will be incurred. The cost estimate and the project schedule—with the scheduled start and finish dates of the different phases, tasks, milestones, and deliverables—are instrumental to developing the project budget. In Project 2010, you can create budget resources that you can maintain as a fixed point of reference to compare against your planned and actual costs to see how well the project is performing against the budget.
- **Cost control** The cost control process manages changes to the project budget. Cost control addresses the manner in which cost variances will be tracked and managed, and how cost information will be reported. A cost management plan can detail cost control procedures and corrective actions.

Planning Resource Costs

The key to planning project costs is entering resource costs to begin with. Typically, the majority of your costs comes from resources carrying out their assignments. When you enter resource cost rates and assign resources to tasks, those resource cost rates are multiplied by the amount of work on assignments. The result is the cost of the assignment.

You can set costs for work resources as well as for material resources. Cost rates might be variable, such as $40/hour or $200/ton, or the rates might be a fixed per-use cost, such as $300 per use.

You can also use cost resources to assign frequently used cost items—for example, facility rentals, permit fees, or travel costs—to certain tasks and then specify the amount for that cost resource on that assigned task.

Setting Costs for Work Resources

You can set pay rates for work resources: people and equipment. When these resources are assigned to tasks, Project 2010 multiplies the pay rates by the amount of assigned work to estimate the planned cost for the assignment. You can also set per-use costs for work resources. If a resource has different costs for different types of assignments or during different periods of time, you can enter multiple costs for one resource.

> **Note**
>
> **You can enter cost information for resources at the same time you add resources to the project. Simply complete all the fields in the Resource Sheet at the same time.**

Specifying Variable Work Resource Costs

To set pay rates for work resources, follow these steps:

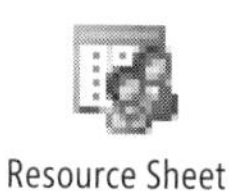
Resource Sheet

1. On the View tab, in the Resource Views group, click Resource Sheet.

   You can also click the Resource Sheet icon in the view shortcuts in the lower-right corner of the Project status bar, next to the Zoom slider.

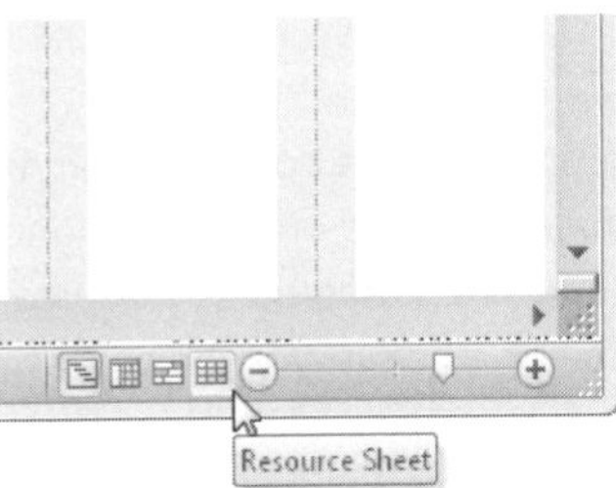

2. Make sure the Entry table is applied to the Resource Sheet.

   You can see the name of the applied table by resting your mouse pointer over the All Cells box where the row and column headings intersect at the upper-left corner of the sheet.

Tables

   If needed, on the View tab, in the Data group, click Tables, and then click Entry.

3. Make sure the work resource is set up.

   Work resources are designated with Work selected in the Type field.

For more information about setting up work resources, see "Adding Work Resources to the Project" on page 250.

4. In the Std. Rate field for the first work resource, enter the resource's standard pay rate—for example, **$30/hour** or **$400/day**.

5. If the resource is eligible for overtime, and if you plan to apply and track overtime in your project plan, enter the resource's overtime pay rate in the Ovt. Rate field. (See Figure 9-1.)

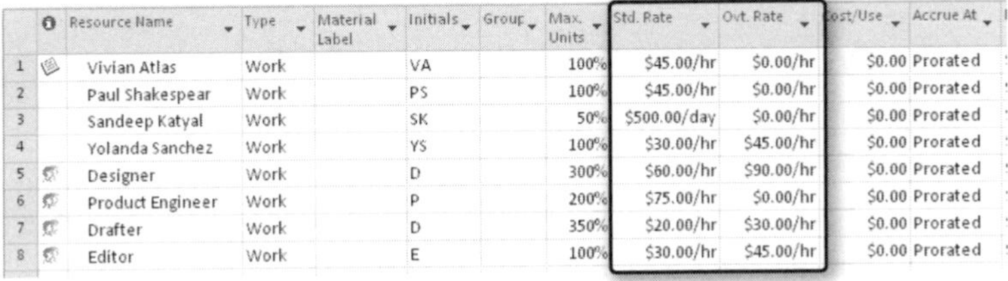

		Resource Name	Type	Material Label	Initials	Group	Max. Units	Std. Rate	Ovt. Rate	ost/Use	Accrue At
1		Vivian Atlas	Work		VA		100%	$45.00/hr	$0.00/hr	$0.00	Prorated
2		Paul Shakespear	Work		PS		100%	$45.00/hr	$0.00/hr	$0.00	Prorated
3		Sandeep Katyal	Work		SK		50%	$500.00/day	$0.00/hr	$0.00	Prorated
4		Yolanda Sanchez	Work		YS		100%	$30.00/hr	$45.00/hr	$0.00	Prorated
5		Designer	Work		D		300%	$60.00/hr	$90.00/hr	$0.00	Prorated
6		Product Engineer	Work		P		200%	$75.00/hr	$0.00/hr	$0.00	Prorated
7		Drafter	Work		D		350%	$20.00/hr	$30.00/hr	$0.00	Prorated
8		Editor	Work		E		100%	$30.00/hr	$45.00/hr	$0.00	Prorated

Figure 9-1 Specify each work resource's standard pay rate and applicable overtime rate in the Resource Sheet.

Set Default Resource Cost Rates

You can set a default standard rate and overtime rate for all work resources in the current project. On the File tab, click Options, and then click Advanced in the left pane. Under General Options For This Project, enter values in the Default Standard Rate and Default Overtime Rate boxes.

Default rates ensure that there's at least an estimated value in the work resource rate fields, which can help you approximate project costs in broad terms until you have confirmed all resource rates.

These values take effect for any new resources you enter but do not change the standard or overtime rate for existing resources, even if their rates show $0.00/hr.

If you're working with Microsoft Project Professional 2010 in an enterprise environment, enterprise resource rate information can be updated by the project server administrator, portfolio manager, or other user with the proper permissions.

For more information about setting up enterprise resource information, see "Creating the Enterprise Resource Pool" on page 838.

INSIDE OUT Specify overtime work yourself

Project 2010 does not automatically assign the overtime pay rate when a resource's work exceeds 8 hours in a day or 40 hours in a week. While it seems as though this overtime assignment would be the expected behavior, Project 2010 can't make that assumption. If it did, the plan might end up showing higher costs than you actually incurred.

For the overtime rate to be used, you must specify overtime work in addition to regular work for the resource. For example, if a person is scheduled to work 50 hours in a week, which includes 8 hours of regular work and 2 hours of overtime work per day, you should assign 10 hours of regular work per day and designate 2 hours of it as overtime work. The cost of the hours specified as overtime work is then calculated with the overtime rate you entered for the resource.

For more information about working with overtime, see "Balancing Resource Workloads" on page 403.

Specifying Fixed Resource Costs

Some work resources incur a cost each time you use them. This *per-use cost* might be instead of or in addition to a cost rate and is often associated with equipment. It's a set, one-time fee for the use of the resource. For example, rental equipment might have a delivery or setup charge every time it's used, in addition to its day rate.

Per-use costs never depend on the amount of work to be done. They're simply one-time costs that are incurred each time the resource is used.

To specify a per-use cost, follow these steps:

1. Be sure the Entry table is applied to the Resource Sheet. If it is not, on the View tab, in the Data group, click Tables, and then click Entry.
2. In the Cost/Use field for the work resource, enter the resource's per-use cost; for example, **$100**.

Setting Costs for Material Resources

To set resource costs for consumable materials, follow these steps:

1. Be sure the Entry table is applied to the Resource Sheet. If it is not, on the View tab, in the Data group, click Tables, and then click Entry.
2. Make sure the material resource is set up in your Resource Sheet.

   Material resources are designated with Material selected in the Type field. Each material resource should also have a unit of measurement—such as yards, tons, or feet—in the Material Label field.

For more information about setting up material resources, see "Adding Material Resources to the Project" on page 258.

3. In the Std. Rate field for the material resource, enter the cost per unit.

   For example, if you have a material resource that is measured in tons, and each ton of this material costs $300, enter **$300** in the Std. Rate field.
4. If there's a per-use cost for the material, such as a setup fee or equipment rental fee associated with using the material, enter it in the Cost/Use field.

   You can have a per-unit cost in the Std. Rate field as well as a per-use cost for the same resource.

TROUBLESHOOTING

You don't see the Material Label field in the Resource Sheet

The Material Label field might be cut off, and you might just see "Material." By default, this is the third column in the Entry table. If the field is cut off, you can widen the column by dragging or double-clicking its right edge. You can also increase the row depth to show the full label. Drag the lower edge of the row header.

Project Management Practices: Procurement Management

When you need to hire contract staff or use vendors for certain phases of your project, procurement management comes into play. Procurement is also necessary when you need to purchase materials and equipment from selected suppliers. Procurement might also be involved in travel planning.

You use procurement planning to identify which project requirements are best satisfied by purchasing products or services outside the project organization. Through procurement planning, you decide what you need, how much you need, when you need it, and who you're purchasing it from.

The procurement process includes the following:

- Plan procurements, including identifying potential suppliers
- Conduct procurements, including soliciting bids, selecting suppliers, and awarding contracts
- Administer procurements, including managing relationships and monitoring performance
- Close procurements

Because contracting and procurement are specialized knowledge areas, it's best to enlist experts and involve them with the project team as soon as possible.

Setting Multiple Costs for a Resource

Suppose you know that certain work resources will get a 5 percent raise on September 1. Maybe the contract for an equipment resource stipulates a discount for the first month of use and then the cost returns to normal for the second month and beyond. Or perhaps a consultant has one rate for one type of work and another rate for another type of work. You can specify different costs at different times by using *cost rate tables*. To specify different costs on a single resource, follow these steps:

1. In the Resource Sheet, click the work or material resource for which you want to specify multiple cost rates.

Information

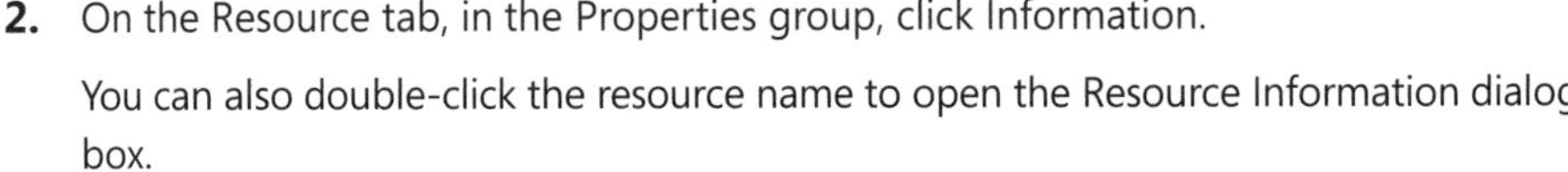

2. On the Resource tab, in the Properties group, click Information.

   You can also double-click the resource name to open the Resource Information dialog box.

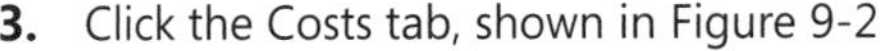

3. Click the Costs tab, shown in Figure 9-2.

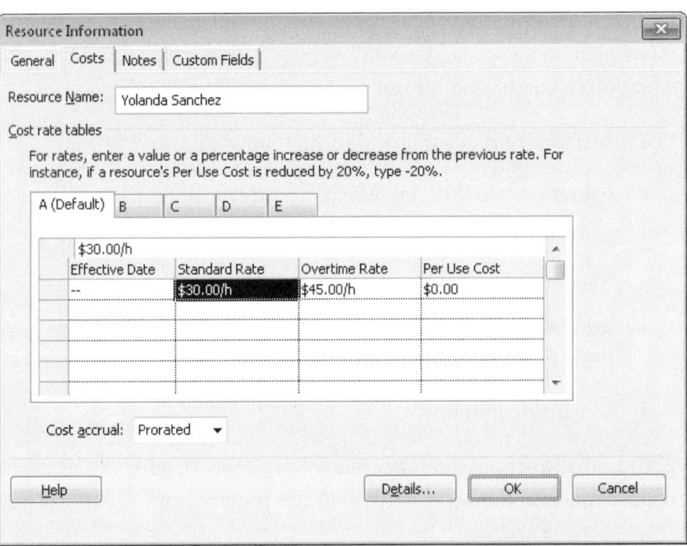

Figure 9-2 Use the cost rate tables in the Resource Information dialog box to specify different resource rates.

4. On the A (Default) tab, in the first row, you see the standard rate, overtime rate, and per-use cost you might have already entered in the Resource Sheet.

5. To specify a change in rate after a certain period of time, still on the A (Default) tab, click in the next blank Effective Date field and enter the date the change is to take effect. Enter the cost changes as applicable in the Standard Rate, Overtime Rate, and Per Use Cost fields, as shown in Figure 9-3.

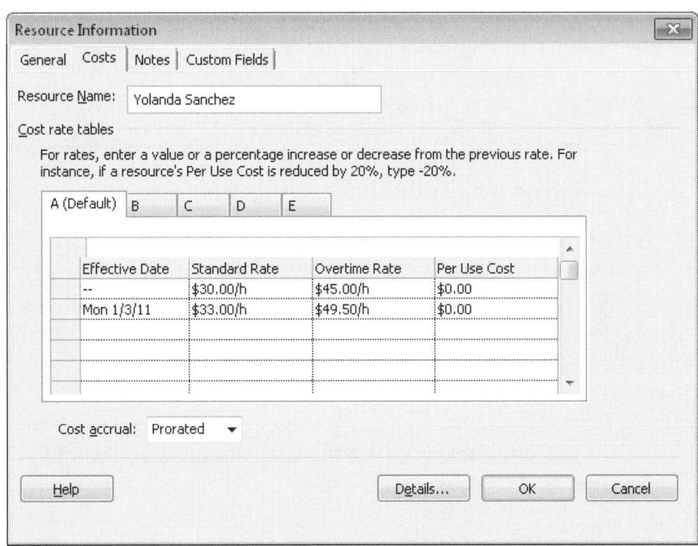

Figure 9-3 If new costs are to take effect on a certain date, add the date and costs to the A (Default) cost rate table.

6. To specify different costs based on different types of activities, enter the different costs in a different tab, such as B or C.

   Click the B tab, for example, and enter the standard rate, overtime rate, and per-use cost for the other activity as applicable. When you assign this resource to a task that uses the different rates, you can specify which cost table to use.

Note

If a percentage rate change goes into effect on a certain date, you can have Project 2010 calculate the new rate for you. Enter the date in the Effective Date field. Then, in the Standard Rate, Overtime Rate, or Per Use Cost fields, enter the percentage change; for example, +10% or -15%. The actual rate representing that change is immediately calculated and entered in the field.

Cost Rate Table A for resources is applied to the resource's assignments by default and is what shows on the Resource Sheet. If you define a different cost rate table on the B or C tab for another category of work, you can specify which cost rate table to use at the assignment level. To do this, follow these steps:

1. In a task view such as the Gantt Chart, use the Assign Resources dialog box to assign the resource to the task.

Task Usage

2. On the View tab, in the Task Views group, click Task Usage.

   Or, on the View tab, in the Resource Views group, click Resource Usage.

   Either of these options presents an assignment view.

Resource Usage

3. Click the assignment that needs a different cost rate table applied.

Information

4. On the Format tab, in the Assignment group, click Information.
5. In the Assignment Information dialog box, make sure that either the General or Tracking tab is active.
6. In the Cost Rate Table list, click the cost rate table you want to apply to this assignment, as shown in Figure 9-4.

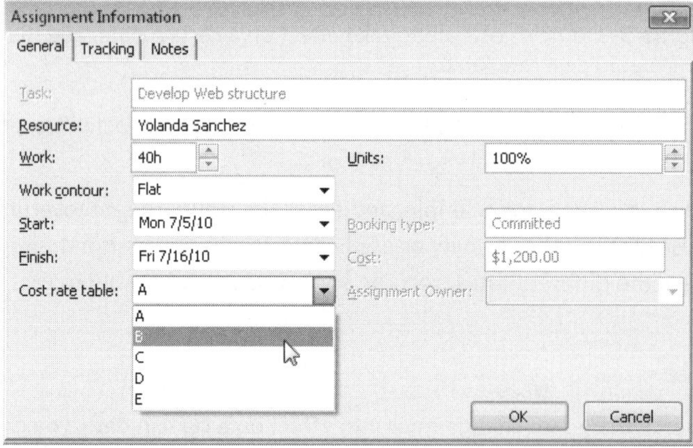

Figure 9-4 In the Assignment Information dialog box, select which cost rate table should be used for this assignment.

You cannot enter a description for the different cost rate tables to explain what each should be used for. Because of this limitation, it's a good idea to enter a resource note for any resource that uses multiple cost rate tables. Simply click the Notes tab in the Resource Information dialog box and enter the note.

Setting Cost Accrual

Cost accrual indicates the point in time when costs are incurred, or charged. You can specify that costs are incurred at the beginning of the assignment or at the end of the assignment. Another option is to *prorate* costs across the time span of the assignment, which is the default method. Specifying the cost accrual method is important for budget cash flow planning.

To specify the cost accrual method, follow these steps:

1. Be sure that the Entry table is applied to the Resource Sheet.
2. In the Accrue At field for the work or material resource, click the method: Start, Prorated, or End.

You can also specify the cost accrual method for a resource on the Costs tab of the Resource Information dialog box.

Note

You can set different cost accrual methods for different resources. However, even if a resource has different cost rate tables, those tables must share a single cost accrual method.

Enter Cost Center Information

Your organization might associate employees and budget items such as materials, equipment, and travel with certain cost centers. To support this, you can add the Cost Center text field to the Resource Sheet or Resource Usage view.

To do this, right-click the column heading next to where you want to insert the Cost Center field, and then click Insert Column on the shortcut menu. In the temporary drop-down menu that appears in the new column, type **cos** to quickly move to the cost fields.

Click Cost Center to apply the field to the new column. Clicking the field also dismisses the drop-down menu. Enter cost center codes in this column for each resource. When the information is in place, you can sort, group, or filter by cost center.

Entering Costs for Cost Resource Assignments

A *cost resource* is a cost item that contributes to the completion of a task but does not affect the schedule when assigned to that task. A cost resource represents a cost item other than a person, a piece of equipment, or a quantity of materials, and the cost item is incurred in the performance of the task. Examples of cost resources are airfare, lodging, and rentals.

When you create a cost resource, you do not enter the cost amount in the Resource Sheet as you do with work or material resources. The cost amount for that resource changes depending on the task to which it is assigned.

For example, suppose you have a cost resource named "Trade Show Registration." Your project plan includes participation in five different trade shows that each have differing registration fees. For the "Plan for Portland trade show" task, you can assign the "Trade Show Registration" cost resource and enter $975. For the "Plan for Las Vegas trade show" task, you can assign the same "Trade Show Registration" cost resource and enter $1,595 for the cost.

The advantage of using the same cost resource for different tasks is that you can summarize your total costs for a particular cost category, such as trade show registration, airfare, or permits.

For more information about setting up cost resources, see "Adding Cost Resources to the Project" on page 259.

To assign a cost resource to a task, follow these steps:

1. Make sure the cost resource is set up in your Resource Sheet.

   Cost resources are designated with Cost selected in the Type field.

2. In the Gantt Chart or other task sheet, click the task to which you want to assign the cost resource.

Assign Resources

3. On the Resource tab, in the Assignments group, click Assign Resources.

4. In the Assign Resources dialog box, click the name of the cost resource you want to assign to the task.

5. Click in the Cost field for the cost resource, and then type the cost amount for this resource on this task. (See Figure 9-5.)

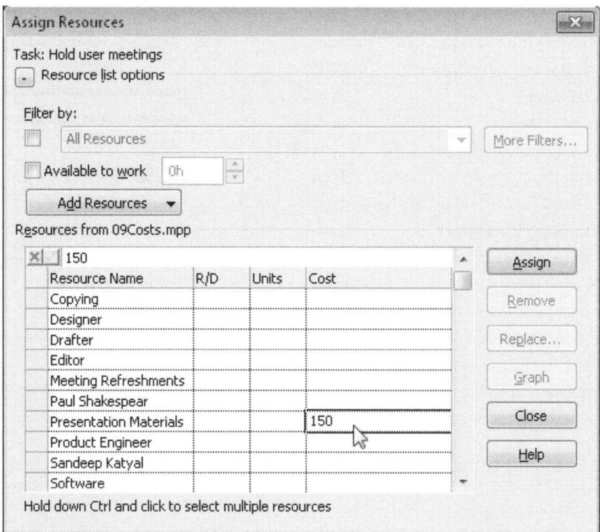

Figure 9-5 Enter the cost amount for this cost resource assigned to this particular task.

6. Click the Assign button.

7. To assign the same cost resource to a different task, click that task. Enter the cost for that cost resource for the newly selected task, and then click the Assign button.

8. When you finish assigning resources to tasks, click the Close button.

   By default, the name of the cost resource as well as the cost amount for the assignment is shown next to the Gantt bar for the task, as you can see in Figure 9-6.

If you need to change the cost you entered on a cost resource assignment, double-click the task to open the Task Information dialog box. Click the Resources tab. In the Cost field for the cost resource, change the amount.

You can also assign cost resources on a timephased basis. Assign the cost resource by using the Assign Resources dialog box as described above. Then go to the Task Usage or Resource Usage view. Add the Cost field to the timesheet area of the view for the assignment, enter an amount for one time period, enter an amount for another time period, and so on. This approach can be useful if you want to show when the costs are incurred. For example, if you want to break down the daily costs on a Catering cost resource at a trade show, you can enter $200 on one day, $150 on the second day, and $225 on the third day.

Chapter 9

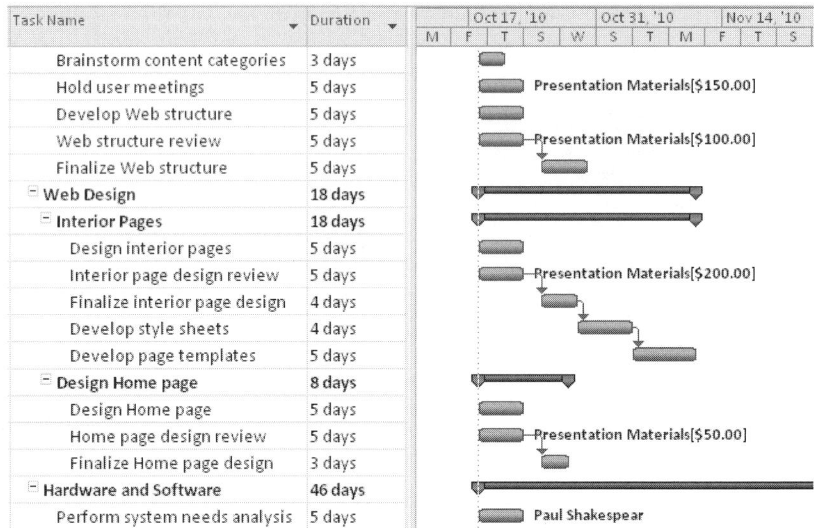

Figure 9-6 The same cost resource can be assigned to multiple tasks for differing cost amounts.

Planning Fixed Costs for Tasks

You might have a task cost that's independent of any resource. For example, the performance of a task might include costs for printing reports for a customer review meeting or the purchase of an external hard drive for transferring the files for the development of a deliverable from one resource to another. Such a task cost can be a "miscellaneous" or incidental cost on the task. If the cost does not need to be tracked as its own category, or if it's only going to be incurred for a single task in the project, it might be a good candidate to be entered as a fixed cost for a task.

To enter a fixed cost for a task, follow these steps:

1. Display the Gantt Chart or other task sheet.
2. On the View tab, in the Data group, click Tables, and then click Cost.

   The Cost table, which includes the Fixed Cost and Fixed Cost Accrual fields, is applied to the task sheet, as shown in Figure 9-7.

Why Use Cost Resources?

In Microsoft Project 2003 and earlier versions, project managers sometimes created work resources such as "Airfare" or "Lodging," with the cost entered in the Cost/Use field. However, the cost could only be a rough estimate if the same resource was to be used for multiple tasks. The alternative was to create a different "Airfare" resource for each instance in which it needed to be used. In addition to being cumbersome, this approach was problematic because it was a work resource, and as such, it adversely affected scheduling. Such a resource had a work calendar, and adding or removing it to a task could change duration or work scheduled for that task.

With cost resources, you can create a resource that is completely independent of task scheduling. You can assign the cost resource to one or more tasks, enter the cost for that resource on each individual task, and then track it thereafter very neatly and accurately.

But then, why not simply enter a fixed cost for a task? Entering fixed costs for tasks does not affect scheduling, and the costs roll up nicely into the project cost summary.

The advantage of using a cost resource instead of a fixed cost for a task is that you can assign multiple cost resources to a single task, whereas you can enter only one amount as a fixed cost for a task. For example, you can assign the "Airfare," "Car Rental," and "Hotel" cost resources to the "Train customer service staff in Dayton" task. This gives you more control, and therefore more accurate cost information, when you apply different types of costs to tasks.

Entering a fixed cost is still quite useful when you want to enter a cost that doesn't need granular tracking or to be summarized with others of its kind. If there's a one-off type of cost associated with the performance of a task, it's still a good technique. But if you have certain costs that you want to track individually or that are used by different tasks throughout the project, the cost resource is the most flexible and accurate alternative.

	Task Name	Fixed Cost	Fixed Cost Accrual	Total Cost
1	**Web Structure**	**$0.00**	**Prorated**	**$12,370.00**
2	Brainstorm content categories	$0.00	Prorated	$4,320.00
3	Hold user meetings	$0.00	Prorated	$1,350.00
4	Develop Web structure	$0.00	Prorated	$1,800.00
5	Web structure review	$0.00	Prorated	$3,100.00
6	Finalize Web structure	$0.00	Prorated	$1,800.00
7	**Web Design**	**$0.00**	**Prorated**	**$15,130.00**
8	**Interior Pages**	**$0.00**	**Prorated**	**$10,040.00**
9	Design interior pages	$0.00	Prorated	$2,400.00
10	Interior page design review	$0.00	Prorated	$1,400.00
11	Finalize interior page design	$0.00	Prorated	$1,920.00
12	Develop style sheets	$0.00	Prorated	$1,920.00
13	Develop page templates	$0.00	Prorated	$2,400.00

Figure 9-7 Apply the Cost table to enter fixed costs for tasks.

3. In the Fixed Cost field for the task, enter the cost.

4. In the Fixed Cost Accrual field, specify when the cost should be accrued: at the beginning of the task, at the end, or prorated throughout the duration of the task. The planned fixed cost for the task is added to the planned cost for the task as derived from the cost of assigned resources and is shown in the Total Cost field.

Note

To set the default fixed cost accrual method, on the File tab, click Options, and then click Schedule in the left pane. Under Calculation Options For This Project, select your preferred default accrual method in the Default Fixed Costs Accrual box. This default accrual method applies only to fixed costs for tasks in this project, not the resource costs.

You can also enter a fixed cost for the project as a whole. To do this, follow these steps:

1. Display the Gantt Chart or other task sheet.

2. Click View, Table, Cost.

   The Cost table is applied.

3. On the Format tab, in the Show/Hide group, select the Project Summary Task check box.

The project summary task row appears at the top of the view and includes rolled-up costs for tasks. (See Figure 9-8.) By default, the name of the project summary is the same as the project file name. However, you can click in the Task Name field and rename it.

	Task Name	Fixed Cost	Fixed Cost Accrual	Total Cost
0	**Web Site Development**	**$0.00**	**Prorated**	**$29,350.00**
1	**Web Structure**	**$0.00**	**Prorated**	**$12,420.00**
2	Brainstorm content categories	$0.00	Prorated	$4,320.00
3	Hold user meetings	$0.00	Prorated	$1,350.00
4	Develop Web structure	$50.00	Prorated	$1,850.00
5	Web structure review	$0.00	Prorated	$3,100.00
6	Finalize Web structure	$0.00	Prorated	$1,800.00
7	**Web Design**	**$0.00**	**Prorated**	**$15,130.00**

Figure 9-8 Add the project summary task to add a fixed cost for the entire project.

4. In the Fixed Cost field for the project summary task, enter the fixed cost for the project.

5. In the Fixed Cost Accrual field, specify when the cost should be accrued: at the beginning of the project, at the end, or prorated throughout the duration of the project.

   The planned fixed cost for the project is added to all other costs calculated for assignments and tasks throughout the project. This total is shown in the Total Cost field of the project summary task.

Chapter 9

As you see, when you enter a fixed cost for a task or the entire project, all there is to do is enter the amount. You're not asked to enter what the cost is for, so it's a good practice to document the fixed cost by entering a note. To enter a note about a fixed cost, follow these steps:

1. Select the task (or the project summary task) for which you entered a fixed cost.

2. On the Task tab, in the Properties group, click Notes.

Notes

3. On the Notes tab in the Task Information (or Summary Task Information) dialog box, enter a note that explains the fixed cost.

To review notes that have been entered on a task, select the task. On the Task tab, in the Properties group, click Notes again. In many tables, including the default Entry table, the notes icon appears in the Indicators column. Rest your mouse pointer over the notes indicator to read the note, as shown in Figure 9-9. You can also double-click the notes indicator to open the Notes tab in the Task Information dialog box.

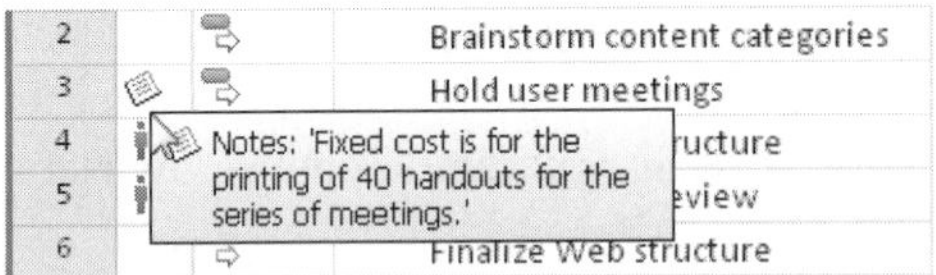

2
Brainstorm content categories
3
Hold user meetings
4
Notes: 'Fixed cost is for the printing of 40 handouts for the series of meetings.'
ucture
5
eview
6
Finalize Web structure

Figure 9-9 Rest your mouse pointer over the notes indicator to read the note explaining details about the fixed cost.

TROUBLESHOOTING

The rolled-up value for fixed costs for tasks looks wrong

If you have fixed costs for individual tasks, and possibly a fixed cost for the project as a whole, these values are not rolled up into the project summary task or outline summary tasks.

Instead, the fixed costs for tasks and any resource costs are calculated and displayed in the Total Cost field for the individual tasks. In turn, the Total Cost field is rolled up in the project summary task, and that's where you can see project cost totals. (See Figure 9-10.)

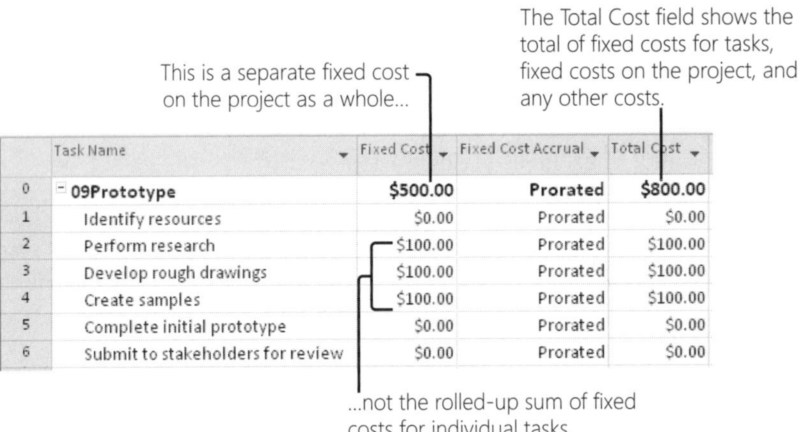

	Task Name	Fixed Cost	Fixed Cost Accrual	Total Cost
0	**09Prototype**	**$500.00**	**Prorated**	**$800.00**
1	Identify resources	$0.00	Prorated	$0.00
2	Perform research	$100.00	Prorated	$100.00
3	Develop rough drawings	$100.00	Prorated	$100.00
4	Create samples	$100.00	Prorated	$100.00
5	Complete initial prototype	$0.00	Prorated	$0.00
6	Submit to stakeholders for review	$0.00	Prorated	$0.00

Figure 9-10 Fixed costs are not rolled up into summary tasks or the project summary task, which enables you to enter a fixed cost for a phase or the project as a whole.

The reasoning is that you might need to enter a fixed cost for a project phase, represented in a summary task. Likewise, you might need to enter a fixed cost for the project as a whole. Not rolling up totals in the Fixed Cost field lets you do this, although at first glance the numbers look wrong. Keep your eye on the Total Cost field instead. Just be aware that the Total Cost field sums resource costs in addition to any fixed costs.

Reviewing Planned Costs

The planned costs for your project become reliable figures that you can use for a budget request or a project proposal when the following information is entered in your project plan:

- All required work and material resources, even if they're just generic resources
- Cost rates and per-use costs for all work and material resources
- Cost resources assigned to tasks with their individual amounts
- All tasks, complete with reliable duration estimates
- Assignments for all tasks
- Any fixed costs for tasks

After this information has been entered, you can review planned costs by various categories, from granular details to a high-level summary: costs for individual assignments, individual tasks or phases, individual resources, and, of course, the entire project.

Reviewing Assignment Costs

Review assignment costs by applying the Cost table to the Task Usage or Resource Usage view, as follows:

1. On the View tab, in the Task Views group, click Task Usage. Or, on the View tab, in the Resource Views group, click Resource Usage.

   Task Usage shortcut

   You can also click the Task Usage icon in the view shortcuts at the lower-right corner of the Project status bar, next to the Zoom slider.

2. On the View tab, in the Data group, click Tables, and then click Cost. The Cost table is applied to the view, as shown in Figure 9-11.

	Task Name	Fixed Cost	Fixed Cost Accrual	Total Cost	Details	M	T	W
0	**Web Site Development**	**$0.00**	**Prorated**	**$60,793.34**	Work	2h	2h	18.67h
1	Web Structure	$0.00	Prorated	$12,973.33	Work	2h	2h	8h
2	Brainstorm content categories	$0.00	Prorated	$5,840.00	Work			
	Sandeep Katyal			*$2,000.00*	Work			
	Designer			*$3,840.00*	Work			
3	Hold user meetings	$0.00	Prorated	$150.00	Work			
	Presentation Materials			*$150.00*	Work			
4	Develop Web structure	$50.00	Prorated	$2,083.33	Work	2h	2h	1.33h
	Vivian Atlas			*$1,200.00*	Work			
	Sandeep Katyal			*$833.33*	Work	2h	2h	1.33h
5	Web structure review	$0.00	Prorated	$3,100.00	Work			6.67h
	Vivian Atlas			*$1,800.00*	Work			5.33h
	Yolanda Sanchez			*$1,200.00*	Work			1.33h
	Presentation Materials			*$100.00*	Work			

Figure 9-11 Apply the Cost table to the Task Usage view to see assignment costs.

In the Task Usage view, you can see individual assignment costs, as well as the total cost for each task. In the Resource Usage view, you can see individual assignment costs with the total cost for each resource.

You can review timephased costs by adding the cost details row to the timesheet area of the Task Usage or Resource Usage view, as follows:

1. Display either the Task Usage or Resource Usage view.
2. On the Format tab, in the Details group, click Cost.

Note

You can also add a row of details by right-clicking in the timesheet area of a usage view and then clicking the name of the detail category—for example, Cost or Actual Work—you want to see.

The Cost field is added to the Work field in the timesheet area of the view, as shown in Figure 9-12.

	Task Name	Fixed Cost	Fixed Cost Accrual	Total Cost	Details	M	T	W
1	Web Structure	$0.00	Prorated	$12,973.33	Work	10h	10h	10h
					Cost	$605.00	$605.00	$605.00
2	Brainstorm content categories	$0.00	Prorated	$5,840.00	Work	10h	10h	10h
					Cost	$605.00	$605.00	$605.00
	Sandeep Katyal			*$2,000.00*	Work	2h	2h	2h
					Cost	$125.00	$125.00	$125.00
	Designer			*$3,840.00*	Work	8h	8h	8h
					Cost	$480.00	$480.00	$480.00

Figure 9-12 Review assignment costs over time by adding the Cost field to the Task Usage or Resource Usage timesheet area of the view.

Zoom

You can adjust the time period detail shown in the timesheet. On the View tab, in the Zoom group, click Zoom, and then click Zoom In or Zoom Out. You can also use the Zoom slider on the status bar. Click the plus button to zoom in, or click the minus button to zoom out.

Reviewing Resource Costs

You can review resource costs to see how much each resource is costing to carry out assigned tasks. To get total costs for a resource's assignments, add the Cost field to the Resource Sheet, as follows:

1. Display the Resource Sheet.
2. Click the column heading next to where you want to insert the Cost field.
3. On the Format tab, in the Columns group, click Insert Column.

   Insert Column

   A new column appears showing a temporary drop-down menu of all available resource fields.
4. Type **cos** to quickly go to the Cost fields in the list. Click Cost to apply the field to the column. Clicking the field also dismisses the drop-down menu.

   The Cost field shows the total planned costs for all assignments for each individual resource.

> **Note**
>
> **Reviewing resource costs is a great way to see how much you're spending on different cost categories as represented by your cost resources. Suppose you have assigned the "Airfare" cost resource to three different tasks. For one task the airfare costs $300, for the second task it costs $700, and for the third task it costs $500. If you add the Cost field to the Resource Sheet, you see that the total cost for airfare in your project is $1,000.**

In the Resource Sheet with the Cost field added, you can sort, filter, or highlight resources by cost information, as follows:

Sort

- **Sort resources by cost** On the View tab, in the Data group, click Sort, and then click By Cost.

  To return the Resource Sheet to its original order, on the View tab, in the Data group, click Sort, and then click By ID.

Filter

- **Filter resources by cost** On the View tab, in the Data group, click the arrow in the Filter box, and then click More Filters. Click Cost Greater Than, and then click Apply. Enter an amount, and then click OK.

  To see all resources again, on the View tab, in the Data group, click the arrow in the Filter box, and then click No Filter.

Highlight

- **Highlight resources by costs** On the View tab, in the Data group, click the arrow in the Highlight box, and then click More Highlight Filters. Click Cost Greater Than, and then click Highlight. Enter an amount, and then click OK.

  To remove the highlights, on the View tab, in the Data group, click the arrow in the Highlight box, and then click No Highlight.

Note

You can group resources by cost, but it's likely that each group would include just a single resource because they would all probably have different totals. Therefore, it's more practical to sort or filter resources by cost than to group them.

For more information about sorting, filtering, and grouping information, see "Rearranging Your Project Information" on page 173.

If you want to see the total resource costs along with the assignments that contribute to that total, use the Resource Usage view with the Cost table applied. The Cost field next to the resource name shows the total cost for the resource, while the assignments listed under each resource name show the component cost for that assignment or the amount that the resource costs for that particular task, as you can see in Figure 9-13.

	Resource Name	Cost	Details		Dec 12, '10		Dec 19, '10
				F	M	T	S
1	Vivian Atlas	$5,880.00	Work	8h	24h	16h	2.67h
	Develop Web structure	*$1,200.00*	Work				
	Web structure review	*$1,800.00*	Work				
	Finalize Web structure	*$1,800.00*	Work	8h	18.67h		
	Assign content owners	*$1,080.00*	Work		5.33h	16h	2.67h
2	Paul Shakespear	$18,360.00	Work		5.33h	16h	16h
	Perform system needs analysis	*$1,800.00*	Work		5.33h	16h	16h
	Evaluate equipment requirements	*$5,400.00*	Work				

Figure 9-13 Review total resource costs along with the individual assignment costs that go into that total by applying the Cost table to the Resource Usage view.

Reviewing Task Costs

You can review the planned task costs to see how much money is required to execute each task. Planned task costs represent the sum for all resources assigned to a task, in addition to any fixed costs for tasks. To view total costs for tasks, do the following:

1. Display the Gantt Chart or other task sheet.
2. On the View tab, in the Data group, click Tables, and then click Cost.
3. Review the Total Cost field to see the cost for each task.

You can run one of two built-in reports that show planned costs: the Budget report and the Cash Flow report. To generate the Budget report, do the following:

1. On the Project tab, in the Reports group, click Reports.
2. Double-click Costs.
3. Double-click Budget.

   NEW! A preview of the Budget report appears next to print and page setup options on the Print Backstage view, as shown in Figure 9-14.

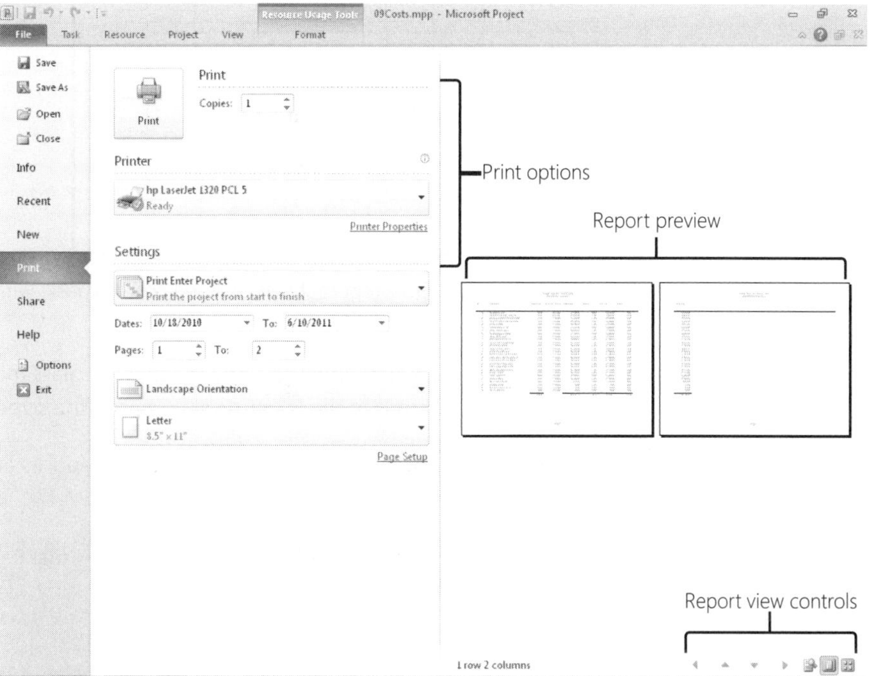

Figure 9-14 The Budget report shows the task name, fixed costs, and total planned costs.

4. To view the report, click the report with the magnifying glass mouse pointer. You can also use the various report viewing controls in the lower-right corner of the screen.

Print

5. To print the report, click the Print button. To close the report, click any of the tabs on the ribbon.

To generate the Cash Flow report, do the following:

1. On the Project tab, in the Reports group, click Reports.

2. Double-click Costs.

3. Double-click Cash Flow.

   A preview of the Cost Flow report appears next to print and page setup options. (See Figure 9-15.)

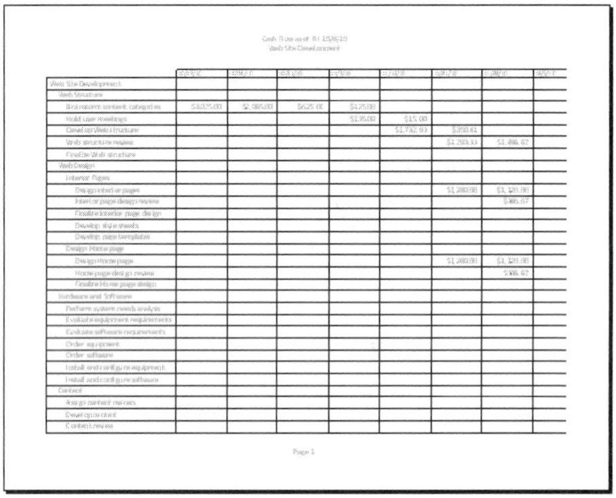

Figure 9-15 The Cash Flow report shows planned costs by task, with totals for tasks and for weekly periods.

4. To view the report, click the report with the magnifying glass mouse pointer or use the report viewing controls in the lower-right corner of the screen.

5. To print the report, click the Print button. To close the report, click any of the tabs on the ribbon.

For more information about reports, see "Generating Text and Visual Reports" on page 534.

In the Gantt Chart or other task sheet with cost information showing, you can sort, filter, or highlight tasks by cost, as follows:

- **Sort tasks by costs** On the View tab, in the Data group, click Sort, and then click By Cost.

  To return the task list to its original sort order, on the View tab, in the Data group, click Sort, and then click By ID.

- **Filter tasks by costs** On the View tab, in the Data group, click the arrow in the Filter box, and then click More Filters. Click Cost Greater Than, and then click Apply. Enter an amount, and then click OK.

  To see all tasks again, on the View tab, in the Data group, click the arrow in the Filter box, and then click No Filter.

- **Highlight tasks by costs** On the View tab, in the Data group, click the arrow in the Highlight box, and then click More Highlight Filters. Click Cost Greater Than, and then click Highlight. Enter an amount, and then click OK.

  To remove the highlights, on the View tab, in the Data group, click the arrow in the Highlight box, and then click No Highlight.

For more information about sorting and filtering information, see "Rearranging Your Project Information" on page 173.

Reviewing the Total Planned Cost for the Project

You can see the total planned cost for the entire project. This cost is the sum of all task costs, as well as any fixed costs you might have entered for the project. To see the total cost for the project, apply the Cost table to the Gantt Chart or other task sheet and show the Project Summary Task, as follows:

1. Display the Gantt Chart or other task sheet.
2. On the View tab, in the Data group, click Tables, and then click Cost.

   The Cost table is applied.
3. On the Format tab, in the Show/Hide group, select the Project Summary Task check box.

   The project summary task row appears at the top of the view. The total project cost is displayed in the Total Cost field.

You can also see the total project cost in the Project Statistics dialog box. To display the Project Statistics dialog box, follow these steps:

1. On the Project tab, in the Properties group, click Project Information.

2. Click the Statistics button. The Project Statistics dialog box appears, as shown in Figure 9-16.

Project Statistics for '09WebDev.mpp'

	Start	Finish
Current	Mon 10/18/10	Fri 6/10/11
Baseline	NA	NA
Actual	NA	NA
Variance	0d	0d

	Duration	Work	Cost
Current	169.33d	1,188h	$60,793.34
Baseline	0d	0h	$0.00
Actual	0d	0h	$0.00
Remaining	169.33d	1,188h	$60,793.34

Percent complete:

Duration: 0% Work: 0%

Close

Figure 9-16 The Project Statistics dialog box shows the overall project cost, as well as the project start and finish dates, total duration, and total work.

Setting Up and Reviewing a Project Budget

If you're concerned with project costs, it's likely that you're working with a budget. It's imperative to always keep an eye on your various budget categories while you're planning and later accruing project costs. If you can easily compare the budget against your planned and actual project costs, you're more likely to stay within your allowed budget.

In Project 2010, a comparison with your budget can be integrated with the project itself. Using the Budget Cost and Budget Work fields, you have the means for setting up and entering values for budget categories within your project plan. You can identify which resources belong under which budget category. You can then group the resources by budget category and compare them against your budget amounts.

Although the initial budget setup is somewhat involved, you have to do the setup only once for a project. After that, you can compare cost amounts against your budget amounts anytime you like.

Creating Budget Resources

Create budget resources that correspond to the budget line items you want to track and compare in your project. Examples of budget categories that might apply to a project plan include Employees, Vendors, Outside Services, Equipment Purchase, Equipment Rental, Materials Inventory, Travel Expenses, and Fees and Licensing. The majority of your costs will come from your resources: human, equipment, material, and cost resources.

> **Note**
>
> **Some costs will come from fixed costs on tasks. This budget process does not factor in these fixed costs.**

To create budget resources, follow these steps:

1. Display the Resource Sheet.
2. In the next available blank row, enter the name of the budget resource in the Resource Name field. You can think of the budget resource as a budget item or category.

   Be sure to name the budget resource item so that it is easily distinguishable from other resources. You might use all caps—for example, EMPLOYEES—if all other resource names are in lowercase letters or initial caps. You might use a budget number as a prefix to the budget resource name—for example, 6220-Vendors. You can also use Budget as part of the budget resource name, as in "Budget-Equipment." This differentiation becomes important later when you're looking at a view that compares the rolled-up numbers in your budget resources next to the numbers for the individual resources.
3. In the Type field, specify whether the budget item is for work, material, or cost resources.

   For work resources, you will eventually express the target budget by the number of hours worked. For cost resources, you will express the target budget by the cost amount.

4. If you are creating a material budget resource, specify the unit of measurement in the Material Label field—for example, packages, pounds, or sets.

   For material resources, you will eventually express the target budget by the number of units. To address this requirement, create a different budget resource for each different material resource that you want to track against the budget.

5. Double-click the name of the new budget resource.

6. On the General tab of the Resource Information dialog box, select the Budget check box.

   Selecting this check box transforms a regular resource into the special budget resource item.

7. Repeat steps 2 through 6 to create all the budget resources you intend to use with your project.

The Budget check box is not available in the Multiple Resource Information dialog box. However, if you have many budget resources, you can designate them more quickly by inserting the Budget column. To do this, follow these steps:

1. With the Resource Sheet showing, right-click the column heading next to where you want to insert the Budget column, and then click Insert Column on the shortcut menu.

2. In the temporary drop-down menu that appears in the new column, type **bu** to quickly move to the Budget fields.

3. Click the Budget field to apply it to the new column. Clicking the field also dismisses the drop-down menu.

4. For each of the budget resources, change the No in the Budget field to Yes. You can click in the field, type **y**, move to the next field, type **y** again, and so on, until all the budget resources are so designated. (See Figure 9-17.)

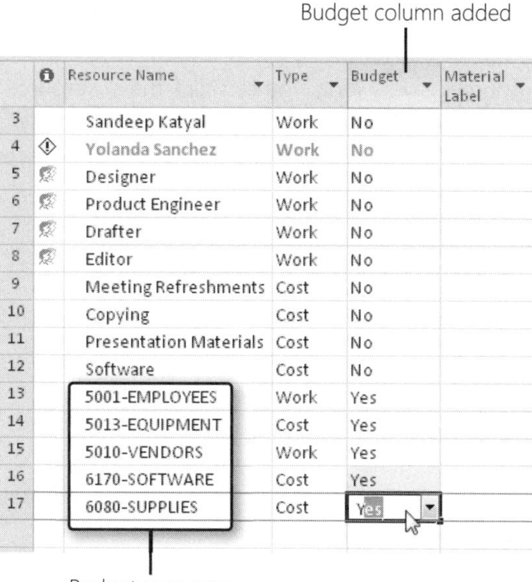

Figure 9-17 You can quickly designate multiple budget resources as such by adding the Budget field to the Resource Sheet and then changing its value from No to Yes.

5. After you designate all your budget resources by using the Budget column, you can hide the column. Right-click the Budget column heading, and then click Hide Column on the shortcut menu.

Assigning Budget Resources to the Project Summary Task

After you create your budget resources, assign them all to your project summary task. The project summary task is the only task to which budget resources can be assigned. To assign budget resources to your project summary task, follow these steps:

1. Switch to the Gantt Chart or other task sheet.

2. On the Format tab, in the Show/Hide group, select the Project Summary Task check box.

   The project summary task now appears at the Task 0 position at the top of the sheet view.

3. Click in the project summary task to select it.

4. On the Resource tab, in the Assignments group, click Assign Resources.

5. Hold down the Ctrl key and click each of your budget resources. If necessary, scroll down through the list of resources to find them all.

   If the list of resources is very long, you can click the + Resource List Options button to show the filter options. Select the check box under Filter By, and then in the drop-down list, click Budget Resources. Be sure that all the budget resources are selected. (See Figure 9-18.)

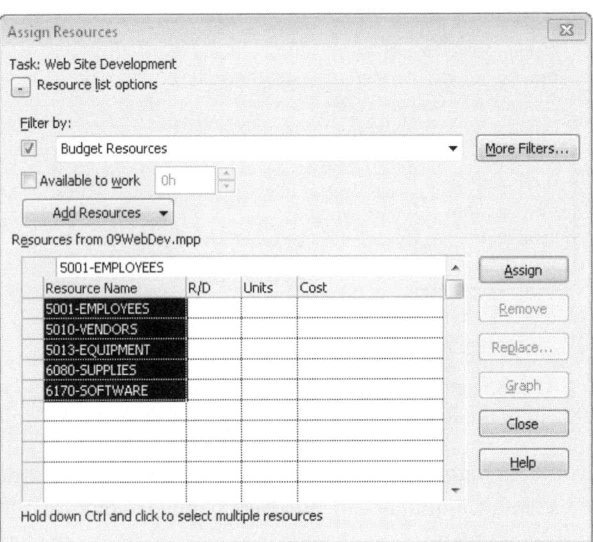

Figure 9-18 If necessary, filter the list of resources to show only budget resources.

6. Click the Assign button, and then click the Close button.

   Unlike regular resources, budget resource names do not appear next to the project summary task bar in the Gantt Chart.

TROUBLESHOOTING

The Assign button is unavailable for a budget resource

If you try to assign a budget resource, but the Assign button is not available in the Assign Resources dialog box (and neither are the Remove and Replace buttons), check the task that's currently selected. If it's any task but the project summary task, the Assign button is unavailable. Select the project summary task, and the Assign button becomes available again.

Entering Budget Values for the Budget Resources

Now that the budget resources are all assigned to the project summary task, you can enter the budget amounts for the work, material, and cost resources in your project. These values represent the cost targets against which you will compare project work and costs. To enter budget values, follow these steps:

1. Switch to the Task Usage view or the Resource Usage view.
2. Right-click the column where you want to insert the Budget Cost column, and then click Insert Column on the shortcut menu.
3. In the temporary drop-down menu that appears in the new column, type **bu** to quickly move to the budget fields.
4. Click the Budget Cost field to apply it to the new column.
5. Repeat steps 2 through 4 to add the Budget Work field to the view.
6. In an assignment row, enter the work or cost value in the Budget Work or Budget Cost field.

   For a budget resource designated as a work resource, express the budget value as a work amount—that is, enter a number of hours in the Budget Work field. This value should be the number of hours (or days or whatever you prefer) that you have budgeted for all work in this category. You might need to extrapolate the number of budgeted hours from a budgeted cost amount, using an average hourly rate, for example.

   For a budget resource designated as a material resource, also use the Budget Work field, but express the value according to the material label—for example, tons, board feet, yards, and so on. This value should be the total amount of material you have budgeted for this category. This figure might also need to be extrapolated from a budgeted cost amount.

   For a budget resource designated as a cost resource, express the budget value as a cost amount in the Budget Cost field, as shown in Figure 9-19. This value should be the total amount of money you have budgeted for this category.

	Resource Name	Type	Budget Cost	Budget Work
13	5001-EMPLOYEES	Work		2,000 hrs
	Web Site Development	*Work*		*2,000 hrs*
14	5013-EQUIPMENT	Cost	$3,000.00	
	Web Site Development	*Cost*	*$3,000.00*	
15	5010-VENDORS	Work		1,500 hrs
	Web Site Development	*Work*		*1,500 hrs*
16	6170-SOFTWARE	Cost	$3,000.00	
	Web Site Development	*Cost*	*$3,000.00*	
17	6080-SUPPLIES	Cost	$1,500.00	
	Web Site Development	*Cost*	*$1,500.00*	

Figure 9-19 Enter the work, material, and cost values for each of your budget resources. These values represent the target budget against which you will compare project costs.

TROUBLESHOOTING

You can't enter a value in the Budget Cost or Budget Work field

For budget resource items designated as cost resources, you can enter a value only in the Budget Cost field, not the Budget Work field. Likewise, for budget resource items designated as work or material resources, you can enter a value only in the Budget Work field and not the Budget Cost field.

If you need to designate a certain budget within a specific period of time—for example, a month or a quarter—you can do so by adding the Budget Cost and Budget Work fields to the timesheet area of the Task Usage or Resource Usage view. To do this, follow these steps:

1. Be sure that the Task Usage or Resource Usage view is displayed.

Add Details

2. On the Format tab, in the Details group, click Add Details.

   The Detail Styles dialog box appears.

3. Under Available Fields, scroll down and click Budget Cost. Hold down the Shift or Ctrl key and also click Budget Work.

   Both fields are selected.

4. Click the Show button to add the fields to the Show These Fields box.

5. Click OK. In the timesheet area of the view, double-click the right edge of the Details column heading to widen the column so that you can see the full field names.

6. On the View tab, in the Zoom group, click Zoom, and then click Zoom In or Zoom Out to see the time unit for which you want to enter timephased budget values.

   For example, the budget for employees might be expressed per week or per month. Zoom the timesheet until it shows weeks or months (rather than days).

   You can also use the Zoom slider on the status bar. Click the plus button to zoom in, or click the minus button to zoom out.

7. In the assignment row under the budget resource for which you want to enter timephased budget values, enter the work or cost value in the Budget Work or Budget Cost field under the appropriate unit of time. (See Figure 9-20.)

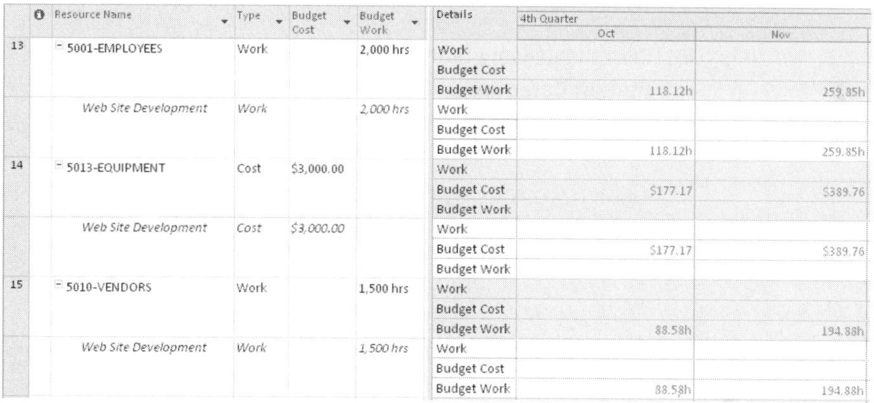

	Resource Name	Type	Budget Cost	Budget Work	Details	4th Quarter	
						Oct	Nov
13	5001-EMPLOYEES	Work		2,000 hrs	Work		
					Budget Cost		
					Budget Work	118.12h	259.85h
	Web Site Development	*Work*		*2,000 hrs*	Work		
					Budget Cost		
					Budget Work	118.12h	259.85h
14	5013-EQUIPMENT	Cost	$3,000.00		Work		
					Budget Cost	$177.17	$389.76
					Budget Work		
	Web Site Development	*Cost*	*$3,000.00*		Work		
					Budget Cost	$177.17	$389.76
					Budget Work		
15	5010-VENDORS	Work		1,500 hrs	Work		
					Budget Cost		
					Budget Work	88.58h	194.88h
	Web Site Development	*Work*		*1,500 hrs*	Work		
					Budget Cost		
					Budget Work	88.58h	194.88h

Figure 9-20 You can enter timephased budget resource values in the timesheet area of the Resource Usage view.

> **Note**
>
> **Even though the Budget Cost and Budget Work fields appear next to all assignments in the view, remember that you can enter budget values only for the budget resources assigned to the project summary task.**

Aligning Resources with Their Budget Resource Type

In this step of the process, you categorize the resources whose costs you want to compare with the budget resource values. You can use an existing text field that isn't being used for anything else, such as the Group or Code field already in the Resource Sheet, or you can create a custom text field. Either way, you create your budget categories and then categorize the resources by using the text field, including the budget resources themselves.

To create a custom text field for your budget categories, follow these steps:

1. Switch to the Resource Sheet.

Custom Fields

2. On the Project tab, in the Properties group, click Custom Fields.

   The Custom Fields dialog box appears.

3. Under Field, be sure that the Resource option is selected.

4. In the Type box, select Text.

5. In the Field box, select the custom text field you want to use; for example, Text1 or Text2.

6. Click the Rename button, and type the name you want for this field—for example, **Budget Category** or **Budget Group**. Click OK.

   The renamed field appears in the Field box, as shown in Figure 9-21.

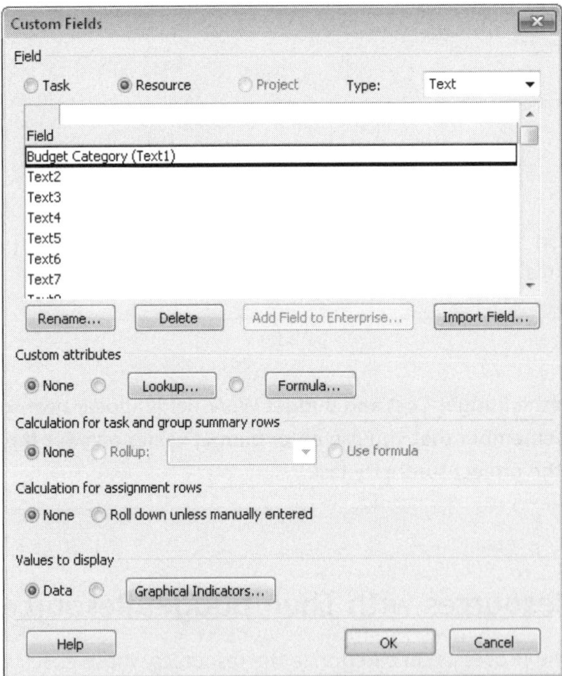

Figure 9-21 Create a custom text field to categorize your resources by their budget types.

7. Under Calculation For Assignment Rows, select the Roll Down Unless Manually Entered option. Click OK.

   This option specifies that the contents of your budget category field should be distributed across assignments in the Task Usage view or Resource Usage view unless you manually enter information in an assignment row.

To add your new text field to the Resource Sheet, follow these steps:

1. Right-click the column heading where you want to insert the text field, and then click Insert Column on the shortcut menu.

2. In the temporary drop-down menu that appears in the new column, type **tex** or the first two or three letters of the name you gave to the text field to quickly find that field in the list.

3. Click the field name to apply it to the new column.

   The text field appears in the Resource Sheet.

Now go down the list of resources and type a budget category for each resource you want to track against the budget. Be sure to also enter a budget category for the budget resources themselves. (See Figure 9-22.) The category names can be whatever you choose; for example, Employees, Vendors, or Equipment. Just be sure to use the same name and same spelling for the same category. This consistency becomes important when you group the resources by their category names in the next step of the process.

		Resource Name	Type	Budget Category	Budget Cost	Budget Work
2		Paul Shakespear	Work	Vendors		
3		Sandeep Katyal	Work	Employees		
4		Yolanda Sanchez	Work	Employees		
5		Designer	Work	Vendors		
6		Product Engineer	Work	Employees		
7		Drafter	Work	Vendors		
8		Editor	Work	Employees		
9		Meeting Refreshments	Cost	Supplies		
10		Copying	Cost	Supplies		
11		Presentation Materials	Cost	Supplies		
12		Software	Cost	Software		
13		5001-EMPLOYEES	Work	Employees		2,000 hrs
14		5013-EQUIPMENT	Cost	Equipment	$3,000.00	
15		5010-VENDORS	Work	Vendors		1,500 hrs
16		6170-SOFTWARE	Cost	Software	$3,000.00	
17		6080-SUPPLIES	Cost	Supplies	$1,500.00	

Figure 9-22 Specify the budget category for each resource you want to track against your budget—possibly all your resources.

Create a Lookup Table for Your Budget Types

You can enter your budget categories in a lookup table so that you can pick categories from a list rather than enter them for each resource. If you have a long list of resources you need to categorize, using a lookup table can save you a lot of time. To create a lookup table for the custom text field you already created, follow these steps:

1. On the Project tab, in the Properties group, click Custom Fields.
2. Under Field, be sure that the Resource option is selected.
3. In the Type box, be sure that Text is selected.
4. In the Field box, select the custom text field you created previously.
5. Under Custom Attributes, click the Lookup button.
6. In the first row of the lookup table, type the first budget category name you want to use, and then press Enter.
7. In the second row, type the second budget category name, and then press Enter.
8. Continue entering budget category names in different rows of the Value column until you enter all your categories.
9. When you have finished, click Close, and then click OK in the Custom Fields dialog box.

Now you can click in your custom text field, click the arrow that appears, and select a budget category from the list.

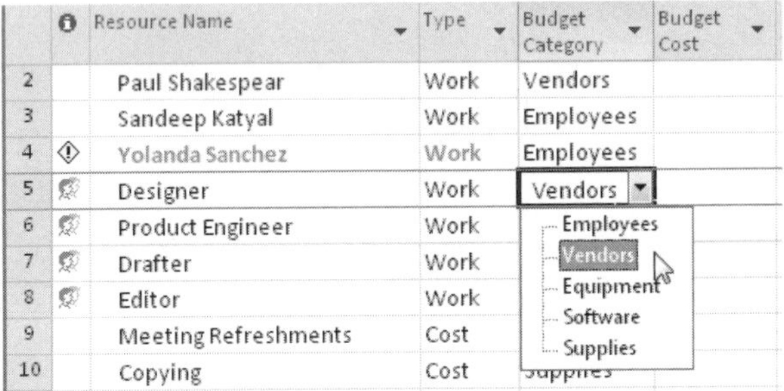

For more information about working with custom fields and lookup tables, see "Customizing Fields" on page 1107.

Note

If you're not using the Group or Code field on the Resource Sheet for any other purpose, you can use either of those fields to categorize your resources instead of going to the trouble of creating a custom text field. Like a custom text field, you can enter any information in the Group or Code field.

At this point, you've completed all the steps necessary for the initial setup of budget resources. Unless you find that you need new budget resources or new resources that you want to track against the budget resources, you're all set to compare project costs against your budget.

Comparing Resource Costs with Budget Resource Values

Now you can compare your resource costs against the values you identified for your budget resources and see where you stand. This comparison is useful in the planning stage, and it will also be useful later when your project is in the monitoring stage, as tasks are being completed and actual costs are being incurred.

1. Switch to the Resource Usage view.
2. If they're not already showing, add the Budget Work, Budget Cost, Work, and Cost fields to the table, as shown in Figure 9-23. To do this, right-click the column where you want to insert the column and then click Insert Column on the shortcut menu. In the temporary drop-down menu that appears, click the field to apply it to the column.
3. On the View tab, in the Data group, click the arrow in the Group By box, and then click New Group By.
4. Click in the Group By field under Field Name, click the arrow that appears in the field, and then click the name of your custom text field (or the Code or Group field) that you used to categorize your resources. (See Figure 9-24.)

		Resource Name	Type	Budget Cost	Budget Work	Cost	Work
1		Vivian Atlas	Work			$5,880.00	130.67 hrs
		Develop Web structure	*Work*			*$1,200.00*	*26.67 hrs*
		Web structure review	*Work*			*$1,800.00*	*40 hrs*
		Finalize Web structure	*Work*			*$1,800.00*	*40 hrs*
		Assign content owners	*Work*			*$1,080.00*	*24 hrs*
2		Paul Shakespear	Work			$18,360.00	408 hrs
		Perform system needs analysis	*Work*			*$1,800.00*	*40 hrs*

Figure 9-23 Show the columns necessary to compare your planned costs against your budgeted costs.

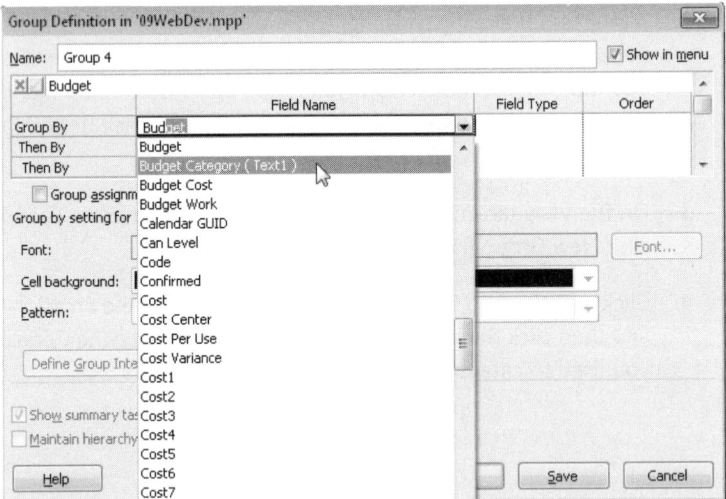

Figure 9-24 Use the Group Definition dialog box to select the name of the field you used to categorize your resources by their budget type.

5. Click Apply.

   The resources in your project are grouped by the budget categories you assigned, as shown in Figure 9-25. Each grouping includes one budget resource. The figures for the budget resource appear in the Budget Cost and Budget Work fields. The figures for all other resources appear in the Cost and Work fields. The total costs for the resources are rolled up in the grouping bar. Compare the rolled-up values with the values for the budget resources to see how the costs in your project are faring against the budget for that category.

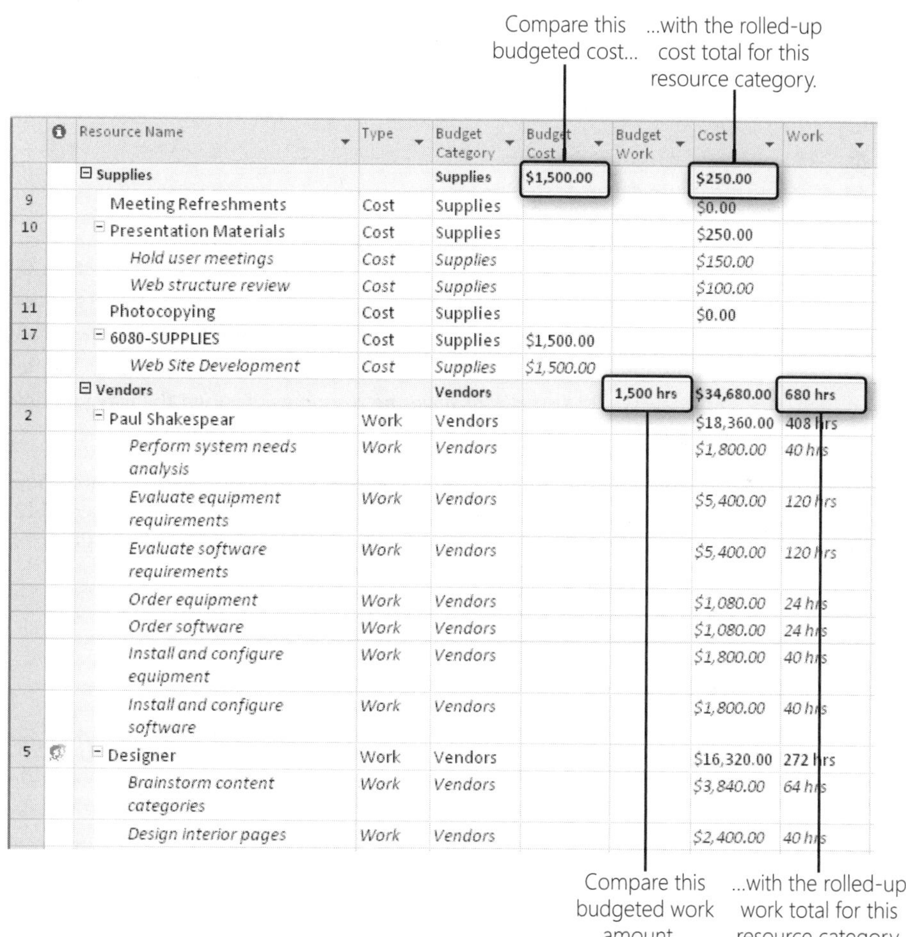

		Resource Name	Type	Budget Category	Budget Cost	Budget Work	Cost	Work
		⊟ Supplies		Supplies	$1,500.00		$250.00	
9		Meeting Refreshments	Cost	Supplies			$0.00	
10		⊟ Presentation Materials	Cost	Supplies			$250.00	
		Hold user meetings	*Cost*	*Supplies*			*$150.00*	
		Web structure review	*Cost*	*Supplies*			*$100.00*	
11		Photocopying	Cost	Supplies			$0.00	
17		⊟ 6080-SUPPLIES	Cost	Supplies	$1,500.00			
		Web Site Development	*Cost*	*Supplies*	*$1,500.00*			
		⊟ Vendors		Vendors		1,500 hrs	$34,680.00	680 hrs
2		⊟ Paul Shakespear	Work	Vendors			$18,360.00	408 hrs
		Perform system needs analysis	*Work*	*Vendors*			*$1,800.00*	*40 hrs*
		Evaluate equipment requirements	*Work*	*Vendors*			*$5,400.00*	*120 hrs*
		Evaluate software requirements	*Work*	*Vendors*			*$5,400.00*	*120 hrs*
		Order equipment	*Work*	*Vendors*			*$1,080.00*	*24 hrs*
		Order software	*Work*	*Vendors*			*$1,080.00*	*24 hrs*
		Install and configure equipment	*Work*	*Vendors*			*$1,800.00*	*40 hrs*
		Install and configure software	*Work*	*Vendors*			*$1,800.00*	*40 hrs*
5		⊟ Designer	Work	Vendors			$16,320.00	272 hrs
		Brainstorm content categories	*Work*	*Vendors*			*$3,840.00*	*64 hrs*
		Design interior pages	*Work*	*Vendors*			*$2,400.00*	*40 hrs*

Figure 9-25 When you group your resources by their budget categories, you can quickly compare the planned costs and planned work for the resources with the budgeted costs and work as shown by the budget resources.

Chapter 9

Note

Your resources initially appear in the order in which they were entered in the project. If you want to see the resource names in alphabetical order, on the View tab, in the Data group, click Sort, and then click By Name. Analyzing your budget performance is easiest if the budget resource appears at the top of each grouping, either because of its name or its ID, which reflects the order in which it was entered.

6. To ungroup the Resource Usage view, on the View tab, in the Data group, click the arrow in the Group By box, and then click No Group.

INSIDE OUT **Create a budget resource view**

If you expect to monitor your budget in this way fairly often, consider creating a custom view. In such a view, you could include a custom table that would always show the Budget Cost, Budget Work, Cost, and Work fields, along with the Resource Name. The view would also always have the resources grouped the way you need them to see the budget comparisons.

For more information about creating a custom budget resource view that includes a custom table and grouping, see "Creating a New Table" on page 1107, "Creating a New Group" on page 1127, and "Creating a New View" on page 1066.

Setting a Different Currency

The currency used in Project 2010 is the one specified in your computer system's regional and language options. However, you can set up your project to work with a different currency, or even to work with multiple currencies in a single plan. These capabilities facilitate cost planning and management for projects that span multiple countries and their currencies.

Setting Up a Different Currency on Your Computer

You can set up a different currency to take effect in all the applications you use on your computer by changing your computer's regional and language options. To do this, follow these steps:

1. On the Windows taskbar, click Start, Control Panel.
2. Click Clock, Language, and Region.
3. Under Region And Language, click Change The Date, Time, Or Number Format. Be sure that the Formats tab is displayed in the Region And Language dialog box that appears.
4. In the Current Format box, click the language and country pairing whose currency you want to use throughout your computer system.

   The formats for date and time for the selected language and country pairing are displayed.
5. Click the Additional Settings button to open the Customize Format dialog box.
6. Click the Currency tab, and check that the currency is displayed the way you want.
7. Click OK in the Customize Format dialog box and again in the Region And Language dialog box.

If you change the country and associated currency, the new setting takes effect for any new projects that you create from this point forward. It does not change the currency settings for existing projects.

Setting Up a Different Currency in Project 2010

If you prefer, you can change the currency settings just in Project 2010 and not for your computer system. Currencies are set for individual plans, not for Project 2010 globally. To apply a new currency in the current project:

1. In Project 2010, open the project in which you want to use a different currency.
2. On the File tab, click Options, and then click Display in the left pane.
3. Under Currency Options For This Project, in the Currency box, select the currency you want to use, as shown in Figure 9-26. You need to know the standard currency abbreviation—for example, GBP for British pounds, EUR for Euros, or USD for American dollars.

   The contents of the Symbol, Placement, and Decimal Digits boxes change to reflect the currency you choose.

4. Make any necessary changes to the Placement or Decimal Digits box, and then click OK.

   Any currencies already entered in the project are changed to the new currency. Note, however, that values are not converted; only the currency symbol is changed.

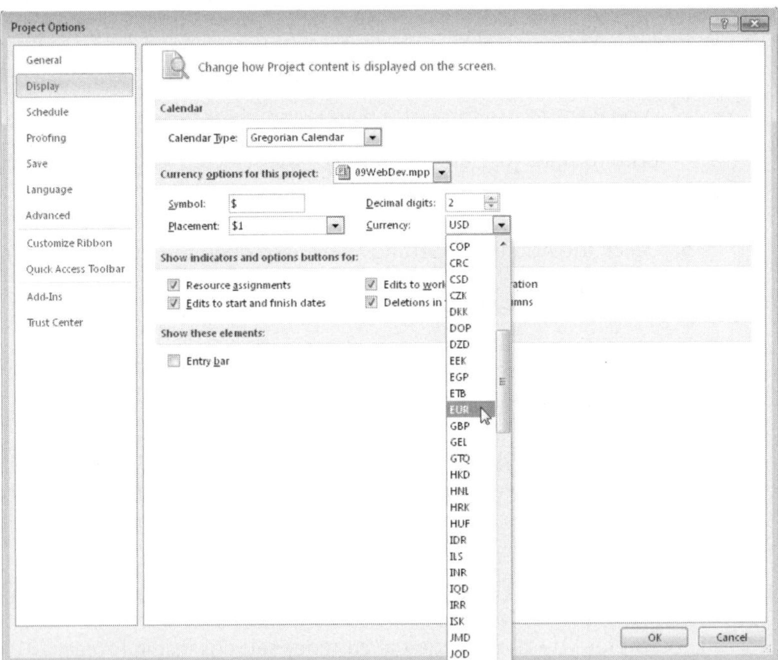

Figure 9-26 Use the Display section in the Project Options dialog box to specify the currency you want to use in this project plan.

Using this method, one currency applies throughout the project plan. If you consolidate projects that use different currencies, be sure to change the settings in each one to a common currency and make the necessary conversions to cost values. Although you can specify different currencies in different projects, only one currency can be in effect for any particular project.

INSIDE OUT Strategies for working with multiple currencies

If you need visibility into multiple currencies in your project, you could create custom fields that include a formula representing an approximation of the exchange rate.

Because exchange rates fluctuate day to day, you might want to add a hyperlink to an exchange rate website so that you have easy access from within your project.

If you have a resource working in more than one country, perhaps being paid differently in those different countries, think about using different cost rate tables for that resource.

For more information about creating a custom cost field that includes a formula, see "Creating a Calculated Field" on page 1112. For information about adding a hyperlink to task information, see "Attaching Project Documentation" on page 94. For information about cost rate tables, see "Setting Multiple Costs for a Resource" on page 328.

CHAPTER 10

Checking and Adjusting the Project Plan

In a perfect world, you'd define the project scope, schedule tasks, assign resources, and presto! The project plan would be finished and ready to execute.

In reality, however, this is rarely the case. After you schedule tasks and assign resources, you generally need to check the results and see whether they meet expectations and requirements. Ultimately, you might need to answer one or all of the following questions—to your satisfaction and to the satisfaction of your managing stakeholders:

- Will the project be finished on time?
- Is the project keeping to its budget?
- Do the resources have the appropriate amount of work?

If you get the wrong answers to any of these questions, you need to adjust your project plan until you get the right answers. For example, if the finish date is too far away, you can add more resources to major tasks.

After you make such adjustments, you need to check the project plan again. Adding resources to tasks might bring in the finish date, but it also might add cost if you have to hire additional resources or authorize overtime. And if you assign more tasks to existing resources, those resources might be overallocated.

To save time as well as money, you might decide to cut certain tasks, a deliverable, or a phase. But if this means you're cutting project scope, you probably need to get approval from your managing stakeholders.

This relationship between time, money, and scope is sometimes referred to as the project triangle, as shown in Figure 10-1. Changing one side of the triangle affects at least one of the other sides of the triangle.

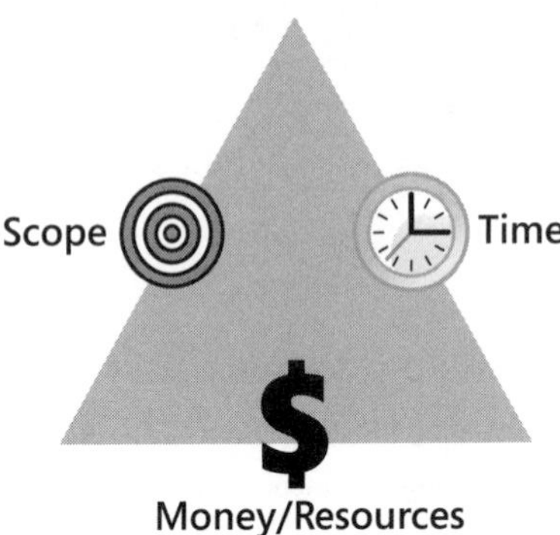

Figure 10-1 Managing your project requires balancing time, money, and scope.

You need to know which side of the triangle is your largest priority. Is it schedule—you definitely have to finish by November 14? Is it budget—there is absolutely $264,300 for this project and not a penny more? Is it scope—it is imperative that each and every task in your project plan be implemented? Only one side of the triangle can be "absolute." The other two sides must be flexible so that you can adjust the project plan to hit that one absolute.

Depending on which side of the project triangle is your absolute, you might adjust your project plan to do one of the following:

- Bring in the project finish date
- Reduce project costs
- Cut project scope

Although resource workloads are not strictly a part of your project triangle, it's likely that you will also check them. Resources are the biggest part of your project costs. If any resources are overallocated, you might be facing more overtime than your budget allows. If resources are grossly overallocated, you run the risk that the tasks won't be done on time and the entire project will slip. If any resources are underallocated, you might be paying more for resources than you should, which also affects your budget.

After you make your adjustments and balance your project triangle to meet the project requirements, you're ready for stakeholder buyoff. After you have buyoff, you're ready to start the execution phase of the project.

Sources of Your Scope, Finish Date, and Budget

Your project scope, finish date, and budget can be imposed on you for various reasons, depending on the type of project and the specific situation. The following are a few examples:

- You are a seller or potential subcontractor bidding on a project whose scope has been defined in the Request for Proposal (RFP). You need to provide the full scope, but your costs and finish date must be competitive with other bidders. If possible, you'll want to include value-added items to give your proposal an advantage while still making a good profit.
- You are a subcontractor and you have been awarded the contract based on a proposal defining broad assumptions of scope, finish date, and cost. Having taken this risk, now you must create a detailed project plan that will actually implement that finish date, cost, and scope.
- You've been assigned as project manager of a project within your company. The scope, budget, or finish date have been handed down as one or more of the project assumptions. Your success is predicated on your ability to implement the project within those limitations.
- You've been assigned as project manager of a project within your company. You and other stakeholders developed the scope to a fair level of detail. It's up to you to propose the budget and finish date for the project.
- You are the project manager, and you've balanced your project triangle the way you believe is best. However, after you submitted the project plan for client review, certain new project requirements or limitations surfaced. You have to readjust the project triangle to take the new limitations or requirements into account.

Working with the Critical Path and Critical Tasks

When optimizing your project plan, it's important to know the critical path through the project. While adjustments to the critical path most obviously affect the project's finish date, such adjustments can also affect budget, resources, and scope.

Most projects have multiple sets of tasks—with task relationships with one another—taking place at any one time. In an office move project, for example, the facilities manager and her team might be researching new office sites and then negotiating the lease. At the same time, the office manager and his team might be ordering new office furniture and equipment and then arranging for movers. These two sets of activities are not dependent on each other and use different sets of resources. Therefore, they can be scheduled on parallel tracks, as shown in Figure 10-2. The project can have any number of sets of tasks on these parallel tracks, or paths, depending on the size and complexity of the project as well as the number of resources involved.

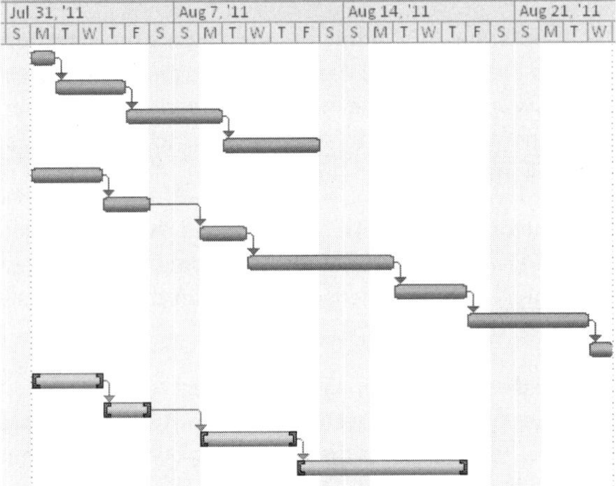

Figure 10-2 Your project is likely to include series of tasks on multiple parallel paths.

At any time, one task has the latest finish date in the project. This task, along with its predecessors, dictates the finish date of the project as a whole. The finish date of this path is critical to the finish date of the project itself; therefore, it's called the *critical path*. In turn, the tasks that make up each step along the critical path are called the *critical tasks*, as shown in Figure 10-3. Because the critical path dictates the finish date of the project, you pay a tremendous amount of attention to it in project management.

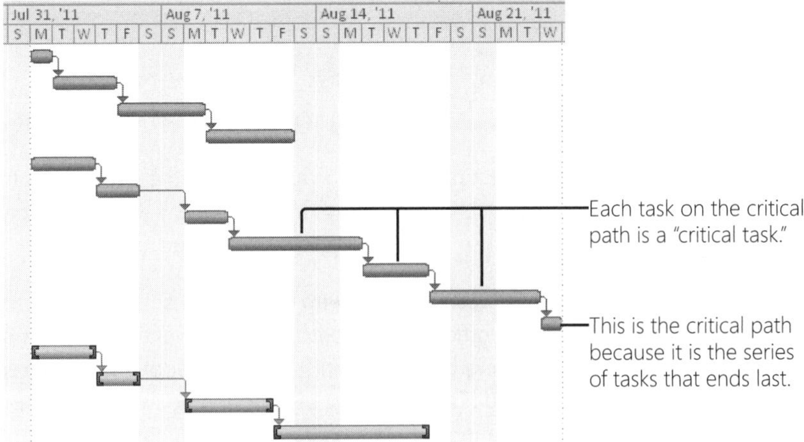

Figure 10-3 The finish date of the last task on the critical path dictates the finish date of the entire project.

> **Note**
>
> **The term *critical task* refers only to tasks that are on the critical path. These terms reflect the scheduling of the tasks, not their relative importance. There can be very important tasks that don't happen to be on the critical path.**

In the planning phase, you identify a particular critical path. After you begin the execution phase and actual progress begins to be reported, the critical path might change from one set of linked tasks to another. For example, task progress is likely to differ in various ways from the original schedule. Perhaps one task in the critical path finishes early, but a task in a second path is delayed. In this case, the second path might become the critical path if it is now the path with the latest finish date in the project.

If you need to bring in the finish date, one of the most effective things you can do is focus on the critical path. If you can make critical tasks along that path finish sooner, you can make the project itself finish sooner.

For more information about strategies to bring in a project's finish date, see "Bringing In the Project Finish Date" on page 383.

Understanding Slack Time and Critical Tasks

Many tasks have some amount of scheduling buffer—an amount of time that a task can slip before it causes a delay in the schedule. This scheduling buffer is called *slack*, or *float*. The following describes the two types of slack:

- **Free slack** The amount of time a task can slip before it delays another task, typically its successor task.
- **Total slack** The amount of time a task can slip before it delays the project finish date, as shown in Figure 10-4.

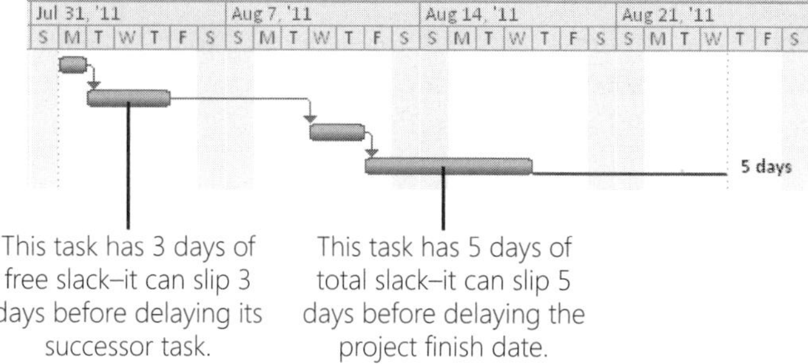
Jul 31, '11
Aug 7, '11
Aug 14, '11
Aug 21, '11
S M T W T F S S M T W T F S S M T W T F S S M T W T F S
5 days
This task has 3 days of free slack–it can slip 3 days before delaying its successor task.
This task has 5 days of total slack–it can slip 5 days before delaying the project finish date.

Figure 10-4 Free slack and total slack show the amount of time a task can slip before it causes a scheduling problem.

Chapter 10

Because critical tasks cannot slip without delaying the project finish date, critical tasks have no slack, and tasks with no slack are critical.

If a noncritical task consumes its slack time, it usually causes its successor to use some or all of its total slack time. The previously noncritical task becomes a critical task and causes its successor tasks to become critical as well.

Negative Slack Situations

Sometimes you run into a situation in which you have negative slack; that is, the opposite of slack time. Negative slack can occur in a task with a finish-to-start task dependency when a successor task is due to begin before the predecessor is finished. This can happen when the task duration of a predecessor task conflicts with a successor task that must begin on a date specified by an assigned constraint. An example is shown in Figure 10-5.

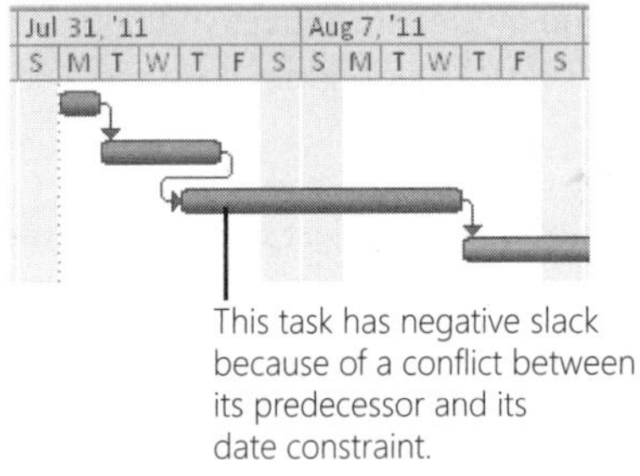
Jul 31, '11
Aug 7, '11
S M T W T F S S M T W T F S
This task has negative slack because of a conflict between its predecessor and its date constraint.

Figure 10-5 In this example, the indicated task has negative slack because although it has a finish-to-start task dependency, its successor is scheduled to begin before the task is finished. As a result, all the task's predecessors also have negative slack.

Negative slack is a problem because it bunches up tasks on each other, essentially indicating that to maintain the schedule, a task needs to start before it should. That is, the task has to be scheduled to start before the conditions of its task dependencies are fulfilled.

Maybe you don't want just those tasks with total slack of 0 to be critical. For example, perhaps you want your critical tasks to be those that still have 1 day of slack. In this case, you can change the definition of a critical task. To do this:

1. On the File tab, click Options, and then click Advanced in the left pane.

2. Under Calculation Options For This Project, enter your preference for a critical task in the box labeled Tasks Are Critical If Slack Is Less Than Or Equal To. (See Figure 10-6.)

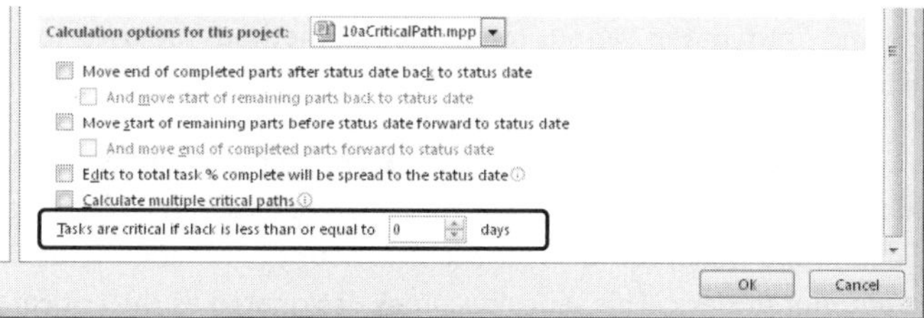

Figure 10-6 Specify the amount of slack that you want to define for a critical task in your project plan.

You can quickly see the amount of slack available in any Gantt chart. With a Gantt view displayed, on the Format tab, in the Bar Styles group, select the Slack check box.

To see more detail about slack—that is, how much free slack and total slack each task has—you can apply the Schedule table to a task sheet, as follows:

Gantt Chart

1. On the View tab, in the Task Views group, click Gantt Chart, or display any other task sheet you want.

Tables

2. On the View tab, in the Data group, click Tables, and then click Schedule.

   The Schedule table is applied, as shown in Figure 10-7. If you're working in the Gantt Chart, you might need to drag the vertical divider to the right to see some of the columns in this table.

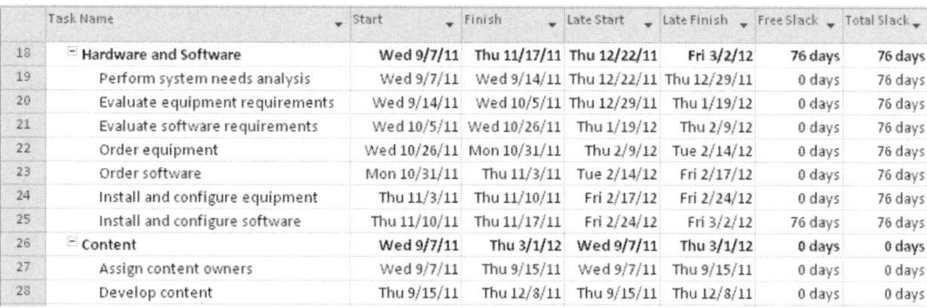

	Task Name	Start	Finish	Late Start	Late Finish	Free Slack	Total Slack
18	**Hardware and Software**	**Wed 9/7/11**	**Thu 11/17/11**	**Thu 12/22/11**	**Fri 3/2/12**	**76 days**	**76 days**
19	Perform system needs analysis	Wed 9/7/11	Wed 9/14/11	Thu 12/22/11	Thu 12/29/11	0 days	76 days
20	Evaluate equipment requirements	Wed 9/14/11	Wed 10/5/11	Thu 12/29/11	Thu 1/19/12	0 days	76 days
21	Evaluate software requirements	Wed 10/5/11	Wed 10/26/11	Thu 1/19/12	Thu 2/9/12	0 days	76 days
22	Order equipment	Wed 10/26/11	Mon 10/31/11	Thu 2/9/12	Tue 2/14/12	0 days	76 days
23	Order software	Mon 10/31/11	Thu 11/3/11	Tue 2/14/12	Fri 2/17/12	0 days	76 days
24	Install and configure equipment	Thu 11/3/11	Thu 11/10/11	Fri 2/17/12	Fri 2/24/12	0 days	76 days
25	Install and configure software	Thu 11/10/11	Thu 11/17/11	Fri 2/24/12	Fri 3/2/12	76 days	76 days
26	**Content**	**Wed 9/7/11**	**Thu 3/1/12**	**Wed 9/7/11**	**Thu 3/1/12**	**0 days**	**0 days**
27	Assign content owners	Wed 9/7/11	Thu 9/15/11	Wed 9/7/11	Thu 9/15/11	0 days	0 days
28	Develop content	Thu 9/15/11	Thu 12/8/11	Thu 9/15/11	Thu 12/8/11	0 days	0 days

Figure 10-7 The Schedule table shows the amount of free slack and total slack as well as late start and late finish dates.

Critical Path Method (CPM)

Schedules are developed from task sequences, durations, resource requirements, start dates, and finish dates. Various mathematical methods are used to calculate project schedules.

The *Critical Path Method*, or *CPM*, is the technique that underlies Microsoft Project 2010 scheduling. The focus of CPM is to analyze all series of linked tasks in a project and determine which series has the least amount of scheduling flexibility; that is, the least amount of slack. This series becomes designated as the critical path.

Four date values are part of the slack calculation for each task:

- Early start
- Early finish
- Late start
- Late finish

The difference between the late start and early start dates is compared, as is the difference between late finish and early finish. The smaller of the two differences becomes the value for total slack.

Viewing the Critical Path

The quickest way to see the critical path is to display the Tracking Gantt. On the View tab, in the Task Views group, click the arrow under Gantt Chart, and then click Tracking Gantt. The Tracking Gantt highlights the critical path in red in the timesheet area of the view, as shown in Figure 10-8.

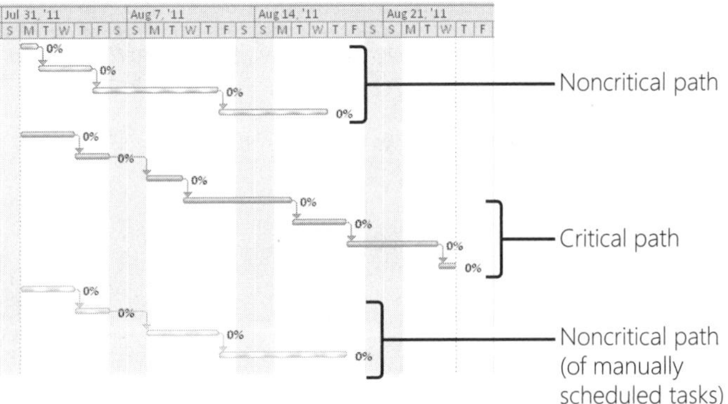

Figure 10-8 The Tracking Gantt highlights the critical path.

Just as in the regular Gantt Chart, the Entry table is the default table for the Tracking Gantt.

There's another quick way to view the critical path in any Gantt chart. With a Gantt chart displayed, on the Format tab, in the Bar Styles group, select the Critical Tasks check box.

Scroll To Task

> **Note**
>
> **When you first open a Gantt chart, the timescale shows today's date. If the tasks you're reviewing are in the past or future, you might not see the Gantt bars in the chart. Click a task whose Gantt bar you want to see. On the Task tab, in the Editing group, click Scroll To Task.**

Although displaying the Tracking Gantt displays the critical path at a glance, you can also look at the details for individual critical tasks. The following list details different methods for viewing critical tasks:

- **Display the Detail Gantt** On the View tab, in the Task Views group, click the arrow next to Gantt Chart. If Detail Gantt does not show in the list, click More Views, and then click Detail Gantt. This view shows the critical path tasks in red Gantt bars, as shown in Figure 10-9. By default, the Delay table is applied to the sheet area of the view.

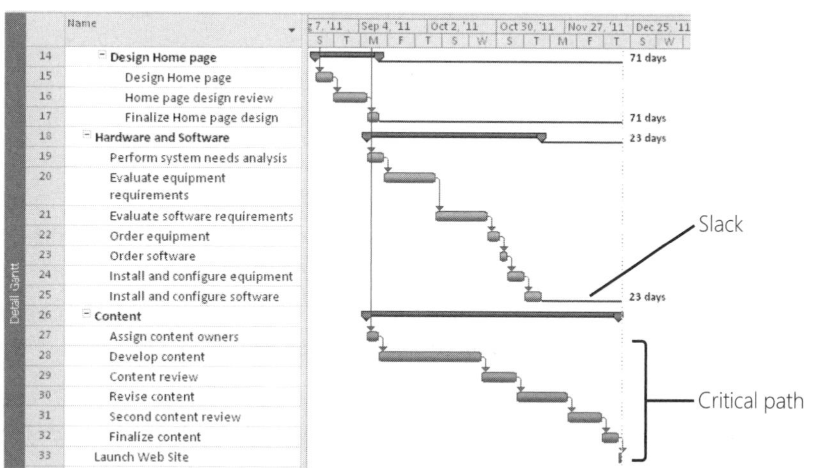

Figure 10-9 The Detail Gantt shows the critical path as well as available slack.

Reports

- **Review the Critical Tasks report** On the Project tab, in the Reports group, click Reports. Double-click Overview, and then double-click Critical Tasks.

INSIDE OUT Format the critical path on the Gantt Chart

Although it's easy enough to highlight critical tasks or switch to the Tracking Gantt or the Detail Gantt to readily see the critical path in red, you can format the critical path on the Gantt Chart any way you like by customizing the bar styles.

To show the critical path in another color or pattern on the Gantt Chart, follow these steps:

1. Display the Gantt Chart.

   Your modifications will apply only to the Gantt bars in the Gantt Chart, and not any other Gantt view.

Format

2. On the Format tab, in the Bar Styles group, click Format, and then click Bar Styles.

   The Bar Styles dialog box lists all the Gantt bar types for the Gantt Chart with the settings for their appearance.

3. Scroll through the table until you see the blank rows, or click where you want to place the new critical task bar definition among the existing Gantt bar definitions. At the top of the dialog box, click Insert Row.
4. In the Name field, type Critical Task or something similar.
5. Click in the Show For … Tasks field for the Critical Task, and then click the arrow that appears in the field.
6. Click Critical.
7. In the lower section of the dialog box under the table, be sure that the Bars tab is active.
8. Under the Middle heading, click the arrow in the Color box, and then click the color you want for critical tasks in the Gantt Chart.

   A preview of the newly formatted Critical bar appears in the Appearance field in the table above.

9. If you want to change the shape or pattern of critical Gantt bars on the Gantt Chart, make your choices in the Shape and Pattern boxes.
10. Click OK.

    The critical path appears as you specified in the chart area of the view.

For more information, see "Formatting the Appearance of Gantt Bars" on page 1072.

Visual Reports

- **Generate the Critical Tasks Status Report** On the Project tab, in the Reports group, click Visual Reports. Click the Task Summary tab, and then double-click either Critical Tasks Status Report (Metric) or Critical Tasks Status Report (US). Microsoft Visio 2010 opens to show the project's critical tasks in a Visio 2010 PivotDiagram, as shown in Figure 10-10.

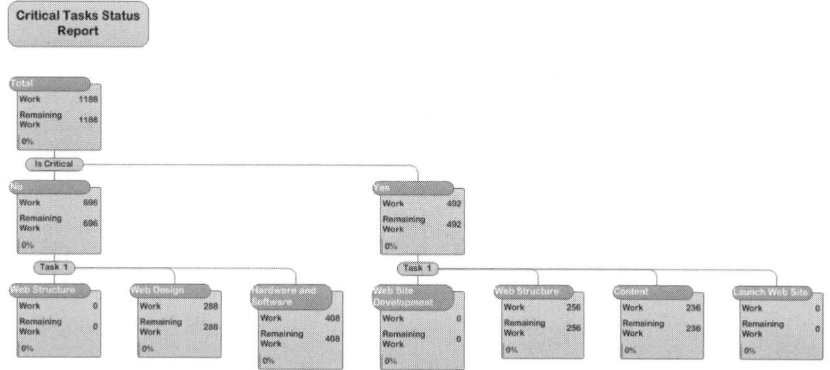

Figure 10-10 The Critical Tasks Status Report diagrams the project's critical tasks in Visio.

Group By

- **Group tasks by critical and noncritical tasks** On the View tab, in the Data group, click the arrow in the Group By box. In the drop-down menu, click Critical. Tasks are grouped by whether they are critical or noncritical, as shown in Figure 10-11.

  To return tasks to their original arrangement, on the View tab, in the Data group, click the arrow in the Group By box, and then click No Group.

	Task Name	Duration	Start	Finish
	⊟ Critical: No	**15d**	**Mon 8/1/11**	**Thu 11/17/11**
3	Hold user meetings	5 days	Mon 8/1/11	Mon 8/8/11
9	Design interior pages	5 days	Wed 8/17/11	Wed 8/24/11
10	Interior page design review	5 days	Wed 8/24/11	Wed 9/7/11
11	Finalize interior page design	4 days	Wed 9/7/11	Tue 9/13/11
12	Develop style sheets	4 days	Tue 9/13/11	Mon 9/19/11
13	Develop page templates	5 days	Mon 9/19/11	Mon 9/26/11
15	Design Home page	5 days	Wed 8/17/11	Wed 8/24/11
16	Home page design review	5 days	Wed 8/24/11	Wed 9/7/11
17	Finalize Home page design	3 days	Wed 9/7/11	Mon 9/12/11
19	Perform system needs analysis	5 days	Wed 9/7/11	Wed 9/14/11
20	Evaluate equipment requirements	15 days	Wed 9/14/11	Wed 10/5/11
21	Evaluate software requirements	15 days	Wed 10/5/11	Wed 10/26/1
22	Order equipment	3 days	Wed 10/26/1	Mon 10/31/1
23	Order software	3 days	Mon 10/31/1	Thu 11/3/11
24	Install and configure equipment	5 days	Thu 11/3/11	Thu 11/10/11
25	Install and configure software	5 days	Thu 11/10/11	Thu 11/17/11
	⊟ Critical: Yes	**15d**	**Mon 7/11/11**	**Tue 12/20/11**
2	Brainstorm content categories	12 days	Mon 7/11/11	Mon 8/1/11
4	Develop Web structure	5.17 days	Mon 8/8/11	Wed 8/17/11
5	Web structure review	7.5 days	Wed 8/17/11	Wed 8/31/11
6	Finalize Web structure	5 days	Wed 8/31/11	Wed 9/7/11
27	Assign content owners	3 days	Wed 9/7/11	Mon 9/12/11
28	Develop content	15 days	Mon 9/12/11	Mon 10/24/1
29	Content review	10 days	Mon 10/24/1	Mon 11/7/11

Figure 10-11 Use the Critical grouping to group critical tasks together and noncritical tasks together.

Filter

- **Filter for critical tasks** On the View tab, in the Data group, click the arrow in the Filter box. In the drop-down menu, click Critical. Only critical tasks are shown.

  To show all tasks again, on the View tab, in the Data group, click the arrow in the Filter box, and then click No Filter.

Highlight

- **Highlight critical tasks** On the View tab, in the Data group, click the arrow in the Highlight box. In the drop-down menu, click Critical. Critical tasks are highlighted in the sheet area of the view.

  To remove the highlight, on the View tab, in the Data group, click the arrow in the Highlight box, and then click No Highlight.

Work with Multiple Critical Paths

By default, you have one path through your project that constitutes your critical path. That one critical path constitutes the series of tasks whose end date is closest to affecting the end date of the project. When the last task is completed, the project is completed.

However, you can display multiple critical paths if you like. Although they might finish earlier than the one "real" critical path, each critical path can show the different networks of tasks throughout your project—for example, for different phases or parallel efforts. To display multiple critical paths, follow these steps:

1. On the File tab, click Options, and then click Advanced in the left pane.
2. Under Calculation Options For This Project, select the Calculate Multiple Critical Paths check box.

To create multiple critical paths, Project 2010 changes the calculation of the critical path so that any task without a successor (that is, the last task in any series of linked tasks) becomes a critical task. The task's late finish date is set to be the same as its early finish date. This setting gives the task 0 slack, which in turn makes it a critical task. Any series of predecessors before this final task becomes a critical path, thereby providing multiple critical paths.

This calculation contrasts with that of a single critical path, in which a task without a successor has its late finish date set to the project finish date. This gives the task slack and, therefore, makes it a noncritical task.

Controlling Schedule Changes with Task Types

As soon as you assign resources to automatically scheduled tasks, two new methods become available to you for controlling how tasks are scheduled: task types and effort-driven scheduling. Use these methods so that as you optimize the project plan to target the required finish date, budget, and scope (or respond to changes after project implementation is under way), automatic task and assignment scheduling happen the way you expect and the way that most closely models reality.

For automatically scheduled tasks to which resources have been assigned, when you change one of the following values, another of the three has to compensate for the change:

- **Assignment units** Reflect the number of resources assigned and to what extent—full time, part time, and so on. Adding or removing resources, or otherwise changing assignment units after the initial assignment, constitutes this type of change.
- **Work** The amount of time (hours, days, and so on) that resources are working on the assigned task.
- **Duration** The time span from the start to the finish of the task. Changing the duration naturally affects the finish date, although it can also affect the start date.

Assignment units, work, and duration are fundamental to how a task with assigned resources is scheduled. The three are interrelated and interdependent. It's another triangle-type relationship. When you change one of the three, at least one of the others is affected. For example, by default, if you revise duration, work is recalculated. If you revise assignment units, duration is recalculated. This is based on the basic Project 2010 scheduling formula:

*Duration * Units = Work*

Whether duration, units, or work changes automatically to compensate for your change depends on the task type and whether the task is effort-driven.

Note

Along with the concept of effort-driven scheduling, the interrelationship between duration, units, and work is a major principle that drives how Project 2010 schedules your project. Commit this formula to memory, write it on a yellow sticky on your computer's monitor, make it your screen saver marquee—anything to help you remember this concept as you work with your project.

So what are the task types? Think of the task type as the one anchor among the three elements of units, work, and duration. When you make a change, the task type dictates which of the three elements must remain fixed, and which of the other two can flex to accommodate the change. (See Figure 10-12.)

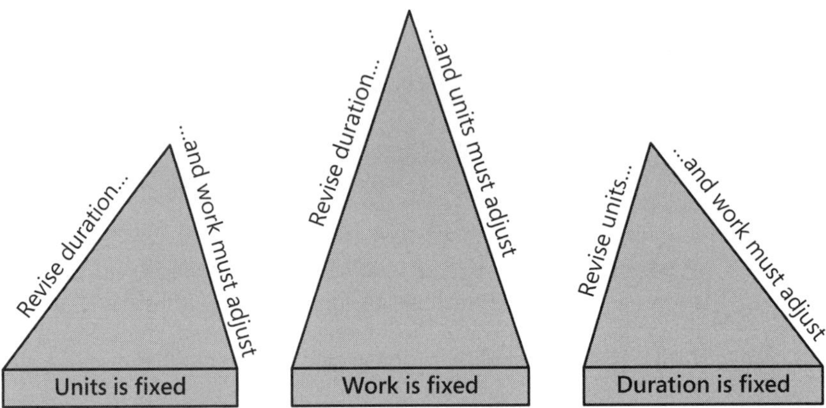

Figure 10-12 When you change one of the three elements, at least one of the others is affected, which changes your task or assignment scheduling.

Setting the task type for each task gives you control over how the schedule is affected when you change units, work, or duration.

The three task types are as follows:

- Fixed Units
- Fixed Work
- Fixed Duration

Which task type you choose for your project default and change for individual tasks has to do with how you develop your project and the scheduling rules you have in mind as you set your task durations and assign your resources.

Because choosing task types is a form of specifying how tasks are automatically scheduled, task types apply only to automatically scheduled tasks.

Should a Task Have Effort-Driven Scheduling?

Before you dive deeper into a discussion of which task types are right for your schedule, you need to understand effort-driven scheduling.

As its name indicates, *effort-driven scheduling* dictates that as more resources are added to a task, there is less work for each resource to perform, although the total work to be done by all assigned resources remains constant. This is the "many hands make light work" principle.

Likewise, if resources are removed from a task, each remaining resource must do more work—again, with the total work for all assigned resources remaining constant.

The results of effort-driven scheduling operate in conjunction with the task type, as follows:

- For an effort-driven, fixed-units task, adding resources decreases the duration.
- For a fixed-work task, adding resources also decreases the duration. By its nature, a fixed-work task is always effort-driven.
- For an effort-driven, fixed-duration task, adding resources decreases the work assigned to each resource.

NEW!

By default, effort-driven scheduling is turned off for all tasks. This is a change from previous versions of Microsoft Project, in which effort-driven scheduling was the default.

This new default gives you more control over your schedule. It's an advantage if the majority of your automatically scheduled tasks should not have their duration, and by extension their finish dates, change when you add or remove assigned resources.

For example, you might have a 4-day architectural drawing review task as part of a construction project. You want all resources assigned to have 4 days to review the drawings. Suppose that you realize later that you forgot a resource who also needs to review the drawings. When you add this resource to the task, you wouldn't want the duration to be reduced—you still want everyone to have 4 days. It isn't the type of task that can be completed more quickly if more resources are added. For these types of tasks, having effort-driven scheduling turned off is best.

On the other hand, suppose that in the same construction project you have a painter assigned to paint the building in 4 weeks. You determine that you need the building to be painted in 2 weeks. You make this an effort-driven task, and when you add a second painter, the task duration is reduced to 2 weeks. In many cases, the primary reason for adding resources to a task is to bring in its finish date.

The upshot is to look at the nature of the task to determine whether it is effort-driven or not, and then set the task accordingly.

To turn on effort-driven scheduling for selected tasks, follow these steps:

1. In the Gantt Chart or other task sheet, click the task for which you want to turn on effort-driven scheduling.

   If you want to turn on effort-driven scheduling for several tasks at one time, click the first task, hold down Ctrl, and then click the other tasks.

Task Information

2. On the Task tab, in the Properties group, click Information.
3. In the Task Information dialog box, click the Advanced tab.
4. Select the Effort Driven check box.

To turn on effort-driven scheduling for all new tasks in the current project plan:

1. On the File tab, click Options, and then click Schedule in the left pane.
2. Under Scheduling Options For This Project, select the New Tasks Are Effort Driven check box.

To turn on effort-driven scheduling for all new tasks in all project plans:

1. On the File tab, click Options, and then click Schedule in the left pane.
2. In the box next to Scheduling Options For This Project, click All New Projects.
3. Select the New Tasks Are Effort Driven check box.

When Should a Task Have Fixed Units?

When you assign a resource to a task, you specify the assignment units in the Units field of the Assign Resources dialog box. As shown in Figure 10-13, you can see the units listed in the chart area of the Gantt Chart. By default, the units appear with the resource name next to the Gantt bar if the units are anything other than 100%.

	Task Name	Duration
100	− Landscaping and Grounds Work	17 days?
101	Pour concrete driveway and sidewalks	1 day
102	Install backyard fence	12 days
103	Sod and complete plantings - front yard	2 days
104	Sod and complete plantings - backyard	1 day

Figure 10-13 Assignment units other than 100% are shown next to the relevant Gantt bars.

The Fixed Units task type dictates that the percentage of assignment units on an assignment should remain constant, regardless of changes to duration or work. This is the default task type because it's the task type that fits the majority of project tasks. If you increase task duration, Project 2010 shouldn't force you to find another resource or force a 50% resource to work 100% on the assignment.

Changes to a fixed-units task have the following results:

- If you revise units, duration also changes, and work is unchanged.
- If you revise work, duration also changes, and units are unchanged because they're fixed.
- If you revise the duration, work also changes, and units are unchanged because they're fixed.

Set a task to the Fixed Units task type if the priority for the task is that its assignment units be constant unless you explicitly change them and if it's okay for duration and work amounts to change. If this is the case for the majority of the tasks in your project, make Fixed Units the default task type for your project.

When Should a Task Have Fixed Work?

When you assign a resource to a task, the task's duration is translated into work. You can see the amount of work in the Task Usage or Resource Usage view.

The Fixed Work task type dictates that the amount of work on an assignment should remain constant, regardless of changes to duration or units.

Changes to a fixed-work task have the following results:

- If you revise units, duration also changes, and work is unchanged because it's fixed.
- If you revise work, duration also changes, and units are unchanged.
- If you revise the duration, units also change, and work is unchanged because it's fixed.

Set a task to the Fixed Work task type if the priority for the task is that its work amounts remain constant unless you explicitly change them, and if it's okay for duration and assignment units to change. If this is the case for the majority of the tasks in your project, make Fixed Work the default task type for your project.

When Should a Task Have Fixed Duration?

When you create a task, you specify the task's duration in the Duration field of the Gantt Chart or other task sheet. The Gantt bar for the task is drawn according to the duration you set.

The Fixed Duration task type dictates that the task duration should remain constant, regardless of changes to units or work.

Changes to a fixed-duration task have the following results:

- If you revise units, work also changes, and duration is unchanged because it's fixed.
- If you revise work, units also change, and duration is unchanged because it's fixed.
- If you revise the duration, work also changes, and units are unchanged.

Set a task to the Fixed Duration task type if the priority for the task is that its duration values remain constant unless you explicitly change them, and if it's okay for work amounts and assignment units to change. If this is the case for the majority of the tasks in your project, make Fixed Duration the default task type for your project.

Understanding Schedule Changes Based on Task Type

Table 10-1 clarifies how Project 2010 reacts when you make certain schedule changes to a task, according to a task's task type or its manual scheduling mode.

Table 10-1 **Task Types and Modes**

Task type or mode	Add or remove resources (units)	Change assignment units	Change work	Change duration
Fixed units (default)	Changed: Work Unchanged: Duration and units	Changed: Duration	Changed: Duration	Changed: Work
Fixed units effort-driven	Changed: Work and duration	Changed: Duration	Changed: Duration	Changed: Work
Fixed work effort-driven	Changed: Duration Unchanged: Work	Changed: Duration Unchanged: Work	Changed: Duration	Unchanged: Work
Fixed duration	Unchanged: Duration, work, and units	Changed: Work Unchanged: Duration	Changed: Work Unchanged: Duration and units	Changed: Work
Fixed duration effort-driven	Changed: Work Unchanged: Duration and units	Changed: Work Unchanged: Duration	Unchanged: Duration and units	Changed: Work
Manually scheduled tasks	Changed: Work	Changed: Work	Unchanged: Duration	Changed: Work
Manually unscheduled task (placeholder)	Changed: Work	Changed: Work	Unchanged: Duration	Changed: Work

Changing the Task Type

As you gain more experience working with Project 2010, you'll see how the changes you make cause schedule recalculations, especially for your automatically scheduled tasks. Specifically, you'll come to appreciate the power of using different task types in different situations. You'll find that although the majority of your tasks are set at the default task type, you'll have a handful of tasks that use different task types because they need to be scheduled differently.

By default, all tasks are Fixed Units. To change the task type for selected tasks, follow these steps:

1. In the Gantt Chart or other task sheet, click the task for which you want to change the task type.

   If you want to change the task type for several tasks at one time, click the first task, hold down Ctrl, and then click the other tasks you want.

2. On the Task tab, in the Properties group, click Information.
3. In the Task Information dialog box, click the Advanced tab.
4. In the Task Type box, click the task type you want to apply to the selected tasks.

To set the default task type for all new tasks in this project plan, follow these steps:

1. On the File tab, click Options, and then click Schedule in the left pane.
2. Under Scheduling Options For This Project, in the Default Task Type box, click the task type you want to apply to all new tasks.

To set the default task type for all new tasks in all project plans:

1. On the File tab, click Options, and then click Schedule in the left pane.
2. In the box next to Scheduling Options For This Project, click All New Projects.
3. In the Default Task Type box, click the task type you want to apply to all new tasks in all new projects.

Bringing in the Project Finish Date

A *time-constrained project* is one in which the project finish date is the most important factor in your project plan. Although you still need to balance budget constraints and satisfy the project scope, the finish date reigns supreme as the top priority.

If your project plan calculates that your finish date will go beyond your all-important target finish date, focus on the critical path. Shorten the critical path and you bring in the finish date.

INSIDE OUT **Save an interim plan before making changes**

Consider saving an interim plan before making changes that affect your project finish date. An interim plan saves a snapshot of the start and finish dates for all your tasks. After you've made some of the changes suggested in this section, you can add these interim start and finish fields as Gantt bars in your Gantt Chart to see the effects of your changes.

For more information about interim plans, see "Saving Additional Schedule Start and Finish Dates" on page 459. For information about creating custom Gantt bars, see "Formatting the Appearance of Gantt Bars" on page 1072.

Viewing Finish Dates and the Critical Path

Before you analyze the critical path, first take a look at your bottom line: what's the project finish date? Follow these steps:

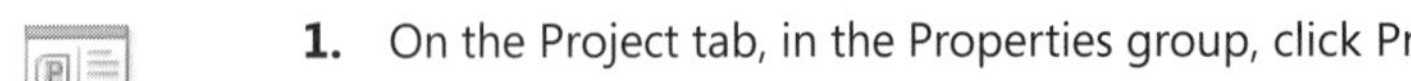

Project Information

1. On the Project tab, in the Properties group, click Project Information.
2. In the Project Information dialog box, click the Statistics button.

   The Project Statistics dialog box appears. The current, or scheduled, finish date appears in the Finish column, as shown in Figure 10-14.

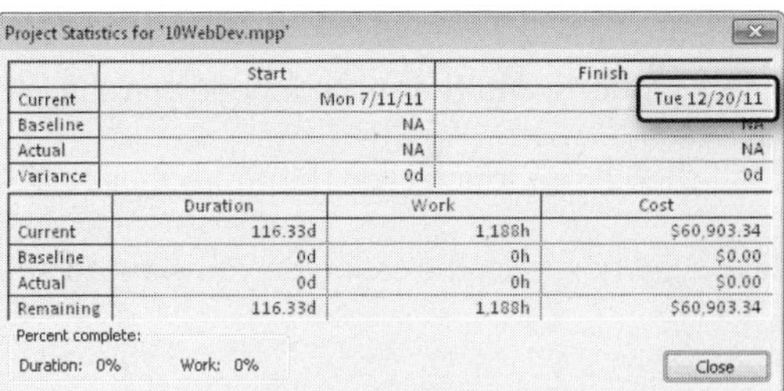

Figure 10-14 The Project Statistics dialog box shows overall project information: project start date, project finish date, total duration, total work, and total cost.

Another way to keep your eye on the project finish date at all times is to add the project summary task row to your project plan. On the Format tab, in the Show/Hide group, select the Project Summary Task check box.

The project summary task appears at the top of any task sheet, including the Gantt Chart, as shown in Figure 10-15. Task information is rolled up for the entire project and its summary total is displayed in the project summary row. Specifically, the Finish field in the project summary row shows the latest finish date in the project.

	Task Mode	Task Name	Duration	Start	Finish
0		Web Site Development	116.33 days	Mon 7/11/11	Tue 12/20/11
1		Web Structure	42.33 days	Mon 7/11/11	Wed 9/7/11
2		Brainstorm content categories	12 days	Mon 7/11/11	Mon 8/1/11
3		Hold user meetings	5 days	Mon 8/1/11	Mon 8/8/11
4		Develop Web structure	5.17 days	Mon 8/8/11	Wed 8/17/11
5		Web structure review	7.5 days	Wed 8/17/11	Wed 8/31/11
6		Finalize Web structure	5 days	Wed 8/31/11	Wed 9/7/11
7		Web Design	28 days	Wed 8/17/11	Mon 9/26/11
8		Interior Pages	28 days	Wed 8/17/11	Mon 9/26/11
9		Design interior pages	5 days	Wed 8/17/11	Wed 8/24/11
10		Interior page design review	5 days	Wed 8/24/11	Wed 9/7/11

Figure 10-15 The project summary row rolls up task information to display the totals for the entire project.

To see the critical path, on the View tab, in the Task Views group, click the arrow in the Gantt Chart button, and then click Tracking Gantt. By viewing the finish date or the critical path, you can easily see whether you're hitting your target finish date.

One efficient way to bring in the finish date is to focus on the critical tasks. You can filter your task sheet to show only critical tasks. On the View tab, in the Data group, click the arrow in the Filter box, and then click Critical. To show all tasks again, on the View tab, in the Data group, click the arrow in the Filter box, and then click No Filter.

For more information, see "Viewing the Critical Path" on page 372.

What If You Have More Time Than Needed?

You reviewed your finish date and got a happy surprise—you have more time available than your schedule says you need. What to do? It depends, of course, on the type of project, the situation, and the amount of surplus time. You can:

- **Use the extra time as buffer against risks or potential problems.**
- **Add scope. Add tasks you were hoping to include but thought you wouldn't have enough time to complete. Build in a higher level of quality. Increase quantities being produced, if applicable.**
- **Use the extra time to save money. For example, you might be able to hire two designers instead of three and have those two designers carry out the design tasks in the longer amount of time that's available.**
- **Inform your manager or client that you can complete the project sooner than expected.**

Checking Your Schedule Assumptions

If you've determined that you need to bring in the finish date, look first at the schedule itself. Be sure that all the scheduling controls you put into place are accurate and required. The fewer controls you impose, the more flexibility Project 2010 can have with scheduling, and that added flexibility can give you an earlier finish date. In the Gantt Chart or other task sheet, review and update the following:

- Date constraints
- Manually entered dates
- Task dependencies
- Durations
- Task calendars

You can look at all tasks in the project, but to affect the finish date, you need only make adjustments to critical tasks. If you shorten the sequence of critical path tasks to the point at which a different sequence is now the critical path, check to see if that path finishes before your target finish date. If it does, switch your focus to that new critical path until you achieve the planned project finish date you need.

In fact, as you make adjustments to tasks and enter actual progress information for tasks, the critical path is likely to change several times throughout the span of the project. Keep a close eye on the critical path as part of your monitoring activities. It's a good idea to apply the Schedule table or show the Total Slack and Free Slack fields in your favorite everyday table. This way you can see how close tasks are to becoming critical.

Note

If you change aspects of your schedule to bring in the finish date, the good news is that you probably won't adversely affect your project triangle. That is, adjusting your schedule to meet your schedule requirements affects only the schedule side of the triangle; costs and scope will probably stay as they are.

Checking and Adjusting Date Constraints

First, look at any date constraints you've set on automatically scheduled tasks in your plan, particularly for your critical tasks. This is where you can potentially make a significant impact on your finish date. To look at the constraints you've applied, follow these steps:

1. Display the Gantt Chart or other task sheet.
2. On the View tab, in the Data group, click Tables, and then click More Tables.
3. In the More Tables dialog box, click Constraint Dates, and then click Apply.

   The table shows the constraint type and constraint dates for all tasks.

If you have the tasks sorted by Task ID—that is, in their outline sequence—you can review constraints for each task within the context of its surrounding tasks. If you like, you can sort the tasks by constraint type, as follows:

1. Apply the Constraint Dates table to the Gantt Chart or other task sheet.

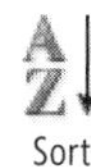
Sort

2. On the View tab, in the Data group, click Sort, and then click Sort By in the drop-down menu.
3. In the Sort By dialog box, click Constraint Type, and then click Sort.

   The tasks are sorted by constraint type, which lets you see where you might have applied a Must Finish On or Start No Later Than constraint, for example. You can also see the constraints' associated dates.

To see only the constraints for critical tasks, follow these steps:

1. Apply the Constraint Dates table to the Gantt Chart or other task sheet.
2. On the View tab, in the Data group, click the arrow in the Filter box, and then click Critical.

   Only critical tasks are shown. When you want to see all tasks again, on the View tab, in the Data group, click the arrow in the Filter box, and then click No Filter.

Be sure that the constraint types and dates you have applied are truly necessary. Wherever you can, change a date constraint to a flexible one such as As Soon As Possible or As Late As Possible. Even changing an inflexible date constraint such as Must Start On or Must Finish On to a moderately flexible date constraint, such as Start No Later Than or Finish No Earlier Than, can improve your schedule. To change the constraint, do the following:

1. Apply the Constraint Dates table to the Gantt Chart or other task sheet.

2. Click in the Constraint Type field, click the arrow, and then click the constraint you want in the list.

Change All Constraints at One Time

Maybe you applied too many date constraints to too many tasks and you just want to start fresh. Select all the tasks in the project by dragging through them or by clicking the Select All box just above the row 1 heading in the upper-left corner of the table. On the Task tab, in the Properties group, click Information. In the Task Information dialog box, click the Advanced tab. In the Constraint Type box, click As Soon As Possible (or As Late As Possible). The constraints on all selected tasks are changed.

For more information about constraints, see "Scheduling Tasks to Achieve Specific Dates" on page 219.

Checking and Adjusting Dates on Manually Scheduled Tasks

When you need to bring in your schedule's finish date, also check the dates set for your manually scheduled tasks. While the dates you enter in the Start and Finish fields do not technically create date constraints, those dates essentially serve the same function.

In a task sheet, either group, filter for, or highlight manually scheduled tasks so that you can see them all together. Review their start and finish dates, paying special attention to any manually scheduled tasks on or near the critical path. Change the dates where you can.

Checking and Adjusting Task Dependencies

The next place to check your schedule for critical path–shortening opportunities is your task dependencies. The Gantt Chart is the best view for reviewing task dependencies and their impact on your schedule. To see critical tasks highlighted, view the Tracking Gantt or Detail Gantt. Focusing on the task dependencies of critical tasks helps you bring in the finish date.

Specifically examine whether the task dependencies are required. If two tasks don't really depend on each other, remove the link. Another option is to consider whether two tasks can begin at the same time. If so, you can change a finish-to-start dependency to a start-to-start dependency. Change a task dependency as follows:

1. Double-click the successor task to open the Task Information dialog box.
2. Click the Predecessors tab.
3. To change the link type, click in the Type field for the predecessor.

4. Click the arrow, and then click the link type you want in the list.

   To remove the link entirely, click anywhere in the predecessor row and press the Delete key.

Remove All Links

If you want to start over with your task dependency strategy, you can remove all links in the project. Be sure that this is really what you want to do because it can erase a lot of the work from your project plan. A safe approach is to make a backup copy of your project before you remove all the links...just in case.

Unlink Tasks

Click the Select All box just above the row 1 heading in the upper-left corner of the table. On the Task tab, in the Schedule group, click Unlink Tasks. All links on all tasks are removed.

For more information about task dependencies, see "Establishing Task Dependencies" on page 206.

Checking and Adjusting Durations

After adjusting date constraints, manually entered dates, and task dependencies, if the finish date is still beyond your target, look at task durations. However, be aware that it's risky to be too optimistic about durations, especially if you used reliable methods such as expert judgment, past project information, or industry metrics to calculate your current durations.

You can look at durations in the Gantt Chart or most task sheets. If your tasks are sorted by Task ID (that is, in their outline sequence), you can review durations for each task within the context of its surrounding tasks. However, you can also sort tasks by duration so you can see the longer durations first. These longer durations might have more buffer built in, so they might be a good place to trim some time. To sort tasks by duration, follow these steps:

1. Display the Gantt Chart with the Entry table applied, or display another task sheet that includes the Duration field.

2. On the View tab, in the Data group, click Sort, and then click Sort By.

   The Sort dialog box appears.

3. In the Sort By box, click Duration, and then click Sort.

   The tasks are sorted by duration.

4. To see only the durations for critical tasks, on the View menu, click the arrow in the Filter box, and then click Critical.

   When you want to see all tasks again, on the View menu, click the arrow in the Filter box, and then click No Filter.

5. To change a duration, simply type the new duration into the task's Duration field.

   The schedule is recalculated with the new duration.

6. To return to the original task order, on the View menu, in the Data group, click Sort, and then click By ID.

For more information about durations, see "Setting Task Durations" on page 196.

Undo

Redo

Note

As you make changes to your project plan, remember that you can undo multiple edits. To undo recent edits, on the Quick Access Toolbar, click Undo. Each time you click Undo, the previous edit is undone. You can press Ctrl+Z to reverse the last edit. The series of operations you can undo goes back to the last time you saved your project.

To redo an edit that you've undone, click Redo on the Quick Access Toolbar. You can also press Ctrl+Y to redo undone edits.

Project Management Practices: Duration Compression

In project management, there are two commonly used methods of shortening a series of tasks without changing the project scope. These two *duration compression* methods are as follows:

- **Crashing the schedule** The schedule and associated project costs are analyzed to determine how a series of tasks (such as the critical path) can be shortened, or *crashed*, for the least additional cost.
- **Fast tracking** Tasks normally done in sequence are rescheduled to be done simultaneously (for example, starting to build a prototype before the specifications are approved).

By their nature, both of these methods are risky. It's important to be aware that these methods can increase cost or increase task rework.

Reviewing Scheduling Factors with the Task Inspector

NEW!

Along with constraints, dates, dependencies, and durations, a number of other factors determine the schedule of any given task. A new tool available in Project 2010 is the Task Inspector. If you used Microsoft Project 2007, you'll see that this is a revamp of the Task Drivers pane. The Task Inspector lists the specific factors responsible for setting the start date of the selected task—for example, the project calendar, a predecessor task, a constraint date, and whether the task is manually or automatically scheduled.

To use the Task Inspector, follow these steps:

1. Open a task view, such as Gantt Chart or Network Diagram.
2. Select the task whose scheduling factors you want to review.
3. On the Task tab, in the Tasks group, click Inspect.

   Inspect

   The Task Inspector appears as a pane to the left of the current view, as shown in Figure 10-16. The Task Inspector lists whether the task is automatically or manually scheduled, its start and finish date, any predecessors or constraints, and more.

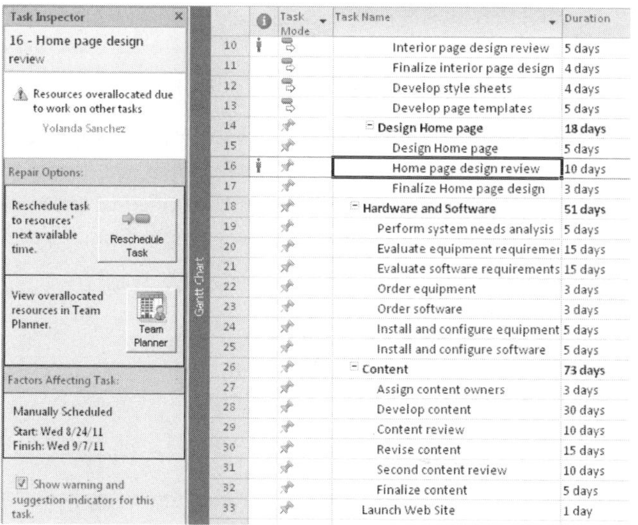

Figure 10-16 Use the Task Inspector to review the factors that determine how a task is scheduled.

You can click the name of a predecessor task to go to that task in the view and to see the task drivers for that task. You can click the name of a calendar listed in the Task Inspector to open that calendar in the Change Working Time dialog box.

4. Keep the Task Inspector open while you click different tasks in the task view and review their task drivers. When you're finished with the Task Inspector, click the X in the upper-right corner of the pane to close it.

Note

If you use task calendars in your schedule, examine the tasks and the task calendars to be sure they're accurately reflecting reality and not impeding progress. Tasks with task calendars assigned display a calendar icon in the Indicators column next to the task name. Place the mouse pointer over the icon to see more information.

For more information, see "Working with Task Calendars" on page 234.

Adjusting Resource Settings to Bring in the Finish Date

Another way to bring in the finish date is to adjust your resource settings. You can check that the resource availability affecting assigned task scheduling is accurate. You can also add resources to tasks to decrease task duration. Be aware that increasing resource availability as well as adding resources to tasks usually means an increase in costs.

Checking and Adjusting Resource Availability

The more availability your resources have, the sooner their assigned tasks can be completed. For example, a 4-day task assigned to a resource who works a regular 5-day week will be completed in 4 days. The same 4-day task assigned to a resource who works a 2-day week will be completed in 2 weeks. For resources assigned to critical tasks, review and update the following:

- Resource calendars
- Maximum (resource) units
- Assignment units

The Task Entry view is best for checking these three items. Apply the view, set the Task Form to show the resource information you need, and then filter for critical tasks, as follows:

1. On the View tab, in the Task Views group, click More Views.
2. In the More Views dialog box, click Task Entry, and then click Apply.

3. To view critical tasks, click in the Gantt Chart—the upper pane of the view. On the View tab, in the Data group, click the arrow in the Filter box, and then click Critical.

   Only critical tasks are displayed. You can also show the Tracking Gantt or Detail Gantt, which display critical tasks in red.

4. Click in the Task Form—the lower pane of the view. On the Format tab, in the Details group, click Work. As shown in Figure 10-17, the Task Form changes to show resource work information, including assignment units and work amounts.

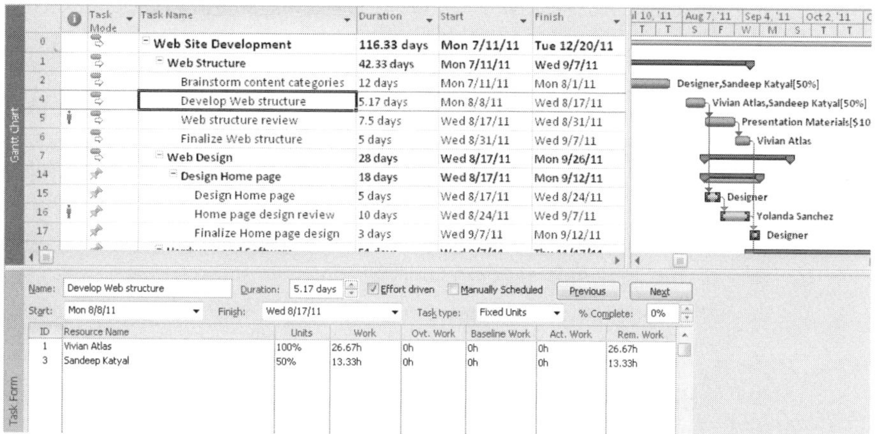

Figure 10-17 The Task Entry view is now set up to check resource assignment units and work amounts.

5. Click a critical task in the Gantt Chart pane.

   The resources assigned to the selected task are listed in the Task Form pane.

6. To check the resource calendar for this assigned resource, double-click the resource name in the Task Form. The Resource Information dialog box appears. On the General tab, click the Change Working Time button. Check the working times set for this resource to verify that they're correct. When you're finished, close the Change Working Time dialog box.

   For more information about resource calendars, see "Setting Working Times and Days Off for Work Resources" on page 267.

7. To check resource units, return to the General tab in the Resource Information dialog box. Under Resource Availability, check the resource units and associated dates, if applicable, and ensure that they're correct. Make any necessary changes, and then click OK.

For more information about resource units, see "Specifying Resource Availability with Max Units" on page 271.

8. To check assignment units, review the Units field next to the resource name in the Task Form to ensure that the setting is correct.

9. To switch the Task Entry combination view to a single-pane view of the Gantt Chart, right-click in the Task Form pane, and then click Show Split to turn the split off.

   If you filtered tasks and want to show all tasks again, on the View tab, in the Data group, click the arrow in the Filter box, and then click No Filter.

Note

You can check your resources' working time calendar, their resource units, and their assignment units—and everything might look correct. A great technique is to scan your project for any assignment units of less than 100%. Find out if the assigned resources can provide any more time on these tasks, especially the critical tasks, to help bring in the finish date. It doesn't hurt to ask, at least.

Adding Resources to Decrease Duration

A key method of shortening the critical path and bringing in the project finish date is to add resources to critical tasks in such a way as to decrease the task's duration. For example, two people working together might be able to complete a development task in half the time it takes either of them, individually. For this to be the case, the task must be either a fixed-units effort-driven task or a fixed-work task. Obviously, the task cannot be a fixed-duration task.

With fixed-units, effort-driven scheduling, when you assign an additional resource to a task that already has assigned resources, the amount of work scheduled for each assigned resource decreases. Likewise, when you remove a resource from an effort-driven task, the amount of work scheduled for each assigned resource increases.

The same is true for fixed-work tasks, which are effort-driven by definition. When you add or remove resources (that is, assignment units) on a fixed-work task, duration changes but work remains fixed, of course.

For more information about task types and effort-driven scheduling, see "Controlling Schedule Changes with Task Types" on page 377.

To check the task type of an individual task, follow these steps:

1. In a task sheet, such as the Gantt Chart, double-click the task.
2. In the Task Information dialog box, click the Advanced tab.
3. Review the Task Type list and the Effort Driven check box. Make any necessary changes.

You can add the task type and effort-driven fields to a task sheet so that you can see the scheduling methods for all tasks at a glance, as follows:

1. Display the task sheet to which you want to add the new columns.
2. Click the column heading to the right of where you want to insert the new column.
3. On the Format tab, in the Columns group, click Insert Column.

Insert Column

4. In the drop-down menu that appears in the new column, type **ty** to move quickly to the Type field in the list.
5. Click the Type field, and the inserted column shows all task types for each task.

   You can use this Type field to quickly change task types.
6. Follow steps 1 through 5 to add the Effort Driven field to the task sheet.

   This field displays Yes or No, indicating whether the task is effort-driven.

When you assign additional resources to your fixed-units, effort-driven or fixed-work critical tasks, the duration of those critical tasks is reduced, which in turn reduces the length of the critical path.

Note

Be aware that as you add resources to critical tasks, you run the risk of reduced productivity. Additional overhead might be associated with bringing on additional resources. More support might be needed to get those resources up to speed on the tasks, and you might lose whatever time savings you thought you might gain. Take care to add resources who are experienced enough to hit the ground running so your efforts don't backfire.

Project Management Practices: Best Resources for Critical Tasks

Having overallocated resources assigned to critical tasks can push out your finish date. If you level overallocated resources, their assignments are rescheduled to times when they can perform them. Even if you do not level overallocated resources, and even if your schedule shows that there's no slip, this doesn't mean it will not happen. An overallocated resource has to let something slip. By leveling, you can see realistically when tasks can be done and make the necessary adjustments to be sure critical tasks are not late.

As much as possible, shift assignments to evenly distribute the resource workload and to ensure that resources working on critical tasks are not overallocated.

For more information about leveling, see "Leveling Assignments" on page 424.

If you have an overallocated resource assigned to critical tasks and an underallocated resource with the right skills and availability, you can switch to or add the underallocated resource to the critical tasks to shorten their durations.

Also, check that the fastest and more experienced resources are assigned to the longer or more difficult critical tasks. Although adjusting assignments might or might not actually reduce the duration, it significantly reduces the risk of critical tasks needing rework or being otherwise delayed.

You can also adjust scope to bring in the finish date. For more information about cutting scope, see "Changing Project Scope" on page 436.

Reducing Project Costs

A *budget-constrained project* is one in which costs are the most important factor in the project plan. Although you still need to balance schedule requirements and satisfy the project scope, in such a project the costs are at the forefront of your decision-making processes as you plan and execute the project.

If your project plan calculates that your total costs are above the allowed budget, you need cost-cutting strategies. Your best approach will involve cutting resources because in projects, resources and costs are often synonymous. As described in the previous section, when you want to bring in the finish date, you focus on tasks in the critical path. In the same way, when you want to cut costs, it's best to focus on resources to gain the biggest cost savings.

Viewing Project Costs

Review your cost picture first, compare it with your budget, and then make any necessary adjustments.

Reviewing Total Cost Using Project Statistics

To review total project costs using project statistics, do the following:

1. On the Project tab, in the Properties group, click Project Information.
2. In the Project Information dialog box, click the Statistics button.

   The Project Statistics dialog box appears. The current, or scheduled, total project cost appears in the Cost column.

Reviewing Costs with the Cost Table

You can review costs for tasks and summary tasks when you apply the Cost table to a task sheet. If you add the project summary task to a sheet view with the Cost table applied, you can see the total project cost as well. To apply and analyze costs in the Cost table, follow these steps:

1. Display the Gantt Chart or other task sheet.
2. On the View tab, in the Data group, click Tables, and then click Cost.

   The Cost table is applied.
3. If the project summary task is not already showing, on the Format tab, in the Show/Hide group, select the Project Summary Task check box.

   The project summary task row appears at the top of the task sheet. The total project cost, as currently scheduled, is displayed in the Total Cost field.
4. Review the Total Cost field for summary tasks. This is the rolled-up total of all assigned resource costs and fixed costs for the subtasks.
5. Review the Total Cost field for individual tasks. This is the sum of all assigned resource costs as well as fixed costs for tasks.

Comparing Resource Costs Against Budget Resource Values

If you are using the budget resource type with the Budget Work and Budget Cost fields, you can group and review predetermined budget values against your planned project costs.

For information about how to create and assign budget resources, enter budget values, and align resources with their corresponding budget resources, see "Setting Up and Reviewing a Project Budget" on page 346.

To group and compare resource costs against budget values, follow these steps:

Resource Usage

1. On the View tab, in the Resource Views group, click Resource Usage.
2. Add the Budget Work, Budget Cost, Work, and Cost fields to the table. To do this, click in the Add New Column heading. Type the first two letters of the field you want to enter, and then click the name.

   A new Add New Column column appears after new columns are defined and inserted.
3. On the View tab, in the Data group, click the arrow in the Group By box, and then click New Group By.
4. In the Group By field under Field Name, select the name of the text field that you're using to categorize your resources. Depending on how you set up your budget categories, this could be a custom text field, the Code field, or the Group field.
5. Click Apply.

   The resources in your project are grouped by the budget categories you assigned. Each grouping includes one budget resource. The figures for the budget resource appear in the Budget Cost and Budget Work fields. The figures for all other resources appear in the Cost and Work fields. The total costs for the resources are rolled up in the grouping bar. Compare the rolled-up values against the values for the budget resources to see how the costs in your project are faring against the budget for that category.
6. To ungroup the Resource Usage view, on the View tab, in the Data group, click the arrow in the Group By box, and then click No Group.

Generating Cost Reports

Five cost reports can help you analyze planned project costs, as follows:

- **Budget report** On the Project tab, in the Reports group, click Reports. Double-click Costs, and then double-click Budget. The Total Cost column is a summary of the resource costs and fixed costs for each task.
- **Cash Flow report** On the Project tab, in the Reports group, click Reports. Double-click Costs, and then double-click Cash Flow. This report forecasts the funding needed for each period of time, enabling you to see whether budgeted costs will be exceeded at a particular point.

- **Cash Flow visual report in Excel** On the Project tab, in the Reports group, click Visual Reports. In the Task Usage tab, double-click Cash Flow Report. As shown in Figure 10-18, Microsoft Excel 2010 opens to show the project's cash flow in a column chart.

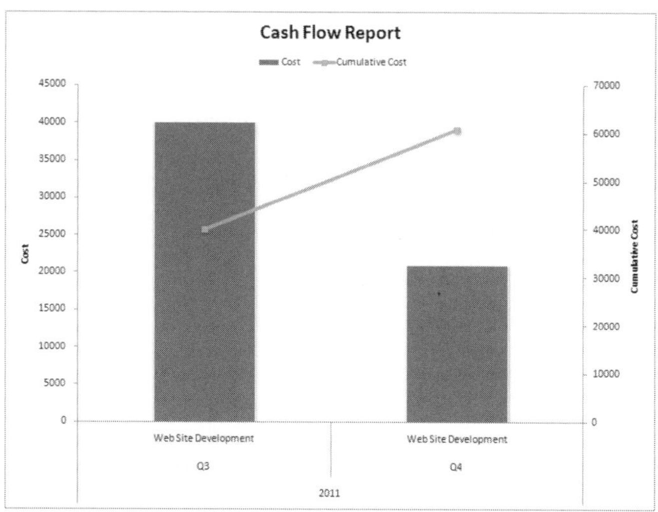

Figure 10-18 Generate the Cash Flow visual report to see cost forecasts by time period in an Excel 2010 column chart.

- **Cash Flow visual report in Visio** On the Project tab, in the Reports group, click Visual Reports. In the Resource Usage tab, double-click Cash Flow Report (Metric) or Cash Flow Report (US). Visio opens to show the project's cash flow in a PivotDiagram, as shown in Figure 10-19.

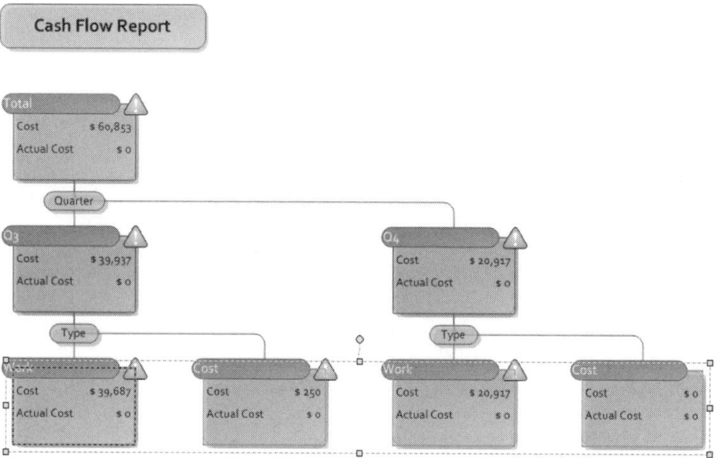

Figure 10-19 Run the Cash Flow visual report to see cost forecasts by time period in a Visio PivotDiagram.

Sorting Tasks or Resources by Cost

You can sort a sheet view by costs. To review task or resource costs in order of amount, do the following:

1. Display a task sheet or resource sheet, depending on whether you want to see costs by resource or by task.
2. On the View tab, in the Data group, click Tables, and then click Cost.
3. On the View tab, in the Data group, click Sort, and then click By Cost.

   The sheet view is sorted by the Total Cost field. To return to the original sort order, click View, Data, Sort, By ID.

Filtering Tasks or Resources by Cost

You can filter a sheet view to display only tasks or resources that have costs exceeding a specified amount. To do this, follow these steps:

1. Display a task sheet or resource sheet, depending on whether you want to see costs by resource or by task.
2. On the View tab, in the Data group, click Tables, and then click Cost.
3. On the View tab, in the Data group, click the arrow in the Filter box, and then click More Filters.
4. In the More Filters dialog box, click Cost Greater Than and then click Apply.
5. In the Cost Greater Than dialog box, enter the amount.

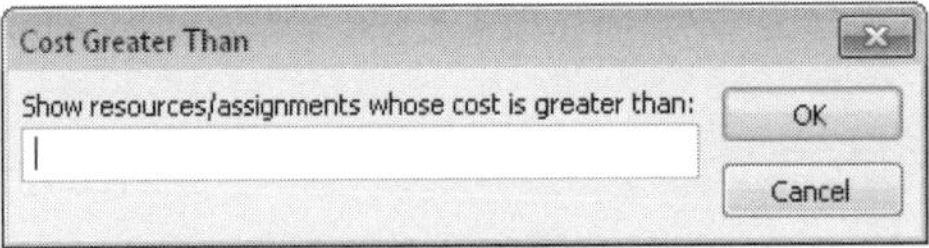

   To see all tasks or all resources again, on the View tab, in the Data group, click the arrow in the Filter box, and then click No Filter.

What If You Have More Money Than You Need?

If you investigate your total project costs and discover that you have more budget than costs, you have some decisions to make. Depending on the type of project, the situation, and the amount of extra budget, you can:

- Reserve the buffer. Use the extra funds as insurance against potential risks.
- Add resources. Use the money to hire resources and take some of the load off overallocated resources or bring in the finish date.
- Add scope. Add tasks you were hoping to include, but thought you wouldn't have enough money to do. Build in a higher level of quality. If applicable, increase quantities being produced.
- Inform your manager or client that you can complete the project well under budget.

Checking Your Cost Assumptions

If you find that your scheduled costs are higher than your budget, first review the individual costs themselves. Check the resource rates as well as fixed costs for tasks and ensure that they're accurate.

To check resource rates, review the Resource Sheet with the Entry table applied. With the default fields in the Entry table, you can see each resource's standard rate, overtime rate, and cost per use.

To check fixed costs for tasks, review a task sheet such as the Gantt Chart with the Cost table applied. The Fixed Cost field displays any costs associated with the tasks that are independent of resource costs.

Adjusting the Schedule to Reduce Costs

If many of your resource costs are based on time periods such as an amount per hour or per day, you might be able to cut costs if you can reduce task durations. For example, suppose that you have a 2-day fixed-units task assigned to a $100/hour resource. By default, this resource is assigned to 16 hours of work, for a cost of $1,600. If you reduce the duration to 1 day, the work is reduced to 8 hours, and the cost is reduced to $800.

When you reduce task duration in a fixed-units or fixed-duration task, the amount of work is also reduced. However, if you reduce duration for a fixed-work task, work stays the same and assignment units increase. In this case, resource costs would not be reduced.

For more information, see "Controlling Schedule Changes with Task Types" and "Checking and Adjusting Durations" on pages 377 and 389, respectively.

Adjusting Assignments to Reduce Costs

Another way to reduce work and therefore cut costs is to reduce work directly. In effect, you're cutting the amount of time that resources are spending on assigned tasks.

The manner in which a work reduction affects your task and resource scheduling depends on the individual task types. When you decrease work in a fixed-units or fixed-work task, duration is reduced. When you decrease work in a fixed-duration task, units are decreased.

To change work amounts for individual resources, display the Task Usage view or Resource Usage view. Then edit the Work field for the assignment.

Adjusting Cost Resources

You might be using cost resources in your project; that is, those cost items that contribute to the completion of a task but—unlike work or material resources—do not affect the schedule when assigned to that task. Examples of cost resources include airfare, lodging, and rentals.

To review the amounts planned for cost resources, switch to the Resource Usage view. Apply the Cost table: click View, Data, Tables, Cost. If you only want to see cost resources in the table, on the View tab, in the Data group, click the arrow in the Filter box, and then click Resources—Cost.

In this way, you can review the costs for each cost resource. If you need to make any adjustments, you can change the Cost field for the assignment under the cost resource.

Note

You can also adjust scope to cut costs. For more information about cutting scope, see "Changing Project Scope" on page 436.

Strategies for Reducing Resource Costs

The following are suggestions for reducing resource costs by adjusting assignments:

- If you have assignments with multiple resources assigned, reduce the work for the more expensive resources and assign the work to less expensive resources. By shuffling work around on an assignment, you won't risk inadvertently changing duration or units.
- If you have resources with the same skills and availability, replace the more expensive work or material resources with less expensive ones. Although this replacement can introduce some risk into your project, it can also ensure that you're using your expensive resources where you really need them.
- If you have resources with the same skills and availability, replace slower work or equipment resources with faster ones. If one resource is faster than another, you might save money, even if the faster resource's rate is higher.
- If you have material resources whose costs are based on assignment units—for example, 3 tons or 100 yards—decrease the assignment units; that is, use less of the material.
- Review your cost resources and see if you can realize any savings there. For example, perhaps you can reduce the amount or cost of travel. Maybe you can try to get discounts on equipment or software that must be purchased for the project.

Balancing Resource Workloads

Although most projects are focused primarily on the finish date or the budget, sometimes a project is defined by its resource limitations, and the use of resources becomes the most important priority in the management of that project. In a resource-constrained project, you need to ensure that all the resources are used well, are doing the right tasks, and are cations and then fix any problems you find. You still need to keep your eye on the schedule and your costs, but schedule and costs are secondary to resource utilization in this type of project.

Balancing resource workloads isn't really part of the project triangle. However, you can adjust scope—add or remove tasks—to balance workload. You can also adjust the schedule—split or delay tasks—until resources have time to work on them. You can adjust costs—add more money—to pay for additional resources to help balance the workload.

Viewing Resource Workloads

When you analyze resource workloads, you're actually reviewing the way resources are assigned. The optimum situation is when all resources in your project are assigned at their full availability, no more and no less, throughout their time on the project.

However, there might be resources for whom you are not able to fill every hour. These resources are said to be *underallocated*. You might have to pay for these resources' time even when they're not directly carrying out project tasks, and this can adversely affect your project budget.

Other resources might consistently have more work than time. These resources are *overallocated*. Such a situation represents risk to the project. If there's more work than available time, it's highly probable that deadlines will be missed, quality will suffer, costs will increase, or scope will have to be cut.

TROUBLESHOOTING

Tasks scheduled at the same time are causing overallocations

You influence how tasks and assignments are scheduled by specifying resource availability through their working time calendars, resource units (maximum units), and assignment units. Within those limitations, however, Project 2010 might still schedule multiple tasks during the same time period, which can cause overallocations.

For example, suppose that a resource has a working time calendar specifying that she works on this project only on Tuesdays. When you assign a task to her, that task is scheduled to accommodate the fact that work will be done only on Tuesdays. When you assign a 5-day task to her, by default, this assignment will take 40 hours, which will stretch across 5 weeks.

Likewise, suppose that another resource works half-time. His resource units are 50 percent. When you assign a task to him, by default his assignment units are also 50 percent. So by default, a 5-day task does not translate to 40 hours in a week, but rather 20 hours.

However, if you have two 1-day tasks assigned to the same resource at the same time, both assignments could be scheduled for the resource at the same time. If that happens, that resource is overallocated.

You can resolve overallocations by following the strategies outlined in "Adjusting Assignments" on page 412 and "Leveling Assignments" on page 424.

At this point in the project, just before work actually begins, you can look at scheduled underallocations and overallocations, make the necessary changes to maximize your resource contributions, and reduce your risk from overallocation. The goal is to balance the workload as much as possible so that you're not wasting resource dollars and burning out your most valuable resources.

You can use one of several Project 2010 views to review how much work is assigned to a resource in any selected time period, as follows:

NEW!

Team Planner

- **Team Planner** On the View tab, in the Resource Views group, click Team Planner, a new view available in Microsoft Project Professional 2010. This view shows the tasks assigned to resources along a timescale grid, making it easy to spot any overallocations, as shown in Figure 10-20.

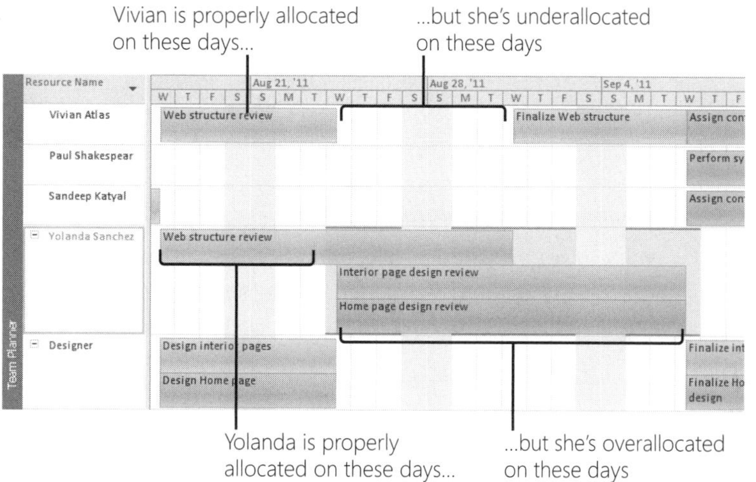

Figure 10-20 The Team Planner in Project Professional 2010 shows the workload of all work resources over time.

Other Views

- **Resource Graph** On the View tab, in the Resource Views group, click Other Views, and then click Resource Graph. In the default Peak Units format, the Resource Graph displays how much the resource is being utilized, in terms of maximum units, for the time period specified in the timescale. This is shown in Figure 10-21.

Chapter 10

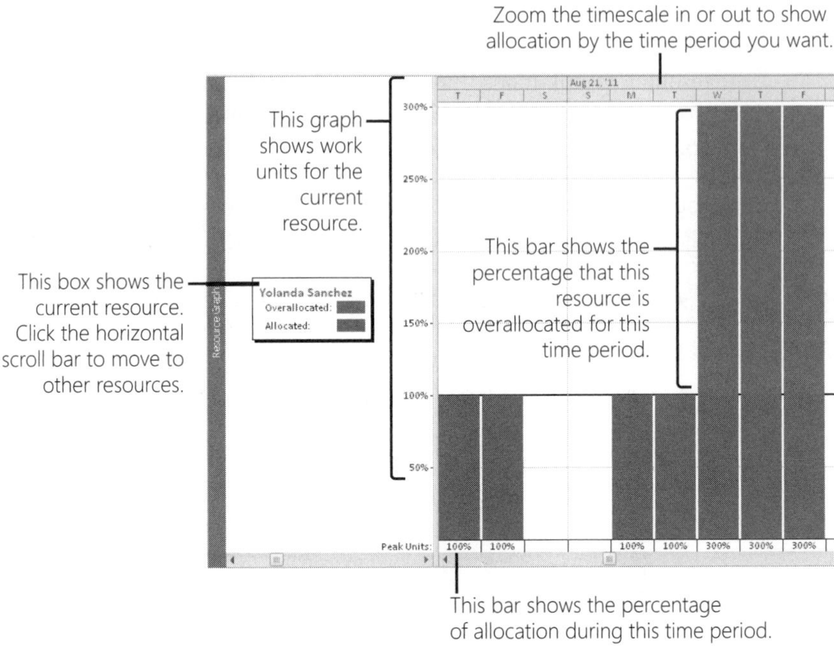
Zoom the timescale in or out to show allocation by the time period you want.
This graph shows work units for the current resource.
This box shows the current resource. Click the horizontal scroll bar to move to other resources.
Yolanda Sanchez
Overallocated:
Allocated:
This bar shows the percentage that this resource is overallocated for this time period.
This bar shows the percentage of allocation during this time period.
Peak Units:

Figure 10-21 The Resource Graph displays resource utilization, one resource at a time.

You can see the resource allocation information by different measures in the Resource Graph. On the Format tab, in the Data group, click the arrow in the Graph box, and then pick a different format, such as Overallocation or Percent Allocation.

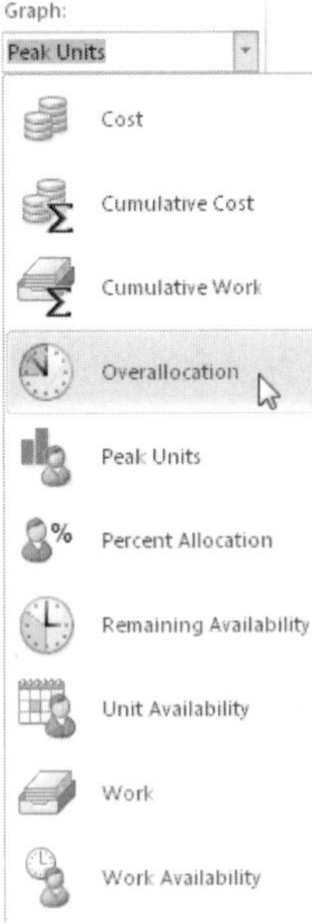
Graph:
Peak Units
Cost
Cumulative Cost
Cumulative Work
Overallocation
Peak Units
Percent Allocation
Remaining Availability
Unit Availability
Work
Work Availability

Zoom

To change the timescale used in the Resource Graph, on the View tab, in the Zoom group, click the Zoom button, and then click Zoom Out or Zoom In. You can also use the Zoom slider in the lower-right corner of the Project 2010 window.

Previous Resource

To see information for a different resource, on the Format tab, in the Navigate group, click Previous Resource or Next Resource. Another method is to simply press the Page Up or Page Down buttons on the keyboard.

Next Resource

- **Resource Usage view** On the View tab, in the Resource Views group, click Resource Usage. Each resource is listed with all assigned tasks, as shown in Figure 10-22. The timesheet area of the view shows how work is allocated over the selected time period. As in all resource views, overallocated resources are shown in red. In the timesheet area, any work that exceeds the resource availability for the time period is also shown in red.

		Resource Name	Work	Details	8/14	8/21	September 8/28
		Revise content	*60 hrs*	Work			
		Finalize content	*20 hrs*	Work			
4		Yolanda Sanchez	120 hrs	Work	9.33h	38.67h	50.67h
		Web structure review	*40 hrs*	Work	9.33h	20h	10.67h
		Interior page design review	*40 hrs*	Work		9.33h	20h
		Home page design review	*40 hrs*	Work		9.33h	20h
5		Designer	272 hrs	Work	42.67h	37.33h	
		Brainstorm content categories	*64 hrs*	Work			
		Design interior pages	*40 hrs*	Work	21.33h	18.67h	
		Finalize interior page design	*32 hrs*	Work			

Figure 10-22 The Resource Usage view can help you find periods of overallocation.

- **Resource Allocation view** On the View tab, in the Resource Views group, click Other Views, and then click More Views. In the dialog box, double-click Resource Allocation. This is a combination view, with the Resource Usage view in the upper portion of the view and the Leveling Gantt in the lower portion, as shown in Figure 10-23.

		Resource Name	Work	Details	9/4	9/11	9/18
1		Vivian Atlas	30.67 hrs	Work	40h	2.67h	
		Develop Web structure	*26.67 hrs*	Work			
		Web structure review	*40 hrs*	Work			
		Finalize Web structure	*40 hrs*	Work	18.67h		
		Assign content owners	*24 hrs*	Work	21.33h	2.67h	
2		Paul Shakespear	408 hrs	Work	21.33h	40h	40h
		Perform system needs analysis	*40 hrs*	Work	21.33h	18.67h	
		Evaluate equipment requirements	*120 hrs*	Work		21.33h	40h
		Evaluate software requirements	*120 hrs*	Work			
		Order equipment	*24 hrs*	Work			
		Order software	*24 hrs*	Work			

		Task Mode	Name
19			Perform system needs analysis
20			Evaluate equipment requirements
21			Evaluate software requirements

Figure 10-23 The Leveling Gantt portion of the Resource Allocation view displays details about the tasks assigned to the resource selected in the Resource Usage view.

Note

When you want to switch to another view from a combination view, remember to first remove the split in the window. Right-click in the timesheet area of the combination view, and then click Show Split to remove the split. You can also simply double-click the split bar. When you switch to the view you want, it appears in the full screen the way you expect.

Find Overallocations Throughout a Task or Resource View

Next Overallocation

Resource views always show overallocated resources in red, making it easy to find them. If you have a long list of resources and you want to examine the overallocations quickly, go to the resource view where you want to review resource or assignment information for overallocated resources. On the Resource tab, in the Level group, click Next Overallocation. Continue to click Next Overallocation to move to the next overallocated resource in turn.

You can even use the Next Overallocation tool in a task view. In the task view, do the same thing: Click Resource, Level, Next Overallocation. You can review each task that has overallocated resources assigned.

- **Resource Form** You get the most information in context when reviewing the Resource Form in a combination view. First display a resource sheet, such as the Resource Sheet or Resource Usage view. If the view includes a timesheet area, such as in the Resource Usage view, right-click in the timesheet area, and then click Show Split. Or, drag the split bar from the lower-right corner of the Project 2010 window, just below the down arrow in the vertical scroll bar. When you split a resource view, the Resource Form appears in the lower portion of the view, with the resource sheet in the upper portion as shown in Figure 10-24.

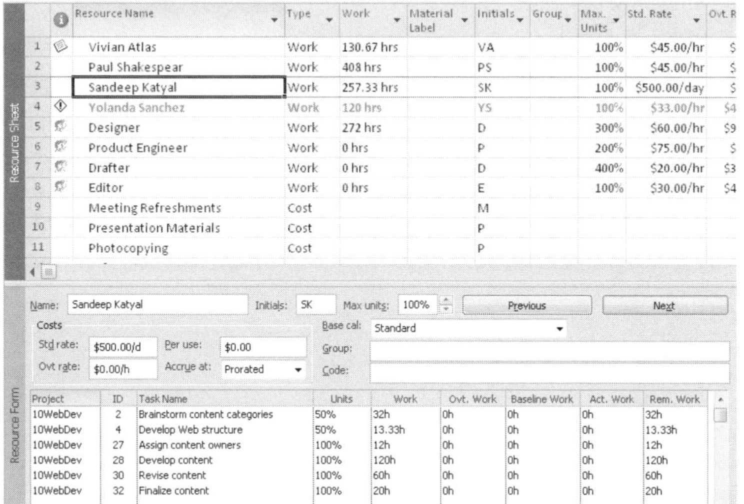

Figure 10-24 The Resource Form displays details about the resource selected in the upper portion of the view.

Another means of seeing how your resources are allocated is to run assignment-related reports, as follows:

- **Who Does What When report** On the Project tab, in the Reports group, click Reports. Double-click Assignments, and then double-click Who Does What When. This report displays the amount of work for each resource by day and by assignment.

- **Overallocated Resources report** On the Project tab, in the Reports group, click Reports. Double-click Assignments, and then double-click Overallocated Resources. This report displays only overallocated resource information. If no resources are overallocated, no report is generated.

- **Resource Usage report** On the Project tab, in the Reports group, click Reports. Double-click Workload, and then double-click Resource Usage. This report displays the amount of work each week by resource and assignment. Totals are included for the resource, assignment, and week.

- **Resource Availability visual report** On the Project tab, in the Reports group, click Visual Reports. Click the Resource Usage tab, and then double-click the Resource Availability Report (Metric) or Resource Availability Report (US). As shown in Figure 10-25, Visio opens to show how much time each resource is working throughout the project and how much time the resource has available.

INSIDE OUT Task views give mixed messages about overallocated resources

NEW!

New in Project 2010 is the Overallocated Resource indicator for task sheets. This indicator appears for any task that has overallocated resources assigned to it. This indicator shows in any task sheet, such as the Gantt Chart or the Task Sheet, that includes the Indicators column (of course, you can add it to any other task table).

		Task Mode	Task Name
4			Develop Web structure
5			Web structure review
6			Finalize Web structure
7			− **Web Design**
8			− **Interior Pages**
9			Design interior pages
10			Interior page design review

If you right-click the Overallocated Resource indicator, you can resolve the overallocation by clicking Fix In Task Inspector or Reschedule To Available Date.

Another way to see if your tasks are assigned to overallocated resources is to add the Overallocated column to a task sheet. To do this, click the column heading to the right of where you want to insert the Overallocated column. On the Format tab, in the Columns group, click Insert Column. In the newly inserted column, type **ov** to quickly scroll through the drop-down menu, and then click Overallocated.

The Overallocated field is a Yes/No field. Yes appears for any tasks to which overallocated resources are assigned. You can sort by the Overallocated field to better focus on balancing the assignments for those tasks. Note that by default, even resources overallocated by a couple of hours in just one week are marked as overallocated.

The problem is that you might see overallocated resource indicators on tasks for which the Overallocated field says No. This occurs because the indicator is looking strictly at the time period for the assigned task and might be showing an overallocation even if the resource is overallocated by just one minute or one hour. By contrast, the Overallocated field might show Yes only for resources that are overallocated across the entire project by as much as a day or even a week. You can just be aware of this, or experiment with how this field reacts to different time settings in the Resource Leveling dialog box (click Resource, Level, Leveling Options). The box labeled Look For Overallocations On A *X* Basis contains the time settings. The default setting is Day By Day, but you might try Week By Week to get more realistic results.

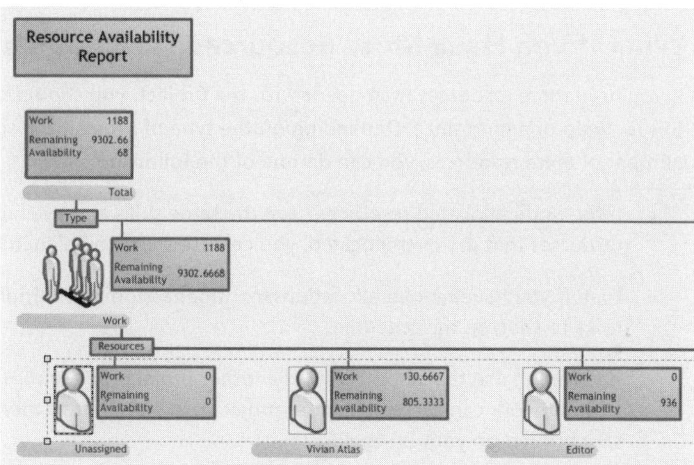

Figure 10-25 The Resource Availability Report diagrams resource usage and remaining availability in a Visio PivotDiagram.

- **Resource Work Availability visual report** On the Project tab, in the Reports group, click Visual Reports. Click the Resource Usage tab, and then double-click the Resource Work Availability Report. Excel opens to show a column chart of collective resource work, availability, and remaining availability in your project.
- **Resource Work Summary visual report** On the Project tab, in the Reports group, click Visual Reports. Click the Resource Usage tab, and then double-click the Resource Work Summary Report. Excel opens to show work, work availability, and remaining availability for each resource in the project.

Reports are particularly useful for resource management meetings or team status meetings.

You can filter a view to examine task allocation, as follows:

- Filter for overallocated resources in a resource sheet such as the Resource Usage view. On the View tab, in the Data group, click the arrow in the Filter box, and then click Overallocated Resources.
- Filter for a specific resource in a task sheet like the Gantt Chart. On the View tab, in the Data group, click the arrow in the Filter box, click Using Resource, and then enter the name of the resource whose assigned tasks you want to see.
- When you want to see all resources or tasks again, on the View tab, in the Data group, click the arrow in the Filter box, and then click No Filter.

What If You Have More Resources Than You Need?

If you have more resources than needed for the project, you should determine whether this is a help or a hindrance. Depending on the type of project, the situation, and the number of extra resources, you can do one of the following:

- **If the underallocated resources have the same skills and availability as other resources that are overallocated, you can use them to balance the workload.**
- **Even if you have no overallocations, consider assigning multiple resources to tasks to shorten the schedule.**
- **If you can't use the resources, find another project for them. Having extra people without work can certainly hinder project progress, not to mention the unnecessary burden on your budget.**

Adjusting Resource Availability

If you find that resources are overallocated or underallocated, check with the resources to see whether their availability can be modified to reflect how they're needed on the project. For example, if a full-time resource is consistently 50 percent underallocated throughout the life of the project, you might consider changing his units to 50 percent and making him available as a 50-percent resource on another project. Or if a part-time resource is consistently 20 percent overallocated, ask her if she can add more time to her availability on the project.

To change resource units, in a resource sheet, double-click the resource name to open the Resource Information dialog box. Click the General tab. In the Resource Availability table, specify the units in the Units field. If necessary, enter the starting and ending dates of the new levels of availability.

To change a resource's working time calendar, click the Working Time tab in the Resource Information dialog box. Make the necessary changes to increase or decrease the resource's working time on the project.

Adjusting Assignments

You can shift assignments around to fix overallocations and underallocations. This shifting assumes, however, that you have resources with similar skills and availability who can fulfill the necessary tasks.

If you can't add or replace resources to take the burden off overallocated resources, you might be able to delay tasks or assignments until the resources have time to work on them. Or you can simply add overtime work to account for the overallocation.

Adding More Resources to Tasks

You can add underallocated resources to tasks to assist overallocated resources. Depending on the task type, you can distribute the work or the assignment units among the assigned resources, thereby better balancing the workload.

For more information about adding resources to tasks, including the impact of effort-driven scheduling and the different task types, see "Adjusting Resource Settings to Bring in the Finish Date" on page 392.

Moving Assignments to Adjust for Overallocations

NEW!

A great way you can use the new Team Planner (available in Project Professional 2010) is to shift assignments around to resolve overallocations. Not only can you easily see when and why overallocations occur, but you can move the assignment from an overallocated resource to another resource or to another time period.

Simply drag the task bar in the timesheet area of the Team Planner to assign it to another resource or to move it to another, less busy time period for the original resource. Dragging the task bar adds a leveling delay value to all tasks, whether they're manually or automatically scheduled.

For more information, see "Using the Team Planner to Assign Resources" on page 296.

Replacing Overallocated Resources

Another way to move assignments from an overallocated resource to one who has more time is to replace the overallocated resource on the task with another resource by using the Assign Resources dialog box. On an assignment, you can replace overallocated resources with underallocated ones as long as they have the same skills and availability. To replace a resource on a task using the Assign Resources dialog box, do the following:

1. In a task sheet such as the Gantt Chart, select the task for which you want to replace resources.

Assign Resources

2. On the Resource tab, in the Assignments group, click Assign Resources.
3. In the Assign Resources dialog box, click the resource you want to replace.

   The currently assigned resources are at the top of the list and have check marks next to their names.

4. Click the Replace button.

   The Replace Resource dialog box appears, as shown in Figure 10-26.

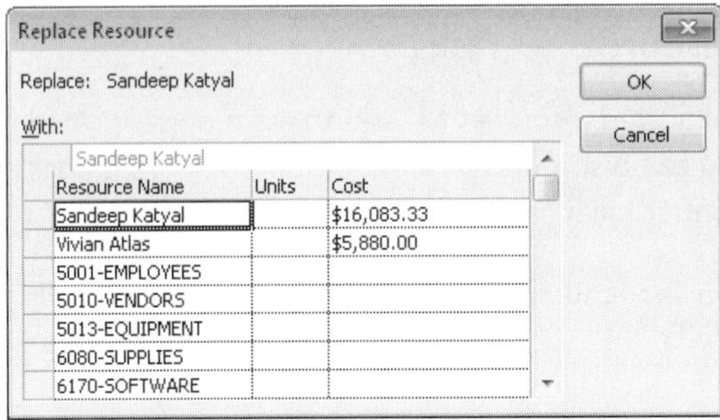

Figure 10-26 Use the Replace Resource dialog box to remove one resource and add a different one in a single operation.

5. Click the resource you want to add to the task, and then click OK.

   The old resource is replaced with the new one.

INSIDE OUT Prevent overallocations in the first place

We often assign resources to tasks and then deal with overallocations later. However, you can try to prevent overallocations at the time you're assigning resources. This works best when you have multiple resources with similar skill sets.

To prevent overallocations when assigning resources to tasks, set up the Assign Resources dialog box to show you only the resources who have time for the task you're assigning. To do this, follow these steps:

1. **In a task view, open the Assign Resources dialog box by clicking Resource, Assignments, Assign Resources.**
2. **Under Resource List Options, select the Available To Work check box.**
3. **In the Available To Work box, enter the amount of time a resource would need to be available to work on this task without being overallocated.**

   Only those resources with at least that amount of available time are listed.

Delaying a Task or Assignment

For an automatically scheduled task, you can delay a task or an assignment until the assigned resource has time to work on it, as follows:

- **Leveling delay** This is a task delay—the amount of time that should pass from the task's automatically scheduled start date until work on the task should actually begin. It delays all assignments for the task. *Leveling delay* can also be automatically calculated and added by the Project 2010 leveling feature.

  For more information about leveling, see "Leveling Assignments" on page 424.

> ### Note
>
> **Don't confuse lag time with task delay. Lag time is the amount of time to wait after the predecessor is finished (or has started, depending on the link type) before a successor task should start. For more information about lag time, see "Delaying Linked Tasks by Adding Lag Time" on page 213.**

- **Assignment delay** This is the amount of time that should pass from the automatically scheduled task's scheduled start date until the assignment's scheduled start date. (See Figure 10-27.)

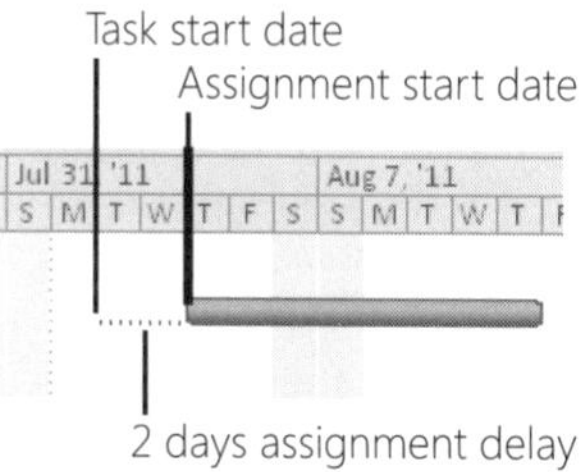

Figure 10-27 Assignment delay is the amount of time from the start date of the task to the start date of the assignment.

Because it's best to delay within available slack time, review the tasks or assignments in context of their slack time and then add delay as time is available. Otherwise, you could push out the finish date of the task (or even of the project) if it's a critical task. To check available slack, do the following:

1. On the View tab, in the Resource Views group, click Other Views, and then click More Views. In the More Views dialog box, click Resource Allocation, and then click Apply.

Chapter 10

2. In the Resource Usage view pane, click the resource or assignment for which you want to examine slack and possibly delay.

3. Click the Leveling Gantt view pane.

4. On the View tab, in the Data group, click Tables, and then click Schedule.

5. Review the Free Slack and Total Slack fields to find tasks that have slack. (See Figure 10-28.)

   You probably will need to drag the vertical split bar to the right to see these fields.

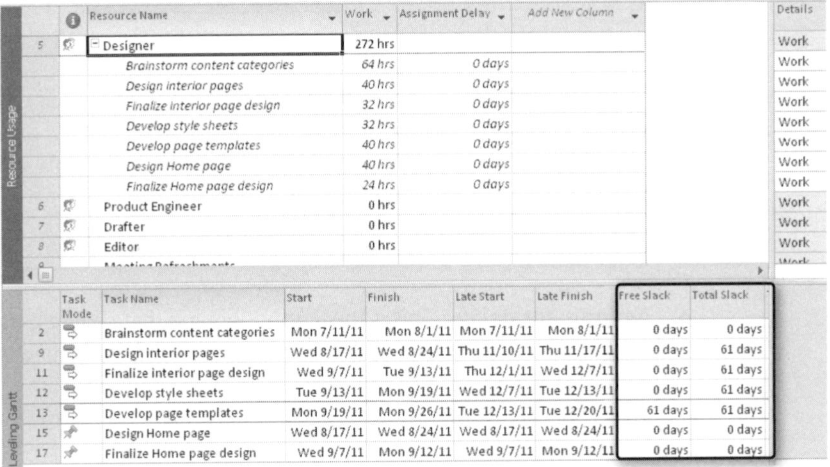

	Resource Name	Work	Assignment Delay	Add New Column	Details
5	Designer	272 hrs			Work
	Brainstorm content categories	*64 hrs*	*0 days*		Work
	Design interior pages	*40 hrs*	*0 days*		Work
	Finalize interior page design	*32 hrs*	*0 days*		Work
	Develop style sheets	*32 hrs*	*0 days*		Work
	Develop page templates	*40 hrs*	*0 days*		Work
	Design Home page	*40 hrs*	*0 days*		Work
	Finalize Home page design	*24 hrs*	*0 days*		Work
6	Product Engineer	0 hrs			Work
7	Drafter	0 hrs			Work
8	Editor	0 hrs			Work

	Task Name	Start	Finish	Late Start	Late Finish	Free Slack	Total Slack
2	Brainstorm content categories	Mon 7/11/11	Mon 8/1/11	Mon 7/11/11	Mon 8/1/11	0 days	0 days
9	Design interior pages	Wed 8/17/11	Wed 8/24/11	Thu 11/10/11	Thu 11/17/11	0 days	61 days
11	Finalize interior page design	Wed 9/7/11	Tue 9/13/11	Thu 12/1/11	Wed 12/7/11	0 days	61 days
12	Develop style sheets	Tue 9/13/11	Mon 9/19/11	Wed 12/7/11	Tue 12/13/11	0 days	61 days
13	Develop page templates	Mon 9/19/11	Mon 9/26/11	Tue 12/13/11	Tue 12/20/11	61 days	61 days
15	Design Home page	Wed 8/17/11	Wed 8/24/11	Wed 8/17/11	Wed 8/24/11	0 days	0 days
17	Finalize Home page design	Wed 9/7/11	Mon 9/12/11	Wed 9/7/11	Mon 9/12/11	0 days	0 days

Figure 10-28 Use the Schedule table in the Leveling Gantt portion of the Resource Allocation view to find available slack in which to add task delay.

6. Also review the timesheet area of the Leveling Gantt. The thin bars to the right of the regular Gantt bars show any available slack, as shown in Figure 10-29.

Figure 10-29 Use the Leveling Gantt portion of the Resource Allocation view to find available slack in which to add task delay.

After you find tasks with slack you can use, add leveling delay as follows:

1. With the Resource Allocation view displayed, click the Leveling Gantt view pane.

2. On the View tab, in the Data group, click Tables, and then click More Tables. In the More Tables dialog box, click Delay, and then click Apply.

3. In the Resource Usage view pane, click the assignment whose task you want to delay.

4. In the Leveling Gantt view pane, in the Leveling Delay field, enter the amount of time you want to delay the task.

If you want to delay an individual assignment for a task that has multiple resources assigned, add assignment delay instead of leveling delay, as follows:

1. With the Resource Allocation view displayed, click the Resource Usage view pane.

2. Click the column heading to the right of where you want to insert the Assignment Delay column.

3. On the Format tab, in the Columns group, click Insert Column.

4. In the newly inserted column, click Assignment Delay.

5. In the Assignment Delay field of the assignment you want to delay, enter the length of the delay.

   This entry indicates how much time after the task's start date the resource is to wait before starting work on this assignment.

Specifying Overtime Work to Account for Overallocations

Often, you can't reassign overallocated work to other resources or delay a task until later. In this case, overtime might be the answer.

Project 2010 does not automatically assign overtime or the associated overtime pay rate when a resource's work exceeds your definition of a normal workday (for example, 8 hours) or a normal workweek (for example, 40 hours). You need to specify overtime work, in addition to total work, for the resource.

For example, suppose a resource is assigned to 10 hours of work in a day. You can specify 2 of those hours as overtime work. The work still totals 10 hours, but 8 hours are regular work and 2 hours are overtime.

Note that overtime can only be entered for automatically scheduled tasks.

Regular Work, Overtime Work, and Total Work

When working with overtime, it's important to keep your work terminology straight; otherwise, it can get confusing. The Work field is actually *total work*; that is, the total amount of time that this resource is assigned to this task.

When you add overtime on an assignment, that amount is stored in the Overtime Work field, and the (total) Work amount stays the same.

Another field, Regular Work, contains the amount of regular (nonovertime) work, based on your amount of total work and overtime work, according to the following calculation:

(total) Work – Overtime Work = Regular Work

You can add the Regular Work field to a sheet view if you want to see the amount of regular work scheduled for a resource in relation to overtime work and (total) work. Note that the Regular Work field is not editable; Project 2010 calculates its value from the Work and Overtime Work fields.

To specify overtime work for overallocated resources on automatically scheduled tasks, first set up a view containing overtime work fields, as follows:

1. On the View tab, in the Resource Views group, click Resource Usage.
2. Be sure the default Usage table is applied. To quickly see which table is applied, rest the mouse pointer in the All Cells box at the upper-left intersection of the table. The pop-up message indicates the name of the table. To change the table, right-click the All Cells box, and then click Usage.
3. Right-click the column heading for the Work field, and then click Insert Column.
4. In the drop-down menu that appears in the new column, type **ov** to quickly move to the Overtime fields. Click Overtime Work.

   The Overtime Work field is added to the Resource Usage view.

Add Details

5. On the Format tab, in the Details group, click Add Details.

   The Detail Styles dialog box appears.
6. In the Available Fields box, click Overtime Work, and then click Show. (See Figure 10-30.)

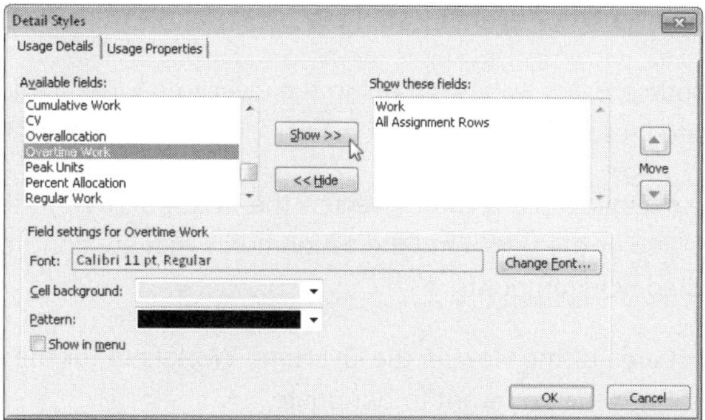

Figure 10-30 Use the Detail Styles dialog box to add another row of timephased information to the timesheet area of the Resource Usage or Task Usage view.

The Overtime Work field appears in the Show These Fields box.

7. Click OK.

   The Overtime Work field is added to the timesheet area of the view, as shown in Figure 10-31.

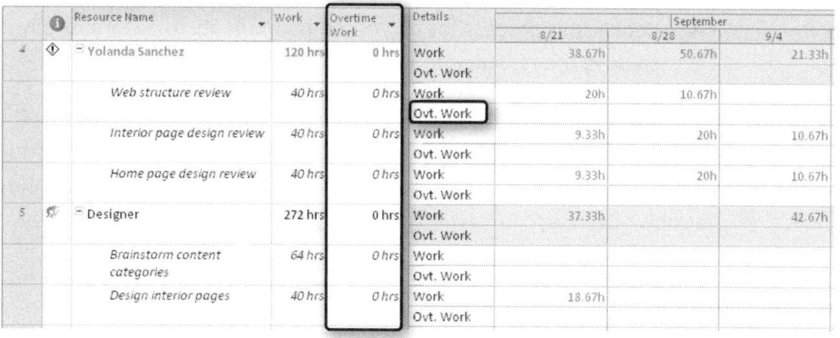

Figure 10-31 Add the Overtime Work field to the sheet and timesheet area of the Resource Usage view.

Note

You might also find it helpful to add the Regular Work field to the sheet area of the Resource Usage view. Right-click the Work field, and then click Insert Column. Type re, click Regular Work, and then click OK.

Chapter 10

To specify overtime work for overallocated resources, follow these steps:

1. In the Resource Usage view containing the Overtime Work field, find the first overallocated resource (highlighted in red) for whom you want to add overtime work.

2. Under the overallocated resource, review the assignments and the hours in the timesheet area of the view. Find the assignments that are contributing to the overallocated work amounts.

3. In the sheet area of the view, in the Overtime Work field for the assignment, enter the amount of overtime you want to designate.

   Don't change the work amount because as the overtime work amount is a portion of the total work. The amount you enter in the Overtime Work field is distributed across the time span of the assignment, which you can see in the timesheet area of the view. For example, if an assignment spans 3 days, and you enter 6 hours of overtime, an amount of overtime is added to each day for the assignment.

   In the timesheet area of the view, you can view how the overtime work you enter is distributed across the assignment's time span. However, you cannot edit the amount of overtime in the individual time periods.

4. Repeat this process for any other assignments to automatically scheduled tasks causing the resource to be overallocated.

When you enter overtime work, the duration of the task is shortened. Overtime work is charged at an overtime rate you enter for the resource in the Resource Sheet or the Resource Information dialog box. The resource name is still shown in red as overallocated, but now you've accounted for the overallocation by using overtime.

Splitting Tasks

Sometimes a resource needs to stop working on one task, start work on a second task, and then return to the first task. This can happen, for example, when an overallocated resource needs to work on a task with a date constraint. In this situation, you can split a task. With a *split task*, you can schedule when the task is to start, stop, and then resume again. As with delay, splitting a task can ensure that resources are working on tasks when they actually have time for them.

Note

In a split task, the task duration is calculated as the value of both portions of the task, not counting the time when the resource is working on something else. However, if you split a task with an elapsed duration, the duration is recalculated to include the start of the first part of the task through the finish of the last part of the task.

To split a task, follow these steps:

1. Display the Gantt Chart.

2. On the Task tab, in the Schedule group, click Split Task. Your mouse pointer changes to the split task pointer, and a small pop-up window explains how to create the split.

3. In the timesheet area of the view, position your mouse pointer on the Gantt bar of the task you want to split; point to the date when you want the split to occur. The date the pointer is resting on shows in the Split Task pop-up window.

4. Drag the Gantt bar to the date when you want the task to resume. The date the split pointer is dragged to also appears in the Split Task pop-up window.

   When you release the mouse, the task is split at your specified dates, as shown in Figure 10-32.

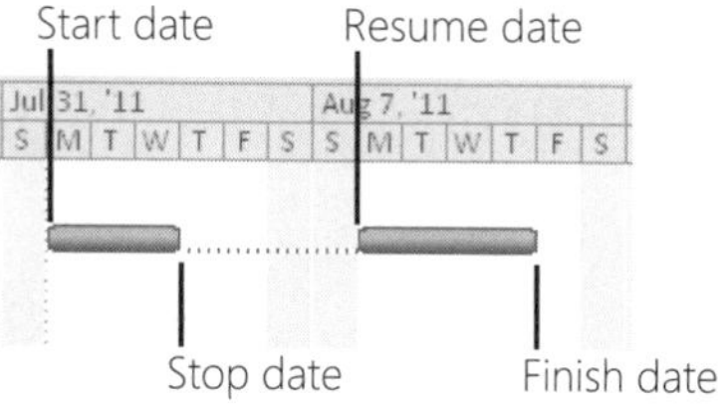

Figure 10-32 Drag the Gantt bar to represent when the task stops and when it resumes.

You can split a longer task multiple times if necessary. Click Task, Schedule, Split Task to activate each new split.

To remove the split in a split task, drag the right portion of the split Gantt bar toward the left portion until both sides of the bar touch and join.

Note

After you begin the execution and tracking phase of the project, you can also split a task on which a resource has started working. For more information on rescheduling, see "Rescheduling the Project" on page 498.

You can also adjust scope to balance the workload. For more information about cutting scope, see "Changing Project Scope" on page 436.

Preventing Overallocations Using the Team Planner

NEW!

You've already seen how you can use the new Team Planner in Project Professional 2010 to review overallocations and move assignments to other resources or other time periods. You can also use the Team Planner to prevent overallocations. In the prevent overallocations mode, the Team Planner moves assignments causing an overallocation to a later time when the assigned resource has time for it. You can think of this as "leveling lite," because Project 2010 uses the same priorities when preventing overallocations as it does when leveling.

For more information, see "Leveling Assignments" in the next section.

To use the Team Planner to prevent overallocations, follow these steps:

1. Display the Team Planner. Any overallocations are highlighted in red, as shown in Figure 10-33.

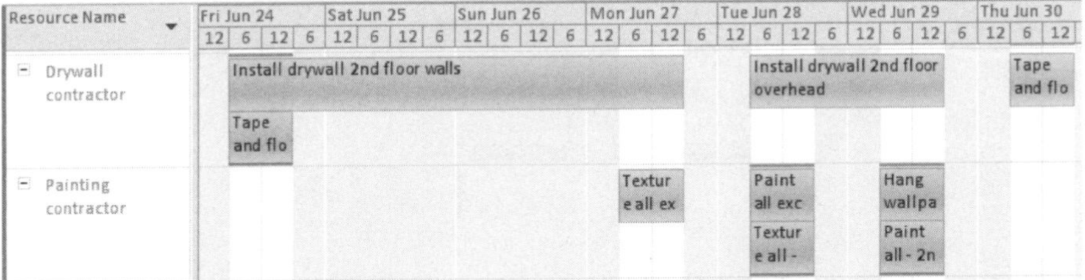

Figure 10-33 The Team Planner shows that the Drywall Contractor and Painting Contractor are both overallocated in late June.

2. On the Format tab, in the Schedule group, click Prevent Overallocations.

Prevent Overallocations

The button changes color to indicate that Team Planner is in the prevent overallocations mode. As shown in Figure 10-34, any tasks causing overallocations are rescheduled for later times when the assigned resource has time for them.

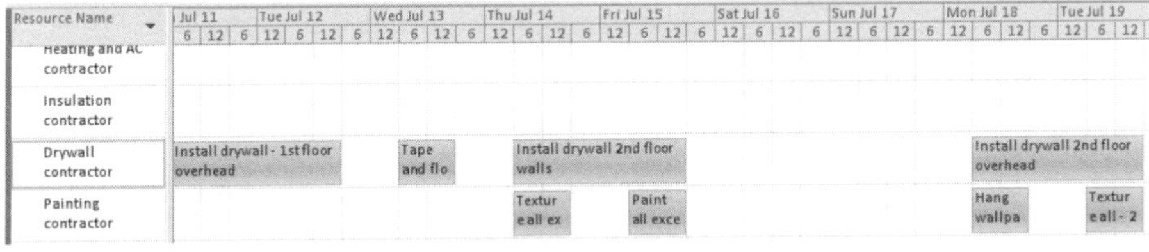

Figure 10-34 The tasks assigned to the Drywall Contractor and Painting Contractor that were causing the overallocation are now rescheduled and spread out to other times.

3. Review the rescheduling of the assignments to be sure you approve of the changes. If you want to move assignments, click Prevent Overallocations again to turn it off.

4. Before leaving the Team Planner, be sure to turn Prevent Overallocations off: click Format, Schedule, Prevent Overallocations.

Note

The prevent overallocations mode in Team Planner reschedules manually scheduled tasks and automatically scheduled tasks and adds leveling delay to both task types.

INSIDE OUT The prevent overallocations mode can cause unintended rescheduling that's hard to undo

As long as the prevent overallocations mode is turned on, whenever you review your schedule in the Team Planner, Project 2010 will automatically reschedule tasks so that there are no overallocations.

Although this rescheduling happens only when you display the Team Planner, it's hard to undo the changes if you don't like them. You can click the Undo button on the Quick Access Toolbar repeatedly to undo the rescheduling and take you back to the previous view. However, as soon as you open the Team Planner again, the rescheduling happens again.

If the unwanted rescheduling happens, and you turn off the prevent overallocations mode, then click Undo. The first thing Undo does is turn the prevent overallocations mode back on. So, you're stuck in a loop and you would have to undo the changes manually, which might be hard to do if you don't remember all the changes you made since the last time you displayed the Team Planner.

So remember—always turn the prevent overallocations mode off before leaving the Team Planner for another view.

For more information about the Team Planner, see "Using the Team Planner to Assign Resources" on page 296.

Leveling Assignments

The previous sections described how you can delay and split tasks to balance or *level* resource assignments based on your own observations, preferences, or date calculations. If you find it tedious or troublesome to do it yourself, Project 2010 can balance the workload for you with the leveling feature, which calculates and implements delay and splits in your project plan according to general specifications that you set.

You can have Project 2010 level assignments whenever you give the command. Although it's often not advisable, you also have the option to keep the leveling feature on all the time. If you leave leveling on all the time, whenever you change the schedule in some way, Project 2010 levels assignments immediately.

Here's a summary of what Project 2010 leveling does and does not do. Leveling:

- Adds delay or splits a task so that the task can be done later when the assigned resources have available time.
- Can balance the workload of resources assigned to manually as well as automatically scheduled tasks.
- Balances the workload of human, equipment, and generic resources.
- Does not reassign tasks or assignment units.
- Does not change work amounts.
- Does not operate on material resources or cost resources.

When you level resources, you carry out some or all of these major process steps, which are detailed in the following sections.

Setting Leveling Priorities

You can set a priority for each task if you like. Priorities range from 0 (the lowest priority) to 1,000 (the highest). All tasks start with a default priority of 500; that is, they are all equal in priority. Project 2010 uses the task priority setting as a leveling criterion. If you have certain tasks that are so important that you never want the leveling feature to split or delay them, you should set them at a priority of 1,000, which ensures that Project 2010 will never use that task to level resources. You might have other tasks that, although important, have more potential flexibility as to when they can be completed. Those tasks can be set at a lower priority, such as 100. Having tasks set at lower priorities gives Project 2010 the flexibility it needs to effectively level resource assignments.

To change the priority of an individual task, do the following:

1. In the Gantt Chart or other task sheet, double-click the task whose priority you want to change from the default of 500.
2. In the Task Information dialog box, click the General tab.
3. In the Priority box, enter the number representing the priority you want for this task.

INSIDE OUT Priorities apply only to resource leveling and substitution

Although it seems that priorities can help influence the way that Project 2010 schedules tasks throughout your project, priorities are actually used only in the context of leveling. (If you're working with Project Professional 2010, priorities also play a part in the Resource Substitution Wizard.) When Project 2010 is determining whether to split or delay one task versus another to level resources, it can use priority as one of its criteria, in addition to the other criteria you set in the Resource Leveling dialog box.

This said, you can still use priorities in your own ways. You can sort and group tasks by priority. You can also create a filter to see only tasks above a certain priority. Just be aware that Project 2010 doesn't use priority values for any other purpose than leveling or resource substitution.

Suppose there are ten tasks throughout your project that you want to set at a higher priority than the average. You can select those tasks and then change their priority in one operation, as follows:

1. In the Gantt Chart or other task sheet, select all the tasks whose priority you want to change to the same number.
2. On the Task tab, in the Properties group, click Information.
3. In the Multiple Task Information dialog box, click the General tab.
4. In the Priority box, enter the number representing the priority you want for all selected tasks.

You can add the Priority field to a task sheet and change the priority for tasks individually throughout the sheet view. To do this, follow these steps:

1. In the Gantt Chart or other task sheet, click the column to the right of where you want the new Priority column to be inserted.

2. On the Format tab, in the Columns group, click Insert Column.

3. In the new column, type **pr** to scroll quickly through the drop-down menu, and then click Priority.

   The Priority column appears in your sheet view, as shown in Figure 10-35.

		Task Mode	Task Name	Duration	Priority	Start
10			Interior page design review	5 days	500	Wed 8/24/11
11			Finalize interior page design	4 days	500	Wed 9/7/11
12			Develop style sheets	4 days	500	Tue 9/13/11
13			Develop page templates	5 days	500	Mon 9/19/11
14			**Design Home page**	**18 days**	**500**	**Wed 8/17/11**
15			Design Home page	5 days	500	Wed 8/17/11
16			Home page design review	10 days	500	Wed 8/24/11

Figure 10-35 Type or select the priority you want in the Priority field.

4. For any task whose priority should be other than the default, enter the number in the Priority field.

Leveling Resources with Standard Defaults

You use the Resource Leveling dialog box to set your leveling preferences and give the command to level. However, the default settings of the dialog box work for the majority of resource-leveling needs. It's a good idea to try leveling with those settings first and see how they work for you. Then you'll have a better idea of the kinds of controls you want to impose on the leveling operation.

Follow these steps to level all resources using the default settings:

Level All

1. On the Resource tab, in the Level group, click Level All.

   This command is available in any view, whether it's a task or resource view.

   If you've done any previous leveling, or if you have added leveling delay manually or by using the Prevent Overallocations feature in the Team Planner, it might look at first like nothing has happened. Another possible result is that it might look like more resources are overallocated than before.

   If either of these is the case, it's likely caused by the fact that by default, any values in the Leveling Delay field must first be cleared. Click Level All a second time.

   Any overallocated resources throughout the project are leveled, as shown in Figure 10-36.

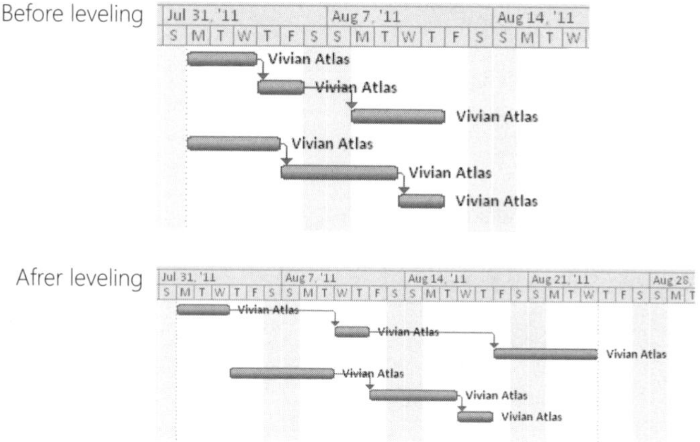

Figure 10-36 The Level All command resolves any overallocations throughout the project according to the settings in the Resource Leveling dialog box.

2. Examine a task view and resource view to see how Project 2010 has distributed assignments to eliminate all overallocations.

3. If you see a change that you don't like, you can change it manually. If you see many changes that you don't like, simply click Undo on the Quick Access Toolbar to undo the leveling operation.

Note

Remember that leveling does not reassign tasks or units. It does not change work amounts. It causes the start date to move later by adding delays, or it splits a task so that it finishes later when the assigned resources have available time.

To see the changes that leveling has made, see "Checking the Results of Leveling" on page 434.

To level one or more selected resources, follow these steps:

Level Resource

1. With any view showing, on the Resource tab, in the Level group, click Level Resource.

2. The Level Resources dialog box appears, listing all resources. If you selected resources, they are selected in the dialog box, as shown in Figure 10-37.

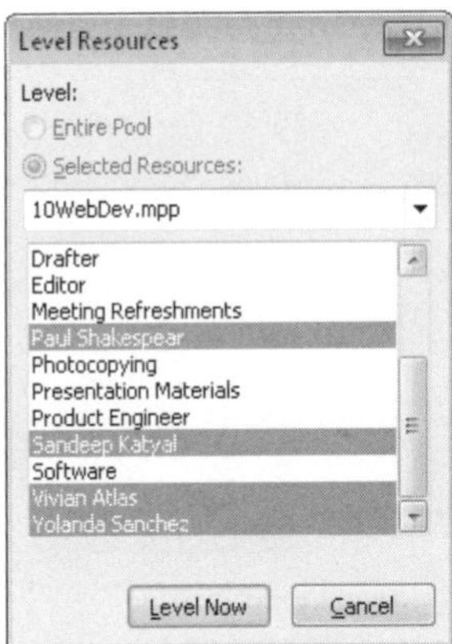

Figure 10-37 The Level Resource command resolves any overallocations for selected resources according to the settings in the Resource Leveling dialog box.

Note that the Entire Pool and Selected Resources options are dimmed when you're working with a standalone file. When you're working with a project file attached to a *resource pool*, the options become available, with Entire Pool being the default. If you click the Selected Resources option, you can choose whether the resources listed are from the resource pool file or from the *sharer file* (the file using the resource pool). Because it's always a good practice to keep the leveling operation as small and contained as possible, selecting certain resources for leveling is recommended over leveling resources in the entire pool.

For more information, see "Sharing Resources by Using a Resource Pool" on page 614.

3. You can change the resources selected in the dialog box.

   To select multiple adjacent resources, drag from the first to the last resource.

   To select multiple nonadjacent resources, click the first resource, hold down the Ctrl key, and then click each of the others.

4. Click Level Now.

   The assignments for the selected resources are leveled as necessary.

Note

You can level selected resources from a task sheet as well. In the Gantt Chart, for example, select one or more tasks that are assigned to overallocated resources. Click Level Resource. All resources assigned to the selected tasks are listed in the Level Resources dialog box. Select the resources you want to level, and then click Level Now.

To level only the assignments on selected tasks, follow these steps:

1. Switch to a task view and select the tasks whose assignments you want to level. Be sure to select more than one task, as leveling selected tasks needs to be done in relation to at least one other task. To select multiple adjacent tasks, drag from the first to the last task.

   To select multiple nonadjacent tasks, click the first task, hold down the Ctrl key, and then click each of the others.

   You can click or drag any field in a task row to select it. You must select at least two tasks for the Level Selection button to become available.

Level Selection

2. On the Resource tab, in the Level group, click Level Selection.

   Any overallocations within the selected tasks are leveled according to the settings in the Resource Leveling dialog box.

   Remember, in this case the leveling is done only on the selected tasks. The resources might still have overallocations elsewhere in the project.

Setting Leveling Options

To see the criteria Project 2010 uses when leveling, open the Resource Leveling dialog box. You can make a variety of adjustments to customize how leveling is done in your project. These settings also control how tasks are moved when you use the Prevent Overallocations mode in the Team Planner.

To set leveling options, follow these steps:

Leveling Options

1. On the Resource tab, in the Level group, click Leveling Options.

   The Resource Leveling dialog box appears, as shown in Figure 10-38.

2. Make any changes to reflect your leveling preferences.

   See "Understanding Leveling Options" in the next section for more details.

3. Click Level All.

   Regardless of whether any tasks or resources are selected, all overallocations throughout the project are leveled according to your settings.

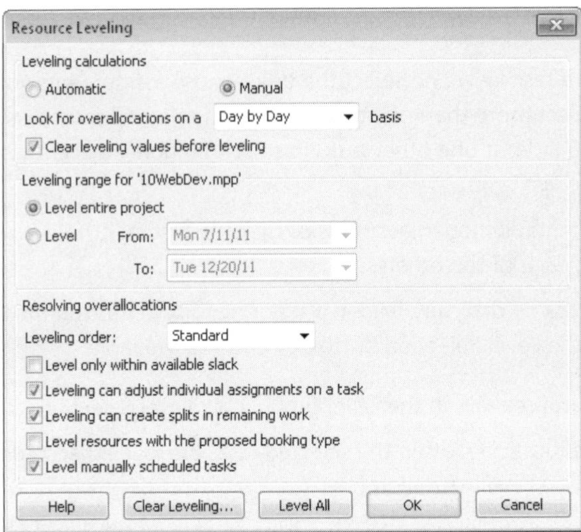

Figure 10-38 You can do a standard leveling operation using the defaults, or you can set your own options in the Resource Leveling dialog box.

INSIDE OUT Rein in the extent of resource leveling

By default, Project 2010 levels on a day-by-day basis. That means even if resources are assigned to a task that goes just one minute over their availability in a day as determined by their resource calendar or maximum units, their assignments will be leveled.

You might think this is somewhat nitpicky, and maybe you'd rather not split tasks or add delays unless there are larger overallocations. If this is the case, click Resource, Level, Leveling Options. Under Leveling Calculations, change the Day By Day setting to Week By Week or Month By Month.

If you set leveling to Week By Week, for example, a resource set up with a 40-hour workweek is only leveled if she is assigned more than 40 hours in a week. However, her assignments are not leveled if she is assigned 14 hours in a single day, as long as the weekly total stays at or below 40 hours.

Understanding Leveling Options

If you've leveled your project a few times and want to take more control over how Project 2010 levels, change the options you want in the Resource Leveling dialog box. The following list details the available options:

- **Calculate automatically or manually** Under Leveling Calculations, be sure that the Manual option is selected. This ensures that resources are leveled only when you explicitly give one of the leveling commands (Level All, Level Resource, or Level Selection).

  The Automatic option is available if you want Project 2010 to level resources whenever you make a change that affects scheduling. However, be aware that this setting can cause Project 2010 operations to become sluggish and therefore this option is not recommended. If you do select the Automatic option, clear the check box labeled Clear Leveling Values Before Leveling to improve performance.

- **Specify the overallocation leveling time period** Resources are considered overallocated if they have even one minute of work scheduled beyond their availability, as determined by their resource calendars and maximum units. You can set the time period at which leveling is triggered in the box labeled Look For Overallocations On A Basis. By default, the time period basis is a day, so if resources are overallocated by one minute within a day, they'll be leveled. If you set the overallocation leveling time period basis to the week, resources that are scheduled for more work than can be accomplished by their weekly availability will be leveled. The choices are Minute By Minute, Day By Day (the default), Week By Week, and Month By Month.

- **Clear leveling** The Clear Leveling Values Before Leveling check box is selected by default. This setting specifies that any delays previously entered as a result of leveling or as a result of manually entering leveling delay are to be cleared before the next leveling operation is performed. The Clear Leveling button does the same thing. Use the check box if you're about to level again and you want to start fresh. Use the button if you're not planning to level right now, but you want to remove any leveling delay from your project plan. If the Clear Leveling button is dimmed, that means there is nothing to clear.

- **Level certain tasks or the entire project** Under Leveling Range, you can specify that only those tasks falling within a date range you enter should be leveled. This can be particularly useful in projects that take place over a long period of time or that are subject to many changes. The default is for all tasks in the project to be leveled.

- **Set the order of leveling operations** When Project 2010 starts to level, it first determines which tasks are causing overallocations. Then Project 2010 works through the project, adding delays and splitting tasks to remove the overallocation. You can control the order in which Project 2010 levels through the project by setting the leveling order. By default, Project 2010 uses the Standard leveling order, which looks at task relationships, slack, start dates, priorities, and constraints to determine whether and how tasks should be leveled. (See Table 10-1.) If you choose the ID Only leveling order, Project 2010 delays tasks with the higher ID numbers before considering any other criteria. If you choose the Priority, Standard leveling order, Project 2010 first looks at any priorities you've set and then all the factors of the Standard leveling order.

- **Level within available slack** By default, the Level Only Within Available Slack check box is cleared. Select this check box if you need to ensure that leveling will not push out the finish date. However, unless your project has a fair amount of built-in slack, if this check box is selected, you might not see many changes to your project.

  Selecting this check box, at least for your first try, can be a good way to see what adjustments can be made by delaying assignments and splitting tasks without pushing out the project finish date. If you don't see many changes as a result, you might realize that you indeed need to add resources, cut scope, or extend the project finish date.

- **Adjust individual assignments on a task** By default, the check box labeled Leveling Can Adjust Individual Assignments On A Task is selected. This setting controls adjustments to when a resource works on a task, independent of other resources working on the same task.

- **Create splits in remaining work** By default, the check box labeled Leveling Can Create Splits In Remaining Work is selected. This means that not only can leveling split tasks that haven't started yet, it can also split tasks that are currently in progress.

- **Level proposed resources** If you're working in Project Professional 2010, you can add resources tentatively to your project and assign them to tasks. Such resources have a proposed booking type. By default, proposed resources are not included in a leveling operation; only committed resources are. If you want to include proposed resources in the leveling operation, select the check box labeled Level Resources With The Proposed Booking Type.

  For more information about working with proposed and committed resources, see "Proposing Tentative Resources" on page 262. If you're working with proposed enterprise resources, see "Building Your Enterprise Project Team" on page 927.

- **Level manually scheduled tasks** By default, the check box labeled Level Manually Scheduled Tasks is selected. This means that if your project includes manually scheduled tasks, they will be leveled along with any automatically scheduled tasks needing to be leveled.

After you change the leveling options to your satisfaction, level the resources in your project plan by clicking the Level All button. To level only selected resources, click OK in the Resource Leveling dialog box, select the resources you want to level, and then use the Level Resource command. To level only assignments within selected tasks, click OK in the Resource Leveling dialog box, selected the tasks, and then use the Level Selection command.

Table 10-2 explains the order in which resource leveling is carried out.

Table 10-2 **Order of Operations for Resource Leveling**

With this leveling order	These fields are examined
Standard	Task relationships Slack Start date Priority Constraint Task ID
ID Only	Task ID
Priority, Standard	Priority Task relationships Slack Start date Constraint Task ID

INSIDE OUT Understanding delay in projects scheduled from the finish date

If you level tasks in a project scheduled from the finish date, negative delay values are applied from the end of the task or assignment, which causes the task or assignment's finish date to occur earlier.

Also, if you switch a project from one to be scheduled from the start date to one that is scheduled from the finish date, any leveling delays and splits are removed.

TROUBLESHOOTING

Leveling delay you entered manually has disappeared

Suppose you entered leveling delay to manually delay tasks. When you use the Project 2010 leveling feature, any previously entered leveling delay is removed by default. This is true whether the delay was entered automatically or manually.

To prevent manual leveling delay from being removed in the future, always clear the Clear Leveling Values Before Leveling check box in the Resource Leveling dialog box. And don't click the Clear Leveling button.

You might also consider entering assignment delay rather than leveling delay when manually entering delay values. Whereas leveling delay values delay all assignments on a task, assignment delay values delay individual assignments. Therefore, it might be a little more cumbersome and repetitious to enter initially, but you never have to worry about losing the values to a new leveling operation.

If you've lost your leveling delay values and want to restore them, click the Undo button on the Quick Access Toolbar as many times as necessary until you get to the point where you have reversed the leveling operation. You can undo operations until the point when you last saved the project file. If you cannot undo, you might need to enter the leveling delay again or use a backup project file.

For more information about manually entering delay, see "Delaying a Task or Assignment" on page 415.

Checking the Results of Leveling

To see the changes made to your project plan as a result of leveling, use the Leveling Gantt. Display the Leveling Gantt as follows:

1. On the View tab, in the Task Views group, click the arrow next to Gantt Chart.

   If Leveling Gantt is not listed, click More Views, and then click Leveling Gantt.

   As shown in Figure 10-39, two sets of Gantt bars in this view show task scheduling before and after leveling, which lets you compare the changes made. The Gantt bars also indicate any task delays and splits created by the leveling operation.

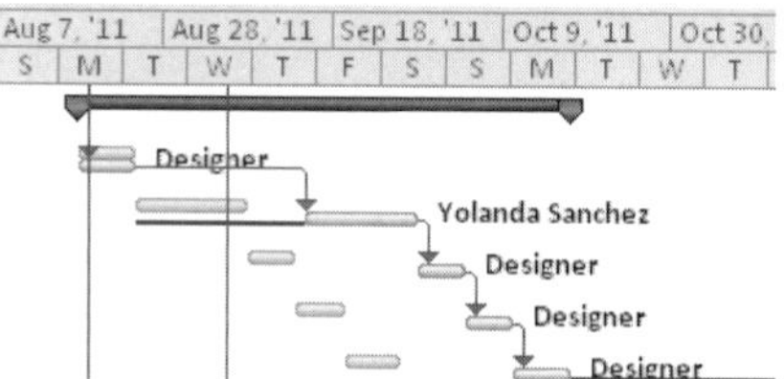

Figure 10-39 The gold Gantt bars show the preleveled task schedule, whereas the blue bars, delays, and splits show the results of the leveling operation.

Clear Leveling

2. If you don't like the results of leveling, click Undo on the Quick Access Toolbar until the leveling is cleared. Or, click Resource, Leveling, Clear Leveling.

TROUBLESHOOTING

Project 2010 performance has slowed since you last leveled

You probably set resource leveling to Automatic. In this mode, each time you make a scheduling change that affects assignments, Project 2010 automatically levels resources. Although this is a nice feature and is sometimes what you might expect Project 2010 to do for you, it can significantly slow performance in larger or more complex projects.

To resolve the slowdown, in the Resource Leveling dialog box, under Leveling Calculations, select the Manual option. Then click Level All, Level Resource, or Level Selection whenever you want resources to be leveled.

Note

If you go to the Leveling Gantt first and then level your project, you can see the results right away in the Leveling Gantt. If you don't like the results, you can immediately click Undo on the Quick Access Toolbar to reverse the changes made by leveling.

TROUBLESHOOTING

You told Project 2010 to level your resources, but nothing changed

One reason this might happen is that the setting under Leveling Calculations might be too broad. If the setting is Look For Overallocations On A Month By Month basis, for example, a resource could be scheduled for 16-hour days in the first two weeks of the month with little to nothing scheduled in the last two weeks, and this resource would not be leveled. Change the setting to a narrower leveling trigger such as Week By Week.

Another reason this might happen is that you chose to level only within available slack. If there is little to no slack in your schedule, then little to no leveling can be done. In the Resource Leveling dialog box, clear the check box labeled Level Only Within Available Slack and try again.

A third reason nothing changed when you gave the leveling command is that you might have clicked OK instead of Level All. If your leveling calculations selection is set to Manual, you need to click Level All. If you don't want to level the entire project, click OK, and then click Resource, Level, Level Resource, or Level Selection.

Remember, leveling does not reassign tasks or units, and it does not change work amounts. It causes the start date to move later by adding delays, or it splits a task so that it finishes later when the assigned resources have available time.

Changing Project Scope

In the course of checking and adjusting your project plan, you might need to cut scope. For example, to meet the finish date, you might need to cut tasks you perceive as optional. To bring project costs in line with your allotted budget, you might cut tasks associated with increased quality or quantity that you think you can live without. Or maybe you need to cut an entire phase or deliverable to alleviate resource overallocation.

Note

Your task list is likely based on the scope statement that all the stakeholders, including customers, originally approved. If you need to cut scope, you might have to go back and obtain stakeholder approval for these changes.

There are two ways to remove tasks from your project. One way is to completely remove the task. In a task sheet, click the task's row heading and then press the Delete key.

NEW!

Inactivate

The other way is to inactivate the task. In a task sheet, select the task. On the Task tab, in the Schedule group, click Inactivate. All information in the task row is dimmed and shown in a strikethrough font, as shown in Figure 10-40.

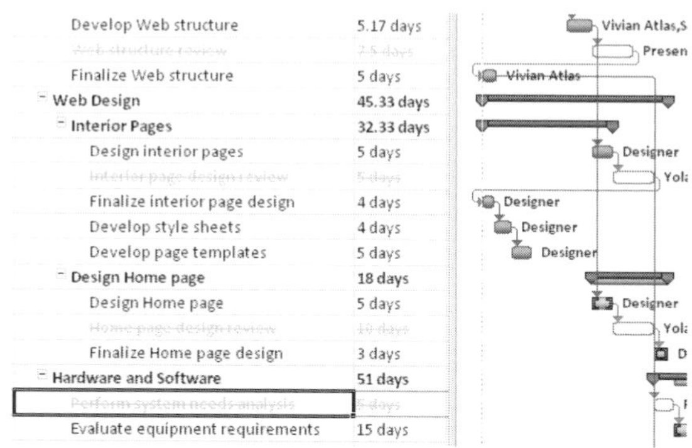

Figure 10-40 Inactivated tasks and their associated Gantt bars still show as "ghost" images in your project plan, and you can reactivate them later if needed.

With inactivated tasks, you can still show tasks in the project plan, even though they're deleted. This is a great way to show managing stakeholders which tasks or deliverables they might or will lose as a result of cutting scope to meet a date or budget. In this way, you can use inactivated tasks to show and schedule what-if scenarios. When you decide on the course you prefer to take, you can reactivate tasks by clicking the Inactivate button again.

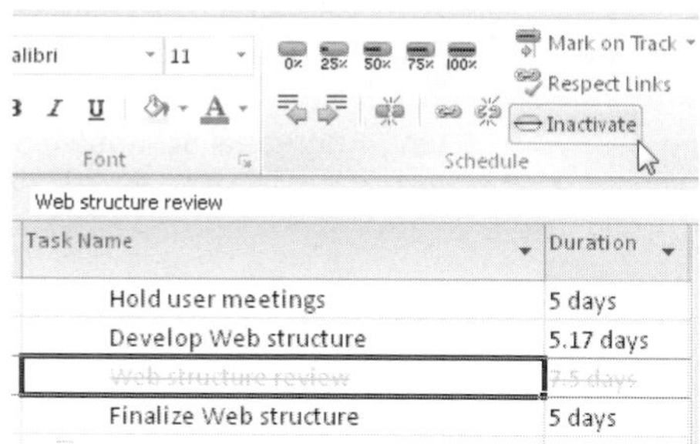

Inactivating tasks is also good historical data. If you later create a new project based on this plan, you'll have the inactivated tasks in place, and you can decide whether to include them in the new project based on your experiences with this project.

An inactivated task behaves exactly like a deleted task. The only difference is that its information, including its Gantt bar, still shows.

CAUTION!

If you delete or inactivate an automatically scheduled task that includes links to predecessors or successors, be sure that the scheduling for the tasks still in place is not adversely affected. If you delete or inactivate a predecessor, for example, the successor could end up being scheduled back at the project start date unless you link it to a different predecessor.

However, this is not true for manually scheduled tasks. If you delete or inactivate a manually scheduled task that's linked to others, the tasks that were previously predecessors or successors tend to remain scheduled where they were.

You can also delete a summary task that represents an entire phase or group of related tasks. To delete a summary task, click its row heading and press the Delete key. A message appears and warns you that deleting the summary task will delete all of its subtasks as well. Click OK to confirm that you want to do this.

Reviewing the Impact of Changes

After you adjust your project plan to bring in your finish date, reduce costs, or balance your workload, check that you've succeeded in hitting your target. Look at the Project Statistics dialog box or review the project summary task, as described earlier in this chapter.

If you created an interim plan to save the task start and finish dates as they were before you started making changes, you can add the interim start and finish fields as Gantt bars in your Gantt Chart to compare them against your new start and finish fields.

For more information about interim plans, see "Saving Additional Scheduled Start and Finish Dates" on page 459. For information about creating custom Gantt bars, see "Formatting the Appearance of Gantt Bars" on page 1072.

When you're content with one aspect of your project plan, such as your finish date, see whether you've "broken" any other aspect of your project, such as your costs. Keep an eye on your finish date, total project costs, and resource allocation while always remembering your highest priority of the three. Continue to adjust and balance until all aspects of the project are just the way you want them.

Obtaining Buyoff on the Project Plan

Typically, before you even start working with Project 2010, you have a defined scope for your project. This scope drives the development of deliverables, milestones, phases, and tasks, and it was also probably developed in conjunction with various stakeholders.

If you are forced to cut scope as a result of adjusting the project plan to meet finish date, cost, or resource requirements, you need to go back to those stakeholders and get their approval for your scope changes.

You might need to justify your changes and specify the tradeoffs that are being made to meet the finish date, reduce costs, or balance workload to a reasonable level. You can also point out that the scope is now defined more precisely, based on the project limitations. With this more precise definition, you lower potential risks. The plan is solid and realistic. The project is now less apt to incur unexpected delays, costs, or other changes that can disrupt the project, cause rework, or lower productivity.

As soon as you obtain buyoff from your stakeholders, you have officially completed the planning phase of your project. You're finally ready to tell your team "Go!" and enter the execution phase of the project.

PART 3

Tracking Progress

Before you can use the sample files for Chapters 11 and 12, you'll need to install them from this book's companion content website. For more information about downloading and installing the sample files, see "About the Companion Content" on page xxviii.

CHAPTER 11

Setting a Baseline and Updating Progress

By now, you've completed the planning phase of your project. The scope is set, along with the project goals and objectives. The tasks and deliverables are scheduled. The budget is approved, and you've procured the necessary human, equipment, and material resources. Your project plan reflects all these details and has been signed off by upper management or by your customers.

After all this, you're ready to charge forward with your team and actually start doing the work prescribed by the project. You are now leaving the planning phase and entering the execution phase.

The execution phase consists of four major activities:

- **Tracking** You track progress on tasks so that you know when tasks are actually completed by the assigned resources.
- **Analyzing** You examine any differences between your original plan and how it's actually progressing. You monitor the differences in schedule or cost to anticipate any potential problems.
- **Controlling** You take any necessary corrective actions to keep the project on a steady course toward completion by its deadline and on its budget.
- **Reporting** You keep stakeholders informed. Whether you're providing task and assignment details to your team members or presenting high-level progress information to executives, you regularly report various aspects of project information.

You used Microsoft Project 2010 in the planning phase to organize, schedule, and budget your project. Now you can use it in the execution phase to enter progress information, analyze performance, and generate status reports. With a close eye on progress and performance, you can adjust the project plan as necessary to ensure that your scope, schedule, costs, and resources are all balanced the way you need.

To execute your project with Project 2010, do two things:

- Save the baseline information of your project as currently planned.
- Enter progress information as your resources complete their assigned tasks.

With both baseline and progress information in hand, you can use the power of Project 2010 to guide your project toward a successful outcome.

INSIDE OUT Are you a charter or a tracker?

Some project managers set up a project plan, painstakingly enter tasks, and create a schedule with meticulously researched durations, task dependencies, and constraints. They acquire and assign exactly the right resources and calculate costs to the last penny. However, after they have their plan perfected, they execute the project and leave the project plan behind. What started out as an excellent roadmap of the project is now little more than a bit of planning history.

To graduate to the next level of project management, take your project plan with you as you move to the execution phase. This means maintaining the plan and entering actual progress information as tasks are being worked on. By tracking progress in this way, your schedule and costs are updated, so you know what to expect as you traverse the weeks and months of your project. Use the calculating power of Project 2010 to:

- Figure variances between your original baseline plan and your current schedule and use these variances to help you adjust upcoming tasks.
- Perform earned value analyses to measure your progress against where you expected to be at a particular point in time.
- Compare resource costs as they are being incurred against your project budget to see if you are on track or whether overruns are on the horizon.
- Generate reports you can share at status meetings to communicate the appropriate level of information.

By entering tracking data in your project plan, you always have the up-to-date details you need at your fingertips. If you need to adjust the plan—either to recover a slipping phase or to respond to a directive to cut 10 percent of the project budget—Project 2010 serves as your project management information system to help you quickly and accurately make those adjustments.

Saving Original Plan Information Using a Baseline

The project plan, having been adjusted to perfection, is considered your baseline. Think of it as your original plan. It represents the most ideal balance between scope, schedule, and cost.

The project plan at this point in time is also your scheduled, or current, plan. This is the only point in the project when the original plan and the current plan are the same.

They're identical only at this time because the current project plan is fluid. For the automatically scheduled tasks in your project, as soon as you enter progress information—such as one task's actual start date or another task's percentage complete—your project plan is recalculated and adjusted to reflect the new information from those actuals.

For example, suppose that Task A has a scheduled finish date of May 3. It's linked with a finish-to-start task dependency to Task B, so Task B's scheduled start date is also May 3. However, Task A finishes 2 days early, on May 1. After you enter the actual finish date of Task A, the scheduled start date of Task B, which has the default ASAP constraint, changes to May 1. The scheduled start dates of any other successor tasks are recalculated as well.

> **Note**
> **If you enter an actual duration, start or finish date, or percentage complete on a manually scheduled task, its information, or the information of any tasks linked to it, is not recalculated.**

This constant recalculation is essential for you to always know where your project stands in current reality. But what if you want to know what your original start dates were? What if you want to compare the original baseline plan with the current schedule to analyze your progress and performance?

The answer is to save baseline information. By setting a baseline, you're basically taking a snapshot of key scheduling and cost information in your project plan at that point in time—that is, before you enter your first actuals and the scheduled plan begins to diverge from the original baseline plan. With the original baseline information saved, you have a basis for comparing the current or actual project plan against your original baseline plan.

The difference between baseline and current scheduled information is called a *variance*. Baselines, actuals, and variances are used in a variety of ways, including earned value analyses, to monitor project schedule and cost performance. In fact, you cannot perform earned value analyses at all unless you have first set a baseline.

Saving a baseline is not the same as saving the entire project plan. When you set a baseline, you copy the contents of the following fields for all tasks, resources, and assignments to their corresponding baseline fields:

- Duration to the Baseline Duration field
- Start to the Baseline Start field
- Finish to the Baseline Finish field
- Work to the Baseline Work field
- Cost to the Baseline Cost field

These are the most frequently used (and useful) baseline fields that will give you a good basis for analyzing schedule and budget performance as you execute your project.

INSIDE OUT

Additional special-purpose baseline fields have limited uses

In addition to the five schedule-related baseline fields (baseline duration, start, finish, work, and cost), nine special-purpose fields are also saved when you set a baseline. (See Table 11-1.) These fields are useful only when your project plan uses certain specific features or meets certain conditions.

Table 11-1 **Special-Purpose Baseline Fields**

Field category	The contents of this field...	which contains the...	are saved in this baseline field...	For more information
Budget resources	Budget Work	Entered budgeted work amounts for comparison against scheduled or actual project work amounts for established budget categories	Baseline Budget Work	"Setting Up and Reviewing a Project Budget" on page 346
	Budget Cost	Entered budgeted costs for comparison against scheduled or actual project costs for established budget categories	Baseline Budget Cost	"Setting Up and Reviewing a Project Budget" on page 346

Field category	The contents of this field...	which contains the...	are saved in this baseline field...	For more information
Deliverable dates	Deliverable Start	Start date for a deliverable in a linked enterprise project	Baseline Deliverable Start	"Depending on Deliverables in Other Projects" on page 921
	Deliverable Finish	Finish date for a deliverable in a linked enterprise project	Baseline Deliverable Finish	"Depending on Deliverables in Other Projects" on page 921
Fixed costs	Fixed Cost	Miscellaneous cost item, typically not associated with a resource cost or regular cost item on a task	Baseline Fixed Cost	"Planning Fixed Costs for Tasks" on page 334
	Fixed Cost Accrual	Entered choice of whether a fixed cost should be recorded at the start or finish of a task or prorated throughout its duration	Baseline Fixed Cost Accrual	"Planning Fixed Costs for Tasks" on page 334
Schedule estimates for manually scheduled placeholder tasks	Estimated Duration	Calculated duration for a placeholder task, with a default of 1 day	Baseline Estimated Duration	"Reviewing Baseline Information" on page 451
	Estimated Start	Calculated start date for a manually scheduled task, typically the same as the project start date	Baseline Estimated Start	"Reviewing Baseline Information" on page 451
	Estimated Finish	Calculated finish date for a manually scheduled task, typically the same as the project start date	Baseline Estimated Finish	"Reviewing Baseline Information" on page 451

Setting a Baseline

You can set a baseline for the entire project and also for additional tasks after they're added.

Setting the Project Baseline

To save the first set of baseline information for your project plan, follow these steps:

Set Baseline

1. On the Project tab, in the Schedule group, click Set Baseline, and then click Set Baseline in the drop-down menu that appears.

   The Set Baseline dialog box appears, as shown in Figure 11-1.

   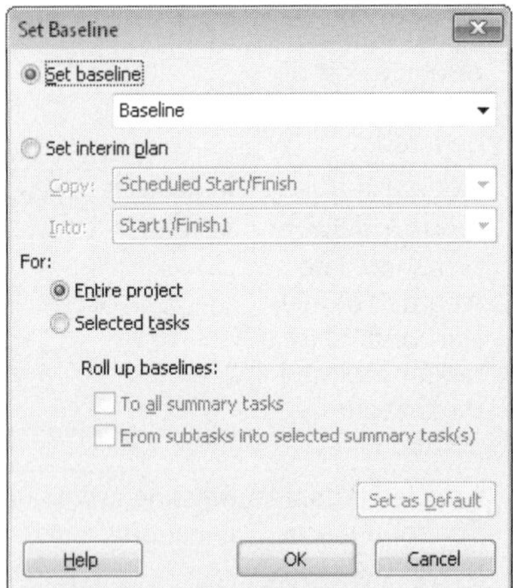

   Figure 11-1 Use the Set Baseline dialog box to save up to 11 baselines and 10 interim plans.

2. Be sure that the Set Baseline option is selected.
3. In the box under the Set Baseline option, verify that Baseline (not Baseline 1 or Baseline 2) is selected.
4. Under For, be sure that the Entire Project option is selected.
5. Click OK.

Although nothing seems to happen, as soon as you click OK, information is copied to the 14 corresponding baseline fields. The value stored in the Cost field is copied to the Baseline Cost field, the value stored in the Work field is copied to the Baseline Work field, and so on.

Setting the Baseline for Newly Added Tasks

But what if you set a baseline and later add another set of tasks? Even after you initially set the baseline, you can still add tasks to it, as follows:

1. In the Gantt Chart or another task sheet, select the tasks that you want to add to the baseline.
2. On the Project tab, in the Schedule group, click Set Baseline, and then click Set Baseline in the drop-down menu that appears.
3. In the dialog box, be sure that the Set Baseline option is selected.
4. Under the Set Baseline option, be sure that Baseline is selected.

   The Baseline box lists the date you last set the baseline. If you want to add tasks to a different baseline—for example, Baseline 1 or Baseline 2—click that baseline in the list.
5. Under For, select the Selected Tasks option.

   When you select the Selected Tasks option, the Roll Up Baselines check boxes become available. (See Figure 11-2.) This option ensures that the summarized baseline data shown in summary tasks is accurate and rolled up the way you expect.

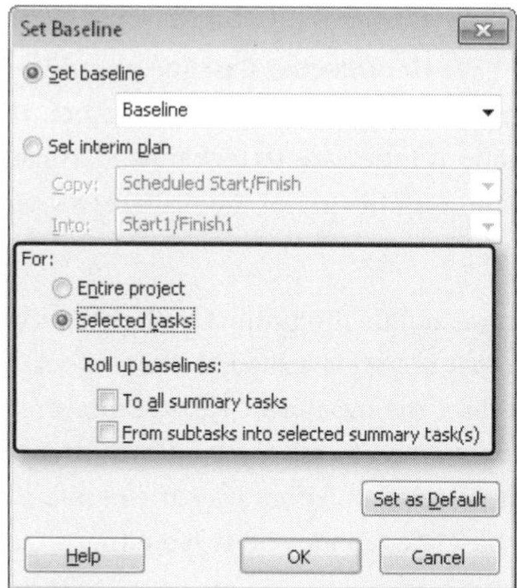

Figure 11-2 When you set a baseline for selected tasks, you can choose how to update the corresponding baseline data on summary tasks.

6. Select the check box that reflects how you want the baseline information of the selected tasks to be rolled up to summary tasks.

   By default, after the initial baseline is set, a summary task is not updated when a subtask is modified, added, or deleted.

   - If you want the selected tasks to be rolled up to all associated summary tasks, select the To All Summary Tasks check box.
   - If you want the selected tasks to be rolled up only to a selected summary task, select the From Subtasks Into Selected Summary Task(s) check box.

7. Click OK, and then click Yes to confirm that you want to change the existing baseline.

Note

When setting a baseline, click the name of the baseline that has a Last Saved date. Under For, select Entire Project or Selected Tasks to specify whether you want to overwrite the baseline information of the entire project or only of selected tasks. The current schedule information in your project plan overwrites the baseline information in the selected baseline.

Protecting Baseline Information

If you're using Microsoft Project Professional 2010 with Microsoft Project Server 2010 and the enterprise project management features, your project server administrator grants or denies the ability to set baselines in enterprise projects. Only those who have the Save Protected Baseline or Save Unprotected Baseline permission set by the administrator can set or potentially overwrite a baseline in your project. This baseline protection feature is used by organizations that want to lock down baseline information and ensure that it's never changed through the life of the project without the proper stakeholders' approvals.

For example, the project manager builds the project and obtains buyoff from all managing stakeholders. When that buyoff is achieved, the project server administrator might check out the project and set the baseline. Or the administrator might temporarily grant the project manager permission to set the baseline. After the baseline is set, the administrator removes that permission. Either way, the baseline is set and cannot be edited or changed. Additional baselines cannot be saved either.

For more information about project server administrator responsibilities, see Chapter 23, "Administering Your Enterprise Project Management Solution."

Reviewing Baseline Information

After you save baseline information, you can review it in various ways. Initially, baseline information is identical to the scheduled information. As your team starts to complete work on the project, the baseline and scheduled information are likely to diverge. It is this deviation—and the amount of it—that you'll be interested in as you monitor and control the project.

The following lists methods for reviewing baseline information:

- **Add the Baseline bar to any Gantt view** Display any Gantt view. On the Format tab, in the Bar Styles group, click Baseline, and then click the Baseline you want to use. (Baselines that have been set are marked with a Last Saved date.) A new bar appears under the Gantt bar showing scheduled values in the chart portion of the Gantt view. For example, in the Gantt Chart, the default is for a gray baseline bar to appear beneath the blue schedule bar, as shown in Figure 11-3.

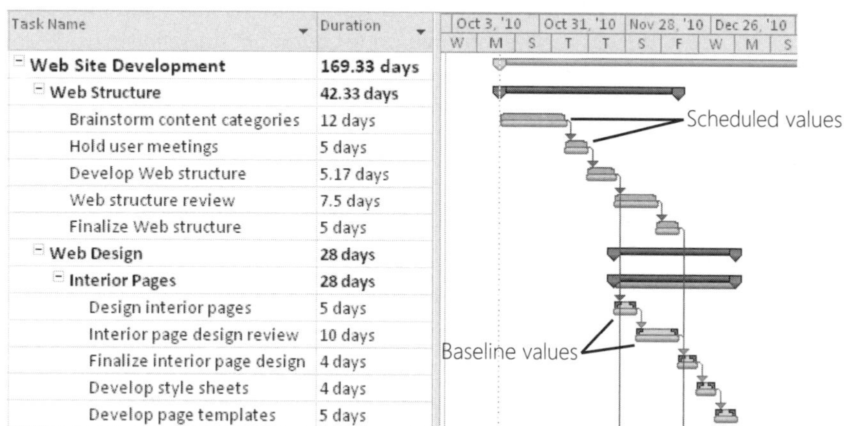

Task Name	Duration
Web Site Development	169.33 days
Web Structure	42.33 days
Brainstorm content categories	12 days
Hold user meetings	5 days
Develop Web structure	5.17 days
Web structure review	7.5 days
Finalize Web structure	5 days
Web Design	28 days
Interior Pages	28 days
Design interior pages	5 days
Interior page design review	10 days
Finalize interior page design	4 days
Develop style sheets	4 days
Develop page templates	5 days

Figure 11-3 Easily add a baseline bar to any Gantt view to quickly see the variance between the original baseline values and the currently scheduled values.

- **Apply the Tracking Gantt** On the View tab, in the Task Views group, click Other Views, and then click More Views. In the More Views dialog box, click Tracking Gantt, and then click Apply. The Tracking Gantt shows the baseline Gantt bars underneath the scheduled Gantt bars. (See Figure 11-4.)

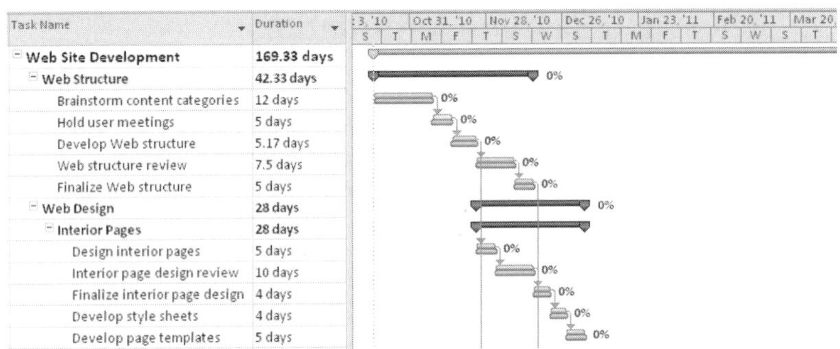

Task Name	Duration
Web Site Development	169.33 days
Web Structure	42.33 days
Brainstorm content categories	12 days
Hold user meetings	5 days
Develop Web structure	5.17 days
Web structure review	7.5 days
Finalize Web structure	5 days
Web Design	28 days
Interior Pages	28 days
Design interior pages	5 days
Interior page design review	10 days
Finalize interior page design	4 days
Develop style sheets	4 days
Develop page templates	5 days

Figure 11-4 The Tracking Gantt shows baseline start, duration, and finish in its Gantt bars in relation to the scheduled Gantt bars.

Another way to apply the Tracking Gantt is to right-click the view bar along the left edge of the Project 2010 window, and then click Tracking Gantt.

Tables

- **Apply the Baseline table to a task sheet** On the View tab, in the Data group, click Tables, and then click More Tables. Click Baseline, and then click Apply. This table shows baseline information for duration, start, finish, work, and cost. (See Figure 11-5.)

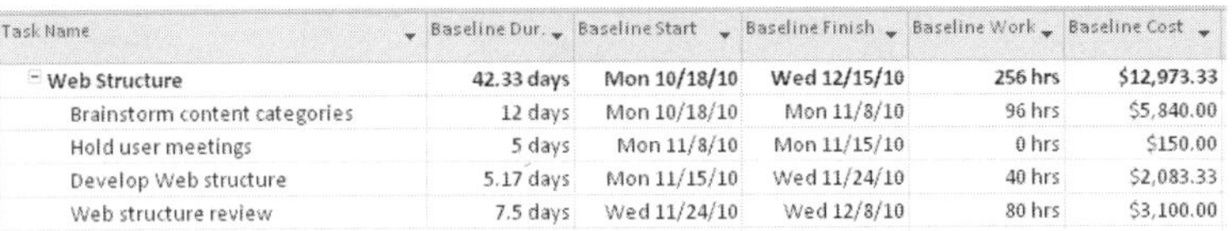

Task Name	Baseline Dur.	Baseline Start	Baseline Finish	Baseline Work	Baseline Cost
Web Structure	42.33 days	Mon 10/18/10	Wed 12/15/10	256 hrs	$12,973.33
Brainstorm content categories	12 days	Mon 10/18/10	Mon 11/8/10	96 hrs	$5,840.00
Hold user meetings	5 days	Mon 11/8/10	Mon 11/15/10	0 hrs	$150.00
Develop Web structure	5.17 days	Mon 11/15/10	Wed 11/24/10	40 hrs	$2,083.33
Web structure review	7.5 days	Wed 11/24/10	Wed 12/8/10	80 hrs	$3,100.00

Figure 11-5 The Baseline table shows many of the baseline fields.

INSIDE OUT Don't mess with the baseline data

You might notice that the fields in the Baseline table are editable. However, even though Microsoft Project lets you edit these fields, that doesn't mean you should.

Frankly, a baseline field should never be edited. The baseline information is a snapshot of the project plan information at a particular point in time. If you change a baseline field, you change a variance or the result of an earned value analysis. You defeat the purpose of saving the baseline if you change it after you start tracking progress.

If you need different values in baseline fields because of changed circumstances, set a new baseline; for example, Baseline 1 or Baseline 2. You can retain the values in your original baseline and choose which baseline to use for earned value analyses.

For more information, see "Saving Additional Baselines" on page 453.

- **Add baseline fields to an existing table** You might find it helpful to add a baseline field next to the equivalent scheduled field in the Entry table, for example. (See Figure 11-6.) You can add the Baseline Duration field next to the Duration field and the Baseline Start field next to the Start field.

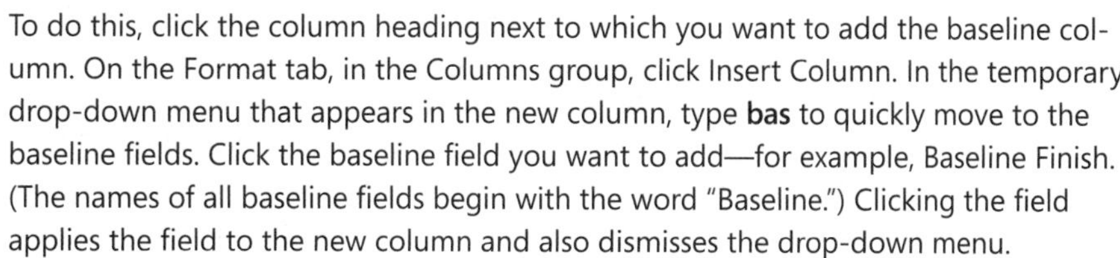

Task Name	Baseline Duration	Duration	Baseline Start	Start	Baseline Finish	Finish
Web Structure	**42.33 days**	**42.33 days**	**Mon 10/18/10**	**Mon 10/18/10**	**Wed 12/15/10**	**Wed 12/15/10**
Brainstorm content categories	12 days	12 days	Mon 10/18/10	Mon 10/18/10	Mon 11/8/10	Mon 11/8/10
Hold user meetings	5 days	5 days	Mon 11/8/10	Mon 11/8/10	Mon 11/15/10	Mon 11/15/10
Develop Web structure	5.17 days	5.17 days	Mon 11/15/10	Mon 11/15/10	Wed 11/24/10	Wed 11/24/10
Web structure review	7.5 days	7.5 days	Wed 11/24/10	Wed 11/24/10	Wed 12/8/10	Wed 12/8/10
Finalize Web structure	5 days	5 days	Wed 12/8/10	Wed 12/8/10	Wed 12/15/10	Wed 12/15/10

Figure 11-6 Showing baseline fields next to the equivalent scheduled fields in a table can help you see at a glance whether and how much of a variance exists.

Insert Column

To do this, click the column heading next to which you want to add the baseline column. On the Format tab, in the Columns group, click Insert Column. In the temporary drop-down menu that appears in the new column, type **bas** to quickly move to the baseline fields. Click the baseline field you want to add—for example, Baseline Finish. (The names of all baseline fields begin with the word "Baseline.") Clicking the field applies the field to the new column and also dismisses the drop-down menu.

> ### Note
> **Open the Project Statistics dialog box to compare current schedule information with baseline schedule information—start, finish, duration, work, and cost. On the Project tab, in the Properties group, click Project Information. In the dialog box that appears, click the Statistics button.**

Saving Additional Baselines

Sometimes you track your project for a period of time and then a big change occurs. Maybe your company undergoes a major shift in priorities. Maybe an emergency project takes you and your resources away from this project. Maybe funding is stalled and then starts up again. In such cases, your original baseline might not be as useful a tool as it once was. And although you don't want to replace it entirely, you want to use a more up-to-date baseline for your everyday tracking requirements.

TROUBLESHOOTING

You see nothing in the baseline fields

Baseline fields show a value of 0 or NA until you set a baseline. If you add baseline fields to a table, apply the Baseline table, or show the Tracking Gantt before you set a baseline, you'll see no information.

To remedy this, on the Project tab, in the Schedule group, click Set Baseline, and then click Set Baseline again. Check the settings in the dialog box, and then click OK. The baseline fields are now populated.

If you set a baseline, but certain baseline fields are still blank, it's probably because you have manually scheduled tasks that are still *placeholder* tasks—that is, tasks that don't have at least two bits of schedule information, such as a duration and a start date, or a start and finish date. You can add the necessary schedule information and then save the baseline again for those tasks, or you can add the Baseline Estimated Duration, Baseline Estimated Start, and Baseline Estimated Finish columns to a task sheet to see "best guesses" of the duration, start, and finish of the placeholder task. By default, Project 2010 sets the task start date as the project start date and uses an estimated duration of 1d?.

For more information about manual scheduling and placeholder tasks, see "Manually Scheduling Tasks" on page 184. For more information about using baseline information to analyze variance and monitor progress, see Chapter 12, "Responding to Changes in Your Project." For more information about earned value, see Chapter 14, "Analyzing Progress Using Earned Value."

Even if nothing catastrophic happens to your project, you might still have good uses for multiple baselines. In addition to taking a snapshot at the beginning of your execution phase, you might want to take snapshots again at the end of each month or each quarter. These snapshots can more precisely show periods of time when you experienced greater variances between baseline and scheduled information.

You can save up to 11 different baselines. To set an additional baseline, do the following:

1. On the Project tab, in the Schedule group, click Set Baseline, and then click Set Baseline again.
2. In the dialog box, be sure that the Set Baseline option is selected.

TROUBLESHOOTING

Your baseline information doesn't roll up

When you first set your baseline, any baseline fields you display show the proper rollup amounts, whether it's duration, start date, finish date, cost, and so on.

As you adjust the schedule or enter tracking information, your scheduled information changes, whereas the baseline information remains the same. It's supposed to stay the same. The job of the baseline is, of course, to always show information from your original plan so you can make the necessary comparisons.

Now suppose that you edit a baseline field, even if you know you shouldn't. Although Project 2010 enables you to edit an individual baseline field, its associated summary task is not recalculated to reflect your edit. Every change that's made to the baseline chips away at the integrity of the baseline information and dilutes the purpose of having the baseline in the first place.

A more likely scenario is that you added or removed tasks in the plan, and these changes are not reflected in the baseline. Strictly speaking again, such changes are not supposed to be in the baseline because it is a change from your original plan.

In any case, if you do have a legitimate reason for updating baseline information, you can add selected tasks to the baseline and have the summary information recalculated, as follows:

1. Select the tasks with the changed information. If applicable, select the summary task(s) you want to update as well.
2. On the Project tab, in the Schedule group, click Set Baseline, and then click Set Baseline again. In the dialog box, be sure the Set Baseline option is selected and that the baseline you want to use is selected in the box.
3. Under For, click the Selected Tasks option.

   The Roll Up Baselines section becomes available.
4. Select the To All Summary Tasks check box if you want all changed information in the selected tasks to roll up to all associated summary tasks.

   Select the check box labeled From Subtasks Into Selected Summary Task(s) if you want the changed information in selected subtasks to roll up only to your selected summary tasks.

INSIDE OUT The estimated baseline fields are useful only for manually scheduled placeholder tasks

NEW!

The estimated baseline fields (Baseline Estimated Duration, Baseline Estimated Start, and Baseline Estimated Finish) do not provide any information that distinguishes them from the regular Baseline Duration, Baseline Start, or Baseline Finish fields. The estimated baseline fields for automatically scheduled tasks are the same as the regular baseline fields, which is expected.

However, the information in the estimated baseline and regular baseline fields are the same for manually scheduled tasks as well.

The only instance in which the estimated baseline field contains information different from the regular baseline fields is in the case of a placeholder task—that is, a manually scheduled task for which there's one or no bits of scheduling information (duration, start date, finish date, or task link).

If only the duration is entered, Project 2010 makes the estimated start date the same as the project start date and calculates the estimated finish date based on the duration. (See Figure 11-7.) This is the same scheduling that would occur if this were an automatically scheduled task.

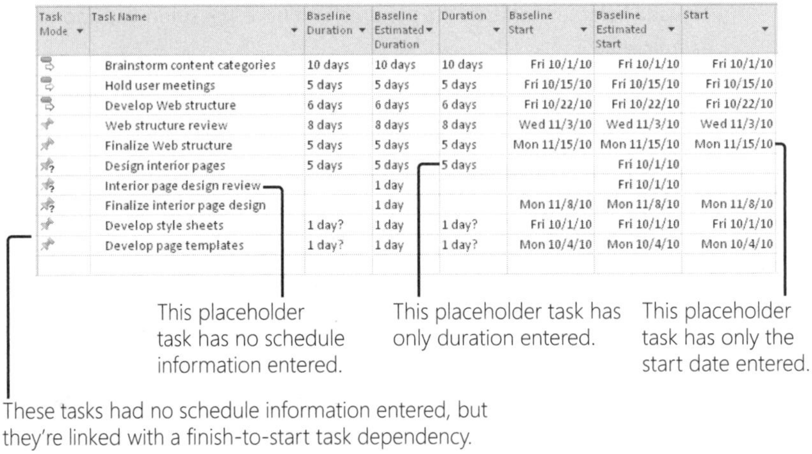

Task Mode	Task Name	Baseline Duration	Baseline Estimated Duration	Duration	Baseline Start	Baseline Estimated Start	Start
	Brainstorm content categories	10 days	10 days	10 days	Fri 10/1/10	Fri 10/1/10	Fri 10/1/10
	Hold user meetings	5 days	5 days	5 days	Fri 10/15/10	Fri 10/15/10	Fri 10/15/10
	Develop Web structure	6 days	6 days	6 days	Fri 10/22/10	Fri 10/22/10	Fri 10/22/10
	Web structure review	8 days	8 days	8 days	Wed 11/3/10	Wed 11/3/10	Wed 11/3/10
	Finalize Web structure	5 days	5 days	5 days	Mon 11/15/10	Mon 11/15/10	Mon 11/15/10
	Design interior pages	5 days	5 days	5 days		Fri 10/1/10	
	Interior page design review		1 day			Fri 10/1/10	
	Finalize interior page design		1 day		Mon 11/8/10	Mon 11/8/10	Mon 11/8/10
	Develop style sheets	1 day?	1 day	1 day?	Fri 10/1/10	Fri 10/1/10	Fri 10/1/10
	Develop page templates	1 day?	1 day	1 day?	Mon 10/4/10	Mon 10/4/10	Mon 10/4/10

This placeholder task has no schedule information entered.

This placeholder task has only duration entered.

This placeholder task has only the start date entered.

These tasks had no schedule information entered, but they're linked with a finish-to-start task dependency.

Figure 11-7 The estimated baseline fields show distinguishing information only for manually entered placeholder tasks.

If no duration is entered, Project 2010 assumes by default an estimated duration of 1 day and makes the estimated start and finish date the same as the project start date.

3. In the Set Baseline list, click Baseline 1, for example. (See Figure 11-8.)

   If a baseline has a Last Saved date after it, you already saved information in that baseline. If you select a baseline with a Last Saved date, you'll overwrite the previous baseline information with current schedule information.

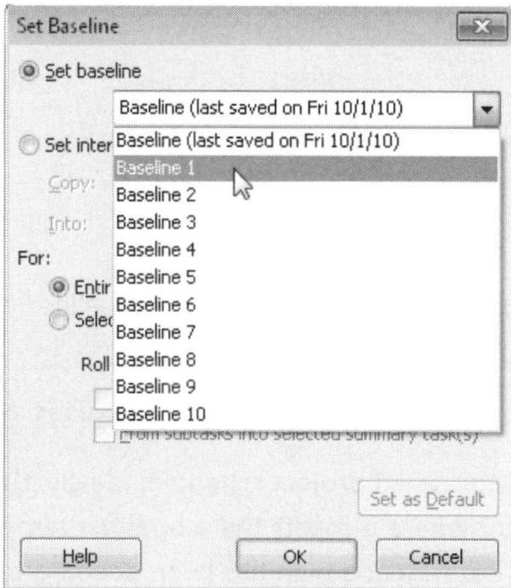

Figure 11-8 To set an additional baseline, choose any of the baselines in the list.

4. Under For, be sure that the Entire Project option is selected.

You can now add columns to a sheet to review the contents of the baseline fields you're now using. Click the column heading next to which you want to add a new baseline column. On the Format tab, in the Columns group, click Insert Column in a task sheet. In the temporary drop-down menu that appears in the new column, type **bas** to quickly move to the baseline fields. Click the name of the baseline field you want to add to the table—for example, Baseline1 Duration or Baseline5 Start. The column and the contents of the field for each task are displayed in the table.

If you use earned value analyses, you can select any of 11 saved baselines for the earned value calculations. For information about earned value analysis, see Chapter 14. For information on selecting which baseline to use for calculating earned value, see "Setting the Baseline" on page 586.

Reviewing Multiple Baselines

By using the Multiple Baselines Gantt, you can view Gantt bars reflecting different baselines. Showing stacked and differentiated Gantt bars for all the baselines you've set provides you with a visual representation of schedule changes from one set of baseline information to another.

On the View tab, in the Task Views group, click the Other Views button, and then click More Views. In the dialog box, click Multiple Baselines Gantt, and then click Apply. Each baseline is represented as a different color Gantt bar, as shown in Figure 11-9.

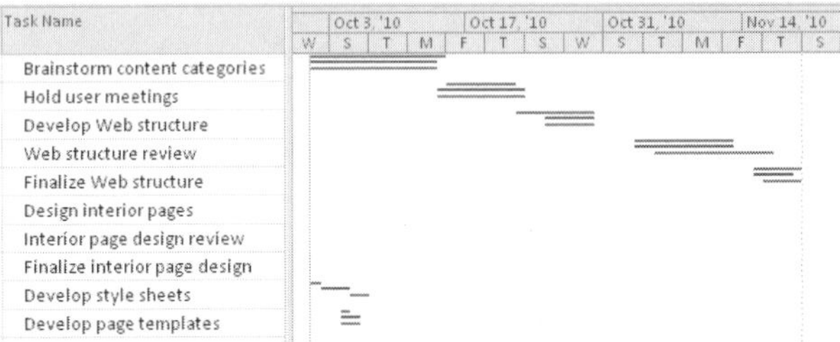

Figure 11-9 Apply the Multiple Baselines Gantt to show all the baselines you have set.

Project Management Practices: Working with the Baseline

The first baseline you set is the approved project schedule. Ideally, this plan has been adjusted and refined to the point where it meets the scope, the targeted finish date, and the budget of the project. The baseline plan has been deemed technically feasible given available resources. The baseline plan has been approved as the plan of record by the managing stakeholders.

This baseline plan is a component of the overall project plan. It provides the basis for measuring the schedule and cost performance of the project. In turn, any variances you find can drive decisions about whether corrective actions should be taken and what those corrective actions should be.

In the course of project execution, if the schedule variance becomes very large—perhaps because of major scope changes or lengthy delays—*rebaselining* might be needed to provide realistic information from which to measure performance. With the ability to save up to 11 baselines in Project 2010, you can save new baselines with a clear conscience. With multiple baselines, you can always retain the original baseline while also having any later baseline information you need because of changed circumstances. Remember that there should always be a single primary baseline that serves as the definitive baseline for analysis and authoritative historical data.

Saving Additional Scheduled Start and Finish Dates

When you set a baseline, remember that it saves duration, work, and cost information, as well as the start and finish information for each task. Because of this, be aware that each baseline you save significantly increases the size of your project file. Setting the first baseline can nearly double the file size. Setting the second baseline can add another third on top of that.

If you have certain situations in which you don't need to save the entire baseline, but could just use a quick snapshot of your start and finish fields at a certain point in time, consider saving an interim plan instead. An interim plan is similar to a baseline plan in that it saves task information at a certain point in time that you can use for comparison purposes later. It differs from a baseline in that it saves only the start and finish fields, and therefore doesn't create such a big hit on your project file size.

If your plan includes manually scheduled tasks, the start and finish dates saved in interim plans are those that you manually entered. If you haven't entered at least two dates or a duration, and if there are no links, Project 2010 makes a "best guess" estimate at a start and finish date, and those are entered as the interim start and finish dates. In other words, the values in the Baseline Estimated Start and Baseline Estimated Finish fields are used for the start and finish dates in the interim plan.

You can save up to 10 different sets of start and finish dates with 10 different interim plans. Think of these interim plans as mini-baselines. An interim plan saves the current start and finish dates and stores them in the custom Start1–10 and Finish1–10 fields.

An interim plan is best used as a quick tool for seeing the effects of a series of changes; for example, a set of progress updates or adjustments you made to bring in the project finish date. Save an interim plan just before making such changes, and then make the changes you want. Set up a Gantt view showing the current start and finish Gantt bars with the Start1 and Finish1 Gantt bars so you can easily see the differences your changes made to the task dates.

To set an interim plan, follow these steps:

1. On the Project tab, in the Schedule group, click Set Baseline, and then click Set Baseline again.
2. Select the Set Interim Plan option.

3. By default, the Copy box displays Scheduled Start/Finish.

   This indicates that the dates in the currently scheduled Start and Finish fields will be saved as this interim plan. If there are no valid values in the Start and Finish fields, as in the case of a manually scheduled placeholder task, the values in the Baseline Estimated Start and Baseline Estimated Finish fields are used. You can copy from a different set of Start and Finish fields. In the Copy list, click the set you want.

4. By default, the Into box displays Start1/Finish1.

   This specifies where the start and finish dates of this interim plan will be stored. You can copy the Start and Finish fields into a different set of Start and Finish fields. In the Into box, click the set you want.

5. Under For, click Entire Project or Selected Tasks.

You can copy start and finish dates from other baselines into an interim plan. This can be useful if you have an old baseline that you want to reuse, but you want to retain its start and finish dates. To do this, click the old baseline in the Copy list, and then click the set of Start and Finish fields in the Into list.

You can also copy start and finish dates from an interim plan to one of the baselines, which can be useful if you used interim plans as a substitute for baselines in the past. You can take advantage of having multiple baselines by using your interim plan information. To do this, click the interim plan containing the start and finish dates in the Copy list. Then, in the Into list, click the baseline to which you want to move the information.

Clearing a Baseline

You can clear baseline and interim plan fields as follows:

1. On the Project tab, in the Schedule group, click Set Baseline, and then click Clear Baseline.

   The Clear Baseline dialog box appears.

2. Select the Clear Baseline Plan or Clear Interim Plan option.

3. In the corresponding box, click the name of the sets of fields you want to clear; for example, Baseline 3 or Start5/Finish5.

4. Select the Entire Project or Selected Tasks option.

5. Click OK.

   The fields are cleared accordingly.

Rename the Fields Used in Your Interim Plan

If you set an interim plan using the Start1 and Finish1 fields, for example, remember that you cannot then use the Start1 and Finish1 fields for any other purpose. It's a good idea to give the fields a name so that you don't forget and try to create another use for them. To name the custom fields used in an interim plan, follow these steps:

Custom Fields

1. On the Project tab, in the Properties group, click Custom Fields.
2. In the Type field, click Start.
3. In the Field list, click the custom start field—for example Start1 or Start4—that you are using for your interim plan.
4. Click the Rename button, and then enter a name for the custom start field; for example, Interim Plan2. (See Figure 11-10.)

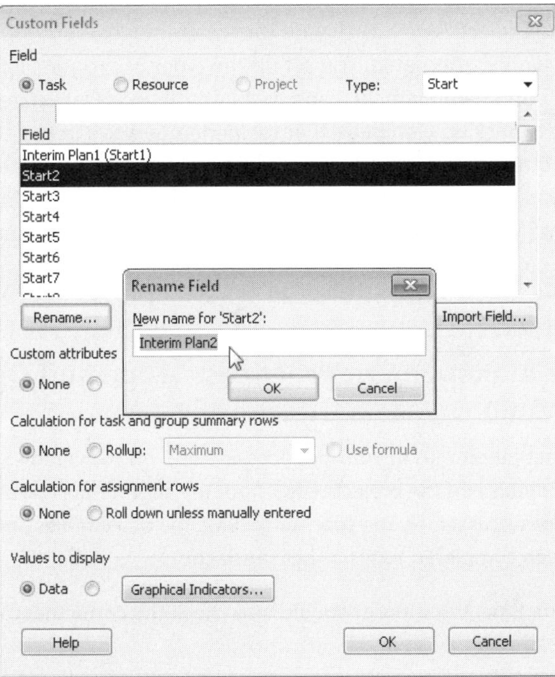

Figure 11-10 To prevent confusion, rename the custom start and finish fields you are using for interim plans.

5. Click OK in the Rename Field dialog box.
6. In the Type field, click Finish.
7. Repeat steps 3–5 for the custom finish field you are using for your interim plan.

Updating Task Progress

So the resources are digging into their assignments, and progress is being made. At regular intervals, you want to record their progress in Project 2010. Depending on how much time you want to spend entering progress information (and how much time you want your team members to spend doing that) and how much detail you or your client need, you can choose a simple, high-level method; a comprehensive, detailed method; or something in between.

Entering actual progress information in Project 2010 ensures that you always know how the project is going. You can keep an eye on the critical path and your budget. You can monitor key tasks and know exactly when you'll be handing off an important deliverable. With actual information coming into your project plan, you can also anticipate potential problems and take corrective actions as necessary.

If you're using Project Server 2010 with Microsoft Project Web App, updating task progress can become highly automated. You set up the types of progress information you want to receive from your team members, and that information is integrated with the assignments in the progress tracking web page that team members use in Project Web App. Every week (or however often you specify), team members send you an update regarding their actual progress toward completing tasks. You can have the progress information automatically integrated into your project plan, or you can review the information before incorporating it.

For more information about exchanging task updates using Project Web App, see Chapter 24.

Project Management Practices: Scope and Quality Verification

As you meet milestones in your project and hand off deliverables, be sure to obtain formal acceptance of the project scope from the appropriate stakeholders—for example, the sponsor or customer. The sponsor reviews the deliverables and signs off that they've been completed to his or her satisfaction.

At the same time, the sponsor should also check the correctness, or quality standards, of the work results.

It's important to have this acceptance process at various intermediate stages throughout the project—for each deliverable or at the end of each major phase, for example—rather than only at the end of the project.

Whether you're exchanging updates electronically, getting a status update in a weekly meeting, using paper timesheets, or making the rounds to hear team members' progress, you can enter the following actual progress information in your project plan:

- Percentage complete
- Actual duration and remaining duration
- Actual start and actual finish
- Percentage work complete
- Actual work complete and remaining work
- Actual work complete by time period

Note

When you enter actuals in your project plan, bear in mind that you're not just keeping your schedule up to date. You're also building historical information that you can use as metrics for other similar project plans. You're recording solid, tested data about how long these tasks actually take.

When you enter one piece of status information, Project 2010 often calculates other pieces of information. Certainly the schedule and costs are automatically recalculated. This is true whether you're working with automatically or manually scheduled tasks.

Even if you're updating a manually scheduled placeholder task, Project 2010 tries to calculate missing schedule information on the basis of any other actual progress information you enter. In the absence of any other scheduling information, Project 2010 assumes that the start date is the same as the project start date and assumes an estimated duration of 1 day.

Choosing the Best Method for Entering Actuals

You have several ways to track actual progress information in your project plan. How do you decide which method to use?

The first consideration is the level of detail you need. Your managing stakeholders might expect you to report a certain level of detail at the weekly status meetings. Or you might need reliable historical information from this project because it's serving as a benchmark for similar future projects.

The second consideration is time. Will you have time to enter detailed progress information, or will you be so busy managing the project and perhaps working on your own assigned tasks that you won't be able to keep track of everything with an adequate amount of detail? What about your team members? Are they going to be too stretched to complete an electronic or paper timesheet? If you're using Project Server and Project Web App, certain processes are automated for you, but they still take time for your team members.

The third consideration is whether you've assigned resources to tasks in your project plan. Obviously, resources carry out the tasks one way or another. But if you chose not to include resources in your project plan, you have fewer available tracking methods.

A fourth and very important consideration is the accuracy and completeness of your progress tracking data. While you can choose a single method, such as entering percentage complete or actual start and actual finish, it's really a combination of methods that result in the most reliably updated project. Whatever combination of methods you choose, be sure you record each of the following types of information:

- Actual start date
- A value of actual work completed, such as percentage complete or actual work
- A value indicating the amount of work yet to be completed, such as remaining duration or remaining work

The following are recommended methods that include these three values:

- Actual start, percentage complete, and remaining duration
- Actual start, actual work, and remaining work
- Actual work and remaining work in the timephased portion of the Task Usage or Resource Usage view

Using one primary method of tracking actuals does not prevent you from using other methods for other tasks. Although you might achieve more consistent results if you stick to one method, sometimes other tasks simply lend themselves to a different type of progress information. Certain tasks are so important that you want to track them very closely. You're free to do that—you're never locked into a single tracking method within a plan.

Updating Progress with Task Scheduling Controls

You can update progress by entering actual information from task scheduling controls such as percentage complete, duration, start date, and finish date. You can use these methods whether or not resources are assigned in your project plan.

Tailor the Progress Fields in Project Web App

If you're using Project Server and Project Web App to collaborate with your team members, your project server administrator can tailor the fields shown in the team members' electronic task progress pages. Depending on the progress information your organization wants to track, you can set up the task tracking method to be one of the following:

- Percent of work complete
- Actual work done and work remaining
- Hours of work done per period
- Free form (team members can report their hours using any method)

These methods have to do with task progress fields, so they can be most useful for helping you and team members track and update assignments. However, any task or assignment field available in Project 2010 can be added. The updated progress information becomes part of the periodic task update that the team members send you.

For more information about how the project server administrator sets up progress fields and timesheets in Project Web App, see "Setting Up Team Member Work Pages" on page 870.

Entering Percentage Complete

One of the simplest methods of tracking task progress is to specify percentage complete. When you enter percentage complete, Project 2010 calculates actual duration and remaining duration.

If you enter percentage complete for one or more tasks in simple increments of 25 percent, it's easiest to use the percentage complete buttons, as follows:

1. In a task sheet view, such as the Gantt Chart or Tracking Gantt, select the task(s) whose percentage complete you want to update.

   You can update multiple tasks at the same time as long as they have the same percentage complete.

50%

2. On the Task tab, in the Schedule group, click 25%, 50%, 75%, or 100%.

   The selected tasks are updated to reflect the percentage complete. In the Gantt Chart, the percentage complete is represented as a thin black line within Gantt bars.

To enter percentage complete other than in 25-percent increments for one or more tasks, do the following:

1. In a task sheet view, such as the Gantt Chart or Tracking Gantt, select the task(s) whose percentage complete you want to update.

Mark on Track

2. On the Task tab, in the Schedule group, click the arrow next to Mark On Track, and then click Update Tasks. The Update Tasks dialog box appears, as shown in Figure 11-11.

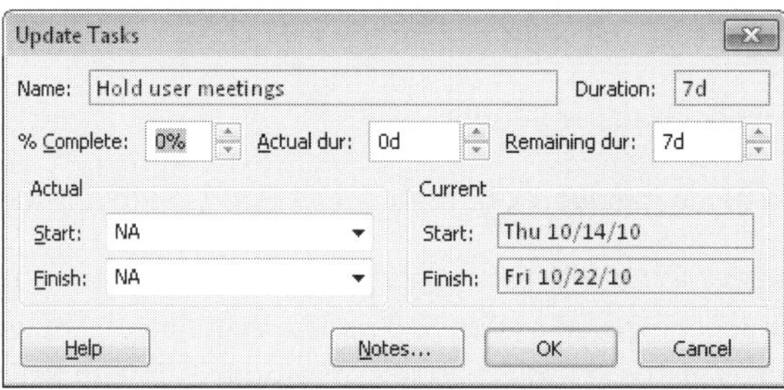

Figure 11-11 Use the Update Tasks dialog box to enter different types of progress information for one or more selected tasks.

3. In the % Complete box, enter the percentage complete that applies to all selected tasks.

4. If you're updating a single task, note the start date under Current. If the actual start date for the selected task is different from the current start date, enter that date in the Start box under Actual.

   If you do not change this start date, the actual start date is recorded as the current or scheduled start date. If you do change the actual start date, that becomes the current scheduled start date.

   The selected tasks are updated to reflect the actual start date and percentage complete. In the Gantt Chart, the percentage complete is represented as a thin black line within Gantt bars. (See Figure 11-12.) If you change the actual start date, the Gantt bar shifts to the new start date, and any successor tasks are also adjusted accordingly.

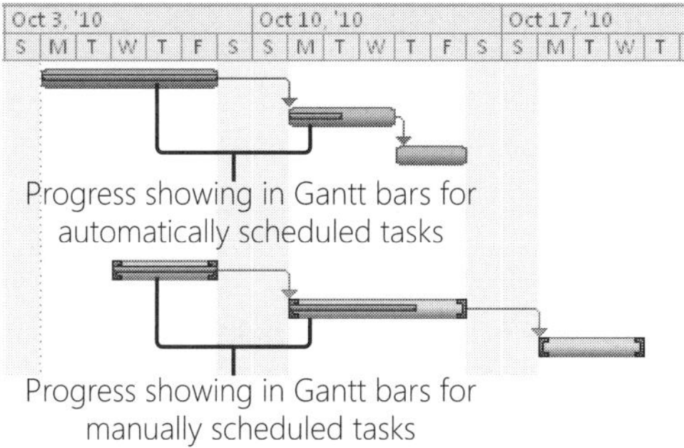

Figure 11-12 Gantt bars display how much of the task is complete.

> **Note**
>
> **If you're updating a manually scheduled placeholder task, Project 2010 tries to calculate missing schedule information based on the percentage complete value you enter. The task is no longer a placeholder task, but becomes a regular manually scheduled task.**
>
> **Project 2010 can do this as long as there is one bit of schedule information—for example, a duration, start date, or finish date. If none of these are present, a placeholder task with an updated percentage complete value remains a placeholder task until it's marked 100 percent complete.**

By default, when you enter the percentage complete for a task, this percentage is distributed evenly across the actual duration of the task. You can change this distribution to the status date instead. On the File tab, click Options, and then click Advanced in the left pane. Under Calculation Options For This Project, select the Edits To Total Task % Complete Will Be Spread To The Status Date check box.

> **Note**
>
> **Progress is shown on all task views, whether a Gantt view, Network Diagram, Calendar, and so on. The one exception is the Timeline view. Although the Timeline shows changes to the task duration and start and finish dates, whether manually or automatically scheduled, it does not reflect progress.**
>
> **For more information, see "Highlighting Tasks with the Timeline" on page 134.**

Entering Actual and Remaining Duration

If you enter the actual duration of a task, Project 2010 calculates the percentage complete. You can change remaining duration, if necessary.

Note

If you update a manually scheduled placeholder task, Project 2010 tries to calculate missing schedule information on the basis of the actual duration you enter. The task is no longer a placeholder task, but becomes a regular manually scheduled task.

Unless you enter a duration for a placeholder task, Project 2010 assumes an estimated duration of 1 day. Therefore, if you enter an actual duration of 1 day or more, the task shows as 100 percent complete. If this is not accurate, be sure to enter a value in the Remaining Duration field.

To enter actual duration for one or more tasks, do the following:

1. In a task sheet view, such as the Gantt Chart or Tracking Gantt, select the task whose actual duration you want to update.
2. On the Task tab, in the Schedule group, click the arrow next to Mark On Track, and then click Update Tasks.
3. In the Actual Dur box, enter the actual duration value.

   Note that when you change a value in the Actual Dur box, the value in the Remaining Dur box is not automatically recalculated unless you click OK and close the dialog box. For example, suppose you enter your first actuals for a 4-day task. When you enter 2d in the Actual Dur box, the Remaining Dur box still shows 4d. If you leave the Remaining Dur box as is and click OK, when you open the Update Tasks dialog box again, the Remaining Dur box now shows 2d.
4. If you expect the task to take more or less time than is currently scheduled, update the remaining duration in the Remaining Dur box.

5. Note the start date under Current. If the actual start date for the selected task is different from the current start date, enter that date in the Start box under Actual.

   If you do not change this start date, the actual start date is recorded as the current or scheduled start date for the task. If you do change the actual start date, that becomes the current scheduled start date for the task.

   The tasks are updated to reflect the actual start date and actual duration, including the calculated percentage complete.

Note

By default, when you enter progress information for tasks, Project 2010 automatically calculates the actual and remaining work and cost for assigned resources. This is the case when you update percentage complete, actual duration, or remaining duration of tasks or assignments.

If you prefer to enter values for actual and remaining work and cost yourself (instead of having Project 2010 calculate these values for you based on entered task progress), you can turn this option off. On the File tab, click Options, and then click Schedule in the left pane. Under Calculation Options For This Project, clear the Updating Task Status Updates Resource Status check box.

Entering Actual Start and Actual Finish

When you enter actual start and finish dates for tasks, you can better monitor the finish date of the project as a whole, especially when you're working with critical tasks. When you enter an actual start date, the scheduled start date changes to match the actual start date. Likewise, when you enter an actual finish date, the scheduled finish date changes to match the actual finish date. Any successor tasks are rescheduled as appropriate.

To enter an actual start or finish date for one or more tasks, do the following:

1. In a task sheet view, such as the Gantt Chart or Tracking Gantt, select the task(s) whose actual start or finish date you want to update.

2. On the Task tab, in the Schedule group, click the arrow next to Mark On Track, and then click Update Tasks.

3. Under Actual, enter the actual start date in the Start box or the actual finish date in the Finish box.

   The scheduled start and finish dates are shown under Current.

TROUBLESHOOTING

Your scheduled start and finish dates change when you enter actuals

When you enter actual start or actual finish dates, your scheduled (current) start or finish dates change to match. This is true for automatically scheduled, manually scheduled, and placeholder tasks. Project 2010 recalculates the scheduled dates so that you can see any effects the change might have on the rest of your schedule. For example, if Task A is scheduled to finish on May 14 but it finishes on May 18 instead, you need to know how its successor Task B is now scheduled. This update is especially important when critical tasks are involved.

If you want to keep your scheduled start and finish dates for comparison purposes, set a baseline or interim plan before you enter the actuals. With a baseline, Project 2010 can not only remember the original start and finish dates; it can also calculate the differences between the original and scheduled information. These differences are stored in the Variance fields, which are empty until you set a baseline and start entering progress information.

Note

In past versions of Microsoft Project, you were able to design a custom tracking view by using the Project Guide. As of Project 2010, the Project Guide has been discontinued. However, you can design a view containing the fields you want to use for tracking by customizing a view.

For information about creating a custom view, see "Creating a New View" on page 1066.

Using Resource Work to Update Progress

If resources are assigned in Project 2010, you can update progress information on the basis of work for the task or the assignment. *Work* doesn't exist in your project plan unless you assign resources, at which time task duration is translated into assignment work time. Work can be further divided among multiple assigned resources, depending on the task type. Using work to update progress can be more precise than updating with percentage complete or actual duration.

INSIDE OUT Add the Update Tasks button to your Quick Access Toolbar

If you expect to use the Update Tasks command frequently to enter % Complete, Actual Start, Actual Finish, Actual Duration, or Remaining Duration values, consider adding the command to your Quick Access Toolbar. It'll save you a lot of extra clicks throughout the life of your project.

To do this, follow these steps:

1. Click the arrow next to the Quick Access Toolbar at the upper-left corner of your Project window, and then click More Commands.

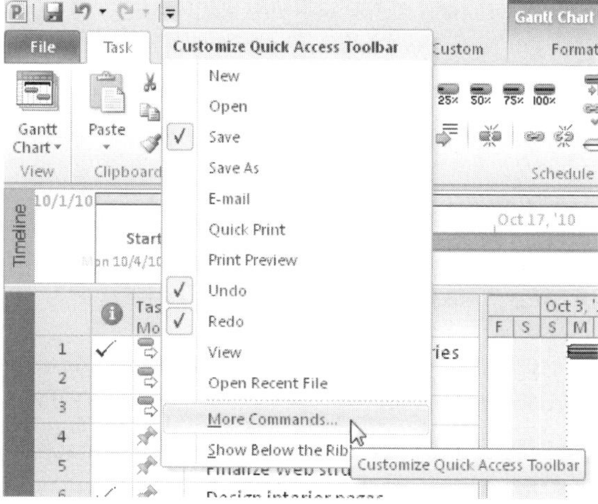

2. In the Choose Commands From box, click Task Tab.
3. In the list of commands that appears, scroll toward the bottom, and then click Update Tasks.
4. Click the Add button, and then click OK.

The work tracking methods described in the following sections are covered from the quickest and simplest to the most sophisticated. Remember that for the most accurate and complete updates of project information, be sure that the method you use includes the actual start date, some indication of actual work completed, and some indication of the remaining work.

Entering Percentage Work Complete

If human resources are assigned in your project plan, you can enter their reports of the percentage of work they've completed so far. Remember, work fields are populated only when work resources (people or equipment) are assigned to tasks. If you want to enter percentage work complete for an entire task (rather than for an assignment), follow these steps:

1. Display a task sheet view, such as the Tracking Gantt or Task Usage view.
2. On the View tab, in the Data group, click Tables, and then click Work.

   The Work table is applied to the current view.
3. In the % W. Comp. field of the task you want to update, enter the value of percentage work complete.

For better progress tracking results, also be sure that the Actual Start field for this task is updated.

Follow these steps to enter percentage work complete for an assignment (rather than for a task):

Task Usage

1. On the View tab, in the Task Views group, click Task Usage.
2. Select the assignment (the resource name beneath the task) whose percentage work complete you want to update.

   If there are several assignments with the same percentage work complete, you can select them and update them all at once.

Information

3. On the Format tab, in the Assignment group, click Information.
4. In the Assignment Information dialog box, click the Tracking tab, as shown in Figure 11-13.
5. In the Actual Start box, enter the date that work on this assignment began.
6. In the % Work Complete box, enter the percentage complete for this assignment.

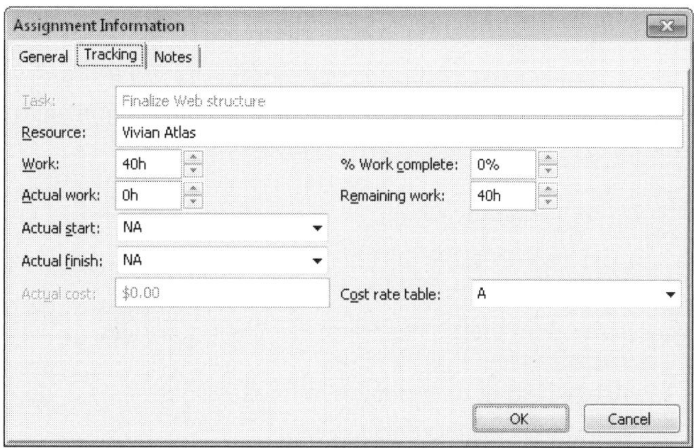

Figure 11-13 Use the Tracking tab in the Assignment Information dialog box to update progress for an assignment.

Entering Actual Work Complete and Remaining Work

As long as resources are assigned in your project plan, you can enter their reports of actual work completed. If they believe that more or less work than originally scheduled remains to be done, you can adjust remaining work as well.

If you have multiple resources assigned to a task and you enter actual work completed for the task, the work amounts are evenly distributed among the assigned resources. To enter total amounts for actual work completed on a task (rather than for an assignment), do the following:

1. Display a task sheet, such as the Task Usage view or Tracking Gantt.
2. On the View tab, in the Data group, click Tables, and then click Work.
3. If necessary, drag the divider bar to see the Actual field. (See Figure 11-14.)

Task Name	Work	Baseline	Variance	Actual	Remaining	% W. Comp.
Hardware and Software	408 hrs	408 hrs	0 hrs	322 hrs	86 hrs	79%
Perform system needs analysis	40 hrs	40 hrs	0 hrs	40 hrs	0 hrs	100%
Evaluate equipment requirements	120 hrs	120 hrs	0 hrs	120 hrs	0 hrs	100%
Evaluate software requirements	120 hrs	120 hrs	0 hrs	120 hrs	0 hrs	100%
Order equipment	24 hrs	24 hrs	0 hrs	24 hrs	0 hrs	100%
Order software	24 hrs	24 hrs	0 hrs	18 hrs	6 hrs	75%
Install and configure equipment	40 hrs	40 hrs	0 hrs	0 hrs	40 hrs	0%
Install and configure software	40 hrs	40 hrs	0 hrs	0 hrs	40 hrs	0%

Figure 11-14 Use the Work table to update actual work on a task.

4. In the Actual field of the task you want to update, enter the actual work value.

   The values in the Remaining and % W. Comp. fields are recalculated.

For better progress tracking results, be sure that the Actual Start field for this task is updated.

To enter total amounts of actual work completed on an assignment (rather than for a task), do the following:

1. Display the Task Usage view.
2. On the View tab, in the Data group, click Tables, and then click Work.
3. If necessary, drag the divider bar to see the Actual field.
4. In the Actual field of the assignment (the resource name under the task) you want to update, enter the actual work value.

   The values in the Remaining and % W. Comp. fields for the assignment are recalculated.

> **Note**
>
> **Another way to update actual work is by using the Assignment Information dialog box. Double-click the assignment to open the dialog box. Click the Tracking tab. Update the value in the Actual Work box. This is also a good method of updating actual work for multiple assignments if they all have the same value.**

This method is considered a happy medium for updating progress information—moderately detailed and moderately time-consuming.

> ## Automate Tracking with Project Web App
>
> **If you use Project Professional 2010 with Project Server and Project Web App, you can automate the gathering and entry of actuals so that you don't have to enter actuals on assignments yourself. Your project server administrator sets up your team members' task progress pages and timesheets in Project Web App so they can periodically enter and submit their actuals.**
>
> **You can then review these actuals and accept them for incorporation into the project plan. If you prefer, you can set a rule to have these actuals automatically accepted and incorporated.**
>
> **For more information about working with team member task updates and timesheets in Project Web App, see "Collaborating with Your Project Team" on page 945.**

Entering Actual Work by Time Period

The most comprehensive method of updating actual progress information is to enter actual and remaining work on assignments by time period. This is the most detailed unit of information you can use because you're entering information about the assignment (rather than the task as a whole), and you're probably entering hours worked in a day.

To enter actual and remaining work in the timesheet area of the Task Usage view, follow these steps:

1. Display the Task Usage view.
2. On the Format tab, in the Details group, select the Actual Work check box.

   The timesheet area of the view changes to include Act. Work as a row under (scheduled) Work.
3. If you also want to show rolled-up actual work totals for assignments, apply the Work table to the sheet area of the view. On the View tab, in the Data group, click Tables, and then click Work. (See Figure 11-15.)

Task Name	Work	Baseline	Variance	Actual	Remaining	% W. Comp	Details	Jan 30, '11 T	F	S
Order equipment	24 hrs	24 hrs	0 hrs	24 hrs	0 hrs	100%	Work	13.33h	10.67h	
							Act. Work	13.33h	10.67h	
Paul Shakespear	24 hrs	24 hrs	0 hrs	24 hrs	0 hrs	100%	Work	13.33h	10.67h	
							Act. Work	13.33h	10.67h	
Order software	24 hrs	24 hrs	0 hrs	18 hrs	6 hrs	75%	Work		24h	
							Act. Work		18h	
Paul Shakespear	24 hrs	24 hrs	0 hrs	18 hrs	6 hrs	75%	Work		24h	
							Act. Work		18h	
Install and configure equipment	40 hrs	40 hrs	0 hrs	0 hrs	40 hrs	0%	Work		13.33h	26.67h
							Act. Work			
Paul Shakespear	40 hrs	40 hrs	0 hrs	0 hrs	40 hrs	0%	Work		13.33h	26.67h
							Act. Work			

Figure 11-15 Use the Task Usage view to enter daily values of actual work on assignments.

4. In the Act. Work field for the assignment and the day, enter the actual work value.

   If you want to enter actual work for different time periods, use the Zoom slider in the lower-right corner of the Project 2010 window to zoom the project plan out or in.

This is considered the most rigorous method for updating progress information—time-consuming yet detailed.

Updating Progress Using a Different Status Date

As you enter actual progress, you can choose the status date to use as the reference point for actual and remaining portions of the task. Changing the status date can be helpful if you receive actuals on Friday, but you don't enter them into the project plan until the next Wednesday. If you use Wednesday's date as the status date, some of your actuals could be skewed. By default, the status date is the current date; that is, today. To set the status date, do the following:

Status Date

1. On the Project tab, in the Status group, click Status Date.
2. In the Select Date box, enter the status date you want to use for the progress information you're about to enter, and then click OK.
3. Enter your actuals as usual. Wherever a current date is needed for an actual date—for example, a finish date—the status date is used.

Be sure to clear the Status Date box when you finish so that you don't use that same date when you update actuals a week later.

You have additional options for how actual progress can be entered in your project plan. On the File tab, click Options, and then click Advanced in the left pane. Under Calculation Options For This Project, the first four check boxes provide options for how actual and remaining task information appears in your schedule in relation to the status date. These options are as follows:

- Move End Of Completed Parts After Status Date Back To Status Date
- And Move Start Of Remaining Parts Back To Status Date
- Move Start Of Remaining Parts Before Status Date Forward To Status Date
- And Move End Of Completed Parts Forward To Status Date

Use these options when you want to move completed or remaining parts in relation to a status date for your entire project. If you want to move completed or remaining parts around a status date for just selected tasks, follow these steps:

1. Select the task(s) whose completed or remaining parts of the schedule you want to move.

Move

2. On the Task tab, in the Tasks group, click Move.

3. In the drop-down menu, click Incomplete Parts To Status Date or Completed Parts To Status Date.

   If you click Incomplete Parts To Status Date, the start of the incomplete portion of the task is rescheduled at the status date (which could be the current date unless you set it otherwise).

   If you click Completed Parts To Status Date, the end of the completed portion of the task is rescheduled to end at the status date.

Whether you move completed or remaining parts around a status date for the entire project or only for rescheduling selected tasks, this setting is likely to create split tasks. However, this is a great way to show real delays affecting in-progress tasks and to reschedule them realistically.

Marking Tasks Exactly on Track

NEW!

If you're looking for an easy, practically automated way to update your tasks, you can use the Mark On Track function. Using this function, which is new in Project 2010, you can specify that any selected tasks are going exactly according to plan up to today's date or your specified status date. The appropriate percentage complete and all actual information for tasks (and assignments, if you have resources assigned) are automatically entered with the click of a single button.

To mark a task as on track, follow these steps:

1. Display a task view, such as the Gantt Chart or Task Sheet.
2. Select the task(s) that you want to mark as progressing exactly as planned.
3. On the Task tab, in the Schedule group, click Mark On Track.

   Progress for all selected tasks is shown as being exactly as planned. Any tasks that should have been completed by today's date or your specified status date are shown as 100 percent complete. Any tasks scheduled to be partially completed by the status date are also shown accordingly. (See Figure 11-16.)

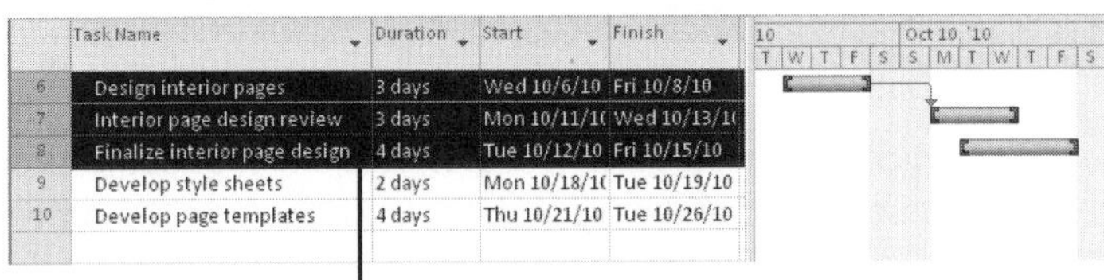

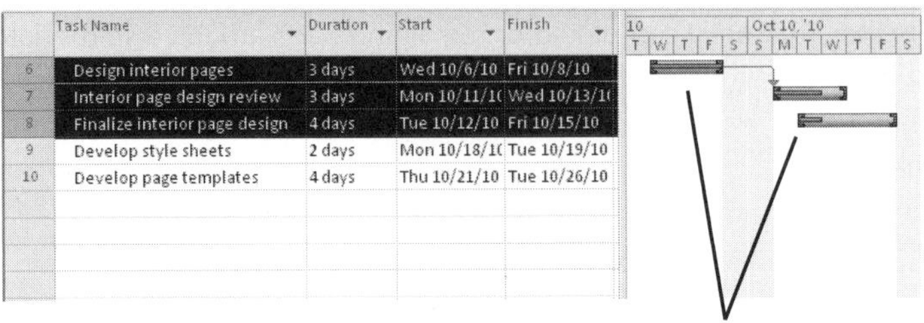

After clicking Mark On Track, actuals are automatically entered to reflect progress as scheduled to the status date of 11/13/2010.

Figure 11-16 Select any tasks that are going exactly as scheduled, and then click Mark On Track to enter current progress information.

Any relevant information for actual start, actual duration, actual finish, actual work, actual cost, and so on are entered in the appropriate fields. An easy way to see this is to apply the Tracking table to a task sheet, as shown in Figure 11-17.

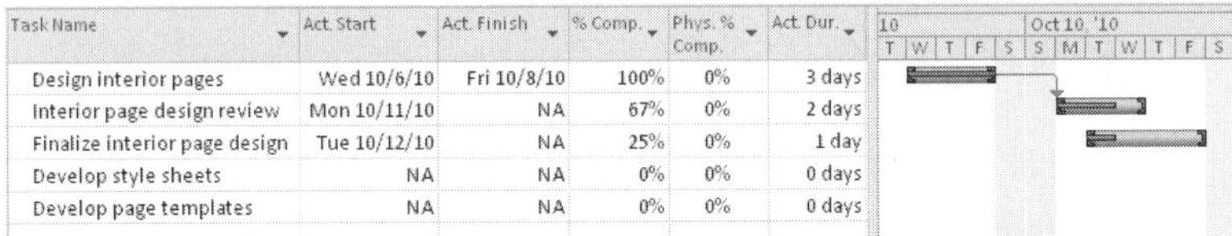

Figure 11-17 The Tracking table includes Actual Start, Actual Finish, % Complete, Actual Duration, Actual Work, and other progress fields. Scheduled information for the task is entered in these fields automatically when you click Mark On Track.

Note

If you select a manually scheduled placeholder task and click Mark On Track, Project 2010 uses the task's estimated schedule information to fill the gaps of any missing schedule information. That is, if there is only a duration but no start or finish date, Project 2010 uses the project start date as the basis. If there is only a start or finish date, Project 2010 assumes an estimated duration of 1 day.

INSIDE OUT Everything is going exactly as planned. Really.

Another way to indicate that certain tasks (or even the entire project) are going completely as originally scheduled is to use the Update Work As Complete Through function in the Update Project dialog box. You can use this function to do a blanket update of all work as complete through a specified status date.

However, because most tasks and projects in the real world do not run according to even the "best-laid plans," this isn't a function you should use too often. If you do, you might be defeating the purpose of tracking progress and not capturing good actuals that could otherwise be very valuable for the next project of this kind.

If you really are too busy and can't be bothered with tracking, you can at least just quickly run through the tasks and mark their percentage complete, or select tasks that really are going according to schedule and use Mark On Track.

However, if you have neglected to enter progress information in your plan that is currently well on its way, you can use this function to help you "catch up" to where the project is now.

Using today's date or another date as the reference complete-through date, you can update tasks as scheduled by following these steps:

Update Project

1. On the Project tab, in the Status group, click Update Project.
2. Be sure that the Update Work As Complete Through option is selected.
3. Enter the complete-through date in the box. By default, today's date appears.
4. Select the Set 0%–100% Complete option if you want Project 2010 to calculate whether the task is not started, 100% complete, or in progress.
   - If a task's scheduled start date is after your complete-through date, the task remains 0 percent complete.
   - If a task's scheduled finish date is before your complete-through date, the task is set to 100 percent complete.
   - If a task's scheduled start date is before your complete-through date and the scheduled finish date is after your complete through date, Project 2010 calculates a percentage complete value.
5. Select the Set 0% Or 100% Complete Only option if you want in-progress tasks to remain at 0 percent. That is, any tasks whose scheduled finish date is after your complete-through date do not have any progress entered for them.

You can use this method to update the entire project or selected tasks. Select the Entire Project or Selected Tasks option to specify your choice.

Updating Actual Costs

When you enter progress information for tasks or assignments, by default the costs associated with those tasks and assignments are calculated accordingly.

Updating Actual Costs for Work Resources

If your assigned work resources (people and equipment) are associated with cost rates or per-use costs, when you enter progress information on their tasks or assignments, actual costs are calculated along with actual work.

Updating Actual Costs for Material Resources

If you entered costs for material resources, actual costs are also calculated based on the completion of the task.

If you need to, in the Actual Work field, you can change the value for the material by specifying the amount of material actually used. Material is measured by its material label—for example, board feet, cubic yards, or cartons—while the Work and Actual Work fields use a time unit such as hours or days for work resources. However, you can edit the Work or Actual Work fields for material resource assignments in the Task Usage view or Resource Usage view or on the Tracking tab in the Assignment Information dialog box, as shown in Figure 11-18.

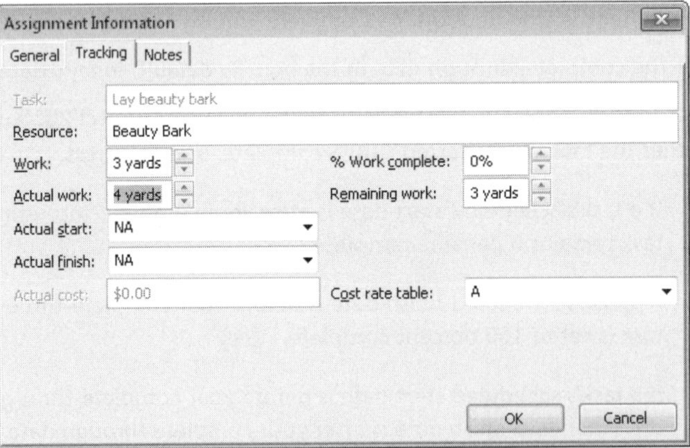

Figure 11-18 You can enter the actual amount of material used or the actual cost for the material on the Tracking tab in the Assignment Information dialog box.

Updating Actuals for Cost Resources

When you specify a percentage complete for a task, the work amount and costs for any assigned work and costs for any material resources are calculated automatically, as are any fixed costs associated with the task.

However, any assigned cost resources are not included in this automatic calculation of actual costs. You can enter progress for cost resources only on the assignment level. To do this, follow these steps:

1. In the Task Usage or Resource Usage view, double-click the assignment of the cost resource to the task.
2. In the Assignment Information dialog box, click the Tracking tab.
3. Even though cost resources are not associated with work, you can enter a percentage in the % Work Complete field, and an actual cost amount will be calculated.

   For example, if a cost resource assigned to a task is set to $100, and you enter 50% in the % Work Complete field, the actual cost is calculated as $50.
4. If the task is 100 percent complete and the total cost for the cost resource has been incurred, enter that cost in the Actual Cost field.

Updating Actuals for Fixed Costs on Tasks

When you enter progress information on a task that includes a fixed cost, the actual fixed cost is calculated with the progress according to the accrual method you selected (start, finish, or prorated).

If a fixed cost has changed from your original setting, simply change the amount. In a task sheet, apply the Cost table, and then change the amount in the Fixed Cost field for the task.

Manually Updating Project Costs

If resources are assigned to tasks in your project plan, and those resources also have their costs entered in Project 2010, costs are updated whenever you enter actual progress information. For example, suppose that a $25/hour resource is assigned to 8 hours of work on a task. When you specify that the task is 50 percent complete, $100 of actual cost is recorded for this task.

If you do not want Project 2010 to calculate costs for you in this manner, you can turn off this option and enter costs yourself. To turn off automatic cost calculation, follow these steps:

1. On the File tab, click Options, and then click Schedule in the left pane.
2. Under Calculation Options For This Project, clear the check box labeled Actual Costs Are Always Calculated By Project.
3. If you prefer to distribute the costs to the status date, select the check box labeled Edits To Total Actual Cost Will Be Spread To The Status Date.

   Otherwise, by default, any edits you make to costs are distributed evenly across the actual duration of a task.

After you turn off automatic cost calculation, you can enter task costs manually. To do this, display a task sheet. On the View tab, in the Data group, click Tables, and then click Cost to apply the Cost table. Enter total actual costs in the Actual field for the task.

To manually enter timephased costs for tasks or assignments, display the Task Usage view. On the Format tab, in the Details group, click Actual Cost. The Actual Cost field is added to the timephased portion of the view. Enter timephased actual costs in the appropriate cells.

INSIDE OUT It's tough to update costs manually

It can be cumbersome and tricky to update costs manually. It's also difficult and time-consuming to maintain this effort throughout the life of a project.

You'll experience more accurate—and automatic—results when you enter work resources and their costs in your project plan, along with any cost resources and fixed costs for tasks. When you assign those resources to tasks, costs are forecasted. When you enter progress on tasks, actual costs are calculated. This is true for automatically or manually scheduled tasks.

CHAPTER 12

Responding to Changes in Your Project

During the execution phase of your project, your resources are working on their tasks, and you're tracking their progress by entering actuals into your project plan. Those actuals, combined with your baseline information, give you the means to compare your current progress against your original plan. As part of your project control responsibilities, you use this information to analyze project performance, see how you're doing, and take any corrective action that you might deem necessary.

In your monitoring and control, you might find that one task finishes a few days early, and this affects its successors and their assigned resources. Maybe another task took longer than expected and went over budget. Possibly various changes in the schedule caused a resource to become overallocated and another one to be underutilized for several weeks.

You might need to adjust your project plan to account for such variances. Sometimes the differences work in your favor, as when a task finishes early. Other times the differences point to a potential problem, which you can prevent if you catch it soon enough.

The nature of the changes you make to your project plan depends on your project priorities. Remember the one fixed side of your project triangle (finish date, budget/resources, or scope) and adjust your project accordingly.

For more information about the project triangle, see the introduction to Chapter 10, "Checking and Adjusting the Project Plan."

In addition to the day-to-day monitoring and adjusting of a project in progress, sometimes large-scale modifications are needed because of external changes imposed on the project. For example, your customers might announce that you must move the finish date up six weeks. Or an unexpected corporate edict might cut $8,000 from your budget or reduce your staff by 10 percent.

Wholesale project modifications can also be indicated because the scheduled finish date, overall cost, or resource allocation has somehow gotten way off track. In this case, radical measures might be needed to bring the project into conformance again.

Whether it's a huge change imposed on you or a project that derails from within, you might need to replan or reschedule the project. The techniques for rescheduling are similar to those you used to hit your targets when you created the project in the first place. In your project plan, you make adjustments to the schedule, costs, resources, or scope, and Microsoft Project 2010 recalculates your schedule so that you can quickly see the results of your replanning. Then you can get back on track.

Baseline, Scheduled, and Actual Project Information

In the course of monitoring project performance, you should keep in mind four terms:

- **Baseline** Baseline dates, costs, durations, and work are your project plan's values at the time you saved baseline information, typically just after you refine the project to reflect all the elements you need, and just before the project begins and you start tracking progress. This is also referred to as *planned* information.
- **Scheduled** The current project combines the project's *actual* performance on past and current tasks with the *planned schedule* for current and future tasks. The combination of the actual and scheduled information forms the current plan as scheduled. In other words, Actual + Remaining = Scheduled. Once you start entering actual progress information, the scheduled information becomes a forecast based on what has already taken place and what's expected to happen from this point forward.
- **Actual** Actual progress information reflects real data about task status. *Actuals* include data such as percentage complete, actual work, actual finish date, and actual costs.
- **Variance** The difference between baseline information and scheduled information is the *variance*. Project 2010 subtracts the baseline value from the scheduled value (which incorporates any actuals you have entered) to calculate the variance. A positive work variance means more work is scheduled than originally planned. A positive finish or duration variance indicates you're behind in your schedule. A positive cost variance signifies that the project is over budget. On the other hand, a negative variance means you're ahead of the game—finishing faster or under budget. A variance of zero indicates that your baseline and scheduled values are the same. If actuals have been entered, this means that everything went exactly according to plan. If the task is still in the future, this means that projections forecast that the task is still going according to plan.

Whether you make large adjustments to respond to big problems or small adjustments to keep a healthy project well on its way, you can always keep a close eye on progress. You can analyze the current status of the project and decide on any necessary corrective actions.

INSIDE OUT **Variances are calculated from scheduled values**

It might seem odd that variances are calculated from scheduled values rather than actual values. However, when you consider that scheduled values incorporate any actual values, it makes sense. And because actual values are not required to make the calculation, you can see variances in future tasks as well. If you see any large variances projected for future tasks or for the project as a whole, you still have time to take corrective action and head off problems.

Monitoring and Adjusting the Schedule

If you're managing a time-constrained project, you'll want to keep a close eye on a few key bits of project information, such as the following:

- Project finish date
- Critical path
- Start and finish dates of critical tasks
- Current progress of critical tasks

Look at these items after you enter actuals. If actuals change task scheduling to the point where your target project finish date is projected to be late, you'll need to adjust the schedule to bring that finish date back in line.

Project Management Practices: Schedule Control

It would be a safe bet to say that no project runs precisely as planned. Tasks take more or less time than planned, resources discover new information, forgotten tasks are remembered, and outside forces influence the project implementation. When changes to the project schedule take place, you might have to revise durations, rearrange task sequences, or analyze what-if scenarios for your project.

Project 2010 is an excellent tool for schedule control because it can calculate and predict the effects of any schedule changes, whether the change comes as a result of entering actual information or what-if information. Project 2010 tracks your planned dates against your actual dates (and other schedule information). This variance analysis is key to schedule control. Analyzing variances in dates, durations, and other schedule information helps you detect where the project is diverging from your original plan. You can then predict possible delays in the schedule further down the line and take corrective actions now to offset those delays.

Monitoring Schedule Progress

Use one or more of the following techniques to help you monitor progress and make adjustments to achieve your finish date:

- Review finish dates and the critical path to see whether you're still on track, or whether the project is slipping behind.
- Check and adjust task constraints, dependencies, and durations as necessary to have the project still finish on time.
- Add resources to tasks to shorten the duration of tasks.

For more strategies about monitoring and adjusting the schedule to achieve a specific finish date, see "Bringing In the Project Finish Date" on page 383.

Another method for monitoring schedule progress is to set a baseline and then compare it against the current schedule. For example, you can see baseline finish dates for tasks next to their scheduled finish dates, based on actuals you entered. Then, you can look at the variances between the baseline and scheduled finish. The finish date variance, for example, is calculated as follows:

(Scheduled/Current) Finish – Baseline Finish = Finish Variance

Note

You can use earned value calculations such as the Schedule Performance Index (SPI) and Schedule Variance (SV) earned value fields to analyze your project performance so far.

For more information on examining project performance, see Chapter 14, "Analyzing Progress Using Earned Value."

Set a Baseline Early On

Because baseline information is vital to tracking and analyzing progress on your project, be sure to set a baseline early in the project. The ideal time to set a baseline is after you build your project plan and adjust all values to hit your target finish date, budget, and resource workload levels.

Even if you're well into tracking progress when you realize you haven't set a baseline, go ahead and set one at that time. Better late than never.

For information about setting a baseline, see "Saving Original Plan Information Using a Baseline" on chapter 445.

Reviewing Overall Schedule Progress

Review your project statistics to get a broad view of how your project status compares with your baseline. Project statistics show your currently scheduled start and finish dates, along with their baseline, actual, and remaining values. To review your project statistics, follow these steps:

Project Information

1. On the Project tab, in the Properties group, click Project Information.

   The Project Information dialog box appears.

2. Click the Statistics button.

   The Project Statistics dialog box appears. The current (scheduled) finish date appears in the Finish column, as shown in Figure 12-1.

Project Statistics for '12NewBiz.mpp'

	Start	Finish
Current	Mon 7/11/11	Thu 12/29/11
Baseline	NA	NA
Actual	NA	NA
Variance	0d	0d

	Duration	Work	Cost
Current	124d	1,368h	$155,400.00
Baseline	0d	0h	$0.00
Actual	0d	0h	$0.00
Remaining	124d	1,368h	$155,400.00

Percent complete:

Duration: 0% Work: 0%

Close

Figure 12-1 The Project Statistics dialog box shows overall project information with its currently scheduled values, baseline values, actual values, and more.

An easy way to keep your eye at all times on the project finish date (along with other key information) is to add the project summary task row, as follows:

1. Display the Gantt Chart or other task sheet.
2. On the Format tab, in the Show/Hide group, select the Project Summary Task check box.

The project summary task appears at the top of any task sheet view, including the Gantt Chart. The Project Summary Task row shows rolled-up task information to display totals for the entire project, as shown in Figure 12-2. Specifically, the Finish field in the project summary row shows the latest finish date in the project. If you add additional fields or apply different tables, information is also rolled up for those fields, as appropriate.

Gantt Chart

By default, the regular Gantt Chart shows progress as a thin black line through the Gantt bar. To also see percentage complete next to the Gantt bars, apply the Tracking Gantt, as shown in Figure 12-2. On the View tab, in the Task Views group, click the arrow next to Gantt Chart, and then click Tracking Gantt. (If Tracking Gantt is not listed, click More Views, and then click Tracking Gantt.)

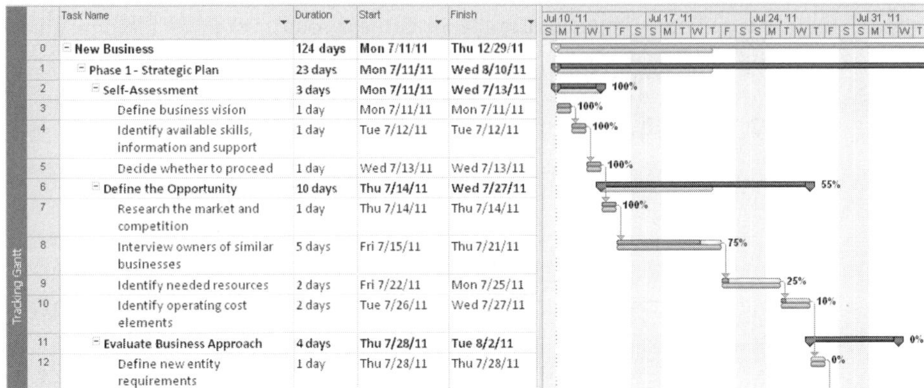

	Task Name	Duration	Start	Finish
0	New Business	124 days	Mon 7/11/11	Thu 12/29/11
1	Phase 1 - Strategic Plan	23 days	Mon 7/11/11	Wed 8/10/11
2	Self-Assessment	3 days	Mon 7/11/11	Wed 7/13/11
3	Define business vision	1 day	Mon 7/11/11	Mon 7/11/11
4	Identify available skills, information and support	1 day	Tue 7/12/11	Tue 7/12/11
5	Decide whether to proceed	1 day	Wed 7/13/11	Wed 7/13/11
6	Define the Opportunity	10 days	Thu 7/14/11	Wed 7/27/11
7	Research the market and competition	1 day	Thu 7/14/11	Thu 7/14/11
8	Interview owners of similar businesses	5 days	Fri 7/15/11	Thu 7/21/11
9	Identify needed resources	2 days	Fri 7/22/11	Mon 7/25/11
10	Identify operating cost elements	2 days	Tue 7/26/11	Wed 7/27/11
11	Evaluate Business Approach	4 days	Thu 7/28/11	Tue 8/2/11
12	Define new entity requirements	1 day	Thu 7/28/11	Thu 7/28/11

Figure 12-2 The Tracking Gantt shows the progress, the percentage complete, the baseline, and the critical path in the chart area of the view. The project summary task shows the rolled-up duration and project start and finish dates.

Reviewing Schedule Variances

To review the differences between your original baseline plan values and your currently scheduled values, apply the Variance table, as follows:

1. Display the Gantt Chart or other task sheet.

Tables

2. On the View tab, in the Data group, click Tables, and then click Variance.

   As shown in Figure 12-3, the Variance table is applied to the current view.

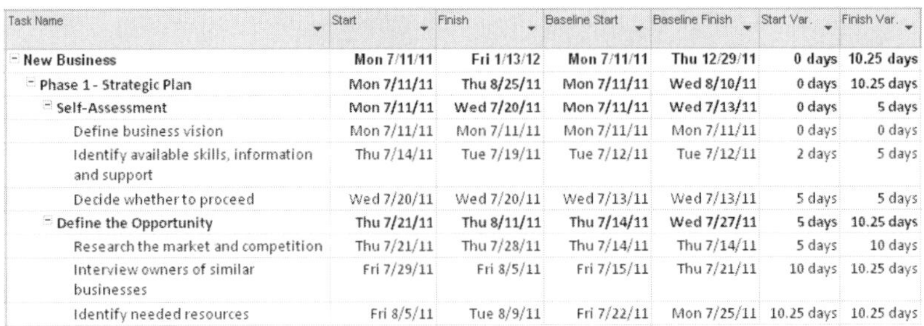

Task Name	Start	Finish	Baseline Start	Baseline Finish	Start Var.	Finish Var.
New Business	Mon 7/11/11	Fri 1/13/12	Mon 7/11/11	Thu 12/29/11	0 days	10.25 days
Phase 1 - Strategic Plan	Mon 7/11/11	Thu 8/25/11	Mon 7/11/11	Wed 8/10/11	0 days	10.25 days
Self-Assessment	Mon 7/11/11	Wed 7/20/11	Mon 7/11/11	Wed 7/13/11	0 days	5 days
Define business vision	Mon 7/11/11	Mon 7/11/11	Mon 7/11/11	Mon 7/11/11	0 days	0 days
Identify available skills, information and support	Thu 7/14/11	Tue 7/19/11	Tue 7/12/11	Tue 7/12/11	2 days	5 days
Decide whether to proceed	Wed 7/20/11	Wed 7/20/11	Wed 7/13/11	Wed 7/13/11	5 days	5 days
Define the Opportunity	Thu 7/21/11	Thu 8/11/11	Thu 7/14/11	Wed 7/27/11	5 days	10.25 days
Research the market and competition	Thu 7/21/11	Thu 7/28/11	Thu 7/14/11	Thu 7/14/11	5 days	10 days
Interview owners of similar businesses	Fri 7/29/11	Fri 8/5/11	Fri 7/15/11	Thu 7/21/11	10 days	10.25 days
Identify needed resources	Fri 8/5/11	Tue 8/9/11	Fri 7/22/11	Mon 7/25/11	10.25 days	10.25 days

Figure 12-3 The Variance table shows the currently scheduled start and finish dates compared with the baseline start and finish dates, including the differences between them.

Note

To quickly change to a different table, right-click the Select All box in the upper-left corner of the table in a sheet view. The list of tables appears.

To quickly see the name of the current view and table, rest your mouse pointer over the Select All box. A ScreenTip lists the name of the current view and table.

TROUBLESHOOTING

Your scheduled values change whenever you enter actuals

Whenever you enter actual progress information, Project 2010 recalculates your scheduled information based on those actuals, so you can see any effect the actual progress information has on the rest of your schedule. This also enables you to continue to see scheduled projections for the project finish date and total cost, based on performance to this point. For example, if Task A was scheduled to finish on May 15, but it finishes on May 20 instead, you'd need to know how its successor, Task B, is now scheduled. This information is especially important if these are critical tasks.

If you want to keep your original start and finish dates for comparison purposes, save a baseline or interim plan before you enter the actuals. Then, add the Baseline Start and Baseline Finish fields to a task sheet, perhaps right next to your scheduled Start and Finish fields. If you're using start and finish dates that you saved with your interim plan, add Start1 and Finish1 (or whichever custom fields you used for your interim plan) to a task sheet.

For more information about setting baselines, setting interim plans, and adding original field information to your task sheet, see "Saving Original Plan Information Using a Baseline" on page 445.

Reviewing the Critical Path

By viewing the finish date or the critical path, you can easily see whether you're still scheduled to hit your target finish date, given the actuals you've entered. To see the critical path, apply the Tracking Gantt or Detail Gantt. Both of these views show the critical path in red by default.

Or, in the Gantt Chart or other Gantt view, on the Format tab, in the Bar Styles group, select the Critical Tasks check box. The critical path turns red.

If you need to bring in the finish date, it's best to start by focusing on those critical tasks.

Filter

You can filter your task sheet to show only critical tasks. On the View tab, in the Data group, click the arrow in the Filter box, and then click Critical. To show all tasks again, on the View tab, in the Data group, click the arrow in the Filter box, and then click No Filter.

Note

After a critical task is completed, it becomes noncritical because it can no longer affect the completion of future tasks.

For more information about viewing the critical path, see "Viewing the Critical Path" on page 372.

Reviewing Task Progress

Reviewing the progress of critical tasks is the most effective means of quickly learning whether your project is staying in line to meet its target finish date.

The easiest place to start is to apply a Gantt view that includes the most progress information.

- The Tracking Gantt stacks the currently scheduled Gantt bars on top of the baseline Gantt bars, so you can quickly see where tasks are shifting away from your original plan. The Tracking Gantt also includes percent complete labels next to each Gantt bar.

Baseline

- In any Gantt view, you can quickly add a baseline bar. On the Format tab, in the Bar Styles group, click Baseline, and then click the baseline whose bars you want to show, typically the first one. Any baseline you have saved shows a date saved next to its name.

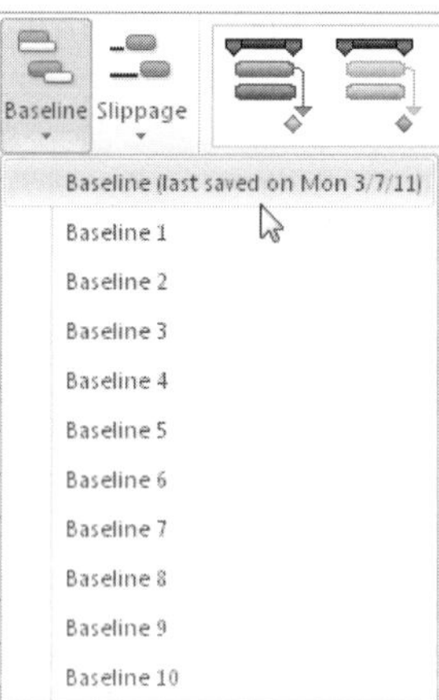

To remove the baseline bars, click Format, Bar Styles, Baselines, and then click the name of the baseline.

- Another way to look at whether tasks are slipping from the original plan is to show slippage lines, which are also created from baseline information. On the Format tab, in the Bar Styles group, click Slippage, and then click the baseline from which you want to show slipped tasks. It's difficult to see slippage bars in a Gantt view that already has baseline bars applied, so choose one or the other.

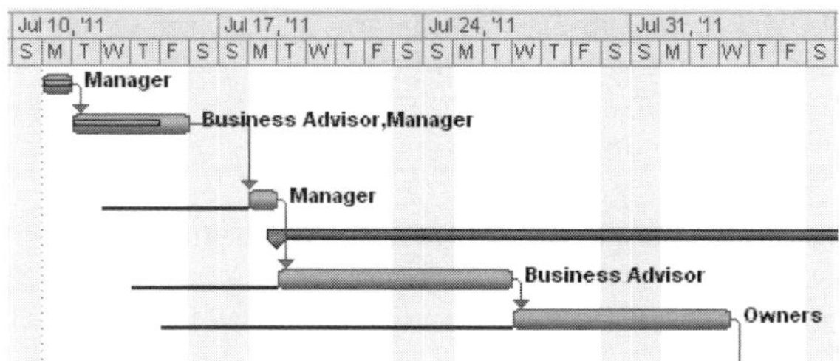

To remove the slippage bars, click Format, Bar Styles, Slippage, and then click the name of the baseline.

- You can highlight any late tasks in a Gantt view. On the Format tab, in the Bar Styles group, select the Late Tasks check box. The Gantt bars for any late tasks are highlighted in black.

If you're working in a very large project, you might prefer to apply a filter to help you focus on potential problem tasks. Choose one of the following filters to highlight task progress:

- Late/Overbudget Tasks Assigned To
- Should Start By
- Should Start/Finish By
- Slipped/Late Progress
- Slipping Tasks (see Figure 12-4)
- Tasks With Deadlines
- Tasks With Fixed Dates

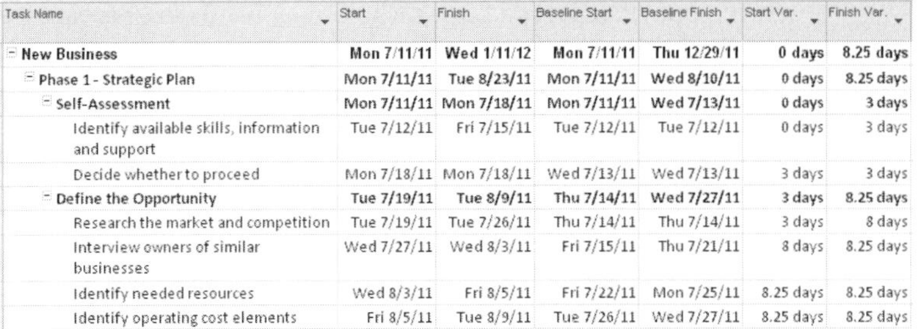

Task Name	Start	Finish	Baseline Start	Baseline Finish	Start Var.	Finish Var.
New Business	**Mon 7/11/11**	**Wed 1/11/12**	**Mon 7/11/11**	**Thu 12/29/11**	**0 days**	**8.25 days**
Phase 1 - Strategic Plan	**Mon 7/11/11**	**Tue 8/23/11**	**Mon 7/11/11**	**Wed 8/10/11**	**0 days**	**8.25 days**
Self-Assessment	**Mon 7/11/11**	**Mon 7/18/11**	**Mon 7/11/11**	**Wed 7/13/11**	**0 days**	**3 days**
Identify available skills, information and support	Tue 7/12/11	Fri 7/15/11	Tue 7/12/11	Tue 7/12/11	0 days	3 days
Decide whether to proceed	Mon 7/18/11	Mon 7/18/11	Wed 7/13/11	Wed 7/13/11	3 days	3 days
Define the Opportunity	**Tue 7/19/11**	**Tue 8/9/11**	**Thu 7/14/11**	**Wed 7/27/11**	**3 days**	**8.25 days**
Research the market and competition	Tue 7/19/11	Tue 7/26/11	Thu 7/14/11	Thu 7/14/11	3 days	8 days
Interview owners of similar businesses	Wed 7/27/11	Wed 8/3/11	Fri 7/15/11	Thu 7/21/11	8 days	8.25 days
Identify needed resources	Wed 8/3/11	Fri 8/5/11	Fri 7/22/11	Mon 7/25/11	8.25 days	8.25 days
Identify operating cost elements	Fri 8/5/11	Tue 8/9/11	Tue 7/26/11	Wed 7/27/11	8.25 days	8.25 days

Figure 12-4 Apply the Slipping Tasks filter to quickly see which tasks are in jeopardy (the summary tasks provide context for the tasks).

To apply one of these filters, follow these steps:

1. Display the Gantt Chart or other task sheet you want to filter.
2. On the View tab, in the Data group, click the arrow in the Filter box, and then click the name of the filter.

   If you don't see the name of the filter you want, click More Filters, and then choose the filter from the More Filters dialog box.
3. When you want to show all tasks again, in the Filter list, click All Tasks.

You can also run text-based and visual reports that provide information about the progress of tasks, such as the following:

- Unstarted Tasks
- Tasks Starting Soon
- Tasks In Progress
- Completed Tasks
- Should Have Started Tasks
- Slipping Tasks
- Critical Tasks Status Report (visual report in Microsoft Visio 2010)
- Task Status Report (visual report in Visio 2010)

To run a text-based report, follow these steps:

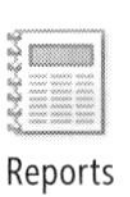
Reports

1. On the Project tab, in the Reports group, click Reports.

2. Double-click Current Activities.
3. Double-click the report you want.
4. If a dialog box asks for more information, enter the information, and then click OK.

   The report appears in the Print Backstage view. You can then print the report for a closer look.

To run a visual report, follow these steps:

1. On the Project tab, in the Reports group, click Visual Reports.
2. On the All tab, double-click the name of the report you want.

   The report is generated from Project 2010 data and displayed in a Visio PivotDiagram.

For more information about reports, see Chapter 13, "Reporting Project Information."

Display Status Icons

You can add the Status Indicator field to any task sheet. This field displays icons that indicate whether a task is completed, on schedule, or behind schedule.

Select the column heading next to where you want to add the Status Indicator column. On the Format tab, in the Columns group, click Insert Column. Type st in the new column that appears, and then click Status Indicator from the drop-down list.

If you prefer to show current task status as text rather than as an icon, insert the Status column instead. For every task, the status of "Future Task," "On Schedule," "Late," or "Complete" appears, as shown in Figure 12-5.

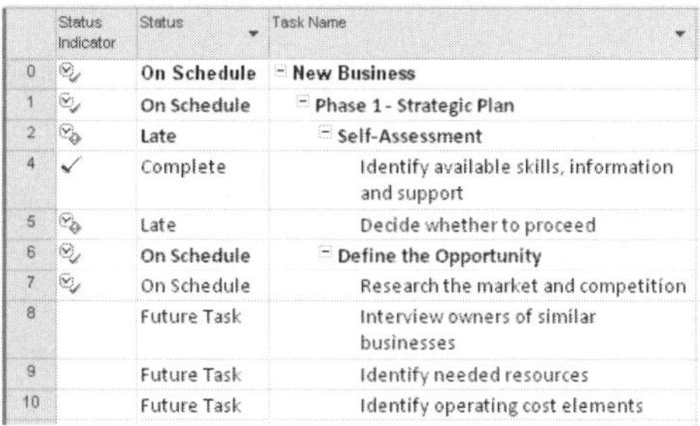

	Status Indicator	Status	Task Name
0		On Schedule	New Business
1		On Schedule	Phase 1 - Strategic Plan
2		Late	Self-Assessment
4	✓	Complete	Identify available skills, information and support
5		Late	Decide whether to proceed
6		On Schedule	Define the Opportunity
7		On Schedule	Research the market and competition
8		Future Task	Interview owners of similar businesses
9		Future Task	Identify needed resources
10		Future Task	Identify operating cost elements

Figure 12-5 Show current status at a glance by adding the Status Indicator or Status column to a task sheet.

Showing Progress Lines

You can add *progress lines* to your Gantt Chart that provide a graphical means of seeing whether tasks are ahead of schedule, behind schedule, or exactly on time. Progress lines are shown for tasks that have been completed, are in progress, or are currently due. They are not shown for tasks in the future.

For any given progress date, which you can set as the status date, you can have Project 2010 draw a progress line connecting in-progress tasks and tasks that should have started. (See Figure 12-6.) You can set the progress date to be the current date, the project status date, or any other date you select. You can also set multiple progress dates at recurring intervals—for example, on the first Monday of every month.

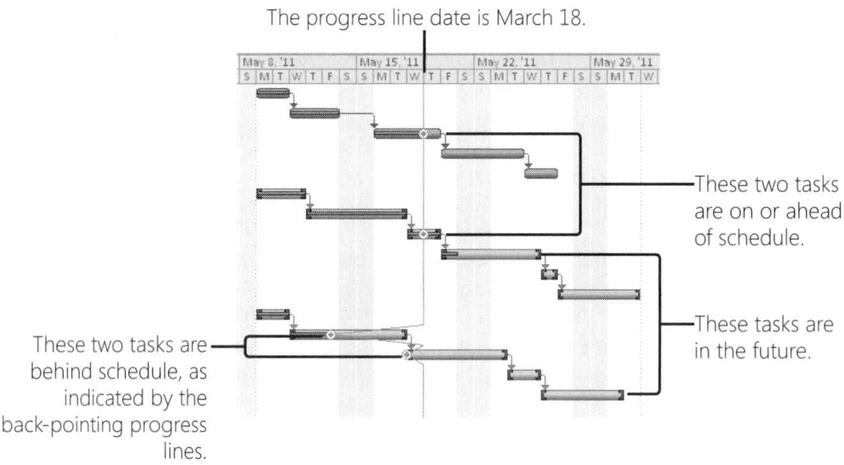

Figure 12-6 The left-pointing peaks indicate a negative schedule variance, whereas straight lines show tasks that are on or ahead of schedule as of the progress line date.

Progress lines create a graph on the Gantt Chart that provides valuable progress information, as follows:

- A progress line angled to the left indicates work that's behind schedule as of the progress line date.
- A straight progress line indicates a task on schedule as of the progress line date.
- Tasks untouched by the progress line are tasks scheduled to start in the future from the progress line date.

To add a progress line to a Gantt chart:

1. Display the Gantt Chart, Tracking Gantt, or any other Gantt view.

Gridlines

2. On the Format tab, in the Format group, click Gridlines, and then click Progress Lines.

   The Progress Lines dialog box appears, as shown in Figure 12-7.

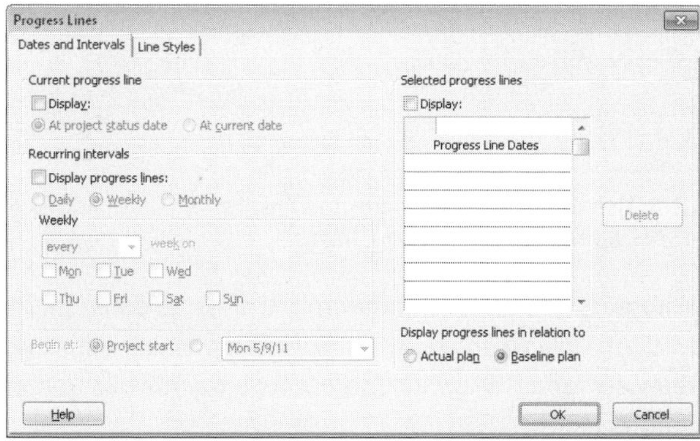

Figure 12-7 Set progress lines in the Gantt Chart by using the Progress Lines dialog box.

3. On the Dates And Intervals tab, under Current Progress Line, select the Display check box. Then select whether you want the progress line to be displayed at the project status date or the current date.

   The project status date, as well as the current date, is set in the Project Information dialog box (click Project, Properties, Project Information). If no status date is set there, the current date (today) is used instead.

4. If you want progress lines to be drawn at regular intervals—for example, once every month—specify this under the Recurring Intervals section.

   If you want progress lines to be drawn on dates that you specify, enter those dates under Selected Progress Lines.

5. Under Display Progress Lines In Relation To, specify whether you want progress lines to reflect the actual plan or your baseline.

6. Click the Line Styles tab, and then set your preferences for how you want the progress lines to appear in the Gantt Chart.

   As shown in Figure 12-8, you can specify the line type and color, and the progress point shape and color for the current progress line and other progress lines.

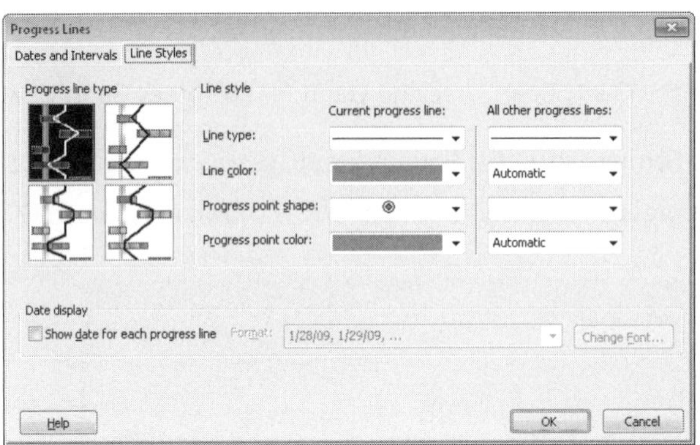

Figure 12-8 Use the Line Styles tab in the Progress Lines dialog box to customize how progress lines appear in your Gantt Chart.

If you defined progress line dates in addition to the status date or current date, you can choose to show them only when you want. For example, you might want to show progress lines in a printed view for a status meeting but hide them while updating progress. To temporarily hide progress lines:

1. On the Format tab, in the Format group, click Gridlines, and then click Progress Lines.
2. On the Dates And Intervals tab, under Current Progress Line, clear the Display check box.

   The defined progress lines are removed from your Gantt Chart, but the dates remain in the Progress Lines dialog box for when you want to show them again.

You can remove one or more of your defined progress lines. To delete a progress line:

1. On the Format tab, in the Format group, click Gridlines, and then click Progress Lines.
2. Be sure the Dates And Intervals tab is showing.
3. Under Selected Progress Lines, select the progress line you want to remove from the Gantt Chart, and then click the Delete button.

To hide the current progress line reflecting the project status date or the current date:

1. On the Format tab, in the Format group, click Gridlines, and then click Progress Lines.
2. On the Dates And Intervals tab, under Current Progress Line, clear the Display check box.

Correcting the Schedule

Let's say you reviewed your schedule details and found that your project isn't going as quickly as planned and the finish date is in jeopardy. Or perhaps upper management has imposed a schedule change, and you need to work toward a different finish date.

If you need to take corrective actions in your project plan to bring in the scheduled finish date, you can do the following:

- Check schedule assumptions—such as duration, constraints, and task dependencies—to see whether any adjustments can be made.
- Add resources to recover a slipping schedule (this will likely add costs).
- Cut scope to recover a slipping schedule (this will probably require stakeholder approval).

For more information about using any of these techniques to adjust the schedule to meet the current or new finish date, see "Bringing In the Project Finish Date" on page 383.

Create a What-If Project

Suppose that an external change is being proposed or you just want to see the effect of a potential change to your project plan. You can save another version of your project plan and make the necessary adjustments to reflect the potential change. You can then examine specifically what the imposed changes will do to your project plan in terms of schedule, cost, and resource allocation.

To save a separate what-if project, first save the project to capture any recent changes. Then click File, Save As. In the File Name box, enter a name for the what-if project, and then click OK.

You can change the what-if project as much as you like because you saved it under a different file name. Your working version of the project plan remains intact, but you gain valuable information about the impact of potential changes. If you or other stakeholders decide to go ahead with the change, you can adopt the what-if project as your new working project.

Compare Projects

With Project 2010, you can compare two projects side by side. This means you can compare your original project against your what-if project and determine what changes you might want to make. On the Project tab, in the Reports group, click Compare Projects.

For more information, see "Compare Project Plans Side by Side" on page 1223.

Inactivate

New in Project 2010 is the ability to deactivate (and reactivate) tasks. Inactive tasks are removed from the schedule, but a dimmed image of their information, including their Gantt bars, remains in place. With deactivated tasks, in many cases you can have a what-if scenario within your working project. Select the task(s) you want to make inactive, and then click Task, Schedule, Inactivate. To reactivate an inactive task, select it and click Inactivate again.

When you adjust your project plan to achieve your finish date, be sure to check costs, resource allocation, and scope. You need to know how your changes affect other areas of the project plan.

You might also need to set a new baseline, especially if there have been major schedule changes.

For more information on new baselines, see "Need a New Baseline?" on page 521.

Rescheduling the Project

Suppose that you and your team started executing a project a few months ago. Some tasks were completed and some were in progress when your team's efforts were redirected to a different, urgent priority. Now you've all returned to the first project, ready to pick up where you left off.

What do you do with your project plan? The scheduled dates of tasks you need to work on now are two months old. Do you have to readjust all the tasks to align them with the current calendar?

No, you just need to do some rescheduling. Depending on the scale, you can:

- Reschedule one or more tasks by a day, a week, a month, or whatever you want.
- Reschedule any uncompleted work to start after a new project resume date.
- Reschedule the entire project, even completed work.

With any of these methods, Project 2010 shifts tasks to the date you specify, and you can continue forward from there.

> **Note**
>
> **When rescheduling on a large scale like this, you'll benefit from setting a new baseline. Keep the old one, but use the new baseline for your everyday variance measurements.**

Rescheduling Selected Tasks

If you just need to reschedule a few tasks, follow these steps:

1. Select the task(s) you want to reschedule by the same amount of time.

NEW!

Move

2. On the Task tab, in the Tasks group, click Move.

   A drop-down menu provides all your task rescheduling choices, as shown in Figure 12-9.

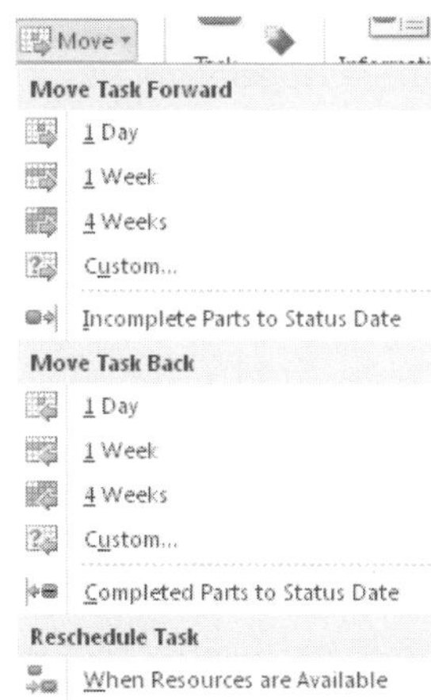

Figure 12-9 You can move selected tasks forward or back by a specified amount of time.

   You can move the selected tasks forward in the schedule by using one of the choices under Move Task Forward. You can move any incomplete parts of the selected tasks to the status date (or today's date) by using Incomplete Parts To Status Date.

   You can move the selected tasks backward in the schedule, which is useful if you find you need to "crash" the schedule and greatly accelerate the project finish date. This is also useful if you need to move a set of tasks all at once, or if you're scheduling from the finish date. Use one of the choices under Move Task Back. You can move any completed parts of the selected tasks to the status date (or today's date) by using Completed Parts To Status Date.

   You can move tasks to wherever they need to be to resolve resource overallocations by using the When Resources Are Available command under Reschedule Task. This operation is essentially the same as using Prevent Overallocations in the Team Planner or leveling selected tasks. An amount of leveling delay is added to tasks as necessary to resolve resource overallocations based on task priority, ID, and other factors in the leveling "engine."

3. Click the rescheduling choice you want for the selected task(s).

   The tasks are rescheduled. If the tasks had any actual progress reported on them, the actuals remain at the dates they took place, and the uncompleted parts of the task are split and moved forward or backward as you specified.

Rescheduling All Uncompleted Tasks

To reschedule uncompleted tasks to resume work after a certain date, follow these steps:

1. Open a task sheet. If you want to reschedule only certain tasks, select those tasks.
2. On the Project tab, in the Status group, click Update Project.

   Update Project

   The Update Project dialog box appears, as shown in Figure 12-10.

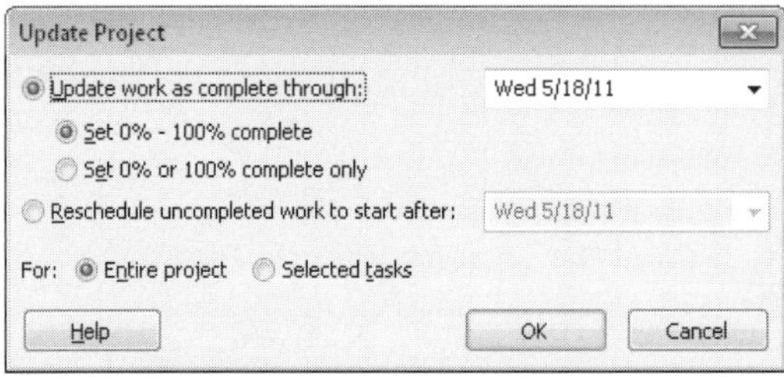

Figure 12-10 Reschedule uncompleted work all at once by using the Update Project dialog box.

3. Select the option labeled Reschedule Uncompleted Work To Start After.
4. In the box, enter the date when you want uncompleted work to start again.

   By default, today's date appears.
5. If you want to reschedule only selected tasks, click the Selected Tasks option. Otherwise, all uncompleted work is rescheduled to start after your specified date.

   The remaining work on tasks is rescheduled to resume after the new start date you specify, as shown in Figure 12-11.

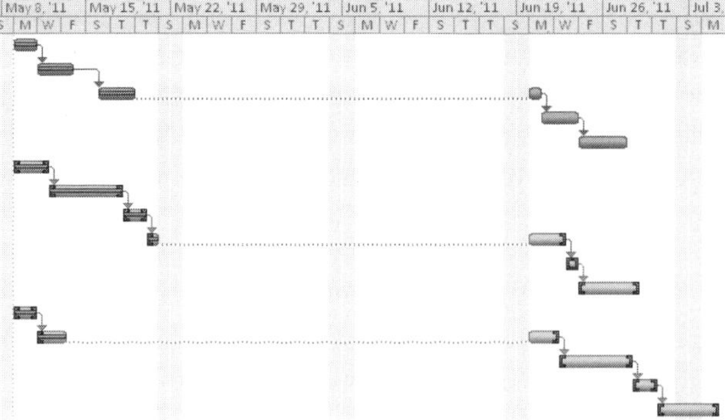

Figure 12-11 This project stalled for about two weeks and then was rescheduled to continue on June 20.

By default, any tasks that were in progress are split so that remaining work is scheduled after the date you specify. If you don't want in-progress tasks to be split, click File, Options, and then click Schedule in the left pane. Under Scheduling Options For This Project, clear the check box labeled Split In-Progress Tasks.

Any uncompleted tasks that have a date constraint (such as Must Start On or Finish No Earlier Than) are not rescheduled, which preserves the constraint and gives you the option of deciding how to handle it.

You can enter any date you want for rescheduling, even one in the past. If a task is in progress, the date does need to be after the task's existing stop date or actual start date.

Manually scheduled placeholder tasks that don't have any start date information are not affected by the reschedule. That is, if a placeholder task includes only a duration or finish date, or no schedule information at all, it does not change. If it includes a start date, that start date is moved to the reschedule date. This is true even after entering actuals for these placeholders.

Rescheduling the Entire Project

To reschedule everything, even completed tasks or other tasks with actuals on them, follow these steps:

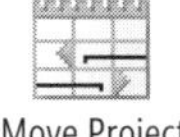

Move Project

1. On the Project tab, in the Schedule group, click Move Project.
2. If any tasks are completed or have other actuals reported on them, an alert message appears. Click Yes to continue with the reschedule operation.

   The Move Project dialog box appears showing the original project start date. (See Figure 12-12.)

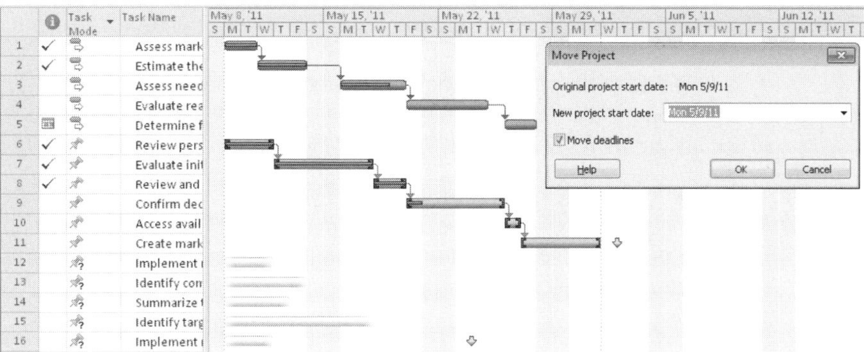

Figure 12-12 Use the Move Project dialog box to specify a new project start date.

3. In the New Project Start Date box, enter the new date, and then click OK.

   All tasks in the project shift to the new start date, as shown in Figure 12-13.

   If there were deadlines in the project, and if the Move Deadlines check box is selected per the default, those deadlines also move in relation to the new start date.

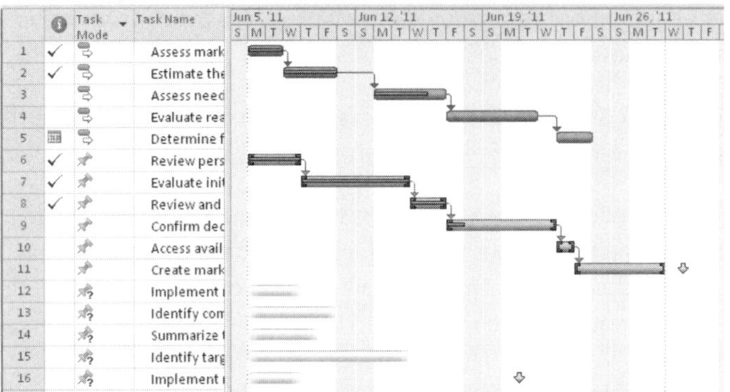

Figure 12-13 When you use Move Project, all tasks shift to a new project start date. This includes completed tasks, tasks with date constraints, and placeholder tasks.

Monitoring and Adjusting Costs

If your project is primarily constrained by budget, you'll want to keep a close eye on resource and task costs and on estimated costs for the project as a whole. You'll also want to adjust your project plan if you receive any actuals that are likely to blow the budget.

Monitoring Project Costs

Use one or more of the following techniques to monitor and adjust costs so that you can continue to work within your budget:

- Display specialized views and tables to review project costs.
- Adjust the schedule to reduce costs.
- Adjust assignments to reduce costs.

For details on techniques for monitoring and adjusting costs to achieve a specific budget, see "Reducing Project Costs" on page 396.

Project Management Practices: Cost Control

Cost control enables a project to stay within the bounds of the prescribed project budget. It involves continual monitoring of the project plan, tracking actual work and cost information, and taking corrective action where needed. If a task early in the project costs more than expected, costs might have to be trimmed in later tasks. In addition, outside forces might affect the project budget. For example, certain material costs might have gone up from the time you developed your plan to the time you actually procure the material. Or your company might undertake a cost-cutting initiative that requires you to cut all project costs by 15 percent.

When changes to project costs take place, you might have to adjust assignments or scope to bring costs in line with the budget. If you have a positive cost variance, the scheduled or current cost is more than your planned baseline cost. If you have a negative cost variance, the scheduled cost is less than your baseline cost. Although you certainly need to know why costs are higher than planned, you also should look into costs that are lower than planned. Lower costs can point to potential problems with increased risk, and perhaps with quality issues.

Earned value analysis is particularly useful for cost control. With variances and earned value analysis, you can assess the differences between planned and scheduled costs, determine their causes, and decide whether corrective actions are needed.

Using baseline information you save, you can review your current costs and compare them with baseline costs. For example, you can see baseline costs for tasks (including their resource costs) next to their scheduled costs, based on actuals you enter. Then you can review the variances between the baseline and scheduled cost. The cost variance is calculated as follows:

(Scheduled/Current) Cost – Baseline Cost = Cost Variance

Note

You can use earned value calculations such as the Budgeted Cost of Work Scheduled (BCWS) and Cost Variance (CV) earned value fields to analyze your project performance against the budget so far.

For more information, see "Generating Earned Value Data" on page 586.

Reviewing Overall Cost Totals

There are two ways to review your overall cost totals.

- **Review project statistics** On the Project tab, in the Properties group, click Project Information, and then click the Statistics button. Under Cost, review the current, baseline, actual, and remaining cost for the project.
- **Add the project summary task row** On the Format tab, in the Show/Hide group, select the Project Summary Task check box. Summary totals for task information in the current table are displayed in the project summary task row at the top of the task sheet. If a table containing cost information is applied, the project summary task row shows project cost totals.

Reviewing Cost Variances

Use the Cost table to review the differences between your original baseline costs and your currently scheduled costs. The Cost table includes fields containing baseline costs, total scheduled costs, actual costs, remaining costs, and cost variances. To apply the Cost table, follow these steps:

1. Display the Gantt Chart or other task sheet.
2. On the View tab, in the Data group, click Tables, and then click Cost.

   As shown in Figure 12-14, the Cost table is applied to the current view.

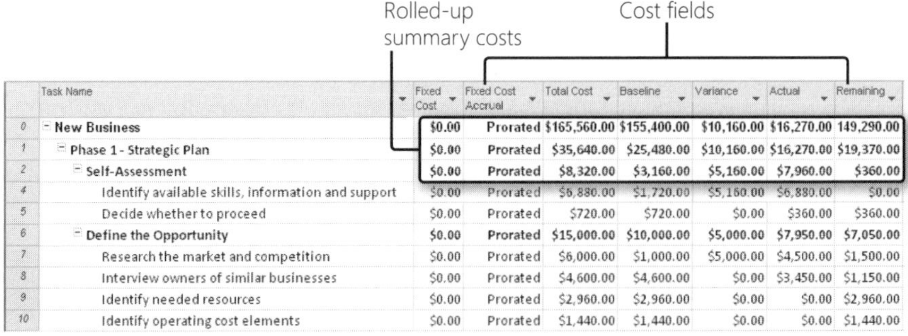

	Task Name	Fixed Cost	Fixed Cost Accrual	Total Cost	Baseline	Variance	Actual	Remaining
0	New Business	$0.00	Prorated	$165,560.00	$155,400.00	$10,160.00	$16,270.00	149,290.00
1	Phase 1 - Strategic Plan	$0.00	Prorated	$35,640.00	$25,480.00	$10,160.00	$16,270.00	$19,370.00
2	Self-Assessment	$0.00	Prorated	$8,320.00	$3,160.00	$5,160.00	$7,960.00	$360.00
4	Identify available skills, information and support	$0.00	Prorated	$6,880.00	$1,720.00	$5,160.00	$6,880.00	$0.00
5	Decide whether to proceed	$0.00	Prorated	$720.00	$720.00	$0.00	$360.00	$360.00
6	Define the Opportunity	$0.00	Prorated	$15,000.00	$10,000.00	$5,000.00	$7,950.00	$7,050.00
7	Research the market and competition	$0.00	Prorated	$6,000.00	$1,000.00	$5,000.00	$4,500.00	$1,500.00
8	Interview owners of similar businesses	$0.00	Prorated	$4,600.00	$4,600.00	$0.00	$3,450.00	$1,150.00
9	Identify needed resources	$0.00	Prorated	$2,960.00	$2,960.00	$0.00	$0.00	$2,960.00
10	Identify operating cost elements	$0.00	Prorated	$1,440.00	$1,440.00	$0.00	$0.00	$1,440.00

Figure 12-14 Apply the Cost table to a task sheet to see the most important cost data for tasks.

With the project summary task row applied, you can also review rolled-up cost totals.

There's also a cost table for resources, which includes cost information for all a resource's assignments. With the Resource Sheet or Resource Usage view displayed, apply the Cost table. The Resource Cost table includes the baseline cost, scheduled cost, actual cost, remaining cost, and cost variance for all the resource's assignments, as shown in Figure 12-15. Cost information is shown for all types of resources—work, material, and cost resources.

	Resource Name	Cost	Baseline Cost	Variance	Actual Cost	Remaining
1	Business Advisor	$60,000.00	$52,000.00	$8,000.00	$8,500.00	$51,500.00
2	Peers	$960.00	$960.00	$0.00	$0.00	$960.00
3	Lawyer	$27,200.00	$27,200.00	$0.00	$0.00	$27,200.00
4	Government Agency	$2,560.00	$2,560.00	$0.00	$0.00	$2,560.00
5	Manager	$52,560.00	$50,400.00	$2,160.00	$4,320.00	$48,240.00
6	Owners	$4,600.00	$4,600.00	$0.00	$3,450.00	$1,150.00
7	Accountant	$10,080.00	$10,080.00	$0.00	$0.00	$10,080.00
8	Banker	$6,000.00	$6,000.00	$0.00	$0.00	$6,000.00
9	Information Services	$1,600.00	$1,600.00	$0.00	$0.00	$1,600.00

Figure 12-15 Apply the Cost table to a resource sheet to see summarized cost data for resources, based on their task assignments.

Review Costs Using Budget Resources

If you are using the budget resource type with the Budget Work and Budget Cost fields, you can group and review predetermined budget values for work and cost against your planned project costs.

Note, however, that the figures for work are expressed as periods of time, such as hours, days, or weeks, rather than dollars. The budget costs apply only to cost resources, not to work or material resources.

For information about how to create and assign budget resources, enter budget values, and align resources with their corresponding budget resources, see "Setting Up and Reviewing a Project Budget" on page 346. To group and compare resource costs and work against budget costs and work, see "Comparing Resource Costs with Budget Resource Values" on page 357.

Reviewing Overbudget Costs

You can apply a filter to a task or resource sheet to see only those tasks or resources associated with overbudget costs, as follows:

1. Display the view and apply the table that contains the information you want to review in the context of overbudget costs.

2. On the View tab, in the Data group, click the arrow in the Filter box, and then click More Filters.
3. In the More Filters dialog box, click Cost Overbudget, and then click Apply.

   Project 2010 filters for any tasks or resources whose scheduled or actual costs are higher than the baseline costs.
4. Review the tasks or resources to analyze the extent of the cost overages.
5. When you finish, show all tasks again. On the View tab, in the Data group, click the arrow in the Filter box, and then click No Filter.

Highlight

If you prefer to highlight rather than filter for overbudget tasks or resources, use the Highlight tool instead. On the View tab, in the Data group, click the arrow in the Highlight box, and then click More Highlight Filters. To remove highlighting, click No Highlight.

Reviewing Cost Performance by Using Earned Value Analysis

If you set a baseline and are entering actuals, you can evaluate current cost and schedule performance by using earned value calculations. To generate most earned value information, you must have the following items in your project plan:

- A saved baseline
- Resources assigned to tasks
- Costs associated with assigned resources
- Actual progress information

To review earned value information, follow these steps:

1. Display the Gantt Chart or other task sheet.
2. On the View tab, in the Data group, click Tables, and then click More Tables.
3. In the dialog box, click Earned Value, Earned Value Cost Indicators, or Earned Value Schedule Indicators, depending on the type of earned value information you want to review.

   The table is applied to the task sheet, as shown in Figure 12-16.

	Task Name	Planned Value - PV (BCWS)	Earned Value - EV (BCWP)	CV	CV%	CPI	BAC	EAC	VAC	TCP
0	**New Business**	**$10,240.00**	**$3,466.67**	**($8,493.33)**	**-245%**	**0.29**	**$155,400.00**	**$536,130.00**	**($380,730.00)**	**1.06**
1	**Phase 1 - Strategic Plan**	**$10,240.00**	**$3,466.67**	**($8,493.33)**	**-245%**	**0.29**	**$25,480.00**	**$87,906.00**	**($62,426.00)**	**1.63**
2	**Self-Assessment**	**$3,160.00**	**$2,800.00**	**($5,160.00)**	**-184%**	**0.35**	**$3,160.00**	**$8,983.43**	**($5,823.43)**	**-0.07**
3	Define business vision	$720.00	$720.00	$0.00	0%	1	$720.00	$720.00	$0.00	1
4	Identify available skills,	$1,720.00	$1,720.00	($5,160.00)	-300%	0.25	$1,720.00	$6,880.00	($5,160.00)	-0
5	Decide whether to proceed	$720.00	$360.00	$0.00	0%	1	$720.00	$720.00	$0.00	1
6	**Define the Opportunity**	**$7,080.00**	**$666.67**	**($3,333.33)**	**-500%**	**0.17**	**$10,000.00**	**$60,000.00**	**($50,000.00)**	**1.56**
7	Research the market and competition	$1,000.00	$666.67	($3,333.33)	-500%	0.17	$1,000.00	$6,000.00	($5,000.00)	-0.11
8	Interview owners of similar businesses	$4,600.00	$0.00	$0.00	0%	0	$4,600.00	$4,600.00	$0.00	1
9	Identify needed resources	$1,480.00	$0.00	$0.00	0%	0	$2,960.00	$2,960.00	$0.00	1

Figure 12-16 The Earned Value Cost Indicators table displays earned value fields related to budget performance.

To learn details about an earned value field and how best to use and interpret it, follow these steps:

1. In a task view with an earned value table applied, rest the mouse pointer over an earned value field column header until the ScreenTip appears.

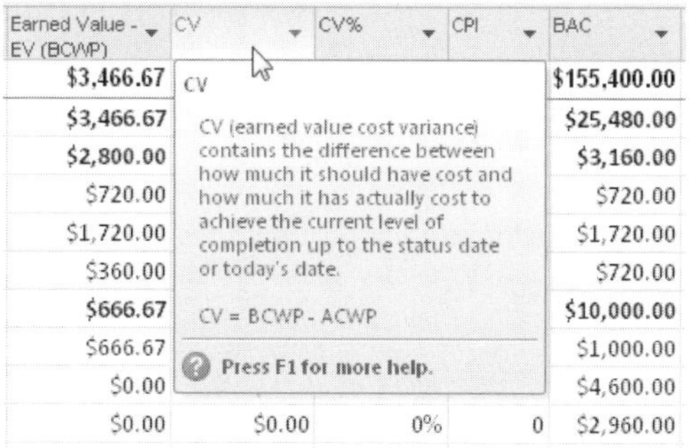

Earned Value - EV (BCWP)	CV	CV%	CPI	BAC
$3,466.67				**$155,400.00**
$3,466.67				**$25,480.00**
$2,800.00				**$3,160.00**
$720.00				$720.00
$1,720.00				$1,720.00
$360.00				$720.00
$666.67				**$10,000.00**
$666.67				$1,000.00
$0.00				$4,600.00
$0.00	$0.00	0%	0	$2,960.00

CV

CV (earned value cost variance) contains the difference between how much it should have cost and how much it has actually cost to achieve the current level of completion up to the status date or today's date.

CV = BCWP - ACWP

Press F1 for more help.

2. Press F1.

   The Project 2010 Help window appears. If necessary, click to expand the category of field you're using—for example, the task field category. (See Figure 12-17.) Information includes a description of that earned value field, how it's calculated, its best uses, and an example of its use.

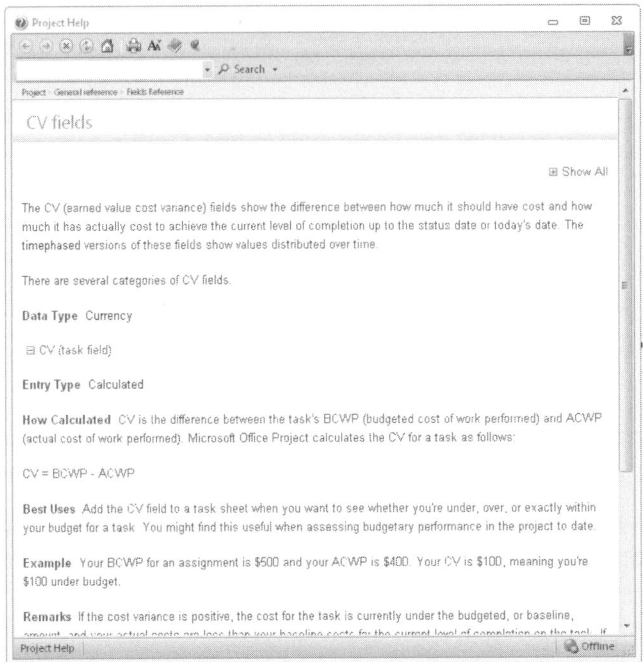

Figure 12-17 Press F1 over any earned value field to get help and detailed information for that field.

For more information about analyzing project performance with earned value, see "Reviewing Earned Value Data" on page 589.

TROUBLESHOOTING

Your earned value fields all show $0.00

If you apply an Earned Value table or insert an earned value field only to find all the values to be $0.00, it's likely that you're missing one or more of the pieces of information needed by Project 2010 to calculate earned value fields.

For earned value to be calculated, you must have all the following items in your project plan:

- A saved baseline
- Resources assigned to tasks
- Costs associated with assigned resources
- Actual progress information
- A status date

Reviewing Budget Status

The following filters can help you focus on any potential problems with project costs and budget:

- Cost Greater Than (see Figure 12-18)
- Cost Overbudget
- Late/Overbudget Tasks Assigned To
- Work Overbudget

	Task Name	Fixed Cost	Fixed Cost Accrual	Total Cost	Baseline	Variance	Actual	Remaining
81	Establish the Operating Control Base	$0.00	Prorated	$18,480.00	$18,480.00	$0.00	$0.00	$18,480.00
83	Obtain required licenses and permits	$0.00	Prorated	$8,960.00	$8,960.00	$0.00	$0.00	$8,960.00
85	Establish security plan	$0.00	Prorated	$5,200.00	$5,200.00	$0.00	$0.00	$5,200.00
86	Develop Marketing Program	$0.00	Prorated	$5,600.00	$5,600.00	$0.00	$0.00	$5,600.00
90	Provide Physical Facilities	$0.00	Prorated	$15,360.00	$15,360.00	$0.00	$0.00	$15,360.00
91	Secure operation space	$0.00	Prorated	$8,000.00	$8,000.00	$0.00	$0.00	$8,000.00
97	Provide Staffing	$0.00	Prorated	$28,800.00	$28,800.00	$0.00	$0.00	$28,800.00
98	Interview and test candidates	$0.00	Prorated	$10,080.00	$10,080.00	$0.00	$0.00	$10,080.00
99	Hire staff	$0.00	Prorated	$7,200.00	$7,200.00	$0.00	$0.00	$7,200.00
100	Train staff	$0.00	Prorated	$11,520.00	$11,520.00	$0.00	$0.00	$11,520.00

Figure 12-18 The Cost Greater Than filter has been applied to this table to focus on those tasks that have the highest costs.

To apply a filter, on the View tab, in the Data group, click the arrow in the Filter box, and then click More Filters. In the dialog box, click the filter you want and then click Apply or Highlight.

To show all tasks again, on the View tab, in the Data group, click the arrow in the Filter box, and then click No Filter. If you used a filter highlight, click the arrow in the Highlight box, and then click No Highlight.

You can also run text-based and visual reports that provide information about costs and budget status, as follows:

- Cash Flow
- Budget
- Overbudget Tasks
- Overbudget Resources
- Earned Value
- Baseline Cost Report (visual report in Microsoft Excel 2010)

- Baseline Report (visual report in Visio)
- Budget Cost Report (visual report in Excel 2010)
- Cash Flow Report (visual reports in Excel or Visio)
- Earned Value Over Time Report (visual report in Excel)
- Resource Cost Summary (visual report in Excel)

To run a text-based cost report, click Project, Reports, Reports. Double-click Costs, and then double-click the report you want. If a dialog box asks for more information, enter the information, and then click OK. The report appears in the Print Backstage view. You can then print the report to study the details.

To run a visual report, follow these steps:

1. On the Project tab, in the Reports group, click Visual Reports.
2. On the All tab, double-click the name of the report you want.

   The report is generated from Project 2010 data and displayed in Visio or Microsoft Excel, as shown in Figure 12-19.

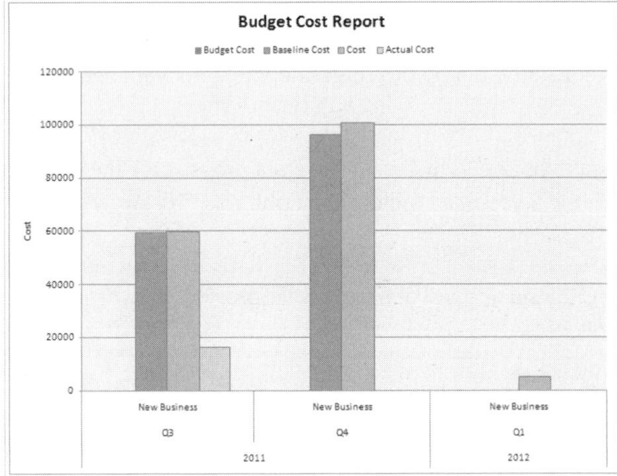

Figure 12-19 Run the Budget Cost visual report in Excel to generate a column chart showing a comparison of budgeted, baseline, scheduled, and actual costs over time.

Realigning the Project with the Budget

Suppose that you reviewed your budget details against the current project costs and found that you will end up significantly over budget. Or perhaps upper management has asked you to cut costs by 10 percent, and you need to work toward a different total project cost.

If you need to take corrective actions in your project plan to reduce project costs, you can do the following:

- Recheck your basic cost assumptions such as resource rates, per-use costs for resources, amounts for cost resources assigned to tasks, and fixed costs for tasks.
- Adjust the schedule to reduce costs. Reducing task durations and adjusting task dependencies can help reduce costs.
- Adjust assignments to reduce costs. Add, remove, or replace resources on assignments as appropriate to cut costs.
- Cut scope to reduce costs (which will probably require stakeholder approval).

When you adjust your project plan to achieve the budget you need, be sure to check your finish date, resource allocation, and scope. You need to know how your changes affect other areas of the project plan.

For more information about using any of these strategies to trim project costs, see "Reducing Project Costs" on page 396.

You might also consider setting a new baseline, especially if major cost or schedule changes have occurred.

For more information on setting a new baseline, see "Need a New Baseline?" on page 521.

Monitoring and Adjusting Resource Workload

If you're a resource manager, or if your biggest project priority is to maintain a balanced workload among your resources, monitor your resources' workload and see if anyone is unexpectedly overallocated or underallocated. As you receive information from resources about their assigned tasks and enter actuals, you can see whether you need to take any action to prevent potential resource allocation problems in the near future.

Monitoring Resource Workload

Do one or more of the following to help you monitor and adjust the schedule to achieve a balanced resource workload:

- Review resource workloads.
- Adjust resource availability.
- Adjust assignments.
- Split tasks to reschedule remaining work for when resources have available time.
- Level assignments.

Because work (in hours, days, weeks, and so on) is the measure of resource effort on tasks, you can use the baseline value for work to help review how well resources are utilized according to actual and scheduled values. For example, you can see one resource's baseline work for tasks next to her values for scheduled work, based on actuals she has submitted regarding her progress. Then you can review the variances between the baseline and scheduled work. Work variance is calculated as follows:

(Scheduled/Current) Work – Baseline Work = Work Variance

If actual work values are considerably higher than originally planned, you can anticipate some problems with resource overallocation now or in the near future.

For more information about adjusting assigned work, see "Balancing Resource Workloads" on page 403.

You can use earned value calculations such as the Budgeted Cost of Work Scheduled (BCWS) and Actual Cost of Work Performed (ACWP) earned value fields to analyze project performance based on resource work. For more information, see Chapter 14.

Reviewing Overall Work Totals

There are two ways to review your overall work totals.

- **Review project statistics** On the Project tab, in the Properties group, click Project Information, and then click the Statistics button. Under Work, review the current, baseline, actual, and remaining work for the project.

- **Add the project summary task row** On the Format tab, in the Show/Hide group, select the Project Summary Task check box. Summary totals for task information in the current table are displayed in the project summary task row at the top of the task sheet. If a table containing work information is applied, the project summary task row shows project work totals.

Reviewing Work Variances

To review the differences between your original baseline work and your currently scheduled work, apply the Work table, as follows:

1. Display the Gantt Chart or other task sheet.
2. On the View tab, in the Data group, click Tables, and then click Work.

   The Work table is applied to the current view, as shown in Figure 12-20.

	Task Name	Work	Baseline	Variance	Actual	Remaining	% W. Comp.
0	**New Business**	**1,456 hrs**	**1,368 hrs**	**88 hrs**	**146 hrs**	**1,310 hrs**	**10%**
1	**Phase 1 - Strategic Plan**	**328 hrs**	**240 hrs**	**88 hrs**	**146 hrs**	**182 hrs**	**45%**
2	**Self-Assessment**	**80 hrs**	**32 hrs**	**48 hrs**	**76 hrs**	**4 hrs**	**95%**
3	Define business vision	8 hrs	8 hrs	0 hrs	8 hrs	0 hrs	100%
4	Identify available skills, information and support	64 hrs	16 hrs	48 hrs	64 hrs	0 hrs	100%
5	Decide whether to proceed	8 hrs	8 hrs	0 hrs	4 hrs	4 hrs	50%
6	**Define the Opportunity**	**136 hrs**	**96 hrs**	**40 hrs**	**66 hrs**	**70 hrs**	**49%**
7	Research the market and competition	48 hrs	8 hrs	40 hrs	36 hrs	12 hrs	75%
8	Interview owners of similar businesses	40 hrs	40 hrs	0 hrs	30 hrs	10 hrs	75%
9	Identify needed resources	32 hrs	32 hrs	0 hrs	0 hrs	32 hrs	0%
10	Identify operating cost elements	16 hrs	16 hrs	0 hrs	0 hrs	16 hrs	0%
11	**Evaluate Business Approach**	**32 hrs**	**32 hrs**	**0 hrs**	**4 hrs**	**28 hrs**	**13%**
12	Define new entity requirements	8 hrs	8 hrs	0 hrs	4 hrs	4 hrs	50%
13	Identify on-going business purchase opportunities	8 hrs	8 hrs	0 hrs	0 hrs	8 hrs	0%
14	Research franchise possibilities	8 hrs	8 hrs	0 hrs	0 hrs	8 hrs	0%

Figure 12-20 Apply the Work table to a task sheet to see scheduled, baseline, and actual work—along with any variances.

With the project summary task row applied, you can also review rolled-up work totals.

Reviewing Overbudget Work

You can apply a filter to a task or resource sheet to see only those tasks or resources that have more actual work reported than was planned, as follows:

1. Display the view and apply the table that contains the information you want to review in the context of overbudget work.
2. On the View tab, in the Data group, click the arrow in the Filter box, and then click More Filters.

3. In the More Filters dialog box, click Work Overbudget, and then click Apply or Highlight.

   Project 2010 filters for any tasks or resources whose actual work reported is higher than the baseline work.

4. Review the tasks or resources to analyze the extent of the work overages.

5. When you finish, show all tasks again.

   On the View tab, in the Data group, click the arrow in the Filter box, and then click No Filter. If you used a filter highlight, click the arrow in the Highlight box, and then click No Highlight.

Reviewing Resource Allocation

The name of any overallocated resource appears in red in any resource view. In the default Entry table of the Resource Sheet, a leveling indicator is also displayed next to the resource name, recommending that the resource be leveled.

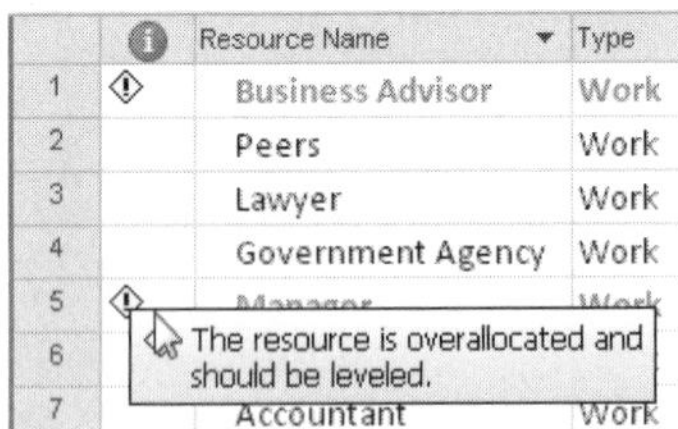

In a task sheet, any task that has an overallocated resource assigned to it displays an overallocated resource icon in the Indicators column.

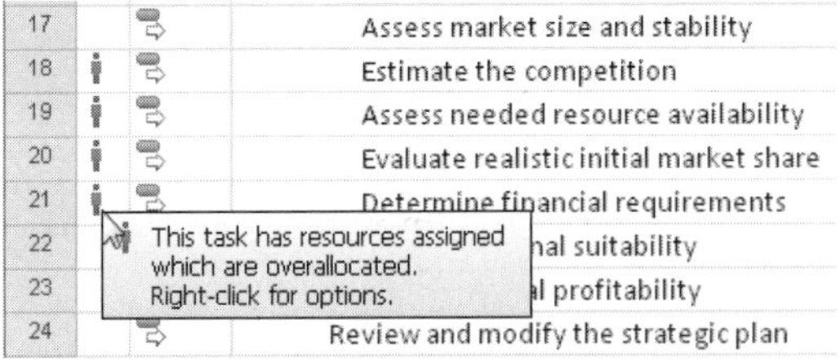

To see the extent of overallocation or underallocation for a resource, use the Resource Graph, as follows:

Other Views

1. On the View tab, in the Resource Views group, click Other Views, and then click Resource Graph.

   The Resource Graph appears, as shown in Figure 12-21.

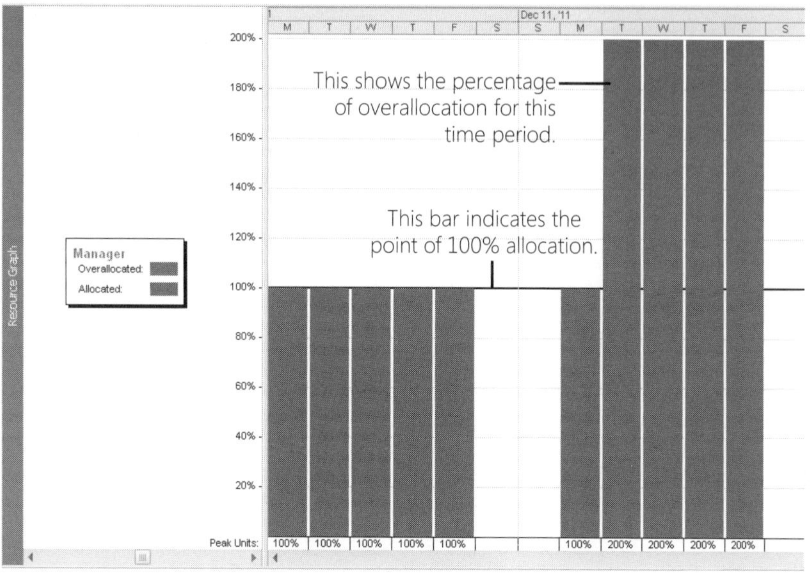

Figure 12-21 The Resource Graph can show whether a resource is fully allocated, overallocated, or underallocated for a selected period of time.

2. Review the allocation for the first resource.

   By default, the Resource Graph shows peak units for each time period, including the percentage allocated and the percentage overallocated. You can show different types of information in the Resource Graph. On the Format tab, in the Data group, click the arrow in the Graph box, and then click another type of information (for example, Work or Remaining Availability).

   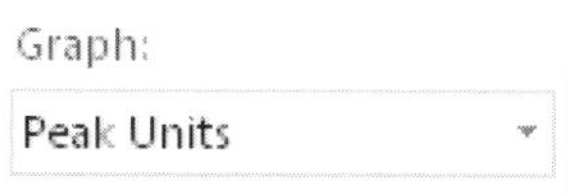

3. Use the Zoom slider in the lower-right corner of the Project 2010 window to zoom the Resource Graph in or out. Zooming in shows details over a shorter period of time. Zooming out shows information across a longer period of time.

   Zoom

   If you prefer, you can also use the zoom buttons on the ribbon. On the View tab, in the Zoom group, click the Zoom button, and then click Zoom In or Zoom Out.

4. To see information for the next resource, press the Page Down key or click in the horizontal scroll bar in the left pane of the view.

Note

Adding the Resource Graph as the lower pane in a combination view can be very useful in finding resource overallocations.

INSIDE OUT Relieve the leveling hair-trigger

The leveling indicator often suggests that the resource be leveled on a day-by-day basis because Project 2010 has found that this resource is overallocated by at least one minute over the resource availability for a day.

You might find that level of detail too fine for your purposes. It might be more effective to level resources on a week-by-week basis or a month-by-month basis. Although the overallocation is still detected when a resource is overallocated by just one minute, looking at the entire week or the entire month instead of just one day provides more of a buffer for overallocations to take care of themselves.

Leveling Options

To change the leveling trigger, click Resource, Level, Leveling Options. In the box labeled Look For Overallocations On A *X* Basis, click Week By Week or Month By Month.

You can also see the details about which assignments are causing resource overallocations (or underallocations) by using the Resource Usage view, as follows:

Resource Usage

1. On the View tab, in the Resource Views group, click Resource Usage.

   The Resource Usage view appears, as shown in Figure 12-22.

		Resource Name	Work	Details	S	M	T	W	T	F	S
					Aug 7, '11						
4		Government Agency	32 hrs	Work							
		Obtain required licenses and permits	*32 hrs*	Work							
5		Manager	584 hrs	Work			6h	8h	8h	8h	
		Define business vision	*8 hrs*	Work							
		Identify available skills, information and support	*32 hrs*	Work							
		Decide whether to proceed	*8 hrs*	Work							
		Define new entity requirements	*8 hrs*	Work			6h	2h			
		Identify on-going business purchase opportunities	*8 hrs*	Work				6h	2h		
		Research franchise possibilities	*8 hrs*	Work					6h	2h	
		Summarize business approach	*8 hrs*	Work						6h	
		Review personal suitability	*8 hrs*	Work							

Figure 12-22 The Resource Usage view shows how resources are allocated for each time period as well as the specific assignments that contribute to that allocation.

Any resource whose name appears in red or with a leveling indicator is overallocated.

2. Review the timesheet area of the view to see where the overallocation occurs.

   You might need to scroll to move to a different time period.

3. Use the Zoom slider in the lower-right corner of the Project 2010 window to zoom the timesheet area in or out.

4. Review the sheet area of the view to see the assignments for each resource.

5. You can add the Overallocation field to the timesheet area of the view. The Overallocation field can help you learn by how many hours or days a resource is overallocated. To add the Overallocation field, on the Format tab, in the Details group, select the Overallocation check box.

   The Overallocation field is added as a new row in the timesheet area of the Resource Usage view, as shown in Figure 12-23.

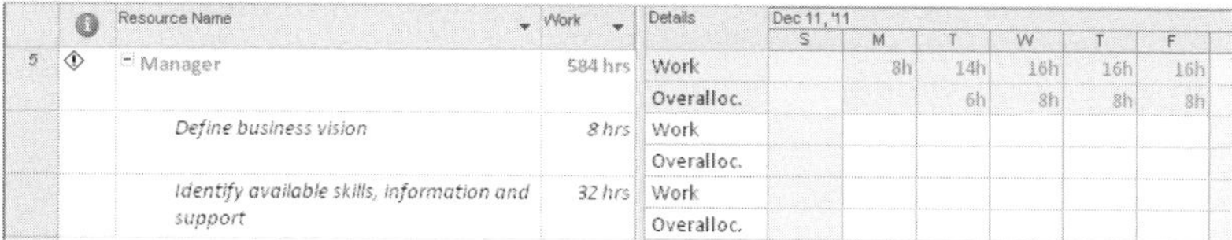

Figure 12-23 Add the Overallocation field to the Resource Usage view to see the number of hours (or other time period) by which each resource is overallocated.

6. To see underallocations or the amount of time that a resource is available for more assignments, add the Remaining Availability field to the timesheet area of the view. On the Format tab, in the Details group, select the Remaining Availability check box.

> ## Note
>
> **If you apply the Work table to the Resource Usage view, you can see work details and tracking information for each resource and assignment—including baseline work, the variance between the baseline and scheduled work, any actual work reported, remaining work, and percentage complete.**

Use the Resource Allocation view to see the Resource Usage view in combination with the Leveling Gantt. This view helps you see which resources are overallocated in conjunction with the tasks that are causing the overallocation. On the View tab, in the Resource Views group, click Other Views, and then click More Views. In the dialog box, click Resource Allocation and then click Apply. Figure 12-24 shows an example of the Resource Allocation view.

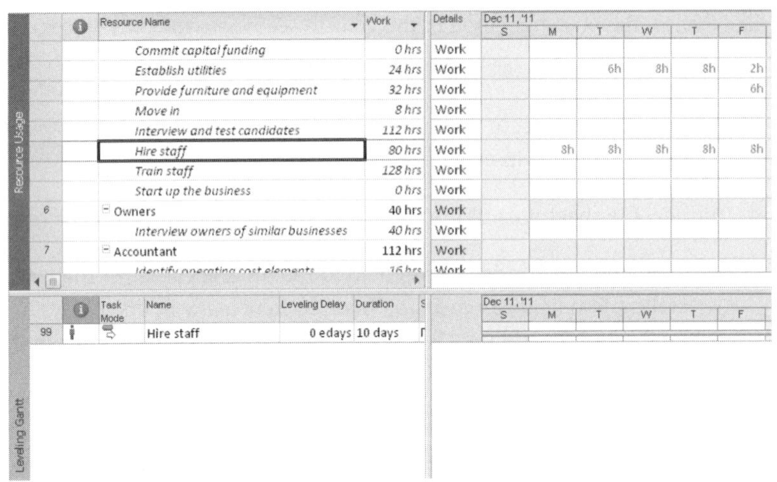

Figure 12-24 With the Resource Allocation view, you can see task information in the lower pane for any assignment you click in the Resource Usage view in the upper pane.

With the Summary table applied to a resource view, you can see the Peak field, which can quickly tell you whether resources are allocated to their maximum availability (100%), overallocated (more than 100%), or underallocated (less than 100%). On the View tab, in the Data group, click Tables, and then click Summary. Figure 12-25 shows an example of the Summary table.

	Resource Name	Group	Max.	Peak	Std. Rate	Ovt. Rate	Cost	Work
1	Business Advisor		100%	200%	$125.00/hr	$0.00/hr	$60,000.00	480 hrs
2	Peers		100%	100%	$60.00/hr	$0.00/hr	$960.00	16 hrs
3	Lawyer		100%	100%	$200.00/hr	$0.00/hr	$27,200.00	136 hrs
4	Government Agency		100%	100%	$80.00/hr	$0.00/hr	$2,560.00	32 hrs
5	Manager		100%	200%	$90.00/hr	$0.00/hr	$52,560.00	584 hrs
6	Owners		100%	100%	$115.00/hr	$0.00/hr	$4,600.00	40 hrs
7	Accountant		100%	100%	$90.00/hr	$0.00/hr	$10,080.00	112 hrs
8	Banker		100%	100%	$150.00/hr	$0.00/hr	$6,000.00	40 hrs
9	Information Services		100%	100%	$100.00/hr	$0.00/hr	$1,600.00	16 hrs

Figure 12-25 By reviewing resources' Peak fields, you can quickly see how many resources are allocated and whether they're available to take on more assignments.

The following filters can help you focus on any potential problems with overallocated resources:

- Overallocated Resources (see Figure 12-26)
- Work Overbudget
- Resources/Assignments With Overtime
- Slipping Assignments

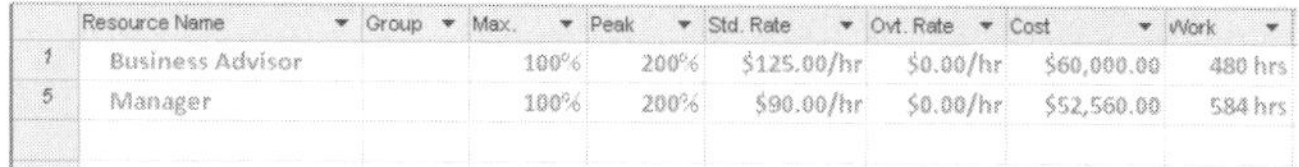

	Resource Name	Group	Max.	Peak	Std. Rate	Ovt. Rate	Cost	Work
1	Business Advisor		100%	200%	$125.00/hr	$0.00/hr	$60,000.00	480 hrs
5	Manager		100%	200%	$90.00/hr	$0.00/hr	$52,560.00	584 hrs

Figure 12-26 Apply the Overallocated Resources filter to a resource view to quickly see a list of resources who have more work assigned than time available for that work.

With a resource view displayed, apply a filter. On the View tab, in the Data group, click the arrow in the Filter box. Then either click the name of the filter you want in the drop-down menu, or click More Filters and find the filter in the dialog box.

You can also generate and print a report. The following reports provide information about resource usage:

- Who Does What
- Who Does What When
- To-Do List
- Overallocated Resources
- Task Usage
- Resource Usage
- Baseline Work Report (visual report in Excel)
- Budget Work Report (visual report in Excel)
- Resource Availability Report (visual report in Visio)
- Resource Remaining Work Report (visual report in Excel)
- Resource Status Report (visual report in Visio)
- Resource Work Availability Report (visual report in Excel)
- Resource Work Summary Report (visual report in Excel)

To run a text-based report about assignments or workloads, click Project, Reports, Reports. Double-click Assignments or Workload, and then double-click the report you want. If a dialog box asks for more, enter the information, and then click OK. The report appears in the Print Backstage view. You can then print the report to study the details.

To run a visual report, follow these steps:

1. On the Project tab, in the Reports group, click Visual Reports.
2. On the All tab, double-click the name of the report you want.

   Project 2010 data is gathered and the report is built and displayed in Visio or Excel.

Balancing the Resource Workload

Suppose that you reviewed information about assignments and workload throughout your project plan and found that some resources are overallocated and others are underallocated. Or perhaps your company had a reduction in force, and your project staffing was reduced by 15 percent.

If you need to take corrective actions in your project plan to balance the resource workload, you can:

- Adjust resource availability.
- Adjust assignments by, for example, adding resources, replacing resources, delaying a task or assignment, or specifying overtime.
- Split tasks to balance the workload.
- Use the Prevent Overallocations feature in the Team Planner to balance the workload.
- Use the Project 2010 leveling feature to balance the workload.
- Adjust scope (this will probably require stakeholder approval).

For more information about using any of these strategies to better allocate your resources, see "Balancing Resource Workloads" on page 403.

When you adjust your project plan to achieve the resource allocation levels you need, be sure to check the scheduled finish date, costs, and scope. You need to know how your changes affect other areas of the project plan.

Need a New Baseline?

If you made substantial changes to the schedule or costs in your project plan, consider whether you should set a new baseline. Your decision depends on how you intend to use baseline information, in terms of variance monitoring, earned value calculations, and archival data. Which will give you the more meaningful data: the original baseline or a new one based on recent changes?

You can retain the original baseline (usually the best idea in terms of project data integrity) and save the new information as Baseline 1, for example.

Another alternative is to copy the original baseline information to Baseline 1, for example, and then make the new baseline the primary. The primary baseline (that is, Baseline—rather than Baseline 1 or Baseline 2) is always used for earned value calculations.

For more information about copying baseline fields, see "Saving Additional Baselines" on page 453.

Reporting and Analyzing Project Information

Before you can use the sample files for Chapter 13, you'll need to install them from this book's companion content website. For more information about downloading and installing the sample files, see "About the Companion Content" on page xxviii.

CHAPTER 13

Reporting Project Information

By this stage of the game, you've built your project plan and you're using it to track progress and display project information. Because you're now in the execution and control processes of the project, you'll need to share important data with stakeholders. For example, your new test procedure might have worked better than expected, but your materials testing ran into some unanticipated slowdowns. All this information is reflected in the project plan. However, for different audiences and different purposes, you want to highlight certain information and filter out other information to represent a certain focus with professional panache.

You can print views and generate reports built in to Microsoft Project 2010 and use them as an integral part of your project communication plan. These views and reports leverage the power of Project 2010 by presenting the specific focus and clarity required by corporate and program departments. By tailoring the views and reports to the interests of different groups (finance, human resources, and procurement, among others), you can feed the right information to the right people, avoid misunderstandings, and mitigate problems. Project 2010 views and reports are often used for:

- Weekly project team meetings
- Monthly department status conferences
- Quarterly or annual executive reviews

In addition to printing views and generating built-in reports, you can design custom reports to meet your specific project communication needs. Many of these are tabular text-based reports. Others are *visual reports* that use project data for graphical display in Microsoft Excel 2010 or Microsoft Visio 2010.

Establishing Your Communications Plan

Reports are instrumental in effective project management. As part of the initial project planning, you'll determine the requirements for reporting, including:

- **Report recipients** Who needs to see the reports? Stakeholders throughout the organization and within the project team need to see certain reports tailored to their areas of responsibility. For example, you might generate one report for your team members, another one for team leads and resource managers, and yet another for executives and customers.
- **Specific content of the reports** What type of information is included? The reports can focus on any aspect of the project; for example, tasks, resource allocation, assignments, costs, and so on. Reports might focus on past successes or current progress. They can provide a forecast of upcoming tasks, costs, or workloads. They might present a high-level summary. They can point out areas of risk or current problems that need resolution.
- **Frequency of report publication** How often should you generate reports? Regularly scheduled project meetings or status reporting often drive the generation of reports. Certain important issues that are being closely watched might warrant report generation more frequently than usual. Be sure to strike a balance between providing up-to-date information often enough and overloading a stakeholder with too detailed or too frequent reporting.

Establishing your communications strategy for a project helps you effectively share realistic progress and estimates. You can point to unexpected changes that present risks. You can avoid larger problems and understand root causes. Specifically, with reports you can:

- Review status
- Compare data
- Check progress on the schedule
- Check resource utilization
- Check budget status
- Watch for any potential problems looming in the future
- Help stakeholders make decisions affecting the project

Using the appropriate Project 2010 views and reports on a regular basis for progress analysis and communication is a key component of effective project management. By implementing a communications plan, including regular presentations of reports to stakeholders, you can keep interested parties aware of crucial information and trends.

Project Management Practices: Communications Management

Communication is a vital element of successful project management. Effective project communication ensures that relevant information is generated, collected, and distributed in a timely manner to the appropriate project stakeholders. Different stakeholders need different kinds of project information—from the team members carrying out the project tasks, to customers sponsoring the project, to executives making strategic decisions regarding the project and the organization. Your stakeholders don't just receive project information; they also generate it. When all your stakeholders share project information, people are linked and ideas are generated—all of which contributes to the ultimate success of the project.

The first stage of effective project communications management is communications planning. This stage should take place in the initiating and planning processes for the project, in conjunction with scope and activity development. As you develop and build your project plan, you also need to determine what types of communication will be necessary throughout the life of the project.

Determine what tools you have at your disposal and how your project team communicates most effectively. You might have weekly meetings and weekly status reports. Perhaps you'll also have monthly resource management and cost management reviews. Other possible communication vehicles include presentations, e-mail, letters, a SharePoint site, or an intranet site. You'll likely use a combination of these vehicles for different aspects of project management and different audiences.

If you're using Microsoft Project Server 2010 and Microsoft Project Web App, you have a very effective means of communicating electronically with your team members and other stakeholders. You can automate the flow of progress information about the project, including progress updates, timesheets, and narrative status reporting. Stakeholders can also review major project views. Because Microsoft SharePoint Server 2010 is integrated with Project Server 2010, you can store reports, manage risks, and track issues.

NEW!

Another excellent means for electronic project communication is the use of SharePoint Server 2010 for nonenterprise workgroup collaboration, which is new in Project 2010. For more information, see Chapter 21, "Collaborating as a Team by Using SharePoint."

Whichever tools you use, you'll be executing your communications plan while the project is being carried out. You'll report on current project status, especially as it relates to the schedule, budget, scope, and resource utilization. You'll also report on overall progress, describing the accomplishments of the project team to date and what is yet to be done. Finally, you'll make forecasts by using project plan information to predict future progress on tasks and anticipate potential problems.

Tasks will be completed, milestones met, deliverables handed off, and phases concluded. Your communications management strategy provides the means for documenting project results and the receipt of deliverables as each stage of the project is completed.

Using Views to Report Project Information

Suppose you've been tracking and managing your project for some time now by using the Gantt Chart, the Resource Sheet, and other Project 2010 views. You can set up one of these views to contain exactly the fields of information you need and then print it to create a kind of interactive report. By printing views, you can share pertinent information with team members and stakeholders. You can include printed views in project status reports and in progress meetings.

Setting Up and Printing Views

To set up, preview, and print a view, follow these steps:

1. Open the view and arrange the data as you want it to appear when it's printed.

   For more information about available views and arranging information in those views, see Chapter 4, "Viewing Project Information."

2. On the File tab, click Print.

   NEW!

   The Print Backstage view appears, as shown in Figure 13-1. The Print Backstage view provides print options and a preview of the view as it will be printed.

INSIDE OUT You can't print just anything

There are some restrictions about which views you can and cannot print, and some guidelines about how to print certain types of views, as follows:

- Form views, such as the Task Form or Resource Form, cannot be printed.
- Combination (split-screen) views, such as the Resource Allocation view made up of the Resource Usage view and the Leveling Gantt, cannot be printed as a combination. However, you can print one part of a split screen at a time. Click in the pane of the view you want to print. The exception, of course, is if the selected pane is a form view.
- If you keep the Timeline above your views, you effectively have a combination view. Click in the main view pane to print that view; click in the Timeline to print the Timeline.
- Divided views, such as Gantt views or the Team Planner (available in Microsoft Project Professional 2010), have a table on the left and a timesheet on the right. Such divided views are not considered combination split-screen views, and therefore the entire view prints.
- A special combination view is the Compare Projects view. The upper pane of the Compare Projects view contains the comparison report showing the differences and similarities between the two projects being compared. The lower pane shows the project files being compared in two pane segments. While you cannot print the entire combination view, you can print any of the three segments individually by clicking in its pane. For more information, see "Comparing Project Plans Side by Side" on page 1223.

3. In the lower-right area of the middle pane of the view, click Page Setup.

   The Page Setup dialog box appears, as shown in Figure 13-2.

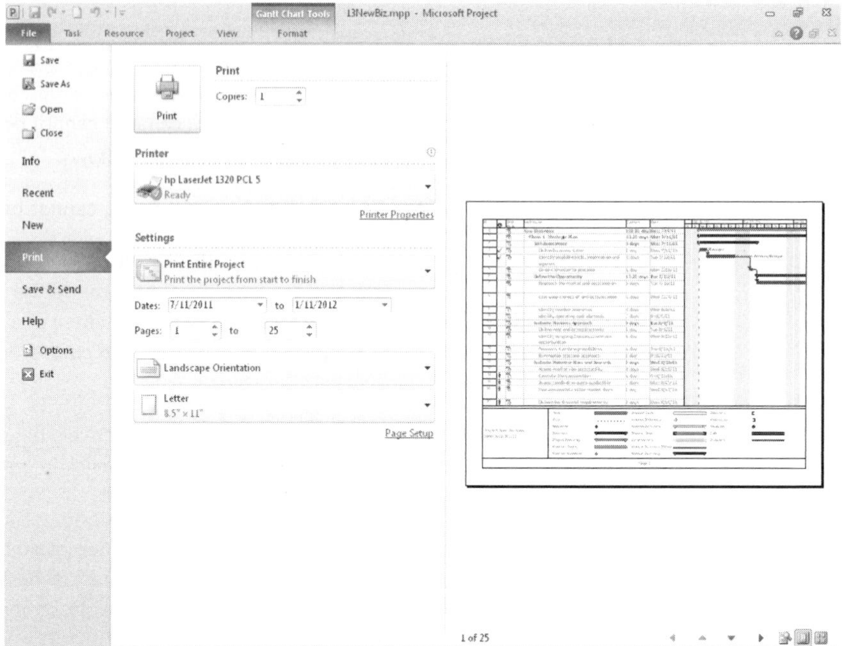

Figure 13-1 The Print Backstage view replaces the old Print dialog box and Print Preview window in a single view.

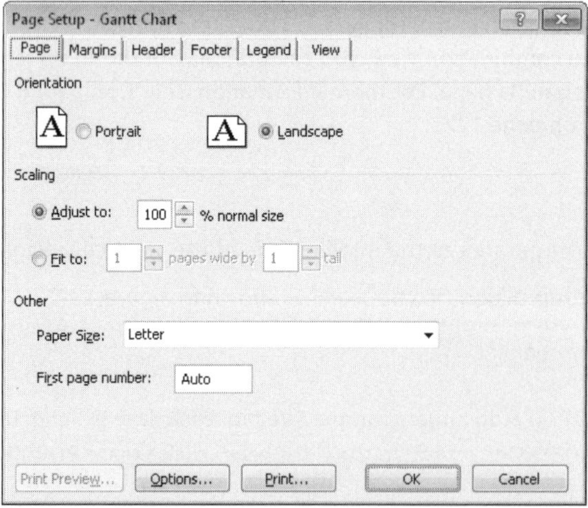

Figure 13-2 Use the Page Setup dialog box to specify page scaling, margins, headers, footers, and more.

4. Specify the options you want for the printed view by using controls on the various tabs.

5. When you are finished, click OK to return to the Print Backstage view.

   The changes you made are reflected in the preview pane on the right.

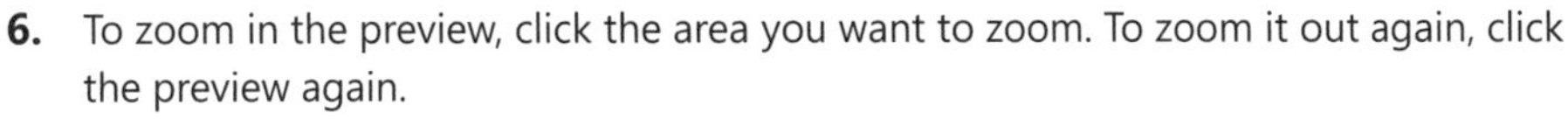

6. To zoom in the preview, click the area you want to zoom. To zoom it out again, click the preview again.

   You can also zoom using the Actual Size, Full Page, and Multiple Pages buttons in the lower-right corner of the preview pane.

Actual Size

Page Down

7. Use the arrow buttons in the lower-right corner of the preview pane to page through the view.

8. To make further adjustments to the page layout, click Page Setup in the middle pane again.

   If you need to adjust the view itself, click one of the other tabs on the ribbon, such as Task or Format, to return to the editable view.

9. In the middle pane, specify any printing options, such as the number of copies, which printer is being used, which pages are being printed, and so on.

Print

10. When you're ready, in the upper-left corner of the middle pane, click Print.

INSIDE OUT The Print Backstage view provides scant preview flexibility

While the new Print Backstage view conveniently puts printer options and the print preview together in one view, this convenience limits flexibility when you are scrutinizing the view being printed. Some limitations are as follows:

- **You can only zoom between actual size (just a fragment), full size (small), and multiple pages (smaller still).**
- **You can't make the preview area larger by dragging the divider between the middle pane; the pane sizes are fixed.**
- **You can't see the preview in a full screen as in previous versions of Microsoft Project.**

Because of this, your best options for closer examination are to just print out the view or save it as a PDF/XPS document.

Create PDF/XPS

To save it as a PDF/XPS document, on the File tab, click Save & Send. Under File Types, click Create PDF/XPS Document. In the right pane, click Create PDF/XPS. Browse to the location where you want to save the file, and then click OK. Make any necessary changes in the Document Export Options dialog box, and then click OK.

You can customize the zoom level and page through the PDF file to see the detail you want. If you need to make changes to the view or the print layout, click the appropriate tab and try again.

For more information, see "Saving a View as a PDF File" on page 579.

Specifying Options for Printed Views

The following list highlights key options available on the six tabs of the Page Setup dialog box, which controls how your view looks when printed. To display this dialog box, click File, Print, and then near the bottom of the middle pane of the Print Backstage view, click Page Setup.

- **Page tab** Specifies whether the view should be printed in portrait or landscape orientation and whether the view should be scaled up or down to fit on a page.
- **Margins tab** Specifies the size of each of the four margins and whether a border should be printed around the page.

Insert File Name

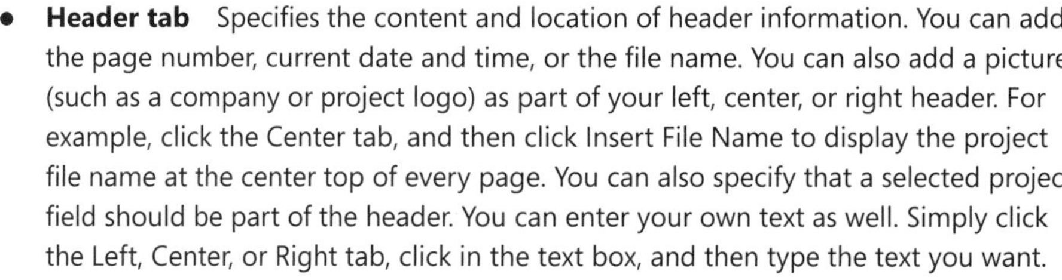

- **Header tab** Specifies the content and location of header information. You can add the page number, current date and time, or the file name. You can also add a picture (such as a company or project logo) as part of your left, center, or right header. For example, click the Center tab, and then click Insert File Name to display the project file name at the center top of every page. You can also specify that a selected project field should be part of the header. You can enter your own text as well. Simply click the Left, Center, or Right tab, click in the text box, and then type the text you want.

Insert Current Date

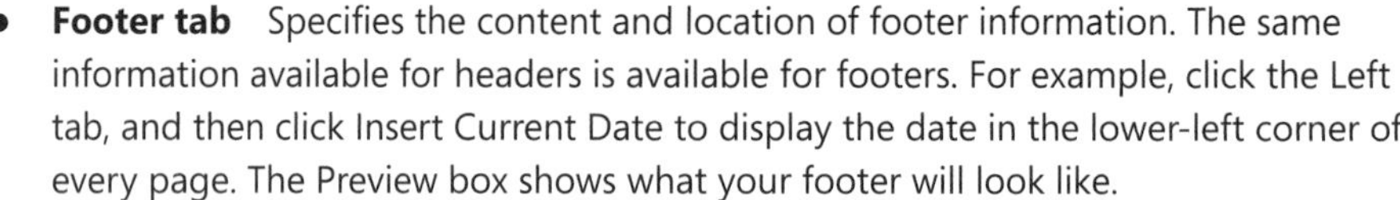

- **Footer tab** Specifies the content and location of footer information. The same information available for headers is available for footers. For example, click the Left tab, and then click Insert Current Date to display the date in the lower-left corner of every page. The Preview box shows what your footer will look like.
- **Legend tab** Specifies the content and location of a view's legend, which specifies what symbols or bars on the view represent. For example, in a print out of the Gantt Chart, the legend includes a key for the task bars, summary bars, deadlines, and milestone symbols. By default, the legend appears on the bottom two inches of every page and includes the project's title and the current date. The options available for headers and footers are also available for legends, and you can also type your own information.
- **View tab** Specifies which elements you want printed on each page—for example, notes, blank pages, or sheet columns. The options available on this tab vary based on the view currently selected for printing.

INSIDE OUT **Be careful when inserting the current date and time in a printed view**

Insert Current Time

The Insert Current Date and Insert Current Time buttons take their information from your computer's system clock. This date and time will change to reflect the date and time when you print the view. However, you might prefer to print a fixed date or time, perhaps one that specifies when the project was last updated, rather than last printed. In this case, in the Alignment area of the Page Setup dialog box, simply type the date or time in the Left, Center, or Right tab text box itself.

Drawing in a Gantt View

NEW!

You might want to highlight certain items in a Gantt view before printing it out. New in Project 2010 is a set of drawing tools similar to those available in other Microsoft Office programs. The only place you can draw in is the chart area of a Gantt view. To mark up a schedule in a Gantt area, do the following:

Drawing

1. On the Format tab, in the Drawings group, click Drawing, and then click the drawing tool you want.

   You can choose from Arrow, Arc, Oval, Polygon, Rectangle, Line, and Text Box.

2. In the chart area of the Gantt view, drag from one point to another to draw the shape, or for polygons, to draw the first segment.

3. If you want to change the order in which elements appear—for example, to display a line in front of a filled rectangle—select the element you want to reorder. Click Format, Drawings, Drawing, and then click Bring To Front, Bring Forward, Send To Back, or Send Backward.

Use a View in Another Application

When reporting on your project, sometimes you might prefer to include a Project 2010 view as part of a Microsoft Word 2010 document or a Microsoft PowerPoint 2010 presentation slide. You can copy a view in Project 2010 and paste it as an image file into another application.

For more information about copying a view and using the graphic in another application, see "Copying a Picture of a View" on page 651.

Generating Text and Visual Reports

In addition to the ability to print views, Project 2010 comes with more than 40 built-in reports that you can simply select, preview, and print. These reports compile the most commonly used sets of information needed to manage a project, coordinate resources, control costs, analyze potential problems, and communicate progress.

When you select and generate a report, information is drawn from selected fields throughout your project. That information is laid out in the predetermined report design or template, in either discrete or summarized form, depending on the specific report. You can generate an up-to-date report minutes before the start of a meeting, and the report instantly reflects the very latest changes you made or that team members have submitted.

You can generate two categories of reports: text-based reports and visual reports. The text-based reports compile information into a tabular format within Project 2010. Visual reports automatically compile and export project information to either Excel or Visio, where it is presented in a graphic such as a column chart or flow diagram.

Working with Text-Based Reports

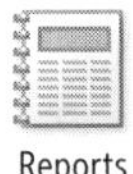
Reports

To see the list of available text-based reports, click Project, Reports, Reports. The Reports dialog box appears, showing six report categories. (See Figure 13-3.)

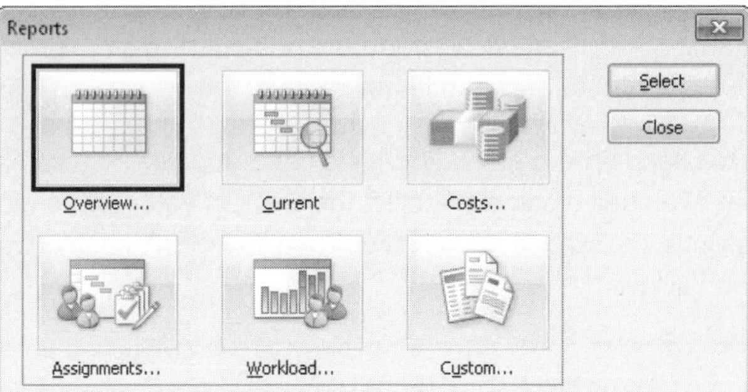

Figure 13-3 There are five categories for 22 built-in text-based reports, plus a Custom category for designing your own report.

The text report categories are:

- Overview
- Current
- Costs

- Assignments
- Workload
- Custom

You might find that reports in a certain category are best suited to one type of audience, whereas reports in another category are better for another type of audience. For example, cost reports might be most appropriate for meetings with the finance department, but you might prefer to distribute assignment reports to team leads.

To generate these reports, Project 2010 gathers information from a particular time period, from certain tables, and with a particular filter applied as appropriate for the requirements of the specific report. Information is formatted with bands, highlights, fonts, and other professional layout considerations.

To select and print a text report, follow these steps:

1. On the Project tab, in the Reports group, click Reports.
2. In the Reports dialog box, double-click the category you want.

   As shown in Figure 13-4, a dialog box appears, listing the available reports in the selected category.

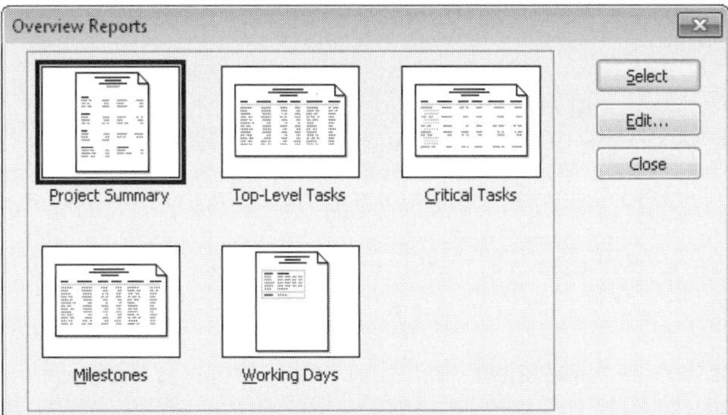

Figure 13-4 The Overview Reports dialog box shows the available summary reports.

3. Double-click the report you want.
4. If a dialog box prompts you for more information, such as a date range, enter the information, and then click OK.

   The report appears in the Print Backstage view, providing print options and a preview of the report as it will be printed, as shown in Figure 13-5.

Indicators Resource Name Work

Business Advisor

ID	Task Name	Units	Work	Delay	Start
4	Identify available skills, information and support	100%	32 hrs	0 days	Tue 7/12/11
7	Research the market and competition	100%	48 hrs	0 days	Tue 7/19/11
9	Identify needed resources	100%	16 hrs	0 days	Wed 8/3/11
17	Assess market size and stability	100%	16 hrs	0 days	Wed 8/10/11
18	Estimate the competition	100%	8 hrs	0 days	Fri 8/12/11
19	Assess needed resource availability	100%	16 hrs	0 days	Mon 8/15/11
20	Evaluate realistic initial market share	100%	8 hrs	0 days	Wed 8/17/11
21	Determine financial requirements	100%	16 hrs	0 days	Mon 8/15/11
28	Access available information	100%	8 hrs	0 days	Tue 8/23/11
29	Create market analysis plan	100%	16 hrs	0 days	Wed 8/24/11
30	Implement market analysis plan	100%	40 hrs	0 days	Fri 8/26/11
31	Identify competition	100%	16 hrs	0 days	Fri 9/2/11
32	Summarize the market	100%	16 hrs	0 days	Tue 9/6/11
33	Identify target market niche	100%	8 hrs	0 days	Thu 9/8/11
46	Confirm decision to proceed	100%	0 hrs	0 days	Thu 9/29/11
49	Describe the vision and opportunity	100%	8 hrs	0 days	Thu 9/29/11
50	List assumptions	100%	8 hrs	0 days	Fri 9/30/11
51	Describe the market	100%	8 hrs	0 days	Mon 10/3/11
52	Describe the new business	100%	8 hrs	0 days	Tue 10/4/11
53	Describe strengths, weaknesses, assets and threats	100%	8 hrs	0 days	Wed 10/5/11
54	Estimate sales volume during startup period	100%	8 hrs	0 days	Thu 10/6/11
55	Forecast operating costs	100%	8 hrs	0 days	Fri 10/7/11
56	Establish pricing strategy	100%	8 hrs	0 days	Mon 10/10/11
57	Forecast revenue	100%	8 hrs	0 days	Tue 10/11/11
58	Summarize pro-forma financial statement.	100%	16 hrs	0 days	Wed 10/12/11
59	Develop break-even analysis	100%	8 hrs	0 days	Fri 10/14/11
60	Develop cash-flow projection	100%	8 hrs	0 days	Mon 10/17/11
61	Identify licensing and permitting requirements	100%	8 hrs	0 days	Tue 10/18/11
62	Develop startup plan	100%	16 hrs	0 days	Wed 10/19/11
63	Develop sales and marketing strategy	100%	8 hrs	0 days	Fri 10/21/11
64	Develop distribution structure	100%	8 hrs	0 days	Mon 10/24/11
65	Describe risks and opportunities	100%	16 hrs	0 days	Tue 10/25/11
66	Publish the business plan	100%	8 hrs	0 days	Thu 10/27/11
67	Confirm decision to proceed	100%	0 hrs	0 days	Fri 10/28/11
85	Establish security plan	100%	16 hrs	0 days	Wed 11/30/11
87	Establish an advertising program	100%	16 hrs	0 days	Tue 11/1/11
88	Develop a logo	100%	8 hrs	0 days	Thu 11/3/11
89	Order promotional materials	100%	8 hrs	0 days	Fri 11/4/11

Peers

ID	Task Name	Units	Work	Delay	Start	Finish
9	Identify needed resources	100%	16 hrs	0 days	Wed 8/3/11	Fri 8/5/11
46	Confirm decision to proceed	100%	0 hrs	0 days	Thu 9/29/11	Thu 9/29/11

Figure 13-5 The Print Backstage view includes at least a partial image of the report showing how it will look when printed.

5. Click an area of the report to zoom in on that area. Click a second time to zoom back out again.

Multiple Pages

You can also zoom by using the Actual Size, Full Page, and Multiple Pages buttons in the lower-right corner of the preview pane.

6. In the lower-right area of the middle pane of the Print Backstage view, click Page Setup to change the page orientation, scaling, margins, header, or footer.

After clicking OK, your changes are reflected in the preview pane for the report.

Page Up

7. Use the arrow buttons in the lower-right corner of the preview pane to page through the view.

8. In the middle pane, specify printing options such as the page range and number of copies.

9. When you're ready, in the upper-left corner of the middle pane, click Print.

Save a Text Report as a PDF File

You can save Project 2010 views as a PDF file without installing any other program. However, you cannot save a Project 2010 text report as a PDF file unless you have an Adobe PDF printer driver installed on your computer.

To print using your Adobe PDF printer driver, in the middle pane of the Print Backstage view, click the arrow next to the name of the currently selected printer. All available printers, including Adobe PDF, are listed. Click Adobe PDF. Click Print. In the Save PDF File As dialog box, browse to the location where you want to save the PDF file, change the file name if you want, and then click OK.

INSIDE OUT Text reports cannot be saved or published to the web as is

Each text-based report in Project 2010 has a preset format and is generated from current project data, so you cannot save a built-in report, as such. Essentially, it's already saved. As long as your project file is saved, you can always quickly generate the report again using current information.

For the same reasons, project text reports cannot be converted to HTML or XML format because the reports are designed only for previewing and printing, and they cannot be saved as a discrete unit.

Copy

However, if you do want to save an instance of a report, perhaps for a historical record of a moment in time or for a series of certain reports throughout the project life cycle, you can periodically copy and save pictures of the tables on which the report is based. First apply the table on which the report is based. On the Task tab, in the Clipboard group, click the arrow next to Copy, and then click Copy Picture. Select the To GIF Image File option, and then click Browse to select the location and enter the file name.

Another good option is to print the report as a PDF file.

If your weekly routine has you generating a particular report and saving it as a GIF file or creating a PDF file, consider creating a macro to do this for you each week.

For more information about creating macros, see Chapter 30, "Automating Your Work with Macros."

Working with Visual Reports in Excel and Visio

Just as text reports present project information in a tabular format, visual reports present project information graphically. When you generate a visual report, specific project data is compiled and sent to Excel or Visio. A PivotTable or PivotDiagram structure specifies how the data is to be displayed in the chart or diagram.

For an Excel visual report, a PivotTable is generated, from which a chart, such as a column or pie chart, is drawn.

A Visio visual report generates a PivotDiagram, a collection of boxes or other shapes arranged in a tree structure.

In either case, you can change the arrangement of the source data to display the information from different perspectives as needed.

Visual Reports

To see the list of built-in visual reports, on the Project tab, in the Reports group, click Visual Reports. The Visual Reports - Create Report dialog box appears, as shown in Figure 13-6.

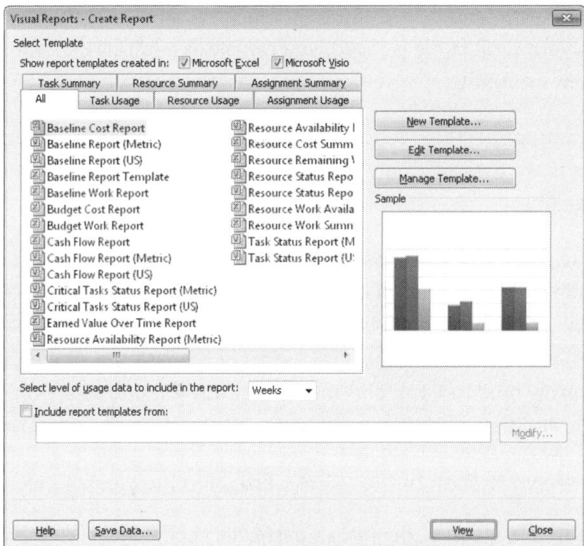

Figure 13-6 There are six categories for 22 built-in visual reports.

The visual report categories are:

- Task Summary
- Resource Summary
- Assignment Summary
- Task Usage
- Resource Usage
- Assignment Usage

The summary reports are more high-level, while the usage reports have specific detail.

To generate a visual report, follow these steps:

1. On the Project tab, in the Reports group, click Visual Reports.
2. In the Visual Reports - Create Report dialog box, click the tab for the report category you want.

   You might find it easier to simply view the All tab and see the list of all 22 visual reports in one place.
3. If you only want to see the list of Excel visual reports, clear the Microsoft Visio check box at the top of the dialog box. If you only want to see the list of Visio reports, clear the Microsoft Excel check box.

   Note that you must have Microsoft Excel or Microsoft Visio installed on your computer to generate the Excel or Visio visual reports. If Visio is not installed, the dialog box only shows the Excel report templates.
4. Click the report you want. Icons next to each report name indicate whether it's an Excel or Visio report template.

   A thumbnail representation of the report appears in the Sample box.
5. In the box labeled Select Level Of Usage Data To Include In The Report, select the period of time you want to use. The default is Weeks.
6. Click View.

   Project 2010 gathers the information required by the selected report template, builds the OLAP (online analytical processing) cube (the set of fields that will be used), opens the template in the target application—either Excel or Visio—and finally displays the visual report in that application, as shown in Figure 13-7.

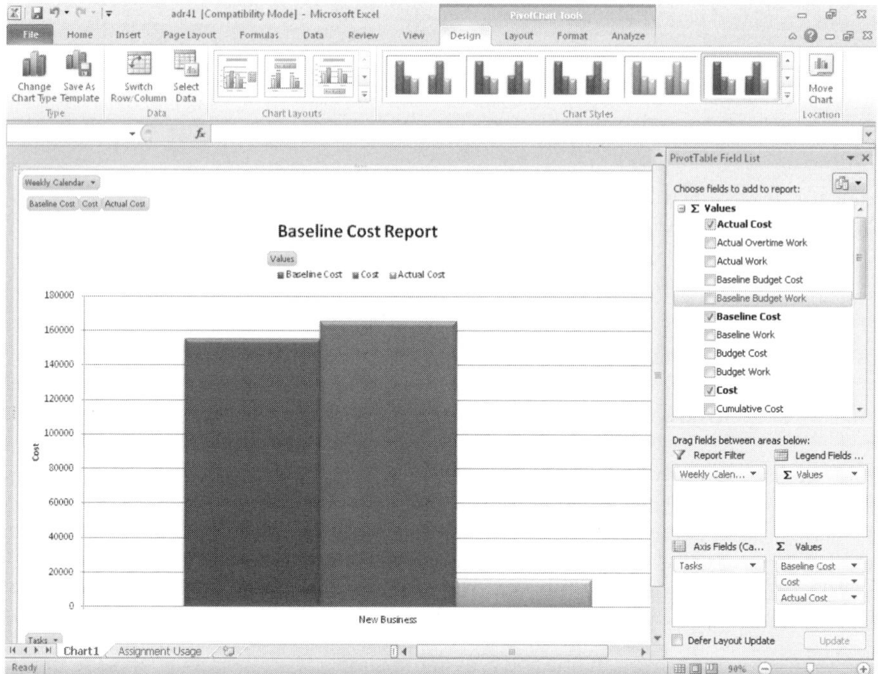

Figure 13-7 When you run an Excel report template, the resulting report is displayed in Excel.

7. In Excel, if you want to view or change the PivotTable on which the report is based, click the second worksheet tab at the bottom of the Excel window. It's named something like Assignment Usage or Task Summary, as shown in Figure 13-8.

8. To print a report in Excel 2010 or Visio 2010, on the File tab, click Print. In the Print Backstage view, make any changes to how the report should look when printed, such as headers or page orientation, specify any print options such as page range and number of copies, and then click the Print button at the top of the center pane.

9. To save a report in Excel 2010 or Visio 2010, on the Quick Access Toolbar, click Save. Specify where you want to save the report, give it a name, and then click Save.

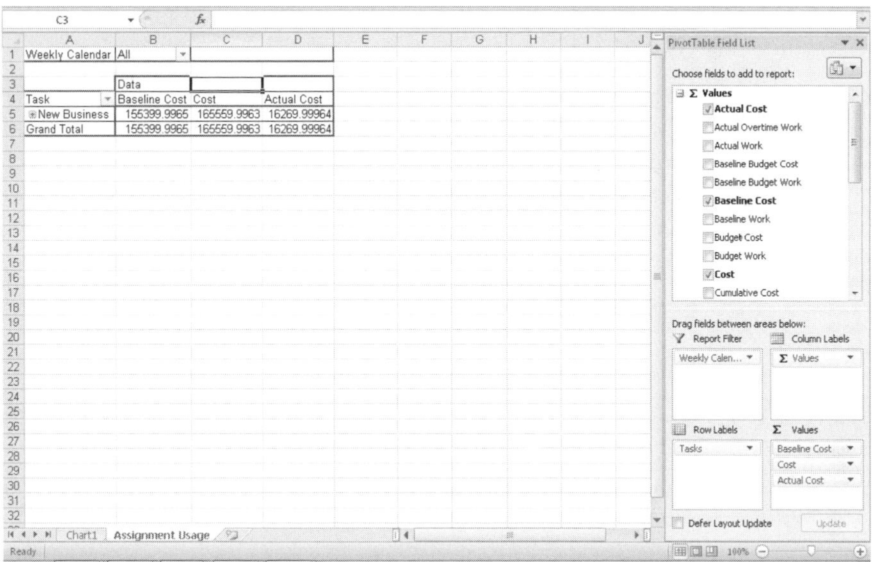

Figure 13-8 The Assignment Usage tab displays the crosstab table on which the Excel chart is based.

Generating the Right Reports

This section categorizes each of the built-in text and visual reports by the activities or requirements that dictate the different ways you might need to present your project information. There are overview reports, reports about current activities, reports about costs, and reports about resource allocation. These groupings can help you determine which report would best suit your needs in a specific situation.

Remember, to generate a text report, click Project, Reports, Reports. To generate a visual report, click Project, Reports, Visual Reports. Each report description in this section indicates whether the report is a text or visual report and also specifies the category in which the report is found.

This section describes the reports provided by Project 2010. Keep in mind, however, that the text reports and visual reports can be modified in a variety of ways. You can also create your own custom reports. Such techniques are described later in "Revising a Built-In Report" on page 564 and "Building a Custom Report" on page 571.

Note

In many cases throughout this section, there is no illustration of a report with its description. This is because many of the reports are so dense with information that to shrink them to illustration size would render them illegible. The best idea is for you to open a project, either a real project or a sample, and generate the reports yourself while you read about them here. You'll see the details of what each report can provide for you, and therefore understand how you might actually use a given report.

INSIDE OUT Sometimes the best report isn't a report

In some cases, a printed view provides information more suited to your requirements or more readily available for printing.

Chapter 10, "Checking and Adjusting the Project Plan," includes information on views to use when reviewing the project plan just before project execution starts. Chapter 12, "Responding to Changes in Your Project," focuses on views most helpful when reviewing project information during project execution.

In these chapters, refer to the following sections, which provide guidance on the right views to use in specific situations:

- **Schedule** "Viewing Finish Dates and the Critical Path" on page 384 and "Monitoring Schedule Progress" on page 486.
- **Costs** "Viewing Project Costs" on page 397 and "Monitoring Project Costs" on page 502.
- **Resources** "Viewing Resource Workloads" on page 404 and "Monitoring Resource Workload" on page 512.

Experiment with the text reports, visual reports, and views. As you familiarize yourself with all the ways in which you can present project information, you'll quickly see which are best for your needs.

Summarizing with Overview Reports

Overview reports are well suited for executives and members of upper management who need more generalized project information and status. Overview reports provide summary project information at a glance.

Using the Project Summary Report

The Project Summary text report, in the Overview category, focuses on the most important information in the project plan and is particularly useful to upper management because of its concise presentation focusing on the "bottom line" of overall project data, including finish dates and costs.

The information in the Project Summary report is the same as that available in the Project Statistics dialog box. It includes a high-level summary of rolled-up dates, duration, work, costs, task status, and resource status, as shown on Figure 13-9. The format is designed for easy comparison of baseline (planned) versus actual data.

Dates		
Start:	Mon 7/11/11	Finish:
Baseline Start:	Mon 7/11/11	Baseline
Actual Start:	Mon 7/11/11	Actual F
Start Variance:	0 days	Finish V

Duration		
Scheduled:	132.25 days	Remainir
Baseline:	124 days	Actual:
Variance:	8.25 days	Percent (

Work		
Scheduled:	1,456 hrs	Remainir
Baseline:	1,368 hrs	Actual:
Variance:	88 hrs	Percent (

Costs		
Scheduled:	$165,560.00	Remainir
Baseline:	$155,400.00	Actual:
Variance:	$10,160.00	

Figure 13-9 The Project Summary report shows overall project information and allows for comparisons with the baseline.

Using the Top-Level Tasks Report

The Top-Level Tasks text report, in the Overview category, presents information about the project plan's summary tasks. It displays the results of the top summary tasks, rolling up all the data from any subtasks. This is most useful for organizations that are clearly divided into functional groups. If each group has its own section at the same level in the project plan, the Top-Level Tasks report quickly shows the status of each group's efforts, as shown in Figure 13-10.

Top Level Tasks as of Mon 8/1/11
New Business

Task Name	Duration	Start	Finish
New Business	132.25 days	Mon 7/11/11	Wed 1/11,
Phase 1 - Strategic Plan	31.25 days	Mon 7/11/11	Tue 8/23/
Phase 2 - Define the Business Op|	27 days	Tue 8/23/11	Thu 9/29/
Phase 3 - Plan for Action	21 days	Thu 9/29/11	Fri 10/28/
Phase 4 - Proceed With Startup P	53 days	Fri 10/28/11	Wed 1/11,

Figure 13-10 The Top-Level Tasks report shows summary task information.

The Top-Level Tasks report is based on the Summary table for tasks, with the Top Level Tasks filter applied. The report includes the top-level summary tasks and their rolled-up durations, start and finish dates, percentage complete, cost, and work.

Using the Critical Tasks Report

The Critical Tasks text report, in the Overview category, filters your project information to show only those tasks that are most likely to affect the project finish date; that is, critical tasks. This report provides a subtable containing successor task information under each task, which shows the other tasks that will be affected by progress on the critical task. The report also lists any notes entered on critical tasks and any indicators from the Task Entry view.

The Critical Tasks report is typically used to explain why problems are occurring in a project. Because task information is always changing as you enter schedule progress, it's a good idea to print the Critical Tasks report just shortly before presenting it for review.

The Critical Tasks report is based on the task Entry table with the Critical filter applied. The report includes durations, start and finish dates, indicators, notes, and successor fields for all critical tasks.

For more information about critical tasks, see "Working with the Critical Path and Critical Tasks" on page 367.

INSIDE OUT Decipher subtables in a text report

Certain text reports include additional task, resource, or assignment information. For example, the Critical Tasks report adds successor information after each critical task listed in the table. The Tasks Starting Soon report adds assignment schedule information after each upcoming task listed.

At first, this additional detail looks like so much clutter in the report. The details are in a subtable below the name of the associated task or resource. This format takes some getting used to, but it's worth the time because it contains such pertinent and useful information.

But if you really hate the additional detail, you can get rid of it. Click the report name, click Edit, and then click the Details tab. Under Task, Resource, or Assignment, clear the check box that represents the additional detailed information you want to remove.

Using the Critical Tasks Status Report in Visio

The Critical Tasks Status Report is a Visio visual report in the Task Summary category. It displays a PivotDiagram showing scheduled work and remaining work for critical and noncritical tasks, as shown in Figure 13-11. The data bar at the bottom of each node specifies the percentage of work complete.

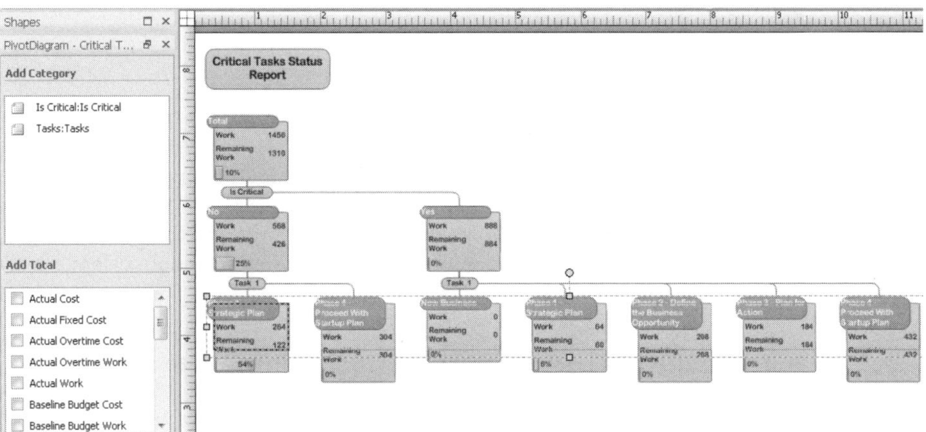

Figure 13-11 The Critical Tasks Status Report shows scheduled work, remaining work, and percentage of work complete for critical and noncritical tasks.

Using the Milestones Report

The Milestones text report, in the Overview category, filters your project tasks to show only milestone tasks and associated information. This high-level report helps you focus on key events and dates in your project.

The Milestones report is based on the task Entry table with the Milestones filter applied. The report includes durations, start and finish dates, indicators, and notes for all milestone tasks.

For more information about milestones, see "Creating Milestones in Your Schedule" on page 231.

Using the Working Days Report

The Working Days text report, in the Overview category, specifies which days are working days and which are nonworking days for each base calendar used throughout the project. (See Figure 13-12.) You might use several base calendars to reflect the scheduled working days of different functional groups or to reflect working times specified by labor contracts.

Base Calendar as of Mon 8/1/:
New Business

BASE CALENDAR:	Standard
Day	Hours
Sunday	Nonworking
Monday	8:00 AM - 12:00 PM, 1:00 PM - 5:00 PM
Tuesday	8:00 AM - 12:00 PM, 1:00 PM - 5:00 PM
Wednesday	8:00 AM - 12:00 PM, 1:00 PM - 5:00 PM
Thursday	8:00 AM - 12:00 PM, 1:00 PM - 5:00 PM
Friday	8:00 AM - 12:00 PM, 1:00 PM - 5:00 PM
Saturday	Nonworking
Exceptions:	None

Figure 13-12 The Working Days report shows working days for each base calendar used in the project, whether for the overall project, for resources, or for tasks.

The Working Days report shows working and nonworking time for each base calendar as well as any exceptions to the norm. **For more information about calendars, see "Setting Your Project Calendar" on page 84.**

Focusing on Tasks with Schedule Progress Reports

Reports that focus on the schedule and current progress of tasks are useful for everyday or weekly checks to make sure that tasks are moving along according to plan. Such reports are designed for more frequent usage and geared toward audiences more directly involved with the work of the project. For example, project teams can use these reports at weekly status meetings. Functional groups in a project can use these reports to quickly check how they are measuring up against the project plan. You might rely on these reports toward the end of projects, when current task status must be monitored frequently.

Text reports specializing in schedule progress are found in the Current Activity Reports dialog box. There are six text reports in the Current category, as shown in Figure 13-13.

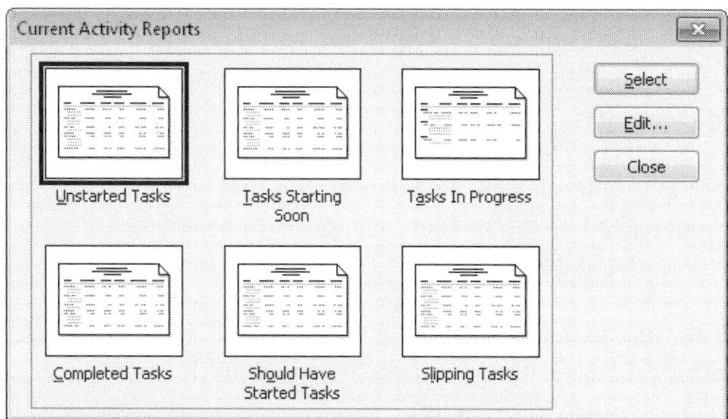

Figure 13-13 The Current Activity Reports dialog box shows the available text reports for the Current category.

Visual reports specializing in schedule progress are found in the Assignment Summary and Assignment Usage categories.

Using the Unstarted Tasks Report

Tasks in the project that have not had any actual progress reported are displayed in the Unstarted Tasks text report, in the Current category. Generally, the number of tasks displayed decreases as the project progresses, so this report can be especially useful toward the end of the project. This information can help with planning expenditures, deploying tools and materials, and quickly assessing the amount of work yet to be done. This report is also effective at showing functional leads and team members the scope of their required efforts.

The Unstarted Tasks report is based on the Entry table with the Unstarted Tasks filter applied. The report includes the task duration, start and finish dates, predecessors, and indicators. Assigned resource schedule information is listed in a subtable under the associated task.

Using the Tasks Starting Soon Report

The Tasks Starting Soon text report, in the Current category, is actually a subset of the Unstarted Tasks report. While the format is similar to that of the Unstarted Tasks report, the difference is that the Date Range filter is applied. You specify the dates for the tasks you want to see in the report.

Using the Tasks In Progress Report

The Tasks In Progress text report, in the Current category, is a handy tool with which you can keep close track of work currently being done. This report quickly shows the amount of work that has started; it also points out tasks that are behind schedule. The in-progress tasks are grouped by month.

Grouping tasks by the month of their start dates helps managers see the longest ongoing tasks that are still unfinished. Using this report regularly helps prevent managers from overlooking (or forgetting) the status updates on lengthy tasks or long-overdue tasks.

The Tasks In Progress report is based on the Entry table with the In Progress Tasks filter applied. The report includes the task duration, start and finish dates, predecessors, indicators, and assignment schedule information.

Using the Completed Tasks Report

The other end of the spectrum of status reports about current progress is the report showing all 100 percent completed tasks, grouped by month, as shown in Figure 13-14.

Completed Tasks as of Mon 8/1/11
New Business

Task Name	Duration	Start	Finish
Define business vision	1 day	Mon 7/11/11	Mon 7/1:
Identify available skills, informati	4 days	Tue 7/12/11	Fri 7/15/:
Decide whether to proceed	1 day	Mon 7/18/11	Mon 7/1ℰ
Research the market and compet	6 days	Tue 7/19/11	Tue 7/26,

Figure 13-14 The Completed Tasks report shows all tasks that are reported as complete so far.

The Completed Tasks text report, in the Current category, is significant for both historical reference and as a record of the team's accomplishments. It provides real data about "lessons learned," helps estimate task durations for future projects, and gives you a general idea of how much work is left to do in the current project. Another important use of this report is to boost team morale, increase motivation, and foster pride in team accomplishments. Although the project goal is paramount, accomplishments and successes to date can be recognized.

The Completed Tasks report is based on the Summary table with the Completed Tasks filter applied. The report includes the task duration, start and finish dates, total cost, and total work.

Using the Should Have Started Tasks Report

The Should Have Started Tasks text report, in the Current category, is most effective when used regularly. This report alerts you to all tasks whose scheduled start dates have passed but for which no progress information has been reported to indicate that work on the task has begun. Sometimes, the data shown in this report reflects missing status updates, making this report an effective tool for improving communication on project progress.

When you select this report, you're prompted to enter a Should Start By date. Any tasks that do not have an actual start date entered and that are scheduled to start on or before a given date (usually the current date) are displayed in this report.

The Should Have Started Tasks report is based on the Variance table with the Should Start By filter applied. Tasks are sorted by start date. The report includes the baseline and scheduled start and finish dates, along with the start variance field. It also includes task notes and subtables for successor tasks to show the tasks immediately affected by those starting late.

Using the Slipping Tasks Report

The Slipping Tasks text report, in the Current category, can only be generated for projects with a baseline saved. The focus of this report is the list of tasks that have started but that will finish after their baseline finish date. The slipping of the finish date can be caused by the start date occurring later than originally planned or by an increase in the duration.

The Slipping Tasks report is based on the Variance table with the Slipping Tasks filter applied. Tasks are sorted by start date. The report includes the baseline and scheduled start and finish dates, along with the start variance field. It also includes task notes and subtables for successor tasks to show the tasks immediately affected by the slipping tasks.

For more information about setting and using a baseline, see Chapter 11, "Setting a Baseline and Updating Progress."

TROUBLESHOOTING

You can't adjust text report column sizes

When you generate a text report, you see the report in the preview area of the Print Backstage view, where you have no control over column widths. There you can specify the content, change font sizes of report elements, adjust the timescale, and modify the headers and footers. This is true whether you're generating a built-in or custom text report.

If you want to change the width of a column in a report, you can do so by changing the width of the column in the table on which the report is based. To find the name of this table, in the Reports dialog box, double-click the category, and then click the name of the report you want to run. Instead of clicking Select, click Edit. On the Definition tab, the Table box shows the name of the table on which the report is based. Apply that table to a task or resource sheet as applicable, and then change the column width of the field by dragging the edges of the column headings. Generate the report, and you'll see that the column width in the report reflects your change.

Remember that you can add and remove fields in a table, and such changes are also reflected in any reports based on that table.

If you find it easier, you might also consider manipulating and printing the sheet view with your table applied.

For more information about printing views, see "Setting Up and Printing Views" on page 528.

You can also adjust the scale of the report so you can fit more columns on a page, or switch the report between portrait and landscape page orientation.

For more information on changing page setup options, see "Adjusting the Page Setup of a Report" on page 569.

For example, suppose that you want to generate the Unstarted Tasks report, but you don't want it to go across two pages. You can change the page setup to reduce the left and right margins to 0.5 inch each, and the scaling to 80 percent.

Using the Baseline Report in Visio

The Baseline Report is a Visio visual report in the Assignment Usage category. It displays a PivotDiagram of the project broken down by quarter and then by task. The diagram compares scheduled work and cost to baseline work and cost for each task. Icons show when scheduled values for work and cost exceed the baseline values.

Using the Baseline Work Report in Excel

The Baseline Work Report is an Excel visual report in the Assignment Usage category. It displays a column chart showing baseline, scheduled, and actual work for each task.

Using the Task Status Report in Visio

The Task Status Report is a Visio visual report in the Assignment Summary category. It displays a PivotDiagram showing work and percentage of work complete for all tasks in the project, as shown in Figure 13-15. Icons show when baseline work exceeds scheduled work, when baseline work equals scheduled work, and when scheduled work exceeds baseline work. The data bar at the bottom of each node indicates the percentage of work complete.

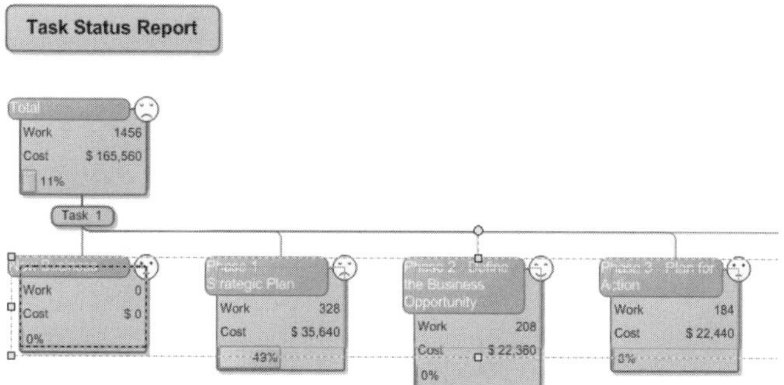

Figure 13-15 The Task Status Report is a Visio diagram that shows work and percentage of work complete for all tasks in the project.

Using the Budget Work Report in Excel

The Budget Work Report is an Excel visual report in the Assignment Usage category. It displays a column chart showing budget, baseline, scheduled, and actual work over time.

Analyzing Budget Status with Cost Reports

Project 2010 cost reports are a powerful and effective means of tracking the fiscal health of a project. By using these reports, you can quickly focus on the pressing cost issues and catch potential problems early. Because the costs are directly tied to the tasks and the resources assigned to those tasks, you can generate these reports without having to rekey or recalculate values—Project 2010 does it all for you.

Text reports specializing in costs are found in the Costs category, where five reports are available for reviewing your project's costs and budget, as shown in Figure 13-16.

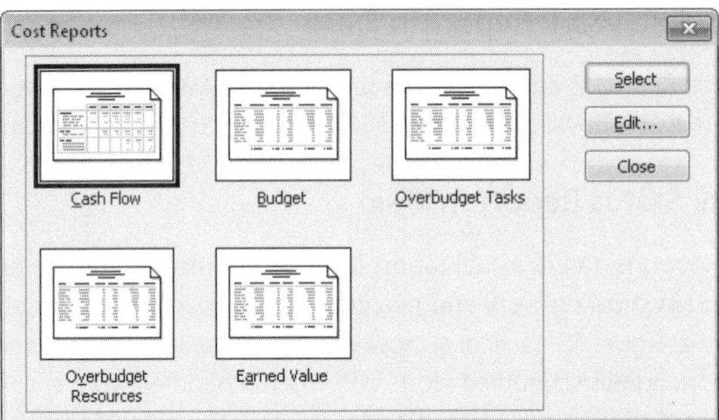

Figure 13-16 Choose one of the available cost-related reports in the Cost Reports dialog box.

Visual reports specializing in costs are found in the Task Usage, Resource Usage, and Assignment Usage categories.

Using the Cash Flow Report

The Cash Flow text report, in the Costs category, is a *crosstab* report that displays total scheduled costs by each task and by each week in the project timespan.

Use this report to see the costs that go into the performance of tasks (assigned human resources, materials, equipment, fees, and fixed costs) per time period. The information shown also enables quick comparisons with baseline budgets or projections, especially when used in conjunction with others, such as the Overbudget Tasks Report, the Tasks In Progress Report, and the Slipping Tasks Report—both to show cost impacts and to clarify budget and earned value figures.

The tasks are listed in order, along with their summary tasks. The costs for each week are totaled in the last column, and the costs for each task are totaled in the last row.

For more information about establishing project costs, see Chapter 9, "Planning Resource and Task Costs."

Using the Cash Flow Report in Excel

The Cash Flow Report in Excel is a visual report in the Task Usage category. Use this report to generate a bar graph with cost and cumulative cost amounts shown over time. This report is based on timephased task data.

Using the Cash Flow Report in Visio

The Cash Flow Report in Visio is a visual report in the Resource Usage category. Use this report to produce a diagram that shows planned and actual costs for your project over time. Costs are broken down by resource type (work, material, cost). An icon displays next to any node in which planned costs exceed baseline costs.

Using the Baseline Cost Report in Excel

The Baseline Cost Report is an Excel visual report in the Assignment Usage category. It displays a column chart comparing baseline, scheduled, and actual costs in groupings by task.

Using the Budget Report

The Budget text report, in the Costs category, lists all project tasks in order of total cost. Use the Budget report to quickly focus on your "big ticket" tasks.

The Budget report is based on the Cost table for tasks. The total scheduled costs for each task are listed, sorted from highest to lowest cost. The total costs include forecasted costs as well as any actual costs that have accrued as a result of tasks started, in progress, or completed. Also included are any task fixed costs and fixed cost accrual (start, end, prorated). The baseline costs and variances between baseline and total costs show whether you're over budget or under budget or exactly as originally planned. The actual and remaining cost fields show costs for completed and in-progress tasks. Each column of cost data is totaled.

Using the Budget Cost Report in Excel

The Budget Cost Report is an Excel visual report in the Assignment Usage category. It displays a column chart showing groupings of budget, baseline, scheduled, and actual costs over time, as shown in Figure 13-17.

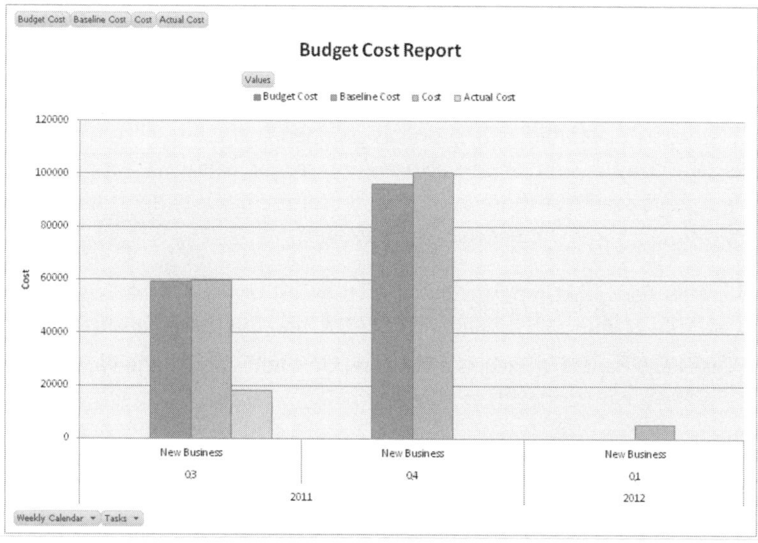

Figure 13-17 The Budget Cost Report shows an Excel column chart of budgeted costs.

Using the Resource Cost Summary Report in Excel

The Resource Cost Summary Report is an Excel visual report in the Resource Usage category. As shown in Figure 13-18, it displays a pie chart representing the distribution of resource costs among the resources assigned to tasks in the project.

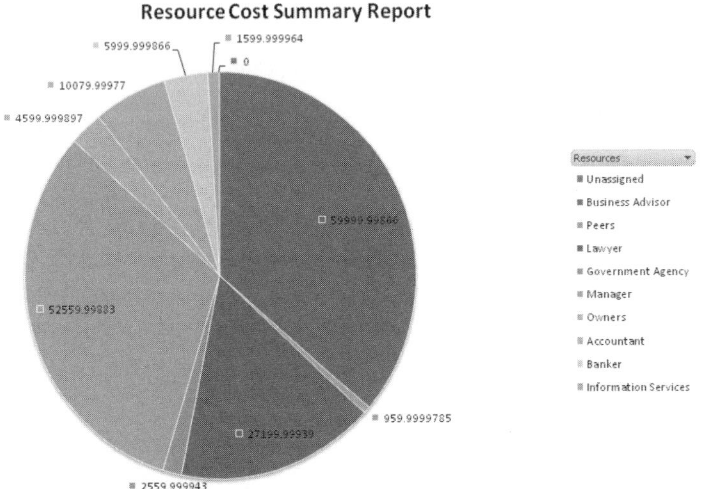

Figure 13-18 In this Resource Cost Summary Report, an Excel pie chart shows that $59,999 is being spent on the business advisor and $10,079 is being spent on the accountant.

Using the Overbudget Tasks Report

The Overbudget Tasks text report, in the Costs category, provides a quick look at all tasks in the project whose actual or scheduled costs are higher than their baseline costs. This includes costs associated with resources assigned to these tasks as well as any fixed costs for tasks. Obviously, this report can be used only for projects with saved baselines. The columns of data are the same as those in the Budget report, but the report filter selects only those tasks whose costs are higher than the baseline.

The Overbudget Tasks report is based on the Cost table with the Cost Overbudget filter applied. The amount of cost variance is listed, and the tasks are sorted in order of the highest variance first. This report is most useful for analyzing the extent of cost overruns for specific tasks.

For more information about adjusting costs to conform to your budget, see "Reducing Project Costs" on page 396.

Using the Overbudget Resources Report

Like the Overbudget Tasks report, the Overbudget Resources report shows the resources whose actual costs exceed those in the baseline plan, as shown in Figure 13-19.

Overbudget Resources as o
New Business

Resource Name	Cost	Baseline Cost	\
Business Advisor	$60,000.00	$52,000.00	
Manager	$52,560.00	$50,400.00	
	$112,560.00	$102,400.00	

Figure 13-19 The Overbudget Resources text report focuses on the resources for which actual and planned costs are exceeding the planned baseline costs.

The Overbudget Resources text report, in the Costs category, is based on the Cost table for resources with the Cost Overbudget filter applied. Tasks are sorted by cost variance. The Cost, Baseline Cost, Variance, Actual Cost, and Remaining Cost columns are included and totaled for all overbudget resources.

Usually, the reason these resources are overbudget is that their tasks are requiring more work than originally planned. This report is most useful for analyzing the extent of cost overruns for specific resources.

For more information about reviewing and controlling costs in your project, see "Monitoring and Adjusting Costs" on page 502.

Using the Earned Value Report

The Earned Value text report, in the Costs category, is based on the concept of comparisons between planned and actual costs. More specifically, *earned value* is the analysis of cost performance based on comparisons between the baseline and actual costs and between the baseline and actual schedule.

Status Date

The earned value analysis always uses a specific date as the reference point for the comparisons being made. This date is referred to as the *status date*, or sometimes the *cutoff date*. To set a status date that's different from today's date, on the Project tab, in the Status group, click the date under Status Date, and then enter a date in the Status Date box.

TROUBLESHOOTING

Project 2010 says there is no data to print

If you try to generate a text report, and a message appears in the preview pane saying that there is no data to print, this typically means that the filter that the report is based on is not returning any fields.

There is no data for you to print.

Most likely, the filter applied to your view or report does not display any tasks or resources. Microsoft Project does not print views or reports on which no tasks or resources are displayed.

Single-click the name of the text report you want, and then select Edit. The dialog box that appears shows how the report is defined, including the fields and filters the report is based on. If there is no data in those fields, or if the applied filter finds no match in your project, this might explain why the report is not generated from your project data.

If you get this message when you're trying to generate the Overbudget Tasks or Overbudget Resources reports, either all your tasks and resources are under budget or right on target. It can also indicate that:

- You haven't entered costs for assigned resources. These costs become a part of your baseline to determine your target budget figures. Display the Resource Sheet and enter costs for resources in the Std. Rate field. You might need to set a new baseline.
- You haven't entered fixed costs for tasks. These costs become a part of your baseline to determine your target budget figures. Apply the Cost table to a task sheet and make any necessary entries in the Fixed Cost field for the tasks. You might need to set a new baseline.

Set Baseline

- You haven't set a baseline yet. The baseline determines your target budget figures. On the Project tab, in the Schedule group, click Set Baseline.

Mark On Track

- You haven't entered any tracking data for in-progress or completed tasks. Select the task(s), and then on the Task tab, in the Schedule group, click the arrow next to Mark On Track, and then click Update Tasks.

The Should Have Started Tasks and Slipping Tasks reports are also based on variances between the current scheduled start dates and the baseline start dates. If no baseline has been saved, or if there is no variance between the baseline start and scheduled start, there is no data to print for this report.

The Earned Value report is based on the Earned Value table for tasks. Every nonsummary task is listed along with its earned value calculations for the following:

- Planned Value (PV), also known as Budgeted Cost of Work Scheduled (BCWS)
- Earned Value (EV), also known as Budgeted Cost of Work Planned (BCWP)
- Actual Cost (AC), also known as Actual Cost of Work Performed (ACWP)
- SV (Schedule Variance)
- CV (Cost Variance)
- EAC (Estimate At Completion)
- BAC (Budget At Completion)
- VAC (Variance At Completion)

Note

By default, the EAC, BAC, and VAC columns of the table flow over onto a second page, even though the report is set up to print in landscape orientation. To adjust the layout so that all columns fit on a single page, click Page Setup in the middle pane of the Print Backstage view. On the Page tab, under Scaling, change the Adjust To percentage to a smaller value, for example 75. (The Fit To option is not available for this report.)

For more information about working with the report layout, see "Adjusting the Page Setup of a Report" on page 569. For more detailed information, including the underlying calculations, about earned value analysis, see Chapter 14, "Analyzing Progress Using Earned Value."

Using the Earned Value Over Time Report in Excel

The Earned Value Over Time Report is an Excel visual report in the Assignment Usage category. It displays a line chart that plots a line each for Earned Value (EV or BCWP), Planned Value (PV or BCWS), and Actual Cost (AC or ACWP). Based on timephased task data, the lines are plotted over time.

Evaluating Resource Allocation with Assignment Reports

Reports that focus on resource assignment work and resource allocation are useful for generating to-do lists for resources and their assigned tasks. This is helping for following up with resources and their current task progress or to determine who has too many assignments in the available time.

As shown in Figure 13-20, four text reports relate to resource assignments.

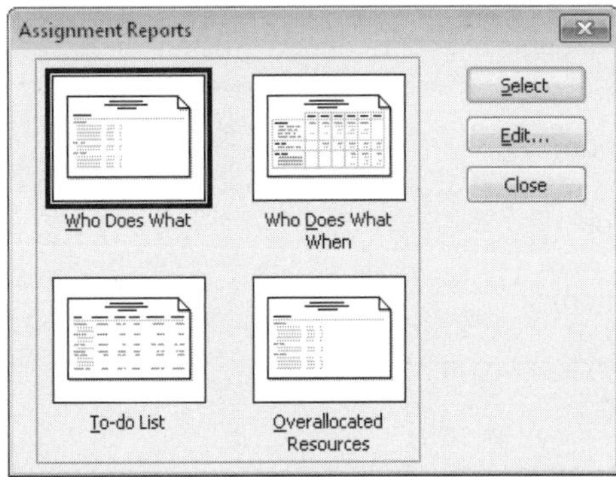

Figure 13-20 The Assignment Reports dialog box lists the reports for resources and their assigned tasks.

Two additional text reports in the Workload report category show assignment work over time either by task or by resource, as shown in Figure 13-21. These reports are excellent tracking tools for seeing the amount of work per task or per resource on a weekly basis. Both are crosstab reports, with a tabular presentation of assigned work by assignment along the left, and by week across the top.

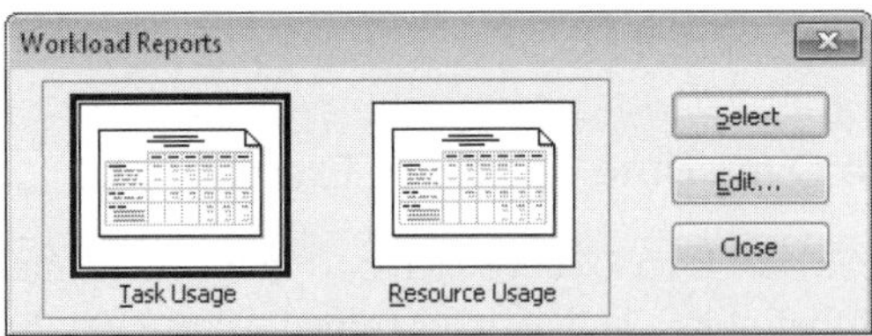

Figure 13-21 The Workload Reports dialog box shows the available reports in this category.

Visual reports specializing in assignments and resource usage are found in the Resource Usage, Resource Summary, and Assignment Summary categories.

Using the Who Does What Report

The Who Does What text report, in the Assignments category, lists the tasks assigned to each resource. It clearly shows the relative number of assignments for all the project resources. This report can also help you or a resource manager plan for coverage when a resource unexpectedly becomes unavailable.

The Who Does What report is based on the Usage table for work resources, and it also shows assignment schedule information.

For more information about making and changing resource assignments, see Chapter 8, "Assigning Resources to Tasks."

Using the Who Does What When Report

The Who Does What When text report, in the Assignments category, is an amplification of the information given in the Who Does What report, adding the daily breakdown of hours of work assigned. And like the Who Does What report, this report can help you plan for coverage when a resource unexpectedly becomes unavailable during a certain period of time.

Who Does What When is a crosstab report that shows a tabular presentation of work assigned by resource, by assignment, and by day.

Down the left side, you see a list of all resources with all their assigned tasks. Across the top is each day in the project. All work hours for each of those assignments are listed by resource and by day. Not only does this show you how resources are assigned, but you can also easily see when a resource is assigned to excessive amounts of work on a given day.

INSIDE OUT **Manage the voluminous Who Does What When report**

Because it is so detailed, the Who Does What When text report requires a lot of paper to print—it can be more than 50 pages for even a smaller project. Because of this, it might be best to use this report less frequently than others. Other alternatives are to view its Print Backstage view preview or create a PDF file rather than print it.

Although it appears that you can specify a date range or page range for this report, when you actually go to print, the entire report prints. This is true for several reports.

You cannot print a date range or page range with this report unless you create a new custom report based on the data this report generates.

INSIDE OUT Reduce the number of pages in the Who Does What When report

You can pull up on the report detail by modifying the report to show work amounts by weeks or by months rather than by days. This significantly reduces the number of pages. To do this, follow these steps:

1. On the Project tab, in the Reports group, click Reports.
2. Double-click Assignments.
3. Click Who Does What When, and then click Edit.

   The Crosstab Report dialog box appears.

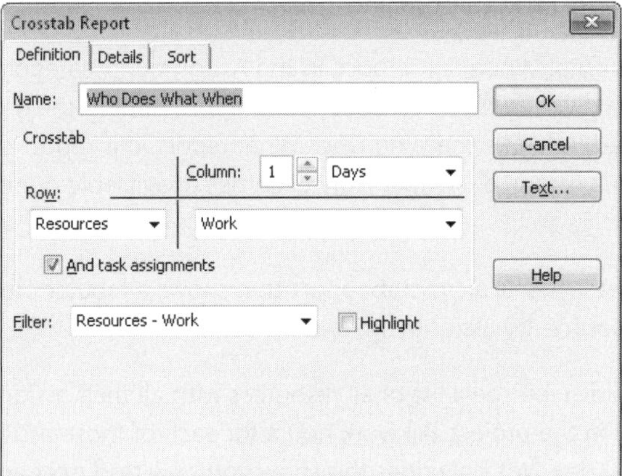

4. Next to Column, change Days to Weeks or Months, for example.

   You can also change the number next to Column to indicate that data should be shown for every two weeks, for example.
5. Click OK.
6. With the Who Does What When report still selected, click Select, and you'll see that your changes have taken effect.

The changes you make to this report are saved with just this project file.

Using the To-Do List

Use the To-Do List to generate a list of tasks to provide to assigned resources, as shown in Figure 13-22.

To Do List as of Mon 8/1/11
New Business

Task Name	Duration	Start
Confirm decision to proceed	0 days	Thu 9/2
Identify implications	1 day	Mon 10/
Research name availability	1 day	Tue 11/1
Develop a logo	1 day	Thu 11/
Choose legal representation	1 day	Wed 11/
Select business tax-basis category	2 days	Thu 11/1
Select business tax-basis category	2 days	Thu 11/1
Obtain required licenses and permits	4 days	Fri 11/1
Obtain required licenses and permits	4 days	Fri 11/1
Establish security plan	2 days	Wed 11/
Secure operation space	5 days	Fri 12/2/
Secure operation space	5 days	Fri 12/2/

Figure 13-22 The To-Do List shows the list of assignments for a selected resource.

This report can be especially useful if you're not using the project team collaboration features in Project Server and Project Web App or in SharePoint to exchange assignment information electronically with your resources.

The To-Do List, a text report in the Assignments category, is based on the Entry table for tasks, with the Using Resource filter applied. It's grouped by week and sorted by task start date. The To-Do List shows the names of all tasks to which the selected resource is assigned, the task durations, and the start and finish dates.

INSIDE OUT Reports can't be e-mailed as is

It would be nice to be able to e-mail a report like the To-Do List to team members or a report like the Project Summary to your boss. But that capability is not available (for many of the same reasons you can't save a report from a moment in time).

The best solution is to save the report as a PDF file. Then you can e-mail the PDF report to team members or other stakeholders. In the middle pane of the Print Backstage view, click the arrow next to the name of the currently selected printer. All available printers, including PDF, are listed. Click Adobe PDF. Browse to the location where you want to save the PDF file, and then click OK. Make any necessary changes in the Document Export Options dialog box, and then click OK.

For more information, see "Saving a View as a PDF File" on page 579. For more information about using e-mail to exchange project information, see "Sending Project File Information" in Chapter 20, "Integrating Project 2010 with Outlook."

Using the Overallocated Resources Report

The Overallocated Resources text report, in the Assignments category, lists only the resources that have been assigned work in excess of their availability, as reflected in their resource calendars. For example, if a resource's availability is based on the default Standard calendar, the resource will become overallocated when scheduled for more than eight hours per day or more than five days per week.

The list includes every task assigned to a resource, not just the tasks for which the resource is overallocated. Overallocated resources have an overallocated indicator by their name, but the report does not show which specific tasks are actually causing the overallocation. Analyze the task start and finish dates and the amount of work scheduled during those timespans to find the periods of overallocation.

The Overallocated Resources report is based on the Usage table for resources, with the Overallocated Resources filter applied. This report includes the resource's name and total work hours on the summary level and the resource's assignment schedule information in a subtable.

For more information about resolving overallocated resources, see "Balancing Resource Workloads" on page 403.

Reports That Identify Problems

Various reports can help you identify problems in the project so that you can mitigate issues before they become disasters. The following reports help you look at potential or current problems:

- Critical Tasks text report (Overview category)
- Critical Tasks Status report (Visio visual report)
- Should Have Started Tasks text report (Current category)
- Overbudget Tasks text report (Costs category)
- Overbudget Resources text report (Costs category)
- Earned Value text report (Costs category)
- Earned Value Over Time report (Excel visual report)
- Overallocated Resources text report (Assignment category)
- Resource Work Summary Report text report (Excel visual report)

For more information about resolving project problems, see Chapter 10 and Chapter 12.

Using the Resource Availability Report in Visio

The Resource Availability Report is a Visio visual report in the Resource Usage category. It displays a PivotDiagram that shows scheduled work and remaining availability for all project resources, broken down by work, material, and cost resources.

Using the Resource Work Availability Report in Excel

The Resource Work Availability Report is an Excel visual report in the Resource Usage category. It displays a column chart showing total capacity in terms of work availability, work, and remaining availability for work resources over time.

Using the Task Usage Report

The Task Usage text report, in the Workload category, emphasizes assignment hours by task and by week. Under the task names are the assignments, shown as the names of the assigned resources.

The Task Usage report is very similar to the Task Usage view. Summary tasks are shown so that the logical groupings of tasks within the project are easy to follow. Totals are shown for each week and each task. This is a clear way to show the full extent of how work and material resources are assigned to every task.

Using the Resource Usage Report

The Resource Usage text report, in the Workload category, emphasizes assignment hours by resource and by week. Under the resource names are the assignments, shown as the names of the tasks to which the associated resource is assigned.

The Resource Usage report is very similar to the Resource Usage view. For each resource, all assigned tasks are listed along with weekly totals of the hours of work assigned for that task. The report layout is the same as the Task Usage report.

Using the Resource Work Summary Report in Excel

The Resource Work Summary Report is an Excel visual report in the Resource Usage category. It displays a column chart showing total capacity, work, remaining availability, and actual work by work units (days, weeks, months, and so on) for each work resource assigned to tasks in your project.

Using the Resource Remaining Work Report in Excel

The Resource Remaining Work Report is an Excel visual report in the Resource Summary category. It displays a column chart showing actual work and remaining work for each work resource by work units (days, weeks, months, and so on).

Using the Resource Status Report in Visio

The Resource Status Report is a Visio visual report in the Assignment Summary category. It displays a diagram of the work and cost for each resource in the project. The percentage of work complete is indicated by shading in each of the nodes, with the shading growing darker as the resource nears completion of total assigned work.

More Built-In Text Reports

Not all text reports are listed in the Reports dialog box. Others are available in the Custom group. These additional reports are as follows:

- Base Calendar
- Resource
- Resource (material)
- Resource (work)
- Resource Usage (material)
- Resource Usage (work)
- Task

To generate these reports, follow these steps:

1. On the Project tab, in the Reports group, click Reports.
2. In the Reports dialog box, double-click Custom.

   The Custom Reports dialog box appears, showing a single list of all built-in reports.
3. In the Reports box, scroll to the report you want to use, and then click Select.

   The report appears in the preview area of the Print Backstage view.

Revising a Built-In Report

After using the standard built-in text and visual reports for several reviews and meetings, you might come up with some new ideas for customizing your presentation and content. You can tweak a built-in report a little (or a lot) to make it better suit your needs. You can either change an existing report or create an entirely new report.

Note

New and modified reports exist only in the current project, by default. If you want to make them available in all your other projects, move the new reports to the project global template by using the Organizer.

For more information, see "Sharing Customized Elements among Projects" on page 1138.

Modifying a Text Report

You can create a new text report by basing it on a copy of an existing report, leaving the original version intact. You can directly modify an existing report. You can also change the page layout of a report so that it prints the way you want.

Copying an Existing Text Report

Copying an existing text report and modifying the copy is the easiest and safest method for creating a new report. The original report remains unfettered, and you can feel free to go wild with the copy. It will probably turn out great, but it's good to know you can experiment without dire consequences. If you get into any trouble, you can always delete the copy and start over again with a fresh copy.

To copy and modify an existing text report, follow these steps:

1. On the Project tab, in the Reports group, click Reports.
2. Double-click Custom.

   The Custom Reports dialog box appears, as shown in Figure 13-23.

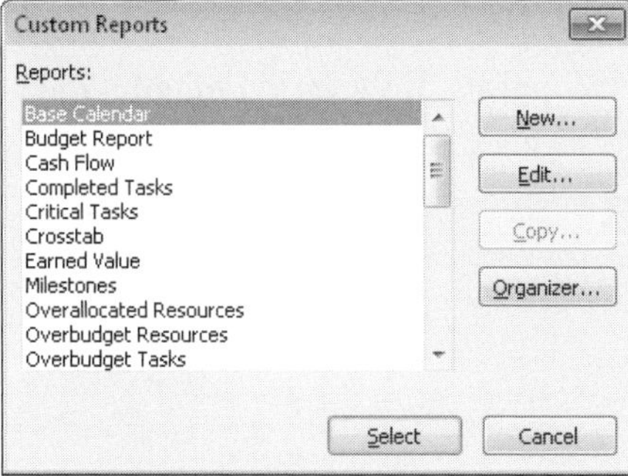

Figure 13-23 The Custom Reports dialog box displays the list of all available built-in text report formats.

3. In the Reports box, click the report you want to copy, and then click Copy.

   One of three possible dialog boxes appears, depending on the format of the report you're copying: Task Report, Resource Report, or Crosstab Report. The Task Report dialog box is shown in Figure 13-24.

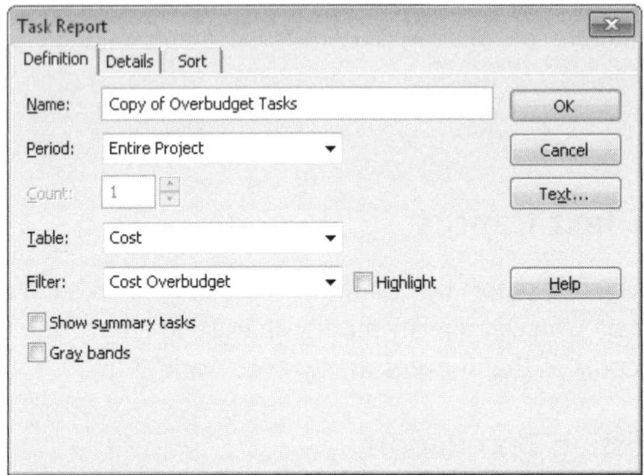

Figure 13-24 The Task Report dialog box appears for any report based on task information.

4. In the Name box, which shows Copy Of <Report Name>, enter the name of your new custom report.

   Be sure it's a name that's different from those already in the Reports list.

5. In the other fields and tabs of the dialog box, make any changes you want to the report content.

   Use the Definition tab to set the fields, time periods, and filters to be used. Use the Details tab to specify additional information you want to add to the report. Use the Sort tab to specify which field should dictate the order of information in the report.

6. Make any changes you want to the report fonts by clicking the Text button.

   The Text Styles dialog box appears, as shown in Figure 13-25.

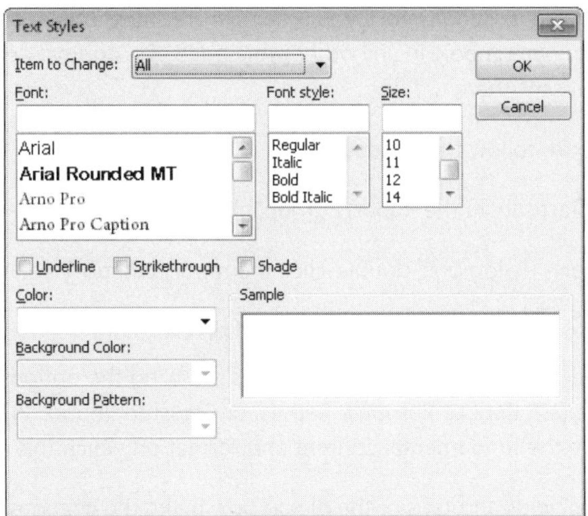

Figure 13-25 Change the font of various items in the report by using the Text Styles dialog box.

In the Item To Change box, click the report element whose text you want to format, and then specify the changes throughout the rest of the dialog box. Click OK.

7. When you are finished making changes to your new report, click OK in the report definition dialog box.

   The name of your new text report appears in the Reports list in the Custom Reports dialog box.

8. Click your new report if necessary, and then click Select to generate the report and see what it looks like in the Print Backstage view.

9. If you want to make further changes, click Project, Reports, Reports. Double-click Custom, select the custom report, and then click Edit.

   The report definition dialog box appears again.

Your new report is saved with your project file and is available whenever you work in this particular project.

Modifying an Existing Text Report

You can directly edit the definition properties of a built-in text report. The elements available for editing vary by report. In some reports, all you can change is the font. In other reports, you can change the reporting period, filter for specific types of information, specify that information be drawn from a specific table, and more.

When you change an existing report, your changes are saved only with the project file. If you open the same text report in any other project file, the original default report properties will still be present there.

To edit a text report, follow these steps:

1. On the Project tab, in the Reports group, click Reports.
2. In the Reports dialog box, double-click the report category you want.
3. Click the report you want to change, and then click Edit.

   One of three possible dialog boxes appears, showing the options available for this report: Task Report, Resource Report, or Crosstab Report. Which one appears depends on the fundamental content and format on which this report is based.
4. In the other fields and tabs of the dialog box, make the changes you want to the report content or format.

   If available, use the Definition tab to set the fields, time periods, and filters to be used. As shown in Figure 13-26, use the Details tab to specify additional information you want to add to the report. Use the Sort tab to specify which field should dictate the order of information in the report.

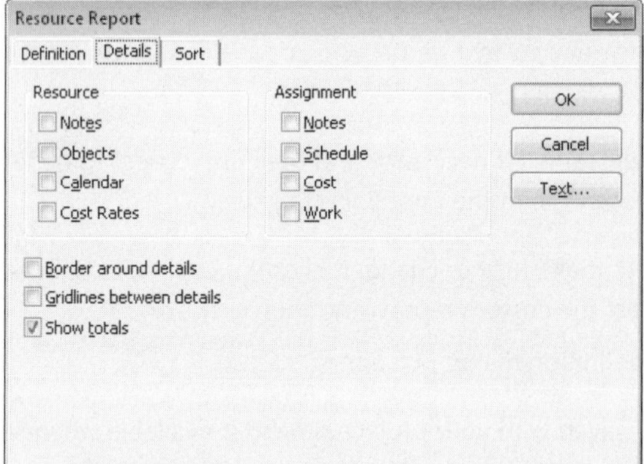

Figure 13-26 You can edit different types of information depending on the report you choose.

5. Make any changes you want to the report fonts by clicking the Text button.
6. When you are finished editing the report, click OK in the report definition dialog box.
7. Click the edited report if necessary, and then click Select to generate the report and see what it now looks like in the Print Backstage view.

8. If you want to make further changes, click Project, Reports, Reports. Double-click the report category, select the modified report, and then click Edit.

   The report definition dialog box appears again.

Your new report is saved with your project file and is available whenever you work in this particular project.

Adjusting the Page Setup of a Report

You can modify the header, footer, page numbering, and other general page setup elements of a built-in report, a copied report, or a brand-new report. To do this, follow these steps:

1. On the Project tab, in the Reports group, click Reports.
2. Double-click the category of the report whose page setup you want to change.
3. Double-click the report to run it.

   The report appears in the Print Backstage view.
4. Near the bottom of the middle pane of the Print Backstage view, click Page Setup.
5. Use the options on the Page, Margins, Header, Footer, and other available tabs to make the changes you want.

For more information about page setup options, see "Specifying Options for Printed Views" on page 531.

The changes you make apply to the selected report in the current project and are saved with the project for the next time you need to print this report.

Modifying a Visual Report

Visual reports are based on *report templates* that specify the data that's being drawn from your project file for the report appearing either in Excel or Visio. To modify a visual report or create your own, you can specify the project fields you want to be available in the Excel or Visio report. Then you work in the Excel or Visio report template to specify how those fields are used. When you save the changes to the Excel or Visio report template, those changes are always available for this or other project files.

To edit a built-in visual report template, do the following:

1. On the Project tab, in the Reports group, click Visual Reports.
2. Click the built-in visual report template you want to edit.

3. If you want to change the project fields that are available in the report template, click Edit Template.

   The Visual Reports - Field Picker dialog box appears, as shown in Figure 13-27.

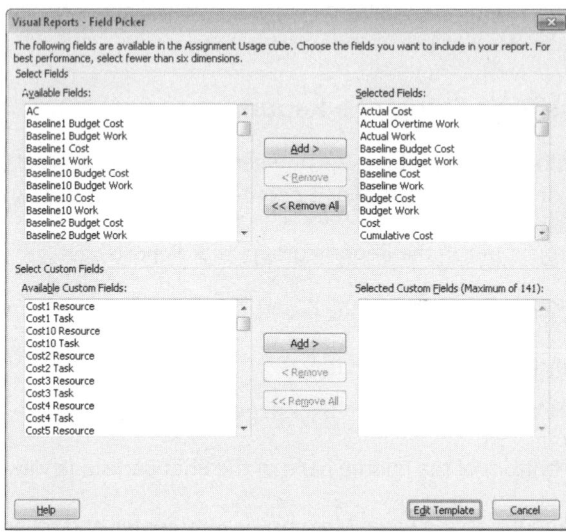

Figure 13-27 When you edit a visual report, you specify which fields you want to be a part of the report.

   To add fields to the OLAP cube for the visual report, select the fields you want in the Available Fields list, and then click Add. The fields appear in the Selected Fields list.

   To remove fields from the Selected Fields list, select the fields, and then click Remove. You can select multiple fields to add or remove by holding the Ctrl key and clicking the fields.

4. If you changed fields in the Visual Reports - Field Picker dialog box, click the Edit Template button.

   If you don't need to add or remove available fields but want to change other aspects of the visual report, click View.

   Either way, Project 2010 builds the OLAP cube for the visual report. Depending on the type of report, Excel or Visio generates the report.

5. Make the changes you want to the PivotTable in Excel or the PivotDiagram in Visio.

6. In Excel or Visio, save the template.

   The changes you've made to the template are saved for future use, replacing the previous version of the template. This modified template is available to any Project 2010 file you use.

For more information, see "Configuring a Visual Report in Excel" on page 738 and "Configuring a Visual Report in Visio" on page 748.

Building a Custom Report

You might have a specialized report requirement that none of the built-in text or visual reports fulfills. The following sections describe how to create a new text report and a new visual report from scratch.

Creating a New Text Report

When you create a new text report, you start with a report template that gives you the framework within which to build a good report. There are four text report templates, or *report types*:

- Task
- Resource
- Monthly Calendar
- Crosstab

If you've edited or copied any existing text reports or just looked at a report's definition out of curiosity, you might already be familiar with some of these report types, as they form the basis for nearly all the built-in text reports.

To build a custom report, follow these steps:

1. On the Project tab, in the Reports group, click Reports.
2. In the Reports dialog box, double-click Custom.
3. In the Custom Reports dialog box, click New.

   The Define New Report dialog box appears, as shown in Figure 13-28.

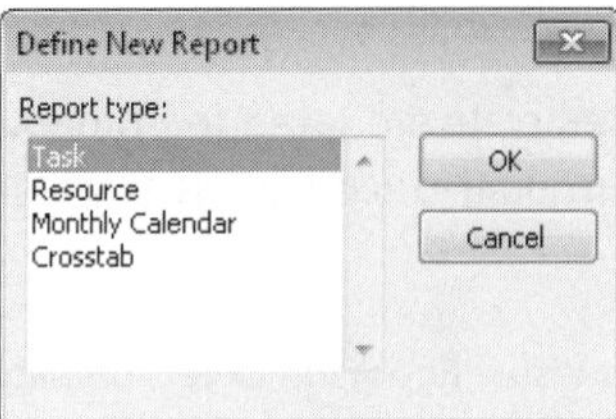

Figure 13-28 Select the format for your new report.

4. In the Report Type box, select the type of report you're creating, and then click OK.

   The report definition dialog box appears, as shown in Figure 13-29. The dialog box you see depends on the report type you select.

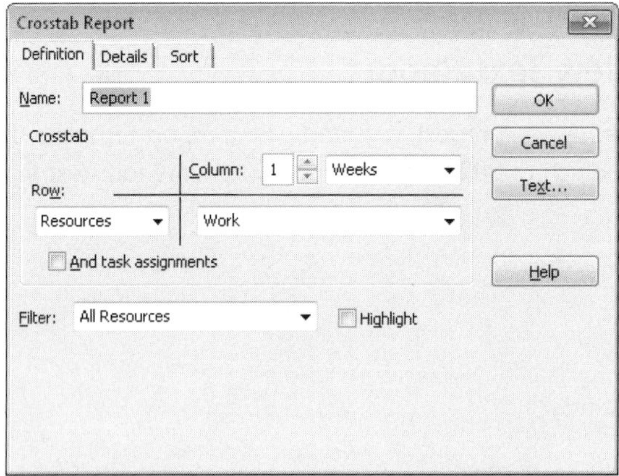

Figure 13-29 The Crosstab Report dialog box appears for any report that displays a tabular format of intersecting information along vertical and horizontal fields of information.

5. In the Name box, enter the name of your new custom report.

   Be sure that it's a unique name in the Reports list.

6. Define your report: Specify any fields, filters, or formatting as the report definition.

   If you're defining a task, resource, or crosstab report, also use the Details tab to specify additional information you want to add to the report. Use the Sort tab to specify which field should dictate the order of information in the report.

7. Make any changes you want to the report fonts by clicking the Text button.

   In the Item To Change box, click the report element whose text you want to format and then specify the changes you want. When you finish, click OK.

8. When you are finished with your new report's definition and changes, click OK in the report definition dialog box.

   The name of your new report appears in the Reports list in the Custom Reports dialog box.

9. Click your new report if necessary, and then click Select to generate the report and see what it looks like in the Print Backstage view.

10. If you want to make further changes, click Project, Reports, Reports. Double-click Custom, click the custom report, and then click Edit.

    The report definition dialog box appears again. Make the changes you want.

Your new report is saved with your project file and is available whenever you work in this particular project.

Creating a New Visual Report Template

When you create a new visual report, you specify the data type, or OLAP cube, such as Task Usage or Assignment Summary. This provides the basis for the visual report, whether it is generated in Excel or Visio.

To create a visual report template from scratch, do the following:

1. On the Project tab, in the Reports group, click Visual Reports.

2. Click New Template.

   The Visual Reports - New Template dialog box appears, as shown in Figure 13-30.

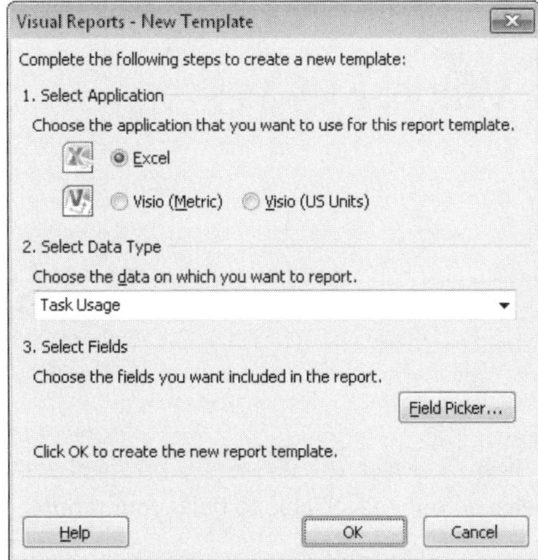

Figure 13-30 When you create a new visual report template, you must specify the application (Excel or Visio), the data type (OLAP cube), and the project fields to be included.

3. Under Select Application, select Excel if you want to create an Excel chart based on a PivotTable from Project 2010 data. Select one of the Visio options if you want to create a flow diagram based on a PivotDiagram from Project 2010 data.

4. Under Select Data Type, choose the type of data you want to use as the basis for your report.

   Visual reports are based on six different sets of information: Task Summary, Task Usage, Resource Summary, Resource Usage, Assignment Summary, and Assignment Usage. These data types determine the fields that Project 2010 adds to the OLAP cube, but you can add or remove fields, as well.

5. To modify the fields to be used in the template, click Field Picker, and then add or remove fields in the Available Fields list.

   To add fields to the new visual report's OLAP cube, select the fields you want from the Available Fields list, and then click Add.

   To remove fields from the Selected Fields list, select the fields, and then click Remove.

6. Click OK in the Visual Reports - Field Picker dialog box, and then click OK in the Visual Reports - New Template dialog box.

   For an Excel template, Excel launches and opens a blank PivotTable, as shown in Figure 13-31.

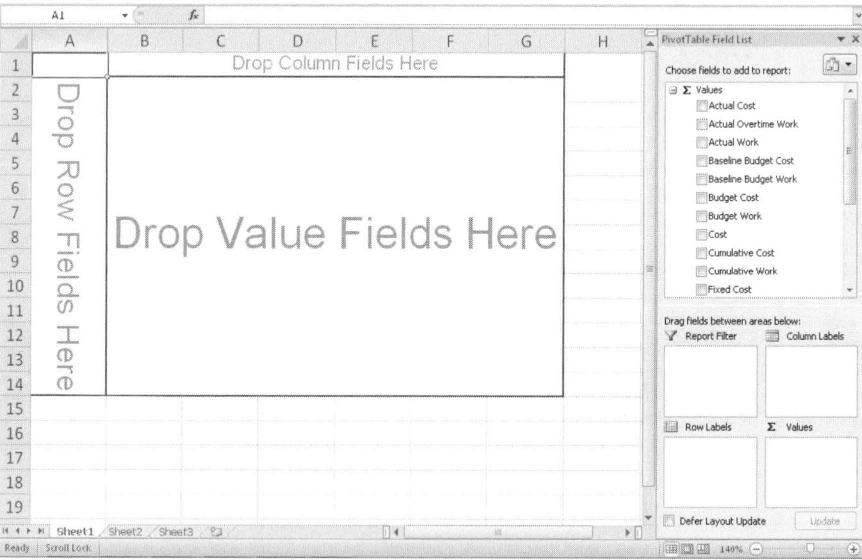

Figure 13-31 Drag fields onto the PivotTable to build your report.

For a Visio template, Visio launches and opens a blank PivotDiagram, as shown in Figure 13-32.

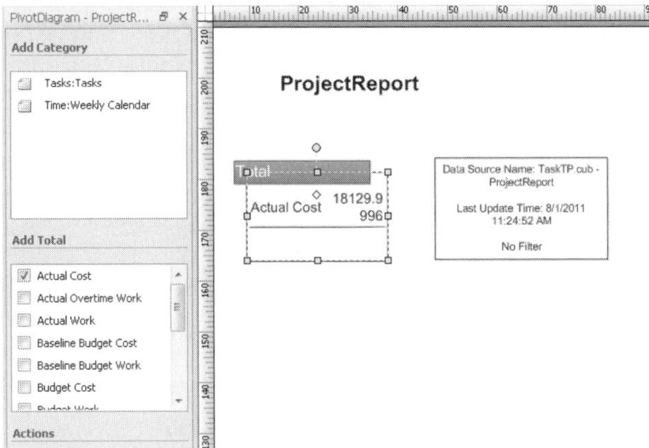

Figure 13-32 Create a PivotDiagram in Visio to use as a custom project visual report.

For details on building a new PivotTable in Excel for a Project 2010 visual report, see "Creating and Editing Visual Report Templates in Excel" on page 740. For details on building a new PivotDiagram in Visio for a Project 2010 visual report, see "Creating and Editing Visual Report Templates in Visio" on page 751.

7. When you have configured the PivotTable or PivotDiagram, save the template. In the Save As dialog box, be sure that the template is being saved to the folder where all the other templates are located, for example the C:\Users\[*username*]\AppData\Roaming\Microsoft\Templates\1033 folder.

Saving the template in this folder ensures that the template appears in the Visual Reports - Create Reports dialog box.

If you save the template in a location other than the default Microsoft templates folder, you can still have it included in the list of visual reports. On the Visual Reports - Create Report dialog box, select the check box labeled Include Report Templates From, click the Modify button, and then browse to the location of your new template. Select the template, and then click OK.

Make New or Changed Reports Available to Other Projects

When you change or create new text reports, they exist only within the current project file. If you want your changed or newly created text reports to be present in all your project files, use the Organizer to copy those reports from your current project to your *global.mpt* project template.

You can go the other direction as well. If you changed a built-in text report and want to return to the original default report, you can copy it from global.mpt back into the project file.

The Organizer is readily available in the Custom Reports dialog box, as follows:

1. On the Project tab, in the Reports group, click Reports.
2. Double-click Custom.
3. In the Custom Reports dialog box, click Organizer.

   The Reports tab in the Organizer dialog box opens.

For more information about copying project elements between an individual project file and the global.mpt project template by using the Organizer, see "Sharing Customized Elements Among Projects" on page 1138.

When you change or create a new visual report, its Excel or Visio template is saved as a separate file. These reports are therefore available to any project file without your needing to use the Organizer.

Saving Project Data Fields

You can save sets of fields or all fields in the current project file. This can be useful if you want to display or analyze project data in another application such as Excel or Microsoft Access 2010.

Saving the Reporting Cube

Six OLAP cubes contain combinations of field data for the current project file. These OLAP cubes are:

- Task Usage
- Resource Usage

- Assignment Usage
- Task Summary
- Resource Summary
- Assignment Summary

If you customize an OLAP cube with a different set of field data, you can save it as a separate cube file. To save a cube file, follow these steps:

1. On the Project tab, in the Reports group, click Visual Reports.
2. Click the Save Data button at the bottom of the Visual Reports - Create Report dialog box.

   The Visual Reports - Save Reporting Data dialog box appears, as shown in Figure 13-33.

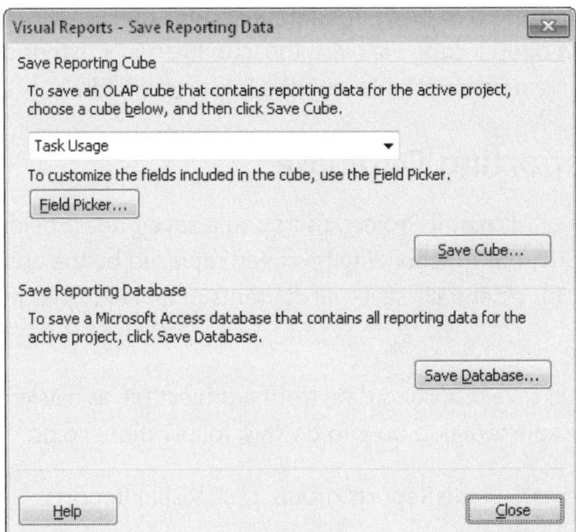

Figure 13-33 Use the Visual Reports - Save Reporting Data dialog box to save a customized OLAP cube.

3. From the drop-down list under Save Reporting Cube, click the cube you want to save—for example, Task Usage or Assignment Summary.
4. If you want to change any of the fields in the cube you have selected, click the Field Picker button.

   The Selected Fields box lists all fields in the selected cube.

5. Change the fields included in the cube as needed.
   - To add fields to the cube, select fields in the Available Fields box, and then click the Add button.
   - To remove fields from the cube, select fields in the Selected Fields box, and then click the Remove button.
   - To add custom fields to the cube, select fields in the Available Custom Fields box, and then click the Add button.
6. Click OK in the Visual Reports - Field Picker dialog box.
7. In the Visual Reports - Save Reporting Data dialog box again, click Save Cube.
8. In the Save As dialog box, browse to the location where you want to save the cube file. Give the file a name if necessary, and then click Save.

   The data in your selected fields are gathered, the cube is built, and the cube file is saved. You can open a cube file (with the .cub file name extension) in Excel, where you can then create a PivotTable with the imported fields.

Saving the Reporting Database

In previous versions of Microsoft Project, users could save project fields to a database. As of Microsoft Project 2007, this functionality has been replaced by the ability to save a project file in XML format. This essentially saves all contents of all fields that make up the project file database.

However, you can still save reporting data from a project file as a Microsoft Access MDB file through the Visual Reports dialog box. To do this, follow these steps:

1. On the Project tab, in the Reports group, click Visual Reports.
2. Click the Save Data button at the bottom of the Visual Reports - Create Report dialog box.
3. Under Save Reporting Database, click Save Database.
4. In the Save As dialog box that appears, browse to the location where you want to save the database. Give the file a name, and then click Save.

   The reporting data in your project file is gathered and saved as an Access (MDB) file. You can then open the file in Access.

Sharing Project Reports Electronically

Project 2010 provides a variety of ways to share views and reports electronically. You can save a view or report as a PDF file and then send it as an e-mail attachment or post it on a SharePoint site or other website. You can save your project as an XML file or save a view as a graphics file and post it to a website.

Share Reports by Using Project Server and SharePoint

If your organization is set up with Project Server and Project Web App, you have a more structured and robust means of sharing reports with team members and stakeholders, not to mention the availability of more reports themselves.

For more information, see "Managing Pages, Views, and Reports" on page 881, "Controlling Project Documents" on page 959, and "Analyzing and Reporting on Project Information" on page 1021.

If your organization manages project workgroup collaboration through SharePoint Foundation or SharePoint Server, you can share reports through the Document Library on your SharePoint site.

Saving a View as a PDF File

You can save a particular view as a PDF (portable document format) file, which you can then save, send, post, or print. To save a view as a PDF file, follow these steps:

1. Open the view and arrange the data as you want it to appear when printed.

   For more information about available views and arranging information in those views, see Chapter 4.

2. On the File tab, click Save & Send.

3. In the Save & Send Backstage view, click Create PDF/XPS Document.

   The right pane shows information about PDF/XPS documents.

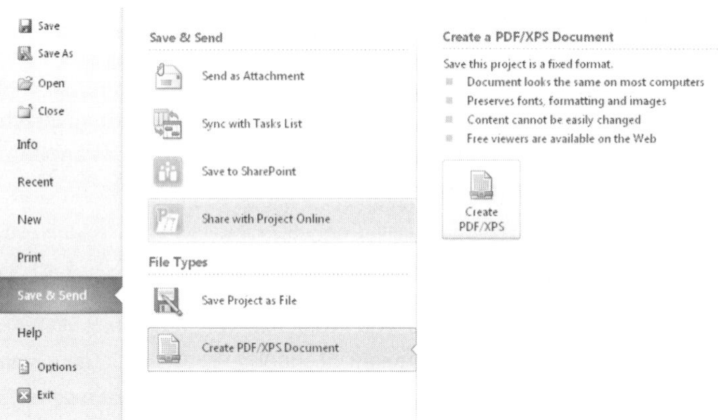

4. In the right pane, click Create PDF/XPS.

5. Browse to the location where you want to save the PDF file. Give the PDF file a name, and then click OK.

6. Make any necessary changes in the Document Export Options dialog box, and then click OK.

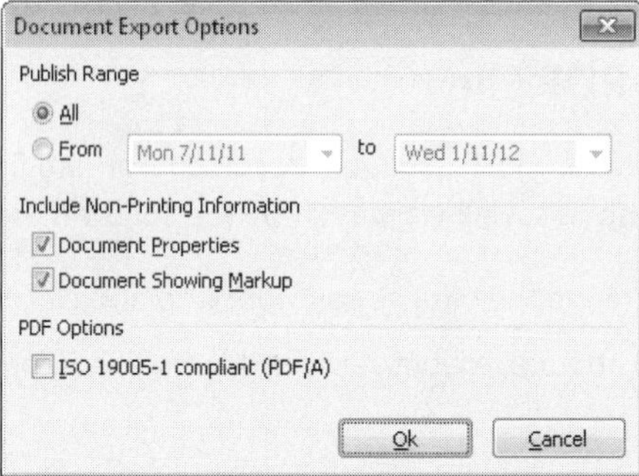

Saving a Report as a PDF File

You can save a text report you have generated as a PDF file. In addition to letting you share the report electronically, saving a report as a PDF file is a good way to save snapshots of project information over time. To save a Project 2010 report as a PDF file, follow these steps:

1. On the Project tab, in the Reports group, click Reports.

2. Select and run the report so that it's showing in the Print Backstage view.

   For more information, see "Working with Text-Based Reports" on page 534.

3. In the middle pane of the Print Backstage view, click the arrow next to the name of the currently selected printer.

   All available printers, including Adobe PDF, are listed.

4. Click Adobe PDF.

5. Click Print.

6. In the Save PDF File As dialog box, browse to the location where you want to save the PDF file. Change the file name if you want, and then click OK.

You can also save a visual report you've generated as a PDF file by using the PDF printing feature in Excel or Visio.

Posting Project Information on a Web Page

As described in the previous sections, you can create a PDF file from a particular project view or report. You can then post that PDF to an intranet site, SharePoint site, or other web-based project information system for team members and other stakeholders to review.

If you want to post project information directly on a web page, though, you can save it as an XML file or save a view as a graphics file.

Saving a Project Plan as an XML File

To do this, follow these steps.

1. Open the project plan you want to save as an XML file.

2. Click File, Save As.

3. In the Save As Type box, click XML Format (*.xml).

4. Navigate to the location where you want to save the new XML file.

5. In the File Name box, type the name for your new XML file.

6. Click Save.

   The file is saved. You can now open it in a markup language editor, apply style sheets, and prepare the information for publication on the web.

Chapter 13

Saving a View as a Graphic Image

Copy Picture is a simple option if you just want to publish a graphic image of a particular view to the web. To use Copy Picture, follow these steps:

1. In your project plan, display the view you want to copy to the other application.
2. Manipulate the view to show the information the way you want it to appear in the destination application.

Copy Picture

3. On the Task tab, in the Clipboard group, click the arrow next to Copy, and then click Copy Picture.

   The Copy Picture dialog box appears.

4. In the Render Image section, click the To GIF Image option, as shown in Figure 13-34. Then click the Browse button to specify the new file's location and name.

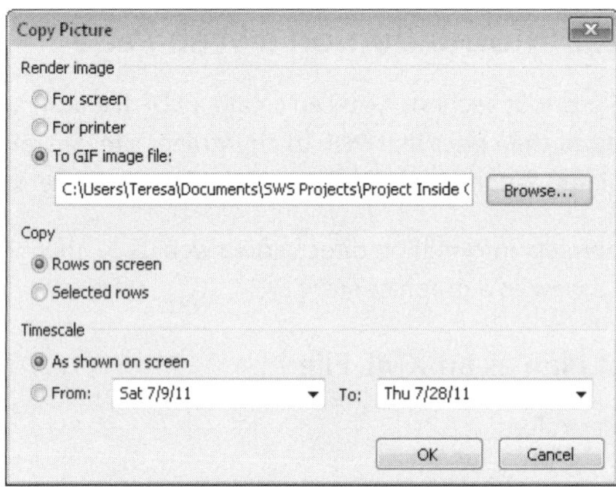

Figure 13-34 Choose the options you want for the picture file you're creating from the current view.

5. In the Copy section, click the Rows On Screen option (the default) if you want the rows currently showing on the screen to be included in the image. Click the Selected Rows option if only selected rows should be included.

6. In the Timescale section, click the As Shown On Screen option (the default) if you want the timescale to be represented as set in the current view.

   Click the From and To option and enter dates in the boxes if you want to specify the timescale and date range to be included in the image.

7. When you are finished setting the Copy Picture options, click OK.

   The view is saved as a GIF image. You can now manipulate it in a graphics program, perhaps to crop the image or add labels. If necessary, you can convert it to another graphics file format, such as JPG, if that makes it easier to post to the website.

CHAPTER 14

Analyzing Progress Using Earned Value

As you track and control your project, you'll probably need to analyze various aspects of project performance. Project analysis, which you might think of as "project data crunching," can give you a closer look at the overall execution of the project. For first-time efforts at managing a particular kind of project or for new variations on an established project theme, you and your stakeholders might want to review key performance indicators and estimates for the remainder of the project. These indicators help assess the effectiveness of the plan and define the amount of corrective action needed to make actual performance in the project conform to the baseline.

A good method for such an examination of project performance is *earned value* analysis, which is a systematic method for measuring and evaluating schedule, cost, and work performance in a project. Microsoft Project 2010 automatically performs a set of calculations on certain types of project data. With the results of these calculations, you can then do earned value analysis. Earned value provides a variety of comparisons between baseline and actual information. The foundations of earned value calculations are the following:

- The project baseline, including schedule and cost information for assigned resources
- Actual work and costs reported
- Variances between actual progress information and baseline information
- A status date

As soon as you set a baseline, Project 2010 begins calculating and storing earned value data. You can view this data by using three built-in earned value tables or two built-in earned value reports. You can also add earned value fields to any sheet view or report.

Generating Earned Value Data

Project 2010 starts to generate earned value information as soon as you set a project baseline. Then, as you start entering progress information such as actual start or finish dates, actual percentage completed, and so on, Project 2010 compares the actuals against the baseline, calculates variances, and plugs those variances into earned value calculations. Three categories of earned value fields are used, each with a different focus:

- Cost
- Schedule
- Work

Setting the Baseline

Set the project *baseline* after you have built and refined the project plan to your satisfaction and just before you start entering progress information against tasks. The project plan should show all tasks and resources assigned, and costs should be associated with those resources. The project plan should reflect your target schedule dates, budget amounts, and scope of work.

Set Baseline

To set a baseline, on the Project tab, in the Schedule group, click Set Baseline, and then click Set Baseline again. In the dialog box that appears, be sure the Set Baseline option is selected, and then click OK.

You can save up to 11 different baselines, which is useful if you want to take a snapshot of key scheduling data at different stages of the project. However, earned value is calculated on only a single baseline. To specify which baseline should be used for earned value analyses, follow these steps:

1. On the File tab, click Options, and then click Advanced in the left pane.
2. Scroll to the section labeled Earned Value Options For This Project, as shown in Figure 14-1.

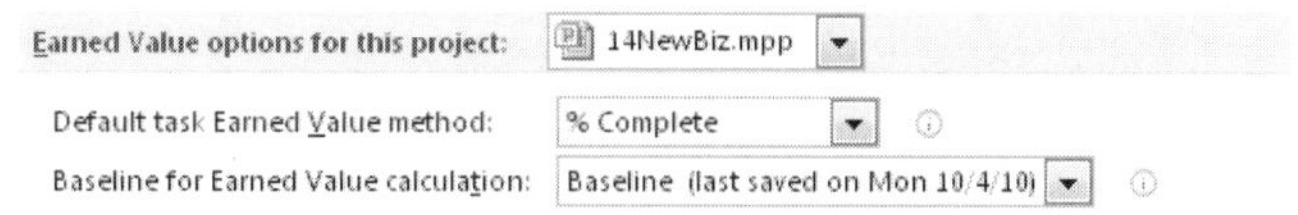

Figure 14-1 Specify which of 11 possible saved baselines should be used for the earned value calculations.

3. In the box labeled Baseline For Earned Value Calculation, click the baseline (Baseline, Baseline1, Baseline2, and so on) that you want to use.

For a complete discussion of baselines, see "Saving Original Plan Information Using a Baseline" on page 445.

Entering Actuals

The counterpart to baseline information for earned value calculations is the *actuals* information. To enter task progress information, follow these steps:

Mark On Track

1. On the Task tab, in the Schedule group, click the arrow next to the Mark On Track button, and then click Update Tasks.
2. In the Update Tasks dialog box, complete one or more of the progress fields indicating percentage complete, actual and remaining duration, or actual start and finish dates.

If you want to enter true *timephased* actuals—that is, the actual amount of work performed per day or other period of time—record them in the timesheet area of the Task Usage or Resource Usage view. Otherwise, Project 2010 derives timephased actuals by dividing any total amount entered in the timespan of the assignment.

For more information about entering actual progress information, see "Updating Task Progress" on page 462.

If you're set up for enterprise project management using Microsoft Project Professional 2010 and Microsoft Project Server 2010, progress information can be updated in your project plan as team members submit task updates via Microsoft Project Web App.

If you and your project server administrator have set up Project Web App to record actual work performed per time period (days or weeks), you receive true timephased actuals from team members. If Project Web App records actuals by percentage complete or total actual work and remaining work, Project 2010 again derives timephased actuals by dividing any total amount entered in the timespan of the assignment.

For more information about working with actuals entered by team members in Project Web App, see "Setting Up Team Member Work Pages" on page 870 and "Collaborating with Your Project Team" on page 945.

Project 2010 can calculate *variances* as soon as your project plan contains baseline as well as actuals information. With variances, the earned value fields begin to populate.

Specifying the Status Date

Earned value data is calculated on the basis of a particular cutoff date, or *status date*. Unless you specify otherwise, the status date is today's date. However, you are likely to specify a different status date, for example, if you want to see figures based on the end of the month, which was last Thursday. Also, the status date is typically the date up to which you have collected status information. A lag almost always exists between the date of the latest status information and the date when you are running your earned value reports.

To enter a status date, do the following:

Status Date

1. On the Project tab, in the Status group, click Status Date.
2. In the Status Date box, enter the status date you want to use.

Because Project 2010 stores timephased data for values such as baseline and actual work, cost, and so on, earned value can be calculated based on the specified status date.

Base Earned Value on Physical Percentage Complete

By default, earned value calculations are based on percentage complete, which in turn is based on task duration or work. However, if your project is geared toward the usage of material, the number of units produced, or some other physical measurement that is not based on the amount of duration or work expended, then it might make more sense for your earned value calculations to be based on physical percentage complete.

For example, suppose your project entails the building of a product and several follow-on support tasks. If you want the earned value to be calculated on the completion of the product itself and not the support tasks, you can use the physical percentage complete method to enter the percentage complete of the product up to the status date. If you specify that the project has a physical percentage complete value of 50 percent, earned value is calculated on how much money you should have spent to get the product to 50 percent versus how much you actually spent to get it to this point.

To set the project to the physical percentage complete method, follow these steps:

1. On the File tab, click Options, and then click Advanced in the left pane.
2. Scroll to the section labeled Earned Value Options For This Project.
3. In the box labeled Default Task Earned Value Method, click Physical % Complete.

Reviewing Earned Value Data

To study and analyze project performance, you can apply one of three earned value tables to a sheet view. You can also run the earned value reports or add selected earned value fields to any sheet view.

Working with Earned Value Tables

With a baseline set and actuals entered, you can evaluate current cost and schedule performance through earned value. To review your earned value information for tasks, do the following:

Other Views

1. On the View tab, in the Task Views group, click Other Views, and then click Task Sheet.

Tables

2. On the View tab, in the Data group, click Tables, and then click More Tables.

   The More Tables dialog box appears.

3. In the Tables list, click Earned Value, and then click Apply.

   The earned value data for your project is displayed, as shown in Figure 14-2.

	Task Name	Planned	Earned Value	AC	SV	CV	EAC	BAC	VAC
0	**14 New Business Startup**	**$69,238.00**	**$12,103.72**	**$12,229.50**	**($57,134.28)**	**($125.78)**	**$0.00**	**$0.00**	**$0.00**
1	**Phase 1 - Strategic Plan**	**$34,550.00**	**$11,063.72**	**$11,189.50**	**($23,486.28)**	**($125.78)**	**$0.00**	**$0.00**	**$0.00**
2	**Self-Assessment**	**$6,816.00**	**$528.00**	**$528.00**	**($6,288.00)**	**$0.00**	**$0.00**	**$0.00**	**$0.00**
3	Define business vision	$528.00	$528.00	$528.00	$0.00	$0.00	$528.00	$528.00	$0.00
4	Identify available skills, information and	$6,288.00	$0.00	$0.00	($6,288.00)	$0.00	$6,288.00	$6,288.00	$0.00
5	Decide whether to proceed	$0.00	$0.00	$0.00	$0.00	$0.00	$0.00	$0.00	$0.00
6	**Define the Opportunity**	**$9,170.00**	**$6,928.00**	**$7,012.50**	**($2,242.00)**	**($84.50)**	**$0.00**	**$0.00**	**$0.00**
7	Research the market and competition	$2,710.00	$468.00	$552.50	($2,242.00)	($84.50)	$4,379.86	$3,710.00	($669.86)
8	Interview owners of similar businesses	$2,640.00	$2,640.00	$2,640.00	$0.00	$0.00	$2,640.00	$2,640.00	$0.00
9	Identify needed resources	$1,920.00	$1,920.00	$1,920.00	$0.00	$0.00	$1,920.00	$1,920.00	$0.00
10	Identify operating cost elements	$1,900.00	$1,900.00	$1,900.00	$0.00	$0.00	$1,900.00	$1,900.00	$0.00

Figure 14-2 Use the Earned Value table to review earned value fields.

> **Note**
>
> **To analyze earned value data by resources instead of tasks, show the Resource Sheet. On the View tab, in the Data group, click Tables, and then click Earned Value.**

Make Earned Value Tables and Views Readily Available

Although the Earned Value table is on the Tables menu for the Resource Sheet, you have to open the More Tables dialog box when you apply the table to a task sheet. If you review the Earned Value table for tasks often enough, you'll do well to add it to the Table menu. To do this, follow these steps:

1. Display the Task Sheet.
2. On the View tab, in the Data group, click Tables, and then click More Tables.
3. In the More Tables dialog box, click Earned Value or one of the other earned value tables you want to add to the Table menu.
4. Click Edit.
5. In the upper-right corner of the Table Definition dialog box, select the Show In Menu check box.

   The selected table is now listed in the Table menu in the current project, and you can get to it with fewer clicks.

You can also create a custom earned value view, perhaps with the Earned Value table applied to the Task Sheet. You can then add your new view to the Views menu as well.

For information about creating a custom earned value view, see "Customizing Views" on page 1062.

Note

When you add the project summary task to a task sheet view with the Earned Value table applied, you can see rolled-up values for the earned value calculations. To add the project summary task, on the Format tab, in the Show/Hide group, select the Project Summary Task check box.

The Earned Value table shows the majority of the earned value fields, and it can be applied to the Task Sheet or Resource Sheet. Also for task sheet views, two other tables are available to help you focus on specific types of earned value information. Apply the Earned Value Cost Indicators table to analyze your project for budget performance. Apply the Earned Value Schedule Indicators table to analyze schedule and work performance. The fields included by default in each of the three earned value tables are shown in Table 14-1.

Table 14-1 **Earned Value Tables**

Table name	Included fields
Earned Value	Planned Value (PV), also known as BCWS (Budgeted Cost of Work Scheduled)
	Earned Value (EV), also known as BCWP (Budgeted Cost of Work Performed)
	Actual Value (AC), also known as ACWP (Actual Cost of Work Performed)
	SV (Schedule Variance)
	CV (Cost Variance)
	EAC (Estimate At Completion)
	BAC (Budget At Completion)
	VAC (Variance At Completion)
Earned Value Cost Indicators	Planned Value (PV), also known as BCWS (Budgeted Cost of Work Scheduled)
	Earned Value (EV), also known as BCWP (Budgeted Cost of Work Performed)
	CV (Cost Variance)
	CV% (Cost Variance Percent)
	CPI (Cost Performance Index)
	BAC (Budget At Completion)
	EAC (Estimate At Completion)
	VAC (Variance At Completion)
	TCPI (To Complete Performance Index)
Earned Value Schedule Indicators	Planned Value (PV), also known as BCWS (Budgeted Cost of Work Scheduled)
	Earned Value (EV), also known as BCWP (Budgeted Cost of Work Performed)
	SV (Schedule Variance)
	SV% (Schedule Variance Percent)
	SPI (Schedule Performance Index)

Insert Column

Note

Add one or more earned value fields to other task or resource tables if you want to keep a close eye on one or two calculations without having to apply an entire earned value table. Display the view and table you want, and then click the column header where you want to add the earned value field. On the Format tab, in the Columns group, click Insert Column. In the temporary drop-down menu that appears, click the earned value field you want. The field is applied to the inserted column and the drop-down menu is dismissed.

Understanding the Earned Value Fields

Measuring earned value helps you see the adherence to the baseline plan or deviation from it, in terms of cost and schedule. But when you review these numbers, what are you actually looking at? Are they good numbers or bad numbers? Or are they just right?

As a general rule, when you see positive numbers in the variance columns of the Earned Value table (that is, the SV, CV, and VAC columns), you're ahead of schedule or under budget so far. When you see negative numbers in these columns, the task is behind schedule or over budget. When you see $0.00 in the SV, CV, or VAC columns, the associated task is exactly on target with the schedule or budget.

The following list can help you understand how earned value fields are calculated in Project 2010 and can also help you interpret the data as part of your analysis. A listing with two names indicates that the calculation can be referred to by either of these names or initials.

- **Planned Value (PV) or Budgeted Cost of Work Scheduled (BCWS)** The original planned cost of a task up to the status date. BCWS indicates the amount of budget that should have been spent by now on this task (or this resource). For example, if a task should be 50 percent finished according to the schedule, the BCWS would be 50 percent of the original planned cost of that task. Project 2010 determines the values by adding the timephased baseline dates for the task up to the status date. Review this amount in conjunction with the BAC and EAC.

- **Earned Value (EV) or Budgeted Cost of Work Performed (BCWP)** The baseline cost of a task multiplied by the calculated percentage complete up to the status date. This reflects the cost of the task work actually done according to the original budget. BCWP indicates the amount of budget that should have been spent by now on this task (or this resource), based on the amount of actual work reported by this date. If the task is 50 percent complete, the BCWP will be the originally planned cost of the work on the task multiplied by 50 percent. For example, if the baseline cost for the task is $1,000, and the task is 50 percent complete, the BCWP is $1,000 times 50% or $500. Because this is a measure of actual work costs incurred, BCWP is sometimes called the earned value of a task. Compare this amount with the EV/BCWS and AC/ACWP.

- **Actual Cost (AC) or Actual Cost of Work Performed (ACWP)** The sum of all costs actually accrued for a task to date. It includes standard and overtime costs for assigned resources, any per-use costs, cost resources, and fixed costs for tasks. ACWP indicates the amount of budget that should have been spent by now on this task (or this resource), based on the actual work reported by this date. Compare this amount with the EV/BCWS and AC/BCWP.
- **Schedule Variance (SV)** The measure of the difference between the cost as planned and the cost as performed (BCWP – BCWS). Even though it's called schedule variance, the variance really calculated is the cost resulting from schedule considerations. The SV dollar amount indicates the difference between the baseline costs for scheduled tasks and actual progress reported on those tasks. A positive SV means that the task is ahead of schedule in terms of cost. A negative SV means that the task is behind schedule in terms of cost. An SV of $0.00 means that the task is exactly on schedule in terms of cost. SV does not necessarily indicate whether you're under or over budget; however, it can be an indicator that the budget should be looked at more closely. SV clearly shows how much schedule slippage and duration increases affect cost. Compare this figure with CV and VAC.
- **Cost Variance (CV)** The difference between the budgeted costs and the actual costs of a task (BCWP – ACWP). The CV dollar amount indicates the difference between the baseline and actual costs for tasks. A positive CV means that the task is currently under budget. A negative CV means that the task is currently over budget. A CV of $0.00 means that the task is exactly on budget. Compare this figure with SV and VAC.
- **Estimate At Completion (EAC)** The projected cost of a task at its completion, also known as Forecast At Completion (FAC). EAC is the amount calculated from the ACWP, BCWP, and the Cost Performance Index (CPI), resulting in a composite forecast total of costs for the task upon completion. This dollar amount indicates the current best guess of what this task will cost by the time it's finished. The projection is based on current schedule performance up to the status date. Compare this amount with the BAC.
- **Budgeted At Completion (BAC)** The baseline cost of a task at its completion. BAC is the cost for the task as planned. BAC is the same as the baseline cost, which includes assigned resource costs and any fixed costs for the task. The budgeted cost is based on the baseline planned schedule performance.

- **Variance At Completion (VAC)** The difference between actual cost at completion and baseline cost at completion, (BAC – EAC). VAC is the cost variance for a completed task. A negative VAC indicates that the forecasted cost for the task is currently over budget. A positive VAC indicates that the forecasted cost for the task is currently under budget. A VAC of $0.00 indicates that the task is right on budget. Compare this figure with SV and CV.
- **Cost Variance Percent (CV%)** The difference between how much a task should have cost and how much it has actually cost to date, displayed in the form of a percentage. CV is calculated as follows: [(BCWP – ACWP)/BCWP] * 100. A positive percentage indicates an under-budget condition, whereas a negative percentage indicates an over-budget condition.
- **Cost Performance Index (CPI)** The ratio of budgeted to actual cost of work performed. CPI is also known as Earned Value for Cost. When the CPI ratio is 1, the cost performance is exactly as planned, according to current work performance. A ratio greater than 1.0 indicates that you're under budget; less than 1.0 indicates that you're over budget. CPI is calculated by dividing BCWP by ACWP.
- **To Complete Performance Index (TCPI)** The ratio of the work yet to be done on a task to the funds still budgeted to be spent on that task. TCPI is calculated as follows: (BAC – BCWP)/(BAC – ACWP). TCPI helps you estimate whether you will have surplus funds or a shortfall. Values over 1.0 indicate a potential shortfall. Increased performance for remaining work would be needed to stay within budget.
- **Schedule Performance Index (SPI)** The ratio of budgeted cost of work performed to budgeted cost of work scheduled. SPI, which is also known as Earned Value for Schedule, is often used to estimate the project completion date. When the SPI ratio is 1.0, the task is precisely on schedule. A ratio greater than 1.0 indicates that you're ahead of schedule; less than 1.0 indicates that you're behind schedule. SPI is calculated by dividing BCWP by BCWS.
- **Schedule Variance Percent (SV%)** The percentage of how much you are ahead of or behind schedule for a task. SV is calculated as follows: (SV/BCWS) * 100. A positive percentage indicates that you're currently ahead of schedule, whereas a negative percentage indicates that you're behind schedule.
- **Physical Percent Complete** This is a user-entered value that can be used in place of % Complete when calculating earned value or measuring progress. It represents a judgment that overrides the calculations based on actual duration or actual work. To use this option, on the File tab, click Options, and then click Advanced in the left pane. Under Earned Value Options For This Project, click the box labeled Default Task Earned Value Method, and then click Physical % Complete.

TROUBLESHOOTING

Your earned value fields are all $0.00

If you applied an earned value table or inserted an earned value field only to find all the values are $0.00, it's likely that you're missing one or more of the pieces of information that Project 2010 needs to calculate earned value fields.

For an earned value to be calculated, you must have all of the following items in your project plan:

- A saved baseline
- Resources assigned to tasks
- Costs associated with assigned resources
- Actual progress information
- A status date

If you set a baseline and you're seeing all zeros except in the EAC and BAC columns, you're probably close to the beginning of your project and haven't entered any tracking information yet. As time goes by and you start entering task progress data, those numbers will start changing to reflect the schedule and current progress.

Another reason for all zeros can be that the status date is set too far in the past.

If you set a baseline and you're seeing all zeros in the SV, CV, and VAC columns, your project is running exactly as planned, with no positive or negative variances recorded at all. Make sure that all your tracking information is entered and up to date. If it is, and you're still seeing all those zeros, you're precisely on schedule and on budget—great job!

Generating the Earned Value Text Report

The Earned Value text report is based on the Earned Value table for tasks. Every nonsummary task is listed, along with its earned value calculations for BCWS, BCWP, ACWP, SV, CV, EAC, BAC, and VAC. To run the Earned Value report, follow these steps:

Reports

1. On the Project tab, in the Reports group, click Reports.
2. Double-click Costs.

3. Double-click Earned Value.

   A preview of the Earned Value report appears in the Print Backstage view, as shown in Figure 14-3.

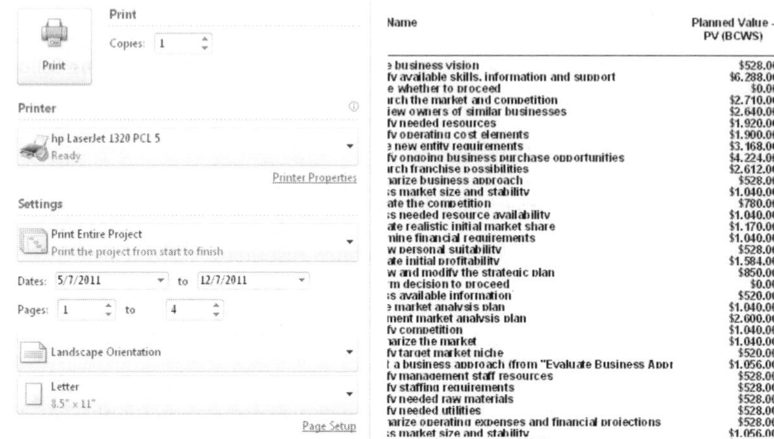

Figure 14-3 The Earned Value report shows earned values for all tasks on the basis of the specified status date.

Print

4. To print the report, click the Print button in the upper-left corner of the Backstage view.

Generating the Earned Value Over Time Visual Report

The Earned Value Over Time Report is a Microsoft Excel chart available within Project 2010. This report plots three lines: for Actual Cost of Work Performed (ACWP or AC), Budgeted Cost of Work Performed (BCWP or planned value), and Budgeted Cost of Work Performed (BCWP or earned value). Based on timephased task data, the lines are plotted over time.

To run the Earned Value Over Time Report, follow these steps:

Visual Reports

1. On the Project tab, in the Reports group, click Visual Reports.

   The Visual Reports–Create Report dialog box appears.

2. On the All tab or the Assignment Usage tab, click Earned Value Over Time Report.

3. Click View.

   Project 2010 gathers the earned value information from your project and sends it to Microsoft Excel 2010, where it plots the information in a line chart for your analysis.

PART 5

Managing Multiple Projects

Before you can use the sample files for Chapters 15 and 16, you'll need to install them from this book's companion content website. For more information about downloading and installing the sample files, see "About the Companion Content" on page xxviii.

CHAPTER 15

Managing Master Projects and Resource Pools

As a project manager, you juggle time, money, resources, and tasks to carry out and complete a project successfully. Often, however, you're not only juggling multiple elements of a single project, you're also juggling multiple projects—each with its own associated challenges. The following are three typical scenarios involving multiple projects:

- Kathryn manages a large project containing many phases or components for which other project managers are responsible. In Microsoft Project 2010, she can set up a master project with subprojects representing those subphases. She can keep an eye on the overall picture while the project managers responsible for the individual phases have complete control over their pieces of the project.

- Frank manages several unrelated projects and keeps the information for each in separate project files. Occasionally, however, he needs to see information about all of them together, perhaps to get accurate availability information about shared resources or to see whether milestone dates in the various projects are coinciding with one another. He might need to print a view or a report that temporarily combines the projects. With Project 2010, Frank can consolidate information from multiple related or unrelated projects, either temporarily or permanently.

- Nicole, Dennis, and Monique are project managers in the same organization. Although they manage different projects, they use many of the same resources. Sometimes, their projects conflict with one another because of demands on the same resources at the same time. In Project 2010, they can create a resource pool file that contains the resources they all use. They can then link their individual project files to that resource pool. The resource availability and usage information is available through that resource pool. When one project assigns tasks to a resource in the resource pool, the resource pool is updated with that resource's allocation information.

Structuring Master Projects with Subprojects

With Project 2010, you can insert one project into another. By default, inserted projects look and act like summary tasks in any task view, with their subordinate tasks readily available. You can view and change all tasks within that inserted project. The task information is changed in the source project file as well, because the two projects are linked by default.

Although you might insert projects for a variety of reasons, the most effective use of this capability is to create a *master project* structure with *subprojects* inserted within that master project. This structure is most useful when you have a large project containing a number of subcomponents, especially if those subcomponents are managed by other project managers. If you're managing the overall project, your master project can give you the view you need into the planning and execution of all the subprojects.

Even if you're the sole project manager, you might find the master project–subprojects structure helpful for alternating between project details and the overall project picture.

Information in the master project and subprojects is interactively linked. When project managers of the subprojects make changes, by default you see those changes reflected in your master project. The reverse is true as well—you can change subproject information in your master project, and those changes are updated in the source subproject.

Your master project can also contain regular tasks. Tasks and subprojects can be organized in relation to one another, and your inserted subprojects can be part of an outline structure and have dependencies, just like regular "native" tasks.

Note

Instead of inserting and linking projects together, you might need to just link an individual task in one project to a task in another project.

For information about linking tasks between projects, see "Linking Information Between Project Plans" on page 663.

Setting Up a Master Project

When you want to set up a master project with subprojects, first decide where all the files are going to reside. If you're the sole user of the projects and subprojects, the files can all be stored on your own computer. If you're handling the master project, and other project managers are responsible for subprojects, you'll need to store the projects on a central file server or in a shared folder to which all the managers have access.

Inserting Projects into a Master Project

Creating a master project is simply a matter of inserting subordinate projects into what you're designating as the central controlling project; that is, the master project. To insert a subproject into a master project, follow these steps:

1. Open the project that you want to become the master project.

2. Display the Gantt Chart or other task sheet.

3. Click the row below where you want to insert the project.

   You can insert the project at any level in an existing outline structure. The inserted project adopts the outline level of the task above the location where it's inserted.

Subproject

4. On the Project tab, in the Insert group, click Subproject.

   The Insert Project dialog box appears, as shown in Figure 15-1.

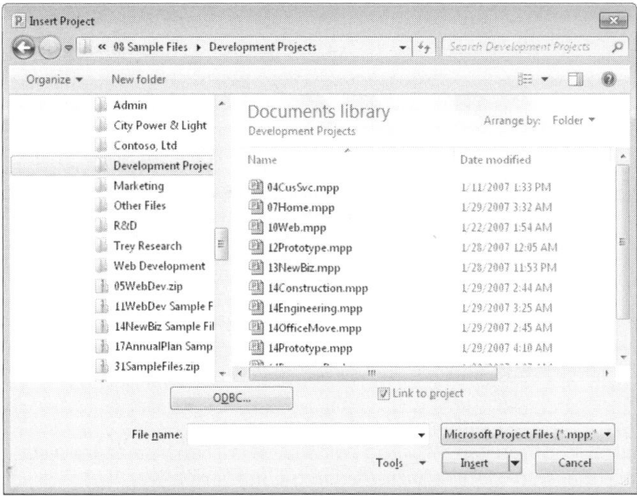

Figure 15-1 Browse in the Insert Project dialog box to find the project you want to insert.

5. Browse to the drive and folder that contains the project file to be inserted.

6. Click the name of the project file that you want to become a subproject, and then click the Insert button.

   The project is inserted, and its file name appears as a collapsed summary task name in the selected row, as shown in Figure 15-2. The Inserted Project icon appears in the Indicators column.

Inserted Project indicator

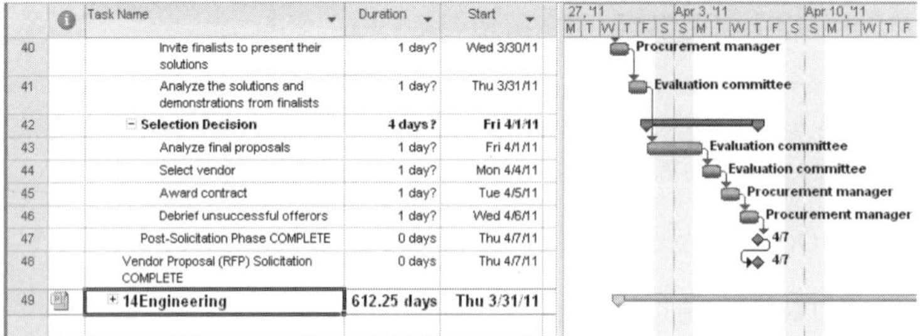

		Task Name	Duration	Start
40		Invite finalists to present their solutions	1 day?	Wed 3/30/11
41		Analyze the solutions and demonstrations from finalists	1 day?	Thu 3/31/11
42		− Selection Decision	4 days?	Fri 4/1/11
43		Analyze final proposals	1 day?	Fri 4/1/11
44		Select vendor	1 day?	Mon 4/4/11
45		Award contract	1 day?	Tue 4/5/11
46		Debrief unsuccessful offerors	1 day?	Wed 4/6/11
47		Post-Solicitation Phase COMPLETE	0 days	Thu 4/7/11
48		Vendor Proposal (RFP) Solicitation COMPLETE	0 days	Thu 4/7/11
49		+ 14Engineering	612.25 days	Thu 3/31/11

Figure 15-2 The inserted project looks like a summary task among your regular tasks.

7. To see the tasks in the inserted project, click the plus sign next to the project name.

   As shown in Figure 15-3, the subproject expands to show all tasks. They look and behave exactly as if you created them in this project.

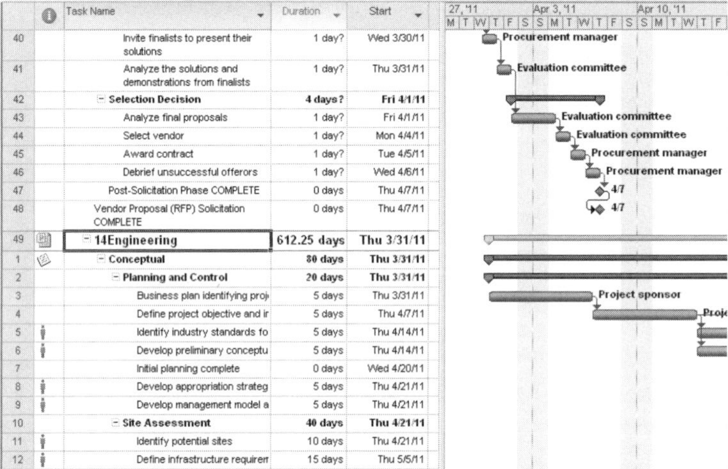

		Task Name	Duration	Start
40		Invite finalists to present their solutions	1 day?	Wed 3/30/11
41		Analyze the solutions and demonstrations from finalists	1 day?	Thu 3/31/11
42		− Selection Decision	4 days?	Fri 4/1/11
43		Analyze final proposals	1 day?	Fri 4/1/11
44		Select vendor	1 day?	Mon 4/4/11
45		Award contract	1 day?	Tue 4/5/11
46		Debrief unsuccessful offerors	1 day?	Wed 4/6/11
47		Post-Solicitation Phase COMPLETE	0 days	Thu 4/7/11
48		Vendor Proposal (RFP) Solicitation COMPLETE	0 days	Thu 4/7/11
49		− 14Engineering	612.25 days	Thu 3/31/11
1		− Conceptual	80 days	Thu 3/31/11
2		− Planning and Control	20 days	Thu 3/31/11
3		Business plan identifying proj	5 days	Thu 3/31/11
4		Define project objective and ir	5 days	Thu 4/7/11
5		Identify industry standards fo	5 days	Thu 4/14/11
6		Develop preliminary conceptu	5 days	Thu 4/14/11
7		Initial planning complete	0 days	Wed 4/20/11
8		Develop appropriation strateg	5 days	Thu 4/21/11
9		Develop management model a	5 days	Thu 4/21/11
10		− Site Assessment	40 days	Thu 4/21/11
11		Identify potential sites	10 days	Thu 4/21/11
12		Define infrastructure requirem	15 days	Thu 5/5/11

Figure 15-3 You can view and edit the tasks of an inserted project in the same way as those that were originally created in the master project.

   To hide the tasks in the inserted project, click the minus sign next to the project name.

8. Repeat steps 3 through 6 for any other projects you want to insert into your master project. (See Figure 15-4.)

   If you're inserting a project immediately after another inserted project, collapse the tasks of the latter subproject before inserting the next one. Otherwise, the newly inserted project will become a subproject within the previous inserted project instead of standing on its own.

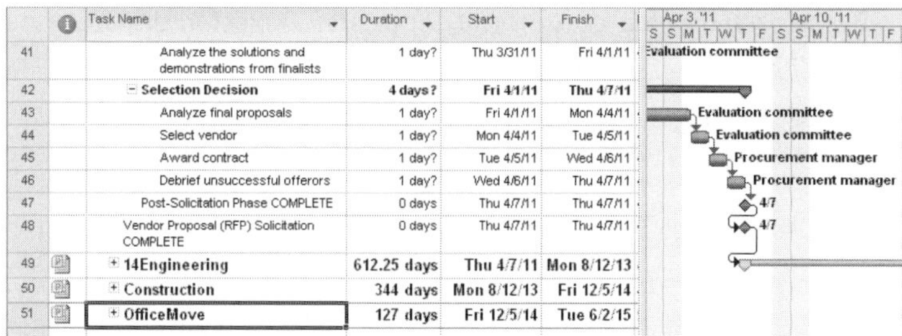

Figure 15-4 This master project contains three subprojects, each one containing the plan for a major project phase.

Indent

Outdent

Link Tasks

9. Indent or outdent the inserted project as needed using the Task, Schedule, Indent Task command or the Task, Schedule, Outdent Task command. Also link inserted projects or tasks to native tasks as appropriate to reflect task dependencies. To do this, click Task, Schedule, Link Tasks.

In the Network Diagram view, the summary task representing the subproject is formatted differently from other tasks and includes the path and name of the source project file. The subproject tasks themselves look the same as regular tasks.

In the Calendar view, the name of the subproject appears with the individual subproject tasks. If you don't see the subproject name, drag the bottom edge of a calendar row to increase its height.

Breaking a Large Project into Subprojects

You might know during the preplanning stage of your project that you want your project set up as a master project with subprojects, which makes things easier. On the other hand, you might not know until you're in the middle of project execution that a master project is just the solution you need. You can still set it up without having to significantly rework your project files.

If you already have multiple project files that you want to bring together with a master project, it's pretty simple. Create a new project file, insert the projects, and you're all set.

If you have a single large project file and you want to break it up into more manageable subproject files, it's a little trickier, but still very doable. In this case, you need to do some reverse engineering. The overall process for doing this is as follows:

Blank Project

1. Using File, New, Blank Project, create and save a blank project file for each new subproject you want to insert.

2. In each new file, click Project, Properties, Project Information to set the project start date (or project finish date if you're scheduling from the finish date) for the project.

   Set the project start date to the current start date of the first scheduled task in the set of tasks you want to move to the new file.

3. Click Project, Properties, Change Working Time to set the project calendar to match the project calendar in the original file.

   For information about copying calendars and other project elements from one project file to another, see "Copying Project Elements by Using the Organizer" on page 630.

4. Move tasks from the large project file into the subproject file by using the Cut or Copy and Paste commands on the Task tab, in the Clipboard group.

   Be sure to select all task information by selecting the row headers, not just the task names. When just the cell is selected, you copy just the contents of the cell; when the entire row is selected, you copy the entire task, which is what you want. Selecting and copying the entire task copies all necessary task information, including any assigned resources, actual progress information, and other information you might not even see in the current view, to the new project file.

   For more information about moving project information, see "Copying and Moving Information Between Projects" on page 625.

5. After you set up the separate project files with their proper project start and finish dates and calendars, you can insert those files as subprojects into your master project.

With Microsoft Project Professional 2010 and Microsoft Project Server 2010, you can insert one enterprise project into another to create a master project-subproject relationship between projects. Using this technique, you can model a program of projects, reflecting all the projects that are being implemented under a specific program in your organization. The overarching program can be represented as the master project, with all the projects within that program set up as subprojects within the master project.

For more information, see "Setting Up a Program of Projects" on page 920.

Working with Subproject Information

You can edit any task, resource, or assignment in a subproject. By default, any change you make to subproject information is instantly made in the source project file. Likewise, any change made in the source project file updates the information in your master project because the subproject and source project are *linked*. This updating is convenient because you never have to worry about whether you're synchronized with the most current subproject information.

TROUBLESHOOTING

Your master project has duplicate resource names

Often, your master project contains a set of tasks and a set of resources assigned to those tasks. When you insert a project, the resources from that inserted project are added to your master project. Resource information appears in the resource views, and task information from the subproject appears in the task views, just as if you had entered it in the master project originally. You can review and edit the information normally.

If you insert a project that contains some of the same resources as your master project, you see the names listed twice in your resource sheets. One instance of the resource name is associated with the master project, and the other instance is associated with the subproject. If that resource is a part of other projects you insert, that name can appear additional times.

You can assign resources from a particular subproject to tasks only in that subproject. That is, you cannot assign resources from one subproject to tasks in a different subproject.

Insert Column

To see which resources are associated with which project, add the Project column to the Resource Sheet or Resource Usage view. Click Format, Columns, Insert Column. Type **pr** to move quickly to the Project field. Select it to insert it into the view.

If you want to work with a single set of resources across all your projects, consider setting up a resource pool.

For more information, see "Sharing Resources by Using a Resource Pool" on page 614.

Changing Subproject Information to Read-Only

In some cases, you might not want subproject information to be changed from the master project. Maybe you want to view it only in the master project—which might be the case when you have several project managers in charge of their own subprojects—and you need to see only the high-level view of all integrated project information. In this case, you can change a subproject to be read-only information in your master project, as follows:

1. Display the Gantt Chart or other task view.
2. Click the subproject summary task name.
3. On the Task tab, in the Properties group, click Information.

Information

4. In the Inserted Project Information dialog box, click the Advanced tab, as shown in Figure 15-5.

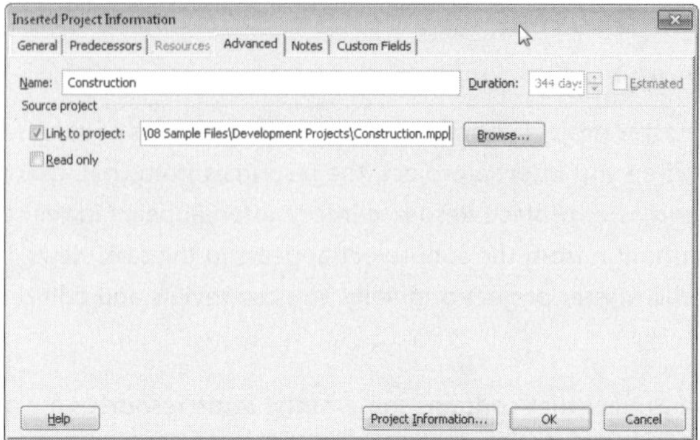

Figure 15-5 Use the Advanced tab in the Inserted Project Information dialog box to change a subproject to read-only or to remove the link to the subproject.

5. Select the Read Only check box.

   Now, if you make changes to any subproject information and then try to save the master project, you'll see a message reminding you that the subproject is read-only.

Whether you make a subproject read-only or not, whenever you change subproject information in a master project and save the master project, you are given the choice to save the subproject information to the subproject file. You can always discard those changes.

INSIDE OUT Is the subproject read-only or isn't it?

If you set your subproject as read-only in your master project, be aware of certain exceptions to read-only subproject enforcement.

If you work in the master project without opening the subproject file, everything behaves as expected: If you change subproject information in the master project, when you try to save the file, Project 2010 reminds you that the subproject is read-only. It also gives you the opportunity to save the subproject as a new file or discard the changes. You can still save changes to other tasks in the master project that are not read-only.

But suppose that you want to open both the master project file and subproject file. The enforcement of the read-only setting depends on which file you open first. If you open the subproject file first and then the master project file, you can make changes to subproject information in the master project. The changes are reflected in the subproject file, and you can save them.

To be sure that your read-only settings are enforced, open only your master project, or open the master project first and then the subproject file. In this case, not only can you not save subproject information changed from the master project, you can't save edits made directly in the subproject file.

Work with Subproject-Related Fields

You might find it helpful to add certain subproject-related fields to a task sheet or the Resource Sheet. You can add the Project, Subproject File, and Subproject Read Only fields to a task sheet. In addition, if you want to know which project a resource is associated with, add the Project field to the Resource Sheet.

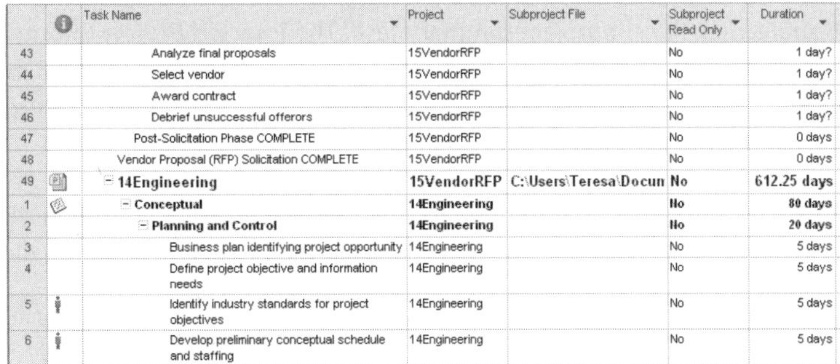

		Task Name	Project	Subproject File	Subproject Read Only	Duration
43		Analyze final proposals	15VendorRFP		No	1 day?
44		Select vendor	15VendorRFP		No	1 day?
45		Award contract	15VendorRFP		No	1 day?
46		Debrief unsuccessful offerors	15VendorRFP		No	1 day?
47		Post-Solicitation Phase COMPLETE	15VendorRFP		No	0 days
48		Vendor Proposal (RFP) Solicitation COMPLETE	15VendorRFP		No	0 days
49		− 14Engineering	15VendorRFP	C:\Users\Teresa\Docun	No	612.25 days
1		− **Conceptual**	**14Engineering**		**No**	**80 days**
2		− **Planning and Control**	**14Engineering**		**No**	**20 days**
3		Business plan identifying project opportunity	14Engineering		No	5 days
4		Define project objective and information needs	14Engineering		No	5 days
5		Identify industry standards for project objectives	14Engineering		No	5 days
6		Develop preliminary conceptual schedule and staffing	14Engineering		No	5 days

To add a field, right-click the column heading to the right of where you want to insert the new field, and then click Insert Column. You might also click in the Add New Column column available on every sheet view. Type the first two or three letters of the field you want, and then select it to insert it into the newly created column.

If you make a subproject read-only, and you add the Subproject Read Only column to a task sheet, you'll see that the subproject summary task is marked Yes, whereas the subtasks are marked No. However, they're all read-only.

You can also sort, group, or filter tasks or resources by these fields.

For more information about the ways you can view project data, see "Rearranging Your Project Information" on page 173.

Viewing the Critical Path in a Master Project

By default, Project 2010 calculates a single critical path across all your projects. If you prefer, you can change your settings to see the critical path for each subproject, as follows:

1. In your master project, click File, Options, and then click Schedule.
2. Under Calculation Options For This Project, clear the check box labeled Inserted Projects Are Calculated Like Summary Tasks.

   This step results in a critical path being calculated for the master project independently of the subprojects. In addition, the critical path for each subproject is shown.

You can easily see the critical path(s) in the Tracking Gantt chart. To see the critical path in any Gantt view, on the Format tab, in the Bar Styles group, select the Critical Tasks check box.

Review Overall Project Information for an Inserted Project

You can review project information and statistics for a subproject in a master project. Double-click the subproject summary task. The Inserted Project Information dialog box appears. Click the Project Information button. The Project Information dialog box appears for the inserted project, showing the project start, finish, and status dates, as well as the name of the project calendar.

To see overall project information for the inserted project—including the project start, finish, and cost—click the Statistics button in the Project Information dialog box.

TROUBLESHOOTING

You lose text and bar formatting when you insert projects

The formatting of the master project is adopted by any inserted projects. If you changed the styles for text, Gantt bars, or Network Diagram nodes in a subproject, you won't see those customizations in the master project. However, formatting changes you made to the master project are adopted by subprojects that you insert. Also, any formatting changes are retained in the subproject file, even if the subproject and master project are linked.

Unlinking a Subproject from Its Source File

You can keep a subproject in a master project but unlink the subproject from its source project file. When you unlink a subproject from its source project file, changes to the source file won't affect the subproject in the master project, and vice versa. To disconnect a subproject from its source, follow these steps:

1. Display the Gantt Chart or other task view.
2. Double-click the subproject summary task.
3. In the Inserted Project Information dialog box, click the Advanced tab.

4. Clear the Link To Project check box.

5. Click OK.

6. If a message asks whether you want to save changes to the subproject, click Yes or No as appropriate.

   The subproject is now disconnected from its source, and all the tasks are adopted as native to the master project. The Inserted Project icon is removed from the Indicators column. Although the project file name still appears in the summary task name field, as shown in Figure 15-6, it's now just a regular summary task—not an inserted project.

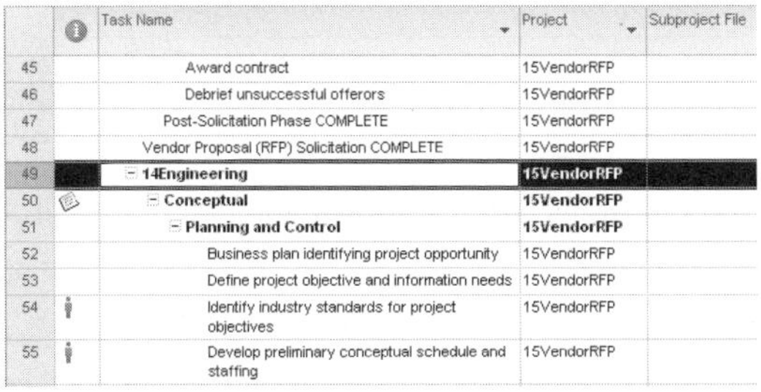

		Task Name	Project	Subproject File
45		Award contract	15VendorRFP	
46		Debrief unsuccessful offerors	15VendorRFP	
47		Post-Solicitation Phase COMPLETE	15VendorRFP	
48		Vendor Proposal (RFP) Solicitation COMPLETE	15VendorRFP	
49		**− 14Engineering**	**15VendorRFP**	
50		**− Conceptual**	**15VendorRFP**	
51		**− Planning and Control**	**15VendorRFP**	
52		Business plan identifying project opportunity	15VendorRFP	
53		Define project objective and information needs	15VendorRFP	
54		Identify industry standards for project objectives	15VendorRFP	
55		Develop preliminary conceptual schedule and staffing	15VendorRFP	

Figure 15-6 The tasks from the disconnected subproject remain in the project, but they no longer have a link to the source project file.

Removing a Subproject from the Master Project

You can completely delete a subproject from the master project and keep the subproject file intact. Note that removing a subproject from the master project cannot be undone. To remove a subproject from the master project:

1. Display the Gantt Chart or other task view.

2. Select the heading of the row containing the subproject summary task.

3. Press the Delete key.

   A Planning Wizard message reminds you that you're about to delete a summary task along with all of its subtasks.

4. Be sure that the Continue option is selected, and then click OK.

   The subproject is removed from the master project. However, the source file for the subproject is still intact.

Consolidating Project Information

You can join information from multiple projects into a *consolidated project*, which can be useful if you're managing several unrelated projects at one time. Sometimes you need to see information from several projects in relation to one another, particularly when you want to view, organize, or work with project information from all projects as a single unit.

You can consolidate projects temporarily, for example, to print a specific view based on information in the projects. You can sort, group, or filter the tasks or resources of the combined projects. If this is a combination you use frequently, you can make it permanent and save the consolidated file for future use.

What's the Difference Between a Consolidated Project and a Master Project?

A consolidated project is simply another implementation of the subprojects feature. The differences are as follows:

- **The consolidated project is not necessarily structured as a hierarchy, as are the master project and subprojects. With a consolidated project, you might bring all the projects together at the same outline level. With subprojects, some projects might be subordinate to others, and you're likely to need to arrange them in a specific sequence.**
- **The projects might be completely unrelated to one another. The consolidated project might simply be a repository for multiple project files.**
- **The consolidation of projects in a single file might be temporary—just long enough for you to review certain information or generate a report.**

To combine multiple projects into a single consolidated project file, follow these steps:

1. On the File tab, click New. In the Backstage view, double-click Blank Project.

   A new project window appears.

2. On the Project tab, in the Insert group, click Subproject.

3. Select all the project files you want to include in the consolidated project.

   If the project files are all stored on the same drive and in the same folder, open that location. Use the Shift key to select multiple adjacent project files. Use the Ctrl key to select multiple nonadjacent project files.

4. Click the Insert button. The projects are inserted into the new file, as shown in Figure 15-7.

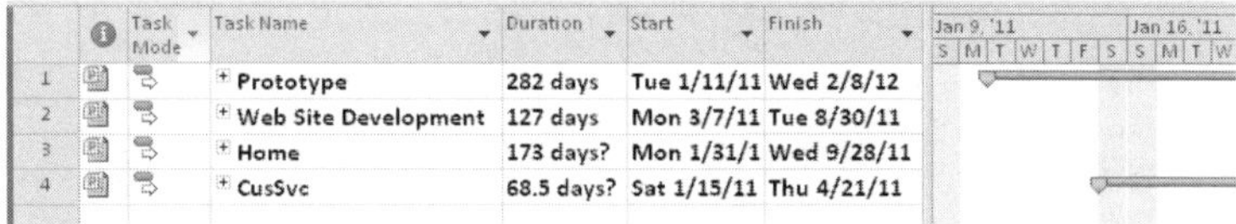

Figure 15-7 The selected projects are inserted into a new window.

5. If you need to consolidate project files located on other drives or folders, repeat steps 2 through 4 until all the files you want are consolidated into your new project file.

6. To keep this file permanently, on the File tab, click Save. Select the drive and folder where you want to store the consolidated file. Enter a name for the consolidated file in the File Name box, and then click the Save button.

   If you're just using this file temporarily, you don't need to save it.

If the project files you want to consolidate are already open, you can use the following alternative method to consolidate them:

1. Be sure that all the project files you want to consolidate are open.

New Window

2. On the View tab, in the Window group, click New Window.

3. In the list of project files that appears in the New Window dialog box, click the names of the open project files you want to consolidate, as shown in Figure 15-8.

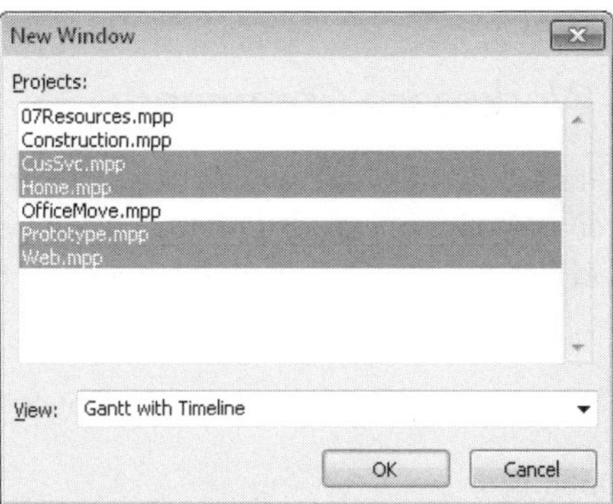

Figure 15-8 In the New Window dialog box, select the names of the project files you want to consolidate.

4. In the View list, click the view in which you want to initially display the consolidated information.

5. Click OK.

   A new project window appears with the project files inserted in alphabetical order and expanded to show all tasks. (See Figure 15-9.)

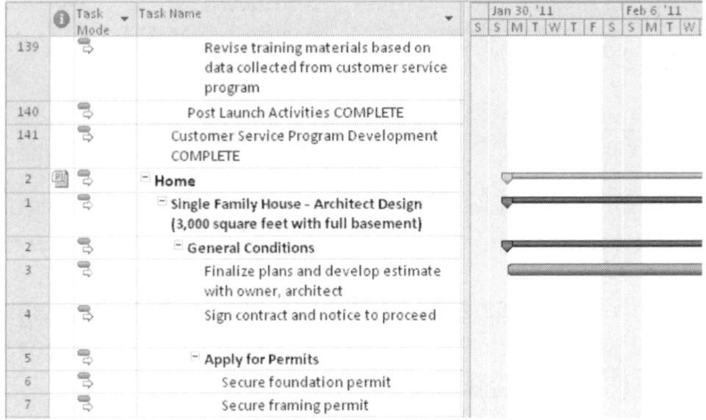

Figure 15-9 The selected projects are inserted into a new window.

Opening Multiple Project Files as a Set

If you always open the same set of project files, you can put those files together in a project *workspace*. Without creating a master project or consolidating the files into a single project file, you can simply associate the projects together. When you open the workspace file, all projects that are a part of that workspace open at once.

You first need to make the Save Workspace command available, and then you can create a workspace file.

Accessing the Save Workspace Command

Earlier versions of Microsoft Project included the Save Workspace command on the File menu. In Project 2010, this command is not included on the ribbon by default. However, it's still available, and you can add it to a custom group on the ribbon or to the Quick Access Toolbar.

To add the Save Workspace command to the Quick Access Toolbar, follow these steps:

1. On the File tab, click Options.
2. In the left pane of the Project Options dialog box, click Quick Access Toolbar.
3. In the Choose Commands From box, click Commands Not In The Ribbon.
4. Scroll down and click Save Workspace.

5. Click the Add button.

   The Save Workspace command is added to the Customize Quick Access Toolbar list on the right.

6. Click OK.

   The Save Workspace command now appears on your Quick Access Toolbar.

Adding a command to the ribbon is more involved than adding it to the Quick Access Toolbar, but doing so can be useful if you want the Save Workspace command on a particular tab. To learn how to add a command to the ribbon, see "Customizing the Project 2010 Ribbon" on page 1153.

Creating the Project Workspace File

After the Save Workspace command is available on the Quick Access Toolbar or the ribbon, you can create a project workspace file.

To save a project workspace, follow these steps:

1. Open all project files you want to be a part of the workspace.

2. Close any project files you do not want to save in the workspace.

Save Workspace

3. On the Quick Access Toolbar (or wherever you added the command), click Save Workspace.

   The Save Workspace As dialog box appears.

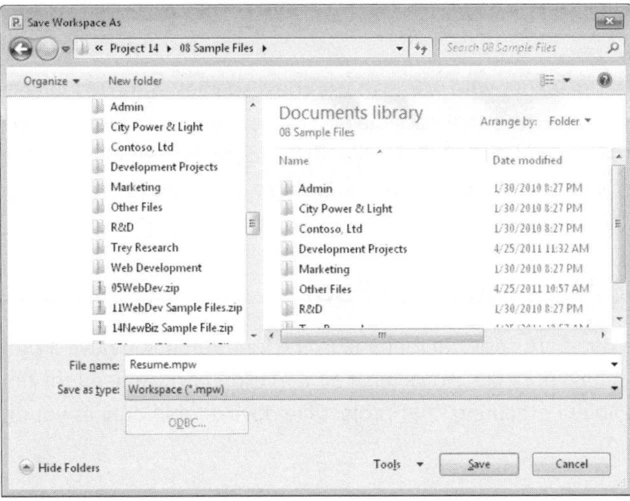

4. Select the drive and folder where you want to save the workspace file, and then enter the name for the workspace in the File Name box.

5. Click the Save button. Workspace files are saved with the *.mpw* extension.

Now, whenever you open the workspace file, all files that are a part of that workspace are opened at the same time. To open a workspace file, on the File tab, click Open. Navigate to the drive and folder where the workspace file resides. In the Files Of Type box, click Workspaces (*.mpw). All project workspace files in that folder are listed. Double-click the one you want to open, and all associated project files open at once.

You can create multiple workspace files to open different sets of project files.

Sharing Resources by Using a Resource Pool

Typically, when you create a project file, you set up and schedule your tasks and then add resources and assign tasks to them. Often, however, resources are assigned to tasks in multiple projects. You might be the manager of these different projects and use the same resources in all of them. Or, multiple project managers might share the same resources for their projects.

To prevent conflicts between projects and avoid resource overallocation among multiple projects, you can create a resource pool. A *resource pool* is a project file that's devoted to maintaining information about resources, including their availability, costs, and current usage or allocation. A resource pool file can be an existing project file whose resources are shared by other projects. More typically, however, a resource pool is a project file without tasks, whose sole purpose is to provide resource information to any number of other projects.

Any project manager who wants to use the resources in the resource pool file can link the project file to the resource pool file and make the project file a *sharer file*. When you link a project file to the resource pool file, the resource names and other information appear in your project file. You can then assign those resources to tasks as if you originally created them in this project file.

Setting Up a Resource Pool

Resource pools are easier to manage in the long run if you have a project file that serves as the resource pool file. However, if all the resources you need for the pool are already in a project you're executing, that project file does double duty as your resource pool file as well.

The Enterprise Resource Pool

Using a local resource pool for multiple projects is similar in concept to using the enterprise resource pool. If you're set up for enterprise project management using Project Professional 2010 and Project Server 2010, your enterprise resource pool consists of all resources identified as part of the organization. With the enterprise resource pool, you can check skill sets, availability, costs, and other resource information to find the right resources for your project.

Because of this access to the enterprise resource pool, whenever you work with enterprise projects, local resource pool functionality is disabled.

To set up the enterprise resource pool, the project server administrator should read "Creating the Enterprise Resource Pool" on page 838. To use the enterprise resource pool, project managers should see "Building Your Enterprise Project Team" on page 927.

To create a resource pool in its own dedicated project file, follow these steps:

1. On the File tab, click New, and then double-click Blank Project.

   A new project window appears.

Resource Sheet

2. On the View tab, in the Resource Views group, click Resource Sheet.
3. Enter the information for all work or equipment resources you want to be included in the resource pool.

   This information should include at least the resource name, maximum units, and standard rate. If different from the default, also enter the cost per use, cost accrual method, and calendar. Enter the initials, group, and overtime rate if such information is applicable to your projects.
4. If you want material resources to be a part of your resource pool, enter at least the material resource names, identify them as material resources, and then enter the material labels and the unit costs.
5. If you want cost resources to be a part of your resource pool, enter at least the cost resource names and identify them as cost resources.

Save

6. On the Quick Access Toolbar, click Save. Select the drive and folder where you want to store the resource pool file.

   If other project managers will be using this resource pool, be sure that you save the file in a location to which you all have access, such as a central file server or a shared folder.

7. Enter a name for the resource pool file in the File Name box, and then click Save.

   Give the resource pool file a name that identifies it as such—for example, **ResPool.mpp** or **Marketing Resources.mpp**.

For more information about entering resource information, see Chapter 7, "Setting Up Resources in the Project."

If you already have resource information in an existing project file, you can use it to create your resource pool file and cut down on your data entry. One method for doing this is to copy the existing project file, and then delete the task information from the file. To do this, follow these steps:

1. Open the project file that contains the resource information you want to use.
2. On the File tab, click Save As.
3. Select the drive and folder in which you want to store the new resource pool file.
4. Enter a unique name for the resource pool file in the File Name box, and then click Save.
5. Display the Gantt Chart or other task sheet.
6. Click the Select All box in the upper-left corner of the sheet view, above the row 1 header.

   The entire sheet is selected.
7. Press the Delete key. If a confirmation prompt appears, click Yes.

   All task information is deleted.
8. Display the Resource Sheet and check the resource information.

   Update any information as necessary, including adding or removing resources.
9. On the Quick Access Toolbar, click Save.

Another method of using existing resource information is to copy and paste information from the existing project files to the new resource pool file. To do this, follow these steps:

1. Open the project file that contains resource information you want to copy.
2. Display the Resource Sheet.

3. Select resource information by selecting the row headers.

   To select adjacent resource rows, drag from the first to the last row header, or click the first row, hold down the Shift key, and then click the last row.

   To select nonadjacent resource rows, click the first row header, and then hold down the Ctrl key and click all other rows you want to select.

   Be sure to select the row headers, not just the task names. Selecting row headers copies all the necessary information—including maximum units and costs—associated with the resource, even if that information isn't displayed in the sheet view.

4. On the Task tab, in the Clipboard group, click Copy.
5. On the File tab, click New, and then double-click Blank Project.
6. In the new project window, display the Resource Sheet.
7. On the Task tab, in the Clipboard group, click Paste.

   The resource information you copied from the other project file is inserted into the appropriate fields in the Resource Sheet.

8. On the Quick Access Toolbar, click Save.
9. Select the drive and folder in which you want to store the resource pool file.

   Enter a name for the resource pool file in the File Name box, and then click Save.

Linking a Project to Your Resource Pool

After the resource pool is set up, you can link project files to it. The project file that uses a resource pool is called the *sharer file*. As long as the resource pool and the sharer file are open at the same time, the resources in the resource pool file appear in the sharer file as if they were originally entered there. Even if you have resources in your project file, you can still use resources from the resource pool.

To link your project to a resource pool, follow these steps:

1. Open the resource pool file.
2. Open your project file that you want to share resources from the resource pool.
3. On the Resource tab, in the Assignments group, click Resource Pool, and then click Share Resources.

   Resource Pool

   The Share Resources dialog box appears, as shown in Figure 15-10.

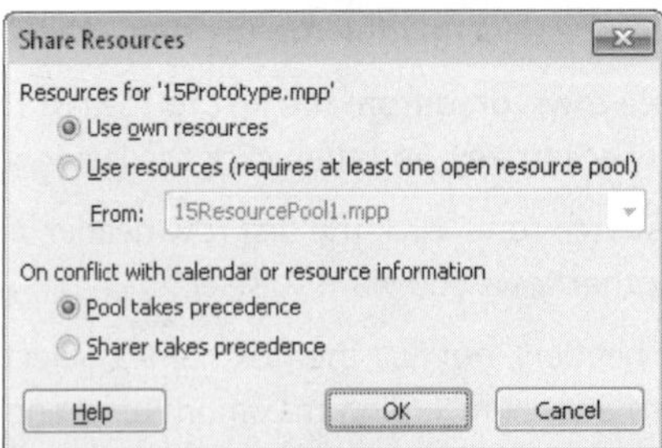

Figure 15-10 Use the Share Resources dialog box to specify that you want your project file to use the resource pool.

4. Select the Use Resources option.

5. In the From list, click the name of the resource pool file. All open files are displayed in this list.

6. Under On Conflict With Calendar Or Resource Information, specify how you want any resource information conflicts to be handled.

   If you want the resource pool information to be the final authority in a conflict, select the Pool Takes Precedence option. This is the default, and it is the recommended option.

   If you want the resource information in the sharer file (your project file) to be the final authority, select the Sharer Takes Precedence option.

7. Click OK.

   Your project file is now designated as a sharer file of the resource pool, thereby linking the two.

   Now all resource information in the resource pool appears in your project file as shown in Figure 15-11. Any resource information in your project file is added to the resource pool.

		Resource Name	Type	Material Label	Initials	Group	Max. Units	Std. Rate
1		Hardware	Cost		H			
2		Supplies	Material	each	S			$200.00
3		Vivian Atlas	Work		V		50%	$70.00/hr
4		Paul Shakespear	Work		P		100%	$65.00/hr
5		Sandeep Katyal	Work		S		50%	$65.00/hr
6		Yolanda Sanchez	Work		Y		100%	$65.00/hr
7		Designer	Work		D		300%	$75.00/hr
8		Product Engineer	Work		P		200%	$90.00/hr
9		Drafter	Work		D		100%	$55.00/hr
10		Editor	Work		E		100%	$65.00/hr
11		Dean Halstead	Work				100%	$65.00/hr
12		Michael Patten	Work				100%	$60.00/hr

Figure 15-11 With the resource pool and sharer file linked, the resource information for both files is merged.

TROUBLESHOOTING

The resource sharing commands are dimmed

If the Resource Sharing and Share Resources commands are unavailable, it indicates that you are working with an enterprise project through Project Professional 2010 and Project Server 2010. Enterprise projects do not use local resource pools. They use the enterprise resource pool instead.

To access the enterprise resource pool, on the Resource tab, in the Assignments group, click Resource Pool, and then click Enterprise Resource Pool.

For more information, see "Building Your Enterprise Project Team" on page 927.

TROUBLESHOOTING

You don't see an open project file in the Share Resources dialog box

Typically, any open project files are shown in the Use Resources From list in the Share Resources dialog box. Sharer files are the exception, however. You are never given the choice to use a sharer file as a resource pool.

You can now work with your project file and the resources as usual, including assigning resources from the pool to tasks. Be sure to save both the sharer file and the resource pool file because you're saving the link between the two. You're also saving any resource information from your sharer file as additional resources in the resource pool.

Note

You can make a regular project file into a resource pool file. Open the project file you want to use as a resource pool file. Also open the project file that is to become the sharer file. In the sharer file, click Resource, Assignments, Resource Pool, Share Resources. Select the Use Resources option, and then select the other project file in the From list.

Although making a regular project file into a resource pool can be convenient at first, keep in mind that when the project ends, the assignments will still be a part of the resource pool file, even though they're no longer relevant.

The next time you open your sharer file, you'll be prompted to also open the resource pool, as shown in Figure 15-12.

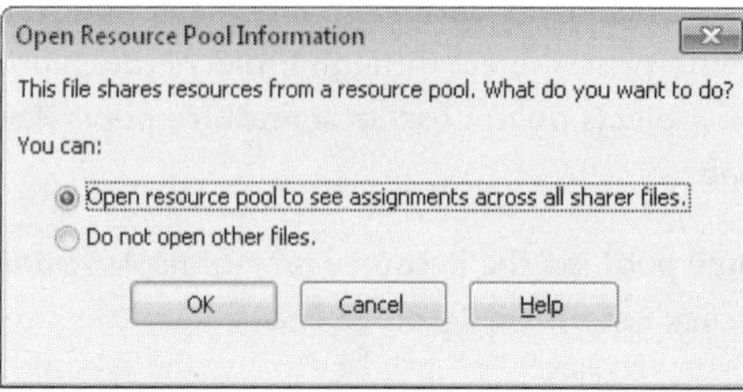

Figure 15-12 If you choose to open the resource file, you'll be able to see all resources, including their assignments, in your sharer file.

Click OK to open the resource file. It opens with read-only privileges. If you select the Do Not Open Other Files option, the resources you're using from the resource pool do not appear.

If you open a resource pool file before opening any of its sharer files, you are prompted to select whether you want read-only or read-write privileges in the resource pool file, as shown in Figure 15-13.

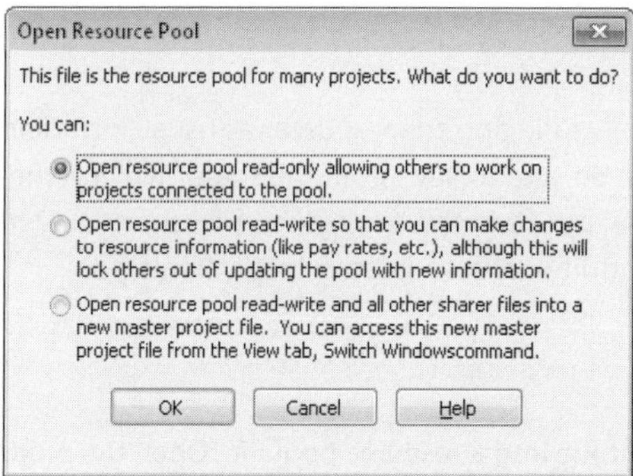

Figure 15-13 You see this alert whenever you directly open a resource pool file. Specify whether you want to open the resource pool as read-only or read-write.

Select the first option to open the resource pool as a read-only file. This is the default, and you should use this option in most cases. You can still update assignment information when working with a read-only resource pool.

Select the second option to open the resource pool as a read-write file. Choose this option when you need to explicitly change basic resource information such as cost or group information. Only one user can open a resource pool as a read-write file at one time.

Select the third option to open the resource pool as a read-write file along with all of its sharer files. These files will be combined into a master project file.

TROUBLESHOOTING

The resources are missing from your sharer file

Suppose that you already linked your project file to a resource pool, thereby making the file a sharer file. But when you close the resource pool, the resources no longer show up in your sharer file. Open the resource pool, and because the two files are linked, the resources appear again in the sharer file.

Checking Availability of Resource Pool Resources

Display the Resource Usage view or the Resource Graph in the resource pool file to check the availability of resources across all sharer projects. In these views, you can see all the assignments for all the resources in the resource pool. You can see the amount of time they're assigned, if they're overallocated, or if they have time available to take on more assignments.

For more information about checking resource allocation, see "Monitoring and Adjusting Resource Workload" on page 511.

INSIDE OUT Where did all these assignments come from?

When you are reviewing assignments across multiple projects in the Resource Usage view of the resource pool file, there's no way to discern which assignments are from which projects.

If you want to see the projects responsible for each assignment, add the Project field to the sheet area of the Resource Usage view. Right-click the Work column heading, for example, and then click Insert Column from the menu that appears. A new column appears to the left of the Work column, with the drop-down menu of all available field names. Type **pr** to quickly scroll through the menu, click Project, and then click OK. The Project field appears in the new column, and the project file name for each assignment is listed.

When assigning resources to tasks, you can also use the filters in the Assign Resources dialog box to find resources with the right skills and availability. (See Figure 15-14.)

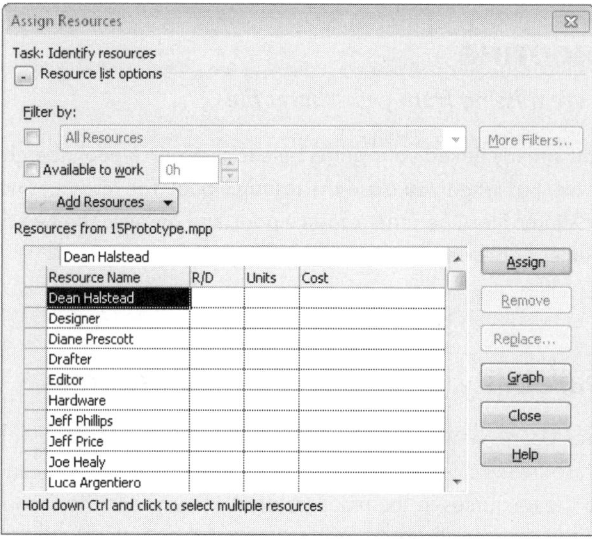

Figure 15-14 Use the Assign Resources dialog box to check resource availability while making assignments.

For example, you can find only those resources from the resource pool who are associated with a particular defined group. Or, you can list only material resources. You can also specify that you just want to see a list of resources who have at least 16 hours of availability across all the projects to which they're assigned.

For more information about filtering resources and reviewing availability graphs, see "Assigning Work Resources to Tasks" on page 283.

Updating Resource Pool Information

If you need to change resource-specific information—such as cost information, notes, maximum units, or working time calendar—you need to open the resource pool file with read-write privileges and change the information. After you save these changes, the next time any users of the sharer files open the resource pool or refresh their resource pool information, they'll see the updated information.

If you're changing resource assignments, there's more flexibility. You can open the resource pool file with read-only privileges, access all your resource information, and change assignment information, as needed. When you start to save the sharer file, a message appears, asking if you want to update the resource pool with your changes, as shown in Figure 15-15. Click OK. Even though the resource pool is read-only, it's updated with your changes at that moment. Any other users of the resource pool will see the changes the next time they open the resource pool or when they refresh the open resource pool.

Figure 15-15 This message appears when you're working with a read-only resource pool and you make changes that affect resources in the pool.

Another way to update the resource pool after making assignment changes is to click Resource, Assignments, Resource Pool, Update Resource Pool.

If you're working with a sharer file and the resource pool that others also use, it's a good idea to periodically refresh the resource pool to be sure that you have the latest changes to resource and assignment information. On the Resource tab, in the Assignment group, click Resource Pool, and then click Refresh Resource Pool.

INSIDE OUT **The resource pool and system performance**

Sometimes project managers find that Project 2010 runs slower when large resource pools are linked with large or complex project files. If you experience system performance problems such as these, open the sharer file without the resource pool file. If you can get by without the resource information, you'll be able to work faster.

Another alternative is to divide your project into a master project with subprojects, and then link the resource pool with the smaller subprojects.

Disconnecting a Resource Pool from a Project Plan

If you no longer need the resource pool and the sharer file to be linked, you can disconnect them as follows:

1. Open both the resource pool and the sharer file.

2. Display the sharer file.

3. On the Resource tab, in the Assignment group, click Resource Pool, and then click Share Resources.

4. Select the Use Own Resources option.

Any resources not assigned to projects in the sharer file disappear from the project file, while the resources assigned to tasks in the sharer project remain. Any assignment information for these resources is removed from the resource pool file.

You can also disconnect the link from within the resource pool as follows:

1. Open the resource pool.

2. On the Resource tab, in the Assignments group, click Resource Pool, and then click Share Resources. The Share Resources dialog box opens, as shown in Figure 15-16.

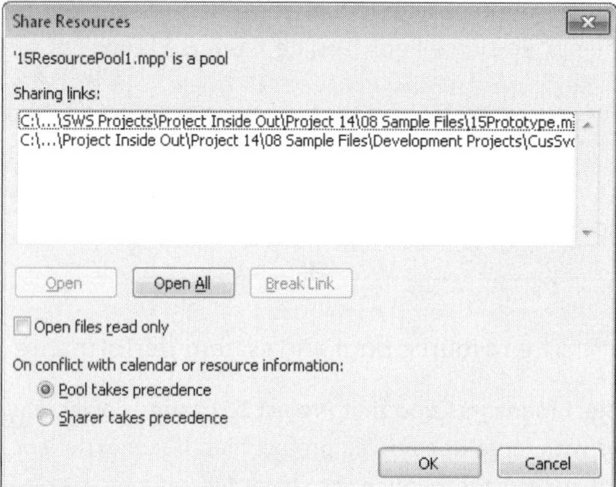

Figure 15-16 In the resource pool, the Share Resources dialog box shows the path of all sharer files.

3. In the Sharing Links box, click the name of the sharer file that you want to disconnect from the resource pool.

4. Click the Break Link button.

CHAPTER 16

Exchanging Information Between Project Plans

IMAGINE that you're starting a new project plan, and you realize there are a series of tasks in another project you worked on that you want to copy over. Or maybe another project has a handful of resources you want to copy and use, along with their accounting codes, calendars, and costs. In Microsoft Project 2010, you can copy task or resource information, or the contents of specific fields, from one project to another. Copying this information can save you a lot of time in data entry.

Another tremendous timesaver is the ability to copy major customizations between two project plans. You might have created a custom view in one project that displays your frequently used columns in the order you like. You can copy that view and make it available in all your other projects. The same goes for many other elements you can customize, including tables, filters, macros, reports, and more.

Beyond copying tasks, resources, fields, or custom elements, another means of exchanging project information is to create links between tasks in different project plans. If the project you're managing is a piece of a much larger project, it might be advantageous to link to dependent tasks in other plans and show the interdependencies that exist. Creating these links can be vital in modeling the schedule when a task in one project depends on the start or finish of a task in another project.

With Microsoft Project 2010, you can easily exchange different types of information between project plans, which enables you not only to model your project appropriately, but also to increase your efficiency by decreasing duplicated entries or development.

Copying and Moving Information Between Projects

Suppose that a project you just finished has a set of resources you want to use in a project you're starting to plan. You can copy the resource information from one project to another by using the Copy and Paste commands.

Maybe you're working with a huge project, and you need to break it up into a master project and subprojects. Or maybe several people are managing different pieces of a single project, and you're trying to pull together fragments of the different project files related to that one project. You can move task information from one project to another by using the Cut and Paste commands.

You can copy or move entire sets of task or resource information. You can also copy individual fields of information, such as task names and durations, or resource names.

INSIDE OUT Deciding how to best take advantage of existing information in other projects

In this section, we're discussing how to copy and paste bits of information from one project to another. This is most useful when you need only certain items in another project but not the bulk of the project itself. Maybe you just need 20 task names in another project that consists of 400 tasks. Or maybe you need those task names along with their durations and dependencies. In this case, it's best to copy the information from the one project to the other.

However, if you think you're going to use about 300 of those 400 tasks (maybe along with their resources) in the new project, it's probably more efficient to make that existing project the basis for the new project. For more information on how to do this, see "Creating a New Project from an Existing Project" on page 81. This approach can be more efficient than copying over items piecemeal.

You might also have access to a similar project that has been made into a template you can use. For information about creating a template from an existing project file, see "Working with Project Templates" on page 1192.

If you're dealing strictly with resource information, you might consider using a resource pool rather than copying and pasting resource information. For more on using resource pools, see "Sharing Resources by Using a Resource Pool" on page 614.

It comes down to efficiency and accuracy. Are you going to spend more time copying and pasting, or would you spend more time deleting extraneous or irrelevant information? Answering that question can help you decide the best method to use.

Copying and Moving Task and Resource Information

When you want to copy or move complete task information—including the task name, duration, predecessors, dates, notes, progress information, resource assignments, and so on—you need to select the entire task. Likewise, you can copy or move complete resource information—including maximum units, availability dates, costs, and calendars—by selecting the entire resource, not just the resource name.

To copy or move task or resource information from one project to another, follow these steps:

1. In the source project, apply a task sheet or resource sheet.

   It doesn't matter whether the sheet contains all the information fields you want to copy or move. All information associated with the task or resource will be copied or moved.

2. Click the row heading for all tasks or resources you want to copy or move.

   If the tasks or resources are adjacent, simply drag across the row headings to select them. You can also click the first row heading, hold down the Shift key, and then click the last row heading. (See Figure 16-1.)

	Task Name	Duration	Start	Finish
33	Order new address labels for notification	1 day	Tue 11/9/10	Tue 11/9/10
34	Obtain estimates from signage companies	7 days	Tue 11/9/10	Wed 11/17/10
35	Order signage for new location	1 day	Thu 11/18/10	Thu 11/18/10
36	Order phone system	1 day	Wed 11/24/10	Wed 11/24/10
37	Order phone lines	1 day	Thu 11/25/10	Thu 11/25/10
38	Order internet phone lines	1 day	Thu 11/25/10	Thu 11/25/10
39	Arrange internal maintenance service	1 day	Thu 11/18/10	Thu 11/18/10
40	Arrange external maintenance service	1 day	Thu 11/18/10	Thu 11/18/10

Figure 16-1 Drag or use the Shift key to select adjacent tasks or resources.

   If the tasks or resources are nonadjacent, click the row heading of the first task or resource you want to select, hold down the Ctrl key, and then click the row headings of all other tasks or resources to be copied or moved. (See Figure 16-2.)

	Resource Name	Type	Material Label	Initials	Group	Max. Units	Std. Rate	Ovt. Rate
1	Vivian Atlas	Work		VA		100%	$45.00/hr	$0.00/hr
2	Paul Shakespear	Work		PS		100%	$45.00/hr	$0.00/hr
3	Sandeep Katyal	Work		SK		50%	$500.00/day	$0.00/hr
4	Yolanda Sanchez	Work		YS		100%	$30.00/hr	$45.00/hr
5	Designer	Work		D		300%	$60.00/hr	$90.00/hr
6	Product Engineer	Work		P		200%	$75.00/hr	$0.00/hr
7	Drafter	Work		D		350%	$20.00/hr	$30.00/hr
8	Editor	Work		E		100%	$30.00/hr	$45.00/hr

Figure 16-2 Use the Ctrl key to select nonadjacent resources or tasks.

Copy

3. On the Task tab, in the Clipboard group, click Copy.

   If you're moving rather than copying the information, on the Task tab, in the Clipboard group, click Cut.

Cut

4. Open the destination project.

5. Display a view compatible with the information you've copied or cut.

   That is, if you're copying or moving task information, display a task sheet view, such as the Gantt Chart or Task Usage view. If you're copying or moving resource information, display a resource sheet view, such as the Resource Sheet or Resource Usage view.

6. Click anywhere in the row where you want to paste the first of your selected tasks or resources.

   When you paste full rows of task information or resource information, they are inserted within existing tasks or resources. No information is overwritten.

Paste

7. On the Task tab, in the Clipboard group, click Paste.

   The copied or cut information is pasted into the cells, starting at your anchor cell.

Copying Fields Between Projects

Instead of copying all information about tasks and resources, you can simply copy the contents of a field, such as task names, resource names, or a custom text field. This procedure can be handy if you need to copy just a set of resource names, for example, or a set of task names with their durations.

> **Note**
>
> **Although you can move (rather than copy) fields from one project to another, it isn't all that useful to do so. For example, if you cut resource names from one project, you'd be left with a set of resource information that has no names associated with it.**

To copy the contents of a field, do the following:

1. In the source project, apply the view containing the fields you want to copy.

2. Select the fields.

   If the fields are adjacent, simply drag to select them, or click the first field, hold down the Shift key, and then click the last field. (See Figure 16-3.)

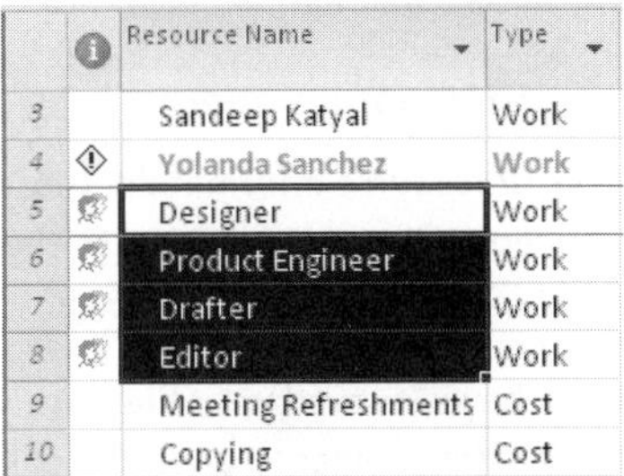

		Resource Name	Type
3		Sandeep Katyal	Work
4		Yolanda Sanchez	Work
5		Designer	Work
6		Product Engineer	Work
7		Drafter	Work
8		Editor	Work
9		Meeting Refreshments	Cost
10		Copying	Cost

Figure 16-3 Drag or use the Shift key to select adjacent fields.

If the fields are nonadjacent, click the first field, hold down the Ctrl key, and then click all other fields to be copied. (See Figure 16-4.)

	Task Name	Duration
27	Order new office equipment	5 days
28	Obtain estimates from moving companies	12 days
29	Hire movers	1 day
30	Evaluate server room needs	2 days
31	Evaluate computer networking needs	2 days
32	Order change of address labels for notifical	1 day
33	Order new address labels for notification	1 day
34	Obtain estimates from signage companies	7 days

Figure 16-4 Use the Ctrl key to select nonadjacent fields.

3. On the Task tab, in the Clipboard group, click Copy.

4. Open the destination project.

5. If necessary, apply a table that contains the same or compatible fields as the information you're pasting.

   For example, if you're pasting text information, such as task names, be sure that the Task Name or another editable text field is available. If you're pasting cost information, you need to paste it into an editable currency field, such as Standard Rate or Cost1. If necessary, add a field to a current table. Click a column heading, and then press the Insert key. Click the name of the field you want to add from the list that appears.

6. Click the anchor cell, which is the cell in which you want to paste the first of your selected fields.

7. On the Task tab, in the Clipboard group, click Paste. The copied information is pasted into the cells, starting at your anchor cell.

   The information overwrites any existing information; it does not insert new cells. In light of this, be sure that you have the right number of blank cells in which to paste the information.

TROUBLESHOOTING

Your pasted information deleted existing information

When you paste selected fields of task or resource information, those fields flow into any existing cells, starting with the anchor cell and continuing to the cells below. If any of those cells contain information, that information is overwritten.

Undo

If this wasn't your intention, and if you haven't saved your file since you inserted the information, click Undo on the Quick Access Toolbar to undo the paste operation. If you have performed other operations since you pasted the fields, repeatedly click Undo until the overwritten information returns.

You cannot undo operations that occurred before the last time you saved the file. If you saved your file after you pasted the fields, you might have to re-create the overwritten information or use your backup project file.

Note

You can copy and paste project information into other applications and paste information from other applications into your project plan. For more information, see "Copying Information" on page 647.

Copying Project Elements by Using the Organizer

In the course of working on a project over a year or so, you're bound to create a number of efficiencies for yourself. For example, you might modify and save a view to display all key cost information at a glance or create a report for a specific meeting you have every other week. Maybe you created a set of macros to automate a number of repetitive task-tracking activities.

When you start a new project and begin work on your new project file, you might think you need to do all that modifying, customizing, and creating all over again. Not so. Just as you can copy task information from one project to another, you can copy customized project elements such as tables, calendars, and fields from one project to another. You do this with the Organizer.

Some elements you change in your project also change your Project 2010 global template, which is applied to all projects on your computer system. Many other elements just stay in the current project. You can use the Organizer to copy elements to the project global template, thereby making them available to all projects. You can also use the Organizer to copy elements from one project to another.

For information about the project global template, see "Working with the Project Global Template" on page 1189. Project managers creating new projects based on the enterprise global template can refer to "Creating a New Enterprise Project" on page 905.

With the Organizer, you can copy the following project elements:

- Views
- Reports
- Microsoft Visual Basic for Applications (VBA) modules and macros
- Tables
- Filters
- Base calendars
- Import/export maps
- Custom fields and outline codes
- Groups

No matter which type of element you copy, the procedure is the same. You select a source file that contains the element you want to copy, select a destination file into which you want to copy the element, and then copy the element.

Note

In earlier versions of Microsoft Project, you could also copy custom toolbars and custom forms. Both of these elements are discontinued as of Project 2010.

Copying an Element from a Project to the Global Template

By default, Project 2010 copies any custom views, tables, filters, and groups to the global template. This means that if you want to copy any of these items from your project plan to the global template, you needn't bother; it's probably already done.

To check whether this setting is in place, or to change the setting, on the File tab, click Options, and then click Advanced in the left pane. Under Display, find the check box labeled Automatically Add New Views, Tables, Filters, And Groups To The Global. The check box indicates whether this setting is on or off.

If you clear this check box, you must use the Organizer whenever you want to copy your custom views, tables, filters, and groups to the global template. Other customized elements, such as reports, calendars, and fields, are not automatically copied under this setting, and you need to perform that operation yourself.

To copy an element from a project to the project global template, follow these steps:

1. Open the project that contains the element you want to copy.

Organizer

2. On the File tab, click Info if necessary, and then click the Organizer button.

   The Organizer dialog box appears, as shown in Figure 16-5.

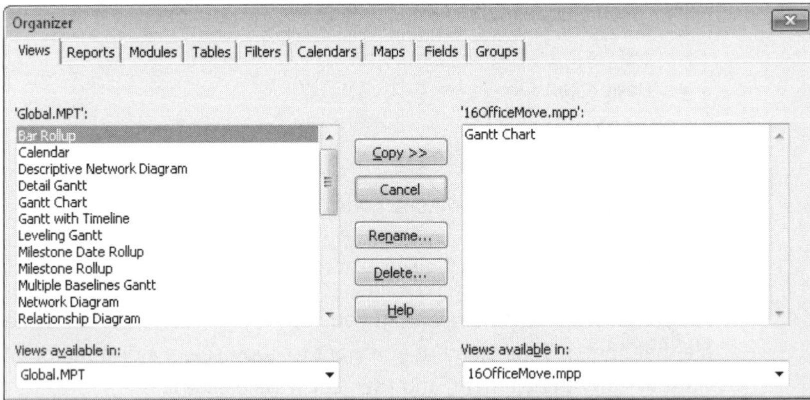

Figure 16-5 Use the Organizer to copy, rename, or delete customized elements between projects or between a project and the project global template.

3. Click the tab for the type of element you want to copy; for example, Views or Reports.

   The name of the current project, along with any customized elements in that project, appears on the right side of the Organizer.

4. If you want to copy a customized element from a different project, in the <Element> Available In list in the lower-right corner of the dialog box, click the name of the individual project that contains the element you want to copy.

   <Element> stands for the name of the current tab.

5. In the list of elements on the right side of the dialog box, click the name of the element you want to copy.

6. Click the Copy button.

   If an element with the same name already exists in the project global template, a confirmation message appears. Click Yes if you want to replace the element in the project global template with the one from the source project.

   To copy the element with a different name, click the Rename button, and then type a new name.

Copying an Element Between Two Projects

To copy an element between two projects, follow these steps:

1. Open both the source and destination projects.
2. On the File tab, click Info if necessary, and then click Organizer.
3. In the Organizer dialog box, click the tab for the element you want to copy.
4. In the <Element> Available In list in the lower-right corner of the dialog box, click the name of the source project.
5. In the <Element> Available In list in the lower-left corner of the dialog box, click the name of the destination project.
6. In the list of elements on the right side of the dialog box, click the name of the element you want to copy.
7. Click the Copy button.

   If an element with the same name already exists in the project global template, a confirmation message appears. Click Yes if you want to replace the element in the project global template with the one from the source project.

   To copy the element with a different name, click the Rename button, and then enter a new name.

Linking Information Between Project Plans

When you link two tasks, you create a task dependency or task relationship between them. In the most common link type (finish-to-start), as soon as a predecessor task finishes, its successor task can start.

Tasks don't have to be in the same project to be linked. You can have *external links*. An *external predecessor* is a task in another project that must be finished (or started) before the current task can start (or finish). Likewise, an *external successor* is a task in another project that cannot start (or finish) until the current task is finished (or started). Creating task relationships with external tasks like these is also referred to as *cross-project linking*.

Linking Tasks Between Different Projects

To link tasks between different projects, you temporarily consolidate the project, link the tasks, and then discard the consolidation. To do this, follow these steps:

1. Open both projects.
2. In either of the two projects, on the View tab, in the Window group, click New Window.

New Window

3. Under Projects, select the two projects that you want to link.

   Use the Ctrl or Shift key to select them both at the same time.
4. In the View list, click the name of the view in which you want the consolidated projects to appear.

   The Gantt With Timeline view is the default.
5. Click OK.

   The two projects are temporarily consolidated into one.
6. Click the task in the project you want to make the external predecessor.
7. Scroll to the task in the other project that you want to become the external successor.
8. When you find the task, hold down Ctrl and click the task.

   Now both the predecessor from one project and the successor from the other project are selected, as shown in Figure 16-6.

Link Tasks

9. On the Task tab, in the Schedule group, click Link Tasks.

   The tasks are linked with a finish-to-start task dependency. You can change the dependency type later.
10. Close the consolidated project without saving it.

    Review the two projects that are still open. You'll see that they now have external predecessors and external successors, as shown by the gray tasks in both projects. (See Figure 16-7.) By default, table text, Gantt bars, and Network Diagram nodes of external predecessors and successors are formatted in gray.

	Task Name	Duration
90	Provide Physical Facilities	15 days
91	Secure operation space	5 days
93	Select computer network hardware	1 day
94	Select computer software	1 day
96	Establish utilities	3 days
97	Provide furniture and equipment	4 days
98	Move in	1 day
99	Provide Staffing	40 days
100	Interview and test candidates	14 days
101	Hire staff	10 days
102	Train staff	16 days
103	Start up the business	0 days
2	16OfficeMove	127 days
1	Office Move	127 days
2	Two To Six Months Before Moving Day	77 days
3	Make list of key needs that must be met by new office space	7 days
4	Identify potential office sites	20 days
5	Make final decision on office space	10 days
7	Finalize lease on office space	10 days
8	Identify major tenant improvement needs	15 days

Figure 16-6 By consolidating projects, you can use the mouse to link tasks in different projects.

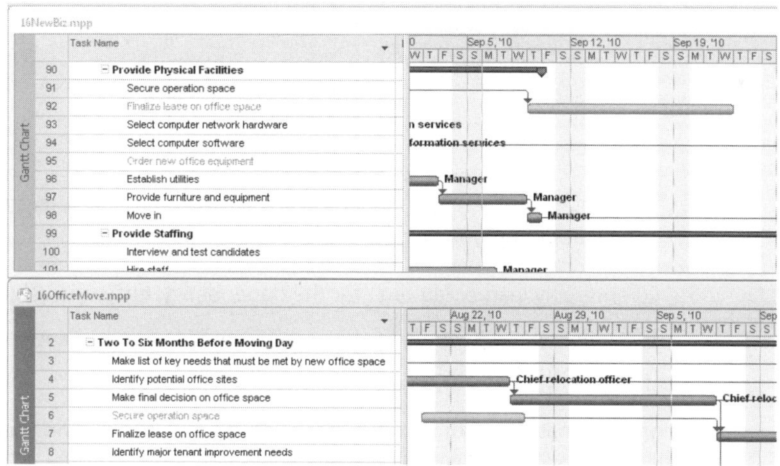

Figure 16-7 Any external predecessors or external successors are displayed in gray.

As you can with regular predecessors, you can change the link type from the default finish-to-start to any of the other three link types (finish-to-finish, start-to-start, or start-to-finish). You can also enter lead time or lag time. Use the Predecessors tab in the Task Information dialog box to do this, as follows:

1. Display the project containing the successor task to the external predecessor.
2. In the Task Name field, double-click the successor task to the external predecessor.
3. In the Task Information dialog box, click the Predecessors tab.

   The path to the external task appears in the ID field, the name of the external task appears in the Task Name field, and the Type and Lag fields are editable. (See Figure 16-8.)

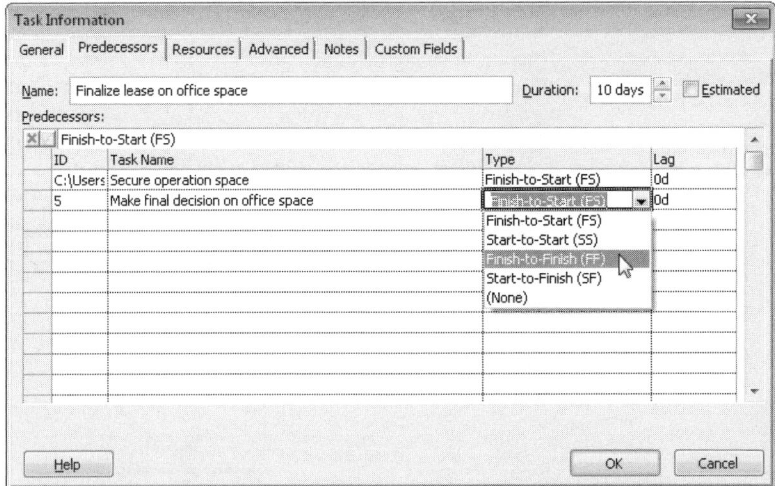

Figure 16-8 The external task name and link information appear in the Predecessors table.

4. To change the task dependency to a type other than finish-to-start, click the entry you want in the Type field.
5. To enter any lead or lag time for the dependency, enter the value in the Lag field.

   Lag time is entered as a positive number, and lead time is entered as a negative number.

For more information about task dependencies in general, including lead and lag time, see "Establishing Task Dependencies" on page 206.

Link Entire Projects

Sometimes, an entire project cannot start or finish until another entire project has finished or started. You can set up this relationship between projects by using a master project and subprojects.

For more information about setting up a master project with subprojects, see "Structuring Master Projects with Subprojects" on page 600.

You can also simply create a task dependency between key tasks in the two projects. For example, if Project1 can't start until Project2 is finished, set up a finish-to-start task dependency from the final task or milestone in Project2 with one of the first tasks in Project1.

Reviewing Cross-Project Links

You can see your external links in the different views throughout your project. Whether they're external predecessors or external successors, by default external tasks are shown in gray type. External tasks are also represented with gray Gantt bars and gray Network Diagram nodes.

If you double-click an external task, the project containing that task opens, and the task is selected. You can then review its task information and current schedule. The other project is still open, and you can return to it by double-clicking the corresponding external task in the second project.

Note

If you don't want external tasks to be visible in your project, you can hide them. On the File tab, click Options, and then click Advanced in the left pane. Under Cross Project Linking Options For This Project, clear the check boxes labeled Show External Successors and Show External Predecessors. By default, this setting applies only to the current project. If you have other projects open, you can choose to which of the open projects the setting should apply.

Links Between Projects

You can review details about all links within your project. On the Project tab, in the Properties group, click Links Between Projects. The External Predecessors tab in the Links Between Projects dialog box, shown in Figure 16-9, shows information about all external predecessors. Likewise, the External Successors tab shows information about all external successors.

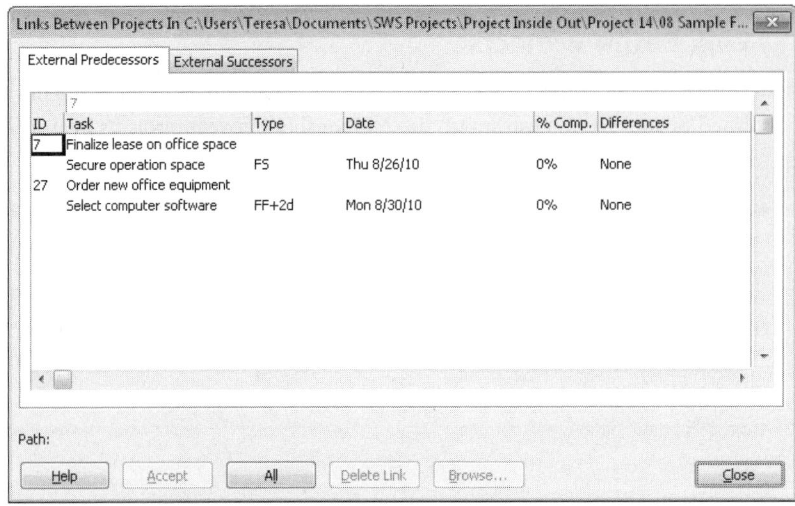

Figure 16-9 The Links Between Projects dialog box shows the pairs of externally linked tasks. It also shows the link types, finish dates, current percentage complete, and any available updates.

The top task in the pair shows the task name in the current project. The bottom task in the pair shows the externally linked task name in the other project, along with the link type, finish date, percentage complete, and any differences since the last time the two projects were synchronized.

To see the path and name of an external task, click its name in the Task field of the Links Between Projects dialog box. The path and name appear at the bottom of the dialog box.

Another way to review information about cross-project links is to add the External Task field or the Project field to a task table. You can also sort, group, or filter by one of these fields.

The External Task field, which is a Yes/No (Boolean) field, simply indicates whether the task is external. The Project field contains the name of the project to which this task belongs. For external tasks, the Project field also contains the full path. (See Figure 16-10.)

	Task Name	External Task	Project	Duration
90	**Provide Physical Facilities**	**No**	**16NewBiz**	**15 days**
91	Secure operation space	No	16NewBiz	5 days
92	Finalize lease on office space	Yes	e Files\16OfficeMove.mpp	10 days
93	Select computer network hardware	No	16NewBiz	1 day
94	Select computer software	No	16NewBiz	1 day
95	Order new office equipment	Yes	e Files\16OfficeMove.mpp	5 days
96	Establish utilities	No	16NewBiz	3 days
97	Provide furniture and equipment	No	16NewBiz	4 days
98	Move in	No	16NewBiz	1 day

Figure 16-10 You can add the External Task or Project fields to a task table to provide information about your cross-project linking.

Chapter 16

To add a field to a task table, first click the column heading next to where you want to insert the new column. On the Format tab, in the Columns group, click Insert Column. In the temporary drop-down menu that appears, type **ex** to scroll quickly to the External Task field or type **pr** to scroll quickly to the Project field. Click the field name to insert it into the new column.

Whether you add the External Task or Project fields to a table or not, you can sort, group, or filter by these fields. This capability can be handy when you want to see all your external tasks together.

For information about sorting, grouping, or filtering by a particular field, see "Rearranging Your Project Information" on page 173 and Chapter 28, "Customizing Your View of Project Information."

Updating Cross-Project Links

By default, the Links Between Projects dialog box appears whenever you open a project file that contains external links that have changed since the last time you opened the file. The Differences field alerts you to any changed information, such as a changed name, schedule change, or new progress information, as you can see in Figure 16-11.

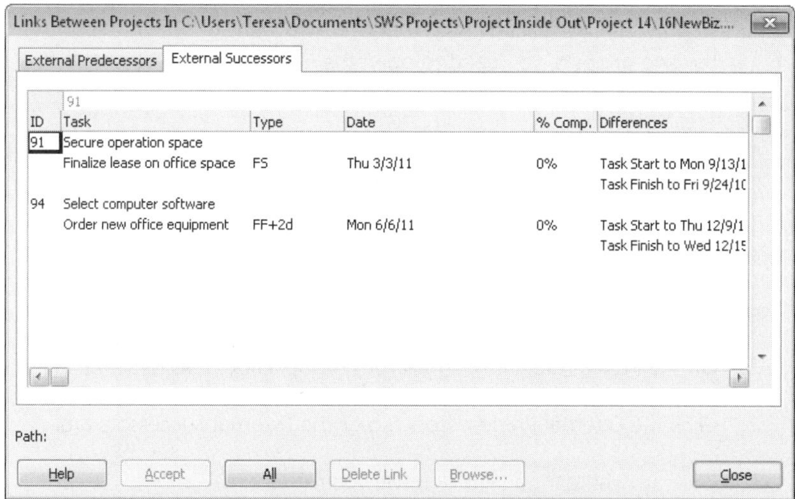

Figure 16-11 The Links Between Projects dialog box appears when you open a project whose external links have changed, and the change is noted in the Differences field.

To incorporate a change from an external task into your project plan, follow these steps:

1. If necessary, click Project, Properties, Links Between Projects to open the dialog box.

   If you open a project file after one of its external links has changed, the Links Between Projects dialog box appears by default.

2. In the Links Between Projects dialog box, review the change in the Differences field.

3. Click the name of the task that has changed, and then click the Accept button.

   To incorporate changes to multiple external links all at once, click the All button.

4. When you finish accepting changes, click the Close button.

   If you click the Close button without accepting the changes, the changes are not incorporated into the project. As long as there are differences between the linked task information in the two projects, this dialog box appears every time you open the project.

You can modify the way differences between projects are updated, as follows:

1. Open the project containing external links.

2. On the File tab, click Options, and then click Advanced in the left pane.

3. Under Cross Project Linking Options For This Project, clear the check box labeled Show Links Between Projects Dialog On Open.

   If this check box is cleared, the Links Between Projects dialog box does not appear when you open the project. Whenever you want to synchronize information between the two projects, you need to open the Links Between Projects dialog box and then accept the differences.

4. If you want to automatically update external task changes in your project, select the check box labeled Automatically Accept New External Data.

Removing Cross-Project Links

To remove an external link, do the following:

1. On the Project tab, in the Properties group, click Links Between Projects.

2. Click the External Predecessors tab or the External Successors tab.

3. Click anywhere in the link you want to remove.

4. Click the Delete Link button.

Identify Deliverables in Other Projects

If you're working with Microsoft Project Professional 2010 and Microsoft Project Server 2010 in an enterprise project management environment, you have the capability to identify deliverables in other projects that affect activities in the current project. You can then set up dependencies to those deliverables in such a way that the deliverable dependency is visible in the current project, but scheduling in this project is not affected.

For more information, see "Depending on Deliverables in Other Projects" on page 921.

PART 6

Integrating Project 2010 with Other Programs

Before you can use the sample files for Chapters 17, 20, and 21, you'll need to install them from this book's companion content website. For more information about downloading and installing the sample files, see "About the Companion Content" on page xxviii.

CHAPTER 17

Exchanging Information with Other Applications

BECAUSE Microsoft Project 2010 is such a specialized application, many of the people you work with on a project might not have it. And even if they have installed it, they might not know how to use it.

But no matter. You can easily exchange data in Project 2010 with other applications.

For example, you might want to provide data from your project plan to a stakeholder who doesn't have access to Project 2010 but does have another compatible application, such as Microsoft Excel 2010 or Microsoft Word 2010.

You might want to send project data to a spreadsheet or database application to manipulate the information in ways in which those applications are especially suited.

In the same way, you can easily bring information into Project 2010 from other applications. If someone has a list of tasks or resources along with associated information that you need in your project plan, copying or importing this information can save you from rekeying the data.

Clearly, the ability to exchange information between applications can save you and other project stakeholders an immense amount of time and effort. More importantly, it also can give you the opportunity to shape data to best present project information for specific purposes.

Several techniques are available for exchanging information between applications. The method you use depends on what you're trying to accomplish with the information. Table 17-1 provides some basic guidelines.

Note

When referring to the exchange of data between applications, the term *source* is used to refer to the originating application. The term *destination* is used to refer to the receiving, or target, application.

Table 17-1 **Appropriate Methods for Information Exchange**

To do this	Use this method
Copy static text or numbers between Project 2010 and another application. The information usually appears as though it were created in the destination application.	Copy
Copy pictures from Project 2010 to another application.	Copy Picture
Add data along with its source application to another program. When you double-click the embedded information, the source application opens, and you can work with it interactively there.	Embed
Create a dynamic connection between the information in the source and destination applications. When the information is updated in one, it's updated in the other, as well.	Link
Reference a file at its source, whether it's a website or file location. Clicking the hyperlink finds and launches the website or the document in its native application.	Hyperlink
Bring information into Project 2010 from another application or in another file format, making the information appear as though it were created in Project 2010 to begin with. Similar to copying, but this method is typically used with entire files or large chunks of data.	Import or Open
Convert Project 2010 information into a file format that can be used by another application, making the information appear as though it were created in that other application to begin with. Has a similar result as copying, but this method is typically used for entire files or large chunks of data.	Export or Save As
Save Project 2010 information as a PDF file to make it easily readable in Adobe Reader on any computer. Note that Adobe Acrobat does not need to be installed on the computer for the project file to be saved as a PDF file.	Save Project 2010 data as a PDF file
Convert Project 2010 information into XML format for use on web pages or in any other application that reads or is based on XML.	Save Project 2010 data as an XML file

It's important to keep in mind that some methods of exchanging data move the data and then freeze it, which means that the information transferred cannot be altered after the exchange. Other methods move the data into the other application and allow it to be dynamically updated and manipulated.

Note

Project 2010 has particularly robust methods for exchanging information with Excel 2010, Microsoft Visio 2010, and Microsoft Outlook 2010.

These methods are covered in their own chapters: Chapter 18, "Integrating Project 2010 with Excel"; Chapter 19, "Integrating Project 2010 with Visio"; and Chapter 20, "Integrating Project 2010 with Outlook."

Integrate with Other Business Applications

If you're set up for enterprise project management using Microsoft Project Professional 2010 and Microsoft Project Server 2010, your organization might take advantage of additional means for working with other applications. Through the Project Server Interface (PSI), you can integrate information between Project Server 2010 and other organizational systems that interact with project management processes such as accounting, procurement, and human resources.

For more information about working with the Project Server Interface, see Chapter 23, "Administering Your Enterprise Project Management Solution."

Copying Information

You can copy textual as well as graphical data between Project 2010 and other applications. With one method, you simply use the Copy and Paste commands. With another method, you use a wizard.

Copying from Project 2010 to Another Application

You can copy field information, such as from a task sheet or resource sheet, to another application, such as Microsoft Access 2010 or Word 2010. When you need a subset of project information in another application, the best transfer method is usually to copy and paste. To copy and paste data from Project 2010 to another application, follow these steps:

1. In Project 2010, display the view and table that contains the information you want to copy. If necessary, insert other columns of information by right-clicking a column and then clicking Insert Column.
2. Select the data you want to copy to the other application. (See Figure 17-1.) You can drag across adjacent items (columns, rows, or fields) or hold down Ctrl while clicking nonadjacent items.

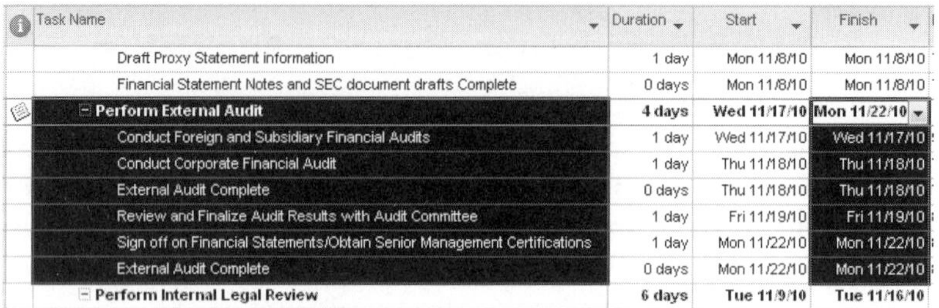

Task Name	Duration	Start	Finish
Draft Proxy Statement information	1 day	Mon 11/8/10	Mon 11/8/10
Financial Statement Notes and SEC document drafts Complete	0 days	Mon 11/8/10	Mon 11/8/10
− Perform External Audit	4 days	Wed 11/17/10	Mon 11/22/10
Conduct Foreign and Subsidiary Financial Audits	1 day	Wed 11/17/10	Wed 11/17/10
Conduct Corporate Financial Audit	1 day	Thu 11/18/10	Thu 11/18/10
External Audit Complete	0 days	Thu 11/18/10	Thu 11/18/10
Review and Finalize Audit Results with Audit Committee	1 day	Fri 11/19/10	Fri 11/19/10
Sign off on Financial Statements/Obtain Senior Management Certifications	1 day	Mon 11/22/10	Mon 11/22/10
External Audit Complete	0 days	Mon 11/22/10	Mon 11/22/10
− Perform Internal Legal Review	6 days	Tue 11/9/10	Tue 11/16/10

Figure 17-1 Select the fields you want to copy to the other application.

Copy

3. On the Task tab, in the Clipboard group, click Copy.

   A copy of the selected data is placed on the Clipboard.

4. Open the application into which you want to paste the project information. Select the area where you want the data to start being inserted.

5. In the destination application, click the application's Paste command.

   Paste

   For example, if you are pasting into a Microsoft Office application, on the Home tab, in the Clipboard group, click Paste.

   Your copied data is inserted at the selection.

If the workspace of the destination application is laid out in columns and rows like Project 2010 tables, as is the case with spreadsheet applications, the pasted project information flows easily into columns and rows. However, if the workspace is open, like a blank page, the incoming project information is likely to run together and look like a bit of a mess. The information is tab-delimited, so if you're pasting into a word-processing program, the program might have a function to convert text to tables, which can make life easier for you.

NEW!

But if you're pasting the Project table data into an Office application, everything is so much easier. In Project 2010, if you copy Project table data to an Excel spreadsheet, the column headings are automatically pasted as well, even if you don't select and copy them. This means you no longer need to worry about leaving space for those headings, you don't need to add them yourself, and there's no guesswork about what those columns are.

Even better, if you paste Project 2010 table data into Microsoft Word or Microsoft Outlook, it's automatically pasted as a table, including the table headings. This is a big improvement over previous versions of Microsoft Project, where the data came in as jumbled tab-delimited text, and you had to convert the text to a table or reformat it by hand.

In addition to automatically pasting the column headings, pasting Project 2010 table data into another Office application retains formatting and outline levels. (See Figure 17-2.)

Copying from Another Application to Project 2010

You can copy table-based or listed information from another application—for example, Access 2010 or Word—and insert it into Project 2010. You select and copy the source data, select the cell in Project 2010 where you want the data to start being inserted, and then paste the data. This is a good way to get project-related information that was created by others in another application into your Project 2010 file. For example, suppose that you asked your manufacturing manager to put together a detailed task list of the process that will be used to manufacture your new product. He completes the list, including tasks and resource assignments, using Access.

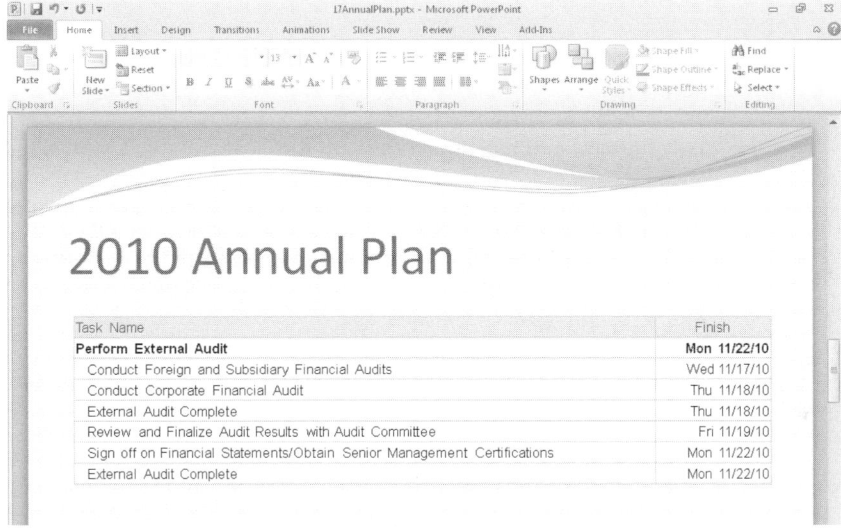

Figure 17-2 Your project data is pasted into the destination application.

If you are copying multiple columns or tabs of information, you do need to be mindful of the order in which data is being pasted and inserted into the project table. The type of data you're pasting must match the field type in which the data is being pasted or you'll get a series of error messages.

For example, if you copy a column of text and try to paste it in the Task Mode or Predecessors column, you'll get an error message because those fields do not accept text content. But if you paste it into the Task Name or Resource Names column, either of which accepts text, it'll work just fine.

As a more complex yet realistic example, imagine you need to copy several columns from another application into Project 2010, such as task names, finish dates, and resource names. To make sure the fields match when you paste the data, you can set up the source information in the proper order (with blank columns in between as necessary) or rearrange columns in a Project 2010 table.

To copy table or list information from another application to Project 2010, follow these steps:

1. Open the source application and file.
2. Select the rows or columns you want to copy, and then click the application's Copy command.

   If you are copying data in an Office application, on the Home tab, in the Clipboard group, click Copy.
3. In Project 2010, open the project plan in which you want to insert the copied information.
4. Apply the view and table that represent the closest match to the types of information you are pasting.

   Insert Column

   If you need to add any columns to match the incoming information, click the column to the right of where you want to insert the new field. On the Format menu, in the Columns group, click Insert Column. In the list of fields that appears, click the name of the field you want.
5. Click the cell in which you want to begin pasting the incoming information.
6. On the Task tab, in the Clipboard group, click Paste.

   The copied information is pasted into the columns you prepared.

   Pasting data into Project 2010 overwrites data in the destination cells. If this is not your intention, insert the appropriate number of empty rows in the sheet before selecting the Paste command.

By default, new tasks inserted are considered manually scheduled tasks. If you changed the default so that new tasks are automatically scheduled, or if you insert information that affects existing automatically scheduled tasks, other project data might be automatically populated and calculated. Review the change highlighting in fields on the current and other tables to be sure the changes are appropriate and make any necessary adjustments.

Note

Any information that can be moved to the Clipboard by using a Copy command can be pasted into Project 2010, but not all views accept all types of data. For example, you can paste objects such as pictures only into the chart area of the Gantt Chart or a task or resource note. Nothing can be pasted into the Network Diagram.

TROUBLESHOOTING

Data doesn't paste into the destination file correctly

When you use the Copy and Paste commands to exchange data, it's important to remember that fields and columns of data stay in the order and format of their source file. Before you paste data from another application into your project file, set up the columns in the source file in the order of the corresponding columns in your project file.

Also be careful that data formats, particularly numbers and dates, are the same in the source file as in your project file. If you want to copy and paste data from another application into a project file that has no project field equivalent, insert columns of generic custom fields (for example, Text1 or Number1) to hold the new data. These extra columns must match the column order in the source file. The matching of compatible columns is called *manual data mapping* and must take place before you select the Paste command. If you paste incompatible data into Project 2010 fields, an error message alerts you that a mismatch has occurred.

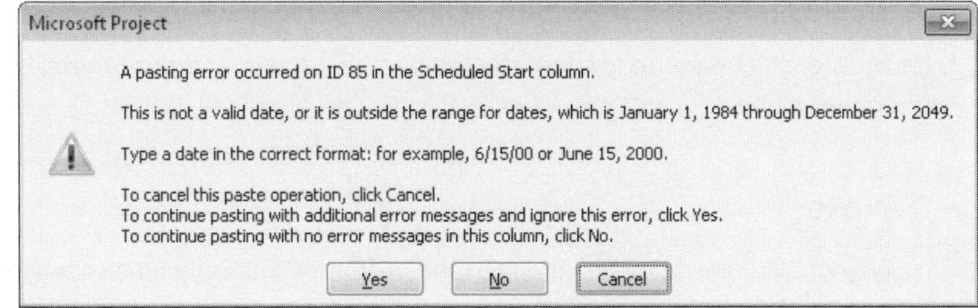

You'll see a separate pasting error for every mismatched field in the paste operation.

For information about copying information from Excel to Project 2010, see "Copying Information from Excel" on page 690.

For information about copying a graphic such as a logo into the Gantt Chart, see "Inserting a Graphic or Other Object in the Gantt Chart" on page 661.

Copying a Picture of a View

Suppose you're creating a formal narrative project status report or preparing a presentation for a high-profile project status meeting. You can take a snapshot of any Project 2010 view and paste it as a graphic into a Word document or a Microsoft PowerPoint presentation slide. You can also copy the project Timeline as a graphic and paste it into another application.

Note

Previous versions of Microsoft Project included the Copy Picture To Office Wizard, which was used to configure and copy information from a Microsoft Project view and paste it into Word, PowerPoint, or Microsoft Visio. Because of the enhanced capabilities of copying and pasting from Project 2010 to Office applications, this wizard is discontinued.

Capturing a View for Other Applications

To capture a view and use it as a graphic in an application such as Word, PowerPoint, or Visio, you can use the Copy Picture function. With this function, you take a snapshot of the current view that you can send in an e-mail message, print, or paste into any application you choose. Copying a picture of a view is a good way to create a simple picture of a view to use on a website or in a report. When configuring the picture, Project 2010 provides choices for the image rendering, the rows to be copied, and the timescale as appropriate to the current view.

Note

Project 2010 creates a GIF image as the output of the Copy Picture function. If you need a different graphics format, you can use any graphics processing software, such as Microsoft Paint, to convert the image.

To copy and paste a picture of a Project 2010 view for use in another application, follow these steps:

1. In your project plan, display the view you want to copy to the other application.
2. Manipulate the view to show the information the way you want it to appear in the destination application.

Copy Picture

3. On the Task tab, in the Clipboard group, click the arrow next to Copy, and then click Copy Picture.
4. In the Copy Picture dialog box, shown in Figure 17-3, select the options you want.

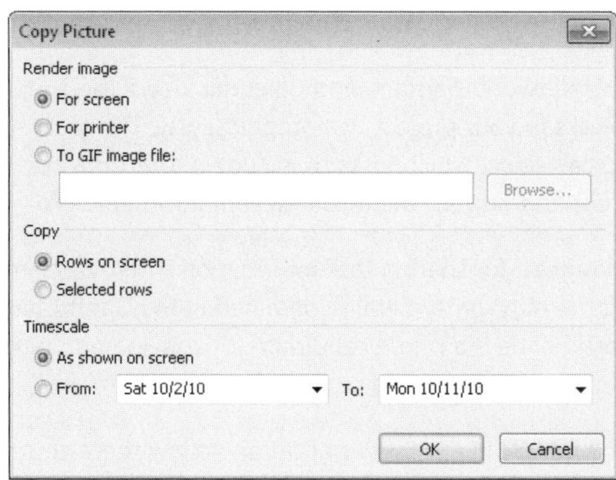

Figure 17-3 Choose the options you want for the picture you're copying.

- In the Render Image section, clicking the For Screen (the default) or For Printer option is similar to pressing the Print Screen key on your keyboard. The view is saved on the Clipboard. When you go to the application where you want to use the image and choose the Paste command, the image appears there, optimized for viewing on the screen or for printing, depending on your choice.

  If you want to save the image as a file rather than paste it as a separate file, click the To GIF Image File option, and then click the Browse button to specify the new file's location and name.

- In the Copy section, click the Rows On Screen option (the default) if you want the rows currently showing on the screen to be included in the image. Click the Selected Rows option if only selected rows should be included.

- In the Timescale section, click the As Shown On Screen option (the default) if you want the timescale to be represented as set in the current view. Click the From and To option and enter dates in the boxes if you want to specify the timescale and date range to be included in the image.

5. When you finish setting the Copy Picture options, click OK.

6. Open the destination application, and click the location where you want to paste the object.

7. Select the application's Paste command.

   If you are pasting into an Office application, on the Home tab, in the Clipboard group, click Paste.

   A static picture of the Project 2010 view as you set it up and specified is pasted into the destination application. If necessary, you can resize the image by dragging any of the edges.

Copying the Timeline for Other Applications

NEW!

Like the Gantt Chart, Network Diagram, and Calendar views, the Timeline view is another way to look at the tasks in your project in a graphical way. The great advantage of the Timeline is that you can select which tasks to include in the Timeline, making it easy for you to control the content and present the most relevant information for your audience.

The Timeline was designed for sharing task information with others involved with the project who don't need the nitty-gritty details contained in the Gantt Chart and other views. Because of this, the Timeline is a prime candidate for copying and pasting into other applications like your e-mail client, PowerPoint, or Visio.

To copy the Timeline for use in another application, follow these steps:

1. In your project plan, be sure the Timeline is showing.

   By default, the Timeline appears above every view. (See Figure 17-4.) If the Timeline is not showing, on the View tab, in the Split View group, select the Timeline check box.

		Resource Name	Type	Material	Initials	Group	Max.	Std. Rate	Ovt. Rate	Cost/Use	Accrue	Base	Code
1		Audit Committee	Work		Audit		100%	$80.00/hr	$0.00/hr	$0.00	Prorated	Standard	
2		Legal Department	Work		Legal		100%	$150.00/hr	$0.00/hr	$0.00	Prorated	Standard	
3		External Auditors	Work		ExtAud		100%	$100.00/hr	$0.00/hr	$0.00	Prorated	Standard	
4		Executive Committee	Work		Exec		100%	$200.00/hr	$0.00/hr	$0.00	Prorated	Standard	
5		CFO/Controller	Work		CFO		100%	$175.00/hr	$0.00/hr	$0.00	Prorated	Standard	
6		Marketing Group	Work		Mkt		100%	$90.00/hr	$0.00/hr	$0.00	Prorated	Standard	
7		Strategic Planning Committee	Work		SPC		100%	$85.00/hr	$0.00/hr	$0.00	Prorated	Standard	
8		PR/IR Dept	Work		PR		100%	$100.00/hr	$0.00/hr	$0.00	Prorated	Standard	
9		Chairman	Work		Chair		100%	$200.00/hr	$0.00/hr	$0.00	Prorated	Standard	

Figure 17-4 By default, the Timeline appears above any view, even resource views.

2. Make any adjustments to the Timeline to reflect what you want to show when you copy it.

For more information about working with the Timeline, see "Highlighting Tasks with the Timeline" on page 134.

Copy Timeline

3. Click anywhere in the Timeline pane, and then on the Format tab, in the Copy group, click Copy Timeline.

4. In the drop-down menu that appears, click For E-mail, For Presentation, or Full Size.

   Nothing appears to happen, although the view is saved on the Clipboard. These commands are similar to pressing the Print Screen key on your keyboard. The e-mail version is small, the presentation version is medium, and full size is large.

5. Go to the application where you want to use the image, click the location where you want the image to appear, and then choose the Paste command.

   If you're pasting the Timeline into an Office application, on the Home tab, in the Clipboard group, click Paste.

   The image is pasted into the document as a static picture, as shown in Figure 17-5.

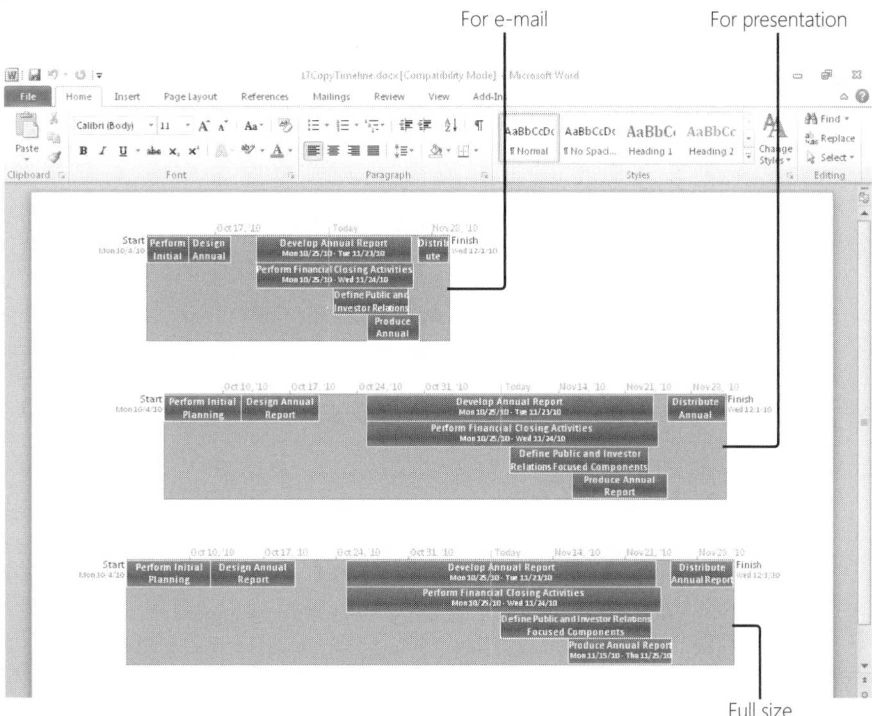

Figure 17-5 Selecting the e-mail, presentation, or full-size version specifies the size at which the Timeline should be copied.

If needed, you can resize the image by dragging any of the handles around the edges. A rotate handle appears at the top center of the image.

Embedding Information

You can insert information from another application into Project 2010 and have that information behave as though that application is resident in Project 2010.

Likewise, you can insert a piece or all of a project plan into another application, such as a PowerPoint presentation or an Excel workbook, and work with that project plan as though you're working in Project 2010.

Whichever the direction, this method of exchanging information is done by embedding an object, which allows for great power and flexibility across different applications.

An *object* is a set of data that gets its format and behavior from another application. When you *embed* an object, you're basically inserting an entire file, with all of its source application's capabilities, into the destination application.

For example, suppose that in Project 2010 you embed a bit of art originally created in a graphics program. The art object appears in Project 2010 as though you created it there. If you double-click the object, the graphics application in which it was created is launched, and you can change the illustration on the spot, save the changes, and close the application. The changes you make are reflected instantly in the art showing in Project 2010.

In order for embedding to work properly, both the source and destination applications must be installed on the same computer or have ready network access to both applications. Also, because embedding inserts an entire file within another file, it uses a large amount of memory while the project is open and makes the destination file much larger.

> **Note**
>
> **Embedding objects between different applications is made possible by *OLE technology*. Any application that employs the OLE standard can embed and link information from another application that also employs that standard.**

Embedding from Project 2010 to Another Application

You can embed a Project 2010 file in another application—for example, Word or PowerPoint. When you double-click the object in the destination application, Project 2010 is launched on the spot, and you can switch views and manipulate data.

Embedding an Existing Project 2010 File

To embed an existing Project 2010 file in another application, follow these steps:

1. Open the destination application and the file in which you want to embed the Project 2010 file.

2. Select the location where you want the Project 2010 object to be embedded.

3. Select the command to insert an object.

   Object

   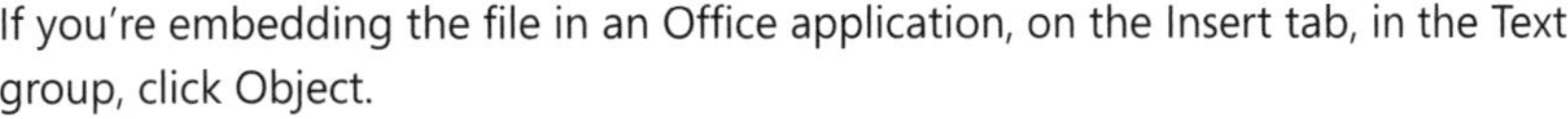

   If you're embedding the file in an Office application, on the Insert tab, in the Text group, click Object.

   If the destination application does not have an Insert Object command, it probably does not support embedding. Look in the application's online Help or other documentation to see whether the command is called something else.

4. In the dialog box, click the Create From File option or tab.

5. Click the Browse button.

   The Browse window appears. Browse through your computer's filing system (and onto your network if applicable) to find the drive and folder in which the project file is located.

6. Double-click the file.

   Its path and name are entered in the File Name box in the dialog box. (See Figure 17-6.)

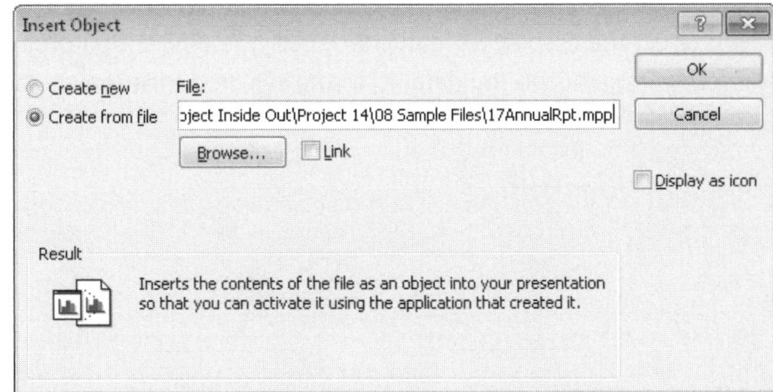

Figure 17-6 Select the project file you want to embed in the other application's file.

7. If you want the embedded object to be linked to the source, select the Link check box.

   - If you link the object, any changes in the original update the embedded object. Likewise, any changes made in the embedded object are reflected in the original.

Chapter 17

- If you don't link the object, you're essentially making a copy of the original object, which becomes a separate entity from the original. You can change the embedded version without affecting information in the original.

8. If you want to display the embedded project as an icon in the destination application, rather than show it in the Gantt Chart or other view, select the Display As Icon check box.

9. Click OK.

   Part of a view of the selected project file appears in the location you selected, as shown in Figure 17-7.

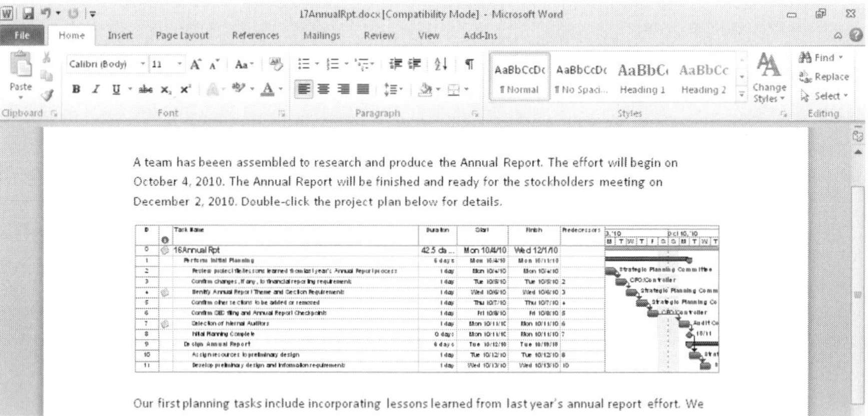

Figure 17-7 The selected project is embedded in the other application, in this case, Word.

If you select the Display As Icon check box, the embedded project file appears as the Microsoft Project icon (by default) in the selected location, as shown in Figure 17-8.

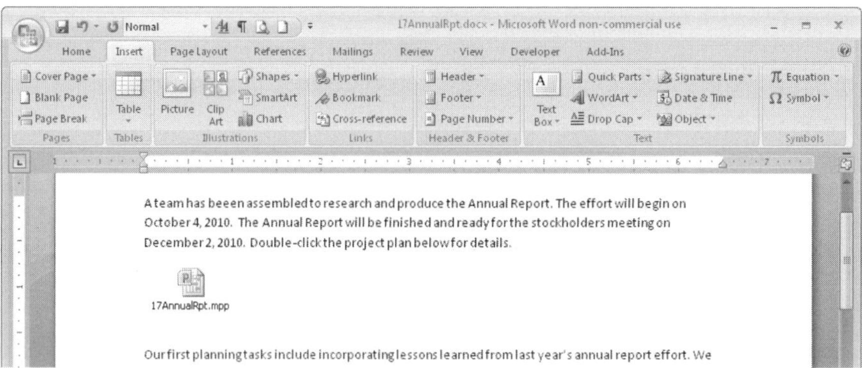

Figure 17-8 The selected project is embedded in Word and displayed as an icon.

> **Note**
>
> **The Display As Icon check box in the Insert Object dialog box is useful when you are embedding a large project file. When the project file is displayed as an icon, you can just double-click the icon to open the embedded file. This might be the most efficient way for you to embed a Project 2010 file in another application. The path and file name appear under the Project icon.**

Creating a New Project 2010 File as an Embedded Object

You can create a new Project 2010 file as an embedded object in another application. In this case, the object exists only within the destination application. To create a new Project 2010 file within another application, follow these steps:

1. Open the destination application and the file in which you want to create a new Project 2010 file as an embedded object.
2. Select the location where you want to embed the new Project 2010 object.
3. Choose the command to insert an object.

   If you're embedding the object in an Office application, on the Insert tab, in the Text group, click Object.
4. In the Insert Object dialog box, click the Create New option or tab.
5. Scroll through the list, and click Microsoft Project Document. (See Figure 17-9.)

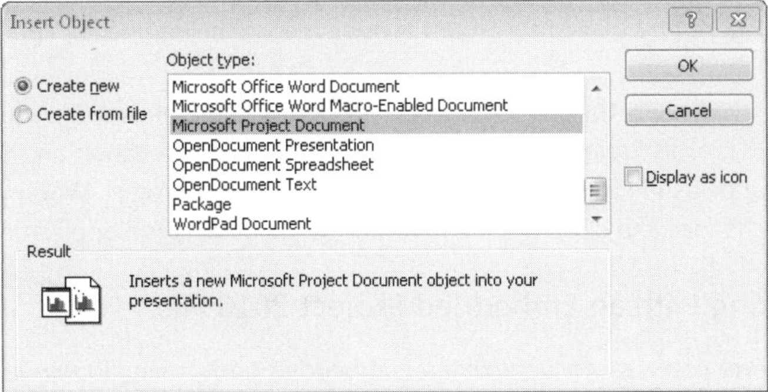

Figure 17-9 Use the Insert Object dialog box to create a new Project 2010 file as an embedded object.

6. If you want to display the embedded project as an icon in the destination application rather than show it in the Gantt Chart or other view, select the Display As Icon check box.

7. Click OK.

   Part of a view of the new project file appears, as shown in Figure 17-10. Double-click the new project to open it and add information to it on the spot. When you finish, save your changes and close the project to return to the destination application.

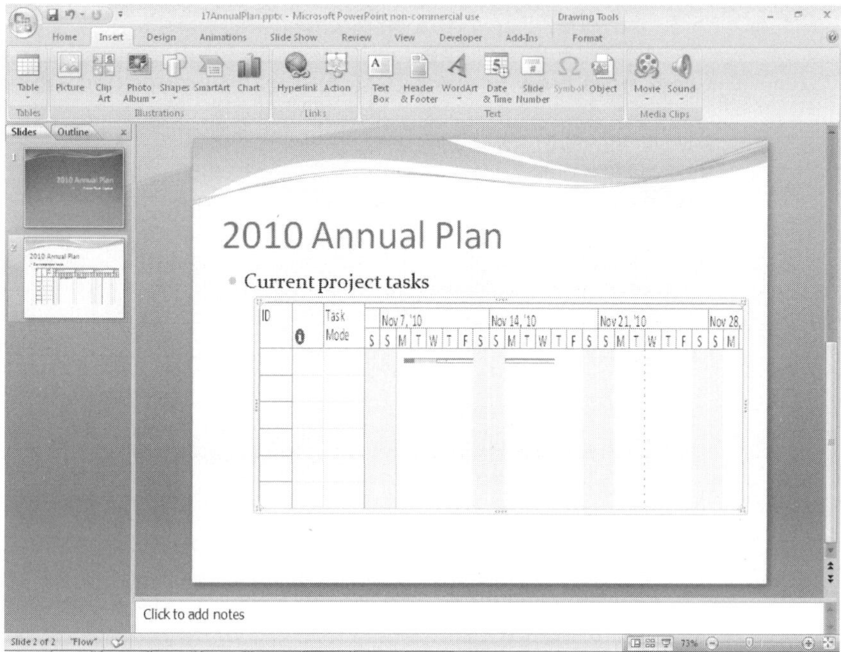

Figure 17-10 The new project is embedded in the destination application, in this case PowerPoint.

If you select the Display As Icon check box, the embedded project file appears as the Microsoft Project icon (by default) in the selected location and the new blank project appears in Project 2010. Add information to the project. When you finish, save your changes and close the file to return to the destination application.

Working with an Embedded Project 2010 File

Whenever you want to work with an embedded project file, double-click the object. Project 2010 opens, and the embedded project file appears. You can use Project 2010 as you usually do, switching views, applying tables and filters, changing data, running calculations, and so on.

For information about embedding a Project 2010 file in Excel, see "Embedding Between Project 2010 and Excel" on page 699.

Embedding from Another Application to Project 2010

You can insert objects from other applications into Project 2010, but only in certain specific places:

- The chart area of a Gantt chart
- The Notes area of the Task Form or Task Information dialog box
- The Notes area of the Resource Form or Resource Information dialog box
- The Notes tab in the Assignment Information dialog box
- The Objects box in the Task Form
- The Objects box in the Resource Form
- Headers, footers, and legends of printable pages

INSIDE OUT **Are your objects so much hidden treasure?**

Most of the places where objects can be embedded are fairly hidden. If you want to be sure that an object like a logo or other graphic has high visibility, insert it in the chart area of the Gantt Chart or in the header, footer, or legend of printable pages.

Inserting a Graphic or Other Object in the Gantt Chart

The chart area of the Gantt Chart is a great location for graphics or other objects you might need to add to Project 2010. The Gantt Chart is often the primary view used by most project managers, and it's also often used for reporting. Because this view is widely used, it's handy to insert objects in an area of the Gantt Chart that's not otherwise occupied, and a well-placed logo can also make the Gantt Chart look all the more professional and finished.

Other objects that might be useful in the Gantt Chart can include bar charts or pie charts of related data, symbols to show significant points, and even simple drawings. Other media forms, such as sounds and video, can be embedded as appropriate.

Note

If you want to add an icon or other graphic to the Gantt Chart, it needs to be in the BMP image format. Other image formats—including TIF, GIF, and JPG—only appear in the Gantt Chart as icons.

To embed an object from another application into the chart area of the Gantt Chart, follow these steps:

1. In Project 2010, display the Gantt Chart of the project plan in which you want to embed the object.

   You can use any of the Gantt views, whether it's the actual Gantt Chart, the Tracking Gantt, or the Detail Gantt, for example.

2. Using Windows Explorer, browse through your computer's filing system to find and select the graphic or other object you want to embed in the Gantt Chart.

   Be sure to use a BMP version of any graphic you want to show in the Gantt Chart. Other graphics formats display only a generic icon when placed in the Gantt Chart.

3. In Windows Explorer or My Computer, click Edit, and then click Copy to copy the object to the Clipboard.

4. Return to Project 2010 and click in the chart area of the Gantt Chart view.

5. On the Task tab, in the Clipboard group, click Paste.

   The object appears in the upper-left corner of the chart area of the Gantt Chart, as shown in Figure 17-11.

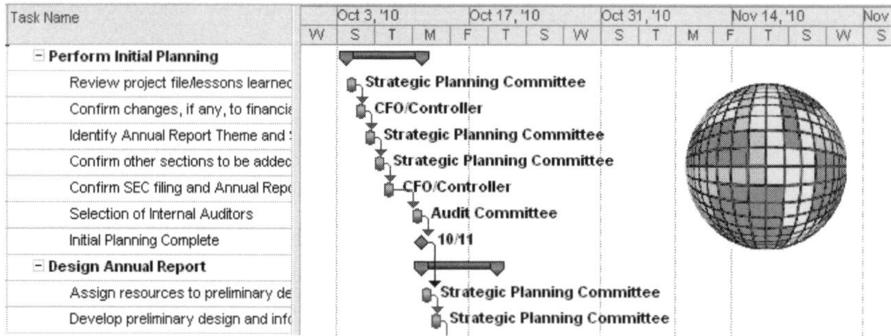

Figure 17-11 Copy and paste a graphic or other object into a Project 2010 Gantt Chart view to embed it.

6. Move the object to the location you want on the Gantt Chart and resize the image as needed.

Chapter 17

Add a Graphic to a Printed View

You can add a graphical object (for example, a company or project logo) to the project file header, footer, or legend so that the object appears when you print a view.

Unlike the other areas in Project 2010 that accept graphics, the file header, footer, or legend areas let you show any graphical format, whether it's BMP, JPG, TIF, GIF, or PNG. However, you cannot adjust the size of the image after it's inserted in the header, footer, or legend, so before inserting it, be sure that the graphic is sized as you want it to appear.

To add a graphic to a header, footer, or legend, follow these steps:

1. On the File tab, click Print.
2. At the bottom of the middle pane of the Print Backstage view, click Page Setup.
3. In the Page Setup dialog box, click the Header, Footer, or Legend tab.
4. Select the location (Left, Center, Right) where you want the graphical object to appear in the printed view.
5. Click Insert Picture.
6. Browse through your system to find the picture, and then double-click it.

Insert Picture

Now when you print the view, the graphic appears in the location you specified.

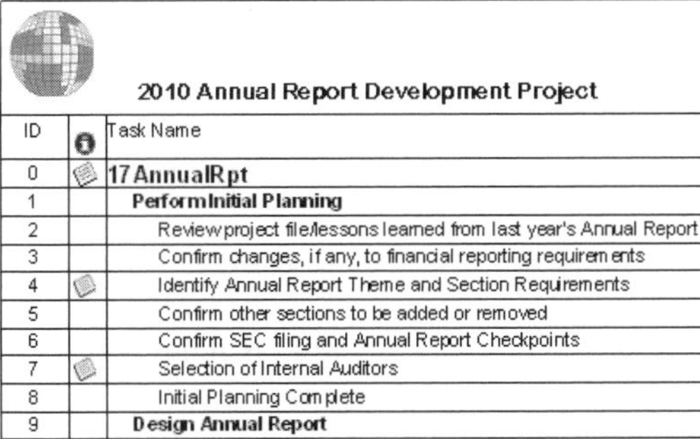
2010 Annual Report Development Project

ID		Task Name
0		17AnnualRpt
1		Perform Initial Planning
2		Review project file/lessons learned from last year's Annual Report
3		Confirm changes, if any, to financial reporting requirements
4		Identify Annual Report Theme and Section Requirements
5		Confirm other sections to be added or removed
6		Confirm SEC filing and Annual Report Checkpoints
7		Selection of Internal Auditors
8		Initial Planning Complete
9		Design Annual Report

For more information about specifying headers and footers for printed views, see "Setting Up and Printing Views" on page 528.

Embedding an Object in a Note

If the object you want to embed is associated with a particular task, resource, or assignment, you might prefer to embed it in a note. To do this, follow these steps:

1. Display a view that contains the task, resource, or assignment you want to associate with an object.

   For example, for tasks, display the Gantt Chart. For resources, display the Resource Sheet. For assignments, display the Task Usage or Resource Usage view.

2. Double-click the task, resource, or assignment with which you want to associate the object.

   The Task Information, Resource Information, or Assignment Information dialog box appears.

3. In the dialog box, click the Notes tab.

Insert Object

4. Click the Insert Object button.

5. In the Insert Object dialog box, select the Create From File option.

6. Click the Browse button. Find the file you want to embed as an object in the note, and then double-click its name.

7. If you want the embedded object to be linked to the source, select the Link check box. If you want to display the object as an icon rather than the object itself, select the Display As Icon check box.

   If you're embedding a graphics object, BMP is the only graphics format that displays the graphic rather than a generic icon.

8. Click OK.

   The object appears in the upper-left corner of the notes area, as shown in Figure 17-12.

   Depending on the object's file type and where you insert it, it might be displayed as the file itself—for example, the actual image or the first page of a presentation—or it might show just the file name. Either way, the object is embedded in your project and is associated with the selected task, resource, or assignment. When you double-click the object, the source application opens and the object is displayed.

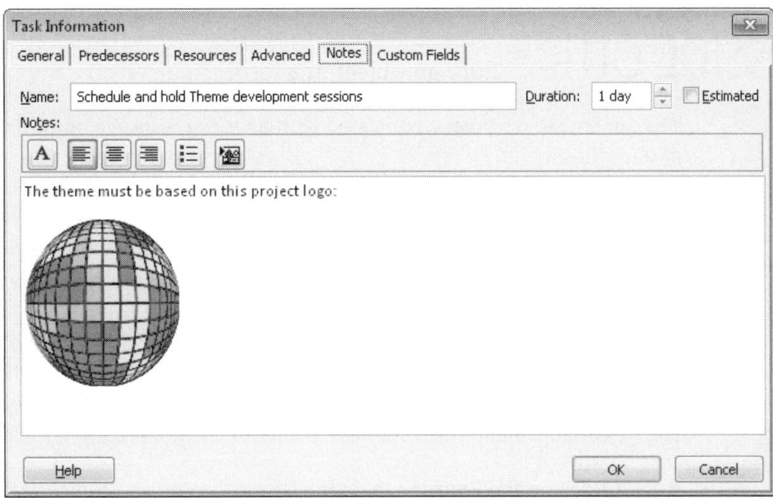

Figure 17-12 Embed an object in a task note, resource note, or assignment note.

Note indicator

As for any note, the Note indicator appears in the Indicators column in a sheet view when a note is present. Double-click the Note indicator to quickly open the Notes tab and see the object.

> **Note**
>
> **You can embed an object in a note associated with the project as a whole. First, add the project summary task: display any task sheet, and then on the Format tab, in the Show/Hide group, click the Project Summary Task check box.**
>
> **Double-click the project summary task. In the Summary Task Information dialog box, click the Notes tab, and then click the Insert Object button and add the object.**

Creating a New Object to Embed in the Project

You can create a new file as an embedded object in your project. In this case, the new object exists only within your project file. To do this, follow these steps:

1. In your project plan, go to the location where you want to embed the object—for example, the Notes area of the Resource Information dialog box.
2. Click the Insert Object button on the dialog box toolbar.
3. In the Insert Object dialog box, be sure that the Create New option is selected.

INSIDE OUT Bury an object in a form

You can embed an object associated with a task or resource in the Task Form or Resource Form.

With any view showing, on the View tab, in the Split View group, click Details. If a task view was showing, the Task Form appears below the task view. If a resource view was showing, the Resource Form appears at the bottom of the split view.

Notes

Select the task or resource to be associated with the embedded object. Click in the form to make it the active view. On the Format tab, in the Details group, click Notes. Click the Insert Object button on the toolbar, and then find and add the object as usual. The object appears in the upper-left corner of the notes area in the form.

If you prefer, on the Format tab, in the Details group, you can click Objects. Because there is no Insert Object button, you need to copy the object using Windows Explorer and then paste it into the object area. Objects pasted into a form are not as flexible as those inserted in the Gantt Chart or in a note. The object cannot be moved or resized. Plus, it takes a lot of clicks to get to it, so it's pretty buried.

4. Scroll through the Object Type box, and click the name of the application with which you want to create the new object—for example, Bitmap Image or Microsoft Visio Drawing.
5. Specify whether you want the new object to be displayed as an icon in the project, and then click OK.

   Depending on your choice, either a miniature version of the application appears in the location you selected, or the application launches immediately. (See Figure 17-13.)
6. If the application is not already open, double-click the application to launch it. Start creating the new file on the spot.
7. On the File menu of the embedded application, choose the command to save or update the object in your project plan. When you finish, choose the command to close the application. The object is updated in the area of the project plan from which you created the object.

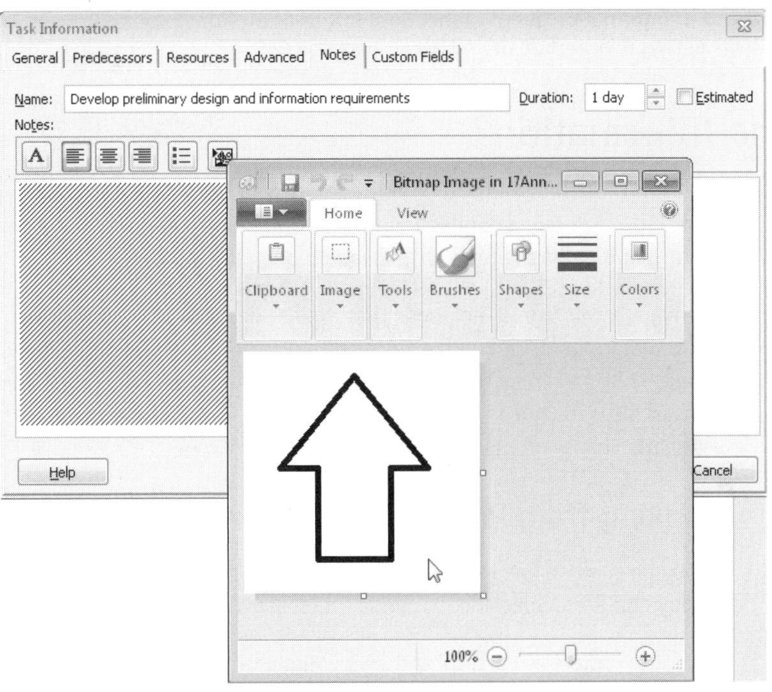

Figure 17-13 In this example, Microsoft Paint launches when you insert a bitmap image as a new object in your note.

Working with the Embedded Object in the Project

If an object embedded in your project is a graphic that's displayed in its proper place, you might never need to do anything with it. With other objects, however, you need to open and work with them. This is particularly true of new objects you create within the project file. They contain nothing until you add your own data.

To open and work with an embedded object, simply double-click the object. The source application opens, and you can use its commands and tools to work with the object as needed. When you finish, choose the save command, and then choose the close or exit command. The source application closes, and the object appears in your project file showing the changes you just made.

Note

To delete an embedded object anywhere in your project plan, simply click it and press the Delete key.

For information about embedding information from Excel to Project 2010, see "Embedding Between Project 2010 and Excel" on page 699.

Linking Information

Linking is another method of exchanging data between applications. By linking information, you maintain a connection to the source application. When a change is made to the information, it's reflected in the destination application.

A major advantage of linking is that the file size is much smaller than it would be if the information in the linked file were embedded. A potential difficulty with linking is that you always need to know the current location of the linked file and its update status. If the linked file is moved, the link is broken. If the information in the linked file becomes obsolete, the linked information also becomes out of date.

Linking from Project 2010 to Another Application

You can create a link from Project 2010 information to another application by using the Copy and Paste Special commands. To create a link, follow these steps:

1. In Project 2010, display the view that contains the information you want to copy and link to another application.

   If the information is text-based—such as tasks, resources, or assignment fields—select the information. If the information is graphical—such as a Gantt chart, Resource Graph, or Network Diagram—arrange the view to contain the information you want to represent in the other application.

2. On the Task tab, in the Clipboard group, click Copy.

3. Open the destination application, for example, Word or PowerPoint. Place the cursor where you want to insert the information.

4. In the destination application, find and click the Paste Special command.

   If you're linking to an Office application, on the Home tab, in the Clipboard group, click the arrow under Paste. In the menu that appears, click Paste Special.

5. In the Paste Special dialog box, select the Paste Link option, as shown in Figure 17-14.

6. Review the choices available in the As box. Click each one to read its description in the Result box, and then select the one that meets your needs.

   The choices vary depending on the type of information copied in Project 2010. One of the choices is always Microsoft Project Document Object, which creates an embedded object that's linked.

It's a good idea to experiment with the different choices in the Paste Special dialog box. You'll get different results depending on the type of data you copy and the nature of the destination application.

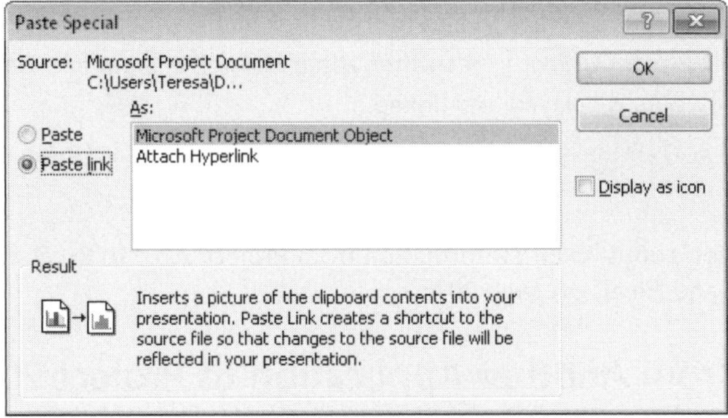

Figure 17-14 Use the Paste Special dialog box to create a link from Project 2010.

7. Click OK.

   The linked information appears in the destination application. (See Figure 17-15.) When changes are made to the information in Project 2010, those changes are reflected in the destination application.

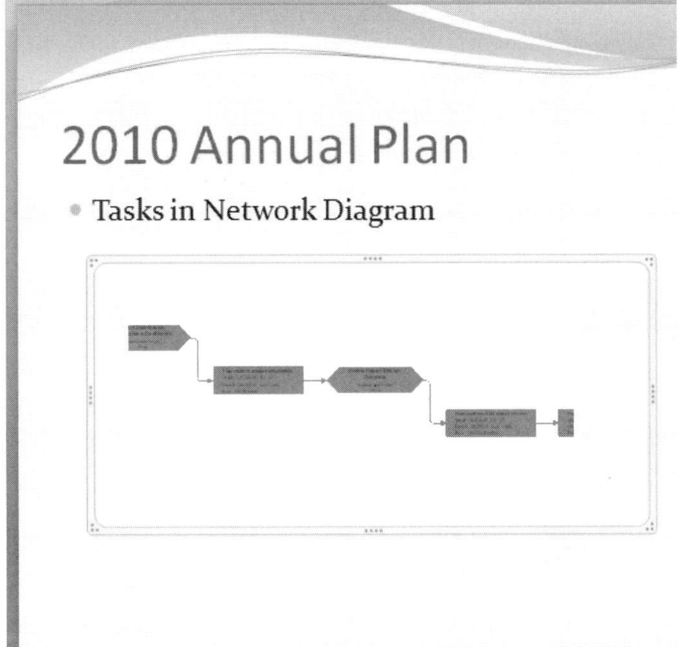

Figure 17-15 Use the Paste Special dialog box to create a link from Project 2010.

Note

If you copy from a Gantt Chart, and you want the bars to show, arrange the view to show as much or as little of the sheet area as you want, then select and copy the rows whose Gantt bars you want to link to the other application. When you paste link as a Microsoft Project Object in the other application, the sheet and Gantt bars of the selected rows are displayed and linked.

For information about linking information from Project 2010 to Excel, see "Linking Between Project 2010 and Excel" on page 707.

Linking from Another Application to Project 2010

You can link an object from another application to specific destination areas in Project 2010. When the information changes in the source file, it changes in its linked area in Project 2010 as well.

Linking Text or Numbers to a Project Table

You can link alphanumeric information from another application to any table in Project 2010. To do this, follow these steps:

1. In the source application, select the text or numbers to be linked to Project 2010, and then choose the application's copy command.

   If you want to copy and link information from an Office application, on the Home tab, in the Clipboard group, click Copy.

2. In Project 2010, display the view and select the sheet view, table, and cell to contain the linked information.

   Be sure that the cell's field type is compatible with the type of information you're linking, whether text or numbers.

   If you're pasting multiple cells of tabular data from the other application, select the cell where you want the paste operation to start flowing in the data. Again, be sure that the incoming data is compatible with the field types in the destination table.

3. On the Task tab, in the Clipboard group, click the arrow under Paste. In the menu that appears, click Paste Special.

4. In the Paste Special dialog box, click the Paste Link option.

   The As box changes to present the options for linking the copied information to the project file.

5. Review the choices available in the As box. Click each one to read its description in the Result box, and then select the one that meets your needs.

   Experiment with the different choices in the Paste Special dialog box. You'll get different results depending on the type of data you're linking and the nature of the source application.

6. Click OK.

   The linked information appears in the selected cell. When changes are made to the information in the source application, those changes are reflected in this cell.

TROUBLESHOOTING

You get an error when you try to link pasted information to your project

If you try to paste information in a cell whose field is not compatible with the type of information you're pasting, you'll see the following error message:

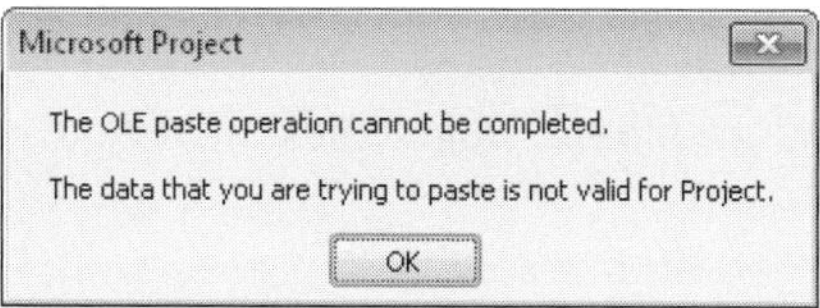

For example, you can paste any text into a Task Name or Resource Name field. However, you can paste numbers only into a number field. And while you can paste any text or numbers into the Duration, Start, or Finish fields of a manually scheduled task, you cannot paste such information into the same fields for an automatically scheduled task.

The error message is misleading, though. While the data might not work in the particular cell that's selected, it doesn't mean it can't be linked anywhere in Project 2010. The data can likely be pasted successfully in another cell with a more open format, such as a Task Name, Resource Name, or custom Text field.

For information about linking information from Excel to Project 2010, see "Linking Between Project 2010 and Excel" in Chapter 18.

Linking a Graphic or Other Object into Your Project Plan

You can link a graphic or other object, such as text or a multimedia file, from another application to specific locations in Project 2010, such as the Notes areas and the Task and Resource Forms. The information needs to exist as its own file, rather than as information copied from a file.

To link a graphic or other object to a note in your project, follow these steps:

1. Display a view that contains the task, resource, or assignment you want to associate with the linked object.

   For example, for tasks, display the Gantt Chart. For resources, display the Resource Sheet. For assignments, display the Task Usage or Resource Usage view. For the entire project, show the project summary task.

2. Double-click the task, resource, assignment, or project summary task with which you want to associate the linked object.

   The Task Information, Resource Information, Assignment Information, or Summary Task Information dialog box appears.

3. In the dialog box, click the Notes tab.

4. Click the Insert Object button on the tab's toolbar.

5. In the Insert Object dialog box, select the Create From File option.

6. Click the Browse button, find the file you want to link in the note, and then double-click its name.

7. Select the Link check box.

   If you're embedding a graphics object, BMP is the only graphics format that displays the graphic rather than a generic icon.

8. Click OK.

   The object appears in the upper-left corner of the notes area. It's linked, so when the source file is updated, the changes appear in the object here in your project plan. It's also embedded, so if you double-click the object, the source application opens and is available for editing and viewing.

In the same way, you can link embedded objects in the Task Form and Resource Form. When inserting the object into the form, select the Link check box, and the object will be dynamically linked. For more information, see "Bury an Object in a Form" on page 666.

INSIDE OUT **You can't link a graphic in the chart area of a Gantt view**

Although you can copy and paste a graphic, such as a logo, into the chart area of a Gantt view, you cannot link the graphic so that it is dynamically updated when changes are made in the source application.

Updating Links in Your Project

By default, whenever you open the project file containing the link, a message appears, asking whether you want to re-establish the link between the files, as shown in Figure 17-16. Clicking Yes re-establishes the link and updates any changed information.

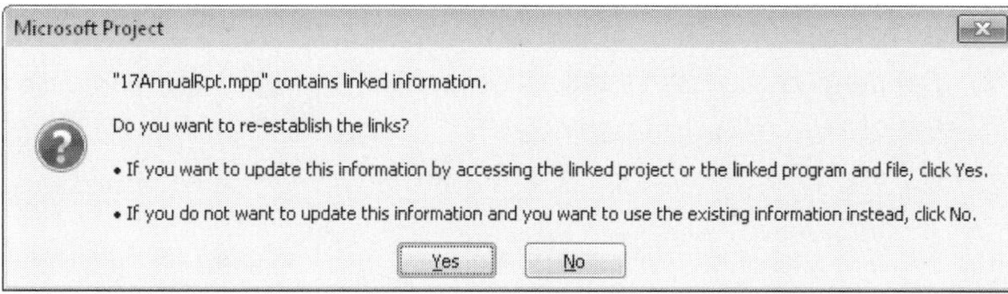

Figure 17-16 Each time you open a linked project, you are prompted to re-establish the link.

If you do not want to see this alert each time you open the project, on the File tab, click Options, and then click Advanced in the left pane. Under Display, clear the check box labeled Show OLE Links Indicators.

If you want to remove linked information, you can simply select it and delete it. You can update the content of the information by editing the source information.

However, if you need to manipulate the links in other ways, such as breaking the link but keeping the information intact, changing the source of the information, or controlling when updates happen, you need to use the Links dialog box.

Unfortunately, the Edit Links command is not available in the Project 2010 ribbon, so you need to make it available before you can use it. The easiest way to do this is to add the command to your Quick Access Toolbar. To do this, follow these steps:

1. On the File tab, click Options, and then click Quick Access Toolbar in the left pane.
2. In the Choose Commands From box, click Commands Not In The Ribbon.
3. Scroll to and click Edit Links, and then click the Add button.
4. Click OK; the Edit Links button is added to the Quick Access Toolbar.

You can also add the Edit Links button to a custom group in the ribbon. For information on how to do this, see "Customizing the Project 2010 Ribbon" on page 1153.

Now you're ready to work with the information linked from other applications. To review and work with links in your project, follow these steps:

Edit Links

1. On the Quick Access Toolbar, click Edit Links.

   The Links dialog box appears, showing all links in your project file. (See Figure 17-17.)

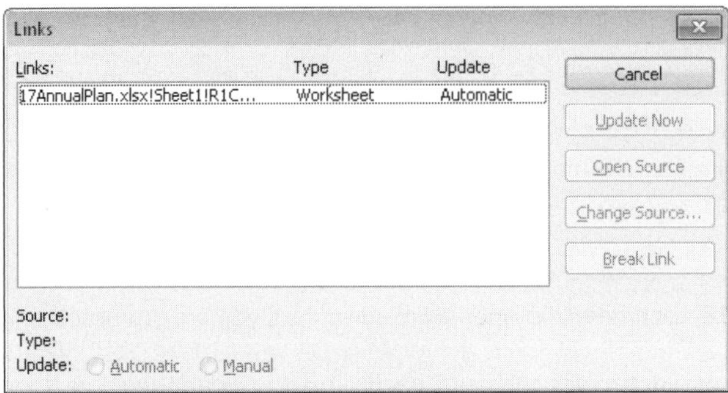

Figure 17-17 Review the status of links in your project file.

2. If you specified not to update a link when you open the project file, or if you're not prompted, you can select a link and click Update Now.
3. If the linked document location has changed, you can update the information in the project by clicking Change Source.
4. To break the link with the source application, click Break Link.

Hyperlinking to Websites or Other Documents

In your project file, you can insert a hyperlink to jump to a website or to a file on your computer or network. Inserting a hyperlink can be useful for including relevant reference material for tasks and resources in your project plan. It's also useful for linking project-related documents, such as the scope document and bill of materials, to your project plan.

Note

Although this method refers to a hyperlink, the item you link to does not have to be a web page and does not have to be in HTML or XML format. It can be any document in any file format. You do need to have the application for that file on your computer, but it does need to be in a stable location.

Creating a Hyperlink

To create a hyperlink in your project, follow these steps:

1. In Project 2010, display the view that contains the task, resource, or assignment to which you want to add a hyperlink.

2. Right-click the task, resource, or assignment name to which you want to add the hyperlink, and then click Hyperlink from the drop-down menu that appears.

   The Insert Hyperlink dialog box appears.

   By default, the Hyperlink command is not available in the ribbon, although you can add it to a custom group or to the Quick Access Toolbar.

4. In the Text To Display box, type a short description of the page you're linking to.

5. If you're linking to a file, in the Look In list, browse to the file on your computer or network system. (See Figure 17-18.)

   If you're linking to a website, enter the web address starting with **http://** in the Address box.

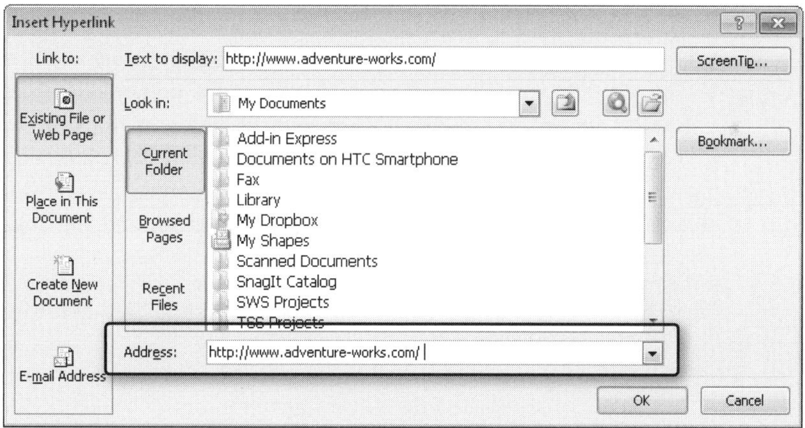

Figure 17-18 The path and name of the selected document appear in the Address box.

Hyperlink indicator

6. Click OK.

   The Hyperlink indicator appears in the Indicators column of the current view. If you rest your mouse pointer over the Hyperlink indicator, the display text for the hyperlink appears.

Following a Hyperlink

To go to the document or website referenced by a hyperlink, click the Hyperlink indicator in the Indicators column. If the Indicators column is not shown, you can apply the Entry table to a task sheet or resource sheet as applicable.

You can also right-click the task, resource, or assignment, point to Hyperlink in the drop-down menu, and then click Open Hyperlink. The hyperlinked document or website appears in its own window.

Tables

If you want to view more details about your hyperlinks, or if you have several hyperlinks throughout your project, you might find it useful to apply the Hyperlink table to a sheet view. On the View tab, in the Data group, click Tables, and then click Hyperlink. To go to the file or website pointed to by the hyperlink, simply click the Hyperlink indicator.

Removing a Hyperlink

To delete a hyperlink, right-click the task, resource, or assignment with which the hyperlink is associated, point to Hyperlink in the drop-down menu, and then click Clear Hyperlinks.

Set Up a Document Library

If you're using Project Professional 2010 with Project Server and Microsoft Project Web App 2010 for enterprise project management, the preferred method for keeping all project documents together is the document library. In Project Web App 2010, you can set up and maintain a document library by using Microsoft SharePoint 2010. This way, all your team members and other stakeholders can view the documents through their web browsers. They can also check documents in and out, providing vital version control.

For more information about setting up a document library, see "Controlling Project Documents" on page 959.

Importing and Exporting Information

When you import or export information between Project 2010 and other applications, the information you transfer appears as though it was created in the destination application. Importing and exporting essentially converts the information from the file format of the source application to that of the destination application.

One particularly useful type of export is to convert a Project 2010 view to a PDF file, which makes the information easily readable by anyone, regardless of whether a user has Project 2010 installed.

Updating Security Settings to Allow Data Import and Export

If you use an older file format when you import and export data between other applications and Project 2010, Project 2010 might block the operation because the default security settings don't allow legacy or non-default file formats to be opened or saved in Project 2010.

Therefore, in most cases you will not be able to finish the import or export operation until you set your Project 2010 security appropriately. To do this, follow these steps:

1. On the File tab, click Options, and then click Trust Center in the left pane.
2. Under Microsoft Project Trust Center, click the Trust Center Settings button.
3. In the left pane of the Trust Center dialog box, click Legacy Formats.

   The default setting is labeled Do Not Open/Save File With Legacy Or Non-Default File Formats In Project. (See Figure 17-19.)

   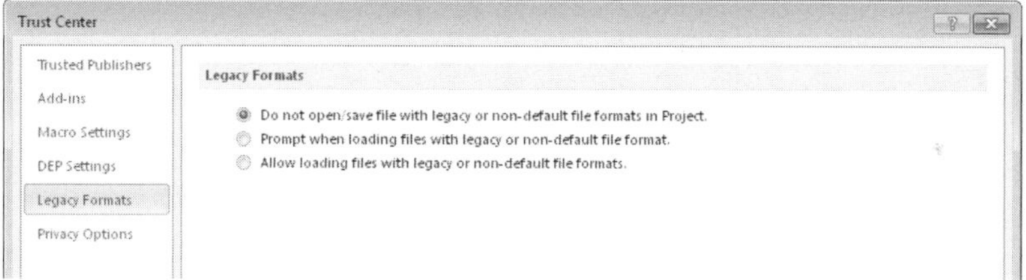

   Figure 17-19 Use the Legacy Formats area in the Trust Center to allow Project 2010 to export information as an older Excel file.

4. Select the option labeled Prompt When Loading Files With Legacy Or Non-Default File Format (medium security) or the option labeled Allow Loading Files With Legacy Or Non-Default File Formats (low security).

Note

Be sure to do this procedure before importing a file. Project 2010 walks you through the entire field-mapping process, which can be lengthy if the file includes many fields. Not until the final step of the mapping wizard does Project 2010 finally alert you that it cannot complete the import operation because the file is in a legacy or non-default file format.

Importing Information into Project 2010

You can bring information into Project 2010 from another application and another file format by importing it. Importing converts another application's file format into the Project 2010 file format. You start an import process simply by using the File, Open command.

You can import the file formats shown in Table 17-2.

Table 17-2 **Supported Import File Types**

File format	File name extension
Project files (for Project 1998 through 2010)	.mpp
Project databases	.mpd
Project templates	.mpt
Project workspaces	.mpw
Project Exchange (for Project versions 4.0 and 98)	.mpx
Microsoft Access databases	.mdb
Excel workbooks	.xlsx
Excel binary workbooks	.xlsb
Excel 97-2003 workbooks	.xls
Text files (tab delimited)	.txt
CSV Text files (comma delimited)	.csv
XML format files	.xml

To import data to Project 2010, follow these steps:

1. On the File tab in Project 2010, click Open.
2. Next to the File Name box, click the file type button, which is labeled Microsoft Project Files by default, and then click the file format of the file you are importing—for example, Microsoft Access Databases or Text (Tab Delimited).
3. Browse to the drive and folder that contain the file you want to import.
4. Click the name of the file you are importing, and then click the Open button.
5. Read the Import Wizard welcome page, and then click Next.
6. On the Import Wizard—Map page, select the New Map option, and then click Next.

7. On the Import Wizard—Import Mode page, select whether you want to import the file as a new project, append it to the current project, or merge it with the current project, and then click Next.

8. On the Import Wizard—Map Options page, under Select The Types Of Data You Want To Import, click the check box labeled Tasks, Resources, or Assignments, as applicable. (See Figure 17-20.)

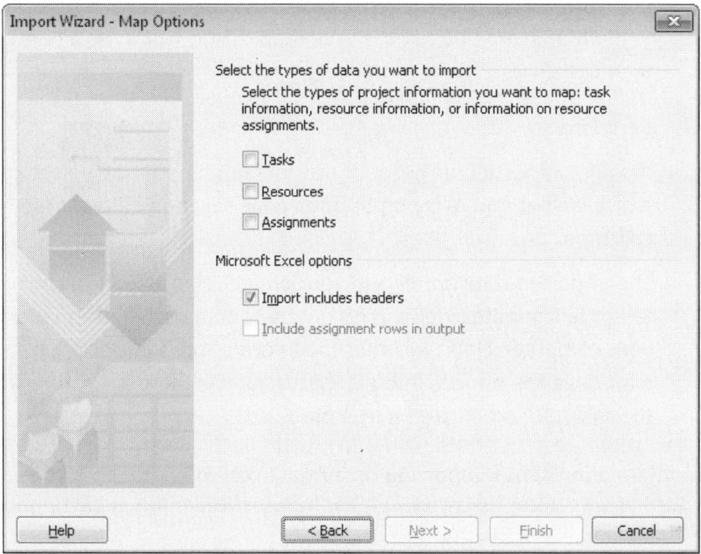

Figure 17-20 Use the Map Options page of the Import Wizard to specify the types of data you are importing.

You will see a separate mapping page for each data type you select on this page—for example, Task Mapping, Resource Mapping, or Assignment Mapping.

9. Under Text File Options, select or clear the check box labeled Import Includes Headers if necessary, and then click Next.

10. On the Mapping page, complete the fields to specify the information to be imported. In the To: Microsoft Project Field column of the table, specify which Project 2010 fields are to be used to store the fields from the source application. Any unmapped data appears in red and will not be imported. Click Next.

When you click the arrow in one of the To: Microsoft Project Field columns, a long list of fields appears. Type the first letter of the field you want to move to it more quickly. For example, type **n** to find and select the Name field, or type **d** to find and select the Duration field.

11. If, on the Map Options page, you selected multiple types of data to import (for example, Tasks and Resources), click Next to proceed to the Mapping page for the next data type. Repeat step 10 for each additional data type.

    You could potentially work through a Task Mapping, Resource Mapping, and Assignment Mapping page.

12. On the Import Wizard—End Of Map Definition page, click Save Map if you want to save the import map you just defined for future use.

    In the Map Name box of the Save Map dialog box, type a name for the map, and then click Save.

13. Click Finish.

    If you're importing an older or non-default file format, you might see a message that indicates that you're trying to open a file saved in an older file format. Click Yes to continue.

    The imported data appears in your project plan as you specified. This process might take a few minutes, depending on the source of the information and the speed of your computer. However, after the information is imported, it's set in your project plan. Save the project, and the information is there for you to work with instantly, as though you had created it in Project 2010.

For information about importing data from Excel to Project 2010, see "Importing and Exporting with Excel" on page 714. For information about exporting information from Visio to Project 2010, see Chapter 19.

Exporting Information from Project 2010

You can use information from Project 2010 in another application and another file format by exporting it. Exporting converts your Project 2010 information to the file format of another application. You start an export process simply by using the File, Save As command.

You can export a project file to the file formats shown in Table 17-3.

Table 17-3 **Supported Export File Types**

File format	File name extension
Project 2007 files	.mpp
Project 2000 to 2003 files	.mpp
Project templates	.mpt
Project 2007 templates	.mpt
PDF files	.pdf

File format	File name extension
XPS files	.xps
Excel workbooks	.xlsx
Excel Binary workbooks	.xlsb
Excel 97-2003 workbooks	.xls
Text files (tab delimited)	.txt
CSV Text files (comma delimited)	.csv
XML format files	.xml

TROUBLESHOOTING

File formats you used to export to are no longer available

In Project 2010, you can no longer use the Save As dialog box to save a project as an Excel PivotTable. However, you can still create visual reports of project data using PivotTables in Excel and PivotDiagrams in Visio.

Also, as of Project 2007, a project cannot be saved as a Microsoft Project database (.mpd), an HTML file, an Access (.mdb) file, or an Open Database Connectivity (ODBC) file for Microsoft SQL Server or Oracle Server.

Instead of saving your project as an MPD or HTML file, you can save your project as an XML file through the Save As dialog box.

For more information about saving project information to XML and working with it in that format, see "Working with Project 2010 and XML Files" on page 684.

To export data from Project 2010, follow these steps:

1. In Project 2010, open the project that contains the information you want to export.
2. On the File tab, click Save As.
3. Browse to the drive and folder where you want to save the exported file.
4. In the File Name box, enter the name for the file.

   By default, the name of the project is adopted, and the extension representing the new file format is added.
5. In the Save As Type list, click the file format to which you want to export your project information. For example, if you want to export your project information to XML, click XML Format (*.xml).

6. Click the Save button.

   Depending on the file format you choose, the export might happen immediately, or you might need to work through the Export Wizard. The Export Wizard opens and guides you step by step through the specifics of data mapping the information you want from Project 2010 to the destination file. (See Figure 17-21.) Some steps and choices in the Export Wizard vary depending on the file type to which you are exporting.

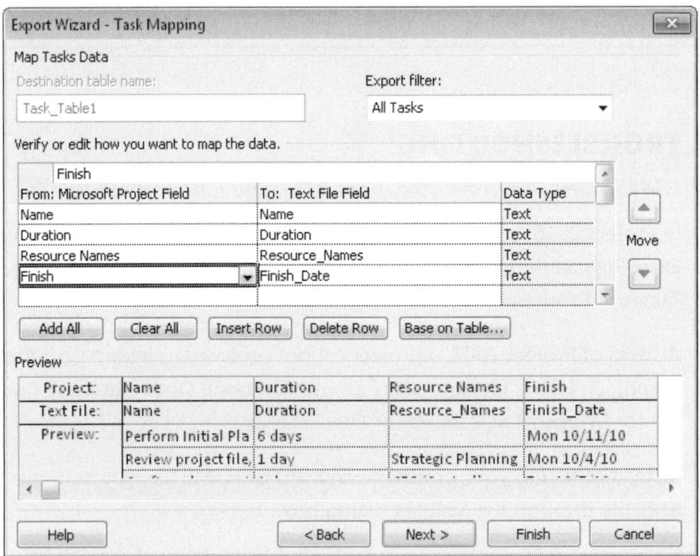

Figure 17-21 Work through the Export Wizard to define the project information that will be available to the destination application.

7. Work through each page of the Export Wizard, clicking Next after making your selections on each page.

8. On the final page, click Finish. Project 2010 exports your project information to the selected file format.

Note

If you want to export a wide and representative range of fields, click in the Export Wizard Task Mapping or Resource Mapping page, click the Base On Table button, and then click Export. The task Export table contains more than 70 task fields. The resource Export table contains more than 20 resource fields.

For information about exporting information from Project 2010 to Excel, see "Importing and Exporting with Excel" on page 714.

Saving Your Project Plan as a PDF File

You can save the current view of your project plan as a PDF file. You do not need to have Adobe Acrobat installed on your computer to save your project plan as a PDF file.

1. In your project plan, display the view you want to save as a PDF file, and then arrange the view in the way you want it to appear.
2. On the File tab, click Save As.
3. In the Save As dialog box, browse to the location where you want to save the new PDF file.
4. In the Save As Type field, click PDF Files (*.pdf).
5. In the File Name box, type the name for the new file.
6. Click Save.

   The Document Export Options dialog box appears, as shown in Figure 17-22.

   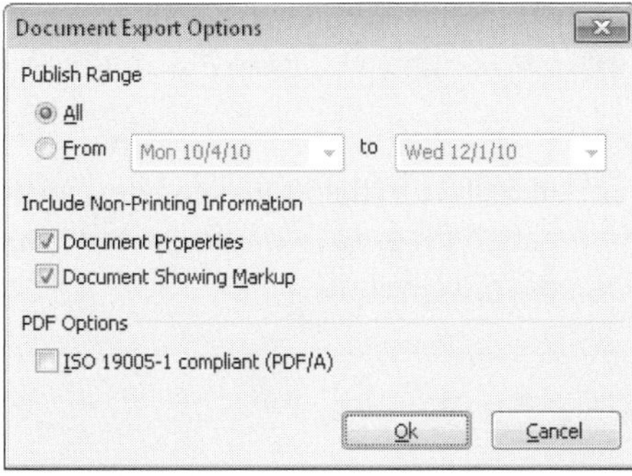

   Figure 17-22 Specify the project information you want to include in the PDF.

7. Specify the options you want for the PDF file, and then click OK.

   The file is saved as a PDF file. You can now send it to anyone, regardless of whether they have Project 2010 installed, because the file can be opened and viewed using Adobe Reader.

> **Note**
>
> **Another way to convert your project plan to a PDF file is by clicking File, Save & Send. The Save & Send Backstage view appears. Click Create PDF/XPS Document, and then click the Create PDF/XPS button that appears. Select the location, enter the file name, and then click OK. Complete the Document Export Options dialog box, and then click OK.**

Working with Project 2010 and XML Files

Project 2010 plans can be saved in XML format. XML is a self-defining, adaptable language that's used to define and interpret data in different applications, particularly in web documents. With XML, you can:

- Define the structure of data used.
- Make your data platform-independent.
- Automatically process data defined by XML.
- Define unique markup tags that hold your data elements.

The simple and consistent nature of XML makes it very useful for exchanging data between many types of applications. You can use project data in XML format in any application that recognizes XML.

By creating and applying an XSL template to the XML data, you can determine which project data is used and how it's formatted for use in a particular application, you can generate a report, or you can publish the data to a website.

> **Note**
>
> **As of Microsoft Project 2007, you can no longer save a project as an HTML or HTM file for an instant web page. Instead, save the project as an XML file and then apply an XSL style sheet.**

To save your project as an XML file, follow these steps:

1. Open the project plan you want to save as an XML file.
2. On the File tab, click Save As.
3. In the Save As Type field, click XML Format.
4. In the Save As dialog box, browse to the location where you want to save the new XML file.
5. In the File Name box, type the name for the file.
6. Click Save.

   The file is saved. You or your organization's webmaster can now open it in a markup language editor, apply style sheets, and prepare the information for publication on the web.

Note

If you just want to show a view of project information in a report or on a website, you can copy a picture of the view by using the Copy Picture function. This creates a GIF graphic file, which you can insert into a report or on a web page. For more information, see "Capturing a View for Other Applications" on page 652.

Importing and Exporting Database Information

As of Microsoft Project 2007, you can no longer save project fields to a database by using the Save As dialog box. This includes the Microsoft Project database (.mpd file) and the ODBC file for SQL Server or Oracle Server. The ability to save a project file in XML format replaces this functionality, because saving the file to XML essentially saves the contents of all fields that make up the project file database.

Although you cannot export to these database formats, you can still open Microsoft Project database and ODBC files to import them into your project plan. ODBC is the protocol used to access data in SQL Server database servers. With ODBC drivers installed, you can connect a Microsoft Project database to SQL Server databases.

To open an ODBC-compliant database file in Project 2010, follow these steps:

1. On the File tab, click Open.
2. In the Open dialog box, click the ODBC button.

   The Select Data Source dialog box appears.
3. On the File Data Source tab, browse to select the file data source for the ODBC driver to which you want to connect.

CHAPTER 18

Integrating Project 2010 with Excel

SOMETIMES the information you use to build a schedule might start in Microsoft Excel 2010. For example, team leaders might use Excel to build task lists for their portion of a project, or detailed information about available resources might be stored in an Excel workbook. Regardless of whether you want to exchange a little or a lot of data with Excel, sharing data between Microsoft Project 2010 and Excel is easy. You can copy data from Excel to Project 2010 or use the Excel-to-Project templates to import information into Project 2010.

Going the other direction, you'll find plenty of reasons to transfer some of your Microsoft Project data to Excel. For example, you can export project cost and earned value data to Excel, where you can create graphs, such as S-curves, to analyze project performance. If you are spoiled by the power of Excel PivotTables and PivotCharts for other kinds of management reporting you do, you can use Project 2010 visual reports to display Microsoft Project data in Excel PivotCharts and control how that data is presented. Then, you can pivot to your heart's content.

In addition, some crucial details are easier to deal with in formats such as text documents, spreadsheets, or databases. For example, information about product defects, their causes, and their resolutions is best suited to a spreadsheet or database file. You might want some information like this available in your project schedule. You can even link Excel information to Project 2010 so that the information is updated automatically. For example, you can update the status of change requests that you've added to your schedule.

For information about exchanging information with applications besides Excel, see Chapter 17, "Exchanging Information with Other Applications."

Whether you want to integrate Excel information into your project plan or feed information from Project 2010 to an Excel workbook, there are several methods for exchanging information. Transferring data between these two programs can simplify aspects of project planning, progress tracking, status reporting, and stakeholder communication.

The methods for transferring information between Project 2010 and Excel, which are described in detail throughout this chapter, are as follows:

- Copy and paste sheet or graphic information.

  You could copy tasks identified by your team leads from an Excel workbook to a Project 2010 file to build your initial task list, or you could copy the calculated costs of phases from a Project 2010 schedule to the project's capital budgeting Excel workbook. You could also paste the Excel cells that summarize software defect status into the Project 2010 Gantt Chart near the testing and debugging tasks.

- Insert, or embed, a Project 2010 file in an Excel file.

  For example, you could embed a Project 2010 file in the Excel file you use to select or prioritize projects.

- Insert, or embed, an Excel workbook or chart in a Project 2010 file.

  This is helpful if you want to review pending change requests in an Excel file while you scan your Project 2010 schedule for resources with available time. You might also refer to your risk management plan in an Excel file to determine how to respond to a problem that has arisen in your project.

- Link information dynamically between Project 2010 and Excel files so that when that information changes in one file, the same information is automatically updated in the other file to reflect that change.

  Linking information is ideal when information changes frequently. For example, linking cost fields in Project 2010 to cells in an Excel cost workbook keeps your cost analyses up to date.

- Open, or import, an Excel file as a Project 2010 file.

  This method comes in handy when you have schedule-related data in Excel, such as an initial task list or a resource list, that you want to use in Project 2010.

- Save, or export, a Project 2010 file as an Excel file. The file is converted to the Excel file format, so it can be opened directly in Excel.

  Saving a Project 2010 file to Excel means you can use Excel's data analysis and formatting capabilities to analyze project information. This is particularly helpful if you don't have access to Microsoft Project Server 2010 and its enterprise project management features.

INSIDE OUT Switch from Excel to Project 2010 for managing projects

Many project managers get their start building simple project schedules in Excel, often because they do not have a copy of Project 2010. Other times, the quantity of features available in Project 2010 and the specialized terminology that come with them is too daunting. Project 2010 includes new features, such as manually scheduled tasks, which help you get started with the program; you'll recoup the purchase price of the software through your increased productivity once Project 2010 starts handling the tasks—and the calculations—you had to perform manually before.

If you use Excel to manage a project, you usually type task names into the cells in the first column of a worksheet. Then, if you type the weeks or months in the first row, you can create something akin to a Gantt chart by highlighting the cells in each task row when work is supposed to take place. If the project plan changes—and, of course, it always does—you have to manually reschedule your tasks if the project starts late or a task takes longer than you estimated. In addition, if you want to track durations, costs, or resource assignments, you have to craft your own formulas to do so. With these challenges, using Project 2010 starts to look like a better idea.

With Project 2010's manually scheduled tasks, you can move effortlessly from Excel to Project 2010. You control the start and finish dates of these tasks, just as you do in Excel. If the plan changes, you change the dates for the affected tasks. For example, you can set up your task list in Project 2010 by importing task names, durations, and start and finish dates as manually scheduled tasks, as described in the section, "Importing and Exporting with Excel" on page 714. If you also include columns for assigned resources, you can import those fields into the corresponding Project 2010 fields as well.

For more information about controlling how tasks are scheduled, see "Manually Scheduling Tasks" on page 184 and "Automatically Scheduling Tasks" on page 185.

The advantage to switching from Excel to manually scheduled tasks in Project 2010 comes when you're ready to take advantage of Project 2010's ability to calculate the schedule. You can create links (dependencies) between the tasks. For example, suppose the "Paint Wall" task has a Finish-to-Start dependency with the "Paint Window Trim" task. If you change your manually scheduled tasks to automatically scheduled tasks and set the start date for the project, Project 2010 calculates the start and end dates for all the tasks—based on the project start date, the task dependencies, and their durations—and automatically recalculates the schedule as you make changes.

For more information about linking tasks, see "Establishing Task Dependencies" on page 206.

After you decide to use Project 2010 to manage projects, the next step is to decide how to transition from Excel to Project 2010. If you manage short projects, the easiest approach is to use your old Excel methods until projects in progress are complete and then start new projects using Project 2010. However, if your projects run longer, or you can't abide your manual management approach one more day, you can transfer some, if not all, of your project information from Excel to Project 2010.

Copying Between Project 2010 and Excel

By using the Copy and Paste commands, you can exchange sheet data and static graphics between Project 2010 and Excel. For example, if you have an Excel file with a proposed list of tasks (with estimated durations) for a project, you can copy the cells for the tasks into a Project 2010 task sheet to get your project schedule started. Similarly, the Copy and Paste commands work well if you want to display a graphic from one program in the other—for example, within the Gantt Chart for an equipment deployment project, you can show an Excel graph of sensors installed each week.

You can also use the Copy command to insert an embedded object. The benefit of embedding an Excel file within a Project 2010 schedule, or vice versa, is that you can open the embedded object without switching programs and you don't have to have access to the original file. Embedded objects are particularly helpful when you send files to someone else.

See "Embedding Between Project 2010 and Excel" on page 699.

Copying Information from Excel

You might want to copy two types of information from Excel worksheets:

- Data from Excel worksheet cells into cells in a sheet view in Project 2010.

  Copying data from Excel cells to Project 2010 cells is a wonderfully simple way to import data from Excel to Project 2010—as long as the columns of information in Excel and Project 2010 line up.

- Images of Excel graphs in graphically-oriented areas in Project 2010.

  Excel is the program of choice when you want to graph numeric data. If you want to display a graph, such as a pie chart or a line graph, within your Project 2010 file, you can copy the graph from Excel to the chart area of a Gantt view or to other non-table areas in Project 2010.

Copying Sheet Information from Excel

Any content within Excel worksheet cells can be copied and pasted into a Project 2010 table. However, the order and data type of the columns of information must match, so some up-front preparation is needed in either the Excel workbook or the Project 2010 table.

Match the Columns

Copying and pasting information is one of the easiest ways to get information from Excel to Project 2010. However, copying and pasting successfully depends on correctly matching up the columns of Excel information you copy and the Project 2010 columns into which you paste.

For example, suppose that your Excel worksheet contains five columns you want to copy to your project plan: Task Name, Resource, Duration, Start Date, and Finish Date. To copy these columns from Excel to Project 2010, you must first make sure that the columns in the Excel worksheet match the order of the columns in a Project 2010 task table. You can rearrange the columns in Excel or in Project.

The following are techniques you can use to arrange your Project 2010 view so that the five Project 2010 columns appear in the same order as the incoming Excel data. (See Figure 18-1.)

- **Move a column to a different location** Click the heading to select the entire column. When the mouse pointer changes to a four-headed arrow, drag to the location where you want the column.
- **Add a column to a Project 2010 table** Right-click in the column to the right of where you want the new column to appear, and then click Insert Column on the shortcut menu. In the drop-down Field Name list, click the field you want to add.
- **Remove a column from a table** Click the column heading, and then press the Delete key.
- **Apply a different table to a Project 2010 sheet view** On the View tab, in the Data group, click the down arrow below the Tables button, and then click the table you want.

Tables

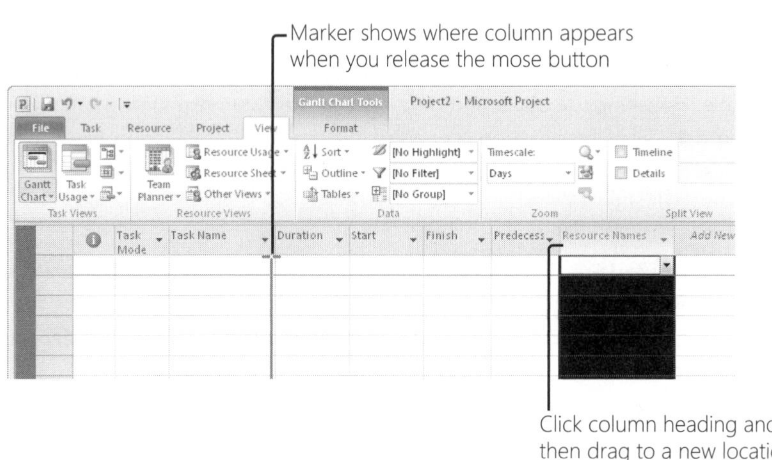
Marker shows where column appears
when you release the mose button
Click column heading and
then drag to a new location

Figure 18-1 Move columns in Project 2010 so that the table columns match the order and type of the Excel data being copied and pasted. A vertical gray marker appears to show where the column will be moved.

To copy and paste Excel worksheet cells into Project 2010, do the following:

1. Arrange the source Excel columns to match the field order and data type in Project 2010, or arrange the destination columns in Project 2010 to match the incoming Excel data.
2. In Excel, select the set of cells to be copied.

Copy

3. On the Home tab, in the Clipboard group, click Copy.
4. In Project 2010, select the *anchor cell* in the table where you want the incoming information to begin to be pasted.

Paste

5. In Project 2010, on the Task tab, in the Clipboard group, click Paste.

   Project pastes the selected Excel data, starting in the anchor cell and then down and to the right to additional cells.

   NEW!

   When you paste data from Excel 2010, by default, Project 2010 retains the formatting that is applied to the data in Excel. For example, if the Excel cells are highlighted with a light blue color and the text is in a bold italic font, the cells in Project 2010 will have the same formatting. A Paste Options indicator appears to the left of the anchor cell. You can choose whether to use the formatting from Excel or the formatting in Project 2010 by clicking the indicator and then choosing the Keep Source Formatting option or the Match Destination Formatting Option, as shown in Figure 18-2.

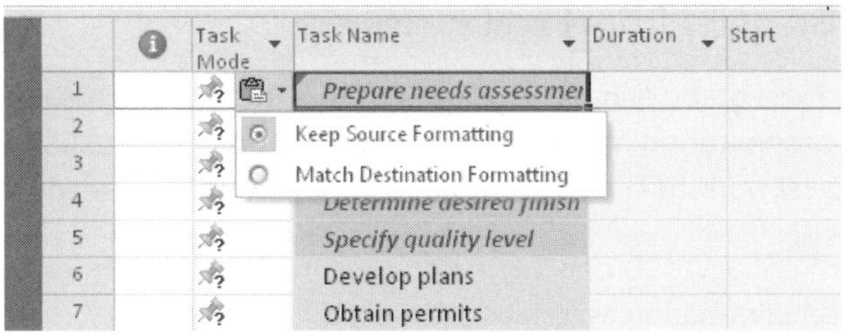

Figure 18-2 Click the option indicator to specify whether you want to keep the formatting from the data in Excel or apply the formatting defined in Project 2010.

Match the Data Types

As far as Project 2010 is concerned, you can paste a set of resource names into any column that represents a text field, such as the Task Name field, the Group field, the Contact field, or even the WBS field. As long as the data type (such as text, date, or number) for the data you are pasting into a field matches the data type for the Project 2010 field, the program obligingly accepts the information. For this reason, you cannot paste a set of resource names into the Work field, for example, because Work is a duration field, and the names are an incompatible data type.

So, matching the columns of information in Excel and Project 2010 really means matching the data types—that is, the kind of information that can be stored in a field (for example, text, number, or date) and the format that information can take (for example, **14d** for a duration field, **1/7/2011** for a date field, or **$35.90** for a cost field).

If you are pasting estimated task duration into Project 2010, chances are you want to use the Duration field. However, you can also paste into custom fields that have a matching data type as well. For example, if you estimate optimistic, most likely, and pessimistic durations, you can paste that data into any custom duration fields, such as Duration 5, Duration 6, and Duration 7.

To add a custom field to a Project 2010 table, right-click the column to the right of where you want the new column to appear, and then click Insert Column on the shortcut menu. In the Field Name drop-down list, click the field you want to add.

For more information about working with custom fields, see "Customizing Fields" on page 1107. For a list of custom fields available in Project 2010, press F1 to open the Help dialog box. Type **fields** in the search box, click Search, and then click one of the field types—for example, Duration1-10 Fields. A complete list of fields of that type appears in the Help pane.

Copying Graphics from Excel

Copying an Excel graph and pasting it as a picture into specific areas of Project 2010 is the most obvious application of copying Excel graphics into Project 2010. However, you can also paste Excel worksheet cells as a picture in Project 2010, instead of pasting those cells into table cells.

To paste Excel information as a static picture, do the following:

1. In Excel, select the chart or other data you want to insert as a picture in Project 2010.
2. On the Home tab, in the Clipboard group, click Copy.
3. In your Project 2010 file, display the location at which you want to place the picture, and click in that location. The following locations in Project 2010 can accept pictures:
   - Chart area of a Gantt chart
   - Notes tab in the Task Information, Resource Information, or Assignment Information dialog box
   - Objects box in the Task Form or Resource Form
   - Notes box in the Task Form or Resource Form
   - Header, footer, or legend of a printable view or report
4. On the Task tab, in the Clipboard group, click the arrow under the Paste button, and then click Paste Special.

   The Paste Special dialog box appears.
5. Select the Paste option.
6. In the As box, click Picture or Picture (Bitmap), as illustrated in Figure 18-3.

   This option ensures that the data, whether it's a chart or a set of worksheet cells, is pasted as a graphic rather than as an embedded object or straight text.

   If the Paste Special command is not available for the location at which you want to paste the picture, press Ctrl+V instead.
7. Click OK.

   The new picture is pasted in Project 2010 at the selected location. (See Figure 18-4.)

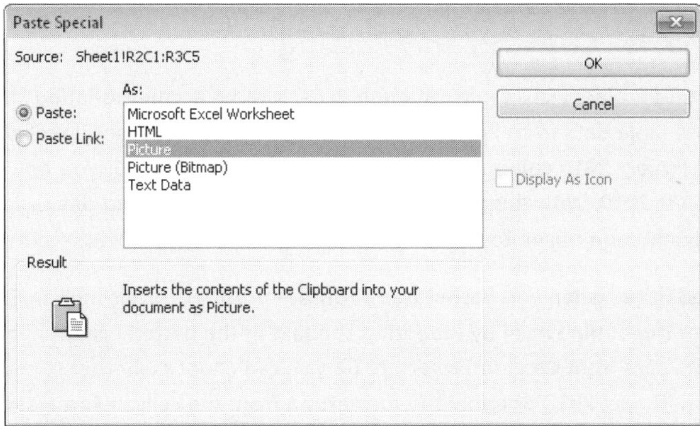

Figure 18-3 Use the As box in the Paste Special dialog box to specify that you want to insert the Excel information as a picture.

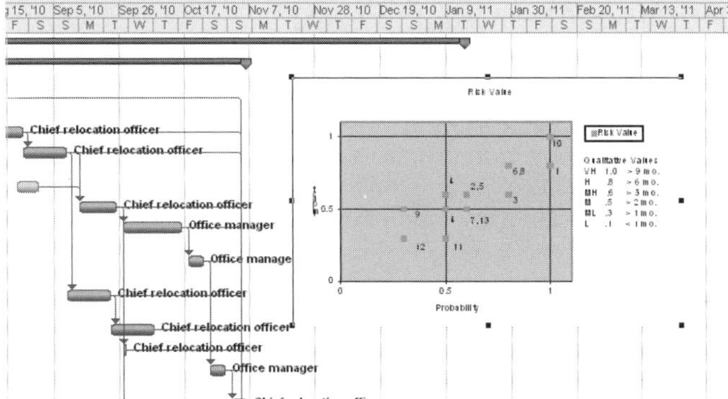

Figure 18-4 The Excel information appears as a picture in the Project 2010 location you selected.

Although static pictures look like embedded objects, you cannot open or edit them. However, you can drag the entire object or a side to move or resize the object.

To learn more about embedded objects, see "Embedding an Excel Object in Project 2010" on page 699.

Copying Information to Excel

Copying information from Project 2010 and pasting it into Excel worksheets is one solution when you need to process project data in a way that Project 2010 doesn't handle easily. Likewise, if you're more comfortable with Excel's sorting, grouping, and formatting features, you can copy data from Project 2010 to Excel to quickly obtain the results you need—for example, when you're rushing to prepare for a hastily convened meeting.

NEW!

Smarter Copying and Pasting

Pasting Project 2010 table data into Excel is more accommodating than before. If you paste table data from Project 2010 into an Excel spreadsheet, Excel automatically pastes the Project 2010 column headings into the first row, even if you don't select them in Project 2010. With this smarter copy and paste, your pasted data is labeled automatically. You don't have to waste time copying Project 2010 headings into Excel.

In addition, when you paste tasks at different outline levels into an Excel file, Excel indicates the outline level by indenting the text in the pasted cells. As you can when you paste data from Excel to Project 2010, you can choose whether to retain the formatting from Project 2010 or apply the formatting from the cells in Excel, as shown in Figure 18-2 earlier in this chapter.

Copying Sheet Information to Excel

Copying and pasting data from a Project 2010 table to Excel worksheet cells is actually easier than the reverse process. Unlike in copying from Excel to Project 2010, the columns or data types don't have to match, because all Excel fields can accept any data type.

To copy Project 2010 table cells and paste them into Excel worksheet cells, follow these steps:

1. In Project 2010, display the view that contains the information you want to copy to Excel.

   If necessary, apply a different table or add columns that contain the information you need.

2. Select the cells or columns you want to copy.

   To select a column, click its heading. Select multiple adjacent columns by dragging across the column headings. Select multiple nonadjacent columns by holding down Ctrl while you click each column heading.

3. On the Task tab, in the Clipboard group, click Copy or press Ctrl+C.

4. In Excel, select the anchor cell in the worksheet where you want the incoming information to begin to be pasted.

5. On the Home tab, in the Clipboard group, click Paste.

   Starting in the anchor cell, Excel pastes the column headings from Project 2010 in the first row and then pastes the selected Project 2010 data to additional cells down and to the right of the anchor cell. Adjust column widths in the worksheet as necessary to see the data. (See Figure 18-5.)

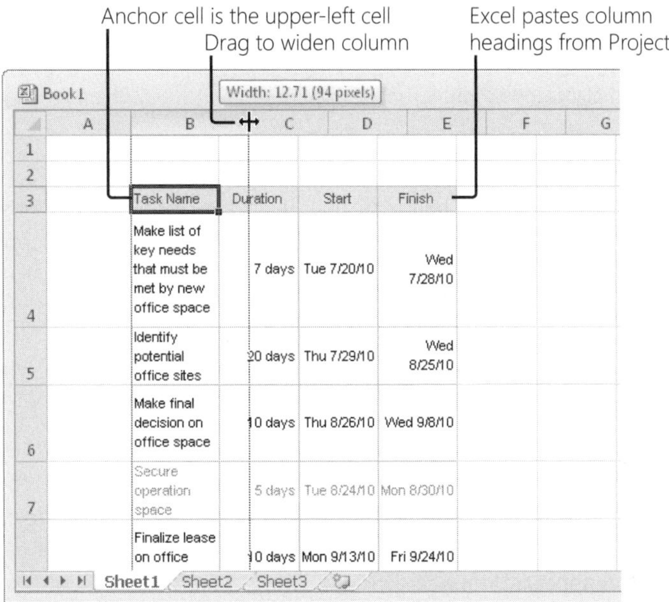

Figure 18-5 Excel pastes the column headings from Project 2010 in the first row and then pastes your project data in cells to the right and down from the anchor cell.

TROUBLESHOOTING

You can't find the Analyze Timescaled Data function

Project 2003 and earlier versions included an Analyze Timescaled Data command. This function, which copied task usage or resource usage over time from Project 2010 to Excel, has been replaced by visual reports for assignment usage. These visual reports can show assignments over a period of time. In fact, if you want to copy timephased data such as resource usage or assignment usage to Excel for further analysis, you can use a visual report to do so.

For more information about visual reports in Excel, see "Producing a Visual Report of Project Data in Excel" on page 734.

Copying Graphics to Excel

You can copy a picture of any Project 2010 view and paste it into Excel. To do this, follow these steps:

1. In Project 2010, display the view you want to capture as a picture for Excel.
2. Manipulate the view to show the information the way you want it to appear in Excel.

Copy Picture

3. On the Task tab, in the Clipboard group, click the arrow next to the Copy button, and then click Copy Picture.
4. In the Copy Picture dialog box, select the options you want.
   - In the Render Image section, select the option for the most likely method for viewing the image: on a computer screen (the default), printed, or a GIF image file (ideal for pictures published to the web).
   - In the Copy section, select the Rows On Screen option (the default) if you want the rows currently showing on the screen to be copied. The Selected Rows option copies the currently selected rows whether or not they appear on the screen.
   - In the Timescale section, select the As Shown On Screen option (the default) if you want the timescale to be represented as set in the current view. Select the From and To boxes if you want to specify a date range different from what appears on the screen.
5. When you've finished setting the Copy Picture options, click OK.
6. In Excel, select the location in the worksheet where you want to paste the picture of the view.
7. On the Home tab, in the Clipboard group, click Paste.

   A static picture of the Project 2010 view appears on the Excel worksheet, as shown in Figure 18-6. You can move the image by dragging it. You can also resize the image by dragging any of the edges.

Copy Timeline

You can also copy a picture of the Project 2010 Timeline view to Excel. With the Timeline active, on the Format tab, in the Copy group, click Copy Timeline, and then choose For Presentation or Full Size. Project 2010 copies the Timeline to the Clipboard. Then you can paste it in an Excel file or in another type of document. For more information on the Timeline, see "Highlighting Tasks with the Timeline" on page 134.

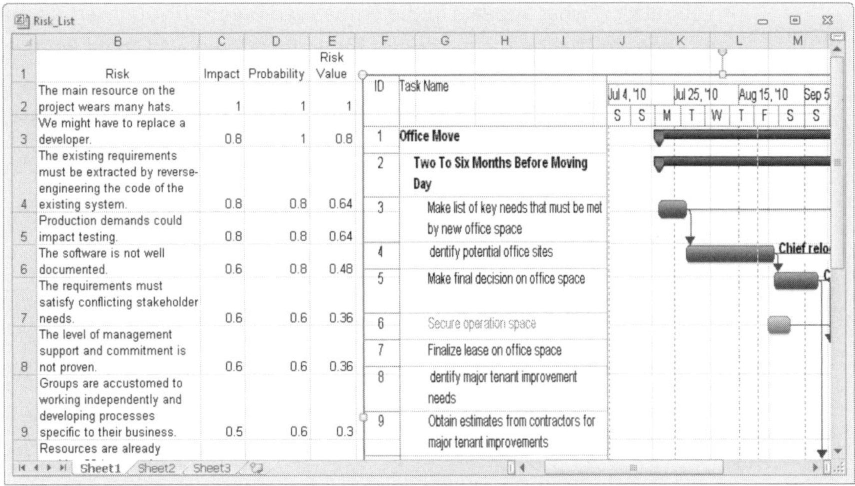

Figure 18-6 The copied picture of your Project 2010 view appears at the position you select in Excel.

Embedding Between Project 2010 and Excel

You can integrate information between Project 2010 and Excel by embedding a source file from one application as an *embedded object* in a file in the destination application. When you embed an object in an application, you're basically inserting an entire file, along with all of its source application's capabilities, into the destination application file. Embedding an object is ideal when you want to send a file to someone who does not have access to the source file or the source application, for example, a team lead for a subcontractor who does not have Project 2010 or access to your file server.

With an embedded object, not only can you have a picture of a Gantt chart in an Excel worksheet, but you can double-click that picture of the Gantt chart to access Project 2010 commands and change the Gantt chart data. You can even switch to a different Project 2010 view, such as the Resource Sheet, and change information there, as well. Likewise, in Project 2010, you can have a picture of an S-curve graph generated by Excel and also double-click it to launch Excel and edit the format of the graph or even the underlying data for the graph.

Embedding an Excel Object in Project 2010

Whether you insert all or part of an Excel worksheet or chart into Project 2010 as an embedded object, when you double-click the object, you can access the entire Excel workbook. The benefit of inserting a portion of an Excel worksheet or chart is that the portion you select is what appears in the embedded object. If you insert an entire file, you can drag its edges to change the portion of the embedded object that's visible.

Embedding Copied Excel Information in a Project 2010 File

To copy and paste selected Excel information as an embedded object, follow these steps:

1. In Excel, select the data or chart you want to insert as an embedded object in Project 2010.
2. On the Home tab, in the Clipboard group, click Copy.
3. In your Project 2010 file, display the location where you want to place the object.

   Only the chart area of a Gantt view and the Objects box in the Task Form or Resource Form can accept a chart or worksheet fragment as an embedded object.

   Objects

   To display the Objects box in the Task Form or Resource Form, click in the form area to make it active (if it's part of a combination view such as the Task Entry view). On the Format tab, in the Details group, click Objects. You can also right-click the form and then choose Objects from the shortcut menu.

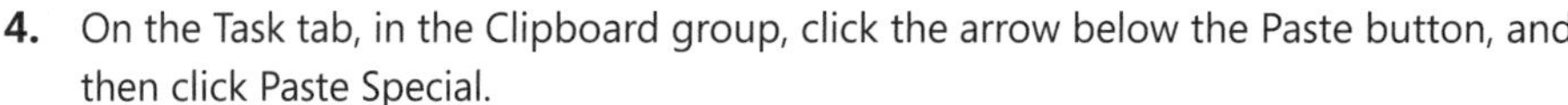

4. On the Task tab, in the Clipboard group, click the arrow below the Paste button, and then click Paste Special.
5. In the Paste Special dialog box, select the Paste option.
6. In the As box, click Microsoft Excel Worksheet or Microsoft Excel Chart.
7. Click OK.

   The data or chart is embedded in Project 2010.

Embedding an Entire Excel File in a Project 2010 File

To embed an entire Excel file into a Project 2010 file, follow these steps:

1. In Project 2010, open the project plan in which you want to embed the Excel file.
2. Display the location at which you want to insert the file.

   Only the chart area of a Gantt chart, the Objects box in the Task Form or Resource Form, and the Notes tab in the Task Information, Resource Information, or Assignment Information dialog box can accept an Excel file as an embedded object.

Insert Object

3. To insert an object into the Notes tab in one of the Information dialog boxes, click the Insert Object button above the Notes area in the dialog box.

   The Insert Object command is not available in the Project 2010 ribbon, so to insert an object into the Objects box in the Task Form, Resource Form, or into the chart area of a Gantt chart, you must first add the Insert Object command to the Quick Access Toolbar. To add the Insert Object command to the Quick Access Toolbar, click the arrow next to the Quick Access Toolbar, and then click More Commands. In the Choose Commands From box, click Commands Not In The Ribbon. Click Insert Object, and then click the Add button. Click OK, and the Insert Object button is added to the Quick Access Toolbar.

You can also add the Insert Object button to a custom group in the ribbon. For information on how to do this, see "Customizing the Project 2010 Ribbon" on page 1153.

4. In the Insert Object dialog box, select the Create From File option.

5. To embed the Excel file, be sure to clear the Link check box.

   By embedding the object, you're essentially making a copy of the original object, and it becomes a separate entity from the original. You can change information in the embedded version without affecting the source data.

   If you select the Link check box, Project 2010 inserts a link to the source file and any changes to the file in Excel update the linked object in Project 2010, as described in section "Linking from Excel to Project 2010" on page 707.

6. If you want the embedded object to be displayed as an Excel icon in your project, rather than be shown as part of the worksheet, select the Display As Icon check box.

7. Click the Browse button, and browse to the location of the Excel file you want to insert. Click the file name, and then click Insert.

   The file's name appears in the File box in the Insert Object dialog box.

8. In the Insert Object dialog box, click OK.

   The Excel file appears in the area you selected. Drag to move or resize the object as needed. (See Figure 18-7.)

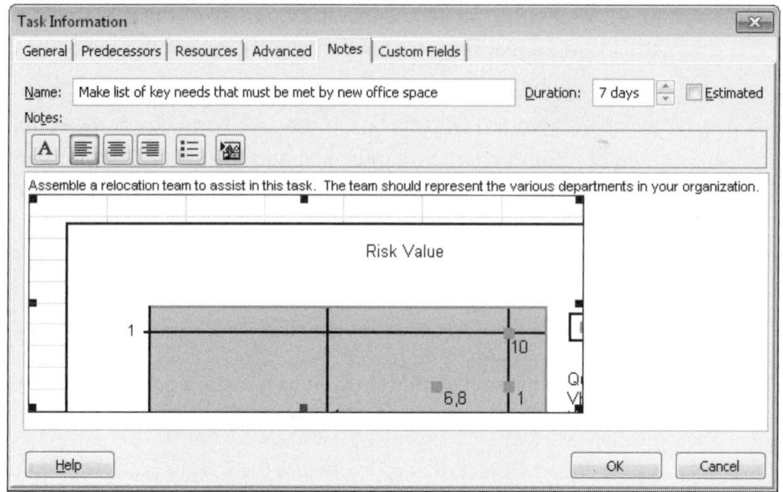

Figure 18-7 The selected Excel file appears embedded in the area you select, such as the Notes tab in the Task Information dialog box.

> **Note**
>
> **You can embed an Excel file in a note associated with the project as a whole. First display the project summary task. On the Format tab, in the Show/Hide group, select the Project Summary Task check box.**
>
> **Double-click the project summary task. In the Summary Task Information dialog box, click the Notes tab. Click the Insert Object button, and then add the Excel file.**

Creating a New Excel Object in Project 2010

You can create a new Excel workbook or chart as an embedded object in your project. In this case, the Excel object exists only within your project file.

> **Note**
>
> **If you think you might sometime want to work on the Excel file outside Project 2010, you should instead create the file in Excel and embed or link it within Project 2010.**

To create an embedded Excel file within Project 2010, follow these steps:

1. In your project plan, display the location at which you want to embed the object.

   Only the chart area of a Gantt chart, the Objects box in the Task Form or Resource Form, and the Notes tab in the Task Information, Resource Information, or Assignment Information dialog box can accept an Excel file as an embedded object.

2. To insert an object onto the Notes tab in one of the Information dialog boxes, click the Insert Object button above the Notes area in the dialog box.

   If you added the Insert Object button to the Quick Access Toolbar, click it to add an object to the chart area of a Gantt chart or to the Objects box in the Task Form or Resource Form.

3. In the Insert Object dialog box, select the Create New option.

4. In the Object Type box, click Microsoft Excel Chart or Microsoft Excel Worksheet.

5. If you want the new object to be displayed as an icon in the project, select the Display As Icon check box.

6. Click OK.

   An Excel worksheet or chart appears in the location you selected. Excel launches if it is not already running and opens the file. The title of the file is Worksheet In <project name>, where <project name> is the name of the file in which you created the object. Start adding your information. On the File tab, click Exit when you are done.

Working with an Embedded Excel Object

To open and work with an embedded Excel object, simply double-click the object. Excel launches and opens the object. When you finish editing the Excel object, on the File tab, click Exit. The Excel window closes, and the modified Excel object appears in Project 2010.

> **Note**
>
> **To delete an embedded object anywhere in your project plan, click it and then press the Delete key.**

Embedding a Project 2010 File in Excel

You can embed a new or existing Project 2010 file as an object in an Excel worksheet. When you double-click the Project 2010 object in Excel, Project 2010 menus and commands temporarily replace those of Excel so that you can create or edit project information without leaving the Excel file.

Embedding an Existing Project 2010 File in Excel

To embed an existing Project 2010 file in Excel, follow these steps:

1. Open the Excel file in which you want to embed the existing Project 2010 file.
2. Select the location at which you want the Project 2010 object to be embedded.
3. On the Insert tab, in the Text group, click Object.
4. In the Object dialog box, click the Create From File tab.
5. Click the Browse button to open the Browse window. Browse through your computer's filing system (and onto your network if applicable) to find the drive and folder where the project file is located.
6. Double-click the file.

   The file's path and name appear in the File Name box in the Object dialog box.
7. To embed the Project 2010 object, make sure that the Link To File check box is cleared.

   If you don't link the object, you're making a copy of the original object, which becomes a separate entity from the original. You can change the embedded project without affecting information in the original project.

   If you select the Link To File check box, the object is linked to the source project plan, as described in "Linking From Project 2010 to Excel" on page 709.
8. If you want the embedded project to be displayed as a Project 2010 icon in Excel, rather than be shown as a part of the Gantt Chart or other view, select the Display As Icon check box.
9. Click OK.

   Part of a view of the selected project file appears in the location you selected. If you selected the Display As Icon check box, the embedded project file appears as the Project 2010 icon (by default) in the selected location. This is particularly useful when your Excel worksheet does not have much empty space.

Creating a New Project 2010 File in Excel

Although you can create a new Project 2010 file as an embedded object in Excel, you should avoid doing so because the Project 2010 object would exist only within the Excel file. Opening Excel to access a Project 2010 object would quickly grow tiresome as you work with your schedule throughout the life of the project. However, if you do decide to create a new Project 2010 file within Excel, follow these steps:

1. Open the Excel file in which you want to create a new Project 2010 file as an embedded object.
2. Select the location at which you want the new Project 2010 object to be embedded.
3. On the Insert tab, in the Text group, click Object.
4. In the Object dialog box, click the Create New tab, if necessary.
5. In the Object Type box, click Microsoft Project Document, as shown in Figure 18-8.

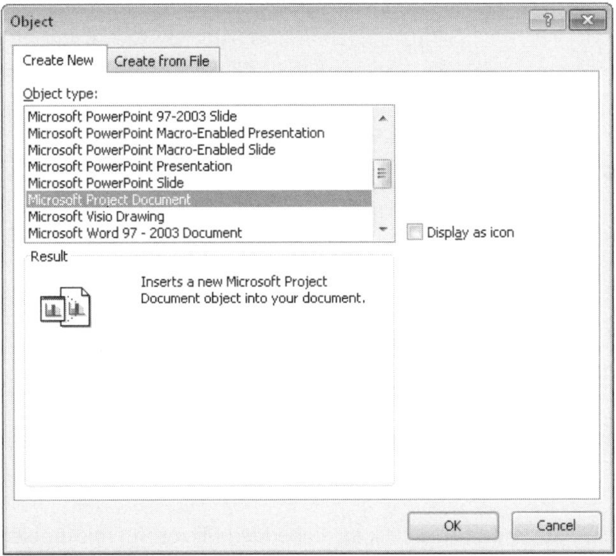

Figure 18-8 Use the Object dialog box to create a Microsoft Project file as an embedded object.

6. If you want the embedded project to be displayed as an icon in Excel, rather than be shown as a part of the Gantt Chart or other view, select the Display As Icon check box.

7. Click OK.

   Part of a view of the new project file appears.

   If you selected the Display As Icon check box, the embedded project file appears as the Microsoft Project icon (by default) in the selected location.

8. Double-click the new project to add information to it on the spot.

Working with the Embedded Project 2010 File

Save

Whenever you want to work with the embedded project file, just double-click the object. The Excel menus change to reflect the relevant Project 2010 menus. (See Figure 18-9.) You can use Project 2010 in the usual way: switch views, apply tables and filters, change data, run calculations, and so on. When you are done working with the embedded Project 2010 file, click File, and then click Save.

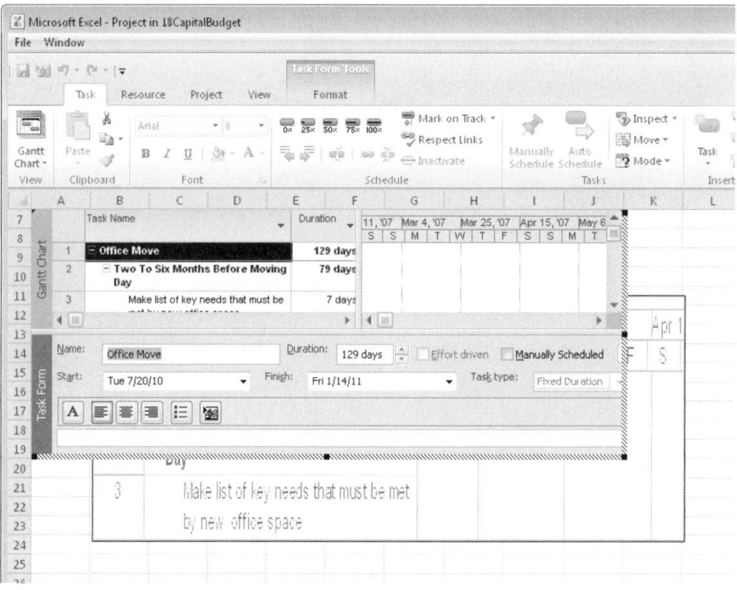

Figure 18-9 When you double-click an embedded Microsoft Project object, the Excel ribbon and tabs change to those of Project 2010.

Linking Between Project 2010 and Excel

You can take the use of embedded objects one step further—by *linking* them to their source. With a dynamic link between source and destination, your linked object is updated whenever the source changes, so the linked information is always up to date. When linked, the source and destination information are the same file, rather than separate copies of one another, which is the case when they are not linked. The advantage of linking objects is that you don't have to worry about maintaining multiple copies of the same information. When you change the original file, those changes appear anywhere that file is linked. The disadvantage is that it's more difficult to distribute file with links. If your recipients do not have access to the source file, you must remember to send the linked files along with the file that contains the links. Depending on where your recipients save the files, they might have to rebuild the links.

Creating a link to embedded objects is as easy as selecting a check box when you're embedding the object, whether it's a fragment you're inserting using the Paste Special dialog box or an entire file you're embedding using the Insert Object command.

Be aware that when you link information between Project 2010 and Excel, you always need to know the current location of the linked file and its update status. Links change automatically if you rename a linked file or move it to a new folder on the same drive. However, if you move a linked file to a different computer, the link is broken.

Linking from Excel to Project 2010

In Project 2010, you can link an Excel worksheet fragment or chart. To do this, follow the steps in "Embedding Copied Excel Information in a Project 2010 File" on page 700. In the Paste Special dialog box, select the Paste Link option.

If you want to link an entire Excel file, follow the steps in "Embedding an Entire Excel File in a Project 2010 File" on page 700. In the Insert Object dialog box, select the Link check box.

You can also copy worksheet cells and link them to Project 2010 table cells. The values look as though they were originally typed in Project 2010, but they are actually linked to Excel data. To link worksheet cell data in a Project 2010 table, follow these steps:

1. In Excel, select the first column of information to be linked in Project 2010, and then, on the Home tab, in the Clipboard group, click Copy. By copying and pasting one column at a time, the Excel columns don't have to be in the same order as the Project 2010 columns. In addition, the paste links will remain in place even if the columns in the Excel worksheet change or move.

2. In Project 2010, display the view, and then click the cell that is to become the anchor cell for the linked information.

   This anchor cell becomes the location of the first cell of data selected in Excel.

3. On the Task tab, in the Clipboard group, click the down arrow below the Paste button, and then click Paste Special.

4. In the Paste Special dialog box, click the Paste Link option.

5. In the As box, click Text Data. (See Figure 18-10.)

   If you select Microsoft Excel Worksheet, an object of the selected cells is embedded and linked, rather than flowing the values into the table cells as text.

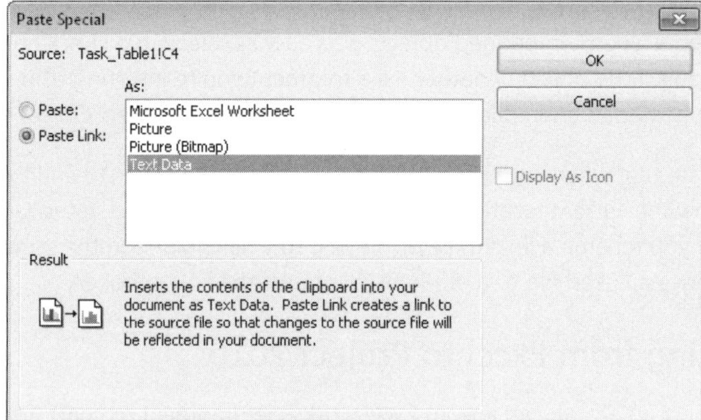

Figure 18-10 Choose these options in the As box in the Paste Special dialog box to link worksheet data with project table data.

6. Click OK.

   The linked information appears at the selection point in your project. When changes occur in the information in the source application, this project file reflects those changes.

7. Repeat steps 1 through 6 for each column in Excel that you want to link to a column in Project 2010.

TROUBLESHOOTING

You're getting paste error messages

Paste error messages are the result of a mismatch between the data type of the incoming Excel data and the Project 2010 columns into which you want them to go. Click through the paste error messages to dismiss them.

Then review the order and type of the Excel data and the order and type of the Project 2010 sheet and see where the problem is. Make any necessary corrections, and then repeat the Copy and Paste Special operation.

See the sidebar, "Match the Data Types" on page 693, to learn more about Microsoft Project data types.

Linking from Project 2010 to Excel

In Excel, you can link to an embedded Project 2010 file. To do this, follow the steps in "Embedding an Existing Project 2010 File in Excel" on page 704. In the Object dialog box, select the Link To File option.

You can also copy a set of table cells in Project 2010 and link them to Excel worksheet cells. The values look as though they were originally typed in Excel, but they are actually linked to Project 2010 data. To link Project 2010 table data to Excel worksheet cells, follow these steps:

1. In Project 2010, select the table data to be linked to Excel.
2. On the Task tab, in the Clipboard group, click Copy.
3. In Excel, click the cell that is to become the anchor cell for the linked information.

   This anchor cell becomes the location of the upper-left cell of the data selected in Project 2010.
4. On the Home tab, in the Clipboard group, click the down arrow below the Paste button, and then click Paste Special.
5. In the Paste Special dialog box, click the Paste Link option.
6. In the As box, click Text.

   If you select Microsoft Project Document Object, an object with the selected project data is embedded and linked rather than flowed into the table cells as text values.

7. Click OK.

The linked information appears at the worksheet selection. (See Figure 18-11.) When changes occur to the data in the project plan, those changes appear in the linked data in Excel.

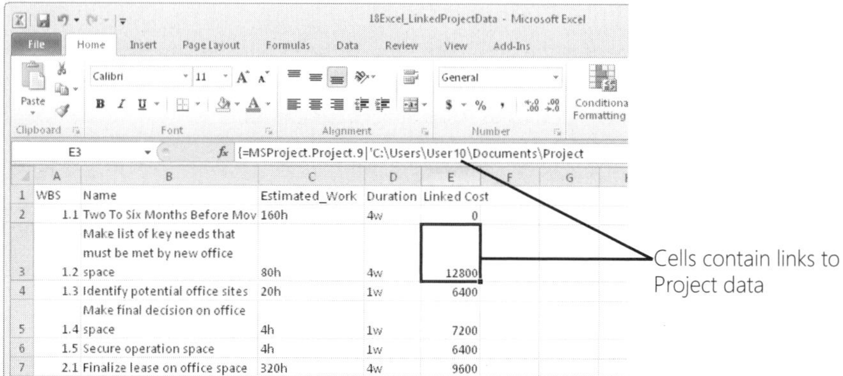

Figure 18-11 When you link Project 2010 data to Excel cells, the cells contain links to fields in Microsoft Project.

Working with a Linked Object

After you have linked information in Microsoft Project or Excel, you can manipulate the information in a couple of ways. You can edit the source information and then accept updates from the source in the destination file, or you can review a list of all linked information in the file and then redirect or break the link if needed.

Editing Linked Information

If you edit the value in a cell that is linked to a source object, the link breaks. If you try to change a value in an array of linked cells, you'll see a message that you can't change part of the array. In both cases, this behavior protects the integrity of the information in the source file.

If you link an entire file, you can double-click the linked object to launch the source file in the source application so you can make the changes you want. When you finish updating the source, click Save, and then return to the destination application to see the changes reflected there.

CAUTION!

Double-clicking a linked object to launch the source file in the source application is different from working with an unlinked embedded object. When you work on an unlinked embedded object, you are working with a copy of the information, not the source file. With linked information, you always need to work in the source because the source updates the destination through the link.

Updating Linked Objects

In both Project 2010 and Excel, when you open a file that contains links, by default you see a dialog box prompting you to update the file by using the links. In Project 2010, click Yes (see Figure 18-12) to re-establish the links and update any information that has changed since the last time you opened and updated this file. The dialog box in Excel includes an Update and Don't Update button. Click Update to re-establish links in the Excel file.

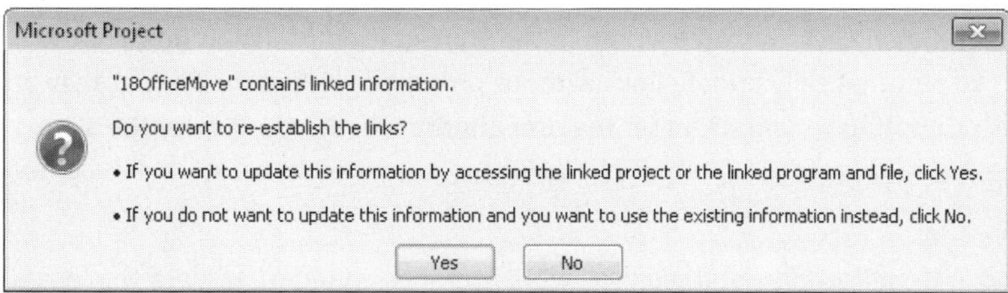

Figure 18-12 When you open a project plan or workbook that contains links, you'll see a message like this.

Viewing Links

Because the Edit Links command is not on the Project 2010 ribbon by default, the easiest way to access the command is to add it to the Quick Access Toolbar. In Project 2010, to review and repair links in your project, follow these steps:

1. On the Quick Access Toolbar, click Edit Links.

   The Links dialog box appears, showing all links existing in your project file.

2. If you know that linked data has changed and you want to update the link immediately, select a link, and then click Update Now.

Edit Links

Showing and Hiding the Update Link Prompt

In Project 2010, you can turn off the Update Link alert so you don't see it each time you open the project containing links. The Edit Links command is not on the ribbon by default, but you can add it to the Quick Access Toolbar or to a custom group on the ribbon. If you add the command to the Quick Access Toolbar, on the toolbar, click Edit Links. In the Links dialog box, be sure to select the link, and then select the Automatic option so that the links update automatically.

You can also add the Insert Object button to a custom group in the ribbon. For information on how to do this, see "Customizing the Project 2010 Ribbon" on page 1153.

In Excel, if you do not want to see the Update Link alert each time you open the workbook, on the File tab, click the Excel Options button at the bottom of the menu. In the Excel Options dialog box, click Advanced. Scroll down to the General section, and then clear the check box labeled Ask To Update Automatic Links. Click OK.

You can further specify when you want the Excel alert to appear. To open the Edit Links dialog box, on the Data tab, in the Connections group, click Edit Links. Select a link, and then click Startup Prompt. In the Startup Prompt dialog box, choose an option to automatically update links without prompting, leave the links as they are without prompting to update, or let the user choose whether to display the alert.

3. If the location of the linked workbook has changed, update the location information in the project by clicking Change Source.

   In the Change Source dialog box, click Browse to locate the file.

4. To break the link with the source application, click Break Link.

   When you break a link, the information remains in the project file as a separate embedded object. You can still view and edit the Excel information; it's simply no longer linked.

To review and work with links in Excel, follow these steps:

1. In Excel, open the workbook containing the links.

2. On the Data tab, in the Connections group, click Edit Links.

   The Edit Links dialog box appears, showing all links existing in the workbook. (See Figure 18-13.)

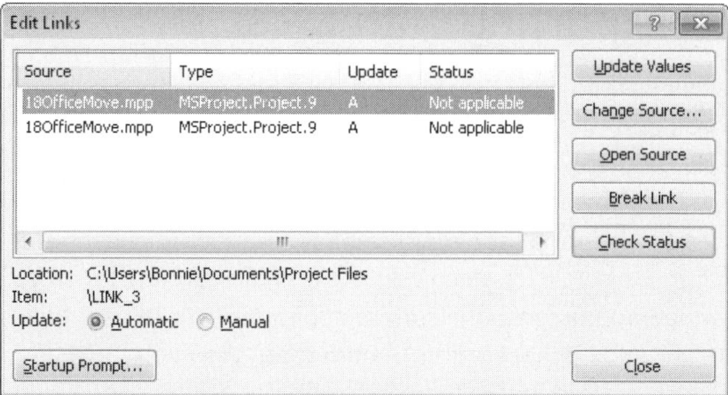

Figure 18-13 Use the Edit Links dialog box in Excel to review and update the links in the current workbook.

3. If you want to update a link immediately, particularly if you have set a link to be updated manually, select it and click Update Values.

4. If the location of the linked project has changed, click Change Source, and then update the location information in the workbook.

5. To break the link with the source application, click Break Link.

   When you break a link, the project information remains in the workbook file as a separate embedded object. The link disappears from the list, but you can still view and edit the project information; it's simply no longer linked.

Note

If you create a link to another Excel file or to a file built with another Microsoft Office application, you can check the status of the link by clicking the Check Status button. When you first open the Excel file, the status for the link shows up as Unknown.

When you click the Check Status button, you might see a status of "Warning: value not updated" to remind you to update values. Or, you might see a status of "Source open" to inform you that the source file is open and might be edited.

However, if the link is to a Project 2010 file, the status shows as "Not applicable." In this case, clicking Check Status does nothing.

Importing and Exporting with Excel

Suppose you want to move larger quantities of information between Project 2010 and Excel, or you don't like having to jockey columns around to make sure data transfers to the right place. For these situations, you can import or export information from Project 2010 to Excel or from Excel to Project 2010. Importing information means bringing information from a foreign file format into the current application (for example, from the Excel XLSX file format to Project 2010, which uses the MPP file format). When you export information, you're saving information in the current application in a different file format so that it can be opened by another application. In both cases, the information will look as though it were originally created in the destination application.

Importing from Excel to Project 2010

With two templates specifically designed for integration, Excel gives you a head start on importing information for tasks, resources, and even assignments from Excel to Project 2010. These templates include commonly used fields, and the fields are already mapped to the corresponding fields in Project 2010. All you have to do is open the Excel file and make a few choices, and the data is imported into your project plan.

One template is designed for importing basic task information into a Gantt chart. Another template allows for more detailed project information, including resources and assignments.

If a team member or other stakeholder has created project information in Excel without using one of these templates, never fear. You can still import any Excel workbook into Project 2010 the "old way."

Building a Project Task List in Excel

Building a project plan doesn't have to be a solitary activity. For example, you might ask others on the project team to create task lists in Excel for their portion of a project, and then you can incorporate their work into Project 2010. The Microsoft Project Task List Import template in Excel, introduced back in Project 2002, simplifies this process.

The standard Project 2010 importing process involves mapping the Excel columns to the corresponding Project 2010 columns to ensure that the right information ends up in the right places in your Gantt Chart task sheet. The Microsoft Project Task List Import template has columns set up to work with the Project 2010 Import Wizard to handle that aspect of the process for you. You can specify a few basic fields for each task, including the task name, duration, start date, deadline date, and resources.

> **Note**
>
> **Although this template includes a Start column, consider leaving the Start fields blank. That way, if you are importing the tasks into an automatically scheduled project, you avoid creating date constraints for the imported tasks. You can fill in the Deadline fields with dates to indicate when the tasks should finish.**

Suppose that the marketing department suggests an addition to the project plan that clarifies their test marketing efforts, but they want to develop the list of detailed tasks in Excel. Have them use the Microsoft Project Task List Template in Excel, as follows:

Sample Templates

1. In Excel 2010, on the File tab, click New.
2. In the Backstage view, under Available Templates, click Sample Templates.
3. Click the Microsoft Project Task List Import Template.
4. Click the Create button.

   The template opens to the Info_Table worksheet, which explains how to use the template.

5. After you read the template information, click the Task_Table tab at the lower-left corner of the worksheet.

   The worksheet appears with columns that map to several standard Project 2010 fields. For example, the ID, Name, Duration, Start, Deadline, Resource Names, and Notes fields are all set up to work with their corresponding Project 2010 fields.

6. Enter the task information in the Task_Table sheet, as shown in Figure 18-14.

   In the template, the columns are labeled so you know where to enter each piece of information. The columns are also formatted to fit the type of data they are to contain. Be sure to enter data valid for the data type that's expected in each column. For example, the Start cells are already set up to display values as dates, but you still must type valid dates if you're importing the tasks into an automatically scheduled project. Likewise, for an automatically scheduled project, the Duration field must contain values that represent a length of time. You can type a value, such as **2d** or **2w**, to represent the duration, but typing words or a date will generate an error when you try to import the file. If you're importing the task sheet into a manually scheduled project, however, you can enter whatever you like into the Start or Duration fields, or you can leave them blank.

To learn how to remove dates constraints, see the sidebar, "Remove the SNET Constraints" on page 723.

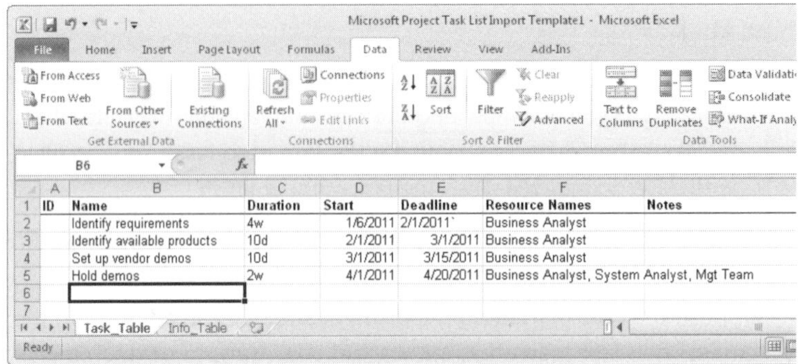

ID	Name	Duration	Start	Deadline	Resource Names	Notes
	Identify requirements	4w	1/6/2011	2/1/2011`	Business Analyst	
	Identify available products	10d	2/1/2011	3/1/2011	Business Analyst	
	Set up vendor demos	10d	3/1/2011	3/15/2011	Business Analyst	
	Hold demos	2w	4/1/2011	4/20/2011	Business Analyst, System Analyst, Mgt Team	

Figure 18-14 Share the Microsoft Project Task List Import template with your team to help build your project plan.

7. When you finish entering task information, on the File tab, click Save.

   Because the file is a template, the Save As dialog box sets the Save As Type box to Excel Workbook.

8. In the Save As dialog box, in the File Name box, type the name of the file, and then click Save.

   At this point, the new Excel task list is ready to be imported into Project 2010.

To learn how to import data from an Excel file into Project 2010, see "Importing from Excel" on page 719.

Note

As an alternative, you can save this file and provide it to your team members to use to enter tasks and task information. The template is typically located on your computer in the Program Files\Microsoft Office\Templates\1033 folder and is named Tasklist.xlt. You can copy this template to a folder you use for custom templates and then e-mail the file to your team members. Have them use this file to enter their task information, save the file, and then send it to you when they're finished.

To open the template in Excel 2007, click the Microsoft Office button, and then click New. In the New Workbook dialog box, under Templates, click Installed Templates. Double-click the Microsoft Project Task List Import Template.

In Microsoft Excel 2003 or earlier, click File, New. In the task pane, click the On My Computer link, click the Spreadsheet Solutions tab, and then double-click the Microsoft Project Task List Import Template.

TROUBLESHOOTING

You can't find the Excel Task List template

There are two reasons why the Task List template might not be available when you click Sample Templates in the Backstage view.

If you are working with Microsoft Excel 2000 or earlier, the template is stored in a different location. In Excel, click File, New. Click the 1033 or Spreadsheet Solutions tab, and then double-click Microsoft Project Task List Import Template.

If you still can't find it, on a computer running Project 2010 and Excel, use Windows Explorer to find the template file. Its typical location is \Program Files\Microsoft Office\Templates\1033 and the file is named TaskList.xlt. Copy the file to a disk or network location so that you can make it available to team members and other stakeholders who would rather use Excel to build their parts of the project schedule.

The other reason you might not see the Task List template is that the computer you're working on does not have Project 2010 installed on it. Although the Task List template is an Excel template, it is installed with Project 2010. If you have Excel installed on the same computer as Project 2010, the Excel-to-Project templates become available in Excel.

Building Detailed Project Information in Excel

If some team members or project stakeholders are doing more than just building a task list in Excel, have them use the Microsoft Project Plan Import Export Template. This template is set up to hold more detailed resource information in the format needed by Project 2010. It includes worksheets for building a project with tasks, resources, and assignments. Each worksheet contains several columns for specifying more detailed information, such as the outline level and predecessors for tasks, and the maximum units and standard rate for resources.

To use this template, make sure that Excel is installed on the same computer as Project 2010 and then follow these steps:

1. In Excel 2010, on the File tab, click New.
2. Below the Available Templates heading in the Backstage view, click Sample Templates.
3. Click Microsoft Project Plan Import Export Template, and then click Create.

   If you don't see the template, close the dialog box. Then, on the File tab, click Open. Browse to the Office template directory, which is typically \Program Files\Microsoft Office\Templates\1033, and then double-click the Projplan.xlt file.

The template creates a new file with one worksheet each for tasks, resources, and assignments. A fourth worksheet, labeled Info_Table, provides general information on how to use the template.

Each worksheet contains columns that correspond to many commonly used fields in Project 2010. The data fields are set up so that when you fill in the worksheets and import them into Project 2010, Project 2010 can map your data without additional instructions from you. If you decide to include additional columns (fields) of data, Project 2010 maps that data to appropriate fields in the Project 2010 data tables for you.

4. At the bottom of the workbook window, click the tab for the worksheet you want to use.

5. Enter the data in the fields you want. You don't have to use all the fields in all the sheets, just the ones you need. (See Figure 18-15.)

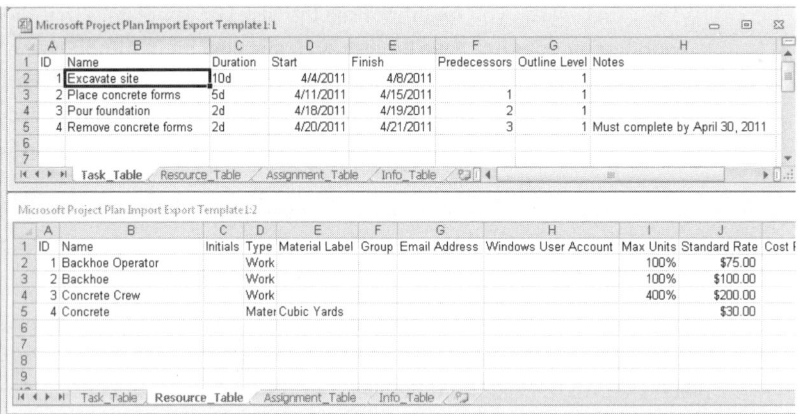

Microsoft Project Plan Import Export Template1:1

ID	Name	Duration	Start	Finish	Predecessors	Outline Level	Notes
1	Excavate site	10d	4/4/2011	4/8/2011		1	
2	Place concrete forms	5d	4/11/2011	4/15/2011	1	1	
3	Pour foundation	2d	4/18/2011	4/19/2011	2	1	
4	Remove concrete forms	2d	4/20/2011	4/21/2011	3	1	Must complete by April 30, 2011

Task_Table / Resource_Table / Assignment_Table / Info_Table

Microsoft Project Plan Import Export Template1:2

ID	Name	Initials	Type	Material Label	Group	Email Address	Windows User Account	Max Units	Standard Rate	Cost F
1	Backhoe Operator		Work					100%	$75.00	
2	Backhoe		Work					100%	$100.00	
3	Concrete Crew		Work					400%	$200.00	
4	Concrete		Mater	Cubic Yards					$30.00	

Task_Table / Resource_Table / Assignment_Table / Info_Table

Figure 18-15 Use the Microsoft Project Plan Import Export Template to develop task, resource, and assignment information in Excel.

6. When you are finished, on the File tab, click Save and give the file a name.

   Make sure you save the file as an Excel workbook and don't overwrite the template.

7. Close the file.

   This workbook is ready to import into Project 2010.

To learn how to import data from an Excel file into Project 2010, see the next section.

Importing from Excel

You can import data from Excel whether you use one of the two Excel templates that Project 2010 provides or you create your own Excel workbook to collect exactly the fields of project information you want to import into Project 2010. In either of these situations, you use the Import Wizard to specify how to import the data into a Project 2010 file and how to map the columns in the workbook to fields in Project 2010.

The standard Microsoft Project import process involves mapping the columns in an Excel worksheet to the corresponding Project 2010 fields to ensure that the right information ends up in the right places in Project 2010. For example, you can set up an Excel workbook with worksheets to collect information about tasks, resources, and assignments. Then, you can import that information to create tasks and resources in a Project 2010 file, link the imported tasks, and then assign resources to them. To import data from an Excel workbook, follow these steps:

1. If you want to import information from Excel into an existing Project 2010 file, first open that Project file.

Open

2. Then, to open the Excel file, in Project 2010, on the File tab, click Open.

3. In the Open dialog box, click the arrow on the button that indicates the current file type, (Microsoft Project Files by default), and then click Excel Workbook.

   If the task list was created using Excel 2003 or earlier, change the file type being shown. To the right of the File Name box, click the arrow in the button labeled Excel Workbook, and then click Excel 97-2003 Workbook in the drop-down list.

CAUTION!

If you don't see Excel workbooks that you've created, the problem might be that they are saved in an earlier Excel format, such as the Excel 97-2003 Workbook format. Project 2010 sets a security option by default that keeps Project 2010 from opening or saving files created in Excel 97-2003 format. In Project 2010, on the File tab, click Options. In the Options dialog box, click Trust Center, and then click the Trust Center Settings button. In the Trust Center dialog box, click Legacy Formats. Select the Allow Loading Files With Legacy Or Non-Default File Formats option.

4. Browse to the folder where the Excel workbook is saved.

   The workbook appears in the list of folders and files.

5. Click the workbook file, and then click Open.

   The Import Wizard appears.

6. Read the Welcome page, and then click Next.

7. On the Map page, keep the New Map option selected, and then click Next.

   If you are a veteran data importer, you might have maps that you created in the past. If the Excel workbook you want to import conforms to the settings in an existing map, select Use Existing Map, and then click Next. On the Map Selection page, select the name of the map you want to use, and then click Next.

8. On the Import Mode page, specify whether you want to import the file as a new project, append the tasks to the currently active project, or merge the data into the active project. (See Figure 18-16.)

   If you built an entire task list in the Excel template, select As A New Project. To add new tasks to the end of the current file, select Append The Data To The Active Project. If you plan to insert the imported tasks somewhere within the current Project 2010 task list, select Merge The Data Into The Active Project.

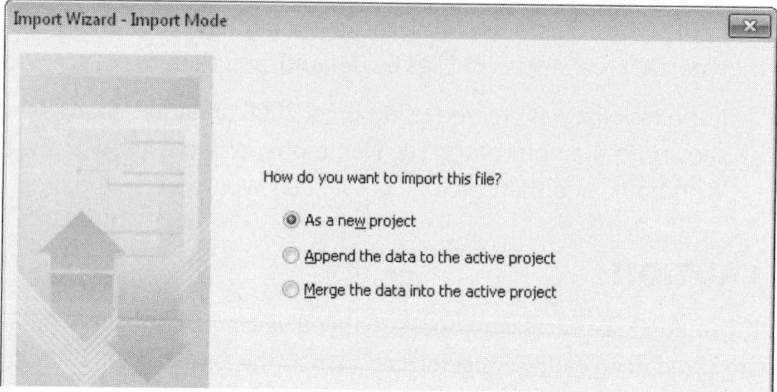

Figure 18-16 You can choose to import the task list template into a new Project 2010 file or the active one.

9. On the Map Options page, select the check boxes (Tasks, Resources, and Assignments) for each type of data you want to import. If your workbook file includes column headings, select the Import Includes Headers check box, and then click Next.

10. On the Mapping page, under Source Worksheet Name, select the sheet that contains the first type of data you're importing, even if it's just Sheet1.

    The fields from the selected Excel sheet appear in the From: Excel Field column. If there is an obvious match to a Project 2010 field, it appears in the To: Microsoft Project Field column. If Project 2010 cannot identify a matching field, the field name appears as (Not Mapped).

11. For any fields that are not mapped, click the box in the To: Microsoft Project Field column and select the Project 2010 field in which you want to store the corresponding imported field. Scroll through the entire table and make sure that all the Excel fields you want to import are mapped to a Project 2010 field.

    The Preview area shows a sample of how your table data is mapped, as shown in Figure 18-17.

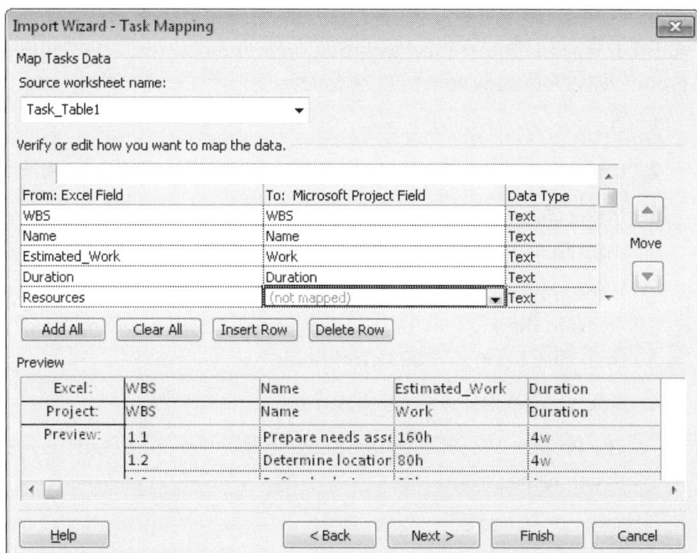

Figure 18-17 Use the Mapping page to match columns in an Excel worksheet with the corresponding Project 2010 fields.

12. If you selected multiple types of data to import on the Map Options page (for example, tasks and resources), click Next to proceed to the Mapping page for the next data type. Repeat steps 10 and 11 for that data type.

    You can potentially work through a Task Mapping, Resource Mapping, and Assignment Mapping page.

13. When you are finished mapping fields, click Next.

14. On the End Of Map Definition page, click Save Map if you want to save the map for future use.

    In the Save Map dialog box, in the Map Name box, type a name for the map, and then click Save.

15. Click Finish.

    If you selected the option to import the data into a new project, Project 2010 creates a new project file and imports the data from the workbook into the fields you specified. Otherwise, Project 2010 imports the data into the active project into the fields you specified.

Variation on an Import Theme

Another way to import Excel information into a new Project 2010 file is to use the New From Excel Workbook function, as follows:

New From Excel Workbook

1. On the File tab, click New.
2. Under New From Existing, click New From Excel Workbook.
3. In the Open dialog box, browse to the folder that contains the Excel file you want to use as the basis for your new project plan.

   If the workbook you want to use was created in Excel 2003 or earlier, click the arrow in the file type drop-down list (currently showing Excel Workbook), and then click Excel 97-2003 Workbook.
4. Double-click the workbook name.

   The Project Import Wizard opens. Follow the same steps as listed earlier to work through the wizard.

Exporting from Project 2010 to Excel

Suppose that your company's accounting department wants to analyze your project cost information in conjunction with those of other projects taking place throughout the company. The department uses Excel to analyze project cost data, so you need to export your Project 2010 information to an Excel workbook.

With the Export Wizard, you can export information you select or export key information from the entire project.

Calculating Project Information by Using Custom Formulas

For certain types of calculation and analysis, you can stay in Project 2010. With custom fields, such as Cost1 or Number3, you can set up formulas to calculate specified data within your project plan. The formula operates on the data in or related to your custom field.

For more information about creating a custom field containing a formula, see "Creating a Calculated Field" on page 1112.

INSIDE OUT Remove the SNET constraints

If new tasks are set to Auto Scheduled, tasks imported with start dates from an Excel file come in to the Project 2010 file with Start No Earlier Than (SNET) constraints. If the Excel workbook's Start field contains a date, that becomes the SNET constraint date. If no date was entered, the SNET date is today's date.

Be sure to review those imported start dates. If any dates besides today's date are entered, check with the person who provided the task list to see if the SNET constraint was intentional. Unless you explain to the people who use an Excel workbook with a Start Date column that Project 2010 figures out start dates for them, they might think they're supposed to enter a start date.

To make a schedule flexible so that Project 2010 can recalculate dates in response to inevitable changes, you need to change those imposed (and arbitrary) date constraints to the most flexible As Soon As Possible constraint. To change the constraints all at once, do the following:

1. In the Gantt Chart, select the names of all tasks with date constraints.

   You can select the Start column if you're changing all tasks in the project to an ASAP constraint.

   If you want to change only certain tasks, click their row headings while holding down the Ctrl key.

Information

2. On the Task tab, in the Properties group, click Information.
3. In the Multiple Task Information dialog box, click the Advanced tab. In the Constraint Type box, click As Soon As Possible.

When you ask others to enter task information, ask them to enter any important finish dates in another column, such as the Deadline column or the Notes column if they use the Microsoft Project Task List Import Template. By doing this, you can change all the SNET constraints to ASAP without having to examine every imported date to see whether it's a real date constraint.

For more information about setting constraints, see "Scheduling Tasks to Achieve Specific Dates" on page 206.

Exporting Selected Data to Excel

Although you can export most information types from Project 2010 to Excel, it's most useful to export numeric data for further analysis in Excel. *Numeric data* is any data that can be used in calculations and mathematical operations, such as cost and work data. Work data (such as hours) can be converted to numeric fields, but it is stored in Project 2010 as text because of the unit labels such as hours, days, or weeks. On the other hand, dates are not considered numeric data, even though they consist mostly of numbers.

When preparing to export information from Project 2010 to Excel for numerical analysis, first decide which tasks, resources, and fields you want to export to Excel. You can export the data for your entire task list or resource list or the data for selected or filtered tasks or resources. You can export all the fields in a given table—such as the Earned Value, Cost, or Tracking table—or you can export just the fields that you select. You can also export a large representation of all your project data with the different types of project, task, resource, and assignment data appearing in different worksheets within an Excel workbook.

To specify the project data you want to export and then send it to Excel, follow these steps:

1. In Project 2010, open the project plan that contains the project information you want to export.

2. Apply the view that contains the task, resource, or assignment information you want to export.

   The table or fields applied to the view do not matter at this point; as part of the export process you choose the fields you want.

3. If you want to export only certain tasks, resources, or assignments, select their rows by using the Shift or Ctrl keys. If you want to export all tasks, all resources, or all assignments, click the Select All cell in the upper-left cell in the view, above the ID number.

   Later, as part of the export process, you can apply a task or resource filter if you want.

4. On the File tab, click Save As.

   The Save As dialog box appears.

5. Browse to the drive and folder where you want to save your information. In the Save As Type list, click Excel Workbook.

   By default, Project 2010 fills in the File Name box with the name of the active project file.

6. In the File Name box, enter a name for your new Excel file, and then click Save.

   The Export Wizard appears.

7. On the Welcome page of the wizard, click Next.

8. On the Export Wizard—Data page, be sure that the Selected Data option is selected, and then click Next.

9. On the Export Wizard—Map page, be sure that the New Map option is selected, and then click Next.

10. On the Export Wizard—Map Options page, select the check box for each type of data you want to map and export: Tasks, Resources, or Assignments. Under Microsoft Excel Options, be sure that the Export Includes Headers check box is selected (see Figure 18-18), and then click Next.

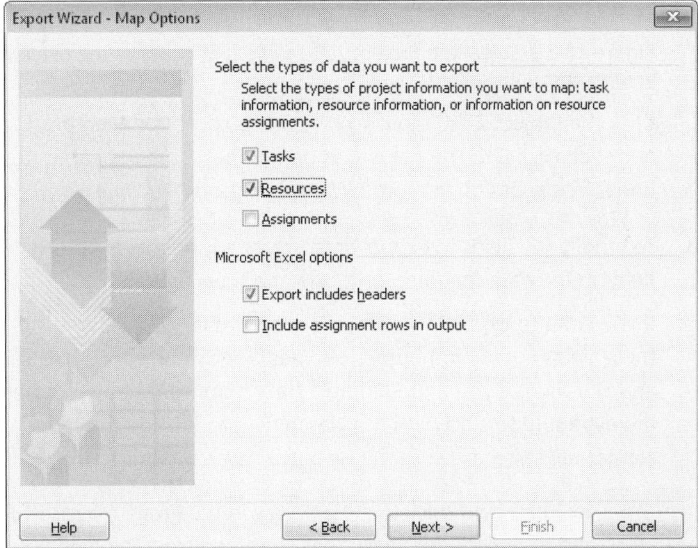

Figure 18-18 In the Export Wizard, select the type of data you're exporting to Excel.

11. On the Mapping page of the wizard, in the Destination Worksheet Name box, you can enter a name for the destination worksheet within the workbook you're creating.

    You can also just use the default name provided—for example, Task_Table1.

12. In the Export Filter box, click any filter you want to apply to the tasks or resources you're exporting.

13. If a Project 2010 table—for example, the Entry table, the Cost table, or the Earned Value table—includes most or all of the fields you want to export, click the Base On Table button.

    The Select Base Table For Field Mapping dialog box appears, as shown in Figure 18-19.

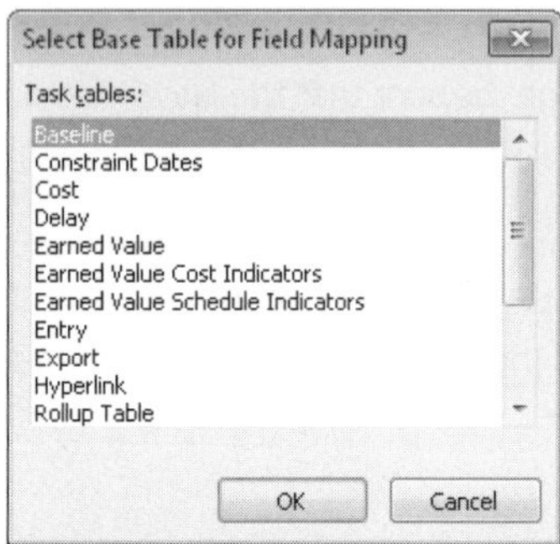

Figure 18-19 Select the Project 2010 table that contains the fields you want to use as your export data source.

    Click the Project 2010 table you want to export (for example, Earned Value or Cost), and then click OK. The fields that define that table appear in the data mapping grid under Verify Or Edit How You Want To Import The Data.

14. To modify the fields to export or to create a list of fields from scratch, add and remove fields in the data mapping grid one at a time, as well.

    If you want to export just numeric project data, you can use this table to select only those fields containing numeric values. For example, you might select Name, Cost, and Duration. If you are building a data map from scratch rather than starting with a table, be sure to start with the Name field to include the task name, or the Resource Names field to make sure the resource name is exported.

    - To add a field, click in a blank row in the From: Microsoft Project Field column, and then click the arrow that appears. Select the field you want from the list that appears. (See Figure 18-20.) Depending on whether you are mapping task data, resource data, or assignment data, the drop-down list displays task, resource, or assignment fields. Type the first two or three characters of the field name to quickly move to it in the list. Press Enter or Tab to select the field. As soon as you enter a field in the From column, its default equivalent appears in the To: Excel Field column, showing the name of the field as it will appear in the Excel workbook column heading. If you want to change the Excel column heading, type the new heading here (for example, from Baseline Cost to Planned Cost).

    - To remove a field from the list, click the field name, and then click Delete Row.

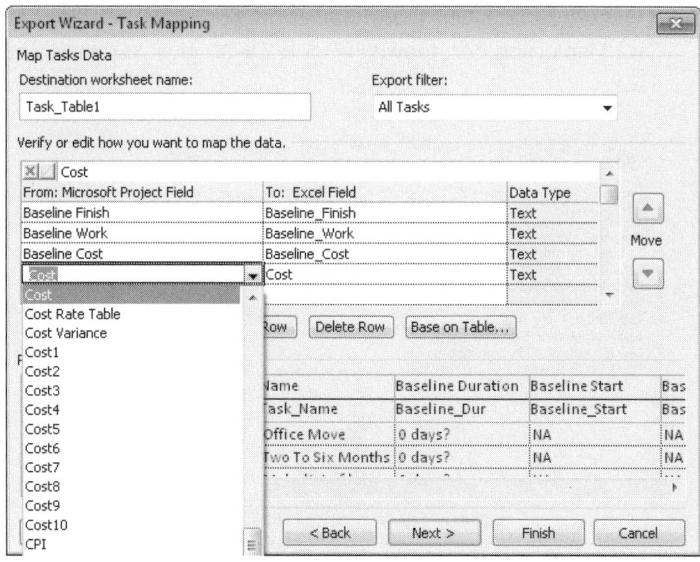

Figure 18-20 On the Mapping page, select the specific fields you want to export.

15. In the table, specify how each field of data should be defined when it is exported to Excel.

The Data Type column shows the data type of the field. Incidentally, this data comes in as Text fields, even though it might really be number, date, or cost fields in Project 2010. To simplify the export process, all fields are changed to text fields. You can then easily convert the data type for any of these fields in Excel, which is especially important for numeric data on which you want to run calculations.

Move Up

Use the Move Up and Move Down buttons to the right of the table to rearrange the order of the fields, which represents the order in which the columns will appear in Excel.

Move Down

In the Preview area at the bottom of the Mapping page, a preview of the data shows how it will appear in Excel. Use the scroll bar to view all the columns.

16. When the map is the way you want it, click Next.

17. If you specified on the Map Options page that you want to export more than one type of data—tasks, resources, and assignments—another Export Wizard mapping page appears for the next data type; for example, the Export Wizard—Resource Mapping page. Repeat steps 11 through 16 for that data type.

Each additional type of data will result in a separate worksheet in the Excel workbook.

When you have defined the data maps for each type of data, the Export Wizard—End Of Map Definition page appears.

18. If you expect to export this same information again, click the Save Map button. In the Save Map dialog box, shown in Figure 18-21, give your map a name, and then click Save.

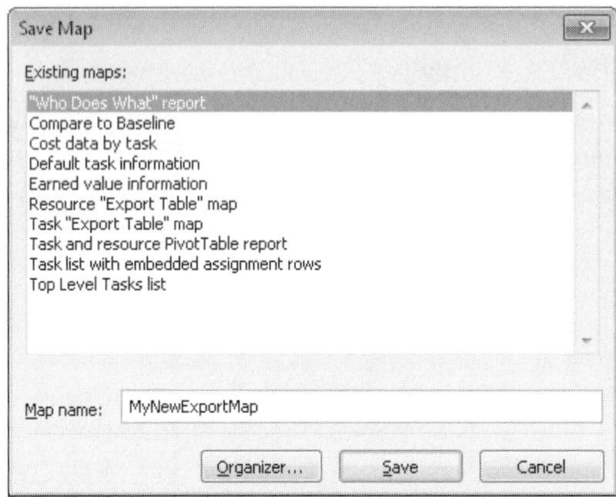

Figure 18-21 The Save Map dialog box shows all built-in export maps and any additional maps that you have created.

Your export map is now saved in the project global template (Global.mpt), so it's available in any project file on your system.

19. Click Finish.

    Your specified project data is exported and saved as a complete Excel workbook in the Excel 2010 format and in the exact layout you defined.

To open and review your exported project data in Excel, follow these steps:

1. In Excel, on the File tab, click Open.
2. In the Open dialog box, browse to the drive and folder in which you saved your exported Excel workbook.
3. Double-click the workbook.

TROUBLESHOOTING

You can't find a field you want in the Mapping table

The list of Project 2010 fields changes depending on whether you're exporting tasks or resources. Tasks and resources have different fields associated with them.

Also, several earned value fields in Project 2010 go by different names than the project management terminology with which you might be familiar. The earned value field names in the Mapping table might even be different than the field names showing in the earned value tables and the rest of Project 2010. Table 18-1 lists these name equivalents and the name you will find in the list of fields.

Table 18-1 **Earned Value Field Names**

If you want this earned value field	Select this equivalent
Budgeted At Completion	Baseline Cost
Planned Value	BCWS (Budgeted Cost Of Work Scheduled)
Earned Value	BCWP (Budgeted Cost Of Work Performed)
Actual Cost	ACWP (Actual Cost Of Work Performed)

If you're looking for a Variance field, look for the specific type of variance—for example, Cost Variance or Earned Value CV (Cost Variance). There's also Work Variance, SV (Schedule Variance), and VAC (Variance At Completion).

Your project data appears in the workbook, using the tasks (or resources or assignments), filter, and table or fields you selected in the export process. (See Figure 18-22.)

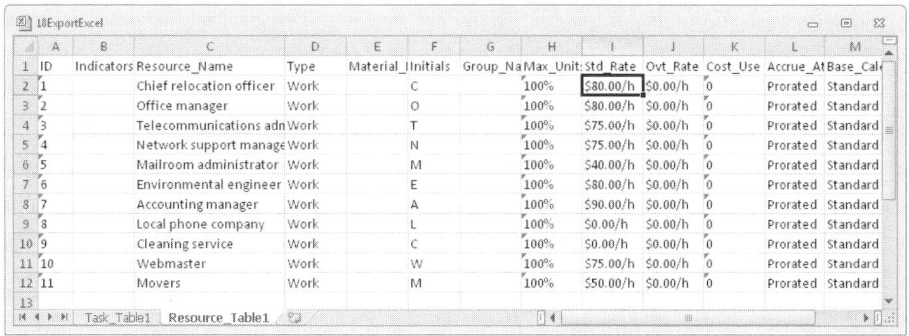

18ExportExcel

	A	B	C	D	E	F	G	H	I	J	K	L	M
1	ID	Indicators	Resource_Name	Type	Material_l	Initials	Group_Na	Max_Unit:	Std_Rate	Ovt_Rate	Cost_Use	Accrue_At	Base_Cal
2	1		Chief relocation officer	Work		C		100%	$80.00/h	$0.00/h	0	Prorated	Standard
3	2		Office manager	Work		O		100%	$80.00/h	$0.00/h	0	Prorated	Standard
4	3		Telecommunications adn	Work		T		100%	$75.00/h	$0.00/h	0	Prorated	Standard
5	4		Network support manage	Work		N		100%	$75.00/h	$0.00/h	0	Prorated	Standard
6	5		Mailroom administrator	Work		M		100%	$40.00/h	$0.00/h	0	Prorated	Standard
7	6		Environmental engineer	Work		E		100%	$80.00/h	$0.00/h	0	Prorated	Standard
8	7		Accounting manager	Work		A		100%	$90.00/h	$0.00/h	0	Prorated	Standard
9	8		Local phone company	Work		L		100%	$0.00/h	$0.00/h	0	Prorated	Standard
10	9		Cleaning service	Work		C		100%	$0.00/h	$0.00/h	0	Prorated	Standard
11	10		Webmaster	Work		W		100%	$75.00/h	$0.00/h	0	Prorated	Standard
12	11		Movers	Work		M		100%	$50.00/h	$0.00/h	0	Prorated	Standard
13													

Task_Table1 | Resource_Table1

Figure 18-22 View and manipulate your project data in Excel.

TROUBLESHOOTING

Project 2010 is not exporting to Excel because of security settings

If you export to an older Excel file format, you might define all your fields in the export map and then click Finish, only to see a security error message and lose all your mapping work. Because of default security settings introduced in Microsoft Project 2007, you cannot save an export map until you have set your security to allow loading and saving of files with legacy or non-default file formats.

To change your security setting, follow these steps:

1. On the File tab, click Options.
2. In the Project Options dialog box, click Trust Center, and then click Trust Center Settings on the right side of the dialog box.
3. Click Legacy Formats.
4. Under Legacy Formats, select the option labeled Prompt When Loading Files With Legacy Or Non-Default File Format (medium security) or the option labeled Allow Loading Files With Legacy Or Non-Default File Formats (low security).

4. Adjust columns, change data types, and do any additional reformatting needed. If you're analyzing numerical data, you can now set up the formulas or charts you want.

   Sometimes, option indicators appear on some cells. For example, you might see an indicator when the export transfers numbers to fields formatted as text. Click an indicator, and, if necessary, click a command to correct an error.

5. On the File tab, click Save.

INSIDE OUT Overwrite Excel format

If you saved your Excel workbook in an older format and then change the contents of the workbook in some way, when you click the Save button, you might see a prompt asking whether you want to overwrite the older Excel format with the current format.

When you begin the process of saving an Excel file in an older format, Excel prompts you to update the format to the current version you have installed on your computer, which might be Excel 2003 or Excel 2010, for example.

Click Yes to update the workbook format, which ensures that you can use the latest features of your current Excel version on your exported project data.

Change the Data Type in an Excel Column

After exporting your project information to Excel, if you need to, you can change the data type of a field of information. For example, Resource Maximum Units fields are exported as text. You can easily change that text to numbers or percentages so that you can run calculations on them.

In Excel, select the column heading. On the Home tab, in the Cells group, click Format, and then click Format Cells. Click the Number tab if necessary. Under Category, select General, Number, or Currency, as appropriate. (See Figure 18-23.) Set any number attributes you want, and then click OK.

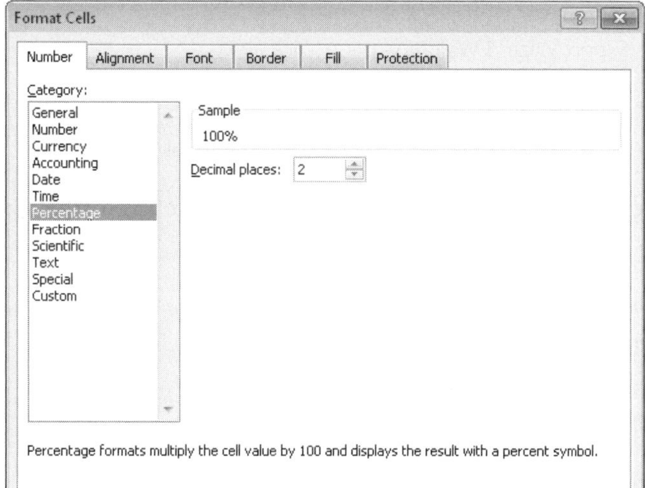

Figure 18-23 Use the Number tab in the Format Cells dialog box in Excel to change the data type or number format of a set of exported project fields.

Even though the Task Mapping page of the Microsoft Project Export Wizard says they're text fields, currency fields (such as Cost and Actual Cost) and earned value currency fields (such as BCWS and VAC) are automatically formatted as currency in Excel.

Exporting Complete Project Data to Excel

Just as you can import information about tasks, resources, and assignments, the Export Wizard helps you export complete project information, organized by Task, Resource, and Assignment data types, which in turn are presented in their own separate worksheets in a single Excel workbook. However, this export procedure does not export timephased information, such as resource usage over time.

To create a complete Excel workbook of project information from your project file, follow these steps:

1. In Project 2010, open the project whose complete information you want to export to Excel.

Save As

2. On the File tab, click Save As.
3. Browse to the drive and folder where you want to save your information.
4. In the Save As Type list, click Excel Workbook.
5. In the File Name box, enter a name for the Excel file, and then click Save.
6. In the Export Wizard Welcome page, click Next.
7. In the Export Wizard—Data page, click Project Excel Template, and then click Finish.

   Your data is saved as an Excel workbook in the Excel 2010 format.

To open and review your exported project data in Excel, follow these steps:

1. In Excel, open the Excel file.

   The workbook contains three worksheets of discrete information: Task_Table, Resource_Table, and Assignment_Table, as shown in Figure 18-24.

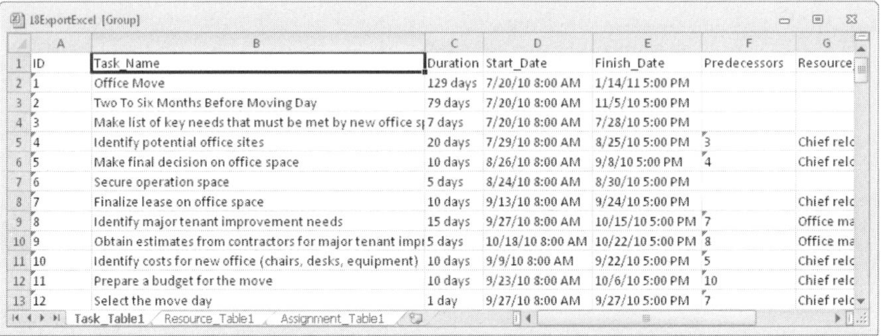
18ExportExcel [Group]

	A	B	C	D	E	F	G
1	ID	Task_Name	Duration	Start_Date	Finish_Date	Predecessors	Resource
2	1	Office Move	129 days	7/20/10 8:00 AM	1/14/11 5:00 PM		
3	2	Two To Six Months Before Moving Day	79 days	7/20/10 8:00 AM	11/5/10 5:00 PM		
4	3	Make list of key needs that must be met by new office s	7 days	7/20/10 8:00 AM	7/28/10 5:00 PM		
5	4	Identify potential office sites	20 days	7/29/10 8:00 AM	8/25/10 5:00 PM	3	Chief relc
6	5	Make final decision on office space	10 days	8/26/10 8:00 AM	9/8/10 5:00 PM	4	Chief relc
7	6	Secure operation space	5 days	8/24/10 8:00 AM	8/30/10 5:00 PM		
8	7	Finalize lease on office space	10 days	9/13/10 8:00 AM	9/24/10 5:00 PM		Chief relc
9	8	Identify major tenant improvement needs	15 days	9/27/10 8:00 AM	10/15/10 5:00 PM	7	Office ma
10	9	Obtain estimates from contractors for major tenant imp	5 days	10/18/10 8:00 AM	10/22/10 5:00 PM	8	Office ma
11	10	Identify costs for new office (chairs, desks, equipment)	10 days	9/9/10 8:00 AM	9/22/10 5:00 PM	5	Chief relc
12	11	Prepare a budget for the move	10 days	9/23/10 8:00 AM	10/6/10 5:00 PM	10	Chief relc
13	12	Select the move day	1 day	9/27/10 8:00 AM	9/27/10 5:00 PM	7	Chief relc

Task_Table1 Resource_Table1 Assignment_Table1

Figure 18-24 By exporting tasks, resources, and assignments to Excel, separate worksheets are created to hold key task, resource, and assignment information from the selected project.

2. Resize and reformat the date fields as necessary.
3. On the File tab, click Save.

> **Note**
>
> **When you export date fields from Project 2010 to Excel, the Excel date fields also include the time. If you prefer, you can change the Excel date format. To do this, first click the column headings for the date fields. On the Home tab, in the Cells group, click Format, and then click Format Cells. In the Format Cells dialog box, click the Number tab if necessary. Under Category, click Date. Click the date format you prefer, and then click OK.**

Reusing a Previously Saved Export Map

If you frequently export the same Project 2010 data to Excel—for example, to run a monthly report—saving the export map and reusing it each time is much easier than having to re-create the map each time you need it. At the end of the export map definition step in the export data process, you click the Save Map button and give your map a name. Then you can call up the map in the future when you need to export the same Project 2010 fields again. To do this, follow these steps:

1. Open the project that contains the data you want to export with your saved export map.
2. If you want to export only certain tasks, resources, or assignments, use the Shift or Ctrl keys to select their rows. If you want to export all tasks, all resources, or all assignments, click the Select All cell in the upper-left cell in the view, above the ID number.
3. On the File tab, click Save As.

   The Save As dialog box appears.
4. Browse to the drive and folder where you want to save your information.
5. In the Save As Type box, select Excel Workbook.
6. In the File Name box, enter a name for your new Excel file, and then click Save.
7. On the Welcome page of the wizard, click Next.
8. On the Export Wizard—Data page, be sure that the Selected Data option is selected. Click Next.
9. On the Export Wizard—Map page, select Use Existing Map, and then click Next.

10. In the Export Wizard—Map Selection page, click your export map in the list (see Figure 18-25), and then click Next.

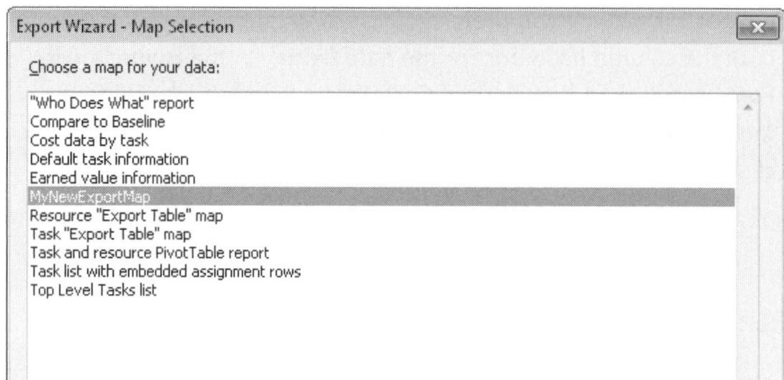

Figure 18-25 The Export Wizard—Map Selection page lists built-in export maps as well as any export maps you have previously saved.

The Export Wizard—Map Options page appears with selections as defined by your saved export map.

11. Click Next.

    The Export Wizard—Task Mapping page appears with the fields defined as you saved them.

12. Click Finish.

    Your project data is exported as an Excel file.

Producing a Visual Report of Project Data in Excel

Visual reports, introduced in Microsoft Project 2007, are easy-to-build report templates that use Microsoft Excel 2003 or later (as well as Microsoft Visio Professional 2007 or later) to transform Microsoft Project task, resource, and assignment information into charts and graphs that communicate your project information more effectively. For example, in earlier versions of Microsoft Project, displaying an Excel graph of earned value required special toolbars and numerous steps to produce the earned value status you wanted. In Project 2010, you simply choose the report labeled Earned Value Over Time, and the graph appears in Excel.

When you first start generating an Excel visual report, Project 2010 gathers the information specified by the selected template and stores it in a database. Then, the visual report template calls on an Excel template to generate the report in an Excel PivotChart. Unlike in the text-based reports of Project 2010, once data is set up for a visual report, you can configure the report to examine different fields over different time periods without generating a brand new report each time. For example, you could begin by analyzing cost overruns for each fiscal quarter and then drill down to view overruns by each week of the project. In addition, you can add, remove, or rearrange the fields you want to analyze, for example, to analyze cost overruns by task.

You can modify existing visual reports or create your own report templates to do exactly what you want. You can use them on your own projects as well as publish them for other team members or project managers to use.

What Are PivotTables?

A powerful method for analyzing project data in Excel is to use crosstab tables of information, which are tabular presentations of intersecting information along vertical and horizontal fields of information. In Excel, these crosstabs are known as PivotTables. Using the flexibility of PivotTables, you can reorganize data in comparative form, with one category of information being filtered and populated into another category of information.

For example, you can use an Excel PivotTable to analyze the relative cost performance of different groups of team members and to also see how that performance varies during different phases of your project.

When you use a visual report template, whether you use one that Project 2010 provides or one you create, the resulting visual report creates a PivotTable that's linked to an OLAP (online analytical process) cube file.

To create a visual report template that sets up an Excel PivotTable you can then configure to display information in a PivotChart, see "Creating and Editing Visual Report Templates in Excel" on page 740.

Note

In previous versions of Microsoft Project, you could save your project file as an Excel PivotTable. This feature is no longer supported because the PivotTable functions are handled through the Excel visual reports.

On the other hand, you can save your Project 2010 file not only as an .xlsx file, but also as an .xlsb file.

Generating a Visual Report from a Built-in Template

Unlike the text reports that are available in Project 2010 and earlier versions, visual reports transfer data to Excel and use Excel's PivotTable feature to categorize and collate results. For example, suppose the executives on your project selection team ask to see cash flow by quarter for potential projects. Rather than use the text report for cash flow, which displays values for cash spent by time period, the Visual Cash Flow report generates an Excel chart that shows cash flows by quarter more clearly, as illustrated in Figure 18-26.

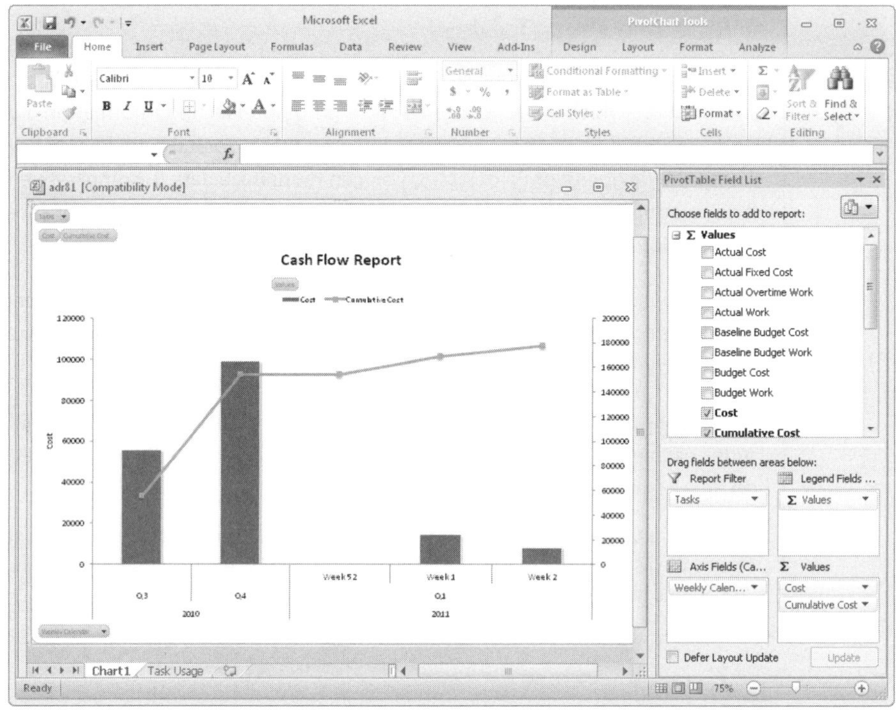

Figure 18-26 Visual reports using Excel can highlight results graphically.

To generate a built-in visual report, do the following:

Visual Reports

1. In Project 2010, on the Project tab, in the Reports group, click Visual Reports.
2. To view only those visual report templates that use Excel, clear the Microsoft Visio check box and be sure to select the Microsoft Excel check box.
3. To view all the visual report templates that come with Project 2010, regardless of the category to which they belong, click the All tab, as shown in Figure 18-27.

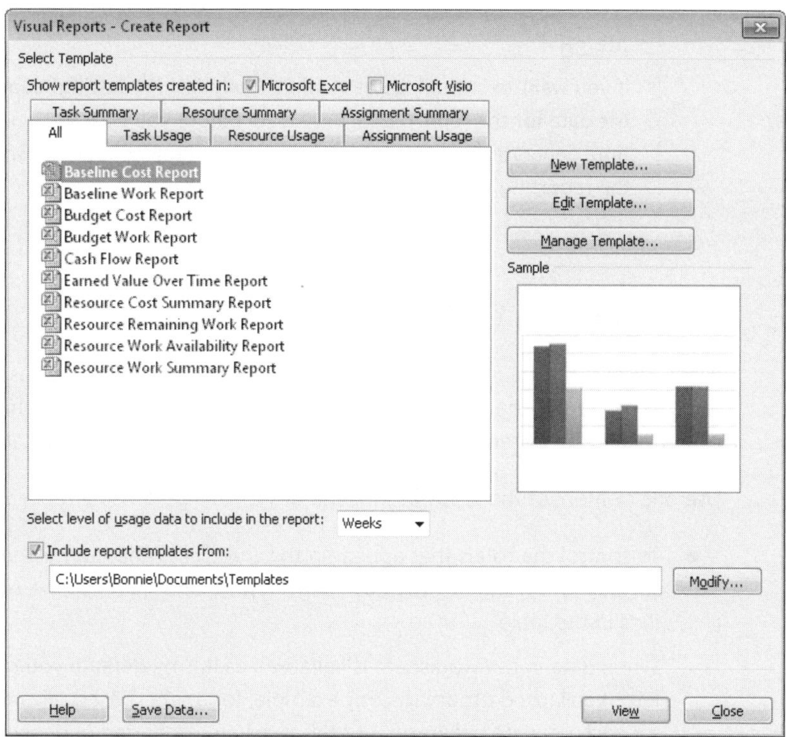

Figure 18-27 Specify whether you want to see report templates based on Excel or Visio and then select the report you want to generate.

Unless you create numerous custom visual report templates, it's easy to find the report you want on the All tab. However, if the list of reports grows unwieldy, select a category tab to see only the reports in that category. For example, the Task Usage category includes the Cash Flow Report template, and the Assignment Usage category includes templates for reporting baseline and budgeted costs and work as well as earned value over time.

4. To specify the level of detail that Project 2010 transfers to Excel, click a time period (Days, Weeks, Months, Quarters, or Years) in the Select Level Of Usage Data To Include In The Report box.

   For projects with shorter durations, choose Days or Weeks. If a project spans a year or more, consider using Months, Quarters, or even Years.

5. To generate the report, click View.

   Excel launches and generates a PivotChart using the data transferred from Project 2010. The first worksheet in the Excel file, which contains the PivotChart, is called Chart1. The second worksheet is labeled with the name of the report category and contains the data for the report.

> **Note**
>
> **If you want to save an OLAP (Online Analytical Processing) cube that contains the data for the report, click Save Data before you click View. This can save you time generating additional reports because Project 2010 doesn't have to gather the reporting data required or transfer it to Excel.**

Configuring a Visual Report in Excel

When Excel is open and displays one of your visual reports, you can use Excel PivotChart tools to configure what you see in the report. For example, you can change the time periods you see, add or remove fields in the chart, or display additional calculations.

Use one or more of the following techniques to change a visual report:

- To control the totals that appear in the chart, click the tab for the data worksheet, such as Task Usage for the Cash Flow Report, and then expand or collapse the groupings in the table.

  When data in the worksheet is collapsed as it is by default, you see plus signs to the left of collapsed groupings. For example, for a time-based report, Q1, Q2, Q3, and Q4 for each year are collapsed, but the years are expanded (indicated by a minus sign to the left). To show more detail for some or all of the report, click the plus sign next to the group you want to expand. (See Figure 18-28.)

- To add fields to the chart, in the PivotTable Field list, select the check box for the field you want to add.

- To remove a field, in the PivotTable Field list, clear its check box.

- To filter the tasks, resources, or assignments included in the report, in the worksheet, click the down arrow in the first row. Expand the drop-down list to the level you want to see, and then select the items you want to include. (See Figure 18-29.)

- To change the calculation that appears in the chart, in the Σ Values section, right click a field, and then click Value Field Settings. In the Value Fields Settings dialog box, in the Summarize Value Field By list, click the type of calculation you want, such as the sum, average, minimum value, maximum value, and so on.

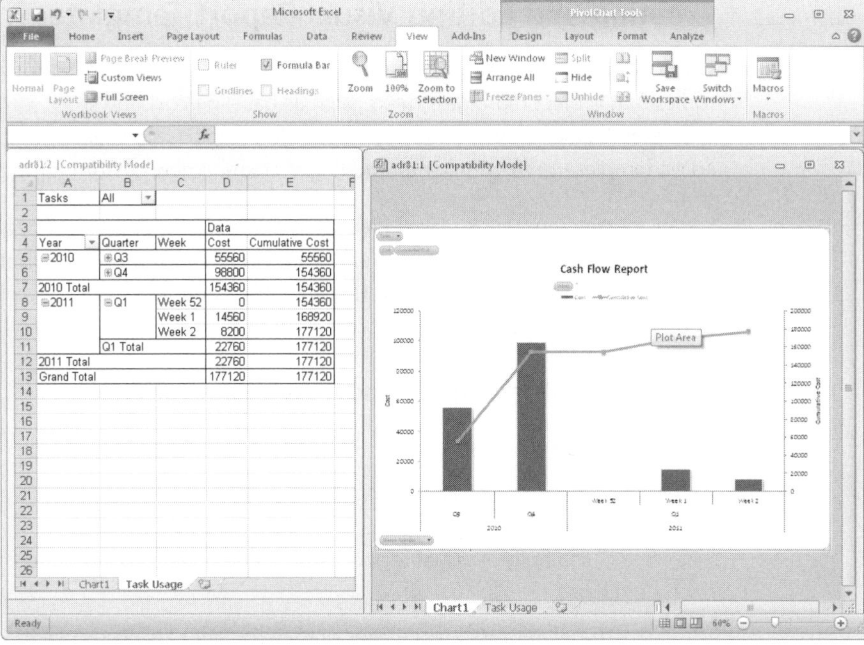

Figure 18-28 Expanding or collapsing time periods or other groups on the data worksheet controls the time periods or groups that appear in a visual report.

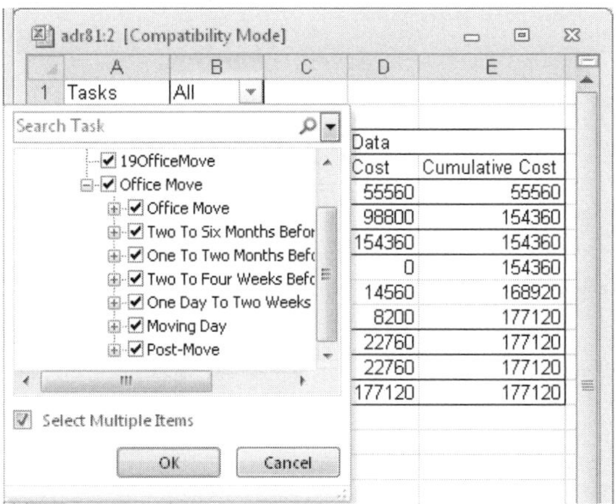

Figure 18-29 Select the tasks, resources, or assignments you want the report to include.

Chapter 18

Creating and Editing Visual Report Templates in Excel

The built-in visual report templates cover many of the project status and performance topics that project managers need, such as baseline cost and work, cash flow, earned value, and resource availability. If none of the built-in reports do exactly what you want, you can edit a template to fit your requirements or create a new custom template.

Because visual reports use Excel PivotCharts or Visio Pivot Diagrams to do the heavy report lifting, visual report templates are either Excel or Visio templates. Whether you edit a built-in template or create your own, you specify the fields you want to work with and the type of data on which you want to report.

Editing a Built-In Visual Report Template for Excel

To edit a built-in visual report template, do the following:

1. On the Project tab, in the Reports group, click Visual Reports.
2. Select the built-in visual report template you want to edit, and then click Edit Template.

   The Visual Reports Field Picker dialog box appears, as shown in Figure 18-30.

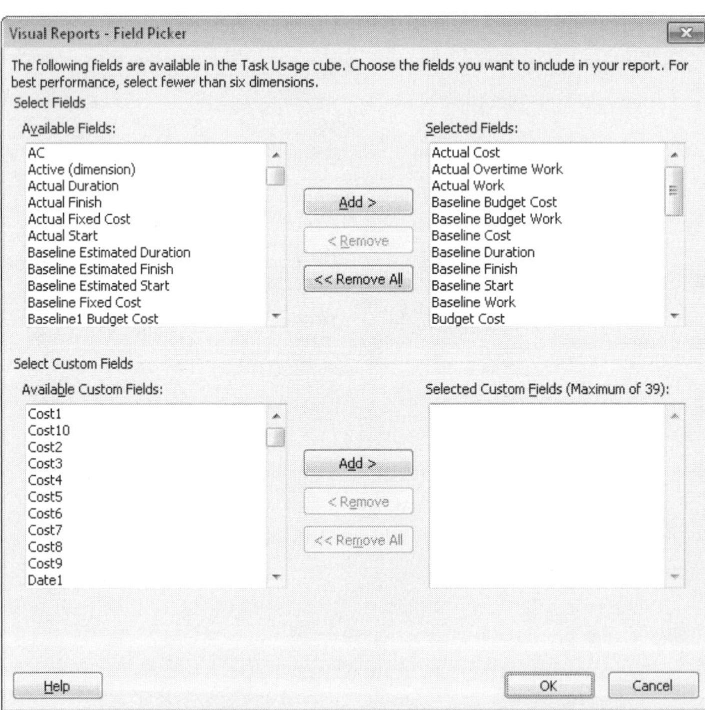

Figure 18-30 You can specify the Project 2010 fields to include in the data cube for a visual report.

3. To add fields to the OLAP cube for the visual report, in the Available Fields list, select the fields you want, and then click Add.

   The fields appear in the Selected Fields list. Remove fields from the Selected Fields list by selecting the ones you want to remove and then clicking Remove. You can select multiple fields to add or remove by holding the Ctrl key and clicking the fields.

4. Click OK to close the Visual Reports - Field Picker dialog box.

5. Click the Edit Template button.

   Project 2010 builds the OLAP cube based on the fields you selected. Excel launches using the built-in Excel template.

6. Make the changes you want to the settings in Excel, and then save the Excel template.

Creating a New Visual Report Template for Excel

To create an Excel visual report template from scratch, do the following:

1. On the Project tab, in the Reports group, click Visual Reports.

2. Click New Template.

   The Visual Reports - New Template dialog box appears with the three basic selections you must make to build a template. (See Figure 18-31.)

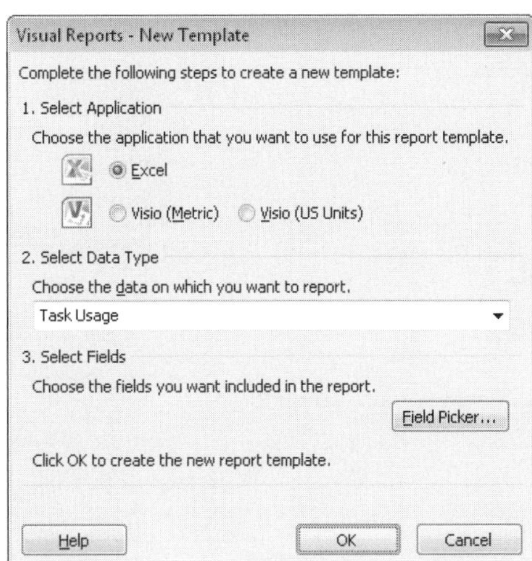

Figure 18-31 When you create a new visual report template, you must specify the application to use, the type of data, and the fields you want to transfer.

3. If necessary, select the Excel option.

4. Under Select Data Type, choose the type of data you want to use as the basis for your report.

   Visual reports are based on six different sets of information: Task Summary, Task Usage, Resource Summary, Resource Usage, Assignment Summary, and Assignment Usage. These data types determine the fields that Project 2010 adds to the OLAP cube, but you can add or remove fields, as well.

5. To modify the fields for the template, click Field Picker, and then add or remove fields in the Available Fields list.

   - To add fields to the new visual report's OLAP cube, select the fields you want in the Available Fields list, and then click Add.

   - To remove fields from the Selected Fields list, select the fields, and then click Remove.

6. Click OK in the Visual Reports - Field Picker dialog box, and then click OK in the Visual Reports - New Template dialog box.

   Excel launches and opens a blank PivotChart, as shown in Figure 18-32.

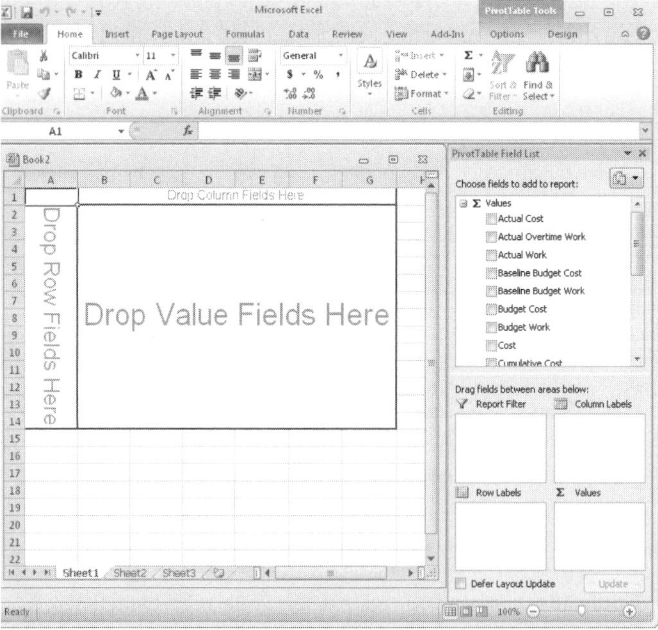

Figure 18-32 Drag fields onto the PivotTable or into the PivotTable configuration boxes to build your report.

7. To build the PivotTable, drag the field you want to use for rows in the table to the area labeled Drop Row Fields here. For example, to produce a resource report, drag the Resources field. Drag the field that you want to use for columns to the area labeled Drop Column Fields here, such as a time period for an earned value report.

8. Drag the Project 2010 fields on which you want to report to the area labeled Drop Value Fields Here.

To learn how to configure your Excel visual report in other ways, see "Configuring a Visual Report in Excel" on page 738.

9. When you finish configuring the PivotTable, on the File tab, click Save. In the Save As dialog box, browse to the folder where you want to save your template.

   To display custom templates in the Visual Reports dialog box, select the Include Reports Template From check box and click Modify to specify the path that contains your custom templates.

CHAPTER 19

Integrating Project 2010 with Visio

Representing your project plan in a graphical format can help others better visualize the project's processes and structures you are trying to communicate. In Microsoft Project 2010, you use Gantt Chart and Network Diagram views to depict your project plan. By using the Microsoft Visio 2010 diagramming software, you can also represent the flows, concepts, structure, and organization involved with your project.

As a project management tool, Project 2010 calculates your task dates, determines resource usage, and maintains a database of the thousands of pieces of data that make up your project plan. Although Project 2010 produces graphical representations of your projects, Visio's diagramming features can take information you select from your project plan and represent it in an easy-to-understand graphic that can clearly communicate project information to wider audiences.

Your favorite point of integration between Project 2010 and Visio is likely to be the visual reports feature. Choose a Visio-based visual report, and Project 2010 transfers the appropriate data to a Visio template, ready for viewing. The Visio templates include commands for configuring which results you see—an indispensable tool when stakeholders question you about different aspects of project performance.

In addition to visual reports, you'll find other reasons to transfer data between Project 2010 and Visio. If the copy of Project 2010 that you requested for your birthday hasn't arrived, you can start building projects using the Visio Timeline, Gantt Chart, and PERT Chart templates. When you switch to Project 2010, you can export your Visio timelines and Gantt charts and start up in Project 2010 where you left off in Visio. Sometimes, the easiest way to summarize project status or highlight problem areas is to export key project information to a Visio timeline or Gantt chart. However, you might not use Visio timelines as often now that Project 2010 includes its own Timeline view.

For more information about the Project 2010 Timeline, see "Highlighting Tasks with the Timeline" on page 134.

You can exchange information between Project 2010 and Visio in several ways:

- **Use a visual report in Project 2010 to analyze data with a Visio PivotDiagram** Each visual report specifies the data to transfer for the report and the Visio PivotDiagram template to use to communicate project information. By letting you swap which fields you use to summarize or total results, Visio PivotDiagrams are perfect when you want to be ready to answer any questions that arise.
- **Import a Project 2010 file to a Visio timeline or Gantt chart** Importing a Project 2010 file into Visio is helpful when you want to take advantage of features in Visio to present project highlights.
- **Import a Visio timeline or Gantt chart into a Project 2010 file** You might not use this method as frequently as transferring information in the other direction, but it's ideal when you want to bring an initial task list into Project 2010 for full-blown project management.

Embed and Link Between Project 2010 and Visio

You can embed or link a Project 2010 file within Visio, and embed or link a Visio file within certain areas of Project 2010. For more information, see "Embedding Information" on page 656 and "Linking Information" on page 668.

Creating a Visual Report of Project Data in Visio

Visual reports, which were introduced in Microsoft Project 2007, use Microsoft Visio Professional 2007 or later or Microsoft Excel 2003 or later to transform Microsoft Project data into easy-to-understand, easy-to-manipulate charts and graphs. Microsoft Project 2010 comes with numerous built-in visual report templates for communicating task, resource, and assignment information.

A visual report assembles the data it needs and stores that data in a database. Then it applies a Visio 2007 or later (or Excel 2003 or later) template to the data to generate the report in a Visio PivotDiagram (or Excel PivotChart). Once you generate the visual report, you can configure the report by using Visio or Excel pivot tools to, for example, examine different fields over different time periods without generating a brand new report. You might begin by analyzing cash flow for each fiscal quarter and then later, when cash flow is tight, expand the report to view cash flow by week or further expand it to view cash flow by task.

If necessary, you can modify any of the existing visual reports or create your own report templates to do exactly what you want. You can add, remove, or rearrange the fields you want to analyze. In addition, you can publish your customized visual reports for team members or other project managers to use.

For more information about creating a visual report in Excel, see "Producing a Visual Report of Project Data in Excel" on page 734.

Generating a Built-in Visual Report for Visio

Visio-based visual reports transfer data to a Visio PivotDiagram for analysis. For example, the Task Status report shows how much money has been spent and the percentage complete for the entire project. You can configure the report to analyze tasks at every layer of the work breakdown structure.

For more information about using the traditional Microsoft Project text-based reports, see "Working with Text-Based Reports" on page 534.

To generate a built-in visual report for Visio, do the following:

1. In Project 2010, on the Project tab, in the Reports group, click Visual Reports.
2. To view visual reports that use Visio, clear the Microsoft Excel check box and be sure to select the Microsoft Visio check box. (See Figure 19-1.)

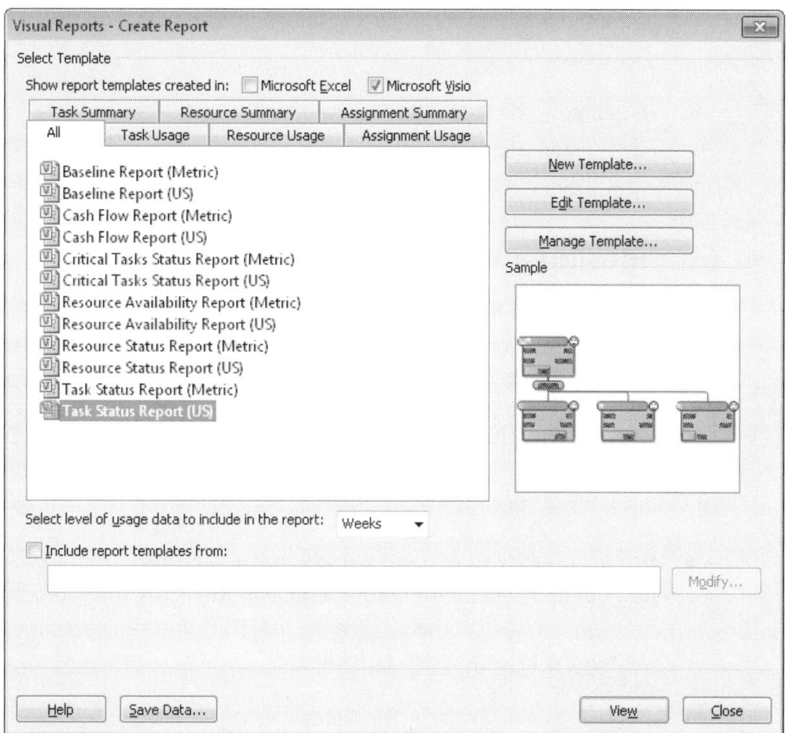

Figure 19-1 Project 2010 comes with several built-in visual reports that use Visio PivotDiagrams.

3. To view the visual reports that come with Project 2010, regardless of the category to which they belong, click the All tab.

   Using the All tab is the easiest way to find the report you want, unless you have created many of your own visual report templates. To see only the reports in a specific category, select the tab for that category. For example, the Resource Usage category includes the Cash Flow Report template, and the Assignment Usage category includes templates for reporting baseline costs.

4. To specify the level of detail that Project 2010 transfers to Visio, click a time period (Days, Weeks, Months, Quarters, or Years) in the Select Level Of Usage Data To Include In The Report box.

   Although any time period can work with any project, the Days or Weeks choices are better for shorter projects, whereas Months or longer periods provide faster reporting for longer projects.

5. If you want to save an OLAP (Online Analytical Processing) cube of the data for the report, click Save Data.

   Saving an OLAP cube makes generating additional reports faster because the step of gathering and transferring data is already complete, and the data is now saved in the OLAP cube.

6. To generate the report, click View.

   Visio launches and creates a PivotDiagram that uses the OLAP cube of data transferred from Project 2010, as shown in Figure 19-2.

Configuring a Visual Report in Visio

When a visual report first opens in Visio, the most detail you see is a box with data for the entire project. (See Figure 19-2.) The tools you need to view the data by different categories or with various calculations are all in the Visio PivotDiagram task pane. For example, you can change the category to view results by tasks, resources, or time periods, and you can add different totals (such as work or cost) or group nodes in different ways.

To modify a visual report to show different results, use any of the following methods:

- **Use a category to expand a node in the diagram** Right-click the node, point to Add Category on the shortcut menu, and then click the category you want for the next level on the submenu. (See Figure 19-3.) You can also click the category you want in the PivotDiagram task pane.

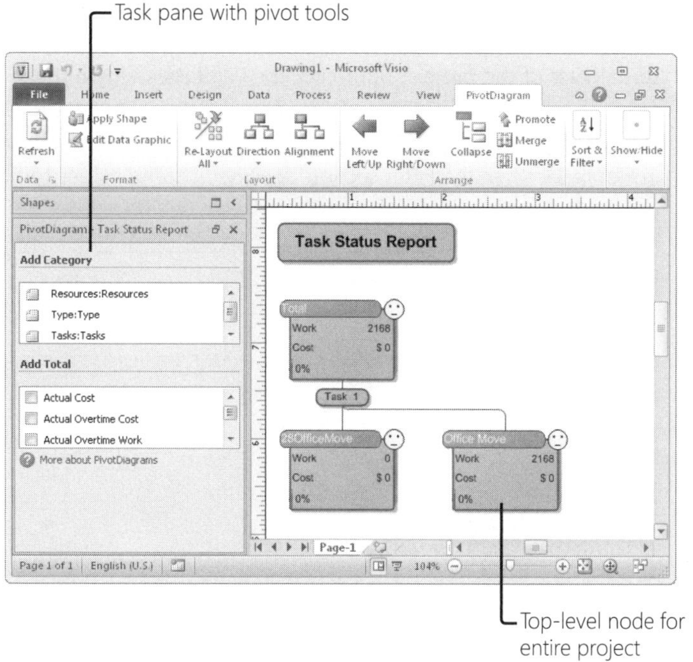

Figure 19-2 A PivotDiagram appears in Visio along with a task pane you can use to further configure the visual report.

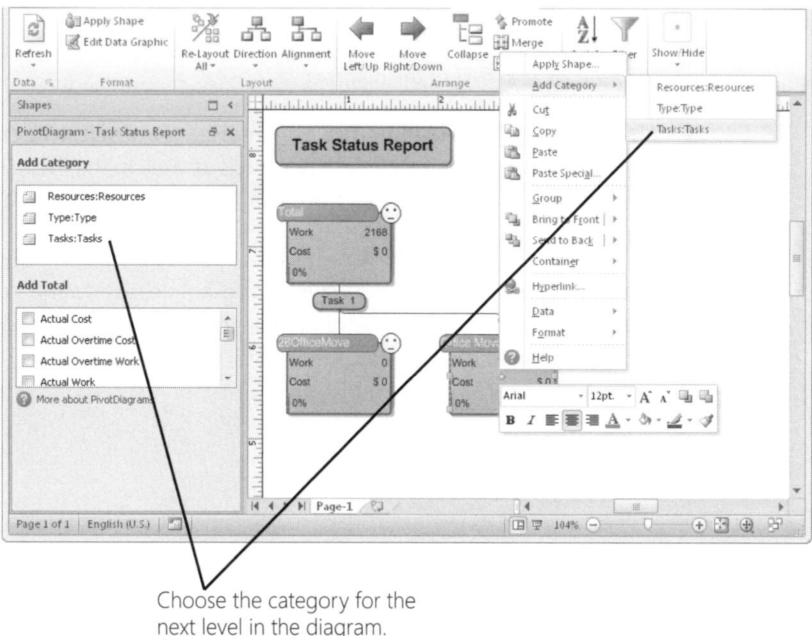

Figure 19-3 You can specify the category to use for the next level in the diagram with each level using a different category.

- **Filter the data that appears at a level** By default, a level in a PivotDiagram includes all the data in the OLAP cube. If you want to display information for only some parts of the project, right-click the Pivot Breakdown shape for that level (the small box that contains the category name, such as Task 2, shown in Figure 19-4) and click Configure Level on the shortcut menu. In the Configure Level dialog box (shown in Figure 19-4), in the Filter section, specify tests and values to filter the data.

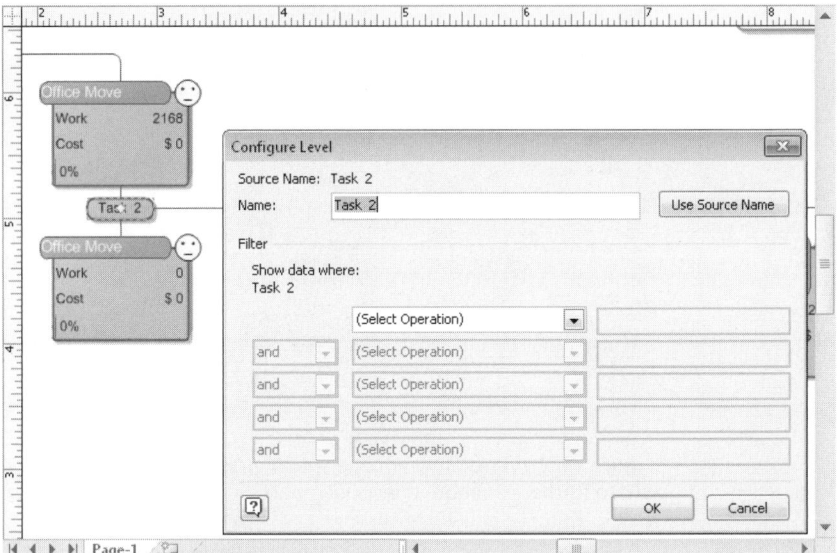

Figure 19-4 In the Configure Level dialog box, you can specify tests to filter the nodes that appear at a level of the diagram.

- **Show different totals in nodes** The nodes for a visual report contain specific totals by default, but you can include other totals as well. In the PivotDiagram task pane, in the Add Total section, select the check boxes for the fields you want to total. (See Figure 19-5.)

- **Combine nodes in different ways** For example, to add the tasks for two summary tasks together, on the PivotDiagram tab, in the Arrange group, shown in Figure 19-6, click a command such as Merge, Promote, or Collapse.

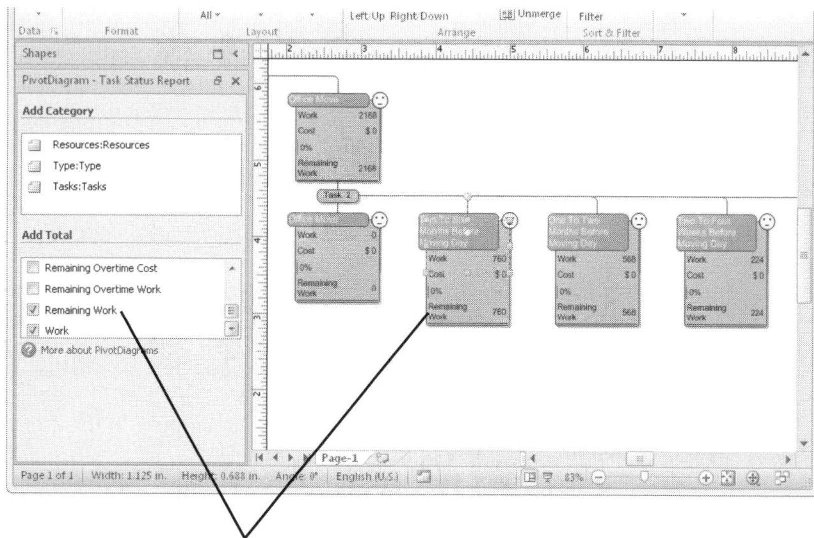

Figure 19-5 To display a field total in the diagram nodes, select the check box for the field in the Add Total section of the PivotDiagram task pane.

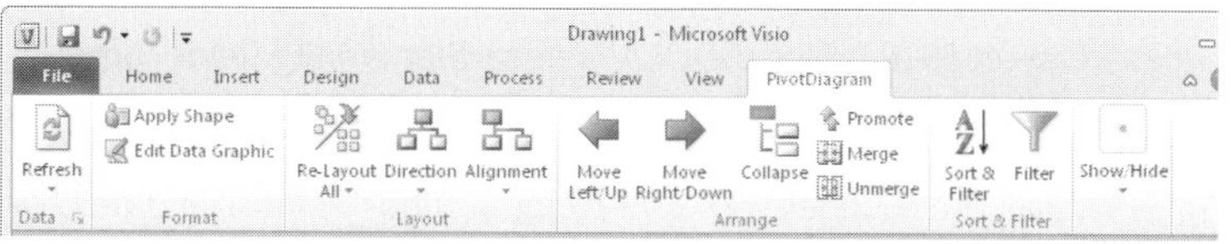

Figure 19-6 The PivotDiagram tab includes commands for fine-tuning the nodes in a PivotDiagram.

Help

Note

For more information on working with Visio PivotDiagrams, click the Help button in the upper-right corner of the Visio window, type PivotDiagram in the Search box, and then press Enter.

Creating and Editing Visual Report Templates in Visio

Although the built-in visual report templates cover many aspects of project performance, from baselines and cash flow to resource availability and task status, you can edit a template to fit your specific requirements. You can even create a new custom visual report template from scratch, which involves only a few more steps than editing a built-in template.

When you choose a visual report template, you are, in effect, specifying the fields you want to work with and the type of data on which you want to report. Because Visio visual reports use PivotDiagrams, you can use pivot features to further fine-tune the report after it's built in Visio.

To edit a built-in visual report template, do the following:

1. On the Project tab, in the Reports group, click Visual Reports.
2. Select the built-in visual report template you want to edit, and then click Edit Template.

   The Visual Reports Field Picker dialog box appears.
3. To add fields to the OLAP cube for the visual report, in the Available Fields list, select the fields you want, and then click Add.

   The fields appear in the Selected Fields list. Remove fields from the Selected Fields list by selecting the ones you want to remove and then clicking Remove. You can select multiple fields to add or remove by holding the Ctrl key and clicking the fields you want to select.
4. Click the Edit Template button.

   Project 2010 builds the OLAP cube based on the fields specified and launches Visio with the built-in Visio template for the selected report.
5. Make the changes you want to the settings in Visio, and then save the Visio template.

To create your own template, do the following:

1. On the Project tab, in the Reports group, click Visual Reports.
2. Click New Template.

   The Visual Reports - New Template dialog box appears with the three basic selections you must make to build a template, as shown in Figure 19-7.
3. To create a Visio-based report, select either the Visio (Metric) or Visio (US Units) option.
4. Under Select Data Type, choose the type of data you want to use as the basis for your report.

   Visual reports are based on six different sets of information: Task Summary, Task Usage, Resource Summary, Resource Usage, Assignment Summary, and Assignment Usage. These data types determine the fields that Project 2010 adds to the OLAP cube, such as resource-related fields for resource reports. You can add or remove fields as well.

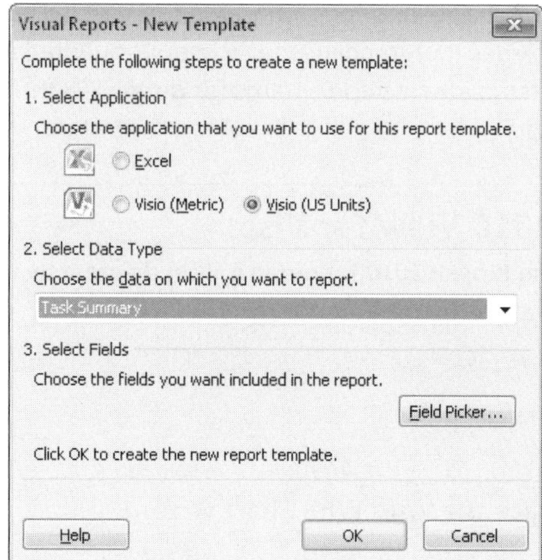

Figure 19-7 When you create a new visual report template, you must specify the application to use, the type of data, and the fields you want to transfer.

5. To modify the fields for the template, click Field Picker.

   You can add or remove fields for the template just as you do for a built-in template, described earlier in this section.

6. Click OK.

   Visio launches, opens a PivotDiagram with a node for the entire project, and sets up a few categories.

7. Configure the diagram by using the techniques described in the section "Configuring a Visual Report in Visio" on page 748.

8. When the PivotDiagram looks the way you want, on the File tab, click Save. In the Save As dialog box, navigate to the folder in which you want to save the template, enter a name for the template, and then click Save.

9. To see your custom templates in the Visual Reports dialog box list, select the Include Reports Template From check box, and click Modify to specify the path that contains your custom templates.

Presenting Project 2010 Data with Visio

If you already have a project schedule built in Project 2010, the main reason to view that data in Visio is to present your project information more effectively. You can transfer all tasks in a project or only top-level tasks, summary tasks, milestones, or any combination of these. Then, you can use the shapes and formatting tools in Visio to highlight crucial information. Although Visio includes four templates for schedule-oriented information, only the Timeline and Gantt Chart templates include wizards for displaying the Project 2010 data you export in Visio diagrams.

Copy a Project 2010 View for Visio

You can capture a view in Project 2010 for use in a Visio diagram by using the Copy Picture feature. For more information, see "Copying a Picture of a View" on page 651.

INSIDE OUT Replace the Visio WBS Chart Wizard

A WBS is frequently shown as a hierarchy that looks like an organization chart. You might remember the Visio WBS Chart Wizard from Microsoft Project 2003. That tool converted tasks in a Microsoft Project file into a hierarchical tree in Visio, but it is not available in Microsoft Project 2010. A visual report that uses a Visio PivotDiagram can generate a hierarchy of tasks similar to a WBS, but Project 2010 doesn't include a built-in visual report for this purpose.

To build a WBS, generate a Visio-based visual report by using the built-in Task Status Report template. In the visual report, select a top-level summary task. As shown earlier in Figure 19-3, in the Add Category section of the PivotDiagram task pane, click Tasks:Tasks to show the subtasks below the selected summary task. Select each summary task you want to expand, and add the Tasks:Tasks category to it.

As described in the section "Creating and Editing Visual Report Templates in Visio" on page 751, you can build your own visual report templates. To approximate a WBS hierarchy, you can set up a Visio PivotDiagram template to display task names and WBS codes in a hierarchical tree.

Showing Project Timeline Information in Visio

NEW!

In Project 2010, you can use the new Timeline view to summarize project information in a timeline to show project phases and key milestones, for example. You can also copy the contents of the Project 2010 Timeline to an e-mail message, a presentation, or another file, such as a Microsoft Word document. With the Project 2010 Timeline, you can select specific tasks to add to the timeline and specify how they appear.

However, a Visio Timeline diagram can still be helpful in a few situations. For example, with the Import Timeline Data Wizard in Visio, you can easily select categories of tasks you want from a Project 2010 file and display them as tasks and events along a horizontal or vertical bar in Visio.

Note

The Project 2010 Timeline displays a project in a horizontal timeline only. By using a Visio Timeline diagram, you can create a horizontal or vertical timeline.

To display Project 2010 information in a Visio timeline, follow these steps:

1. Make sure that the Project 2010 file that you want to present is not open in Project 2010.
2. In Visio, create a new Timeline drawing or open an existing one.

   To create a new Timeline drawing using the Timeline template, on the File tab, click New. Under Template Categories, click Schedules, click Timeline, and then click Create.

   For more information about using the Timeline template, see "Using the Visio Timeline Template" on page 761.

Import Data

3. On the Timeline tab, in the Timeline group, click Import Data.

CAUTION!

If the Timeline tab in Visio doesn't include the Import Data command, Project 2010 is not installed on the computer you are using.

4. On the wizard's first page, click Browse. Navigate to the Project 2010 file that you want to display in Visio. Select the file, and then click Open. Click Next to proceed to the next wizard page.
5. On the page titled Select Task Types To Include, select the type of tasks you want to display in Visio and then click Next.

By default, All is selected, which builds a timeline of the entire project. For presentations, especially to upper-management stakeholders who need a high-level view, you might build a summary timeline by choosing Top Level Tasks And Milestones.

6. On the page titled Select Shapes For Your Visio Timeline, select the shapes you want to use on the timeline if they differ from the ones selected by default. (See Figure 19-8.) Click Next.

   The wizard transfers the overall project schedule information into a Timeline shape. Milestones in your Project 2010 schedule (and any tasks with a duration of zero) become Visio Milestone shapes. Summary tasks in your project schedule become Interval shapes.

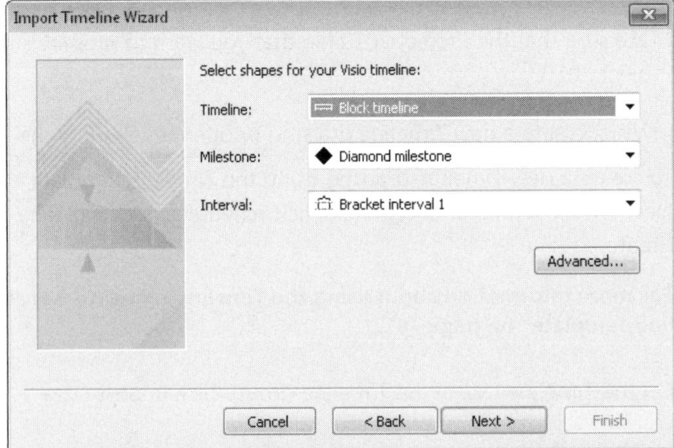

Figure 19-8 In the Import Timeline Wizard, you can choose the Visio shapes to use for the overall schedule, summary tasks, and milestones.

7. If you're ready to specify the timescale and data settings for the timeline, click Advanced.

   However, a better approach is to wait until after the timeline is created to set these options. That way, you can see right away whether the settings in place do what you want.

8. On the final wizard page, review the import properties you selected. If you decide to change any of the properties, click Back until you get to the appropriate page.

9. When the import properties are set the way you want, click Finish.

   Visio transfers the information from the selected Project 2010 tasks (see Figure 19-9) to Visio shapes. If you opened an existing Timeline drawing, Visio creates the new timeline on a new page.

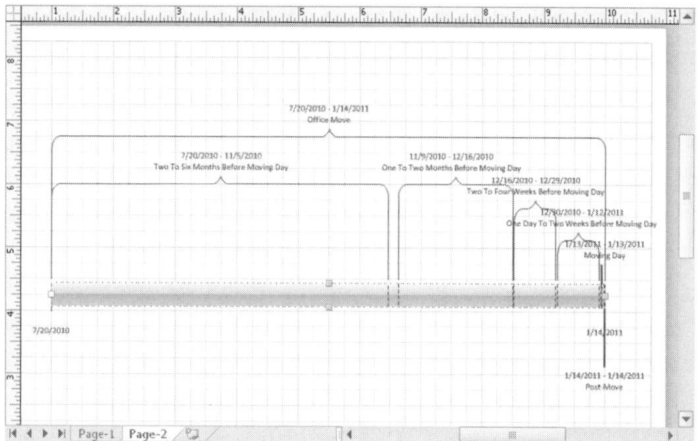

Figure 19-9 If shapes in the diagram overlap, select and drag them to another location.

10. If you display summary tasks, and the intervals or their annotations overlap, select a shape and drag its yellow control handle to reposition the label.

11. To change the shape for a task, right-click it and then click Set Timeline Type, Set Interval Type, or Set Milestone Type on the shortcut menu.

12. To configure other aspects of a shape, right-click it and choose a command from the shortcut menu, such as Set Percent Complete or Change Date/Time Formats.

Displaying Project Information in a Visio Gantt Chart

To display Project 2010 data in a Visio Gantt chart, follow these steps:

Create

1. In Visio, on the File tab, click New. On the Choose A Template screen, double-click Schedule, click the Gantt Chart icon, and then click Create.

   In the Gantt Chart Options dialog box, click OK to close the dialog box. You can configure the Gantt chart after you import the tasks from Project 2010.

   You can also import Project 2010 data into an existing Gantt chart drawing.

Import Data

2. On the Gantt Chart tab, in the Manage group, click Import Data.

   The Import Project Data Wizard launches.

3. On the page titled I Want To Create My Project Schedule From, select Information That's Already Stored In A File, and then click Next.

4. On the page titled Select The Format Of Your Project Data, select Microsoft Project File, and then click Next.

5. On the page titled Select The File Containing Existing Project Schedule Data, click Browse, navigate to the directory that contains the file you want to import, select the file, and then click Open. Click Next.

6. On the Time Scale page, specify the major and minor timescale units, as well as the time units you want to use for duration. Click Next.

7. If you want to specify the shapes for the Gantt chart, on the Time Scale page, click Advanced. You can also change shapes after the schedule is imported.

8. On the page titled Select Task Types To Include, select the type of tasks (All, Top Level Tasks Only, Milestones Only, Summary Tasks Only, or Top Level Tasks And Milestones) you want to import from Project 2010 to Visio. Click Next.

9. On the final wizard page, review the import properties you selected.

   To change any properties, click Back until you get to the appropriate page.

10. When the import properties are set the way you want, click Finish.

    The selected tasks are imported into tasks in a Gantt chart in Visio. If you import data into an existing drawing, Visio creates a new page for the imported chart.

11. To configure the chart, on the Gantt Chart tab, in the Manage group, click Chart Options, which opens the Gantt Chart Options dialog box, shown in Figure 19-10.

    On the Date tab, you can specify the start and finish dates for the timescale, the units to use for duration, and the time units for the timescale. On the Format tab, you can specify the shapes for task bars, summary bars, and milestones, as well as the text that appears as labels on the bars.

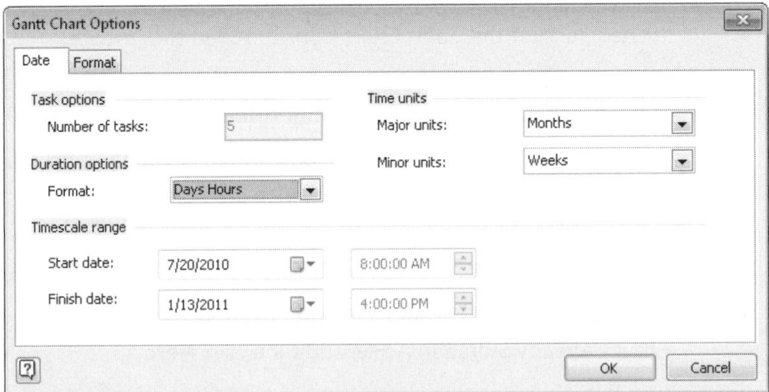

Figure 19-10 After you transfer the schedule information into a Visio Gantt chart, you can set Visio Gantt chart options to configure the appearance of the chart.

Exporting Data from Visio to Project 2010

Although you're not likely to transfer data from Visio to Project 2010 as often, the process is even easier than going from Project 2010 to Visio. If you build draft schedules in Visio as timelines or Gantt charts, it's easy to bring that information into Project 2010 for further work.

Exporting Timelines from Visio to Project 2010

As long as Project 2010 and Visio are both installed on your computer, you can transfer timeline data from Visio to Project 2010 or vice versa. For example, suppose you built a simple Visio timeline to present a potential project at a project selection committee meeting. The project is approved, and now you want to use the Visio timeline to build the basic schedule in Project 2010. When you export a timeline from Visio to Project 2010, intervals turn into tasks with start dates, finish dates, and durations.

To export information from a Visio timeline to Project 2010, follow these steps:

1. In Visio, open the timeline drawing and select the timeline shape.

Export Data

2. On the Timeline tab, in the Timeline group, click Export Data.

   If the timeline you select is associated with expanded timelines, Visio asks if you want to export markers on the expanded timelines. To export only the overview timeline, click No. To export all information, click Yes.

3. In the Export Timeline Data window that appears, navigate to the folder in which you want to save the new project file, type the project file name in the File Name box, make sure that the Save As Type box is set to Microsoft Project File, and then click Save.

   A message box appears telling you that the project has been successfully exported. Click OK.

4. Open the file in Project 2010.

Note

When you export timeline information to Project 2010, the start and finish dates that are created set task constraints of Start No Earlier Than for all the tasks. The easiest way to change these to As Soon As Possible is to insert the Constraint Type column into the Task Sheet.

Right-click a column heading in the Task Sheet, and then click Insert Column on the shortcut menu. In the Field Name drop-down list, click Constraint Type. In the Constraint Type column for the first task, click As Soon As Possible, and then drag that value down through the rest of the tasks.

Exporting Visio Gantt Charts to Project 2010

To export project information from a Visio Gantt chart to Project 2010, follow these steps:

1. In Visio, open the Gantt chart drawing and select the Gantt chart frame.

Export Data

2. On the Gantt Chart tab, in the Manage group, click Export Data. The Export Project Data Wizard launches.
3. On the page titled Export My Project Data Into The Following Format, select Microsoft Project File, and then click Next.
4. On the page titled Specify The File To Enter Project Schedule Data, click Browse, open the folder in which you want to save the project file, type the project file name in the File Name box, and then click Save.
5. Back in the wizard, click Next.
6. On the final wizard page, review the export properties, and then click Finish to export the data. A message indicates that the project has been successfully exported. Click OK.

   If you want to change any properties, click Back until you get to the appropriate page.
7. In Project 2010, open the project file you just created.

Copy Elements Between Project 2010 and Visio

As described in Chapter 17, you can copy Visio diagrams and paste them into Project 2010 schedules or copy portions of a Project 2010 schedule and paste them into Visio diagrams. For example, you could build a Visio organization chart to show the reporting structure of a team and then embed it in the Notes box of the Resource Information dialog box for the resource who acts as the team lead. You could also take a picture of a Project 2010 view and embed it in a Visio file to show, for instance, the high-level project schedules for each business unit in a Visio organization chart.

By using the Copy command in Visio in conjunction with the Paste or Paste Special command in Project 2010, you can embed a Visio diagram as an object or as a picture in a vacant area of your Gantt Chart or in the Notes box of the Task Information or Resource Information dialog boxes.

Representing Project Data in a Visio Diagram

If you decide to build a project directly in Visio, or if you plan to export Project 2010 information to a Visio diagram, it's helpful to understand how the four Visio templates for schedules work. The templates that apply to projects or other date-related information include the following:

- **Timeline** The Timeline template displays tasks and events along a horizontal or vertical bar. A timeline of a project can be useful, for example, to summarize the phases of a multiyear project and key milestones toward its completion. A Visio timeline is helpful when you want to include categories of tasks, such as top-level summary tasks and milestones. On the other hand, in Project 2010 you can display a project in a horizontal timeline using the Timeline and select specific tasks you want to add to the timeline to emphasize key tasks and milestones.
- **Gantt Chart** Although you can use Visio to build simple Gantt charts, it is more useful as a presentation tool when you're using data exported from Project 2010.
- **PERT Chart** The Project 2010 Network Diagram view is a much better option than its Visio PERT Chart counterpart, because Project 2010 calculates start and finish dates for tasks in addition to showing the hierarchy of tasks.

  For more information about using the PERT Chart in Project 2010, see "Flowcharting with Network Diagrams" on page 147.

- **Calendar** Although the Calendar template is a member of the Schedule category in Visio, it doesn't integrate with Project 2010. You can build calendars for special events within a project, but, to show the work that's scheduled for a project, the Calendar view in Project 2010 is a better tool.

  For more information about the Project 2010 Calendar view, see "Visualizing the Project with the Calendar" on page 138.

Using the Visio Timeline Template

The Visio Timeline template summarizes the time span for phases and tasks and highlights milestones along the horizontal or vertical timeline. By expanding portions of a timeline, you can emphasize critical portions of a project.

Configuring the Time Period and Time Format

Configure the time period and time format for a timeline by doing the following:

1. Right-click a timeline shape, such as Block Timeline or Cylindrical Timeline, and then click Configure Timeline on the shortcut menu.

2. In the Configure Timeline dialog box, shown in Figure 19-11, under Time Period, type the start and finish dates for the time period that the timeline represents. If the timeline spans a short period, you can specify the start and finish times, too.

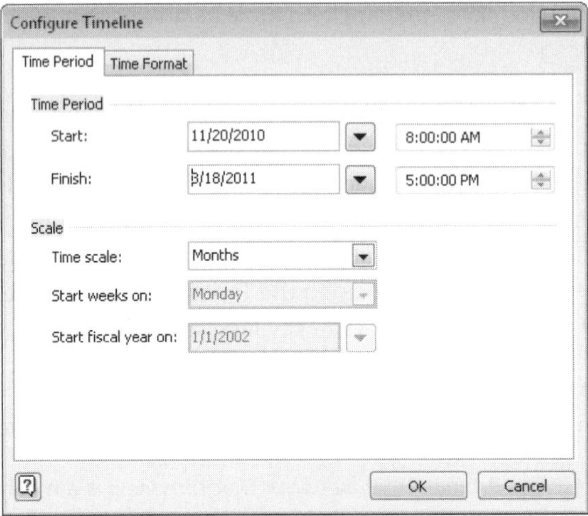

Figure 19-11 The Configure Timeline dialog box contains controls for specifying the start and finish dates and time intervals for a timeline.

3. In the Time Scale drop-down list, choose the time interval to show on the timeline, such as Months. When you select Quarters, you can also specify the Start Fiscal Year On date. For Weeks, you can specify the first day of the week.

4. Specify the date format by choosing a language in the Timeline Language box on the Time Format tab.

5. Control whether dates and times appear on a timeline by clicking the Time Format tab and then selecting the check boxes that control whether the start date, finish date, and interim time scales appear. In addition, you can select the date format for dates and specify whether interim marks show the date or only tick marks.

Configuring a Timeline Interval

Configure an interval within a timeline—for example, to adjust the phases of a project or the duration of a task—by doing the following:

1. Right-click an Interval shape, such as Block Interval, and then click Configure Interval on the shortcut menu.

2. In the Configure Interval dialog box, specify the start date and finish dates and, optionally, the start and finish times.
3. In the Description box, type the text that you want within the interval.

Configuring Milestones

Configure milestones for events or key dates by doing the following:

1. Right-click a Milestone shape, such as Diamond Milestone, and then click Configure Milestone on the shortcut menu.
2. In the Configure Milestone dialog box, specify the date (and, optionally, the time) in the Milestone Date box.
3. In the Description box, type the text for the milestone.

Expanding a Portion of a Timeline

For a multiyear project, activities that span only a few days or weeks are barely visible in a timeline, but they might nevertheless be essential to success. By adding Expanded Timeline shapes to a timeline diagram, you can display more detail for a small portion of the total project. Furthermore, you can expand a timeline to more than one level.

To expand a timeline, follow these steps:

1. From the Timeline Shapes stencil, drag the Expanded Timeline shape onto the drawing.
2. In the Configure Timeline dialog box, specify the start and finish dates for the expanded timeline and, optionally, the start and finish times as well. The dates that you specify for the expanded timeline must be within the date range of the overview timeline.
3. In the Time Scale box, select the time intervals the expanded timeline covers.
4. Click OK to add the expanded timeline to the drawing. Visio adds milestones, intervals, and date markers that occur during the expanded time period.

Synchronizing Milestones and Intervals

Visio synchronizes milestones and intervals between higher-level and expanded timelines, but you can synchronize milestones and intervals across any number of timelines on a page. To synchronize a milestone or interval with another, follow these steps:

1. Select the milestone or interval you want to synchronize, or drag the Synchronized Milestone or Synchronized Interval shape onto the timeline.

Synchronize

2. On the Timeline tab, in the Milestone group, click Synchronize, or, in the Interval group, click Synchronize.

3. In the Synchronize With drop-down list, select the milestone or interval with which to synchronize.

4. Select the date format, if necessary, and then click OK. A gray dotted line shows the synchronization between the milestones or intervals.

Using the Gantt Chart Template

Just as in Project 2010, in a Visio Gantt chart, task data appears in a table as well as in a chart of task bars, milestones, and other symbols that represent the relationships and schedule of project tasks. The major difference, of course, is that a Visio Gantt chart does not calculate start and finish dates, resource assignments, costs, and other project management information. For this reason, the Visio Gantt Chart template is best for presentations or status reports. If you don't have easy access to Project 2010, you can add shapes to a Visio drawing to build a Gantt chart.

Whether you import a Gantt chart from Project 2010 into Visio or build one from scratch, you can modify the Gantt chart in Visio in the following ways:

- Add task bars and milestones by dragging Row, Task Bar, and Milestone shapes onto a Gantt chart frame or by clicking Gantt Chart, Tasks, New. Type the name of the new task along with the start date, finish date, duration, and any other task information.
- Delete tasks by selecting the tasks and then clicking Gantt Chart, Tasks, Delete.
- Rename a task by double-clicking the task name, typing the new name, and pressing Esc.
- Add project fields, such as Resource Names or % Complete, in the table area of the Gantt chart by right-clicking a Gantt chart frame and then clicking Insert Column on the shortcut menu. In the Insert Column dialog box, click the field you want to add.
- Remove a column from the table by clicking anywhere in the column and then clicking Gantt Chart, Columns, Hide.
- Indent and outdent tasks to specify summary tasks and their subtasks.

- Link tasks by using the Link Lines shape to show dependencies between predecessor and successor tasks.

Configure Working Time

- Specify the working days and hours for your project team. On the Gantt Chart tab, in the Manage group, click Configure Working Time. The Configure Working Time dialog box appears, as shown in Figure 19-12. Select the check boxes for work days, and click the times in the Start Time and Finish Time boxes.

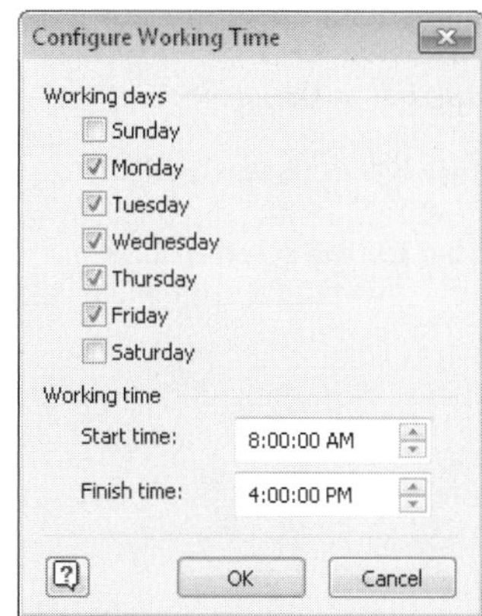

Figure 19-12 You can specify working days and times in the Configure Working Time dialog box.

- Annotate the Gantt chart for presentations by adding Title, Legend, Text Block, and Horizontal Callout shapes.
- Configure the Gantt chart time units, duration, and timescale. On the Gantt Chart tab, in the Manage group, click Chart Options. Click the Date tab, and then choose the settings you want, such as the start and finish dates for the Gantt chart.
- Format task bars, milestones, and summary task bars. On the Gantt Chart tab, in the Manage group, click Chart Options, and then click the Format tab.
- Change start date, finish date, and duration by typing values in the fields in the table within the Gantt Chart shape or by dragging task bars in the chart area. Dragging task bars is quick, but it is typically not as accurate as typing values. You can also show progress by dragging the yellow control handle on the left side of a task bar toward the right.

Navigating Within Visio Gantt Charts

The Navigation group on the Visio Gantt Chart tab, shown in Figure 19-13, includes commands for finding task bars and dates in a Gantt chart. The following tools help you navigate within the chart area of your Visio Gantt chart:

- **Previous** Displays the time period immediately prior to the current period
- **Next** Displays the time period immediately after the current period
- **Go To Start** Jumps to the first task bar in the project
- **Go To Finish** Jumps to the last task bar in the project
- **Scroll To Task** Displays the task bar for the selected task

Figure 19-13 The Gantt Chart tab offers a fast way to navigate to the task you want.

Using the PERT Chart Template

Program Evaluation and Review Technique (PERT) charts display project tasks as a network or hierarchy of boxes, much like a work breakdown structure. However, always keep in mind that the Visio PERT chart is primarily designed for presentation, not actual project management. It does not calculate start dates, finish dates, or durations. If you need to use a PERT chart as a project management tool rather than just a communications tool, use the Network Diagram in Project 2010.

To build a PERT chart in Visio, drag shapes onto the drawing and type values in the boxes. There's no wizard for transferring information between Project 2010 and Visio PERT charts. However, you can use the data features in Visio Professional to link boxes on a diagram to data in a Microsoft Project database.

CHAPTER 20

Integrating Project 2010 with Outlook

MICROSOFT Project 2010 and Microsoft Outlook 2010 are well suited for one another. A Project 2010 plan is made up of tasks, and Outlook 2010 includes the Tasks list. Project 2010 schedules when tasks should start and finish; Outlook has its calendar to show when the items on its Tasks list are scheduled to occur. In Project 2010, you specify information about resources who will work on tasks; Outlook has its address book that lists information about people in your organization and beyond. You need to communicate project information to team members and other stakeholders; Outlook can send messages and files to these people.

When you use Project 2010 and Outlook together, you can do the following:

- Import tasks from your Outlook Tasks list to your Project 2010 plan or include tasks from a Project 2010 plan in your Outlook Tasks list.
- Copy tasks from an Outlook e-mail message to create tasks in your Project 2010 plan, or copy tasks from a Project 2010 plan to an Outlook e-mail message.
- Add resource information to your project plan from your Outlook address book.
- Send or route an entire project file to others.
- Publish a project file to an Exchange folder.

Some of these techniques work only with Outlook. With other techniques, you can use any 32-bit Messaging Application Programming Interface (MAPI)–based e-mail system. These distinctions are made throughout the chapter.

Exchanging Task Information with Outlook

You can pull tasks from your Outlook Tasks list into your project plan. This technique is helpful when you initially identify tasks in Outlook and then realize that they represent work you need to track in your project plan. You can also copy a task from your project plan and add it as a task in your Outlook To-Do List, which comes in handy when you want a reminder about work you need to perform and when it is due. If you're like many users and keep Outlook open throughout the workday, you can maintain visibility to your most pressing project tasks.

Integrate Project Web App Tasks with Outlook

If you're working in an enterprise project management environment with Microsoft Project Professional 2010 and Microsoft Project Server 2010, your team members can add nonproject tasks from their Outlook calendar to their task list in Microsoft Project Web App. This process works the other way as well: Team members can send assigned tasks from Project Web App to their Outlook calendar and work with them there.

For more information about how team members using Project Web App in an enterprise environment can integrate their Outlook calendar with their assigned tasks, see "Working with Project Tasks in Outlook" on page 998.

Adding Outlook Tasks to Your Project Plan

Suppose you started brainstorming tasks for a new project in your Outlook Tasks list, and you're now ready to import those tasks into Project 2010. (See Figure 20-1.)

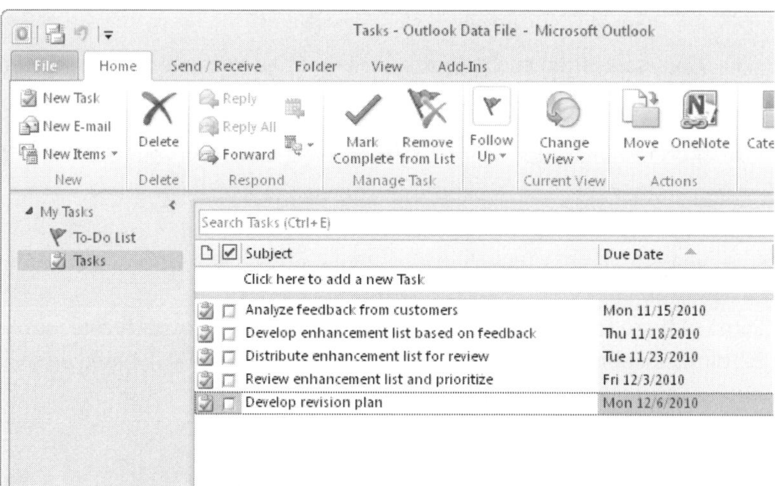

Figure 20-1 Tasks entered in your Outlook Tasks view can be imported to your project plan.

Details

> **Note**
>
> **If you want to specify the hours of work in Outlook, double-click the task to edit it. On the Task tab, in the Show group, click Details. Type the work value in the Total Work field. Click Save & Close to save the task.**

To import Outlook tasks into your project plan, follow these steps:

1. In Project 2010, open the project plan into which you want to import the Outlook tasks.

Insert Task

2. On the Task tab, in the Insert group, click the down arrow below the Task button, and then click Import Outlook Tasks.
3. If a security alert appears, click Allow.

   As long as at least one incomplete task is present in your Outlook Tasks list, the Import Outlook Tasks dialog box appears (see Figure 20-2), even if Outlook is not already running. Any tasks marked complete in Outlook are not listed in the dialog box.

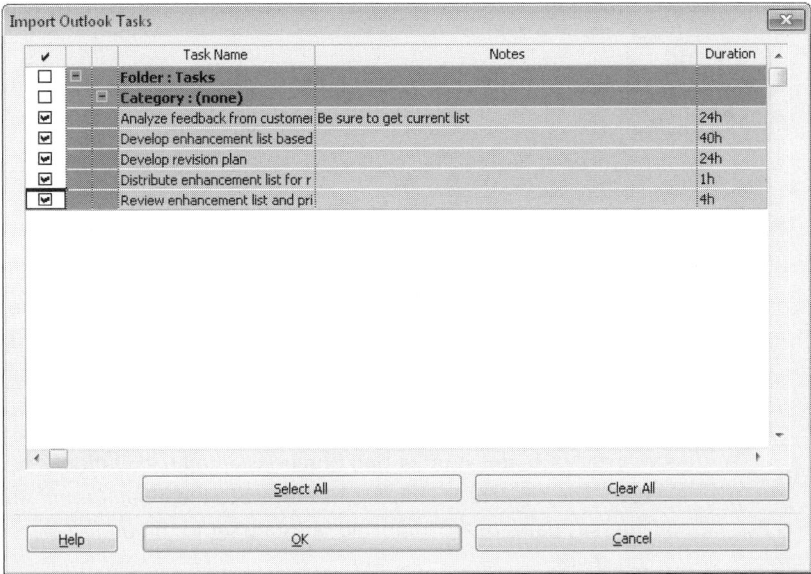

Figure 20-2 Use the Import Outlook Tasks dialog box to import tasks from your Outlook Tasks list to your project plan.

4. Select the check box for each task you want to import. Click the Select All button to import all listed tasks.

   Items displayed with a darker background are folders or summary tasks, and you might not want to import them. If the same tasks are saved in multiple folders, be careful to select just one instance of the task for import. Clear the check box for any Outlook tasks not relevant to your project plan.

5. After selecting the tasks you want, click OK.

   The tasks you selected are appended after the last task in your project plan. (See Figure 20-3.)

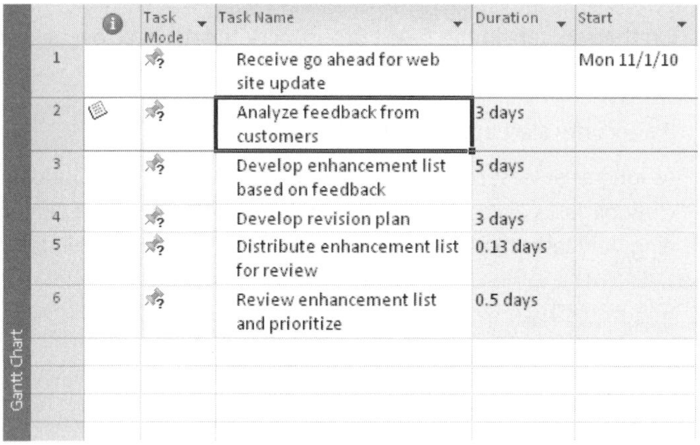

		Task Mode	Task Name	Duration	Start
1			Receive go ahead for web site update		Mon 11/1/10
2			Analyze feedback from customers	3 days	
3			Develop enhancement list based on feedback	5 days	
4			Develop revision plan	3 days	
5			Distribute enhancement list for review	0.13 days	
6			Review enhancement list and prioritize	0.5 days	

Gantt Chart

Figure 20-3 The selected Outlook tasks and associated notes are appended to the current project plan.

The imported Outlook tasks have the following characteristics:

- If the task mode for new tasks is set to Manually Scheduled, the tasks are created as manually scheduled tasks, and durations from the Outlook tasks are copied to the Project 2010 Duration field. The Start field for these tasks remains empty.
- If the task mode for new tasks is set to Auto Scheduled, the tasks are created as automatically scheduled tasks, and durations entered in Outlook are not copied to Project 2010. The imported Outlook tasks revert to the default estimated duration of 1 day. The start dates of the imported tasks are set to the project start date with the ASAP constraint.
- There are no links, predecessors, or assigned resources.

Note indicator

- Any notes entered in Outlook become task notes. Double-click the Note indicator in the Indicators column to review the note.

NEW!

Copy Tasks To and From Outlook E-mail Messages

Suppose you ask team leads to identify tasks for their portions of your project. They send you e-mail messages with the tasks they identified listed in the body of the message. When you use Project 2010 and Outlook 2010, you can copy these tasks to your Project 2010 file simply by copying the text of the message and pasting it into the Task Name column of a Project 2010 table.

In the opposite direction, you can paste Project 2010 task information into an Outlook e-mail message. The information that you copy is automatically pasted as a table with the headings from the Project 2010 table in the first row. The Project 2010 table data that you paste into an Outlook e-mail message also retains the formatting you applied in Project 2010.

For more information about copying and pasting between Project 2010 and other applications, see "Copying from Project 2010 to Another Application" on page 647 and "Copying from Another Application to Project 2010" on page 649.

Adding Project 2010 Tasks to Outlook Tasks

Adding Outlook tasks to your project plan can help you quickly create tasks necessary to your project. Going the other direction—that is, adding key project tasks from your project plan to your Outlook Tasks list—is helpful when you want to keep a closer eye on critical tasks or milestone tasks, for example. Adding project tasks to your Outlook Tasks list is also helpful when you want to monitor tasks that you're assigned to.

In Project 2010, you can send several tasks and some of their associated information to your Outlook Tasks list by using the Set Reminder command. However, this command is not on the ribbon by default.

If you plan to frequently add Project 2010 tasks to your Outlook Tasks list, add the Set Reminder command to the Quick Access Toolbar. To do this, follow these steps:

1. Click the arrow next to the Quick Access Toolbar, and then click More Commands.
2. In the Choose Commands From box, click Commands Not In The Ribbon.
3. Click Set Reminder, and then click the Add button.
4. Click OK.

   The Set Reminder button is added to the Quick Access Toolbar.

Set Reminder

You can also add the Set Reminder button to a custom group in the ribbon. For information on how to do this, see "Customizing the Project 2010 Ribbon" on page 1153.

Now that the Set Reminder button is on the Quick Access Toolbar, you can send Project 2010 tasks to your Outlook Tasks list by following these steps:

1. Open the project plan that contains the tasks you want to track in Outlook.
2. Select the tasks you want to send to Outlook.

   Drag to select multiple adjacent tasks, or hold down the Ctrl key to select multiple nonadjacent tasks.
3. On the Quick Access Toolbar, click Set Reminder.
4. Specify when you want the reminder to alert you. You can set the reminder for a number of minutes, hours, days, or another period of time before the start or finish date of the selected tasks.
5. Click OK.

   The selected tasks are added to your Tasks list in Outlook. (See Figure 20-4.) The start date, reminder time, and due date (finish date) are included.

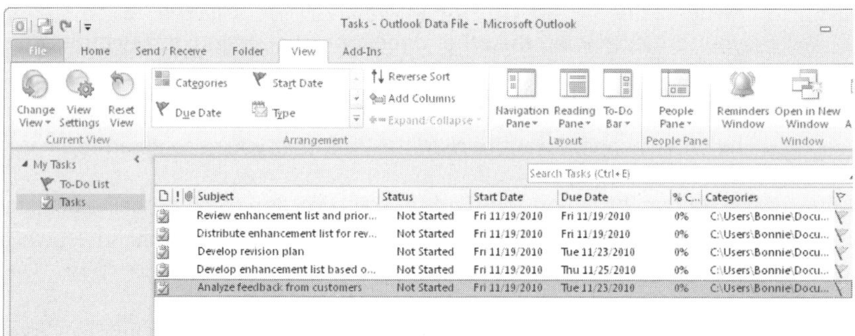

Figure 20-4 Use the Set Reminder command in Project 2010 to add project tasks and some associated data to Outlook.

Another way to add project tasks to Outlook is to use the Copy and Paste commands. However, you can copy only the task name, and you have to copy the tasks one at a time. To copy and paste a task name to your Outlook task list, follow these steps:

1. In your project plan, display a task view such as the Gantt Chart.

2. Select the name of the task you want to copy to Outlook.

   You can copy and paste only one task at a time from your project plan to Outlook. Be sure to select only the task name. If you select multiple fields, all the information is pasted together in the task's Subject field in Outlook.

Copy

3. On the Task tab, in the Clipboard group, click Copy.
4. Switch to Outlook and display the Tasks view or the To-Do list.
5. Right-click in the Subject entry box labeled Click Here To Add A New Task, and then click Paste.

   The task you copied from your project plan appears in the box.

6. Press Enter.

   The task is added to the Tasks list.

7. Repeat steps 2 through 6 for any additional tasks you want to copy to Outlook.

Building Your Resource List with Outlook

You can quickly and accurately add resource names and e-mail addresses to your project plan by pulling them from your Outlook address book or Contacts list.

> **Note**
> **If you're set up for enterprise project management using Project Professional 2010 and Project Server 2010, don't use the Outlook address book or Contacts list to build your resource list. Use the enterprise resource pool instead.**

To import resource names from Outlook into your project plan, follow these steps:

1. In Project 2010, open the project in which you want to add resources from Outlook.
2. On the View tab, in the Resource Views group, click Resource Sheet.
3. Select the first row to which you want to add the resources.

Add Resources

4. On the Resource tab, in the Insert group, click the down arrow to the right of the Add Resources button, and then click Address Book.

   The Select Resources dialog box appears, as shown in Figure 20-5. Under Address Book, select Outlook Address Book, Contacts, or any other folder where the resources you need are stored.

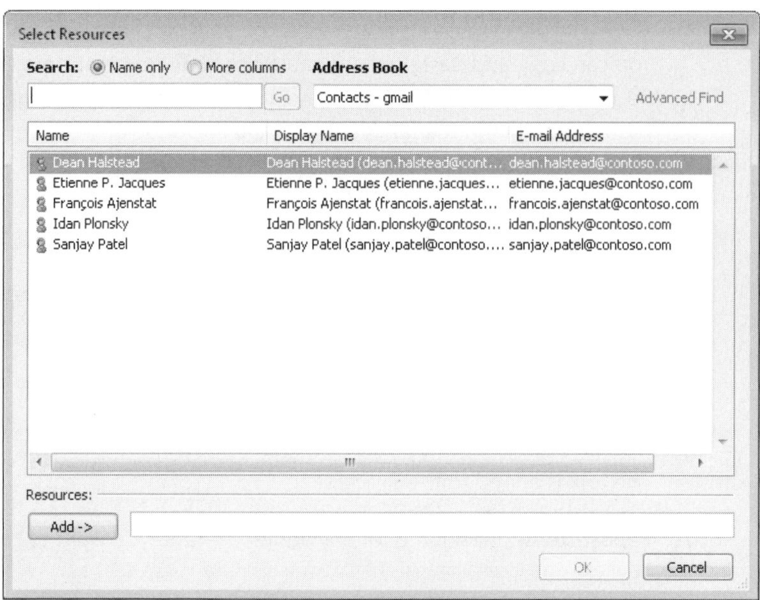

Figure 20-5 Use the Select Resources dialog box to select resources from your e-mail address book.

5. Select the names of the resources you want to add to your project. Drag to select multiple adjacent resources, or hold down the Ctrl key to select nonadjacent resources.

6. Click the Add button, and then click OK.

   The selected resources are added to your project and listed in the Resource Sheet.

Sending Project File Information

You can send information from your project file to people who have Outlook or any other MAPI-based e-mail system, including Microsoft Exchange, Microsoft Mail, Novell Group-Wise, or Lotus Notes. You can send project file information in the following ways:

- Send the entire project file as an attachment.
- Send a selected set of tasks or resources as a Project 2010 file attachment.
- Send a set of tasks or resources as a picture to a set of predefined recipients.
- Route a project file to a group of recipients to obtain their input.
- Publish a project file to a Microsoft Exchange public folder.

Sending an Entire Project File

You can quickly send an entire file to selected recipients directly from your project file. To do this, follow these steps:

1. In Project 2010, open the project file you want to send.
2. On the File tab, click Save & Send, and then click Send As Attachment.

   Your MAPI e-mail application is launched, if necessary. A new e-mail message form appears, with your project file attached and the name of the project in the Subject field.
3. In the To box (and Cc box, if necessary), add the e-mail addresses of the recipients.
4. In the message area, add any necessary comments regarding the project file.

   The e-mail message should look similar to the example in Figure 20-6.

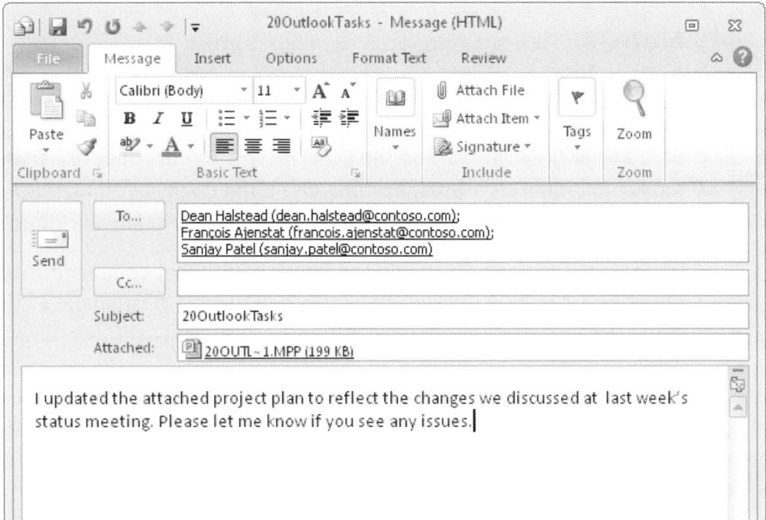

Figure 20-6 Quickly send the project file as an e-mail attachment.

5. Click the Send button.

   Your message and the attached project file are sent to the specified recipients.

Routing a Project File

> **Note**
>
> **You can route a project file if you're using Outlook or any other 32-bit MAPI-based e-mail program.**

Sometimes you need to send project information to several individuals. Maybe you need feedback from each of your team leads about the task list and resource assignments for your project. Or, perhaps one team member is developing the task list, someone else is adding the resources, and someone else is assigning those resources to tasks. One way to share your work with several people is to route your project plan through e-mail to a list of individuals. You can specify whether your addressees receive your e-mail message one by one or at the same time.

> **Note**
>
> **The Routing Recipient command is not available on the Project 2010 ribbon by default. However, you can add it to the Quick Access Toolbar or to a custom group on the ribbon. To add the command to the Quick Access Toolbar, click the arrow next to the toolbar and then click More Commands. In the Choose Commands From list, click Commands Not In The Ribbon, click Send To Routing Recipient, click Add, and then click OK.**
>
> **For information for how to add the Routing Recipient command to a custom group in the ribbon, see "Customizing the Project 2010 Ribbon" on page 1153.**

To route a project file, follow these steps:

1. In Project 2010, open the project file you want to route.

Send To Routing Recipient

2. On the customized Quick Access Toolbar, click Send To Routing Recipient. If a security alert appears, click Allow.

   The Routing Slip dialog box appears.

3. Click the Address button.

   The Address Book dialog box appears.

4. Click the names of the individuals you want on the distribution list, and then click the To button. Click OK.

   Note that to open the project file, each individual on the distribution list must have access to Project 2010 on their computer.

5. If you're routing the project to one recipient at a time, use the Move buttons to designate the order of the recipients.

6. In the Subject field, change the subject if necessary.

7. In the Message Text box, enter any comments or instructions to accompany the attached project file. (See Figure 20-7.)

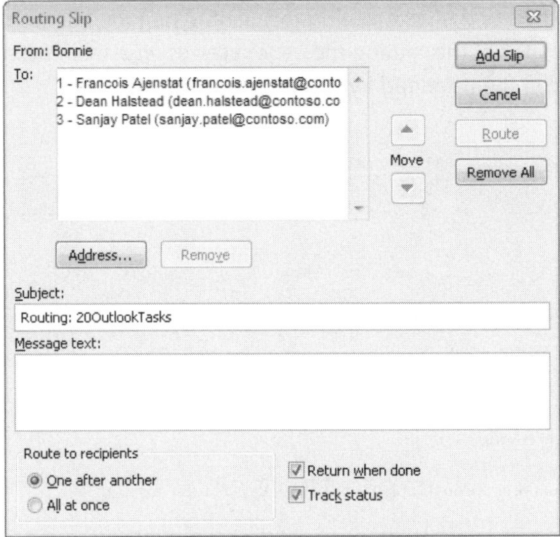

Figure 20-7 Complete the Routing Slip dialog box to send the project file to multiple recipients.

8. Under Route To Recipients, select the One After Another option (the default) or the All At Once option.

   Although sequential routing can be time-consuming and impractical for urgent information, it can work well for review and evaluation, especially when reviewers are in widely dispersed locations. Each recipient edits the project file and adds comments to the routing message. To send it to the next designated addressee, the recipient clicks File, Send To, Next Routing Recipient.

9. Select the Track Status check box to keep an eye on the progress of the project routing and make sure it doesn't get stuck too long with any one recipient. Select the Return When Done check box to make sure the file comes back to you so that you can see everyone's changes and comments.

10. Click the Route button.

    The message with the project file is routed to your designated recipients through e-mail.

The routing e-mail has the project file attached (see Figure 20-8), although the instructions it provides for the recipients aren't accurate. When a recipient finishes reviewing the project, he or she uses the Send To Routing Recipient command as described in the steps above. The person can add comments to the message and click Route to send an e-mail with the file attached to the next routing recipient. When the last recipient has reviewed the project, the originator of the routing message receives an e-mail message with the attached project and any comments added by previous recipients.

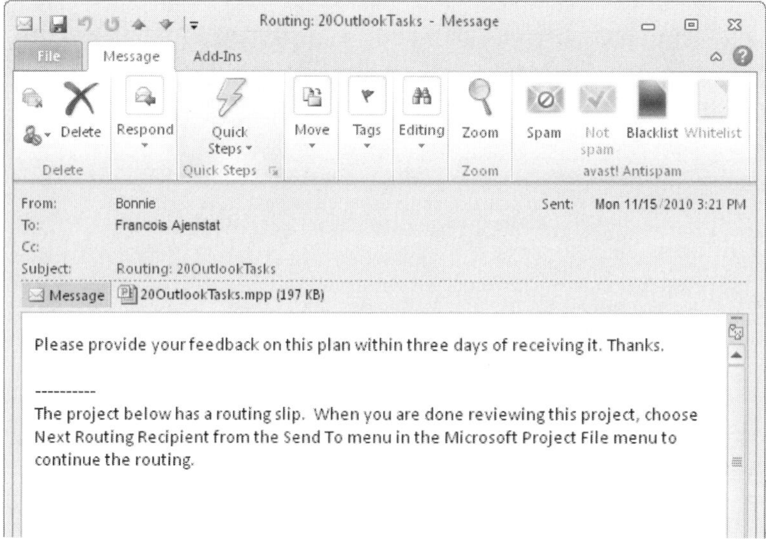

Figure 20-8 The routing e-mail provides instructions to each recipient, along with the attached project file.

Publishing the Project File to an Exchange Folder

> **Note**
>
> You can publish a project file to an Exchange folder if you're using Microsoft Exchange Server and if you have permission to use public folders.
>
> You can send your project file to an Exchange folder, which is especially useful for making the project file available to a large number of stakeholders. The Send To Exchange Folder command is not available on the Project ribbon by default, but you can add it to the Quick Access Toolbar or to a custom group on the ribbon.
>
> For information on how to add a command to the ribbon, see "Customizing the Project 2010 Ribbon" on page 1153.

To send the file to an Exchange folder, do the following:

1. In Project 2010, open the project file you want to publish to an Exchange folder.

Send To Exchange Folder

2. On the Quick Access Toolbar or the custom group on the ribbon, click Send To Exchange Folder.

   The Send To Exchange Folder dialog box appears, displaying the folders available to you.

3. Click the folder to which you want to send the project file, and then click OK.

   Your project file is copied to the selected folder.

Workgroup Messaging Is Done with Project Web App or SharePoint

In past versions of Microsoft Project, an e-mail workgroup messaging solution existed in which users of 32-bit MAPI-based e-mail systems could exchange project workgroup messages, including task assignments and progress updates, with project team members. E-mail workgroup messaging started out as a forerunner to Project Web App. Although it was a simple, low-end method for team collaboration on a project, e-mail workgroup messaging became outmoded, particularly with the advent and increasing usage of Project Server and Project Web App. Therefore, e-mail workgroup messaging has been unavailable for a while.

However, Project 2010 offers a new way to collaborate with your project team. You can synchronize tasks between a Project 2010 schedule and a SharePoint Tasks list. With this approach, you can publish tasks for your team members to see or bring tasks added to the SharePoint Tasks list into your Project 2010 plan. You can also publish changes from your Project 2010 file to SharePoint to communicate status or bring progress updates from SharePoint tasks into your Project 2010 file.

For information on synchronizing tasks between Project 2010 and a SharePoint Tasks list, see Chapter 21, "Collaborating as a Team by Using SharePoint."

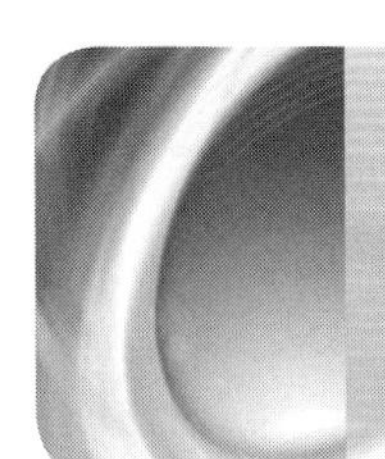

CHAPTER 21

Collaborating as a Team by Using SharePoint

You and your project team might need more methods for collaborating and sharing files than are afforded by Microsoft Project 2010 as a standalone program. Yes, you can share project files and convert views to PDF. Indeed, you can exchange project information with Microsoft Word, Excel, Visio, Outlook, and other programs. However, you might feel you need a greater level of workgroup collaboration—a way by which you can share project files and task lists in a central location with users who don't use Project 2010. You might want to make task assignments and receive progress updates that can be synchronized with the main project file.

In your case, the whole enterprise project management solution with Microsoft Project Server 2010 and Microsoft Project Web App might be overkill, especially because you're working with a smaller team and you're certain you won't need to synchronize more than one thousand tasks. You need an in-between solution.

NEW! New in Project 2010 is the ability to upload and synchronize a project file to a SharePoint site; this might just be that middle ground you're looking for.

With SharePoint, organizations can create web-based solutions for workgroup collaboration. A team can use SharePoint to create a website to share information with others on the team, create a document library, publish reports, track issues and risks, and create and track project tasks lists.

Two products are available: Microsoft SharePoint Foundation 2010 and Microsoft SharePoint Server 2010. SharePoint Foundation 2010 is the new version of Microsoft Windows SharePoint Services and provides the basic infrastructure for SharePoint Server 2010. While SharePoint Foundation is designed for smaller organizations as an entry-level solution, SharePoint Server is the full-featured business collaboration platform. The workgroup collaboration features for synchronizing project schedules and task lists between Project 2010 and SharePoint sites are available in both SharePoint Foundation and SharePoint Server.

With Microsoft Project Standard 2010, you can save a project file to a SharePoint Server or SharePoint Foundation site. Microsoft Project Professional 2010 takes it much further, giving project managers the ability to do the following:

- Publish a Project schedule to a SharePoint project tasks list.
- Create a project from a SharePoint project tasks list and convert it to a Project schedule.
- Synchronize schedule information in the SharePoint tasks list and Project schedule.
- Receive progress updates on task assignments from team members, and synchronize those updates into the Project schedule.

Creating a Project Tasks List on a SharePoint Site

SharePoint 2010 gives you the ability to create a *project tasks list*, which is a mini-Gantt chart complete with task names, start dates, due dates, and more. Team members who are part of the workgroup using the SharePoint site can be assigned to tasks in the tasks list.

Project managers and team members can work with their project tasks list in SharePoint. Project tasks lists can also be synchronized with Project 2010 for integration with a project schedule. In this way, team members can help create task information that becomes part of a larger project schedule. The project manager and the team can assign tasks to the appropriate team members, and then together, they can track progress and keep each other updated.

Note

The SharePoint steps in the procedures throughout this chapter are based on default SharePoint site settings. Your SharePoint site might be extensively customized and therefore commands might be in different places. If you can't find a command or window referenced in any of these procedures, check with your SharePoint administrator.

To create a project tasks list in SharePoint, follow these steps:

1. On your organization's SharePoint site, click Site Actions, View All Site Content.

   Alternatively, you can click Lists, and then click Create.

   The Site Actions menu is often in the upper-left corner of the SharePoint window, as shown in Figure 21-1.

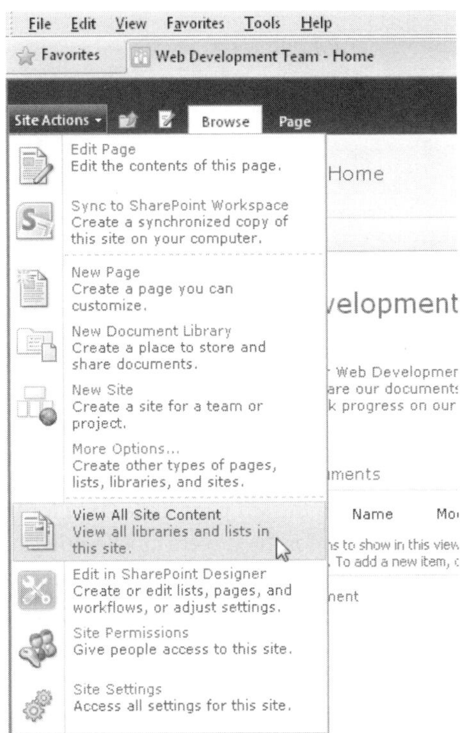

Figure 21-1 Click Site Actions, View All Site Content to start creating a project tasks list in SharePoint.

2. Near the top of the All Site Content page, click the Create button.

   The All Create dialog box appears, showing all content types available to be created, including library, list, page, and site items.

3. Scroll down in the Create dialog box, and then click Project Tasks.

   The right pane shows a description of the Project Tasks content type, as shown in Figure 21-2.

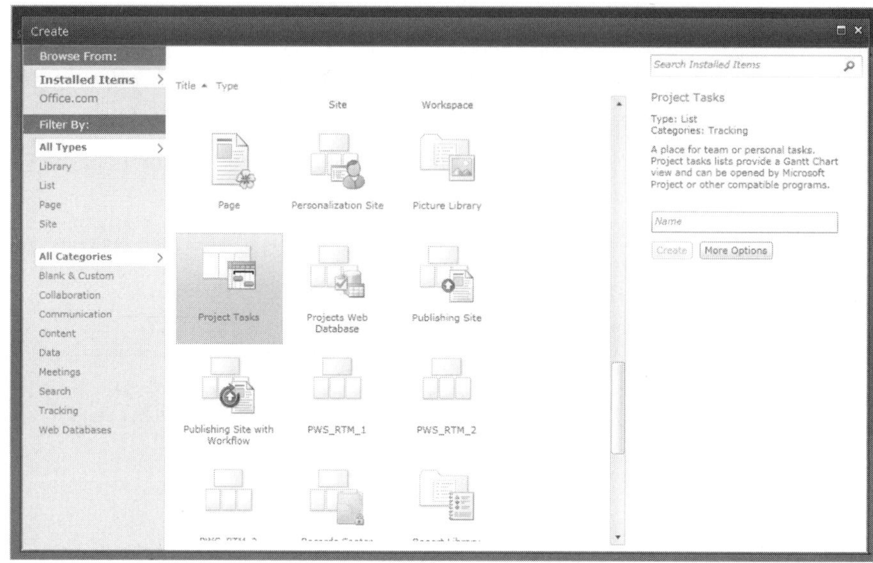

Figure 21-2 With Project Tasks selected, use the right pane to create the new project tasks list.

4. In the right pane, type a name for your new project tasks list in the Name box, and then click Create.

   Note that the name will appear in the left pane under Lists for the site. The name also becomes part of the web address for the project tasks list page. Although you can change the name of a list, the web address always remains the same.

   The new project tasks list is created and appears as a new window, as shown in Figure 21-3.

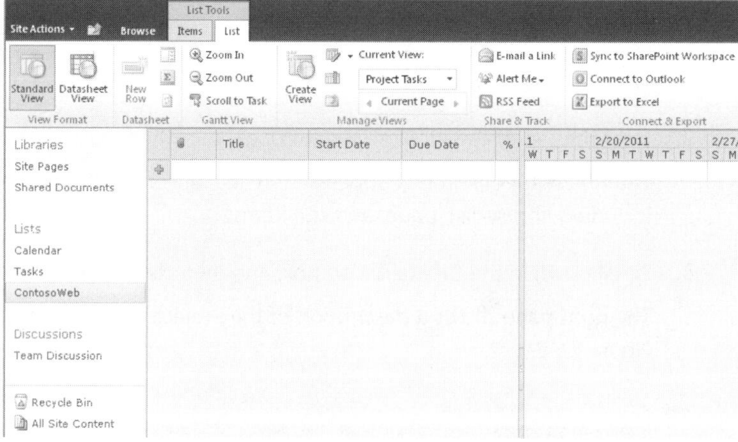

Figure 21-3 When you create a new project tasks list, it appears as a blank mini-Gantt chart view, and its name appears in the left pane under Lists.

5. Click in the Title field, type the first task name, and then fill in any of the other fields you want. Click in other cells or press the Tab key to move to other cells. Press Enter to move to the next row and enter the next task name.

   As you enter start dates and due dates, symbols and Gantt bars appear in the chart area of the Project Tasks view. (See Figure 21-4.)

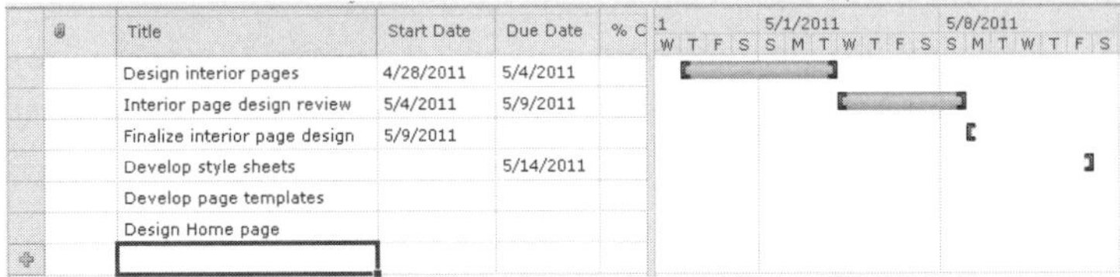

Figure 21-4 As you enter task information into the table, the Gantt area starts to fill in.

By default, you can review the project tasks list in the standard Gantt-like view or in the Datasheet view. You can also customize the view or create an entirely new view that meets the needs of the team and the project.

You can use SharePoint features to link tasks and create a hierarchy of summary tasks and subtasks. You can connect with Microsoft Outlook for reminders and alerts and integrate with SharePoint Workspace through Microsoft Office.

For more information about working with SharePoint project tasks and views, see SharePoint online Help.

Exchanging Project Information with SharePoint

You can exchange project information between a SharePoint project tasks list and a Project schedule. Information can be appended to an existing project plan or tasks list, or it can be used to create a new plan or tasks list. Whether you're saving an existing SharePoint project tasks list into Project, or saving a Project plan as a SharePoint tasks list, the process is the same.

After the information is saved between Project and SharePoint, the project information can then be synchronized in both places, providing for project information visibility across the team as well as up-to-the-minute progress updates.

> **Note**
>
> **If you're using Project Professional 2010 with Project Server 2010 as part of an enterprise project management solution, you probably do not need to synchronize with SharePoint tasks lists because you have more sophisticated methods for synchronizing and sharing task information with Project Server.**
>
> **However, if you are using both, note that the option to synchronize with a SharePoint tasks list is available only when you're not connected to your project server.**

Saving and Synchronizing SharePoint Tasks List Project

To save and synchronize a SharePoint project tasks list in Project, follow these steps:

1. In Project 2010, open the project plan in which you want to add the SharePoint project tasks list to be synchronized. This can be an existing project plan or a new blank project.
2. On the File tab, click Save & Send.

   The Save & Send Backstage view appears.

Sync With Tasks Lists

3. Click Sync With Tasks Lists.

   The Sync With Tasks Lists information appears in the right pane of the Backstage view, as shown in Figure 21-5.

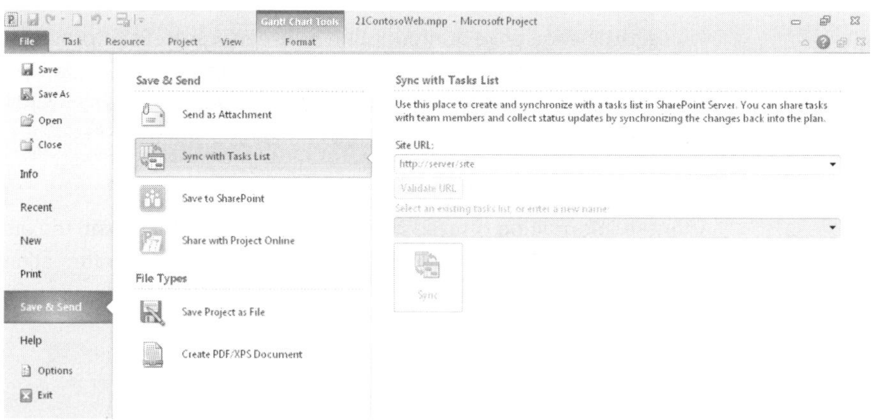

Figure 21-5 Enter and validate the SharePoint web address by clicking Sync With Tasks Lists in the Backstage view.

4. In the Site URL box, type the web address of the SharePoint site that contains the project tasks list you want to save in Project.

   This should be the web address of the SharePoint site, not that of the project tasks list page.

   The easiest thing to do is to copy and paste the web address. To do this, click in the address box of the browser showing the SharePoint site, and then press Ctrl+C. Click in the Site URL box on the Save & Send Backstage view, and then press Ctrl+V.

Validate URL

5. Click Validate URL.

6. If prompted, enter your SharePoint user name and password.

Sync

7. After the SharePoint location is validated, click in the box labeled Select An Existing Tasks List, Or Enter A New Name, then click the name of your SharePoint project tasks list, and then click Sync.

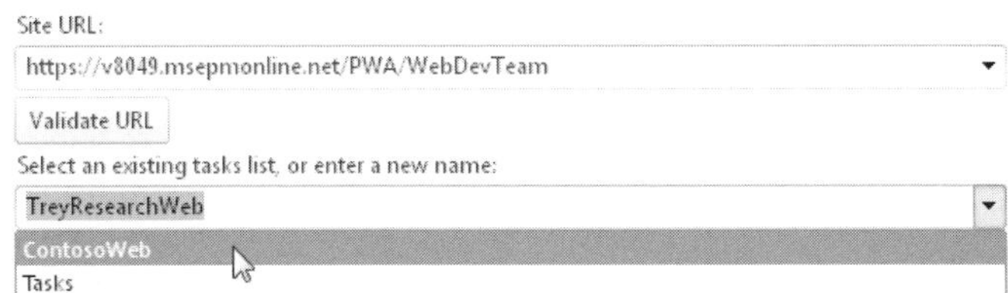

A message indicates progress for the synchronization. If another message states that automatically scheduled tasks will be changed to manually scheduled tasks, click OK.

If the current project includes existing tasks, the imported SharePoint tasks are appended after them, as shown in Figure 21-6. If any of the existing tasks in the current project are automatically scheduled tasks, they are changed to manually scheduled tasks by the synchronization process. Because the SharePoint site does not have a scheduling engine, all dates and durations are interpreted as manually scheduled upon synchronization.

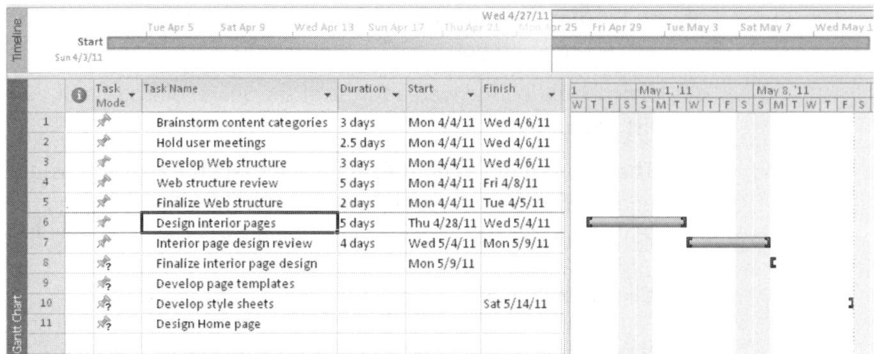

Figure 21-6 After synchronizing with SharePoint, the project tasks list is appended to any existing tasks in the project plan.

Creating a New SharePoint Tasks List from a Project Plan

If you need to create a new SharePoint tasks list from an existing project plan and have the two connected for synchronization, follow these steps:

1. In Project 2010, open the project plan you want to synchronize with your SharePoint site.
2. On the File tab, click Save & Send.
3. In the Save & Send Backstage view, click Sync With Tasks Lists.
4. In the Site URL box, type the web address of the SharePoint site in which you want to create a project tasks list from your information in Project.

   This should be the address of the SharePoint site, not that of the project tasks list page.
5. Click Validate URL.
6. If prompted, enter your SharePoint user name and password.
7. After the SharePoint location is validated, click in the box labeled Select An Existing Tasks List, Or Enter A New Name. Click the name of the SharePoint project tasks lists to which you want to append the tasks in your project plan, or type a name to create a new SharePoint project tasks list.

8. Click Sync.

   The tasks from the project plan are saved to the SharePoint project tasks list you indicated. If a message states that automatically scheduled tasks will be changed to manually scheduled tasks, click OK.

   After the synchronization is done, go to your SharePoint site. Check the project tasks list to see that the tasks from your Project 2010 schedule are now added. If you created a new project tasks list, its name appears under Lists in the left pane of the SharePoint window.

INSIDE OUT Save a project to SharePoint by using Project Standard 2010

If you're working with Project Standard 2010, you can still post a project file to a SharePoint site, but the features are more limited.

To save a project file to a SharePoint site, follow these steps.

1. **Open the file in Project 2010.**

Save To SharePoint

2. **On the File tab, click Save & Send, and then click Save To SharePoint.**

   The Save To SharePoint information appears in the right pane of the Backstage view.

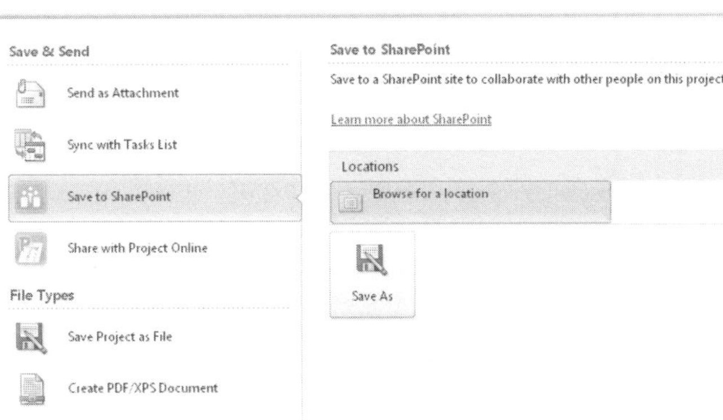

Browse For A Location

3. **In the right pane, double-click Browse For A Location.**

Saving a project file in this way is the only interaction available between Project Standard 2010 and your SharePoint site. You cannot import a project tasks list from SharePoint into Project Standard 2010, and synchronization of changes is not available.

Synchronizing Changes Between Project and SharePoint

After you create the connection between your project plan and the SharePoint project tasks list, when information in one or the other changes, you can synchronize them to be sure the changes are reflected in both places.

Synchronizing Changes and Resolving Sync Conflicts

To synchronize changes between your project plan and the SharePoint project tasks list, follow these steps:

1. Open the project plan that's connected to SharePoint.
2. On the File tab, click Info, and then click Sync.

   The information in the two locations is synchronized.

   Note that the SharePoint site does not need to be open on your computer when you do the synchronization.

   Sometimes you might get a synchronization conflict. This happens if a field has changed in both the SharePoint version and in the Project version. In such cases, a dialog box provides information about the conflict and asks you to choose whether to keep the SharePoint version or the Project version.

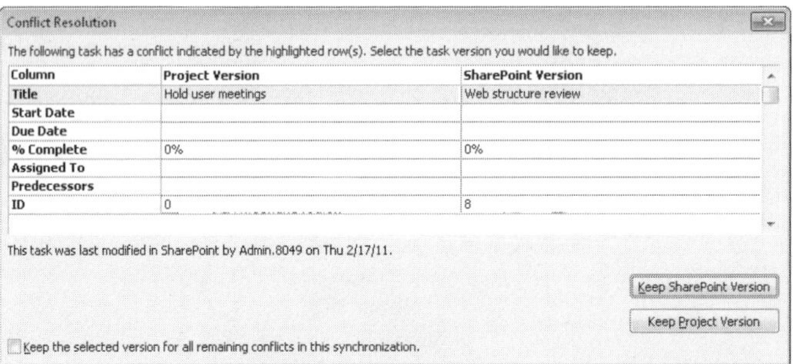

Mapping Fields Between Project and SharePoint

If you want to show a column of information from your Project 2010 plan in your connected SharePoint project tasks list, or vice versa, the fields need to be mapped. Project 2010 does a good job of identifying which fields are included and how they map. You can change the mapping, which can be necessary if certain fields are not showing up or they're appearing in unintended columns.

To review and change field mapping in your project plan in Project 2010, follow these steps:

1. On the File tab, click Info.

Manage Fields

2. In the Information Backstage view, under Sync To Tasks List, click the Manage Fields button.

   The Manage Fields dialog box appears, as shown in Figure 21-7. The dimmed fields are the standard synchronized fields; they cannot be changed. Below those are any additional fields being used in the SharePoint project tasks list.

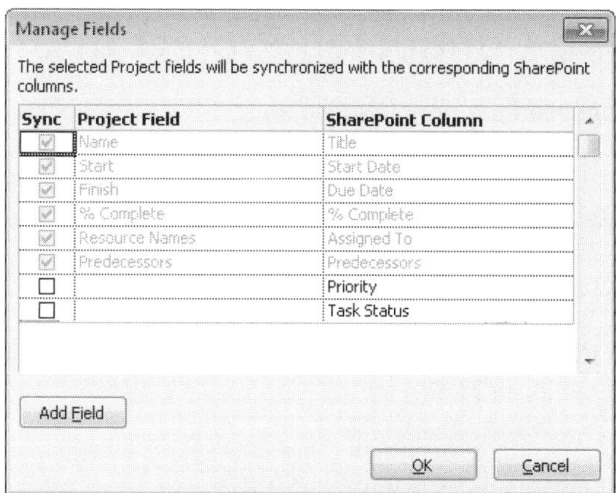

Figure 21-7 Identify the pairings of fields between the project file and the connected SharePoint project tasks list by using the Manage Fields dialog box.

3. If additional SharePoint fields are showing without a Project 2010 field pairing, and you want them to be part of the synchronization, click in the Project Field cell, and then click the arrow to show all available Project fields. Click the field you want to associate with the SharePoint field.

   The field is entered in the cell, and the Sync check box is selected.

4. To add a new Project field for synchronization, click Add Field. In the Add Field dialog box, shown in Figure 21-8, click the arrow in the Project Field box to see all available Project fields. Click the field you want to add to the synchronization. The corresponding SharePoint field appears in the SharePoint Column box. Click OK.

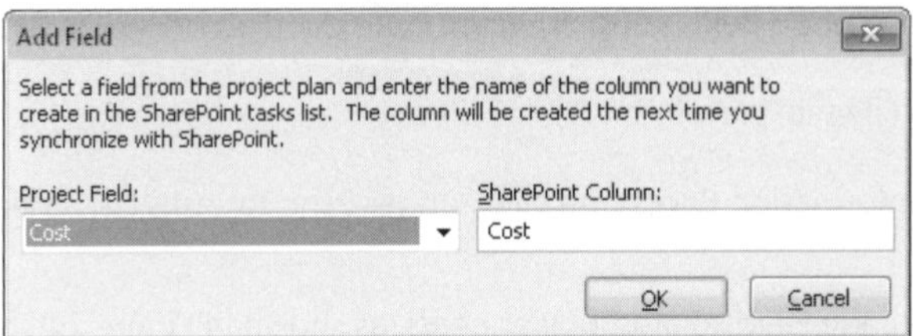

Figure 21-8 Create new, more meaningful pairings of fields by using the Add Fields dialog box.

Opening and Viewing Connected Project Information

With a connection between the project schedule and the SharePoint site, you can open one from the other.

To open the connected SharePoint site from the project file, follow these steps:

1. With the file open in Project 2010, click File, Info.
2. In the Information Backstage view, under Sync To Tasks Lists, click the SharePoint Site link, as shown in Figure 21-9.

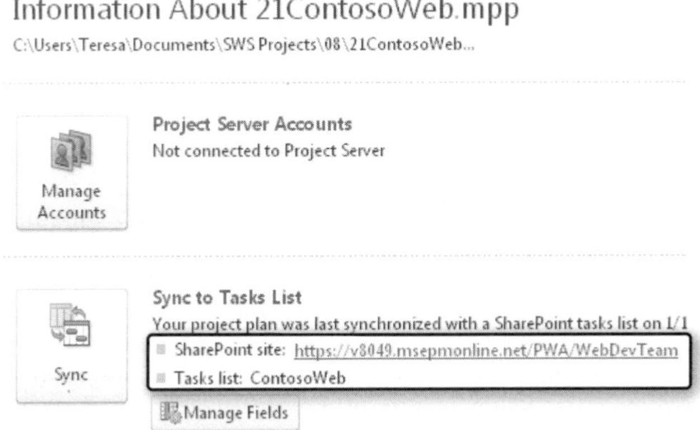

Figure 21-9 Click the SharePoint link on the Information Backstage view to open the connected SharePoint site.

The SharePoint site opens to its Home page. You can then browse to the project tasks list, typically by clicking its name under Lists in the left pane.

To open the connected Project file from the SharePoint site, follow these steps:

1. On the SharePoint site, open the project tasks list.

2. On the List tab, in the Connect & Export group, click Open Schedule.

Open Schedule

If a message asks you to confirm that you want to open the project file, click Yes.

The files are synchronized, and the project file opens in Project 2010.

Collaborating with Team Members on Task Updates

The convenience of synchronizing project information between Project and SharePoint becomes evident when you assign tasks to team members and start tracking progress on those assigned tasks.

Assigning Tasks to Team Members

Before you start assigning tasks to team members, set up SharePoint and your project file with the names of all team members. Be sure that the names are in the same form in both places, as SharePoint doesn't allow any resources to be assigned that are not members of the SharePoint group.

To ensure that you have the same resource names in SharePoint and your project file, it's best to use one of the following techniques:

- Set up all resources in SharePoint, and then copy and paste their names from a table in SharePoint into the Resource Sheet in Project 2010.
- Assign resources only in SharePoint, at least at first. When the project tasks list is synchronized, the resources show up in the project plan, not only on the assigned tasks, but also in the Resource Sheet. They can then be used for future task assignments within Project.

Other Types of Resources

You might need to assign tasks to resources other than SharePoint team members. Examples can include the following types of resources:

- **Generic resources such as "Equipment Technician" or "Marketing Specialist"**
- **Outside consultants or vendors**
- **Equipment resources**
- **Material resources for consumable supplies**
- **Cost resources such as "Airfare" or "Printing"**

For such resources, add their names to the SharePoint list to be sure their assignment can be recorded and tracked.

Assigning Resources in SharePoint

To assign a resource in SharePoint, follow these steps:

1. In your SharePoint project tasks list, click in the Assigned To cell for the task you want to assign to a team member.

Browse

2. Click the Browse button that appears when you click in the cell.

   The Select People And Groups dialog box appears, as shown in Figure 21-10.

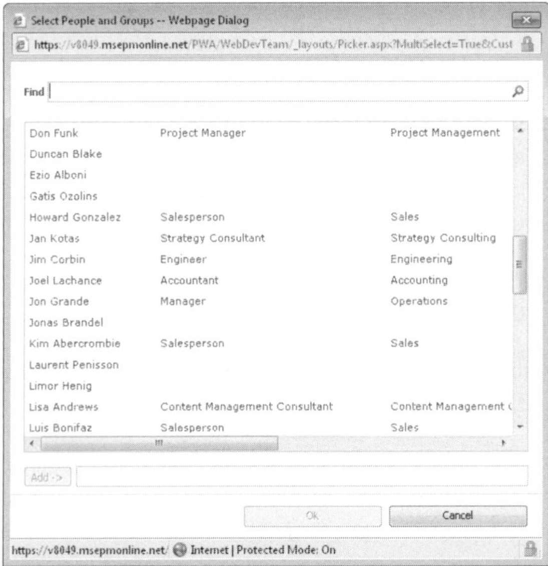

Figure 21-10 Assign resources to tasks in SharePoint by using the Select People And Groups dialog box.

Search

3. If necessary, type a name in the Find box, and then click the Search button. In the list, click the name of the resource you want to assign to the current task.

Instead of browsing in the Select People And Groups dialog box, you can type a resource name directly in the Assigned To box. However, you need to be careful that you use the proper form of the name so that SharePoint recognizes it. If SharePoint doesn't recognize the name, you'll see an error on the task, as shown in Figure 21-11.

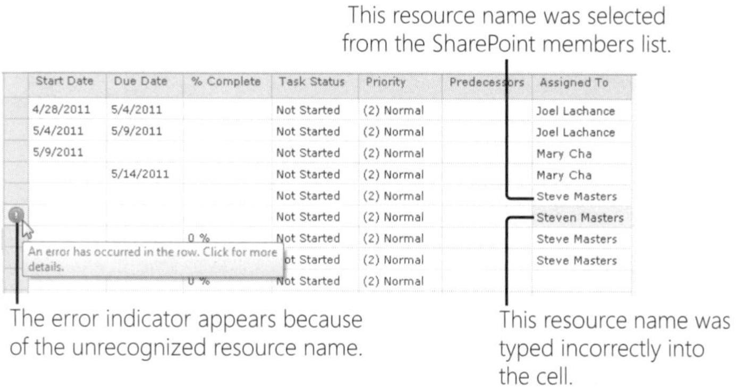

This resource name was selected from the SharePoint members list.

Start Date	Due Date	% Complete	Task Status	Priority	Predecessors	Assigned To
4/28/2011	5/4/2011		Not Started	(2) Normal		Joel Lachance
5/4/2011	5/9/2011		Not Started	(2) Normal		Joel Lachance
5/9/2011			Not Started	(2) Normal		Mary Cha
	5/14/2011		Not Started	(2) Normal		Mary Cha
			Not Started	(2) Normal		Steve Masters
			Not Started	(2) Normal		Steven Masters
		0 %	Not Started	(2) Normal		Steve Masters
			ot Started	(2) Normal		Steve Masters
		0 %	Not Started	(2) Normal		

An error has occurred in the row. Click for more details.

The error indicator appears because of the unrecognized resource name.

This resource name was typed incorrectly into the cell.

Figure 21-11 An error appears for any task that has unrecognized resources assigned.

For more information about working with resources in SharePoint, see SharePoint online Help.

Assigning Resources in Project

To assign a resource in your project plan, follow these steps:

1. In your project plan, first be sure that the Resource Sheet reflects the resource names as they are entered in SharePoint.
2. Switch to the Gantt Chart or other task sheet.
3. Select the task to which you want to assign a resource.
4. On the Resource tab, in the Assignments group, click Assign Resources.

Assign Resources

5. Click the resource name(s) you want to assign to the selected task, and then click Assign.
6. With the Assign Resources dialog box still open, select other tasks and continue to assign resources to them. (See Figure 21-12.)
7. When you are finished assigning tasks, click Close.

Chapter 21

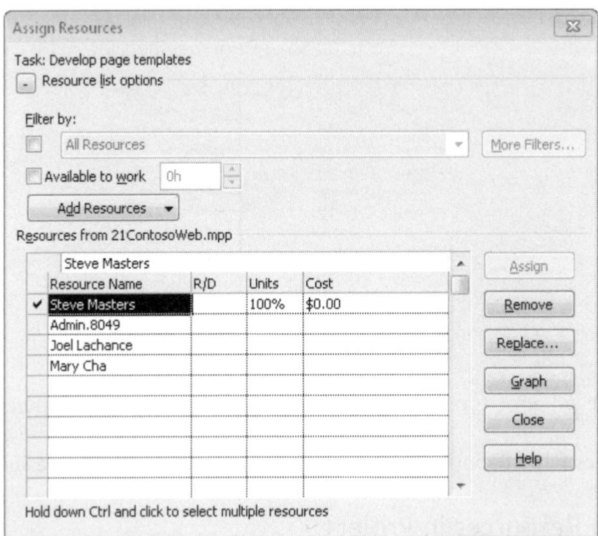

Figure 21-12 Assign resources to tasks by using the Assign Resources dialog box in Project 2010.

Whether you assign resources in SharePoint or Project, the next time you give the Sync command, the assignments are synchronized across the two locations.

For more information about working with resources in Project 2010, see Chapter 8, "Assigning Resources to Tasks."

Updating Task Progress

Although a custom solution could be designed, there is no formal mechanism for using SharePoint to request task updates from team members. However, team members can update their assigned tasks in SharePoint. When you synchronize the project tasks list with Project 2010, the updates can appear in the project plan. Likewise, if you include progress tracking in the project plan, this information can be included in the SharePoint project tasks list. For progress information to appear in both places when synchronized, be sure that the progress fields are mapped and showing in both places.

Updating Task Progress in SharePoint

The default view for the project tasks list shows the % Complete and Task Status columns for entering task updates. To update progress in the SharePoint project tasks list using these fields, follow these steps:

1. In your SharePoint project tasks list, click in the % Complete cell for the task.

2. Type the percent complete for the task.
3. Press Tab to move to the Task Status cell.

   Note that the Task Status cell does not change when you enter a percent complete.
4. Click the arrow in the Task Status cell, and then select one of the choices: In Progress, Completed, Deferred, Waiting On Someone Else.

For more information about working with columns in a SharePoint list, see SharePoint online Help.

Updating Task Progress in Project

To update progress in your project plan, first decide what kinds of progress information you want to use. You have many choices, from the very broad to the very detailed, as follows:

- Percentage complete
- Actual duration and remaining duration
- Actual start and actual finish
- Percentage work complete
- Actual work complete and remaining work
- Actual work complete by time period

Your update progress choice is not an all-or-nothing decision; you can use any combination of these methods that suit the purposes of your project, your team, and the individual tasks.

For more information about progress tracking in Project 2010, see "Updating Task Progress" on page 462.

When you decide which types of progress tracking information you and your team want to use, you can map those fields to be sure there are corresponding pairs in Project and SharePoint that always synchronize with each other.

For information about properly synchronizing fields between SharePoint and Project, see "Mapping Fields Between Project and SharePoint" on page 790.

When the fields are mapped, you can add columns as necessary and enter progress information. When you give the Sync command, progress entered in either SharePoint or Project is reflected in both locations.

PART 7

Managing Projects Across Your Enterprise

CHAPTER 22

Understanding Enterprise Project Management

ENTERPRISE *project management (EPM)* refers to the framework of tools used for managing projects, and entire portfolios of projects, within an organization in a collaborative way. This chapter provides a high-level overview of the benefits of enterprise project management, the roles and components of the Microsoft enterprise project management solution, and an introduction to the new project portfolio management features.

Over the past 30 years, companies have evolved through the use of technology, globalization, and working in distributed teams. Information sharing and communication are key enablers for achieving success in managing major projects.

To satisfy the needs of large organizations for managing and communicating information about multiple projects across multiple sites, Microsoft developed an enterprise project management solution. This solution is made up of the following components:

- **Microsoft Project Professional 2010** The desktop project management application.
- **Microsoft Project Server 2010** The engine powering the enterprise project management solution. Project Server 2010 stores and processes all project information.
- **Microsoft Project Web App (PWA)** The scalable and customizable web-based interface to Project Server that is used for project management and portfolio management (PPM).

Why Use Enterprise Project Management?

This section details the advantages of using the Microsoft enterprise project management solution over the standalone desktop project management solution provided by Microsoft Project Standard 2010 or Project Professional 2010:

- Team members can view and update the progress of their assigned tasks in the Tasks page of Project Web App, shown in Figure 22-1. They can also create new tasks and delegate tasks to other team members.

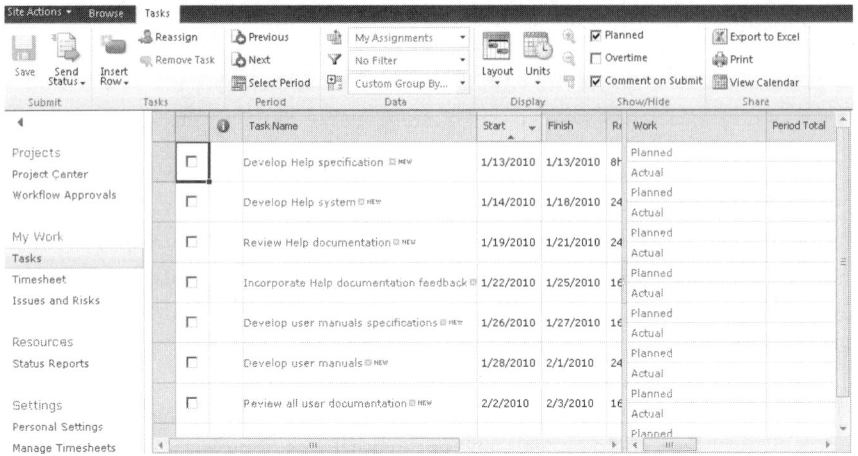

Figure 22-1 Team members can view tasks, timesheets, issues, and risks.

- Project managers can create and initiate projects, which are then analyzed by the portfolio manager or project management office (PMO) in terms of their value for organizational strategy. They can enter the project schedule (as illustrated in Figure 22-2), select resources, estimate costs, enter issues and risks, and check task status in Project Web App or in Project Professional. They can also review and approve task updates from team members.

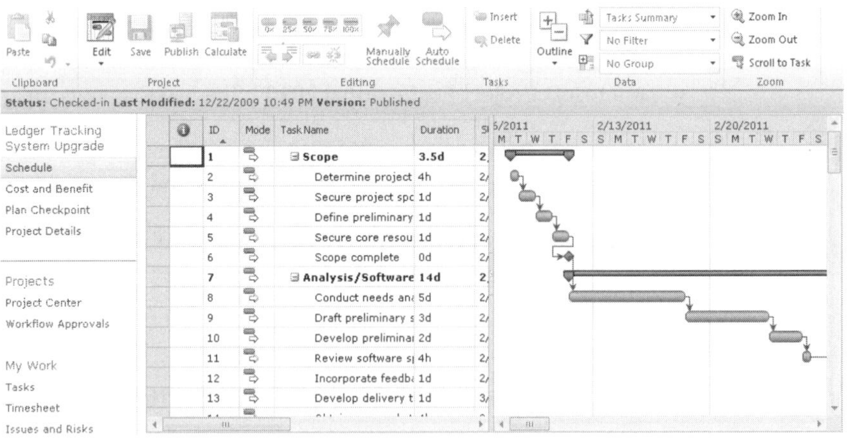

Figure 22-2 Project managers can enter the project schedule, assign resources, and analyze costs in Project Web App.

NEW!

- New in Project 2010 is the addition of a powerful portfolio management module, replacing what used to be the separate functionality of Microsoft Office Project Portfolio Server 2007. Each project proposal can determine the start of a workflow in the system, based on the standard project management methodology. The project manager can track the status of the project in all the phases of the workflow. An example of a project life-cycle workflow can be seen in Figure 22-3. A *workflow* essentially reflects the project life cycle. You can have different workflows for different project types. A workflow consists of *stages* within *phases*. You can customize and configure each phase and each stage, including the placement of approval steps.

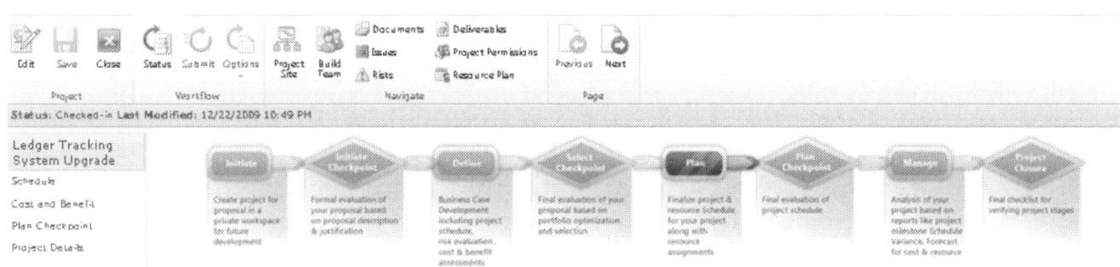

Figure 22-3 New in Project Web App is the ability to enforce the phases and stages in a project life cycle.

- Portfolio managers and executives can analyze the portfolio of projects, as shown in Figure 22-4, and decide on the projects that are likely to garner the greatest business value. They can factor in changes to the project key performance indicators and perform what-if analyses on the projects.

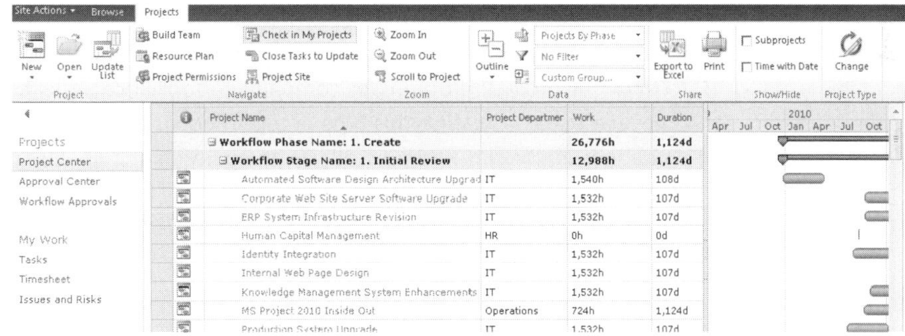

Figure 22-4 The Project Center shows information about all projects, their costs, risks, and workflow status

- Executives can define the company strategy or business drivers for their organization, as shown in Figure 22-5. *Business drivers* are a translation of the aligned company business strategy into measurable objectives.

Chapter 22

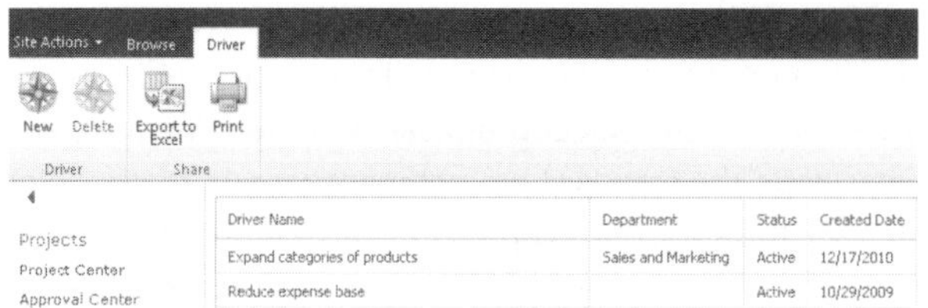

Figure 22-5 You can use the new demand management feature set to define and prioritize business drivers.

- Because Project Server 2010 is built on top of Microsoft SharePoint Server 2010, Project Server takes advantage of important features, like building project or program SharePoint sites, where relevant information—including documents, issues, and risks—about the project or program can be stored.
- Project Web App facilitates the communication of task assignments among the members of a team. Hundreds, even thousands, of projects or programs can be managed in a consistent manner throughout an organization. In Project Web App, such elements as views, the ribbon, macros, reports, and workflows can be customized and standardized across projects.
- Resource information can be managed in Project Web App. The skill sets, cost, availability, and other information can be built into the enterprise resource pool that all project managers use to build their teams.

NEW!

- New in Project Server 2010 is the reporting module, built using the Microsoft Business Intelligence platform. The reporting functionality is built as a SharePoint subsite and is highly customizable. This new reporting module provides you with the ability to track key project, program, or company performance indicators, such as cost or time, in a visual way. With this type of reporting visibility, you can react to changing conditions in projects and portfolios with agility, as shown in Figure 22-6.

As shown in Figure 22-7, the Project Web App interface for editing schedule information or tasks is similar to the Project Professional interface. This makes updating information more intuitive and efficient.

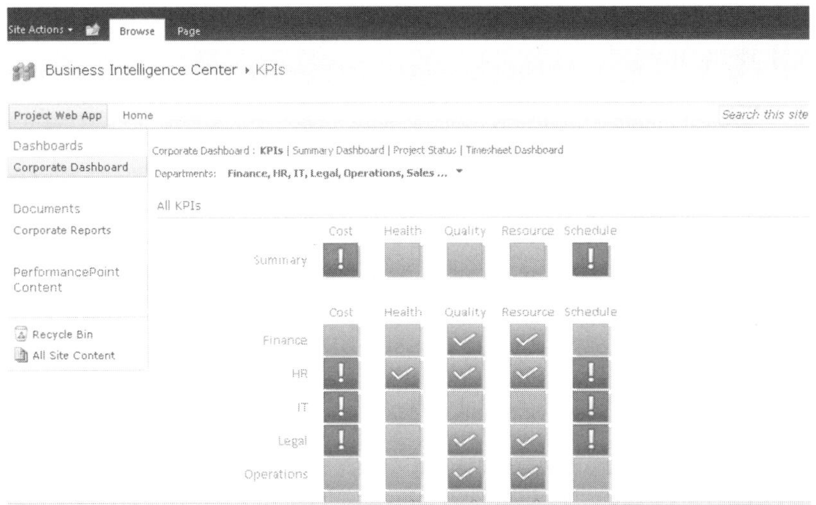

Figure 22-6 In Project Server 2010, visibility on the status of key performance indicators is now available.

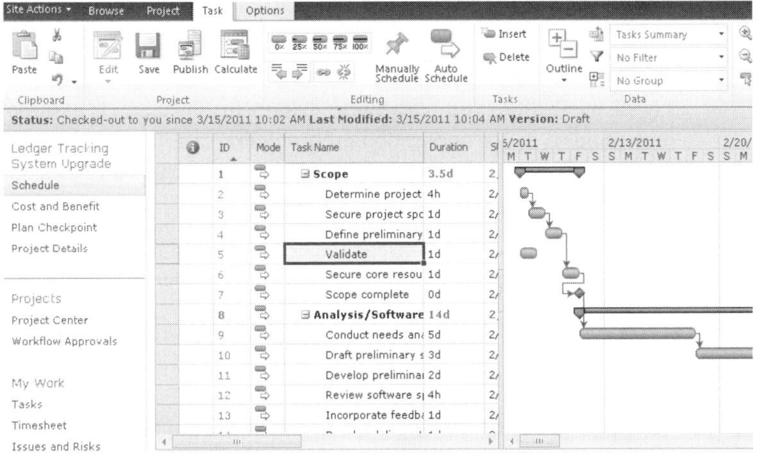

Figure 22-7 You can edit the project schedule in Project Web App by using an interface similar to Project Professional.

With the Project 2010 enterprise project management solution, programs and projects at all levels of complexity can be centrally managed and controlled.

INSIDE OUT What's new in Project Server 2010 and Project Web App

Several modules were improved or redesigned in Project Server and Project Web App, and new features were introduced, as follows:

- **Integrated project and portfolio management** Microsoft has developed a new *demand management* module in Project Server that helps initiate projects and specifies their business case for more detailed analysis of what projects to include in the portfolio.
- **New resource capacity module** Resource capacity planning can now be done by using the resource capacity module across the organization, ensuring maximum resource utilization.
- **Project workflows** New in Project Server 2010 is the option to configure clear life-cycle workflows for managing different types of projects, with actions required from the different parties involved. These workflows, typically established by the project server administrator and portfolio manager, help ensure that the right level of governance over the projects in your organization.
- **Enhanced user experience** In Project Web App, Microsoft has replaced the toolbar with the ribbon for easier access and grouping of the main features.
- **Easy customization and scalability** Easier customization is ensured by enhancements to the application programming interface (API) called *Project Server Interface (PSI)* and also to SharePoint Server 2010 and Microsoft Visual Studio 2010.

A complete version comparison between Project Server 2003, 2007, and 2010 is available at *www.microsoft.com/project/en/us/project-server-2010-versions.aspx*.

Who's Who in Enterprise Project Management

In enterprise project management, the following roles are reflected:

- **Project manager** The traditional user of Microsoft Project, the project manager is the person responsible for the success or failure of the assigned project, and as such, all the other roles revolve around this one. The project manager typically uses Project Professional 2010 as well as Project Web App. The project manager builds the project schedule, creates and assigns resources, creates the change management plan, manages issues and risks, manages project costs, and communicates with all project stakeholders.

- **Resource manager** Although the role of the resource manager is often fulfilled by the project manager, Project Web App and Project Professional include distinctive resource management features. The resource manager works closely with the project manager to ensure that all projects are staffed with the right resources. The resource manager can manage resource information in the enterprise resource pool, review timesheets, and create custom resource-related reports.

- **Team leader** The team leader manages resource notifications, views team member task status, and reports to the project manager. Team leaders can assign tasks to their team members and view existing assigned tasks.

- **Team member** The team member carries out the day-to-day activities of projects to which they're assigned. Team members can report progress and provide status updates to their team leader and project manager, as shown in Figure 22-8.

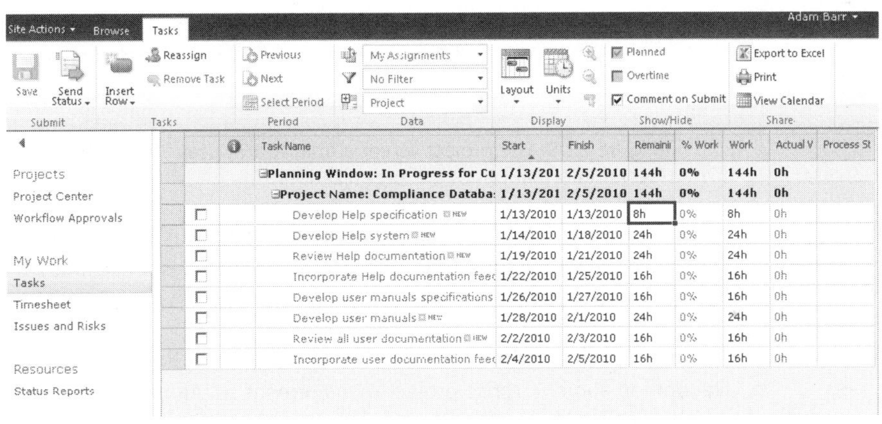

Figure 22-8 Team members can update their progress on tasks using the Tasks page.

- **Portfolio manager** The portfolio manager analyzes the project portfolio and makes decisions and recommendations on projects in various stages of the project life cycle. The portfolio manager is instrumental in designing the demand management system, including project workflows and business drivers, to ensure that the right projects are selected for the organization's portfolio. The portfolio manager can also create custom views, fields, and reports to standardize project management practices throughout the entire enterprise.

- **Executive** Upper management, customers, and other managing stakeholders provide high-level direction for a project, a portfolio of projects, or an entire program. They might also fulfill the role of the project sponsor. These executives can keep an eye on the progress of milestones, deliverables, costs, and other concerns through the use of specialized views in Project Web App. They can also compare aspects of multiple projects by using sophisticated modeling or analysis, leading to informed decisions for the organization.

- **Project server administrator** The project server administrator configures the project server for the organization, including user permissions, roles, custom fields, calendars, look and feel, reporting, and more. The project server administrator works primarily in Project Web App, as shown in Figure 22-9.

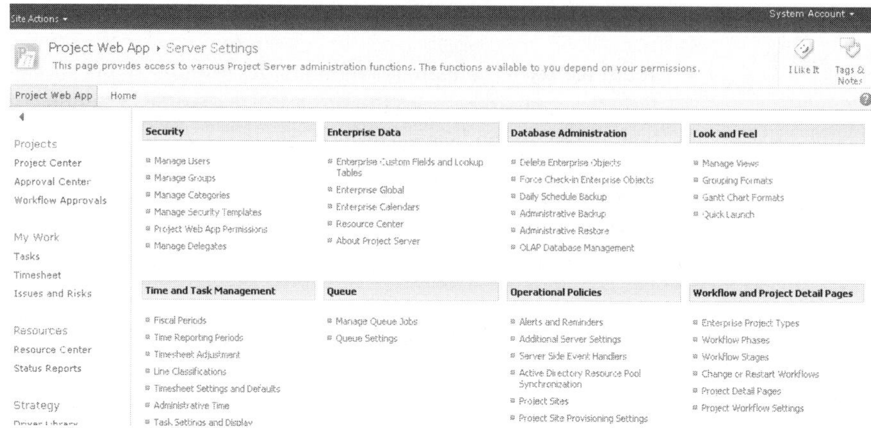

Figure 22-9 The project server administrator uses Project Web App to configure project server information for the organization.

Although these roles are distinct, one person might fulfill two or more overlapping roles and have the permissions that reflect these multiple responsibilities. It is also possible to customize functionalities down to user-group level, allowing for maximum flexibility.

The rest of this chapter provides a broad overview of the Microsoft Project workgroup collaboration and enterprise project management solution, establishing the context of how all the components work together. Succeeding chapters are designed for specific enterprise project management stakeholders who work with aspects of Project Server and Project Web App in specialized ways, according to their role in the organization. These chapters and their intended audiences are as follows:

- Chapter 23, "Administering Your Enterprise Project Management Solution," is designed for the project server administrator. This chapter presents general guidelines on configuring and tailoring Project Server and Project Web App for enterprise project management in a specific organization. It also includes step-by-step instructions for completing typical system administration duties such as adding new users and setting up security permissions. In addition, the chapter covers the creation of customized elements for standardization as well as the setup for the enterprise resource pool, timesheets, and reports. Chapter 23 should also be reviewed by project managers and portfolio managers who want a clearer picture of the capabilities that are implemented by the project server administrator.

- Chapter 24, "Managing Enterprise Projects and Resources," is the project manager's chapter. In this chapter, you learn how to set up a project, build the project plan, define issues and risks, and build your team. This chapter also covers collaboration with team members and other project stakeholders, and it details enterprise project management procedures in Project Web App as well as in Project Professional.
- Chapter 25, "Participating on a Team Using Project Web App," is intended for team members, team leaders, and resource managers who use Project Web App to track and manage their work on projects. This chapter includes information about creating and accepting project tasks, reporting progress, working with timesheets, and viewing the overall project picture.
- Chapter 26, "Making Executive Decisions Using Project Web App," is directed at project executives and other managing stakeholders who need to see the overall picture of proposals and projects, as well as resource and cost information. In this chapter, managing stakeholders learn how to use Project Web App to work with the portfolio, view the enterprise resource pool, and analyze the project and portfolio performance information.
- Chapter 27, "Managing and Analyzing Project Portfolios," is designed for portfolio managers who set up the governance processes for portfolio and project management, focusing on selecting the right projects for the portfolio. This chapter describes designing the demand management system including workflows, optimizing the project portfolio by using strategic business drivers, and viewing and communicating portfolio information.

Understanding the Components of Enterprise Project Management

There are different ways to look at the pieces that contribute to the Project Server enterprise project management solution. You can look at them from an architectural standpoint or from a data flow standpoint. In this section, however, we'll review the components of the Microsoft enterprise project management solution from the point of view of its component applications. These applications are Project Server, Project Professional, Project Web App, and SharePoint Server.

Understanding Project Server Architecture

Project Server stores all the data associated with your enterprise projects, portfolios, and programs. It also stores the information related to user access, security settings, administrative settings, and so on.

The Project Server architecture is multi-layered. The layers are as follows:

- Project Professional and Project Web App (displayed in Internet Explorer 7 or later), act as clients in the front-end layer. Third-party applications and line-of-business (LOB) applications can also access Project Server as clients. The front-end applications communicate with the middle layer through the Project Server Interface (PSI) Web Services, as illustrated in Figure 22-10. The Project Web App pages use standard SharePoint Server 2010 Web Parts as well as Web Parts that communicate with the PSI. You can install one or more Project Web App servers, depending on capacity needs.

- The middle layer includes the PSI and the business-objects logic layer, in which objects such as Project, Resource, Task, and so on, are present. All information from the databases is made available through the data access layer, which is another middle layer. This middle layer makes the translation from the database objects to the business object layer.

- The third layer is the database layer, which includes several databases: a Draft database for projects that are not published but locked for editing by a user; a Published database for projects that are open for editing; an Archive database for historical projects; and the Reporting database, which is the staging area for generating reports and online analytical processing (OLAP) cubes. The Reporting database is updated in almost real time from the Published database.

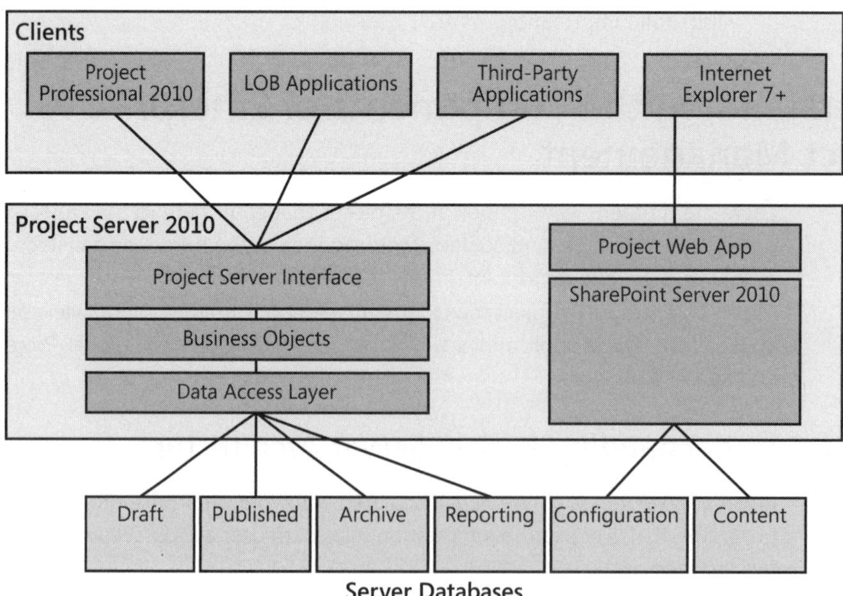

Figure 22-10 Project Server 2010 is a layered application including a database layer, a middle layer, and a presentation or client layer.

The Project Server functionality allows for customization through the PSI in the same way that SharePoint Web Parts do. For easy customization you can use technologies and programs like Windows Communication Foundation, Business Connectivity Services, Microsoft Visual Studio 2010, and Microsoft SharePoint Designer 2010.

Understanding the Role of Project Professional

While Project Web App is intended to be used by a variety of project stakeholders, Project Professional is the project management application designed for project managers. Project Professional is one of the primary client applications for Project Server and is a major source of project data—projects, tasks, resources, assignments, scheduling dates, costs, and tracking information.

Because Project Professional and Project Server are interconnected, the project manager can choose project templates from the project server (as shown in Figure 22-11), choose which fields to synchronize on the project server, publish schedules, and collaborate with the team. Project managers can also see which other projects the resources allocated to their projects are working on. (See Figure 22-12.)

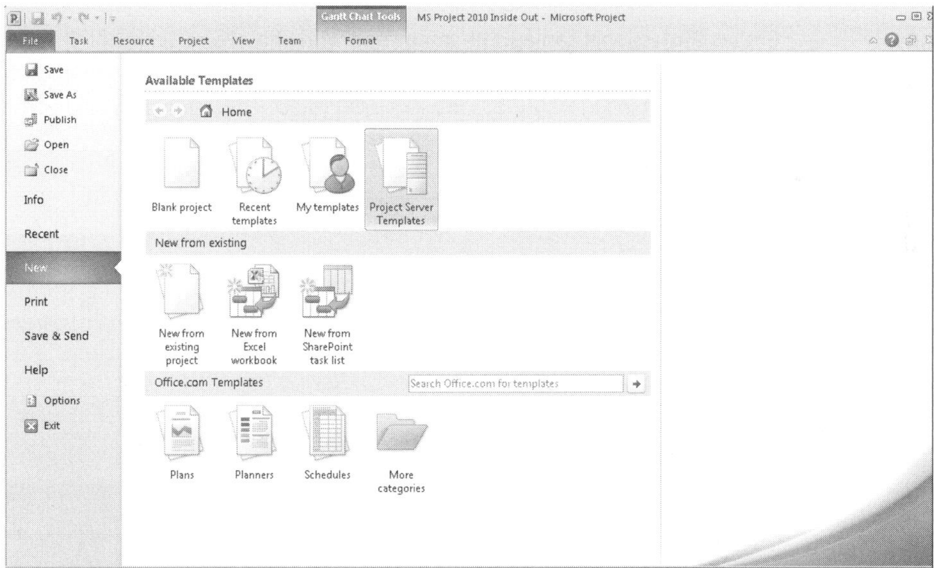

Figure 22-11 Create a new project in Project Professional by using a project server template.

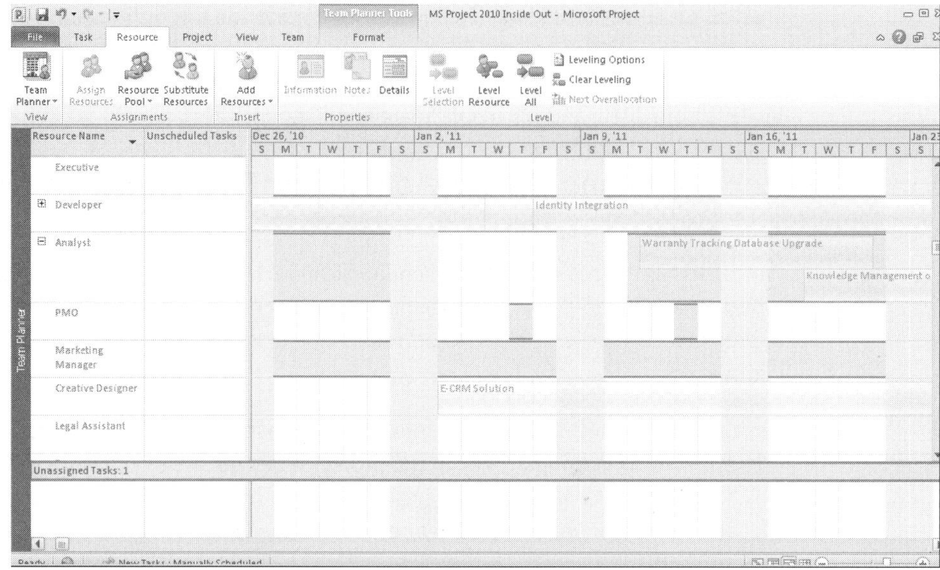

Figure 22-12 Use Project Professional to see details about overallocated resources.

Project Professional can also be integrated with SharePoint Server or SharePoint Foundation 2010, allowing project managers to create projects from task lists entered on a SharePoint site, as shown in Figure 22-13. You can use Project Professional to map corresponding fields between SharePoint lists and project task fields.

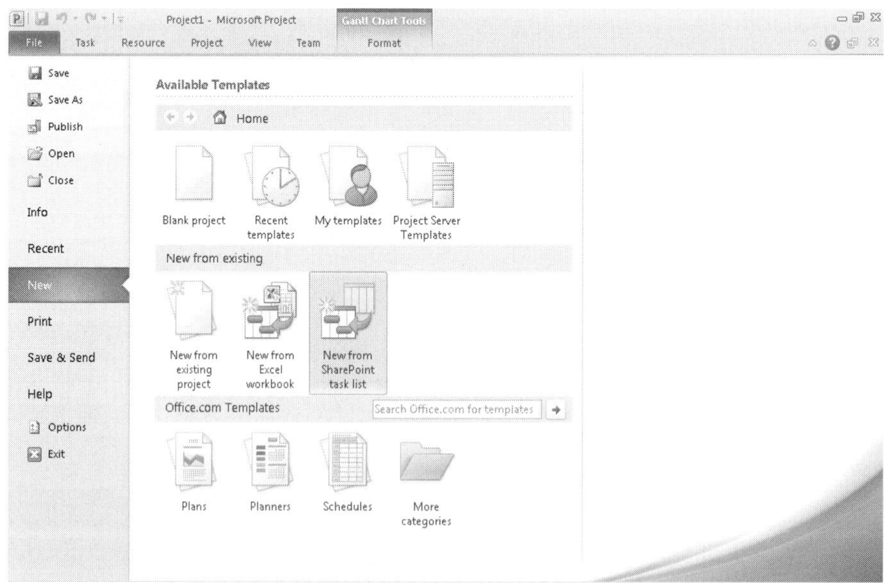

Figure 22-13 You can create a new project starting with a list of SharePoint tasks.

In most cases, if you're using the Microsoft enterprise project management features, you don't need to use the SharePoint integration features for sharing tasks lists with Project Professional. For more information, see Chapter 21, "Collaborating as a Team by Using SharePoint."

Understanding the Role of Project Web App

Project Web App is the web-based interface for entering and displaying project data, including tasks, resources, assignments, scheduling dates, costs, and tracking information. Project Web App is also the interface for the new project portfolio management features. It is the view into your project server and the underlying project databases.

This web application typically lives on your organization's intranet or extranet and is accessed by all project stakeholders. Project Web App can also be accessed from Project Professional.

Putting the Components Together

Here's a simplified example of a sequenced enterprise project management interaction between Project Server, Project Professional, and Project Web App:

1. Project data that is entered in either Project Professional or Project Web App is saved to a project database that's part of your project server architecture.
2. When projects are published (rather than simply saved), their data is saved in the Published database and the Reporting database. Whenever a project is saved, it is saved to the Draft database. Whenever a project is published, it is also saved to the Published database. The data in the Published database is then transformed and added to the Reporting database for analysis purposes.
3. When a user needs to see project, task, resource, or assignment information in Project Web App or Project Professional, Project Server calls up this information from the appropriate database and displays it in pages created through the Project Server Interface (PSI).

Understanding Project Portfolio Management

Project portfolio management (PPM) is a term used to describe the methods with which you can analyze, prioritize, and optimize proposed projects within an organization. Not all projects that are proposed within an organization can be undertaken, considering ever-present budgetary and resource constraints. The objective of project portfolio management, therefore, is to ensure that the ideal mix of projects is selected that will enable your organization to achieve its strategic goals.

NEW!

Project portfolio management features are now available from within Project Web App. These features are designed to be used primarily by portfolio managers and secondarily by executives.

The first step in project portfolio management is to define business drivers—the key strategic objectives for your organization. These drivers can include market expansion, profit or share growth, or reduction of operational costs. A comprehensive business driver definition and prioritization by the company's leadership team enables company executives and the portfolio manager to select only those projects that maximize the return on investment.

Whenever a project is proposed, the project should be rated against all business drivers relevant for that project. Portfolio analysis can also be performed for in-progress projects and can provide a basis for decisions such as moving more funding to higher priority projects, reallocating resources, or even shutting down a project.

Portfolio analysis considers a number of variables, including the following:

- **Business drivers** To what degree is a project maximizing the probability of achieving the business drivers? The assessment for each business driver should be entered when the project proposal is added.
- **Cost** Because all companies have limited budgets and resources dedicated to achieving strategic goals through projects, portfolio analysis takes into consideration each project's cost.
- **Resources** For each project proposal, a resource plan can be entered. For example, suppose you will need a project manager, an architect, and ten construction workers for your project. Project proposals might be rejected if there are not enough of the needed resources available.

You can at any time add projects or remove projects from the analysis in Project Web App. After the portfolio of projects has been selected and communicated, project managers can start the planning process for those projects.

To learn more about portfolio analysis, see "Understanding Project Portfolio Management" on page 1029 and "Designing Your Demand Management System" on page 1032.

Understanding the Enterprise Project Management Project Life Cycle

The enterprise features of Project Professional can extend the scope of Project 2010 beyond individual projects to multiple departments and groups in a midsize to large, multiple-project business, and can even handle a complex program of projects that are distributed across various global locations. With enterprise project management, information stored in your project server database for every resource and every project in the entire company can be quickly collated and reported.

For any business that works on multiple projects, rich customization, resource management, reporting, and portfolio analysis capabilities become possible through enterprise project management. Executives, customers, and other managing stakeholders can review and analyze information on all projects and resources in their organization, providing for a comprehensive understanding of the nature and progress of the activities within the organization. In addition, the enterprise features help individual project managers plan and control their projects within the context of their organization.

The following steps detail a typical enterprise project life cycle:

1. Early on, as part of the Project Server configuration process, the project server administrator, possibly in conjunction with the portfolio manager, uses Project Professional to create the enterprise global template—the basis for all project plans to be created throughout the enterprise.

   This global template contains standardized project elements such as custom views and fields, custom reports, currency format, tables, formulas, and Microsoft Visual Basic for Applications (VBA) modules created to reflect the organization's requirements. The use of the enterprise global template propagates the custom elements as the organizational standard for all projects.

2. Also early in the process, the project server administrator or resource manager sets up the enterprise resource pool, which includes vital information about the organization's resources, such as skills, costs, and availability.

3. The project server administrator and portfolio manager can also define the standard life cycle or workflow that a project must follow through to completion. The workflow can include approvals, verifications, milestone checkpoints, and so on.

4. The enterprise project life cycle typically starts with the creation of a project in Project Professional or Project Web App, using a standard project template from a library of best practice templates, from Excel data, a SharePoint list, or from scratch. Once the project is saved, you can also create a team workspace that is used for collaboration by the project stakeholders. This functionality can be configured by the project server administrator.

5. After the project is created, a project life-cycle workflow can be applied, as defined by a portfolio manager. Depending on the workflow, a request for approval might be sent to the portfolio manager, who can evaluate the project based on the initial data.

6. Depending on the approver's action, the status of the project is updated. If the project is approved, the requestor enters a business case for the project, which contains the project schedule, resource estimates, strategic impact on business drivers, and risks. The project is resubmitted to the portfolio manager.

7. The portfolio manager and other managing stakeholders of the organization determine what the optimal portfolio of projects is based on the projects' impact, the company budget, and resource constraints. This enables the company to focus only on the projects that bring the most benefits to the company. The best portfolio is selected, and the projects are assigned to the project managers.

8. If the business case for the project is approved, the project manager enters the planning stage of the project and starts to build the project team. The project manager views resource availability and assigns resources to the project schedule. After all planning is complete, with resources allocated, risks entered, and deliverables specified, the project manager can submit the project for the necessary approvals to start project execution.

9. The portfolio manager receives the request to approve the project plan and can undertake a further analysis of its impact on company costs, resources, and key business drivers.

10. Should the project plan be approved, project execution can start, and the project manager will allocate the tasks to team members and other stakeholders and will monitor and control the project. The project manager, resource manager, portfolio manager, and all project stakeholders can use business intelligence functionality to gain insights about the progress on the project.

11. After project execution is complete, the final step is the project closure.

Keep in mind that there can be multiple project life cycles that apply to different types of projects depending on your project server configuration.

Collaborating as a Project Team

Communication is a critical component of effective project management. There's no question that establishing an effective two-way information flow prevents a host of problems.

Project Server and Project Web App provide a highly efficient process for exchanging project information with team members. As the project manager working in Project Professional and Project Web App, you can communicate project information to achieve the following:

- Submit assignments and task changes to assigned resources.

- Request assignment actuals from assigned resources.
- Request, receive, and compile narrative status reports.
- Incorporate actuals submitted by assigned resources directly into the project plan.
- Publish the full project plan for review by team members and other stakeholders.

For details on workgroup collaboration information for the project manager, see "Collaborating with Your Project Team" on page 945.

With Project Web App, team members can see all the relevant project information for their assignments. Project Web App has an easy-to-navigate user interface that simplifies information flow. Figure 22-14 shows an example of how team members might see their tasks.

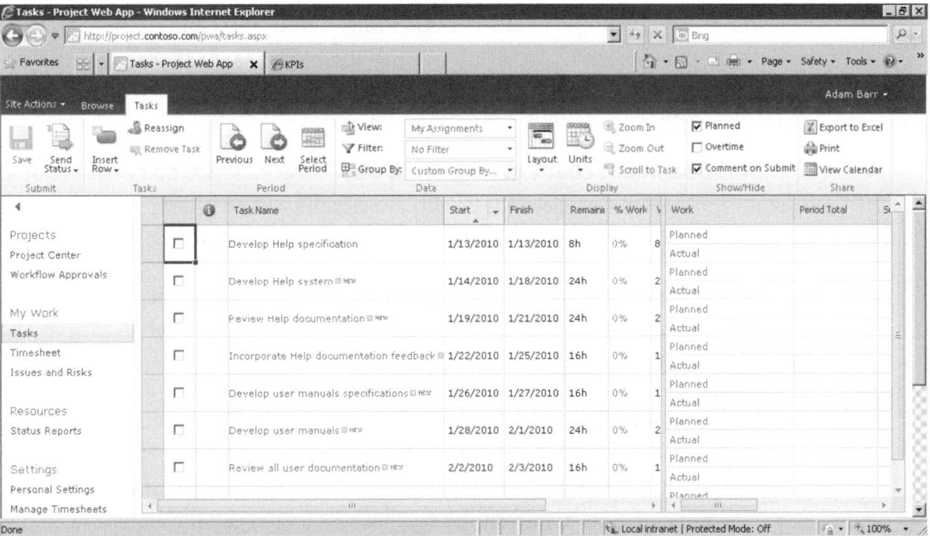

Figure 22-14 Team members use the Assignment Details page to review specifics about assigned tasks.

Using Project Web App, team members can:

- Accept (or reject) task assignments.
- Create and self-assign new tasks for addition to the project plan.
- Add comments to assignments that become part of the project task record.
- Update task information so that it is reflected in the project plan.

- Enter daily or weekly actuals, specify percentage complete for a task, or indicate the amount of completed and remaining work to report progress on assignments, and then submit this information to the project manager for incorporation into the project plan.
- Review assignments in different views, with applied filters, groupings, and sorting.
- Review the entire project plan to see the context of individual assignments.

Information updated or changed by team members is stored in the project server databases.

The project manager can accept or reject changes. If the project manager accepts an update, it can be incorporated immediately into the project plan. The project server databases are then updated to show that the change has been accepted, and team members who review the project plan through Project Web App can see the updates.

Because Project Web App is built on SharePoint, the following functions are included in the Project Web App experience:

- **Document check in and check out** You can include project-related documents and even associate them with individual tasks or phases. You can implement version control through document check-in and check-out processes.
- **Issues tracking** You can record issues associated with a task or phase. You can then track the issues, assign responsibility, and close them when they're resolved. The issue becomes a part of the task history.
- **Risk tracking** You can record potential risks associated with a task or phase, along with mitigation plans should the risk become a reality. You can assign responsibility and track the risk and then close the risk record when appropriate. The risk information becomes a part of the task history, which can be especially helpful when planning another similar project.

Standardizing Enterprise Projects

A key element of effective management and control systems is standardization. One purpose of standardization is to ensure that one project is operating with the same ground rules as any other project of the same type. Another purpose is consistency throughout the organization.

A standardized project life cycle can also ensure better governance of projects throughout the organization.

If all projects follow the same structure and life cycle, they can be read and modified in a way that is easy to understand by the entire organization.

The portfolio manager is responsible for establishing these standards and working with the project server administrator to implement the standards.

You can standardize and customize the use of Project 2010 for the way your enterprise does business, as follows:

- Tailored fields, reports, calendars, views, VBA modules, and other Project 2010 elements are applied to all projects through the use of the enterprise global template. Individual project templates are also available.
- Your project server administrator can use enterprise custom fields and create formulas, outlines, and pick lists for skill codes or titles.
- Custom pages can be created that include standard project, task, or resources Web Parts as well as custom Web Parts.

In these ways, your project management efforts can be tailored to the specific processes of your organization.

Managing Enterprise Resources

The lack of a skilled worker for a job can cause serious delays or loss of business. Likewise, having underutilized resources can be an unnecessary drain on the organization's treasury and can severely reduce profits.

As organizations become more and more distributed across the globe, having a centralized resource pool that includes all relevant information on resources is vital.

You can use the Microsoft enterprise project management solution to view and understand resource allocation, utilization, and availability throughout the enterprise. Although it is not a human resources tool, Project 2010 features help project managers, resource managers, portfolio managers, and functional managers maximize their resource usage while they keep an eye on overallocations.

Because people are not the only type of resource that needs to be managed within a project, Project 2010 also supports nonhuman work resources, such as machinery and other fixed assets, and material resources, such as consumable supplies and components.

You can use Project 2010 features to connect to other resource management systems to get up-to-date information on resources. You can also use Active Directory to help create the enterprise resource pool.

With Project 2010 enterprise project management, you can obtain up-to-date information about the availability and utilization of thousands of resources in an enterprise as follows:

- Project managers and resource managers can define resource requirements early in the project, either in the resource plan or in the Project Web App schedule.
- Depending on the available resources, the new capacity planning module can be used to reschedule projects in order to maximize resource allocations.
- Managers can search for the right skills and location by using Resource Center and Team Builder functionality.
- Once project managers have identified the appropriate resources, they can use the Resource Assignment or Availability views to understand when resources are able to work on their projects.
- Resource availability graphs enable project managers to quickly identify when and why resources might be underallocated or overallocated.
- With workgroup collaboration features, project managers and team members can automate their communications with each other and get the assignments and actual skills they need.

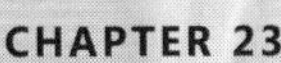

CHAPTER 23

Administering Your Enterprise Project Management Solution

MICROSOFT Project Server 2010 is a complex application to deploy and manage. We recommend having a trained IT professional who is dedicated to planning the deployment or upgrade of your installation of Project Server 2010 and in charge of ongoing operations. This project server administrator is the expert who can provide the proper assessment of your organization's needs in terms of the number of projects and project types, security needs for Project Server and Microsoft SharePoint Server, and business intelligence and reporting. Your project server administrator can ensure that performance or configuration issues are kept to a minimum.

This chapter is designed especially for the project server administrator. Project server administration responsibilities include but are not limited to:

- Planning for the Project Server deployment.
- One-time configuration after Project Server installation.
- Managing security by setting up users and permissions.
- Establishing the enterprise resource pool and associated resource information.
- Standardizing project elements included in the enterprise global template.
- Customizing views and pages for the requirements of the enterprise or a particular project.
- Customizing workflows for projects.
- Customizing the time periods and time reporting.
- Customizing reports.

Although this chapter is targeted to project server administrators, project managers and portfolio managers might find this chapter helpful for understanding available enterprise project management capabilities and configuration.

For an overview of enterprise project management concepts, see Chapter 22, "Understanding Enterprise Project Management."

Project Server 2010 Installation Guidelines

This chapter covers setup and administrative procedures performed by the project server administrator after the server equipment and software are in place, including the operating system, database, and client applications. This chapter does not cover planning for Project Server installation.

You can find issues and guidelines regarding Project Server installation, including system software and hardware requirements, in Appendix A, "Installing Microsoft Project 2010."

For details on Project Server architecture, deployment planning, performance, security, and upgrading to Project Server 2010, go to *technet.microsoft.com/en-us/library/cc197605.aspx*.

After you develop the deployment plan and install Project Server, you'll need to configure business intelligence and reporting services such as Excel Services, PerformancePoint Services, and Secure Store Services. You also need to configure time-reporting periods and integration with other systems, such as a Microsoft Exchange server.

For a comprehensive description of post-installation configuration of Project Server, see the Microsoft TechNet article at *technet.microsoft.com/en-us/library/gg263353.aspx*.

Signing In and Out

To sign in to Microsoft Project Web App, follow these steps:

1. Open your web browser. In the Address bar, enter the URL for the location of your project server.
2. On the sign-in page, enter the user ID and password that were set up for you as the project server administrator.

   The Home page of Project Web App appears.

INSIDE OUT **Claims-based authentication**

Claims-based authentication **is a new authentication method available in Project Server 2010 through Microsoft SharePoint Server 2010 and Microsoft SharePoint Foundation 2010. Claims-based authentication uses federated authentication services like** ***single sign-on*** **or Active Directory authentication. In essence, a security token composed of several user attributes is assigned to a user for the purposes of authentication. This method of authentication is more flexible.**

Note

If single sign-on (SSO) is enabled in your environment, the system does not prompt you for a user name and password. Once you enter the Project Web App URL in the address bar, you are automatically signed in.

To sign out from Project Web App, follow these steps:

1. In the upper-right corner of the Project Web App window, click your user name.
2. In the drop-down list that appears, click Sign Out.

Configuring Project Server Security

As the project server administrator, you configure enterprise project management options on the Server Settings page in Project Web App. Links to all pages are listed on the *Quick Launch* located in left pane of the Project Web App window. On the Quick Launch, under Settings, click Server Settings. The Server Settings page appears, as shown in Figure 23-1. Only users with administrative permissions can open the Server Settings page.

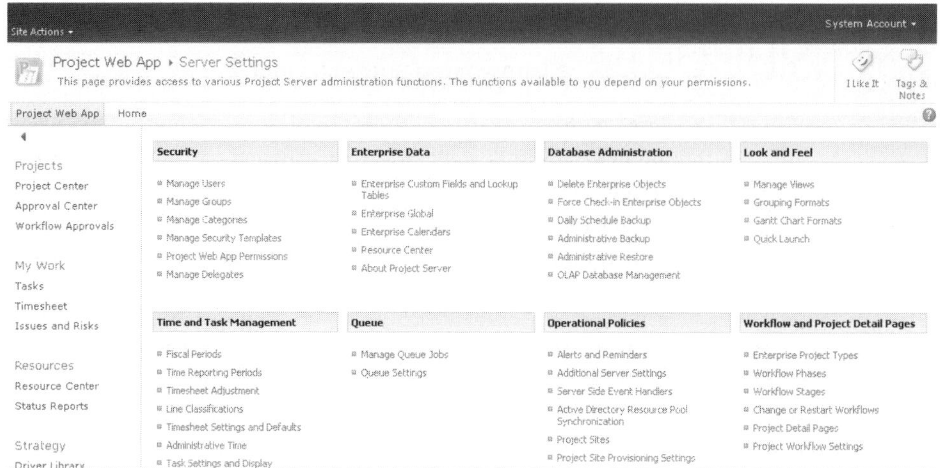

Figure 23-1 Set up enterprise project management options on the Server Settings page in Project Web App.

Carry Out Administrative Duties

The Server Settings page in Project Web App contains all the tools and commands you need to administer enterprise project management features for your organization, as follows:

- **Security**
- **Enterprise data**
- **Database administration**
- **Look and feel**
- **Time and task management**
- **Queues**
- **Operational policies**
- **Workflow and project detail pages**

To allow people throughout the organization to use the Microsoft Project 2010 enterprise project management features they need, you first need to identify them as users of your project server. At the same time, you also specify user permissions that enable each user to carry out his or her responsibilities according to the user's role.

Help

Note

If you ever need assistance while using Project Web App, click Help in the upper-right corner of the Project Web App page. Project Web App Help appears in a separate window.

Understanding Groups, Categories, and Permissions

Project Server security is based on users, groups, and categories. *Groups* contain a set of users who have the same permissions—they need to access the same data in the same way (for example, all project managers, all portfolio managers, all executives in your organization). *Categories* provide access to different items, such as projects and resources, based on defined parameters.

The security model for Project Server is inherited from SharePoint Server. This allows you, as project server administrator, to manage user and group access to objects such as projects, tasks, resources, the strategy section, reporting, and so on. You can manage security efficiently by employing *user groups*, to which you can assign the same security level.

Project Server comes with a robust set of built-in user groups and categories, each of which is associated with a set of permissions related to various aspects of enterprise project management.

You can look at *permissions* as having authority to perform a specific action in Project Server—for example, to add a project or add a task.

There are two types of permissions:

- **Global permissions** These permissions give users and groups the ability to perform actions in Project Web App. Global permissions are assigned on a user or group basis.

  For a full list of user permissions, see *technet.microsoft.com/en-us/library/cc197631.aspx*.

- **Category permissions** These permissions allow users or groups to perform actions at a category level. Category permissions are groupings of global permissions (for example, task permissions, resource permissions, and so on).

The default groups in Project Server are typically sufficient for managing security permissions for the different roles in your organization. It is recommended that you do not change the default security settings. If you need to configure special security exceptions, you can create new security objects.

The built-in user groups, also known as *roles,* are as follows:

- **Administrators** Users who have all global permissions as well as category permissions.
- **Executives** Users who have access to view project and Project Server data. These users need to be able to access project and portfolio information.
- **Portfolio Managers** Users who can create projects and teams. They can also perform portfolio analysis in the Strategy section.
- **Project Managers** Users who have project-related permissions and certain resource permissions. These users maintain project information such as schedule, costs, and so on, and they can receive progress updates.
- **Resource Managers** Members of this group have resource-related global and category-level permissions. They can manage and assign resources.
- **Team Leads** Users who have limited access for task creation and status reports.
- **Team Members** Users who can update task progress and suggest task changes. Typically all Project Web App users have this basic but limited permission set.

Each of the user groups can be associated with a security template that includes the set of permissions most likely to be needed by everyone in that group.

In addition to setting the permissions for a new user, you also set the categories of information that can be associated with a user group, to which users are then assigned.

Although you can create your own categories, the built-in categories are:

- **My Direct Reports** Gives users permission to approve timesheets and status updates.
- **My Organization** Contains all project-level and resource-level permissions. This category is intended to give users visibility into all data and tools available in Project Web App.
- **My Projects** Allows users access to project-related data.
- **My Resources** Allows resource-level permissions, filtered on users.
- **My Tasks** Allows users to see projects to which they are assigned. This category is associated with the Team Members group.

It is not recommended that you change the built-in categories. Instead, add new categories that you can configure and use.

To further understand the differences between groups and categories, think of groups as collections of users and think of categories as collections of data. User groups can be granted access to categories. For example, you can grant the Project Managers group access to My Projects.

For more information, see the full list of default group and category associations at *technet.microsoft.com/en-us/library/cc197658.aspx*.

Creating a User Account

To create a user account in Project Web App and set the user's permissions, follow these steps:

1. On the Quick Launch, under Settings, click Server Settings.
2. Under Security, click Manage Users.

   The Manage Users page appears, as shown in Figure 23-2.

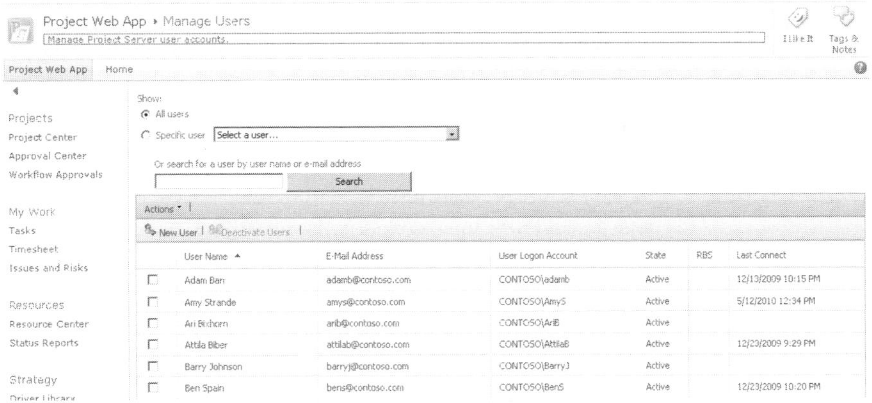

Figure 23-2 Open the Manage Users page to add a new user account.

New User

3. In the toolbar above the table, click New User.

   The New User page appears, as shown in Figure 23-3.

Chapter 23

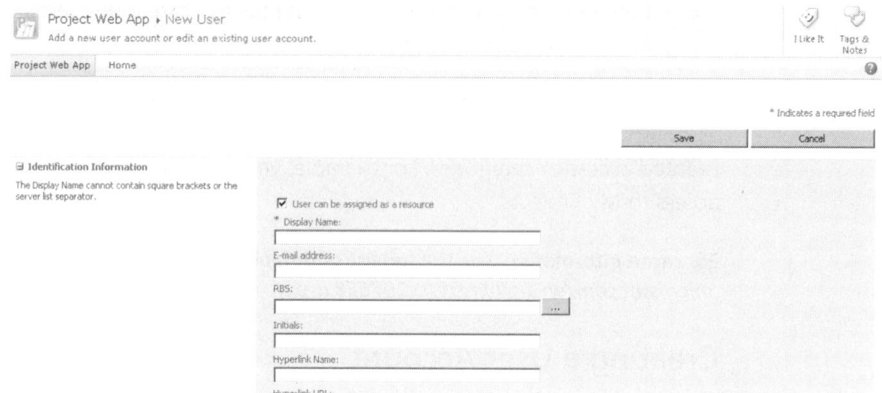

Figure 23-3 On the New User page, specify the new user's account name, group, permissions, and other information.

4. In the Identification Information section, be sure that the check box labeled User Can Be Assigned As A Resource is selected if the user is to be part of your enterprise resource pool.

5. Enter at least the user's display name, which is typically the person's first and last name. If you complete the E-mail Address box, type the address in the format of *someone@microsoft.com*.

6. Under User Authentication, enter the user ID. You can also select the option to not synchronize with Active Directory.

7. In the Assignment Attributes section, select or clear the Resource Can Be Leveled check box. Enter the calendar type, timesheet manager, assignment owner, availability and cost rates.

8. You can also select the option to synchronize the resource's tasks with Microsoft Exchange Server tasks. This allows users to update their tasks using Microsoft Outlook.

9. Select the department to which the resource belongs.

10. Select the security group, the user's role, security categories, and which menu options the user is able to see—for example, My Direct Reports, My Tasks, and so on.

11. Select the group fields. These fields apply if your organization groups resources for cost tracking. Type the codes in the group codes fields.

12. In the Team Assignments section, specify whether this person is part of a team. Type the name of the team or select it from the list. The project manager will be able to assign resources to the team as well.

13. In the System Identification section, specify an external ID. This information might be used to link the user account you are currently creating to information in the human resources department for reporting and data consolidation.

14. When you are done entering all the information, click Save at the bottom or top of the page.

After you set up user accounts, team members and other Project Web App users need only to use their web browser to go to the URL for your project server location. They enter their user name (and password, if necessary), and their own view of Project Web App appears.

The Differences Between Users and Resources

There is a difference between Project Server users and enterprise resources. Project Server users are any individuals who can sign in to Project Server and use Project Web App or Microsoft Project Professional 2010.

On the other hand, enterprise resources are people, equipment, and materials who can be assigned to project tasks.

You are likely to have certain Project Web App users such as executives, accountants, and other managing stakeholders who need access to project information but who are not themselves available to be assigned to a project team.

You might also have enterprise resources who are not users of Project Web App. In addition to the obvious cases of equipment and material resources, examples include team members who carry out project tasks but who do not have access to a computer to enter progress information in Project Web App.

By default, users are automatically identified as enterprise resources. You can control this on the New User page, by selecting or clearing the check box labeled User Can Be Assigned As A Resource.

Enterprise Resource Information

When you identify a Project Server user as an enterprise resource in the New User page, you can enter resource and assignment information, as follows:

- **Resource Can Be Leveled** Specify whether this resource's assignments can be split or delayed to resolve overallocations. By default, this check box is selected.
- **Base Calendar** Select the base calendar to be used to schedule this resource's working and nonworking times. By default, the Standard calendar is selected.
- **Default Booking Type** Specify whether this resource should show as a committed or proposed resource by default.
- **Timesheet Manager** Enter the name of the user responsible for receiving this resource's timesheets. You can click Browse to select the user's name from a list.
- **Default Assignment Owner** Enter the name of the user who is responsible for entering progress information for this resource's assignments. By default, the current resource is the assignment owner. You can click Browse to select another resource from a list.
- **Earliest Available** Enter the soonest date this resource is available to accept assignments. If you leave this box blank, Project 2010 assumes that this resource is currently available.
- **Latest Available** Enter the latest date that this resource is available to accept assignments. If you leave this box blank, Project 2010 assumes that this resource has open-ended availability.
- **Standard Rate and Overtime Rate** Enter the cost rates for this resource. These fields are used for cost calculation and analysis.
- **Resource Custom Fields** If any custom fields have been created for resources, they are listed here for you to enter the information applicable to the current resource.
- **Team Assignment Pool** If the current resource is a member of a team that can carry out tasks assigned to the team as a whole, select the Team Assignment Pool check box.
- **Team Name** If the Team Assignment Pool check box is selected, enter or click the name of the team to which the current resource belongs.

Project managers using enterprise project management features in Project Professional 2010 and Project Web App should refer to Chapter 24, "Managing Enterprise Projects and Resources." Team members and resource managers needing information about using Project Web App should refer to Chapter 25, "Participating on a Team Using Project Web App." Executives and other managing stakeholders using Project Web App should refer to Chapter 26, "Making Executive Decisions Using Project Web App."

Deactivating a User

You can deactivate a user—for example, one who has left the company after working on several projects. When you deactivate a user, the information about that user's assignments remain intact. When a user is deactivated, he or she can no longer send status updates, request status reports, and edit/delegate tasks.

When a user is deactivated, the project manager is prompted to reassign the user's work.

To deactivate a user, follow these steps:

1. On the Quick Launch, under Settings, click Server Settings.
2. On the Server Settings page, under Security, click Manage Users.
3. Select the check box next to the name of the user you want to deactivate.

   You can select several check boxes to deactivate multiple users at once.
4. In the toolbar above the table, click Deactivate Users.

   Deactivate Users

   In the alert that appears, click OK. The selected user is deactivated and can no longer sign in to the server.

If you need to reactivate a deactivated user, in the Manage Users page, click the user's name to open the Edit User page. In the Identification Information section in the Account Status box, click Active. Click the Save button.

Viewing or Changing Permissions for User Groups

You can review the sets of permissions assigned to a particular user group. You can also modify the set of permissions for a user group. To do this, follow these steps:

1. On the Quick Launch, under Settings, click Server Settings.

2. Under Security, click Manage Security Templates.

   Click the name of the template whose permissions you want to see—for example, Executives or Portfolio Manager. As discussed at the beginning of this chapter, each security group has an associated security template containing the group's permissions.

3. In the Add Or Edit Template page, scroll through the Category Permissions and the Global Permissions lists to see the permissions for the selected group.

   Make any changes by selecting or clearing the Allow or Deny check boxes next to permissions. By selecting the Allow check box, you grant the user group access to this functionality. By selecting the Deny check box, you restrict that user group from using that functionality.

4. When you are finished, click the Save button.

Creating a Security Template

A security template is a collection of permissions that can be associated with a user group or a category. By using a security template, you can standardize security across your organization.

Project Server comes with seven built-in security templates, one for each of the seven built-in user groups, from Team Member to Administrator. You can also set up your own security templates with entirely different sets of permissions. You can then assign the new set of permissions to users, groups, and categories in a single step.

To create a new security template, follow these steps:

1. On the Quick Launch, under Settings, click Server Settings.
2. Under Security, click Manage Security Templates.

New Template

3. In the toolbar above the table, click New Template.

   The Add Or Edit Template page appears.

4. In the Name section, type a name in the Template Name box. You can also type a description.
5. If you want to base your new security template on an existing template, click the name of the template in the Copy Template box.
6. In the Category Permissions section, select or clear the Allow or Deny check boxes next to the permissions listed.

7. In the Global Permissions section, select or clear the Allow or Deny check boxes next to the permissions listed.

8. When you have finished, click the Save button.

> **Note**
>
> **To delete a security template, on the Server Settings page, under Security, click Manage Security Templates. Select the check box next to the name of the security template you want to delete, and then in the toolbar above the table, click Delete Template.**

Creating a Group

Each group, or role, defined in Project Web App is identified by a set of permissions. You can specify which users belong to which group, the categories of information they have access to, and the permissions for what they can do with that information. If your organization uses different roles from those identified as groups in Project Web App (for example, Project Managers and Team Leaders), you can create your own. To do this, follow these steps:

1. On the Quick Launch, under Settings, click Server Settings.

2. Under Security, click Manage Groups.

   The Manage Groups page appears, as shown in Figure 23-4.

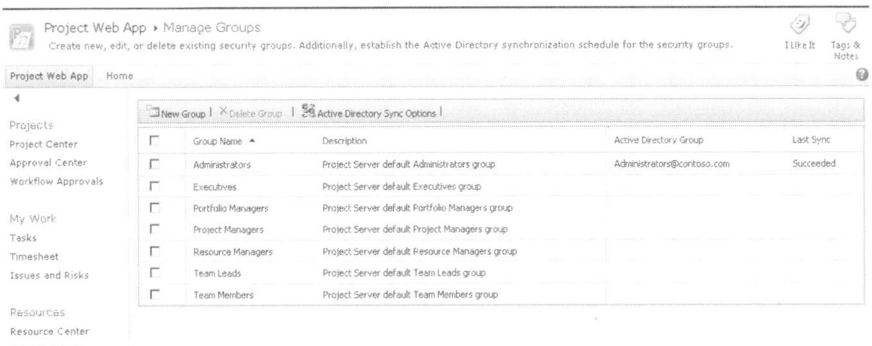

Figure 23-4 Use the Manage Groups page to review, modify, add, or delete groups (roles).

New Group

3. In the toolbar above the table, click New Group.

   The Add Or Edit Group page appears.

4. In the Group Information section, enter the group name and description in the first two boxes.

5. In the Users section, click the users you want to add to the group, and then click the Add button.

   You can also add users after you finish defining the group.

6. In the Categories section, click any categories (for example, My Tasks or My Resources) that members of this group should have access to, and then click the Add button.

7. In the Selected Categories box, select each category in turn. Then, in the Permissions box that appears, set the permissions for the selected category. Repeat this process for each category in the Selected Categories box.

   If you want to use a security template to set permissions for a category, scroll to the bottom of the page, click in the Set Permissions With Template box, and then select the template. Click Apply. Make any adjustments to the permissions as necessary for the selected category.

8. Click the plus sign next to the Global Permissions label to expand the list. Specify the global permissions that you want to apply to your new group.

   If you prefer to use a security template to set global permissions for a category, scroll to the bottom of the page, click in the Set Permissions With Template box, and then select the template. Click Apply. Make any necessary adjustments to the permissions for the selected category.

9. When you have finished defining the new group, click the Save button.

To edit an existing group, on the Server Settings page, under Security, click Manage Groups. In the table, click the name of the group you want to change. In the Add Or Edit Group page, you can edit the group by modifying which users are in the group, changing the categories associated with the group, or changing permissions for the group.

Delete Group

Note

To delete a group, on the Server Settings page, under Security, click Manage Groups. Select the check box next to the name of the group you want to delete, and then click Delete Group.

> **Permissions Shown Are Specific to the Group and Category**
>
> **When you select a category in the Selected Categories box on the Manage Groups page, remember that the set of permissions displayed are specific to the group/category combination and do not cover all the categories. Each category has its own set of permissions for this group. This concept is key to understanding Project Server security.**

Customizing Categories

Categories are clusters of information, such as My Tasks, My Projects, or My Resources. Some user groups should have access to all categories, whereas other groups need access to only two or three categories.

If the built-in categories don't quite fit the way your organization works with projects, you can customize them or create entirely new ones. To create a new category, follow these steps:

1. On the Quick Launch, under Settings, click Server Settings.
2. Under Security, click Manage Categories.

   The Manage Categories page appears.

New Category

3. In the toolbar above the table, click New Category to open the Add Or Edit Category page.
4. In the Name And Description section, enter a name and description for your new category.
5. In the Users And Groups section, select the users and groups you want to add to the category, and then click the Add button.
6. Select the first user or group in the Users And Groups With Permissions box.

   In the Permissions box that appears, specify the permissions for users in this category, and then repeat this process for each user and group you added to the category. To move from one user group to the next, simply select the name of the user group in the Users And Groups With Permissions box.
7. In the Projects section, specify which projects the users in this category should be able to access: all projects in your project server database or just selected projects. Select or clear the project-related check boxes to further define the category.

8. Click the plus sign next to Resources to expand the Resources section.

   Specify which resources the users in this category should be able to view: all current and future resources in your project server database or just selected resources. (See Figure 23-5.) Select or clear the resource-related check boxes to further define the category.

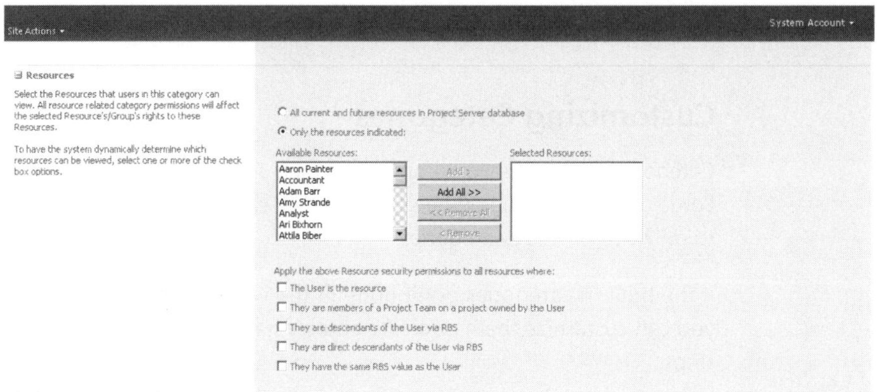

Figure 23-5 Specify the resources whose information can be accessed by users in this category.

9. In the Views - Add To Category section, select the check box for the views that the users in this category should be able to use.

   To select all views in a group of views, such as Project or Resource Center, select the check box next to that name, and all the views within that group are selected.

10. When you have finished, click the Save button.

    Your new category is added to the table in the Manage Categories page.

To modify an existing category, click the category name in the Manage Categories page—for example, My Direct Reports or My Tasks. Review the information on the Add Or Edit Category page, and make the changes you want. When you have finished, click the Save button.

Delete Categories

Note

To delete a category, on the Server Settings page, under Security, click Manage Categories. Select the check box next to the category you want to delete, and then in the toolbar above the table, click Delete Categories.

Administering the Enterprise Resource Pool

The enterprise resource pool is the set of people, equipment, and materials that can be assigned to carry out the work of projects throughout an organization. The organization can be as compact as a small department or as wide ranging as all employees in all regions of a worldwide corporation. The enterprise resource pool contains fundamental information about resources, such as skill sets and availability, which helps project managers find the right resources for their projects.

The enterprise resource pool also contains cost information, which not only helps project managers work within their allotted budgets, but also helps accounting and human resource departments figure costs from their points of view.

With the enterprise resource pool, high-level visibility of resource availabilities, skills, roles, and utilization is now possible. Project managers as well as upper management can see when additional staff is needed and where there are underutilized resources. They also can view the basic data for all project resources in one place.

Furthermore, project managers can plan for project staffing needs with accurate and current resource information from the entire enterprise instead of from just their own team or group. The advantages of the multiple project resource pool, such as resource sharing between project managers, are magnified when applied to the entire enterprise.

Resource managers can use the enterprise resource pool to staff, plan, and budget with more accuracy and confidence. They can see resources by skill level and definition, availability, and organizational hierarchy (Resource Breakdown Structure). In addition, they can assist project managers with current and anticipated resource requirements by analyzing the enterprise resource database. Together with project managers, resource managers can work with generic resources in the enterprise resource pool as well as with roles and departments to perform planning and contingency analyses.

The project server administrator is often the one who sets up and maintains the enterprise resource pool. However, because of the specialized information related to resource skills, costs, and availability, specialists such as a portfolio manager, resource manager, or human resources representative might also be involved in the setup. By default, the project server administrator, portfolio manager, and resource managers are given the permission to add and edit enterprise resource data.

A user with the permission to edit enterprise resource data can do the following:

- Create and add users to the enterprise resource pool.
- Update information on resources in the enterprise resource pool.

- Customize resource fields for use in the enterprise resource pool.
- Specify multiple properties for resources in the enterprise resource pool.

For more information about working with a resource pool, see "Sharing Resources by Using a Resource Pool" on page 614.

Creating the Enterprise Resource Pool

After you create the enterprise resource pool, project managers can access it and build project teams from it. If you want to, you can add the bulk of your resources at one time. You can, however, always add individual resources as time goes on. Project managers who have been working with their own resources can also import those local resources into the enterprise resource pool. You can add a team resource such as Accounting or Research. You can also associate resources to roles so that the project manager can plan for a role instead of a specific resource, and you can add generic resources. Any individual enterprise resource that's a member of that team can do the work on tasks assigned to the team resource.

Adding Multiple Enterprise Resources

If you want to add several resources at one time to your enterprise resource pool, along with information about each resource, you can use the Project 2010 Resource Sheet. Be sure that your user profile allows the Edit Enterprise Resource Data permission in your project server. If you are the project server administrator or portfolio manager, you have this permission by default.

To add multiple enterprise resources, follow these steps:

1. On the Quick Launch, under Resources, click Resource Center.

   Here you can see the list of all the enterprise resources.

Open

2. On the Resources tab, in the Editing group, click Open.

   Project Professional opens.

3. In Project Professional, display the Resource Sheet by clicking View, Resource Views, Resource Sheet.

   The Resource Sheet appears, labeled as Checked-Out Enterprise Resources window, as shown in Figure 23-6. If you did not select any resources in the Resource Center, the sheet is empty.

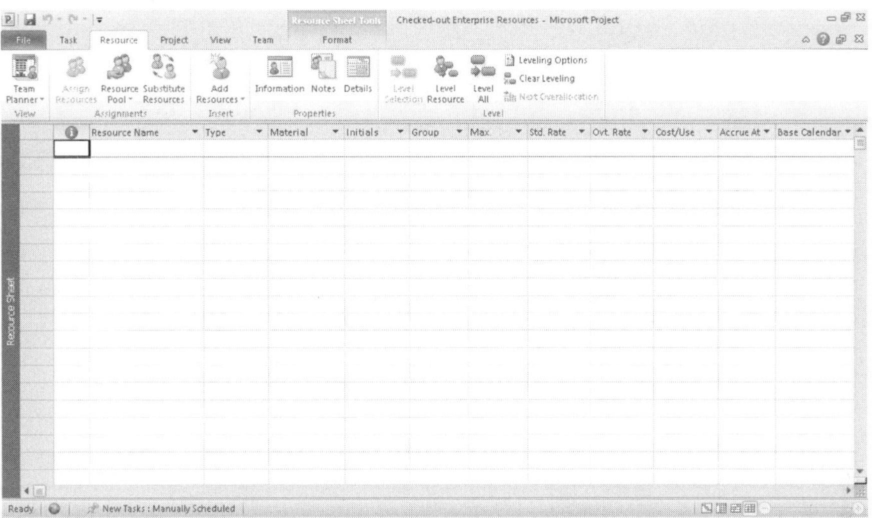

Figure 23-6 The Checked-Out Enterprise Resources window shows the enterprise resource pool in the Resource Center.

> ## Note
>
> **When you are adding a new resource to an existing enterprise resource pool, it might seem odd to see a blank Resource Sheet.**
>
> **In reality, however, you never really check out the entire resource pool unless you select all resources and then click the Open button. Typically, you come here to add several new resources or edit information for a select group of resources, while the rest of the resources are still safely checked in.**

4. In the Resource Sheet, enter the names and information for the new enterprise resources you want to add.

   You can enter the resource type, group, maximum units, cost rates, and base calendar. (See Figure 23-7.)

   Information

   If you want to add more complete resource information, on the Resource tab, in the Properties group, click Information. On the various tabs of the Resource Information dialog box, enter information as appropriate to this resource. When you have finished, click OK.

   For more information about the different types of resource information that can be added to the Resource Sheet and Resource Information dialog box, see Chapter 7, "Setting Up Resources in the Project."

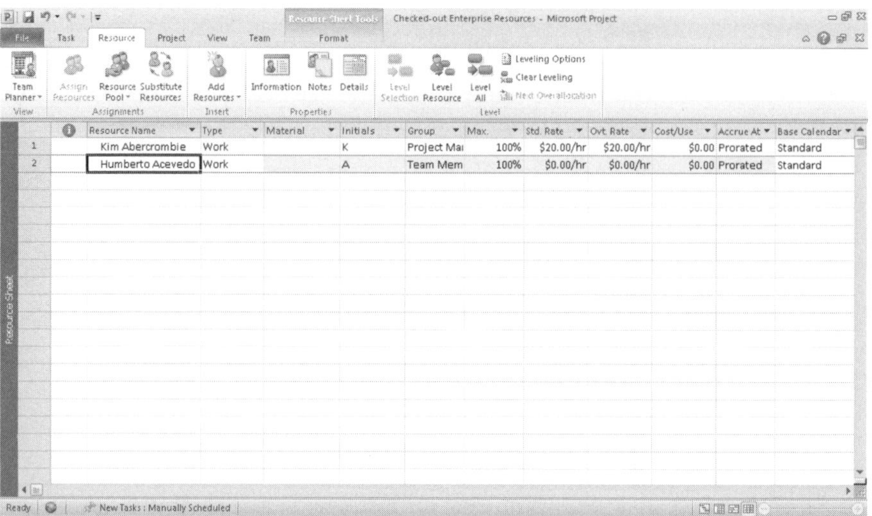

Figure 23-7 Enter resource names and associated information in the Checked-Out Enterprise Resources window.

Save

5. To save changes, on the File tab, click Save.

6. When you are finished adding resources and want to check in the enterprise resource pool and its new information, click File, Close.

7. If a prompt asks whether you want to save your changes, click Yes. When you return to Project Web App and click Resource Center, you'll see that the new resources have been added to the enterprise resource pool.

Note

Just as you can open Project Professional from Project Web App, you can open Project Web App from Project Professional. Make sure Project Professional is connected to your project server. On the Resource tab, in the Assignments group, click Resource Pool, and then click Enterprise Resource Pool. A new browser opens to the Resource Center in Project Web App.

TROUBLESHOOTING

Your new resources are not added as Project Server users

Although it might be convenient to quickly enter resources in the Resource Sheet of Project Professional, the drawback is that resources entered in this manner are not added as Project Server users. To add these resources as Project Server users, follow these steps:

1. In the Resource Center, select the check boxes next to the names of the resources you want to add as users.
2. On the Resource tab, in the Editing group, click Edit Resource.

   The Edit Resource page appears for the first resource.
3. In the Identification Information section, select the check box labeled Resource Can Logon To Project Server.
4. Complete the User Authentication, Security Groups, Security Categories, and Global Permissions sections for this resource.
5. When you have finished editing the information for the first user, click the Save And Continue button.

   The second selected resource appears. Repeat steps 3 through 5 for that resource and all succeeding resources.

Adding Resources by Synchronizing with Active Directory

If your organization uses Active Directory, you have at your fingertips the easiest method for generating your enterprise resource pool. You can synchronize Active Directory security groups with those in your project server. In this way, resources from a specific Active Directory group are instantly mapped to the enterprise resource pool. Not only does this add the resources to your server, but the periodic synchronization helps keep your list of users and resources up to date. If the resource exists in Active Directory, the resource is automatically added to the enterprise resource pool upon the next scheduled Active Directory update to your project server.

Resources that no longer exist in Active Directory are likewise removed from the project server. This is a one-way synchronization, from Active Directory to your project server.

The Active Directory synchronization options are set as part of your project server configuration. These options can be set during initial configuration, or they can be set anytime afterward. To synchronize project server with Active Directory, follow these steps:

1. On the Quick Launch, under Settings, click Server Settings.

2. Under Operational Policies, click Active Directory Resource Pool Synchronization.

   The Active Directory Enterprise Resource Pool Synchronization page appears. (See Figure 23-8.)

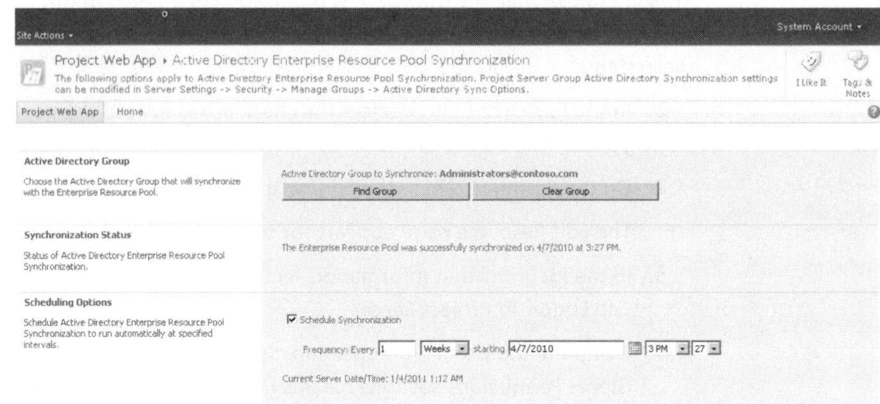

Figure 23-8 Set scheduling and resource options to synchronize an Active Directory group with your enterprise resource pool.

3. In the Active Directory Group section, click the Find Group button, and then select the Active Directory group you want to synchronize with your enterprise resource pool. You can search for the group by entering all or part of the group name.

4. In the Scheduling Options section, select the Schedule Synchronization check box, and then specify the frequency at which your project server should be synchronized with Active Directory—for example, every week or every 2 months. Specify the date when updates should begin and the time of day when updates should occur.

5. When you have finished, click Save And Synchronize Now or click Save.

Note

Your organization might have information about your enterprise resource pool in another system—for example, your human resources or general ledger system. The Project Server Interface (PSI) can be used to develop an application programming interface (API) that interacts with that system to help you create your enterprise resource pool.

Adding an Individual Enterprise Resource

To add an individual resource to the enterprise resource pool, follow these steps:

1. On the Quick Launch, under Resources, click Resource Center.
2. On the Resources tab, in the Editing group, click New Resource.
3. In the New Resource page, complete all the sections as they apply to the resource you're creating.
4. If this resource should also be a user of your project server, be sure to select the check box labeled Resource Can Logon To Project Server.
5. When you have finished, click Save.

   The new resource is saved as a new member of the enterprise resource pool.

Add Enterprise Resources as Project Web App Users

When you add work resources from within Project Web App, you have the choice of making them Project Server users at the same time. On the New Resource page, in the Identification Information section, be sure that the Resource Can Logon To Project Server check box is selected. When this check box is selected, you can enter logon and permissions information, as follows:

- **User Authentication** **Enter the user's logon account name.**
- **Security Groups** **Select and add the user group(s) of which this user should be a member.**
- **Global Permissions** **In the Set Permissions With Template box, select the template that represents this user's role, and then click Apply. In the Global Permissions list, select or clear individual check boxes to tailor the permissions for this user.**

Adding a Team Resource

Suppose your organization has several resources in the product testing department who are all capable of carrying out the same tasks. The project manager could assign Chris to do one task, Sam to do another, and Maria to do a third. But it might be easier to assign all three tasks to a resource named Product Testing Team, and let Chris, Sam, and Maria decide among themselves who should do what.

You can create a resource that represents a group of resources—that is, a team. A project manager can then assign tasks to the team. Resources that are identified as part of that team can assign themselves to a team task, report on it, and complete it.

To create a team resource in Project Web App, follow these steps:

1. On the Quick Launch, under Resources, click Resource Center.
2. On the Resources tab, in the Editing Group, click New Resource.
3. In the Type section, be sure that the Generic check box is cleared.
4. In the Identification Information section, clear the check box labeled Resource Can Logon To Project Server.
5. In the Display Name box, enter the name of the team resource—for example, Drafters or Writers.
6. In the Assignment Attributes section, specify the options for leveling, base calendar, default booking type, and availability dates for the collective resources that will make up this team. Enter a resource in the Timesheet Manager and Default Assignment Owner boxes.
7. Complete the fields in the Resource Custom Fields and Group Fields sections as applicable to this team resource.
8. In the Team Details section, select the Team Assignment Pool check box.
   This identifies this resource as a team resource.
9. When you have finished, click Save.

   The team resource is created as part of your enterprise resource pool in your project server, and project managers can now assign tasks to this team resource.

Note

You can also create team resources in Project Professional. Add the Team Assignment Pool field to the Resource Sheet and change the field to Yes to mark your team resources.

To create the list of teams in your enterprise, you can use a built-in custom field named Team Name. You create and associate a lookup table with the Team Name field. The lookup table of teams becomes available in the Team Name drop-down list in the Edit Users and Edit Resources pages in Project Web App.

To create your list of teams for the Team Name field, follow these steps:

1. On the Quick Launch, under Settings, click Server Settings.
2. On the Server Settings page, under Enterprise Data, click Enterprise Custom Fields and Lookup Tables.
3. Scroll down below the Enterprise Custom Fields table to get to the Lookup Tables For Custom Fields table.
4. In the toolbar above the table, click New Lookup Table.
5. In the Name field, enter a name for your team lookup table—for example, Team Pools.
6. Scroll down to the Lookup Table section.
7. To define a new team, click in an available row, and then type the name of the team. (See Figure 23-9.)
8. To insert a team name between two others, click the team name below which you want to insert a new team, and then click the Insert Row button. Type the name of the team.

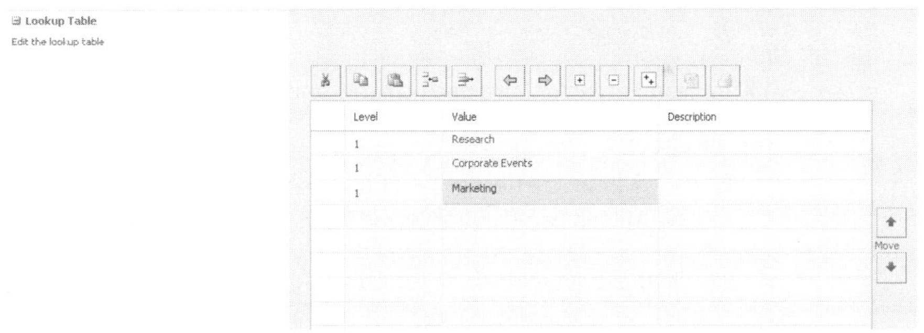

Figure 23-9 Define your teams on the New Lookup Table page, and then associate that lookup table with the Team Name built-in custom field.

9. To edit an existing team name, drag across a team name, and then type to make the change you want.

Outdent

Indent

10. Use the Outdent and Indent buttons to specify the team position in the hierarchy, if applicable.
11. Use the Move buttons to change the sequence of the team names as necessary.

12. To delete a team name, click in its row, and then click Delete Row.

13. Click Save.

To associate the Team Name enterprise custom field with your team lookup table, follow these steps:

1. On the Enterprise Custom Fields And Lookup Tables page, in the Enterprise Custom Fields table, scroll down and click Team Name.

   Team Name is the built-in custom field designed for the team resource function.

   The Edit Custom Field: Team Name page appears.

2. In the Custom Attributes section, in the Lookup Table box, select the name of your team definition lookup table.

   > **Note**
   >
   > **Once you associate the team lookup table with the Team Name field, this association becomes permanent. However, you can always change the content of the lookup table.**

3. Click Save.

After team resources have been created and identified as such, you need to identify the resources that belong to each team. To do this, follow these steps:

1. In the Resource Center, select the check boxes next to the names of the resources that should be identified as members of a particular team.

2. On the Resources tab, in the Editing group, click Edit Resource.

3. In the Edit Resource page for the first selected resource, scroll down to the Team Details section. In the Team Name box, select the name of the team to which this resource belongs.

4. Click the Save And Continue button. The second selected resource appears.

5. Repeat steps 3 and 4 for that resource. Continue in this manner until all appropriate resources have been associated with their team resource.

Resources who want to assign themselves to a team task can follow these steps:

1. On the Quick Launch, click My Work.
2. Select the team task to which you want to assign yourself.
3. On the Tasks tab, in the Tasks group, click Insert Row, and then click Add Yourself To A Task.
4. Select the project, the phase, and the task. Modify the start and end date if needed.
5. On the Tasks tab, in the Submit group, click Send Status, and then click Selected Tasks.

   The request to assign yourself to a team task is sent to the manager.

For more information about how team members work with tasks and assignments, see "Working With Your Assignments" on page 973.

What's the Difference Between a Generic Resource and a Team Resource?

A generic resource is a placeholder for work or cost resources that will be added to a project at a later date, typically after the project has been approved and can be staffed up. A generic resource provides a means for estimating resource requirements and costs. Generic resources typically have job title names such as Engineer, Trainer, Architect, or Graphic Designer.

A team resource represents a group of people, each of whom are capable of carrying out tasks to which the team resource is assigned. Use of the team resource provides the project manager or resource manager with more flexibility in making assignments. Use of the team resource method also provides members of the team with the freedom to choose which assignments they take on. Team resources typically have team or department names, such as Quality Assurance Team, Maintenance Crew, or Sales and Marketing.

Importing Existing Local Resources to the Project Server

A number of resources, complete with reliable availability and cost information, might already exist in enterprise and nonenterprise projects. You can easily open those projects and import the resources into the enterprise resource pool by using the Import Resource Wizard.

Local resources are flagged with the Local Resource icon in the Indicators field of the Resource Sheet.

Follow these steps to import local (nonenterprise) resources from an existing project to the enterprise resource pool:

1. Be sure you're signed in to the project server through Project Professional. It doesn't matter whether the project containing the local resources is open.

2. On the Resource tab, in the Insert group, click Add Resources, and then click Import Resources To Enterprise.

3. If the resources you want to import are in an enterprise project, click the name of that project, and then click Open.

   If the resources are in a local project stored on your computer or network, find its general location in the Look In task pane. Browse to the file, and then double-click the file to open it.

   The Import Resources Wizard appears. (See Figure 23-10.)

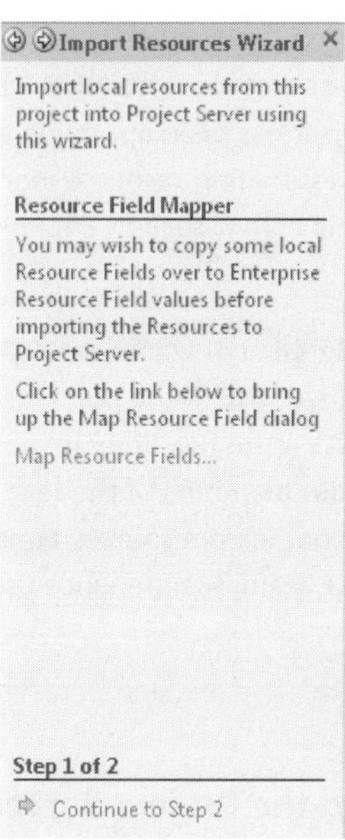

Figure 23-10 The Import Resources Wizard helps you import local resources to your project server.

4. If any custom resource fields in this project also need to be imported with the resources, click the Map Resource Fields link.

Map any custom resource fields from the original project to the enterprise resource pool. (See Figure 23-11.) This step ensures that all the necessary information associated with the resource is imported to the enterprise resource pool. When you have finished, click OK.

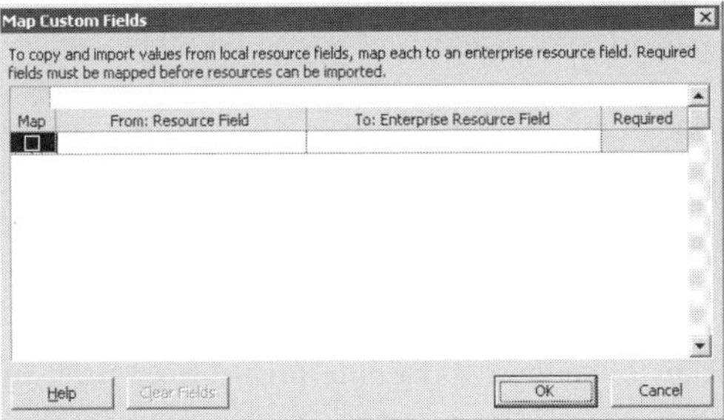

Figure 23-11 Map any custom resource fields to the enterprise resource pool.

5. Click the Continue To Step 2 link to open the Confirm Resources task pane.

   This task pane lists the number of local resources to be imported and the number of import errors that are anticipated. The nature of any errors is listed in the Errors column next to the resource name in the Import Resource sheet.

6. If there are any resources you do not want to import, click No in the Import field for that resource.

7. To resolve any errors, double-click the resource name to make the necessary changes in the Resource Information dialog box.

8. To check for errors again, click the Validate Resources button in the task pane.

9. When all errors are resolved, click the Save And Finish link.

   The resources and their associated calendar, cost, and other information are imported to the project server to become part of your enterprise resource pool.

Import Projects and Resources at Once Using the Import Projects Wizard

If you want to import resources from a nonenterprise project that you need to import to the Project Server as an enterprise project, you can do both at the same time. The primary job of the Import Projects Wizard is to import tasks from an existing project into a new enterprise project. If you want to, you can specify that the resources in that project also be added to the enterprise resource pool and assigned to the newly created enterprise project.

Updating Resource Information

After resources are added to the enterprise resource pool, you can edit their resource information by making the necessary changes in the Edit Resource page in Project Web App.

You can also edit resource information in the Project Professional Resource Sheet by checking the resources out, making the necessary changes, and then checking them in again.

Any resource information—such as base calendar, group name, and resource custom fields—can be edited this way.

> **Note**
>
> **Assignment information is changed in the enterprise project itself, not in the enterprise resource pool.**

Resource information cannot be changed casually by project managers. Only those users granted the Edit Enterprise Resource Data permission can check out and edit resource information. By default, the project server administrator, portfolio manager, and resource managers are the only ones granted this permission.

Finding and Selecting Resources

When working with an enterprise resource pool that supports even a handful of projects, you might soon find that your enterprise resource pool is quickly filled with dozens if not hundreds of resources. Because of this, it's important to be able to deftly find and select the resources you need in the Resource Center without too much scanning and scrolling.

The Resource Center contains controls for helping you look at resources the way you need to and therefore find the resources you want to modify, as follows:

- **Select a view** On the Resources tab, in the Data group, click in the View box to see a list of available resource views. For information about creating additional views, see "Creating and Managing Views" on page 887.

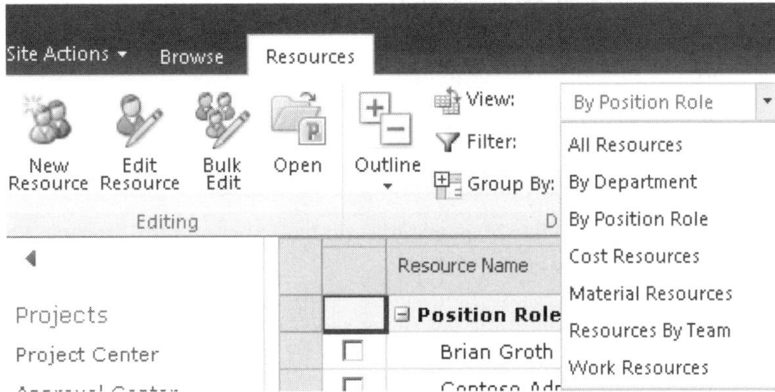

- **Filter for resources** On the Resources tab, in the Data group, click in the Filter box to show available resource filters. Using Custom Filter, you can create a custom filter and add it to the Filter box.
- **Group resources** On the Resources tab, in the Data group, click in the Group By box to see available groupings. You can group resources by fields such as resource type, cost center, timesheet manager, and more. You can also create your own custom groupings.

To select all resources in the view, move your mouse pointer over the first column heading (above the check boxes). Click the arrow that appears in the heading, and then click Select All. To clear all selected resources, click Clear All.

These controls are fairly standard throughout Project Web App, and they apply to project views and task views as well.

Modifying Enterprise Resource Information

To modify enterprise resource information in Project Web App, follow these steps:

1. In the Resource Center, select the check boxes next to the resources whose information you want to change.

Bulk Edit

2. If you're changing the department or the content of custom fields, on the Resources tab, in the Editing group, click Bulk Edit.
3. Make the changes on the Bulk Edit page, and then click Save.

   You only need to make the change once on this page, and the change is applied to all selected resources.

Edit Resource

4. For any other changes, on the Resources tab, in the Editing group, click Edit Resource.
5. In the Edit Resource page for the first resource, make your changes.
6. Click the Save And Continue button.
7. Repeat steps 5 and 6 for the second resource.

   Continue in this manner until you have changed the resource information for all selected resources.
8. When you finish the last resource, click the Save button.

If you prefer, or if it's easier given the accessibility of certain resource information fields, you can change resource information in Project Professional. To do this, follow these steps:

1. In Project Web App, select the check boxes next to the resources whose information you want to change.

Open

2. On the Resource tab, in the Editing group, click Open.

   Project Professional opens.
3. On the View tab, in the Resource Views group, click Resource Sheet.
4. Make the changes you want to the enterprise resources.
5. If you need to work with additional resource information, double-click the resource name to open the Resource Information dialog box. Enter information on the various tabs as appropriate to this resource. When you have finished, click OK.
6. Whenever you want to save changes, on the File tab, click Save.
7. When you're finished modifying the resource information, and you want to check the enterprise resources back into your project server, on the File tab, click Close.
8. If a prompt asks whether you want to save your changes, click Yes.

If an enterprise resource is checked out by another user and you need to check this resource back into the enterprise resource pool (usually because of some extenuating circumstance), you can force a resource check-in as follows:

1. On the Quick Launch, under Settings, click Server Settings.
2. Under Database Administration, click Force Check-In Enterprise Objects.

3. In the box labeled Select The Type Of Object You Want To Force Check-In, click Enterprise Resources. All resources that are currently checked out are listed in the table.

4. Select the check boxes for the resources you want to check in, and then click Check-In.

Removing a Resource from the Enterprise Resource Pool

Although you can delete a Project Server user, it's best to deactivate resources instead, as even obsolete resources are probably associated with assignments and actuals that are best retained for your archival project data. You can deactivate a resource by using the Edit Resources page in Project Web App or by checking out the enterprise resource in Project Professional.

To deactivate a resource with Project Web App, follow these steps:

1. In the Project Web App Resource Center, select the check box next to the name of the resource(s) you want to deactivate.

2. On the Resources tab, in the Editing group, click Edit Resource.

   The Edit Resource page appears.

3. In the Identification Information section, in the Account Status box, click Inactive.

4. Click Save. If you selected multiple resources, click Save And Continue.

The selected resource is deactivated. The deactivated user cannot sign in to your project server, and other users cannot send updates, tasks, or requests to the deactivated user. By default, the resource is still listed in the resource table, but its active flag has been changed from Yes to No. If you want to, you can create a filter or an autofilter that does not show inactive resources in the Resource Center.

Note

If you really must, you can completely remove a resource—for example, to delete resources mistakenly added. To do this, on the Quick Launch, under Settings, click Server Settings. Under Database Administration, click Delete Enterprise Objects. In the first section, select the Resources And Users option. Select the check boxes for the resources you need to delete. Click Delete, and then click OK. If these resources own any projects, these projects will be assigned to your account.

Establishing the Enterprise Portfolio

The enterprise portfolio is the full set of projects that is stored on your project server. Individual project managers initially add their projects to the project server, and then they check their own projects out and in. Team members might participate on one, two, or more projects in the enterprise portfolio at one time, or transition from one to another over time. Executives, portfolio managers, and other managing stakeholders can review aspects of some or all projects in the portfolio.

Individual project managers are responsible for adding projects to the project server. They can create a new enterprise project entirely from scratch. They can also import a local project—that is, one they've been working on that's stored on their own computer or elsewhere on the network.

After a project is published to the project server, it is considered published to the enterprise. The new enterprise project becomes available to be viewed and checked out by users with the proper permissions.

Project managers needing more information about creating a new enterprise project can refer to "Creating a New Enterprise Project" on page 905.

If a published project is checked out by a project manager or other user, and you need to check it in (usually because of some extenuating circumstance), you can force a project check-in as follows:

1. In the Project Web App Quick Launch pane, under Settings, click Server Settings.
2. Under Database Administration, click Force Check-In Enterprise Objects.
3. In the box labeled Select The Type Of Object You Want To Force Check-In, click Enterprise Projects.

   All projects that are currently checked out are listed in the table.
4. Select the check boxes for the projects you want to check in, and then click Check In.

Setting Up Project Workflows

NEW!

Project Server 2010 has integrated the capability provided by Microsoft Office Project Portfolio Server 2007 to offer extensive portfolio analysis and project selection functionality.

In Project Server 2010, the project server administrator and the portfolio manager(s) can configure standard project life cycles, or workflows, for the organization, and they can decide which approvals a project has to go through to reach completion.

Project managers can create projects inside Project Web App that, depending on the project type, follow a specific *project workflow*. This control ensures that the right portfolio of projects—the one that creates the biggest return on investment—is selected.

The process of gathering and managing all project proposals, from when a proposal is created to when a project is closed, is called *demand management*. The typical demand management phases in Project Server are Create, Select, Plan, and Manage. Project workflows can be created only by using Visual Studio 2010, through the Project Server Interface (PSI). Although you cannot create workflows in Project Web App, you can configure the following elements:

- **Enterprise project type (EPT)** The *enterprise project type* reflects the project template and a combination of project phases, project stages, a project workflow, and project detail pages. You can create a new enterprise project type from the Server Settings page. Under the Workflow And Project Detail Pages section, click Enterprise Project Types.
- **Workflow phase** Workflow *phases* are categories describing the development point the project is in. In the default workflow provided with Project Server, phases include Create, Select, Plan, Manage, and Finished. Each phase contains a series of steps or stages. You can create new phases from the Server Settings page. Under the Workflow And Project Detail Pages section, click Workflow Phases link.
- **Workflow stage** A workflow *stage* is a subcategory within a phase that describes the detailed condition of a project in that phase. The stage is associated with steps or activities. For example, in the default workflow provided with Project Server, the Create phase includes stages named Initial Review, Define (Major Project), Automated Rejection, Define (Minor Project), Initial Proposal Details, and more. You can create new phases from the Server Settings page. Under the Workflow And Project Detail Pages section, click Workflow Stages.
- **Project Detail Pages (PDPs)** The *project detail pages* are pages in which you can view or enter project information. One or more project detail pages are available for each phase. Examples of project detail pages are the Project Schedule, Project Cost, and so on. You can edit existing pages or upload new pages from the Server Settings page. Under the Workflow And Project Detail Pages section, click Project Detail Pages.

For more information, see "Designing Your Demand Management System" on page 1032.

Managing Workflow Phases

To add or edit a workflow phase, follow these steps:

1. On the Quick Launch, under Settings, click Server Settings.
2. Under Workflow And Project Detail Pages, click Workflow Phases.

   The Workflow Phases page appears, which lists the following phases by default:

   - Create
   - Select
   - Plan
   - Manage
   - Finished

New Workflow Phase

3. To define new workflow phases, click New Workflow Phase in the toolbar above the table.

   To edit an existing phase, simply click its name.

4. In the page that appears, specify the new workflow phase name and description, as shown in Figure 23-12.

   If you're editing an existing phase, make the changes you want to the current information.

5. When you are finished, click the Save button.

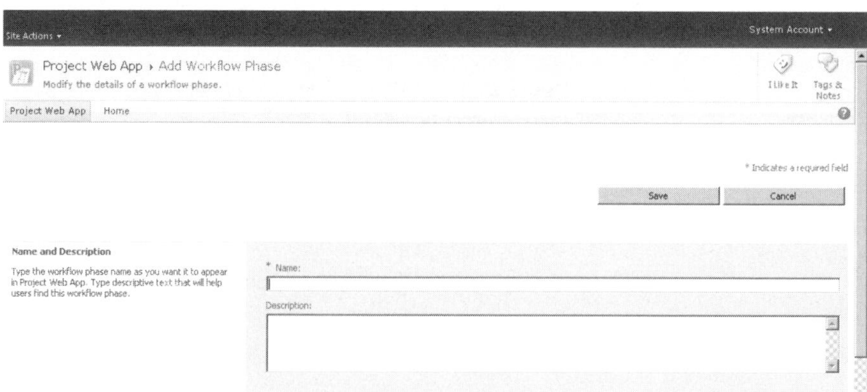

Figure 23-12 Enter the workflow phase name and description, and then click Save

The new phase is added to the list.

Managing Workflow Stages

Workflow stages are a set of activities related to a workflow phase. You can add or modify a workflow stage by following these steps:

1. On the Quick Launch, under Settings, click Server Settings.
2. Under Workflow And Project Details, click Workflow Stages.

   The Workflow Stages page appears, listing all stages for all phases, as shown in Figure 23-13.

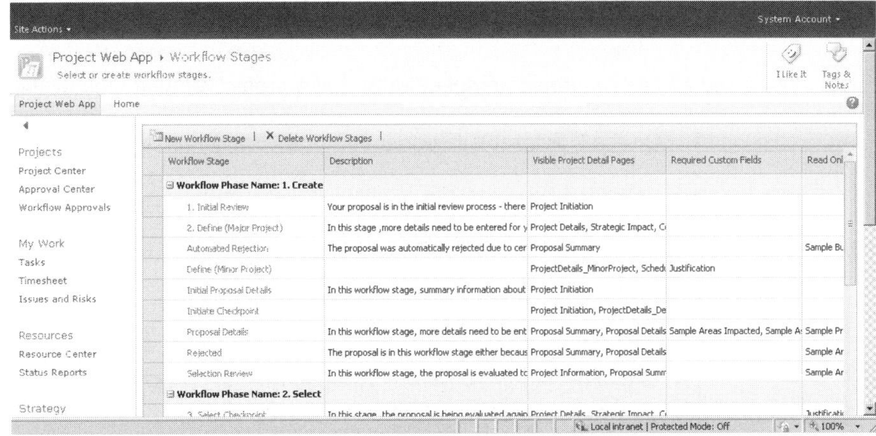

Figure 23-13 Use the Workflow Stages page to add, edit, or delete workflow details.

New Workflow Stage

3. To create a new stage, in the toolbar above the table, click New Workflow Stage.

   To edit an existing stage, simply click its name in the table.

4. In the page that appears, in the Name And Description section, enter a name and description for the new workflow stage.

   In the Description For Submit section, enter the description users see when the workflow is submitted.

   In the Workflow Phase box, specify the phase this stage is associated with.

   In the box labeled Choose Workflow Stage Status Project Detail Page box, select the project detail page that should appear as the introduction for this workflow stage.

   In the Visible Project Detail Pages, select and add the other project detail pages to be associated with this workflow stage.

   In the Required Custom Fields section, select any custom fields to be used for this workflow stage.

Select or clear the check box labeled Project Check In Is Required as appropriate.

If you are editing an existing stage, make the changes you want to the current information.

5. When you are finished, click the Save button.

   The new stage is added to the list.

Configuring Enterprise Project Types

The project server administrator and portfolio manager typically manage *enterprise project types*, which are essentially templates for different types of projects. Each template is a project type, made up of project phases and stages.

To add a new project template or to edit a project template follow these steps:

1. On the Quick Launch, under Settings, click Server Settings.
2. Under Workflow And Project Details, click Enterprise Project Types.

   The Enterprise Project Types page appears, listing all defined enterprise project types.
3. To create an enterprise project type, in the toolbar above the table, click New Enterprise Project Type.

   To edit an existing enterprise project type, simply click its name in the table.
4. In the page that appears (see Figure 23-14), enter the name and description of the project type you're adding.

   In the Site Workflow Association box, select the name of the workflow this enterprise project type is to be associated with.

   In the New Project Page box, click the project detail page that should appear as the introduction for this enterprise project type.

   Use the Default check box to specify whether this is the default project type.

   In the Departments box, enter the departments to which this project type applies.

   In the Project Plan Template box, click the name of any templates to be used for this project type.

   In the Project Site Template box, click the name of any workspace template that should be used when a project is created using this enterprise project type.

   If you are editing an existing enterprise project type, make the changes you want to the current information.

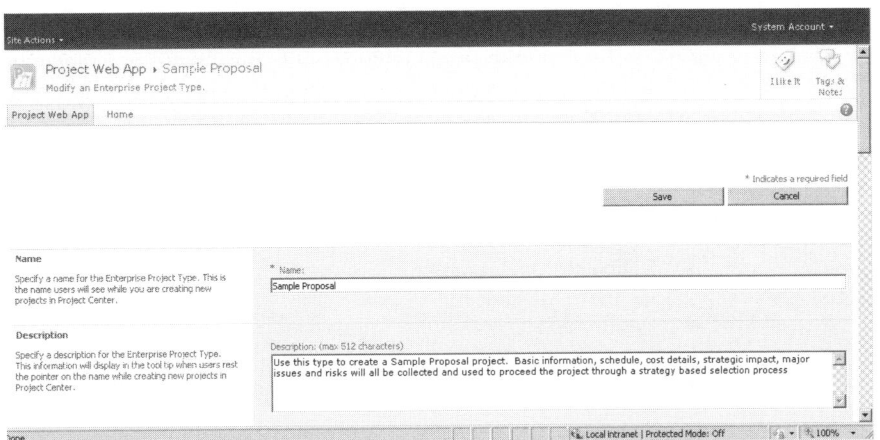

Figure 23-14 Use the Add Enterprise Project Type page to create a new enterprise project template.

5. When you are finished, click the Save button.

   The new enterprise project type is added to the list.

Standardizing Enterprise Project Elements

As the project server administrator, you have the authority to define customizations needed by your organization and then propagate those customizations to all enterprise projects as the accepted project management standards.

To create and disseminate custom project elements, you use the *enterprise global template*, also simply known as the enterprise global. You check out the enterprise global and then customize any number of Project 2010 elements as necessary. You can define views, tables, filters, macros, custom fields, and more. When you check in the enterprise global with your changes, the elements you changed become part of all projects throughout the enterprise.

Working with the Enterprise Global Template

When a project manager or other authorized user checks out an enterprise project, the latest update of the enterprise global is automatically attached. The enterprise global is akin to a global template, or the "global global," over the regular project global template. The enterprise global dictates standards being enforced and customizations made available to Project 2010 interface elements in projects throughout the enterprise.

These standards provide for customization and consistency across all projects in an organization. The standards propagated through the enterprise global template also make it possible for project information throughout the enterprise to be compared and analyzed in meaningful ways.

The following list contains examples of the tailoring and standardizing you might do for projects in your enterprise:

- Define custom views
- Design reports
- Build and apply macros to enterprise data
- Set up custom calendars
- Define and customize information tables

Table 23-1 shows the Project 2010 elements that can be modified in the enterprise global and integrated with all enterprise projects. The table also provides cross-references to sections in this book where you can find more information about customizing these interface elements.

Table 23-1 **Customizable Project 2010 Elements**

Project elements	For more information
Filters	"Customizing Filters" on page 1129
Groups	"Customizing Groups" on page 1124
Macros	"Creating Macros" on page 1171
Reports	"Building a Custom Report" on page 571
Tables	"Customizing Tables" on page 1103
Ribbon	"Customizing the Project 2010 Ribbon" on page 1153
Views	"Customizing Views" on page 1062

Changing the Enterprise Global

By default, only the project server administrator and portfolio manager have the Save Enterprise Global permission which allows updates to the enterprise global.

To use Project Professional to check out and change the enterprise global, follow these steps:

1. Be sure you're logged in to the project server through Project Professional.

Manage Global Template

2. In Project Professional, on the File tab, click Info, click Manage Global Template, and then click Open Enterprise Global.

   The enterprise global opens as a special project plan called Checked-Out Enterprise Global. (See Figure 23-15.)

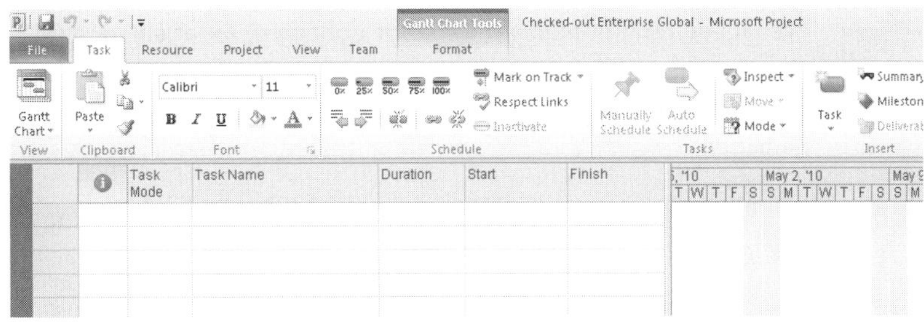

Figure 23-15 The Checked-Out Enterprise Global is a special project plan you use to standardize elements of all project plans used throughout your organization.

3. Define and customize Project Professional elements for the enterprise as needed. Refer to Table 23-1 to find specific instructions for customizing a specific element.

4. When you're finished working with the enterprise global and you want to check it back in to the project server, on the File tab, click Close.

5. In the prompt that appears, click Yes to save your changes. The updated enterprise global is checked in to the project server and is now available to all project managers.

Note

You can also check out the enterprise global and open Project Professional starting from within Project Web App. On the Server Settings page, under Enterprise Data, click Enterprise Global. Click the Configure Project Professional button. The enterprise global is checked out to you and appears in Project Professional. You can now make the changes you need as described above. When you have finished, save your changes and check the enterprise global back into the project server.

Create an Enterprise Global Change Process

It's likely that project managers will have a number of good ideas regarding items that should become part of the enterprise global. They are also likely to have thoughts about custom fields and calendars. Your organization might do well to develop a consistent process for handling such suggestions. It might be something as simple as having project managers submit a written suggestion to the project server administrator showing an example of the proposed change. The process might be as formal as a periodic change review meeting. It depends entirely on your organization.

Even if you can't implement a change right away (or at all), remind project managers that they can still create and use their own project global templates, as long as there's no conflict between elements in the project global and elements in the enterprise global.

For more information, see "Working with the Project Global Template" on page 1189.

Copying a Custom Element from a Project to the Enterprise Global

You might find it a great idea to experiment with certain customized changes by applying them to a regular enterprise project or even a local project before checking out the enterprise global and making the changes there. But you don't have to make the change twice. You can simply copy the custom change from the regular project to the enterprise global by using the Organizer.

To copy custom elements from a regular project to the enterprise global, follow these steps:

1. Log in to the Project Server through Project Professional.
2. In Project Professional, open the regular enterprise or nonenterprise project that contains the element you want to copy to the enterprise global.
3. On the File tab, click Info, click Manage Global Template, and then click Open Enterprise Global.

   The enterprise global opens as Checked-Out Enterprise Global.
4. On the File tab, click Info, click Manage Global Template, and then click Organizer.

   The Organizer dialog box appears, as shown in Figure 23-16.

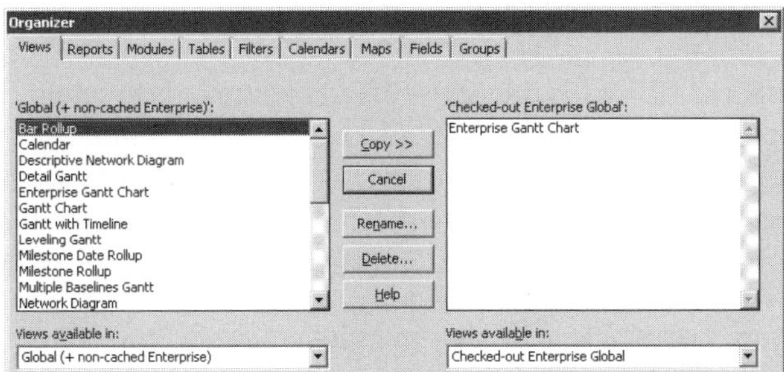

Figure 23-16 Copy customized elements from a project and the enterprise global.

5. Click the tab for the type of element you want to copy—for example, Views.

6. In the <Element> Available In box in the lower-right corner of the dialog box, click the project that contains the element you want to copy, if necessary.

   (<Element> stands for the name of the current tab). The name of the project from which you want to copy the element might already be showing in the box.

7. Be sure the box in the lower left of the dialog box is labeled Global (+Non-Cached Enterprise).

   If this item is not currently showing, select Global (+Non-Cached Enterprise) from the <Element> Available In box. This is the name of the enterprise global template.

8. From the list of elements on the right side of the dialog box, click the name of the element you want to copy.

9. Click Copy. If an element with the same name already exists in the enterprise global, a confirmation message asks you to confirm that you want to replace the element in the enterprise global. Click Yes to replace the element in the enterprise global with the one from the source project.

   To copy the element with a different name, click Rename, and then type a new name.

10. Check the enterprise global to be sure that your new element is present.

11. When you finish working with the enterprise global, on the File tab, click Close.

12. In the prompt that appears, click Yes to save your changes and check the enterprise global in to the project server.

Customizing Enterprise Project Fields

Another responsibility of the project server administrator is to set up custom fields for enterprise projects as a whole as well as for individual enterprise tasks, resources, and assignments. You can define these custom fields to hold special information, such as a specific category of costs, dates, or text that is not provided by built-in Project 2010 fields. You can also create lookup tables for all custom field types except for Yes/No fields.

You can create a custom field in any enterprise project in Project Professional. You then choose a command to add the field to the enterprise, and it becomes part of the project global template. However, note that you cannot create fields in the checked-out global template itself.

In Project Server, you can create an unlimited number of custom fields for enterprise projects. However, because of the impact on performance and usage, we do not recommend this. Use as many custom fields as you need, but be aware of possible tradeoffs.

For example, you can use the Duration1 custom field to create an enterprise task field. As soon as you add the field to the project server, it changes to Enterprise Duration1, and the Duration1 field in Project 2010 becomes available for another use.

You can define the following custom field types for projects as a whole and for tasks, resources, and assignments:

- Cost
- Date
- Duration
- Finish
- Flag
- Number
- Start
- Text

Establishing Custom Fields

For enterprise projects, you can create a wide range of custom fields. There are different sets of custom fields for the different types of project database information, as follows:

- **Project fields** Store summary project information. Custom project fields can be viewed as part of the project summary row in an individual project plan.
- **Task fields** Store information about the tasks in a project. Similar to the other types of fields, this information can include, for example, cost, date, text, and number information.
- **Resource fields** Store information about the resources in a project.

NEW!

In Project 2010, departmental custom fields are available. Each department can manage its own project, task, or resource custom field. Departmental custom fields can also be shared across departments.

In Project Web App, you can restrict the access of a user who can edit one department's custom fields from editing the custom fields of another department.

Custom fields can be defined in Project Web App or Project Professional. To use Project Web App to define a custom enterprise field, follow these steps:

1. On the Quick Launch, under Settings, click Server Settings.
2. Under Enterprise Data, click Enterprise Custom Fields And Lookup Tables.
3. To create a single-value custom field, in the toolbar above the Enterprise Custom Fields table, click New Field.

   In the New Custom Field page, complete the fields to specify the details for the new custom field. When you are finished, click the Save button.
4. To create a custom field with a lookup table of multiple values, scroll down to the Lookup Tables For Custom Fields table. In the toolbar above the table, click New Lookup Table.

   In the New Lookup Table page, complete the fields to specify the details for the new custom field and its lookup table. When you are finished, click the Save button.

To use Project Professional to define a custom field for enterprise projects, follow these steps:

1. With Project Professional logged on to your project server, show a task view if you want to define a custom task field. Show a resource view to define a custom resource field.

2. On the Project tab, in the Properties group, click Custom Fields.

   The Custom Fields dialog box appears.

3. In the Type box, select the type of custom field you want to add—for example, Text or Date.

4. In the Field box, click the next available custom text field—for example, Text1. (See Figure 23-17.)

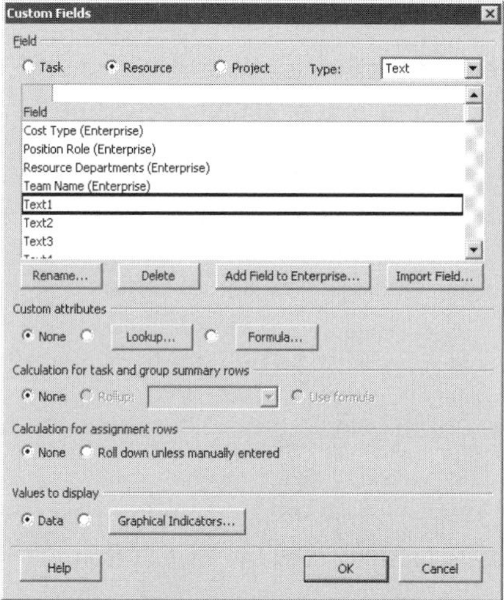

Figure 23-17 Use the Custom Fields dialog box to define custom enterprise fields.

5. Click the Rename button, type a descriptive name for your new custom resource field, and then click OK.

6. If you want to specify a formula or graphical indicator for the custom field, use the sections in the lower half of the dialog box.

7. If you want this custom field to include a lookup table—that is, a drop-down list of preset values—click the Lookup button under Custom Attributes. In the Value column of the table, enter the items that comprise the drop-down list. (See Figure 23-18.)

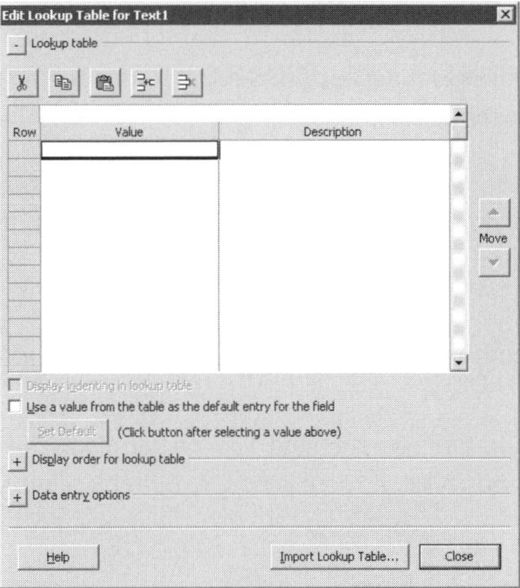

Figure 23-18 Use the Edit Lookup Table dialog box to define the items that should appear in a custom field's drop-down list.

8. Make any other changes you want to the definition of the lookup table for the new custom field, including a default value or the display order. When you have finished, click Close.

9. In the Custom Fields dialog box, click the Add Field To Enterprise button.

10. In the Field Name box, enter the name of the custom field as you want it to appear in a table in Project Professional or a custom view in Project Web App. In the Lookup Table Name box, enter the name of the custom field as you want it to appear in a drop-down list of custom enterprise fields. Click OK.

11. In the alert that indicates that the field has been added to your project server, click OK. The new field does not appear in Project Professional until you restart the application. However, it does become available in Project Web App immediately.

12. Click OK in the Custom Fields dialog box.

13. Restart Project Professional to see and use the new field.

For more information about defining custom fields and outline codes, including lookup tables, formulas, and graphical indicators, see "Customizing Fields" on page 1107.

Associating Resource Codes with Resources

After you define an enterprise resource custom field, associate the field and its values with enterprise resources by following these steps:

1. In the Resource Center of Project Web App, select the check boxes next to the names of the resources for whom you want to enter resource custom fields and values.
2. On the Resources tab, in the Editing group, click Edit Resource.
3. In the Resource Custom Fields section, enter the appropriate value in the custom resource field.

   If you created a lookup table for the field, click the arrow in the field and then click an entry in the drop-down list. If there is no lookup table, simply type the value in the field.
4. Click the Save And Continue button.
5. Enter the value in the custom resource field for the next resource.

   Repeat steps 3 and 4 until you've entered values in the custom resource fields for all selected resources.

Note

If you're making the same change to custom resource fields for multiple resources, you can select the resources, and then click Resources, Editing, Bulk Edit. Your custom fields appear in the Resource Custom Fields section. Enter the value in the custom resource field that applies to all selected resources. Select the Apply Changes check box next to the custom resource field, and then click the Save button. The change is applied to all selected resources at once.

Use Regular Custom Fields

Only the project server administrator or another user with the proper permissions can create and save custom enterprise fields to the enterprise. If for individual project plans, custom fields are needed that don't affect the enterprise, project managers can define custom fields for their own use in enterprise projects. Instead of using the enterprise custom fields such as Enterprise Cost1-10, they can use Cost1-10, Date1-10, Text1-30, and so on.

For more information about regular custom fields, see "Customizing Fields" on page 1107.

Creating Calendars to Reflect Nonworking Times

In addition to standardizing elements such as views and fields to reflect the operations of your organization, you can also create enterprise-level working times calendars that dictate how projects and resources are scheduled. By default, resources are assigned to the Standard working times base calendar, which reflects a schedule of Monday through Friday, 8:00 A.M. to 5:00 P.M., with an hour off for lunch. You can customize the Standard calendar to reflect your organization's holidays, company meetings, offsite conferences, and other events to be sure that project tasks are not scheduled for work during those times.

To change the Standard base calendar that is the starting point for working and nonworking times for all projects in your organization, follow these steps:

1. On the Quick Launch, under Settings, click Server Settings.
2. Under Enterprise Data, click Enterprise Calendars.

Edit Calendar

3. Click Standard in the Enterprise Calendars table, and then in the toolbar above the table, click Edit Calendar.

   The Change Working Time dialog box opens in Project Professional. (See Figure 23-19.)

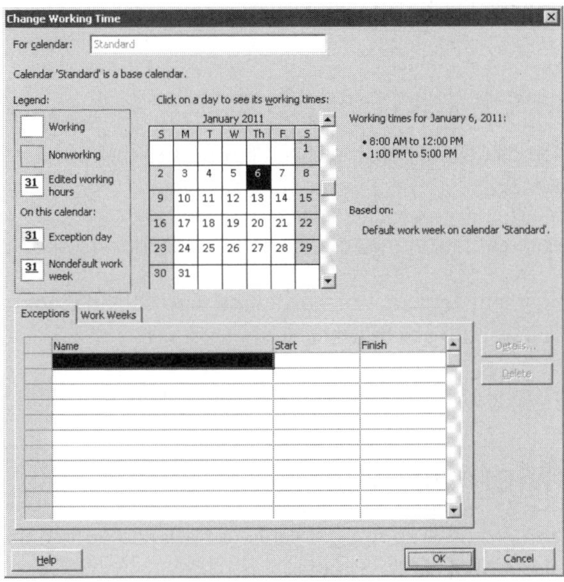

Figure 23-19 Use the Change Working Time dialog box to edit the enterprise calendar.

4. Change the Standard working time calendar by entering exceptions or by creating alternative workweeks.

For detailed information about changing a working time calendar, see "Modifying a Base Calendar" on page 85.

5. When you've made all the changes you want, click OK. The Standard working times calendar is applied to all enterprise projects and resources. The next time project managers check out any enterprise project that uses the Standard working times calendar, the changes take effect.

Copy Calendar

You can create a new base calendar that uses an existing calendar as its starting point. In the table on the Enterprise Calendars page, click the name of the calendar that you want to copy, and then click Copy Calendar. Enter a name for the new calendar, and then click OK. The copied calendar appears in the list of calendars. Select it, click Edit Calendar in the toolbar, and make the changes you want.

You can also create a new base calendar from scratch—that is, with no exceptions or alternative workweeks defined other than the defaults. The new base calendar is essentially the built-in Standard base calendar, with working times of Monday through Friday, 8:00 A.M. to 5:00 P.M., with an hour off for lunch. To create a new calendar, on the Enterprise Calendars page, click New Calendar in the toolbar. In the For Calendar box in the Change Working Time dialog box, enter a name for your new calendar. Make the changes you want, and then click OK.

To assign a base calendar to a resource, follow these steps:

1. In the Resource Center, click the check box next to the resource to which you want to apply a calendar.
2. On the Resources tab, in the Editing group, click Edit Resource.
3. In the Assignment Attributes section, in the Base Calendar box, click the name of the calendar you want to assign to the current resource.
4. Click Save, or click Save And Continue if you're editing multiple resources.

Setting Up Team Member Work Pages

Team members use Project Web App primarily to track and update their assigned tasks for one or more projects. They do this on the Tasks page.

Team members and managers also have the ability to submit timesheets that track different categories of time—for example, billable time, nonbillable time, billable overtime, and non-billable overtime. They perform this activity on the Timesheet page.

Team members can also use the Microsoft SharePoint features built in to Project Web App to manage issues and risks that have been assigned to them for resolution. To do this, they use the Issues And Risks page in the Project SharePoint page.

These three pages are available under My Work in the Quick Launch pane.

What's the Difference Between Tasks and Timesheets?

Your organization might choose to use just the Tasks page, or it might decide to implement the Tasks page in conjunction with the Timesheet page. To use either or both of these pages successfully, you must understand the differences between the two as well as how they work together.

Understanding the Tasks Page

The Tasks page, also referred to as the *task progress page,* is the page that team members work with to track and update the tasks assigned to them from one or more projects. (See Figure 23-20.) As the project server administrator, you can customize the Tasks page to suit the needs of your organization.

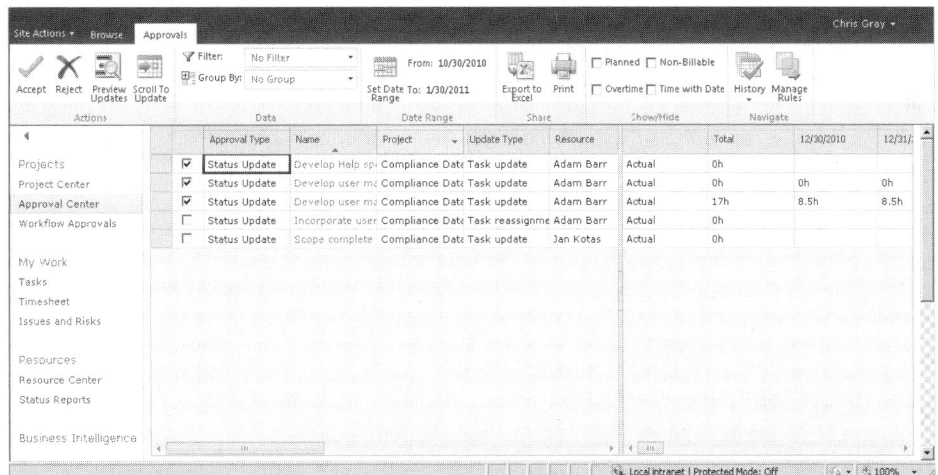

Figure 23-20 The Tasks updates can be approved or rejected by the team managers or project managers.

Chapter 23

Team members use the Tasks page to see the tasks assigned to them, the scheduled start and finish dates for the tasks, and other assignment information. They also use this page to periodically report on current progress, submitting this progress information to their project manager for incorporation into the project plan.

Understanding the Timesheet Page

The Timesheet page is used in organizations that have specific time-reporting requirements. For example, use the timesheet when you want visibility into certain time categories, such as billable and nonbillable time, scheduled and actual time, overtime, and so on. Default time categories are provided, but you can set up custom time categories as needed. The timesheet is especially useful when you need to integrate information about resource time with an accounting or general ledger system, particularly for client billing purposes.

In the timesheet, team members can also set up and use the administrative time feature, in which they can identify instances of nonproject working time or nonworking time.

Similar to their work with task progress on the Tasks page, team members submit timesheets to their designated timesheet managers on a periodic basis.

Working with Task Progress and Timesheets

You do not have to use both task progress and timesheets. If you do not have specialized time-reporting needs outside the project plan, just use the task progress page to update the project plan. Use both, however, if you need to update the project plan as well as an accounting or general ledger system.

Remember that the task progress page indicates status on how complete a task assignment is, while the timesheet indicates the number of hours spent per day or per week doing various activities. The two are often, but not always, related.

For example, suppose the project team is working for a customer who is to be billed 8 hours per day (40 hours per week) for the contracted work. The timesheet would reflect this, and invoices would be generated for the customer from the timesheet showing 8 hours per day for 5 days per week. However, the resource might actually be working 10 hours per day to complete the tasks by a certain deadline. The task progress page would show this, and the information would be reflected in project actuals but would have no impact on the timesheet or the customer billing.

Working with Timesheet Single-Entry Mode

NEW!

New in Project Server 2010 is the timesheet *single-entry mode*, which unifies the data entered in the Timesheet and Tasks pages in Project Web App.

As the project server administrator, you can establish whether timesheet and task progress information should be unified in single-entry mode or kept separate. To do this, follow these steps:

1. On the Quick Launch, under Settings, click Server Settings.
2. Under Time And Task Management, click Timesheet Settings And Defaults.
3. Scroll to the bottom of the page to the Single Entry Mode section.
4. Select or clear the Single Entry Mode check box.
5. Click the Save button.

Defining the Task Progress Page

To set up the task progress page (the Tasks page), you need to establish the update method and rules used by your organization. If you need to, you can also change the fields and the type of Gantt Chart used on the page.

For more information about how team members work with the Tasks page, see "Working with Your Assignments" on page 973.

Setting the Update Method and Restrictions

With your project server administrator privileges, you define the assignment progress tracking method that is reflected on the Tasks page. The tracking method can be as simple as noting whether an assignment is not started, in progress, or completed. It can be as detailed as tracking every hour devoted to each assignment.

Depending on the level of project management control that your organization needs, you can set up a number of assignment update restrictions. For example, you can:

- Specify whether time should be reported every day or just once per week.
- Specify whether project managers have the capability to edit updates submitted by team members.
- Close tasks to further update by anyone after a certain period of time.

Work with the project managers, the portfolio manager, and the requirements of the organization to determine the most appropriate default tracking method. After setting the default, project managers might still be able to switch to a different tracking method for their own projects, but only if you allow that possibility in your project server configuration.

The three tracking methods are as follows:

- **Percentage of work complete** This is the least restrictive and least time-consuming tracking method. The Tasks page includes a field that team members use to update how far along they are with their assignments.
- **Actual work done and remaining work** This tracking method provides a medium level of detail. With this method, the Tasks page includes fields for total actual work and remaining work for each assignment. Team members enter these total amounts for each progress update requested.
- **Hours of work done per time period** This is the most detailed tracking method.

The Tasks page includes a field for each time period, either days or weeks, for the duration of the project. Team members enter the number of hours worked per day or per week and submit this information with each progress update.

In addition to the default tracking method, you can also control when actuals are accepted and whether they can be changed after they've been submitted to the project server.

To set the default tracking method and certain update restrictions, follow these steps:

1. On the Server Settings page, under Time And Task Management, click Task Settings And Display.

   The Task Settings And Display page appears, as shown in Figure 23-21.

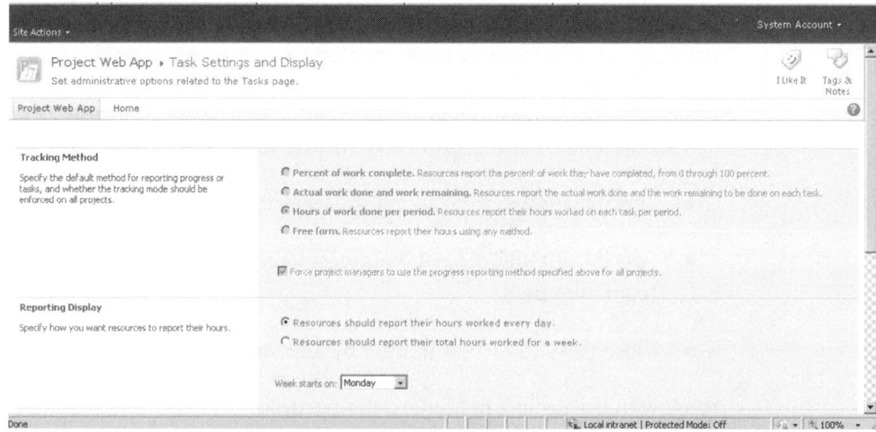

Figure 23-21 Use the Task Settings And Display page to set the default work-tracking method for the team member task progress page.

Chapter 23

2. In the Tracking Method section, select the option for the tracking method that represents the default for your organization: Percent Of Work Complete, Actual Work Done And Work Remaining, or Hours Of Work Done Per Period, or Free Form.

3. Select or clear the check box labeled Force Project Managers To Use The Progress Reporting Method Specified Above For All Projects.

   If this check box is cleared, project managers are allowed to change the tracking method in their individual projects. If this check box is selected, project managers must always use the default method selected on this page.

4. Work through the other options on this page, reading the information in the left pane of each section for additional guidance.

   Options include whether team members should report their hours each day or at the end of the week, and whether the project manager is permitted to change actual time worked as reported by the team members.

5. When you have finished, click the Save button.

Closing Tasks Against Further Reporting

Another restriction you can apply to protect actual progress information is to close completed tasks to prevent any further updates from being submitted on them. This is also known as *locking down* the tasks.

To do this from the Server Settings page, follow these steps:

1. On the Server Settings page, under Time And Task Management, click Close Tasks To Update.

2. In the Select A Project box, click the name of the project that contains the tasks you want to lock down.

   The tasks in that project are listed in the Select Tasks section.

3. Select the Lock check box next to the task(s) for which you want to close further reporting.

   If you want to select all tasks, click Select All below the table.

4. Click the Publish or Submit button.

To lock down the tasks from within a project detail page, follow these steps:

1. On the Quick Launch, under Projects, click Project Center.

2. Click the name of the project that contains the tasks you want to lock down.

3. At the top of the Quick Launch, under the project name, click Schedule.
4. On the Options tab, in the Tasks group, click Close To Updates.
5. In the Close Tasks To Update page that appears, be sure that the current project is selected in the Select A Project box.
6. Select the Lock check box next to the tasks(s) for which you want to close further reporting.
7. Click the Publish or Submit button.

What's the Difference Between Save, Submit, and Publish?

In several pages throughout Project Web App, both Save (or Submit) and Publish buttons are available to you. Clicking the Save (or Submit) button saves the changes from that page in the Draft (Working) database, but they are not available to other users.

On the other hand, clicking the Publish button saves the changes and locks them down in the Published database. Changes that are published can be accessed by other users with the appropriate permissions.

Setting the Fields

The Tasks page is set up with a standard set of task and assignment fields. That set of fields changes according to the tracking method chosen. You can change the fields that team members see on their task progress page. As the project server administrator, you can choose from the full set of Project 2010 fields to establish the set of available timesheet fields.

If you have defined any custom enterprise fields, including custom fields with a drop-down "pick list" or lookup table, you can include them in the set of default task progress fields, as well.

For more information about defining custom enterprise task fields, including defining drop-down lookup tables, see "Customizing Enterprise Project Fields" on page 864.

To modify the set of default task progress fields, follow these steps:

1. On the Server Settings page, under Look And Feel, click Manage Views.

   The Manage Views page appears, as shown in Figure 23-22.

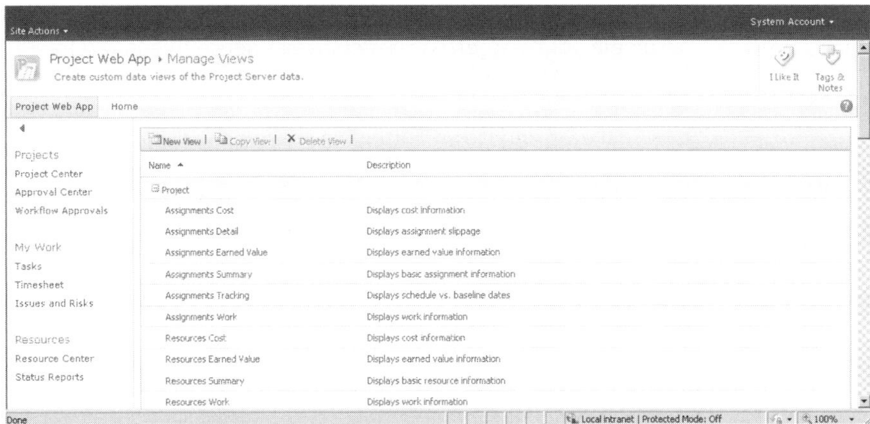

Figure 23-22 Use the Manage Views page to modify, add, or remove views in Project Web App.

2. Scroll about halfway down the table and click the My Assignments view under the My Work category.

   The Edit View: My Assignments page appears, as shown in Figure 23-23.

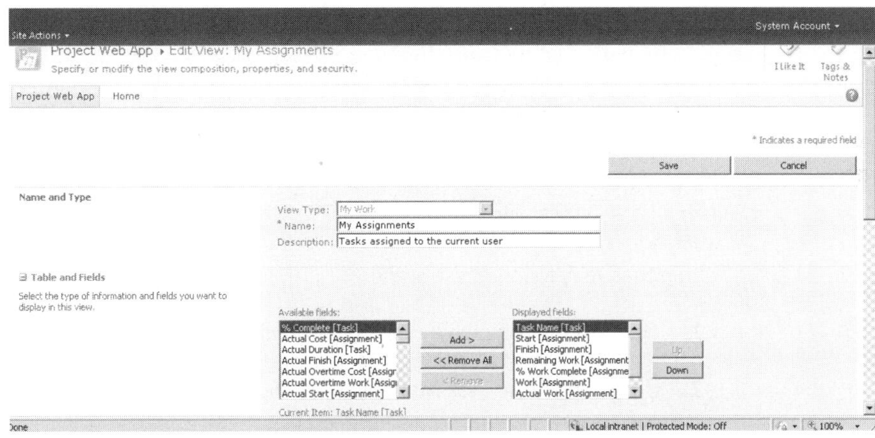

Figure 23-23 Details for the selected view appear on the Edit View page.

3. In the Table And Fields section, select one or more fields in the Available Fields box, and then click Add to move them to the Displayed Fields box on the right.

   This process specified which fields should show on the task progress page. If you have defined any custom enterprise fields, they are also part of the list of available fields.

4. If you need to delete any fields from the view, select those in the Displayed Fields box on the right, and then click Remove to delete them from the set of fields shown in the task progress page.

5. Use the Up and Down buttons to arrange the fields in the order you want them displayed in the view.

6. When you have finished, click the Save button.

Your changes are saved to the project server. The next time team members click their Tasks page, they will see your new version of the page.

Defining the Timesheet Page

To set up the Timesheet page, you establish the fiscal year and reporting periods for your organization. You set up the categories of time to be reported and set any necessary timesheet update rules.

For more information about how team members work with the timesheet, see "Logging Time by Using Timesheets" on page 992.

Identifying the Reporting Periods

Because team members use the timesheet to report on their progress, you can be sure that the time periods for which they report map not only to your organization's fiscal year but also to the reporting periods you need—whether that's weekly, biweekly, or monthly.

The first step is to set up your fiscal year and define your monthly periods within that year—for example, calendar months, four-week periods, or four-week periods with a five-week adjustment period. To set up your organization's fiscal year and the reporting periods within that year, follow these steps:

1. On the Quick Launch, under Settings, click Server Settings.

2. Under Time And Task Management, click Fiscal Periods.

3. In the Manage Fiscal Period section, click the year you are defining, and then click Define.

   The Define Fiscal Year Parameters page appears.

4. Follow the instructions in the left pane to complete this page and define the fiscal year start date, the fiscal period model, and the fiscal period naming conventions.

5. Click the Create And Save button.

   The Fiscal Periods page appears again, this time showing the table of fiscal periods you have just specified.

6. If you need to make any adjustments, click in the End Date field for a period. Using the date picker icon that appears, click the date for the fiscal period.

   Repeat this for any other fiscal periods you want to adjust.

7. Click the Save button.

Setting Timesheet Defaults and Update Restrictions

As the project server administrator, you are responsible for defining defaults and updating rules for the timesheets used by resources.

To set timesheet defaults and additional update restrictions, follow these steps:

1. On the Server Settings page, under Time And Task Management, click Timesheet Settings And Defaults.

2. Work through the options on this page, reading the information in the left pane of each section for additional guidance.

   Options include what information can be displayed in the Microsoft Outlook timesheet, whether the Project Web App timesheet should include fields for overtime and nonbillable time, how timesheets are created, whether tracking units are days or weeks, and whether future time reporting is allowable.

3. When you have finished, click the Save button.

Setting Categories for Administrative Time

Each team member is associated with a working times calendar. However, team members can also designate administrative time to schedule vacation or nonbillable working time—that is, time spent not working directly on project tasks. Project managers and resource managers can then approve and incorporate administrative time into project scheduling.

As the project server administrator, you can set up categories for administrative time—for example, vacation, company meetings, and training. You specify whether the administrative time is a working or nonworking time and whether it requires approval by the team member's manager.

To add a new administrative time category, follow these steps:

1. On the Server Settings page, under Time And Task Management, click Administrative Time.

   The Edit Or Create Administrative Time page shows the list of categories. Default categories are Administrative, Jury Duty, Sick Time, and Vacation.

New Category

2. In the toolbar above the table, click New Category.
3. In the new row that's added to the table, type a name for the new category.
4. In the Status field, specify whether the category is open or closed.

   With an open category, team members can record time against the category. A closed category is not shown in the team member's Administrative Time dialog box.

5. In the Work Type field, specify whether the category is Working or Non Work.

   For example, a category called Nonproject Meeting would be a Working type, while the Personal Time Off category would be Non Work.

6. In the Approve field, specify whether the category requires approval by the team member's manager.
7. In the Always Display field, select the check box if the category should appear in the team member's Administrative Time dialog box. Clear the check box if it should not appear.

   Turning the Always Display field on or off can be useful if your organization wants to make a category available only during a certain period of the year.

8. When you have finished, click the Save button.

To edit an existing category, simply click in the field and make the changes you want. To delete an existing category, click the name of the category, and then in the toolbar above the table, click Delete Category.

For more information about how project managers work with administrative time, see "Tracking Billable and Nonbillable Time by Using Timesheets" on page 954.

Setting the Billing Categories

Built in to Project Server is a standard billing category for project work as well as four billing categories for administrative work (Administrative, Jury Duty, Sick Time, and Vacation).

You can add different billing categories as needed. To do this, follow these steps:

1. On the Server Settings page, under Time And Task Management, click Line Classifications.
2. Click New Classification.
3. In the row that's added to the table, type a name for the new billing category.
4. In the Description field, type an explanation for the use of the category.
5. Click the Save button.

The new line classification becomes available in the timesheet. When a resource working in the timesheet clicks Timesheet, Tasks, Insert Row to add an existing assignment or other item, the new category is listed in the Line Classification box. The category then appears in the Billing Category field for the new row.

Managing Pages, Views, and Reports

Project server administrators have the capability to create custom pages, views, and reports for Project Web App users. You do this so that Project Web App clearly reflects your organization and also to provide users with information where and when they need it.

Pages are the major screens you see as you move from area to area within Project Web App. For example, Server Settings is a page, Project Center is a page, and Resource Center is a page. You can add and remove elements on most pages by editing the page's Web Parts, which are the content components that make up the page.

On the other hand, views are subsets of pages. Views specify a certain collection or arrangement of information within a page. For example, the default view for the Project Center page is the Summary view, but you can switch to the Cost view or the Tracking view.

Creating and Managing Pages with Web Parts

Project Web App is essentially a website made up of a series of pages. The elements on these pages come from a collection of predesigned Web Parts. Web Parts are a feature of Microsoft SharePoint, the platform on which Project Web App is built. Web Parts are self-contained, reusable components that consist of types of information, varying from sophisticated, dynamic web page content embedded in a frame to simple, concise text messages. Generally, most features and content that can be seen on a web page can be included as a Web Part. Web Parts group and position all key information logically and consistently; the information is accessed through hyperlinks.

You can use Web Parts in Project Web App to develop web page components that convey key project information efficiently for your team or organization. For example, the Tasks page is made up of the Tasks Web Part, and the Project Center is made up of the Project Center Web Part. But you can put the two Web Parts together to create another page. You can add the Reminders Web Part to the Timesheet page if you learn that's what your users need.

Modifying a Built-In Page

You can modify the structure and content category of any Project Web App page, including the Home page. To do this, follow these steps.

1. In Project Web App, navigate to the page you want to change.
2. Click Site Actions in the upper-left corner of the window, and then on the drop-down menu, click Edit Page.

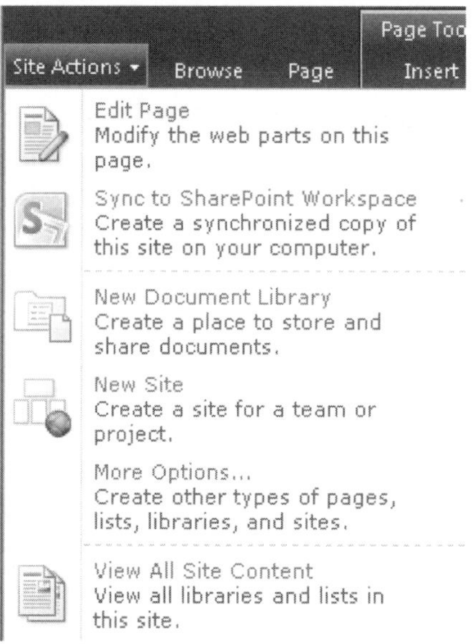

The page is redrawn to show each Web Part element on the page. An Add A Web Part control (see Figure 23-24) shows at the top of the page. The Page Tools and Web Part Tools tabs appear on the ribbon.

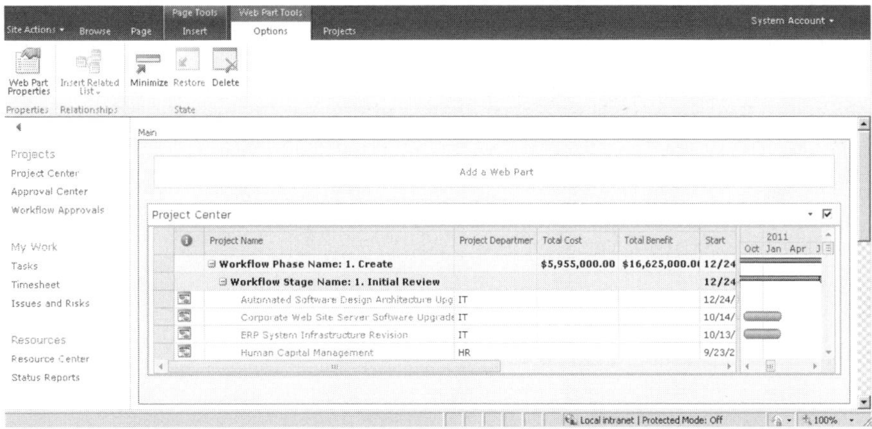

Figure 23-24 When you edit a page, Web Part controls appear directly on the page.

3. Using the Web Parts controls, edit the page:

- To add a new Web Part, click the Add A Web Part control. In the Add Web Parts pane that appears, select the Web Part category from the Categories box on the left. Under Web Parts, select the name of the Web Part you want to add; for example, Project Detail Pages or Reporting Services Reports. When you click the name of a Web Part, a description appears in the About The Web Part pane on the right. Click the Add button. The Web Part is added to the page. A new Add A Web Part control appears at the top in case you want to add another.

- To edit an existing Web Part, click the arrow near the upper-right edge of the Web Part's title bar, and then from the drop-down menu that appears, click Edit Web Part. Or, you can click in the Web Part, and then on the Options tab, in the Properties group, click Web Part Properties. A task pane appears on the right side of the window, as shown in Figure 23-25. Specify how you want to modify the Web Part. The choices differ depending on the nature of the Web Part. However, most Web Parts provide choices such as Appearance, Layout, and Advanced. Click OK or Apply at the bottom of the Web Part pane to implement your changes on the page.

Figure 23-25 Use the Web Part task pane to edit a Web Part on the page.

- To remove a Web Part from a page, click the arrow near the upper-right edge of the Web Part and click the Close option. The page is redrawn with that Web Part removed. Don't use the Delete command because that will remove the Web Part entirely from Project Server.

4. When you have finished making changes to Web Parts on the current page, on the Page tab, in the Edit group, click Stop Editing, as shown in Figure 23-26. The Web Part controls disappear, and the changes you made are shown on the page.

Figure 23-26 When you're done editing the Web Parts, click Stop Editing on the Page tab of the ribbon.

Creating a Page

You can create an entirely new page and arrange the Web Parts you want on it. To do this, follow these steps:

1. On any page in Project Web App, click the Site Actions button in the upper-left corner of the window, and then from the drop-down menu, click More Options.

2. In the Create window that appears, scroll down and click Web Part Page.

3. In the right pane, click the Create button.

4. On the New Web Part page, enter the name that you want to appear in headings and links throughout Project Web App when you refer to this page.

5. In the Layout section, in the Choose A Layout Template box, click the page layout you want for the new page. (See Figure 23-27.)

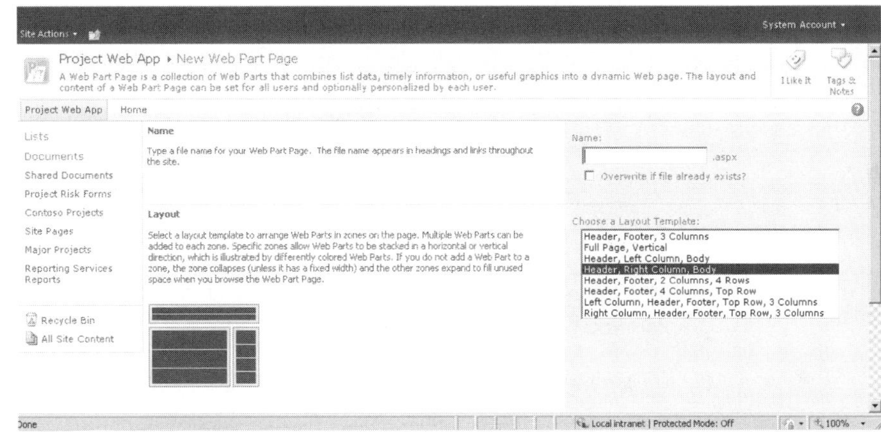

Figure 23-27 Specify the layout for your new page.

6. In the Save Location section, click the document library where you want to save this web page. This is the category that will contain the Web Part page.

7. Click Create.

   The page is created and appears as a page filled only with Web Parts controls, as shown in Figure 23-28.

Figure 23-28 When you create a new Web Part page, a series of Web Part controls appears to help you start building the content for the page.

8. Click one of the Add A Web Part controls.
9. In the pane that appears, under Categories, click the category that contains the Web Part you want to add.
10. Under Web Parts, click the Web Part you want to add.

    A description of the selected Web Part appears in the About The Web Part section on the right.
11. Under About The Web Part, in the Add Web Part To box, click the location on the page where you want the new Web Part to be added.

    The location choices correspond with the layout you chose for this page.
12. Click Add.

    The Web Part is added to the page in the location you specified.
13. Repeat steps 8 through 12 for additional Web Parts you want to add to this page.
14. When you have finished adding Web Parts to the new page, on the Page tab, in the Edit group, click Stop Editing.

    Your changes are saved and the new page appears according to your specifications.

Deleting a Custom Page

To delete custom web page you've created in Project Web App, follow these steps:

1. On the Quick Launch in Project Web App, under Documents, click the category name of the document library in which the Web Part page was created—for example, Shared Documents or Project Risk Forms.

   Any pages you have created are listed.

2. Move your mouse pointer to the left of the name of the page you want to delete, and then select the check box that appears.

3. On the Documents tab, in the Manage group, click Delete Document, and then click OK.

   The page is moved to the Recycle Bin.

4. To return to Project Web App, click the Navigate Up button in the upper-left corner of the page, and then click Project Web App.

Creating and Managing Views

Many pages throughout Project Web App need to display only a single view of project data. Examples of such pages include the Home page and the Personal Settings page.

The use of other pages, however, benefit from the availability of different views of project data. Such pages include:

- Tasks
- Timesheets
- Project Center
- Resource Center
- Business Intelligence

A *view* is a collection of selected fields, filtered in a particular way, laid out in a certain format, and with certain permissions applied on a page. For example, the Project Center page includes the Cost, Projects by Phase, Summary, Tracking, and Work views, among others. To see the views available for a page, the user clicks in the View box, typically located in the Data group on the page's ribbon.

You can modify existing Project Web App views or create new views to add to a page. When defining a view, you can specify the following types of information:

- View name and description.
- The fields to be displayed in the view's table.
- Formatting for the view, including Gantt Chart format if applicable, outline levels, grouping format, and sort order.
- The filter to be applied to the view's information.
- The security categories that the view belongs to.

Modifying a Built-In View

To modify an existing view, follow these steps:

1. On the Quick Launch, under Settings, click Server Settings.
2. Under Look And Feel, click Manage Views.

   All views used throughout Project Web App are listed under their categories.
3. Click the name of the view you want to change. The Edit View page appears.
4. Go to the section that contains the aspect of the view you want to change—for example, the fields included in the view are in the Table And Fields section, and the filter applied to this view is in the Filter section.
5. Click the Save button.

   The view is now changed for all Project Web App users.

Creating a New View from a Copied View

You can create a view that uses an existing view as its starting point. To do this, follow these steps:

1. On the Server Settings page, under Look And Feel, click Manage Views.
2. On the Manage Views page, click somewhere to the right of the name of the view you want to copy. Don't click the name of the view itself, or you'll open the Edit View page.

3. In the toolbar above the table, click Copy View.
4. In the dialog box that appears, enter a name for the new view, and then click OK.

   The copied view appears in the list.
5. Click the name of the copied view to open the Edit View page, and then make the changes you want.
6. Click the Save button.

Creating a View from Scratch

If you prefer, you can create a view from a completely clean slate. To do this, follow these steps:

1. On the Server Settings page, under Look And Feel, click Manage Views.
2. In the toolbar above the table, click New View.
3. In the Name And Type section, click the type of view you want from the View Type drop-down list. The view type determines the page on which your new view becomes available.
4. Work through the sections of the New View page to define the view.
5. Click the Save button.

   The new view is added to the list and is also now available to apply to the page you specified through the Views drop-down list.

Deleting a View

You can delete a view you created. To do this, follow these steps:

1. On the Server Settings page, under Look And Feel, click Manage Views.
2. On the Manage Views page, click somewhere to the right of the name of the view you want to delete.

   Don't click the name of the view itself, or you'll open the Edit View page.
3. In the toolbar above the table, click Delete View, and then click OK.

   The view is deleted from the list.

Customizing the Quick Launch

To change the Quick Launch pane to better suit the needs and preferences of your organization, follow these steps:

1. On the Quick Launch, under Settings, click Server Settings.
2. On the Server Settings page, under Look And Feel, click Quick Launch.
3. In the Configure Quick Launch Behavior section, specify how menu items should be expanded or collapsed within their sections.
4. In the Set Menu Item Details section, you can do the following:
    - Edit the name or web address of a link appearing on the Quick Launch. Click the link name to open the Add Or Edit Link page. Enter a different name in the Custom Link Name field, or enter a different URL in the Custom Web Address field.
    - Hide a link on the Quick Launch. Click the link name to open the Add Or Edit Link page. In the Display Links In Quick Launch box, click No.

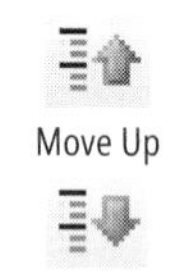

Move Up

Move Down

    - Change the order of links on the Quick Launch. Click anywhere to the right of the link whose position in the list you want to change. Don't click the name of the item itself or you'll open the Add Or Edit Link page. On the toolbar above the table, click the Move Up or Move Down button until the link appears in the position you want.
    - Create a link. On the toolbar, click New Link to open the Add Or Edit Link page. In the URL section, enter the name of the link as it should appear on the Quick Launch. Also enter the web address for the link. In the Heading section, select the location where the new link should appear on the Quick Launch.
    - Delete a link you created. Click anywhere to the right of the link to select it, and then click Delete Link.
5. When you have finished, click the Save button.

Sending Automated Alerts and Reminders to Users

You can have Project Server automatically send e-mail messages to team members and project managers to remind them about assignments and status reports that are due. To set up automated alerts and reminders, follow these steps:

1. On the Quick Launch, under Settings, click Server Settings.
2. Under Operational Policies, click Alerts And Reminders.
3. Complete the fields in the Notification E-Mail Settings section. (See Figure 23-29.)

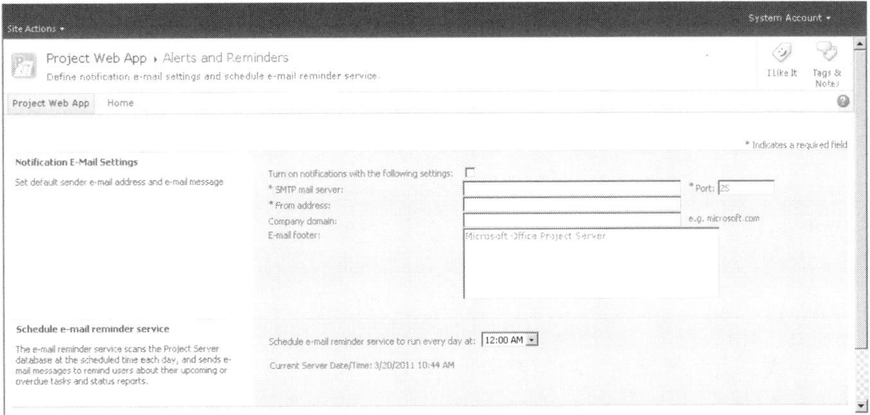

Figure 23-29 Use the Alerts And Reminders page to send e-mail reminders to users about their assignments and status reports.

4. In the Schedule E-Mail Reminder Service section, specify the time of day that the reminder should be sent.
5. Click the Save button.

CHAPTER 24

Managing Enterprise Projects and Resources

As a project manager using Microsoft Project 2010 or the earlier versions, you have probably created projects, assigned resources, tracked progress, and generated your fair share of reports. If you are working with enterprise project management and collaborating with your project team through Microsoft Project Server 2010, there are differences in how you work with your projects and resources.

This chapter is designed especially for the project manager working in an enterprise project management environment. You'll learn how you can best make use of the Microsoft enterprise project management (EPM) solution as a project manager, so that you can maximize the probability of delivering successful projects and spend the right amount of time at each project stage.

Project server administrators and portfolio managers should see Chapter 23, "Administering Your Enterprise Project Management Solution." Team members can refer to Chapter 25, "Participating on a Team Using Project Web App." Executives and project sponsors can find pertinent information in Chapter 26, "Making Executive Decisions Using Project Web App." Portfolio managers or the project management office (PMO) can refer to Chapter 27, "Managing and Analyzing Project Portfolios" for information about demand management and optimizing the portfolio.

The Microsoft enterprise project management solution is a framework of project management processes and collaboration tools that with which project managers can manage and coordinate a great number of projects and resources. All project stakeholders can connect to the project server and obtain the information they need very quickly, as follows:

- Portfolio managers and executives can revise the project portfolio and can notify project managers of approved projects.
- Project managers can create and maintain their project plans.
- Team members and team leaders can see assigned tasks and provide status updates and timesheet information.

Through Project Server 2010, the collaboration between the project manager and all other project stakeholders is structured and easy to manage.

For you as the project manager, Project Server 2010 and the enterprise project management features include the following:

NEW!

- **Demand management** In Project Server 2010, you get an unified view of all projects being undertaken by the organization, including the projects that you manage. You can group projects by the phase they are in, see the status of all the projects in one glimpse, and drill down to see the details of the projects you manage. You can add new projects by specifying the project details.
- **Schedule management** With Microsoft Project Web App, you can create your project plan directly in the web browser and display the schedule as a Gantt chart. You can enter tasks in Project Web App, create outlines, link tasks, and set the Manually Schedule or Auto Schedule task modes just as you can in Microsoft Project Professional 2010.
- **Resource management** You can add resources to your project using the enterprise resource pool. You can check resource availability and assignments, directly from Project Web App.
- **Issues and risk management** In Project Server 2010, you can leverage the full power of Microsoft SharePoint Server 2010 to create project workspaces to which you can upload all relevant project files, specify issues and risks.
- **Financial management** Project Web App gives you the option to enter cost and benefit information for your projects, and using Microsoft Excel Web App or InfoPath Forms Services.
- **Team communication and status updates** Through the use of the Tasks and Timesheet pages, team members can report on the status of their assigned tasks and submit these updates to you on a regular basis. As the project manager, you can approve or reject these updates. Upon approval, the status updates are incorporated into the project, thereby automating your progress tracking efforts. Also through Project Web App, you can request regular text-based status reports from team members that you can compile into a periodic status report.

NEW!

- **Business intelligence** The new business intelligence functionality in Project Server can help your organization see both standardized reports and views in your project pages as well as configure on-demand reports.

INSIDE OUT **Project management standards can be configured in Project Server 2010**

In Project Server 2010, the standard Project Management Institute (PMI) framework for managing projects can be incorporated as part of the Project Server configuration. Such configuration can go a long way toward ensuring high standards and adherence to project management best practices throughout the organization.

Because Project Server is so readily customizable, the project manager can choose among several project plan templates and project workflows (life cycles) that reflect the scale and priority of the project.

Because the software is only one piece of the overall project management framework, it is up to you as the project manager and your portfolio manager to determine how best to employ and implement the enterprise project management components.

Connecting to Your Project Server

After your project server administrator adds you as a user with project manager permissions in the project server, you can configure Project Professional to connect to the server. Then you have all the allowed enterprise project management features at your disposal.

In this section, you'll learn how to set up Project Professional to connect with your project server. You'll learn how to sign in to your project server from Project Professional and Project Web App. You'll also learn the basics of navigating around Project Web App to carry out your project management activities.

Setting Up Project Professional with Project Server

To get started with enterprise project management, you need to be sure that the project server administrator has added you as a project server user. You'll be provided with the project server web address, and possibly with a project server user name and password.

To set up your project server account in Project Professional, follow these steps:

1. Start Project Professional.
2. On the File tab, click Info, and then click the Manage Accounts button, as shown in Figure 24-1.

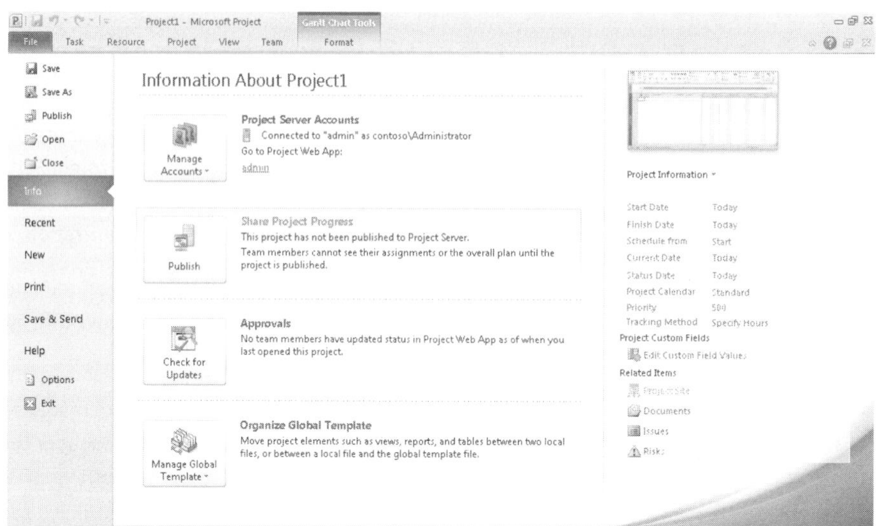

Figure 24-1 Use the Information Backstage view to start setting up your Project Server connection in Project Professional.

3. In the Project Server Accounts dialog box, click Add.

   The Account Properties dialog box appears, as shown in Figure 24-2.

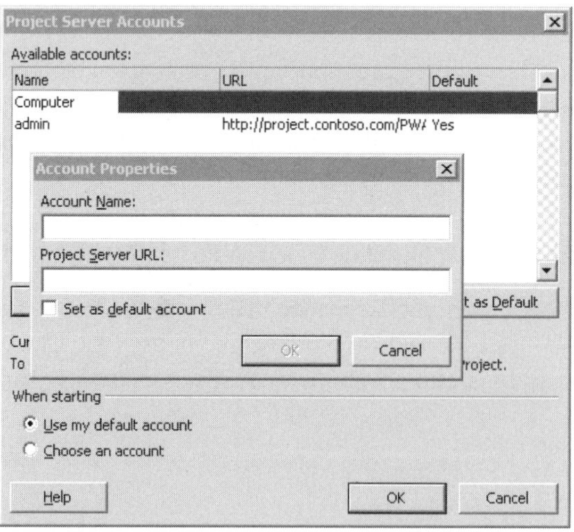

Figure 24-2 In the Account Properties dialog box, enter the new account name and the web address of your project server.

4. In the Account Name box, enter any name you want to identify the project server for yourself.

5. In the Project Server URL field, enter the web address of your organization's project server in the format *http://servername/PWA*. Your project server administrator can provide this information.

6. Click OK.

   The Project Server Accounts dialog box is updated with the new information, as shown in Figure 24-3.

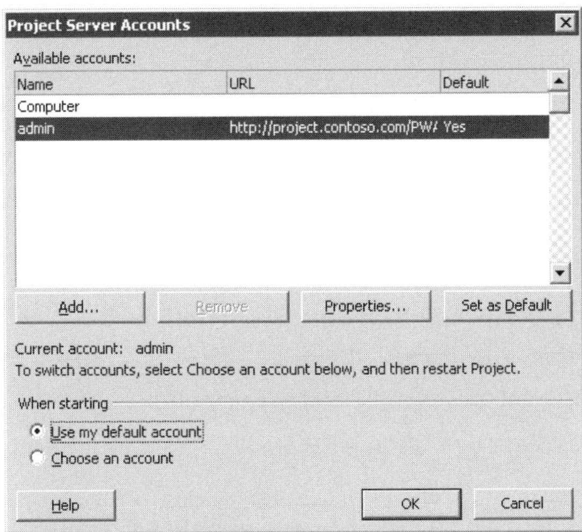

Figure 24-3 If you select Use My Default Account, the system automatically connects to your default account whenever you open Project Professional.

7. Under When Starting, select Use My Default Account if you want Project Professional to always connect to the account you designate as the default. To set an account as the default, click its name in the Available Accounts box, and then click Set As Default.

   If you instead prefer to choose the account or sometimes work offline when starting up Project Professional, select Choose An Account.

   With this option, every time you open Project Professional, the system will prompt you to select the account.

8. Click OK.

   You are now set up to log on to your project server through Project Professional. If you want to log on immediately, exit Project Professional, and then start it up again.

Logging On via Project Professional

If you specified in the Project Server Accounts dialog box that you want to automatically connect to your project server, all you need to do to log on to your project server from Project Professional is to start Project Professional. The specified project server location is found, and Project Professional logs you on immediately. Depending on your configuration, you might be prompted for a user name and password.

The project server administrator must set up your user account before you can successfully log on to the project server. If you have problems logging on, check with your project server administrator.

For more information on adding user accounts see "Creating a User Account" on page 827.

If you specified that you want to manually connect to the project server, follow these steps:

1. Start Project Professional.
2. In the Login dialog box that appears, click in the Profile box, and then click the project server account name.

   If instead you want to work offline, click Computer.
3. Click OK.
4. If you are prompted for a user name and password, enter them, and then click OK.

Signing In via Project Web App

Many of your project management responsibilities are best carried out from within your familiar Project Professional window. Nevertheless, other responsibilities are best performed from within Project Web App. Many tasks can be done in either place, and it is just a matter of which application is more convenient at the time or which method you find more efficient.

To sign in to Project Web App, follow these steps:

1. Start Internet Explorer.
2. In the address box, type the URL of your project server, and then press Enter.

   This URL is the one you enter in the Account Properties dialog box in Project Professional. However, you do not need to have the account set up in Project Professional to sign in to Project Web App directly using Internet Explorer.

   Depending on your server configuration, Project Web App might prompt you for your user name and password, as shown in Figure 24-4.

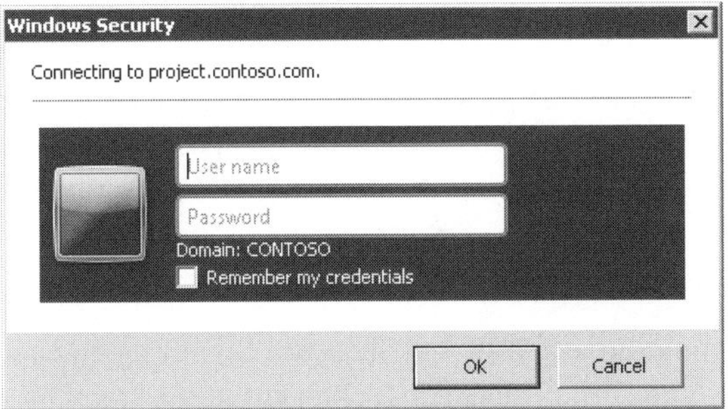

Figure 24-4 Depending on your configuration, you might be prompted to enter your user name and password to sign in to Project Web App.

3. If necessary, enter your user name and password, and then click OK.

> ### Note
>
> **If single sign-on (SSO) is enabled in your environment, the system does not prompt you for a user name and password. Once you enter the Project Web App URL in the address bar, you are automatically signed in.**

Your Project Web App Home page appears. (See Figure 24-5.)

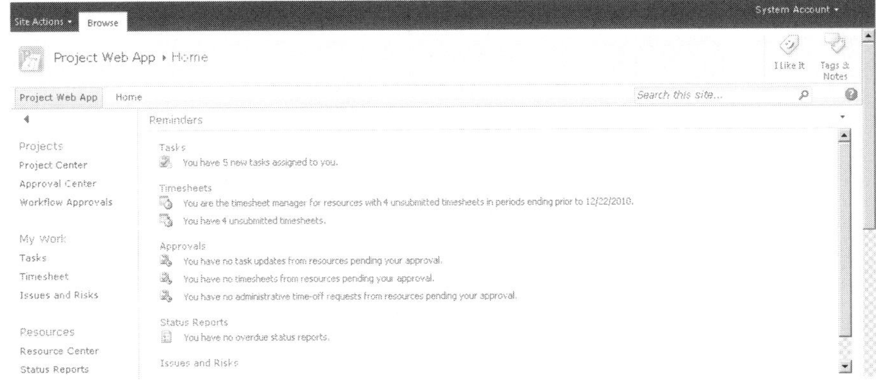

Figure 24-5 After a successful sign-in, the Project Web App Home page appears.

To sign out of Project Web App, follow these steps:

1. In the upper-right corner of any Project Web App window, click your account name.
2. In the drop-down menu that appears, click Sign Out.

Finding Your Way Around

Once you sign in to Project Web App, take a moment to click around and orient yourself to the content and controls. If you have used previous versions of Microsoft Project Server or Microsoft SharePoint, much of Project Web App will feel familiar to you.

Using the Quick Launch

Most pages throughout Project Web App show the Quick Launch pane on the left side of the window. (See Figure 24-6.) The Quick Launch includes all relevant groupings for each user type, including the project manager user type. This means you only see Quick Launch items that you, as a project manager, are likely to find applicable to your needs.

Projects
Project Center
Approval Center
Workflow Approvals

My Work
Tasks
Timesheet
Issues and Risks

Resources
Resource Center
Status Reports

Strategy
Driver Library
Driver Prioritization
Portfolio Analyses

Figure 24-6 The Quick Launch is your command center to all the areas of Project Web App to which you have access.

The Quick Launch includes the following items:

- **Projects** Includes links for reviewing project information. Using this section, you can see all enterprise projects and drill down to a specific project and review and update information regarding the schedule, resources, costs, and more.
- **My Work** Displays current tasks assigned to you. This section also includes your current timesheet and the issues and risks assigned to you.
- **Resources** Focuses on the enterprise resource pool. In this area, you can add new resources and manage existing ones. You can check resource assignment and availability.

- **Strategy** Designed for executives and the portfolio manager, this section is used to define the organizational strategy and analyze the portfolio of projects in relation to that strategy.
- **Business Intelligence** Provides tools for generating reports and viewing dashboards that provide insights into key performance indicators for projects and the portfolio.
- **Settings** Lets you modify your personal settings in Project Web App. If you have certain access permissions, you might also be able to update server settings.
- **Lists** Shows any SharePoint lists that you create, including tasks lists.
- **Documents** Contains links to project-related document libraries and risk-tracking forms and lists.

Working with Pages and Controls

The Home page is the first Project Web App page you see when you sign in. By default, it includes a list of items that need your attention—for example, approvals you need to process or status reports that are coming due. Your project server administrator can set up your Home page to include the content most appropriate for your organization.

Most Project Web App pages include the ribbon of commands rather than toolbars or menus. (See Figure 24-7.) The commands on the ribbon are organized on multiple tabs and groups.

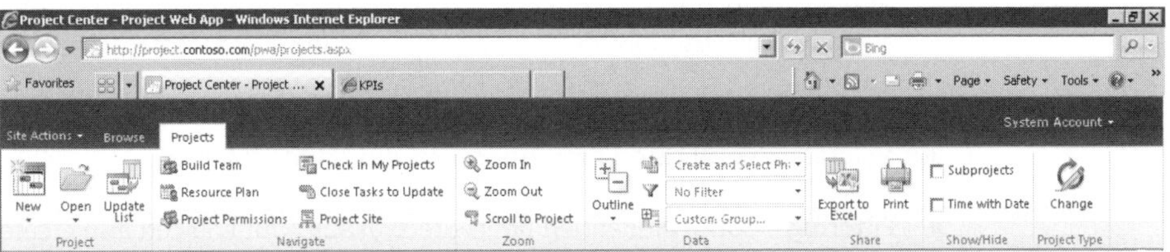

Figure 24-7 Use the ribbon on most Project Web App pages to find and execute commands.

All pages throughout Project Web App have certain standard controls, as follows:

- **User account controls** Your account name appears in the upper-right corner of the Project Web App page. Click your account name to display a drop-down menu that includes the commands My Settings, My Profile, Sign In As A Different User, Sign Out, and Personalize This Page.
- **Browse tab** Every page includes a Browse tab that contains standard controls, as shown previously in Figure 24-7. While other context-sensitive tabs are often present, you can always count on the Browse tab to be there to provide standard controls to help you navigate the site or find content. The Browse tab includes:

Project Web App

  - **Project Web App** This button is a link to the Project Web App Home page.

Home

- **Home** This button is a link to the site's Home page, which can be the same or different from your Project Web App Home page, depending on your configuration.

- **Search** In the Search box, type a word or phrase you want to find throughout this site, and then click the Search button.

Help

- **Help** Click the Help button to get assistance while using Project Web App. The Project Server Help window appears. A Help topic pertaining to the current page appears, but you can find other Help topics by typing a phrase or question in the Search For box. You can also click the Home button in the Help window and browse through the table of contents.

I Like It

- **I Like It** This button is a SharePoint 2010 social media feature. Use the I Like It button to tag a Project Web App or SharePoint page. The page is bookmarked so that you can easily find it, and you can receive newsfeed updates about the page.

Tags & Notes

- **Tags & Notes** Another SharePoint social feature, use Tags & Notes to add a name or keyword and description to a page that becomes visible to other users. The system can create tag clouds so that you can view all the pages that have a particular tag.

- **Site Actions** Like the Browse tab, the Site Actions tab is visible on every page. Click the Site Actions tab to access a menu for creating or editing web pages or managing settings on the Project Web App site. Project server administrators and portfolio managers typically use this menu to customize Project Web App.

Most major Project Web App pages, such as the Project Center and Resource Center, include standard controls on their ribbon, including the following:

- **Filtering** Some predefined filters are available, but you can also create custom filters.

Export to Excel

Print

- **Share options** Use options to export data to Excel and to print.
- **Zoom options** You can zoom in and out of a Gantt chart and other views.

Zoom In

Zoom Out

> **Note**
>
> You can customize the version of pages you use throughout Project Web App. To do this, click your account name in the upper-right corner of the page, and then in the drop-down menu, click Personalize This Page. You can also ask your project server administrator to customize elements of pages that are available for your role.

Working with Tables

Several pages in Project Web App include a grid, or table, that lists information such as projects, tasks, or resources. (See Figure 24-8.)

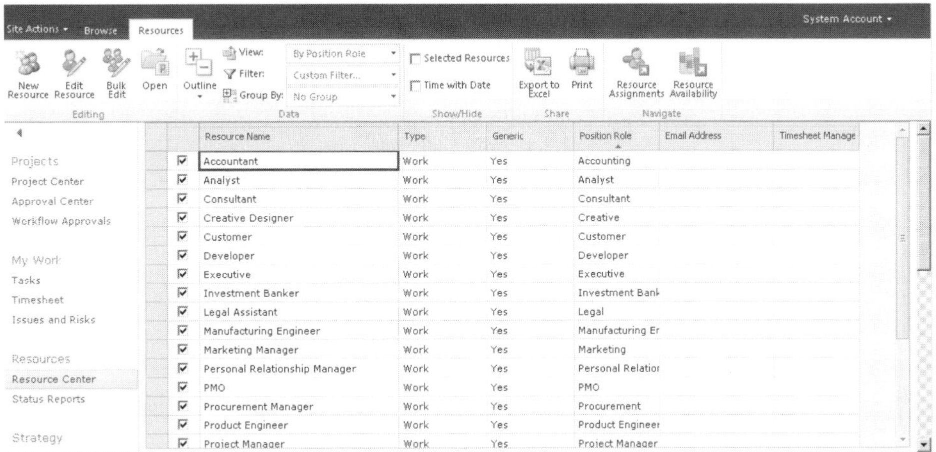

Figure 24-8 You use tables throughout Project Web App to view and edit information related to project, tasks, resources, and more.

The following elements are present for most tables:

- **List items** The main feature of a table is the list of items. In most cases, you can click an item to drill down to see more information, be it project or task details or resource information. For example, in the Project Center, you can click the name of the project; you can see the workflow status, project plan, and so on.
- **Check boxes** Some tables include check boxes next to each listed item. Clicking the check box selects the item for further action, such as editing or deleting. Selecting multiple items allows you to perform bulk or multiple operations at the same time.

- **Ribbon** One or more tabs are typically available on the ribbon above the table. For example, when you are editing a project schedule, the ribbon includes the Project, Task, and Options tabs. (See Figure 24-9.)

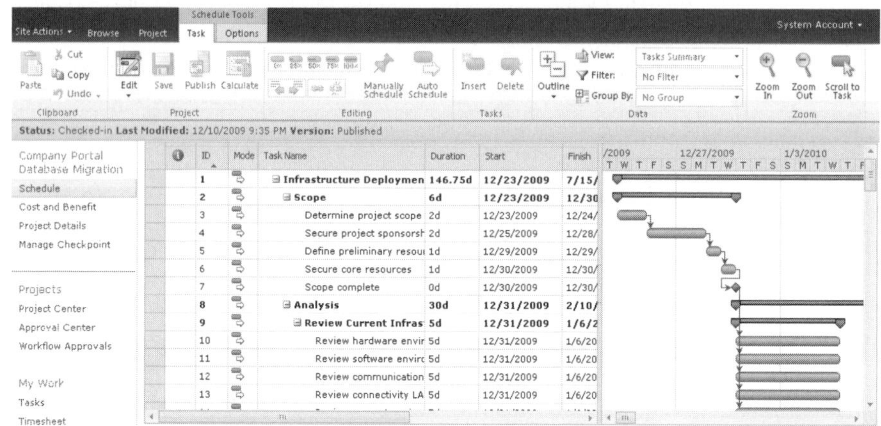

Figure 24-9 Edit the project tasks in a table.

- **Status bar** Before editing a project, the project manager checks out the project. The status bar indicates that the project is checked out, when it was last modified, and the version.

Status: Checked-in **Last Modified:** 12/10/2011 9:35 AM **Version:** Published

Working with Enterprise Projects

With your user account set up and Project Professional connected successfully to the project server, you are ready to get down to business and start creating enterprise projects.

You can create your enterprise projects from within Project Web App or Project Professional. Although there are some differences, many of the basic project management features are available in both places.

You can save a new project to the project server or import an existing local project. Either way, your new enterprise project is associated with the enterprise global template, which sets the project management standards for your organization and the project workflow.

You manage your enterprise project files in specific ways. You check out a project from the project server, work on it, and then check it back in. You can save your project to the project server as often as you like and publish the project only when you are ready to make the information available to assigned resources and other Project Web App users.

NEW!

Demand Management Helps Evaluate New Projects

Even after you add your project to the project server, you might not be able to start planning the project. Project Server 2010 integrates capabilities for demand management and portfolio management. *Demand management* is the process of gathering and managing all project proposals, from when a proposal is initiated until a project is closed. Demand management is used to capture organizational demands and give the portfolio manager and executives the option to implement only those projects that bring the most value to the organization in a structured process.

Typically, the portfolio manager defines the approval process that a certain type of project must go through to receive the permission to start. This process is referred to as the *project workflow*, also known as the project life cycle.

For more information about how project managers work with workflows, see "Following a Project Workflow" on page 923. For more information about how demand management is implemented through Project Server 2010, see "Designing Your Demand Management System" on page 1032.

Talk with your portfolio manager to get more information about the project workflows and demand management details being implemented in your organization.

After your enterprise projects are published on the project server and the project has received all the necessary approvals, you can carry out your day-to-day project management tasks. With the project checked out, you can add new tasks, modify existing tasks, work with resources, update progress-tracking information, review and add information in custom enterprise fields, generate reports, and more.

Creating a New Enterprise Project

You can choose one of two methods for creating an enterprise project. One way is to start a new project plan in Project Professional or Project Web App, being sure you are connected to the project server, and then save the project plan to the project server. The other way is to open an existing local project and import it to the project server.

As soon as the project is saved to the project server, the enterprise global template is applied to the project, and accordingly, enterprise standards apply.

Creating an Enterprise Project by Using Project Professional

To create a new enterprise project and save it to the project server using Project Professional, follow these steps:

1. Start Project Professional 2010 and connect to the project server.

2. On the File tab, click New.

3. In the Backstage view that appears, click Blank Project or click the name of the existing project or template you want to use as the basis for the new project, and then click the Create button in the right pane.

4. Enter tasks or adapt information for your new project.

For more information about creating a project, see "Creating a Project File" on page 74.

5. On the File tab, click Save As.

   The Save To Project Server dialog box appears. (See Figure 24-10.)

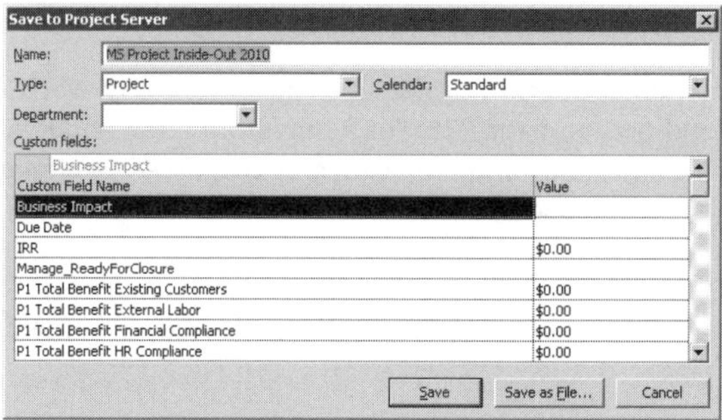

Figure 24-10 When you save a new file while connected to the project server, the Save To Project Server dialog box appears.

6. In the Name box, type the project file name.

7. In the Calendar box, specify the base calendar being used as the project calendar.

   This project calendar is the one specified in the Project Information dialog box.

8. In the Department box, select the department this project pertains to, if applicable.

9. Enter the value for any of the custom enterprise project fields listed in the Custom Fields table.

   These fields have been created for your organization to establish standards and points of comparison among multiple projects.

10. Click Save.

    Your new project is saved as an enterprise project on the project server.

11. When you close the new enterprise project, a message asks whether you want to check the project into the project server.

    When you check the project in, you are publishing it. Click Yes to check the project in (publish it on the project server). Click No to keep the project checked out to you (others cannot see or modify the project).

    You can publish projects on the project server from Project Professional by clicking File, Publish.

    Learn more details about checking project files in and out in "Managing Your Files on the Project Server" on page 912.

Saving Projects Locally

If you want to save the project but do not want to save it to the project server just yet, in the Save To Project Server dialog box, click Save As File and then click OK. In the Save As dialog box, enter the file name, select the location on your local hard disk where you want to save the project and then click Save. Later, when you are ready, you can import the project to the server.

Creating an Enterprise Project by Using Project Web App

To create a new project and save it to the project server by using Project Web App, follow these steps:

1. On the Quick Launch, under Projects, click Project Center.

   The Project Center appears, showing the list of all enterprise projects.

2. On the Projects tab, in the Project group, click New, and then select the project template (also known as *enterprise project type*) you want to use to create the new project. (See Figure 24-11.)

   You can also open Project Professional or add a project from a SharePoint list to create the project by selecting one of those commands on the New drop-down menu.

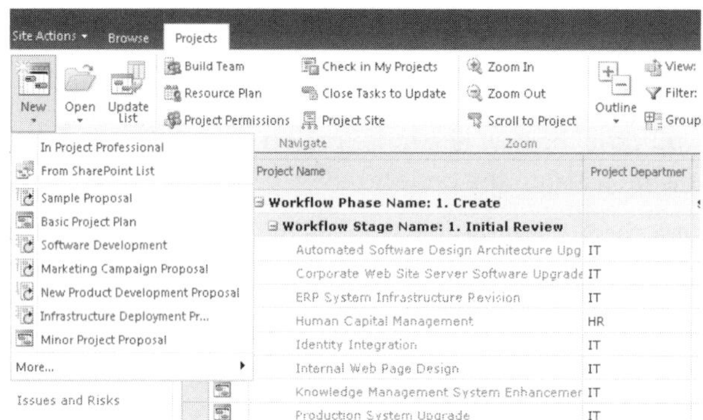

Figure 24-11 Select the project template from the New drop-down menu on the Projects tab.

Note

Each project template is associated with a *workflow* of project phases and approvals. Depending on the project template you select, you manage different checkpoints throughout the project life cycle.

For more information, see "Following a Project Workflow" on page 923.

3. After selecting the project template, enter project information on the project detail page that appears, as shown in Figure 24-12. The information includes details such as the project name, description, and start date.

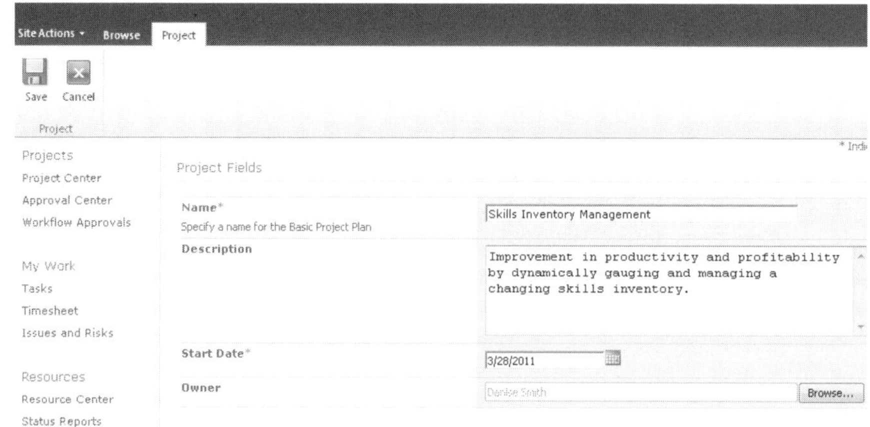

Figure 24-12 Enter the new project information in the project detail page.

4. On the Project tab, in the Project group, click Save.

   The new project is created and saved, and then the Schedule project detail page appears. In this page, you can start entering task names and other task information. Many of the project plan controls in the Schedule project detail page are similar to those in Project Professional.

   For more information about creating a project, see "Creating a Project File" on page 74. For more information about entering project information, see Chapter 5, "Scheduling Tasks Manually or Automatically," and Chapter 6, "Building Your Schedule."

Your Actions Are Queued in Project Web App

Project Server has implemented queuing services to better service user actions. This means that requests performed in Project Web App—for example, creating a project, saving information, and checking in a project—might not be performed immediately but are queued instead until the project server has sufficient capacity.

Upon selecting an action, the project server displays its status in the upper-right corner of the page.

Saving Changes for Your Enterprise Project

Whenever you save an enterprise project, changes are saved to the project server. Until you give the command to publish the project, it is considered a working draft, and no one but you can see it or work with it. You can build your draft project by using the enterprise global template and the enterprise resource pool, but it is all your own business and no one else's yet. The project is listed in the Project Center, but it does not have any details.

To create a working draft version of a project, simply click the File tab, and then Save to save it to the project server in Project Professional.

Publishing Project Information to the Project Server

When your project is ready for public consumption and analysis by the rest of your organization, it is ready to be published to the project server.

As soon as you publish a new project, it is listed in Project Center. Any task assignments are made available to the assigned resources. By default, a web-based SharePoint workspace is created to view the details of the newly published project.

INSIDE OUT **Project Server maintains four project databases**

Your project server maintains four project databases, each containing different versions of enterprise project files:

- **Draft** The Draft database, also known as the working store, contains projects that have been saved to the project server but not published.
- **Published** The Published database contains projects that have been published. It also contains project templates. When a project is published, task assignments are made available to the assigned resources.
- **Reporting** As soon as you publish your project, data from the project is added to the Reporting database in a format that is conducive to creating reports. As your project is updated, those updates are also reflected in the Reporting database. As reports and views are created, the most up-to-date information from your project is used. This database is optimized for reporting.
- **Archive** The Archive database saves backup versions of projects and other data.

Publishing a Project In Project Professional

To publish a project for the first time from Project Professional, follow these steps:

1. Be sure that Project Professional is connected to the project server.
2. On the File tab, click Save to save the project to the project server.
3. On the File tab, click Publish.
4. Review the Publish Project dialog box to be sure that all the specifications are as they should be. (See Figure 24-13.)

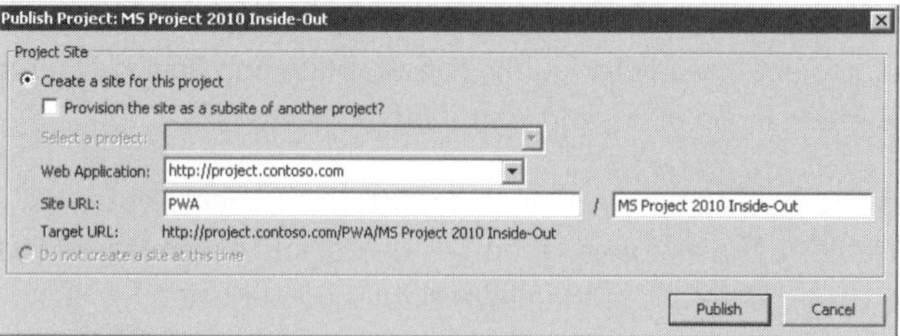

Figure 24-13 Use the Publish Project dialog box to make your project available to other enterprise users through Project Web App.

5. Click Publish.

   The project is now published to the project server and is available to other Project Web App users. If you switch over to Project Web App, you'll see that your published project is now listed in the Project Center.

After you first publish your project to the project server, other users do not automatically see any further changes you make. You always have a choice about whether any new changes are published to the project server. To publish recent changes on an already-published project, click File, Publish. The latest version of your project is made available to others who need to view details about your project in Project Web App.

Exclude Tasks from a Published Project

You can exclude selected tasks from being published to the project server. This can be useful if you are working on what-if scenarios with various tasks and are not ready to make those tasks known to the organization.

To exclude tasks from being published to the project server, follow these steps:

1. **In Project Professional, in a task sheet such as the Gantt Chart, right-click the column heading next to where you want to insert the Publish column.**
2. **In the shortcut menu that appears, click Insert Column.**
3. **In the drop-down fields list that appears, type pu to quickly find and click the Publish field.**
4. **For the tasks you do not want to publish to the project server, change the Publish field to No.**

Publishing a Project In Project Web App

To publish your project while working in Project Web App, follow these steps.

1. On the Quick Launch, under Projects, click Project Center.
2. Click the name of the project.

   The project detail page for the project appears.
3. On the Task tab, in the Project group, click Publish, as shown in Figure 24-14.

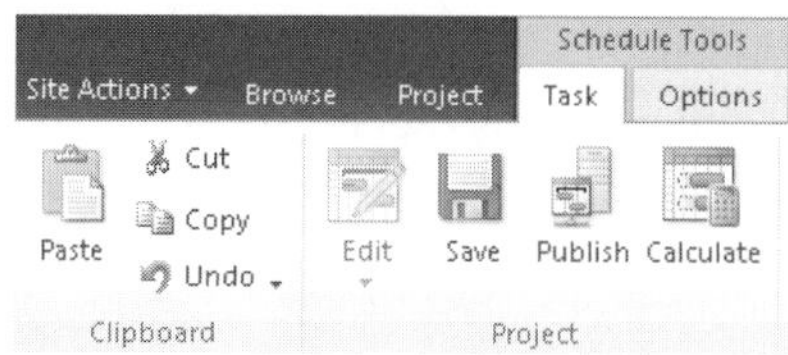

Figure 24-14 On the Task tab of the project detail page, in the Project group, click Publish.

The project is published and now all users with proper permissions can see the project.

Managing Your Files on the Project Server

There are three aspects of file management on the project server as you open, close, and save your project files:

- Checking project files out and in
- Saving changes in a project file
- Publishing project information to the project server

You've already learned about saving and publishing files on the project server in the previous section. In this section, you'll learn about checking enterprise project files out and in on the project server.

Checking Out an Enterprise Project

As soon as you open a project, either in a project detail page in Project Web App, or with Project Professional, the project is checked out to you. When you close the project, you are asked whether you want to check in the project.

It's good practice to check out a project from the project server when you want to work on it and check it back in when you are done for the day. This is typically done when updating plans, costs, and resource requirements.

To check out an enterprise project in Project Professional, follow these steps:

1. With Project Professional connected to the project server, click File, Open.

   The Open dialog box appears, showing the list of enterprise projects that have previously been opened on this computer. (See Figure 24-15.)

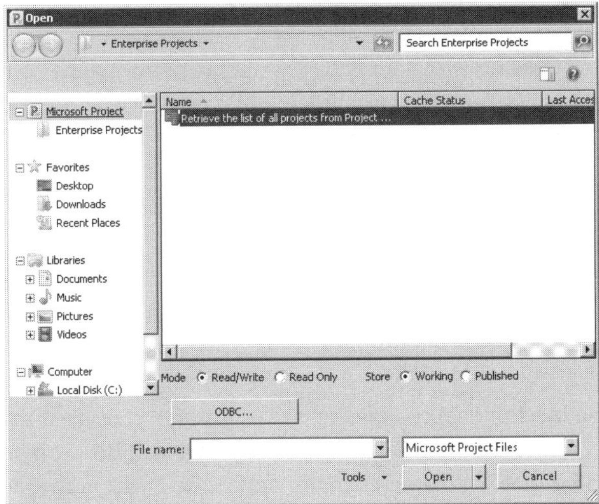

Figure 24-15 The Open dialog box presents a list of recently accessed projects and the option to retrieve the full list of projects from the project server.

2. Click the name of the project you want to check out.

   If the project you are looking for is not listed, double-click Retrieve The List Of All Projects From Project Server at the top of the list of files. The Group By control appears. Click the arrow in the Group By box to choose a property by which to categorize the projects so that you can more quickly find what you are looking for. Any project you open in Project Professional is copied to your active cache.

3. Be sure that the project you want to check out is not already checked out by someone else.

   A project can be checked out by only one user at a time. You can see if the project is checked out in the Cache Status column in the Open dialog box.

4. Next to Mode, ensure that the Read/Write option is selected, which is the default.

   If someone else has checked out the project you want, you can still open it if you select the Read Only option.

5. To see the list of published projects, next to Store, select the Published option. To see the list of published as well as draft (not published) projects to which you have access, select the Working option.

   The Working option is selected by default.

6. Click Open.

   The project opens. The enterprise global template is attached to the project, and the enterprise resource pool is available for use in the project.

Checking In Projects from Project Professional

When you finish working with your enterprise project for the time being, you check it back in to the project server. Your organization might have specific rules for when you need to check in your projects.

To check in an enterprise project from Project Professional, follow these steps:

1. Be sure that Project Professional is connected to the project server.
2. On the File tab, click Save to save your final changes.
3. On the File tab, click Close.

   If you made additional changes since the last time you saved the file, the Close dialog box appears, as shown in Figure 24-16. In this dialog box, you have the choice not only to save or discard your changes, but also to check in the file or not.

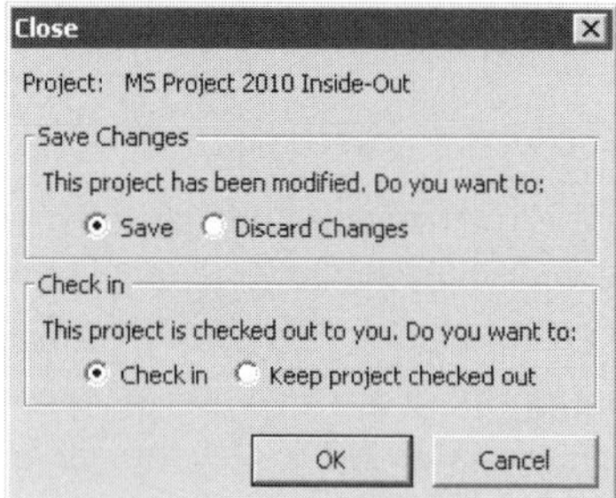

Figure 24-16 Select the Save option to save the changes to your project, and select the Check In option to release the editing rights on the project and check in the project with your most recent changes.

Note

If you have not entered values for any required custom enterprise fields, you see a prompt reminding you to do so. You must complete these fields before you can successfully check in the project.

For more information about custom enterprise fields, see "Working with Custom Enterprise Fields" on page 919.

Checking In Projects in Project Web App

If you use Project Web App to edit project information, you need to check in your project after you finish making changes to it.

You typically make your changes in one of the project detail pages for the project. Examples of project detail pages include Schedule and Cost And Benefit.

To check in your project, be sure the project is open in one of its project detail pages. On the Project tab, in the Project group, click Close, as shown in Figure 24-17.

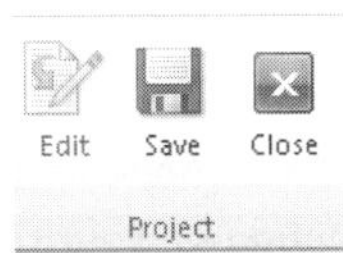

Figure 24-17 In Project Web App, click Project, Project, Close to check in the project.

The project server prompts you to confirm whether you want to check in the project or cancel the action, as shown in Figure 24-18. Click Yes, and the project is checked in.

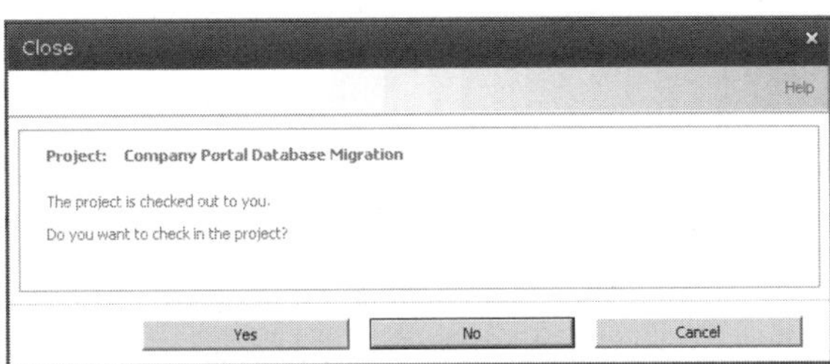

Figure 24-18 Your confirmation in the Close dialog box completes the check-in process.

The status of the check-in action appears in the top-right corner of the screen until the check-in is complete.

After you check in your project, if it is published, other project server users with the proper permissions can view your changes and edit the project.

Working Offline with Enterprise Projects

You do not always need to be connected to the project server to work with projects. Moreover, you do not always need to work with enterprise projects when you are connected to the project server. Working offline is particularly helpful if you are traveling or in some other situation without easy Internet access and need to continue to work on your project files. Working offline can also be handy if you want to try some contingency scenarios with an enterprise project.

To work offline with an enterprise project, in Project Professional, check out the enterprise project. On the File tab, click Info, Manage Accounts, Work Offline.

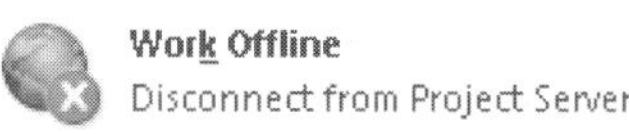

When you are ready to connect to the project server again, on the File tab, click Info. Under Project Server Accounts, click Connect To Server.

Note

You can be connected to the project server and also open a local, nonenterprise project. To do this, on the File tab, click Open. Browse to the location on your computer or network that contains the non-enterprise project. Select the local project, and then click Open.

Refining Your Enterprise Projects

Now that your projects are stored on the project server, you can work with them as enterprise projects. What does that mean to you?

Essentially, it means that you are now using the enterprise global template, which contains any standard project elements that have been defined for your organization, including macros, views, toolbars, and so on. You also have access to enterprise resources and tools for working efficiently with those resources. In the wider view, your enterprise projects can be reviewed and analyzed by others so that they can see the full portfolio of projects taking place throughout the organization.

Reviewing the Enterprise Global Template

When you start Project Professional and connect to your project server, the latest update of the enterprise global template is automatically attached. The enterprise global template is akin to a global template or the "global global" over the standard project global template. The enterprise global template dictates standards being enforced and customizations made available to Project 2010 interface elements in projects throughout the enterprise. These standards provide for customization and consistency across all projects in an organization. The standards propagated through the enterprise global template also make it possible for project information throughout the enterprise to be compared and analyzed in meaningful ways.

By default, the portfolio manager and project server administrator are the only users with permission to modify the enterprise global template. However, as a project manager, you have permission to view the enterprise global template so that you can see the controls behind your individual enterprise projects. The following list details the project elements that can be modified and propagated as standards via the enterprise global template:

- Views
- Reports
- Visual Basic modules
- Tables
- Filters
- Calendars
- Import and export maps
- Fields
- Groups

To review the enterprise global template and see the specific elements that are set up for your organization, follow these steps:

1. Be sure that Project Professional is connected to the project server. As soon as it is connected, the enterprise global template is loaded for use with your enterprise projects.
2. On the File tab, click Info. In the Organize Global Template section, click Manage Global Templates, and then click Open Enterprise Global.

   An enterprise project plan, which appears to be empty, is displayed. The title bar shows "Checked-out Enterprise Global." (See Figure 24-19.)

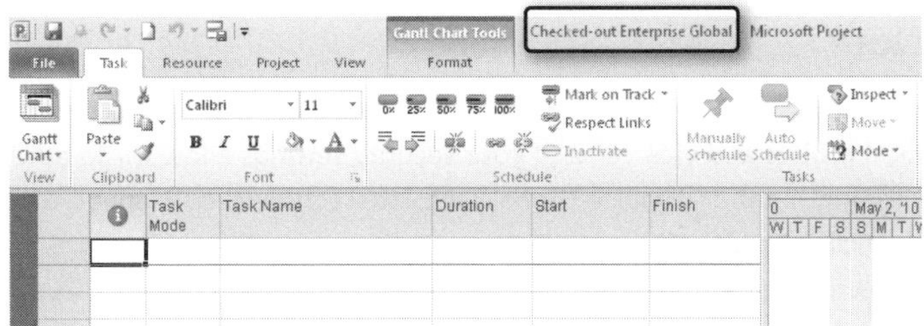

Figure 24-19 Review features in the enterprise global template to see your organization's standards.

The enterprise global template is not checked out to you in the sense that you can make changes to it, but rather that you are using it as the structure for your own checked-out enterprise projects.

1. You can browse around the various interface features—such as the view definitions, filter definitions, custom toolbars, and so on—to see how the enterprise global template has been customized.

2. When you have finished reviewing the enterprise global template, close it.

   Although you can inadvertently enter data in the enterprise global template, the data is not saved when you close it. Only specific elements (views, groups, macros, currency formats, and so on) can be saved to the enterprise global template, and only by those who have the proper permissions. Tasks or assignments are never saved with the enterprise global template.

The global standards are present in any enterprise projects you currently have checked out. In fact, if you browse the interface elements in your own enterprise project, you'll see the same customizations present there that are in the enterprise global template.

If the enterprise global template changes after you connect to the project server, you see those changes only after you close Project Professional and reconnect.

It is likely that your organization has a system—whether formal or informal—for project managers to suggest changes to the enterprise global template. Find out from the project server administrator or portfolio manager how you can suggest changes you want to see implemented. When the enterprise global template is updated, you see the changes take effect the next time you check out an enterprise project.

Even though the enterprise global template affects all your enterprise projects, you can still use your own project global template on projects on your own computer. As long as elements in the project global template do not conflict with elements in the enterprise global template, you can create your own sets of standards for all your own projects.

For more information, see "Working with the Project Global Template" on page 1189.

Note

You can view template elements and move elements from the enterprise project to a local project and vice versa (if your security settings allow it). To do this, on the File tab, click Info. In the Organize Global Template section, click Manage Global Template, and then click Organizer.

Remember that you can change interface elements to apply only to an individual project without them being a part of the enterprise global template or your own project global template.

Working with Custom Enterprise Fields

Custom enterprise fields often constitute a major area of customization and standardization implemented via the enterprise global template. Custom fields can be designed to store a specific category of numbers, durations, or text not provided by built-in Project 2010 fields. Custom fields of different data types are available for assignments, tasks, and entire projects. The portfolio manager or project server administrator defines these fields as part of the enterprise global template, and then the fields become part of your project. These fields can also be used, for reporting purposes.

Local custom fields are available on your local computer, while enterprise custom fields are available on your project server. Examples of local custom fields include Text1 or Cost5. Examples of enterprise custom fields include Enterprise Text7 or Enterprise Cost3.

There are three categories of custom enterprise fields:

- Custom enterprise project fields, such as Enterprise Project Cost or Enterprise Project Duration
- Custom enterprise task fields, such as Enterprise Date or Enterprise Flag
- Custom enterprise resource fields, such as Enterprise Text or Enterprise Number

NEW!

Although local, non-enterprise projects impose a limit on the number of custom fields you can create, in Project Server 2010, an unlimited number of custom fields can be created for each field type (Cost, Date, Text, and so on).

Another major fields improvement in Project Server 2010 is that custom fields can be associated with departments. Permission to use department-level custom fields is also restricted only to the users in that department.

Generally, the responsibility for adding custom fields to the enterprise global template falls to the project server administrator or the portfolio manager. After custom fields have been defined, you can add them to tables in Project Professional and in Project Web App. They're also available in certain project detail pages in Project Web App.

For more information about custom fields, see "Customizing Enterprise Project Fields" on page 864 and "Customizing Fields" on page 1107.

Setting Up a Program of Projects

You can insert one enterprise project into another to create a master project/subproject relationship. Using this technique, you can model a program that reflects all projects being implemented under a specific program in your organization. The overarching program can be represented as the master project, with all the projects within that program set up as subprojects of the master project. As implemented through Project Server, a program is a set of related projects that is often set up in a hierarchical relationship.

For more information about inserting one project into another, see "Structuring Master Projects with Subprojects" on page 600.

By contrast, a portfolio is a collection of enterprise projects being implemented by an organization as reflected in the project server. They might or might not be related to one another, and they might or might not be set up in a hierarchical relationship.

All enterprise projects are listed in the Project Center in Project Web App, whether they are part of a program, whether they are a master project or a subproject, or whether they are projects unrelated to any others except that they're being implemented within the same organization.

Setting up programs in Project Server by using master projects and subprojects supports large organizations that need to implement a number of large projects and subprojects that often take place at various locations around the world.

When you open a master project, all the subprojects are listed (and checked out) as tasks in any task view. You can then drill down by clicking one of the subprojects to see the tasks within that project.

If you want to distinguish between master projects and subprojects on the Project Center page, work with your project server administrator or portfolio manager to create and add a custom field to the table in the Project Center. For example, a text field called Master-Subproject could be created in which project managers would indicate whether a project is a master project, a subproject, or neither. That field could then be added to a Project Center view. Another field for subprojects could specify the name of the master project.

You can set up dependencies and deliverables (or commitments) between the projects within a program, providing visibility to when a key deliverable that affects related projects is coming due.

The program hierarchy can be maintained and its status summarized in reports that are generated in the Business Intelligence Center.

Depending on Deliverables in Other Projects

Through Microsoft enterprise project management features, you can manage dependencies on deliverables among projects in your organization. By managing these dependencies, you can keep an eye on commitments in other projects without necessarily affecting the scheduling of your project.

Of course, you can still create links—task dependencies—from one project to another. Doing so is still necessary when there is a true relationship between tasks, such as the common finish-to-start task relationship in which a task in one project cannot begin until a task in another project has been completed. This type of structure does affect scheduling because if the predecessor task slips, the successor task slips as well.

For information about linking tasks between projects, see "Linking Information Between Project Plans" on page 633.

However, if you're working in an enterprise project management environment and you want to be alerted to the status of deliverables in one enterprise project that affect the outcome but not necessarily the scheduling of another enterprise project, you might consider setting up deliverable dependencies.

Setting Up a Dependency on a Deliverable

To set up a dependency on a deliverable, follow these steps:

1. Be sure that Project Professional is connected to your project server.
2. In Project Professional, open the enterprise project that is dependent on a deliverable in another enterprise project.
3. If you want to link a task to the deliverable in the other project, select the task.
4. On the Task tab, in the Insert group, click Deliverable, and then click Manage Dependencies.

   Deliverable

   The Dependency task pane appears on the left side of the project window.
5. In the Dependency task pane, click Add New Dependency.
6. In the Select Project box, click the name of the project that contains the deliverable.

   The Select Deliverable pane appears. As you roll your mouse over each deliverable task, a pop-up shows the full name of the deliverable and its start and finish dates.
7. Click the name of the deliverable you want to include as a dependency with the current project.

8. If you want to create a link (task dependency) with the deliverable, select the Link To Selected Task check box.

9. Click Done.

Checking the Status of a Deliverable

To see an update about a deliverable, follow these steps:

1. Be sure that Project Professional is connected to your project server.

2. Open the enterprise project that is dependent on a deliverable in another enterprise project.

3. On the Task tab, in the Insert group, click Deliverable, and then click Manage Dependencies.

   The Dependency task pane appears, showing the names of the deliverables in other projects you have set up.

4. At the bottom of the Dependency task pane, click Accept All Server Changes if that option is present. Also click Get Updates.

   Information about the deliverable's finish date is updated in the task pane.

Creating a Deliverable

In addition to creating dependencies to deliverables in other projects, you can create deliverables in your own projects. To do this, follow these steps.

1. Be sure that Project Professional is connected to your project server, and then open the enterprise project that is to contain the deliverable.

2. If the deliverable is a particular task, or if you want to associate a deliverable with a task in your project, select that task. However, the deliverable can be independent of any task in the project and be associated only with the project as a whole.

3. On the Task tab, in the Insert group, click Deliverable, and then click Add New Deliverable.

4. Complete the fields in the Add Deliverable task pane.

5. If you are associating the deliverable with a selected task, select the Link To Selected Task check box.

   The fields under Deliverable Details are filled in with information from the selected task.

6. If the deliverable is to be associated with the project but not a particular task, enter a title for the deliverable as well as start and finish dates.

7. Click Done.

Following a Project Workflow

NEW!

New in Project Server 2010 is a powerful portfolio management module, replacing what used to be the separate functionality in Microsoft Office Project Portfolio Server 2007. With the integrated portfolio management features, including demand management, workflow, and business drivers, your organization can be more focused on project management governance, standardization, and approvals.

The *project workflow* steps refer to the project life cycle or the phases and stages a project should go through to reach completion. Project Server includes a predefined project workflow, which consists of the phases of Create, Select, Plan, Manage, and Close. Your portfolio manager can create other workflows for various types of projects for your organization.

The use of the project workflow affects how you manage projects from start to finish. With checkpoints at various stages in the workflow, projects can have a closer and more standardized means for governance and control. In addition, the workflow ensures that the right projects are selected for the strategic benefit to the organization.

A project life cycle, or workflow, typically starts with the creation of a project proposal based on an established template, or *enterprise project type*. Depending on the enterprise project type, a workflow is automatically integrated with the new proposal. As the project manager, you'll be prompted for various approvals at specific checkpoints along the way. If the proposal is approved, you convert the proposal into a project.

One of the key checkpoints is for you to enter a structured business case for the project, which includes the schedule, resource estimates, risks, and strategic impact of the project on established business drivers for the organization.

Based on this information, the portfolio manager and other managing stakeholders determine whether this project has a place in the organization's optimal portfolio of projects. If the project is selected, you get the "green light" to move forward with planning and executing the project. Throughout the rest of the project's life cycle, other checkpoints in the project workflow ensure that the project is continuing to fulfill its expected benefit to the organization, and this project governance continues until the project is complete and closed.

This process of gathering and managing all projects, from proposal creation to project closure, is called *demand management*.

For more information about project workflows, phases, stages, and enterprise project types, see "Setting Up Project Workflows" on page 854.

Initiating a Project Proposal

A proposal is a simple way to define some basic project details for a potential project without investing a lot of time in it. If the project is approved, you can convert it into a real project plan that can be opened in Project Professional with the groundwork already done. You do not need to do any converting or importing; you just need to add detail.

Submitting the proposal is part of the Create phase in the project workflow.

To create a proposal, follow these steps:

1. On the Quick Launch, under Projects, click Project Center.
2. On the Projects tab, in the Project group, click New, and then select Sample Proposal.

   The Project Information page appears, as shown in Figure 24-20.

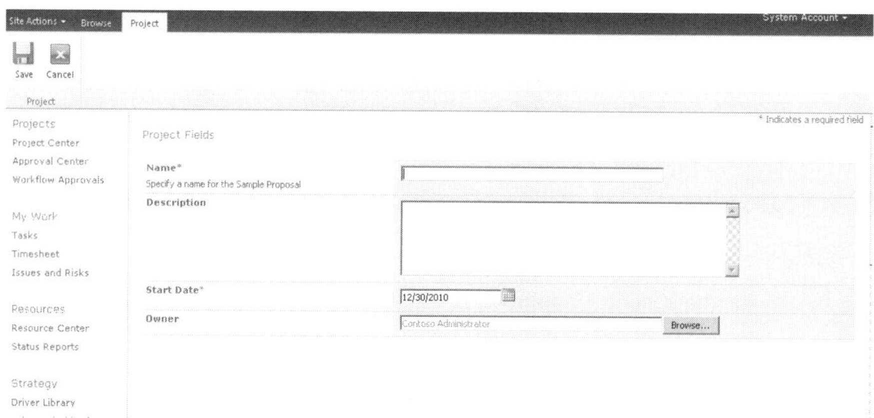

Figure 24-20 Start creating a proposal on the Project Information page.

3. Complete the information on the page.
4. On the Project tab, in the Project group, click Save.

   The proposal file is created and saved. Your proposal name appears at the top of the Quick Launch. On the project detail page that appears, you can see the workflow step the proposal is in along with additional information about the next steps. Figure 24-21 shows an example.

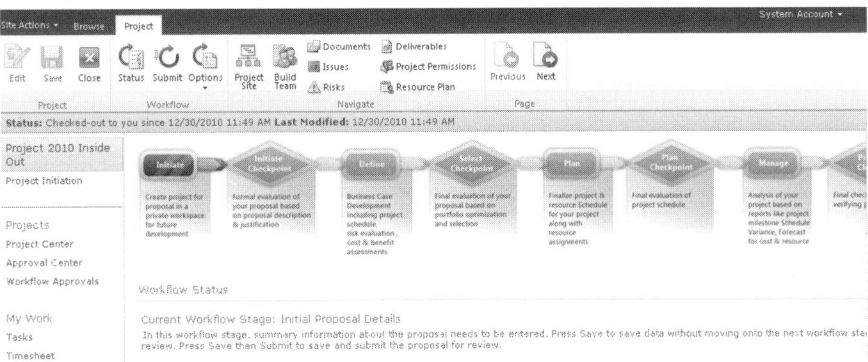

Figure 24-21 In the project detail page, you see the workflow step your project is in.

The proposal is in the Initiate phase of the workflow.

5. Scroll down and click All Workflow Stages.

   This shows the next workflow steps your project has to go through.

6. After you enter the necessary information for the Initiate phase, on the Project tab, in the Workflow group, click Submit. Read the message that appears, and then click OK.

   According to the workflow, the proposal is evaluated by the portfolio manager and possibly by executive stakeholders. If your project is approved, it moves from the Initiate phase it to the Define phase.

Working Through the Define Phase and Beyond

When a proposal reaches the Define phase of the project, you need to enter more details about the project. Such details include weighing the project against the organization's business drivers so that the strategic impact of the project can be measured. You'll also be prompted to enter information about cost, benefit, and risks.

To fulfill the default workflow steps in the Define phase, follow these steps:

1. On the Quick Launch, under Projects, click Project Center.

2. On the Projects tab, in the Project group, click the name of your proposal.

   The project detail page for your proposal appears.

3. At the top of the Quick Launch, under the proposal name, click Strategic Impact.

   The Strategic Impact page is displayed.

4. On the Project tab, in the Project group, click Edit.

5. As shown in Figure 24-22, select the rating of each business driver for this project.

For more information about business drivers, see "Reflecting Strategy by Defining Business Drivers" on page 1037.

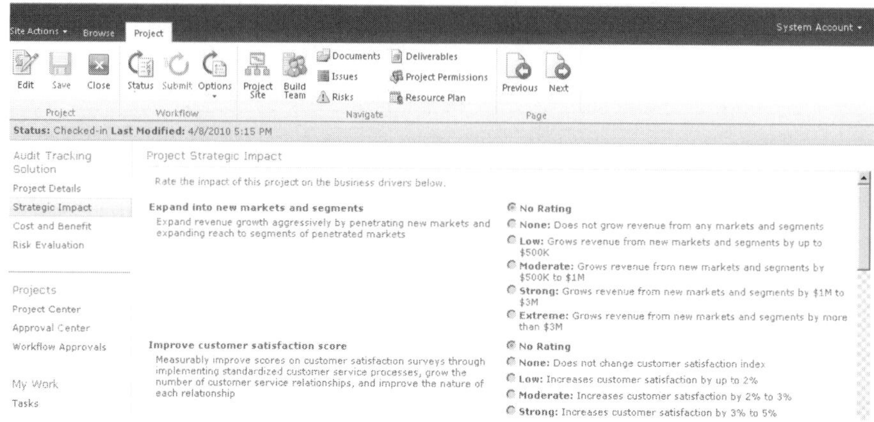

Figure 24-22 Select the impact this project has on each business driver listed on the Project Strategic Impact page.

6. On the Project tab, in the Project group, click Save.
7. On the Project tab, in the Page group, click Next.

   The Cost And Benefit page appears.
8. Enter the necessary information, including the cost, benefit, and cash flow information for the next five years.

   This information gives the portfolio manager the information needed to determine whether the project should be included in the portfolio.
9. On the Project tab, in the Project group, click Save.
10. On the Project tab, in the Page group, click Next.

    The Risk Evaluation page appears.
11. Enter the necessary risk information.
12. On the Project tab, in the Project group, click Save.

13. After you enter the necessary information for the Define phase, on the Project tab, in the Workflow group, click Submit. Read the message that appears, and then click OK.

    According to the default workflow, the project is evaluated further by the portfolio manager. If your project is approved again, it moves to the Select phase. At this checkpoint, the portfolio manager and executives make the decision whether to include the project in the portfolio. The analysis they make can be based on costs, resource constraints, risks, and strategic impact.

    If the project passes the Select checkpoint, it enters the Plan phase. At this point, you can start to enter the schedule in Project Web App or in Project Professional.

If your project makes it through the Select phase, then you enter the Plan phase. Here's where you convert your proposal to a full-fledged project.

For more information about creating a project, see "Creating an Enterprise Project by Using Project Web App" on page 907.

After you save and publish the project plan, the project might be submitted for a planning checkpoint. The portfolio manager reviews your project plan to see whether it adheres to the project management standards and follows the costs and schedule specified at the project proposal initiation.

Should the project pass the planning checkpoint, it proceeds to the Manage phase. In this phase, project execution actually begins. Resources carry out their assigned tasks and submit task updates for incorporation and tracking in the project plan. When the project is completed, the project enters the Close phase.

Note

The workflow phases and checkpoints described in this section might be different for certain projects or for all projects in your organization. Contact your portfolio manager or project server administrator for more information.

Building Your Enterprise Project Team

Among the advantages of enterprise project management is the capability to work with the enterprise resource pool and its associated functions. The enterprise resource pool is the set of people, equipment, and materials available to be assigned and carry out the work required in projects throughout an organization. It contains fundamental information about resources, such as skill sets and availability, which helps you find the right resources for your projects. The enterprise resource pool also contains cost information, which not only helps you work within your allotted budget but also helps accounting and human resources figure costs from their points of view.

With the enterprise resource pool comes a high level of visibility into resource availabilities, skills, roles, and utilization. Project managers as well as upper management can see when additional staff is needed and where there are underutilized resources. They also can view the basic data for all project resources in one place. Resource managers can also use the enterprise resource pool to staff, plan, and budget with more accuracy and confidence. They can see resources by skill level and definition, availability, and organizational hierarchy. In addition, they can assist project managers with current and anticipated resource requirements by analyzing the enterprise resource database. Together with project managers, resource managers can create and modify generic resources in the enterprise resource pool to perform planning and contingency analyses.

Finding Resources to Meet Your Needs

You can have Project 2010 mine the entire enterprise resource pool to find resources that have the exact skills, availability, and other traits you need for your project.

Specifically, in the planning processes of your project, when putting together the perfect team to carry out your project, you can:

- Find and add resources by name.
- Find resources associated with a certain title, code, skill set, or other attribute.
- Use a generic resource as a placeholder.
- Add a team assignment pool to your project.
- Find resources that are available for work during a certain period of time.
- Replace a resource already on your team with another enterprise resource.
- Find more resources that have the same traits as a resource already on your team.
- Match and replace generic resources in your project with real enterprise resources.
- Propose tentative resources to your project.

This section details all these techniques for using the Build Team process to find the right enterprise resources to add to your project.

Building Your Project Team in Project Professional

You might already know exactly which enterprise resources you need to add to your team. If this is the case, you can find and add the resources in Project Professional by following these steps:

1. Be sure that Project Professional is connected to the project server, and then check out the project to which you want to add resources.

2. On the Resource tab, in the Insert group, click Add Resources, and then click Build Team From Enterprise.

   If there are more than one thousand resources in the enterprise resource pool, a dialog box appears to help you filter the enterprise resources. In the custom enterprise resource field that appears, select a code or other attribute to help define the list of resources you'll be working with, and then click OK.

   The Build Team dialog box appears. (See Figure 24-23.) The upper portion of the dialog box contains filters and options for finding resources that meet certain criteria. The Enterprise Resource table in the lower-left area of the dialog box contains the list of enterprise resources. When no filter is applied, the table lists all members of your organization's enterprise resource pool. The Project Resources table in the lower-right area of the dialog box lists any enterprise and nonenterprise resources you have already added to the current project.

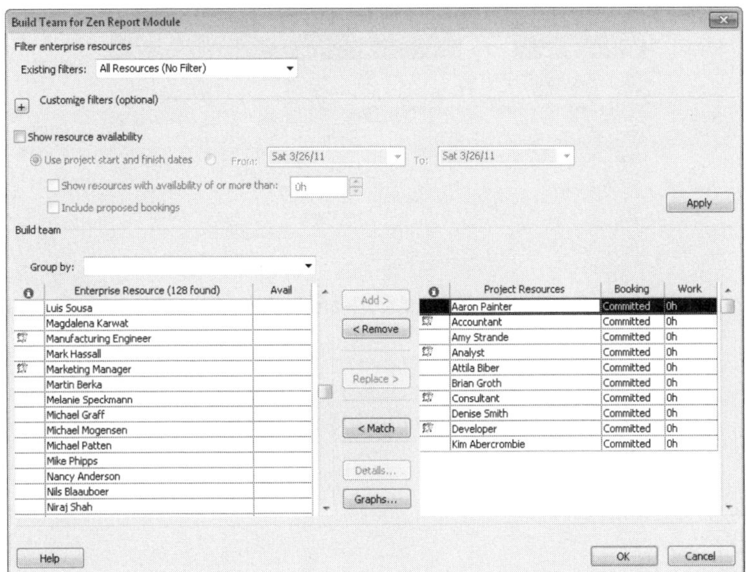

Figure 24-23 Use the Build Team dialog box in Project Professional to add enterprise resources to your project.

By default, enterprise resources are listed alphabetically by name. You can re-sort the list by clicking the Enterprise Resource column heading.

3. Scroll through the Enterprise Resource table to find and select a resource by name. You can select multiple resources at once. Use Shift to select multiple adjacent resources; use Ctrl to select multiple nonadjacent resources.

4. Click Add to add a resource.

   The selected resources are added to the Project Resources table.

Building Your Project Team in Project Web App

If you prefer, you can build your enterprise resource team for your project in Project Web App. To add resources in Project Web App, follow these steps:

1. On the Quick Launch, under Projects, click Project Center.

2. In the Project Center, click the name of the project for which you want to build your resource team.

3. At the top of the Quick Launch, under the project name, click Schedule to open the Schedule project detail page.

4. On the Project tab, in the Navigate group, click Build Team, as shown in Figure 24-24.

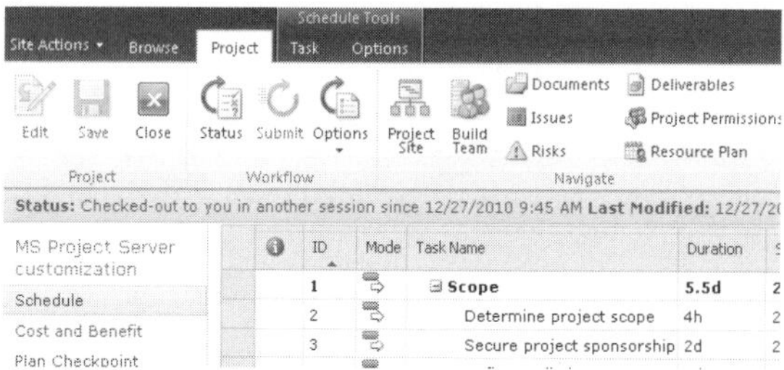

Figure 24-24 Access the Build Team function from the Project tab of the project detail page.

5. On the Build Team page shown in Figure 24-25, select the check boxes next to the resource names you want to add to your project.

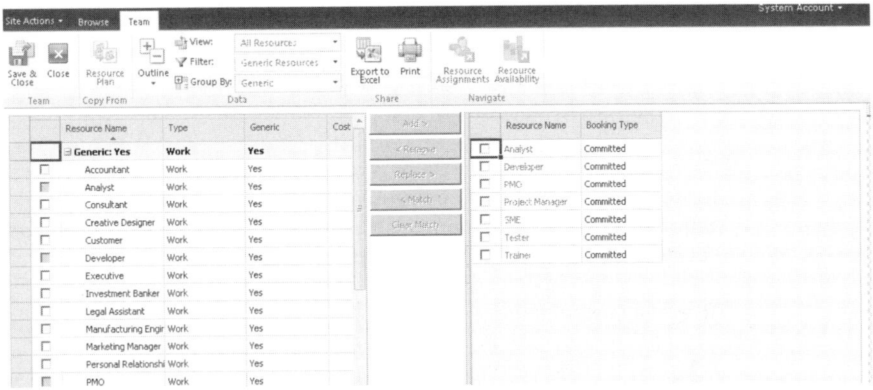

Figure 24-25 Use the Build Team page in Project Web App to find resources and add them to the project.

6. Click the Add button.

   The selected resources are added from the enterprise resource pool table on the left to the project table on the right.

7. When you're finished using the Build Team page, on the Team tab, in the Team group, click Save & Close.

Identifying Resource Attributes by Using Custom Enterprise Fields

Custom fields for identifying enterprise resource attributes can be defined by your project server administrator or another user with the proper permissions.

After the custom resource fields are defined, the project server administrator (or other user) associates resources in the enterprise resource pool with the custom resource fields that define those resources. In this way, the enterprise resources are defined by their job code, qualifications, specialties, locations, or any other attributes needed by an organization.

For more information about custom enterprise fields, see "Working with Custom Enterprise Fields" on page 919.

You can use the custom enterprise resource fields to do the following:

- Match or replace resources in your project with others associated with the same values in their custom fields. You do this by using the Build Team process.
- Substitute generic or enterprise resources in your project with enterprise resources possessing matching values in their custom fields. You do this by using the Resource Substitution Wizard.

- Arrange enterprise resources in your project by their custom fields so that you can review your project team by your organization's resource breakdown structure (RBS) or another resource hierarchy. You do this by sorting, filtering, or grouping by the custom field.

Your project server administrator is responsible for creating your enterprise resource pool and for setting up the custom enterprise resource fields, according to the needs of your organization. For more information, see "Creating the Enterprise Resource Pool" on page 838 and "Customizing Enterprise Project Fields" on page 864.

To add a custom enterprise resource field to your enterprise project, follow these steps:

1. With Project Professional connected to the project server, check out the enterprise project to which you want to add the custom enterprise resource field that has been established for your organization.
2. Display the Resource Sheet and table to which you want to add the custom enterprise field.
3. Right-click the column heading next to where you want to insert the custom enterprise field, and then click Insert Column.
4. In the drop-down list of fields that appears, type the first two letters of the custom enterprise field name to quickly scroll to and click it.

   You should know the name of the field from information you received from your project server administrator.

   The selected custom enterprise resource field appears in the newly inserted column.

Using Generic Resources as Placeholders

You can use *generic resources* to help you define resources of a particular role or skill set—for example, Visual Basic Programmer Expert. The project manager can create generic resources.

Generic resources can also be created and added to the enterprise resource pool by the project server administrator or another user with the proper permissions. For best results, an organization should define a generic resource for every classification in its resource breakdown structure. Project managers and resource managers can then use those generic resources in their projects for planning and modeling purposes.

Because generic resources are just placeholders for real resources, they are not associated with any availability status. They can be used in as many projects by as many project managers as needed.

Generic resources are invaluable for helping project managers identify team requirements and ultimately find real resources. Generic resources are typically defined by a job title or function rather than a person's name. What makes generic resources truly useful is their association with custom enterprise resource fields, which go a long way toward defining the attributes of the resource.

With generic resources associated with custom fields that define resource attributes, you can populate your project team by using the Build Team process.

Note

Your organization might have established a set of generic resources as part of the enterprise resource pool. If this is the case, rather than create your own, use the Build Team process to find the generic resources you want, and then add them to your project team.

If you're not sure whether generic resources have been defined for your organization, check with your project server administrator, or just filter and browse the enterprise resource pool in the Build Team process.

Adding a Team Assignment Pool to Your Project Resource List

Sometimes you don't need to add specific enterprise resources to your project; sometimes you just need a collection of people from a particular department or group to carry out certain tasks. You can assign tasks to the group, and members of the group can assign themselves to the tasks, report on them, and complete them.

This is the idea behind *team assignment pools*, also known as *team resources*. A team assignment pool might be a department such as Marketing or a group of individuals doing the same job such as editors.

Use Team Assignment Pools

The project server administrator can create team assignment pools in Project Web App as part of your enterprise resource pool. After this is done, you can add team assignment pools to your project teams.

For more information, see "Adding a Team Resource" on page 843.

To find team assignment pools and add them to your list of project resources, do the following:

1. With Project Professional connected to the project server, open your enterprise project.

2. On the Resource tab, in the Insert group, click Add Resources, and then click Build Team From Enterprise.

3. In the Build Team dialog box, click the plus sign next to Customize Filters to expand the section.

4. Click in the Field Name column of the first row, type **te** to scroll quickly through the list, and then click Team Assignment Pool.

5. In the Test column, click Equals.

6. In the Value(s) field, click Yes. (See Figure 24-26.)

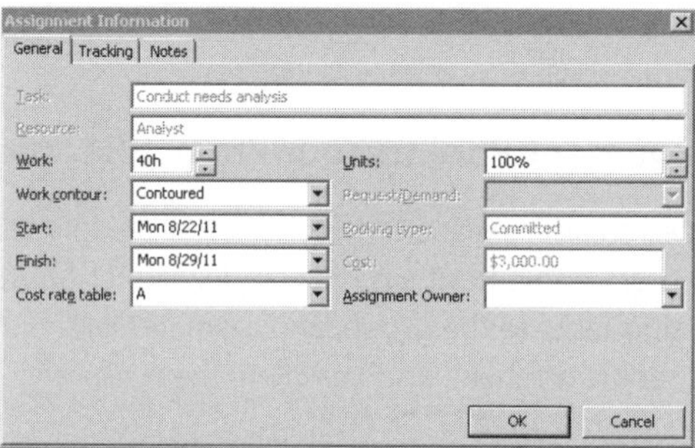

Figure 24-26 Create a custom filter to find all team assignment pools, and then add the one you want to your project.

7. Click the Apply button.

   All enterprise resources that are identified as team assignment pools (team resources) are listed in the Enterprise Resource table.

8. Click a team resource you want, and then click Add to add it to your project resource list.

   You can now assign tasks to the team assignment pool.

Finding Enterprise Resources That Meet Specific Criteria

If you're looking for a set of enterprise resources that fits a certain set of criteria, you can use the various built-in filters, groups, and other controls in the Build Team dialog box to narrow your search.

To use Project Web App to find and add resources who possess certain attributes, follow these steps:

1. In the Project Center, click the name of the project for which you want to find resources.
2. At the top of the Quick Launch, under the project name, click Schedule to open the Schedule project detail page.
3. On the Project tab, in the Navigate group, click Build Team.

   The Build Team page appears.
4. One of the easiest ways to narrow the enterprise resource pool is to switch to a different view on the Build Team page. On the Team tab, in the Data group, click in the View box.

   Typical views for this page include All Resources, Cost Resources, Material Resources, and Work Resources.
5. To further narrow the list of enterprise resources, apply a built-in filter. On the Team tab, in the Data group, click in the Filter box. On the drop-down menu, click a filter name.

   Only those enterprise resources who meet the criteria of the filter are listed in the Enterprise Resource table. This not only reduces your choices to a more manageable level, but it also shows you just the resources that are most useful for your project's purposes.

   If you need to create your own filter based on different criteria than what's provided, click Custom Filter in the menu.
6. You can group the resources in the table by a particular resource field. On the Team tab, in the Data group, click in the Group By box, and then click the field you want to group by.

   For example, you might find it helpful to group resources by Cost Center or Earliest Available.

   The list of enterprise resources is rearranged according to your selected grouping.

   If you need to create your own group based on different criteria than what's provided, click Custom Group in the menu.

For more information about using existing filters and groups, see "Rearranging Your Project Information" on page 173.

To use Project Professional to find and add resources who possess certain attributes, follow these steps:

1. Be sure that Project Professional is connected to the project server, and then check out the project to which you want to add resources.
2. On the Resource tab, in the Insert group, click Add Resources, and then click Build Team From Enterprise.
3. At the top of the Build Team dialog box, click in the Existing Filters box.
4. Click a filter that will narrow the enterprise resource list the way you need it.
5. If you need to create your own filter, if necessary, click the plus sign next to Customize Filters to expand the section.

   A filter definition table appears.
6. Click in the Field Name column of the first row, and select the field on which you want to filter.
7. In the Test column, click the test you want to use, such as Equals or Is Greater Than.
8. In the Value(s) field, enter the value that should be stored in the field for the resources found by the filter.
9. If you need to define another set of criteria, in the second row of the table, click in the And/Or field and then click And or Or.
10. Select the field, test, and value for the second set of criteria.
11. When you have finished defining the filter, click Save Filter if you want to save it for future use. Otherwise, click Apply.

You can combine the application of your filter with other criteria, including an existing filter or work-availability criteria. When you click the Apply button, the list of enterprise resources changes to show only those resources who meet the criteria of your filter(s).

Creating your own Build Team filter is particularly useful if you want to find resources that are associated with a certain value in a custom enterprise field such as Enterprise Resource Text or Enterprise Resource Number. Likewise, if RBS codes have been set up and applied to enterprise resources, you can filter for a particular RBS code.

For more information about creating filters, see "Customizing Filters" on page 1129.

Review Resource Assignments and Availability

If you find a resource you want to add or replace in your project, you can get more information about that resource's availability and workload. This can help you decide whether this resource really has the time to work on your project.

To do this, follow these steps:

1. In Project Center, click the name of the project for which you want to find the resource.
2. At the top of the Quick Launch, under the project name, click Schedule.
3. On the Project tab, in the Navigate group, click Build Team.
4. Select the check box next to the resource name in either the enterprise resource pool table on the left or the project resource table on the right.
5. On the Team tab, in the Navigate group, click Resource Availability.

   You can also get to this graph from Project Professional. In the Build Team dialog box, select the names of the resources for whom you want to see availability graphs, and then click Graphs. The Resource Availability page in Project Web App opens.
6. Review the availability information.

   To switch to a different view, on the Availability tab, in the Views group, click in the View box and select one of the other views; for example, Availability Work By Project, Remaining Availability, and Work.

   If you selected multiple resources, you can switch to another resource's graph by clicking the check box under the graph's legend.

   You can see the resource's current and upcoming assignments. On the Availability tab, in the Navigate group, click Resource Assignments.
7. When you are finished reviewing availability and assignment information for the selected resources, on either the Availability tab or the Assignments tab, in the Navigate group, click Resource Center.

Replacing an Existing Project Resource with an Enterprise Resource

You can use the Build Team process in Project Professional or Project Web App to replace a resource on your project team with one from the enterprise resource pool. This step is useful if you have a local resource in the project that you know has been added to the enterprise resource pool.

It is also useful if you want to replace generic resources in your project with real enterprise resources or if you want to replace resources who have the same role.

To replace an existing project resource with an enterprise resource, follow these steps:

1. In the Build Team dialog box in Project Professional or on the Build Team page in Project Web App, apply the filters or groupings you need to find the replacing resource.

2. In the Project Resources table on the right, click the name of the resource you want to replace.

3. In the Enterprise Resource table on the left, click the name of the replacing resource.

4. Click Replace.

   The resource selected in the Enterprise Resource table replaces the one selected in the Project Resources table. If the original resource has reported any actual work on assigned tasks, the original resource remains in the project plan as associated with those assignments. Any remaining work on any tasks assigned to the original resource is now assigned to the replacing resource.

Matching an Existing Project Resource

Suppose that you have a resource who has the perfect combination of qualifications for certain tasks in your project, and everything is great—except that you need five more resources just like him. If the existing resource and enterprise resources have attributes defined for them—such as role, RBS codes, skill sets, or certifications—you can use the Build Team process to find other resources who have the same attributes.

To find more enterprise resources whose defined traits match those of an existing project resource, follow these steps:

1. In the Build Team dialog box in Project Professional or on the Build Team page in Project Web App, apply any filters or groups you need to define matching resources.

2. In the Project Resources table on the right, click the name of the resource whose traits you want to match to additional enterprise resources.

3. Click Match.

   The list of filtered enterprise resources is searched for resource matches. The resulting list of resources represents resources whose attributes match those of your selected resource.

4. If you want to add any of these resources, click their names, and then click Add.

Matching and Replacing Generic Resources

You can combine the Match and Replace functions in the Build Team dialog box to help you find enterprise resources to replace generic resources, as follows:

1. In the Build Team dialog box in Project Professional or on the Build Team page in Project Web App, apply any filters to better focus the list of resources.
2. In the Project Resources table on the right, select the generic resource you want to match and replace with an actual resource, and then click Match.

   Project 2010 finds all the resources in the enterprise resource pool who have the same attributes as the ones you defined for your generic resource. Those matching resources are listed in the Enterprise Resource table on the left.
3. Select the matching resource who you want to replace the generic resource, and then click Replace.

   The matching enterprise resource is added to your project team. If you assigned any tasks to the generic resource, the enterprise resource is now assigned to those tasks.
4. Repeat steps 2 and 3 to match and replace any other generic resources in your project plan.

INSIDE OUT Use the Build Team dialog box instead of the Resource Substitution Wizard

Just as you can use the Build Team dialog box to match and replace generic or other placeholder resources in your project plan with real enterprise resources who have matching attributes, you can use the Resource Substitution Wizard in Project Professional to find, match, and replace placeholder resources that have been assigned to tasks. The Resource Substitution Wizard is available by clicking Resource, Assignments, Substitute Resources.

However, the wizard is cumbersome to use and often does not provide satisfactory assignment results.

For more control over the outcome, use the match and replace features in the Build Team dialog box to narrow down the list of resources in the enterprise resource pool. You can use the Build Team dialog box to replace the generic resource, or you can do so manually.

Proposing Tentative Resources

As soon as you add enterprise resources to your project team and assign tasks to those resources, their availability information changes in the enterprise resource pool. This availability update ensures, for example, that a single resource is not inadvertently booked full-time for two or three different projects.

Sometimes, however, you need to build a project and its team as a proposal or estimate. You might want to show actual resources in the project to demonstrate the skill level as well as to calculate real costs. However, if the project is just an estimate or model, you probably don't want to tie up the resource's availability in case the project does not actually happen.

In another scenario, you might be working with an approved project and want to run a what-if analysis on the impact of adding certain resources to the project.

For either of these cases, you can "soft-book" resources on your project by adding them as proposed rather than committed resources on your team.

Note

The booking type, proposed or committed, applies to the resource as a whole on your project. The booking type does not apply to individual assignments within the project.

By default, all resources are booked as committed. To specify that a resource you're adding be booked as a proposed resource on your project team, do the following:

1. In the Build Team dialog box in Project Professional or on the Build Team page in Project Web App, apply any filters or groups you might need to find the resources you want.
2. In the Enterprise Resource table on the left, click the name of the resource you want to add as a proposed resource.
3. Click Add.
4. In the Project Resources table on the right, click in the Booking field for the resource, and then click Proposed.

   This resource is now considered soft-booked. As you work through your project, you can choose to consider resources' booking types when you assign tasks to resources in your project and when leveling assignments to resolve overallocations.

> **Note**
>
> **When you're searching for resources who meet certain availability criteria in Project Professional, you can choose whether proposed resource information should be considered. In the Build Team dialog box, select the Show Resource Availability check box, and then select or clear the Include Proposed Bookings check box.**
>
> **A resource's booking type becomes part of the resource information. When you're ready to confirm a resource's place in your project, display the Resource Sheet or other resource view. Double-click the proposed resource's name to open the Resource Information dialog box. On the General tab, in the Booking Type box, change Proposed to Committed.**

Assigning Tasks to Enterprise Resources

Once you have built your project team, you're ready to assign tasks to those team members. You can assign tasks to regular resources, team resources, or generic resources.

Assign Resources

In Project Professional, on the Resource tab, in the Assignments group, click Assign Resources. The Assign Resources dialog box appears. Assign your project tasks to the resources in your list.

For more information, see Chapter 8, "Assigning Resources to Tasks."

To assign resources to tasks in Project Web App, follow these steps:

1. On the Quick Launch, under Projects, click Project Center.
2. In the Project Center, click the name of the project.
3. At the top of the Quick Launch, under the project name, click Schedule to open the Schedule project detail page.
4. Apply a view that includes the Resource Names column by default. On the Task tab, in the Data group, click in the View box, and then click Tasks Summary, Tasks Schedule, or Tasks Detail. (See Figure 24-27.)

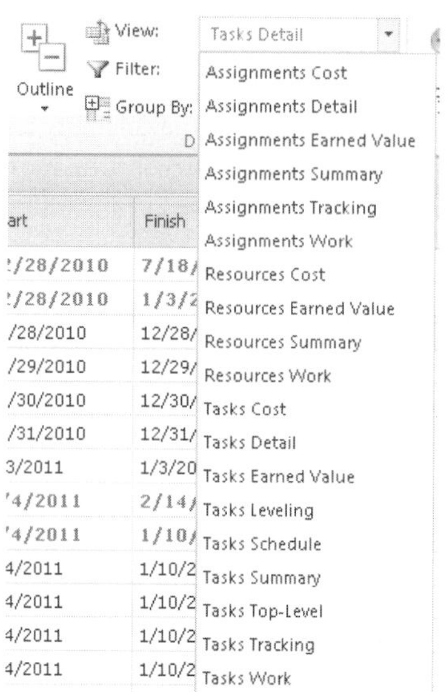

Figure 24-27 Apply a view to help you assign resources to tasks in Project Web App.

5. Drag the split bar to the right until the Resource Names column is visible.
6. Double-click in the Resource Names column.

   A list of your team's resource names appears.
7. Select the check boxes for the resources you want to assign to each task.
8. Continue assigning resources in this manner until all assignments are in place, as shown in Figure 24-28.

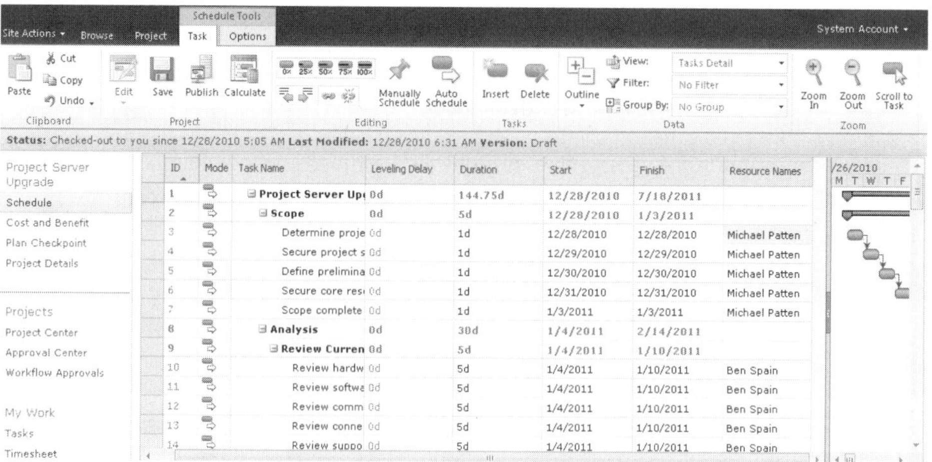

Figure 24-28 The Tasks Detail page is useful for assigning resources directly in the table.

9. To periodically save your changes, on the Task tab, in the Project group, click Save. When you're ready to publish the project with the new resource assignments, on the Task tab, in the Project group, click Publish.

Identifying Assignment Owners

When you assign a task to a work resource, by default that resource becomes the *assignment owner*—that is, the person responsible for providing progress updates about the assignment. However, what if certain resources do not have Project Web App readily available to them, or for some other reason they can't provide progress updates? Or, what if the work resource is a piece of equipment?

In such cases, you can identify a different assignment owner. Even though the assigned resource is still responsible for carrying out the assignment itself, the assignment owner becomes responsible for the progress updates on the assignment.

> **Note**
>
> **Assignments to material resources and generic resources are owned by the default assignment owner, which is typically the person who created the project plan. That's probably you. Cost resources do not have assignment owners.**

To identify an assignment owner different from the assigned resource in Project Professional, follow these steps:

1. With Project Professional connected to the project server and your enterprise project open, be sure that the resource has been assigned to tasks.
2. Open one of the two assignment views: Task Usage or Resource Usage. To do this, click View, Task Views, Task Usage or View, Resource Views, Resource Usage.
3. Double-click the assignment for which you want to designate a different assignment owner. In the Task Usage view, the assignment is the resource name under the task name. In the Resource Usage view, the assignment is the task name under the resource name.

   The Assignment Information dialog box appears, as shown in Figure 24-29.

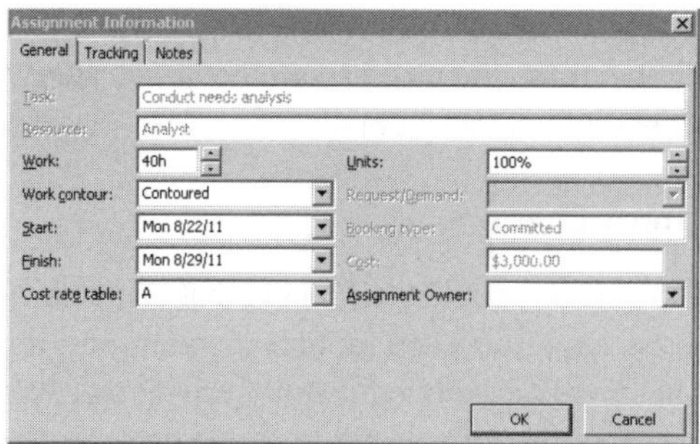

Figure 24-29 Use the Assignment Information dialog box to change the assignment owner.

4. On the General tab, in the Assignment Owner box, select the name of the resource to be responsible for submitting status updates for this assignment.

   All enterprise resources added to this project, as well as the project manager who originally published this project, are listed as possible assignment owners.

In Project Web App, the assignment owner receives the assignment information and the reminders to submit updates and status reports on this assignment.

Each work resource has a *default assignment owner*. Typically, that default is the resource himself. Otherwise, the default assignment owner is the project manager who generated the current project. The default assignment owner for any enterprise work resource on your project team can be changed by the project server administrator or another user with the permission to edit enterprise resource information.

Although you cannot change the default assignment owner, in Project Professional you can see who it is on the General tab in the Resource Information dialog box. Likewise, in Project Web App, you can see assignment owners for each task by applying the Assignments Tracking view to the Schedule page.

The project server administrator can change the default assignment owner in the Resource Center. Select the check box next to the resource name, and then on the Resources tab, in the Editing group, click Edit Resource. The Default Assignment Owner field is available in the Assignment Attributes section.

Assigning Status Managers

The flip side of the assignment owner is the status manager. Just as a resource needs to be responsible for submitting status information about an assignment, another person needs to be responsible for receiving that status information. That person is the *status manager*.

The default status manager for a task is the person who originally published the task to the project server. There can be different status managers for different tasks. To see or change the status manager for tasks, add the Status Manager field to a task sheet in Project Professional as follows:

1. With Project Professional connected to the project server and your enterprise project open, switch to a task sheet such as the Gantt Chart.

2. Right-click the column heading next to where you want to insert the Status Manager field.

3. In the shortcut menu that appears, click Insert Column.

4. In the drop-down list that appears, type **stat** to quickly find and click the Status Manager field.

   The Status Manager field appears in the newly inserted column.

5. To change a status manager for a task, click in the field, and then click the arrow. In the list of status managers for the current project, click the status manager you want for this task.

Collaborating with Your Project Team

After you set up your enterprise project team, you have powerful methods of project collaboration and communication at your fingertips. Using Project Professional and Project Web App, you can assign tasks to resources, receive progress updates, and request narrative status reports—all electronically via publication of information to your project server.

This collaboration process automates the gathering and entry of actuals so that you don't have to enter actuals on assignments yourself. Your project server administrator or portfolio manager sets up your resources' task progress pages in Project Web App so that the resources can enter and submit their actuals on a periodic basis. You can then review these actuals and accept them for incorporation into the project plan.

To keep a close eye on time usage and project availability, you can also track nonproject tasks and time through the use of timesheets and administrative time such as nonproject meetings, training, or nonworking time requested by resources.

Because Project Server is built on SharePoint Server, you can also control project-related documents, track project issues, and manage project risks.

Who Designs the Tasks Page?

In Project Web App, the Tasks page, also known as the task update page, is the central view used by project resources. It contains the assignments for each individual resource. The Tasks page also includes fields that resources use to enter progress information—their actuals—which they periodically submit to the project server for you to then incorporate into the project plan.

The project server administrator or portfolio manager is responsible for setting the fields in the Tasks page used by resources to report. This simplifies tracking and also ensures that the same fields of information are available for all projects across the enterprise so that reliable reporting across multiple projects is possible.

Work with your project server administrator to help determine the default Tasks page fields and permissions so that your needs as a project manager are met while the organization's reporting and billing requirements are fulfilled as well.

For more information about setting up the task update and timesheet pages for resources, see "Setting Up Team Member Work Pages" on page 870.

When collaborating with your resources on their project assignments, three basic activities are at work:

- You publish project information, thereby making project and assignment information available on the project server for resources and other Project Web App users.
- You request information such as task updates, timesheets, and status reports from resources.
- You review and accept information such as task updates, timesheets, and status reports from resources and then incorporate that information into the project plan.

Before you start doing any of these, it's a great idea to set up options that govern the details of how these activities are done.

INSIDE OUT The Collaborate toolbar no longer exists

As with all toolbars throughout Project Professional 2010, the Collaborate toolbar you might have used in Microsoft Office Project 2007 no longer exists. You can find its commands on the File, Info Backstage view or on the Resource tab in Project Professional or in the Resource Center and elsewhere in Project Web App.

Publishing Project Information for Resources

Your enterprise project plan is built, resources are added to the project, and those resources are assigned to tasks. Furthermore, your options for team collaboration using Project Web App are set up. You are ready to start moving forward on your project.

Although all the information about your project is published on the project server, the four primary types of information you are exchanging with your resources are:

- Task assignments and progress updates on those assignments
- Narrative status reports about assigned tasks
- Issues, risks, and project document updates
- Nonproject information such as timesheets and administrative time

Merely saving a project to the project server does not make it available for other users to see and work with. You must explicitly give the Publish command in Project Professional or the Publish command on the Project tab in Project Web App for the project information to be published to the project server and become usable to your resources and other users of the project server with the right permissions.

When you publish your project, changes you have made since the last time you published are made public on the project server. Although you can explicitly exclude certain tasks from being published, typically all changes in your project are published at the same time. This includes new assignments, changed assignments, and any other information changed throughout the entire project.

For more information about publishing your project and excluding certain tasks from being published, see "Managing Your Files on the Project Server" on page 912.

When you publish a project, assignments from the project appear on the Project Web App Tasks page for the assigned resources. By default, the assigned resources see an alert on their Home pages indicating that new tasks have been assigned to them. On their My Work pages, the new assignments are marked with the New! icon. A resource can view details about the assignment, including the start and finish date, the amount of scheduled work, other resources assigned, predecessor and successor tasks, and notes.

If you publish a project that includes changed assignments, those assignments are marked with the Assignment Updated icon in the assigned resources' Tasks page. Resources can also see details of the entire project by clicking its name in the Project Center. This is helpful for resources who want to see the overall context of their assignments.

For details about how resources and resource managers work with assigned tasks, see Chapter 25.

Exchanging Task Progress Information

While your resources are working on their assignments, you periodically need progress updates of actual work on assignments. You can request progress updates and then accept and incorporate those updates into your project plan.

Setting Up Task Updates

As soon as you publish a project and task lists on the project server, team members to whom you assigned tasks are notified of their assignments on their Tasks page and can start executing the work.

It's best for you and your project team to agree on when task updates should be submitted—for example, every Monday morning or every other Wednesday by noon. You might also want them to send you a task update whenever a task is completed, whenever a major milestone or deliverable has been fulfilled, or whenever there is a significant change or accomplishment.

Task updates consist of some measure of how much work has been done per day or per week on assigned tasks. This measure can be one or more of the following:

- Percent of work complete
- Actual work done and work remaining
- Hours of work done per period

It is the responsibility of the project server administrator or portfolio manager to set up the assignment tracking method, the layout of the resources' Tasks page to accommodate the preferred tracking method, and the frequency of task update reporting. This is done on the Task Settings And Display page, as described in "Setting Timesheet Defaults and Update Restrictions" on page 879.

Reviewing Task Updates from Resources

Just as you publish information for resources to see on the project server, resources submit information to keep you informed. Whenever they change a task assignment in some way—whether to update their progress, reassign it to someone else, or reject it—they can save it or they can submit it. When they submit it, the information is essentially published, and you are notified. Upon submitting the information, they can enter a comment about the transaction.

When your resources submit updates about their assignments, by default a reminder appears on your Project Web App Home page—for example, "You have 3 task updates from resources pending your approval." Click the link in that reminder to go to the Approval Center in Project Web App. Or, on the Quick Launch, under Projects, click Approval Center.

Check For Updates

Update notifications also appear in Project Professional. On the File tab, click Info. In the Approvals section, see whether any updates have been submitted. If they have, click Check For Updates. The Approval Center in Project Web App opens in a new browser window.

In the Approval Center, you can review the information that your project team members submit. You can also decide whether to accept the information and incorporate it into your project plan or take some other action. (See Figure 24-30.)

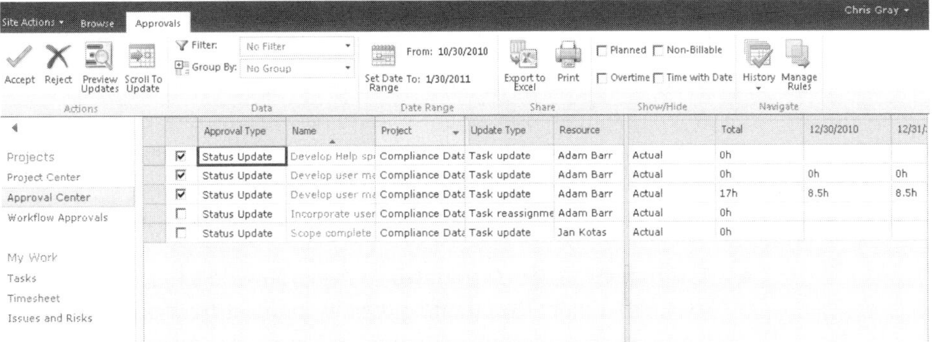

Figure 24-30 The Approval Center shows any assignment information that has been submitted by a resource assigned to tasks in one of your projects.

Resources typically submit three types of task update information to the project server for you to review, accept, and incorporate, as appropriate:

- **Rejected assignments** When you publish new assignments to the project server, resources see their assignments on their Tasks pages. If necessary, resources can delete, or reject, an assignment. Project Web App prompts resources to type a comment when they submit assignments, generally to explain why they have rejected the assignment. You see any deleted assignments, along with the comment, listed in the Approval Center. (See Figure 24-31.)

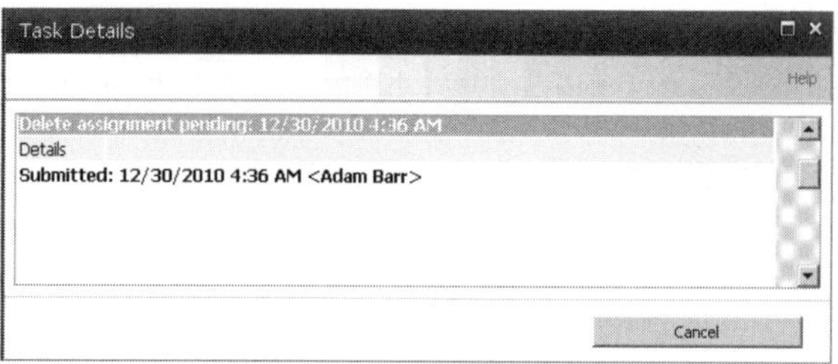

Figure 24-31 Click the assignment name to read the comment.

- **New self-assigned or reassigned tasks** Resources can create new tasks, assign themselves to them, and submit them to the project server for inclusion in the project plan, if you approve. This is particularly helpful when you are relying on your resources to fill in the details of tasks that are needed for their areas of expertise. If your resources are members of a team assignment pool, they can assign themselves to a team task. If you allow it, your resources can reassign tasks to other resources on your team.

  When resources assign themselves to newly created tasks, assign themselves to team tasks, or reassign tasks to other resources, you are notified in the Approvals Center. This way you always know of any new tasks and the specific resources working on those tasks.

- **Assignment progress updates** When you send a request for progress information, resources respond by updating their assignment-tracking information according to the tracking method set up by the project server administrator. They might update percentage complete on their current assignments, enter total work and remaining work hours on assignments, or enter the number of hours per day or per week they've spent on each assignment. Such updates are one of the primary reasons for using Project Web App. They keep your project tracking up to date, and you always know the current status of tasks without having to collect and enter the information manually. Review the task update and any comments from the Approvals Center.

Incorporating Task Updates into the Project

Once you have reviewed the task update information submitted by your resources, you can decide whether to incorporate the information into the project plan or return it to the resource who sent the update.

To accept a task update, follow these steps:

1. On the Approval Center, select the check box next to the name of the assignment(s) you want to accept and incorporate into your project plan.

Preview Updates

If you're not sure whether you want to accept or reject an update, select the assignment in question, and then on the Approvals tab, in the Actions group, click Preview Updates. A separate Approval Preview window appears with a Gantt chart showing how the schedule will look if you accept the update. Using this window, you can see the updated schedule in a web browser before you commit to the changes the update would cause.

Accept

Reject

2. On the Approvals tab, in the Actions group, click Accept or Reject.

3. In the dialog box that appears, you have another chance to view an approval preview. You can also enter a transaction comment that becomes part of the assignment for the resource to see. Click Accept or Reject.

   If you click Accept, the information is submitted to the project server, and your project plan is updated accordingly. If the update was an assignment rejection, the resource is removed from the task. If the update was a reassigned task, the new resource is shown as assigned to the task in the project plan. If it was a progress update, the tracking information is incorporated into the project plan. Accepted task updates are removed from the Task Updates table.

   If you click Reject, your project plan is unchanged, and the task update is removed from your Approval Center page. The task is updated on the Tasks page of the resource with a reject icon.

4. After you accept or reject the task updates, publish them to the project server. To do this, on the Approvals tab, in the Navigate group, click History, and then click Status Updates.

   The Status Updates page appears, as shown in Figure 24-32.

   Select the check boxes for all the updates listed. On the Status Updates tab, in the Actions group, click Publish.

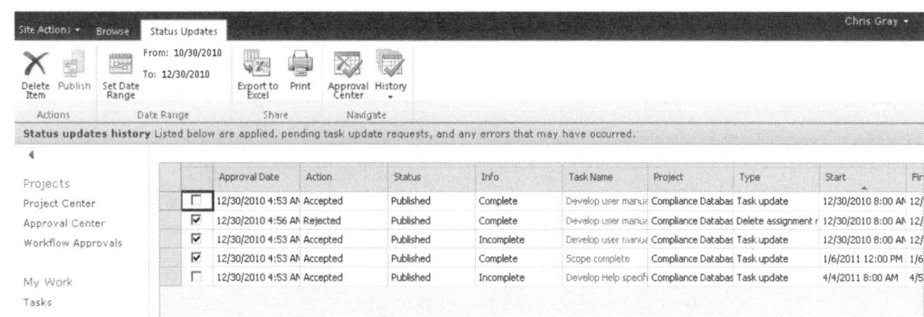

Figure 24-32 Use the Status Updates History page to select and publish the updates to the project server.

Requesting and Receiving Text-Based Status Reports

It's great to get task updates specifying the percentage complete or the number of hours worked each day on a task. However, often you want more detail about task progress. That's where narrative status reports come in.

You can design a status report for resources to complete and submit periodically. You set up how often the status report should be submitted. You also set up the topics that the resources should report on. At the designated time periods, your resources write their status reports and submit them to the project server. When the resources' reports are in, the project server automatically compiles them into a full team status report.

You need to request the status report only when you first set it up. Resources see automated reminders on their Project Web App Home page when a status report is coming due.

Requesting Text-Based Status Reports

To set up the format and request that your resources submit regular text-based status updates, follow these steps:

1. On the Quick Launch, under Resources, click Status Reports.
2. In the Requests section, in the toolbar, click New, and then click New Request.

   The Status Report Request page appears as shown in Figure 24-33.

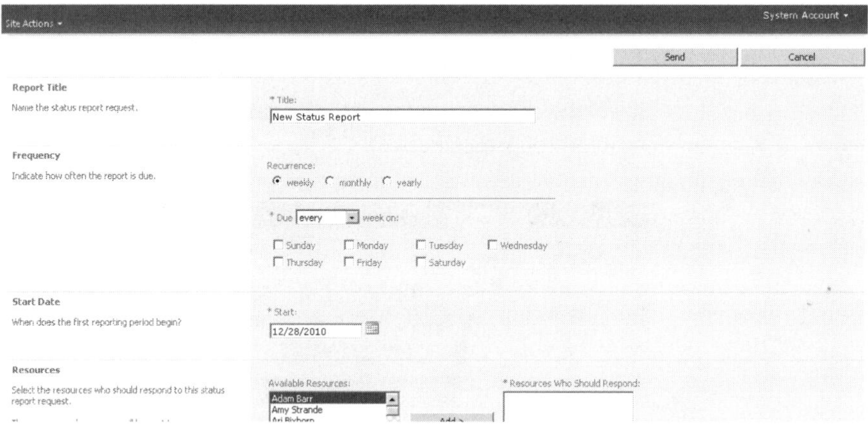

Figure 24-33 Use the Status Report Request page to design a periodic narrative status report for resources to send to you.

3. Work through the page to specify the design and frequency of your status report.

4. In the Frequency section, specify how often and when the status report is to be submitted.

5. In the Resources area, select the resources who are to receive this status report request and who will be responsible for submitting the status report.

6. In the Sections area, specify the headings for the status report. Your resources will report information using these headings.

   To add a new heading, click Insert Section in the toolbar above the table. A new row appears in the table. Click in the row, and then type the heading you want.

   To remove a heading, click it, and then click Delete Section.

7. When you have finished designing the status report, click Send.

   The status report request, details, and schedule are sent to the resources you selected. They will see reminders on their Project Web App Home page about status reports coming due. They will also see the name of the status report listed on their Status Reports page, which they can see on the Quick Launch under Resources.

   For more information about how resources work with their status reports, see "Submitting Text-Based Status Reports" on page 990.

Reviewing Text-Based Status Reports

Project Web App automatically merges the status reports from all resources for a given time period. To review the combined status reports that have been submitted, follow these steps:

1. In Project Web App, on the Quick Launch, under Resources, click Status Reports.

2. Under Requests, click the name of the status report whose responses you want to review.

   The View Responses page appears.

3. To specify the time period of status reports you want to see, set the dates in the View Status Reports From boxes, and then click Apply.

4. Under Group Merged Reports By, specify whether you want the merged report to be grouped by resource name or response date.

5. In the table, click the icon for the status report.

   The merged status report appears. The responses from each resource are grouped under the section headings you identified, as shown in Figure 24-34.

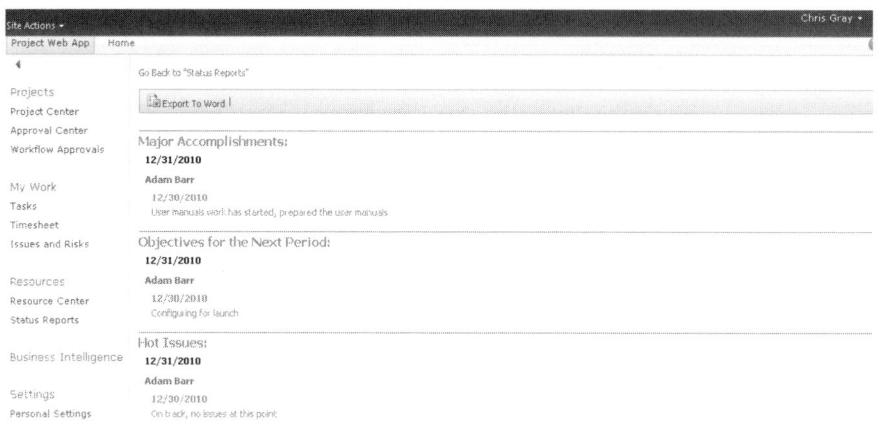

Figure 24-34 The status report contains the headings you specified.

6. If you want to include the status report in a Microsoft Word document for printing or for inclusion in a project status report, in the toolbar above the status report, click Export To Word.

Tracking Billable and Nonbillable Time by Using Timesheets

Timesheets are used for tracking nonproject working time and time off in conjunction with time spent on projects. With timesheets, an organization can essentially account for every hour of every resource's day, even time that's spent in meetings, in training, on different projects, or on time off.

Such detailed tracking is important in organizations that have specific time-reporting requirements. For example, certain organizations need visibility into certain time categories—for example, billable and nonbillable time, scheduled and actual time, or overtime. Default time categories are provided with the timesheet in Project Web App, but your project server administrator can set up custom time categories as appropriate.

The timesheet is especially useful when you need to integrate information about resource time with an accounting or general ledger system, particularly for client-billing purposes.

If your organization does not need such tight time tracking, you can simply ignore the timesheet feature and use just the Tasks page to keep the project plan up to date. In fact, the project server administrator could set up Project Web App in such a way as to remove the timesheet pages and links.

NEW!

New in Project Server 2010 is the timesheet single-entry mode, which unifies the data entered in the Timesheet and Tasks pages. The project server administrator can establish whether timesheet and task progress information should be unified in single-entry mode or kept separate.

However your organization decides to use timesheets, here are some key points to understand:

- Your project server administrator or portfolio manager sets up the timesheet format. This includes the fiscal year and reporting periods, accounting classifications, billing categories, and any rules and restrictions for how timesheets are updated.

  For information about what's involved in setting up the timesheet format, see "Setting Up Team Member Work Pages" on page 870.

- Timesheets can be updated independently of the task progress page, or they can be set up to be one and the same in single-entry mode.
- Resources can identify and report administrative time, which is used to account for nonproject working time such as meetings and classes. Administrative time can also be used to account for nonworking time, such as vacations and personal time off.
- If your organization uses timesheets, all resources using Project Web App are associated with a timesheet manager. This could be the resource's supervisor, the resource manager, or the project manager. The timesheet manager is responsible for reviewing and approving the resource's periodic timesheets and any administrative time that requires approval. The project server administrator or another user with permissions to edit resource information identifies each resource's timesheet manager.

Reviewing and Approving Timesheets

Similar to how they update tasks from the Tasks page, resources submit timesheets to their designated timesheet managers on a periodic basis. If you are serving as a timesheet manager, you will receive timesheets for review and approval. Timesheets can be set up for automatic approval.

To review and approve timesheets, follow these steps:

1. On the Quick Launch, under Projects, click Approval Center.
2. On the Approvals tab, in the Data group, click in the Filter box, and then click Timesheet or Timesheet Lines.

   The timesheet might contain project work, administrative work, and so on.
3. To approve a timesheet, select the check box next to the timesheet, and then click Approve.

   To reject the timesheet items, select the check box next to the timesheet items, and then click Reject.

For information about how resources work with their timesheets, or if you need to submit timesheets yourself, see "Logging Time by Using Timesheets" on page 992.

> **Note**
>
> **In Project Server 2010, you can have multilevel timesheet approvals. The project manager, functional manager, and others can approve the timesheet in phases.**

Reviewing and Approving Administrative Time

No matter how dedicated and conscientious, no one can spend every minute of the workday or workweek devoted to project assignments. They need to take some time for nonproject and nonbillable tasks such as handling e-mail, attending staff meetings, and participating in training workshops.

In addition, some nonworking time is bound to happen during the course of a project, such as sick time, vacation time, and holidays.

Through the use of timesheets in Project Web App, *administrative time* can be used to account for and even track nonproject time. Resources can assign themselves to an administrative time category in the timesheet. These categories are typically set up by the project server administrator.

Resources can also create additional administrative time tasks as needed on their timesheets. As the project manager, you might need to submit your own timesheets as well, depending on your organization's reporting and billing requirements.

Configuring Task Update Options

The project server administrator or portfolio manager often configures how progress reporting on team member's task assignments is done throughout the enterprise. However, as the project manager, you have some choices about how to support your resources in their work as well as which efficiencies you need to help you manage the flow of information between you and your resources.

Setting Up E-Mail Notifications and Reminders

To help manage the communication between you and your resources, you can specify that alerts, reminders, and e-mail messages automatically be sent to you or your resources under certain conditions. Such conditions might include when a resource updates assignments, when a resource's assignment is about to start, or when a status report is due.

To set up automated alerts and reminders, follow these steps:

1. In Project Web App, on the Quick Launch, under Settings, click Personal Settings.
2. On the Personal Settings page, click Manage My Resources' Alerts And Reminders.
3. On the page that appears, work through the fields to specify which alerts and reminders should be sent under which conditions. (See Figure 24-35.)

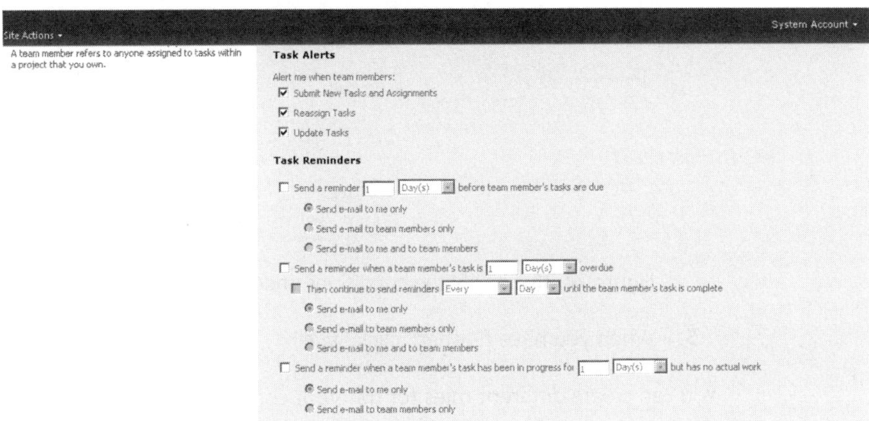

Figure 24-35 You can have alerts and reminders sent to your resources and to yourself regarding assignment updates and status reports.

4. Click Save.

Setting Rules for Accepting Updates

As resources execute, update, and complete their assigned tasks, they submit their task updates to you through the project server on a periodic basis. You can manually review each task update and accept the information into your project plan or not. You can also set up rules to specify which updates are safe to automatically incorporate into your project plan.

Using rules can help keep your project plan up to date while significantly reducing the number of updates you have to manually handle.

To set up rules for accepting changes to the project plan, follow these steps:

1. In Project Web App, on the Quick Launch, under Projects, click Approval Center.
2. On the Approvals tab, in the Navigate group, click Manage Rules.
3. On the Rules tab, in the Rule group, click New.

Manage Rules

4. On the Edit/Create Rule page, specify the rules you want for managing assignments and updates. (See Figure 24-36.)

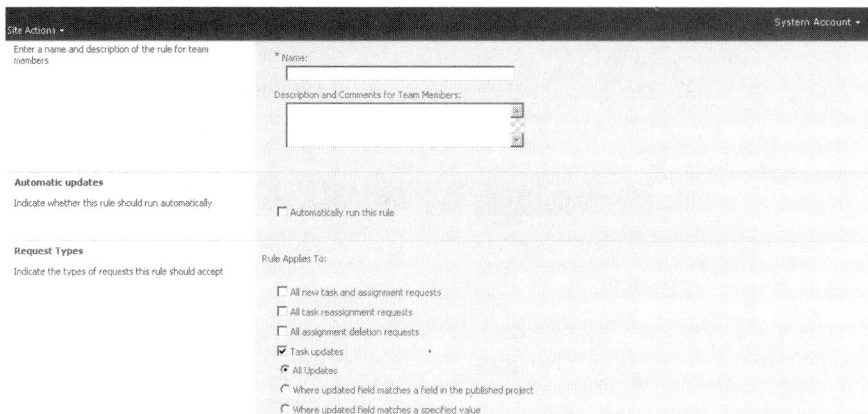

Figure 24-36 Specify the conditions under which updates can be automatically accepted.

5. When you have finished, click Save.

You can create different rules for different conditions. All the rules you create are listed on the Rules page.

Managing Documents, Risks, and Issues

Because Project Server is built on SharePoint Server 2010, you have the following collaboration features available in Project Web App:

- Document control
- Risk management
- Issue tracking
- Deliverables
- Team calendars
- Announcements
- Team discussions

Documents, risks, and issues can be added, tracked, linked with tasks, assigned responsibility, and eventually closed. These all become an important aspect of managing the project as well as capturing important project archival information for use in planning future projects.

Each project has an associated SharePoint project site that can serve different collaboration purposes for the project team and stakeholders.

Controlling Project Documents

Through SharePoint project sites and Project Server, you can establish a document library associated with your project. The Project Web App document library can be an excellent repository for project-related documents, including needs analyses, scope definition, product specifications, deliverable documents, team contact information, change control plan, and status reports.

By creating a central location for public documents related to the project, you can enhance collaboration and the project management process, ensuring that resources and other stakeholders have essential information at their disposal.

Taking advantage of SharePoint 2010, you can also customize project sites to meet your specific project needs, control them through document workflows (for example, by requiring document approvals and versioning), and effectively collaborate on documents.

Depending on permissions, you and your resources can add documents, view documents, and search for documents in the document library. When adding a new document, you enter the file name and location for the document, specify the owner and status (for example, Draft, Reviewed, Final), and enter any pertinent comments. You can also associate a document with specific tasks, if you want to.

Document versions can be controlled by using check-in and check-out processes. If a document is checked out, only the user who has checked it out can save to it. Multiple versions of a document can be compared and archived separately. When a document is linked to a project or to individual tasks, the most current version of the document is linked.

To work with the generic document library, follow these steps:

1. On the Quick Launch, under Documents, click Shared Documents.
2. Move the mouse pointer over the name of the document you want to work with. Click the arrow that appears, and select how you want to work with the document.

   You can view the document in the web browser, edit it in its source application, check it out, and so on.
3. To return to Project Web App, on the Browse tab, click Home or Project Web App.

You can also associate project and task-specific documents. To do this, follow these steps:

1. On the Quick Launch in Project Web App, under Projects, click Project Center.
2. In the Project Center, click the name of the project you want to associate with a document.
3. On the Project tab, in the Navigate group, click Project Site.

Project Site

The project workspace site is displayed, as shown in Figure 24-37. It might include information about the workflow steps the project is going through. It also includes links to issues, risks, deliverables, calendars, and other items associated with the project.

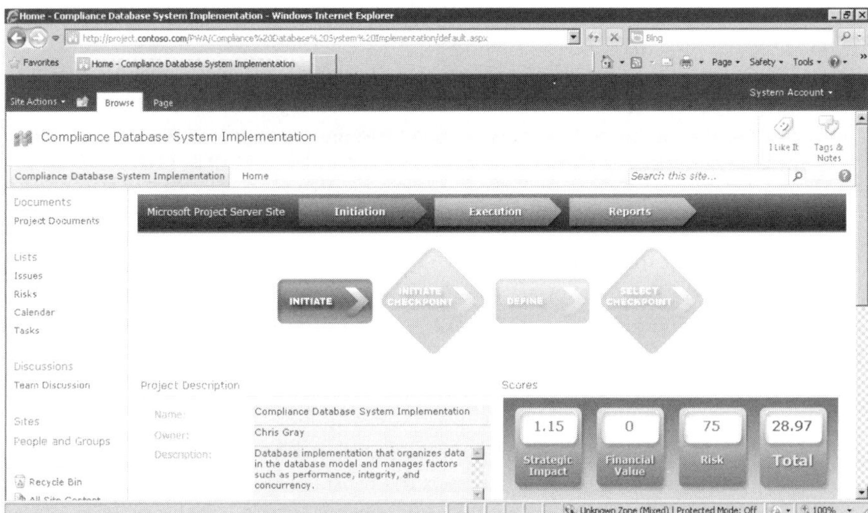

Figure 24-37 Click items on the project site Quick Launch to access project issues, risks, team discussions, calendars, and more.

Mitigating Project Risks

Risks are events or conditions that can have a positive or negative impact on the outcome of a project. As a result, project management and risk management go hand in hand.

Risks can be recorded by any stakeholder: you as the project manager, the project team, team managers, and your project sponsor. After they are recorded, risks are analyzed in light of their probability (likelihood) and proximity. The risk impact is assessed, and if the risk might have a high impact, you as a project manager should mitigate risks that are expected to have a negative impact and enhance the probability of risks that have an expected positive impact on the project.

Much of what you do in project management is essentially managing risk. Straightforward risk-management functionality is provided in Project Web App through the project SharePoint site. Users can record information about risks, update this information, and track risks. Risks can be escalated to the right person for mitigation.

Risks can also be associated with specific tasks, resources, documents, issues, and other risks.

Note

Project Server 2010 provides a variety of ways to capture risks across projects by standardizing the risk information entry forms. Risk can be captured by entering a score—for example, from 0 to 100 or a risk rating from low to high.

Portfolio managers can standardize the definition of risk entry forms and can afterward analyze the risks for the purpose of making decisions about competing projects. Risk reporting is available, including scorecards and visual reports.

To log a risk against a project or even against a task within a project, follow these steps:

1. On the Quick Launch in Project Web App, under Projects, click Project Center.
2. In the Project Center, click the name of the project for which you want to log a risk.
3. On the Project tab, in the Navigate group, click Project Site.

   You can also open the Risks page directly from the project detail page by clicking Project, Navigate, Risks.

   You can navigate to the project risks page when the project is open in Project Professional. On the File tab, click Info, and then click Risks in the right pane of the Backstage view.
4. On the Quick Launch of the SharePoint project site page, click Risks.
5. In the Risks page that appears, click Add New Item.

   The Risks - New Item page appears, as shown in Figure 24-38.

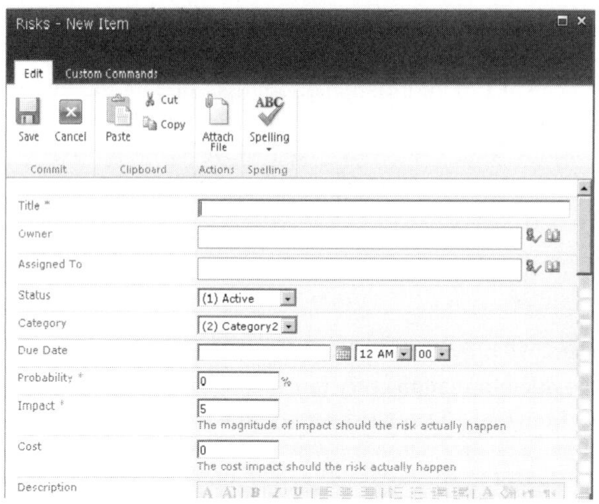

Figure 24-38 Enter risk information in the Risks - New Item page.

6. Define the information about the risk by completing the fields throughout the page. Enter the title, select the owner (the person accountable for the risk), and select the person to whom the risk is assigned. Also specify its status, due date, probability, a mitigation plan, impact, and information about the trigger of the risk.

7. To link the risk to items like tasks, issues, or documents, on the Custom Commands tab, in the Custom Command group, click Link Items.

8. Click Save.

Although the risk is linked to the task, the task is not linked to the risk. The project plan contains no indication about the risk. Because of this, it is worth your while to enter a task note referring to the risk.

Monitoring Project Issues

Issues tracking is integral to project management and team communication because most issues either arise from task activity or will affect task activity. By tracking issues related to a project, you can improve communication on project-related issues and ensure that problems are handled before they become crises.

With the issue tracker, resources can enter issues, assign ownership, track progress, record resolutions, and create related reports. The issues are stored on your project server and are accessible through Project Web App on the project workspace site.

Depending on permissions, you and your resources can create an issue, set its priority, and assign responsibility. The issue page includes a due date, discussion of the issue, and date of resolution. Issues can be associated with affected tasks, content in the document library, or other related issues.

To log an issue against a project task, follow these steps:

1. On the Quick Launch in Project Web App, under Projects, click Project Center.
2. Click the name of the project for which you need to log an issue.

   The project detail page appears.
3. On the Project tab, in the Navigate group, click Issues.

   You can get to the project issues page when the project is open in Project Professional. On the File tab, click Info, and then click Issues in the right pane of the Backstage view.
4. In the Issues page that appears, click Add New Item.

   The Issues - New Item page appears, as shown in Figure 24-39.

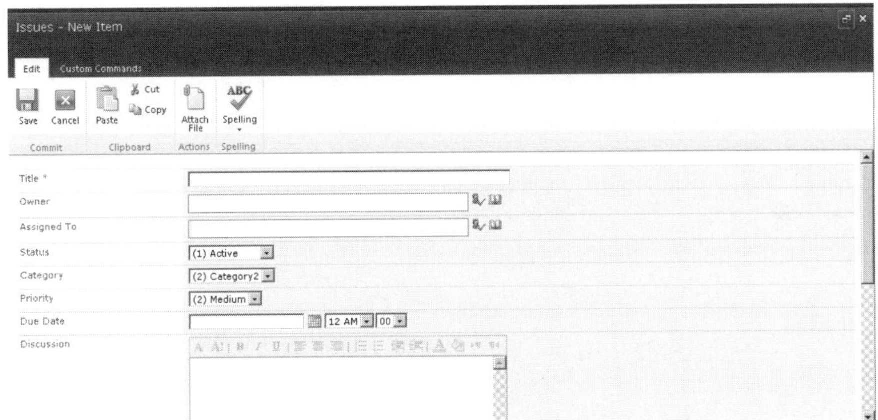

Figure 24-39 Document all details about an issue in the Issues - New Item page.

5. Complete the fields on the Issues - New Item page. The fields include the issue title, owner, its status and priority, discussion of the issue, and resolution.
6. You can link tasks, risks, or documents to the issue. On the Custom Commands tab, in the Custom Commands group, click Link Items.
7. Click Save.

CHAPTER 25

Participating on a Team Using Project Web App

A project plan might make an impressive report or boardroom presentation, but without resources to implement the tasks, that lovely project plan is nothing more than fiction. As a project team member, you know that it falls to you to help achieve the goals of the project. You also know that you must regularly inform the project managers about your progress so that they understand how the projects are coming along.

This is where you and Microsoft Project Web App come on the scene. You use Project Web App, the web-based application for all project stakeholders, to view the tasks allocated to you and to update the status of the tasks in a timely manner, but also to see overall project information, giving you a bigger picture of the project's purpose and status.

Project Web App doesn't limit you to just one project either; you can use it for as many projects as you're contributing to. And if you're working for two or three project managers at a time on these multiple projects, you can use Project Web App to keep all this information straight and keep all project managers well informed.

You can use Project Web App to log the time you're spending on project tasks, as well as time for nonproject or nonbillable tasks such as meetings, training, vacation, and sick leave.

With project management automated like this, you can spend more time working on your tasks and less time worrying about keeping management up to date. In situations where project execution can be done by geographically distributed teams, the Microsoft Project Server 2010 collaboration features, such as task updates, timesheets, project workspaces, issues, and risk tracking are vital for sharing project information and files to ensure that everyone is on the same page.

This chapter is designed for project team members, team leads, and resource managers—all of whom use Project Web App to carry out their project-related responsibilities.

If you're curious about the structure and flow of information in Project Server 2010 and how Project Web App and Microsoft Project Professional 2010 work together, see Chapter 22, "Understanding Enterprise Project Management."

To start using the Project enterprise and team collaboration features, use your web browser to connect to your organization's installation of Project Server 2010. You can then sign in to Project Web App.

After the project manager publishes a project to the project server, you use Project Web App to see and update the list of tasks to which you're assigned. Depending on the security permissions that have been set up for you, you can add more tasks and assign yourself to existing tasks as needed. Project Web App is the central location for all your project tracking activities.

With your assignments in place, your way is set to start working on those assignments, according to the established start and finish dates. While you work, you can record how far along you are on each assignment or even how much time you're spending on each assignment. You can make notes about any potential problems, significant accomplishments, issues, or changes. In this way, all pertinent information about your tasks is in one central location when your project managers ask for a progress update or status report. You can work on assignments from different projects and update them in one single view.

The microcosm of your own tasks draws your focus most of the time. But sometimes it helps to see the tasks that others on the project team are working on at the same time. Depending on your security settings, you can use Project Web App to review the full project schedule, which shows who's doing what, when. You have access to collections of project-related documents, issues, and risks, as well.

In addition to everything else you do, you might have resource management responsibilities. This might be something as simple as reassigning a few tasks to peers on your project team, or as involved as being the team lead or supervisor over a larger group of project resources. You might be a resource manager responsible for building teams and managing all resources on one, two, or many projects in your organization. Resource management features in Project Web App make sure that you have the tools you need.

Getting Started with Project Web App

You use your web browser (Internet Explorer version 7 or later) to connect to your organization's installation of Project Server. You then sign in to the project server from Project Web App with the user name and password that has been set up for you by your project server administrator.

After you're signed in, browse around to orient yourself to the layout of Project Web App. This will give you some idea of how you can use Project Web App as a partner in your project assignment and time-tracking activities.

INSIDE OUT Improvements to time and task management

If you've worked with previous versions of Project Web App, you might be interested in the following improvements in Project 2010:

- **One-stop reporting for task progress and timesheet information** The Tasks page and Timesheet page are redesigned to combine content between the two. That is, you can enter timesheet information such as nonproject working time on your Tasks page. Likewise, you can enter task update information such as percentage complete on assignments on your Timesheet page. The project server administrator sets whether your organization uses this single-entry mode.
- **Improved Tasks and Timesheet pages** The Tasks and Timesheet pages are split into two sections to provide you with more information. Use one side for viewing assignment details, and use the other side for viewing or updating hours in a timesheet. You can update your task progress in both sides, depending on how you're asked to report on each assignment—for example, percentage complete, actual and remaining hours, or hours per day.
- **Task and Timesheet approvals come in to a single Approval Center** The approvals for task updates and timesheets are now done on a single page. While this is mostly useful for project managers and resource managers, this will be convenient for you if find yourself in a team lead position for which you need to approve team members' task updates and timesheets.
- **Exchange and Outlook integration** You can now update your tasks from your Exchange client (Microsoft Outlook or Outlook Web App) without needing to install an add-in.

Project server administrators and portfolio managers should read Chapter 23, "Administering Your Enterprise Project Management Solution." Project managers can refer to Chapter 24, "Managing Enterprise Projects and Resources." Executives and other managing stakeholders can find pertinent information in Chapter 26, "Making Executive Decisions Using Project Web App." Portfolio managers can refer to Chapter 27, "Managing and Analyzing Project Portfolios."

Signing In and Out of Project Web App

To sign in to Project Web App, follow these steps:

1. Start Windows Internet Explorer (version 7.0 or later).

2. In the address box, type the URL for your organization's project server, and then press Enter.

   Your project manager or project server administrator provides you with the URL you need.

   Depending on the project server settings, the system might display a dialog box for entering your project server user name and password, as shown in Figure 25-1.

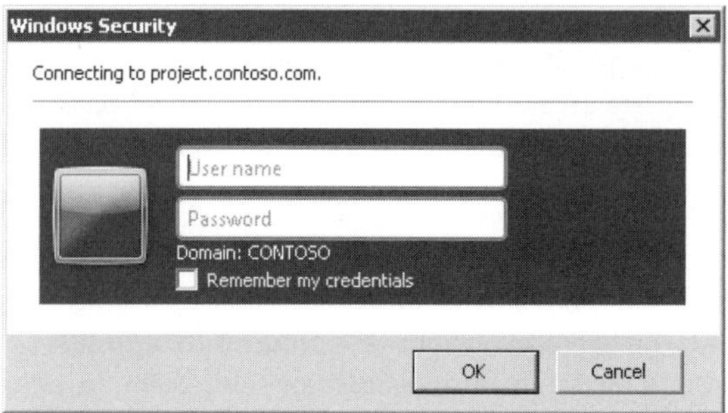

Figure 25-1 If necessary, enter your user credentials, and then click OK to sign in to Project Web App.

3. If necessary, enter your user name and password, and then click OK.

   If single sign-on is enabled, you are signed in to the application without needing to enter a user name or password.

   Your Project Web App Home page appears. (See Figure 25-2.)

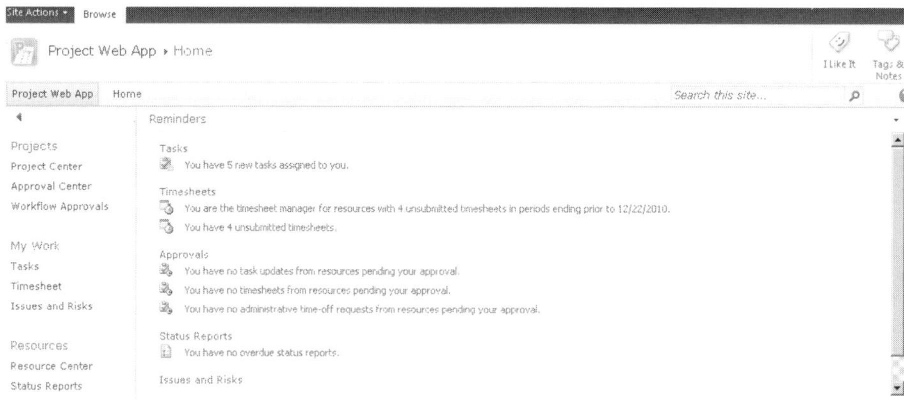

Figure 25-2 After successfully signing in, the Project Web App Home page appears.

To sign out of Project Web App, follow these steps:

1. In the upper-right corner of any Project Web App window, click your account name.
2. In the menu that appears, click Sign Out.

Finding Your Way Around

Once you are signed in to Project Web App, take a moment to click around and orient yourself to the content and controls. If you have used previous versions of Microsoft Project Server or Microsoft SharePoint, much of Project Web App will seem familiar.

Using the Quick Launch

The Project Web App Home page and other major pages show the Quick Launch on the left side of the screen. The Quick Launch includes relevant groupings for each user type, including the team member or team lead user type. This means you only see Quick Launch items that you are likely to find applicable to your needs.

Depending on your user security, you might be able to see one or more of the items described in the following list or shown in Figure 25-3.

Projects
Project Center
Approval Center
Workflow Approvals

My Work
Tasks
Timesheet
Issues and Risks

Resources
Resource Center
Status Reports

Strategy
Driver Library
Driver Prioritization
Portfolio Analyses

Figure 25-3 The Quick Launch is your command center to all the available areas in Project Web App.

The most relevant items on the Quick Launch for team members and team leads are the My Work, Lists, and Documents sections. You might also find the Projects and Settings sections useful on occasion. The sections on the Quick Launch include:

- **Projects** Includes links for reviewing project information. This section is used most by project managers. However, as a team member, you can click Project Center to get a high-level overview of all the company's projects and also to see details about projects to which you're assigned.
- **My Work** Displays current tasks assigned to you. This section also includes your timesheet and the issues and risks assigned to you.
- **Resources** Focuses on the enterprise resource pool. This section is used mostly by project managers, resource managers, portfolio managers, and the project server administrator to add, view, or modify resource information.
- **Strategy** Designed for executives and portfolio managers, this section is used to define the organizational strategy and analyze the portfolio of projects for the organization.
- **Business Intelligence** Designed for executives and portfolio managers, this section provides tools for generating reports and dashboards that provide information and insights about projects.
- **Settings** You can use this section to modify your personal settings in Project Web App.
- **Lists** Shows any SharePoint lists associated with projects to which you are assigned.
- **Documents** Contains links to project-related document libraries and risk-tracking forms and lists.

Working with Pages and Controls

The Home page is the first Project Web App page you see when you sign in. By default, it includes a list of items that need your attention—for example, tasks that have been recently assigned to you or status reports that are coming due. Your project server administrator can set up your Home page to include the content most appropriate for your organization.

Most Project Web App pages include the ribbon of commands rather than menus and toolbars. (See Figure 25-4.) The commands on the ribbon are organized on multiple tabs and groups.

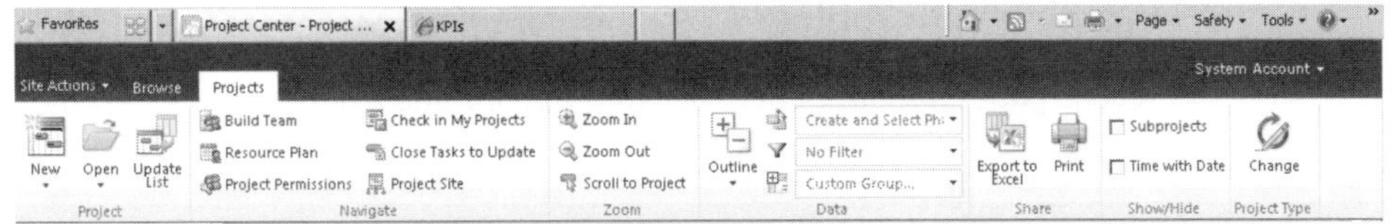

Figure 25-4 Use the ribbon on most Project Web App pages to find and execute commands.

All pages throughout Project Web App have certain standard controls you can use to browse, find content, or personalize your pages. The following list highlights some of the most useful control:

- **User account controls** Your account name appears in the upper-right corner of the Project Web App page. Click your account name to display a drop-down menu that includes the commands My Settings, My Profile, Sign Out, and Personalize This Page.
- **Browse tab** Every page includes a Browse tab. While other context-sensitive tabs are often present, you can always count on the Browse tab to be there to help you browse the site or find content. The Browse tab includes:
    - **Project Web App** This button is a link to the Project Web App Home page.
    - **Home** This button is a link to the site's Home page, which can be the same or different from your Project Web App Home page, depending on your configuration.
    - **Search** In the Search box, type a word or phrase you want to find throughout this site, and then click the Search button.
    - **Help** Click the Help button to get assistance while using Project Web App. The Project Server Help window appears. A Help topic pertaining to the current page appears, but you can find other Help topics by typing a phrase or question in the Search For box. You can also click the Home button in the Help window and browse through the table of contents.

Note

You can customize your version of pages you use throughout Project Web App. To do so, click your account name in the upper-right corner of any page, and then in the menu, click Personalize This Page.

Working with Tables

Several pages throughout Project Web App include a grid, or table, that lists information such as tasks and timesheets. (See Figure 25-5.)

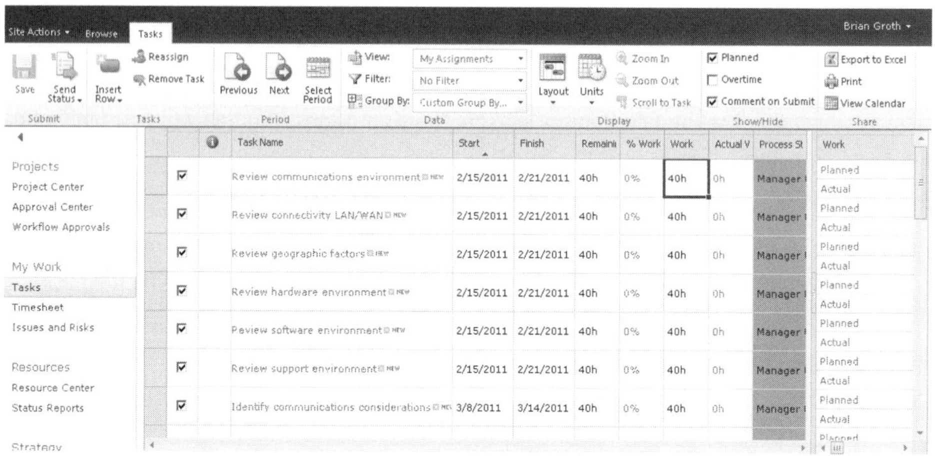

Figure 25-5 You use tables throughout Project Web App to view and edit task-related information.

The following elements are present for most tables:

- **List items** The main feature of a table is the list of items. In most cases, you can click an item to drill down to see more information, whether it is project or task details or resource information. For example, you can click the name of the task to see the details of the task.
- **Check boxes** Some tables include check boxes next to each listed item. Clicking the check box selects the item for further action, typically by using a tab item on the ribbon. Selecting multiple items allows for bulk or multiple operations. For example, after you select multiple tasks, you can click Reassign. This operation applies to all selected tasks.
- **Ribbon** One or more tabs are typically available on the ribbon above the table. When you're working on your assignments in the Tasks page, the ribbon includes the Tasks tab containing a variety of commands for your assignments. (See Figure 25-5).

- **Status bar** When you save or submit changes to your tasks and timesheets, the status bar, which appears above the current table, notifies you when the action is complete. The status bar might show a message such as "Saving," "Updates have been saved," or "There are unsaved updates."

Working with Your Assignments

When the project plan is developed and tasks are assigned to resources, the project manager publishes the project plan to the project server.

Then, when you sign in to Project Web App, you see project tasks that have been specifically assigned to you. These are your assignments.

When working with your assignments, you can:

- Review your new assignments and any changes to existing assignments.
- Assign yourself to team tasks or reassign your tasks to other resources.
- View the full project plan to see the context of your work.
- Enter and submit progress information about your assignments.

INSIDE OUT Differences between tasks and assignments

Projects are made up of hundreds, sometimes thousands, of tasks. When a resource is assigned to a task, that intersection of task and resource is considered an *assignment*. Each assignment is stored as a separate entity, or record, in the project server database, and is tracked separately.

If the project manager assigns multiple resources to a single task, there are multiple assignments for the one task. Each of the assigned resources is responsible for their own part in completing the work of the task.

For example, suppose that a business analyst and technical writer have both been assigned to a "Gather requirements" task. The business analyst might be responsible developing the tools and methods for gathering requirements, both of them might conduct research, and the technical writer might write the resulting requirements document.

This means that what we refer to as "tasks" on the Tasks (or Timesheet) page are really assignments. The items you see on the Tasks page are only those project tasks to which you have been assigned, that is, your "assignments." In the context of this chapter, the term "tasks" and "assignments" are used interchangeably.

Reviewing New and Changed Assignments

As soon as you sign in to Project Web App, your Home page lists any new notifications that require your attention. Notifications come from new or changed assignments or progress requests published to the project server for you by the project manager. The following are examples of notifications or reminders you might see in the Project Web App Home page. (See Figure 25-6.)

- New tasks have been assigned to you.
- Task information on an existing assignment has changed.
- The project manager is requesting a progress update on your assignments.
- A status report is coming due.

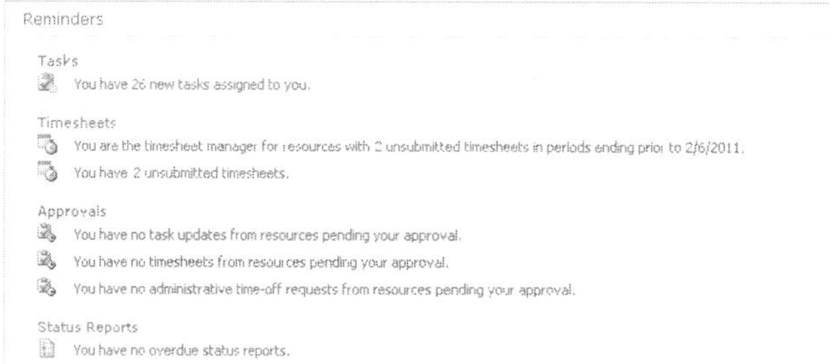

Figure 25-6 You can find all notifications on the Project Web App Home page.

When you want to see more details about one of the notifications, simply click the notification link. The page containing the details of the notification appears.

Reviewing New Assignments

The Home page always includes notifications when a new task has been assigned to you. Click the notification link (for example the "26 new tasks" link in Figure 25-6), and the Tasks page appears. Or, on the Quick Launch, under My Work, click Tasks.

The Tasks page shows your list of assignments along with the fields appropriate to the progress-tracking method that has been chosen by the project server administrator and your project manager. Typical fields might include the amount of scheduled work for each assignment, scheduled start date, scheduled finish date, and percentage complete.

NEW

When you receive a new task assignment, it is marked with the New icon next to the task name. You don't need to take any further action to accept your new assignments. You can review the summary information on the page, or you can click the task name and review additional assignment details, such as other resources assigned, predecessor and successor tasks, and notes. (See Figure 25-7.)

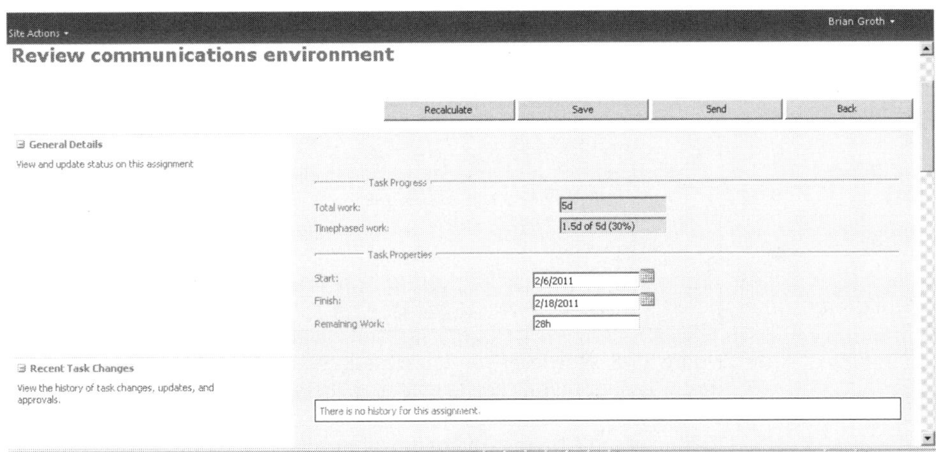

Figure 25-7 Click an assignment name to see additional information on the Assignment Details page.

All assignments you are working on, even those owned by different project managers, are shown on your Tasks page. By default, all your assignments are grouped by project. If you prefer, you can group tasks by status. On the Tasks tab, in the Data group, click in the Group By box, and then click Status. You can also click Custom Group By to create a different grouping.

Rejecting an Assignment

On occasion, you might find it necessary to reject an assignment. Maybe the assignment is a duplicate of another one you already have. Maybe you feel you're not qualified to carry out the assignment. Maybe you have a scheduling conflict and cannot do it during the required time. Whatever the reason, if you need to reject an assignment, follow these steps:

1. On the Quick Launch, under My Work, click Tasks.
2. On the Tasks page, select the check box next to the assignment(s) you need to reject.
3. On the Tasks tab, in the Tasks group, click Remove Task, and then click OK in the message that appears.

   Remove Task

   A strikethrough line appears in the task row.

   The status bar shows the message, "There are unsaved updates."
4. If necessary, select the check box next to the task name, and then on the Tasks tab, in the Submit group, click Send Status, and then click Selected Tasks.

   Send Status

   Submitting the task update ensures that your project manager or team lead will be notified of your request to be removed from this assignment.

The Submit Changes dialog box appears, as shown in Figure 25-8.

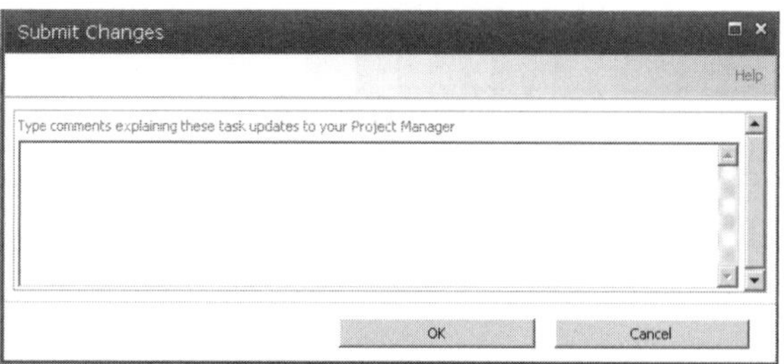

Figure 25-8 Whenever you submit task changes, you are prompted to enter a comment. It's always a good practice to enter specifics about the changes you're submitting.

5. In the Submit Changes dialog box, enter a comment to explain why you need to be removed from this assignment, and then click OK.

   Entering a comment is not required to reject an assignment; however, it is a good communications practice.

   This comment will be stored as a transaction comment with the assignment and can be seen on your Assignment Details page in the Recent Task Changes And Notes section.

This task update and your comment appear on the project manager's Approval Center page. If the project manager approves your update, the project plan is changed to remove you as an assigned resource on the task. At that point, the task is removed from your task list. The project manager will then likely assign another resource to the task.

However, if the project manager rejects your update, the assignment comes back to you. In this case, the project manager is, in effect, rejecting your rejection of the assignment, and the project plan remains unchanged in this regard. The strikethrough line is removed from the assignment on your Tasks page, and the assignment is marked with the Update Rejected icon and remains in your task list.

Reviewing Changed Assignments

During the course of a project, task information often changes. New tasks are added, durations change, and then there is a ripple effect for related tasks throughout the project.

When the project manager publishes the project with the changed tasks, if any of your assignments are affected, they are marked with the Assignment Updated icon next to the task name, on the Tasks page.

Review the assignment information in the table—the cells which contain changed information are highlighted with another color. You can also click the assignment name to review the details.

Reassigning a Task to Another Resource

By default, resources can transfer an assignment to another resource. This can be useful in groups that are used to shifting workload according to the skills, availability, and preferences of members in the group. This can also be useful in organizations in which a team lead or resource manager decides who should handle a particular assignment. In such a case, the project manager can assign the task to the team lead or resource manager, and that individual then reassigns the task to the right person.

The ability to reassign tasks to other resources is made possible by permissions set by the project server administrator.

If you have the capability to reassign tasks, do so by following these steps:

1. On the Quick Launch, under My Work, click Tasks.
2. Select the check boxes next to the task(s) you want to reassign.

   If you do not select any check boxes, all your assignments will be available for reassignment.
3. On the Tasks tab, in the Tasks group, click Reassign.

   Reassign

   The Task Reassignment page appears, as shown in Figure 25-9.

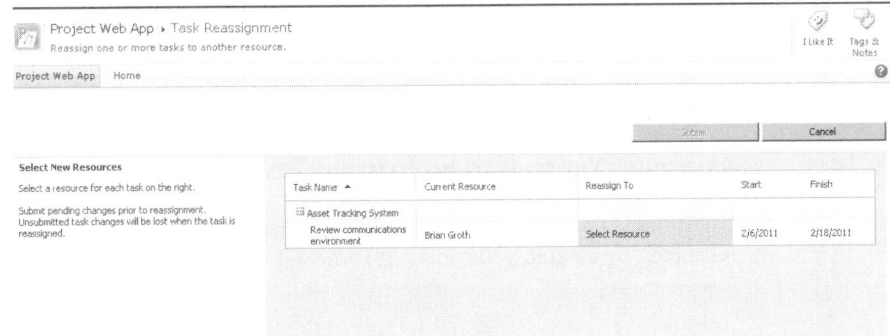

Figure 25-9 Select the resource you want to reassign the task to, select the start date, enter your comments, and then click Submit.

4. On the Task Reassignment page, in the table in the Select New Resources section, find the task you want to reassign.

   If you selected tasks, only those tasks are listed in the table.

   If you had not selected tasks, all your assigned tasks are listed.

5. Double-click the Select Resource cell to see the list of resources assigned to this project. Click the name of the resource to whom you want to reassign this task.

6. If necessary, in the Start Date section, enter the date on which you want the reassigned resource(s) to start working on these tasks.

7. In the Comments section, enter a note about the reassignment.

   The project manager sees your comment when he or she reviews the task update reflecting this reassignment. Unless the reassignment is routine, it's a good idea to explain your reason for the reassignment.

8. Click Submit to save and publish the reassignment.

   This task update, including your comment, appears on the project manager's Approval Center page as a task reassignment request. If the project manager accepts the update, the project plan is changed to show the reassigned resource on the task. If the project manager rejects the update, the assignment returns to you, and the project plan remains unchanged.

Assigning Yourself to New Tasks

You can assign yourself to existing tasks that you want to work on in the project. If you're a member of a team assignment pool, you can assign yourself to a task assigned to that pool.

You can also propose an entirely new task for a project you're working on and assign yourself to it.

Assigning Yourself to an Existing Task

Your project manager might have published project information without assigning tasks to resources. By default, you can assign yourself to tasks in a published project for which you are a resource.

To see all the tasks in a project, on the Quick Launch, under Projects, click Project Center. Click the name of the project. The project detail page appears, showing all project tasks. If necessary, at the top of the Quick Launch, under the project name, click Schedule.

Take note of the summary task that contains the task to which you want to assign yourself. Once you have this information, you can assign yourself to the task by following these steps:

1. On the Quick Launch, under My Work, click Tasks.

2. On the Tasks tab, in the Tasks group, click Insert Row, and then click Add Yourself To A Task.

Insert Row

   The Add Task page appears. (See Figure 25-10.)

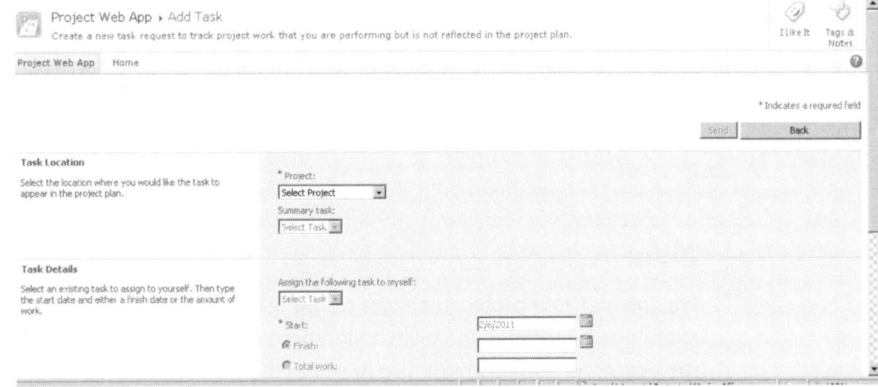

Figure 25-10 Use the Add Task page to assign yourself to an existing task.

3. In the Task Location section, click in the Project box, and then click the name of the project that contains the task.

   Only the projects to which you are assigned are listed in the Project box.

4. Click in the Summary Task box, and then click the summary task that contains the task to which you want to assign yourself.

5. In the Task Details section, click in the Select Task box, and then click the task to which you want to assign yourself.

6. Update the start and finish dates if needed.

7. In the Comments box, add a note.

8. Click Submit.

   Your request appears in the project manager's Approval Center as a new assignment request. If the project manager approves your request, the project plan is changed to show you as an assigned resource on the task.

Assigning Yourself to a Team Task

Instead of selecting and assigning an individual to a task, sometimes a project manager prefers to specify that a particular department or group be responsible for the task. Members of that group can then decide for themselves who will actually carry out the assignment.

A *team assignment pool* might be a department, such as Business Development, or a group of individuals doing the same job, such as Analysts. When a project manager assigns a task to a member of the team assignment pool, or *team resource*, that task is considered a *team task*.

Note

For you and your project manager to use team resources, your project server administrator needs to define the team assignment pool in the enterprise resource pool. The project server administrator also needs to identify you as a member of the team assignment pool.

To assign yourself to a team task, follow these steps:

1. Display the Tasks page.
2. On the Tasks tab, in the Tasks group, click Insert Row, and then click Insert Team Tasks.

   The Team Tasks page appears.

   Any tasks that are assigned to the team to which you belong are listed in the table on the Team Tasks page.

   Select the check box next to the team task you want to assign yourself to.
3. On the Tasks tab, in the Tasks group, click Assign To Me.

4. To return to the Tasks page, on the Tasks tab, in the Navigate group, click Tasks.

   The team task is now listed as one of your assignments. The project manager is notified in the Approval Center page.

Proposing a New Project Task

Suppose that you're working on a project and you see that a task should be added. To propose the task to your project manager and to ensure that your work on the project is accounted for, you can create and submit a new task to the project manager.

To propose a new project task, do the following:

1. Identify where the new task might belong in the context of the whole project. On the Quick Launch, under Projects, click Project Center. In the Project Center, click the name of the project. The project detail page appears, showing all project tasks. Take note of the summary task that should contain the new task you are proposing.
2. On the Quick Launch, under My Work, click Tasks.
3. On the Tasks tab, in the Tasks group, click Insert Row, and then click Create a New Task.

   The New Task page appears.
4. In the Task Location section, click in the Project box, and then click the name of the project to which you want to add the task.
5. Click in the Summary Task box, and then click the summary task under which you want to add the new task.
6. In the Task Details section, enter the task name in the Task Name box.
7. Enter the task start and finish dates in the appropriate fields.
8. In the Comments box, add a note about the new task.
9. Click Send.

The new task appears in your task list. Your request also appears on the project manager's Approval Center page as a new task request. If the project manager approves your request, the new task is added to the project plan with you as the assigned resource.

INSIDE OUT **The activity plan feature is discontinued**

In Microsoft Project 2007, you could use activity plans to create a to-do list or a mini-project just for your own uses. Activity plans are discontinued in Project 2010.

However, if you want to create a to-do list or simple project for yourself, and if you have the rights to do so, you can create a basic project plan. On the Quick Launch, under Projects, click Project Center. On the Projects tab, in the Project group, click New, and then click Basic Project Plan or Minor Project Proposal. These are standard project plan templates that are not associated with a structured project workflow.

Working with Your Task Information

The Tasks page is the hub for your project assignment information and is likely the place where you spend the most time when working in Project Web App.

On the Tasks page, you can view and arrange your assignments in different layouts, different views, or with an assortment of filters or groups applied. You can view and update information about the assignment, including your progress toward completion.

Viewing and Arranging Your Tasks

You can view your tasks in one of three predefined layouts. To do this, follow these steps:

1. On the Quick Launch, under My Work, click Tasks.
2. On the Tasks tab, in the Display group, click Layout, and then click the layout you want—Gantt Chart, Timephased Data, or Sheet, as follows:
   - **Gantt Chart** Displays your assigned tasks in a Gantt chart view, with the sheet area listing the task names and other field information and the chart area showing Gantt bars indicating the start date, duration, and finish date for each task.
   - **Timephased Data** Displays your assigned tasks in a timephased view. The sheet area on the left lists the task names and other field information. The timephased area on the right displays certain task fields—such as planned and actual work—by day, by week, or other time increment. You can use the timephased area to update your task progress for the defined time period.

- **Sheet** Displays your task information in a simple table format. You can directly update the Remaining Work, % Work Complete, and Actual Work fields, and you can see the current status.

In addition to choosing your preferred page layout, you can also customize the Tasks page to show, hide, group, or sort information as follows:

- **Filter** You can apply a filter to see only those tasks that meet certain criteria. On the Tasks tab, in the Data group, click in the Filter box, and then click the filter you want. For example, you can apply a filter to see only your incomplete tasks, overdue tasks, newly assigned tasks, or completed tasks. To see all tasks again, click Tasks, Data, click in the Filter box, and then click No Filter.
- **Time Period** When working in the Timephased Data layout, you can specify the time period for which you want to see your task information. On the Tasks tab, in the Period group, click Select Period. In the Timesheet Period box, select a predefined time period. If you want to enter a custom time period, enter the dates in the From and To boxes.
- **Group** By default, your assignments are grouped by project. If you prefer, you can group tasks by status. On the Tasks tab, in the Data group, click in the Group By box, and then click Status. You can also click Custom Group By to create a different grouping.
- **Sort** By default, tasks are sorted by their start dates. You can also sort by any column in the table. Simply click in the heading of the column you want to sort by, click the arrow that appears, and then click Sort Ascending or Sort Descending. For example, you can sort start dates of your task from earliest to latest. You can also sort by remaining work, from highest to lowest. To return to the original order, click Sort Ascending in the Start column heading.

Viewing or Updating Task Fields

You can see and update task fields in two ways: from the Tasks page directly by double-clicking a column such as Remaining Work and entering the information, or by clicking the task name and displaying the task details page.

To update a task field on the Tasks page, simply double-click in the table cell for the task, and then make your change. You can update any field that is not dimmed. If you're working in the Timephased Data or Gantt Chart page layout, you can drag the split bar to the right to view and update more fields.

You can add, remove, and rearrange the columns. Move your mouse pointer over any column heading until the arrow appears. Click the arrow, and then click Configure Columns. In the Configure Columns dialog box, select the check boxes for the columns you want to show and clear the check boxes for the columns you want to hide. Select a column and click Move Up or Move Down to change its position in the table. Click OK. The changes you made apply to all layouts: Gantt Chart, Timephased Data, or Sheet.

On this page you can do the following:

- Update progress information
- Review the history of communications on this assignment between you and the project manager
- Review any issues, risks, or documents associated with this task
- See the project manager contact and the team's components
- Review this task's predecessors and successors
- Read and respond to task notes stored together with the task in the project plan

Certain types of custom fields might have been created and added to your Task page by the project manager or project server administrator. If this is the case, you see the custom fields on the task details page, and probably also directly on the Tasks page.

Some of these custom fields can contain a value list from which you can choose an appropriate option. If such a custom field is part of your Tasks list, and if you have read-write permission for the field, click in the field. A drop-down list shows all the choices. Click a choice, and that value now appears in the field. This procedure makes it easy for you to enter the correct form of information while maintaining project data integrity.

When you finish changing the task details page, click Save to save your changes and return to the Tasks page. If you want to save your changes and immediately publish them to the project server so your project manager will see your changes right away, click Send.

Glimpsing the Big Project Picture

By default, you can review complete project information for all the published projects for which you're a resource. This is helpful to see the overall context of your assignments.

To review information about projects you're working on, follow these steps:

1. On the Quick Launch, under Projects, click Project Center.

   The Project Center page appears, listing all enterprise projects.

2. Click the name of the project whose tasks you want to review.

   The project detail page appears. If the project is not already showing as a task listing and schedule, at the top of the Quick Launch, under the project name, click Schedule.

   The tasks are listed along with their durations, start and finish dates, and current progress.

3. Depending on your user permissions and how your project server administrator has set up views, you might be able to apply different views to the project schedule page. On the Task tab, in the Data group, click in the View box, and then click the view you want.

   The Tasks Summary view presents the project schedule as a Gantt chart showing summary information. Experiment with other views to see which ones are most useful to you.

Tracking Assignments and Updating Progress

After your assignments are established, you're ready to work on them. Of course, your project manager wants to be informed periodically of what you're accomplishing as well as of any snags you might be running into. You will provide up to three categories of progress information, depending on your organization's requirements for time and status tracking:

- Specific work hours or percentage complete on your individual assignments, also known as *actual work*, or just *actuals*
- Text-based status reports in a format set up by your project manager
- Hours or days spent on different categories, such as billable and nonbillable time, nonproject administrative time, nonworking time, and so on

Tracking Progress Information

While you work on your assignments, its good practice to keep your Tasks page updated. At the end of each day, for example, you can log the percentage complete, the remaining time on an assignment, or the number of hours worked on each task. Which of these three you update depends on how your Tasks page has been set up by your project server administrator.

If all the fields you need to update are showing on the Tasks page, you can double-click the value in a particular field and type the new value. You can also click the task name to open the task details page. In the General Details section, update the appropriate fields. When you are finished, on the Tasks tab, in the Submit group, click Save . This saves your information without submitting it for review by your project manager just yet.

Keeping your assignment progress information up to date each day makes it all the easier for you to quickly send a progress update when your project manager asks for it.

Working with Progress Update Requests

As soon as you have assignments on your Tasks page, you have the ability to submit progress updates. Your project manager and the rest of the project team might have agreed on when progress updates should be submitted—for example, every Friday at noon or the last day of each month. Your project manager might submit a project update request at those times or just expect you to submit a project update without a reminder.

Your project manager can also explicitly request progress updates at any time. Either way, such requests appear as a reminder on your Project Web App Home page, and you might also receive an automated notification via e-mail.

Whenever your project manager submits a progress update request, a question mark icon appears next to the assignment on the Tasks page.

Note

The project manager who created the project is typically the project owner. By default, this project manager is also the status manager. A status manager different from the project manager can be designated for a project. This person is responsible for reviewing and accepting or rejecting progress updates and status reports for a project. You can see who the project manager and status manager are in the Contacts section of the task details page.

Submitting Progress Information

Submitting your progress updates, or actuals, on your individual tasks is the heart of the Project Web App functions. Submitting your assignment actuals ensures that your project manager is well informed about how you're doing on your tasks and knows whether you have too much work or whether you need more time or assistance.

In addition, the actuals you submit help everyone on the project team anticipate potential problems or bottlenecks and come up with solutions before they become crises.

You've already seen how you submit changes to your assignments, such as when you reassign a task to another resource or when you create a new task for the project. The project manager is notified of your task update and decides whether to reject your change or accept it for incorporation into the project plan.

Submitting progress updates containing your actuals works the same way. You enter your actuals on your assignments and then submit them to the project server. Your project manager reviews your actuals and accepts them. This acceptance then updates the progress information in the project plan.

You can update the assignment status all at once in the Tasks page or individually by opening each task. When you've updated your assignment information, you can save and submit them to your project manager.

Updating Progress in the Tasks Page

Directly updating progress information in the Tasks page is the fastest and easiest approach. To do this, simply double-click in the table cell for the task you want to update. If you're working in the Timephased Data or Gantt Chart page layout, you can drag the split bar if necessary to view and update fields. (See Figure 25-11.)

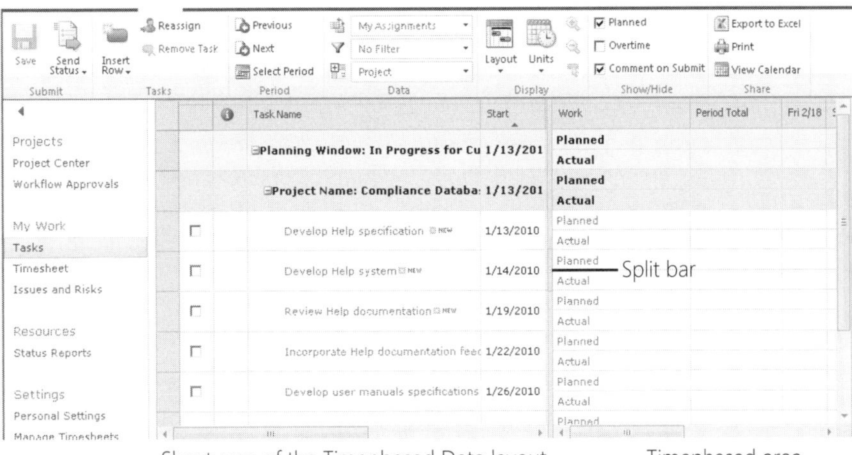

Figure 25-11 Double-click in the cell in which you want to update information. If you're working in the Timephased Data or Gantt Chart layout, you can drag the split bar to see the columns you need.

Depending on how you're asked to report progress, you might update the Actual Work and Remaining Work fields, or the % Work field. You might need to change the Start and Finish fields. You can update any fields in the table that are not dimmed. The same fields are available in any of the three layouts: Gantt Chart, Timephased Data, or Sheet.

If you're asked to report the number of hours worked on a task per day, per week, or other time period, apply the Timephased Data layout, and then enter your hours in the timephased area of the page in the Actual field for the task and the time period. If you enter hours in each individual time increment (for example, each day), the total hours are updated in the Period Total field. If you enter a value in the Total Period field, the work amount is divided across each individual time increment.

Updating Progress on the Task Details Page

Although not as efficient as updating progress on the Tasks page, you can use the task details page to enter progress information. This is useful when you need to review details about the assignment at the same time.

To enter progress information about an individual assignment using the task details page, follow these steps:

1. On the Tasks page, click the assignment name to open the task details page.
2. In the General Details section, under Task Progress or Task Properties, enter actuals for your assignments in the fields designated for this purpose. (See Figure 25-12.)

   If your project tracks work amounts, the Task Progress section includes the Total Work and Timephased Work fields. If your project tracks percentage of work complete, the Task Progress section includes the Percent Complete field. Use this field to report percentage complete on each of your assignments at this point—for example, 15%, 50%, or 100%.

   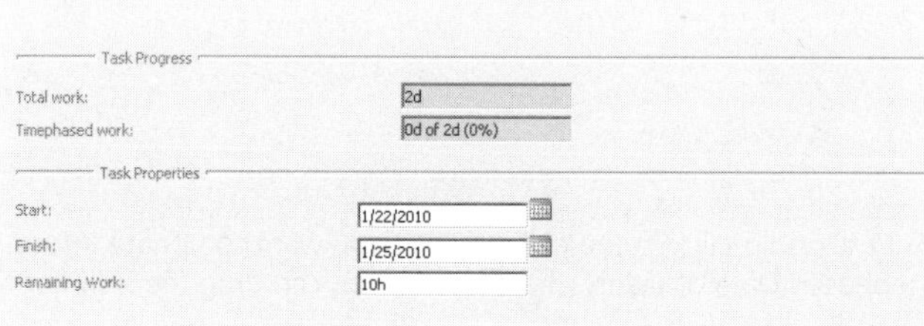

   Figure 25-12 On the task details page, update the task progress and properties sections.

   If your project tracks total actual work and remaining work for the reporting time period, the section includes the Actual Work and Remaining Work fields. In the Actual Work field, enter the amount of time you spent on each assignment. In the Remaining Work field, enter the estimated number of hours needed to complete the assignment.

   If your project tracks hours of work done per time period, time periods such as days or weeks are provided. In the timephased fields for each time period (day or week), type the amount of time you spent on each assignment.

Saving and Submitting Progress Information

As you make changes to your task information, remember to periodically save your work. The status bar indicates "There are unsaved updates" if you have changes that have not been saved. To save changes, on the Tasks tab, in the Submit group, click Save.

You can submit your progress information to the project server and your project manager for all your changed assignments or for just those assignments marked with the question mark update request icon. It's perfectly fine to report on more assignments than the project manager requested. In fact, it's good practice to submit an update whenever there is a significant change or accomplishment on an assignment.

When working on the task details page, you can click Save to save your changes and submit them later, or you can click Send to submit them immediately to the project server and your project manager.

When working on the Tasks page, you can submit your changes to the project server and your project manager by following these steps:

1. On the Tasks page, select the check boxes for all the tasks you want to submit.

   If you want to submit changes to all tasks, you don't need to select any check boxes.

2. On the Tasks tab, in the Submit group, click Send Status , and then click Selected Tasks.

3. In the Submit Changes dialog box, type a comment regarding the task update of all assignments in the group you're submitting.

   The progress updates for your selected assignments are submitted to the project server and your project manager. When your project manager reviews and accepts your update, your actuals update the task progress information in the project schedule.

> **Note**
>
> **If you're updating assignments from multiple projects or multiple project managers, you don't need to do anything special. When you submit updates from multiple projects or for different project managers, the project server makes sure that the information is distributed to the correct managers and ultimately updates the correct project schedules.**

Own Another Resource's Assignments

When the project manager assigns a task to a team member, by default that resource becomes the assignment owner—that is, the person responsible for providing status updates about the assignment.

However, certain resources do not have Project Web App readily available to them or have some other reason that they cannot provide status updates. Sometimes the resource responsible for carrying out a task is a piece of equipment, and status updates are required on the progress of that equipment.

In these cases, the project manager can designate an assignment owner who is different from the assigned resource. If you are designated as an assignment owner for another resource's assignments, those assignments appear on your Tasks page. If the Resource Name field is present in the table, it shows the other resource name. Click an assignment name, and the Contact section on the task details page shows the name of the assigned resource.

As the assignment owner, you are not responsible for carrying out the other resource's assignments, but you are responsible for providing progress updates and status reports to the project manager about these assignments.

Submitting Text-Based Status Reports

Your project manager might design a status report for you and the other resources to complete and submit periodically. This is different from your progress updates, which deal strictly with assignment information such as actuals, new assignments, or reassigned tasks. Status reports are completely text-based and are not incorporated into the project plan. The project manager sets up the time period and the topic headings, such as "Accomplishments", "Goals," and "Potential Problems." At the designated time periods, you write your status report and submit it to the project server. When everyone's status reports are in, the project manager can review the compiled team status report.

After the project manager first sets up the status report, you'll see an automated reminder notification on your Project Web App Home page whenever a status report is coming due.

To create and submit your text-based status report, follow these steps:

1. On the Quick Launch, under Resources, click Status Reports.

   The Status Reports page appears, showing a table of status reports for different projects. (See Figure 25-13.)

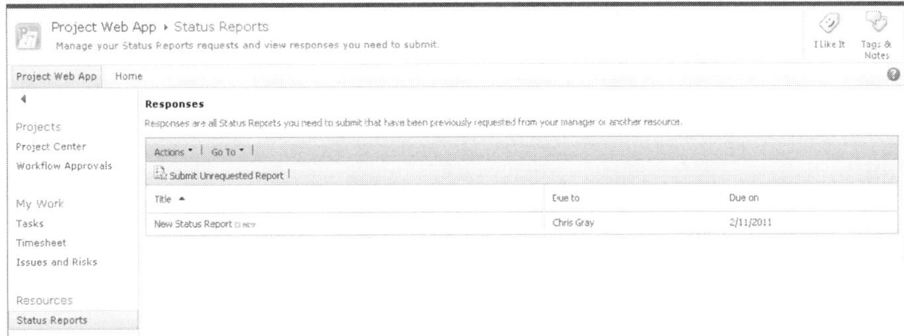

Figure 25-13 The Status Reports page shows all status reports for your various projects, which project manager receives them, and when the next one is due.

2. In the table, click the name of the status report you want to write.

   The Status Report Response page appears.

3. Change fields in the To and Period sections if needed.

4. In the Sections area, type your status report in the boxes provided.

   The headings of the boxes reflect the points that the project manager wants all resources to report on for each status report.

5. If you want to add another section of information, click the Click To Add Section button. Type a title for the section, and then click OK. In the new box, enter your additional information.

6. If you just want to save your report and update the project server later, click Save.

   This option is useful if you're not quite finished with your status report, or if it's not time to submit the report yet. It's a good idea to enter status information whenever you have a significant accomplishment or encounter a possible blocking problem. Then, when the status report comes due, you'll have most of your information in place already.

7. When you're ready to submit your status report to the project server and your project manager, click Send.

   Your status report is submitted to the project server. The project server automatically merges your status report with the status reports from the other resources for the same time period for your project manager to view.

Submit Unrequested Report

You can also send a status report that's separate from the normal status report format or that's going to a different resource. You can specify your own status report title, the resources who should receive the status report, and which sections it should contain. To do this, on the Status Reports page, in the toolbar in the Responses section, click Submit Unrequested Report.

Complete the fields on the Unrequested Status Report page. In the Sections area, click the Click To Add Section button. Type a title for the section, and then click OK. In the new box, enter your additional information. When you're finished, click Save or Send.

Logging Time by Using Timesheets

Not every minute of every day can be devoted to your project assignments. You know that you have to take time for nonproject tasks such as attending staff meetings and participating in training workshops. And then there are also vacations, holidays, and personal time off.

Project Web App has a method for tracking different categories of time—*timesheets*. With timesheets, you can log how you spend your time throughout the workday and a standard reporting period (for example, a week), whether it's on project tasks, nonproject working time, or nonworking time.

Such detailed tracking is important in organizations that have specific time-reporting requirements, either for their own internal billing purposes or for working with their customers.

For example, certain organizations need to see all billable and nonbillable time, scheduled and actual time, overtime, and so on. Your project server administrator sets up the format for the timesheet as it is to be used for your organization's needs.

Note

If your organization does not need such exact time tracking, it might not have implemented the timesheet feature. If this is the case, you will not see it in Project Web App or it will be an empty page.

Reviewing and Submitting a Timesheet

You submit timesheets to your timesheet managers on a periodic basis, based on your organization's reporting period. Common reporting or fiscal periods include calendar months or four-week periods. When you sign in to Project Web App, your list of reminders includes any timesheets that are coming due.

To see the timesheet for the current reporting period, on the Quick Launch, under My Work, click Timesheet. The timesheet appears, listing incomplete tasks from past periods and tasks from the current period. (See Figure 25-14.)

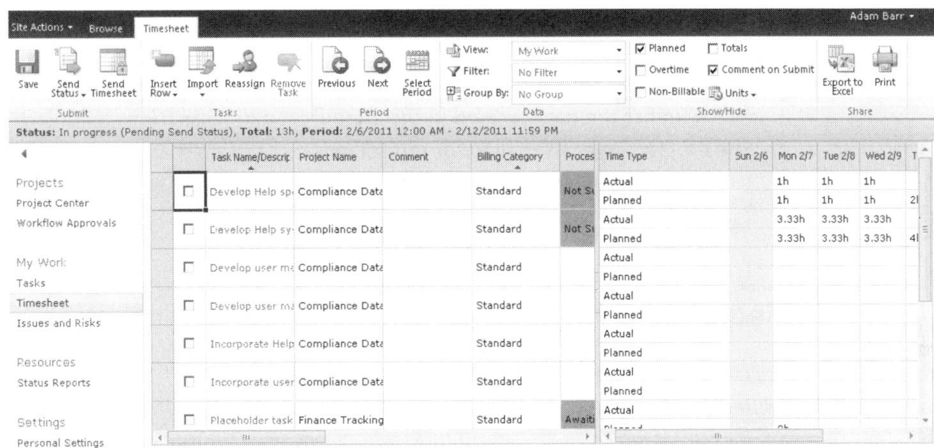

Figure 25-14 When you open your timesheet, you can report the status of the current tasks, independent of project and nonbillable time like vacation, sick leave, and so on.

The status bar might show information about the status of the timesheet, the time reported, and the time period.

This view is very similar to the Tasks page. You can enter the actual time spent on a task, plus time spent on nonbillable activities.

From the timesheet you can also update the status of regular assignments and submit the changes in the same way that you do on the Tasks page, by clicking Tasks, Submit, Send Status. Then, on the Timesheet tab, in the Submit group, click Send Timesheet.

Select Period

If you want to work on the timesheet for a different period, on the Timesheet tab, in the Period group, click Select Period. A drop-down list appears in which you can select the time period.

The table lists information about in-progress tasks and the projects they belong to. Nonbillable work is associated with the word "Administrative" in the Project Name column instead of with a project name.

The Billing Category column indicates the type of billing the task or administrative work falls under—for example, it can be Standard, Administrative, Jury Duty, Sick Time, Vacation, and so on. Your project server administrator defines additional billing types as needed.

NEW!

> **One-Stop Reporting for Tasks and Timesheet Information**
>
> **New in Project Server 2010 and Project Web App is the timesheet single-entry mode, which unifies the data entered in the Timesheet and Tasks pages in Project Web App. The project server administrator can set whether the Tasks and Timesheet pages are set to single-entry mode, or whether their information should be entered separately.**

Requesting Nonproject or Nonworking Time

If you are planning a vacation or an upcoming week of training, for example, you can account for this in your timesheet by requesting *administrative time*. Certain categories of administrative time are set up by your project server administrator to reflect common types of nonproject working time or nonworking time. You can specify when you plan to need administrative time, and it becomes a part of your timesheet. Some categories require management approval; others do not.

To specify administrative time, follow these steps:

1. On the Quick Launch, under My Work, click Timesheet.

Insert Row

2. On the Timesheet tab, in the Tasks group, click Insert Row, and then click Insert Administrative Tasks.

   The Administrative Time dialog box appears.

3. Click in the Category box, and then click the category Administrative Work, for example, Vacation.

4. In the Description box, enter an explanation as necessary.

5. Click OK.

   The new administrative item is added to your timesheet.

You can also request personal time in a similar way, as follows:

1. On the Timesheet tab, in the Tasks group, click Insert Row, and then click Insert Personal Task.

   The Add New Personal Task dialog box appears.

2. Enter the name of the new timesheet line, the classification, and comments as appropriate.

3. Click OK.

   The item is added to your Timesheet.

Just as on the Tasks page, you can do the following on the Timesheet page:

- Create new tasks.
- Add existing tasks.
- Assign yourself to a task or to a team task.
- Reassign a task to someone else.

Working with Issues and Risks

Issues are certain events or decisions that need to be taken that have a certain effect on the course of a project and that the project manager cannot solve independently. For example, an issue can occur if one of the assumptions made at the beginning of the project proves to be false.

Risks are uncertain events that might have a negative or positive influence on your project if they occur. Typically, a risk is characterized by an impact (which can be rated numerically or from low to high) and a probability. What you want to do for a project is minimize or eliminate the occurrence of negative risks and maximize the probability of positive risks. It is the job of the project manager, but also of all the project stakeholders, to gather and report project risks.

As team members on a project team, it is the expectation that you also report issues and raise possible risks. You might also be the owner of issues and risks that others have reported; this means you have to solve the issue or perform risk prevention or enhancement (for positive risks).

Issues and risks are managed in the project-specific SharePoint *workspaces*, or *project sites*, which are typically created whenever a new project is published. The project workspace includes links to issues, risks, documents, discussions, and other items associated with the project.

To see any issues and risks assigned to you, on the Quick Launch, under My Work, click Issues And Risks. The issues and risks are grouped by project and indicate a status of Active, Postponed, or Closed, as shown in Figure 25-15.

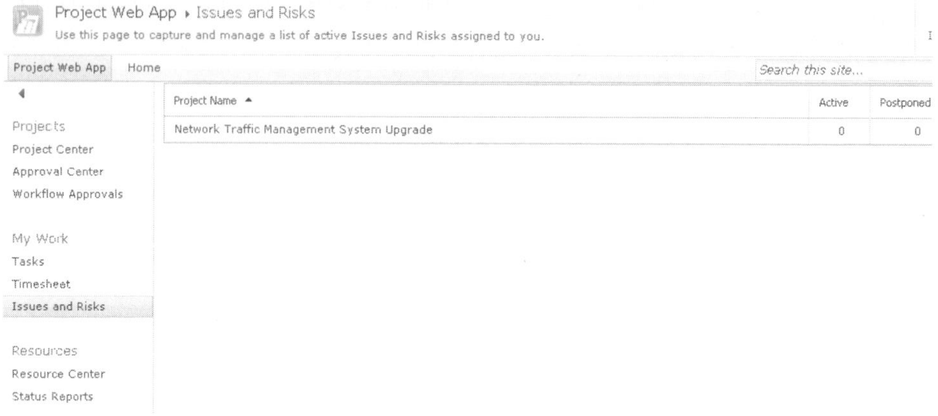

Figure 25-15 Use the Issues And Risks page to review issues and risks that are assigned to you for resolution or monitoring.

By clicking the project name, the project-specific SharePoint workspace site appears, where all details about the project's issues and risks are logged.

On the Quick Launch of the project site, under Lists, click Issues. The full list of project issues appears. (See Figure 25-16.) Click the name of the issue to open it and see details.

Documents
Project Documents

Lists
Issues
Risks
Calendar
Tasks

ID	Title	Assigned To	Status	Priority	Category	Due Date
Count= 3						
1	Unable to update theme	Adam Barr	(2) Postponed	(2) Medium	(2) Category2	
2	Broken Pipe	Mike Shughrue	(1) Active	(2) Medium	(2) Category2	
3	test 1	Carol Philips	(1) Active	(2) Medium	(2) Category2	

Add new item

Figure 25-16 Review the Issues area to see the list and status of issues for the project.

To edit an existing issue, follow these steps:

1. On the Quick Launch of the project site, under Lists, click Issues.

   The full list of project issues appears.

2. Click the name of the issue you want to edit.

3. On the View tab, in the Manage group, click Edit Item.

4. Update any of the fields as necessary. You can change the status, for example, from Active to Closed. You might also want to add information to the Discussion box or the Resolution box.

5. On the Edit tab, in the Commit group, click Save.

To log a new issue, follow these steps:

1. On the Quick Launch, under Lists, click Issues.
2. Click Add New Item.

   The Issues - New Item page appears.
3. In the appropriate fields, enter basic information about the issue, including the title, owner, and assignment.
4. In the next set of fields, enter the status, category, priority, and due date for the issue.
5. In the Discussion field, enter the background and facts about the issue.
6. In the Resolution field, enter details about how the issue will be resolved.
7. On the Edit tab, in the Commit group, click Save.

   The issue is added to the site. The project manager and other team members working on this project are now able to see the new issue.

To view, edit, or add a risk item for tracking, open the project site. On the Quick Launch for the project site, under Lists, click Risks.

Issues and risks should be regularly reviewed during team meetings and project reviews to ensure that issues are being resolved and risks are being monitored.

Setting Up E-Mail Reminders and Outlook Tasks

Through Project Web App, you have tools at your disposal for making your life a little easier. You can set up automated notifications so that you can receive e-mail messages reminding you about various aspects of your project and progress tracking. You can specify when you want to see reminders appear on your Project Web App Home page regarding your assignments and status reports. You can also integrate your project tasks into your Microsoft Outlook calendar.

Setting Your Alerts and Reminders

As a team member or team lead, you have the option to configure your own alerts and reminders. These configurations are beyond the page configurations set up by the project server administrator and the project manager.

To configure automated e-mail alerts and reminders to yourself, follow these steps:

1. On the Quick Launch, under Settings, click Personal Settings.

2. Click Manage My Alerts And Reminders.

3. Review the options in the Tasks and Status Reports sections, and then select the check boxes and make further specifications for the events for which you want to be notified via e-mail (Task Alerts and Status Report Alerts) and see reminders on your Project Web App Home page (Task Reminders and Status Report Reminders).

   Clear the check boxes for events for which you do not want an e-mail notification or reminder on the Project Web App Home page.

   You can set up notification and reminder options for new or changed tasks, upcoming tasks, overdue tasks, and for status reports, as shown in Figure 25-17.

4. In the Queue Job Failures section, specify whether you want an alert if a queue job fails.

   Whenever you save changes to your tasks or timesheet page, or submit changes to the project server, a *queue job* is started. Some queue jobs are carried out right away; others might take several minutes or longer, depending on the volume of activity of all Project Web App users.

5. When you are finished, click Save.

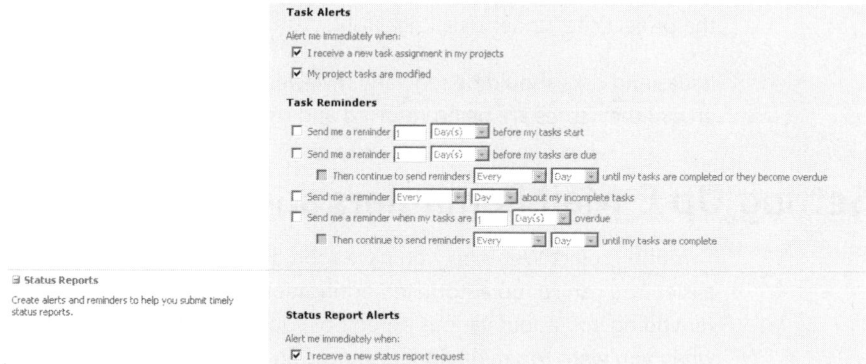

Figure 25-17 On the Manage My Alerts and Reminders page, you can set up e-mail alerts and Project Web App reminders for changed tasks, upcoming tasks, overdue tasks, and more.

Working with Project Tasks in Outlook

Project Server 2010 is integrated with Microsoft Exchange Server, which ensures that team members can view and update their project tasks directly in Outlook or Outlook Web App.

Project server tasks are displayed in Outlook 2007 or Outlook 2010 as tasks, and they are grouped by project name. Team members can receive notifications and update their server tasks directly in Outlook.

In Outlook 2010, you no longer need to install an Outlook add-in to see your tasks from Project Web App.

For more details about integrating your project tasks with Outlook, contact your project server administrator.

Managing Resources in Project Web App

If you're a resource manager supporting a project, additional capabilities are available to you in Project Web App. You can add to and edit the enterprise resource pool. You can build a project team based on skill sets. You can assign tasks to the right resources, and you can review and approve task progress reports and timesheets.

For detailed information about the different resource management functions in Project Web App and Project Professional 2010, refer to the appropriate section in Table 25-1.

Table 25-1 **Resource Management References**

Section	On Page
"Creating the Enterprise Resource Pool"	838
"Finding Resources to Meet Your Needs"	928
"Finding Enterprise Resources That Meet Specific Criteria"	935
"Assigning Tasks to Enterprise Resources"	941
"Exchanging Task Progress Information"	948
"Requesting Text-Based Status Reports"	952
"Tracking Billable and Nonbillable Time by Using Timesheets"	954
"Setting Up E-Mail Notifications and Reminders"	956

CHAPTER 26

Making Executive Decisions Using Project Web App

As an executive, you need a high-level overview of the portfolio of projects that are taking place now and in the near future. Such summary information should clearly indicate the status of projects and the associated costs, resources, and risks. You should be able to obtain the information you need to make sound decisions and take action when necessary.

Executives and other managing stakeholders can use the project portfolio management (PPM) features in Microsoft Project Web App to define and communicate the organization's business strategy. With a clear definition of the organizational goals, you can be sure that only the right mix of projects that fulfills that strategy is selected in the project portfolio. With the enterprise project management (EPM) features, you can monitor and measure projects and resources throughout the entire organization. You can see information about dozens of projects and resources presented in a manner most relevant to your requirements.

This chapter focuses on the features applicable to executives and other stakeholders who use Project Web App to work with strategic business drivers, review project portfolio information, and work with enterprise resource information.

NEW!

Business Strategy Definition and Portfolio Analysis

New in Microsoft Project Server 2010 are business strategy and portfolio analysis features, including the following:

- **Strategy definition through business drivers or key company development directions.**
- **Business driver prioritization for the organization, whether it's the entire company or a single department.**
- **Portfolio analysis considering important aspects, such as cost, risk, and resources.**

When you are a managing stakeholder vested with executive-level permissions in Project Web App, you can sign in to Project Web App and see your entire portfolio of projects in one place, view all enterprise resource information, and arrange information in views or reports so that you can analyze, compare, and evaluate data.

You can use Project Web App to visualize the strategic value of your selected portfolio. Also, through the portfolio analysis tools, you can analyze resource requirements and allocations to ensure that the portfolio of projects that brings the most value is selected under the existing resource constraints.

You can use the portfolio analysis feature in Project Web App to introduce or eliminate projects. You can save analysis results for later reference.

As projects are selected and travel through their life cycle, you can compare hundreds of projects, one project against another, and check whether there are new projects that might bring more value, or whether some of the projects in the portfolio are adrift and should be shut down. Your high-level views of the project portfolio and enterprise resources can be easily adapted and tailored to what you need to see for your particular focus.

Because Project Server 2010 is integrated with Microsoft SharePoint Server 2010, you have additional project collaboration and analysis information at your fingertips through workspace features that include discussions, calendars, risk management, issues tracking, and document management.

Through all these features, Project Web App provides clear visibility into your organization's project and portfolio management efforts. You can access vital information that helps you prevent problems and ensure smooth operations. Through the Microsoft enterprise project management features, you can see the big project picture, use resources wisely, and make sound decisions for the future of your organization.

Getting Started with Project Web App

This section covers signing in and out of Project Web App, using the Quick Launch task bar, and becoming oriented to the pages containing the information you need.

More About Enterprise Project Management

This chapter is designed to stand alone, providing executives and other managing stakeholders everything they need to view and analyze project and portfolio information in Project Web App.

However, if you have a wider interest, you can find more details about Microsoft enterprise project management in other chapters, as follows:

- For an overview of the enterprise project management and project portfolio management solutions provided through Project Server 2010, Microsoft Project Professional 2010, and Project Web App, read Chapter 22, "Understanding Enterprise Project Management."
- For information about the responsibilities of the project server administrator, see Chapter 23, "Administering Your Enterprise Project Management Solution."
- Details about how project managers work with enterprise projects and the enterprise resource pool are covered in Chapter 24, "Managing Enterprise Projects and Resources."
- For a deep dive into project and portfolio management, read Chapter 27, "Managing and Analyzing Project Portfolios," which is designed for portfolio managers. Although portfolio managers have more responsibilities in Project Web App, and therefore more functionality available to them, executives typically need to work closely with portfolio managers when setting up the business drivers to reflect organizational strategy and also when prioritizing the business drivers and the projects for the portfolio.

Signing In and Out

Use your web browser to connect to your organization's installation of Project Server. In the address box, type the address of your project server as provided by your project server administrator, and then press Enter.

Depending on your project server settings, a dialog box might ask for your Project Web App user name and password.

After you sign in, your Project Web App Home page appears, as shown in Figure 26-1.

To sign out of Project Web App, find and click your user name in the upper-right corner of the Project Web App window. In the drop-down menu that appears, click Sign Out.

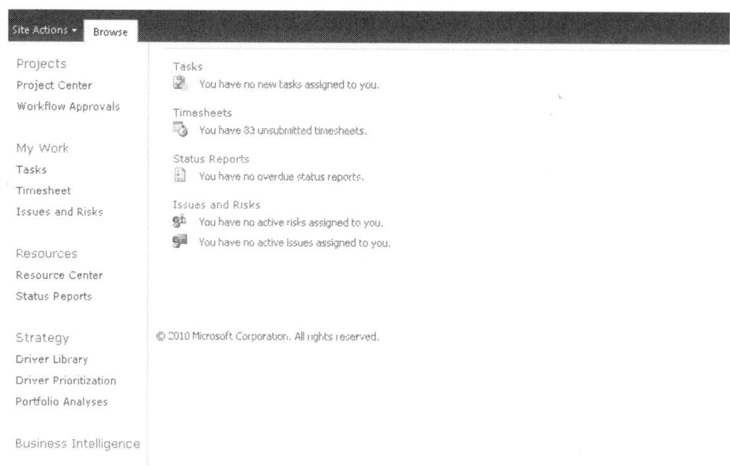

Figure 26-1 After signing in, the Project Web App Home page appears.

Navigating Project Web App

The best way to get to know where you can find the information and tools you need in Project Web App is to simply browse around the various pages. You'll become oriented to the layout and get a good idea of how you can use Project Web App for your executive analysis activities.

When you first sign in, you see the Home page. By default, the Home page lists items that need your attention, for example, status reports that have been submitted to you, dashboards that have been updated, or reports you have requested. Your project server administrator sets up your Home page to include the content most appropriate for you as an executive and for your organization as a whole.

Most pages throughout Project Web App show the Quick Launch task pane on the left side of the window. The Quick Launch includes all relevant groupings of activities for each user type, including the executive user type. This means you see only Quick Launch items that you, as an executive, are likely to find applicable to your needs.

As shown in Figure 26-2, the Quick Launch includes the following items:

- **Projects** Includes links for reviewing project information. Using this section, you can drill down in project information, check the approval status of each project, review financial information, and see project progress information.

- **Resources** Focuses on resource management. In this area, you can ask for status reports from project managers, portfolio managers, or key stakeholders, and you can also review status reports you've received.
- **Strategy** Designed especially for you, as an executive. This is where you and others in the leadership team can use business drivers to reflect organizational strategy in the projects chosen for the portfolio.
- **Business Intelligence** Provides tools for generating reports and viewing dashboards that give you insights into the company or department's key performance indicators.
- **Settings** Lets you modify your personal settings in Project Web App as well as project server settings in accordance with your access rights.
- **Lists** Shows any SharePoint lists that you create, including tasks lists.
- **Documents** Contains links to project-related document libraries, issues, and risk-tracking forms and lists.

Projects
Project Center
Workflow Approvals

My Work
Tasks
Timesheet
Issues and Risks

Resources
Resource Center
Status Reports

Strategy
Driver Library
Driver Prioritization
Portfolio Analyses

Business Intelligence

Figure 26-2 The Quick Launch is your command center to all the areas of Project Web App.

Many pages are built around a grid or table in which you can drill down to see more information. Many pages also include a ribbon of commands rather than toolbars or menus. The commands on the ribbon are organized on multiple tabs and groups.

Understanding Project Portfolio Management

Project management is focused on delivering projects with quality within multiple project management constraints. However, for the sake of the overall organization, it is important that executives ask key questions, such as:

- Are we focusing on the projects that deliver our company's strategic goals?
- Do we have enough information to include a project in the portfolio?
- Will we be able to complete all the selected projects in the portfolio, considering the existing budget and resources? Do we need to shut down a project that has already started?
- Do we have enough flexibility to accommodate changes and meet any possible new opportunities?

Through *project portfolio management*, you can answer these questions, and you can have full visibility into your organization's entire portfolio of projects. Project portfolio management ensures that you, as an executive, go beyond just successfully delivering projects and instead create an ongoing, dependable process that facilitates your ability to achieve your strategic vision through the projects being selected and executed. Rather than focusing only on the details of project execution, with project portfolio management the focus shifts to the overall benefits of projects to the organization.

Project Server 2010 reflects a portfolio management life cycle, as shown in Figure 26-3.

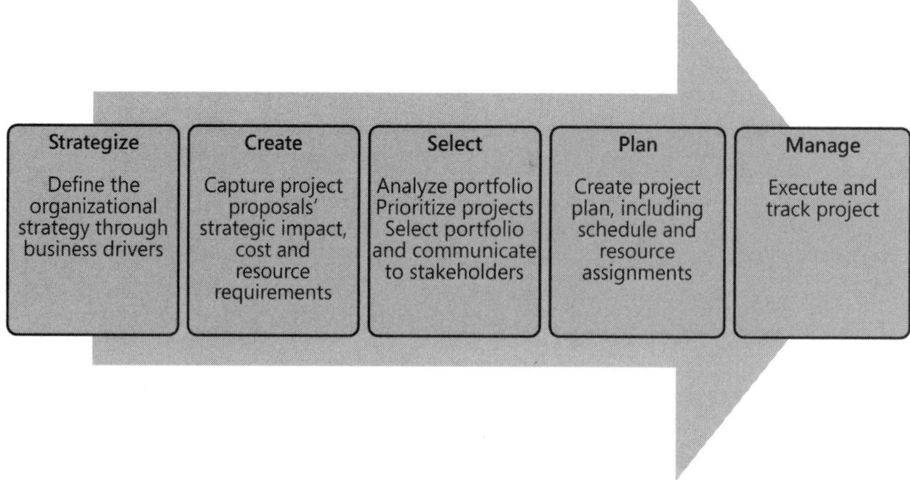

Figure 26-3 The project portfolio management life cycle is a five-phase process that starts with business driver definition and ends with project execution.

Reviewing and Prioritizing Business Drivers

NEW!

New in Microsoft Project 2010 is the ability to use strategic planning and portfolio analysis tools in Project Web App to develop *business drivers* and prioritize projects to select the right mix of projects for your organization.

It is the responsibility of the executive leadership team to define the organization's business strategy in terms of its vision, mission, and goals.

Working with your portfolio manager, you and your leadership team can then translate those strategic elements into specific business drivers entered into Project Web App. These business drivers are measurable objectives that can also be prioritized. Proposed projects are then assessed as to their alignment with one or more of the business drivers, and that assessment feeds the decision as to whether the project is a good candidate for the organization's project portfolio.

With the business driver tools in Project Web App, you can do the following:

- **Translate the organizational strategy** Break down the organization strategy into defined, measurable, and actionable objectives.
- **Reflect the consensus on organizational priorities** Ensure that the executives from different departments or teams—who might have different priorities—are on the same page regarding the most important business drivers for the entire organization.
- **Prioritize competing projects** Use the business drivers to prioritize projects that might compete for budget or resources, based on criteria such as business value, risk, cost, and more.
- **Shape the portfolio of projects** Identify the right portfolio on varying conditions. Because your budget and resource constraints might vary throughout the year, in Project Web App you have the ability to create what-if scenarios. Through the use of such scenarios, you can predict conditions if you need to add or cut certain projects.

Viewing Your Business Drivers

You can view the business drivers set up for you in Project Web App. These business drivers can start out being a sample set, or they might be the business drivers tailored to your organization's specific strategic goals.

To see your business drivers, on the Quick Launch, under Strategy, click Driver Library. The business driver library appears, as shown in Figure 26-4.

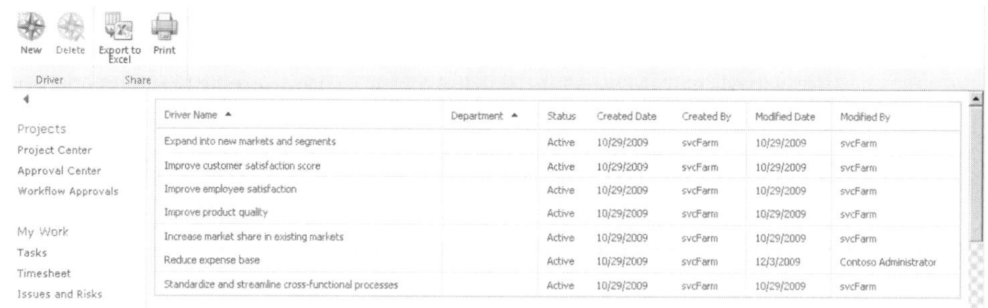

Figure 26-4 Review your business driver library in Project Web App.

If you find you need to modify, add, or remove your business drivers, check with your portfolio manager or project server administrator.

For more information, see "Changing the Business Drivers" on page 1038.

Sharing Your Business Drivers

It's often helpful to share the list of business drivers with others, especially others on your executive leadership team.

To print the list, on the Driver tab, in the Share group, click Print.

To export the list to Microsoft Excel, on the Driver tab, in the Share group, click Export To Excel.

Prioritizing Business Drivers

After you and your leadership team have developed your business drivers and your portfolio manager has entered them into Project Web App, the next step is to *prioritize* them. The best approach is to work with the leadership team and portfolio manager, perhaps in a workshop setting, during which you can come to consensus about the priorities.

Project Web App provides the tools necessary for an objective prioritization. The Driver Prioritization function in Project Web App walks you through prioritization by using the *pairwise comparison* method. The outcome is a relative priority for all business drivers, along with a consistency ratio score that is used later as you rate and rank projects for possible inclusion in your organization's portfolio of projects.

Creating a prioritization is a three-step process in which you define the details of the prioritization, prioritize the drivers, and then review the priorities.

New

To create a new prioritization, on the Quick Launch, under Strategy, click Driver Prioritization. On the Prioritizations tab, in the Prioritizations group, click New. Complete the fields, and then work through the pages to complete the prioritization of drivers.

For more information, see "Prioritizing Business Drivers" on page 1040.

Analyzing Your Portfolio to Select the Best Projects

At this point, working with the portfolio manager, you and the others on the executive leadership team have translated the organization's strategy into the business drivers in Project Web App, and those business drivers are also prioritized against one another. The workflow ensures that individuals creating proposals and project plans establish the business case for those projects by scoring them against each of the business drivers.

You can now analyze those proposals and plans to determine which ones are the most necessary and appropriate projects to become part of your project portfolio mix. These will be the projects that help you make the most progress toward your organization's strategic goals.

You can use the portfolio analysis engine in Project Web App to rate selected projects and help you make your decisions about the portfolio.

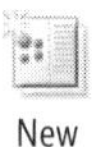
New

To analyze selected projects against the prioritized business drivers, on the Quick Launch, under Strategy, click Portfolio Analyses. On the Analysis tab, in the Analysis group, click New. Work through the New Portfolio Analysis Wizard.

After working through the portfolio analysis wizard, you see clearly where the selected projects stand against different criteria, including business drivers, cost, resources, and other criteria you might choose. You can force projects in or out of the portfolio mix as needed, so you have the flexibility you need to ensure that your portfolio includes the proper projects.

Once your decisions have been made about which projects are in and out, it's important to communicate this information to all stakeholders. The projects that have gotten the green light can now move forward with planning and execution.

For more information, see "Selecting the Best Projects for the Portfolio" on page 1044.

Working with the Portfolio of Projects

Although business drivers and portfolio analysis information alone might be sufficient for you to make business decisions as an executive, sometime you might want also to become involved in the task progress and resource details of the project. You might even want to propose a new project yourself.

The Project Center is your hub of information for your project portfolio. This is where you can inspect the details of an individual project or analyze aspects of multiple projects to get the high-level and low-level pictures you need of projects.

You can see the projects that are taking the bulk of your resources' time. This can help you determine whether you need to shift resource allocation and to ramp up or ramp down on hiring or the use of vendors.

You can use specialized views to look at overall costs of entire projects. You can combine projects in different ways to see those costs from various angles.

Most importantly, you can get that vital "view from 30,000 feet" into the collection of your organization's projects and gain insight into the key scope and activities of the organization. This can help you understand where your organization is now so that you can make strategic decisions about where you want it to go.

Reviewing Project Information

As an executive, you are required to make decisions at all project phases and stages and to make sure you have a balanced portfolio of projects that does not exceed the budgeted costs and can be fulfilled with the budgeted resources. It is important that you have the ability to make data-based decisions regarding projects at any point along a project's life cycle.

To this end, Project Server 2010 introduces the concept of the project *workflow*, which reflects phases, stages, and checkpoints along a project's life cycle. The phases of the workflow can be configured with the help of your project server administrator or portfolio manager. For example, you can establish that projects that require minimal effort in terms of costs and resources move directly to the planning stage, while projects that require a budget above a threshold you determine need to go through an initial approval process.

It is important that an executive, together with the portfolio manager, define the right project phases, depending on project type or department. It is also important to decide when review and approval stages in the process are required. Approval checkpoints are important to ensure that:

- Only the right projects are selected.
- Due diligence is performed for projects that have significant increases in cost or scope, delays in schedule, or are not meeting customer needs. Such projects need to be reworked or possibly even canceled before going any further and increasing company costs with little to no return.

- Projects with significant risks are reviewed regularly and that those risks are mitigated or eliminated.
- Governance over project performance is established and that the right level of quality is built in to the projects.

Understanding Project Workflow Phases and Stages

The following list explains Project Server's default *phases* in the project workflow. Each phase consists of multiple stages. *Stages* are steps that define the activities for that phase. (See Figure 26-5.)

- **Initiation** The project requestor defines the high-level details of the project, which might be project name, project manager, cost, and start date. After the project proposal is added, the proposal is sent to the portfolio manager and possibly to executives for approval. If the proposal is approved, it goes to the next phase; otherwise, the project is rejected.
- **Define** The project is defined in more detail. After more details are entered, the project is sent again to the portfolio manager and possibly to executives for selection. If the project is selected, it moves to the Plan and Manage phases. If not, the project is rejected.
- **Plan** During planning, the project manager enters the detailed schedule of tasks, selects the resources for the project, assigns them to tasks, and puts together the overall plan. The project manager also enters detailed costs based on the resource selection. After planning, the project can be sent for another review. If approved, the project goes to execution (the Manage phase).
- **Manage** In the Manage phase, the project is being executed. Team members and team managers report progress on current tasks and update their timesheets. The project manager tracks the schedule and costs. At certain checkpoints during the Manage phase, the project can be sent for review to ensure that it's meeting the initial criteria for cost, scope, and time and that it's following the internal project management standards.
- **Close** The final phase in the project workflow is project closure. In the Close phase, documents are archived and the lessons learned report can be drafted and posted on the project SharePoint site.

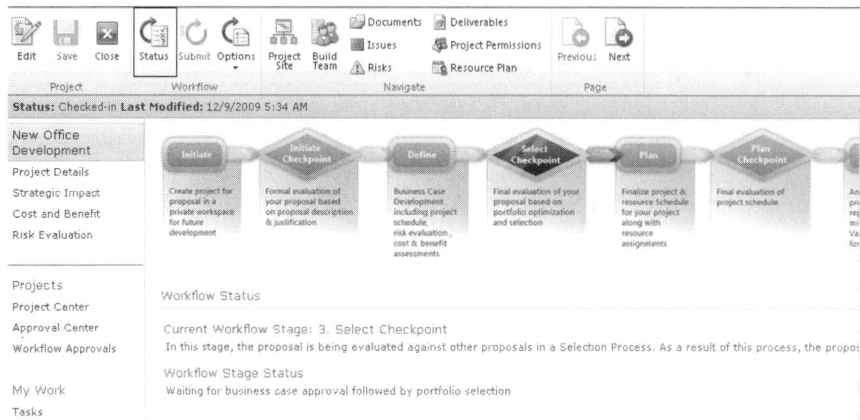

Figure 26-5 On the Stage Status page, you can see details about the current stage and the upcoming stages in the project workflow. In this example, the project is in the Define phase at stage 3, awaiting approval of the business case.

To learn more about portfolio analysis and demand management, see Chapter 27.

Viewing Project Summary Information

You can see the summary list of all published enterprise projects and then drill down to examine the details of an individual project. To see the summary of enterprise projects, follow these steps:

1. On the Quick Launch, under Projects, click Project Center.

   The Project Center appears. The table lists all enterprise projects, with each project occupying a single row and showing summary data for that project in the table and in the Gantt chart area.

   If proposals are configured in your installation of Project Server, the Project Center also lists any published project proposals.

2. Arrange the Project Center table to see the information you want. To do this, on the Projects tab, in the Data group, click in the View box.

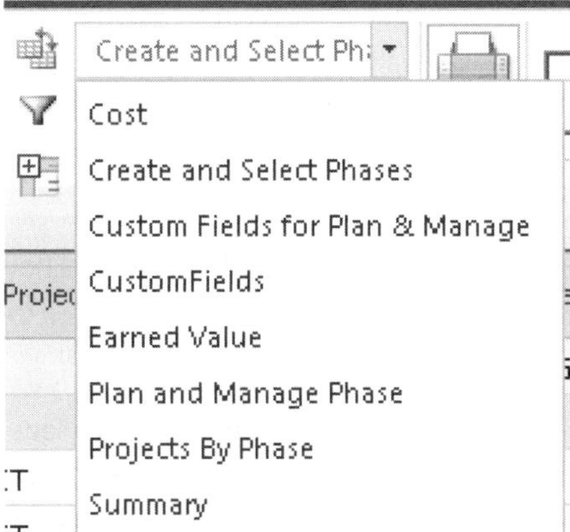

3. In the View drop-down menu, click the view that reflects the type of information you want to see.

The views available on this list depend on how your project server administrator has configured Project Server for your organization. The following list highlights the available default views:

- **Cost** Shows scheduled costs, baseline costs, fixed and variable costs, actual costs, and remaining costs. This is a good view for keeping a close eye on the budget.
- **Earned Value** Shows the calculated earned value indicators such as BCWP (Budgeted Cost of Work Performed), BCWS (Budgeted Cost of Work Scheduled), SV (Schedule Variance), CV (Cost Variance), and more. From this view, you can see how well a project is performing against its planned schedule or budget.
- **Summary** Shows an invaluable high-level overview of all projects, which can be an excellent starting place for monitoring the status of all projects in the portfolio. The view includes project start and finish dates, percentage complete, progress indicators, project owner, and the enterprise project type on which it is based.
- **Work** Shows the amount of work scheduled, baseline work, actual work, remaining work, and more. This is a good view for keeping an eye on resource requirements.
- **Create And Select Phases** Shows all projects in the Create and Select phases of the workflow. The view groups the projects by the phases and stages they're in. Fields include the project cost and estimated benefit. This view is helpful for seeing the projects in the portfolio pipeline coming up for consideration.

- **Plan And Manage Phase** Shows all projects in the Plan and Manage phases of the workflow. The view groups the projects by the phases and stages they're in. In addition to the project cost and estimated benefit, this view includes a series of graphic indicators for the project cost, health, quality, resources, and schedule. Another field indicates the probability of success for this project.

- **Projects By Phase** Shows all projects grouped by the workflow phases and stages they're in, from Create through Manage. This view also shows the project cost and estimated benefit, the project department, and risk indicator.

You can sort, filter, or group information from different points of view. You can move the split bar between the table and chart to show more of one side or the other. Scroll through the table or chart. Compare values in a field of information among the various projects.

As needed, the project server administrator or portfolio manager can create and add custom views to the Project Center.

Viewing Project Details

To see detailed information for any one of your enterprise projects, follow these steps:

1. On the Quick Launch, under Projects, click Project Center.

   The Project Center appears, showing a list of all published enterprise projects for your organization.

2. In the Project Center, click the name of the project you want to review.

   A page appears for the selected project. Which page appears depends on which workflow the project is following. For projects in the Plan and Manage phases, Project Web App displays the project schedule in the form of a Gantt chart, as shown in Figure 26-6.

   For projects in the Initiate phase, Project Web App shows the workflow stage the project is in and a graphical representation of the next steps.

Whether you're working on the Project Center page or the Schedule page, the default view is a Gantt chart. In a Gantt chart, the left side of the view displays a table, and the right side displays the Gantt bars showing the start, duration, and finish of each item (project, task, or assignment) across the timescale. The current date is shown as a dashed vertical line. You can see more or less timescale detail in the chart area by zooming. On the Tasks tab, in the Zoom group, click Zoom In or Zoom Out.

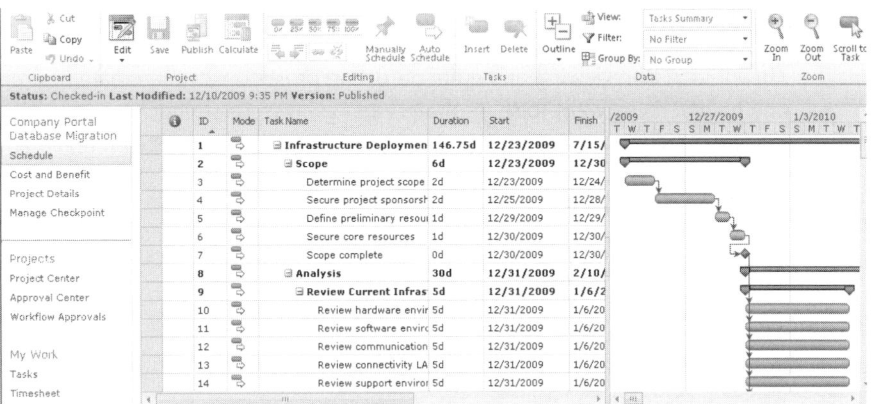

Figure 26-6 In the Quick Launch under the project name, you can select whether you want to see the schedule, cost and benefit information, project details, or checkpoint information for the selected project.

Reviewing Project Workspaces

Documents, issues, and risks can be added, tracked, linked with tasks, assigned responsibility, and eventually closed. They all become an important aspect of seeing the project through to a successful completion. They are also instrumental in capturing project archival information for use in planning future projects.

The lists of documents, issues, and risks associated with a project are maintained in the *project workspace*, which is essentially a SharePoint site for the project. You can create a project workspace when a project is created or anytime afterward. In addition to documents, issues, and risks, the site can include announcements from team members, a calendar of upcoming events, a list of deliverables between related projects, and team discussions.

To open the workspace for a project, follow these steps:

1. On the Quick Launch, under Projects, click Project Center.
2. If there is a folder icon next to the name of a project, this indicates that the project has an associated project workspace.
3. Click the folder.

   The project workspace appears in a separate window.

For details about creating project workspaces and viewing documents, risks, and issues in a project SharePoint site, see "Managing Documents, Risks, and Issues" on page 958.

Creating a New Project

In addition to reviewing and editing existing projects, you can create new projects. This can be helpful if you want to share project ideas with your staff or set up the vision of a new program that portfolio managers and project managers can then implement.

To create a new project, follow these steps:

1. On the Quick Launch, under Projects, click Project Center.
2. On the Project tab, in the Project group, click New.

New

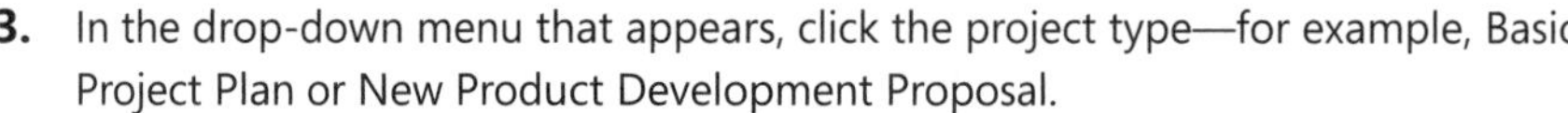

3. In the drop-down menu that appears, click the project type—for example, Basic Project Plan or New Product Development Proposal.

   The project types will differ depending on how your project server administrator has configured Project Server for your organization.

   A page appears in which you can start entering the project details.

For more information about creating a new project in Project Web App, see "Creating a New Enterprise Project" on page 905. To learn how to save, publish, and check in your new project, see "Managing Your Files on the Project Server" on page 912.

Working with Resource Information

The Resource Center is where executives and resource managers can keep a close eye on the performance of enterprise resources. In the Resource Center, you can review skills and other identifying attributes for resources, their current assignments, their current or future workload allocation, and their current or future availability for additional work.

Viewing the Enterprise Resource Pool

You can see the entire enterprise resource pool and then examine details for an individual resource. To see the enterprise resource pool, follow these steps:

1. On the Quick Launch, under Resources, click Resource Center.

   The Resource Center appears, showing the enterprise resource pool. Each resource occupies a single row that shows basic resource information. (See Figure 26-7.)

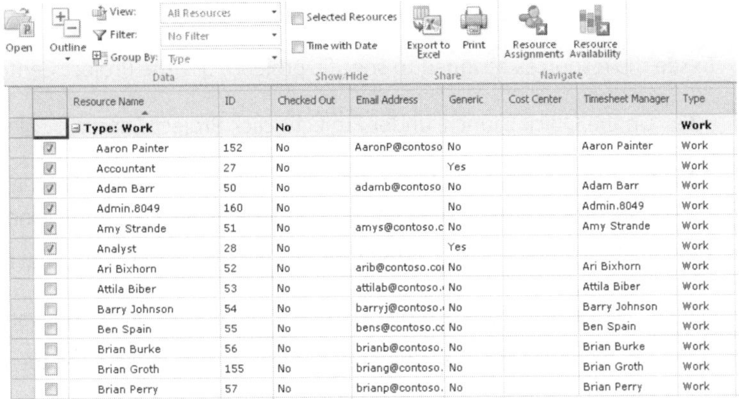

Figure 26-7 The Resource Center displays the enterprise resource pool.

2. If you want, on the Resource tab, in the Data group, click in the View box, and then click the view that shows the type of resource information you want to see.

   The project server administrator or portfolio manager can create and add different views to the Resource Center.

   You can also sort, filter, or group resource information.

To view detailed information for a particular enterprise resource, follow these steps:

1. In the Resource Center, select the check box next to the name of the resource for which you want to see details. If you want to see details for multiple resources one after another, select the check boxes for each of them.

2. On the Resources tab, in the Editing group, click Edit Resource.

Edit Resource

3. Scroll through the Edit Resource page to see resource details. Included on the page are the resource's contact information, assignment attributes, and availability dates, as well as the contents of any custom fields that have been designed.

   By default, executive privileges do not include the ability to edit resource information. However, if you need that capability, talk with your project server administrator.

4. If you selected multiple resources, when you're finished with the first resource, click the Save And Continue or Continue Without Saving button.

   The Edit Resource page for your second selected resource appears.

5. Continue in this manner until you get to the last resource. On the page for the last resource, click Save or Cancel. To return to the Resource Center at any time, you can also click the Cancel Remaining button.

   The Resource Center showing all enterprise resources appears.

Viewing Resources for Specific Projects

To see the resources assigned to specific projects, use the Project Center, as follows:

1. On the Quick Launch, under Projects, click Project Center.
2. Show the projects that are in the Plan or Manage phase: On the Projects tab, in the Data group, click in the View box, and then click Plan And Manage Phase.

   Typically only projects in the Plan or Manage phases would have resources assigned.
3. Click the name of the project whose assigned resources you want to see.

   The names of the available project detail pages are listed at the top of the Quick Launch.
4. In the Quick Launch, under the project name, click Schedule.

   The Schedule project detail page appears.
5. If the Resources Summary view is not already showing, on the Task tab, in the Data group, click in the View box, and then click Resources Summary.

   The Resources Summary view lists all resources assigned to the selected project, as shown in Figure 26-8.

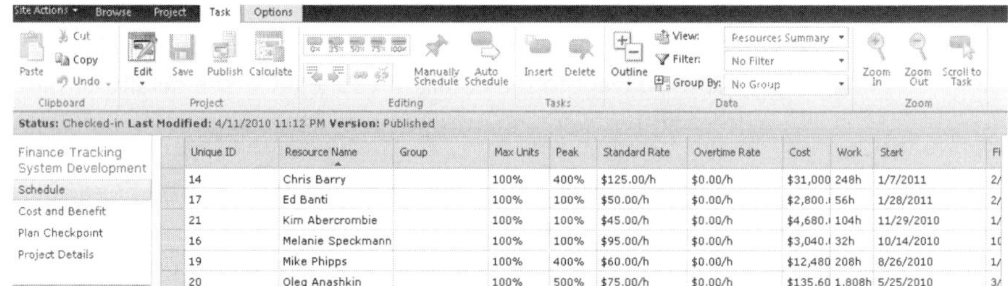

Figure 26-8 In the View drop-down menu in the Data group, select Resources Summary.

Reviewing Resource Assignments

To review resource assignments, follow these steps:

1. On the Quick Launch, under Resources, click Resource Center.
2. In the Resource Center, select the check box next to the name of the resource whose assignments you want to see. If you want to see assignments for multiple resources at once, select the check boxes for each of them.

Resource Assignments

3. On the Resources tab, in the Navigate group, click Resource Assignments.

   The Resource Assignments page appears, as shown in Figure 26-9. In a Gantt chart format, the assignments for the selected resources are listed, grouped by resource name and then by project name.

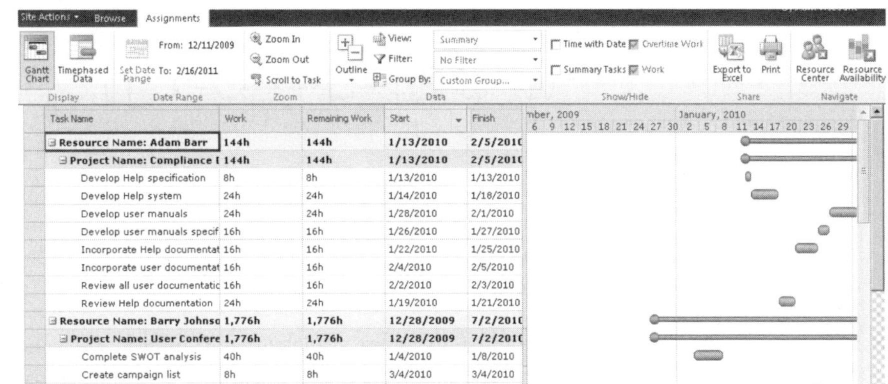

Figure 26-9 The assignments for the selected resources appear on the Resource Assignments page.

4. Scroll through the table and the chart to view the information you want.
5. When you are finished, on the Assignments tab, in the Navigate group, click the Resource Center button.

Reviewing Resource Availability

To review resource availability, follow these steps:

1. On the Quick Launch, under Resources, click Resource Center.
2. In the Resource Center, select the check box next to the name of the resource whose availability you want to see. If you want to see availability for multiple resources, select the check boxes for each of them.

Resource Availability

3. On the Resources tab, in the Navigate group, click Resource Availability.

   The Resource Availability page appears, as shown in Figure 26-10. The availability, as measured by work amounts over time, is drawn in a column chart for each selected resource. Availability and capacity information are shown for each resource in a table below the chart.

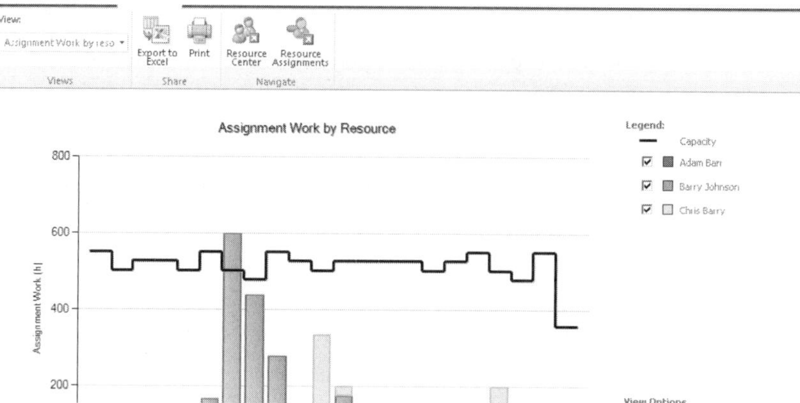

Figure 26-10 Availability graphs for the selected resources appear on the Resource Assignments page.

4. If you want to hide a resource's availability information, clear the check box next to the resource's name in the legend. Select the check box to show the availability information again.

5. On the Availability tab, in the Views group, click in the View box to select other resource availability views—for example, Assignment Work By Project, Remaining Availability, or Work.

6. When you are finished, on the Assignments tab, in the Navigate group, click the Resource Center button.

   The Resource Center appears again.

Reviewing Resource Plans

With a resource plan, project managers and resource managers can estimate potential resource requirements associated with proposals or new projects. You can review resource plans if you want to see how resources are being used for other nonproject activities.

To see a resource plan, follow these steps:

1. On the Quick Launch, under Projects, click Project Center.

2. In the table, select the name of the project or proposal whose resource plan you want to review. Do not click the project name; click in any other cell or the row heading for the project.

Resource Plan

3. On the Projects tab, in the Navigate group, click Resource Plan.

   The resource plan for the selected project appears.

4. When you are finished, on the Plan tab, in the Plan group, click Close.

   The Project Center appears again.

Analyzing and Reporting on Project Information

Having accurate information about the status of the company's key project-related performance indicators is vital for executives. With the new business intelligence suite of tools available in Project Server 2010, you can easily find relevant information in the immense amount of data that is stored on your project server.

With the Project 2010 business intelligence features you can:

- Standardize the way reporting is done with the help of the project server administrator. You can base reporting on standard metrics.
- Create automated processes for reporting. You can have predefined reports that you and the project managers can easily access.
- Easily drill down in data through the use of the reporting services provided in the Business Intelligence Center.

The Business Intelligence library in Project Server includes a standard set of templates. Users can open the template in Excel and create new reports from the template.

Based on these reports, your portfolio manager or your project server administrator can build standard reports that you can use regularly. Figure 26-11 shows a standard list of sample reports and templates.

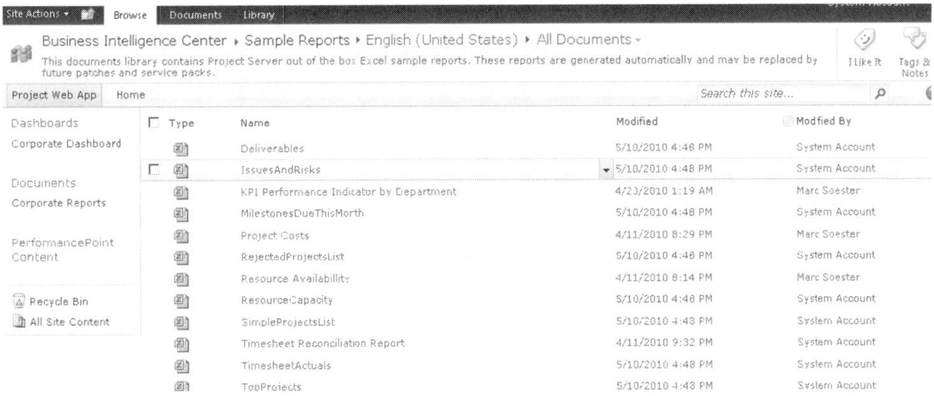

Figure 26-11 Click the template name to create a new report based on that template.

Besides these reports, you can also create dashboards. *Dashboards* are views that provide instant information about your key performance indicators. Your portfolio manager can set up dashboards for you, showing the most relevant key performance indicators. Details can be shown in dashboards by department, program, and project, and they can help you identify issues that need your attention.

Dashboards visually highlight the status of the key performance indicators. Figure 26-12 shows an example of a configured dashboard.

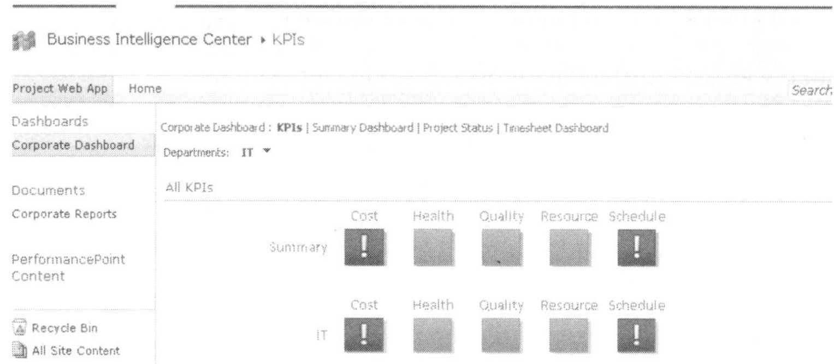

Figure 26-12 Dashboards provide visual snapshots of your projects' key performance indicators.

Understanding the Portfolio Analysis Tools

In the Project Web App Business Intelligence Center, you can leverage a whole set of tools to build your reports. Depending on the report type, you can use one or several of these tools to obtain the information you are interested in. The tools include:

- **Online Views** These are used for the Quick Online Views, and they can be seen in several pages in Project Web App, such as the Project Center, Resource Center, and others.

  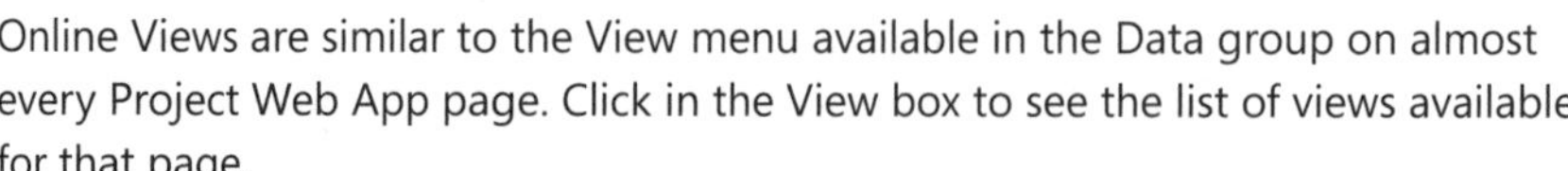

  Online Views are similar to the View menu available in the Data group on almost every Project Web App page. Click in the View box to see the list of views available for that page.

  You can export a view to Excel. On the current tab, in the Share group, click Export To Excel. This quickly generates an Excel report in which you can drill down and analyze your data.

- **Excel Services** Through Excel Services, you can view sample reports or already-created Excel reports in the web browser. This functionality enables you to drill down in the data through standard Excel filters directly in the browser, as shown in Figure 26-13. You can start building Excel reports based on existing samples or templates.

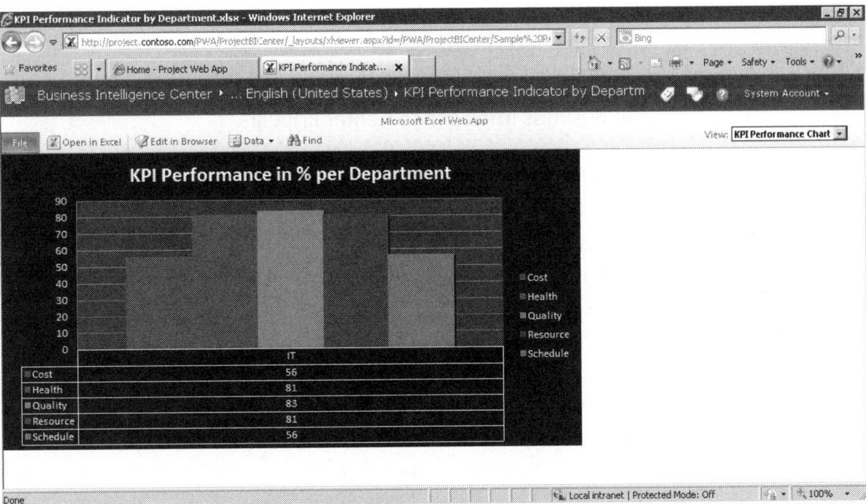

Figure 26-13 Select the view in the View box in the upper-right corner of the page to switch between viewing the chart or PivotTable and the raw data.

- **PerformancePoint Services** This tool is the engine that drives the creation of the dashboard and the key performance indicator (KPI) reports. In dashboards, you can combine different types of data. PerformancePoint Services also provides access to the Dashboard Designer.
- **Visio Services** This tool facilitates the visualization of project management processes by generating timeline views, dynamic timelines, and so on.
- **SQL Reporting Services** You can use the SQL Reporting Services to create standard printable reports.

Generating Reports

There are various ways in which you can create new reports in Project Web App. You can start with a sample or template already existing in the Business Intelligence Center, or you can create a report from scratch. In this section, you'll learn how to create reports using the samples that come with your installation of the Business Intelligence Center.

> **Note**
>
> **The templates available depend on your administrator's configuration of the business intelligence functionality.**

To create a new report based on a sample report, follow these steps:

1. On the Quick Launch, click Business Intelligence.

   The Business Intelligence Center appears.

2. In the left pane, click Documents.

3. Under Document Libraries in the page that appears, click Sample Reports.

   The Business Intelligence Center displays the list of available sample reports, as shown in Figure 26-14.

Figure 26-14 The Sample Reports library displays the predefined reports that are installed with Project Web App. You can customize these reports to your needs.

4. Click the arrow to the right of the sample report you want to customize, and then in the drop-down menu that appears, click Edit In Microsoft Excel. If a security alert appears, click OK.

   The report opens in Excel, as shown in Figure 26-15.

5. Modify the report as needed, adding fields or creating filters or whatever you might need to show the information you want for this report.

   You need to name the filter as well as the PivotTable and the chart for the report to work. You will then be able to select them from the Excel Services drop-down list. To name the filter, select the filter cell and enter a name. (See Figure 26-16.)

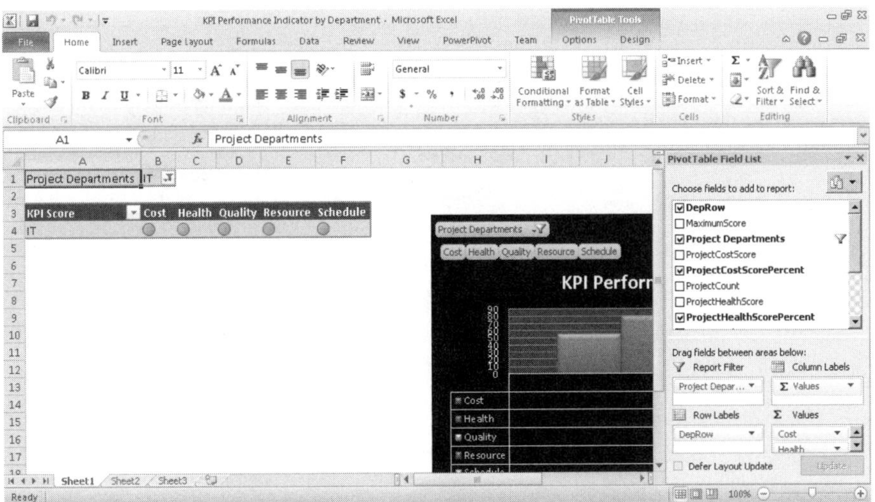

Figure 26-15 The data is displayed as a PivotTable and chart in Excel. You can configure the contents of the PivotTable and change the chart options.

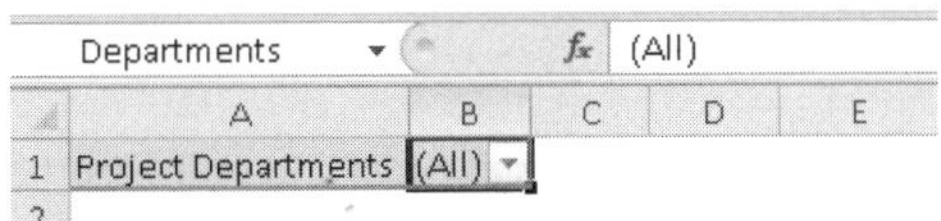

Figure 26-16 Select the different parts in the file (PivotTable, filter, and chart) and name them.

6. When you have finished your modifications, publish the report. On the File tab in Excel, click Save & Send, and then click Save To SharePoint.

7. In the right pane of the Backstage view, click the Publish Options button.

8. In the Publish Options dialog box, select or clear the check boxes to specify the items included in the report, as shown in Figure 26-17.

9. Click OK in the Publish Options dialog box.

10. Save the report in the location you want.

    After the report is saved, you can view it using Excel Services by accessing the location you specified.

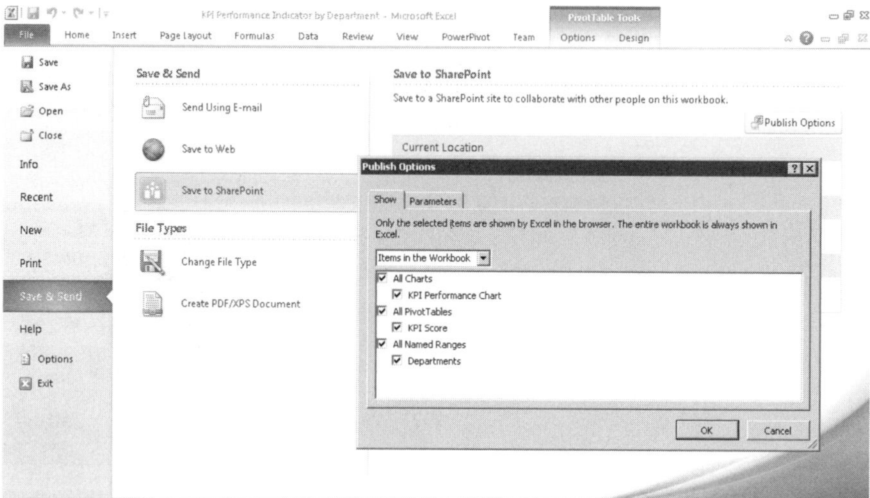

Figure 26-17 Use the Publish Options dialog box to specify the items to include in the report.

Note

You can also create reports using templates as a starting point. In the Documents area of the Business Intelligence Center, click Templates. The templates are predefined reports based either on the relational database or on OLAP (online analytical processing) cubes.

Using Dashboards

Dashboards are generally created and configured by the project server administrator or the portfolio manager.

To view available dashboards, follow these steps:

1. On the Quick Launch, click Business Intelligence.
2. In the left pane, click Dashboards.

   A list of all dashboard items appears.
3. Click folders or items to open them.

For more information about dashboards and using the Dashboard Designer, see "Creating Dashboards" on page 1055.

CHAPTER 27

Managing and Analyzing Project Portfolios

Nearly all organizations have their available time stretched and budgets squeezed by undertaking more projects than they should. Even well-chosen projects can be poorly executed and cost more than they should. Projects that have no business seeing the light of day do not deliver value or help to advance the organization's strategic goals. This is not a sustainable situation for any organization.

The solution is to have a process that allows for a clear-eyed, objective look at the organization's proposed projects and ensures that only the right projects get the green light to move forward and be carried out. Which are the right projects? They're the ones that have "the right stuff," the characteristics to satisfy the organization's strategic vision and goals in terms of profit potential, customer service, quality, compliance, and so on. The collection of projects undertaken by an organization is its *project portfolio.*

NEW!

Integrated into Microsoft Project Server 2010 are new project portfolio management features. These features provide for proposed project evaluation and selection, workflow capabilities, and business intelligence and analysis across all projects in the portfolio. This means that you now have a single platform for comprehensive project portfolio management as well as enterprise project management.

Project portfolio management (PPM) encompasses the methods by which an organization can centrally collect, analyze, prioritize, and select proposed projects, and then execute the selected projects while being ever mindful of the overall progress, cost, and resource utilization throughout. While project management focuses on executing an individual project, the objective of project portfolio management is to achieve the ideal mix of projects that can enable the organization to achieve its strategic goals.

The project portfolio management features in Project Server 2010 include the following:

- **Integrated project and portfolio management** In Microsoft Project 2007, the portfolio management features were handled on a separate add-on server platform. In Project Server 2010, project portfolio management functionality is now completely integrated with enterprise project management in the Microsoft Project Web App user interface. The result is a common and interconnected user experience throughout the entire project portfolio management life cycle.

- **Demand management system** The heart of the project portfolio management features implemented in Project Server 2010 is the demand management system. In this context, *demand management* is the system for selecting project proposals that align with the organization's strategic business objectives and then governing the execution of selected projects against a defined workflow that ensures the fulfillment of key indicators at identified checkpoints in the project life cycle. Different enterprise project categories can be defined and associated with a workflow, a project, and a template.

- **Workflow configuration** As a major component of the demand management system, the *workflow* defines each step in the life cycle of a project. In fact, the workflow essentially implements the demand management system. The portfolio manager can configure all aspects of the workflow to reflect the characteristics of the organization and to ensure the appropriate level of governance. The workflow typically begins with the initial project proposal and includes all approval steps along the way through to project selection, execution, and closure. The project manager can track the status of the project in all the steps of the workflow. You can use the Project Web App workflow module to define one or more workflows for the different categories of projects in your organization.

- **Business driver definition** The identification and prioritization of *business drivers*—that is, key business objectives or development areas for an organization—is another significant component of the demand management system. Examples of business drivers include: increase profit, expand into new markets, or enhance customer satisfaction. The portfolio manager and members of the executive leadership team can objectively weigh and prioritize proposed projects against the defined business objectives and more quickly come to a consensus about which projects have the most merit and have the most potential for fulfilling the organization's strategic goals. Project Web App includes an intuitive visual interface for defining and prioritizing business drivers.

- **Portfolio analysis tools** In Project Web App, portfolio managers and executives can use the business drivers, the optimizer, and planning tools to analyze the projects in the portfolio. They can see which projects hit the target for the key business drivers. They can analyze which projects are best meeting the business drivers for that function within given cost and resource constraints. They can optimize portfolios based on different filters, such as strategic value, financial value, resource utilization, and risk.

This chapter is designed especially for the portfolio manager or project management office (PMO) responsible for managing the organization's project portfolio. The portfolio manager works closely with the project server administrator, with key project managers, and with executives to configure the demand management system with its workflow and business drivers so that the project portfolio can be effectively and efficiently selected, managed, and analyzed.

For an overview of how Project Server 2010 implements the end-to-end enterprise project management solution, see Chapter 22, "Understanding Enterprise Project Management." For an understanding of the responsibilities of the project server administrator and how Project Server can be configured to support the requirements of the portfolio manager and project manager, see Chapter 23, "Administering Your Enterprise Project Management Solution." For details about working with individual projects in the enterprise project management environment, see Chapter 24, "Managing Enterprise Projects and Resources."

Understanding Project Portfolio Management

As implemented in Project Server 2010, the project portfolio management life cycle consists of five stages. In Project Web App, a default but customizable workflow reflects these five stages, as follows:

- **Strategize** The executive leadership team defines the organization's business strategy in terms of its vision, mission, and goals.

  The portfolio manager can work with the leadership team to translate the defined business strategy into business drivers, which are entered in Project Web App. The business drivers are prioritized to reflect department, group, and overall priorities.

- **Create** Project managers, executives, and others create project proposals or complete project plans.

  Using Project Web App or Microsoft Project Professional 2010, proposals and plans are created, captured, and added to the project server. As part of the project plan development workflow, project managers not only develop the project plan, but also create the business case for each project. In this way, there is clear visibility into whether and how a proposed project satisfies one or more business drivers. In this way, the estimated strategic impact of each project is measured against each of the business drivers.

- **Select** The executive leadership team and portfolio manager analyzes the proposed projects and selects the projects that most closely align with the organization's strategic objectives.

  Through the use of the portfolio analysis tools in Project Web App, the proposed projects are analyzed and prioritized. They're given an empirical score that helps you and the leadership team objectively determine how well each project meets your strategic goals, given the limitations in place related to cost, resource availability, compliance requirements, risk, and more. This prioritization process helps the leadership team arrive at consensus more quickly, and possibly less painfully, by showing clearly how the projects align with the organization's strategic business drivers. This phase ensures that the right projects are selected, and the right mix of projects is developed. At this point, the project portfolio is set, and the decisions are communicated to all project stakeholders.

- **Plan** The projects selected to be part of the portfolio are given the "green light," and the project plans are fully developed. Project managers are assigned, resources are acquired, and budgets and schedules are locked into place. The customized project planning workflow can include checkpoints that ensure the project plan meets key performance indicators.

- **Manage** Project managers execute the planned projects, using Project Professional 2010 and Project Web App as their tools for managing, tracking, and reporting. As in the Plan phase, the customized workflow can include checkpoints for key performance indicators as project milestones are met.

  After the projects are under way, the portfolio manager works closely with the project managers to keep a constant eye on issues or risks that have larger implications for the success of individual projects and the portfolio as a whole. The portfolio manager also ensures that members of the executive leadership team have reports and dashboard information at their fingertips so that they can quickly access the high-level project and portfolio information they need to stay up to date and to make decisions at critical junctures.

  The portfolio manager also subjects the projects to regular portfolio analysis to monitor whether the project is living up to its potential for delivering the intended benefit toward strategic goals.

This process is not necessarily linear, but is actually more iterative. Depending on the needs of the organization, you might find yourself traversing various phases as the portfolio is continually refined. For example, you might switch back and forth between the Select and Plan phases several times until you have sufficient information to include or exclude proposed projects in the portfolio.

Figure 27-1 shows the portfolio management life cycle in relation to the project management life cycle.

Project Portfolio Management Life Cycle

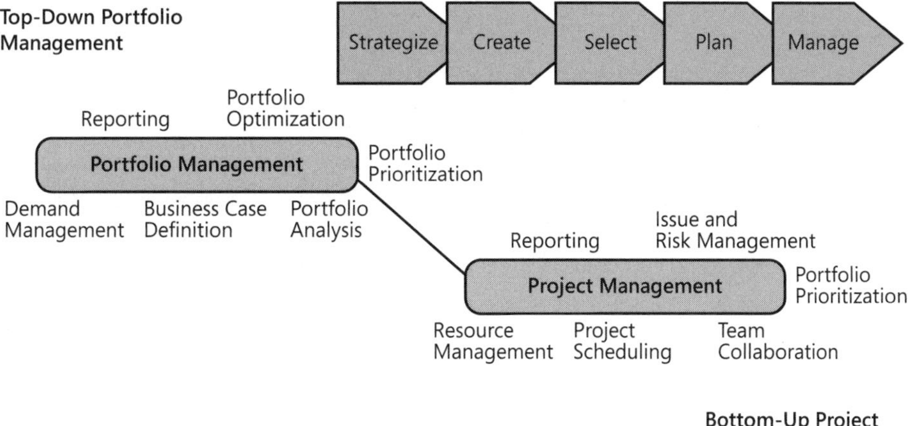

Figure 27-1 The portfolio management life cycle is a five-step iterative process.

The phases of the portfolio management life cycle map to the project management life cycle as shown in Figure 27-2. For example, after the project is proposed in the Initiate phase, it's included in the portfolio analysis as part of the Create phase.

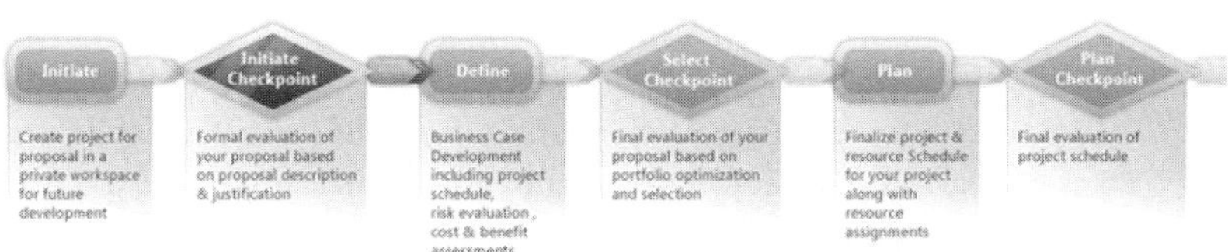

Figure 27-2 The phases of the project life cycle map to the phases in the portfolio life cycle.

Just as Project 2010 provides tools for each phase of project management, Project Server 2010 offers tools for managing each phase of the project portfolio management process. These tools—graphs, diagrams, and scoring calculations—help in your implementation and decision making in a manner that reflects professional best practices for project portfolio management and can be customized to your organization's needs.

Designing Your Demand Management System

Demand management is the system in Project Server 2010 that helps you capture and select project proposals that align with your organization's strategic business objectives and then govern the execution of the selected projects against a workflow, including key checkpoints through project execution and closure.

Demand management ensures that all projects are managed centrally and all stakeholders have access to a holistic view of all projects taking place from beginning to end.

The workflow is essentially the "engine" for the demand management system; it is the means by which the demand management system is implemented. The workflow defines each step in the life cycle of a project. As the portfolio manager, you configure the workflow to reflect where in the project life cycle you need certain checkpoints that determine the health and progress of that project, and even whether the project is meeting the necessary criteria to continue.

Although you can customize workflows however you need to, a typical workflow starts with a project proposal, entails various approval steps to selection, and includes the standard project management phases of planning, management, controlling, and closure.

You can use the Project Web App workflow module to define one or more workflows for your organization. This section defines basic concepts about workflows, explains the default workflow provided in Project Server 2010, provides instruction on customizing an existing workflow, and describes how a workflow is associated with enterprise project types.

Note

By default, portfolio managers do not have rights to create and revise project workflows. Work with your project server administrator to ensure that you have the rights you need to customize your organization's workflows.

Understanding Workflow Basics

In previous versions, the governance imposed on projects published to the project server consisted of the contents of the enterprise global template, which might include required custom fields or provide views and reports of special use in the organization. With the enterprise resource pool, all projects in the organization had a common set of rules that dictated how resources were assigned and availability tracked.

This is all still true. Now, with the additional demand management features as implemented through the use of workflows, organizations have more control over how projects are executed.

As with the model of the project life cycle, the workflow consists of phases and stages within a project to enforce project governance. The following are some basic workflow terms you need to understand:

- **Workflow phase** A workflow *phase* is a major category describing the point of development that a project is in. In the default workflow provided with Project Server, phases include Create, Select, Plan, Manage, and Finished. A phase contains a series of steps or stages.
- **Workflow stage** A workflow *stage* is a subcategory within a phase that describes the detailed condition of a project in that phase. The stage is associated with steps or activities. For example, in the default workflow provided with Project Server, the Create phase, includes stages named Initial Review, Define (Major Project), Automated Rejection, Define (Minor Project), Initial Proposal Details, and more. (See Figure 27-3.)

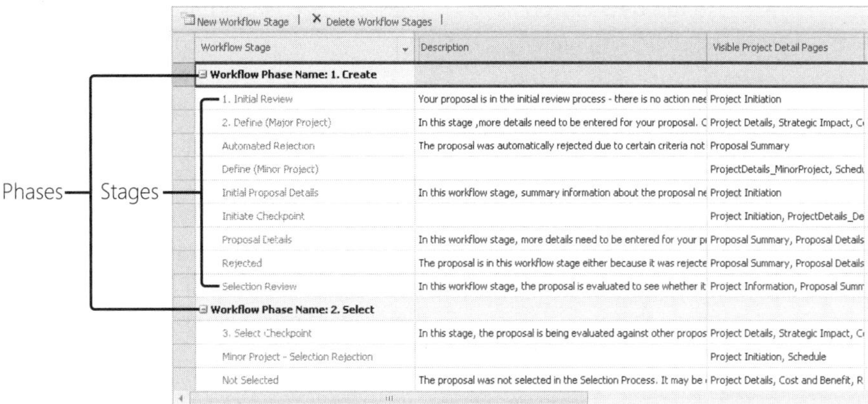

Figure 27-3 A workflow phase indicates the level of project development, and workflow stages describe the detailed condition of the project in that phase.

Using the Default Workflow

Project Server 2010 proposes a default project workflow that you can use as a starting point. This workflow consists of five phases: Create, Select, Plan, Manage, and Finished. Figure 27-4 models the interactions within the first four phases.

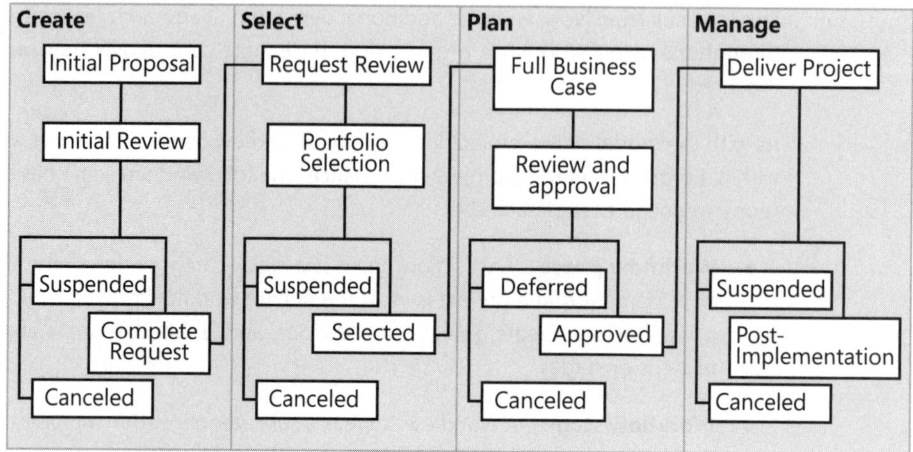

Figure 27-4 Project Server 2010 provides a default project workflow that can be easily adapted by many organizations. (From *"Project 2010: Introducing Demand Management," MSDN Blog, blogs.msdn.com/b/project/archive/2009/11/13/project-2010-introducing-demand-management.aspx, November 13, 2009.*)

In this default workflow, the phases, stages, enterprise project type, and project detail pages are fully configured.

For more information about enterprise project types and project detail pages, see "Initiating a Project Proposal" on page 924.

Customizing an Existing Workflow

You can easily customize the default workflow provided by Project Server 2010. You can add, change, or remove phases as well as stages. For example, you might need to add a stage that provides a notification regarding an approval or a step reflecting an interaction with another system such as the company's accounting system.

Changing a Workflow Phase

To make changes to existing workflow phases, follow these steps:

1. On the Quick Launch in Project Web App, under Settings, click Server Settings.
2. Under Workflow And Project Detail Pages, click Workflow Phases.
3. To add a new phase, on the toolbar above the table, click New Workflow Phase. Type the name and description of the new phase in the Name and Description boxes. Note that the name appears in alphabetical order in the phases list. Click Save.

   To edit an existing phase, click the name of the phase. Modify the name or description, and then click Save.

New Workflow Phase

Delete Workflow Phases

To remove an existing phase, click the phase description so that the item is selected rather than opened. On the toolbar, click Delete Workflow Phases, and then click OK.

Adding a New Workflow Stage

To add a new workflow stage, follow these steps:

1. On the Quick Launch, under Settings, click Server Settings.
2. Under Workflow And Project Detail Pages, click Workflow Stages.
3. To add a new stage, on the toolbar above the table, click New Workflow Stage.

   New Workflow Stage

   The Add Workflow Stage page appears.
4. Type the name and description of the new stage in the Name and Description boxes. Note that the name will appear in alphabetical order within the workflow phase.
5. In the Description For Submit box, type the description you want users to see when they click Submit in a project detail page.
6. In the Workflow Phase box, click the phase with which this new stage should be associated.
7. As appropriate, select information associated with the project detail pages and custom fields in the remaining fields.
8. When finished, click Save.

Changing an Existing Workflow Stage

To modify an existing workflow stage, follow these steps:

1. On the Quick Launch, under Settings, click Server Settings.
2. Under Workflow And Project Detail Pages, click Workflow Stages.
3. Click the name of the stage you want to modify.
4. In the page that appears, modify any of the fields that define the selected stage.
5. When you are finished, click Save.

Removing a Workflow Stage

To remove a workflow stage, follow these steps:

1. On the Quick Launch, under Settings, click Server Settings.

2. Under Workflow And Project Detail Pages, click Workflow Stages.
3. Click the stage description so that the item is selected rather than opened.
4. On the toolbar above the table, click Delete Workflow Stages, and then click OK.

Associating a Workflow with an Enterprise Project Type

When project managers and other users create a new project proposal or plan, they select from an *enterprise project type*. When an enterprise project type is associated with a workflow, that workflow governs the checkpoints to which that project must adhere.

To associate a workflow with an enterprise project type, follow these steps:

1. On the Quick Launch in Project Web App, under Settings, click Server Settings.
2. Under Workflow And Project Detail Pages, click Enterprise Project Types.
3. Click the name of the enterprise project type you want to associate with a workflow.
4. In the page that appears, click in the Site Workflow Association field, and then click the workflow you want to associate with this enterprise project type.
5. Make any necessary changes to the New Project Page, Available Project Detail Pages, and Default fields.
6. When you finish making changes, click Save.

For more information, see "Configuring Enterprise Project Types" on page 858.

A project is governed by a workflow when it is based on a particular enterprise project type.

Creating a New Workflow

New project workflows can be created in Microsoft Visual Studio 2010 through the Project Server Interface (PSI). You must have administrative rights to your project server to create a new project workflow.

For best results, plan the new workflow by identifying the phases, stages, activities, and associations. Obtain feedback on the new workflow before implementing it. After you create the new workflow, you can associate it with a category and enterprise project type.

For more information about creating a new workflow, see your project server administrator.

Optimizing Your Project Portfolio

You can use strategic planning and portfolio analysis tools in Project Web App to develop business drivers and prioritize projects to select the right mix of projects for your organization.

Reflecting Strategy by Defining Business Drivers

It is the responsibility of the executive leadership team to define the organization's business strategy in terms of its vision, mission, and goals.

The portfolio manager, working with the leadership team, can then translate those strategic elements into specific business drivers entered into Project Web App. These business drivers are measurable objectives that can also be prioritized. Proposed projects are then assessed as to their alignment with one or more of the business drivers, and that assessment feeds the decision as to whether the project is a good candidate for the organization's project portfolio.

With the business driver tools in Project Web App, you can do the following:

- **Translate the organizational strategy** You can break down the organization strategy into defined, measurable, and actionable objectives.
- **Reflect the consensus on organizational priorities** Ensure that the executives from different departments or teams—who might have different priorities—are on the same page regarding the most important business drivers for the entire organization.
- **Prioritize competing projects** Use the business drivers to prioritize projects that may compete for budget or resources based on criteria such as business value, risk, cost, and more.
- **Shape the portfolio of projects** Identify the right portfolio on varying conditions. As your budget and resources constraints might vary throughout the year, in Project Web App you have the ability to create what-if scenarios. Through the use of such scenarios, you can predict conditions if you need to cut or add certain projects.

Viewing Existing Business Drivers

You might have a sample set of business drivers in Project Web App. This gives you a good place to start.

To review the existing business drivers library, on the Quick Launch, under Strategy, click Driver Library. The Driver Library page appears, as shown in Figure 27-5. Note that these might be a sample set, or they might reflect your organization's actual business drivers, based on its strategic plan.

Driver Name ▲	Department ▲	Status	Created Date	Created By	Modified Date	Modified By
Expand into new markets and segments		Active	10/29/2009	svcFarm	10/29/2009	svcFarm
Improve customer satisfaction score		Active	10/29/2009	svcFarm	10/29/2009	svcFarm
Improve employee satisfaction		Active	10/29/2009	svcFarm	10/29/2009	svcFarm
Improve product quality		Active	10/29/2009	svcFarm	10/29/2009	svcFarm
Increase market share in existing markets		Active	10/29/2009	svcFarm	10/29/2009	svcFarm
Reduce expense base		Active	10/29/2009	svcFarm	12/3/2009	Contoso Administrator
Standardize and streamline cross-functional processes		Active	10/29/2009	svcFarm	10/29/2009	svcFarm

Figure 27-5 Review the driver library which lists business drivers.

It's often helpful to share the list of drivers with others, especially the executive leadership team.

Print

To print the list, on the Driver tab, in the Share group, click Print.

Export to Excel

To export the list to Microsoft Excel, on the Driver tab, in the Share group, click Export To Excel.

Changing the Business Drivers

For demand management to work appropriately, it's vital that you create business drivers that correspond with your organization's strategic goals.

To add a new business driver, follow the steps below:

1. On the Quick Launch, under Strategy, click Driver Library.

New

2. On the Driver tab, in the Driver group, click New.

   The New Business Driver page appears, as shown in Figure 27-6.

3. In the Name box, enter the driver name.

   The driver name should reflect a high-level strategic objective for the organization.

4. In the Description box, be specific with an explanation of the new business driver.

5. In the Department(s) box, select the department(s) to which the new business driver is relevant.

6. In the Status box, select whether the driver is active or inactive.

   Active drivers appear on appropriate pages and are required. Inactive drivers do not appear. If you are drafting the driver and are not ready for it to go "live," make it inactive for now. If you are ready, make it active.

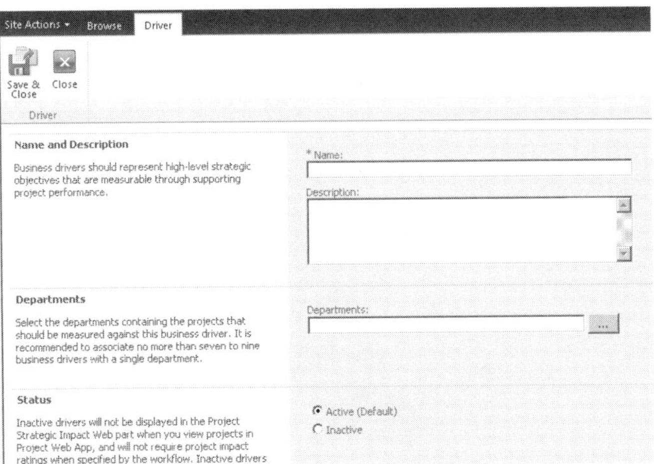

Figure 27-6 Use the New Business Driver page to create a new business driver that reflects one of your organization's strategic goals.

7. In the Project Impact Statement boxes, enter an impact statement for the new business driver in each of the five boxes, as shown in Figure 27-7. The impact ratings describe how strongly a project contributes to the business driver; they are used by the project manager when creating the business case for a proposed project.

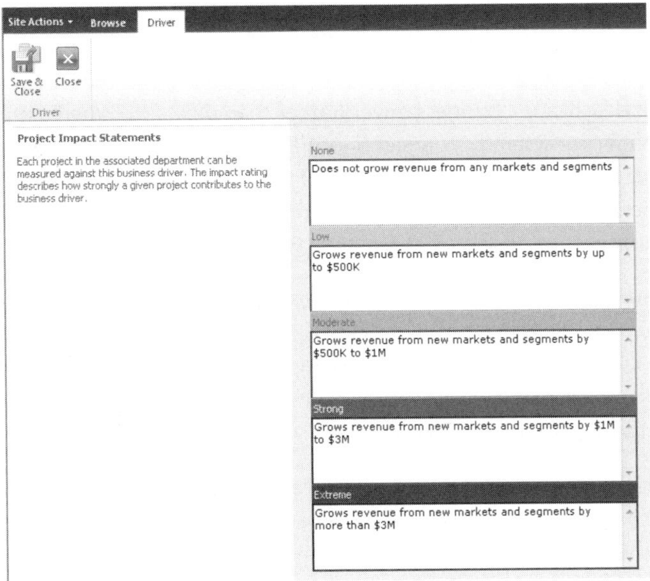

Figure 27-7 The Project Impact Statements help the project manager gauge how well the proposed project aligns with this business driver.

After the business drivers and their project impact statements are established, anyone proposing a new project needs to rate the project against the business drivers, as shown in Figure 27-8.

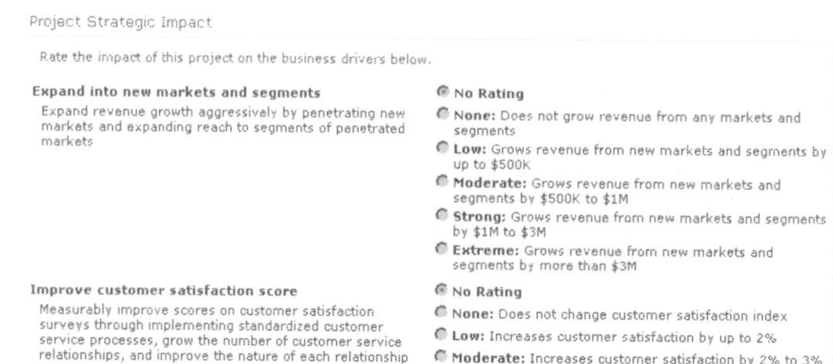

Figure 27-8 Upon initiating a new project, a project manager must work through the Project Strategic Impact pages to indicate how well the proposed project meets the requirements of the business drivers.

Save & Close

8. On the Driver tab, in the Driver group, click Save & Close.

   The new driver is added to the driver library. Repeat this process for all additional business drivers until they are all present.

To modify existing business driver information, click the driver name. The Edit Business Driver page appears. Change any of the fields as needed. When you are finished, click Driver, Driver, Save & Close.

You can deactivate a business driver (rather than delete it). When a driver is deactivated, it is no longer considered in project prioritizations. For historical purposes, it's preferable to deactivate a driver rather than delete it if you have used it in prioritizations. To deactivate a business driver, click the driver name. In the Edit Business Driver page, in the Status field, select the Inactive option. Click Driver, Driver, Save & Close.

Delete

To delete a business driver, select the row containing the driver information. Just don't click the driver name itself; otherwise, you'll open the Edit Business Driver page. When the driver row is selected, click Driver, Driver, Delete.

Prioritizing Business Drivers

After business drivers are developed and agreed upon by the leadership team, the next step is to prioritize them. The best approach is to work with the leadership team, perhaps in a workshop setting, during which you can come to consensus about the priorities.

You can perform the prioritization in Project Web App. The Driver Prioritization function walks you through prioritization by using the *pairwise comparison* method. The outcome is a relative priority for all drivers, along with a consistency ratio score.

Creating a prioritization is a three-step process in which you define the details of the prioritization, prioritize the drivers, and then review the priorities.

To create a new prioritization, follow these steps:

1. On the Quick Launch, under Strategy, click Driver Prioritization.

   The Driver Prioritization page appears, as shown in Figure 27-9.

Name ▲	Department ▲	Type	Complete	Created Date	Created By	Modified Date	Modified By
CIO Priortization		Calculated	Yes	11/18/2009	Contoso Administrator	11/18/2009	Contoso Administrator
COO Priortization		Calculated	Yes	11/18/2009	Contoso Administrator	11/18/2009	Contoso Administrator
Executive Consensus		Calculated	Yes	11/21/2009	Contoso Administrator	11/21/2009	Contoso Administrator
HR Priortization		Calculated	Yes	11/18/2009	Contoso Administrator	11/21/2009	Contoso Administrator

Figure 27-9 Use the New Business Driver Prioritization page to start working through the driver prioritization process.

New

2. On the Prioritizations tab, in the Prioritizations group, click New.

   The New Prioritization page appears.

3. Complete the Name and Description fields.

4. In the Department field, select the departments to which this driver prioritization applies.

5. In the Prioritization Type field, specify whether the prioritization should be calculated or manually entered.

6. Select the drivers that you would like to include in this prioritization.

   You must select at least two drivers, and it's best to include from five to twelve drivers in the prioritization.

7. In the lower-left corner of the page, click the Next: Prioritize Drivers button.

   Project Web App takes you through multiple screens in which you can prioritize each driver against all the rest, as shown in Figure 27-10. Each driver is rated from Is Extremely Less Important Than to Is Extremely More Important Than.

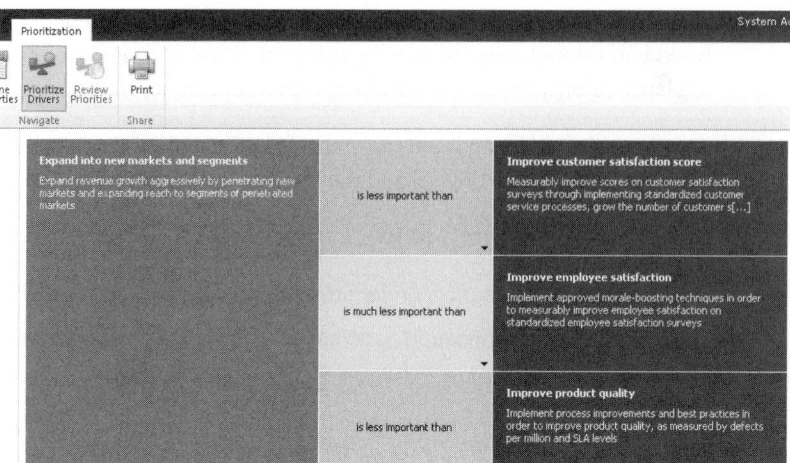

Figure 27-10 On the Prioritization page, rate each driver against all the rest.

8. In the lower-right corner of the page, click the Next: Review Priorities button.

   Project Web App generates the relative priority score for each of the driver. This is automatically calculated based on an algorithm.

9. Review the priorities and score.

10. If you want, review the consistency ratio by clicking the plus sign next to Consistency Ratio at the bottom of the screen.

    The consistency ratio indicates the consistency of your ranking and prioritization of the business drivers. It is recommended that the consistency ratio be above 70 percent.

Close

11. On the Prioritization tab, in the Prioritization group, click Close.

    The Driver Prioritization page appears, with your new prioritization listed with the others.

You can create multiple prioritizations that you can later apply in different situations, depending on the department or role.

INSIDE OUT Driver prioritization logic

When you choose the calculated prioritization type, Project Web App puts you through the built-in pairwise comparison method for your selected business drivers.

The logic used is based on a method for making complex decisions called *Analytical Hierarchy Process (AHP)*. As in this case, AHP applies to prioritization situations when the priority of an individual item is compared to the rest and no item is ignored.

Each one of the drivers is associated with a weight or a numeric value that substitutes the analytical prioritization (Extremely More, Strongly More, Equal, Moderately More, and so on) as shown in Figure 27-11.

	Driver A	Driver B	Driver C	Driver D
Driver A		Equal	Strongly More	Extremely More
Driver B			Moderately Less	Strongly Less
Driver C				Moderately More
Driver D				

	Driver A	Driver B	Driver C	Driver D
Driver A	1	1	6	9
Driver B	1	1	3	1/3
Driver C	1/6	1/3	1	1/6
Driver D	1/9	1	1/6	1

Figure 27-11 Each of the analytical comparison results is allocated a number within the matrix.

This is the process for the algorithm:

- The business drivers are placed in a matrix according to the values entered by the user.
- Each of the prioritizations is given a numeric weight. For example, Equal is 1, Extremely More equals 9, while Extremely Less equals 1/9. Strongly More equals 6, while Strongly Less equals 1/6.
- The diagonal is allocated the value of 1 as each driver equals itself.
- After the matrix above the diagonal is filled in, the matrix below the diagonal is calculated, with the opposite values filled in. For example, if Driver A compared to Driver C equals 6, than Driver C compared to Driver A equals 1/6.

After the matrix is calculated, the icon value for the matrix is calculated, and the values are displayed.

Selecting the Best Projects for the Portfolio

At this point, you and the executive leadership team have translated the organization's strategy into the business drivers in Project Web App, and those business drivers are also prioritized against one another. The workflow ensures that those creating proposals and project plans establish the business case for those projects by scoring them against each of the business drivers.

You can now analyze those proposals and plans to determine which ones are the most necessary and appropriate projects to become part of your project portfolio mix. These will be the projects that further the most progress toward your organization's strategic goals.

You can use the Portfolio Analysis engine in Project Web App to rate selected projects and help you make your decisions about the portfolio. To do this, follow these steps.

1. On the Quick Launch, under Strategy, click Portfolio Analyses.

   The Driver Prioritization page appears.

New

2. On the Analyses tab, in the Analysis group, click New.

   The New Portfolio Analysis Wizard launches.

3. In the Define Properties page that appears, enter the name and description you want for the analysis in the Name and Description fields.

4. In the Department field, select the department(s) to which this analysis should pertain.

5. In the Prioritization Type area, select whether you want to prioritize based on your business drivers or based on custom fields.

   If you have entered and prioritized your business drivers, select the option labeled Prioritize Projects Using Business Drivers, and then click the name of the prioritization you did on your business drivers.

   If you have not entered or prioritized your business drivers, or if you want to analyze the project portfolio based on entries in custom fields, select the option labeled Prioritize Projects Using Custom Fields.

6. In the Prioritize These Projects area, click the Selected Projects button.

   A list of all projects and proposals entered in your project server appears, as shown in Figure 27-12.

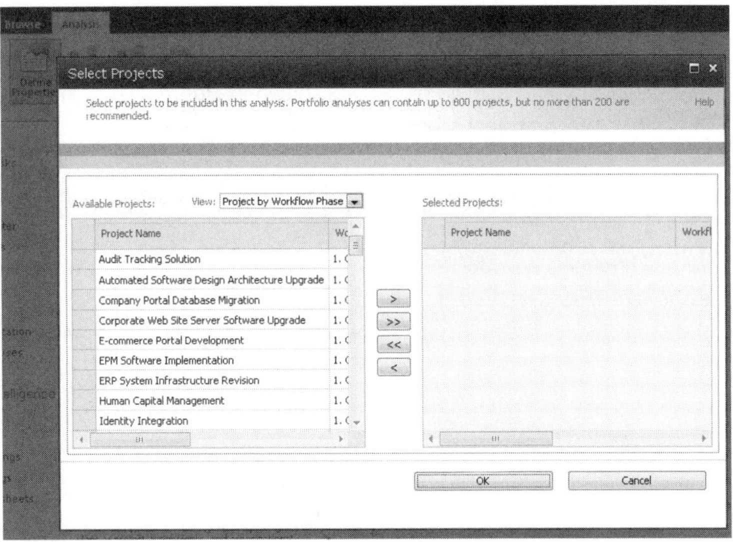

Figure 27-12 Use the Select Projects dialog box to specify which projects stored in your project server should be included in the portfolio analysis.

7. Select the projects you want to be part of the portfolio analysis.

Move All Items

Move Selected Items

To add all the projects, click the Move All Items button.

To add selected projects, select the projects you want to add, and then click the Move Selected Items button. Drag across the rows or hold down the Shift key while clicking the first and last items to select adjacent items. Hold down the Ctrl key while clicking to select nonadjacent items.

8. When you finish adding projects for the analysis, click OK in the Select Projects dialog box.

9. In the Analysis Primary Cost Constraint box, select the primary budget constraint to be used in this analysis.

10. In the Time-Phased Resource Planning section, select the check box if you want the analysis to consider resource requirements.

    Only select this check box if all the projects selected for analysis have had resources assigned or a resource plan developed. Note that once you have selected and saved the analysis with this check box selected, it cannot be changed.

11. In the lower-right corner of the page, click the Next: Prioritize Projects button.

    The Prioritize Projects page appears, showing your selected projects in a matrix against your business drivers. As shown in Figure 27-13, this reflects how the generator of each project scored the project against your business drivers.

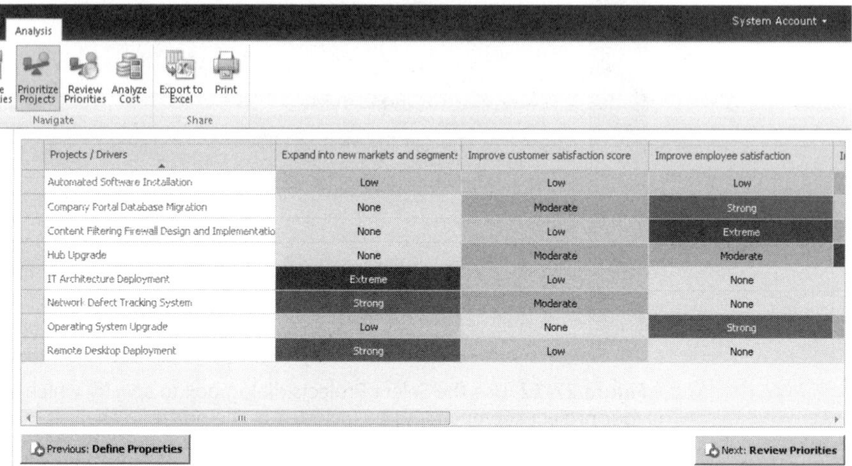

Figure 27-13 The Prioritize Projects page shows a matrix of how closely each of the selected projects meets your business drivers.

12. In the lower-right corner, click Next: Review Priorities.

    The Review Priorities page shows the overall score of each of the selected projects. The score indicates an overall rating of how closely the project maps to your overall business strategy based on your prioritized business drivers. The projects are listed in order from highest to lowest score.

13. In the lower-right corner, click Next: Analyze Cost.

    The Analyze Cost page shows the cost analysis for each of the projects based on the primary budget constraint you selected in the Define Properties page. (See Figure 27-14.)

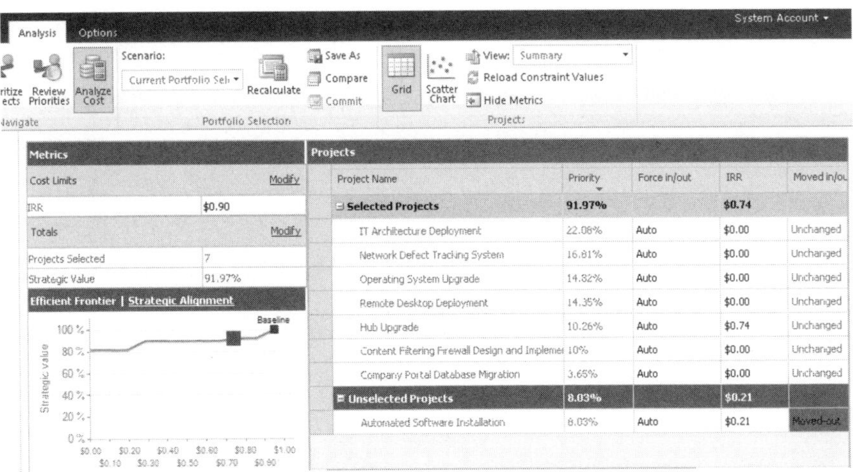

Figure 27-14 The Analyze Cost page shows the cost information together with the priority scores for each of the selected projects.

You can modify the Metrics section to see the analysis based on different criteria. Under Metrics, click Modify. In the Modify Constraints dialog box that appears, select a constraint, click Add, and then click OK. The Analyze Cost page is recalculated to show results with the new constraint.

On this page, you can force a project in or out of the portfolio mix regardless of its score or performance against other constraints. You might want to do this if a project has too low a score with too high a cost and is being recommended to be removed from the portfolio but you know that you need to include it because of a compliance or legal mandate or another compelling reason. Click in the Force In/Out cell, then click the button that appears. Click Forced-In. In the same way, you can force a project out of the portfolio mix if needed, perhaps as a tradeoff for including a forced-in project.

14. If you chose to include resource analysis, a fifth page of the wizard appears: Analyze Resources, as shown in Figure 27-15.

    The Analyze Resources page shows which of the selected projects can be done based on current resources. On this page, you can also perform what-if analyses by adding new resources.

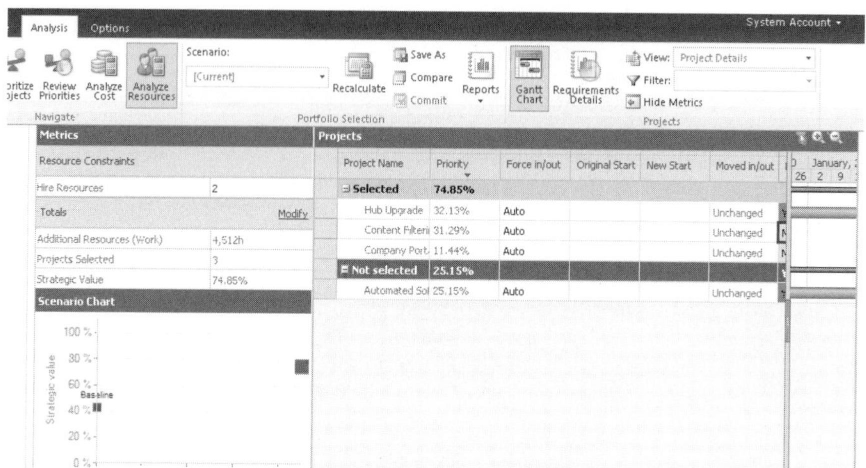

Figure 27-15 You can specify that resources be considered as part of your portfolio analysis, in which case the Analyze Resources page shows your options.

15. When you are finished, on the Analysis tab, in the Analysis group, click Close.

    This saved analysis is added to any other analyses listed on the Portfolio Analysis page. You can return to it as needed, compare it with others, and make other changes.

After working through the Portfolio Analysis Wizard, you see clearly where the selected projects stand against different criteria, including business drivers, cost, resources, and other criteria you might choose. You can force projects in or out of the portfolio mix as needed, so you have the flexibility you need to ensure that your portfolio includes the proper projects.

Once your decisions have been made about which projects are in and out, communicate this information to all stakeholders. The projects that have received the green light can now move forward with planning and execution.

Viewing Project Information

While the selected projects in your ideal portfolio mix are being planned and executed, your job as the portfolio manager is to keep a vigilant eye on the projects as they progress. You need to see how the various projects might impact one another and be aware of any large issues or risks you need to attend to. While typically you might be satisfied to look at the high-level summary information of individual projects, on occasion you'll need to drill down into the project details.

The Project Center is your hub of information for your project portfolio. This is where you can inspect the views of an individual project or analyze aspects of multiple projects to get the high-level and low-level picture of projects you need.

You can see the projects that are taking the bulk of your resources' time. This can help you determine whether you need to shift resource allocation and to ramp up or ramp down on hiring or the use of vendors.

You can use specialized views to look at overall costs of entire projects. You can combine projects in different ways to see those costs from various angles.

This section includes details about the best views for getting the summary and detailed project information you need to manage the organization's project portfolio.

Seeing Project Summary Information

You can see the summary list of all published enterprise projects and then drill down to examine the details of an individual project.

To see the summary of enterprise projects, on the Quick Launch, under Projects, click Project Center. By default, a Gantt chart view of all projects and proposals published in your project server appears, as shown in Figure 27-16.

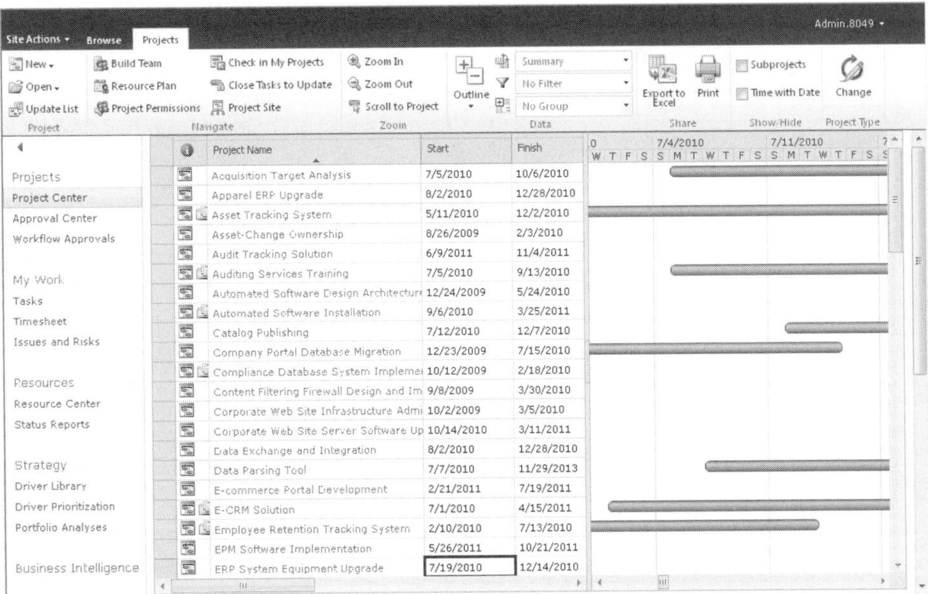

Figure 27-16 The Project Center appears as a Gantt chart listing all your enterprise projects.

Chapter 27

View

Each project occupies a single row and shows summary data for that project.

To see more or less detail in the time span shown in the chart area, zoom the time span in or out. On the Projects tab, in the Zoom group, click Zoom In or Zoom Out.

You can change the Project Center view to show different types of information. On the Projects tab, in the Data group, click the arrow in the View box, and then click the view that shows the information you want to see, as shown in Figure 27-17.

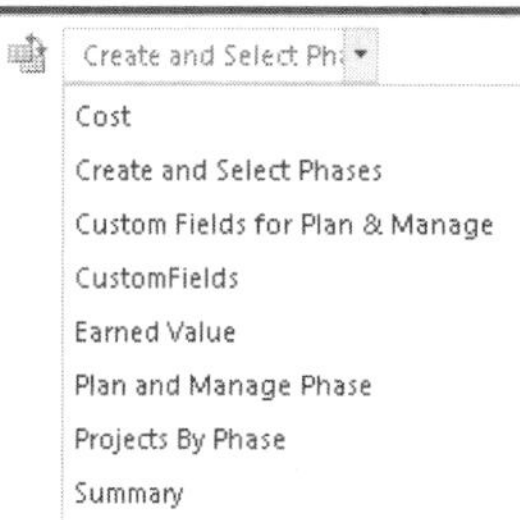

Figure 27-17 The Project Center view shows the information you want to see.

The following list points out some highlights of these views:

- **Cost** Shows scheduled costs, baseline costs, fixed and variable costs, actual costs, and remaining costs. This is a good view for keeping a close eye on the budget.
- **Earned Value** Shows the calculated earned value indicators such as BCWP (Budgeted Cost of Work Performed), BCWS (Budgeted Cost of Work Scheduled), SV (Schedule Variance), CV (Cost Variance), and more. From this view you can see how well a project is performing against its planned schedule or budget.
- **Summary** Shows an invaluable high-level overview of all projects, which can be an excellent starting place for monitoring the status of all projects in the portfolio. The view includes project start and finish dates, percentage complete, progress indicators, project owner, and the enterprise project type on which it is based.
- **Work** Shows the amount of work scheduled, baseline work, actual work, remaining work, and more. This is a good view for keeping an eye on resource requirements.
- **Create And Select Phases** Shows all projects in the Create and Select phases of the workflow. The view groups the projects by the phases and stages they're in. Fields include the project cost and estimated benefit. This view is helpful for seeing the projects coming up for consideration in the portfolio pipeline.

- **Plan And Manage Phase** Shows all projects in the Plan and Manage phases of the workflow. The view groups the projects by the phases and stages they're in. In addition to the project cost and estimated benefit, this view includes a series of graphic indicators for the project cost, health, quality, resources, and schedule. Another field indicates the probability of success for this project.

- **Projects By Phase** Shows all projects grouped by the workflow phases and stages they're in, from Create through Manage. This view also shows the project cost and estimated benefit, the project department, and risk indicator.

You can work with the project server administrator to create and add different views to the Project Center that suit the types of information you need to see most frequently.

Viewing Project Details

To see detailed information for any of the enterprise projects, in the Project Center, simply click the name of the project. Depending on the workflow the project is associated with, and which phase the project is in, a project detail page appears. For projects in the Plan or Manage phase, the project schedule in the form of a Gantt chart appears, as shown in Figure 27-18.

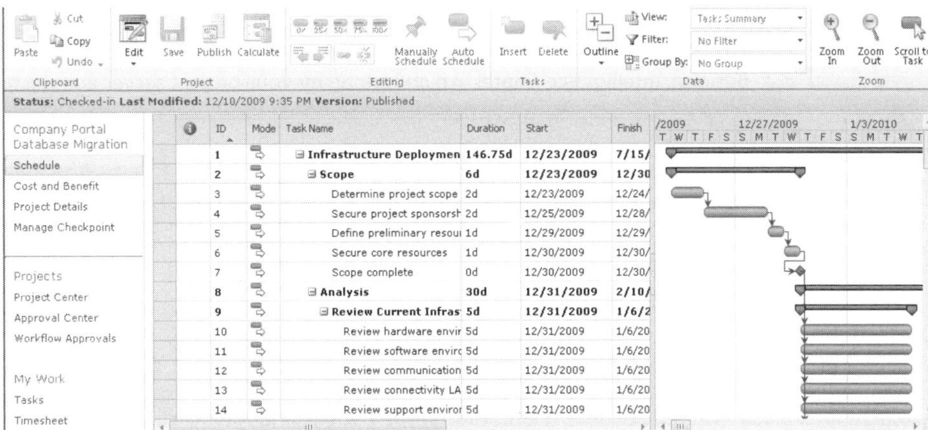

Figure 27-18 Review the details of an individual project.

To see other details about the project, click other links, such as Cost And Benefit or Project Details, under the project name on the Quick Launch.

Communicating Portfolio Information

As the portfolio manager, you need to be sure that stakeholders, especially executives and other managing stakeholders, get the information they need about the portfolio to stay informed and make necessary decisions.

One easy method for providing portfolio information is to directly use the information in any view by printing or exporting it to Excel. Nearly all table-based views throughout Project Web App include the Print and Export To Excel commands. For example, in Project Center, on the Projects tab, in the Share group, click Print or click Export To Excel.

Using the Business Intelligence Center in Project Web App, you can use a variety of tools to design reports and dashboards to provide others with the necessary information.

Creating Reports

You can create new reports based on a sample or template in the Business Intelligence Center, or you can create one entirely from scratch. The reports in the Business Intelligence Center are created using Excel Services.

Note

The templates available depend entirely on your organization's configuration of the Business Intelligence Center, which is done by your project server administrator.

To create a report based on a sample report in Excel, follow these steps:

1. On the Quick Launch, click Business Intelligence.

   The Business Intelligence Center appears.

2. In the left pane, click Documents.

3. Under Document Libraries on the page that appears, click Sample Reports.

   The Business Intelligence Center displays the list of available sample reports, as shown in Figure 27-19.

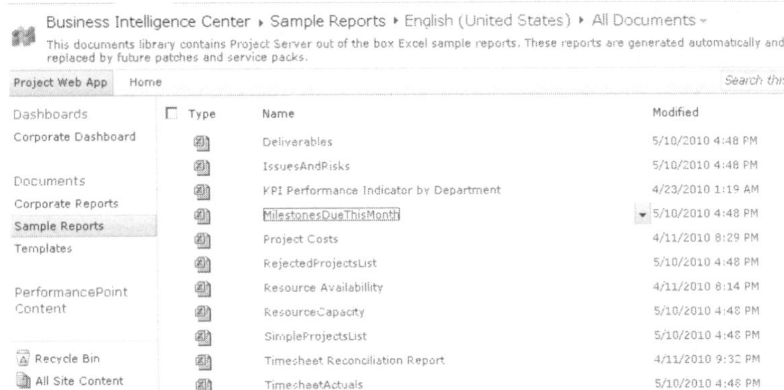

Figure 27-19 The Sample Reports library displays the predefined reports installed with Project Web App. You can customize these reports to your needs.

4. Click the arrow to the right of the sample report name you want to customize, and then click Edit In Microsoft Excel in the drop-down menu that appears. If a security alert appears, click OK.

   The report opens in Excel, as shown in Figure 27-20.

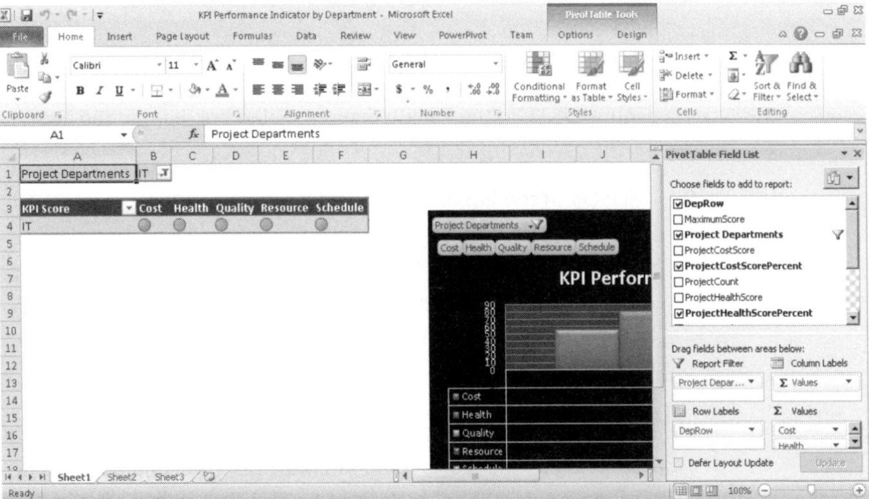

Figure 27-20 The selected sample report is shown in Excel as a PivotTable and chart. You can configure the contents of the PivotTable and change the chart options.

5. Modify the report as needed, adding fields or creating filters or whatever you might need to show the necessary information you want for this report.

   You need to name filters, as well as the PivotTable and chart, for the report to work. You can then select them from the Excel Services drop-down menu.

Save To SharePoint

6. When you are finished modifying the report, publish the report. On the File tab in Excel, click Save & Send, and then click Save To SharePoint.
7. In the right pane of the Backstage view, click the Publish Options button.
8. In the Publish Options dialog box, select or clear the check boxes to specify the items to be included in the report, as shown in Figure 27-21.

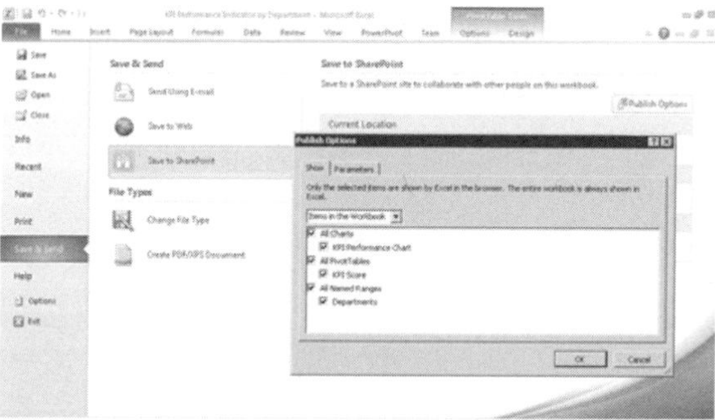

Figure 27-21 In the Publish Options dialog box, specify the items to be included in the report.

9. Click OK in the Publish Options dialog box.
10. Save the report in the location you want.

    After the report is saved, you can view it using Excel Services by accessing the location you specified.

Note

You can also create reports using templates as a starting point. In the Documents area of the Business Intelligence Center, click Templates. The templates are predefined reports based on the relational database or on OLAP (online analytical processing) cubes.

INSIDE OUT **The Project Server data source structure**

Project Server 2010 includes four databases for storing project data. While the user interacts with Project Web App and makes transactions in the user interface, the data is stored in the Draft database, the Publish database, or the Archive database.

The fourth database is the Reporting database, which takes data from the Publish database and is the source for all reports. See Figure 27-22 for a diagram of the database structure.

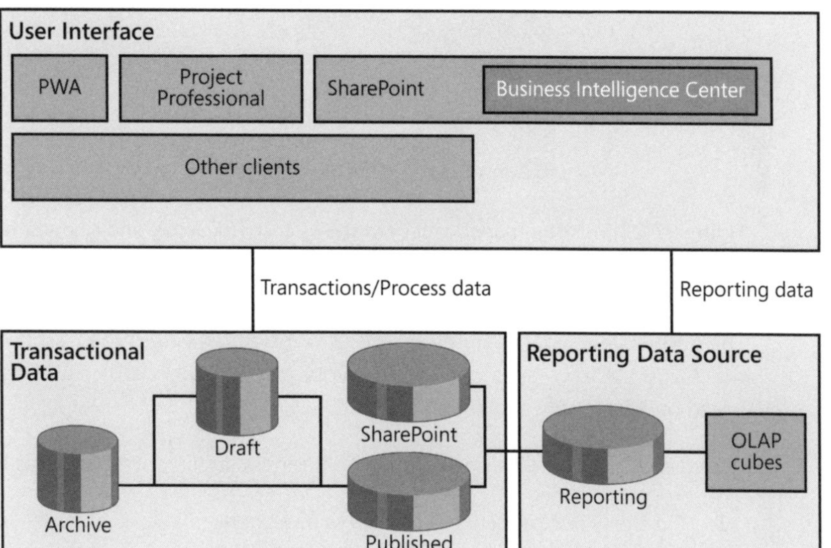

Figure 27-22 The Project Server Reporting database holds all transactional data, which is then used as the source for reports generated by the Business Intelligence Center.

The Reporting database also includes objects such as Project Schedule Data, Global Resource Data, and Timesheet Data. Data for demand management and business drivers is also included in the Reporting database.

Data from the Reporting database is built into OLAP cubes.

Creating Dashboards

Project dashboards are graphically-oriented interactive sources for seeing certain types of project information at a glance. You can design dashboards for key performance indicators on the portfolio, project dashboards, resource information dashboards, and more.

You can create dashboards for yourself and for use by executive stakeholders. Figure 27-23 shows an example of a project dashboard.

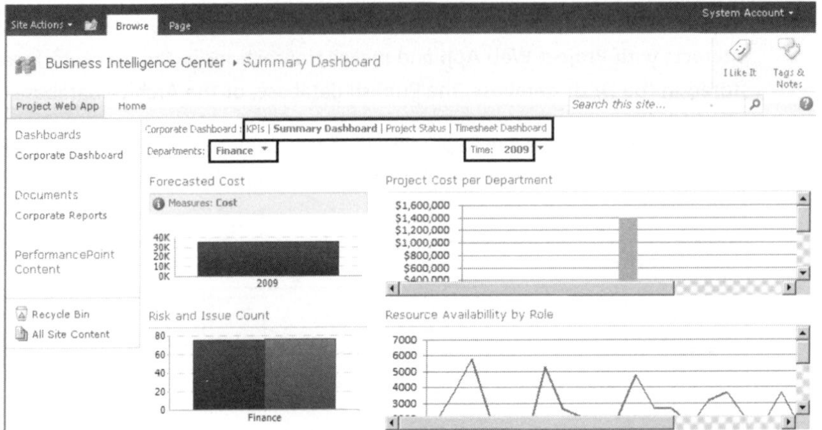

Figure 27-23 This Summary Dashboard shows cost, risk, issue, and resource availability information at a glance. Built-in controls, such as the Departments and Time fields, allow the data to be changed and refreshed instantly.

The Business Intelligence Center in Project Web App includes the Dashboard Designer, which you use to create and customize your project dashboards. Dashboard Designer is based on PerformancePoint Services.

Access the Dashboard Designer from the Business Intelligence Center, as follows:

1. On the Quick Launch, click Business Intelligence.

   The Business Intelligence Center appears, as shown in Figure 27-24.

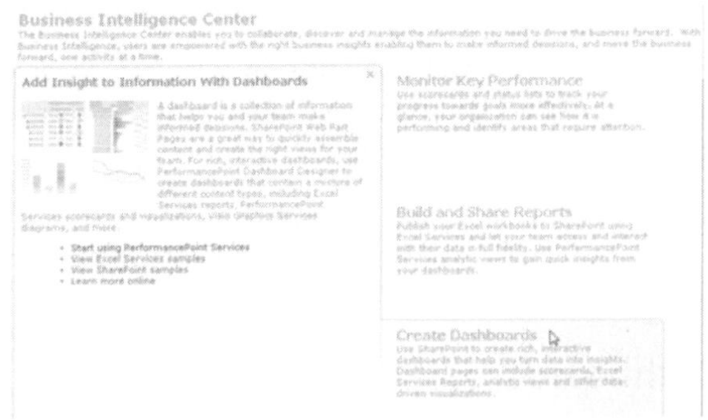

Figure 27-24 Launch PerformancePoint Services and the Dashboard Designer from the Business Intelligence Center.

2. On the Business Intelligence Center page, point to Create Dashboards, and then click Start Using PerformancePoint Services.

Run Dashboard Designer

3. Click the Run Dashboard Designer button.

   Follow the prompts to install Dashboard Designer.exe on your computer. The program is about 15 MB in size. You need to do this only the first time you access Dashboard Designer on your computer.

   The Dashboard Designer application appears.

4. Configure the data connections so that you can connect to your database. To do this, double-click Data Connections under Untitled Workspace and add a data source.

   After you configure the data source, you can edit or create pages.

5. In the Dashboard Designer, on the Create tab, in the Dashboard Items group, click the type of dashboard you want to create—for example, a dashboard, scorecard, or KPI (key performance indicator). (See Figure 27-25.)

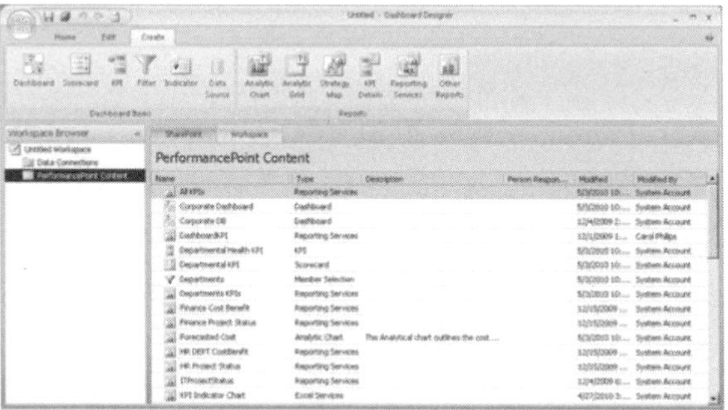

Figure 27-25 Using the Dashboard Designer, you can create your dashboards, scorecards, KPIs, filters, and indicators.

   You can select from various dashboard layouts and Excel reports to create your items.

   After you create a new dashboard item, it becomes available in the Project Web App Business Intelligence Center. You can quickly add reports to the dashboards by linking existing Excel Services reports or by adding new KPI reports.

You can also use the Dashboard Designer to configure dashboards from components created in other tools, such as Excel Services.

For more details about working with the Dashboard Designer for Project Server, see the Microsoft TechNet site titled "Business Intelligence in Project Server 2010" at *technet.microsoft.com/en-us/projectserver/ff513702*

To view dashboards in Project Web App, follow these steps:

1. On the Quick Launch, click Business Intelligence.
2. In the left pane, click Dashboards.

   A list of all dashboard items appears.
3. Click folders or items to open them.

As you develop and refine dashboards, be sure to let other stakeholders know of their existence and location in Project Web App.

PART 8

Customizing and Managing Project Files

Before you can use the sample files for Chapters 28, 31, and 32, you'll need to install them from this book's companion content website. For more information about downloading and installing the sample files, see "About the Companion Content" on page xxviii.

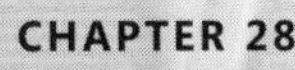

CHAPTER 28

Customizing Your View of Project Information

Organizations are as unique as people, and each project that an organization manages has its own particular needs. Each step in managing a project requires a specific set of information, as does responding to each new challenge that arises. In Microsoft Project 2010, you can control what information you see and how it is formatted, whether these customizations are to satisfy your own preferences or meet the specialized needs of a particular project or situation. Almost every aspect of viewing information in Project 2010 can be molded to your specifications, including the following:

- Views
- Tables
- Fields
- Groups
- Filters

You can also customize text-based and visual reports. For more information, see "Generating Text and Visual Reports" on page 354. The ribbon interface is customizable, too. To learn more, see "Customizing the Project 2010 Ribbon" on page 1153.

If you use codes to categorize information—for example, accounting codes to assign tasks to budget line items or skill codes to identify resources—customized outline codes in Project 2010 can fulfill this purpose. You can adapt these codes to your organization's standards, apply them to project tasks and resources, and then use them to sort, group, or filter information.

When you customize Project 2010, you can choose to keep your customizations in one project or make them available to every project you create. In addition, with the Organizer, you can manage customized elements and copy them to share with others. This chapter describes how to customize all these features and use them in your projects.

Customizing Views

The right perspective on the right data can simplify your project management tasks, uncover potential problems, or show the way to potential solutions. Each view in Project 2010 gives you a different point of view on project information. You can specify the views you want to see, and you don't have to stick with the views that come with the program. Change the tables and fields that a view displays, rearrange the organization of information, and control its appearance to peruse your project information the way you want. For example, with Background Cell Highlighting, you can apply highlight colors or patterns to the cells in the view tables to make key tasks stand out, similar to highlighting cells in a Microsoft Excel spreadsheet.

For more information about working with built-in Project 2010 views, see "Using Views" on page 131.

Changing the Content of a View

Project 2010 comes with numerous standard views that present task, resource, and assignment information. When these standard views don't meet your needs, you can customize their content or create new views that are more suitable. For example, if you like to take into account the amount of work that tasks require, you can change your Gantt Chart to show a table with the Work field. In single-pane views, you can specify which screen, table, group, and filter to apply when the view appears. For combination views, you can designate the views that appear in the primary pane on the top and the Details pane on the bottom.

Note

Even though views such as the Gantt Chart and Task Usage view are made up of two panes, one on the left and one on the right, they're still considered single-pane views.

Note

If you plan to use new tables, groups, or filters in a view, you must create those elements before you use them in a customized view. You must also create new single-pane views before you can include them in a combination view.

For elements that already exist, it doesn't matter whether you customize them or assign them to customized views first.

To customize the content of an existing single-pane view—for example, the Gantt Chart, Resource Sheet, or Task Usage view—do the following:

Other Views

1. On the View tab, in the Resource Views group, click the arrow next to Other Views, and then click More Views.

2. In the More Views dialog box, in the Views list, click the view's name. (See Figure 28-1.)

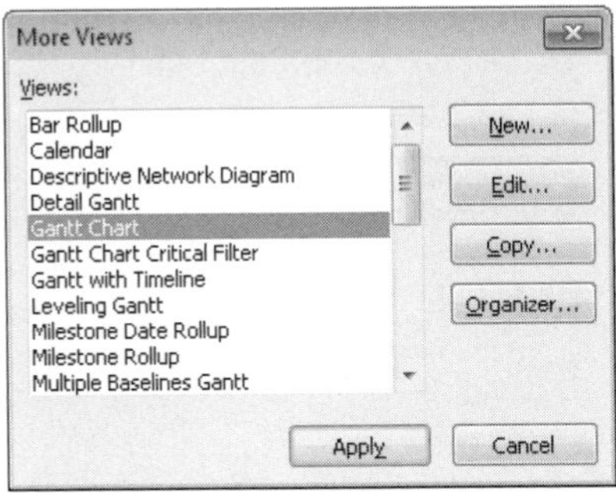

Figure 28-1 You can edit an existing view, copy an existing view, or create a completely new view.

3. To change the selected view, click the Edit button. The View Definition dialog box appears, as shown in Figure 28-2.

   To create a view that is similar to the selected view, click the Copy button in the More Views dialog box. Type a new name in the Name box of the View Definition dialog box.

   When you edit an existing single-pane view, the View Definition dialog box displays the screen used, such as Gantt Chart, but you can't modify it. When you create a new single-pane view from scratch, you can choose which type of screen to use.

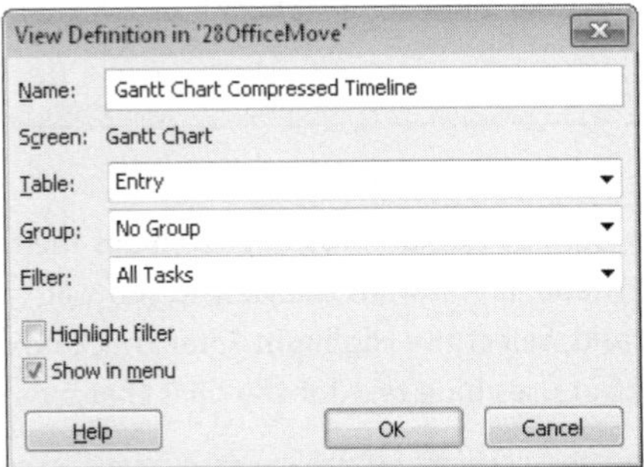

Figure 28-2 When you customize a single-pane view, you choose a table, group, and filter.

NEW!

Project 2010 differentiates customized views from standard ones by listing customized views at the top of a view drop-down menu under the Custom heading. Likewise, built-in views appear under the Built-In heading, as you can see in Figure 28-3.

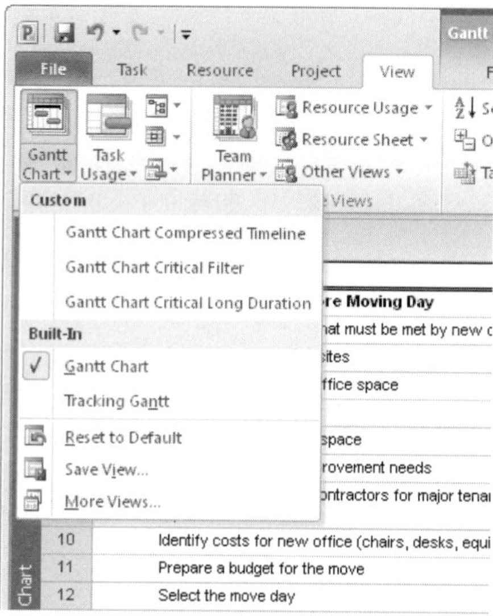

Figure 28-3 In Project 2010, the views you create appear under the Custom heading, while built-in views appear under the Built-In heading.

4. In the Table box, click the table you want to appear in the customized view.
5. In the Group box, click the group you want to use.

   If this view doesn't need a group, choose No Group.
6. In the Filter box, click the filter you want to apply.

   If this view doesn't need a filter, choose All Tasks (for a task view) or All Resources (for a resource view).

Note

When you apply a filter to a view, by default Project 2010 hides the tasks or resources that don't meet the filter's criteria. If you want the view to show all tasks or resources but emphasize the filtered tasks, select the Highlight Filter check box. This setting displays all tasks and resources but uses blue text for the ones that pass the filter tests.

INSIDE OUT Tired of clicking More Views?

By default, the view drop-down menus on the Task, Resource, and View tabs include the views used most frequently by the majority of Project 2010 users. However, if you take the time to customize views or simply prefer other standard views, such as the Task Details Form, you might get tired of clicking a tab on the ribbon, clicking the arrow next to a view button, and then clicking More Views every time you want to use them.

Fortunately, the views that appear on the view drop-down menus are within your control. To include a view on a view drop-down menu, click the arrow next to any view button on the Task tab, the Resource tab, or the View tab, and then click More Views. Click the view you want to add, and then click Edit. In the View Definition dialog box, select the Show In Menu check box. To remove a view that you don't use, clear its Show In Menu check box.

You can also modify the order in which views appear—for example, you can move the Task Sheet to the top of the list. By default, task views appear first in alphabetical order, followed by resource views in alphabetical order. Custom views appear above built-in views. In the More Views dialog box, click the view you want to move and then click Edit. In the Name box, change the view name in some way. This copies the original view and adds it to the top of the list under the Custom heading. Note that your custom views appear in alphabetical order. By using certain letters or numbers, you can control the order in which the views are listed.

To customize the content of an existing combination view—for example, the Task Entry view or Resource Allocation view—follow these steps:

Gantt Chart

1. On the Task tab, in the Task Views group, click the arrow next to Gantt Chart, and then click More Views. (You can also click the arrow next to any view button on the Task tab, the Resource tab, or the View tab, and then click More Views.)
2. In the More Views dialog box, in the Views list, click the name of the combination view you want to customize.
3. To change the existing view, click the Edit button.

   To create a new view based on the existing view, click the Copy button. In the View Definition dialog box, in the Name box, type a new name for the view.
4. In the Primary View box, click the name of the view that you want to appear in the top pane. (See Figure 28-4.)

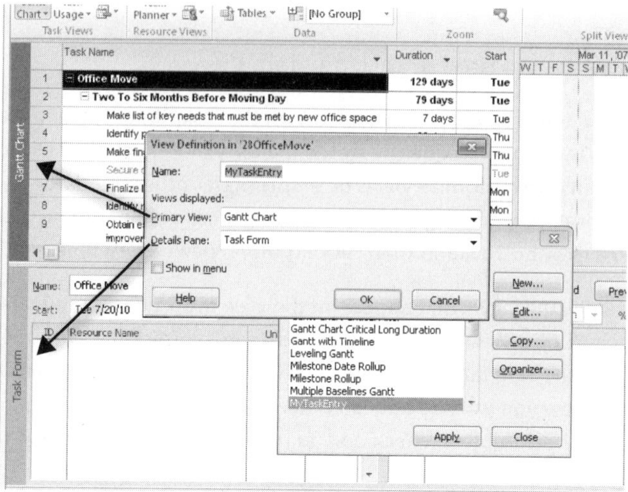

Figure 28-4 For combination views, you specify which single-pane view appears in the top pane (Primary View) and which appears in the bottom pane (Details Pane).

5. In the Details Pane box, click the view you want to appear in the bottom pane.

INSIDE OUT **Change the table and view definition**

When you are using a view and choose a different table to display, you also change the table for the definition of that view. In Project 2010, applying a group or filter to a view also changes the group or filter applied in the View Definition dialog box. The next time you display that view, the table uses its new table, group, and filter .

Creating a New View

If none of the existing views comes close to meeting your needs, you can craft an entirely new single pane or combination view. To do this, follow these steps:

1. On the Task, Resource, or View tab, click the arrow next to one of the view buttons, and then click More Views.

2. In the More Views dialog box, click New.

3. In the Define New View dialog box, select either the Single View or Combination View option and then click OK.

   The View Definition dialog box for the type of view you selected appears and fills in the Name box with a default name, such as View 1.

4. If you are creating a new single-pane view, in the View Definition dialog box, choose the type of screen you prefer—a built-in view layout or form such as Gantt Chart or Task Form.

   The only time you can choose the screen for a single-pane view is when you create a new one. When you edit a single-pane view, the View Definition dialog box displays the type of screen, but you can't modify it.

5. Specify the rest of the contents of the view, as described in the previous section, "Changing the Content of a View."

NEW!

Automatically Add New Elements to the Project Global

Project 2010 includes an option that automatically adds new views, tables, filters, and groups to the project global template, which makes them available to other project files. If you want new items to be available only in the project file in which you create them, you must turn off this option. To do this, on the File tab, click Options, and then click Advanced. Under Display, clear the check box labeled Automatically Add New Views, Tables, Filters, And Groups To The Global.

Apply a View Quickly

Keyboard fans can choose a view from a drop-down view menu by assigning a keyboard shortcut. In the View Definition dialog box for the view, type an ampersand (&) before the letter in the view name that you want to use for the shortcut and then save the customized view.

When you want to use your keyboard shortcut, press Alt to display keyboard shortcuts on the ribbon. Press the shortcut letter to select the ribbon tab. For example, press H to select the Task tab, press G to display the drop-down menu of task views, and then press the shortcut letter for the view you want, such as N for the Tracking Gantt view. This works for built-in views as well as your custom views.

Use a different letter for each keyboard shortcut. If you choose a letter that is already in use by another menu entry, you might have to press the letter more than once to apply the view you want.

Saving a View

NEW!

You might alter a view in several ways—for example, by changing the table that appears, modifying the contents of the table in the view, applying a filter, applying a group, or some combination of all of these. In Project 2010, you can quickly save these customizations to a new view and a new table. To do this, follow these steps:

1. On the Task, Resource, or View tab, click the arrow next to one of the view buttons, and then click Save View. The Save View dialog box appears.
2. In the Name box, type a name for the new view. Click OK.

   Project 2010 saves the new view. The program also saves the new table, adopting its name from the name of the new view. For example, if you named the new view MyNewView, the table name would be MyNewView Table1.

> **Note**
>
> **If you choose the Save View command again while the same view is displayed, the Save View dialog box appears with two options. To update the current view with the changes you made, select the Update Current View option. To save the view as another new view, select the Save As A New View option, and then, in the Name box, type the name for the view.**

Changing Text Formatting in Views

By default, the font used throughout Project 2010 views is 8-point Arial. If your reading glasses nudge you toward a different font or larger size for text, you can adjust both the font and size for one or more elements in a particular view. By changing the formatting for a text style, you can alter the appearance of entire categories of elements in a view. For example, you can change the text for critical tasks in a sheet view to bold and red. In addition, you can customize the formatting for individual instances of text, such as the text in a single row or even a single table cell, to emphasize a few key pieces of information.

Changing Text Formatting for a View

By modifying a text style, you can adjust both the font and size for one or more elements in a particular view. To select the elements to change and the font and size to use, follow these steps:

Text Styles

1. On the Format tab, in the Format group, click Text Styles.
2. To change the characteristics for all text, in the Item To Change box, be sure that All is selected.

   This changes the font for all text elements in the current view in this project, including column and row headings, Gantt bar text, and all field data such as task and resource names. If you want to change the text for a specific element, such as Summary Tasks, in the Item To Change box, click the element. If you want the text displayed on all critical Gantt bars to be 16-point red type, start by clicking Critical Tasks in the Item To Change box. To specify the text style for text at a specific position on all bars, in the Item To Change box, choose the position, such as Bar Text-Left or Bar Text-Inside.
3. In the Font list, choose the font you want.
4. To apply bold or italic to the text, in the Font Style list, choose the formatting you want.
5. In the Size list, choose the font size for the text.

   You can also apply a color to the text, which can emphasize important tasks. For instance, you might apply a bright blue or maroon color to the text for critical tasks so that they stand out in the task list as well as in the Gantt Chart.
6. To apply the changes, click OK.

Highlight the Background in Cells

You can revise the background color of cells, for example, by choosing a light red background color to make critical tasks in a table stand out.

In the Text Styles dialog box, in the Item To Change drop-down list, choose the category of task to highlight, such as critical tasks, summary tasks, or changed cells. You can choose the font, font style, and size of the text for the selected item, such as Arial Italic 8-point. To choose a color for the text, choose the color in the Color drop-down list. Then, to highlight the cell background, in the Background Color drop-down list, choose the color you want, and Project 2010 highlights cell backgrounds with that color.

INSIDE OUT **No way to set an overall default font style**

Suppose you have used the Text Styles dialog box to apply specific fonts to row and column titles in the Gantt Chart, used another style to milestone tasks, and yet another to critical tasks. When you switch from the Gantt Chart to the Task Usage view, you find that the fonts revert to their default style in that view.

Text styles apply only to the current view in the current project. If you want those text styles to appear in other views, you need to make the same changes in each view in which you want them to appear.

If you take the time to make all those text style changes, you can increase the benefit by making them available to all your projects. To do this, use the Organizer to copy your modified views to the global template (global.mpt).

For information about copying views to the global template for use in other projects, see "Copying Customized Elements" on page 1140.

Changing the Format of Individual Text

When you want to adjust the font and size for text that doesn't fall into a specific category, you can select the text you want to format and change its font, size, and other types of formatting. You can format the text for several rows in a table, all the cells in a single row of a table, or even a single cell. To select the text to change and the font and size to use, follow these steps:

1. To format a single cell of text, right-click the cell. To format more than a single cell, select all the text that you want to format, and then right-click somewhere within the selected text.

   A mini-toolbar appears above the cell you right-click. (See Figure 28-5.)

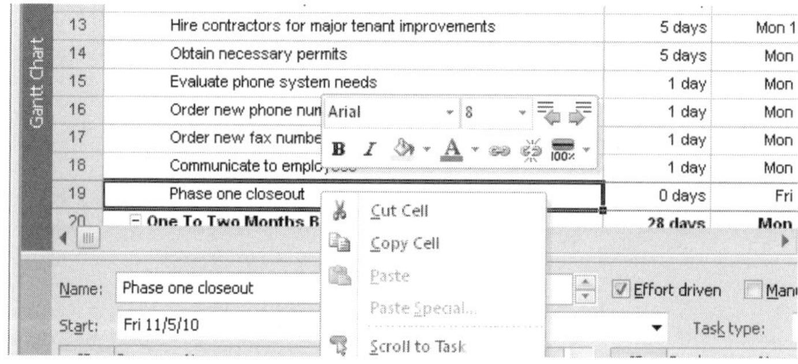

Figure 28-5 In Project 2010, right-clicking text displays a mini-toolbar with commands for formatting individual text elements.

2. To change the font for the selected text, click the arrow next to the current font name, and then choose the new font from the drop-down list.

3. To change the size of the selected text, click the arrow next to the current font size, and then choose the font size.

4. To apply bold or italic to the text, click the Bold or Italic button in the mini-toolbar.

5. To apply a color to the text, click the arrow next to the Font Color button, and then choose the color you want to apply. To apply a cell background color to the cell, click the arrow next to the Background Color button, and then choose the background color.

   Font color is helpful for emphasizing important tasks. For instance, you might apply a bright blue or maroon color to the text for the payment milestones in your schedule so that they stand out in the task list as well as in the Gantt Chart.

Format Painter

Copy Formatting

Suppose you apply several types of formatting to text, such as a 16-point Calibri font with red color, bold, and with a gray cell background, and now you want to apply those formats to other text in a table. You can copy formatting from one element to another. Select the formatted text. On the Task tab, in the Clipboard group, click the Format Painter button, and then select the text to which you want to apply the formatting.

Formatting a Gantt Chart View

The chart area on the right side of a Gantt chart provides a graphical representation of your project schedule. You can emphasize information in your schedule by formatting individual Gantt bars or all Gantt bars of a certain type. Similarly, you can apply formatting to different categories of text or only to the text that is selected. Link lines and gridlines communicate important schedule information, but for high-level views, they might get in the way. Gantt chart layout options and formatting for gridlines control how much you see of these elements.

Quick Formatting with the Gantt Chart Wizard

There's an easy way to format the primary elements in a Gantt chart. The Gantt Chart Wizard steps you through settings that specify the information you see in your Gantt chart and how the elements are formatted. You can choose a standard type of Gantt chart such as Critical Path or Baseline, choose from several predefined Gantt chart styles, or create a custom Gantt chart.

If you opt for a customized Gantt chart, you can control which types of Gantt bars appear and customize the color, pattern, and end shapes for each type. The customized settings in the Gantt Chart Wizard include whether to display resources and dates on the taskbars, exactly which fields to display, and whether to show or hide the link lines between dependent tasks.

In Project 2010, the Gantt Chart Wizard is not available on the ribbon by default. However, you can add the Gantt Chart Wizard to a custom group on the ribbon. For information about adding commands to the ribbon, see "Adding Commands to a Custom Group" on page 1155. In the Project Options dialog box, in the Choose Commands From drop-down list, click Commands Not On The Ribbon, and then click Gantt Chart Wizard in the list of commands.

Formatting the Appearance of Gantt Bars

The shape, fill pattern, and color of types of Gantt bars or individual bars are customizable. You can also customize the marks that appear at the beginning and end of those bars. For example, you can change the mark that designates milestone tasks, add color to summary task bars, or accentuate critical tasks that aren't complete by making them red with red stars at each end of task bars.

Note

In Project 2010, some of the most common Gantt bar formatting commands are available on the Format tab. For example, to display critical tasks with red task bars, on the Format tab, in the Bar Styles group, select the Critical Tasks check box.

You can also choose a set of color-coordinated Gantt bars from the Gantt Chart Style gallery. On the Format tab, in the Gantt Chart Style group, click the color theme you want. The top Gantt bar in the theme represents manually scheduled tasks, while the bottom Gantt bar shows the color for auto-scheduled tasks.

To change the appearance of all Gantt bars of a particular type, follow these steps:

1. Display the Gantt chart whose bars you want to customize. On the Task tab, in the View group, click the arrow next to the Gantt Chart button, and then click the Gantt chart you want—for example, the Gantt Chart or the Tracking Gantt. You can also click More Views to open the More Views dialog box to select any Gantt chart.

   Your modifications apply only to the Gantt bars in this specific Gantt chart.

Format

2. On the Format tab, in the Bar Styles group, click the arrow under the Format button, and then click Bar Styles. (You can also open the Bar Styles dialog box by double-clicking the background in the right pane of a Gantt chart.)

   The Bar Styles dialog box lists the Gantt bar types for the current view with the settings for their appearance. (See Figure 28-6.) For example, Gantt bars appear blue for automatically scheduled normal tasks, whereas summary Gantt bars are solid black with black end marks at both ends.

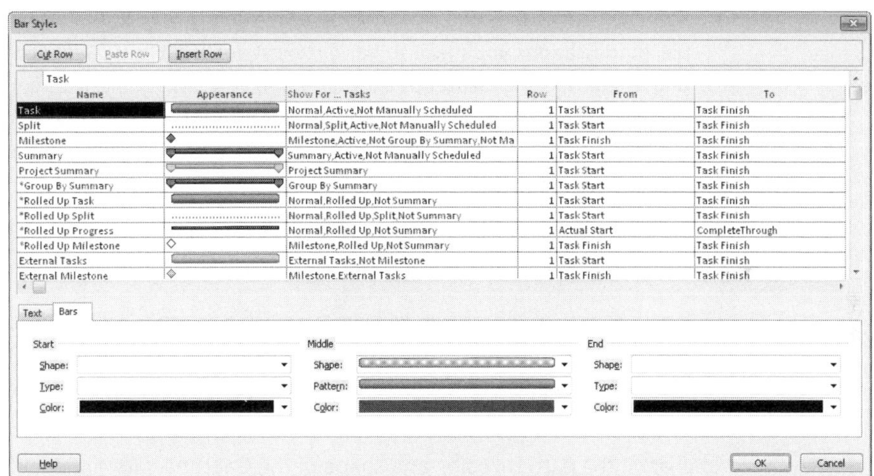

Figure 28-6 You can customize the appearance of the Gantt bar as well as markers at its start and end.

3. To select the Gantt bar to format, click its name in the table.

4. Click the Bars tab, and then make the changes you want to the start, middle, and end of the bar.

   The settings for the start and end determine the appearance of the markers at the beginning and end of the bar, whereas the settings for the middle control the appearance of the bar itself.

5. For the start and end, begin with the Shape box and choose the mark to add to the start or end of the bar, such as the downward pointing arrows for summary tasks. In Project 2010, the mark drop-down list includes shapes for manually scheduled tasks, such as the brackets for Gantt bars without start or finish dates. Then, in the Type box, choose whether the mark should be a solid color, framed with a line, or outlined with a dashed line. Finally, choose the color for the mark.

6. For the bar itself, under the Middle heading, choose the shape of the bar, such as a full rectangle for regular tasks, a half-height rectangle to show a baseline bar, or a thin rectangle to show progress. In the Pattern and Color boxes, select the pattern and color for the bar.

   For solid colors, in the Pattern box, choose the solid blue entry near the top of the drop-down list.

Change the Format of a View

Format changes that you make within a view apply only to the active view. For example, modifications you make to bar or text styles, individual Gantt bars, or text formatting in the Tracking Gantt appear only when you display the Tracking Gantt. Although this separation means that you must repeat formatting in each view that you want to modify, the advantage is that you can customize the formatting for any view without worrying about modifying others.

Changes you make to views in one project file apply only to that project file. When you create a new project file, it uses the default views.

If you want to make customized views available to other project files, see the section "Sharing Customized Elements Among Projects" on page 1138.

To change the pattern, color, and shape of the Gantt bars for an individual task (rather than all tasks of a particular type), do the following:

1. In the sheet area of the view, click the task or tasks whose Gantt bar format you want to change.

2. On the Format tab, in the Bar Styles group, click the arrow under the Format button, and then click Bar.

3. In the Format Bar dialog box, click the Bar Shape tab.

4. Make the changes you want in the Start (beginning mark), Middle (the bar itself), and End (ending mark) areas.

NEW!

Note

To quickly change the color of an individual Gantt bar, right-click the Gantt bar whose color you want to change. On the mini-toolbar that appears above the Gantt bar, click the arrow next to the bar color button, and then choose the color you want. The drop-down panel offers color-coordinated theme colors and several standard colors. To specify the exact hue you want, click More Colors, and then specify the color you want in the Colors dialog box.

TROUBLESHOOTING

Changing the bar style for one task changes the Gantt bars for all tasks

The Bar and Bar Styles commands on the Format drop-down menu sound similar and even perform similar functions, but their scope is quite different. The Bar command applies the changes you make to only the tasks that are currently selected. The Bar Styles command applies changes to all Gantt bars of a particular type—for example, critical tasks, incomplete tasks, or milestones.

This distinction is analogous to changing the formatting in a word-processing document. You can select an individual paragraph and change the formatting to Arial 14 bold. But if you want all headings to use this formatting, you can save time by creating a style and applying it to each heading paragraph.

Creating a Gantt Bar

In addition to changing the styles of Gantt bars, you can also define new types of Gantt bars. For example, if you use the Marked field to flag high-risk tasks, you can set up a special bar style to show marked tasks in lime green. To format your own type of bar, follow these steps:

1. Apply a Gantt chart.
2. On the Format tab, in the Bar Styles group, click the arrow under the Format button, and then click Bar Styles.
3. Scroll to the end of the list of Gantt bar types and click in the first blank row.

   If you want to insert the new Gantt bar type earlier in the list, click the row immediately below where you want to insert the type, and then click Insert Row. Project 2010 inserts a blank row above the selected row.

4. In the Name field, type the name of your new Gantt bar.

5. Click the cell in the Show For ... Tasks column.

6. Click the arrow in the box, and then click the category of task for which this bar should be displayed. For example, if you're creating a style for tasks that are not finished, click Not Finished.

   If you want a Gantt bar style to appear when a task satisfies more than one condition, click the first condition, type a comma, and then click the second condition, such as Critical, Not Finished. You can also create a Gantt bar that appears when a condition is not true. Type **Not** in front of a selected task condition, such as Not Milestone or Critical, Not In Progress.

7. In the From and To columns, click the date fields that determine the beginning and end of the Gantt bar. For example, you might draw a progress bar from the Start date to the Complete Through date, or a bar from the Actual Start date to the Deadline date for critical tasks that aren't yet finished.

8. Click the Bars tab, and then specify the appearance for the start, middle, and end of the bar.

9. If you want to display text on the bar, click the Text tab, and then click the box for the position where you want text to appear for the Gantt bar, such Left, Top, or Inside.

10. Click the arrow in the box, and then click the name of the task field whose content you want to appear for this Gantt bar type.

Note

If you want to call attention to tasks that don't meet any of the task conditions listed in the Show For... Tasks field, you can create a new bar style that applies only to marked or flagged tasks. When you set a task's Marked field or the appropriate flag field to Yes, its Gantt bar appears in that bar style.

You can add the Marked field to the sheet area of your Gantt chart and then set the value to Yes for each task you want to mark. If you are already using the Marked field, insert a column for one of the custom flag fields, such as Flag1, and set it to Yes for those tasks. In the Bar Styles dialog box, create a new bar style to specify the bar appearance and associated text for marked or flagged tasks.

TROUBLESHOOTING

A Gantt bar doesn't appear in the chart

Gantt charts display bars in the order that they appear in the Bar Styles dialog box. If Gantt bar styles with a narrower shape, such as progress bars, appear above the full-height Gantt bars in the list, the wider Gantt bars hide the narrower ones.

To see all the bars, be sure to rearrange the order so that narrower Gantt bars appear below the wider ones in the Bar Styles list.

INSIDE OUT Stack the Gantt bars

Some tasks meet the conditions for several types of Gantt bars. For example, suppose that you have set multiple baselines and want to use the Multiple Baselines Gantt view to review trends in baseline dates. If you create a bar style for each baseline, Project 2010 draws a Gantt bar for the task for each condition that it satisfies—in this example, for each baseline it contains.

Because multiple bars are likely to overlap each other, you can make them all visible at the same time by stacking up to four Gantt bars, one above the next. To do this, in the Bar Styles dialog box, in the Row field, specify 1, 2, 3, or 4 to indicate the position for that bar style in the stack.

Formatting the Appearance of Gantt Bar Text

Displaying task field values next to Gantt bars makes it easy to correlate task information with bars in the chart. In addition, displaying text next to Gantt bars might reduce the number of columns needed in the sheet area of the Gantt chart, leaving more room on the screen to show the chart area of the view.

To specify the text for all Gantt bars of a particular type, follow these steps:

1. On the Format tab, in the Bar Styles group, click the arrow under the Format button, and then click Bar Styles.
2. Click the name of the Gantt bar style whose text you want to change.
3. Click the Text tab.

4. Click the box for the position, such as Left or Right, at which you want the text to appear for the Gantt bar style.

5. Click the arrow in the box, and then click the name of the task field whose content you want to appear for this Gantt bar type. (See Figure 28-7.)

   For example, if you want the percentage of completion to appear inside the Gantt bar, click the Inside box, click the arrow, and then click % Complete. To remove text from a position, select the box for that position and then press the Backspace key.

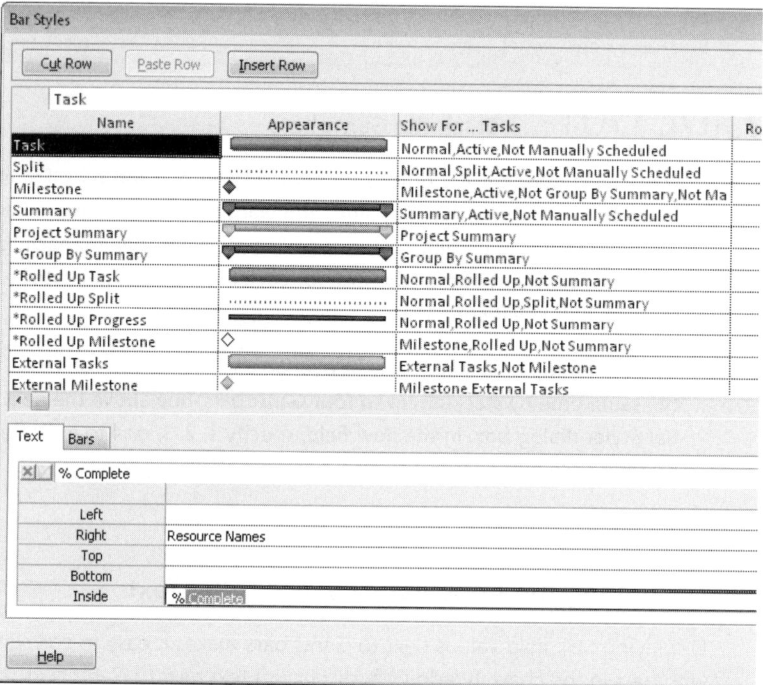

Figure 28-7 You can display project information at the left, right, top, or bottom and inside of Gantt bars by specifying fields to display as text.

6. When you're done, click OK to close the Bar Styles dialog box.

To change the text accompanying the Gantt bar for selected tasks, do the following:

1. In the sheet area of the view, click the task or tasks whose Gantt bar text you want to change.

2. On the Format tab, in the Bar Styles group, click the arrow under the Format button, click Bar, and then click the Bar Text tab in the Format Bar dialog box.

3. On the Bar Text tab, click the box for the position—such as Left, Right, Top, or Bottom—where you want the text to appear for the Gantt bar.

4. Click the arrow next to the box, and then click the name of the task field whose content you want to appear for this Gantt bar.

Although you can't change the font, style, or color of the text for individual Gantt bars, you can change the text style for all Gantt bars of a particular type or the text style for the text at a specific position on a bar. For more information about working with built-in Project 2010 views, see "Changing Text Formatting for a View" on page 1068.

Formatting the Layout of Gantt Bars

Link lines between dependent tasks show how tasks relate to each other. However, too many link lines can obscure the very information you are trying to communicate. If the schedule is too cluttered, you might want to modify the appearance of link lines, the height of Gantt bars, or whether splits and rolled-up bars are displayed. To change the layout of links and bars in a Gantt chart, do the following:

Layout

1. On the Format tab, in the Format group, click Layout.

2. In the Layout dialog box, select the option for how you want the links between dependent tasks to appear.

   For example, you can hide the link lines, draw them as S shapes between the ends of tasks, or display them as L shapes from the end of one task to the top of another task.

3. If you display date fields on Gantt bars, choose a date format to use.

   For example, to keep text for dates to a minimum, choose a format that shows only the numeric month and day. If time or day of week is important, choose a format with these elements shown.

4. If you want to make Gantt bars thicker or thinner, in the Bar Height box, choose a number between 6 and 24, with 12 being the default thickness.

5. Choose other layout options to roll up Gantt bars, draw the bar length in increments of whole days, or show splits.

   For example, select the Always Roll Up Gantt Bars check box if you want summary tasks to display information about their subordinate tasks. If you are fine-tuning your project schedule, you might want to view where splits occur or see the duration of tasks down to the hour.

Formatting the Appearance of Gridlines

Gridlines separate elements such as columns and rows in the sheet area of a Gantt chart or the dates and Gantt bars in the chart area. For example, you might want to add horizontal lines to the chart to help correlate Gantt bars with their associated tasks in the sheet area. To change the gridlines in a Gantt chart, follow these steps:

Gridlines

1. On the Format tab, in the Format group, click Gridlines.
2. In the Line To Change box, click the element for the gridlines you want to add, remove, or change.

   Elements for both the sheet area and chart area of the Gantt chart appear in the Line To Change list. For example, Gantt Rows represents the horizontal lines between each row in the chart area of the Gantt chart. Sheet Rows are the horizontal lines between rows in the sheet area of the view.

   The Normal area shows the settings for the currently selected line to change.
3. In the Normal section, change the line type in the Type box and the color in the Color box.
4. If you want to display lines at certain intervals, such as after every fourth item, click the interval in the At Interval section.

Marking Up a Schedule with Drawing Tools

Project 2010 comes with a set of drawing tools, such as Arrow, Line, Arc, Polygon, and Text Box, similar to the tools available in other Microsoft Office programs. The only area that you can draw on is the chart area of a Gantt view. To mark up a schedule in a Gantt area, do the following:

1. **On the Format tab, in the Drawings group, click Drawing, and then click the drawing tool you want. You can choose from Arrow, Arc, Oval, Polygon, Rectangle, Line, and Text Box.**
2. **In the chart area of the Gantt view, drag from one point to another to draw the shape or for polygons, to draw the first segment.**
3. **If you want to change the order in which elements appear—for example, to display a line in front of a filled rectangle—select the element you want to reorder. Click Drawing, and then click Bring To Front, Bring Forward, Send To Back, or Send Backward.**

Modifying the Timescale

The timescale is a prominent feature in many Project 2010 views, such as Gantt chart and usage views. A view can contain up to three timescales. For instance, a view can show the fiscal year and fiscal quarters on two timescales or the year, months, and days on three timescales. You can customize the units, the labels for time periods, and the label alignment for each timescale. In addition, you can choose how many timescales you want to use as well as the width of each period in the timescale.

Changes you make to the timescale apply only to the active view, but those changes become a permanent part of that view definition. Your timescale customizations appear each time you display that view.

To set the options for one or more tiers in the timescale, do the following:

1. Display a view that contains a timescale, such as the Gantt Chart, Task Usage view, or Resource Graph.
2. Right-click the timescale heading, and then click Timescale on the shortcut menu.

   The Timescale dialog box appears.
3. The Timescale dialog box has four tabs: Top Tier, Middle Tier, Bottom Tier, and Non-Working Time. (See Figure 28-8.) The Middle Tier tab is displayed by default. In the Show list below Timescale Options, click the number of tiers you want to display (one, two, or three).

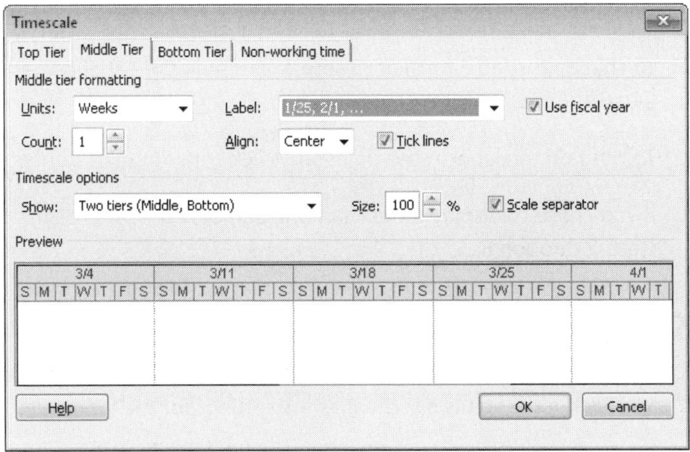

Figure 28-8 Customize the time periods that appear in a timescale in a view, such as the Gantt Chart, Task Usage view, or Resource Graph.

4. To change the width of the timescale columns, click a percentage in the Size box.

   If you use small time periods, choose a smaller percentage to fit a longer overall period in the view. If the values in the view appear as hash (#) marks, choose a larger percentage to display the values.

5. If you want lines drawn between each timescale tier, select the Scale Separator check box.

To set the options for each timescale tier, follow these steps:

1. In the Timescale dialog box, click the tab for the timescale tier you want to customize.

2. In the Units box, specify the time unit you want to display for the current tier. For example, you might choose Quarters for the top tier if your organization's financial performance depends on this project.

   The time unit in a lower tier must be shorter than the unit for the tier above it. For example, if the top tier time unit is months, the middle tier can't be years.

3. To display the fiscal year in the timescale, select the Use Fiscal Year check box.

   If you clear the Use Fiscal Year check box, the timescale displays the calendar year.

4. To display an interval of more than one unit, choose the number of units in the Count box.

   For example, to display two-week intervals, click Weeks in the Units box and 2 in the Count box.

5. To change the label format, choose a format in the Label box, for example, 1st Quarter, Qtr 1, 2004, or 1Q04.

6. To position the label in the timescale, click Left, Right, or Center in the Align box.

7. If you chose to display more than one tier, click the tabs for the other tiers and repeat steps 2 through 6.

CAUTION!

Clicking the Zoom command in the Zoom group on the View tab or dragging the Zoom slider in the status bar changes the settings for the timescale.

You can also control how nonworking time appears in the timescale. To set the nonworking time options in the timescale, do the following:

1. In the Timescale dialog box, click the Non-Working Time tab.
2. To hide nonworking time, select the Do Not Draw check box.
3. If you display nonworking time, choose the color and pattern for the nonworking time shading.
4. Choose the calendar whose nonworking time you want to display in the Calendar box.

> **Note**
>
> **The Non-Working Time tab in the Timescale dialog box changes only the appearance of nonworking time in the timescale. To modify the schedule for nonworking time, on the Project tab, in the Properties group, click Change Working Time. Alternatively, right-click the timescale heading, and then click Change Working Time.**
>
> **For more information about changing working and nonworking time for the project, see "Setting Your Project Calendar" on page 84.**

Modifying a Network Diagram

Network diagrams display tasks as boxes, or nodes, with link lines showing task dependencies. Because a network diagram doesn't include a task sheet like a Gantt chart, it's important to choose wisely when you select the fields that you want to appear inside the boxes. In addition, you can customize the appearance of the boxes and how they are arranged within the diagram.

Formatting the Content and Appearance of Boxes

Boxes in a network diagram are the equivalent of Gantt bars in a Gantt chart, so it should be no surprise that you can change the appearance of boxes in a network diagram associated with a category of tasks. Similar to selecting the fields that appear around or inside Gantt bars, the task fields that appear inside network diagram boxes are customizable as well.

Network Diagram

To change the appearance and content for all boxes of a particular type, do the following:

1. On the View tab, in the Task Views group, click Network Diagram.
2. On the Format tab, in the Format group, click Box Styles.

Box Styles

The Box Styles dialog box, shown in Figure 28-9, lists all the box types for the current view and the settings for their appearance.

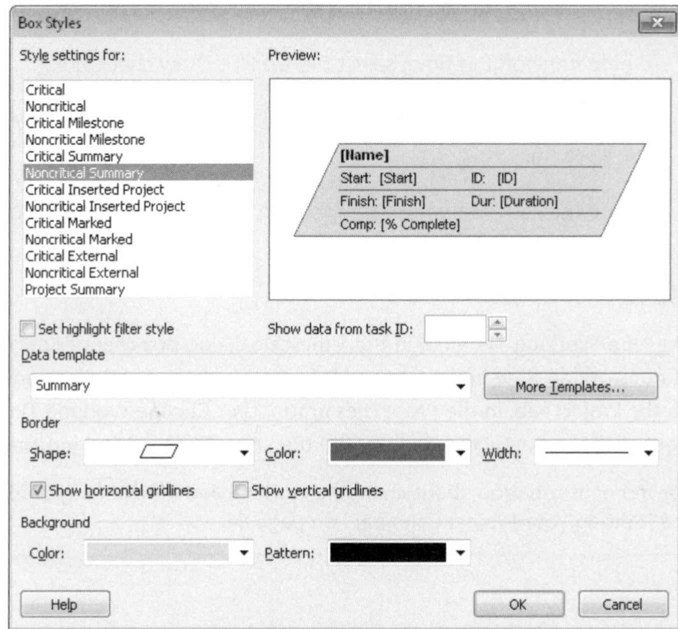

Figure 28-9 You can customize the appearance of a network diagram box as well as specify what task information appears inside each box.

3. To customize a specific type of box, click its name in the Style Settings For list.
4. To change the fields that appear within the box, in the Data Template box, click a data template.

   The Preview area shows the box with the fields that the selected data template specifies.
5. In the Border area, you can change the shape, color, and width of the box border.
6. If you want to display horizontal or vertical gridlines between the fields inside a box, select the Show Horizontal Gridlines or Show Vertical Gridlines check box.
7. If you want a color or pattern other than the default, choose a background color and pattern.

   Although you can select different colors and patterns for the box background, be aware that dark colors make reading the task information difficult.

Note

To show exactly the fields you want, you can modify or create new data templates for the boxes in a network diagram. For example, you might want to include a custom field in a data template. Templates can contain fields that display graphical indicators.

To modify or create a template, click More Templates, click a template name, and then click Edit or Copy. To create a new template, click New. To insert a field into the data template, in the Choose Cells section, click the cell where you want to insert the field, click the arrow, and then click the name of the field in the list.

To change the displayed fields and border appearance for individual boxes (rather than all boxes showing a particular type of project information), follow these steps:

1. In the network diagram, click the box(es) you want to format.

Box

2. On the Format tab, in the Format group, click Box.

   The Format Box dialog box appears.

3. In the Data Template box, click the data template you want to use.

   A preview of the box with the selected data template appears.

4. Make the changes you want to the shape, color, and width of the border.

5. Make the changes you want to the background color and pattern for the box.

Note

You can open the Format Box dialog box by double-clicking the border of a box. Double-clicking the background of a network diagram opens the Box Styles dialog box.

Changing the Layout of Boxes

The network diagram is much like a flowchart of the tasks in a project. The layout options for a network diagram control how boxes are positioned and aligned, the distance between the boxes, the appearance of links, and other settings.

To change the layout of a network diagram, do the following:

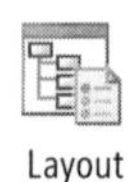

Layout

1. On the Format tab, in the Format group, click Layout.

   The Layout dialog box appears.

2. To position boxes manually by dragging, select the Allow Manual Box Positioning option.

   If you're happy to delegate layout choices to Project 2010, select the Automatically Position All Boxes option. The program uses the settings you choose to reposition the boxes in the network diagram.

3. In the Arrangement box, choose the order in which sequential boxes appear in the diagram.

   For example, you can arrange the boxes from the top left to the bottom right of the diagram. Another popular choice is Top Down-Critical First, which arranges boxes from the top down but also places critical tasks before others.

4. With the Row and Column boxes, specify the alignment, distance between rows and columns, and the width and height of the boxes.

   The numbers in the Spacing boxes represent the number of pixels between boxes and must be between 0 and 200.

5. In the Link Style section, select how lines should be drawn between boxes and specify whether arrows and link labels should be included.

6. If you want to show links in different colors, in the Link Color section, choose the colors you want for your links.

   By default, network diagrams display noncritical links in blue and critical links in red, similar to noncritical and critical bars in a Gantt chart.

Fine-Tune the Display of the Network Diagram

If you select the option to position boxes automatically, it's a good idea to also select the Adjust For Page Breaks check box in the Box Layout section. Otherwise, boxes located across a page break are printed on two pages in the diagram.

Summary tasks are difficult to distinguish in a network diagram, so you might want to clear the Show Summary Tasks check box. If you display summary tasks, it's best to select the Keep Tasks With Their Summaries check box.

> **Note**
>
> **In Project 2010, the ribbon includes a few commands for changing the display of a network diagram. For example, to turn off summary tasks, on the Format tab, in the Show/Hide group, clear the Summary Tasks check box. To display link lines as straight lines, select the Straight Links check box.**

Modifying the Timeline

NEW!

The Timeline condenses a project into a linear diagram. By default, the bar in the Timeline shows the date range that is visible in the timescale of the current view, such as the Gantt Chart or Task Usage view. You can change the date range or alter the date format. If you add tasks or milestones to the timeline, you can control whether they appear as bars or as callouts. The number of lines of text and the detail shown in the Timeline are customizable. Just as you can with other types of views, you can format categories of text with text styles or apply formatting to individual text that you select.

For more information about the Timeline, see "Highlighting Tasks with the Timeline" on page 134.

> **Note**
>
> **You can display either the Timeline or the Details pane but not both. To display the Timeline, on the View tab, in the Split View group, select the Timeline check box. If you select the Details check box, Project 2010 automatically clears the Timeline check box.**

Changing the Appearance of a Task on the Timeline

If you add tasks to the Timeline, they appear in both the Timeline and the view in the primary pane. You can emphasize tasks in the Timeline by showing them as bars or as callouts, as shown in Figure 28-10. Callouts are helpful for showing longer spans of time, such as project phases or significant summary tasks. You might use bars to show lower-level tasks that you add to the Timeline. You can show some tasks as callouts and others as bars, which is helpful when you want to add several tasks that occur during the same timeframe.

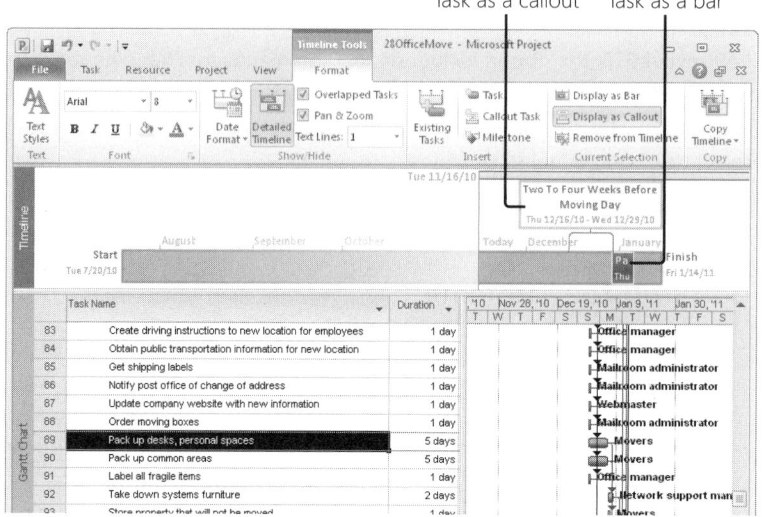

Figure 28-10 A task shown as a bar appears within the Timeline bar. A callout appears above the Timeline bar with a bracket to show the date range of the task.

To change the appearance of a task on the Timeline, do the following:

Display as Bar

Display as Callout

1. Click in the Timeline to make it active.
2. Click the task you want to change.
3. On the Format tab, in the Current Selection group, click Display As Bar or Display As Callout.

You can format categories of text or individual text in the Timeline. To alter the formatting for a category of text, on the Format tab, in the Text group, click Text Styles. To format individual text, select the text, and then, in the Font group on the Format tab, choose the command you want. To learn more about formatting text, see "Changing Text Formatting in a View" on page 1068.

Changing the Content of the Timeline

You can change the amount of information you see in the Timeline. For example, you can format dates to show only the month and day or the full date and time. You can also control how much text appears in tasks and how many tasks you see.

You can change the amount of information that appears in the Timeline. Format the Timeline in any of the following ways:

Date Format

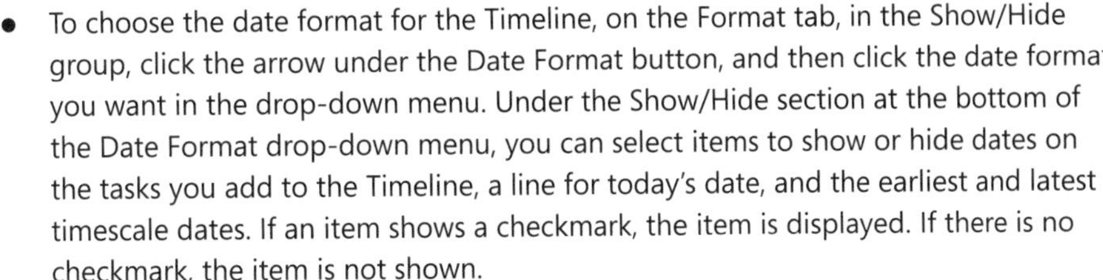

- To choose the date format for the Timeline, on the Format tab, in the Show/Hide group, click the arrow under the Date Format button, and then click the date format you want in the drop-down menu. Under the Show/Hide section at the bottom of the Date Format drop-down menu, you can select items to show or hide dates on the tasks you add to the Timeline, a line for today's date, and the earliest and latest timescale dates. If an item shows a checkmark, the item is displayed. If there is no checkmark, the item is not shown.

Detailed Timeline

- To show or hide the task names and dates for tasks you add to the Timeline, on the Format tab, in the Show/Hide group, click Detailed Timeline. The Detailed Timeline button, which is orange when it is selected, displays task names and dates in task bars and above callouts. If you hide details, the Timeline displays only task bars without names and dates and also hides callouts.
- If you want to see all the tasks you add to the Timeline, even if they occur during the same timeframe, select the Overlapped Tasks check box. When you select this check box, the Timeline displays each overlapping task in its own row. If you clear this check box, the Timeline shows the first task for a date range.
- The Pan & Zoom check box is selected by default. This setting lets you drag the blue bar at the top of the Timeline to change the dates that appear in the timescale in the Primary pane. If you clear this check box, the Timeline displays the full project date range.
- To choose the number of text lines for task names in task bars, click the arrow next to the Text Lines box, and choose the number of lines. By default, the task name uses only one line of text.

Modifying the Team Planner

The Team Planner, available in Project Professional 2010, shows the assignments within a project, resource by resource. The modifications you can make to the Team Planner are similar to those for other views. You can format categories of text with text styles, format the gridlines in the view, and alter the appearance of different types of tasks, such as automatically scheduled tasks, manually scheduled tasks, or late tasks. You can also control whether you see unassigned or unscheduled tasks.

Changing the Appearance of Team Planner Elements

Text styles, gridlines, and types of tasks are all customizable in the Team Planner. To alter the appearance of Team Planner elements, do the following:

Team Planner

1. On the View tab, in the Resource Views group, click Team Planner.

Text Styles

2. To alter the appearance of categories of text, on the Format tab, in the Format group, click Text Styles.

3. In the Text Styles dialog box, choose the item to change and specify the settings you want.

   To control the number of lines of text in assignment bars, click the arrow next to the Text Lines box and click the number of lines.

4. If you want to modify the gridlines, on the Format tab, in the Format group, click Gridlines.

To learn more about text styles and formatting gridlines, see "Changing Text Formatting for a View" on page 1068 and "Formatting the Appearance of Gridlines" on page 1080.

5. To change the border color or fill color for different categories of tasks, on the Format tab, in the Styles group, click the arrow next to one of the task type buttons, and then choose the border color or fill color. You can change the colors for auto-scheduled tasks, manually scheduled tasks, tasks with actual work, external tasks, and tasks that are late.

   If you select tasks, click the arrow next to the Selected Tasks button, and then choose the border color or fill color for those tasks.

Changing the Information in the Team Planner

You can control whether the Team Planner shows unassigned tasks or unscheduled tasks. You can also choose the outline level for the tasks that appear. If resources often work on several tasks at once, you can expand resource rows to show all concurrent tasks.

To change the information in the Team Planner, do the following:

1. On the View tab, in the Resource Views group, click Team Planner.

Roll-Up

2. To summarize your project, on the Format tab, in the Format group, click the arrow under the Roll-Up button, and then choose the outline level you want to see.

   Bars show the parent task name for the outline level you choose. By default, the Team Planner shows all subtasks, so each bar in the view displays the name of the actual task.

3. If you want to see all the assignments for a resource even if they occur simultaneously, select the Expand Resource Rows check box.

   If you clear the check box, only the first assigned task for a date range appears.

4. By default, the Team Planner shows unassigned tasks, which is helpful when you want to find tasks that don't yet have resources assigned. (See Figure 28-11.) To hide the Unassigned Tasks section, clear the Unassigned Tasks check box.

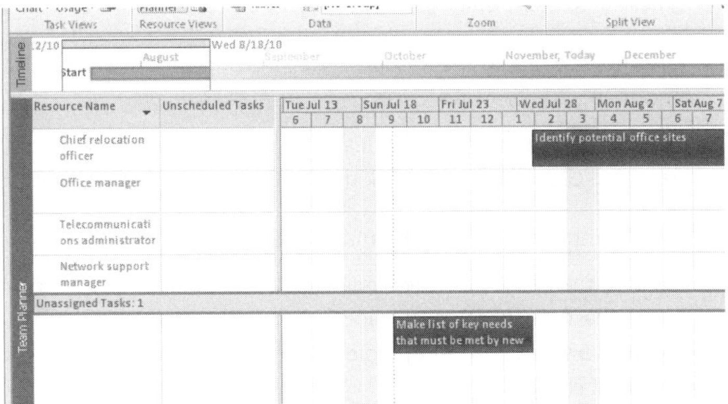

Figure 28-11 You can control whether the Team Planner displays the Unassigned Tasks section and the Unscheduled Tasks column.

5. The Unscheduled Tasks check box is selected by default, so manually scheduled tasks without dates appear in the Unscheduled Tasks column. To hide the Unscheduled Tasks column, clear the Unscheduled Tasks check box.

Modifying the Resource Graph

The Resource Graph shows resource allocation, cost, or work over periods of time, which is helpful when you're looking for resource overallocations you need to balance or costly resources you want to replace with less expensive ones. The horizontal axis represents time, and the vertical axis represents units, such as resource availability, allocation, cost, or work. In addition to choosing the fields that appear in the graph, you can modify the appearance of bars and text of particular types as well as change the gridlines in the graph. Unlike with Gantt charts, you cannot modify the appearance of individual bars or text.

Modifying the Appearance of Resource Graph Bars

The Bar Styles dialog box for the Resource Graph contains six areas, each of which controls the appearance of bars for different sets of information. For example, if you graph overallocations, the two top areas display overallocations, whereas the middle areas display allocations less than or equal to the maximum available units. The bottom areas show proposed assignments.

The areas on the left side of the dialog box control the appearance of data for an entire group, such as all tasks or filtered resources. The areas on the right side of the dialog box control the appearance of data for selected tasks or a single selected resource.

Follow these steps to modify the appearance of Resource Graph bars of a particular type:

1. On the View tab, in the Resource Views group, click the arrow next to Other Views, and then click Resource Graph.

   You can also open the Bar Styles dialog box by right-clicking the background of the Resource Graph and then clicking Bar Styles on the shortcut menu.

2. On the Format tab, in the Format group, click Bar Styles.

   Because the bars in the Resource Graph represent information you don't see in a Gantt chart, the Bar Styles dialog box for the Resource Graph, shown in Figure 28-12, contains a set of choices completely different from the Bar Styles dialog box options for Gantt charts.

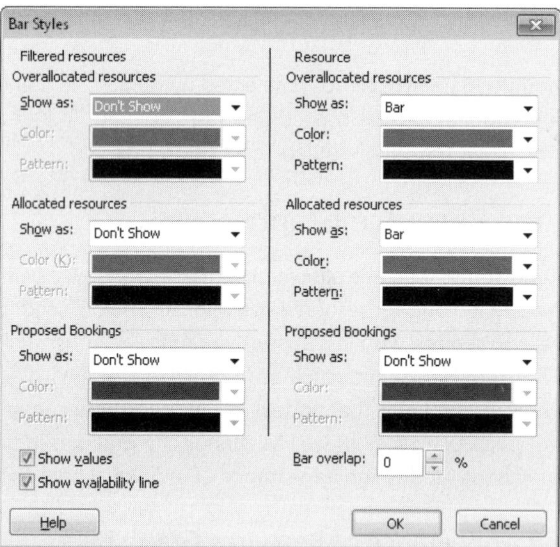

Figure 28-12 The Bar Styles dialog box for the Resource Graph includes choices for showing allocations for individual resources and groups of resources.

3. In the Bar Styles dialog box, choose the types of data you want to show—for example, allocated resources or proposed bookings.

   For example, you can view overallocations for the selected resource and others in the same resource group. (See Figure 28-13.) For any information you do show, specify the color and pattern for its representative bars.

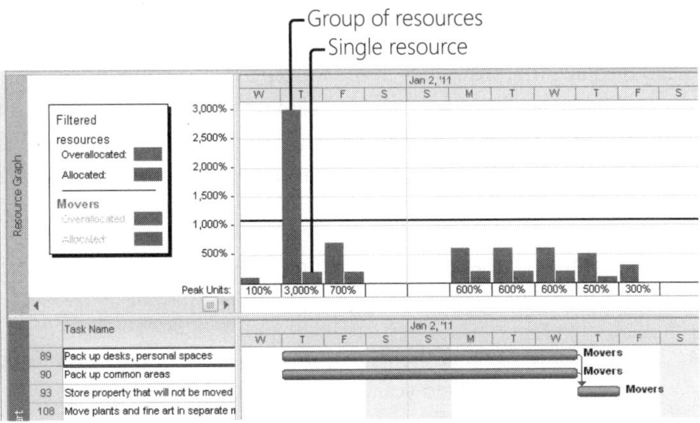

Figure 28-13 The Resource Graph can show information for a selected resource and a group of resources.

INSIDE OUT Determine what the Resource Graph shows

When the Resource Graph appears in the Details pane below a task view in the Primary pane, the graph shows the values for only one resource, but it shows all tasks to which that resource is assigned. However, when the Resource Graph appears in the Primary pane or in the Details pane below a resource view, it displays the values for all tasks. It can display the data for one resource or a group of resources or compare one resource's data to a group's data.

If you want to see the data for only the selected resource, click Don't Show in the Show As box for Filtered Resources. However, if you want to compare the values of the selected resource to other resources in a filter, in the Filtered Resources area, click one of the other graph methods, such as Bar or Step.

By default, the Resource Graph shows overallocations in red and regular assignments in blue, but you can change the methods, colors, or patterns for either. In addition, when you view any of the fields that relate to work or resource availability, you can select the Show Availability Line check box to display resource availability on the graph. Seeing the amount of time that a resource has available is helpful when you are trying to find someone to work on a task or you want to know how much more you can assign to someone.

Changing the Fields that Appear in the Resource Graph

You can display different values in the Resource Graph depending on what you are trying to do. For example, if you are trying to eliminate overallocations for a resource, you can display Overallocation or Percent Overallocation. On the other hand, if you are looking for an available resource, the Remaining Availability or Work Availability fields might be more beneficial.

You can use either of the following methods to choose which values appear in the Resource Graph:

Graph:
Peak Units

- On the Format tab, in the Data group, click the arrow in the Graph box. In the drop-down list, click the field you want to display.
- Right-click the background of the Resource Graph, and then click the field to display.

You can display the following fields in the Resource Graph:

- **Peak Units** Represents the highest percentage of units assigned to a resource during each period on the graph. Units that exceed the maximum units for the resource appear as an overallocation.

INSIDE OUT **Peak units can be misleading**

Peak units are particularly helpful when you look at the allocation for a resource that represents more than one person, such as Painters, which might have maximum units of 400 percent for a four-person painting team. Peak units show the highest allocation during a period. Suppose one resource is assigned concurrently to two 2-day tasks during one week. Peak Units equals 200 percent (two tasks multiplied by 100 percent allocation). However, if you shift one of the tasks, that person can complete 4 days of work during 1 week and would not use up more than 100 percent allocation during the period.

- **Work** Displays the amount of work assigned to a resource during the period. If the hours exceed the number of hours available for the resource, the excess hours appear as an overallocation. The hours available for a resource take into account both the resource calendar (working and nonworking time) and the resource's maximum units.
- **Cumulative Work** Displays the total work assigned to the resource since the project began.

- **Overallocation** Includes only the hours that the resource is overallocated during the period, not work hours that fit in the resource's workday.
- **Percent Allocation** Represents the work assigned as a percentage of the resource's available time.
- **Remaining Availability** Shows the number of hours that the resource is available during a period. This graph is helpful when you are trying to find someone to work on a new task.
- **Cost** Displays the total of the labor cost and per-use cost of a resource for the period. The total cost of a task appears in the period in which the task begins or ends, depending on whether resource costs accrue at the start or end. If resource costs are prorated, the costs are distributed over the time periods spanned by the task.
- **Cumulative Cost** Shows the running total of the cost since the start of the project. This choice shows the total cost of a project when you display the value for a group that includes all the project resources.
- **Work Availability** Represents the number of hours that a resource could work during a period based on his or her maximum units and resource calendar. It doesn't take into account any existing assignments. This field is helpful for identifying whether you have correctly created a resource calendar.
- **Unit Availability** Displays the same information as Work Availability, formatted as a percentage.

Note

You can control how values are presented in the Resource Graph. To change the unit for work, on the File tab, click Options, and then click Schedule in the left pane. In the Work Is Entered In box, select the time unit you prefer to represent work values. For example, in a large project, you might choose Days, whereas in a short project, Hours might be more useful.

To change the currency format for costs, on the File tab, click Options, and then click Display in the left pane. Under Currency Options For This Project, specify the currency format you want. If you want to change the currency format for a project other than the active project, click the arrow next to the box, click the project you want, and then change the currency format.

To modify the text styles or gridlines in the Resource Graph, follow the steps described in the sections "Changing Text Formatting for a View" on page 1068, "Changing the Format of Individual Text" on page 1070, and "Formatting the Appearance of Gridlines" on page 1080.

Modifying the Calendar

You can change the Calendar to display one week, several weeks, or a month. The bar styles, text styles, layout, gridlines, and timescale for task bars in the Calendar are all customizable.

To choose the time period to display, use one of the following methods:

Zoom

- On the View tab, click the arrow next to the Zoom button, and then click Zoom In or Zoom Out.

  By default, the Calendar displays one month at a time. If you click Zoom In, Project 2010 displays two weeks. Click Zoom In once more to show only one week. Click Zoom Out to switch from one week, to two weeks, to a full month.

- Above the Calendar, click the button for a time period.

  Click Month to display an entire month. Click Week to show one week. To show a specific time period, click Custom. In the Zoom dialog box, select the Number Of Weeks option and type the number in the box. You can also choose a start date and end date for the period.

- On the right side of the status bar, drag the Zoom slider to the left or right to zoom out or in, respectively.

Note

To navigate to the next or previous time period, above the Calendar, click the left arrow or right arrow. For example, if the Calendar shows one week, clicking the right arrow moves to the next week. Clicking the left arrow shows the previous week.

To display a monthly preview pane, do the following:

1. Right-click the Calendar, and choose Timescale on the shortcut menu.
2. On the Week Headings tab, select the Display Month Pane check box.
3. Click OK.

   To the left of the Calendar, Project 2010 displays a pane that shows the current, next, and previous months.

To modify the bar styles for a particular type of task, do the following:

1. On the Task tab, in the View group, click the arrow next to the Gantt Chart button, and then click Calendar.

Bar Styles

2. On the Format tab, in the Format group, click Bar Styles.

   Because the Calendar presents information that you don't see in a Gantt chart, the Bar Styles dialog box for Calendars contains different settings from the Bar Styles dialog box for Gantt charts.

3. To change the appearance of a specific type of Calendar bar, in the Task Type list, click its name—for example, Noncritical or Inactive.

4. In the Bar Shape section, specify the bar type, pattern, color, and split pattern for the Calendar bar.

5. In the Text section, in the Field(s) box, click the field that you want to appear inside the Calendar bar.

   If you want to show the contents of multiple fields with the Calendar bar, separate each field with a comma. For example, to see the task name and resource initials, select the Name field, type a comma, and then select Resource Initials. (See Figure 28-14.)

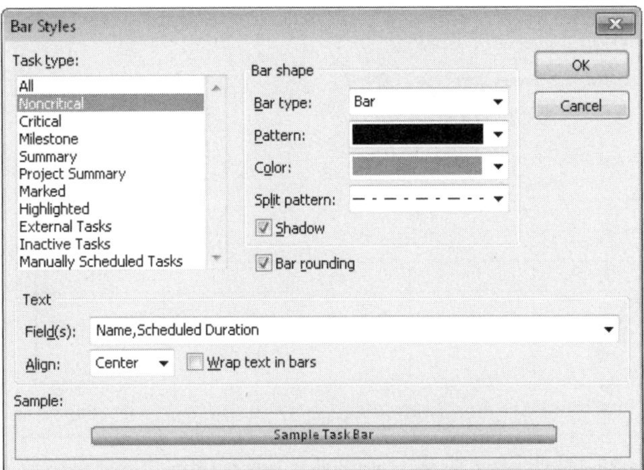

Figure 28-14 Use the Bar Styles dialog box for the Calendar to specify bar formatting and field content for various types of Calendar bars.

To modify the arrangement of tasks in the Calendar, follow these steps:

1. On the Format tab, in the Layout group, click the arrow in the lower-right corner of the group.

   The Layout dialog box for the Calendar appears.

2. To display as many tasks as you can in the Calendar boxes, select the Attempt To Fit As Many Boxes As Possible option.

   This option sorts tasks by Total Slack and then by Duration. Otherwise, tasks appear in the current sort order.

3. Select the Automatic Layout check box to reapply the layout options as you add, remove, or sort tasks.

To modify the timescale in the Calendar, do the following:

1. Right-click a heading in one of the Calendar date boxes, and then click Timescale on the shortcut menu.

2. In the Timescale dialog box, shown in Figure 28-15, click the Week Headings tab, and then choose the titles that you want to appear for months, weeks, and days in the calendar.

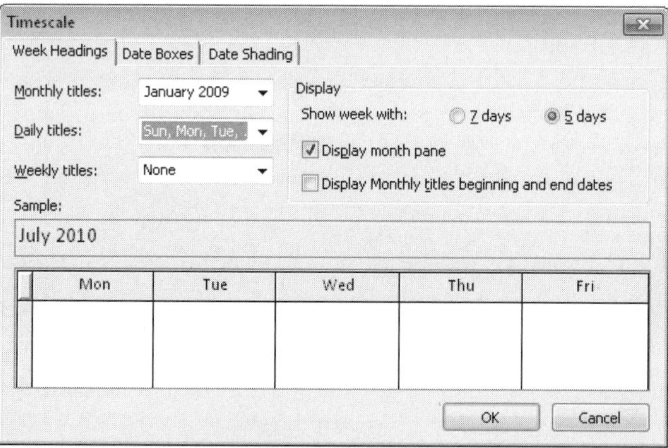

Figure 28-15 Use the Time-scale dialog box for the Calendar to specify the Calendar timescale's appearance.

3. Select the 7 Days option to display all days in a week. Select the 5 Days option to display only the workdays.

4. Select the Display Month Pane check box to include a preview of the previous and following months in the view.

5. Click the Date Boxes tab to specify the information you want to appear in the heading for each date box.

   For example, by default, the day of the month appears at the top-right corner of the box, and the overflow indicator is in the top-left corner. You can choose the format for the date and display the date in a different corner. Alternatively, you can show portions of the date in separate corners, such as the month in the upper left and the day in the upper right.

6. Click the Date Shading tab to customize how working and nonworking time for base and resource calendars appear on the calendar.

For information about modifying the text styles in the Calendar, refer to "Changing Text Formatting for a View" on page 1068. To change gridlines in the Calendar, follow the steps described in the section "Formatting the Appearance of Gridlines" on page 1080.

Modifying a Sheet View

The Resource Sheet and the Task Sheet use a tabular layout to display information about your project resources and tasks. The Task Sheet appears as the sheet area of a Gantt chart. It's easy to change the table that appears in the sheet view along with the height of rows and width of columns.

To change the table in the sheet view, use one of the following methods:

- On the View tab, in the Resource Views group, click the arrow next to Other Views, and then click More Views. In the More Views dialog box, click a sheet view, for example, Task Sheet or Resource Sheet, and then click Apply.
- Right-click the Select All box in the upper-left corner of the table (above row 1). A shortcut menu appears with tables for the sheet view. Click the name of the table that you want to apply.

  For example, to see costs in the Task Sheet, click Cost on the shortcut menu. If the table you want doesn't appear on the shortcut menu, click More Tables, and then double-click the table you want in the Tables list.

To resize a column in the sheet, use one of the following methods:

- To resize the column to fit all the values in the column, position the mouse pointer between two column headings until it changes to a two-headed arrow and then double-click the column edge.

- To resize a column to the width you need, position the mouse pointer between two column headings until it changes to a two-headed arrow, and then click and drag until the column on the left is the width you want it to be.
- Right-click the column heading, and then click Field Settings on the drop-down menu to display the Field Settings dialog box. Click the column width in the Width box or click Best Fit.

Tables

Note

You can wrap text in a table's column headings by adjusting the column heading row's height. To adjust the row height automatically to display the entire column title, on the View tab, click the arrow next to the Tables button, and then click More Tables. Click the table you want to modify, and then click Edit. In the Table Definition dialog box, select the Auto-Adjust Header Row Heights check box. You can also drag to adjust the column heading row height.

NEW!

In Project 2010, you can also wrap text in the cells within a column, which is helpful if your task names are long. In the Table Definition dialog box, click the Text Wrapping cell for the field you want to wrap. Click the arrow in the box, and click Yes.

Chapter 28

You can change the height of one or more rows in a sheet. To change the height of a row, position the mouse pointer between the two row headings (beneath the row's ID number) until the mouse pointer changes to a two-headed arrow, and then click and drag upward or downward to make the row shorter or taller, respectively.

For information about resizing all rows in a table, as well as inserting, deleting, moving, and copying rows and columns in a table, see "Customizing Tables" on page 1103.

Modifying a Usage View

Usage views, such as the Resource Usage and Task Usage view, display information divided across time periods. Usage views include a sheet view in the left pane and a timephased grid (the timesheet area of the view) with field details in the right pane. You can customize the sheet and the timescale for the timesheet area as you can in the Gantt Chart and other views. You can also choose which fields you want to see in the timesheet area of the view.

To select and format the timephased fields shown in the timesheet area of a usage view, follow these steps:

Task Usage

1. On the View tab, in the Task Views group, click Task Usage, or, in the Resource Views group, click Resource Usage.

2. On the Format tab, in the Details group, click Add Details, and then click the Usage Details tab to open the Detail Styles dialog box. You can also right-click the timesheet area of the view and click Detail Styles.

   The Usage Details tab, shown in Figure 28-16, lists the different timephased fields that you can display in the timesheet area of the view, such as Work, Actual Work, Overtime Work, and Cost.

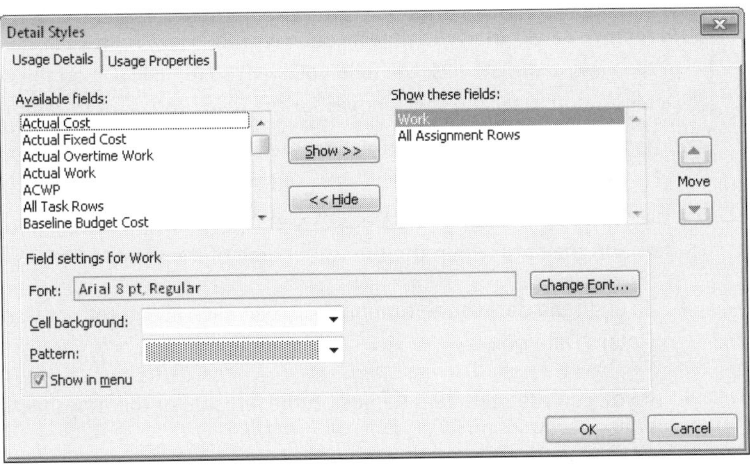

Figure 28-16 Choose the fields to display as well as their formatting in the Detail Styles dialog box.

3. In the Available Fields list, click the field you want to add to the timesheet area of the Usage View, and then click Show.

   To include multiple fields, hold down Ctrl and click each field to add it to the selection. Then click Show to add them all to the Show These Fields list.

4. To remove a field from the timesheet area of the view, click its name in the Show These Fields list and then click Hide.

5. To change the order in which fields appear, click a field in the Show These Fields list and then click the Move Up or Move Down arrow buttons.

6. If you want to change a field's appearance in the timesheet area of the view, choose the font, color, and pattern for the selected field.

Note

To quickly add a field, right-click the timesheet area of the view and then click the field you want to add. A check box appears in front of the field name on the shortcut menu, and another row of timephased information appears in the timesheet area of the view for each task. In Project 2010, you can also add fields from the Format tab. In the Details group, select the check boxes for the fields you want to add.

To remove a field from the timesheet area of the view, right-click the timesheet area of the view, and then click the field you want to remove. Or, on the Format tab, in the Details group, clear the check boxes for the fields you want to remove.

The Usage Properties tab in the Detail Styles dialog box enables you to format the detail headers and the data within the timesheet area of the view:

- To align the data in the timephased cells, click Right, Left, or Center in the Align Details Data box.
- If you can't see the field names on the left side of the timesheet area of the view, click Yes in the Display Details Header Column box.
- If the field names are missing in some of the rows, select the Repeat Details Header On All Assignment Rows check box.
- If the field names take up too much space, select the Display Short Detail Header Names check box.

For information about modifying the text styles or gridlines in a Usage view, follow the steps described in "Changing Text Formatting for a View" on page 1068 and "Formatting the Appearance of Gridlines" on page 1080. For information about formatting the sheet area of the Usage view, see "Modifying a Sheet View" on page 1099, and "Customizing Tables" on page 1103. For information about formatting the timescale, see "Modifying the Timescale" on page 1081.

The values in the timesheet area of the view often exceed the width of the columns. Instead of adjusting the width of columns in the Timescale dialog box, you can use the mouse to resize them in the timesheet area of the usage view timesheet. To resize columns in the timesheet area of the view, follow these steps:

1. In the timesheet area of the view, position the mouse pointer between two column headings until it changes to a two-headed arrow.

2. Click and then drag the pointer to the left or right until the columns are the width you want.

   If the usage view is part of a combination view that's displaying a timesheet area in both panes, changing the column width in one pane changes the width in the other pane so that the timephased columns always line up.

Customizing Tables

Many views—such as the Gantt Chart, Task Usage view, and Resource Usage view—display a table of data as a major section. A few views, like the Task Sheet and the Resource Sheet, consist entirely of one big table of data. If the information you want doesn't appear in the current table, you can switch tables or modify the table contents. You can customize the contents of a table directly in the view or through the Table Definition dialog box.

For information on switching the table applied to a sheet view, as well as working with tables in general, see "Using Tables" on page 150.

INSIDE OUT **Table modifications update the table definition**

Table changes you make in the view change the table definition. If you insert or remove columns, modify the column attributes in the Field Settings dialog box, or use the mouse to adjust the column width, the table definition changes to reflect those modifications.

Because it is so easy to make changes to a table in a view, it's important to remember that those changes become a permanent part of that table's definition. If you want to keep the current table the way it is, make a copy of it, and then make your modifications to the copy.

Many of the customizations you can make in the Table Definition dialog box are also available directly within a table in a view. You can insert, remove, and edit columns in a view. To learn more about modifying a table in a view, see "Using Tables" on page 150.

Modifying the Columns in a Table

You can add, move, remove, or modify columns in any table. To modify the definition of an existing table, follow these steps:

1. Right-click the Select All cell in the upper-left corner of the sheet (above the task ID cells) and then click More Tables on the shortcut menu.

   The More Tables dialog box appears with the current table selected.

2. Click the Edit button.

   To use the current table as a foundation for a new table, click Copy instead of Edit.

   To use a different table as a basis for a new table, in the More tables dialog box, click that table's name and then click Copy.

3. The Table Definition dialog box, shown in Figure 28-17, appears. If necessary, type a descriptive name in the Name box.

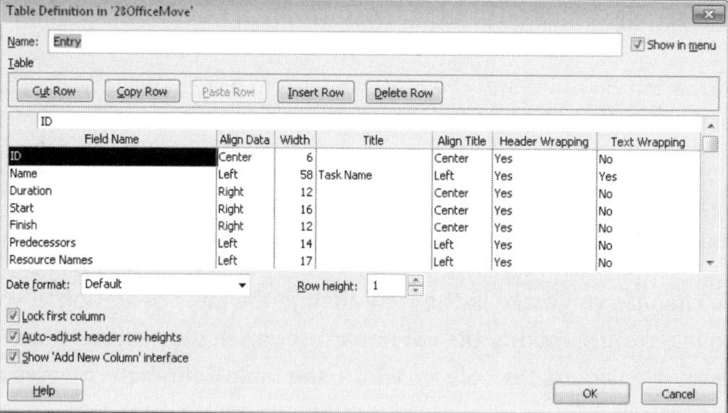

Figure 28-17 Use the Table Definition dialog box to customize the columns for a table.

4. If you want this table to appear on the table drop-down menus, select the Show In Menu check box.

5. To move a column in the table, click the field name you want to move, and then click Cut Row.

   You move columns in a table by moving fields in the rows in the table definition grid.

6. Click the row above which you want to insert the field.

7. Click Paste Row to insert the field at the new location.

You can add columns to the end of the table definition grid or insert them where you want. To insert a column into the table, follow these steps:

1. In the Table Definition dialog box, click the row in the grid above which you want to insert the field.

2. Click Insert Row to insert a blank row in the list.

3. Click the Field Name cell, click the arrow that appears in the cell, and then click the field name you want in the list.

4. Specify the alignment of the data and the column heading as well as the width of the column.

   If you want the column heading text to wrap, click Yes in the Header Wrapping cell. If you want the contents of cells to wrap, click Yes in the Text Wrapping cell.

5. To display text in the column header—other than the field name—in the Title cell, type the text you want to appear.

CAUTION!

Pressing Enter is the same as clicking OK—either action closes the Table Definition dialog box. To complete a row with default entries, press Tab or click another cell in the list.

TROUBLESHOOTING

The Field Name list doesn't show the field you want to add

When you're editing a task table, only task fields appear in the Field Name list. Likewise, when you edit a resource table, you can add only resource fields. Assignment fields appear only when you edit usage views.

Similarly, if you can't find the table you want to modify, you might have the wrong type of view displayed. In the More Tables dialog box, select the Task or Resource option to display the list of task or resource tables.

Note

You can turn the current table into a new table directly in a view. On the View tab, in the Data group, click the arrow next to the Tables button, and then click Save Fields As A New Table. In the Save Table dialog box, type the name for the table and click OK.

To remove a column from a table, follow these steps:

1. In the Table Definition dialog box, click the field name for the column you want to remove.
2. Click Delete Row.

Modifying Other Table Options

You can customize other properties of a table by using the Table Definition dialog box. For example, you can specify the format of dates or set a row height for all rows.

To set other table options, do the following:

1. In the Table Definition dialog box, in the Date Format box, click the format you want for any date fields.

   If you don't specify a format, the table uses the default date format for the entire project.

2. To change the height of the rows in the table, click a number in the Row Height box.

   This number represents a multiple of the standard row height.

3. To adjust the height of the header row to make room for the full column title, select the Auto-Adjust Header Row Heights check box.
4. To include the Add New Column column as the rightmost column in the table, select the Show 'Add New Column' Interface check box.

To learn more about the Add New Column interface option, see "Using Tables" on page 150.

INSIDE OUT Lock the first column for scrolling

If a table includes numerous columns, you might have to scroll in the sheet area of the view to see them all. But it's difficult to enter data in the correct cells when you can't see the Task Name column. You can keep a column in view by moving it to the first column and then selecting the Lock First Column option in the Table Definition dialog box.

To lock the Task Name column, in the Table Definition dialog box, click Name in the Field Name column and then click Cut Row. Click the first row in the Field Name list, and then click Paste Row to insert the Name field in the first row in the list. Select the Lock First Column check box, and click OK. Task Name is the first column, shaded to indicate that it's locked in place. It does not disappear as you scroll.

Creating a New Table

If none of the existing tables even come close to meeting your needs, you can create a completely new table. To do this, follow these steps:

1. Right-click the Select All cell in the upper-left corner of the sheet (above the task ID cells), and then click More Tables on the shortcut menu.
2. In the More Tables dialog box, select the Task or Resource option to create a task or resource table, respectively.
3. Click New.

   The Table Definition dialog box appears with a default name in the Name box.
4. Enter a new descriptive name in the Name box.
5. If you want this table to appear in table menus, select the Show In Menu check box.
6. Continue by adding the fields you want to appear in the table.

For information about how to add fields to a table, see "Modifying the Columns in a Table" on page 1103.

Customizing Fields

Project 2010 comes with a robust set of fields of several data types. When you right-click a column heading and then click Field Settings on the shortcut menu, the Field Settings dialog box appears with a few modifiable attributes, such as the title or alignment. However, you cannot change what these built-in fields represent or how they are calculated. If you want to track information that Project 2010 does not monitor, such as defect rates during testing, you can create your own custom fields and add them to tables in your views.

For more information about adding fields to tables, see "Using Fields" on page 160. For more information about Project 2010 fields, on the File tab, click Help, and then click Microsoft Office Help. In the Project Help dialog box, click the General Reference link. Click the Fields Reference link. A complete list of fields appears in the Help pane.

Project 2010 provides a set of several custom fields of each data type for tasks and another set of custom fields of each data type for resources. The number of custom fields varies for data type. For example, there are 10 fields for start and finish dates, 20 fields for flags and numbers, and 30 fields for custom text. In addition, there are 10 sets of custom outline codes for both tasks and resources. Microsoft Project Professional 2010 provides similar sets of enterprise-level custom codes. With Project Professional 2010, you can define project-related custom fields in addition to task and resource fields.

The custom fields in both Microsoft Project Standard 2010 and Project Professional are as follows:

- **Cost** Cost1 through Cost10 expressed in currency
- **Date** Date1 through Date10 expressed as a date
- **Duration** Duration1 through Duration10 expressed as time
- **Finish** Finish1 through Finish10 expressed as a date
- **Flag** Flag1 through Flag20 expressed as a Yes/No flag
- **Number** Number1 through Number20 expressed as numeric data
- **Start** Start1 through Start10 expressed as a date
- **Text** Text1 through Text30 expressed as alphanumeric text up to 255 characters
- **Outline Code** Outline Code1 through Outline Code10 (the outline code format is defined by a code mask)

CAUTION!

Even though the Start and Finish fields appear in the Custom Field list, Project 2010 uses these fields to store the dates for interim plans. If you intend to save interim plans in your project, don't use the custom Start and Finish fields, because information in those fields is overwritten when you save an interim plan. Instead, use custom Date fields for your customized dates.

For more information about interim plans, see "Saving Additional Scheduled Start and Finish Dates" on page 459.

Customizing a Field

Custom fields already exist; you can't introduce new fields into the Project 2010 database. What you can do is modify the valid values for custom fields or specify how their values are calculated. You can control how their summary values are determined. You can also substitute graphical indicators for the values for a custom field to make information easier to digest.

An outline code uses a lookup table to define the valid values for the field. **See the section "Working with Outline Codes" on page 1116, to learn how to create outline codes.**

Follow these steps to customize a field of any type other than outline code:

Custom Fields

1. On the Project tab, in the Properties group, click Custom Fields.

   The Custom Fields dialog box appears, as shown in Figure 28-18.

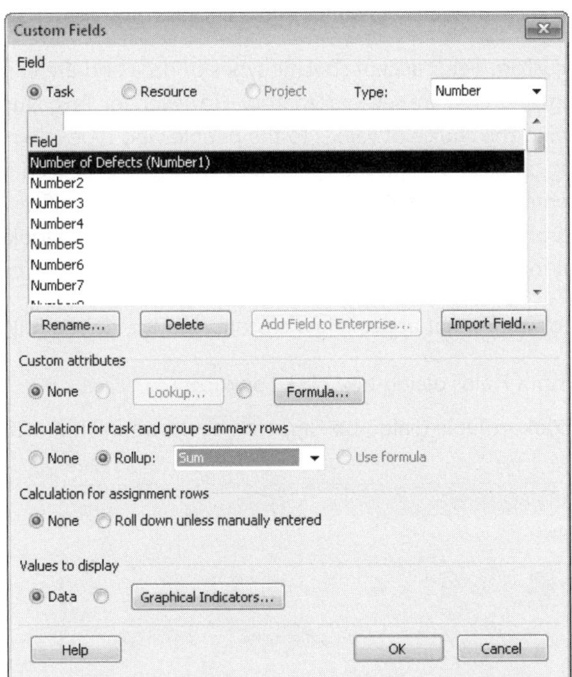

Figure 28-18 Create an alias, a list of values, or a formula for calculation. You can also set additional options for a custom field.

2. Select the Task or Resource option to specify whether this is a task or resource field.

3. In the Type box, choose the type of custom field you want to customize.

4. To communicate the purpose of the custom field, click Rename.

   Custom field names, such as Cost 1 or Date5, tell you mainly what type of field you're dealing with. Although you can change the title that appears in a column heading in a table, creating an alias for a custom field is a better approach. By creating an alias, the name you choose appears instead of the field name each time you use the field. In addition, the alias and the original field name both appear in field lists.

5. In the Rename Field dialog box, enter a descriptive name for the field.

Specifying Lookup Values for a Custom Field

With custom fields, you can control the values that they accept, as well as whether those values are identified in a list of valid values or calculated by a formula. If you do not specify values in some way, the custom field accepts any entry as long as it meets the requirements for the data type—for example, a Number field accepts numbers, not text or dates.

Some types of custom fields accept specific types of data and are easy to fill in—Start, Finish, Date, Flag, and Cost are self-explanatory. However, for Text, Number, and Outline Code fields, leaving the choice of values to the people who type in data could lead to gibberish. By setting up a list of values for people to choose from, called a lookup table, you can help them enter the right values. And, if valid values are specific, you can set up a custom field to accept only the values you specify. You can identify a lookup table for any custom field except for a Flag field, because that type of custom field accepts only Yes or No.

To specify a list of values that appears in a custom field list, do the following:

1. In the Custom Fields dialog box, click Lookup.

   The Edit Lookup Table dialog box appears, as shown in Figure 28-19.

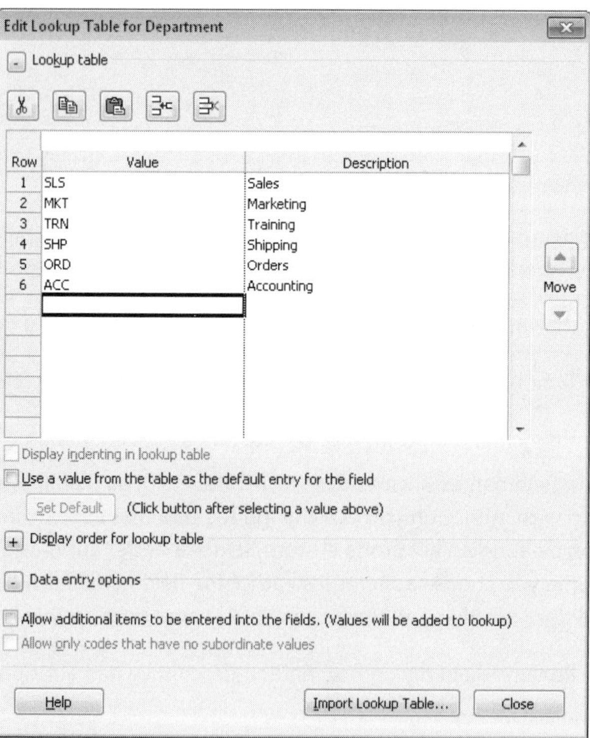

Figure 28-19 Specify the values to appear in a list for a custom field.

2. Click a blank cell in the Value column, and then type the value. In the Description cell in the same row, add a description of what the value represents.

   For example, if you use a custom text field to store department abbreviations, the Description field can hold the full department name. When you display the drop-down list of values in a task sheet, the value and its description appear in the list.

3. To specify one of the values as the default, select the Use A Value From The Table As The Default Entry For The Field check box. Click the cell that contains the default value, and then click Set Default.

   The default value appears in bold and in blue.

4. To insert new values, remove existing values, or rearrange the values in the lookup table, click Cut Row, Copy Row, Paste Row, Insert Row, or Delete Row.

   You can also rearrange the order of the values by clicking a value and then clicking the up and down arrows to the right of the lookup table.

5. To order the values, click the plus sign to the left of the Display Order For Lookup Table label.

   The By Row Number option displays the values in the order you enter them in the list. You can also sort the values in ascending or descending order. If you choose the Sort Ascending or Sort Descending option, click Sort to rearrange the rows.

6. To allow users to enter values not in the lookup table, click the plus sign to the left of the Data Entry Options label and select the Allow Additional Items To Be Entered Into The Fields check box.

   In Project 2010, this check box is cleared by default so that the lookup table values you specify are the only valid values unless you say otherwise. If you allow other entries in the custom field, Project 2010 adds those values automatically to the lookup table.

Note

If another custom field (in the current project or another project) contains a lookup table with the entries you want, click Import Lookup Table. If the lookup table resides in another project, open the project file. Then, in the Import Lookup Table dialog box, click the project that contains the lookup table, select the option for the type of field (Task, Resource, or Project), and then click the name of the custom field that contains the lookup table.

Creating a Calculated Field

You can set up a custom field to calculate its value by using formulas that contain functions and other fields in the Project 2010 database. For example, you might set up a field to show productivity by dividing the number of actual hours worked by the number of lines of code written (stored in another custom field).

To define a formula for a calculated field, follow these steps:

1. In the Custom Fields dialog box, click the Formula option.

   A message box appears telling you that any data in the field will be discarded because the formula will determine the field values. If the field is empty or contains data you don't care about, click OK to continue. To keep the data in the field, click Cancel, and then choose a different field to customize.

2. Click the Formula button.

   The Formula dialog box appears and displays the custom field name followed by an equal sign above the Edit Formula box.

3. To add a field to the formula, click Field, point to the field category, and then click the field you want to add. (See Figure 28-20.)

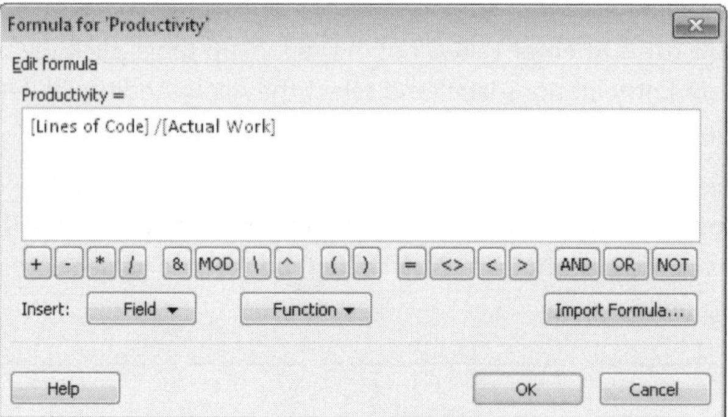

Figure 28-20 Build a formula by using functions, values, and any field in the Project 2010 database.

4. To add a function to the formula, click one of the function buttons.

   Alternatively, click Function, point to the function category, and then click the function you want to add.

5. To type a value in the formula, click the location in the formula where you want to insert the value, and then type the text or number.

6. To direct the order in which functions execute, insert parentheses in the formula.

Share Formulas with Other Projects

You can share most customized elements between projects by copying them with the Organizer, but the Organizer doesn't include a tab for formulas. One way to copy a formula between projects is to copy the custom field whose definition contains the formula.

If you want to bring a formula into your current project from another one, you can also import the formula from a custom field in the other project. First, open the project that contains the custom field with the formula you want. Make the project into which you want to import the formula the current project. On the Project tab, in the Properties group, click Custom Fields. In the Custom Fields dialog box, select the custom field into which you want to import the formula. Click Formula. In the Formula dialog box, click Import Formula. In the Import Formula dialog box, click the project that contains the formula, select the option for the type of field (Task, Resource, or Project), and then click the name of the custom field that contains the formula.

For more information about sharing elements, see "Sharing Customized Elements Among Projects" on page 1138.

Calculating Group and Summary Values

By default, Project 2010 does not calculate values for custom fields for summary tasks or for the rows containing rolled-up values for groups. However, you can choose the type of calculation for summary tasks and group summary rows or use the formula you defined for the field. To use the same formula that you defined for the custom field, in the Custom Fields dialog box, under Calculation For Task And Group Summary Rows, select the Use Formula option.

If you select the Rollup option, you can choose from several built-in calculations in the Roll-up drop-down list, including the following:

- **Average** The average of all nonsummary values underneath the summary task or group
- **Average First Sublevel** The average of all the values of tasks one level below
- **Maximum** The largest value of all nonsummary values
- **Minimum** The smallest value for all nonsummary values
- **Sum** The sum of all nonsummary values underneath the summary task or group

When you work with a custom number field, the following calculations also appear when you select the Rollup option:

- **Count All** The number of summary and nonsummary tasks at all levels below the summary task or group
- **Count First Sublevel** The number of nonsummary and summary tasks one level below the summary task or group
- **Count Nonsummaries** The number of nonsummary tasks below the summary task or group

Calculating Values for Assignment Rows

In Project 2010, you can control how values in a task custom field are distributed to the assignments within the task. For example, if you set up a number field, you can apportion the value to each assignment. Click the Roll Down Unless Manually Entered option to apportion the contents of the custom field to assignments. Project 2010 divides the value across assignments unless you manually enter values into the custom field in an assignment row. Click the None option if you do not want to distribute the contents of the custom field to assignments.

Working with Graphical Indicators

Graphical indicators in place of custom field values can make values easier to interpret. At the same time, if you want your audience to see status without the actual results, you can use graphical indicators to hide the actual numeric values. For example, you might want to display a green light when a task is ahead of schedule, a yellow light when a task is slightly behind schedule, and a red light when a task is more than 2 weeks late.

To display graphical indicators instead of values, follow these steps:

1. Open the Custom Fields dialog box and choose the custom field to which you want to apply graphical indicators.
2. Under Values To Display, select the Graphical Indicators option, and then click the Graphical Indicators button.

   The Graphical Indicators dialog box appears.
3. To assign graphical indicators to nonsummary rows, select the Nonsummary Rows option.
4. In the table, click the first empty cell in the Test column, click the arrow, and then click the test you want to apply for an indicator—for example, Equals or Is Less Than.

5. Enter the value for the test in the Value(s) cell.

   You can enter a number or other string, or you can select a field whose contents become the comparison value. For example, to display an indicator when a custom number field has a negative value, click Is Less Than in the list in the Test cell and then type 0 in the Value(s) cell. To display an indicator when a custom date field is greater than the baseline finish, click Is Greater Than in the Test cell and then click [Baseline Finish] in the Value(s) field.

6. Click the Image cell, click the arrow, and then click the graphical indicator to display when the condition is true. (See Figure 28-21.)

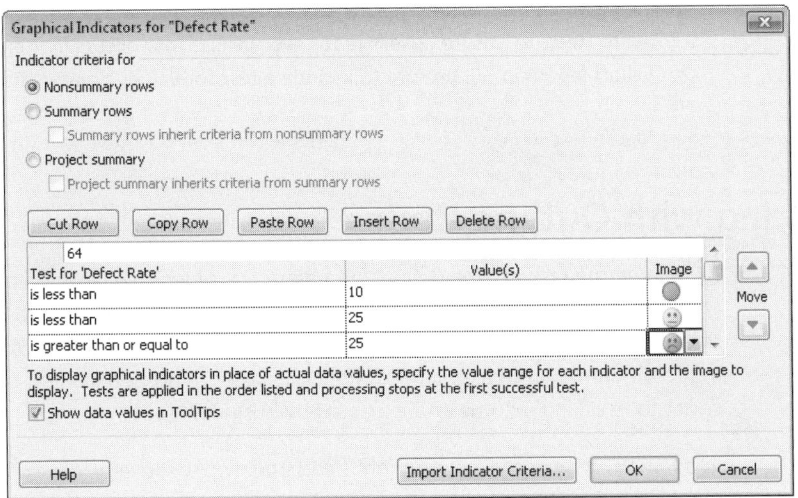

Figure 28-21 Set up criteria for displaying an icon that alerts you to specific conditions in the project.

7. To define graphical indicators when other conditions are true, repeat steps 4 through 6 in the next blank row in the table.

Note

By default, summary rows and the project summary row both inherit the same conditions that you specify for nonsummary rows. If you want to use different conditions for summary rows, select the Summary Rows option and then clear the Summary Rows Inherit Criteria From Nonsummary Rows check box. Define the tests and indicators for summary rows as you would for nonsummary rows. To specify different conditions for the project summary row, select the Project Summary option and then clear the Project Summary Inherits Criteria From Summary Rows check box. Define the tests and indicators for the project summary row.

INSIDE OUT **Define graphical indicator tests carefully**

With graphical indicators, Project 2010 compares the field value against the first test you define. If the value passes the test, the graphical indicator for that test appears. If the value doesn't pass the test, Project 2010 continues to check it against each subsequent test until it passes.

You must be careful to set up your tests to include all possible outcomes. For example, if you have two "if greater than" tests, be sure to test for the largest value first—for example, values greater than 50 before values greater than 25. If you test for values greater than 25 first, values greater than 50 pass that test as well. Be careful to include "equal to" tests to ensure coverage for every value that occurs. For example, if you test for values less than 50, be sure to include a test for values greater than or equal to 50.

Working with Outline Codes

By default, the task outline delineates a hierarchy of tasks. A work breakdown structure (WBS) is a special hierarchy that divides the work for your project into manageable pieces that you can assign to project resources. But you might need to structure your tasks according to different hierarchies. For example, the accounting department might have a set of codes for tracking income and expenses by business unit.

In addition, your organization might need one, two, or several ways of looking at resource hierarchies. For example, your organization's resource manager might want to review the resource breakdown structure, whereas the procurement manager might require a bill that itemizes the materials for the project.

Using custom outline code fields in Project 2010, you can create up to 10 sets of custom task codes and 10 sets of resource codes, in much the same way you set up WBS codes. You can then sort, group, or filter your tasks or resources by any of these outline codes to see the tasks or resources displayed in that structure.

For information about setting up a task outline of summary tasks and subtasks, see "Sequencing and Organizing Tasks" on page 109. To set up and apply work breakdown structure codes, see "Setting Up Work Breakdown Structure Codes" on page 122.

Setting Up Outline Codes

Outline codes are customizable alphanumeric codes that are helpful for categorizing project tasks and resources in numerous ways. Project 2010 does not recalculate custom outline codes as you modify the location or indentation of a task or resource because only you know the structure of tasks or resources you want to represent. To help others use your custom outline codes properly, you can create a lookup table so that users can choose values from a list. You can eliminate invalid codes by restricting users to choosing only the predefined values.

An outline code can consist of several levels of uppercase or lowercase letters, numbers, or characters, along with a symbol to separate the levels of the code. The maximum length for an outline code is 255 characters.

Selecting the Outline Code

Follow these steps to select the custom outline code you want to start defining:

1. On the Project tab, in the Properties group, click Custom Fields.
2. Select the Task or Resource option to specify whether you're creating a task or resource outline code.
3. In the Type box, click Outline Code.
4. Click the name of the outline code that you want to modify in the field list—for example, Outline Code1 or Outline Code8.
5. To rename the custom outline code, click the Rename button, and then type the new name in the Rename Field dialog box.

   This name and the original field name appear in lists where the outline code appears.

Defining a Code Mask

The code mask is the template that delineates the format and length of each level of the outline code as well as the separators between each level. For example, if your building name standard is a two character identifier followed by a hyphen and then a three digit number, the code mask identifies those criteria. To define the code mask, do the following:

1. In the Custom Fields dialog box, click the outline code for which you want to define a code mask.

2. Click the Lookup button.

   The Edit Lookup Table dialog box appears.

3. Click the plus sign to the left of the Code Mask label to display the code mask options.

4. Click Edit Mask.

   The Code Mask Definition dialog box appears.

5. In the first row of the Sequence column, choose whether the first level of the code (or hierarchy) is a number, uppercase letters, lowercase letters, or alphanumeric characters.

6. In the Length field of the first row, specify the length of the first level of the code.

   A number in the Length cell indicates a fixed length for that level. For example, if you choose 3, the values at that level must be three characters. If the level can contain any number of characters, click Any in the list.

7. In the Separator field of the first row, specify the character that separates the first and second levels of the code.

   You can use a comma, hyphen, plus sign, or forward slash as a separator.

8. Repeat steps 5 through 7 until all the levels of your custom outline code are set up. (See Figure 28-22.)

   As you enter the code mask for each succeeding level, the Code Preview box shows an example of the code.

With the code mask defined, your custom outline code is ready to use. If you click OK and then save the custom outline code, any sequence of characters that fits your code mask can be entered as a valid value for that outline code field.

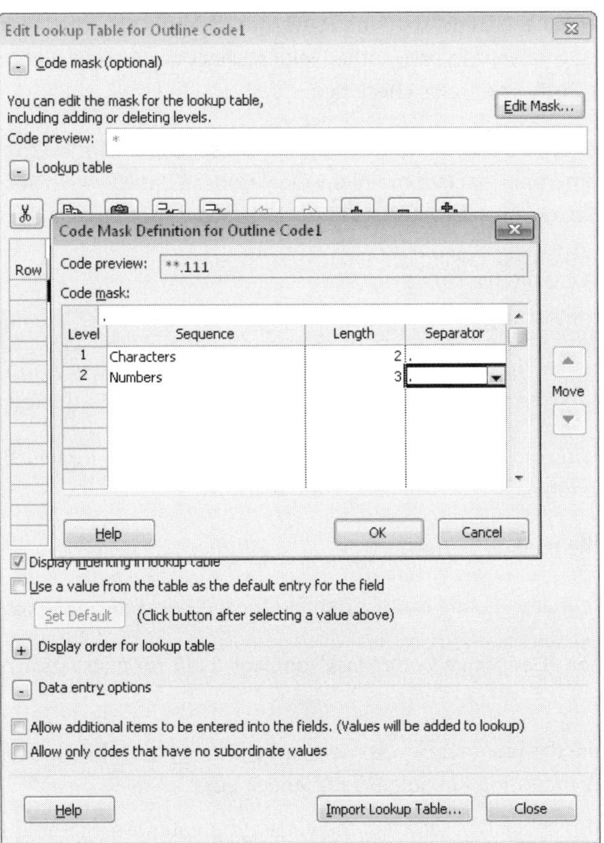

Figure 28-22 Open the Code Mask Definition dialog box to define the format of each level of an outline code.

Controlling Outline Code Values

To obtain the best results, you should provide users with some hints about the correct values and format for outline codes. And, if your custom outline code has specific valid values, you can ensure that users enter only those values. To do this, follow these steps:

1. Be sure that the Edit Lookup Table dialog box is open and that the code mask is defined for the selected outline code.

   In the Edit Lookup Table dialog box, the Code Preview box shows a sample of the code mask set up for the field.

2. You don't have to do anything to restrict codes to only those listed in the lookup table. If you want to allow other values, select the Allow Additional Items To Be Entered Into The Fields check box.

3. To restrict codes to the ones with all levels specified—for example, both building ID and number—select the Allow Only Codes That Have No Subordinate Values check box.

Defining a Lookup Table

If you want more control over the values that you or other users enter in the outline code fields, you can set up a lookup table for the outline code values. A lookup table comprises a list of values for the outline code. To define a lookup table, do the following:

1. In the Custom Fields dialog box, click the outline code for which you want to create a lookup table.

2. Click the Lookup button.

3. Be sure that the code mask is defined for the selected outline code.

See the section "Defining a Code Mask" on page 1117 for instructions on setting up the code mask.

4. To make the hierarchy levels more apparent as you define lookup values, select the Display Indenting In Lookup Table check box.

   With this check box selected, the values you enter are indented according to their level in the hierarchy.

5. Click the first blank cell in the Value column.

6. Type a value in the Outline Code cell.

   The format and length of this value must match the first level of your defined code mask. For example, if you specified that the first level in the outline code's hierarchy must be two characters in length and then enter a three-character code, the entry appears in red.

7. Click the Description cell and type a meaningful description of the entry.

8. In the Value cell in the second row, enter a value that conforms to the second level in the code mask. Click the Indent button to demote the entry to the next level of the code.

   The character types (number, uppercase letters, and so on) and length of each entry must match your code mask for the level. If the value you enter doesn't conform to the code mask defined for the outline level, the entry appears in red.

9. If you want to promote the entry one level higher in the code, click the Outdent button.

10. Repeat steps 5 through 8 to define additional values in the lookup table. (See Figure 28-23.)

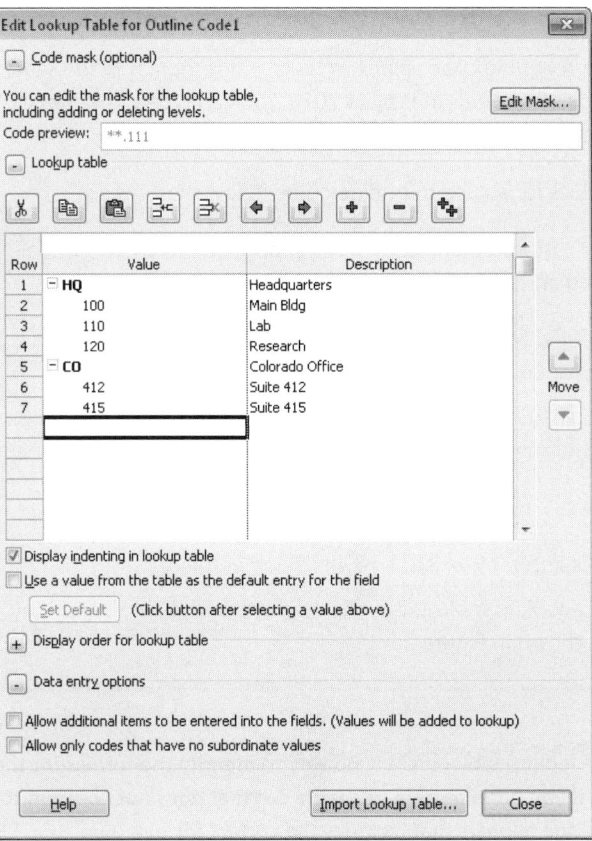

Figure 28-23 Define values in a lookup table to simplify outline code data entry.

11. To expand or collapse the outline levels, click the plus and minus signs that precede higher-level values.

12. When you are finished defining the lookup table, click Close.

    The lookup table is saved with the outline code definition and code mask.

> **Note**
>
> **To insert a value in the outline, click the Insert Row button. You can also use the Delete Row, Cut, Copy, and Paste buttons to edit the values that already exist in the list.**

Assigning Outline Codes

You can assign outline code values to tasks and resources in the same manner as you enter values for any other fields in Project 2010. You can type the values or, if you created a lookup table, choose the values from a list.

To assign values for a custom outline code, follow these steps:

1. If your custom outline code doesn't appear in the current table, right-click a column heading and then click Insert Column on the shortcut menu.

2. In the Field Name list, click the outline code field (for example, Outline Code1), and then click OK.

   If you renamed the outline code in the Custom Fields dialog box, you'll see the field listed both by its new name and its underlying custom field name.

3. Click a cell in the custom outline code column.

4. If no lookup table exists, type the value in the cell.

   When a lookup table exists, click the arrow in the cell, and then click an entry in the list, as shown in Figure 28-24.

> **Note**
>
> **Without a lookup table, there is no way to identify the format for the outline code. However, if you enter a value in a table cell that does not conform to the code mask, an error message appears that includes the correct format.**

2	**Two To Six Months Before Moving Day**		**79 days**	**Tue 7/20**
3	Make list of key needs that must be met by new office space		7 days	Tue 7/20
4	Identify potential office sites		20 days	Thu 7/29
5	Make final decision on office space		10 days	Thu 8/26
6	Secure operation space		5 days	Tue 8/24
7	Finalize lease on office space		10 days	Mon 9/13
8	Identify major tenant improvement needs			Mon 9/27
9	Obtain estimates from contractors for major tenant improvements			Mon 10/18
10	Identify costs for new office (chairs, desks, equipment)			Thu 9/9
11	Prepare a budget for the move			Thu 9/23
12	Select the move day			Mon 9/27
13	Hire contractors for major tenant improvements			Mon 10/25
14	Obtain necessary permits		5 days	Mon 11/1
15	Evaluate phone system needs		1 day	Mon 9/27
16	Order new phone number		1 day	Mon 9/27

HQ Headquarters
100 Main Bldg
110 Lab
120 Research
CO Colorado Office
412 Suite 412
415 Suite 415

Figure 28-24 Click the arrow in the outline code field to choose from the lookup table.

Reviewing Your Tasks or Resources by Outline Code

Grouping, filtering, and sorting by outline codes is similar to processing tasks and resources based on values in other fields. You simply apply a group, filter, or sort criterion that uses the custom outline code.

To quickly use a custom outline code to group tasks or resources, do the following:

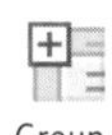
Group

1. On the View tab, in the Data group, click the arrow next to the Group box, and then click New Group By.

   If the outline code appears in the table, click the arrow next to the column heading, and then click Group On This Field.

2. In the Group Definition dialog box, click the arrow in the Field Name cell, and then click the name of the outline code.
3. If necessary, change the value in the Order cell, the color and pattern of the group, and other group settings.
4. Click Apply.

For information about customizing a group, see "Modifying a Group" on page 1125.

To quickly use a custom outline code to filter tasks or resources, follow these steps:

1. Display the sheet view whose rows you want to filter.
2. Click the arrow next to the column heading for the outline code.

3. In the drop-down menu, select the check box for the value by which you want to filter and clear the check boxes for values you want to hide.

   If you want to create a custom filter based on the outline code, on the drop-down menu, point to Filters, and then click Custom.

> **Note**
>
> **To turn off the AutoFilter arrows, on the View tab, click the arrow next to the Filter box, and then click Display AutoFilter.**

For information about customizing a filter, see "Customizing Filters" on page 1129.

To use an outline code to sort your tasks or resources, do the following:

Sort

1. On the View tab, in the Data group, click the arrow next to Sort, and then click Sort By.
2. In the Sort dialog box, click the arrow in the Sort By box and then click the name of the outline code in the list.
3. If necessary, select the Ascending or Descending option to change the sort order.

Customizing Groups

In Project 2010, groups can collate tasks, resources, or assignments that meet a set of conditions. For example, you might group tasks by their schedule variance so that you can concentrate on the ones furthest behind schedule. You might group resources by their level of availability so that you can assign the resources who have the most free time. You can also choose to group assignments instead of tasks or resources, for example, to see which assignments are running over on the targeted hours.

Group summary rows show subtotals for the values in the numeric fields for the group. For example, assignments grouped by salaried employees, hourly employees, and contractors can show the total hours of work performed by each group. When you group these elements, subtotals for the groups appear in the Task and Resource Sheet as well as in the timesheet area in usage views.

For information about applying built-in groups, see "Grouping Project Information into Categories" in Chapter 4.

Modifying a Group

If one of the existing groups doesn't meet your needs, you can modify a built-in group or create your own. If you want to keep the original group definition intact, simply copy an existing group and then modify the copy with the criteria you want. Do the following to customize a group:

1. On the View tab, in the Data group, click the arrow next to the Group box, and then click More Groups.

2. In the More Groups dialog box, click either the Task or Resource option to display the existing task or resource groups.

3. Click the group you want to modify in the list, and then click Edit or Copy.

   The Group Definition dialog box appears.

4. If you have copied an existing group, in the Name box, change the name of the group.

5. Click the first empty cell in the Field Name column, click the arrow, and then click the name of the field by which you want to group.

   The category for the field (Task, Resource, or Assignment) appears in the Field Type cell, as you can see in Figure 28-25.

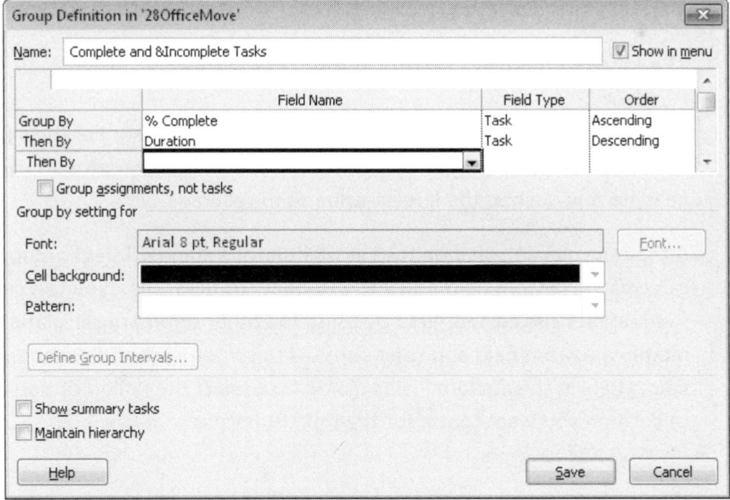

Figure 28-25 Group tasks, resources, or assignments by one or more fields.

6. If necessary, change the grouping order.

   Choose Ascending to show the smallest numbers first—for example, to see the tasks that have the least amount of completed work as shown in the % Complete field. Descending order shows the largest values first, which is ideal for locating the resources with the most availability.

7. To change the font for group rows, click Font. In the Font dialog box, choose a font, font style, font size, and color.

8. To change the background color for cells in group rows, click a color in the Cell Background box.

9. To change the pattern for the group headings, click a pattern in the Pattern box.

Note

For task usage views, you can group by tasks or assignments. If you want to see groupings by individual assignments within a task group, select the Group Assignments, Not Tasks check box. For resource usage, you can group by resources or assignments by selecting the Group Assignments, Not Resources check box for a resource group.

TROUBLESHOOTING

You can't change the calculation for the value that appears in the group heading row

The group heading rows for standard fields display the sum of the values for the entries in the group. However, you might want to use a different calculation for the group heading row, such as the largest value or the average.

Although you can't change the calculation for a standard field group summary, you can create a custom field equal to the standard field. Then you can calculate the group summary for the custom field by using the other summary calculations. To do this, first modify a custom field and use a formula to set the custom field equal to the standard field. Then, in the Custom Fields dialog box, select the Rollup option and choose the calculation you want to use for the rolled-up value.

Groups often display elements in small sets, one set for each discrete value that exists for the field that you grouped. This process works well for fields such as Milestones that have only two values. For groups based on cost or work, the number of discrete values can seem endless. The solution to this dilemma is to define intervals for groups—for example, to group tasks by % Complete equal to 0%, from 1% to 50%, from 51% to 99%, and finally 100%. To do this, follow these steps:

1. In the Group Definition dialog box, click the field for which you want to define intervals.
2. Click Define Group Intervals. The Define Group Interval dialog box appears, as shown in Figure 28-26.

   The default selection for Group On is Each Value, which creates a separate group for each discrete value in the field.

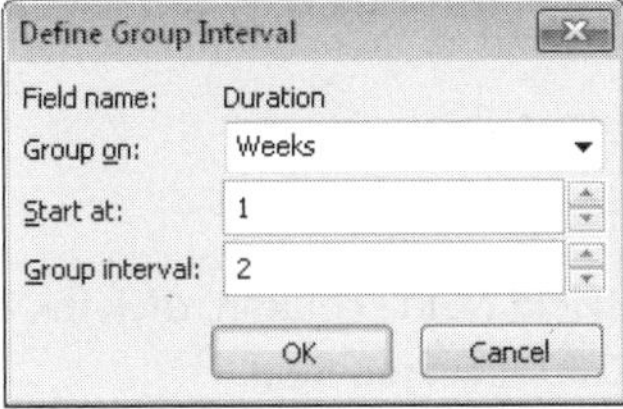

Figure 28-26 Set the starting value and size for group intervals.

3. Click the arrow in the Group On box, and then click the interval you want to use in the list.

   The intervals listed depend on the type of field. For example, the intervals for a field that represents work include units in which work is measured, such as hours, days, weeks, and months. For % Complete, the list includes several common sets of intervals.

4. To start the interval at a specific number, type the number in the Start At box.
5. To define the interval size, type the number in the Group Interval box. To group assignments in intervals of 2 weeks worth of work, type 2.

Creating a New Group

When no groups exist that are similar to what you want, you can create a new group. To create a new group, do the following:

1. On the View tab, in the Data group, click the arrow next to the Group box, and then click More Groups.

2. In the More Groups dialog box, select the Task or Resource option to specify whether you're creating a task or resource group, and then click New.

3. In the Name box, type a descriptive name for the new group.

4. To define the group, follow the steps described in "Modifying a Group" on page 1125.

Group Tasks with Overallocated Resources

You can create and apply a custom group that shows which tasks have overallocated resources assigned to them. This can help you determine which tasks are more at risk of missing their dates or generating overtime costs. To do this, complete these steps:

1. On the View tab, in the Data group, click the arrow next to the Group box, and then click More Groups.
2. In the More Groups dialog box, select the Task option and then click New.
3. In the Name box, type Overallocated.
4. Select the Show In Menu check box.
5. Click in the Group By row in the Field Name column, click the arrow, and then type **ov** to scroll directly to the Overallocated field.
6. Click in the Order cell in the same row, click the arrow, and then click Descending to show the overallocated group first.
7. Click Save to save the group.

   Your new group appears in the More Groups dialog box. Because the Overallocated field is a Yes/No field, the view is divided into two groups: those tasks that have overallocated resources assigned and those that do not.
8. Click Apply to initiate the Overallocated grouping to the current view. Click Close to close the dialog box without grouping.

Any time you want to apply the Overallocated grouping to a task view, on the View tab, in the Data group, click the arrow next to the group box, and then click Overallocated.

INSIDE OUT **Different "groups" in Project 2010**

Project 2010 uses the term "group" to describe several different features. Each feature serves a different purpose, so it's important to choose the correct one.

A group resource represents several interchangeable resources. For example, you might define a resource called Carpenters, which represents five carpenters who can do basic carpentry. The maximum units for this resource would be the sum of the maximum units for each individual in the group resource, 500 percent in this example.

A resource group represents a category of individual resources. You might define a resource group for employees and another for contractors so that you can sort, filter, and view assignments that are performed in-house versus those that are outsourced.

Throughout Microsoft Office, each subsection on the ribbon is referred to as a group. For example, the Task tab of the Project 2010 ribbon contains the View group, the Schedule group, and so on.

Finally, a group that you apply using the Group command on the View tab categorizes and sorts tasks, resources, or assignments based on the values in any field in Project 2010.

Customizing Filters

Projects contain so much information that data that isn't pertinent can simply get in the way. Filters restrict the tasks or resources that appear so that you can more easily analyze a situation. Project 2010 provides a number of standard filters that you can use as-is to hide information you don't need to see in a given situation. For example, the Incomplete Tasks filter displays only those tasks that are either in progress or not yet started so that you can focus on work yet to be done. These filters work equally well as templates for your own customized filters. You can create a filter based on the Incomplete Tasks filter to display incomplete tasks that are behind schedule. This enables you to see what kind of course correction you need.

For more information about working with the built-in Project 2010 filters, see "Seeing Only What You Need by Filtering" on page 178.

Modifying a Filter

You can modify an existing filter, but it's better to keep the original filter intact by copying the filter and then modifying the copy. To customize a filter, follow these steps:

Filter

1. On the View tab, in the Data group, click the arrow next to the Filter box, and then click More Filters.
2. In the More Filters dialog box, select the Task or Resource option to display the existing task or resource filters.
3. Click the filter you want to modify, and then click Edit or Copy.
4. In the Name box, change the name to indicate what the filter shows.
5. Click the Field Name cell you want to change, click the arrow, and then click the name of the field by which you want to filter. (See Figure 28-27.)

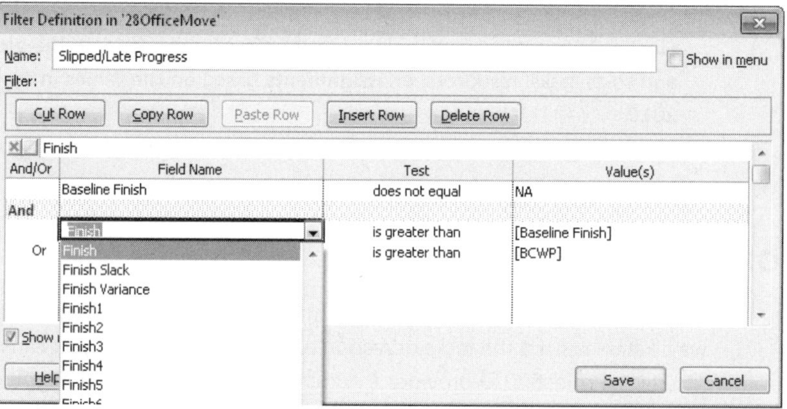

Figure 28-27 Modify the fields, tests, and values for a filter to display only the tasks that meet your criteria.

6. Click the Test cell, click the arrow, and then click the name of the test you want to use for the filter.

   Table 28-1 describes the tests you can use within a filter and provides an example of each.

7. In the Value(s) cell, specify the value you want to use for the filter test.

   You can type a value, click a field name from the list, or type a prompt to define an interactive filter.

8. To display the summary tasks for tasks that pass the filter criteria, select the Show Related Summary Rows check box.

For information about creating an interactive filter, see "Creating Interactive Filters" on page 1136.

TROUBLESHOOTING

A filter doesn't display the correct tasks

Project 2010 doesn't automatically update filter results when you make changes to your project, which can produce what appear to be incorrect filter results. If you make changes to your project after a filter is applied, elements that no longer meet the filter criteria don't disappear until you reapply the filter. The fastest way to reapply the current filter is by pressing Ctrl+F3.

Table 28-1 **Filters**

Filter test	How you can use it
Equals	The values must be equal. For example, to filter for milestones, test whether the Milestone field equals Yes.
Does Not Equal	The values are different. For example, to show tasks with overtime, test whether the Overtime Work field does not equal 0.
Is Greater Than	The value in the field is greater than the entry in the Value(s) cell. For example, to show tasks that are late, test for the Finish field greater than the Baseline Finish field.
Is Greater Than Or Equal To	The field value is greater than or equal to the entry in the Value(s) cell. For example, to show tasks at least 50 percent complete, test whether the % Complete field is greater than or equal to 50 percent.
Is Less Than	The field value is less than the entry in the Value(s) cell. For example, to show tasks that are ahead of schedule, test for the Finish field less than the Baseline Finish field.
Is Less Than Or Equal To	The field value is less than or equal to the entry in the Value(s) cell. For example, to show tasks that are within budget, test whether the Cost Variance field is less than or equal to 0.

Filter test	How you can use it
Is Within	The Field Name value is between or equal to the boundary values in the Value(s) cell. For example, to find the tasks within a range, test whether the ID is within the range specified in the Value(s) cell. To specify a range, type the starting value, type a comma, and then type the last value, such as 100,200.
Is Not Within	The Field Name value is outside the boundary values in the Value(s) cell. For example, to find the tasks that are not in progress, test whether the % Complete value is not within 1%–99%.
Contains	The field value is text that contains the string in the Value(s) cell. For example, to find the tasks to which resources from any development group are assigned, test whether the Resource Group field contains the word "Development."
Does Not Contain	The field value is text that does not contain the string in the Value(s) cell. For example, to find resources not in a resource group, check whether the Resource Group does not contain the name.
Contains Exactly	The field value is text that must exactly match the string in the Value(s) cell. For example, to find tasks to which only a particular resource is assigned, check whether the Resource Name field contains exactly the resource's name.

Note

When you use the Equals or Does Not Equal test, you can compare a text field value to a string with wildcard characters. Wildcard characters include the following:

- *** represents one or more characters.**
- **? represents any single character.**

For example, DB* matches DB Developer, DB Administrator, and DB Designer. Des??? matches Design but does not match Describe.

Creating Filters

If you can't find a filter similar to what you want, you can create one and filter on any field or combination of fields in Project 2010, including custom fields that you define. To create a new filter, follow these steps:

1. On the View tab, in the Data group, click the arrow next to the Filter box, and then click More Filters.

2. In the More Filters dialog box, select the Task or Resource option to create a task or resource filter and then click New.
3. In the Filter Definition dialog box, type a descriptive name for the filter in the Name box.
4. If you want the new filter to appear on the Filtered For menu, select the Show In Menu check box.
5. Enter the field, test, and values that define your filter criteria.
6. To include the summary rows for the tasks or resources that meet the filter criteria, select the Show Related Summary Rows check box.

Create a Filter for Resource Booking Type

If you're using Project Professional, you might have added some resources to your project as proposed resources—that is, resources you would like to use but who haven't yet been committed to your project. You can create a filter to find proposed resources—for example, to see which managers you still need to convince—or just committed resources when you want to focus on fulfilled assignments. Creating such a filter can be particularly helpful when you're finalizing your project team or the task assignments.

To create a filter for a booking type, follow these steps:

1. On the View tab, in the Data group, click the arrow next to the Filter box, and then click More Filters.
2. In the More Filters dialog box, select the Resource option and then click New.
3. In the Name box, type a descriptive name for the filter—for example, Proposed Resources or Committed Resources.
4. Select the Show In Menu check box.
5. Click in the first row of the Field Name column, and then type bo to scroll quickly through the list of fields. Click Booking Type.
6. Click in the Test column, and then click Equals.
7. Click in the Value(s) column, and then click Proposed or Committed.
8. Click OK. Your new filter appears in the More Filters dialog box.
9. Click Apply or Highlight to apply your new filter to the current view. Otherwise, click Close.

Any time you want to apply your new filter to a resource view, on the View tab, in the Data group, click the arrow next to the Filter box, and then click Proposed or Committed.

Creating Comparison Filters

Some of the handiest filters use criteria that compare the values in two different fields for the same task or resource. For example, to look for tasks that haven't started on time, you can filter for tasks in which the Actual Start date is greater than the Baseline Start date.

To define a test that compares two fields, do the following:

1. In the Filter Definition dialog box, click the Field Name cell, click the arrow, and then click the name of the field by which you want to filter—for example, Actual Start.
2. Click the Test cell, click the arrow, and then click the name of the test you want to use—"is greater than," in this example.
3. Click the Value(s) cell, click the arrow, and then click the name of the field with which you want to compare the first field (see Figure 28-28)—in this example, [Baseline Start].

   A field name in the Value(s) cell is enclosed in square brackets [ ].

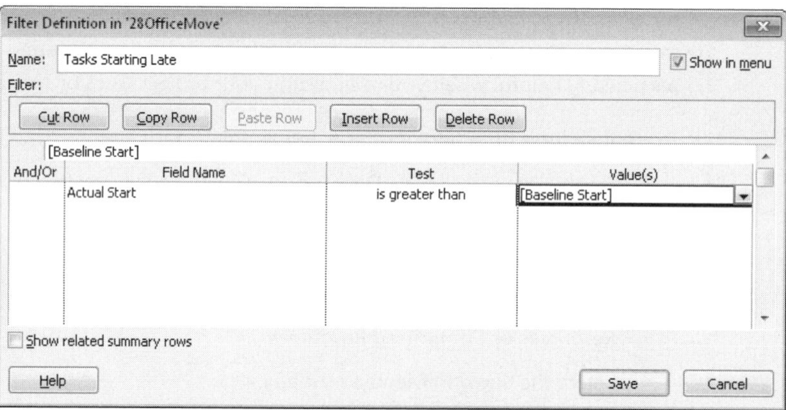

Figure 28-28 Create a filter that compares the value in one field against the value in another field.

Creating Filters with Multiple Tests

Sometimes it takes more than one or two criteria to filter the list to your satisfaction. You can create filters in which tasks or resources must meet at least one of the criteria or all of the criteria.

To define multiple filter criteria, follow these steps:

1. In the Filter Definition dialog box, in the Name box, type a descriptive name for the filter.
2. In the first row in the table, specify the field, test, and value for the first set of filter criteria.
3. In the second row, click the And/Or cell in the second row, and then click And or Or.

   If you click And, the resulting filter displays elements only if they meet both criteria. If you click Or, the filter displays tasks that meet one or both of the criteria.
4. In the second row, specify the field, test, and values for the second set of filter criteria.
5. Repeat steps 2 through 4 for any additional tests you want to define for the filter, defining each test on a separate row in the table and relating them with an And or Or.

With more than one test, filters evaluate tests in the order in which they occur in the filter definition. The filter restricts elements to those that pass the first test and then compares those results to the outcome of the next test. The filter continues until there are no further tests to evaluate.

In some cases, you might want to adjust the order in which the tests are evaluated. For example, you might want to filter tasks first for those that use a particular resource and that aren't yet complete. Then you can filter the list for tasks that start and finish within a particular date range. You can control the order that Project 2010 evaluates tests by inserting an And or Or test in an otherwise empty row. Including a test in an empty row is the equivalent of placing parentheses around the tests that occur before and after the empty row.

Do the following to group criteria within a filter:

1. Define one or more tests for the first group of filter criteria.
2. In the next blank row after the first group of criteria, click the And/Or cell, and then click And or Or. Keep the rest of this row blank.

   This blank row containing only And or Or creates the grouping between the first set of filter criteria and the second set.
3. In the next row, define the tests for one or more additional filter criteria. (See Figure 28-29.)

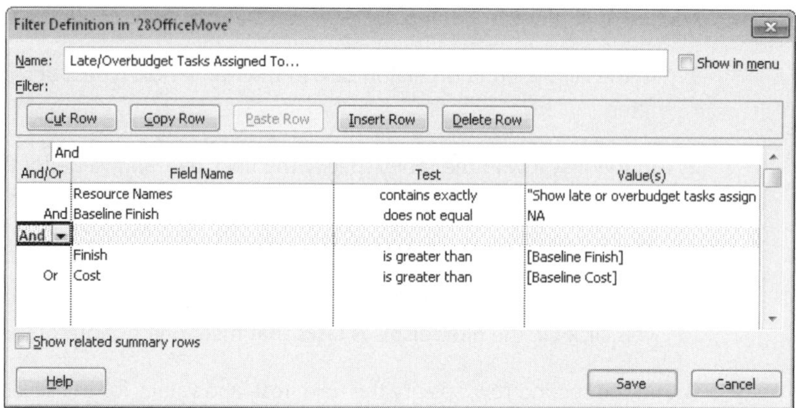

Figure 28-29 Use And or Or operators in otherwise empty rows to control the order of test evaluation for a filter.

Creating Interactive Filters

In many cases, you want to supply different values each time you apply a filter. For example, you might want to filter the task list by different resources to produce a list of assignments for each resource assigned to your project. Interactive filters request values and then filter based on the values you provide.

To create an interactive filter, follow these steps:

1. In the Filter Definition dialog box for a new filter, in the Name box, type a descriptive name for the filter.
2. Click the field and test for the filter.
3. In the Value(s) cell, type a text string within quotation marks followed by a question mark.

When you apply your new interactive filter, the text string you entered appears as a prompt in a dialog box. (See Figure 28-30.) The question mark instructs Project 2010 to display the prompt and wait until the user enters the value.

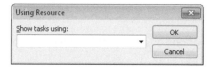

Figure 28-30 When you create an interactive filter, a dialog box appears, asking for the information you specified.

Customizing AutoFilter Criteria

AutoFilter is an easy way to filter by values in a single field. For example, to show tasks assigned to a specific resource, click the arrow in the Resource Names column heading, point to Filters, and then select the check boxes for the resources by which you want to filter and clear the check boxes for the resources you don't want to see. If the filter you want has only one or two conditions, you don't have to turn to the Filter Definition dialog box. You can create a custom AutoFilter instead. In addition, you can quickly create custom filters by saving an AutoFilter test.

Note

By default, AutoFilter is turned on. However, if you don't see arrows next to each column heading, you have to turn AutoFilter on. On the View tab, in the Data group, click the arrow next to the Filter box, and then click Display AutoFilter.

Keeping AutoFilter turned on makes it easy to filter your views. However, you can turn off AutoFilter for new projects. On the File tab, click Options. In the Project Options dialog box, click Advanced in the left pane, and then, below the General heading, clear the check box labeled Set AutoFilter On For New Projects.

To use AutoFilter to create a custom filter:

1. Display the sheet view whose rows you want to filter.

   The AutoFilter arrows appear in the column headings for each field in the sheet view, as shown in Figure 28-31.

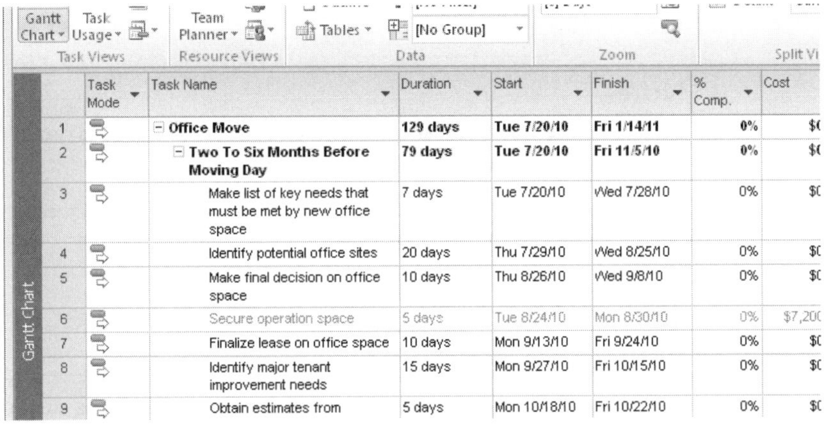

Figure 28-31 By default, AutoFilter arrows appear in every column heading.

2. Click the arrow next to the column heading for the column whose information you want to filter by, point to Filters, and then click Custom.

   The Custom AutoFilter dialog box appears with the field set to the current column.

3. Click the arrow in the first test box, and then click the test you want to use, such as Is Greater Than.

4. In the first value box, click the arrow and then enter a value or field name.

5. To add a second test, select the And or Or option.

6. Click the test and value for the second test. (See Figure 28-32.)

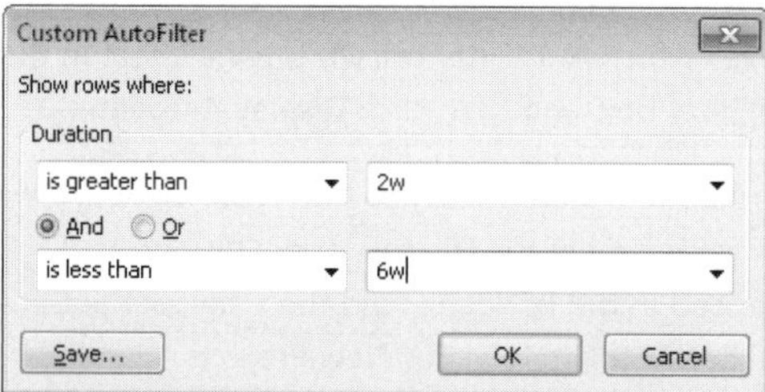

Figure 28-32 Customize and save an AutoFilter.

7. To save the AutoFilter test, click Save.

   The Filter Definition dialog box appears with the tests that you defined via AutoFilter. You can enter a filter name and make other changes before you click Save to save the filter.

To learn more about applying AutoFilters to a table, see "Seeing Only What You Need by Filtering" on page 178.

> **Note**
>
> **To turn off the AutoFilter arrows, on the View tab, in the Data group, click the arrow next to the Filter box, and then click Display AutoFilter.**

Sharing Customized Elements Among Projects

If you customize elements—such as tables, views, fields, or filters—in one project, you will probably want to use those elements in new projects. Some customized elements are stored in the project in which you create them, whereas others are stored in the global template. In either case, you can copy elements to other projects or templates by using the Organizer. If you want a customized element available to every new project, use the Organizer to copy the element to the global template. In addition, you can use the Organizer to rename or remove elements from a project or template.

For information about using the global template, see "Working with the Project Global Template" on page 1189. To use the enterprise global template, see "Standardizing Enterprise Project Elements" on page 859.

Working with the Organizer

The Organizer includes tabs for almost every type of customizable element in Project 2010 (custom formulas belong to the custom fields in which you define them). By clicking a tab, you can see the elements of that type that are available in two project files. These project files can be active projects or templates, so you can copy customized elements between active projects or from a project to a template, or you can restore the original element from a template to a project.

NEW!

Copying Elements to the Global Template Automatically

By default, Project 2010 automatically copies new views, tables, filters, and groups to the global template, so they are available to other Project files. This setting works well when you don't share your global template with others and you use the same customizations in all your projects. However, if you do share your global template with other project managers, you might not want to copy your new elements to the global template.

To change this setting, on the File tab, click Options. In the Project Options dialog box, click Advanced in the left pane. Under Display, clear the check box labeled Automatically Add New Views, Tables, Filters, And Groups To The Global. When you clear this check box, you must use the Organizer to copy new customizations to the global template.

You can copy, delete, or rename the following customizable elements:

- Calendars of working time
- Filters
- Forms
- Fields

- Groups
- Maps for importing and exporting data
- Tables
- Reports
- Modules of Microsoft Visual Basic for Applications (VBA) code and macros
- Views

To open the Organizer, on the File tab, click Info, and then click Organizer. An Organizer button to open the Organizer dialog box is also available in the following dialog boxes:

- More Filters
- More Groups
- More Tables
- More Views
- Custom Reports

Copying Customized Elements

No matter which type of element you copy, the procedure is the same. You choose a source file that contains the element you want to copy, choose a destination file into which you want to copy the element, and then copy the element.

Follow these steps to copy an element from a project to the global template:

1. Open the project that contains the element you want to copy.
2. On the File tab, click Info, and then click Organizer to open the Organizer dialog box, shown in Figure 28-33.

Organizer

3. Click the tab for the type of element you want to copy.
4. In the <Element> Available In box on the right side of the dialog box, click the project that contains the element you want to copy.

   <Element> stands for the name of the current tab. The <Element> Available In box lists all open projects.

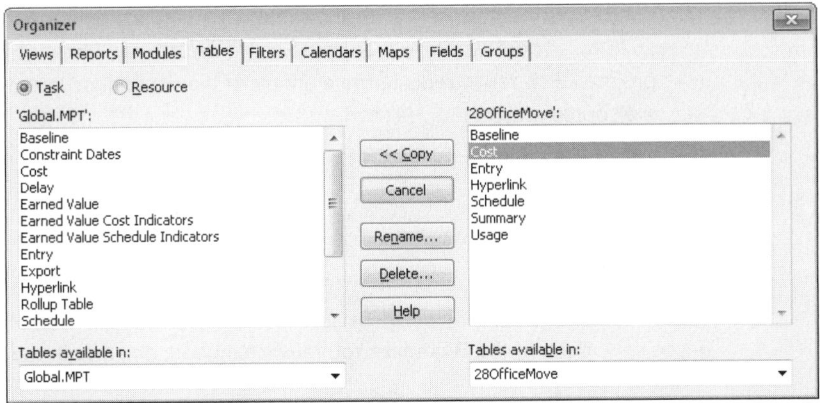

Figure 28-33 Copy customized elements between projects and templates, or rename and delete existing elements.

5. Click the name of the element you want to copy from the list of elements on the right side of the dialog box.

6. Click Copy.

7. If an element with the same name already exists in the global template, Project 2010 asks you to confirm that you want to replace the element in the global template. Click Yes to replace the element in the global template with the one from the source project.

   If you do not want to replace the element, click Rename and then type a new name. When you click OK, Project 2010 copies the renamed element to the global template.

To copy an element between two projects, do the following:

1. Open both the source and destination projects.

2. On the File tab, click Info, and then click Organizer.

3. Click the tab for the type of element you want to copy.

4. In the <Element> Available In box on the right side of the dialog box, click the source project.

5. In the <Element> Available In box on the left side of the dialog box, click the destination project.

6. Click the name of the element you want to copy from the list of elements on the right side of the dialog box.

7. Click Copy. If an element with the same name already exists in the destination, Project 2010 asks you to confirm that you want to replace the element in the destination project. Click Yes to replace the element in the destination project with the one from the source project.

   To copy the element with a different name, click No. Then click Rename and enter a new name.

CAUTION!

You can't rename some built-in elements. In addition, you can't rename fields when you're working in the Organizer. You must change field names in the Custom Fields dialog box.

Removing Customized Elements

Although customized elements can simplify your work, extraneous elements in projects and templates can be distracting. When you copy a customized element to the global template, you no longer need it in the project in which you created it. Similarly, if you create a customized element by accident, you can remove it using the Organizer. To do this, follow these steps:

1. Open the project that contains the element you want to delete.
2. If you want to delete a view, you must first apply a different view.

   If you try to delete the view that is currently displayed, Project 2010 warns you that the view is in use. Switch to a different view and then you can delete the view.
3. On the File tab, click Info, and then click Organizer.
4. Click the tab for the type of element that you want to delete.
5. In the <Element> Available In box on the right side of the dialog box, click the project that contains the element you want to delete.

   <Element> stands for the name of the current tab.
6. Click the name of the element you want to remove from the list of elements on the right side of the dialog box.
7. Click Delete. In the confirmation box, click Yes to delete the element.

Renaming Customized Elements

You can use the Organizer to rename customized elements. For example, you should rename a customized element in your project if you want to copy it to the global template without overwriting the original element in the global template. You can't rename some built-in elements. For example, fields are renamed in the Custom Fields dialog box.

Do the following to rename a customized element:

1. Open the project that contains the element that you want to rename.
2. On the File tab, click Info, and then click Organizer.
3. Click the tab for the type of element that you want to rename.
4. In the <Element> Available In box on the right side of the dialog box, click the project that contains the element you want to rename.

   <Element> stands for the name of the current tab.
5. Click the name of the element in the list of elements on the right side of the dialog box.
6. Click Rename.

   The Rename dialog box appears.
7. Type the new name for the element.

Restoring Customized Elements to their Default State

If you forget that changes you make to a table in a view modify that table's definition, you might customize a standard table accidentally. You can reverse the changes you made, but if you made a lot of changes before you realized your mistake, it's easier to restore the standard table. You can restore standard elements by using the Organizer to copy them from the global template to your active project.

> **Note**
>
> **You can't restore a table if it appears in the current view. Either switch to a view that does not use that table or right-click the Select All box (the blank cell above the ID numbers) and click another table name on the shortcut menu.**

Follow these steps to restore a standard element:

1. Open the project to which you want to restore a standard element.
2. On the File tab, click Info, and then click Organizer.
3. Click the tab for the type of element that you want to restore.
4. In the <Element> Available In box on the right side of the dialog box, click the project to which you want to restore the standard element.

   <Element> stands for the name of the current tab. The global template appears on the left side of the dialog box by default.
5. Click the name of the element you want to restore in the list of elements in the global template on the left side of the dialog box.
6. Click Copy. When the confirmation dialog box appears asking you to confirm that you want to replace the element in the project, click Yes.

Note

You can restore a table to its default definition from the ribbon. On the View tab, in the Data group, click the arrow next to Tables, and then click Reset to Default.

CHAPTER 29

Customizing the Project 2010 Interface

Microsoft Project 2010 introduces the Microsoft Office ribbon and Quick Access Toolbar to the Project 2010 user interface. This is a radical change to the way you access the many Microsoft Project features needed to pilot your projects to successful completion. Instead of arranging commands in menus and toolbars, the Office ribbon, shown in Figure 29-1, presents commands graphically and logically organized in tabs and groups.

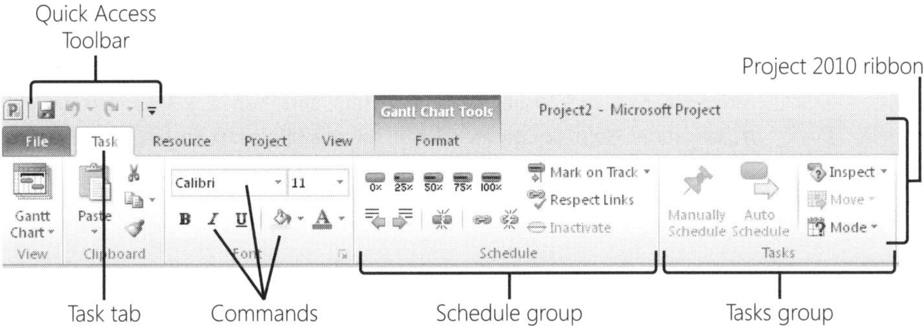

Figure 29-1 The Project 2010 ribbon replaces the menus and toolbars in previous versions of Microsoft Project.

The built-in tabs, groups, and commands on the Project 2010 ribbon reflect how most project managers prefer to work, but you might have different requirements and inclinations. Maybe the commands you use frequently are not organized on the tabs or in the groups you expect or prefer, or your favorites are scattered across different tabs or groups.

As you use Project 2010 and begin to identify commands you call on most often, you can customize the ribbon in a variety of ways by adding, changing, or removing elements. Customizing the ribbon can be as simple as adding a single command to an existing tab. It can be as elaborate as creating your own custom tabs, with custom groups arranged on them containing commands you select from the hundreds of built-in features or with new commands you create from macros.

Above the ribbon, the Quick Access Toolbar shows commonly used commands. You can customize the Quick Access Toolbar with the commands you use most frequently.

If you and your co-workers want to share customized ribbons and Quick Access Toolbar settings, you can do so by importing or exporting these settings and sending them to each other.

INSIDE OUT **Custom forms are no longer available**

Previous versions of Microsoft Project included capabilities for creating forms to enter data into fields. As of Project 2010, custom forms are no longer available.

However, if you do a lot of data entry, you can easily arrange or create a custom table to include fields in the order you need.

If you want to create a custom form as an alternative to working in tables or to replace those you created in earlier versions of Microsoft Project, you can use Visual Basic for Applications (VBA).

Macros

To find information about VBA, on the View tab, in the Macros group, click the arrow under Macros, click Visual Basic, click Help, and then click Microsoft Visual Basic for Applications Help. For greater detail, see the Microsoft Project 2010 Software Development Kit (SDK), available at *http://msdn.microsoft.com/en-us/library/ms512767.aspx*.

Customizing the Quick Access Toolbar

The Quick Access Toolbar is a convenient spot that always shows the same set of commands, regardless of which Project 2010 view is active or which tab is showing on the ribbon. By default, the Quick Access Toolbar shows the Save, Undo, and Redo commands, as shown in Figure 29-2.

Figure 29-2 By default, the Quick Access Toolbar shows the Save, Undo, and Redo commands as some of the most frequently used commands in Project 2010.

You can customize the Quick Access Toolbar in the following ways:

- Add your own frequently used commands.

- Remove commands that you don't use much.
- Rearrange the order of commands.
- Reset the Quick Access Toolbar to its original settings.
- Display the toolbar below the ribbon.

Note

The customizations you make apply only to the Project 2010 Quick Access Toolbar and not to the Quick Access Toolbar in other Office 2010 applications you might be using.

Adding a Command to the Quick Access Toolbar

You can add a command to the Quick Access Toolbar by selecting it from the ribbon or by searching for it in a list of commands.

To use the ribbon to add a frequently used command to the Quick Access toolbar, follow these steps:

1. On the ribbon, navigate to and right-click the command you want to add to the Quick Access Toolbar.
2. In the shortcut menu that appears, click Add To Quick Access Toolbar.

   The icon for the command you selected is added as the right-most command on the Quick Access Toolbar.

To add a command to the Quick Access Toolbar by finding it in a list of commands, follow these steps:

1. On the File tab, click Options.
2. In the left pane of the Project Options dialog box, click Quick Access Toolbar.

   You can also right-click anywhere in the Quick Access Toolbar or the ribbon. In the shortcut menu that appears, click Customize Quick Access Toolbar.
3. In the Choose Commands From box, click the category that contains the command you want to add to the Quick Access Toolbar—for example, Commands Not In The Ribbon or Gantt Chart Tools, Format Tab. Figure 29-3 shows all the categories.

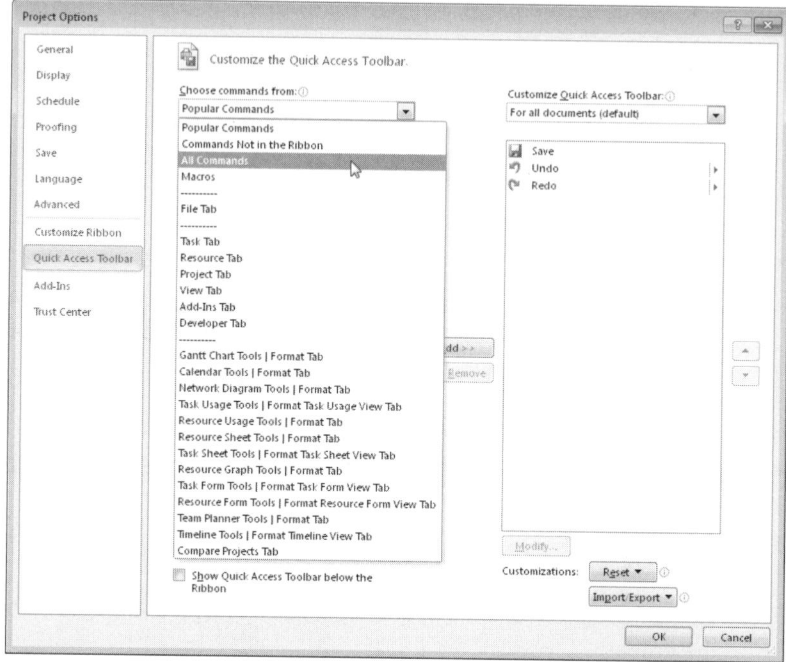

Figure 29-3 Find the command you want to add to the Quick Access Toolbar in any of the categories shown in the Choose Commands From drop-down menu.

4. Click the command you want to add, and then click the Add button.

   The command name is added to the Customize Quick Access Toolbar list on the right.

Move Up

Move Down

5. You can change the position of the command by using the Move Up or Move Down arrow button to the right of the Customize Quick Access Toolbar list.

6. Click OK.

   The command now appears in your Quick Access Toolbar.

Note

If you click the arrow just to the right of the Quick Access Toolbar, you'll see a list of frequently used commands. The commands with a checkmark are those that are showing on the Quick Access Toolbar. To add one of the other commands, simply click it. It's added to the end of the Quick Access Toolbar. To see the full list of commands, click More Commands. The Customize The Quick Access Toolbar page appears, and you can search for and add a command.

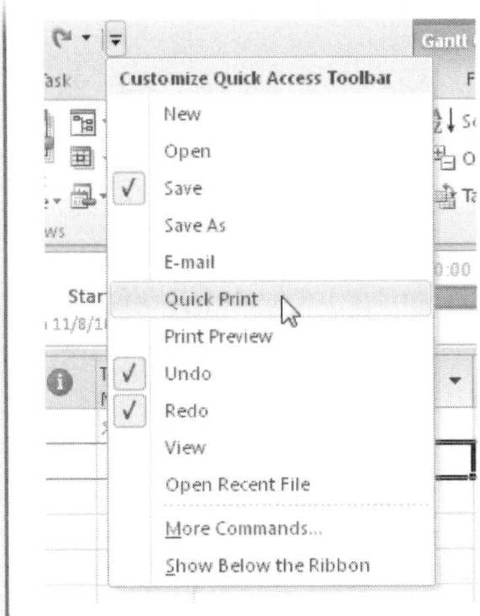

Rearranging Commands on the Quick Access Toolbar

To change the order of commands on the Quick Access Toolbar, follow these steps:

1. On the File tab, click Options.
2. In the left pane of the Project Options dialog box, click Quick Access Toolbar.

   You can also click the arrow to the right of the Quick Access Toolbar, and then click More Commands.

   The Customize The Quick Access Toolbar dialog box appears.
3. In the list of commands on the right, click the name of the command you want to move to a different location on the Quick Access Toolbar.
4. Click the Move Up or Move Down arrow button to the right of the list.
5. Click OK.

   The Quick Access Toolbar commands are listed in the order you specify.

If you have many commands on the Quick Access Toolbar, you might want a vertical line separator between groups to help you find commands more quickly. To add a separator to the Quick Access Toolbar, follow these steps:

1. Click the arrow to the right of the Quick Access Toolbar, and then click More Commands.

   The Customize The Quick Access Toolbar dialog box appears.

2. In the Choose Commands From box on the left, make sure that Popular Commands is selected.

3. In the list of commands, select <Separator>, and then click Add.

4. To the right of the Customize Quick Access Toolbar list, click the Move Up or Move Down arrow button to position the separator where you want it.

   If you first select the command below which you want to add the separator, when you click Add, the separator appears below the selected command. (See Figure 29-4.)

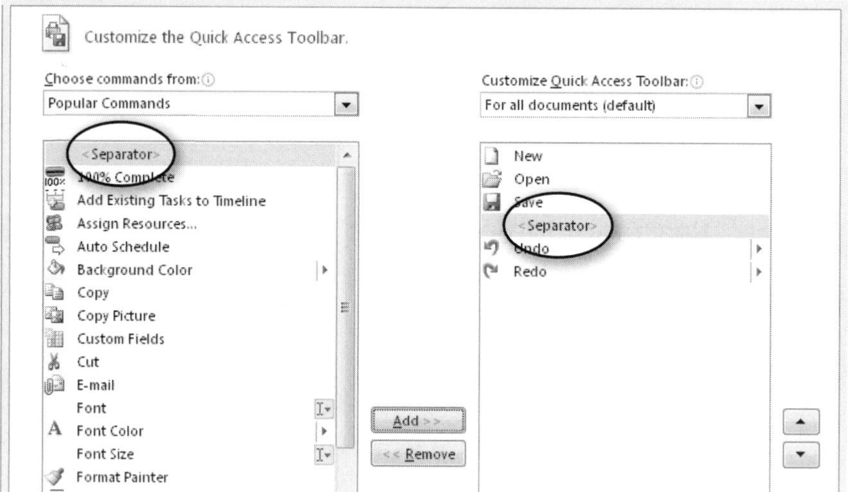

Figure 29-4 Add the separator to the location you want in the Quick Access Toolbar.

5. Click OK.

   The separator appears in the Quick Access Toolbar as you specified, as you can see in Figure 29-5.

Figure 29-5 A separator helps group commands on the Quick Access Toolbar.

Create a Quick Access Toolbar for a Specific Project Plan

By default, all changes to the Quick Access Toolbar apply to all project plans that you open on a specific computer. But you can create a specialized Quick Access Toolbar for a particular project plan.

To do this, open the project plan, and then open the Customize The Quick Access Toolbar dialog box. In the Customize Quick Access Toolbar box, change the setting from For All Documents (Default) to For <ProjectName>. Now add and arrange the commands you want. This Quick Access Toolbar will apply only to the current project plan. If you move the project plan to another computer, its Quick Access Toolbar moves with it.

Removing a Command from the Quick Access Toolbar

Your Quick Access Toolbar is most effective when you use it only for your most frequently used commands. If the toolbar becomes cluttered with commands you don't use much, you can easily remove them by following these steps:

1. Click the arrow to the right of the Quick Access Toolbar.
2. If any of the extraneous commands are checked in the drop-down menu that appears, click its name to clear the checkmark. The command is immediately removed from the Quick Access Toolbar.

   Otherwise, click More Commands to open the Customize The Quick Access Toolbar dialog box.
3. In the Customize Quick Access Toolbar list on the right, click the command you want to remove, and then click the Remove button.
4. Click OK.

Note

You can share customized Quick Access Toolbar settings with your co-workers. For more information, see "Sharing a Custom Ribbon and Quick Access Toolbar" on page 1166.

Resetting the Quick Access Toolbar

You can restore the Quick Access Toolbar to its default settings. Resetting the Quick Access Toolbar removes any commands you added or any rearranging you've done. To do this, follow these steps:

1. Click the arrow to the right of the Quick Access Toolbar, and then click More Commands.
2. Near the lower-right corner of the dialog box, click the Reset button, and then click Reset Only Quick Access Toolbar.
3. In the message that appears, click Yes.

   The commands showing in the Customize Quick Access Toolbar list change to the default commands of Save, Undo, and Redo.
4. Click OK.

   The Quick Access Toolbar is now returned to its default settings.

Moving the Quick Access Toolbar

By default, the Quick Access Toolbar sits above the ribbon. However, you can move it below the ribbon.

To do this, click the arrow to the right of the Quick Access Toolbar, and then click Show Below The Ribbon.

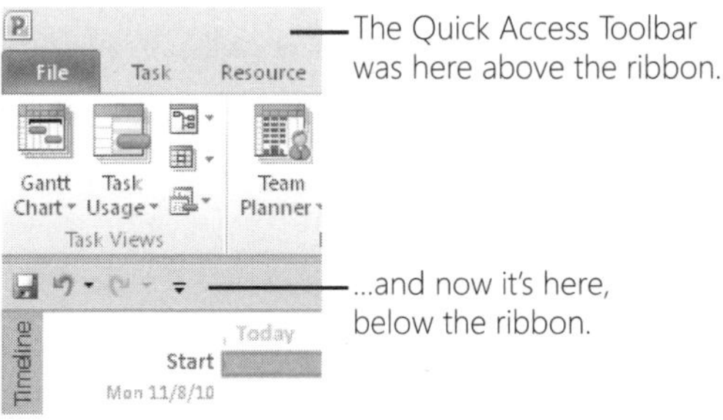

Moving the toolbar can be helpful if you prefer to have your most frequently used commands directly above your project plan, which lets you access them more quickly with your mouse.

Customizing the Project 2010 Ribbon

NEW!

The Project 2010 ribbon contains the commands for the features you use every day to plan and track your projects. You can customize the Project 2010 ribbon in the following ways:

- Add a custom tab, group, or command.
- Change the name, order, and content of existing tabs, groups, and commands.
- Remove a tab, group, or command from the ribbon.

When you customize the ribbon, be aware of the following characteristics and guidelines:

- The ribbon shows one active tab at a time.
- Tabs contain groups.
- Groups contain commands.
- Commands can be added only to custom groups. This is true for built-in commands and macro commands that you create.
- The customizations you make to the Project 2010 ribbon apply only to Project 2010 and not to any other Office applications.

Minimize or Expand the Ribbon

You can hide the ribbon so that only the tabs are showing, without a tab's groups or buttons. When you click a tab in the minimized ribbon, the full ribbon appears. After you click a button, the ribbon is minimized again. This is a great way to give yourself more working space in the project plan, either temporarily or after you're familiar with where commands are on the ribbon.

Minimize The Ribbon

In the upper-right corner of the Project 2010 window, click the Minimize The Ribbon icon.

Expand The Ribbon

To show the full ribbon again, in the upper-right corner of the Project 2010 window, click the Expand The Ribbon icon.

Adding a Custom Group or Tab to the Ribbon

You can create a custom group on any existing tab and add commands to that group. You can even create a custom tab and add custom groups of commands to it.

Creating a Custom Group

If you want to add commands (either built-in commands or macros) to the ribbon, you must first create a custom group to contain them. Because the commands in existing groups are fixed, you can add commands only to a custom group you create. However, you can add that custom group to an existing tab, such as the Task tab or the View tab, or you can add it to a custom tab you create.

To create a custom group on the ribbon, follow these steps:

1. On the File tab, click Options.
2. In the left pane of the Project Options dialog box, click Customize Ribbon.

   You can also right-click anywhere in the ribbon and then click Customize The Ribbon.
3. In the Customize The Ribbon box on the right side of the dialog box, make sure that Main Tabs is selected.
4. In the Main Tabs list, click the plus sign next to the tab where you want to add your custom group.

   The tab expands to show the existing groups on that tab.
5. In the expanded list of groups, click the name of the group after which you want to add your custom group.
6. Click the New Group button below the list.

   The label New Group (Custom) appears below the group you selected, as shown in Figure 29-6.
7. With New Group (Custom) still selected, click the Rename button below the list.

   The Rename dialog box appears, showing a gallery of buttons. Ignore the buttons for now. You're just creating the group name.
8. In the Display Name box, type the name you want for your custom group, and then click OK.

   The new name appears in the list, with (Custom) after the name. This helps you distinguish your custom groups from the built-in groups.

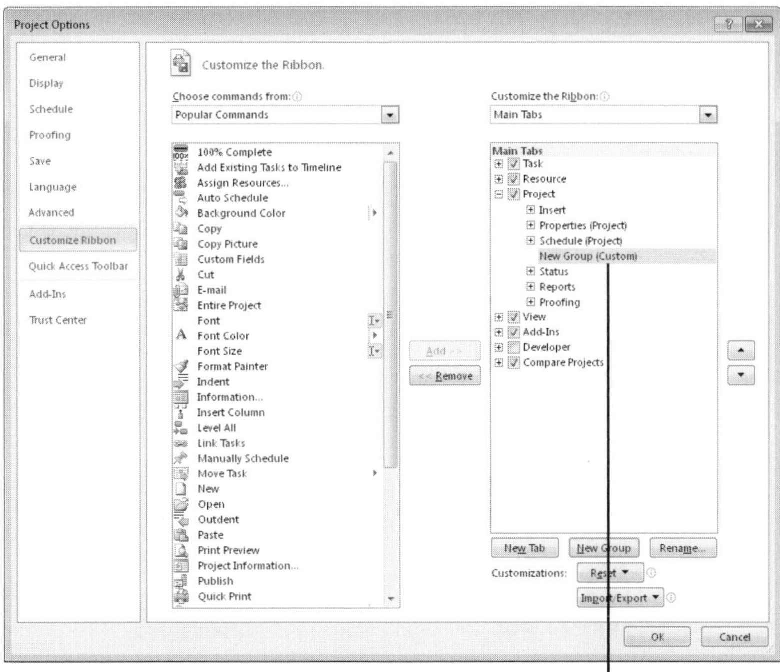

After clicking the New Group button, the new group label appears below the group selected in the list.

Figure 29-6 You can only add commands to a custom group on the ribbon.

9. If you want to change the position of the custom group, click its name, and then click the Move Up or Move Down arrow button to the right of the box until the group is located where you want it.

Adding Commands to a Custom Group

After you create a custom group, you have a place to add commands. You can add built-in commands or custom commands (macros) to your custom group. You can also change the name or button icon associated with any command you add to the custom group.

To add an existing command to a custom group, follow these steps:

1. Be sure that the Project Options dialog box is still open.
2. Click the arrow in the Choose Commands From box, and then select the category from which you want to choose your command—for example, All Commands, Commands Not In The Ribbon, or Tool Tabs.

   The commands in the category you select are listed in the box on the left.

3. In the Main Tabs box on the right, click the name of the custom group to which you want to add the command.

4. In the command list on the left, click the name of the command you want to add to the custom group, and then click the Add button.

   The command name appears under the custom group name, as shown in Figure 29-7.

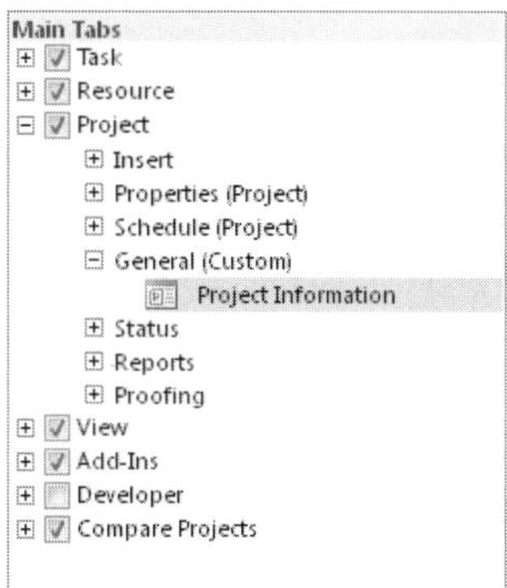

Figure 29-7 Add the command to your custom group.

5. Repeat steps 2 through 4 to add any other commands you want to the custom group.

   It's okay to have a group containing just a single command. Keep in mind that as a group grows larger, it's more likely to affect the visibility of other groups on that tab. Buttons might become smaller, and groups on the far right might "fall off" the ribbon.

6. When you are finished adding commands, click OK in the Project Options dialog box.

7. Navigate to the tab where you added the custom group.

   You'll see your custom group with the commands you've added (see Figure 29-8).

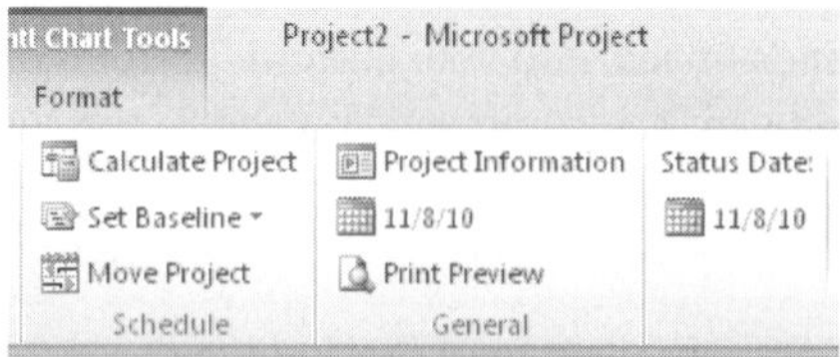

Figure 29-8 Your custom group appears with its commands on the tab you specified.

For information on adding a macro command to a custom group, see "Adding Macros to a Custom Group" on page 1184.

Find Commands

Suppose you used a certain command in earlier versions of Microsoft Project, and now you can't find it on the Project 2010 ribbon. You can search for it by following these steps:

1. Right-click anywhere in the ribbon or Quick Access Toolbar, and then click Customize Quick Access Toolbar or Customize The Ribbon. The Project Options dialog box appears.
2. In the Choose Commands From box, click All Commands. All commands in Project 2010 are listed.
3. Scroll through the list to find the command.
4. To find where the command is located on the ribbon, rest the mouse pointer over the command name. The location of the command appears, including the name of the tab, group, and command.

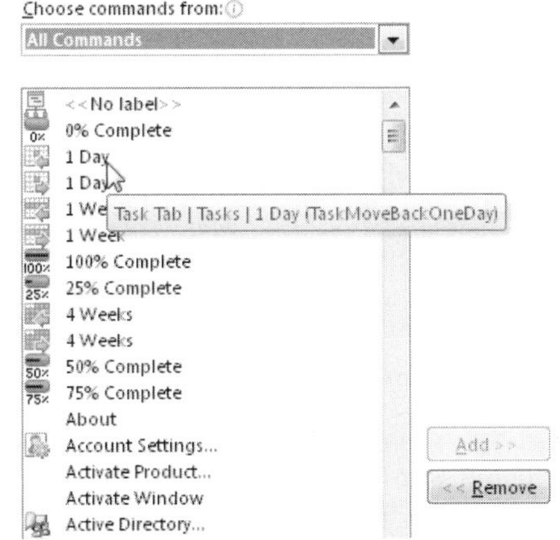

The commands are listed in alphabetical order. You might need to look in different places if you're not sure of the exact command name.

You might also try clicking Commands Not In The Ribbon in the Choose Commands From box. If you need to use a command that's not on the ribbon, you can add it to a custom group or to the Quick Access Toolbar.

INSIDE OUT **Decide whether to add a command to the Quick Access Toolbar versus a custom group**

Commands you use that are buried, or that have no home on the default ribbon at all, are great candidates for being added to a custom group or to the Quick Access Toolbar.

The question is, which location is more appropriate?

The answer is all about how often you use the command and how accessible you need it to be.

Consider these three scenarios:

- If you use a command occasionally but it's not represented on the ribbon, create a custom group, add the command to it, and place that group on an appropriate tab.
- If it's truly a command you use frequently—one you use about every day—by all means add it to the Quick Access Toolbar. You'll find that locating it there will save you a lot of clicks.
- If it's a command you're just using today for a single purpose, and you don't expect to use it much again during the life of the project, consider adding it temporarily to the Quick Access Toolbar. When you're done using it, remove it from the Quick Access Toolbar.

As you continue to use Project 2010, you'll get more of a feel for where you like your commands to be and under which conditions.

Creating a Custom Tab

You might find it advantageous to add your custom groups to a custom tab rather than to a built-in tab. You can move built-in groups from other tabs to your custom tab and really customize the layout of commands on the Project 2010 ribbon.

To create a custom tab, follow these steps:

1. Right-click anywhere in the ribbon, and then click Customize The Ribbon in the shortcut menu that appears.
2. In the Customize The Ribbon box, make sure that Main Tabs is selected.
3. In the Main Tabs list, click the tab after which you want the custom tab to appear.

4. Below the Main Tabs list, click the New Tab button.

   The new tab is added, and it contains one new custom group. (See Figure 29-9.) You can now add commands to the custom group, rename the custom group, add other groups to the tab, and rearrange the position of the custom groups and the custom tab.

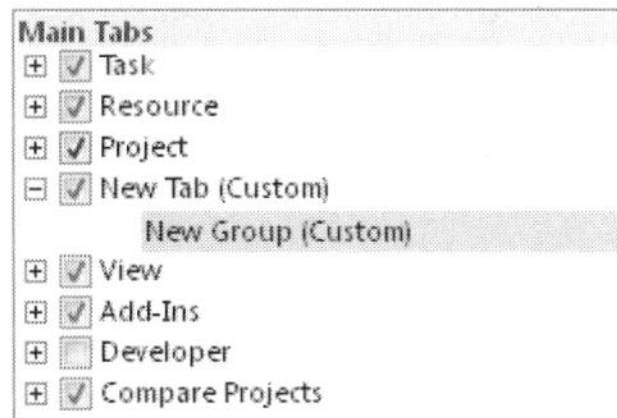

Figure 29-9 The custom tab is inserted after the selected tab and includes a blank custom group.

Changing Tabs, Groups, and Commands

Whether custom or built-in, the tabs, groups, and commands on the Project 2010 ribbon can be modified in several ways. You can rearrange the order of tabs and groups, and you can rename tabs and groups as well.

Rearranging Tabs and Groups

Using the Move Up and Move Down arrow buttons in the Customize The Ribbon dialog box, you can rearrange tabs, groups, and, in certain cases, commands.

First open the dialog box by right-clicking anywhere in the ribbon, and then clicking Customize The Ribbon in the shortcut menu. In the Customize The Ribbon box, make sure that Main Tabs is selected.

Rearrange ribbon elements as follows:

- **Change the order of tabs** In the Main Tabs list, click the tab you want to move to a different location, and then click the Move Up or Move Down arrow button until the tab is positioned where you want it.

- **Change the order of groups** In the Main Tabs list, click the group you want to move to a different location on the tab, and then click the Move Up or Move Down arrow button until the group is positioned where you want it.

- **Move a group to a different tab** In the Main Tabs list, click the group you want to move to a different tab, and then click the Move Up or Move Down arrow button until the group moves to the adjacent tab. Keep clicking Move Up or Move Down until it's located on the tab and in the position you want.

- **Rearrange commands in a custom group** Although you cannot rearrange commands in a built-in group, you can rearrange commands in a custom group. This is true for built-in commands and for macro commands you create yourself. In the Main Tabs list, navigate to and expand the tab and custom group that contain the commands you want to rearrange. Commands in built-in groups are dimmed and unavailable for any changes; commands in custom groups are shown in black. Click the command you want to move, and then click the Move Up or Move Down arrow button until the command is located where you want it within the custom group.

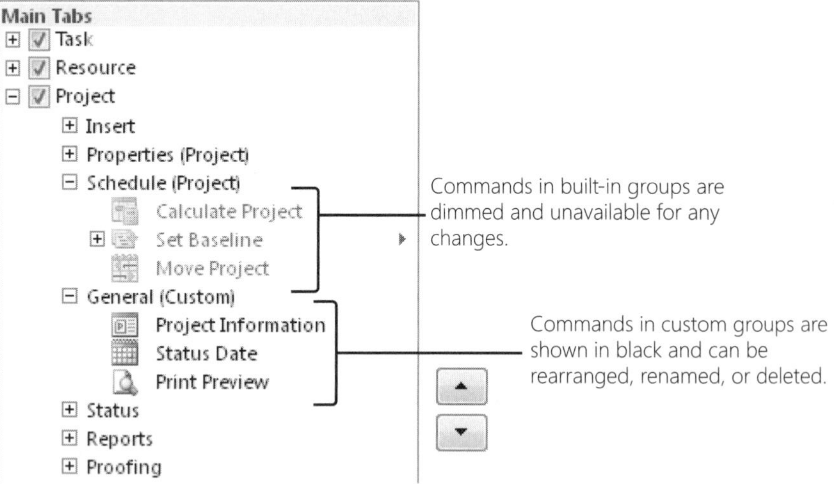

Renaming Tabs and Groups

You can rename built-in or custom tabs, as well as built-in or custom groups.

To start, open the Customize The Ribbon dialog box by right-clicking anywhere in the ribbon and then clicking Customize The Ribbon in the shortcut menu. In the Customize The Ribbon box, make sure that Main Tabs is selected.

To rename a tab or a group, select the item in the Main Tabs list, and then click the Rename button located near the lower-right corner of the dialog box. The Rename dialog box appears.

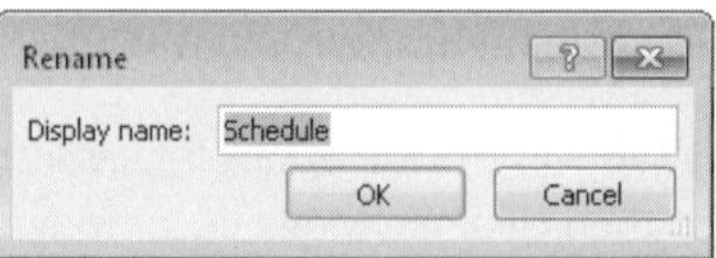

Type the new name in the Display Name box, and then click OK. Click OK in the Customize The Ribbon dialog box, and you're done.

Changing the Name or Button Icon for a Command

Along with renaming tabs and groups, you can rename commands added to custom groups. This means that the only elements you cannot rename are commands in built-in groups. You can also change the button icon for commands added to custom groups. This is true for built-in commands as well as for macro commands you've created. If it's in a custom group, the command is fair game for you to change.

To change the name and button icon of a command in a custom group, follow these steps:

1. Right-click anywhere in the ribbon, and then click Customize The Ribbon in the shortcut menu that appears.
2. In the Customize The Ribbon box, make sure that Main Tabs is selected.
3. In the Main Tabs list, expand the tab and custom group to navigate to the location of the command you want to change.
4. Click the name of the command whose name or icon you want to change.

   Remember, you can change the name or icon only for a command you've added to a custom group. Commands in built-in groups cannot be changed.
5. Below the tab listing, click the Rename button.

   The Rename dialog box appears, as shown in Figure 29-10. The Rename dialog box includes not only the Display Name box but a symbol gallery of options for the command's button icon.

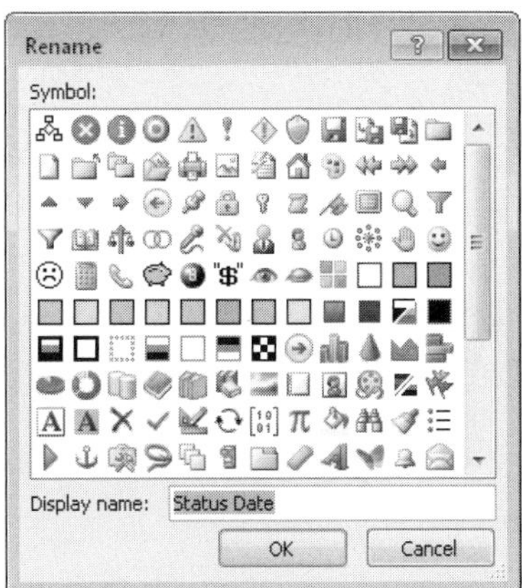

Figure 29-10 Use the Rename dialog box to change the name or button icon for the command in your custom group.

6. If you want to change the display name of the command, type the new name in the Display Name box.

   If you want to change the icon shown for the command, find and click the icon you want in the symbol gallery.

7. Click OK in the Rename dialog box, and then click OK in the Project Options dialog box.

8. In the ribbon, navigate to the tab where the custom group resides.

   You'll see that the command name or icon has been updated according to your specifications. (See Figure 29-11.)

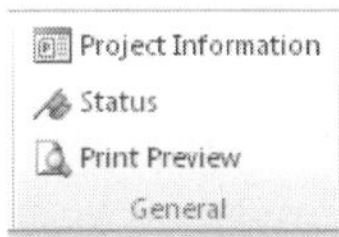

Figure 29-11 The command appears with its new name and button icon.

For specifics on naming and assigning a button icon to a macro command, see "Changing the Macro Icon or Display Name" on page 1185.

Removing Tabs, Groups, and Commands

You can remove a built-in tab or group and easily add it back later should the need arise. This can help remove clutter from your ribbon or make room for your own custom groups of commands. You can replace a built-in group that doesn't quite have the combination of commands you prefer with a custom group that has exactly the commands you want.

You can remove any tab, any group, and certain commands from the Project 2010 ribbon. The following rules apply:

- You can remove a built-in tab from the ribbon. When you do this, all the groups and commands it contains are also removed. A built-in tab can easily be added back if needed.

- You can delete a custom tab, along with any groups and commands it contains.

- You can remove built-in groups from a tab. They can easily be added back if needed.
- You can delete custom groups from a tab.
- You can remove commands only from a custom group. Commands in a built-in group are always dimmed and unavailable for any changes.

Note

An easy way to see whether you can remove a ribbon element is to click it in the Main Tabs list in the Customize The Ribbon dialog box. If the Remove button is available when you click an element, you can remove that element. If the Remove button is dimmed, you cannot remove that element. The Remove button should be dimmed only for commands in built-in groups.

To remove any tab, any group, or a command in a custom group, follow these steps:

1. Right-click anywhere in the ribbon, and then click Customize The Ribbon in the shortcut menu to open the Customize The Ribbon dialog box.
2. In the Customize The Ribbon box, make sure that Main Tabs is selected.
3. In the Main Tabs list, navigate to and click the name of the tab, group, or command you want to remove.

   Remember that only commands in a custom group can be removed. Commands in built-in groups cannot be changed in any way.

<< Remove

4. Click the Remove button, which is located between the two list boxes.

   The item selected in the Customize The Ribbon list is removed from the box. If it's a built-in tab or group, it's still available in the Choose Commands From box. Whether it's a built-in command or a macro, it also remains available in the Choose Commands From box. However, if it's a custom tab or custom group, clicking the Remove button completely deletes it.
5. When you are finished removing ribbon elements, click OK in the Customize The Ribbon dialog box.

   Your changes are shown in the Project 2010 ribbon.

INSIDE OUT

Replace a built-in group with a custom group

By now it's very clear that you can't customize commands in a built-in group. You can't add or remove them. You can't rename them or change their button icons. You can't even rearrange their order.

However, you can work around this limitation. You can create a custom group and essentially replicate a built-in group with the same or similar commands. Then you can remove the built-in group and add the custom group in its place. In this group, you're free to change the commands however you want to.

This replication and replacement might take a bit of work, but for certain groups you use a lot it can be worth the effort.

Restore a Removed Tab or Group

When you remove a built-in tab or group, it remains available in the Choose Commands From box in the Customize The Ribbon dialog box. A removed tab retains all its properties and contents, including its component groups. Likewise, a removed group retains all its commands.

To restore a removed tab or group, follow these steps:

1. Open the Customize The Ribbon dialog box.
2. In the Choose Commands From box, click either All Tabs or Main Tabs.
3. Navigate to and click the tab or group you want to restore to your ribbon. If a tab or group is not already on the ribbon, when you click its name in the Choose Commands From list, the Add button between the two list boxes becomes available. If the Add button is dimmed, this means the selected tab or group is already on the ribbon, and you don't need to restore it after all.
4. In the Customize The Ribbon list, navigate to and click the element below which you want to add the tab or group you are restoring. If you're restoring a tab, click the name of the tab that should come before the restored tab. If you're restoring a group, expand the tab and click the name of the group that should come before the restored group.
5. Click the Add button between the two list boxes.
6. The selected tab or group is restored to the ribbon, just below the element you selected in the Customize The Ribbon list.
7. When you are finished restoring elements to the ribbon, click OK.

Resetting Ribbon Defaults

It's safe to experiment with the ribbon because you can always reset it to its default configuration. You can reset just a selected tab or the entire ribbon. When you reset defaults, any changes you made to the tabs, groups, or commands are reversed. This includes any custom tabs, groups, or commands you added, so be sure to reset with care.

Resetting the Selected Tab

To reset the selected tab, follow these steps:

1. Right-click anywhere in the ribbon, and then click Customize The Ribbon in the shortcut menu.
2. In the Customize The Ribbon box, be sure that Main Tabs is selected.
3. In the Main Tabs list, navigate to and click the name of the tab you want to reset to its original default settings.
4. Click the Reset button, which is located below the Customize The Ribbon list.
5. In the menu that appears, click Reset Only Selected Ribbon Tab.

   The selected tab is reset to its original defaults.
6. Click OK in the Customize The Ribbon dialog box.

Resetting the Ribbon to All Default Settings

When you choose to reset the entire ribbon to all default settings, you lose any customizations you made to the ribbon. This includes any custom tabs, any custom groups, and any commands added to those groups. Resetting the entire ribbon also resets the Quick Access Toolbar to its default commands.

To reset the entire ribbon to all default settings, follow these steps:

1. Right-click anywhere in the ribbon, and then click Customize The Ribbon in the shortcut menu.
2. Click the Reset button, and then click Reset All Customizations.

   A message appears that confirms that you want to remove all customizations for the ribbon and Quick Access Toolbar.
3. Click Yes.

   The entire ribbon and the Quick Access Toolbar are reset to their original defaults.
4. Click OK in the Customize The Ribbon dialog box.

Note

If either the Reset Only Selected Ribbon Tab or the Reset All Customizations command is dimmed, this means there's nothing to reset. These features have been reset already or no customizations have been made.

Sharing a Custom Ribbon and Quick Access Toolbar

NEW!

If you create a customized ribbon and Quick Access Toolbar that can help your team work with Project 2010 more effectively, you can export those settings. Your co-workers can then import the settings into their installation of Project 2010 and use the same customized ribbon you're using. You share a custom ribbon by exporting and importing custom ribbon settings.

Note

In previous versions of Microsoft Project, the Organizer was used to share custom menus and toolbars. In Project 2010, the Organizer is not used for sharing ribbon customizations; instead, the Import/Export button in the Customize The Ribbon dialog box performs this function.

Exporting a Custom Ribbon for Another User

To export ribbon and Quick Access Toolbar customizations for another user, follow these steps:

1. Right-click anywhere in the ribbon, and then click Customize The Ribbon in the shortcut menu to open the Customize The Ribbon dialog box.
2. Click the Import/Export button near the lower-right corner of the dialog box, and then click Export All Customizations.

   The File Save dialog box appears.
3. Navigate to the drive and folder where you want to save your customizations file. In the File Name box, change the name of the file if necessary.

   By default, the file name is Project Customizations.exportedUI.

4. Click the Save button.

   The customization file is saved in the location you specified. You can now make that file available to your co-workers, for example, by placing it on a shared network drive or by e-mailing the file to them.

Importing a Custom Ribbon from Another User

To import a custom ribbon and Quick Access Toolbar file from a user who has exported his or her customizations, follow these steps:

1. Obtain the ribbon customization file from the other user, and place the file on your computer or network file system where you can find it.

2. In Project 2010, right-click anywhere in the ribbon, and then click Customize The Ribbon in the shortcut menu.

3. Click the Import/Export button near the lower-right corner of the dialog box, and then click Import Customization File.

   The File Open dialog box appears.

4. Navigate to the drive and folder where the exported customizations file is stored.

   By default, the file name is Project Customizations.exportedUI.

5. Click the customizations file, and then click Open.

   A message asks if you want to replace all current ribbon and Quick Access Toolbar customizations.

6. Click Yes.

   The customizations from the imported file are now applied to your ribbon and Quick Access Toolbar.

CHAPTER 30

Automating Your Work with Macros

One of the easiest ways to increase your day-to-day productivity with Microsoft Project 2010 is to use macros. A macro can automate repetitive, tedious, or complex tasks, which frees your time and brainpower for actually managing your projects.

This chapter provides a basic understanding of what macros are and how you can create them to automate tasks you need to do frequently. Typically, you create a macro by recording the incremental steps in any given activity in Project 2010. This means that little (if any) programming is required to create a macro.

Understanding Macros

Washing the dishes—what a chore. Pick up a dirty plate, wash it with soapy water, rinse it off, and then dry it. It's the same every time. But with a dishwasher, all the tedium of washing, rinsing, and drying is handled by the machine, leaving you free to do better things with your time. In much the same way, suppose you need to format and print a certain report every Friday. You don't want to perform the same tedious series of commands week after week; you just want your report ready before the meeting. What you need is a macro.

What Is a Macro?

Basically, a *macro* is a shortcut that performs a series of commands. Rather than manually performing each step necessary to complete a task, you tell the software what each step is, what needs to be accomplished in each step, and in what order the steps must occur. Then you designate a way to set this series of commands in motion.

To do this in Project 2010, you have Microsoft Visual Basic for Applications (VBA), a subset of the highly popular Microsoft Visual Basic programming language. VBA is a macro language that is not only powerful but easy to understand and use. What's more, the tools available in Project 2010 make creating macros as easy as can be. Most macros can be created without ever seeing, much less writing, VBA code.

Why Use Macros?

When you use Project 2010 (or any other business productivity software), you use it because it makes doing your job easier and more efficient. One of the reasons that software can make you more productive is that its features and commands are, in a sense, a collection of macros that accomplish tasks associated with the business of the software. These "macros" perform tasks that software designers learned their customers want to do. But what the designers can't do is create all the features that every customer wants. This is where macros can prove so useful.

Because individual users can create a macro to accomplish some particular task, you can essentially customize the software by adding features that support the particular way you do your job.

For example, let's say that you have to print that report every Friday. Before you can print anything, you have to do the following:

- Choose the appropriate view of your project data.
- Choose among several filters to exclude unwanted tasks.
- Choose how to sort the data.
- Choose the report format you need.

After you open the project plan, you might have to click your mouse well over a dozen times before you can print the report. With a macro to perform all those steps for you, printing the report is reduced to just a few mouse clicks.

Just because macros can be used to perform a complex series of steps doesn't mean that every macro has to be elaborate. Maybe you have certain simple things you do in Project 2010 all the time, such as turn the Planning Wizard on or off. By recording a macro and adding it to a custom group on the ribbon, you have a convenient one-click method for turning the Planning Wizard on or off.

For more information about adding a macro to a custom group on the ribbon, see "Adding Macro Commands to the Ribbon" on page 1182.

Creating Macros

The easiest and quickest way to create a macro, especially one that you will use to automate a lengthy series of steps, is to record the steps that make up the activity. Recording a macro is just what it sounds like: Start the macro recorder, perform the series of actions you want the macro to do, and then stop the recorder. In most cases, there's no need to edit the VBA code generated by the recorder.

For more information about creating macros by writing VBA code directly, including how to edit macros, see the Microsoft Project 2010 Software Development Kit (SDK), available online at *http://msdn.microsoft.com/en-us/library/ms512767.aspx*.

Understanding the Record Macro Dialog Box

Before you record a macro, you must first prepare your Project 2010 environment for recording by setting the conditions required for the steps in the macro to occur. Such conditions might include something obvious, such as opening a particular project file, but they can also include steps such as selecting a certain task or resource. You should also have a clear plan for what you want to record. Any mistakes you make while the macro recorder is running are included in the macro. After you set the conditions and make your plan, you're ready to begin recording.

Macros

On the View tab, in the Macros group, click the arrow under Macros. In the menu that appears, click Record Macro. The Record Macro dialog box appears (see Figure 30-1), in which you enter information about the macro (such as a name and a description) and assign it a shortcut key if you like.

Figure 30-1 The decisions you make in the Record Macro dialog box determine when you can use a macro as well as aspects of how it behaves when it runs.

For more information about macro keyboard shortcuts, see "Creating Keyboard Shortcuts" on page 1180.

Three settings in the Record Macro dialog box are even more important than the name of the macro or the keyboard shortcut you might use to run it:

- **Store Macro In** Use the choices in the Store Macro In box to specify whether to store the macro in this project only or in the project global template. If you choose This Project, the macro is stored in the file with the project that is currently open and is available only when that project is open. If you choose Global File (the default), the macro is stored in the project global template file (global.mpt) and is available whenever Project 2010 is running, regardless of whether a particular project (or any project at all) is open.
- **Row References** Accept the default setting of Relative if you want Project 2010 to record relative row references. With this setting, when the macro runs, it always attempts to move the same number of rows from the selected cell when the macro encounters the command to select a new cell.

  For example, suppose that a cell in row 1 is selected and you select a cell in row 4 while recording the macro. From then on, every time the macro runs and encounters the command to select a new cell, it moves three rows from whatever cell was selected before the macro was run.

  Select the Absolute option if you want to be certain that a particular row—based on the selected cell's row ID—is selected when a macro runs. In the example just given, your macro will always select a cell in row 4, regardless of which cell is selected before the macro is run.
- **Column References** Unlike row references, the default setting for column references is Absolute, based on the selected field. No matter where fields are positioned, absolute column references select the same column every time. Relative column references work just like relative row references.

Where the Macros Are: In the Project or the Global

When creating a new macro, you need to decide whether you want to store the macro in the current project or in the project global template file. Which is best? Well, that depends. Table 30-1 lays out the conditions and recommendations for different situations.

Table 30-1 **Where to Store the Macros**

Store the macro in the project if	Store the macro in the global if
Certain very specific conditions must be met in the project plan for the macro to run successfully. For example, you might need to select a particular task before running your macro, or you might need to select a varying group of resources.	Conditions aren't as stringent for the macro. Many formatting macros can fit this category.
You're distributing the project to others and want the project to be fully self-contained, without also having to provide the project global template.	The macro is entirely for your own use, for the use of individuals using the same project plan on the same computer, or for the use of individuals who all have access to the project global template, through a network share, for example.
You're not expecting to edit the macro.	The macro is used in multiple projects or by multiple users, and you know you might need to adjust the macro and want to make the change just once. When you edit a macro in the project global template, the change is implemented the next time any user accesses the global template to open his project. That is, you don't have to edit the macro 30 times for 30 different users on 30 different computers.
You've set up a number of keyboard shortcuts, and you're concerned about the limited number of keyboard shortcuts in the global template and keyboard shortcuts in the project getting in each other's way.	Keyboard shortcuts are not a big issue for your macros, or you're certain that macros in the project plan and the global template use different keyboard shortcuts.

Share Keyboard Shortcuts between the Global and the Project

Because all the macros in a particular project must share the available keyboard shortcuts and macro names, only one macro in a project can use Ctrl+A as a keyboard shortcut, for example. This rule also applies to the project global template file, which is open whenever Project 2010 is running.

This means if you use Ctrl+A as a keyboard shortcut in the project global template, no other macro in the global template can use that shortcut. If you store your Ctrl+A macro in the project file, however, you can store another macro in another project and assign Ctrl+A as its keyboard shortcut as well.

INSIDE OUT **Absolute column references can be trickier than expected**

The decision to use absolute column references might seem like the best solution in all cases, but absolute column references are based on the selected field. Because fields can be moved, you might sometimes get unexpected results.

For example, suppose that you record a macro using absolute column references in a project you share with someone else. When you record the macro, you select the third column, which contains the Start field. At some point, however, your co-worker opens the project and inserts the Duration field as the third column.

The next time you run the macro, the fourth column is selected because that's the new location of the Start field. If you assumed that the third column would always be selected because absolute column references are "safe" and that's where you always put the Start field, your macro is now broken.

Knowing When to Say "When"

Knowing when to stop the recorder can be as important as the recording environment itself. For an automatic procedure like a macro to be truly trustworthy—and therefore useful—it should have an ending point that is intuitive, or at least easy to remember.

For example, the Bold button in the Font group of the Task tab is basically a macro to automate clicking Bold in the Font Style list in the Font dialog box. If you have already selected a word, you know that clicking the Bold button formats the word a certain way and then stops. If you haven't selected a word, you know that the Bold button turns on bold formatting for anything you type until you click it again to turn bold formatting off. Both endings are so easy to remember that they've probably become intuitive for you.

The same should be true for any macro you record. It should be easy for you to remember what conditions must be met before you can run the macro, what the macro will do, and when it will stop. A macro that performs a 20-step procedure for you is no good if you're afraid to run it because you can't remember what it might do along the way.

Recording a Macro

Suppose you need to generate that weekly report. The report you print every Friday requires you to do the following:

- Change the view to the Tracking Gantt.
- Apply a filter to display only incomplete tasks.

- Sort the tasks by finish date in ascending order.
- Print the view.

> **Note**
>
> **Before recording a macro, make sure that all your planned steps will take you successfully through to the end of the process you want to program. In other words, make sure that any required conditions are met for the macro to be completed.**

You've decided to automate the steps needed to print your Friday report by recording them in a macro. Follow these steps to record the macro:

1. On the View tab, in the Macros group, click the arrow under Macros, and then click Record Macro.

   The Record Macro dialog box appears.

2. In the Macro Name box, enter a name for your new macro; for example, Friday_Report.

   A macro name cannot contain spaces, but you can use the underscore character to represent a space if you want. Although the macro name can contain letters, numbers, and the underscore character, the name must begin with a letter. Also, the macro name cannot use any word that Project 2010 reserves as a keyword.

3. In the Store Macro In box, click This Project.
4. In the Description box, change the first line to a descriptive name; for example, **Weekly task report**.
5. Because this macro won't select cells, be sure that the Row References option is set to Relative, and the Column References option is set to Absolute (Field).
6. Click OK to begin recording.

   There's no visible indication that you're in the macro recording mode. However, on the View tab, in the Macros group, click the arrow under Macros, and you can see that the Record Macro command has changed to Stop Recording.

   > **Note**
   >
   > **Remember, everything you do when recording is written into the macro that you are creating, including any mistakes.**

Gantt Chart

7. On the View tab, in the Task Views group, click the arrow next to Gantt Chart, and then click Tracking Gantt.

Filter

8. On the View tab, in the Data group, click the arrow in the Filter box, and then click Incomplete Tasks.

Sort

9. On the View tab, in the Data group, click Sort, and then click By Finish Date.

Print

10. On the File tab, click Print, and then click the Print button.

11. On the View tab, in the Macros group, click the arrow under Macros, and then click Stop Recording.

Note

In this example, we chose to store the macro in the current project, but this would be a good candidate for a macro that could be stored in the project global template file as well. Because all this macro does is change the way the data in a particular project is displayed and then print a report, you could record the steps to open the correct project at the beginning of the macro. You could then print the report whenever Project 2010 is running without having to open the project first yourself.

TROUBLESHOOTING

Your macro doesn't select the correct cell

If your macro is supposed to select cells as it runs, but it selects the wrong ones or even causes an error, one of the following items may be the cause:

- The macro was recorded using one combination of settings for absolute or relative column or row references, but the actual conditions under which the macro is run require a different combination.

  You can re-record the macro by using a combination that better suits the situation under which the macro is run, or you can edit the macro code in the Visual Basic Editor (VBE) and then change the combination manually.

  Table 30-2 shows the different values that should be used when changing the type of column and row references, if you change the reference settings manually:

Table 30-2 **Absolute and Relative References**

Reference	Absolute	Relative
Column	The value for the Column argument is the name of the field in quotation marks.	The value for the Column argument is a positive number, indicating the number of the column.
Row	The value for the Row argument is a positive number, indicating the number of the row, and the RowRelative argument is False.	The value for the Row argument may be either a negative or positive number. The RowRelative argument is either True or is missing (the default value is True).

The columns for the row number and the Indicators field (if showing) are both counted when using relative column references. When you are manually editing column references in a macro, keep in mind that the first "normal" column is actually column 3.

- The macro assumes that a particular cell or item has been selected before the macro is run.

  You could try to remember to check that the proper cell is selected before you run the macro, but re-recording the macro (or editing it in the Visual Basic Editor) to select the proper cell before the macro does anything else solves the problem and also makes the macro more robust.

- The column (or row, if it is for a subtask) containing the cell to select may have been hidden, or the row may have been deleted.

  Most of the solutions to this problem involve writing complicated Visual Basic code, so the best solution, until you're more comfortable editing your macros in the Visual Basic Editor, is to be sure that the proper conditions are met before running your macro. Using column references can also help you spot this problem early on because your macro will cause an error on the line that refers to the missing column, which makes it easier for you to guess what the problem is.

Looking at Macro Code

For many people, knowing how to record and play back a macro is sufficient for most of their needs. But what if you make a minor mistake while recording a macro? What if you record a complex macro that references a project by file name and then the file name is changed? Although you might not ever need to know how to write VBA code, much less create an entire macro with it, the first step to making simple changes or corrections is to understand how simple and logical the macro code can be.

For more information about the Visual Basic Editor, refer to its Help system. On the View tab, in the Macros group, click the arrow under Macros, and then click Visual Basic. Click Help, Microsoft Visual Basic for Applications Help.

If you were to start the Visual Basic Editor included as part of Project 2010 and open the Friday_Report macro, the code would look similar to the following:

```
Sub Friday_Report()
' Macro Weekly task report
' Macro Recorded Tue 11/2/10 by Steve Masters.
    ViewApplyEx Name:="Tracking Ga&ntt", ApplyTo:=0
    FilterApply Name:="Incomplete Tasks"
    Sort Key1:="Finish", Renumber:=False
    FilePrint
End Sub
```

The code is short and reasonably simple. You might already have some guesses about what different sections of the code mean, such as information that also appears in the Project 2010 interface. Table 30-3 describes each line in the VBA code.

Table 30-3 **Breakdown of Code in the Friday_Report Macro**

Macro code	What it means
`Sub Friday_Report()`	It's the beginning of the macro. *Sub* is short for subroutine, which is what a macro really is. The text that follows is the name of the macro.
`' Macro Weekly task report` `‘ Macro Recorded Tue 11/2/10 by Steve Masters.`	Any line that starts with an apostrophe is a comment and is ignored by Visual Basic. You can use comments anywhere in a macro to remind yourself of what the different parts do.
`ViewApplyEx Name:= “Tracking Ga&ntt”`	This line changes the view to the Tracking Gantt. The ampersand (&) comes before the letter that acts as an access or shortcut key for the view.
`FilterApply Name:= “I&ncomplete Tasks”`	This line applies a filter to display only incomplete tasks.
`Sort Key1:= “Finish”, Ascending1:=True Renumber:=False`	This line sorts the tasks by finish date in ascending order without renumbering the task IDs.
`FilePrint`	This line prints the view.
`End Sub`	It's the end of the macro, like the period at the end of a sentence.

If, after recording the macro, you decide that you prefer to sort the tasks in descending order, it doesn't take much time or trouble to record the macro all over again. But it takes even less time to edit the macro and change True to False in the line *Sort Key1:= "Finish", Ascending1:=True*.

Follow these steps to start the Visual Basic Editor so that you can edit the macro code:

1. On the View tab, in the Macros group, click the Macros.

   Pressing Alt+F8 is another way to quickly display the Macros dialog box.

2. In the Macro Name list, click the name of the macro you want to edit.

3. Click the Edit button.

   The Visual Basic Editor starts and displays your macro code. (See Figure 30-2.) You can now begin editing the macro code.

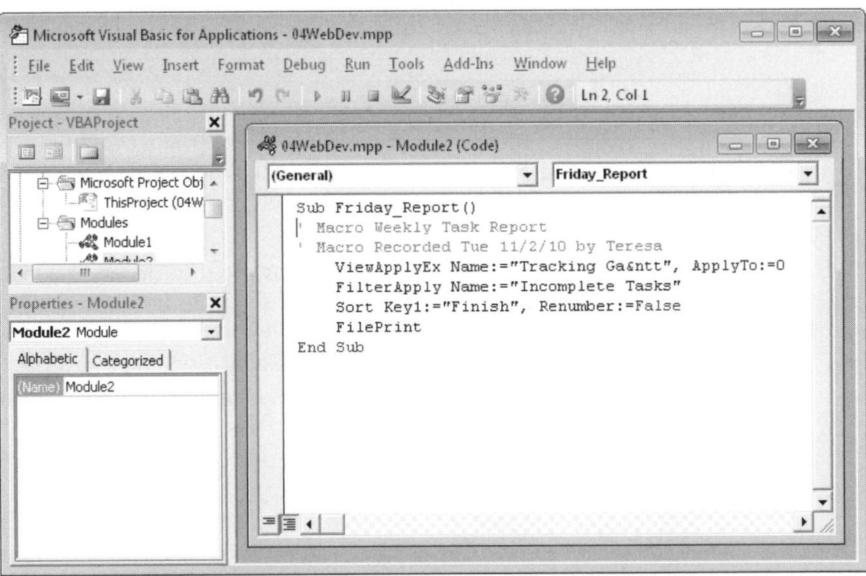

Figure 30-2 Open the Visual Basic Editor to review and edit your macro code.

Running Macros

To run a macro, select it from the list of available macros in the Macros dialog box, as follows:

1. On the View tab, in the Macros group, click Macros.

2. In the Macro Name list, click the name of the macro you want to run. (See Figure 30-3.)

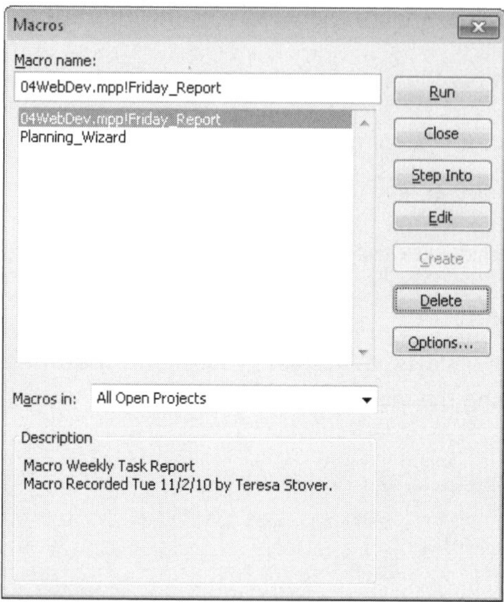

Figure 30-3 Select the macro you want to run from the Macros dialog box.

3. Click the Run button.

   The macro runs according to the steps you recorded in that macro.

It's certainly easy enough to press F8 and then select and run your macro. However, you can make your macro more readily accessible by assigning a keyboard shortcut or by adding a command to the ribbon. Either of these methods can be handy for macros you use fairly often.

Creating Keyboard Shortcuts

Key commands such as Ctrl+C are the oldest and most common shortcuts to access software features, especially for displaying dialog boxes or performing some quick action. Unfortunately, as more and more keyboard shortcuts are assigned to software features, fewer of these simple combinations are left for macros.

In Project 2010, a keyboard shortcut for a macro must be a combination of the Ctrl key and a letter. Because Project 2010 has many built-in keyboard shortcuts, the only letters available for macro shortcuts are A, E, J, M, Q, T, and Y.

Note

If you use other letters, such as Ctrl+B or Ctrl+C, that are already used by the software, you don't get an error message, and it appears that you're allowed to use them. However, the keyboard shortcut is not applied to your macro, and it retains its original coding; for example, Bold for Ctrl+B or Copy for Ctrl+C.

You can assign a keyboard shortcut to a macro when you record it, as described in "Creating Macros" on page 1171. You can also assign a keyboard shortcut to a macro any time after you create it by using the Macro Options dialog box.

Follow these steps to open the Macro Options dialog box:

1. On the View tab, in the Macros group, click Macros.
2. In the Macro Name list, click the name of the macro you want to modify.
3. Click the Options button.

   The Macro Options dialog box appears, as shown in Figure 30-4.

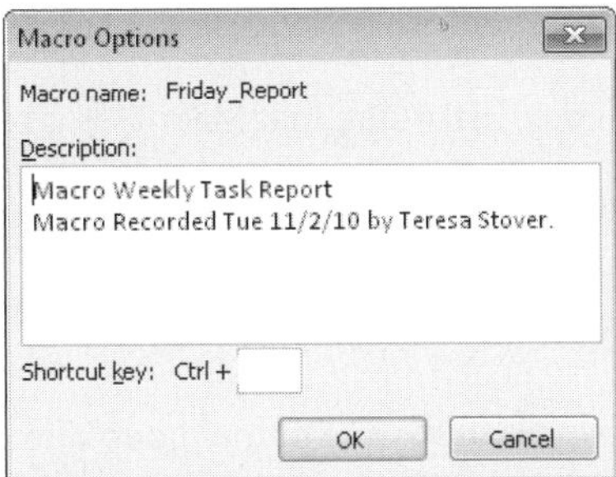

Figure 30-4 Change a macro's description or shortcut key in the Macro Options dialog box.

4. In the Shortcut Key box, type the letter you want to use.

   You can also edit the macro description if you want.

Note

To take the most advantage of the quick access provided by keyboard shortcuts, assign them to frequently used macros that perform simple tasks such as opening a dialog box.

Adding Macro Commands to the Ribbon

You can add a macro as a command on the ribbon. This can be very convenient, especially if you don't care to rely on your memory and want the macro always at your fingertips. By placing a macro on the ribbon, you can:

- Forget the keyboard shortcut.
- Display the name of the macro as part of the button.
- Add it to a custom group on any tab (or a custom tab), and group it with other related commands.

Creating a Custom Group to Hold Your Macros

Because the commands in existing groups are fixed, you can add a macro command only to a custom group you create. However, that custom group can be on an existing tab, such as the Task tab or the View tab, or you can create a custom tab instead.

To create a custom group on the ribbon, follow these steps:

1. On the File tab, click Options.
2. In the left pane of the Project Options dialog box, click Customize Ribbon.
3. In the Customize The Ribbon box, make sure that Main Tabs is selected.
4. In the Main Tabs box, click the plus sign next to the tab where you want to add your custom group.

   The tab expands to show the existing groups on that tab.
5. In the expanded list of groups, click the name of the group after which you want to add your custom group.
6. Click the New Group button below the list.

   New Group (Custom) appears below the group you selected, as you can see in Figure 30-5.

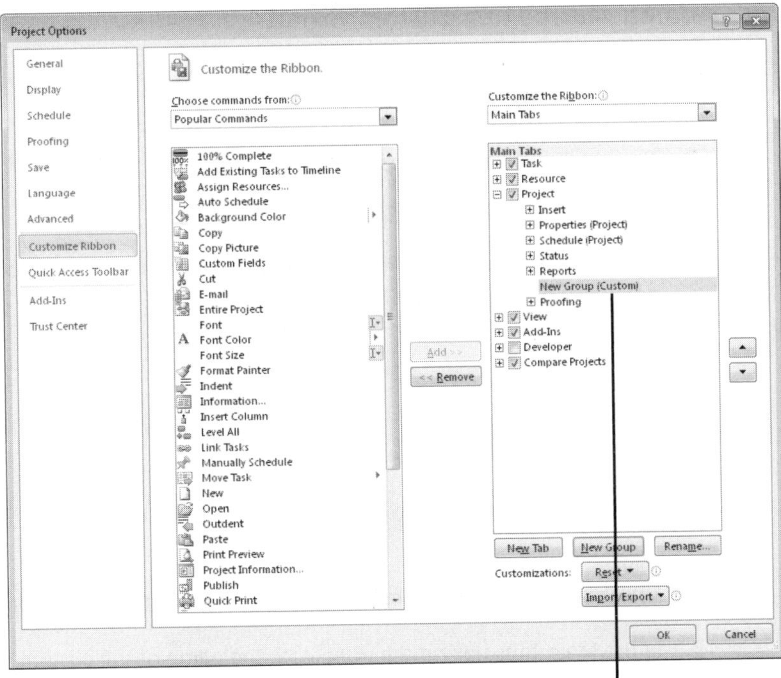

After clicking the New Group button, the new group label appears below the group selected in the list.

Figure 30-5 Create a custom group to contain your macros on the ribbon.

7. With New Group (Custom) still selected, click the Rename button below the list.

   The Rename dialog box appears, showing a gallery of buttons.

8. In the Display Name box, type the name you want for your custom group, and then click OK.

   Ignore the buttons in the gallery for now. You're just creating the group name.

9. If you want to change the position of the custom group, click its name, and then click the up or down arrow until it's located where you want.

Note

If you need to remove a custom group name from the list, click the name and then click the Remove button in the middle of the dialog box.

Adding Macros to a Custom Group

After you create a custom group, you have a place to add your macro. To add a macro to a custom group on the ribbon:

1. Be sure the Project Options dialog box is still open.
2. In the Choose Commands From box, click Macros.

   All macros available from the project global template or from the current project plan are listed. (See Figure 30-6.)

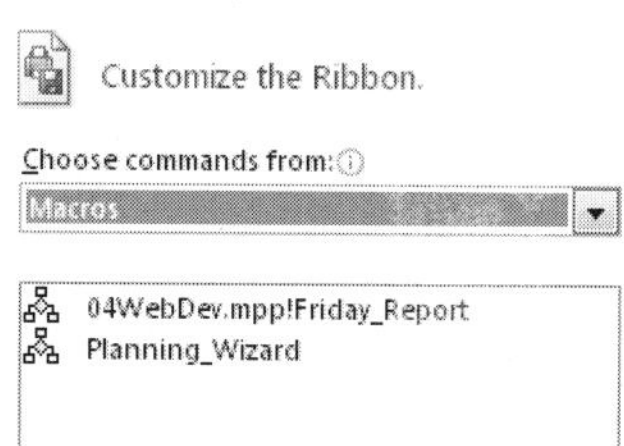

Figure 30-6 Your macros are listed, ready to be added to the custom group.

3. In the Main Tabs box on the right, click the name of the custom group to which you want to add the macro.
4. In the Macros list on the left, click the name of the macro you want to add to custom group, and then click the Add button.

   The macro name appears under the custom group name, as shown in Figure 30-7.

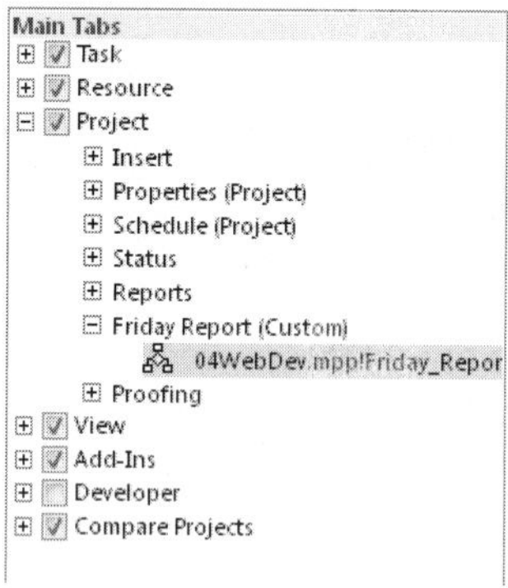

Figure 30-7 Add your macro to the custom group.

5. Click OK in the Project Options dialog box.

6. Navigate to the tab where you added the custom group that now contains your macro.

   You'll see your macro name and the generic macro icon in your custom group. (See Figure 30-8.)

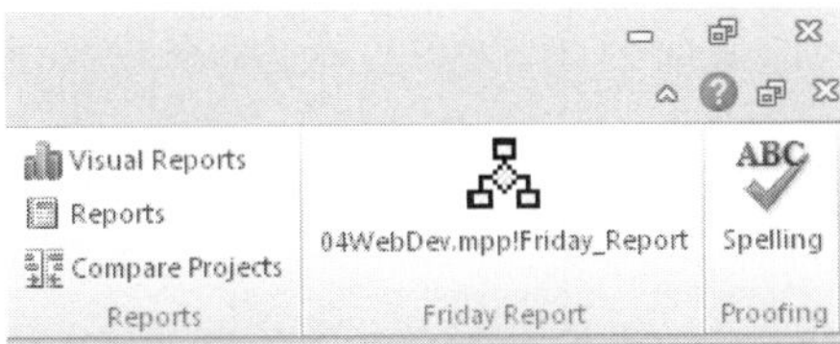

Figure 30-8 Your macro appears in your custom group on the tab you specified.

Changing the Macro Icon or Display Name

When you add a macro to a custom group, you initially see the generic macro icon and the name of the macro. To change to a different icon or display name for the macro, follow these steps:

1. On the File tab, Options.

2. In the left pane of the Project Options dialog box, click Customize Ribbon.

3. In the Customize The Ribbon box, make sure that Main Tabs is selected.

4. In the Main Tabs box, expand the appropriate tab and custom group where your macro resides.

5. Click the name of the macro whose icon or name you want to customize.

6. Below the tab listing, click Rename button.

   The Rename dialog appears, as shown in Figure 30-9.

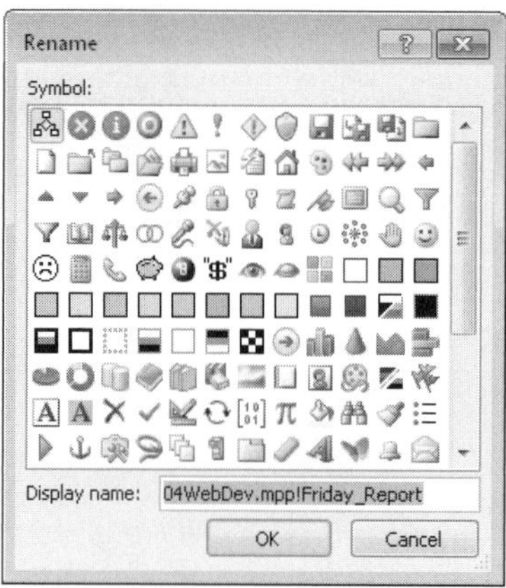

Figure 30-9 Use the Rename dialog box to change the macro or display name for your macro on the ribbon.

7. If you want to change the icon shown for your macro, find and click the icon you want.

   If you want to change the display name of the macro, type the new name in the Display Name box.

8. Click OK in the Rename dialog box, and then click OK in the Project Options dialog box.

9. Navigate to the tab where you added your macro.

   You'll see that the macro name or icon has been updated according to your specifications. (See Figure 30-10.)

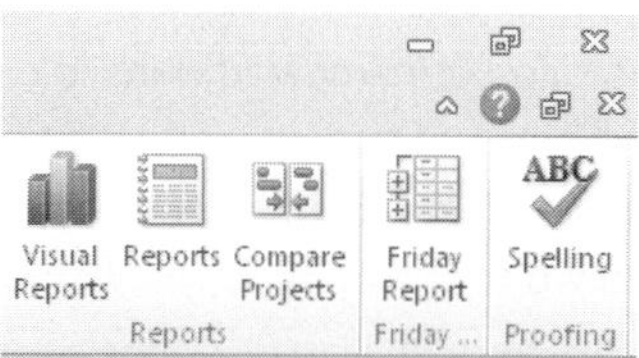

Figure 30-10 Your macro appears with its new name and icon.

For more information about customizing the ribbon, see "Customizing the Project 2010 Ribbon" on page 1153.

CHAPTER 31

Standardizing Projects by Using Templates

With each project you manage, you learn more and more. You practice effective project management methods and see what works and what doesn't, especially for your particular organization and your brand of projects. You gain more knowledge about project management in your specific discipline or industry. Likewise, as you continue to manage projects with Microsoft Project 2010, you increase your proficiency with it as a productivity tool for planning, tracking, and communicating project information.

You can record some of the knowledge you gain from hard-won project management experience by using Project 2010 templates. As you enter the closing stages of a project, saving the project file as a template for future use can be one of your most valuable activities because of the tremendous efficiencies the template can provide for future projects. Templates are special project files in which various types of project information can be stored for use with future projects, either by you or by other project managers.

You can also use templates to save yourself from reinventing that old wheel. Obtain project templates developed by industry experts and adapt them for your project requirements. This can save you time and give you a leg up on planning your next project. You might also find some new approaches to consider that you hadn't thought of before.

Whether a template is based on your own project experiences or someone else's, it can contain the following types of information:

- Tasks
- Durations
- Task sequencing
- Task dependencies
- Phases
- Deliverables

- Milestones
- Generic work, equipment, and cost resources
- Resource assignments
- Average resource rates
- Custom project, task, and resource fields

Templates are also a great means for setting standards and ensuring that you adhere to best practices. If your organization follows a specific methodology in each project, if certain review processes are required at certain stages, or if a specific format is mandated for deliverables, those requirements can be reflected in the template. Similarly, any custom features—including custom fields, tables, views, filters, and so on—that reflect organization standards or that create project conveniences can also become a part of your template.

Understanding the Template Types

Project 2010 has three types of templates:

- **Project template** The *project template* might contain task and resource information that you can use as a basis for starting a new project. It's often based on past project experiences in the organization or the industry. For example, you can find product development templates, commercial construction templates, software project templates, ISO 9001 management templates, and so on.

  A wide variety of project templates are available within Project 2010 and from third-party sources. You can use such a project template as the basis for a new project you're creating. If you're closing a project, you can save and adapt your plan as a project template file for you or others to use and benefit from your experience.

- **Project global template** The *project global template*, also referred to as the *global.mpt file*, is a template that contains elements and settings pertinent to how you use Project 2010. Such elements include views, tables, groups, filters, and reports for customized ways of looking at project information. The project global template can include calendars and macros for specific methods of executing Project 2010 commands and functions. The project global template can also include Project 2010 program settings that define the defaults for editing, scheduling, and calculations, to name a few.

  The project global template is automatically attached to every project file you work with. As the user and project manager, you have control over the content of your project global template, and you can share it with others if you want to.

- **Enterprise global template** If you're set up for enterprise project management using Microsoft Project Professional 2010 and Microsoft Project Server 2010, the *enterprise global template* is automatically attached to every enterprise project you check out or create while Project Professional 2010 is connected to your project server. Think of the enterprise version as being the global template over the project global template, or the "global global."

  This template dictates standards being enforced and customizations made available throughout the enterprise—for example, custom fields, views, and macros. These standards provide for customization and consistency across all projects in an organization. The standards propagated through the enterprise global template also make it possible for project information throughout the enterprise to be compared and analyzed in meaningful ways.

  Because the enterprise global template affects all projects throughout the enterprise, only users who have certain permissions can check out and modify the enterprise global template. Many organizations give that responsibility to one or two project server administrators or portfolio managers.

  The enterprise global template and your local project global template can work together. As long as there's no conflict between elements in your project global template and elements in the enterprise global template, you can create your own standards and customizations for all your own projects. If a conflict exists in such a situation, the enterprise global template takes precedence.

For more information, see "Working with the Enterprise Global Template" on page 859.

Working with the Project Global Template

The project global template—global.mpt—is loaded every time Project 2010 starts. Essentially, the project global template is a collection of custom elements and default settings that are in effect throughout a project file.

Customized Elements Controlled by the Organizer

You can move the following elements between the project global template and the local project file:

- Views
- Reports
- Macros and Microsoft Visual Basic for Applications (VBA) modules
- Tables

- Filters
- Base calendars
- Import/export maps
- Custom fields, including outline codes
- Groups

As you alter settings in your project by customizing views and calendars, modifying tables, and creating sets of custom fields, for example, those changes initially apply to just the current project. If you want your custom settings available to any project opened on your local computer, you can add them to the project global template by using the Organizer, shown in Figure 31-1. Those new settings become your new defaults.

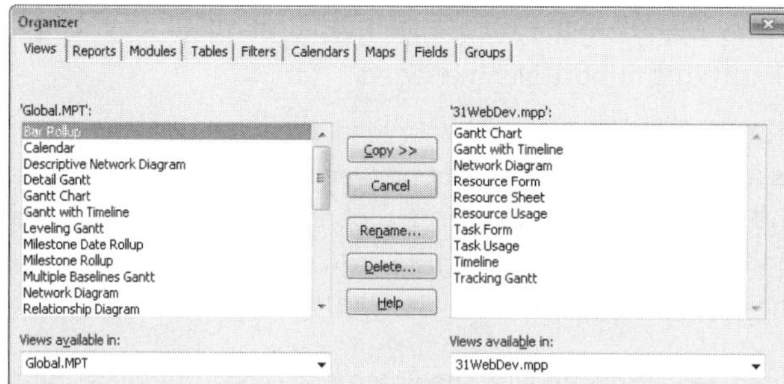

Figure 31-1 Use the Organizer to copy customized elements to the project global template and make those elements available to other projects.

When you create a new view, table, filter, or group, they're added by default to the project global template. If you don't want to use the default setting, you can change it so that you control whether any of these items are added to the project global template. On the File tab, click Options, and then click Advanced in the side pane. Under Display, clear the check box labeled Automatically Add New Views, Tables, Filters, And Groups To The Global.

For more information about the Organizer, see "Sharing Customized Elements Among Projects" on page 1138.

Customized Project Options

The project global template also contains your Microsoft Project–wide settings, which you access by clicking File, Options. In the Project Options dialog box, various categories of options are available—Display, Schedule, Proofing, and so on. Certain settings apply just to the current project file; others apply to Project 2010 as a whole and change the project global template.

In many cases, you can select whether a setting should apply to the current project file or to all project files on this computer. You can use the All New Projects setting to apply specific project settings to your project global template. (See Figure 31-2.)

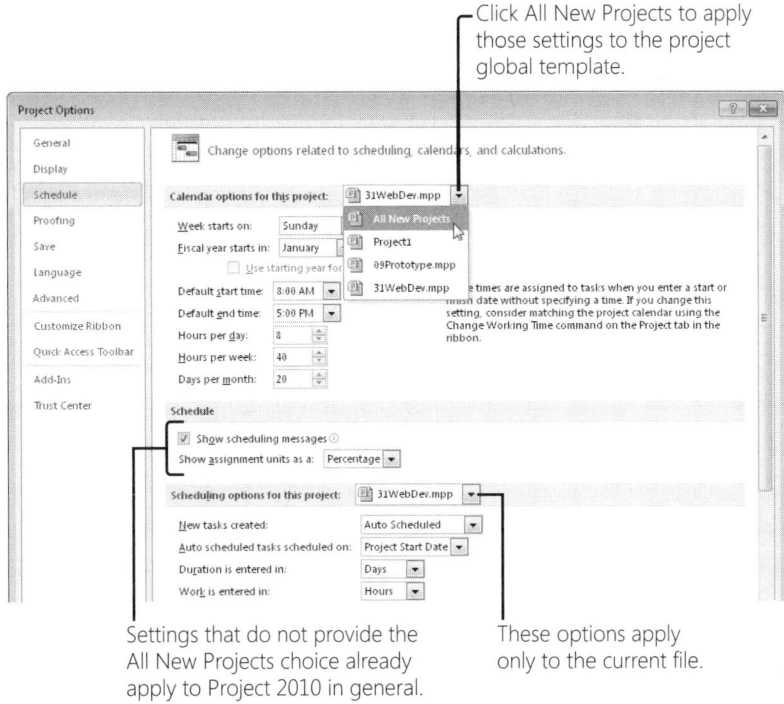

Figure 31-2 Settings that include the Options For This Project menu apply by default only to the current project file. However, you can set those options as a general Project-wide default by clicking All New Projects.

When you change a Project 2010 setting, every new file you open from that point on will reflect that change. When you change a local project setting and then indicate that this applies to all new projects, the project global template is updated for new projects, but that setting is not changed for existing projects.

The Customized Ribbon and Quick Access Toolbar

The project global template also contains your ribbon and Quick Access Toolbar customizations. Any changes you make to the Project 2010 ribbon are universal—you see the same ribbon with every project you open on your computer.

However, you do have a choice with the Quick Access Toolbar. Although the default is for customizations to apply to all projects on your computer, you can choose to make a Quick Access Toolbar customization apply only to the current project.

For more information about customizing the ribbon and Quick Access Toolbar, see Chapter 29, "Customizing the Project 2010 Interface."

Working with Project Templates

A project template is a standardized starting point for a new project. A template can contain task information, resource information, or both. It might be very broad in scope, showing just major phases and generic resource names, for example. Or, the template can be highly detailed, with multiple outline levels for tasks, task durations, task dependencies, and specific resource information.

> **Note**
>
> **Because the terms *project template* and *project global template* are so similar, often you'll hear people refer to the latter simply as the "project global," the "global," or the "global MPT file."**

Project 2010 makes available an ever-growing set of templates for a variety of industries and applications. While many of these templates are designed by Microsoft, many others are designed by third-party sources, such as project management consulting firms, professional societies, and standards organizations.

To supplement these canned templates, you can create your own templates, basing them on previous projects you have completed. It's good practice to adapt and save the plan for a completed project as a template for future use in your organization, either by yourself or by others.

A project template serves as a knowledge base for a certain type of project. It is meant to save you time when planning your new project and to let you build on past project experiences. The project template can also help set and enforce organizational standards. It can disseminate custom features and elements, such as specially designed reports, company-specific base calendars, and modified views.

Starting a New Project from a Template

Whenever you start a new project, you're given the opportunity to choose a template. If you start a project with a template, your project file is populated with information from that template. You then adapt that information to meet your project's specific requirements. When you save the file, you save a new project file and don't overwrite the existing template file. This way, the template remains available for use in its more generic format.

Available Templates

Previous versions of Microsoft Project had a built-in set of templates. In Project 2010, the template list comes directly from Office.com. You can browse through thumbnails of dozens of templates that are provided by Microsoft and third-party sources. When you find one that meets your needs, you can download it to your local computer and start to adapt it immediately.

The following are the categories in which the templates are provided:

- Business development
- Customer service
- Construction and facilities
- Finance and accounting
- General business
- Human resources
- Information technology
- Standards and processes

Examples of specific templates you can download include training rollout, insurance claim processing, ISO 9001 management review, direct mail marketing campaign, Six Sigma DMAIC cycle, SOX (Sarbanes-Oxley Act) compliance and technology options, and vendor evaluation. You can even find templates for Project Management Institute (PMI) process, Project Office plan, and Microsoft Project Server deployment. More templates are being added all the time.

You can see the complete list of the templates on the Backstage view. On the File tab, click New. Under Available Templates, Office.com Templates, click any of the categories; for example, click Plans. Browse through the template thumbnails.

Creating a New Project with a Template

To create a new project from a template, follow these steps:

1. On the File tab, click New.

   The Available Templates Backstage view appears, as shown in Figure 31-3.

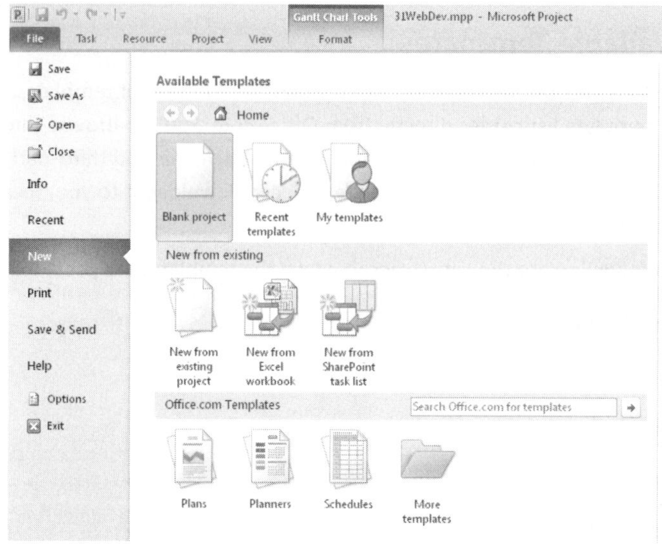

Figure 31-3 Available templates either on your computer or on Office.com are listed in the Backstage view when you click New on the File tab.

2. If the template you want is already on your computer, you can find it by clicking Recent Templates or My Templates.

   Otherwise, click one of the categories under Office.com Templates, and then browse through the templates from Office.com.

3. When you find the template you want and click Download, Create, or OK, the template opens as a new project plan. (See Figure 31-4.)

   Whenever you download a template from Office.com, it becomes available on your computer, and you can find it under My Templates on the Available Templates Backstage view.

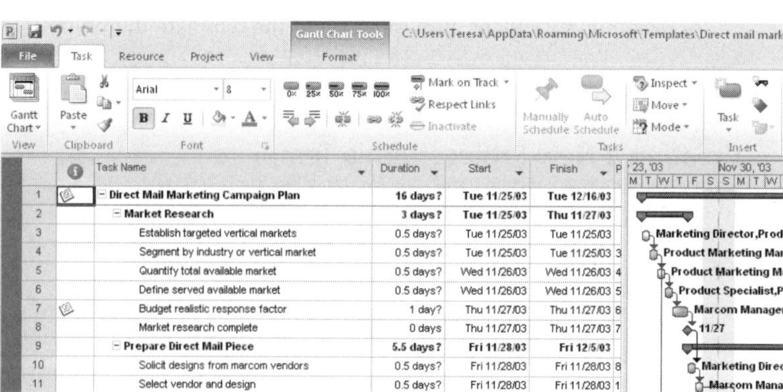

Figure 31-4 A new project file is created based on your selected template.

INSIDE OUT **Project templates are not well-organized**

While the Office.com Templates page offers certain conveniences, it's a pain to scroll through. It's a rather long list, the templates are not in any particular order—neither alphabetical or disciplinary—and there's no way to sort or search. You just have to browse the titles until you find something that might work.

An alternative is to go to *http://office.microsoft.com/en-us/templates*, click See All Categories, and then click Plans. Click the subcategory you want, for example, Business, and then browse through the list. When you go to the Office.com Templates page like this, you can sort the available templates by title or rating.

Also on this web page, you can enter keywords in the search box and find the type of template you need. It might help to use "Project" as one of the keywords because templates for various Microsoft Office programs are included here.

Also be aware that some of the templates are a bit dated or refer to older technology, like Microsoft Project 2003. But many of the templates were created with Project 2007 or Project 2010, so you have a wide variety of more current templates from which to choose.

Saving Your New Project

The original template file has an extension of .mpt, indicating that it is a Project 2010 template file type. When you save a new project file based on a template, the file is saved by default as a normal MPP (Microsoft Project plan) file. To save a project based on a template, do the following:

Save

1. On the File tab, click Save.
2. In the Save As dialog box, choose the drive and folder where you want to save the new project.
3. In the File Name box, enter a descriptive name for your project, and then click the Save button.

Adapting the Template to Your Project

Review your new project file for the types of information included and the level of detail. Review as follows:

- In the Gantt Chart or other task sheet, review the list of tasks. Determine whether you need to add more tasks or remove extraneous ones.

- Check to see whether durations are filled in for the tasks. If they are, see whether they seem close to the durations you expect in your new project. Most templates include durations as estimated durations, as indicated by the question mark (?).
- See whether any automatically scheduled tasks should be switched to manually scheduled tasks. Most templates are created with automatically scheduled tasks. This might be because the template was created in an earlier version of Microsoft Project, before the advent of manually scheduled tasks. This might also be because the template was created from a finished project, and by the time a project reaches its end, most or all of its tasks are automatically scheduled.
- Examine the chart area of the Gantt Chart or the Network Diagram and see whether task dependencies have been set up. Review their appropriateness and their complexity.
- Display the Resource Sheet. If generic resources are listed, start considering real resources who can replace the generic ones. If you're using a template generated within your organization, you might see names of actual individuals.

Based on this review, you can see how much adaptation you need to do to tailor this template to your project.

Move Project

Whether you're building a new project plan based on a template or on an existing plan, you'll need to change the project start date. On the Project tab, in the Schedule group, click Move Project. The Move Project dialog appears, as shown in Figure 31-5.

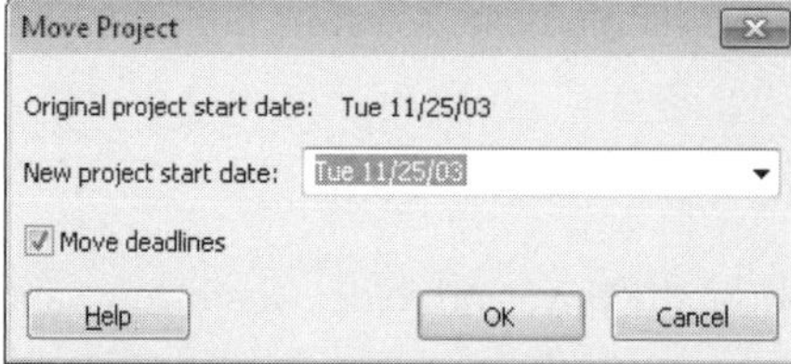

Figure 31-5 Use the Move Project dialog box to set the start date for the new project based on a template or other existing plan.

If you want any existing deadlines to be moved in relation to the new start date, be sure that the Move Deadlines check box is selected.

INSIDE OUT Create a new project from an existing one

New From Existing Project

You can use an existing project as the basis for a new project. To do this, on the File tab, click New. Under New From Existing, click New From Existing Project. Browse to find the project you want to use as the basis for your new project, and then open it. When you save this file, Project 2010 makes sure that you give it a different name, so the original file remains intact.

When you use an existing project file as the basis for a new project plan, you often need to do a little more adaptation than with a regular template because the original file contains extraneous information, such as actuals, that you won't need in your new project.

A quick way to remove the bulk of this historical information while keeping the good stuff is to first save the file as a template, as follows:

Save As

1. On the File tab, click Save As.
2. In the Save As Type list, click Project Template (*.mpt). The folder location changes to your computer's default location for Microsoft Project templates.
3. Keep or change this location, and then type a name in the File Name box.
4. Click Save.
5. In the Save As Template dialog box, select all the check boxes to remove baselines, actuals, cost information, and whether tasks have been saved to Project Server. Click Save. The file is saved as a template, minus the data that pertained only to the progress of that particular project.
6. On the File tab, click Save As again. This time, save the file as a regular Project (*.mpp) file in the folder you want. The default location showing is the Microsoft Templates folder. You probably don't want to save your regular project files there.

You're now set to go. There might be additional information still to remove, such as date constraints or certain resource information, but you've already taken care of the bulk of it.

Creating Your Own Project Template

After you plan and track a few projects to completion using Project 2010, you'll see that you're recording valuable information in your project plans. Of course, you'll archive your project plan for historical purposes. However, you can also use an existing or completed project plan as the basis for a template, which saves you and others a great deal of time in planning future projects.

By creating your own template, you can save task and resource information, format settings, project-specific options, calendars, macros, and other elements that you've used successfully in other projects. Any Microsoft Project file can be saved as a template.

To save an existing project file as a template for future use by you or other project managers, follow these steps:

1. Open the project file you want to save as a template.
2. On the File tab, click Save As.
3. In the Save As Type list, click Project Template (*.mpt).

   The file name changes from the .mpp extension to .mpt, indicating that a copy of the regular project plan file will be saved as a template file. Also, the file is moved to the Templates folder. As long as your template is stored in this folder, the template will be listed in the New dialog box when you click My Templates on the Available Templates Backstage view.
4. Click the Save button.

   The Save As Template dialog box appears. (See Figure 31-6.)

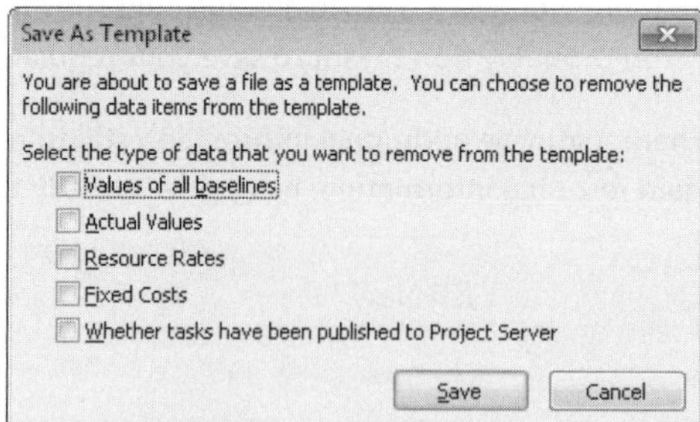

Figure 31-6 The file might include tracking and other specific information not appropriate for a template. Select the information you want to exclude from the template.

5. Select the check box for any item you do not want to save as part of the template, and then click the Save button.

The file is saved as a template in your Microsoft Templates folder on your computer's hard disk.

Copy Templates That Others Have Created

If you want to use templates that others in your organization have created, or if you obtain templates from a third-party source or an industry standards organization, copy the files to your Microsoft Templates folder. Storing the templates in the appropriate folder ensures that you'll see the templates listed in the Templates dialog box.

To see or change the default location that Project 2010 is using to store templates, on the File tab, click Options, and then click Save in the left pane. Under Save Templates, find the path for User Template.

For Project 2010 running on Windows 7, the default path is C:\Users\<Name>\AppData\Roaming\Microsoft\Templates.

By default, the Application Data folder is hidden in your Windows file system. To show hidden files and folders, follow these steps.

1. In Windows 7, open Windows Explorer.
2. Click Organize on the toolbar, and then click Folder And Search Options.
3. Click the View tab.
4. In the Advanced Settings box, double-click Hidden Files And Folders if necessary to show its options.
5. Select the Show Hidden Files, Folders, And Drives option, and then click OK.

Note that these steps are for Windows 7. If you're running Windows XP or Windows Vista, the steps might be slightly different.

To check that your new template appears in the New dialog box when you click My Templates on the Available Templates Backstage view, follow these steps:

1. In Project 2010, on the File tab, click New.
2. Under Available Templates, click My Templates.

   The New dialog box appears, and your new template should be listed. (See Figure 31-7.)

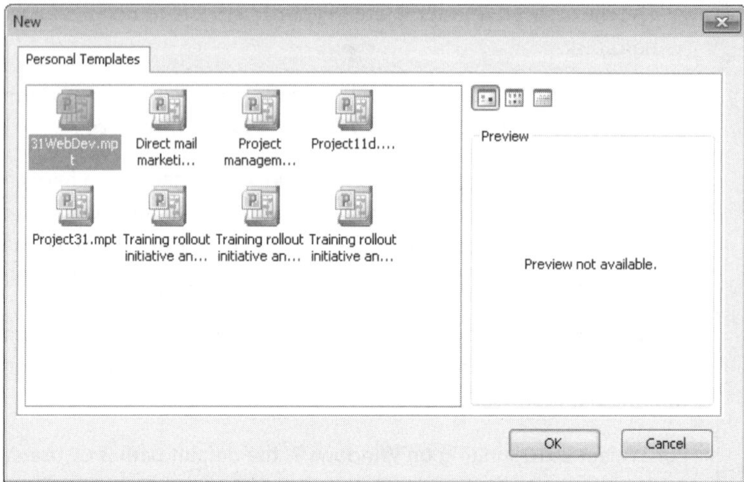

Figure 31-7 The New dialog box contains any templates you've created or downloaded, as long as they're saved in the Microsoft Templates folder on your computer.

Move the Templates Folder

By default, templates stored in the Microsoft Templates folder appear on the Personal Templates tab in the New dialog box. You can store templates in a different folder, however, and direct the Templates dialog box to find them in the new location. Changing the location of the templates can be useful if a set of templates has been developed for your organization and they've been placed on a file server for multiple project managers to use and perhaps update.

To change the location of the Microsoft Templates folder, on the File tab, click Options, and then click Save in the left pane. Under Save Templates, click the Browse button. Browse to the new location for templates, and then click OK.

Review the new template file to see whether any other information should be removed. Here are some suggestions:

- Display the task sheet and apply the Constraints table. See if any date constraints should be changed to As Soon As Possible or As Late As Possible.
- Review the task dependencies shown in the template. Determine whether they're useful or should be removed.

- Determine whether tasks should be automatically or manually scheduled.
- If there are any inactive tasks, determine whether they should be activated or deleted.
- Review the Resource Sheet. Decide whether you want to keep specific resource information or replace it with generic resource names. Also decide whether you should change maximum units and other availability information, and whether the cost information should be retained or deleted.
- Review tasks, resources, and assignments to see whether any notes should be removed.

After you finish adapting the template, on the File tab, click Save As. Be sure that the Save As Type box shows Project Template (*.mpt). Click Save. Your changes are made to the template.

Updating an Existing Template

If you need to update the information in an existing template, you cannot simply open the template and save it. If you do, Project 2010 will try to save a copy of the template as a regular project (MPP) file. To update and save information in the template itself, follow these steps:

1. Open the template you want to update.
2. Make the changes you want.
3. On the File tab, click Save.

   The Save As dialog box opens because you're saving from a project template.
4. In the Save As Type list, click Project Template (*.mpt).

   The current folder switches to the Microsoft Templates folder. The template you just edited should appear in the list of files.
5. Click the template, and then click the Save button.

   A prompt appears, indicating that you're about to replace the existing file. And that's exactly what you want to do.
6. Click OK. The Save As Template dialog box appears.
7. Click the Save button. Your changes are saved to the template file.

CAUTION!

If several project managers use the same project template, be careful when you're updating templates because your changes can affect many projects.

Closing a Project

After you and your team have worked through the planning, executing, and controlling processes of the project, the final process is closing the project. At this point, you've fulfilled the goals of the project and it's complete. In the closing stages of the project, you can analyze project performance with concrete data about schedule, cost, and resource use. You can also identify lessons learned and save acquired project knowledge.

Analyzing Project Performance

Review your overall project and compare your baseline plan to your actual plan. You can review variances in the schedule, in costs, and in assignment work. Any large variances can help point out problem areas in the project. Some helpful reports for such analysis include the following:

- Project Summary
- Overbudget Tasks
- Top-Level Tasks
- Overbudget Resources
- Milestones
- Earned Value
- Budget

Reports

To generate one of these reports, on the Project tab, in the Reports group, click Reports. Double-click Overview or Costs, and then double-click the name of the report.

For more information about generating reports, see "Generating the Right Reports" on page 541.

Recording Lessons Learned

Whether or not you continue to be involved in this type of project, others are likely to benefit from the experience and knowledge you gained. At the end of your project, gather your team together and conduct a "postmortem" session, in which you can objectively discuss what went well with the project and what could be improved next time.

It's often helpful to have team members prepare notes in advance. For larger projects, you might find it practical to conduct a series of meetings with different groups of team members and stakeholders, perhaps those who were responsible for different aspects of the project.

Be sure to have a concrete method for recording the discussion points. After the session(s), compile the lessons learned report, including solutions to identified problem areas.

If the project plan is your repository for project-related documents, add your lessons-learned report to the closed project. You can embed the document in the plan or create a link to the document. If you're using Microsoft SharePoint or working in an enterprise environment with Project Server 2010, you can add the report to the project's document library.

For more information about adding a document to a project, see "Attaching Project Documentation" on page 94. For information about using the document library, see "Controlling Project Documents" on page 959.

In addition to archiving the document with the rest of the project's historical records, include it with your planning materials for the next project. Be sure to keep your solutions in the forefront so that you can continue to improve your project management processes.

Saving Acquired Project Knowledge

Through the planning and tracking of your project, it's likely that you've recorded a mass of valuable information about the following:

- Task durations
- Task and resource costs
- Work metrics (units per hour completed, and so on)

You might want to collect information about planned or actual durations, work, and costs to use as standards for planning future projects.

Project Management Practices: Administrative Closure

As you complete each major milestone or phase, you probably receive formal acceptance of that phase by the sponsor or customer. The sponsor reviews the deliverables and checks that the scope and quality of work are completed satisfactorily, and then signs off the acceptance of that phase.

When you reach the end of the project, you obtain your final acceptance and signoff, which at this point should be a formality because the sponsor has been involved and has signed off on the interim deliverables all along.

This final project acceptance is part of the administrative closure of the project. Administrative closure also includes analyzing project success and effectiveness and archiving documents and results. At this point, contracts are closed and budget records are archived. Employees should be evaluated, and their skills in your organization's resource pool should be updated to reflect the increase in skills and proficiencies they've gained as a result of working on this project.

A complete set of project records should make up the project archives, and these archives should be readily available as a reference for future similar projects.

These durations and work metrics can be included in a project template based on the closing project. Save the project plan as a project template for use by you or other project managers who will be working on a similar type of project in the future. In your template, you can remove actuals, resource names, and constraint dates, for example. But the tasks, durations, task dependencies, base calendars, and generic resources can be invaluable in a project template. In addition, any custom solutions you've developed—such as views, reports, filters, and macros—can also become a part of your template. Through the efficiencies you built into your project plan, you're laying the groundwork for future efficiencies.

CHAPTER 32

Managing Project Files

YOUR project files are the heart of your project management efforts. As the project manager, these are the files you find yourself "living in" the most. Because of this, it's essential that your project files are properly saved, that you can easily find and open them, and that they're properly safeguarded with the necessary backups and security.

Sometimes you need to save all or part of a project file in another format—such as PDF or XLSX—to make it easier for others to read your project information or so you can manipulate or present project information in a different way. Likewise, sometimes you need to open a file created in another type of application—for example, a Microsoft Access database or an XML file—to import information from that source for use as part of your project plan.

NEW!

Now built in to Microsoft Project 2010—rather than being a separate add-in—is the ability to compare two project files side by side and see their differences.

These issues and features are all part of basic project file management, which is covered in this chapter.

Saving Project Files

Saving a project file ensures that it's stored on a hard disk for future access. The hard disk might be on your own computer or on your organization's network. It can be your project server as an enterprise project. Saving files to consistent locations makes finding your files logical and as quick as you need it to be.

If you're running Microsoft Project Professional 2010, you can also open an enterprise project file stored in the Microsoft Project Server 2010 database. For more information about saving, publishing, and checking project files in to your organization's project server, see "Creating an Enterprise Project by Using Project Professional" on page 905 and "Managing Your Files on the Project Server" on page 912.

Saving a New Project

Saving a project file is the same in Project 2010 as in any other Microsoft Office application. To save a new project file to a drive on your local computer or to a network drive, follow these steps:

1. On the File tab, click Save As.

   The Save As dialog box appears, showing the contents of the most recently used folder or your default file location, as shown in Figure 32-1. Unless you explicitly change it, this default file location typically is your Documents folder.

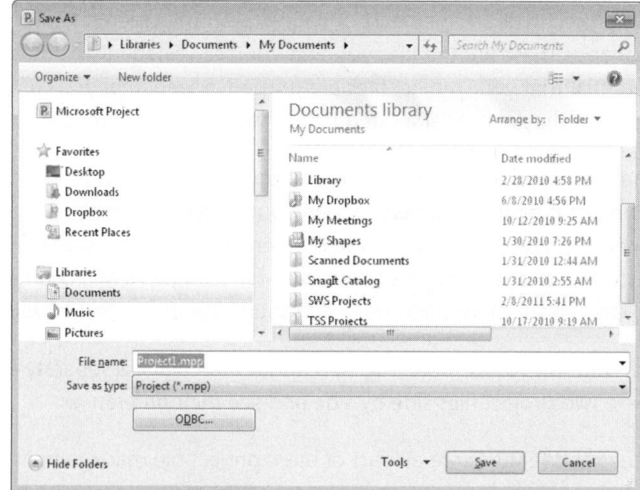

Figure 32-1 Use the Save As dialog box to browse to the folder where you want to save your new project file.

2. In the dialog box, double-click the drive or folder where you want to save the new project file. Continue double-clicking folders until you get to the location where you want to save the file.

3. In the File Name box, type the name of the file.

4. Click Save.

A Project By Any Other Name

In Project 2010, you can name a project just about anything you want, as long as the name doesn't exceed 255 characters. Any combination of uppercase and lowercase letters can be used; Project 2010 does not recognize case in file names. However, the following symbols cannot be used in a file name:

- Asterisk (*)
- Less-than symbol (<)
- Backward slash (\)
- Question mark (?)
- Colon (:)
- Quotation mark (")
- Forward slash (/)
- Pipe symbol (|)
- Greater-than symbol (>)
- Semicolon (;)

Save

After saving a file with a name and in a specific location, be sure to save frequently during your work session. A good rule of thumb is to save about every five minutes or whenever you make significant changes that you wouldn't want to lose in the event of a system failure or power outage. On the Quick Access Toolbar, click Save. You can also press Ctrl+S.

Saving Project Files Automatically

Although it's not so difficult to remember to click the Save button every few minutes while working, sometimes all your powers of concentration are devoted to an activity such as adjusting the project schedule to achieve a changed project finish date. It's only after the power outage that you realize that you haven't saved your file for more than an hour, and anguish ensues.

Save Options

Depending on what you're trying to do, there are different ways to save your project file:

- **Save** When you click File, Save for a new, unsaved project, the Save As dialog box appears. You can select the file's storage location and name the file. For projects that are already saved, clicking the Save command quickly saves your changes to the existing file without opening the Save As dialog box.
- **Save As** When you click File, Save As in any project file, the Save As dialog box appears. You can select the file's storage location and name the file. Use this dialog box to save new project files or create an alternate or backup copy of your project. You can also use this dialog box to save the project as a different file type.
- **Save Workspace** You can save multiple project files as a workspace that saves and opens the identified project files as a unit. The project files are still individual files that can be opened singly. However, when the workspace file is opened, all project files associated with that workspace are opened at the same time.

Save Workspace

For more information about saving a workspace, see "Opening Multiple Project Files as a Set" on page 612.

To provide that extra assistance that everyone needs from time to time, you can have Project 2010 remember to save the file automatically every few minutes. To do this, follow these steps:

1. On the File tab, click Options, and then click Save in the left pane.
2. Under Save Projects, select the Auto Save Every check box.
3. In the Auto Save Every box, enter the number of minutes after which you want Project 2010 to automatically save your file, as shown in Figure 32-2.

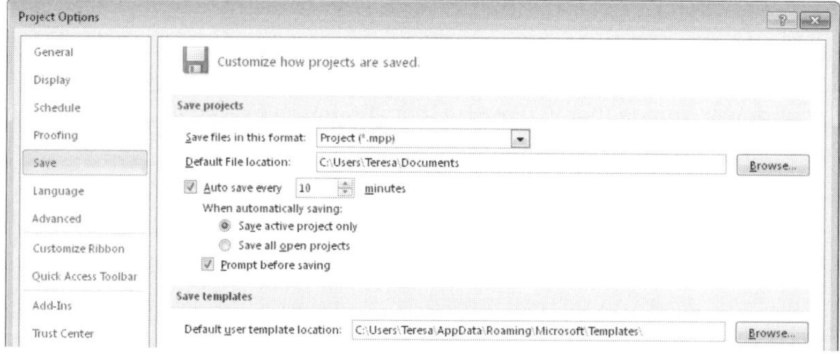

Figure 32-2 Set your automatic save preferences in the Save page of the Project Options dialog box.

4. Under When Automatically Saving, specify which project files should be automatically saved.

   To have Project 2010 automatically save only the active project, select the Save Active Project Only option, which is the default.

   To have Project 2010 automatically save the active project along with any other open projects, select the Save All Open Projects option.

5. Select or clear the Prompt Before Saving check box according to your preference.

INSIDE OUT **Turn the Prompt Before Saving prompt on or off**

It can be handy to be notified when your application is about to perform an action that you might not otherwise be aware of. However, you might find the Prompt Before Saving feature annoying. You've already instructed Project 2010 to save your file at a frequency that you specified. If you don't want to be asked at every specified interval (which could be every five minutes!) whether you want to save, clear the Prompt Before Saving check box.

However, if you frequently experiment with what-if scenarios in your project file, you might want to be prompted before Project 2010 saves one of your experiments and you can't revert back to your original.

Specifying the Default Save Location

If you have a drive or folder dedicated to your project management files, you might want to make that your default save location instead of using the typical Documents folder. This default location is the folder presented first whenever you open or save a project file. To set the default folder, follow these steps:

1. On the File tab, click Options, and then click Save in the left pane.
2. In the Default File Location, click the Browse button.
3. In the Modify Location dialog box, browse to the drive and folder you want to see first when you are saving or opening project files. Click OK.
4. In the Project Options dialog box, click OK.

Note

If you regularly save your project files as something other than an MPP file (for example, a Microsoft Project 2007 file), you can change the default file format. On the File tab, click Options, and then click Save in the left pane. Click in the box labeled Save Files In This Format, and then click the file format you want to use as the default.

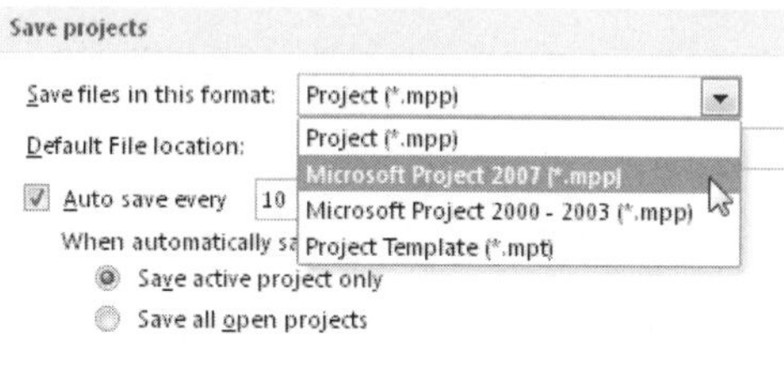

Opening Project Files

Opening project files from your local computer or network drive is the same in Project 2010 as in any other Microsoft Office application. In addition, you can:

- Quickly open a project from an extensive list of recently opened files.
- Open a project saved in a previous version of Microsoft Project.
- Find a project file based on your search criteria, and then open it when it's found.

If you're running Project Professional 2010, you can also open an enterprise project file stored in the Project Server 2010 database. For more information about checking out and opening an enterprise project file, see "Logging On via Project Professional" on page 898 and "Checking Out an Enterprise Project" on page 912.

Opening a Saved Project

You typically open a saved project by browsing for it in the Open dialog box. You can also find and open a recently opened file from the list of recent projects.

Opening a Project

To open a project from your local computer or a network drive, follow these steps:

Open

1. On the File tab, click Open.

   The Open dialog box opens to your default file location or to your most recently used folder, as shown in Figure 32-3. Unless you explicitly change it, this default file location typically is your Documents folder.

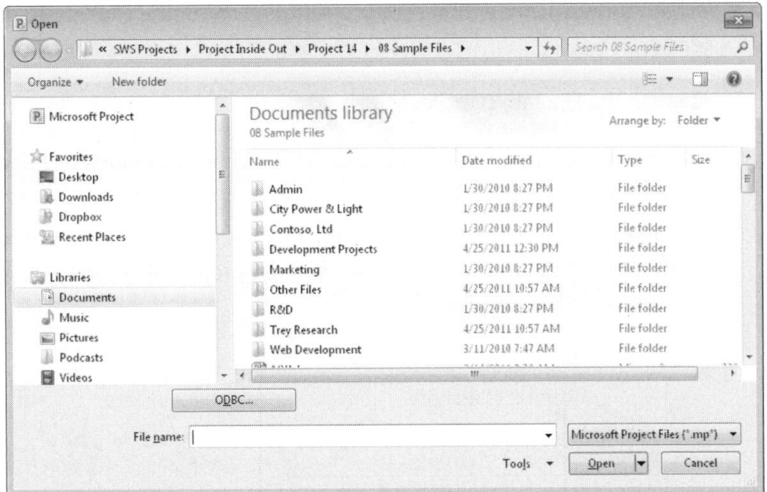

Figure 32-3 See your list of folders and files and open your project files by using the Open dialog box.

2. In the dialog box, double-click the drive or folder where the project file resides. Continue double-clicking folders until you get to the location of the project file you want to open.

3. Double-click the project file you want to open.

Opening a Recent Project

Project 2010 can maintain a long list of recently opened project files. This can be one of the most convenient ways to open your projects. To open a recently opened project file, follow these steps:

1. On the File tab, click Recent.

   The list of about 15 of your most recently opened project files appears. They are listed in order of access, with the most recently opened file on top.

2. Click the name of the recent project to open it.

Unpinned indicator

Pinned indicator

If you want a certain project file to never cycle off the Recent Projects list, you can "pin" it. Next to its name in the Recent Projects list, click the pin icon. When you click the pin icon, the file is moved to the top of the list and the pin icon changes to indicate that it's a pinned file.

You can show a number of recent projects directly on the File tab. To do this, follow these steps:

1. On the File tab, click Recent.
2. At the bottom of the window, select the check box labeled Quickly Access This Number Of Recent Projects.

   Because the default number in the box is 4, as soon as you select the check box, the names of the four most recently opened project files appear on the File menu, as shown in Figure 32-4.

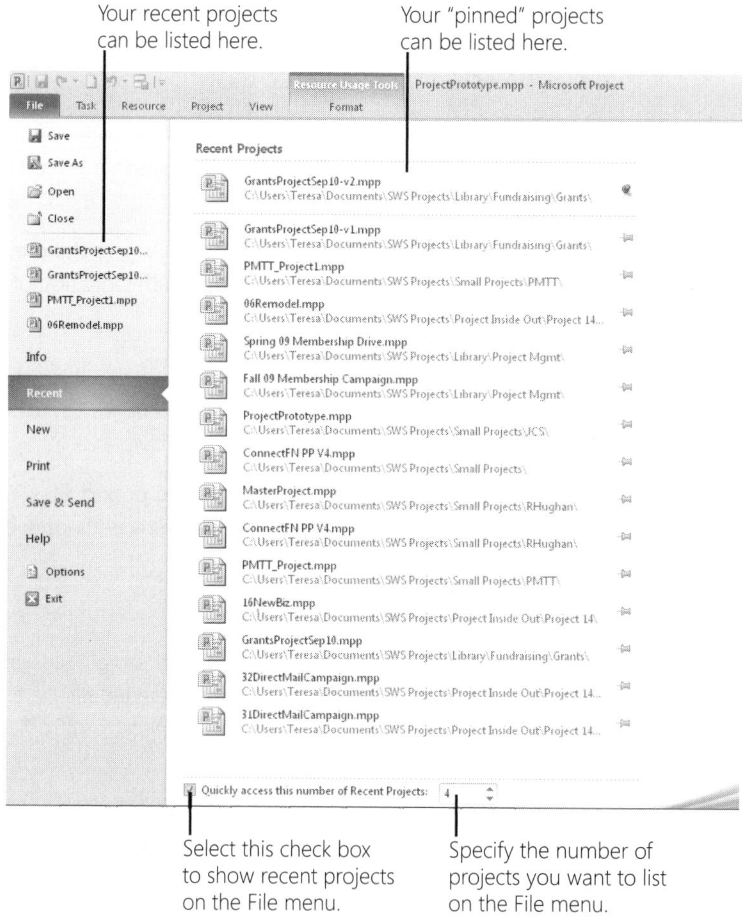

Figure 32-4 Open recently opened files from the Recent Projects list.

3. If you want to change the number of recent project files listed on the File tab, change the number in the box labeled Quickly Access This Number Of Recent Projects.

   You can list as many as 17 files.

4. To remove the list of recent projects from the File tab, clear the check box.

Searching for Files

Searching for a lost project file can be frustrating and time-consuming. You can use the search tool in Windows Explorer to find a lost file. To do this, follow these steps:

1. In Windows, click Start, All Programs, Accessories, Windows Explorer.

2. Browse to the drive or folder where you want the search to begin.

   The Search box is located in the upper-right corner and reflects the name of the current drive or folder.

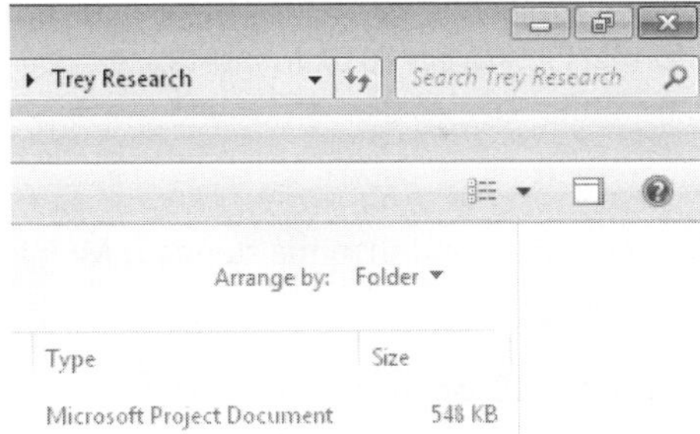

3. Click in the Search box and type a portion of the file name for which you're searching.

   For example, if you know that your file name contains the word **software** or **deployment**, as in "Software Deployment Project," enter one or more of these words.

   As you type, results start to appear in the window.

   If there are many results, you can change your search term to narrow the focus. You can also click in the Arrange By box and select a criterion such as Top Results or Date Modified to specify how the results should be sorted.

4. When you find the file you're looking for, double-click it to open it.

   Unlike for Word, Excel, or .jpg files, clicking a Project file does not show a preview in the Windows Explorer preview pane.

> **Note**
>
> **The same search box used in Windows Explorer also appears in the Open dialog box. You might experiment with it. However, it doesn't seem to work as well as the Windows Explorer version.**

Saving and Opening with Different File Formats

A file format is an arrangement of data in a file that specifies the file type and defines the file properties in such a way that its resident application or any compatible application can open the file correctly. When you create and save a regular Microsoft Project file, it's saved as an MPP file. The file name's .mpp extension indicates that this is indeed a regular Microsoft Project file.

However, you can save, or *export*, project files to other file formats. You can also open, or *import*, files from other file formats in Project 2010. In most cases, you carry out, or at least start, the exporting process from the Save As dialog box and the importing process from the Open dialog box.

To save a project file as a different file format than the standard MPP format, follow these steps:

1. With the file open in Project 2010, on the File tab, click Save As.

   If the file format converts a single view rather than the entire file, display the view you want to export.

2. Browse to the drive and folder where you want to save the file.
3. Click the arrow in the Save As Type box.
4. Click the file format you want.

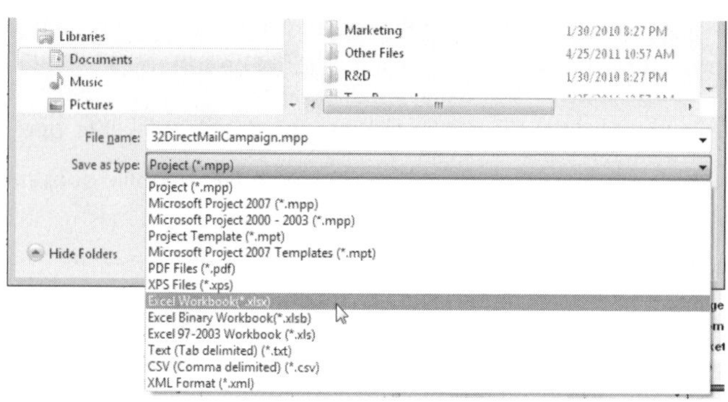

5. Click Save.

   In some cases, another process such as export mapping might start. In other cases, you might see a dialog box asking for more information. In most cases, however, the file or view is simply saved in the selected format.

To open a file in Project 2010 that's in a different file format than MPP, follow these steps:

1. In Project 2010, on the File tab, click Open.
2. Browse to the drive and folder that contain the file you want to import into Project 2010.
3. Click the arrow in the button currently labeled Microsoft Project Files (*.mp*) next to the File Name box.
4. Click the file format of the file you want to import.

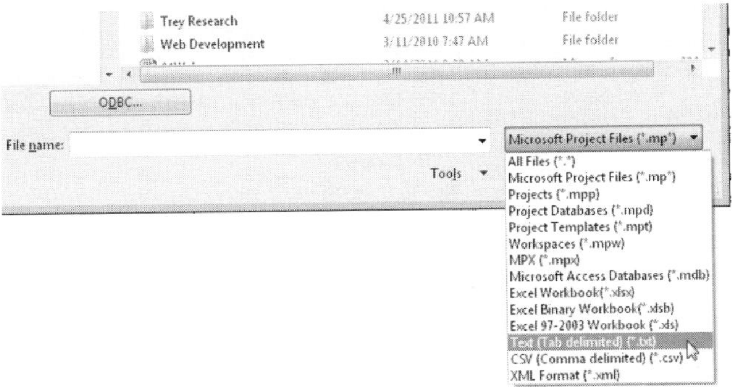

5. All files of that format in the current folder are listed in the dialog box.
6. Double-click the file you want to import.

   In some cases, another process such as import mapping might start. In most cases, however, information from the imported file simply opens in Project 2010.

Table 32-1 details the file formats supported by Project 2010 for saving, opening, or both. Unless otherwise noted, the file formats listed can be accessed from the Save As Type box on the Save As dialog box or the Files Of Type box on the Open dialog box.

Chapter 32

Table 32-1 **Supported File Formats**

File format	Extension	Save or Open	Notes
Project	.mpp	Save Open	Saves or opens the file as a Microsoft Project Plan file, which is the default file type for projects being opened or saved in Project 2010.
Microsoft Project 2007	.mpp	Save Open	Saves or opens the file as a Microsoft Project Plan file using the file format from Microsoft Project 2007.
Microsoft Project 2000-2003	.mpp	Save Open	Saves or opens the file as a Microsoft Project Plan file using the file format from Microsoft Project 2000, 2002, and 2003.
MPX	.mpx	Open	Opens a Microsoft Project Exchange (MPX) file created in Microsoft Project 98 or an earlier version. This is a record-based ASCII text-file format that Project 2010 can read, allowing earlier Microsoft Project files to be opened and converted to Project 2010 files.
Project Template	.mpt	Save Open	Saves the file as a Microsoft Project template file that can then be used as a basis for new projects. Opens a template file. You can change and save those changes to the template file.
Microsoft Project 2007 Templates	.mpt	Save Open	Saves the file as a Microsoft Project 2007 template file that can then be used as a basis for new projects in Microsoft Project 2007. Opens a template file. You can change and save those changes to the template file.
Project Workspaces	.mpw	Save Open	Saves all open project files as a Microsoft Project workspace file. Available through the Save Workspace command that can be added to the Quick Access Toolbar or ribbon. Opens a Microsoft Project workspace file, which opens all associated projects in a single step.
PDF Files	.pdf	Save	Saves the current view as a PDF (Portable Document Format) file. Ensures that the view is preserved with its original formatting and is not editable. A PDF file is also easy to open and read using a free downloadable reader on any computer.
XPS Files	.pdf	Save	Saves the current view as an XPS (XML Paper Specification) file. Ensures that the view is preserved with its original formatting and is not editable. An XPS file is also easy to open and read on any computer by using a free downloadable XPS viewer.
Excel Workbook	.xlsx	Save Open	Saves specified project fields as Microsoft Excel data so that the file can then be opened in Microsoft Excel 2007 or 2010. Opens, through the import process, an Excel 2007 or 2010 workbook in Project 2010.
Excel Binary Workbook	.xlsb	Save	Saves specified project fields in the Excel 2007 Binary File Format (BIFF12). Opens a file saved in the Excel 2007 Binary File Format.

File format	Extension	Save or Open	Notes
Excel 97-2003 Workbook	.xls	Save Open	Saves specified fields as Microsoft Excel data so that the file can then be opened in Microsoft Excel 97-2003. Opens, through the import process, an Excel 97-2003 workbook in Project 2010.
Text (Tab Delimited)	.txt	Save Open	Saves fields from a single Project 2010 table as a text file. A tab-delimited text file uses tabs to separate fields of data in a record. Opens a tab-delimited text file which can be imported into a Project 2010 table. This is ideal for using project information in a third-party application or on another operating system.
Text (Comma Delimited)	.csv	Save Open	Saves fields from a single Project 2010 table as a text file. A comma-delimited text file uses commas to separate fields of data in a record. Opens a comma-delimited text file that can be imported into a Project 2010 table. This is ideal for using the project information in a third-party application or on another operating system.
XML Format	.xml	Save Open	Saves a project file as eXtensible Markup Language (XML) data. The structure of the resulting file is determined by the Project 2010 XML schema. Opens an XML file in Project 2010. For Project 2010 to understand and open it, an XML file must conform to the Project 2010 XML schema.
Project Databases	.mpd	Open	Opens a legacy Microsoft Project database.
Microsoft Access Databases	.mdb	Open	Opens a Microsoft Access database file in Project 2010.
Open Database Connectivity		Open	Opens a database file created in ODBC-compliant Microsoft SQL Server databases. To open an ODBC file, click the ODBC button in the Open dialog box and follow the instructions in the Select Data Source dialog box.

Note

Previous versions of Microsoft Project provided the ability to save Project data to an Excel PivotTable. This feature is no longer available in Project 2010. However, you can still create Excel visual reports that use your project data in an Excel PivotTable format. For more information, see "Producing a Visual Report of Project Data in Excel" on page 734.

Chapter 32

Working with Microsoft Project File Formats

In Project 2010, the MPP file format for regular project files is updated. However, you can easily open project files created in earlier versions of Microsoft Project. If the file was created in Microsoft Project 98 through Microsoft Project 2007, you can open it in Project 2010 with no conversion required.

If the project file was created in a version earlier than Microsoft Project 2000, the file must first be saved in the MPX (Microsoft Project eXchange) format. Project 2010 can then open the MPX file and save it as a Project 2010 file. The MPX file format is a record-based ASCII text-file format and is available in the Save As and Open dialog boxes.

To open a Project 2010 file in an earlier version of Microsoft Project, the file must first be saved in the appropriate Microsoft Project file format. In the Save As dialog box, you can specify that a file be saved in the Microsoft Project 2007 format or the Microsoft Project 2000-2003 format.

You can save a project file as a template file (MPT), which can then be used as a basis for new projects.

For more information about working with project templates, see "Working with Project Templates" on page 1192.

INSIDE OUT The Save Workspace command is not readily available

If you always like to have certain project files open at one time—for example, a resource pool with the project files that use them, or the subprojects associated with a master project—you can save them as a Microsoft Project Workspace (MPW) file. Then you can conveniently open all associated projects in a single step by just opening the project workspace file.

However, the Save Workspace command is not available on the ribbon, although it still lurks behind the scenes in Project 2010. You have to find it and then add it to the Quick Access Toolbar or to a custom group on the ribbon before you can use it to save a workspace.

For details about finding, adding, and using the Save Workspace command, see "Opening Multiple Project Files as a Set" on page 612.

Fortunately, the process for opening a project workspace file is as straightforward as it should be, because you can do it from the Open dialog box. On the File tab, click Open. Browse to the drive and folder where the workspace file resides. In the Files Of Type box, click Workspaces (*.mpw). All project workspace files are listed. Double-click the one you want to open, and all associated project files open all at once.

Exporting and Importing with Excel

You can export project information to an Excel spreadsheet. This process starts in the Save As dialog box and ends up in the Export Wizard, where you map corresponding fields between Project and Excel.

Likewise, you can import Excel information into a project plan. The process starts in the Open dialog box and ends in the Import Wizard, again to map pairs of corresponding fields between Project and Excel.

For more information about importing and exporting with Excel and other applications, see "Importing and Exporting Information" on page 676.

Exchanging Project Information with Databases

Because a project file is essentially a database collection of fields and records, it makes sense that you can convert Project 2010 information to and from database applications.

There are three ways to exchange project information with a database:

- Save the project file in XML format
- Save to or open from an ODBC (Open Database Connectivity) database file
- Save the project file as a Microsoft Access (MDB) file

Saving a Project File to XML Format

To save a project file in XML format for subsequent use in a database, follow these steps:

1. With the project file open in Project 2010, on the File tab, click Save As.
2. Browse to the drive and folder where you want to save the new XML file you'll be creating.
3. Click the arrow in the Save As Type box, and then click XML Format.
4. If you want, change the name in the File Name box.
5. Click Save.

   The structure of the resulting file is determined by the Project 2010 XML schema.

Saving and Opening with an ODBC Database

To save a project file as an ODBC database, first open the project file you want to convert. On the File tab, click Save As. Click the ODBC button, and then work through the Select Data Source dialog box.

To open an ODBC database, on the File tab in Project 2010, click Open. Click the ODBC button, and then work through the Select Data Source dialog box.

Saving and Opening with a Microsoft Access Database

You can save reporting data from a project file as a Microsoft Access MDB file through the Visual Reports dialog box. To do this, follow these steps:

Visual Reports

1. On the Project tab, in the Reports group, click Visual Reports.
2. Click the Save Data button at the bottom of the Visual Reports - Create Report dialog box.
3. Under Save Reporting Database, click Save Database.
4. In the Save As dialog box that appears, browse to the location where you want to save the database. Give the file a name, and then click Save.

   The reporting data in your project file is gathered and saved as an Access (MDB) file. You can then open the file in Access.

To open a Microsoft Access MDB file in Project 2010, follow these steps:

1. In Project 2010, on the File tab, click Open.
2. Browse to the drive and folder that contain the Access database file you want to import into Project 2010.
3. Click the arrow in the button currently labeled Microsoft Project Files (*.mp*) next to the File Name box.
4. Click Microsoft Access Databases (*.mdb).
5. All MDB files in the current folder are listed in the dialog box.
6. Double-click the file you want to open.

> **Note**
>
> **You can also open a legacy Microsoft Project database (MPD) file in Project 2010 by using this procedure. In the list of file types, click Project Databases (*.mpd).**

Working with Common Cross-Application File Formats

You can save or open information from several file formats especially designed to work across different applications and even different operating systems. This means that you can still exchange information with a program for which there is not an explicit file format. These common cross-application file formats available in Project 2010 are:

- TXT (tab-delimited text)
- CSV (comma-separated value text)
- XML (eXtensible Markup Language)
- PDF (Portable Document Format)
- XPS (XML Paper Specification)

Both the TXT and CSV text file formats allow for text transfer between applications. If the text is in table format, the TXT format separates the fields with tabs, whereas the CSV format separates the fields with commas. When you import a TXT or CSV file into a table format, the fields separate into columns according to the tabs or commas.

The XML format provides a self-defining, adaptable language that's used to define and interpret data in different applications, particularly in web-based documents. An accompanying XSL style sheet is used to work with and interpret the XML file.

For more information about working with the XML file format, see "Working with Project 2010 and XML Files" in Chapter 17.

NEW!

New in Project 2010 is the ability to save an active view as a PDF or an XPS file. No other program needs to be installed to create these files. With either of these programs, you can ensure that your file preserves its original formatting and is not editable. You can save, send, post, or print these views.

A PDF file can be opened by any computer using the free, downloadable Adobe Reader. An XPS file opens in the browser of most Windows computers. This makes these files easy to open and read on any computer. This is especially important because you can't assume that everyone who needs to see your project information has access to Project 2010.

To save a view as a PDF or an XPS file, follow these steps:

1. In Project 2010, open the view and arrange the data as you want it to appear when its printed.

   For more information about available views and arranging information in those views, see Chapter 4, "Viewing Project Information."

2. On the File tab, click Save & Send.
3. In the Save & Send Backstage view, click Create PDF/XPS Document.

   The right pane displays information about PDF/XPS documents, as shown in Figure 32-5.

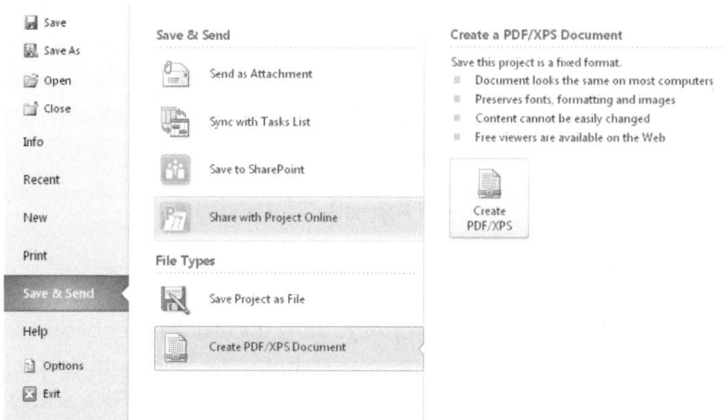

Figure 32-5 Create a PDF or an XPS file by using the Save & Send Backstage view.

Create PDF/XPS

4. In the right pane, click Create PDF/XPS.
5. Browse to the location where you want to save the file.
6. Enter a name in the File Name box.
7. If you want to create an XPS file instead of the default PDF file, click in the Save As Type box, and then click XPS Files (*.xps).
8. Click OK.
9. Make any necessary changes in the Document Export Options dialog box, as shown in Figure 32-6, and then click OK.

Instead of using the Save & Send Backstage view, you can also save a project view as a PDF or an XPS file by clicking File, Save As, and then selecting PDF Files (*.pdf) or XPS Files (*.xps) in the Save As Type box.

For information about PDF reports, see "Saving a Report as a PDF File" on page 579.

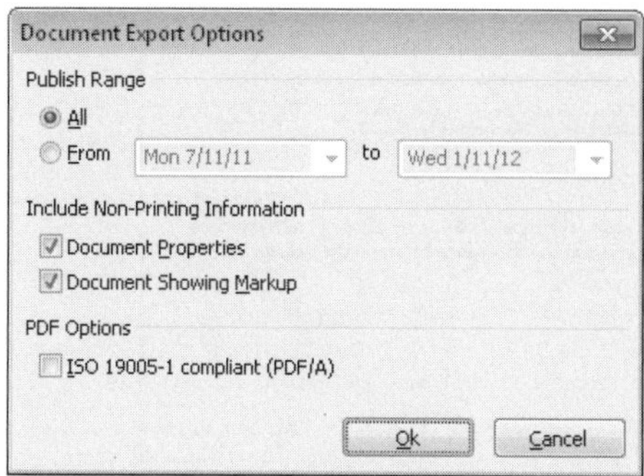

Figure 32-6 Specify options for the PDF or XPS file in the Document Export Options dialog box.

Comparing Project Plans Side by Side

In previous versions of Microsoft Project, the Compare Projects feature was an add-in. Now the feature is built in to Project 2010, and it provides a comprehensive view that shows differences between two projects line by line. You might want to compare projects in the following situations:

- You've sent a preliminary project plan for others to review, edit, and return to you. You can compare a reviewer's edited version with your original version to see exactly where changes were made.
- You've created a "what-if" version of your project plan, and now you want to compare the two versions to start implementing some of the changes.
- You saved an earlier version for historical purposes, kind of like an extensive baseline. Now you want to compare versions to see the differences in the project plan from the original.
- You have two versions of the project plan, and it's not clear what the differences are between them, or which one contains the most current information. Comparing the two will make this evident.

To compare the contents of two project files, follow these steps:

1. Open the two projects you want to compare; and be sure that one of the comparison projects is the active project.

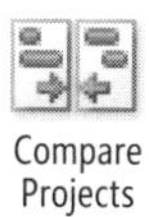

2. On the Project tab, in the Reports group, click Compare Projects.

   The Compare Project Versions dialog box appears, as shown in Figure 32-7.

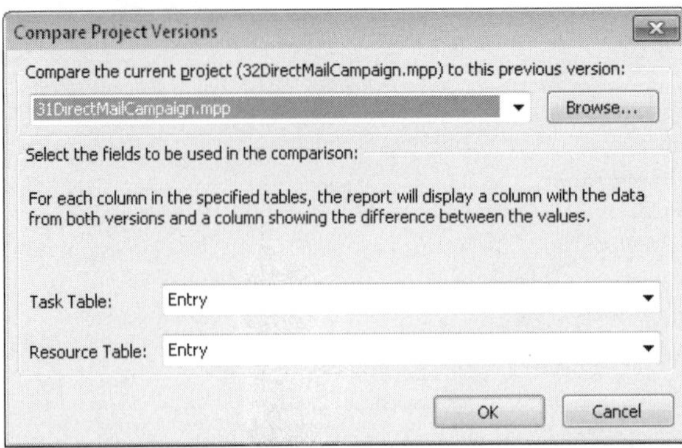

Figure 32-7 Specify the projects and fields you want to compare by using the Compare Project Versions dialog box.

3. Click in the box labeled Compare The Current Project (*projectname*.mpp) To This Previous Version, and then click the name of the other project in the drop-down menu.

   If you didn't open the comparison project, you can click Browse to find and select it.

4. In the Task Table box, select the name of the table you want to use to compare task information.

5. In the Resource Table box, select the name of the table you want to use to compare resource information.

6. Click OK.

   Project 2010 creates the comparison report, which is a combination view, as shown in Figure 32-8. The upper pane shows information from both projects temporarily merged. A legend indicates the differences in the information. The divided lower pane shows the same table in the two projects.

Compare Projects

The Task Comparison report shows first. To switch to view resources, click Compare Projects, View, Resource Comparison.

In either report, use the commands on the Compare Projects tab to filter data or to show or hide columns.

Close Comparison

When you are finished reviewing the comparison report, click Compare Projects, Compare, Close Comparison. The combination view closes, but the Comparison Report remains open. You can save it as its own project file if you want.

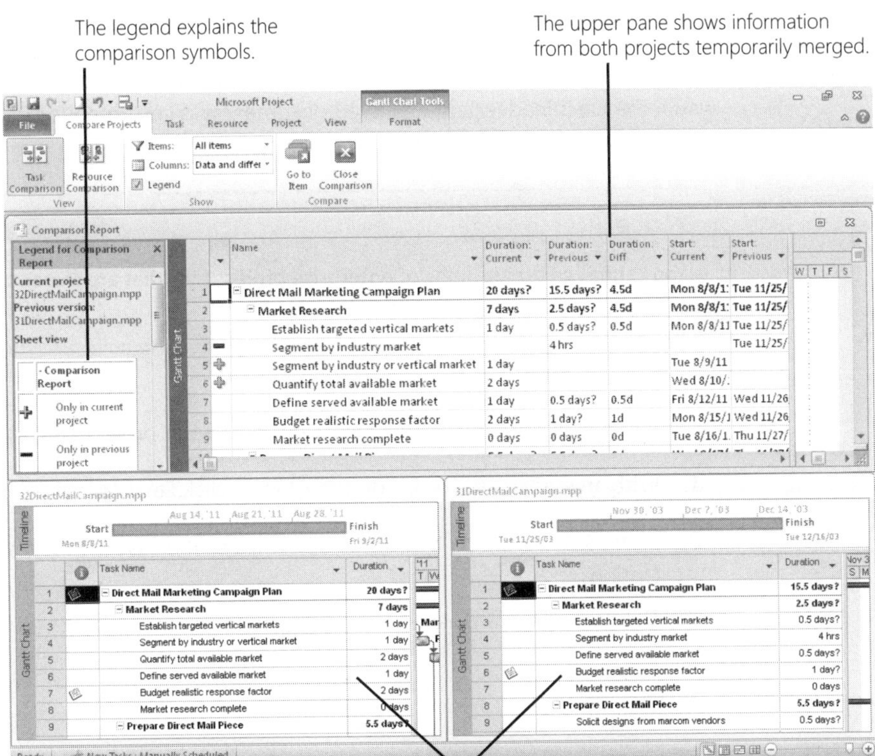
The legend explains the comparison symbols.
The upper pane shows information from both projects temporarily merged.
The lower pane shows both projects side by side.

Figure 32-8 The Compare Projects report shows differences between two project files.

Safeguarding Your Project Files

As you work hard creating, updating, and tracking your project file, you want to make the file as secure as possible. The further you travel through the life cycle of the project, the more valuable is the information you have in the project plan, and therefore, the more devastating a file loss can be.

This section discusses various methods for protecting your files from different types of loss or corruption.

Backing Up Your Project Files

It's always a good policy to have at least two copies of any important computer file. This way, if the file is inadvertently deleted or somehow is corrupted (or if you get a little crazy with your what-if scenarios), you have another file to return to.

Note

You cannot create backups of enterprise project files that are stored on your project server.

To specify that automatic backups be saved for all your project files, follow these steps:

1. With any project file open, on the File tab, click Save As.
2. In the Save As dialog box, click Tools (next to the Save button), and then click General Options.

   The Save Options dialog box appears, as shown in Figure 32-9.

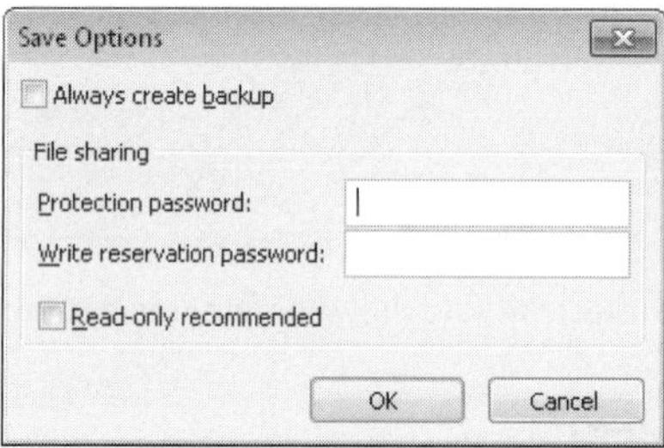

Figure 32-9 Set file backups and passwords in the Save Options dialog box.

3. Select the Always Create Backup check box.
4. Click OK in the Save Options dialog box. Click Save in the Save As dialog box.
5. Click OK in the message to confirm that you're saving changes in the active file.

   A backup file of the active project is saved. The backup copy adopts the same file name as the original, but it has an extension of BAK. For example, the backup file for deployment.mpp is deployment.BAK.

   The backup file is not identical to the active file; rather, it lags by one Save operation. That is, when you save the active file, the previous version is saved as the backup file.

   From now on, as long as the Always Create Backup check box is set, whenever you save any project, a backup of that file is created.

To restore a backup file as a regular project file, follow these steps:

1. On the File tab, click Open.
2. In the Open dialog box, browse to the drive and folder where the backup file is located.
3. Click the arrow in the file type button next to the File Name box, and then click All Files (*.*).

   This ensures that files ending in .BAK are shown in the list.
4. Double-click the backup file you want to restore as a regular project file.

   The backup file opens.
5. On the File tab, click Save As.
6. If necessary, browse to the location where you want to save the restored project file.
7. In the File Name box, enter a new file name for the restored backup file.

   Note that by default, the file name appends .BAK.mpp. It's a good idea to remove the .BAK from the file name.
8. Be sure that Project (*.mpp) is selected in the Save As Type box.
9. Click Save.

Note

Your project BAK file is a great contingency in case your project file is accidentally deleted or corrupted. However, if both the project and the backup are saved on the same drive and that drive crashes, your backup will be lost as well. Remember to periodically save your files to an alternate drive.

Protecting Your Project Files with a Password

If you are not working in an enterprise project management environment that uses a project server as a central location for your company's project files, saving your project files to a public network folder is one way to have centralized project files. This enables your company to back up critical files more regularly and reliably. It also provides a convenient location for your coworkers to collaborate on projects.

However, storing your project files on the network can also enable unauthorized individuals to access files that contain sensitive or confidential information. Perhaps your project is in its initial phase, and you aren't ready to share it with the rest of the company. Or maybe a project has information that should be seen only by a small group of people in your organization. In this case, assigning a *protection password* is a great idea. With a protection password, no one can open and view the project file unless he or she knows the password.

On the other hand, maybe you don't mind who sees the project, but you want to be sure that only a select few ever change the file. In this case, you can assign a *write reservation password*.

> **Note**
>
> **You cannot assign a password to an enterprise project file stored on the project server.**

To assign a password to a project, follow these steps:

1. Open the project file for which you want to set a password.
2. On the File tab, click Save As.
3. In the Save As dialog box, click Tools, and then click General Options.
4. To set a password for opening and viewing the project file, type the password in the Protection Password box.

   To set a password for editing the project file, type the password in the Write Reservation Password box.

   You can set both passwords on the same file if you want.
5. Click OK.
6. In the Confirm Password dialog box, type the password again.

   If you set both kinds of passwords, the first Confirm Password dialog box is for the protection password, and the second is for the write reservation password.

7. Click OK.

8. In the Save As dialog box, click Save, and then click OK.

> **Note**
>
> **If you want to remind users to open the project as read-only without locking out users who might have forgotten the password, consider selecting the Read-Only Recommended check box. If you select this check box, the next time a user begins to open this file, a message suggests that the user open the file as read-only unless they need to change the file. It then provides the option of opening the file as read-only.**

Opening Files Safely

Project 2010 includes a set of security options related to opening files from older file formats. By default, files from older file formats or nondefault file formats are not opened. If you need to open such a file—for example, when you're bringing older project files into Project 2010 or when you're importing an Excel file—you must change this security setting.

To change the security setting for legacy files, follow these steps:

1. On the File tab, click Options, and then click Trust Center in the left pane.

2. Click the Trust Center Settings button.

3. In the left pane, click Legacy Format.

4. Select the option labeled Prompt When Loading Files With Legacy Or Non-Default File Formats In Project or the option labeled Allow Loading Files With Legacy Or Non-Default File Formats.

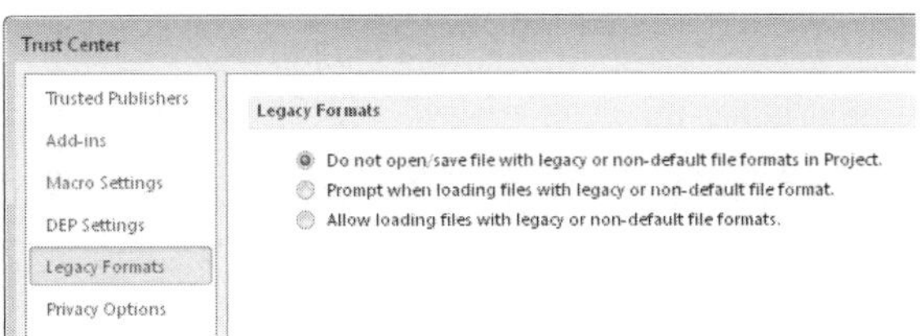

You can also set the security level for opening files that contain macros. Still in the Trust Center, click Macro Settings in the left pane. Select the security option you want.

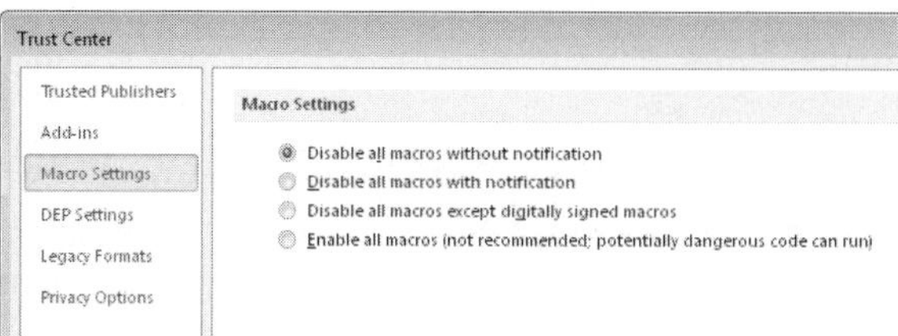

INSIDE OUT File properties are on the Info Backstage view

As in previous versions, with Project 2010 you can associate a project file with a title, subject, author, manager, and other information.

To do this, on the File tab, click Info. In the right pane, click Project Information, and then click Advanced Properties.

The Properties dialog box for the current project file appears. In the Summary tab, enter or view the file properties.

PART 9

Appendixes

APPENDIX A

Installing Microsoft Project 2010

This appendix describes system requirements, procedures, and guidelines for installing and activating the standalone desktop editions of Microsoft Project 2010.

This appendix also includes system requirements for implementing Microsoft Project Server 2010 for enterprise project management. It includes general guidelines to consider when planning an enterprise project management installation and provides resources for more detailed information.

Setting Up Project Standard or Project Professional 2010

You can install Microsoft Project Standard 2010 and Microsoft Project Professional 2010 as your standalone desktop project management solution. Project Professional 2010 has certain additional features for team planning and collaboration beyond the features included in Project Standard 2010.

For details about the new features in Project Standard 2010 and Project Professional 2010, see "What's New in Project 2010" on page 9.

When Project Professional 2010 is connected to Project Server 2010, additional features are made available to facilitate enterprise project management.

See "Understanding Issues for Project Server 2010 Setup" on page 1239 for more information.

Understanding System Requirements

Before you install Project Standard 2010 or Project Professional 2010, be sure that your system meets the minimum requirements. Table A-1 shows the minimum system requirements for a computer running Project Standard or Project Professional.

Table A-1 **Minimum System Requirements for Project 2010**

Component	Requirement or specification
Processor speed	700 MHz or higher
Random access memory (RAM)	512 MB or more
Hard disk space	2.5 GB available disk space
Media drive	DVD drive
Monitor display	1024×768 pixel resolution or higher
Graphics	DirectX 9.0C–compatible graphics card with drivers dated 11/1/2004 or later; required for graphics hardware acceleration
Operating system	One of the following: • Windows XP with Service Pack SP3 (32-bit) • Windows Vista SP1 • Windows Server 2003 with SP2 • Windows Server 2008 or later (32-bit or 64-bit) • Windows 7 or later
Internet	Internet access and a web browser such as Windows Internet Explorer 7 or later; needed to use Internet functions such as Office.com or online activation and registration

Table A-2 shows the minimum system requirements for using certain features of Project Standard or Project Professional.

Table A-2 **Project 2010 System Requirements for Specific Features**

Feature	Requirement or specification
Visual reports	Before installing Project 2010 to use visual reports with Office 2010, you must install: • Office 2010 • Visio 2010 • Microsoft SQL Server 2008 Analysis Services 10.0 OLE DB provider (available as a free download from Microsoft SQL Server 2008 Feature Pack, October 2008: *go.microsoft.com/fwlink/?LinkID=110393*
Visual reports feature with Excel PivotTables	Microsoft Excel 2003 SP2 or later

Appendix A

Feature	Requirement or specification
Visual reports feature with Visio PivotDiagrams	Microsoft Office Visio Professional 2007 or later
Import Outlook Tasks	Microsoft Outlook 2003 SP2 or later
Save to SharePoint (Std) or SharePoint synchronization (Pro)	Windows Server 2008 with SP2 (64-bit) or later running Microsoft SharePoint Server 2010
SharePoint synchronization (Pro)	Microsoft Access 2010 or Microsoft Visio 2010
Certain online functionality, such as participation in Microsoft Project forums	Windows Live ID

Setting Up Project 2010

To set up Project Standard or Project Professional on your computer, follow these steps:

1. Insert the Project Standard or Project Professional DVD in your computer's DVD drive.

   The AutoPlay window appears. Click Run SETUP.EXE. Then click Continue in the next security alert that appears.

   If the Project Setup program does not start automatically, click the Windows Start button, and then click Run. Type ***X*:\setup.exe** (where *X* is the name of your DVD drive), and then click OK. An alternative method is to use Windows Explorer to open the contents of the DVD, and then double-click the setup.exe file.

   If a message asks to confirm that you want to make changes to this computer, click Yes.

   The Microsoft Project 2010 window appears, asking for your 25-character product key.

2. Type your product key. It is either on the DVD case or provided as part of your license agreement.

   You do not need to enter the dashes, but it doesn't matter if you do. After you type the final digit, the key is validated.

3. Click Continue.

4. Read the Microsoft software license terms, and then select the check box labeled I Accept The Terms Of This Agreement. Click Continue.

5. On the next page, choose the type of installation you want.

- If no previous version of Microsoft Project is present on your computer, the choices are Install Now or Customize. If you click Install Now, installation begins immediately.
- If you are upgrading from a previous version of Microsoft Project, the choices are Upgrade or Customize. If you click Upgrade, installation begins immediately.
- If you click Customize, a window with five tabs appears. The Upgrade tab gives you a choice between removing or keeping the previous version of Microsoft Project on your computer. The Installation Options tab lets you specify which individual features should be installed. The File Location tab lets you specify the location where the project program files should be installed. The User Information tab provides fields for you to enter your name, initials, and organization. The Platform tab specifies your choices having to do with 32-bit and 64-bit applications on Windows. When you are finished with the customized settings, click Install Now.

The Installation Progress window shows the progress bar for the installation of Project 2010.

When the installation process is complete, a window appears telling you how to start the program.

6. Click Close.
7. Click Start, All Programs, Microsoft Office, Microsoft Project 2010.

   The Welcome To Microsoft Office 2010 window appears.
8. Choose the option you prefer regarding updates and downloads, and then click OK.

   If you had a previous version of Microsoft Project installed, a Planning Wizard appears, asking whether you want to copy your previous global settings to your new project global template.
9. Select the option you prefer regarding your previous global settings, and then click OK.

   Project 2010 opens.

Activating Project 2010

After installing Project 2010, you can use it with full functionality for a period of time before it requires activation. After this activation grace period expires, Project 2010 transitions to reduced functionality mode, in which it operates like a viewer. You cannot create new projects or save changes to existing project files. When you obtain and enter your product key and activate Project 2010 after the grace period expires, you can restore it to full functionality again.

The activation process is designed to verify that your installation of Project 2010 is properly licensed. It also checks that your product key is not in use on more computers than are permitted by the software license.

Until you activate Project 2010, the Activation Wizard appears each time you open Project 2010. This wizard guides you through the activation process, which takes just a minute or so. You can activate Project 2010 over the Internet or by phone.

To activate Project 2010, do the following:

1. Start Project 2010. The Microsoft Project 2010 Activation Wizard appears each time you start Project 2010 until you have activated it.

   You can also click File, Help to open the Help Backstage view.

   If you see an Activate Product Key button, you need to activate Project 2010.

   If you do not see this button, and if the Help Backstage view says Product Activated in the right pane, no further action is needed.

2. Follow the steps in the wizard to activate Project 2010. Select whether you want to activate over the Internet or by telephone. Click the Next button and follow the instructions.

3. On the next page, click Register Now to register your copy of Project 2010.

   Registering Project 2010 is an optional step. It is recommended, however, so that you can be notified of any important patches or other product information.

4. Click Close to finish activating Project 2010.

Changing Your Project 2010 Setup

After Project 2010 has been installed successfully, you can add or remove optional features, repair any program files that might have become corrupted, or remove the entire application.

Adding or Removing Features

To add or remove Project 2010 features, do the following:

1. Insert your Project 2010 DVD into your computer's DVD drive.

2. In the AutoPlay dialog box that appears, click Run SETUP.EXE, and then click Yes if necessary.

3. In the Microsoft Project 2010 window, select the Add Or Remove Features option, and then click Continue.

   The Installation Options window appears.

4. To add a feature, click the plus sign next to the feature name—for example, Microsoft Project. Then change Run All From My Computer, Installed On First Use, or Not Available.

   Installed On First Use makes the feature available. The setup program uses your Project 2010 DVD to install the added feature.

   Run From My Computer installs the feature on your computer's hard disk.

5. To remove a feature, click the arrow next to the feature you want to remove and change the Run From My Computer or Installed On First Use setting to Not Available. This will remove the feature from your setup.

6. Click Continue.

   The Configuration Progress window shows the current status of the changes that are being made.

7. When the changes are complete, click Close.

Repairing Project 2010

If you notice that Project 2010 isn't running as well as it should, or if a particular feature has stopped working correctly, you might need to repair some Project 2010 program files. To repair Project 2010 files by reinstalling them, follow these steps:

1. Insert your Project 2010 DVD into your computer's DVD drive.

2. In the AutoPlay dialog box that appears, click Run SETUP.EXE, and then click Yes if necessary.

3. In the Microsoft Project 2010 window, select the Repair option, and then click Continue.

   The Configuration Progress window shows the status of repairs to the Project 2010 files. The setup file detects any problems with the files and replaces those files, as needed.

4. When the repairs are complete, click Close.

   In some cases, your system might need to be restarted to make the repairs take effect. In the message that appears, click Yes to restart your computer.

Removing Project 2010 from Your Computer

Use the Project 2010 DVD again if you ever need to uninstall Project 2010. To do this, follow these steps:

1. Insert your Project 2010 DVD into your computer's DVD drive.
2. In the AutoPlay dialog box that appears, click Run SETUP.EXE, and then click Yes if necessary.
3. Select the Remove option, and then click Continue.
4. In the message that appears, click Yes to remove Project 2010.

   The Configuration Progress window shows the status of Project 2010 files being removed from your system.
5. When Project 2010 has been completely removed, click Close.
6. In the message that appears, click Yes to restart your computer. This completes the uninstall process.

Issues for Project Server 2010 Setup

This section includes general information and considerations for setting up Project Server 2010 together with Project Professional 2010 and Microsoft Project Web App for enterprise project management.

The individuals responsible for installing and configuring Project Server 2010 and the enterprise project management solution should have a solid working knowledge of Microsoft SQL Server and skills and knowledge as a system administrator. In addition, your organization should commit resources—including project managers, resource managers, and portfolio managers—to planning your enterprise project implementation to ensure that you get the maximum benefit from your Project Server deployment.

Understanding the Components of EPM

The following applications are used to implement the Microsoft enterprise project management solution, which runs on the Windows Server 2008 operating system.

- **SQL Server** As the foundation of Project Server and the enterprise project management solution, SQL Server is responsible for the project server databases. There are four project databases: Draft (or Working), Published, Archive, and Reporting.
- **Project Server** Project Server is the server that manages all data associated with your enterprise projects, portfolios, and programs. Project Server provides timesheet, reporting, team collaboration, and data analysis tools. Project Server provides the new project portfolio management capabilities, including demand management, workflow configuration, portfolio analysis, and business intelligence. Project Server also manages the global settings and information related to user access, security settings, and other administrative settings.

  All this information, which is generated either in Project Professional or Project Web App, is stored in the project databases powered by SQL Server.

  Project Server is protected by a security layer that restricts access to only those authorized to send and receive data from the database.
- **Microsoft SharePoint Server** Project Server is built on the SharePoint Server 2010 platform, which provides the administrative and user interface framework, the infrastructure for user management, logon capabilities, layout and content of pages and views, team collaboration, and integration with the reporting features of Project Server.

  Specifically, the integration with SharePoint Server enables the project collaboration workspace, document library, and risk-tracking and issue-tracking features of Project Web App and Project Professional.
- **Project Server Interface** Project Server uses the Project Server Interface (PSI) as its application program interface (API), which is the means through which Project Professional and Project Web App have a view into and interact with Project Server. The PSI enables tasks, resources, assignments, and entire projects to be manipulated—created, viewed, edited, or deleted.

  In addition, developers can use the PSI to create methods for interacting with line-of-business applications (for example, human resources, procurement, and accounting systems) and other third-party applications.
- **Project Professional** Project Professional is the primary client application interface for Project Server. Users with appropriate permissions can use the enterprise global template and enterprise resource pool to build their projects and resource teams, publish project plans to Project Server, and perform other enterprise project and resource management tasks.

Project Professional is the major source of project data, including projects, tasks, resources, assignments, scheduling dates, costs, and tracking information that is served by the project server.

When Project Professional is part of an enterprise project management solution, collaboration options become available, making it convenient for project managers to move back and forth between the Project Professional environment and the Project Web App environment.

- **Project Web App** The web-based user interface for project data, Project Web App shows tasks, resources, assignments, scheduling dates, costs, and tracking information. It also is the interface for the new project portfolio management capabilities. Project Web App runs on Internet Explorer and provides unique capabilities to work specifically as a client for Project Server and display targeted project data. Project Web App is the view into the project server and the underlying project database.

  Project Web App is accessed by users who are authenticated through Windows or through the project server. Such users typically include team members, team leads, resource managers, project managers, portfolio managers, executives, and project server administrators.

  For more information about the users and components of the Microsoft enterprise project management solution, see Chapter 22, "Understanding Enterprise Project Management."

Analyzing Your Project Server Requirements

Before the enterprise project management components are installed, your organization needs to articulate how it manages projects, portfolios, and programs. It should also examine various line-of-business processes and determine how these interact with project management and resource management processes. This analysis will help you make the right decisions toward ensuring that the architecture and configuration of Project Server and its components correspond to the way your organization does business.

The following are some questions to consider:

- How many people do you expect to use Project Server, including from Project Professional and from Project Web App?
- What are the roles that members of the project team play, and what kinds of responsibilities and privileges do they need?

- What types of projects does your organization implement?
- What kind of security do you need to implement?
- Which enterprise features do you expect to use?
- What categories of time-tracking information do you need employees to track and submit?
- What kind of reporting and business intelligence are you going to need?
- How do you want to implement demand management for your organization?
- How might you want to customize the Project Web App interface?

For a series of articles, white papers, videos, and webcasts that can help your organization answer these types of questions and more, go to Microsoft TechNet at *www.technet.microsoft.com*. In the Search box, type **Planning Project Server 2010**, and then click the Search button. The article titled "Planning and Architecture for Project Server 2010" should appear. Click the link.

Understanding Project Server System Requirements

With the Microsoft enterprise project management capabilities afforded by Project Professional connected to Project Server, you have access to powerful standardization, customization, resource management, project portfolio management, and executive analysis capabilities across your entire organization.

Project Server can be set up in several ways:

- As a single server that uses built-in database installations
- As a single-server farm installation
- As a multiple-server farm installation

Table A-3 lists the minimum server requirements for these three configurations. In addition, through one of several Microsoft Project partners, you can access and configure web-based server hosting for your enterprise project management solution. Through a third-party hosting provider such as Project Hosts, you can speed up enterprise project management deployment for your organization without needing to purchase, configure, and maintain the IT infrastructure yourself.

Table A-3 **Minimum Server Requirements for Project Server Configurations**

Configuration type	Minimum server requirements
Single server installation with built-in database	Server with a 64-bit, four-core processor 4 GB of RAM for developer or evaluation installation 8 GB of RAM for production use 80 GB hard disk space for installation; additional free space (at least 16 GB recommended) for day-to-day operations in production environments DVD drive
	Windows Server 2008 Standard, Enterprise, Data Center, or Web Server, SP2, 64-bit Or Windows Server 2008 R2 Standard, Enterprise, Data Center, or Web Server
Single-server farm installation	Server with a 64-bit, four-core processor 4 GB of RAM for developer or evaluation installation 8 GB of RAM for production use 80 GB hard disk space for installation; additional free space (at least 16 GB recommended) for day-to-day operations in production environments DVD drive
	Microsoft SQL Server 2008, SP1, 64-bit and Cumulative Update 2 Or Microsoft SQL Server 2008, R2, 64-bit Or Microsoft SQL Server 2005 with SP3, 64-bit
Multiple-server farm installation	Server with a 64-bit, four-core processor (for small deployments) Server with 64-bit, eight-core processor (for medium deployments) 8 GB of RAM for production use (for small deployments) 16 GB of RAM for production use (for medium deployments) 80 GB hard disk space for installation; additional free space (at least 16 GB recommended) for day-to-day operations in production environments DVD drive
	Microsoft SQL Server 2008, SP1, 64-bit and Cumulative Update 2 Or Microsoft SQL Server 2008, R2, 64-bit Or Microsoft SQL Server 2005 with SP3, 64-bit

In addition to these requirements, additional software requirements for a computer running Project Server are listed in Table A-4.

Table A-4 Project Server Software Requirements

System requirement	Minimum specification
Server software and associated services	Microsoft Project Server 2010
	Microsoft SharePoint Server 2010 Enterprise edition
	Microsoft .NET Framework 3.5 for the Resource Substitution Wizard
Client software	Microsoft Office Project Professional 2007 or Microsoft Project Professional 2010
	Microsoft Project Web App
	Internet Explorer 7 or 8 for Microsoft Project Web App user access

Users such as project managers and resource managers who need to run Project Professional and Project Web App should be sure their computers meet the minimum system requirements outlined in Table A-5.

Table A-5 Minimum System Requirements for Client Users of Project Professional with Project Web App

System requirement	Minimum specification
Processor speed	700 MHz or higher
Random access memory (RAM)	512 MB or more
Hard disk space	2.5 GB available disk space
Media drive	DVD drive
Monitor display	1024×768 pixel resolution or higher
Graphics	DirectX 9.0C–compatible graphics card with drivers dated 11/1/2004 or later Required for graphics hardware acceleration
Operating system	One of the following: • Windows XP with Service Pack SP3 (32-bit) • Windows Vista SP1 • Windows Server 2003 with SP2 • Windows Server 2008 or later (32-bit or 64-bit) • Windows 7 or later
Internet	Internet access and a web browser such as Internet Explorer 7 or later; needed to use Internet functions such as Office.com or online activation and registration

For more details about hardware and software system requirements for your Project Server installation and deployment, go to Microsoft TechNet at *www.technet.microsoft.com*. In the Search box, type **Project Server 2010 system requirements**, and then click the Search button. The article titled "Hardware and Software Requirements (Project Server 2010)" should appear. Click the link.

Finding Resources for Project Server Setup

The following list includes articles and downloadable documents that can help you plan, configure, and install the hardware and software necessary to implement your organization's enterprise project management solution. Links to the web pages and files for the downloadable books are also included on the Microsoft Project 2010 Inside Out companion website at *oreilly.com/catalog/9780735626874/*.

- Project Server 2010 Product Information
  www.microsoft.com/project/en/us/project-server-2010.aspx
- Microsoft Enterprise Project Management (EPM) Solution
  www.microsoft.com/project/en/us/solutions.aspx
- Project Server Help and How-to
  office2010.microsoft.com/en-us/project-server-help
- Project 2010 and Project Server 2010 (MSDN Library)
  msdn.microsoft.com/en-us/library/ee758031.aspx
- Microsoft Project 2010 MSDN Blog
  blogs.msdn.com/b/project/
- Project Server 2010 (TechNet Library)
  technet.microsoft.com/en-us/library/cc303399.aspx
- Project Server TechCenter
  technet.microsoft.com/en-us/projectserver/default.aspx
- Project 2010 Overview for Developers
  msdn.microsoft.com/en-us/library/ee767697.aspx
- Project 2010 SDK (Software Developer Kit) Documentation
  msdn.microsoft.com/en-us/library/ms512767.aspx

APPENDIX B

Online Resources for Microsoft Project 2010

This appendix includes a listing of web resources related to Microsoft Project 2010 and project management.

This information and links are all on the Microsoft Project 2010 Inside Out companion website at *http://go.microsoft.com/FWLink/?Linkid=218006*. Other resources are available on the companion website as well.

Microsoft-Sponsored Resources

The following is a list of Microsoft websites that can provide further assistance and information in your work with Project 2010.

Project Desktop Basics

- **Project 2010 Version Comparison**
  www.microsoft.com/project/en/us/project-standard-2010-versions.aspx
  Comparison of features in Microsoft Project 2003, 2007, and 2010. Also shows distinctions between Microsoft Project Standard 2010 and Microsoft Project Professional 2010.

- **Project Help and How-to**
  office.microsoft.com/en-us/project-help/
  The overview page for Project 2010 help articles and other resources for learning how to use the product. Also includes links to discussion forums, technical resources, templates, and training programs.

- **Getting started: Get to know Project 2010**
  office.microsoft.com/en-us/project-help/getting-started-get-to-know-project-2010-HA010355886.aspx
  An introduction to new, changed, and discontinued features of Project 2010. A clearinghouse for resources to help you start learning about project management and Project 2010.

- **Getting started: Microsoft Project basics**
  office.microsoft.com/en-us/project-help/getting-started-microsoft-project-basics-HA010355887.aspx
  If you've never used any version of Microsoft Project, this page and its links are a great starting point.

- **Getting started: Introduction to project management**
  office.microsoft.com/en-us/project-help/getting-started-introduction-to-project-management-HA010359477.aspx
  An overview of project management principles and how to apply these principles using Project 2010.

- **Learn the Project 2010 Ribbon**
  office.microsoft.com/en-us/project-help/learn-the-project-2010-ribbon-HA010359476.aspx
  An online Help article that provides an overview of each tab on the Project 2010 ribbon, along with sample uses of each tab and links to other articles with in-depth information about related features.

- **Learn where menu and toolbar commands are in Project 2010**
  www.microsoft.com/project/en/us/ribbon_guide.aspx
  This interactive guide maps menus and commands from previous versions of Microsoft Project to the commands on the new Project ribbon.

Project Server Basics

- **Microsoft Project Server 2010 Product Information**
  www.microsoft.com/project/en/us/project-server-2010.aspx
  Broad overview information about Microsoft Project Server 2010, including what's new, benefits, feature comparisons, and more.

- **Microsoft Enterprise Project Management (EPM) Solution**
  www.microsoft.com/project/en/us/solutions.aspx
  Overview information about the Microsoft EPM solution through Project Server 2010, Microsoft Project Web App, and Project Professional 2010. Includes demos, training, and case studies, as well as details about demand management, portfolio analytics, time and task management, and business intelligence and reporting.

- **Project Server Help and How-to**
  office2010.microsoft.com/en-us/project-server-help
  Comprehensive set of online Help articles and videos for using Project Server 2010 and Project Web App. Topics include managing portfolios, reporting on projects, and submitting time and status.

Discussion Forums and Social Media

- **Project Forum on Microsoft Answers**
  social.answers.microsoft.com/Forums/en-US/addbuz/threads
  Discussion forum for Microsoft Project users. You can find answers to your questions and learn from questions posed by other users.

- **Project Professional Forum on TechNet**
  social.technet.microsoft.com/Forums/en-us/projectprofessional2010general/threads
  Discussion forum for more advanced users of Project Professional.

- **Project Server Forum on TechNet**
  social.technet.microsoft.com/Forums/en-us/category/projectserver2010
  Discussion forum for more advanced users of Project Server. Includes forums for general questions and answers, setup and operation, and customization and programming.

- **Microsoft Project on Facebook**
  www.facebook.com/pages/Microsoft-Project/95221953802
  Official page of Microsoft Project on Facebook. Includes tips, techniques, and updated information about Project 2010 and project management.

- **Microsoft Project Help Team on Twitter**
  twitter.com/ProjectHelpTeam
  Official page of Microsoft Project Help writers. Includes links to online Help articles on tips, techniques, and news about Project 2010 and project management.

- **Microsoft Developer Network (MSDN) blog on Project 2010**
  blogs.msdn.com/b/project/
  Official blog for the Microsoft Project product development group. Includes entries from product managers, program managers, and online Help writers.

Developer Information

- **Project Server 2010 (TechNet Library)**
  technet.microsoft.com/en-us/library/cc303399.aspx
  TechNet library of content for Project Server 2010. Includes information on evaluation, planning, architecture, deployment, operations, security, troubleshooting, and more.

- **Project Server 2010 TechCenter**
  technet.microsoft.com/en-us/projectserver/ee263909
  Clearinghouse for Project Server 2010 information. Includes news, resources, case studies, downloads, blogs, forums, and more.

- **Planning and architecture for Project Server 2010**
  technet.microsoft.com/en-us/library/cc197605.aspx
  A series of articles, white papers, videos, and webcasts that can help your organization analyze and plan your Project Server installation and configuration.

- **Hardware and software requirements (Project Server 2010)**
  technet.microsoft.com/en-us/library/ee683978.aspx
  Details about system requirements for Project Server 2010 installation and deployment, whether it's a single server using a built-in database installation, a single-server farm installation, or a multiple-server farm installation.

- **On-Demand Hosting Services for Project Server 2010**
  www.microsoft.com/project/en/us/on-demand-hosting.aspx
  Provides information and links about third-party hosting services for Project Server 2010 and the Microsoft enterprise project management solution.

- **Project 2010 and Project Server 2010 (MSDN Library)**
  msdn.microsoft.com/en-us/library/ee758031.aspx
  Developer information for creating and configuring enterprise project management solutions. Includes the Project 2010 developer reference and SDK documentation.

- **Project 2010 SDK (Software Development Kit) Documentation**
  msdn.microsoft.com/en-us/library/ms512767.aspx
  Software development kit for Project 2010, including documentation, code samples, how-to articles, and programming references to help customize and integrate Project 2010 and Project Server 2010.

Project Certification

- **Microsoft Certified Technology Specialist (MCTS) Exam 70-178: Managing Projects with Microsoft Project 2010**
  www.microsoft.com/learning/en/us/exam.aspx?ID=70-178
  Microsoft Learning site providing an overview, objectives, preparation materials, and online community resources for the MCTS 70-178 exam.

- **MCTS Exam 70-177: Configuring Microsoft Project Server 2010**
  www.microsoft.com/learning/en/us/exam.aspx?ID=70-177
  Microsoft Learning site providing an overview, objectives, preparation materials, and online community resources for the MCTS 70-177 exam.

Independent Resources

The following is a list of independent websites of organizations that can provide further assistance and information in your work with Project 2010 and project management.

Organizations

- **Project Management Institute (PMI)**
  www.pmi.org/
  Project Management Institute is a nonprofit professional organization for project managers. PMI establishes industry-recognized project management standards and provides training. PMI also sponsors the Project Management Professional (PMP) certification, which is the most recognized professional credential for project managers. PMI publishes "A Guide to the Project Management Body of Knowledge (PMBOK)," which details generally accepted project management standards, practices, knowledge areas, and terminology.

- **MPUG, the Official Industry Association for Microsoft Project**
  www.mpug.com/Pages/Home.aspx
  MPUG is an independent professional users group of Microsoft Project users. The website offers information about a variety of Microsoft Project and project management resources, with a goal to improve the understanding and use of Microsoft Project and related products. The site includes a calendar of MPUG events, a directory of MPUG chapters around the world, MPUG blogs, job board, newsletter, library, and more.

Experts and Resources

- **Microsoft Project Most Valuable Professionals (MVPs)**
  mvp.support.microsoft.com/communities/mvp.aspx?product=1&competency=Project
  A directory of Microsoft Project MVPs, who are "super users" recognized by Microsoft as providing exceptional service to the Microsoft Project user community.

- **Project Hosts**
  www.projecthosts.com/
  Website of a Microsoft partner that provides a browser-based hosted solution for Microsoft enterprise project management and SharePoint Server. For a monthly per-user subscription, users can accelerate enterprise project management deployment and reduce IT infrastructure costs, for purposes of either evaluation or ongoing operations.

Blogs and Discussions

- **Christophe Fiessinger's Blog**
  blogs.msdn.com/b/chrisfie/about.aspx
  A blog about the Project Server enterprise project management and project portfolio management solutions, hosted by Christophe Fiessinger, senior technical product manager for Microsoft. Includes white papers, case studies, training and certification information, demos, and related blogs.
- **Projectified**
  www.projectified.com/
  A blog about Microsoft Project and Project Server hosted by Microsoft Project consultant Brian Kennemer.
- **ProjHugger**
  www.projhugger.com/
  A blog for Microsoft Project enthusiasts published by Carl Chatfield, coauthor of *Project 2010 Step by Step*.
- **MPUG Blogs**
  www.mpug.com/blogs/default.aspx
  Blog about Microsoft Project hosted by MPUG and contributed by various MPUG members.
- **Corporate Geek**
  corporategeek.info/Project-Management
  Blog about project management basics and techniques, with contributions from project managers Ciprian Rusen, Richard Newton, and Andreea Marinescu.
- **Project Manager Network for Project Managers on LinkedIn**
  www.linkedin.com/groups/Project-Manager-Network-1-Group-37888?mostPopular=&gid=37888
  Discussion group about project management topics hosted on the LinkedIn professional networking site.
- **MPUG Global (Microsoft Project Users Group) on LinkedIn**
  www.linkedin.com/groups/Project-Manager-Network-1-Group-37888?mostPopular=&gid=37888
  Discussion group about project management topics hosted on the LinkedIn professional networking site.

APPENDIX C

Keyboard Shortcuts

This appendix lists Microsoft Project 2010 keyboard shortcuts for commonly used commands and operations that you can otherwise carry out by using the mouse. In addition to the reference tables of commonly used shortcuts, lists of other techniques for finding keyboard shortcuts are included.

Keyboard Shortcut Reference Tables

Table C-1 provides keyboard shortcuts for common file management commands. Table C-2 provides keyboard shortcuts for commands that control views and windows. Table C-3 lists keyboard shortcuts for commands that allow you to quickly move around a project view. Table C-4 lists keyboard shortcuts for commonly used editing commands. Table C-5 lists keyboard shortcuts for commands used while outlining project tasks. Table C-6 lists keyboard shortcuts for special-use commands.

Table C-1 **Working with Files**

Action	Keyboard shortcut
Save	Ctrl+S
Open the Save As dialog box	Alt+F2 or F12
Open the Open dialog box	Ctrl+O
Close the current file	Ctrl+F4
New	Ctrl+N or F11
Open the Print Backstage view	Ctrl+P
Exit Project 2010	Alt+F4

Table C-2 **Working with Views and Windows**

Action	Keyboard shortcut
Activate the other pane in a combination view	F6
Activate the next project window	Ctrl+F6
Activate the previous project window	Ctrl+Shift+F6
Activate the split bar	Shift+F6

Action	Keyboard shortcut
Zoom in (show smaller time units)	Ctrl+/
Zoom out (show larger time units)	Ctrl+Shift+*
Open a new window	Shift+F11 or Alt+Shift+F1
Close the current project file	Ctrl+F4
Close Project 2010	Alt+F4

Table C-3 **Navigating in a Project View**

Action	Keyboard shortcut
Move to the first field in the current row	Home or Ctrl+Left Arrow
Move to the first row	Ctrl+Up Arrow
Move to the first field of the first row	Ctrl+Home
Move to the last field in the current row	End or Ctrl+Right Arrow
Move to the last row	Ctrl+Down Arrow
Move to the last field of the last row	Ctrl+End
Move the timescale to the left	Alt+Left Arrow
Move the timescale to the right	Alt+Right Arrow
Move to the start of the timescale in a project	Alt+Home
Move to the end of the timescale in a project	Alt+End

Table C-4 **Editing in a Sheet View**

Action	Keyboard shortcut
Undo the last edit	Ctrl+Z
Redo the last item undone	Ctrl+Y
Cancel an entry	Esc
Clear or reset the selected field	Ctrl+Delete
Cut selected data	Ctrl+X
Copy selected data	Ctrl+C
Paste selected data	Ctrl+V
Delete selected data	Delete
Open the Find dialog box	Ctrl+F or Shift+F5
Find again	Shift+F4
Open the Go To dialog box	F5
Check spelling	F7
Select a column	Ctrl+Spacebar
Select a row	Shift+Spacebar
Select all rows and columns	Ctrl+Shift+Spacebar

Table C-5 **Outlining Tasks**

Action	Keyboard shortcut
Indent	Alt+Shift+Right Arrow
Outdent	Alt+Shift+Left Arrow
Hide subtasks	Alt+Shift+Minus Sign
Show subtasks	Alt+Shift+=
Show all tasks	Alt+Shift+*

Table C-6 **Giving Specialized Commands**

Action	Keyboard shortcut
Link tasks	Ctrl+F2
Unlink tasks	Ctrl+Shift+F2
Change to a manually scheduled task	Ctrl+Shift+M
Change to an automatically scheduled task	Ctrl+Shift+A
Scroll to show Gantt bar of current task (Scroll To Task)	Ctrl+Shift+F5
Open the Assign Resources dialog box	Alt+F10
Open an Information dialog box (Task, Resource, Assignment)	Shift+F2
Switch between automatic and manual calculation	Ctrl+F9
Reset sort to ID order or remove grouping	Shift+F3
Remove a filter and show all tasks or all resources	F3
Calculate scheduling changes in all open projects	F9
Calculate scheduling changes in the active project	Shift+F9
Open Project Help	F1

Finding More Keyboard Shortcuts

You can find information about additional keyboard shortcuts in Project 2010 Help. Click the Help icon in the upper-right corner of the Project 2010 window to open the Project Help window (or click File, Help, Microsoft Office Help). In the search box, type keyboard shortcuts and then click Search. Click the topic titled "Keyboard Shortcuts For Project 2010."

Another way to find keyboard shortcuts is to rest your mouse pointer over the command in the ribbon. The ScreenTip for the command appears. If there's a keyboard shortcut for the command, it appears next to the command name in the ScreenTip.

If you want a keyboard shortcut for a command you use frequently, but there isn't one built in, consider creating a macro for the command and then associating the macro with a keyboard shortcut. For more information, see "Creating Keyboard Shortcuts" on page 1130.

Using Ribbon KeyTips to Access Commands

You can use the keyboard to execute any menu command on the ribbon by using KeyTips, as follows:

1. Press and release the Alt key.

   KeyTips are displayed above each feature in the current view.

2. Press the letter shown in the KeyTip that corresponds with the tab you want to use. Do this even if the tab you want is already showing.

   The tab you select becomes active, and the KeyTips for the features showing on that tab appear.

3. Press the letter shown in the KeyTip that corresponds with the command you want.

   Depending on the command, a dialog box might open, a drop-down menu might appear, or the command might be executed.

> **Note**
>
> **To cancel the use of the KeyTips, press and release the Alt key or the Esc key.**

To use access keys to execute a command on the Quick Access Toolbar, follow these steps:

1. Press and release the Alt key.

2. Press the KeyTip number that corresponds with the command you want.

   The command is executed.

Index to Troubleshooting Topics

Index

A

B

D

H

I

N

O

S

W

X

Z

About the Authors

Teresa S. Stover has worked more than 20 years as a technical communications and project management consultant for software, manufacturing, business, and education. She specializes in Microsoft Project and project management for entrepreneurial startups, nonprofit organizations, and content development.

Her clients have included Apple Computer, National Semiconductor, Boeing, MetLife, and the Puyallup School District. Most significantly, she has worked with the Microsoft Project product team for every release since Project 4.0 in the early 1990s.

Teresa has won several awards from the Washington School Public Relations Association and the Society for Technical Communications, including Best in Show. She has written 13 other books, including titles on Windows, Office, Team Manager, and Microsoft Money, and periodically conducts workshops on software, project management, business, and writing topics. Recent achievements include recognition for her work in instructional design, web content, and nonprofit organizational development.

Typically ensconced in her Victorian home office in southern Oregon, like a content Rapunzel in the tower, she emerges to volunteer for Josephine Community Libraries as project manager and webmaster. She hangs out with her husband, Craig, Draco the German shepherd, and Tique the cat. She looks forward to more travels around the country with Craig in their new camper van.

Learn more at Teresa's website, *www.stoverwriting.com*. Teresa welcomes e-mails from readers sent to *teresa@stoverwriting.com*.

Bonnie Biafore has always been good at getting things done, but a few decades passed before she realized that she was "managing projects." She earned her PMP and has run her own company, MonteVista Solutions, offering project management and consulting services to clients in a variety of industries for the last 14 years.

On a parallel course, writing and ferocious editing have been a lifelong habit. She's written award-winning books about project management, investing, personal finance, and several commercial software programs (Microsoft Project, Quicken, QuickBooks, and Visio). Bonnie also writes the Project Certification Insider column for the Microsoft Project User Group (MPUG).

When she isn't meeting deadlines, she walks her Bernese mountain dogs, cooks gourmet meals, or hikes in the nearby mountains. You can learn more about Bonnie and her books at her website, *www.bonniebiafore.com*.

Andreea Marinescu is passionate about helping others understand new concepts. After managing multiple IT development projects with ups and downs, she discovered the magic that a project management framework brings. With a Project Management Professional (PMP) certification from the Project Management Institute (PMI) and a Prince 2 Practitioner certificate from the APM Group in the UK, she is now a team manager, project manager, and trainer at one of the biggest multinational corporations in the world.

In addition to her normal work, Andreea has participated in multiple nongovernmental organizations and enjoys coaching, organizing events, and helping to build diversity and inclusion networks in her community.

As a respite from leading teams or training in the corporate world, Andreea enjoys live concerts at home as part of a musical family. She has eight years of music school training and a piano degree.

What do you think of this book?

We want to hear from you!

To participate in a brief online survey, please visit:

microsoft.com/learning/booksurvey

Tell us how well this book meets your needs—what works effectively, and what we can do better. Your feedback will help us continually improve our books and learning resources for you.

Thank you in advance for your input!

Stay in touch!

To subscribe to the *Microsoft Press® Book Connection Newsletter*—for news on upcoming books, events, and special offers—please visit:

microsoft.com/learning/books/newsletter